**O'REILLY®**

# Strata
Making Data Work

# Learn how to turn data into decisions.

From startups to the Fortune 500, smart companies are betting on data-driven insight, seizing the opportunities that are emerging from the convergence of four powerful trends:

- New methods of collecting, managing, and analyzing data

- Cloud computing that offers inexpensive storage and flexible, on-demand computing power for massive data sets

- Visualization techniques that turn complex data into images that tell a compelling story

- Tools that make the power of data available to anyone

Get control over big data and turn it into insight with O'Reilly's Strata offerings. Find the inspiration and information to create new products or revive existing ones, understand customer behavior, and get the data edge.

**O'REILLY®**

**Visit oreilly.com/data to learn more.**

# Oracle PL/SQL Programming

FIFTH EDITION

# Oracle PL/SQL Programming

*Steven Feuerstein*
*with Bill Pribyl*

O'REILLY®

Beijing · Cambridge · Farnham · Köln · Sebastopol · Tokyo

**Oracle PL/SQL Programming, Fifth Edition**

by Steven Feuerstein with Bill Pribyl

Published by O'Reilly Media, Inc., 1005 Gravenstein Highway North, Sebastopol, CA 95472.

O'Reilly books may be purchased for educational, business, or sales promotional use. Online editions are also available for most titles (*http://my.safaribooksonline.com*). For more information, contact our corporate/institutional sales department: (800) 998-9938 or *corporate@oreilly.com*.

**Editors:** Deborah Russell and Julie Steele
**Production Editor:** Loranah Dimant
**Production Services:** Newgen, Inc.

**Indexer:** Ellen Troutman Zaig
**Cover Designer:** Karen Montgomery
**Interior Designer:** David Futato
**Illustrator:** Robert Romano

| | |
|---|---|
| September 1995: | First Edition. |
| September 1997: | Second Edition. |
| September 2002: | Third Edition. |
| August 2005: | Fourth Edition. |
| September 2009: | Fifth Edition. |

**Revision History for the Fifth Edition:**

| | |
|---|---|
| 2011-05-06 | Fifth release |
| 2011-12-16 | Sixth release |
| 2012-10-12 | Seventh release |

See *http://oreilly.com/catalog/errata.csp?isbn=9780596514464* for release details.

ISBN: 978-0-596-51446-4

[M]

1349986604

*To my father, Sheldon Feuerstein, whose intellectual curiosity, personal integrity, and devotion to family inspire me daily.*

—Steven Feuerstein

*To my father.*

—Bill Pribyl

# Table of Contents

Preface .................................................................... xxv

## Part I.  Programming in PL/SQL

1. **Introduction to PL/SQL** ..................................................... 3
   What Is PL/SQL?                                                        3
   The Origins of PL/SQL                                                  4
      The Early Years of PL/SQL                                           4
      Improved Application Portability                                    5
      Improved Execution Authority and Transaction Integrity             5
      Humble Beginnings, Steady Improvement                              6
   So This Is PL/SQL                                                      7
      Integration with SQL                                               7
      Control and Conditional Logic                                      8
      When Things Go Wrong                                               9
   About PL/SQL Versions                                                 10
      Oracle Database 11g New Features                                   12
   Resources for PL/SQL Developers                                       17
      The O'Reilly PL/SQL Series                                         17
      PL/SQL on the Internet                                             18
   Some Words of Advice                                                  19
      Don't Be in Such a Hurry!                                          20
      Don't Be Afraid to Ask for Help                                    21
      Take a Creative, Even Radical Approach                             22

2. **Creating and Running PL/SQL Code** ...................................... 23
   Navigating the Database                                               23
   Creating and Editing Source Code                                      24
   SQL*Plus                                                              25
      Starting Up SQL*Plus                                               26
      Running a SQL Statement                                            28

Running a PL/SQL Program                                             28
Running a Script                                                    30
What Is the "Current Directory"?                                     31
Other SQL*Plus Tasks                                                32
Error Handling in SQL*Plus                                          36
Why You Will Love and Hate SQL*Plus                                 37
Performing Essential PL/SQL Tasks                                    38
Creating a Stored Program                                          38
Executing a Stored Program                                         41
Showing Stored Programs                                            42
Managing Grants and Synonyms for Stored Programs                   43
Dropping a Stored Program                                          44
Hiding the Source Code of a Stored Program                         44
Editing Environments for PL/SQL                                     45
Calling PL/SQL from Other Languages                                 46
C: Using Oracle's Precompiler (Pro*C)                              47
Java: Using JDBC                                                   48
Perl: Using Perl DBI and DBD::Oracle                              49
PHP: Using Oracle Extensions                                      50
PL/SQL Server Pages                                               51
And Where Else?                                                   52

3.  **Language Fundamentals** . . . . . . . . . . . . . . . . . . . . . . . . . . . . . . . . . . . . . . . . . **53**
PL/SQL Block Structure                                              53
Anonymous Blocks                                                  54
Named Blocks                                                      56
Nested Blocks                                                     57
Scope                                                             58
Qualify all References to Variables and Columns in SQL Statements 59
Visibility                                                        61
The PL/SQL Character Set                                            64
Identifiers                                                         66
Reserved Words                                                    68
Whitespace and Keywords                                           69
Literals                                                            70
NULLs                                                             71
Embedding Single Quotes Inside a Literal String                   72
Numeric Literals                                                  73
Boolean Literals                                                  74
The Semicolon Delimiter                                             74
Comments                                                            75
Single-Line Comment Syntax                                        75
Multiline Comment Syntax                                          75

The PRAGMA Keyword                                              76
Labels                                                          77

## Part II.   PL/SQL Program Structure

**4.  Conditional and Sequential Control** ....................................... **81**
IF Statements                                                  81
   The IF-THEN Combination                      82
   The IF-THEN-ELSE Combination                 84
   The IF-THEN-ELSIF Combination                85
   Avoiding IF Syntax Gotchas                   86
   Nested IF Statements                         88
   Short-Circuit Evaluation                     89
CASE Statements and Expressions                                90
   Simple CASE Statements                       91
   Searched CASE Statements                     93
   Nested CASE Statements                       95
   CASE Expressions                             95
The GOTO Statement                                             97
The NULL Statement                                             98
   Improving Program Readability                99
   Using NULL After a Label                     99

**5.  Iterative Processing with Loops** ........................................ **101**
Loop Basics                                                   101
   Examples of Different Loops                 102
   Structure of PL/SQL Loops                   103
The Simple Loop                                               104
   Terminating a Simple Loop: EXIT and EXIT WHEN   105
   Emulating a REPEAT UNTIL Loop               106
   The Intentionally Infinite Loop             106
The WHILE Loop                                                108
The Numeric FOR Loop                                          109
   Rules for Numeric FOR Loops                 110
   Examples of Numeric FOR Loops               111
   Handling Nontrivial Increments              112
The Cursor FOR Loop                                           112
   Example of Cursor FOR Loops                 114
Loop Labels                                                   115
The CONTINUE Statement                                        116
Tips for Iterative Processing                                 119
   Use Understandable Names for Loop Indexes   119

The Proper Way to Say Goodbye . . . . . . . . . . . . . . . . . . . . . . . . . . . . . . . . . . . 120
Obtaining Information About FOR Loop Execution . . . . . . . . . . . . . . . 121
SQL Statement as Loop . . . . . . . . . . . . . . . . . . . . . . . . . . . . . . . . . . . . . . . . 122

6. **Exception Handlers** . . . . . . . . . . . . . . . . . . . . . . . . . . . . . . . . . . . . . . . . . . . . . **125**
Exception-Handling Concepts and Terminology . . . . . . . . . . . . . . . . . . 125
Defining Exceptions . . . . . . . . . . . . . . . . . . . . . . . . . . . . . . . . . . . . . . . . . . . 128
Declaring Named Exceptions . . . . . . . . . . . . . . . . . . . . . . . . . . . . . . . . 128
Associating Exception Names with Error Codes . . . . . . . . . . . . . . . 129
About Named System Exceptions . . . . . . . . . . . . . . . . . . . . . . . . . . . . 132
Scope of an Exception . . . . . . . . . . . . . . . . . . . . . . . . . . . . . . . . . . . . . . . 134
Raising Exceptions . . . . . . . . . . . . . . . . . . . . . . . . . . . . . . . . . . . . . . . . . . . . 135
The RAISE Statement . . . . . . . . . . . . . . . . . . . . . . . . . . . . . . . . . . . . . . . 136
Using RAISE_APPLICATION_ERROR . . . . . . . . . . . . . . . . . . . . . . . . . 137
Handling Exceptions . . . . . . . . . . . . . . . . . . . . . . . . . . . . . . . . . . . . . . . . . . 138
Built-in Error Functions . . . . . . . . . . . . . . . . . . . . . . . . . . . . . . . . . . . . 139
Combining Multiple Exceptions in a Single Handler . . . . . . . . . . . 144
Unhandled Exceptions . . . . . . . . . . . . . . . . . . . . . . . . . . . . . . . . . . . . . . 145
Propagation of Unhandled Exceptions . . . . . . . . . . . . . . . . . . . . . . . 145
Continuing Past Exceptions . . . . . . . . . . . . . . . . . . . . . . . . . . . . . . . . . 148
Writing WHEN OTHERS Handling Code . . . . . . . . . . . . . . . . . . . . . 150
Building an Effective Error Management Architecture . . . . . . . . . . . . 152
Decide on Your Error Management Strategy . . . . . . . . . . . . . . . . . . 153
Standardize Handling of Different Types of Exceptions . . . . . . . . 154
Organize Use of Application-Specific Error Codes . . . . . . . . . . . . . 157
Use Standardized Error Management Programs . . . . . . . . . . . . . . . 157
Work with Your Own Exception "Objects" . . . . . . . . . . . . . . . . . . . 159
Create Standard Templates for Common Error Handling . . . . . . . 162
Making the Most of PL/SQL Error Management . . . . . . . . . . . . . . . . . 164

## Part III. PL/SQL Program Data

7. **Working with Program Data** . . . . . . . . . . . . . . . . . . . . . . . . . . . . . . . . . . . . . **167**
Naming Your Program Data . . . . . . . . . . . . . . . . . . . . . . . . . . . . . . . . . . . 167
Overview of PL/SQL Datatypes . . . . . . . . . . . . . . . . . . . . . . . . . . . . . . . . 169
Character Data . . . . . . . . . . . . . . . . . . . . . . . . . . . . . . . . . . . . . . . . . . . . . 170
Numbers . . . . . . . . . . . . . . . . . . . . . . . . . . . . . . . . . . . . . . . . . . . . . . . . . . . 170
Dates, Timestamps, and Intervals . . . . . . . . . . . . . . . . . . . . . . . . . . . . 172
Booleans . . . . . . . . . . . . . . . . . . . . . . . . . . . . . . . . . . . . . . . . . . . . . . . . . . . 172
Binary Data . . . . . . . . . . . . . . . . . . . . . . . . . . . . . . . . . . . . . . . . . . . . . . . . 172
ROWIDs . . . . . . . . . . . . . . . . . . . . . . . . . . . . . . . . . . . . . . . . . . . . . . . . . . . 173
REF CURSORs . . . . . . . . . . . . . . . . . . . . . . . . . . . . . . . . . . . . . . . . . . . . . 173

Internet Datatypes                                                    174
"Any" Datatypes                                                      174
User-Defined Datatypes                                               174
Declaring Program Data                                               175
Declaring a Variable                                                 175
Declaring Constants                                                  176
The NOT NULL Clause                                                  177
Anchored Declarations                                                177
Anchoring to Cursors and Tables                                      179
Benefits of Anchored Declarations                                    180
Anchoring to NOT NULL Datatypes                                      181
Programmer-Defined Subtypes                                          182
Conversion Between Datatypes                                         183
Implicit Data Conversion                                             183
Explicit Datatype Conversion                                         185

8. Strings . . . . . . . . . . . . . . . . . . . . . . . . . . . . . . . . . . . . . . . . . . . . . . . . 191
String Datatypes                                                     191
The VARCHAR2 Datatype                                                192
The CHAR Datatype                                                    193
String Subtypes                                                      194
Working with Strings                                                 195
Specifying String Constants                                          195
Using Nonprintable Characters                                        197
Concatenating Strings                                                198
Dealing with Case                                                    199
Traditional Searching, Extracting, and Replacing                     202
Padding                                                              205
Trimming                                                             206
Regular Expression Searching, Extracting, and Replacing              207
Working with Empty Strings                                           218
Mixing CHAR and VARCHAR2 Values                                      219
String Function Quick Reference                                      222

9. Numbers . . . . . . . . . . . . . . . . . . . . . . . . . . . . . . . . . . . . . . . . . . . . . . 231
Numeric Datatypes                                                    231
The NUMBER Type                                                      232
The PLS_INTEGER Type                                                 237
The BINARY_INTEGER Type                                              238
The SIMPLE_INTEGER Type                                              239
The BINARY_FLOAT and BINARY_DOUBLE Types                             241
The SIMPLE_FLOAT and SIMPLE_DOUBLE Types                             246
Numeric Subtypes                                                     246

Number Conversions 247
   The TO_NUMBER Function 247
   The TO_CHAR Function 251
   The CAST Function 256
   Implicit Conversions 257
Numeric Operators 259
Numeric Functions 260
   Rounding and Truncation Functions 260
   Trigonometric Functions 261
   Numeric Function Quick Reference 261

**10. Dates and Timestamps** ..................................................... **267**
Datetime Datatypes 267
   Declaring Datetime Variables 270
   Choosing a Datetime Datatype 271
Getting the Current Date and Time 272
Interval Datatypes 274
   Declaring INTERVAL Variables 275
   When to Use INTERVALs 276
Datetime Conversions 278
   From Strings to Datetimes 279
   From Datetimes to Strings 281
   Working with Time Zones 284
   Requiring a Format Mask to Match Exactly 287
   Easing Up on Exact Matches 288
   Interpreting Two-Digit Years in a Sliding Window 288
   Converting Time Zones to Character Strings 290
   Padding Output with Fill Mode 291
Date and Timestamp Literals 291
Interval Conversions 292
   Converting from Numbers to Intervals 293
   Converting Strings to Intervals 294
   Formatting Intervals for Display 295
Interval Literals 295
CAST and EXTRACT 297
   The CAST Function 297
   The EXTRACT Function 299
Datetime Arithmetic 300
   Date Arithmetic with Intervals and Datetimes 300
   Date Arithmetic with DATE Datatypes 301
   Computing the Interval Between Two Datetimes 302
   Mixing DATEs and TIMESTAMPs 304
   Adding and Subtracting Intervals 305

|  | Multiplying and Dividing Intervals | 306 |
|  | Using Unconstrained INTERVAL Types | 306 |
|  | Date/Time Function Quick Reference | 308 |

| **11.** | **Records** | **311** |
|  | Records in PL/SQL | 311 |
|  | Benefits of Using Records | 312 |
|  | Declaring Records | 314 |
|  | Programmer-Defined Records | 315 |
|  | Working with Records | 318 |
|  | Comparing Records | 325 |
|  | Trigger Pseudo-Records | 326 |

| **12.** | **Collections** | **327** |
|  | Collections Overview | 328 |
|  | Collections Concepts and Terminology | 328 |
|  | Types of Collections | 330 |
|  | Collection Examples | 331 |
|  | Where You Can Use Collections | 335 |
|  | Choosing a Collection Type | 340 |
|  | Collection Methods (Built-ins) | 341 |
|  | The COUNT Method | 343 |
|  | The DELETE Method | 343 |
|  | The EXISTS Method | 345 |
|  | The EXTEND Method | 345 |
|  | The FIRST and LAST Methods | 346 |
|  | The LIMIT Method | 347 |
|  | The PRIOR and NEXT Methods | 348 |
|  | The TRIM Method | 349 |
|  | Working with Collections | 350 |
|  | Declaring Collection Types | 350 |
|  | Declaring and Initializing Collection Variables | 355 |
|  | Populating Collections with Data | 359 |
|  | Accessing Data Inside a Collection | 364 |
|  | Using String-Indexed Collections | 365 |
|  | Collections of Complex Datatypes | 370 |
|  | Multilevel Collections | 374 |
|  | Working with Collections in SQL | 382 |
|  | Nested Table Multiset Operations | 387 |
|  | Testing Equality and Membership of Nested Tables | 389 |
|  | Checking for Membership of an Element in a Nested Table | 390 |
|  | Performing High-Level Set Operations | 390 |
|  | Handling Duplicates in a Nested Table | 392 |

Maintaining Schema-Level Collections                      393
   Necessary Privileges                              393
   Collections and the Data Dictionary              394

**13. Miscellaneous Datatypes** . . . . . . . . . . . . . . . . . . . . . . . . . . . . . . . . . . . . . . . . . . **395**
The BOOLEAN Datatype                                      395
The RAW Datatype                                          396
The UROWID and ROWID Datatypes                            397
   Getting ROWIDs                                   398
   Using ROWIDs                                     398
The LOB Datatypes                                         400
Working with LOBs                                         401
   Understanding LOB Locators                       403
   Empty Versus NULL LOBs                           405
   Writing into a LOB                               407
   Reading from a LOB                               409
   BFILEs Are Different                             411
   SecureFiles Versus BasicFiles                    415
   Temporary LOBs                                   418
   Native LOB Operations                            421
   LOB Conversion Functions                         425
Predefined Object Types                                   426
   The XMLType Type                                 426
   The URI Types                                    430
   The Any Types                                    431

## Part IV.  SQL in PL/SQL

**14. DML and Transaction Management** . . . . . . . . . . . . . . . . . . . . . . . . . . . . . . . . . . **439**
DML in PL/SQL                                             440
   A Quick Introduction to DML                      440
   Cursor Attributes for DML Operations             444
   RETURNING Information from DML Statements         445
   DML and Exception Handling                       446
   DML and Records                                  447
Transaction Management                                    450
   The COMMIT Statement                             451
   The ROLLBACK Statement                           451
   The SAVEPOINT Statement                          452
   The SET TRANSACTION Statement                    453
   The LOCK TABLE Statement                         454
Autonomous Transactions                                   454

Defining Autonomous Transactions                                    455
Rules and Restrictions on Autonomous Transactions                   456
Transaction Visibility                                              457
When to Use Autonomous Transactions                                 458
Building an Autonomous Logging Mechanism                            459

**15. Data Retrieval** ...............................................  **463**
Cursor Basics                                                       464
Some Data Retrieval Terms                                           465
Typical Query Operations                                            466
Introduction to Cursor Attributes                                   467
Referencing PL/SQL Variables in a Cursor                            470
Choosing Between Explicit and Implicit Cursors                      471
Working with Implicit Cursors                                       471
Implicit Cursor Examples                                            472
Error Handling with Implicit Cursors                                473
Implicit SQL Cursor Attributes                                      476
Working with Explicit Cursors                                       477
Declaring Explicit Cursors                                          479
Opening Explicit Cursors                                            482
Fetching from Explicit Cursors                                      483
Column Aliases in Explicit Cursors                                  484
Closing Explicit Cursors                                            485
Explicit Cursor Attributes                                          487
Cursor Parameters                                                   489
SELECT...FOR UPDATE                                                 492
Releasing Locks with COMMIT                                         494
The WHERE CURRENT OF Clause                                         495
Cursor Variables and REF CURSORs                                    496
Why Cursor Variables?                                               497
Similarities to Static Cursors                                      498
Declaring REF CURSOR Types                                          498
Declaring Cursor Variables                                          499
Opening Cursor Variables                                            500
Fetching from Cursor Variables                                      501
Rules for Cursor Variables                                          504
Passing Cursor Variables as Arguments                               507
Cursor Variable Restrictions                                        509
Cursor Expressions                                                  509
Using Cursor Expressions                                            510
Restrictions on Cursor Expressions                                  512

**16. Dynamic SQL and Dynamic PL/SQL** ..................................... 513

| | |
|---|---|
| NDS Statements | 514 |
| The EXECUTE IMMEDIATE Statement | 514 |
| The OPEN FOR Statement | 517 |
| About the Four Dynamic SQL Methods | 523 |
| Binding Variables | 525 |
| Argument Modes | 526 |
| Duplicate Placeholders | 527 |
| Passing NULL Values | 528 |
| Working with Objects and Collections | 529 |
| Dynamic PL/SQL | 531 |
| Build Dynamic PL/SQL Blocks | 532 |
| Replace Repetitive Code with Dynamic Blocks | 534 |
| Recommendations for NDS | 535 |
| Use Invoker Rights for Shared Programs | 535 |
| Anticipate and Handle Dynamic Errors | 536 |
| Use Binding Rather Than Concatenation | 538 |
| Minimize the Dangers of Code Injection | 540 |
| When to Use DBMS_SQL | 543 |
| Parse Very Long Strings | 543 |
| Obtain Information About Query Columns | 544 |
| Meet Method 4 Dynamic SQL Requirements | 546 |
| Minimize Parsing of Dynamic Cursors | 552 |
| Oracle Database 11g New Features | 554 |
| DBMS_SQL.TO_REFCURSOR Function | 554 |
| DBMS_SQL.TO_CURSOR Function | 556 |
| Enhanced Security for DBMS_SQL | 558 |

## Part V.  PL/SQL Application Construction

**17. Procedures, Functions, and Parameters** ................................... 565

| | |
|---|---|
| Modular Code | 566 |
| Procedures | 567 |
| Calling a Procedure | 568 |
| The Procedure Header | 569 |
| The Procedure Body | 570 |
| The END Label | 570 |
| The RETURN Statement | 571 |
| Functions | 571 |
| Structure of a Function | 571 |
| The RETURN Datatype | 573 |
| The END Label | 575 |

| | |
|---|---|
| Calling a Function | 575 |
| Functions Without Parameters | 576 |
| The Function Header | 576 |
| The Function Body | 577 |
| The RETURN Statement | 578 |
| Parameters | 579 |
| Defining Parameters | 580 |
| Actual and Formal Parameters | 580 |
| Parameter Modes | 581 |
| Explicit Association of Actual and Formal Parameters in PL/SQL | 585 |
| The NOCOPY Parameter Mode Qualifier | 589 |
| Default Values | 589 |
| Local or Nested Modules | 590 |
| Benefits of Local Modularization | 591 |
| Scope of Local Modules | 594 |
| Sprucing Up Your Code with Local Modules | 594 |
| Module Overloading | 595 |
| Benefits of Overloading | 596 |
| Restrictions on Overloading | 599 |
| Overloading with Numeric Types | 600 |
| Forward Declarations | 601 |
| Advanced Topics | 602 |
| Calling Your Function From Inside SQL | 602 |
| Table Functions | 605 |
| Deterministic Functions | 615 |
| Go Forth and Modularize! | 616 |
| **18. Packages** | **617** |
| Why Packages? | 617 |
| Demonstrating the Power of the Package | 618 |
| Some Package-Related Concepts | 621 |
| Diagramming Privacy | 623 |
| Rules for Building Packages | 624 |
| The Package Specification | 624 |
| The Package Body | 626 |
| Initializing Packages | 627 |
| Rules for Calling Packaged Elements | 632 |
| Working with Package Data | 633 |
| Global Within a Single Oracle Session | 633 |
| Global Public Data | 634 |
| Packaged Cursors | 635 |
| Serializable Packages | 639 |
| When to Use Packages | 642 |

Encapsulate Data Access      642
Avoid Hardcoding Literals      645
Improve Usability of Built-in Features      647
Group Together Logically Related Functionality      648
Cache Static Session Data      649
Packages and Object Types      650

**19. Triggers** ................................................................. **651**
DML Triggers      652
DML Trigger Concepts      653
Creating a DML Trigger      655
DML Trigger Example: No Cheating Allowed!      660
Multiple Triggers of the Same Type      665
Who Follows Whom      666
Mutating Table Errors      668
Compound Triggers: Putting It All In One Place      669
DDL Triggers      673
Creating a DDL Trigger      673
Available Events      676
Available Attributes      676
Working with Events and Attributes      678
Dropping the Undroppable      681
The INSTEAD OF CREATE Trigger      682
Database Event Triggers      683
Creating a Database Event Trigger      683
The STARTUP Trigger      685
The SHUTDOWN Trigger      685
The LOGON Trigger      685
The LOGOFF Trigger      686
The SERVERERROR Trigger      686
INSTEAD OF Triggers      690
Creating an INSTEAD OF Trigger      690
The INSTEAD OF INSERT Trigger      692
The INSTEAD OF UPDATE Trigger      694
The INSTEAD OF DELETE Trigger      695
Populating the Tables      695
INSTEAD OF Triggers on Nested Tables      696
AFTER SUSPEND Triggers      697
Setting Up for the AFTER SUSPEND Trigger      698
Looking at the Actual Trigger      700
The ORA_SPACE_ERROR_INFO Function      701
The DBMS_RESUMABLE Package      702
Trapped Multiple Times      703

To Fix or Not to Fix? 704
Maintaining Triggers 705
Disabling, Enabling, and Dropping Triggers 705
Creating Disabled Triggers 706
Viewing Triggers 706
Checking the Validity of Triggers 707

**20. Managing PL/SQL Code** ............................................... **709**
Managing Code in the Database 710
Overview of Data Dictionary Views 711
Display Information About Stored Objects 712
Display and Search Source Code 713
Use Program Size to Determine Pinning Requirements 715
Obtain Properties of Stored Code 715
Analyze and Modify Trigger State Through Views 716
Analyze Argument Information 717
Analyze Identifier Usage (Oracle Database 11g's PL/Scope) 719
Managing Dependencies and Recompiling Code 721
Analyzing Dependencies with Data Dictionary Views 722
Fine-Grained Dependency (Oracle Database 11g) 726
Remote Dependencies 727
Limitations of Oracle's Remote Invocation Model 730
Recompiling Invalid Program Units 731
Compile-Time Warnings 735
A Quick Example 735
Enabling Compile-Time Warnings 736
Some Handy Warnings 738
Testing PL/SQL Programs 746
Typical, Tawdry Testing Techniques 747
General Advice for Testing PL/SQL Code 751
Automated Testing Options for PL/SQL 752
Testing with utPLSQL 753
Testing with Quest Code Tester for Oracle 755
Tracing PL/SQL Execution 756
DBMS_APPLICATION_INFO 759
Quest Error Manager Tracing 761
The DBMS_TRACE Facility 763
Debugging PL/SQL Programs 766
The Wrong Way to Debug 767
Debugging Tips and Strategies 769
Protecting Stored Code 774
Restrictions on and Limitations of Wrapping 774
Using the Wrap Executable 775

Dynamic Wrapping with DBMS_DDL ............................. 775
Guidelines for Working with Wrapped Code ..................... 776
Introduction to Edition-Based Redefinition (Oracle Database 11g Release
2) .................................................................... 777

**21. Optimizing PL/SQL Performance** ........................................ **781**
Tools to Assist in Optimization ................................... 783
Analyzing Memory Usage ...................................... 783
Identifying Bottlenecks in PL/SQL Code ....................... 783
Calculating Elapsed Time ...................................... 788
Choosing the Fastest Program ................................. 790
Avoiding Infinite Loops ....................................... 792
Performance-Related Warnings ................................. 793
The Optimizing Compiler .......................................... 793
Insights on How the Optimizer Works .......................... 795
Runtime Optimization of Fetch Loops .......................... 798
Data Caching Techniques .......................................... 799
Package-Based Caching ........................................ 800
Deterministic Function Caching ................................ 805
Function Result Cache (Oracle Database 11g) .................. 807
Caching Summary ............................................. 819
Bulk Processing for Multirow SQL ................................. 820
High Speed Querying with BULK COLLECT ...................... 821
High Speed DML with FORALL ................................. 828
Improving Performance With Pipelined Table Functions ............ 838
Replacing Row-Based Inserts with Pipelined Function-Based Loads 839
Tuning Merge Operations with Pipelined Functions ............. 846
Asynchronous Data Unloading with Parallel Pipelined Functions 848
Performance Implications of Partitioning and Streaming Clauses in Par-
allel Pipelined Functions ...................................... 851
Pipelined Functions and the Cost-Based Optimizer ............. 853
Tuning Complex Data Loads with Pipelined Functions .......... 859
A Final Word on Pipelined Functions .......................... 866
Specialized Optimization Techniques .............................. 866
Using the NOCOPY Parameter Mode Hint ..................... 867
Using the Right Datatype ...................................... 870
Stepping Back for the Big Picture on Performance ................. 871

**22. I/O and PL/SQL** ......................................................... **873**
Displaying Information ............................................ 873
Enabling DBMS_OUTPUT ..................................... 874
Write Lines to the Buffer ...................................... 874
Read the Contents of the Buffer ............................... 875

Reading and Writing Files     876
    The UTL_FILE_DIR Parameter     877
    Work with Oracle Directories     879
    Open Files     880
    Is the File Already Open?     882
    Close Files     882
    Read from Files     883
    Write to Files     885
    Copy Files     888
    Delete Files     889
    Rename and Move Files     890
    Retrieve File Attributes     890
Sending Email     891
    Oracle Prerequisites     893
    Configuring Network Security     893
    Send a Short (32,767 or Less) Plaintext Message     894
    Include "Friendly" Names in Email Addresses     896
    Send a Plaintext Message of Arbitrary Length     897
    Send a Message with a Short (< 32,767) Attachment     898
    Send a Small File (< 32767) as an Attachment     900
    Attach a File of Arbitrary Size     900
Working with Web-Based Data (HTTP)     903
    Retrieve a Web Page in "Pieces"     903
    Retrieve a Web Page into a LOB     905
    Authenticate Using HTTP Username/Password     906
    Retrieve an SSL-Encrypted Web Page (Via HTTPS)     906
    Submit Data to a Web Page via GET or POST     908
    Disable Cookies or Make Cookies Persistent     912
    Retrieve Data from an FTP Server     912
    Use a Proxy Server     913
Other Types of I/O Available in PL/SQL     913
    Database Pipes, Queues, and Alerts     914
    TCP Sockets     914
    Oracle's Built-in Web Server     914

**Part VI. Advanced PL/SQL Topics**

**23. Application Security and PL/SQL** ........................................ **919**
Security Overview     919
Encryption     921
    Key Length     922
    Algorithms     923

Padding and Chaining                                    924
The DBMS_CRYPTO Package                                  925
Encrypting Data                                         926
Encrypting LOBs                                         929
SecureFiles                                             930
Decrypting Data                                         930
Performing Key Generation                               932
Performing Key Management                               932
Cryptographic Hashing                                   938
Using Message Authentication Codes                      940
Using Transparent Data Encryption (TDE)                 941
Transparent Tablespace Encryption                       944
Row-Level Security                                      945
Why Learn About RLS?                                    947
A Simple RLS Example                                    949
Using Dynamic Policies                                  953
Using Column-Sensitive RLS                              957
RLS Debugging                                           960
Application Contexts                                    964
Using Application Contexts                              965
Security in Contexts                                    966
Contexts as Predicates in RLS                           967
Identifying Non-Database Users                          970
Fine-Grained Auditing                                   972
Why Learn About FGA?                                    973
A Simple FGA Example                                    974
Access How Many Columns?                                976
Checking the Audit Trail                                977
Using Bind Variables                                    978
Using Handler Modules                                   979

24. **PL/SQL Architecture** .................................................. **981**
Who (or What) is DIANA?                                 981
How Does Oracle Execute PL/SQL Code?                    982
An Example                                             983
Compiler Limits                                        986
The Default Packages of PL/SQL                          987
Execution Authority Models                              990
The Definer Rights Model                                990
The Invoker Rights Model                                995
Combining Rights Models                                 997
Conditional Compilation                                 998
Examples of Conditional Compilation                     999

The Inquiry Directive ................................................... 1000
The $IF Directive ..................................................... 1004
The $ERROR Directive ................................................. 1005
Synchronizing Code with Packaged Constants ............................ 1006
Program-Specific Settings with Inquiry Directives ...................... 1006
Working with Postprocessed Code ...................................... 1008
PL/SQL and Database Instance Memory .................................. 1009
PGA, UGA, and CGA ................................................. 1010
Cursors, Memory, and More .......................................... 1011
Tips on Reducing Memory Use ........................................ 1013
What to Do if You Run Out of Memory ................................ 1024
Native Compilation .................................................... 1027
When to Run Interpreted Mode ....................................... 1027
When to Go Native .................................................. 1028
Native Compilation and Database Release .............................. 1028
What You Need to Know ............................................... 1029

**25. Globalization and Localization in PL/SQL** ................................... **1031**
Overview and Terminology ............................................. 1033
Unicode Primer ....................................................... 1034
National Character Set Datatypes ..................................... 1036
Character Encoding .................................................. 1036
Globalization Support Parameters .................................... 1037
Unicode Functions ................................................... 1038
Character Semantics ................................................... 1045
String Sort Order ..................................................... 1049
Binary Sort ......................................................... 1049
Monolingual Sort .................................................... 1050
Multilingual Sort ................................................... 1052
Multilingual Information Retrieval ..................................... 1054
IR and PL/SQL ...................................................... 1056
Date/Time ............................................................ 1059
Timestamp Datatypes ................................................ 1059
Date/Time Formatting ............................................... 1060
Currency Conversion .................................................. 1064
Globalization Development Kit for PL/SQL ............................. 1066
UTL_I18N Utility Package ............................................ 1066
UTL_LMS Error-Handling Package ................................... 1069
GDK Implementation Options ........................................ 1070

**26. Object-Oriented Aspects of PL/SQL** ...................................... **1073**
Introduction to Oracle's Object Features .............................. 1073
Object Types by Example .............................................. 1076

Creating a Base Type                                                      1076
Creating a Subtype                                                        1078
Methods                                                                   1079
Invoking Supertype Methods in Oracle Database 11g                         1084
Storing, Retrieving, and Using Persistent Objects                        1085
Evolution and Creation                                                    1093
Back to Pointers?                                                         1095
Generic Data: The ANY Types                                              1102
I Can Do It Myself                                                        1106
Comparing Objects                                                        1110
Object Views                                                              1115
A Sample Relational System                                               1116
Object View with a Collection Attribute                                  1118
Object Subview                                                            1121
Object View with Inverse Relationship                                    1122
INSTEAD OF Triggers                                                      1123
Differences Between Object Views and Object Tables                       1125
Maintaining Object Types and Object Views                                1127
Data Dictionary                                                          1127
Privileges                                                               1128
Concluding Thoughts from a (Mostly) Relational Developer                 1130

A.  Regular Expression Metacharacters and Function Parameters . . . . . . . . . . . . . . .  1133

B.  Number Format Models . . . . . . . . . . . . . . . . . . . . . . . . . . . . . . . . . . . . . . . . . .  1139

C.  Date Format Models . . . . . . . . . . . . . . . . . . . . . . . . . . . . . . . . . . . . . . . . . . . .  1143

Index . . . . . . . . . . . . . . . . . . . . . . . . . . . . . . . . . . . . . . . . . . . . . . . . . . . . . . . . . . .  1149

# Preface

Millions of application developers and database administrators around the world use software provided by Oracle Corporation to build complex systems that manage vast quantities of data. At the heart of much of Oracle's software is PL/SQL—a programming language that provides procedural extensions to Oracle's version of SQL (Structured Query Language) and serves as the programming language within the Oracle Developer toolset (most notably Forms Developer and Reports Developer).

PL/SQL figures prominently as an enabling technology in almost every new product released by Oracle Corporation. Software professionals use PL/SQL to perform many kinds of programming functions, including:

- Implementing crucial business rules in the Oracle Server with PL/SQL-based stored procedures and database triggers
- Generating and managing XML documents entirely within the database
- Linking web pages to an Oracle database
- Implementing and automating database administration tasks—from establishing row-level security to managing rollback segments within PL/SQL programs

PL/SQL was modeled after Ada,[1] a programming language designed for the U.S. Department of Defense. Ada is a high-level language that emphasizes data abstraction, information hiding, and other key elements of modern design strategies. As a result of this very smart design decision by Oracle, PL/SQL is a powerful language that incorporates many of the most advanced elements of procedural languages, including:

- A full range of datatypes from number to string, and including complex data structures such as records (which are similar to rows in a relational table), collections (which are Oracle's version of arrays), and XMLType (for managing XML documents in Oracle and through PL/SQL)

---

[1]. The language was named "Ada" in honor of Ada Lovelace, a mathematician who is regarded by many to have been the world's first computer programmer. Visit *http://www.adahome.com* for more information about Ada.

- An explicit and highly readable block structure that makes it easy to enhance and maintain PL/SQL applications
- Conditional, iterative, and sequential control statements, including a CASE statement and three different kinds of loops
- Exception handlers for use in event-based error handling
- Named, reusable code elements such as functions, procedures, triggers, object types (akin to object-oriented classes), and packages (collections of related programs and variables)

PL/SQL is integrated tightly into Oracle's SQL language: you can execute SQL statements directly from your procedural program without having to rely on any kind of intermediate API (Application Programming Interface) such as JDBC (Java Database Connectivity) or ODBC (Open Database Connectivity). Conversely, you can also call your own PL/SQL functions from within a SQL statement.

Oracle developers who want to be successful in the 21st century must learn to use PL/SQL to full advantage. This is a two-step process. First, you must become familiar with and learn how to use the language's ever-expanding set of features; and second, after gaining competence in the individual features, you must learn how to put these constructs together to build complex applications.

For these reasons and more, Oracle developers need a solid, comprehensive resource for the base PL/SQL language. You need to know the basic building blocks of PL/SQL, but you also need to learn by example so that you can avoid some of the trial and error. As with any programming language, PL/SQL has a right way and many wrong ways (or at least "not as right" ways) to handle just about any task. It is my hope that this book will help you learn how to use the PL/SQL language in the most effective and efficient way possible.

## Objectives of This Book

What, specifically, will this book help you do?

*Take full advantage of PL/SQL*

Oracle's reference manuals may describe all the features of the PL/SQL language, but they don't tell you how to apply the technology. In fact, in some cases, you'll be lucky to even understand how to use a given feature after you've made your way through the railroad diagrams. Books and training courses tend to cover the same standard topics in the same limited way. In this book, I'll venture beyond the basics to the far reaches of the language, finding the nonstandard ways that a particular feature can be tweaked to achieve a desired result.

*Use PL/SQL to solve your problems*

You don't spend your days and nights writing PL/SQL modules so that you can rise to a higher plane of existence. You use PL/SQL to solve problems for your company or your customers. In this book, I try hard to help you tackle real-world problems, the kinds of issues developers face on a daily basis (at least those problems that can be solved with mere software). To do this, I've packed the book with examples—not just small code fragments, but substantial application components that you can apply immediately to your own situations. There is a good deal of code in the book itself, and much more on the accompanying web site. In a number of cases, I use the code examples to guide you through the analytical process needed to come up with a solution. In this way you'll see, in the most concrete terms, how to apply PL/SQL features and undocumented applications of those features to a particular situation.

*Write efficient, maintainable code*

PL/SQL and the rest of the Oracle products offer the potential for incredible development productivity. If you aren't careful, however, this capability will simply let you dig yourself into a deeper, darker hole than you've ever found yourself in before. I would consider this book a failure if it only helped programmers write more code in less time; I want to help you develop the skills and techniques to build applications that readily adapt to change and that are easily understood and maintained. I want to teach you to use comprehensive strategies and code architectures that allow you to apply PL/SQL in powerful, general ways to the problems you face.

## Structure of This Book

Both the authors and O'Reilly Media are committed to providing comprehensive, useful coverage of PL/SQL over the life of the language. This fifth edition of *Oracle PL/SQL Programming* describes the features and capabilities of PL/SQL up through Oracle Database 11*g* Release 2. I assume for this edition that Oracle Database 11*g* is the baseline PL/SQL version. However, where appropriate, I reference specific features introduced (or only available) in other, earlier versions. For a list of the main characteristics of the various releases, see the section "About PL/SQL Versions" on page 10 in Chapter 1.

PL/SQL has improved dramatically since the release of Version 1.0 in the Oracle 6 database so many years ago. *Oracle PL/SQL Programming* has also undergone a series of major transformations to keep up with PL/SQL and provide ever-improving coverage of its features.

The fifth edition offers the following new content:

*Oracle Database 11g new features for PL/SQL*

As explained above, this book incorporates all new PL/SQL features in Oracle Database 11*g* Releases 1 and 2. The major features are summarized in Chapter 1, along with references to the chapters where these features are discussed in detail.

*Optimizing PL/SQL Performance*

Chapter 21 is new in the fifth edition. It collects together previous content in this book on optimizing the performance of PL/SQL code, and then adds lots of new information not previously available in *Oracle PL/SQL Programming*.

I am very happy with the results and hope that you will be too. There is more information than ever before, but I think we managed to present it without losing that "trademark" sense of humor and conversational tone that readers have told me for years make the book readable, understandable, and highly useful.

One comment regarding the "voice" behind the text. You may notice that in some parts of this book we use the word "we," and in others "I." One characteristic of this book (and one for which readers have expressed appreciation) is the personal voice that's inseparable from the text. Consequently, even with the addition of coauthors to the book (and, in the third, fourth, and fifth editions, significant contributions from several other people), we've decided to maintain the use of "I" when an author speaks in his own voice.

Rather than leave you guessing as to which lead author is represented by the "I" in a given chapter, we thought we'd offer this quick guide for the curious; you'll find additional discussion of our contributors under the Acknowledgments.

| Chapter | Author | Chapter | Author |
|---------|--------|---------|--------|
| Preface | Steven | 15 | Steven |
| 1 | Steven | 16 | Steven |
| 2 | Bill and Steven | 17 | Steven |
| 3 | Steven and Bill | 18 | Steven |
| 4 | Steven, Chip, and Jonathan | 19 | Darryl and Steven |
| 5 | Steven and Bill | 20 | Steven |
| 6 | Steven | 21 | Steven and Adrian |
| 7 | Chip, Jonathan, and Steven | 22 | Bill and Steven |
| 8 | Chip, Jonathan, and Steven | 23 | Arup |
| 9 | Chip, Jonathan, and Steven | 24 | Bill, Steven, and Chip |
| 10 | Chip, Jonathan, and Steven | 25 | Ron |
| 11 | Steven | 26 | Bill and Steven |
| 12 | Steven and Bill | 27 | Bill and Steven |
| 13 | Chip and Jonathan | 28 | Bill and Steven |
| 14 | Steven | | |

# About the Contents

The fifth edition of *Oracle PL/SQL Programming* is divided into six parts:

Part I, *Programming in PL/SQL*

I start from the very beginning in Chapter 1: where did PL/SQL come from? What is it good for? I offer a very quick review of some of the main features of the PL/SQL language. Chapter 2 is designed to help you get PL/SQL programs up and running as quickly as possible: it contains clear, straightforward instructions for executing PL/SQL code in SQL*Plus and a few other common environments. Chapter 3 reviews fundamentals of the PL/SQL language: what makes a PL/SQL statement, an introduction to the block structure, how to write comments in PL/SQL, and so on.

Part II, *PL/SQL Program Structure*

Chapter 4 through Chapter 6 explore conditional (IF and CASE) and sequential (GOTO and NULL control statements; loops and the CONTINUE statement introduced for loops in Oracle Database 11g; and exception handling in the PL/SQL language. This section of the book will teach you to construct blocks of code that correlate to the complex requirements of your applications.

Part III, *PL/SQL Program Data*

Just about every program you write will manipulate data, and much of that data will be local to (defined in) your PL/SQL procedure or function. Chapter 7 through Chapter 13 concentrate on the various types of program data you can define in PL/SQL, such as numbers, strings, dates, timestamps, records, and collections. You will learn about the new datatypes introduced in Oracle Database 11g (SIMPLE_INTEGER, SIMPLE_FLOAT, and SIMPLE_DOUBLE), as well as the many binary, date, and timestamp types introduced in other recent releases. These chapters also cover the various built-in functions provided by Oracle that allow you to manipulate and modify data.

Part IV, *SQL in PL/SQL*

Chapter 14 through Chapter 16 address one of the central elements of PL/SQL code construction: the connection to the underlying database, which takes place through the SQL language. These chapters show you how to define transactions that update, insert, merge, and delete tables in the database; how to query information from the database for processing in a PL/SQL program; and how to execute SQL statements dynamically, using native dynamic SQL (NDS).

Part V, *PL/SQL Application Construction*

This is where it all comes together. You know about declaring and working with variables, and you're an expert in error handling and loop construction. Now, in Chapter 17 through Chapter 22, you'll learn about the building blocks of applications, which include procedures, functions, packages, and triggers, and how to move information into and out of PL/SQL programs. Chapter 20 discusses managing your PL/SQL code base, including testing and debugging programs and managing dependencies; it also provides an overview of the edition-based redefinition capability introduced in Oracle Database 11g Release 2. Chapter 21, new in the fifth edition, focuses on how you can use a variety of tools and techniques to get the best performance out of your PL/SQL programs. Chapter 22 covers I/O techniques for PL/SQL, from DBMS_OUTPUT (writing output to the screen) and UTL_FILE (reading and writing files) to UTL_MAIL (sending mail) and UTL_HTTP (retrieving data from a web page).

Part VI, *Advanced PL/SQL Topics*

A language as mature and rich as PL/SQL is full of features that you may not use on a day-to-day basis, but that may make the crucial difference between success and failure. Chapter 23 explores the security-related challenges we face as we build PL/SQL programs. Chapter 24 contains an exploration of the PL/SQL architecture, including PL/SQL's use of memory. Chapter 25 provides guidance for PL/SQL developers who need to address issues of globalization and localization. Chapter 26 offers a guide to the object-oriented features of Oracle (object types and object views).

Appendixes A through C summarize the details of regular expression syntax and number and date formats.

In this fifth edition, the chapters on invoking Java and C code from PL/SQL applications, which were part of the hardcopy fourth edition, have been moved to the book's web site.

If you are new to PL/SQL, reading this book from beginning to end should improve your PL/SQL skills and deepen your understanding of the language. If you're already a proficient PL/SQL programmer, you'll probably want to dip into the appropriate sections to extract particular techniques for immediate application. Whether you use this book as a teaching guide or as a reference, I hope it will help you use PL/SQL effectively.

## What This Book Does Not Cover

Long as this book is, it doesn't contain everything. The Oracle environment is huge and complex, and in this book we've focused our attention on the core PL/SQL language itself. The following topics are therefore outside the scope of this book and are not covered, except in an occasional and peripheral fashion:

*The SQL language*

I assume that you already have a working knowledge of the SQL language, and that you know how to write SELECTs, UPDATEs, INSERTs, MERGEs, and DELETEs.

*Administration of Oracle databases*

While database administrators (DBAs) can use this book to learn how to write the PL/SQL needed to build and maintain databases, this book does not explore all the nuances of the Data Definition Language (DDL) of Oracle's SQL.

*Application and database tuning*

I don't cover detailed tuning issues in this book, although Chapter 21 does discuss the many tools and techniques that will help you to optimize the performance of your PL/SQL programs.

*Oracle tool-specific technologies independent of PL/SQL*

This book does not attempt to show you how to build applications in a tool like Oracle's Forms Developer, even though the implementation language is PL/SQL. I have chosen to focus on core language capabilities, centered on what you can do with PL/SQL from within the database. However, most everything covered in this book is applicable to PL/SQL inside Forms Developer and Reports Developer.

## Conventions Used in This Book

The following conventions are used in this book:

*Italic*

Used for file and directory names and for emphasis when introducing a new term.

`Constant width`

Used for code examples.

**`Constant width bold`**

Indicates user input in examples showing an interaction. Also, in some code examples, highlights the statements being discussed.

`Constant width italic`

In some code examples, indicates an element (e.g., a parameter) that you supply.

*UPPERCASE*

In code examples, generally indicates PL/SQL keywords or certain identifiers used by Oracle Corporation as built-in function and package names.

*lowercase*

In code examples, generally indicates user-defined items such as variables, parameters, etc.

*Punctuation*

In code examples, enter exactly as shown.

*Indentation*

In code examples, helps to show structure but is not required.

--

In code examples, a double hyphen begins a single-line comment that extends to the end of a line.

*/\* and \*/*

In code examples, these characters delimit a multiline comment that can extend from one line to another.

*.*

In code examples and related discussions, a dot qualifies a reference by separating an object name from a component name. For example, dot notation is used to select fields in a record and to specify declarations within a package.

[ ]

In syntax descriptions, square brackets enclose optional items.

{ }

In syntax descriptions, curly brackets enclose a set of items from which you must choose only one.

|

In syntax descriptions, a vertical bar separates the items enclosed in curly brackets, as in {TRUE | FALSE}.

...

In syntax descriptions, ellipses indicate repeating elements. An ellipsis also shows that statements or clauses irrelevant to the discussion were left out.

Indicates a tip, suggestion, or general note. For example, I'll tell you if a certain setting is version-specific.

Indicates a warning or caution. For example, I'll tell you if a certain setting has some kind of negative impact on the system.

# Which Platform or Version?

In general, all the discussions and examples in this book apply regardless of the machine and/or operating system you are using. In those cases in which a feature is in any way version-dependent—for example, if you can use it only in Oracle Database 11*g* (or in a specific release such as Oracle Database 11*g* Release 2)—I note that in the text.

There are many versions of PL/SQL, and you may find that you need to use multiple versions in your development work. Chapter 1 describes the various versions of PL/SQL and what you should know about them; see "About PL/SQL Versions" on page 10.

# About the Code

All of the code referenced in this book is available from:

> *http://www.oreilly.com/catalog/9780596514464*

Click on the Examples link to go to the book's web companion. You will also find information about all of Steven's books and accompanying resources at:

> *http://www.stevenfeuerstein.com/*

As mentioned earlier, you will also find the contents of some of the chapters from earlier editions that we removed or condensed in the different editions of the book. These may be especially helpful to readers who are running older versions of Oracle.

You might also want to visit PL/SQL Obsession (Steven Feuerstein's PL/SQL portal) at:

> *http://www.ToadWorld.com/SF*

where you will find training materials, code downloads, and more.

To find a particular example on the book's web site, look for the filename cited in the text. For many examples, you will find filenames in the following form provided as a comment at the beginning of the example shown in the book, as illustrated here:

```
/* File on web: fullname.pkg */
```

If the code snippet in which you are interested does not have a "File on web" comment, then you should check the corresponding chapter code file.

A chapter code file contains all the code fragments and examples that do not merit their own file, but may prove useful to you for copy-and-paste operations. These files also contain the DDL statements to create tables and other objects on which the code may depend.

Each chapter code file is named *chNN_code.sql*, where *NN* is the number of the chapter.

Finally, the *hr_schema_install.sql* script will create the standard Oracle Human Resources demonstration tables, such as employees and departments. These tables are used in examples throughout the book.

# Using Code Examples

This book is here to help you get your job done. In general, you may use the code in this book in your programs and documentation. You do not need to contact us for permission unless you're reproducing a significant portion of the code. For example, writing a program that uses several chunks of code from this book does not require permission. Answering a question by citing this book and quoting example code does not require permission. On the other hand, selling or distributing a CD-ROM of examples from O'Reilly books does require permission. Incorporating a significant amount of example code from this book into your product's documentation does require permission.

We appreciate, but do not require, attribution. An attribution usually includes the title, author, publisher, and ISBN. For example: *Oracle PL/SQL Programming*, Fifth Edition, by Steven Feuerstein with Bill Pribyl. Copyright 2009 Steven Feuerstein and Bill Pribyl, 978-0-596-51446-4.

If you think your use of code examples falls outside fair use or the permission given here, feel free to contact us at *permissions@oreilly.com*.

## Safari® Books Online

Safari Books Online is an on-demand digital library that lets you easily search over 7,500 technology and creative reference books and videos to find the answers you need quickly.

With a subscription, you can read any page and watch any video from our library online. Read books on your cell phone and mobile devices. Access new titles before they are available for print, and get exclusive access to manuscripts in development and post feedback for the authors. Copy and paste code samples, organize your favorites, download chapters, bookmark key sections, create notes, print out pages, and benefit from tons of other time-saving features.

O'Reilly Media has uploaded this book to the Safari Books Online service. To have full digital access to this book and others on similar topics from O'Reilly and other publishers, sign up for free at *http://my.safaribooksonline.com*.

## Comments and Questions

We have tested and verified the information in this book and in the source code to the best of our ability, but given the amount of text and the rapid evolution of technology, you may find that features have changed or that we have made mistakes. If so, please notify us by writing to:

O'Reilly Media, Inc.
1005 Gravenstein Highway
Sebastopol, CA 95472
800-998-9938 (in the United States or Canada)
707-829-0515 (international or local)
707-829-0104 (fax)

You can also send messages electronically. To be put on the mailing list or request a catalog, send email to:

*info@oreilly.com*

To ask technical questions or comment on the book, send email to:

> *bookquestions@oreilly.com*

As mentioned in the previous section, we have a web site for this book where you can find code, updated links, chapters from previous editions of the book, and errata (previously reported errors and corrections are available for public view). You can access this web site at:

> *http://www.oreilly.com/catalog/9780596514464*

For more information about this book and others, see the O'Reilly web site:

> *http://www.oreilly.com*

# Acknowledgments

Since *Oracle PL/SQL Programming* was first published in 1995, it has had a busy and productive history as the "go to" text on how to use the PL/SQL language. For that, I first of all express our appreciation to all our readers.

Maintaining *Oracle PL/SQL Programming* as an accurate, readable, and up-to-date reference to PL/SQL has been, from the start, a big (all right, I admit it—sometimes overwhelming) job; it certainly would not have been possible without the help of many Oracle specialists, friends, and family, and of course the incredible staff at O'Reilly Media.

You will find below rather detailed thank yous for those who helped pull together the fifth edition of *Oracle PL/SQL Programming*. Following that, you will find an acknowledgment of the many people who were instrumental in the earlier editions.

First and foremost, I thank those who contributed chapters and/or substantial content for the book; listed alphabetically, they are Adrian Billington, Chip Dawes, Jonathan Gennick, Ron Hardman, Darryl Hurley, and Arup Nanda. As of this edition, Chip Dawes has taken over responsibility for updating a half-dozen chapters. Jonathan wrote or substantially updated six chapters in past editions. Darryl has updated the fine chapter on database triggers for several editions and contributed insights on Oracle's internationalization features. Arup Nanda wrote the excellent chapter on security. Ron Hardman stepped up to the plate and wrote the chapter on globalization and localization. Adrian Billington provided excellent material in Chapter 21 on pipelined table functions.

New to the fifth edition, I have also invited each of our contributors to say a few words about themselves:

**Adrian Billington** is a consultant in application design, development, and performance tuning who has been working with Oracle databases since 1999. He is the man behind *oracle-developer.net*, a web site full of SQL and PL/SQL features, utilities, and techniques for Oracle developers. Adrian is also an Oracle ACE and a member of the

OakTable Network. He would like to thank James Padfield (Padders), Tom Kyte, and Steven Feuerstein for inspiring him to become a better developer during his impressionable early years as an Oracle professional. He lives in the UK with his wife Anji and three children, Georgia, Oliver, and Isabella.

**Chip Dawes** has been building and maintaining systems on relational databases since 1988 and with Oracle since 1990. He is currently a consultant with Piocon Technologies, a Chicago-based consultancy. He enjoys working with, lecturing on, and writing about Oracle database administration, PL/SQL programming, and Business Intelligence systems. Chip is an Oracle Certified Professional and has earned computer science and aerospace engineering degrees from St. Louis University.

**Jonathan Gennick** is an experienced technology professional who is well-known for his Oracle database expertise. His past experience encompasses both software development and database administration. As a developer, he has always enjoyed troubleshooting and debugging. He loves working with SQL and PL/SQL, and is well-known for his books and articles on those topics. In his off hours, Jonathan enjoys a rather low-tech approach to life. He serves actively in his local church where you'll often find him putting together crazy props such as floor-sized crossword puzzles for the class he teaches each week. He is an avid mountain-biker, riding even in the dead of winter on very cool, studded bicycle tires imported from Finland. He assists in cooking lunch at his local school. And he serves his local community as an Emergency Medical Technician for the Alger County Ambulance Service.

**Ron Hardman** owns AcademyOnDemand.NET, a software company for the K-12 education community. He also consults around the world on Oracle Text and Oracle globalization technologies, and has been working with Oracle both as an employee and as a customer for more than 13 years. Ron is an Oracle ACE and teaches Oracle Text, Application Express (APEX), and PL/SQL classes at his offices in Colorado Springs, Colorado. He enjoys writing about more than technology, and he will release his first historical fiction title in the spring of 2010 through his FoxRunPress.com publishing company.

**Darryl Hurley** has been working with Oracle technology for 20-plus years, focusing on PL/SQL and DBA work. He lives in Richmond, BC, Canada with his lovely wife Vanessa and beautiful daughter Bianca. He can be reached at *opp@implestrat.com*.

**Arup Nanda** has been an Oracle DBA since 1993, touching all aspects of the job—modeling, performance troubleshooting, PL/SQL coding, backups, disaster recovery, and more. He works as a Lead DBA at a major corporation, has written about 300 articles, coauthored four books, and presented several times at conferences. He offers training sessions, engages in special projects like audits and DR, and writes about Oracle technology. He was *Oracle Magazine*'s 2003 DBA of the Year and is an OCP, an OTN ACE Director, and a member of the OakTable Network. He lives in Connecticut, USA, with his wife Anu and son Anish.

With such a big book, we needed lots of reviewers, especially because we asked them to test each code snippet and program in the book to keep to an absolute minimum the number of errors that made it into the printed version. I am deeply grateful to the following men and women of the Oracle PL/SQL world, who took time away from the rest of their lives to help make *Oracle PL/SQL Programming* the best book that it could be.

For this fifth edition, I first thank our full-book reviewers: Robert A. G. Cook and Edward Wiles. They actually read and reviewed all the chapters and measurably improved the quality of the book.

Next, I offer my deep appreciation to Bryn Llewellyn, Oracle's PL/SQL Product Manager, and other members of the PL/SQL development team, most notably Charles Wetherell. Bryn provided crucial information and feedback on Oracle Database 11g's new features and answered endless questions about various PL/SQL features with bottomless patience. There is no doubt that my understanding of PL/SQL and the accuracy with which I present it owe a great debt to Bryn.

I also give thanks to our other, deeply appreciated technical reviewers: Patrick Barel, Daniel Cronk, Shelley Johnson, Dwayne King, Andrew McIlwrick, Dan Norris, Alex Nuijten, Drew Smith, Mark Vilrokx, and Daniel Wong. From a non-Oracle perspective, grateful thoughts go to Joel Finkel, my favorite jack-of-all-trades who makes up for the narrow specialization that simultaneously benefits and constrains my capabilities when it comes to computers and software.

Of course, that's just the technical content. Once I feel that we've got our treatment of PL/SQL "right," it's time for the remarkable crew at O'Reilly Media, led by my good friend, Deborah Russell, to transform our many chapters and code examples into a book worthy of the O'Reilly imprint. Many thanks to Julie Steele, editor and Loranah Dimant, production editor for the book; Rob Romano, who created the excellent figures; and the rest of the crew.

I have now had the pleasure and honor of working with Deborah Russell for 16 years, since I started cranking out pages for the first edition of *Oracle PL/SQL Programming* back in 1993. Surely, Debby, you must know more about PL/SQL than almost any developer in the world. If you ever need a programming job, be sure to give me a call! It has been a real joy to work with Debby, and I look forward to producing at least ten more editions of this book with her guiding the way.

And here are the many people we thanked (and continue to be grateful to) for their contributions to the first four editions of this book:

Sohaib Abassi, Steve Adams, Don Bales, Cailein Barclay, John Beresniewicz, Tom Berthoff, Sunil Bhargava, Jennifer Blair, Dick Bolz, Bryan Boulton, Per Brondum, Boris Burshteyn, Eric Camplin, Joe Celko, Gary Cernosek, Barry Chase, Geoff Chester, Ivan Chong, Dan Clamage, Gray Clossman, Avery Cohen, John Cordell, Steve Cosner, Tony Crawford, Ervan Darnell, Lex de Haan, Thomas Dunbar, Bill Dwight, Steve Ehrlich,

Larry Elkins, Bruce Epstein, R. James Forsythe, Mike Gangler, Beverly Gibson, Steve Gillis, Eric Givler, Rick Greenwald, Radhakrishna Hari, Gerard Hartgers, Donald Herkimer, Steve Hilker, Bill Hinman, Gabriel Hoffman, Chandrasekharan Iyer, Ken Jacobs, Hakan Jakobsson, Giovanni Jaramillo, Dwayne King, Marcel Kratochvil, Thomas Kurian, Tom Kyte, Ben Lindsey, Peter Linsley, Vadim Loevski, Leo Lok, Debra Luik, James Mallory, Raj Mattamal, Nimish Mehta, Ari Mozes, Steve Muench, Jeff Muller, Kannan Muthukkaruppan, James Padfield, Rakesh Patel, Karen Peiser, Fred Polizo, Dave Posner, Patrick Pribyl, Nancy Priest, Shirish Puranik, Chris Racicot, Sri Rajan, Mark Richter, Chris Rimmer, Alex Romankevich, Bert Scalzo, Pete Schaffer, Scott Sowers, JT Thomas, David Thompson, Edward Van Hatten, Peter Vasterd, Andre Vergison, Zona Walcott, Bill Watkins, Charles Wetherell, Solomon Yakobson, Ming Hui Yang, and Tony Ziemba.

Finally, I thank my wife, Veva Silva, and two sons, Christopher Tavares Silva and Eli Silva Feuerstein, for their support and tolerance of so much of my time and attention.

# Programming in PL/SQL

This first part of this book introduces PL/SQL, explains how to create and run PL/SQL code, and presents language fundamentals. Chapter 1 asks the fundamental questions: Where did PL/SQL come from? What is it good for? What are the main features of the PL/SQL language? Chapter 2 is designed to get you and up and running PL/SQL programs as quickly as possible; it contains clear, straightforward instructions for executing PL/SQL code in SQL*Plus and a few other common environments. Chapter 3 answers basic questions about the language structure and keywords: What makes up a PL/SQL statement? What is the PL/SQL block structure all about? How do I write comments in PL/SQL?

Chapter 1, *Introduction to PL/SQL*
Chapter 2, *Creating and Running PL/SQL Code*
Chapter 3, *Language Fundamentals*

# Introduction to PL/SQL

PL/SQL stands for "Procedural Language extensions to the Structured Query Language." SQL is the now-ubiquitous language for both querying *and* updating—never mind the name—of relational databases. Oracle Corporation introduced PL/SQL to overcome some limitations in SQL and to provide a more complete programming solution for those who sought to build mission-critical applications to run against the Oracle database. This chapter introduces PL/SQL, its origins, and its various versions. It offers a quick summary of PL/SQL in the latest Oracle releases, Oracle Database 11*g* Release 1 and Release 2. Finally, it provides a guide to additional resources for PL/SQL developers and some words of advice.

## What Is PL/SQL?

Oracle's PL/SQL language has several defining characteristics:

*It is a highly structured, readable, and accessible language*
> If you are new to programming, PL/SQL is a great place to start. You will find that it is an easy language to learn and is rich with keywords and structure that clearly express the intent of your code. If you are experienced in other programming languages, you will very easily adapt to the new syntax.

*It is a standard and portable language for Oracle development*
> If you write a PL/SQL procedure or function to execute from within the Oracle database sitting on your laptop, you can move that same procedure to a database on your corporate network and execute it there without any changes (assuming compatibility of Oracle versions, of course!). "Write once, run everywhere" was the mantra of PL/SQL long before Java appeared. For PL/SQL, though, "everywhere" means "everywhere there is an Oracle database."

*It is an embedded language*
> PL/SQL was not designed to be used as a standalone language, but instead to be invoked from within a host environment. So, for example, you can run PL/SQL programs from within the database (through, say, the SQL*Plus interface).

Alternatively, you can define and execute PL/SQL programs from within an Oracle Developer form or report (this approach is called *client-side PL/SQL*). You cannot, however, create a PL/SQL executable that runs all by itself.

*It is a high-performance, highly integrated database language*

These days, you have a number of choices when it comes to writing software to run against the Oracle database. You can use Java and JDBC; you can use Visual Basic and ODBC; you can go with Delphi, C++, and so on. You will find, however, that it is easier to write highly efficient code to access the Oracle database in PL/SQL than it is in any other language. In particular, Oracle offers certain PL/SQL-specific enhancements such as the FORALL statement that can improve database performance by an order of magnitude or more.

# The Origins of PL/SQL

Oracle Corporation has a history of leading the software industry in providing declarative, non-procedural approaches to designing both databases and applications. The Oracle Server technology is among the most advanced, powerful, and stable relational databases in the world. Its application development tools, such as Oracle Forms, offer high levels of productivity by relying heavily on a "paint-your-screen" approach in which extensive default capabilities allow developers to avoid heavy customized programming efforts.

## The Early Years of PL/SQL

In Oracle's early years, the declarative approach of SQL, combined with its groundbreaking relational technology, was enough to satisfy developers. But as the industry matured, expectations rose, and requirements became more stringent. Developers needed to get "under the skin" of the products. They needed to build complicated formulas, exceptions, and rules into their forms and database scripts.

In 1988, Oracle Corporation released Oracle Version 6, a major advance in its relational database technology. A key component of that version was the so-called "procedural option" or PL/SQL. At roughly the same time, Oracle released its long-awaited upgrade to SQL*Forms Version 2.3 (the original name for the product now known as Oracle Forms or Forms Developer). SQL*Forms V3.0 incorporated the PL/SQL engine for the first time on the tools side, allowing developers to code their procedural logic in a natural, straightforward manner.

This first release of PL/SQL was very limited in its capabilities. On the server side, you could use PL/SQL only to build "batch-processing" scripts of procedural and SQL statements. You could not construct a modular application or store business rules in the server. On the client side, SQL*Forms V3.0 did allow you to create procedures and functions, although support for functions was not documented, and was therefore not used by many developers for years. In addition, this release of PL/SQL did not implement array support and could not interact with the operating system (for input or output). It was a far cry from a full-fledged programming language.

But for all its limitations, PL/SQL was warmly, even enthusiastically, received in the developer community. The hunger for the ability to code a simple IF statement inside SQL*Forms was strong. The need to perform multi-SQL statement batch processing was overwhelming.

What few developers realized at the time was that the original motivation and driving vision behind PL/SQL extended beyond the desire for programmatic control within products like SQL*Forms. Very early in the life cycle of Oracle's database and tools, Oracle Corporation had recognized two key weaknesses in their architecture: lack of portability and problems with execution authority.

## Improved Application Portability

The concern about portability might seem odd to those of us familiar with Oracle Corporation's marketing and technical strategies. One of the hallmarks of the Oracle solution from the early 1980s was its portability. At the time that PL/SQL came along, the C-based database ran on many different operating systems and hardware platforms. SQL*Plus and SQL*Forms adapted easily to a variety of terminal configurations. Yet for all that coverage, there were still many applications that needed the more sophisticated and granular control offered by such host languages as COBOL, C, and FORTRAN. As soon as a developer stepped outside the port-neutral Oracle tools, the resulting application would no longer be portable.

The PL/SQL language was (and is) intended to widen the range of application requirements that can be handled entirely in operating system-independent programming tools. Today, Java and other programming languages offer similar portability. Yet PL/SQL stands out as an early pioneer in this field and, of course, it continues to allow developers to write highly portable application code.

## Improved Execution Authority and Transaction Integrity

An even more fundamental issue than portability was execution authority. The database and the SQL language let you tightly control access to, and changes in, any particular database table. For example, with the GRANT command, you can make sure that only certain roles and users can perform an UPDATE on a given table. On the other hand, this GRANT command can't ensure that the full set of UPDATEs performed by a user or application is done correctly. In other words, the database can't guarantee the integrity of a transaction that spans more than one table, as is common with most business transactions.

The PL/SQL language provides tight control and management over logical transactions. One way PL/SQL does this is with the implementation of execution authority. Instead of granting to a role or user the authority to update a table, you grant privileges only to execute a procedure, which controls and provides access to the underlying data structures. The procedure is owned by a different Oracle database schema (the "definer" of the program), which, in turn, is granted the actual update privileges on those tables needed to perform the transaction. The procedure therefore becomes the "gatekeeper" for the transaction. The only way that a program (whether it's an Oracle Forms application or a Pro*C executable) can execute the transfer is through the procedure. In this way, the overall application transaction integrity is guaranteed.

Starting with Oracle8i Database, Oracle added considerable flexibility to the execution authority model of PL/SQL by offering the AUTHID clause. With AUTHID, you can continue to run your programs under the definer rights model described earlier, or you can choose AUTHID CURRENT_USER (invoker rights), in which case the programs run under the authority of the invoking (current) schema. Invoker rights is just one example of how PL/SQL has matured and become more flexible over the years.

## Humble Beginnings, Steady Improvement

As powerful as SQL is, it simply does not offer the flexibility and power developers need to create full-blown applications. Oracle's PL/SQL language ensures that we can stay entirely within the operating system-independent Oracle environment and still write highly efficient applications that meet our users' requirements.

PL/SQL has come a long way from its humble beginnings. With PL/SQL 1.0, it was not uncommon for a developer to have to tell his or her manager, "You can't do that with PL/SQL." Today, that statement has moved from fact to excuse. If you are ever confronted with a requirement and find yourself saying, "There's no way to do that," please don't repeat it to your manager. Instead, dig deeper into the language, or explore the range of PL/SQL packages offered by Oracle. It is extremely likely that PL/SQL today will, in fact, allow you to do pretty much whatever you need to do.

Over the years, Oracle Corporation has demonstrated its commitment to PL/SQL, its flagship proprietary programming language. With every new release of the database, Oracle has also made steady, fundamental improvements to the PL/SQL language itself. It has added a great variety of supplied (or *built-in*) packages that extend the PL/SQL language in numerous ways and directions. It has introduced object-oriented capabilities, implemented a variety of array-like data structures, enhanced the compiler to both optimize our code and provide warnings about possible quality and performance issues, and in general improved the breadth and depth of the language.

The next section presents some examples of PL/SQL programs that will familiarize you with the basics of PL/SQL programming.

# So This Is PL/SQL

If you are completely new to programming or to working with PL/SQL (or even SQL, for that matter), learning PL/SQL may seem an intimidating prospect. If this is the case, don't fret! I am confident that you will find it easier than you think. There are two reasons for my optimism:

- Computer languages in general are not that hard to learn, at least compared to a second or third "human language." The reason? It's simply that computers are not particularly smart (they "think"—perform operations—rapidly, but not at all creatively). We must rely on a very rigid syntax in order to tell a computer what we want it to do. So the resulting language is also rigid (no exceptions!) and therefore easier for us to pick up.

- PL/SQL truly is an easy language, compared to other programming languages. It relies on a highly structured "block" design with different sections, all identified with explicit, self-documenting keywords.

Let's look at a few examples that demonstrate some key elements of both PL/SQL structure and functionality.

## Integration with SQL

One of the most important aspects of PL/SQL is its tight integration with SQL. You don't need to rely on any intermediate software "glue" such as ODBC (Open Database Connectivity) or JDBC (Java Database Connectivity) to run SQL statements in your PL/SQL programs. Instead, you just insert the UPDATE or SELECT into your code, as shown here:

```
 1   DECLARE
 2      l_book_count INTEGER;
 3
 4   BEGIN
 5      SELECT COUNT(*)
 6        INTO l_book_count
 7        FROM books
 8       WHERE author LIKE '%FEUERSTEIN, STEVEN%';
 9
10      DBMS_OUTPUT.PUT_LINE (
11         'Steven has written (or co-written) ' ||
12         l_book_count ||
13         ' books.');
14
15      -- Oh, and I changed my name, so...
16      UPDATE books
17         SET author = REPLACE (author, 'STEVEN', 'STEPHEN')
18       WHERE author LIKE '%FEUERSTEIN, STEVEN%';
19   END;
```

Let's take a more detailed look at this code in the following table:

| Line(s) | Description |
|---|---|
| 1–3 | This is the declaration section of this so-called "anonymous" PL/SQL block, in which I declare an integer variable to hold the number of books that I have authored or coauthored. (I'll say much more about the PL/SQL block structure in Chapter 3.) |
| 4 | The BEGIN keyword indicates the beginning of my execution section—the code that will be run when I pass this block to SQL*Plus. |
| 5–8 | I run a query to determine the total number of books I have authored or coauthored. Line 6 is of special interest: the INTO clause shown here is actually not part of the SQL statement but instead serves as the "bridge" from the database to local PL/SQL variables. |
| 10–13 | I use the DBMS_OUTPUT.PUT_LINE built-in procedure (i.e., a procedure in the DBMS_OUTPUT package supplied by Oracle) to display the number of books. |
| 15 | This single-line comment explains the purpose of the UPDATE. |
| 16–18 | I have decided to change the spelling of my first name to "Stephen", so I issue an update against the books table. I take advantage of the built-in REPLACE function to locate all instances of "STEVEN" and replace them with "STEPHEN". |

## Control and Conditional Logic

PL/SQL offers a full range of statements that allow us to very tightly control which lines of our programs execute. These statements include:

*IF and CASE statements*
 These implement conditional logic; for example, "If the page count of a book is greater than 1000, then...."

*A full complement of looping or iterative controls*
 These include the FOR loop, the WHILE loop, and the simple loop.

*The GOTO statement*
 Yes, PL/SQL even offers a GOTO that allows you to branch unconditionally from one part of your program to another. That doesn't mean, however, that you should actually *use* it.

Here is a procedure (a reusable block of code that can be called by name) that demonstrates some of these features:

```
1   PROCEDURE pay_out_balance (
2      account_id_in IN accounts.id%TYPE)
3   IS
4      l_balance_remaining NUMBER;
5   BEGIN
6      LOOP
7         l_balance_remaining := account_balance (account_id_in);
8
9         IF l_balance_remaining < 1000
10        THEN
11           EXIT;
12        ELSE
13           apply_balance (account_id_in, l_balance_remaining);
14        END IF;
```

```
15        END LOOP;
16   END pay_out_balance;
```

Let's take a more detailed look at this code in the following table:

| Line(s) | Description |
|---------|-------------|
| 1–2 | This is the header of a procedure that pays out the balance of an account to cover outstanding bills. Line 2 is the parameter list of the procedure, in this case consisting of a single incoming value (the identification number of the account). |
| 3–4 | This is the declaration section of the procedure. Notice that instead of using a DECLARE keyword, as in the previous example, the keyword IS (or AS) is used to separate the header from the declarations. |
| 6–15 | Here is an example of a simple loop. This loop relies on an EXIT statement (see line 11) to terminate the loop; FOR and WHILE loops specify the termination condition differently. |
| 7 | Here, I call to the account_balance function to retrieve the balance for this account. This is an example of a call to a reusable program within another reusable program. Line 13 demonstrates the calling of another procedure within this procedure. |
| 9–14 | Here is an IF statement that can be interpreted as follows: if the account balance has fallen below $1,000, stop allocating funds to cover bills. Otherwise, apply the balance to the next charge. |

## When Things Go Wrong

The PL/SQL language offers a powerful mechanism for both raising and handling errors. In the following procedure, I obtain the name and balance of an account from its ID. I then check to see if the balance is too low; if it is, I explicitly raise an exception, which stops my program from continuing:

```
 1   PROCEDURE check_account (
 2      account_id_in IN accounts.id%TYPE)
 3   IS
 4      l_balance_remaining       NUMBER;
 5      l_balance_below_minimum   EXCEPTION;
 6      l_account_name            accounts.name%TYPE;
 7   BEGIN
 8      SELECT name
 9        INTO l_account_name
10        FROM accounts
11       WHERE id = account_id_in;
12
13      l_balance_remaining := account_balance (account_id_in);
14
15      DBMS_OUTPUT.PUT_LINE (
16         'Balance for ' || l_account_name ||
17         ' = ' || l_balance_remaining);
18
19      IF l_balance_remaining < 1000
20      THEN
21         RAISE l_balance_below_minimum;
22      END IF;
23
24   EXCEPTION
```

```
25      WHEN NO_DATA_FOUND
26      THEN
27         -- No account found for this ID
28         log_error (...);
29
30      WHEN l_balance_below_minimum
31      THEN
32         log_error (...);
33         RAISE;
34   END;
```

Let's take a more detailed look at the error-handling aspects of this code in the following table:

| Line(s) | Description |
|---------|-------------|
| 5 | I declare my own exception, called l_balance_below_minimum. Oracle provides a set of predefined exceptions, such as DUP_VAL_ON_INDEX, but I need something specific to my application, so I must define it myself in this case. |
| 8–11 | This query retrieves the name for the account. If there is no account for this ID, the database raises the predefined NO_DATA_FOUND exception, causing the program to stop. |
| 19–22 | If the balance is too low, I explicitly raise my own exception because I have encountered a serious problem with this account. |
| 24 | The EXCEPTION keyword denotes the end of the executable section and the beginning of the exception section in which errors are handled. |
| 25–28 | This is the error-handling section for the situation in which the account is not found. If NO_DATA_FOUND was the exception raised, it is trapped here, and the error is logged with the log_error procedure. |
| 30–33 | This is the error-handling section for the situation in which the account balance has gotten too low (my application-specific exception). If l_balance_below_minimum is raised, it's trapped here, and the error is logged. Then, due to the seriousness of the error, I raise the same exception again, propagating that error out of the current procedure and into the PL/SQL block that called it. |

Chapter 6 takes you on an extensive tour of PL/SQL's error-handling mechanisms.

There is, of course, much more that can be said about PL/SQL—which is why you have hundreds more pages of material to study in this book! These initial examples should, however, give you a feel for the kind of code you will write with PL/SQL, some of its most important syntactical elements, and the ease with which one can write—and read—PL/SQL code.

# About PL/SQL Versions

Each version of the Oracle database comes with its own corresponding version of PL/SQL. As you use more up-to-date versions of PL/SQL, an increasing array of functionality will be available to you. One of our biggest challenges as PL/SQL programmers is simply "keeping up." We need to constantly educate ourselves about the new features in each version—figuring out how to use them and how to apply them to our applications, and determining which new techniques are so useful that we should modify existing applications to take advantage of them.

Table 1-1 summarizes the major elements in each of the versions (past and present) of PL/SQL in the database. (Note that in early versions of the database, PL/SQL version numbers differed from database release numbers, but since Oracle8 Database, they have been identical.) The table offers a very high-level glimpse of the new features available in each version. Following the table, you will find more detailed descriptions of "what's new" in PL/SQL in the latest Oracle version, Oracle Database 11g.

 The Oracle Developer product suite also comes with its own version of PL/SQL, and it generally lags behind the version available in the Oracle database itself. This chapter (and the book as a whole) concentrates on server-side PL/SQL programming.

*Table 1-1. Oracle database and corresponding PL/SQL versions*

| Oracle Database release | PL/SQL version highlights |
| --- | --- |
| 6.0 | The initial version of PL/SQL (1.0) was used primarily as a scripting language in SQL*Plus (it was not yet possible to create named, reusable, and callable programs) and also as a programming language in SQL*Forms 3. |
| 7.0 | This major upgrade (2.0) to PL/SQL 1.0 added support for stored procedures, functions, packages, programmer-defined records, PL/SQL tables (now known as collections), and many package extensions. |
| 7.1 | This PL/SQL version (2.1) supported programmer-defined subtypes, enabled the use of stored functions inside SQL statements, and offered dynamic SQL with the DBMS_SQL package. With PL/SQL 2.1, you could execute SQL DDL statements from within PL/SQL programs. |
| 7.3 | This PL/SQL version (2.3) provided enhanced functionality of collections, offered improved remote dependency management, added file I/O capabilities to PL/SQL with the UTL_FILE package, and completed the implementation of cursor variables. |
| 8.0 | The new version number (8.0) for PL/SQL reflected Oracle's effort to synchronize version numbers across related products. PL/SQL 8.0 is the version of PL/SQL that supported enhancements of Oracle8 Database, including large objects (LOBs), object-oriented design and development, collections (VARRAYs and nested tables), and the Oracle/Advanced Queuing facility (Oracle/AQ). |
| 8.1 | The first of Oracle's *i* series, the corresponding release of PL/SQL offered a truly impressive set of added functionality, including a new version of dynamic SQL, support for Java in the database, the invoker rights model, the execution authority option, autonomous transactions, and high-performance "bulk" DML and queries. |
| 9.1 | Oracle 9*i* Database Release 1 came fairly quickly on the heels of its predecessor. The first release of this version included support for inheritance in object types, table functions and cursor expressions (allowing for parallelization of PL/SQL function execution), multilevel collections, and the CASE statement and CASE expression. |
| 9.2 | Oracle 9*i* Database Release 2 put a major emphasis on XML (Extensible Markup Language) but also had some treats for PL/SQL developers, including associative arrays that can be indexed by VARCHAR2 strings in addition to integers, record-based DML (allowing you to perform an insert |

| Oracle Database release | PL/SQL version highlights |
|---|---|
| | using a record, for example), and many improvements to UTL_FILE (which allows you to read/write files from within a PL/SQL program). |
| 10.1 | Oracle Database 10g Release 1 was unveiled in 2004 and focused on support for grid computing, with an emphasis on improved/automated database management. From the standpoint of PL/SQL, the most important new features, an optimized compiler and compile-time warnings, were transparently available to developers: |
| 10.2 | Oracle Database 10g Release 2, released in 2005, offered a small number of new features for PL/SQL developers, most notably support for preprocessor syntax that allows you to conditionally compile portions of your program, depending on Boolean expressions you define. |
| 11.1 | Oracle Database 11g Release 1 arrived in 2007. The most important feature for PL/SQL developers was the function result cache, but there are also some other goodies like compound triggers, the CONTINUE statement, and native compilation that produces machine code. |
| 11.2 | Oracle Database 11g Release 2 became available in the fall of 2009. The most important new feature overall is the edition-based redefinition capability, which allow administrators to "hot patch" applications while they are being executed by users. |

## Oracle Database 11g New Features

Oracle Database 11g offers a number of new features that improve the performance and usability of PL/SQL. It also rounds out some "rough edges" of the language. Here is a summary of the most important changes for PL/SQL developers (all features are available in both Release 1 and Release 2 unless otherwise noted).

### Edition-based redefinition capability (Release 2 only)

Historically, applications built on Oracle Database had to be taken offline while the application's database objects were patched or upgraded. Oracle Database 11g Release 2 introduces revolutionary new capabilities that allow online application upgrades with uninterrupted availability of the application. Existing sessions can continue to use the pre-upgrade application until their users decide to finish; and, at the same time, new sessions can use the post-upgrade application. When there are no sessions using the pre-upgrade application any longer, it can be retired. The application as a whole therefore enjoys hot rollover from the pre-upgrade version to the post-upgrade version.

This new capability relies on a number of database features, but the biggest one is edition-based redefinition. While application architects will be responsible for most of the edition-based redefinition tasks, this capability will also be of great interest to developers.

The edition-based redefinition capability is introduced in Chapter 20.

### FORCE option with CREATE TYPE (Release 2 only)

You can now specify that you want to force the "CREATE OR REPLACE" of a new type, even if it has other types that depend on it. In earlier versions, such an attempt would raise the ORA-02303 exception.

See Chapter 26 for more information on the FORCE option.

### Function result cache

Prior to the release of Oracle Database 11g, package-based caching offered the best, most flexible option for caching data for use in a PL/SQL program. Sadly, the circumstances under which it can be used are quite limited, since the data source must be static, and memory consumption grows with each session connected to the Oracle database.

Recognizing the performance benefit of this kind of caching, Oracle implemented the function result cache in Oracle Database 11g Release 1 and enhanced it in Release 2. This feature offers a caching solution that overcomes the weaknesses of package-based caching and offers performance that is almost as fast. When you turn on the function result cache for a function, you get the following benefits:

- The Oracle database stores both inputs and the return value in a separate cache for each function. The cache is shared among all sessions connected to this instance of the database; it is *not* duplicated for each session.
- Whenever the function is called, the database checks to see if it has already cached the same input values. If so, then the function is not executed. The values in the cache are simply returned.
- Whenever changes are made to tables that are identified as dependencies for the cache, the database automatically invalidates the cache. Subsequent calls to the function will then repopulate the cache with consistent data.

You will definitely want to seek out opportunities to apply this outstanding feature, which is described in much more detail in Chapter 21.

### CONTINUE statement

Oracle Database 11g offers a new feature for loops: the CONTINUE statement. Use this statement to exit the current iteration of a loop and immediately continue on to the *next* iteration of that loop. This statement comes in two forms, just like EXIT: the unconditional CONTINUE and the conditional CONTINUE WHEN.

Here is a simple example of using CONTINUE WHEN to skip over loop body execution for even numbers:

```
BEGIN
   FOR l_index IN 1 .. 10
   LOOP
      CONTINUE WHEN MOD (l_index, 2) = 0;
```

```
      DBMS_OUTPUT.PUT_LINE ('Loop index = ' || TO_CHAR (l_index));
   END LOOP;
END;
```

The CONTINUE statement is described in detail in Chapter 5.

### Sequences in PL/SQL expressions

You can now reference the *sequence_name*.CURRVAL and *sequence_name*.NEXTVAL elements natively in PL/SQL. A SELECT FROM SYS.dual is no longer necessary.

See Chapter 14 for more details.

### Dynamic SQL enhancements

The PL/SQL development team has greatly increased the interoperability between the two types of dynamic SQL (DBMS_SQL and native dynamic SQL), as well as improved the completeness of feature coverage. You can, for example, now convert between a DBMS_SQL cursor number and a cursor variable. You can also EXECUTE IMMEDIATE a CLOB.

Oracle Database 11g also has enhanced the security of DBMS_SQL. The package now protects against the situation in which a program that uses DBMS_SQL and raises an exception allows an attacker to use the unclosed cursor to compromise the security of the database. Security enhancements include the generation of unpredictable (probably randomized) cursor numbers, restriction of the use of DBMS_SQL whenever an invalid cursor number is passed to a DBMS_SQL program, and rejection of a DBMS_SQL operation when the current user attempting to use the cursor has changed from the user that opened the cursor.

See Chapter 16 for information about these features.

### New native compilation and SIMPLE datatypes

The PL/SQL native compiler now generates native machine code directly, instead of translating PL/SQL code to C code and having the C compiler generate that machine code. Working with native compilation is now also simpler: an individual developer can compile PL/SQL units for native execution without any intervention by a DBA. With natively compiled code, you can expect to see substantial improvement in execution speed, perhaps by as much as an order of magnitude. With native compilation turned on, you can also benefit from improved performance with several new, specialized numeric datatypes: SIMPLE_INTEGER, SIMPLE_FLOAT, and SIMPLE_DOUBLE.

Native compilation is described in Chapter 24. The new numeric types are described in Chapter 9.

## SecureFiles

The terminology for the LOB implementation has changed in Oracle Database 11*g*. Oracle has re-engineered the implementation of LOBs using a technology called *SecureFiles*. SecureFiles improves many aspects of managing LOBs, including disk format, caching, locking, redo, and space management algorithms. This updated technology significantly improves performance and allows LOBs to be deduplicated, compressed, and encrypted using simple parameter settings.

For more information on using SecureFiles, see Chapters 13 and 23.

## Trigger enhancements

You can now create a *compound trigger* that allows you to combine what were previously distinct triggers (BEFORE and AFTER events) into a single body of code with separate event sections. This trigger will make it easier to maintain complex trigger logic, especially for mutating table trigger errors. You can also now explicitly specify the order of executions when you have more than one trigger defined on the same event (and the same database object).

Compound triggers are described in detail in Chapter 19.

## Automatic subprogram inlining

A new level of compiler optimization (3) now implements automated subprogram inlining, which means that the compiler replaces a local subprogram call (to a subprogram declared in the same PL/SQL unit) with a copy of the code implementing that subprogram. This optimization reduces runtime execution since a "lookup" to find and execute that subprogram is no longer needed.

Chapter 21 describes the optimization levels and other aspects of PL/SQL performance.

## PL/Scope

PL/Scope is a compiler-driven tool that collects and organizes data about user-defined identifiers from PL/SQL source code, and makes that information available through the ALL_IDENTIFIERS data dictionary view. PL/Scope makes it much easier to build automatic, sophisticated quality assurance and search processes for your applications. You will most likely take advantage of PL/Scope through the PL/SQL editor you are using, but you can also write (somewhat complex) queries against ALL_IDENTIFIERS to "mine" your code base.

See Chapter 20 for a more detailed description of PL/Scope.

### PL/SQL hierarchical profiler

In Oracle Database 11g, Oracle complements the existing PL/SQL Profiler (DBMS_PROFILER) with a new hierarchical profiler. By using the supplied DBMS_HPROF package, you can obtain information about the dynamic execution profile of your PL/SQL code, organized by *subprogram calls*. This profiler accounts for SQL and PL/SQL execution times separately. Each subprogram-level summary in the dynamic execution profile includes key data, including the number of calls to a subprogram, how much time is spent in the subprogram, how much time is spent in the subprogram's *subtree* (any subprograms it calls), and detailed parent-children information.

Chapter 21 discusses both the traditional profiler and the hierarchical profiler.

### Fine-grained dependency tracking

Prior to Oracle Database 11g, dependency information was recorded only with the granularity of the object as a whole. If *any* change at all was made to that object, all dependent program units were marked INVALID, *even if the change did not affect that program unit*. In Oracle Database 11g, Oracle has fine-tuned its dependency tracking down to the element within an object. In the case of tables, for example, the Oracle database now records that a program unit depends on specific columns within a table. With fine-grained dependency tracking, the database can avoid the recompilation that was required in earlier versions of the database, making it easier for you to evolve your application code base.

See Chapter 20 for more discussion of fine-grained dependency tracking.

### Supertype invocation from subtype

One restriction in Oracle's object-oriented functionality that has been lifted in Oracle Database 11g is the ability to invoke a method of a supertype that is overridden in the current (or higher-level) subtype. Prior to Oracle Database 11g, if you overrode a supertype's method in a subtype, there was no way that you could call the supertype's method in an instance of the subtype. This is now possible. In Oracle's implementation of supertype invocation, you don't simply refer to the supertype with a generic SUPERTYPE keyword, as is done in some other object-oriented languages. Instead, you must specify the specific supertype from the hierarchy. This approach is more flexible (you can invoke whichever supertype method you like, but it also means that you must hardcode the name of the supertype in your subtype's code.

See the further discussion of this feature in Chapter 26.

# Resources for PL/SQL Developers

O'Reilly published the first edition of this book back in 1995. At that time, *Oracle PL/SQL Programming* made quite a splash. It was the first independent (i.e., not emanating from Oracle) book on PL/SQL, and it fulfilled a clear and intensely felt need of developers around the world. Since that time, resources—books, development environments, utilities, and web sites—for PL/SQL programmers have proliferated. (Of course, this book is still by far the most important and valuable of these resources!)

The following sections describe very briefly many of these resources. By taking full advantage of these resources, many of which are available either free or at a relatively low cost, you will greatly improve your development experience (and resulting code).

## The O'Reilly PL/SQL Series

Over the years, the Oracle PL/SQL series from O'Reilly has grown to include quite a long list of books. Here we've summarized the books currently in print. Please check out the Oracle area of the O'Reilly web site (*http://oracle.oreilly.com*) for much more complete information.

*Oracle PL/SQL Programming, by Steven Feuerstein with Bill Pribyl*
> The 1,200-page tome you are reading now. The desk-side companion of a great many professional PL/SQL programmers, this book is designed to cover every feature in the core PL/SQL language. The current version covers through Oracle Database 11g Release 2.

*Learning Oracle PL/SQL, by Bill Pribyl with Steven Feuerstein*
> A comparatively gentle introduction to the language, ideal for new programmers and those who know a language other than PL/SQL.

*Oracle PL/SQL Best Practices, by Steven Feuerstein*
> A relatively short book that describes dozens of best practices that will help you produce high-quality PL/SQL code. Having this book is kind of like having a "lessons learned" document written by an in-house PL/SQL expert. The second edition features completely rewritten content that teaches best practices by following the challenges of a development team writing code for the make-believe company, MyFlimsyExcuse.com.

*Oracle PL/SQL Developer's Workbook, by Steven Feuerstein with Andrew Odewahn*
> Contains a series of questions and answers intended to help PL/SQL programmers develop and test their understanding of the language. Covers PL/SQL features through Oracle8i Database, but of course most of those exercises apply to later versions of the database as well.

*Oracle Built-in Packages, by Steven Feuerstein, Charles Dye, and John Beresniewicz*
> A reference guide to the prebuilt packages that Oracle supplies with the core database server. The use of these packages can often simplify the difficult and tame

the impossible. This book covers features through Oracle8 Database, but the in-depth explanations of and examples for the included packages is still very helpful in later releases.

*Oracle PL/SQL for DBAs, by Arup Nanda and Steven Feuerstein*
The PL/SQL language becomes and more important to Oracle DBAs with each new version of the database. There are two main reasons for this. First, large amounts of DBA functionality are made available through a PL/SQL package API. To use this functionality, you must also write and run PL/SQL programs. Second, it is critical that DBAs have a working knowledge of PL/SQL so that they can identify problems in the code built by developers. This book offers a wealth of material that will help DBAs get up to speed quickly on fully leveraging PL/SQL to get their jobs done.

*Oracle PL/SQL Language Pocket Reference, by Steven Feuerstein, Bill Pribyl, and Chip Dawes*
A small but very useful quick-reference book that might actually fit in your coat pocket. It summarizes the syntax of the core PL/SQL language through Oracle Database 11*g*.

*Oracle PL/SQL Built-ins Pocket Reference, by Steven Feuerstein, John Beresniewicz, and Chip Dawes*
Another helpful and concise guide summarizing built-in functions and packages through Oracle8 Database.

## PL/SQL on the Internet

There are also many online resources for PL/SQL programmers. This list focuses pri-marily on those resources to which the coauthors provide or manage content.

*Steven Feuerstein's PL/SQL Obsession web site*
PL/SQL Obsession is Steven's online portal for PL/SQL resources, including all of his training presentations and supporting code, freeware utilities (some listed be-low), video recordings, and more. See *http://www.ToadWorld.com/SF*.

*I Love PL/SQL And*
"I Love PL/SQL And" is a web site that makes it very easy for any PL/SQL developer to communicate to the PL/SQL development team her priorities regarding future changes to the PL/SQL language. Provided by Steven with the support and coop-eration of Bryn Llewellyn, the PL/SQL Product Manager, this site lets you choose from a list of commonly-requested enhancements and send an email to Bryn adding your vote to those features most important to you. See *www.iloveplsqland.net*.

*Oracle Technology Network*
Join the Oracle Technology Network (OTN), which "provides services and re-sources that developers need to build, test, and deploy applications" based on Oracle technology. Boasting membership in the millions, OTN is a great place to download Oracle software, documentation, and lots of sample code. See the main

page at *http://otn.oracle.com*. The PL/SQL page on OTN may be found at *http://www.oracle.com/technology/tech/pl_sql/index.html*.

*PL/Net.org*

PLNet.org is a repository of open source software, maintained by Bill Pribyl, that is written in PL/SQL or is otherwise for the benefit of PL/SQL developers. You can read more about the project's background or check out the Frequently Asked Questions (FAQs). You will also be directed to a number of utilities, such as utPLSQL, the unit-testing framework for PL/SQL developers. Check out *http://plnet.org*.

*Open Directory Project*

Courtesy of the "dmoz" (Directory Mozilla) project, here you can find a choice set of links to PL/SQL sites. There is also a subcategory called "Tools" with a fairly comprehensive set of links to both commercial and noncommercial developer tools. See *http://dmoz.org/Computers/Programming/Languages/PL-SQL/*.

*Quest Error Manager*

The Quest Error Manager (QEM) is a framework that will help you standardize the management of errors in a PL/SQL-based application. With QEM, you can register, raise, and report on errors through an API that makes it easy for all developers to perform error management in the same way, with a minimum amount of effort. Error information is logged into the instance (general information about the error) and context (application-specific name-value pairs) tables. Go to *http://toadworld.com/Downloads/ExclusiveToadWorldFreeware/tabid/78/Default.aspx*.

*Quest CodeGen Utility*

Quest CodeGen Utility is a very flexible code generator and repository for reusable code. With CodeGen, you can generate table APIs that will automatically execute the most common SQL operations against your tables (using the most advanced features of PL/SQL and with very robust error management). You can also generate all sorts of useful PL/SQL code from the "PL/SQL by Feuerstein" script library. Check out *http://toadworld.com/Downloads/ExclusiveToadWorldFreeware/tabid/78/Default.aspx*.

# Some Words of Advice

Since 1995, when the first edition of this book was published, I have had the opportunity to train, assist, and work with tens of thousands of PL/SQL developers. In the process, I have learned an awful lot from our students and readers, and have also gained some insights into the way we all do our work in the world of PL/SQL. I hope that you will not find it too tiresome if I share some advice with you on how you can work more effectively with this powerful programming language.

# Don't Be in Such a Hurry!

We are almost always working under tight deadlines, or playing catch-up from one setback or another. We have no time to waste, and lots of code to write. So let's get right to it—right?

Wrong. If we dive too quickly into the depths of code construction, slavishly converting requirements to hundreds, thousands, or even tens of thousands of lines of code, we will end up with a total mess that is almost impossible to debug and maintain. Don't respond to looming deadlines with panic; you are more likely to meet those deadlines if you do some careful planning.

I strongly encourage you to resist these time pressures and make sure to do the following before you start a new application, or even a specific program in an application:

*Construct test cases and test scripts before you write your code*
> You should determine how you want to verify a successful implementation before you write a single line of a program. By doing this, you are more likely to get the interface of your programs correct, and be able to thoroughly identify what it is your program needs to do.

*Establish clear rules for how developers will write the SQL statements in the application*
> In general, I recommend that individual developers not write a whole lot of SQL. Instead, those single-row queries and inserts and updates should be "hidden" behind prebuilt and thoroughly tested procedures and functions (this is called *data encapsulation*). These programs can be optimized, tested, and maintained much more effectively than SQL statements (many of them redundant) scattered throughout your code.

*Establish clear rules for how developers will handle exceptions in the application*
> All developers on a team should raise, handle, and log errors in the same way. The best way to do this is to create a single error-handling package that hides all the details of how an error log is kept, determines how exceptions are raised and propagated up through nested blocks, and avoids hardcoding of application-specific exceptions. Make sure that all developers use this package and that they do *not* write their own complicated, time-consuming, and error-prone error-handling code.

*Use "stepwise refinement" (a.k.a. top-down design) to limit the complexity of the requirements you must deal with at any given time*
> If you use this approach, you will find that the executable sections of your modules are shorter and easier to understand, which makes your code easier to maintain and enhance over time. Local or nested modules play a key role in following this design principle.

These are just a few of the important things to keep in mind *before* you start writing all that code. Just remember: in the world of software development, haste not only makes waste, it virtually guarantees a generous offering of bugs and lost weekends.

## Don't Be Afraid to Ask for Help

Chances are, if you are a software professional, you are a fairly smart individual. You studied hard, you honed your skills, and now you make a darn good living writing code. You can solve almost any problem you are handed, and that makes you proud. Unfortunately, your success can also make you egotistical, arrogant, and reluctant to seek out help when you are stumped. This dynamic is one of the most dangerous and destructive aspects of software development.

Software is written by human beings; it is important, therefore, to recognize that human psychology plays a key role in software development. The following is an example.

Joe, the senior developer in a team of six, has a problem with his program. He studies it for hours, with increasing frustration but cannot figure out the source of the bug. He wouldn't think of asking any of his peers to help because they all have less experience then he does. Finally, though, he is at wits' end and "gives up." Sighing, he picks up his phone and touches an extension: "Sandra, could you come over here and take a look at my program? I've got a problem I simply cannot figure out." Sandra stops by and, with the quickest glance at Joe's program, points out what should have been obvious to him long ago. Hurray! The program is fixed, and Joe expresses gratitude, but in fact he is secretly embarrassed.

Thoughts like "Why didn't I see that?" and "If I'd only spent another five minutes doing my own debugging I would have found it" run though Joe's mind. This is understandable but also very thick-headed. The bottom line is that we are often unable to identify our own problems because we are too close to our own code. Sometimes, all we need is a fresh perspective, the relatively objective view of someone with nothing at stake. It has nothing to do with seniority, expertise, or competence.

We strongly suggest that you establish the following guidelines in your organization:

*Reward admissions of ignorance*
> Hiding what you don't know about an application or its code is very dangerous. Develop a culture that welcomes questions and requests for help.

*Ask for help*
> If you cannot figure out the source of a bug in 30 minutes, immediately ask for help. You might even set up a "buddy system," so that everyone is assigned a person who is *expected* to be asked for assistance. Don't let yourself (or others in your group) go for hours banging your head against the wall in a fruitless search for answers.

*Set up a formal peer code review process*
> Don't let any code go to QA or production without being read and critiqued (in a positive, constructive manner) by one or more other developers in your group.

## Take a Creative, Even Radical Approach

We all tend to fall into ruts, in almost every aspect of our lives. People are creatures of habit: you learn to write code in one way; you assume certain limitations about a product; you turn aside possible solutions without serious examination because you just *know* it cannot be done. Developers become downright prejudiced about their own programs, and often not in positive ways. They are often overheard saying things like:

- "It can't run any faster than that; it's a pig."
- "I can't make it work the way the user wants; that'll have to wait for the next version."
- "If I were using X or Y or Z product, it would be a breeze. But with this stuff, everything is a struggle."

But the reality is that your program can almost always run a little faster. And the screen can, in fact, function *just* the way the user wants it to. And although each product has its limitations, strengths, and weaknesses, you should never have to wait for the next version. Isn't it so much more satisfying to be able to tell your therapist that you tackled the problem head-on, accepted no excuses, and crafted a solution?

How do you do this? Break out of the confines of your hardened views and take a fresh look at the world (or maybe just your cubicle). Reassess the programming habits you've developed. Be creative—step away from the traditional methods, from the often limited and mechanical approaches constantly reinforced in our places of business.

Try something new: experiment with what may seem to be a radical departure from the norm. You will be surprised at how much you will learn and grow as a programmer and problem solver. Over the years, I have surprised myself over and over with what is really achievable when I stopped saying "You can't do that!" and instead simply nodded quietly and murmured, "Now, if I do it this way...."

# CHAPTER 2

# Creating and Running PL/SQL Code

Even if they never give a second thought to tasks such as system design or unit testing, all PL/SQL programmers must be familiar with some basic operational tasks:

- Navigate the database.
- Create and edit PL/SQL source code.
- Compile the PL/SQL source code, correcting any code errors (and, optionally, warnings) noted by the compiler.
- Execute the compiled program from some environment.
- Examine results of program execution (screen output, changes to tables, etc.).

Unlike standalone languages such as C, PL/SQL is hosted inside an Oracle execution environment (it is an "embedded language"), so there are some unexpected nuances to all of these tasks: some are pleasant surprises; others, consternations. This chapter will show you how to accomplish these tasks at the most basic level (using SQL*Plus), with a brief tour of the nuances sprinkled in. It concludes with some drive-by examples of making calls to PL/SQL from inside several common programming environments such as PHP and C. For more detailed information about compilation and other more advanced tasks, see Chapter 20.

## Navigating the Database

Everybody who chooses to write PL/SQL programs does so to work with the contents of an Oracle database. It is, therefore, no surprise that you will need to know how to "get around" the Oracle database where your code is going to run. You will want to examine the data structures (tables, columns, sequences, user-defined types, etc.) in the database, as well as the signatures of any existing stored programs you will be invoking. You will probably also need to know something about the actual contents (columns, constraints, etc.) of the tables.

There are two distinct approaches you can take to database navigation:

1. Use an IDE (integrated development environment, a fancy name for a fancy editor) like Toad, SQL Developer, PL/SQL Developer, SQL Navigator, etc. They all offer visual browsers which support point and click navigation.

2. Run scripts in a command-line environment like SQL*Plus that queries the contents of data dictionary views like ALL_OBJECTS or USER_OBJECTS (demonstrated later in this chapter).

I strongly recommend that you use a graphical IDE. If you have been around Oracle long enough, you might be addicted to and fairly productive with your scripts. For the rest of us, a graphical interface is much easier to work with and understand—and much more productive—than scripts.

Chapter 20 also offers examples of using several data dictionary views for working with your PL/SQL code base.

## Creating and Editing Source Code

These days, programmers have many, many choices for code editors, from the simplest text editor to the most exotic development environments. And they do make very different choices. One of the authors of this book, Steven Feuerstein, is rather addicted to the Toad IDE. He is a very typical user, familiar with perhaps only 10% of all the functionality and buttons, but relying heavily on those features. Bill Pribyl, on the other hand, describes himself as "something of an oddball in that I like to use a fairly plain text editor to write PL/SQL programs. My one concession is that it automatically indents code as I type, and it displays keywords, comments, literals, and variables in different colors."

The most sophisticated programmer's editors will do much more than indentation and keyword coloring; they will also offer graphical debuggers, perform keyword completion, preview subprograms of packages as you type their name, display subprogram parameters, and highlight the specific row and column where the compiler reported an error. Some editors also have "hyperlinking" features that allow you to quickly browse to the declaration of a variable or subprogram. But the need for most of these features is common across many compiled languages.

What is unique about PL/SQL is the fact the source code for stored programs must be loaded into the database before it can be compiled and executed. This in-database copy can usually be retrieved by a programmer who has sufficient permissions. We can immediately recognize a host of code management issues, including:

- How and where does a programmer find the "original" copy of a stored program?
- Does it live on disk or does it just live in the database?
- How and how often do we perform backups?
- How do we manage multi-developer access to the code? That is, do we use a software version control system?

These questions should be answered before you begin development of an application, most preferably by making choices about which software tools will do this work for you. While there is no single set of tools or processes that work best for all development teams, I can tell you that I always store the "original" source code in files—I strongly suggest that you *not* use the RDBMS as your code repository.

In the next section I will demonstrate how you can use SQL*Plus to accomplish many basic tasks for PL/SQL development. These same tasks can be completed in your IDE.

# SQL*Plus

The granddaddy of Oracle frontends, Oracle's SQL*Plus provides a *command-line interpreter* for both SQL and PL/SQL. That is, it accepts statements from the user, sends them off to the Oracle server, and displays the results.

Often maligned for its user interface, SQL*Plus is one of my favorite Oracle tools. I actually *like* the lack of fancy gizmos and menus. Ironically, when I started using Oracle (circa 1986), this product's predecessor was boldly named UFI—*User Friendly Interface*. Two decades later, even the latest version of SQL*Plus is still unlikely to win any user friendliness awards, but at least it doesn't crash very often.

Oracle has, over the years, offered different versions of SQL*Plus, including:

*As a console program*
> This is a program that runs from a shell or command prompt[1] (an environment that is sometimes called a *console*).

*As a pseudo-GUI program*
> This form of SQL*Plus is available only on Microsoft Windows. I call it a "pseudo-GUI" because it looks pretty much like the console program but with bitmapped fonts; few other features distinguish it from the console program. Beware: Oracle has been threatening to desupport this product for years, and it hasn't really been updated since Oracle8i Database.

*Via iSQL*Plus*
> This program executes from a web browser connected to a middle-tier machine running Oracle's HTTP server and *i*SQL*Plus server.

Starting with Oracle Database 11g, Oracle ships only the console program (*sqlplus.exe*).

Figure 2-1 is a screenshot of a SQL*Plus console-style session.

Usually, I prefer the console program because:

* It tends to draw the screen faster, which can be significant for queries with lots of output.

---

1. Oracle calls this the "command-line interface" version of SQL*Plus, but I find that somewhat confusing, because two of the three styles provide a command-line interface.

- It has a more complete command-line history (on Microsoft Windows platforms, at least).
- It has a much easier way of changing visual characteristics such as font, color, and scroll buffer size.
- It is available virtually everywhere that Oracle server or client tools are installed.

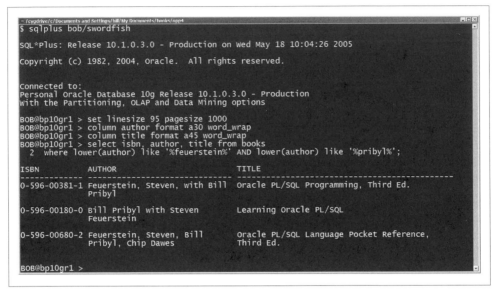

*Figure 2-1. SQL\*Plus in a console session*

## Starting Up SQL\*Plus

To start the console version of SQL\*Plus, you can simply type "sqlplus" at the operating system prompt (designated by "OS>"):

```
OS> sqlplus
```

This works for both Unix-based and Microsoft operating systems. SQL\*Plus should display a startup banner and then prompt you for a username and password.

```
SQL*Plus: Release 11.1.0.6.0 - Production on Fri Nov 7 10:28:26 2008

Copyright (c) 1982, 2007, Oracle.  All rights reserved.

Enter user-name: bob
Enter password: swordfish

Connected to:
Oracle Database 11g Enterprise Edition Release 11.1.0.6.0 - 64bit

SQL>
```

Seeing the "SQL>" prompt is your cue that your installation is set up properly. (The password won't echo on the screen.)

You can also launch SQL*Plus with the username and password on the command line:

```
OS> sqlplus bob/swordfish
```

I do *not* recommend this, because some operating systems provide a way for other users to see your command-line arguments, which would allow them to read your password. On multiuser systems, you can instead use the /NOLOG option to start SQL*Plus without connecting to the database, and then supply the username and password via the CONNECT command.

```
OS> sqlplus /nolog

SQL*Plus: Release 11.1.0.6.0 - Production on Fri Nov 7 10:28:26 2008

Copyright (c) 1982, 2007, Oracle.  All rights reserved.
SQL> CONNECT bob/swordfish
SQL> Connected.
```

If the computer you're running SQL*Plus on also has a properly configured Oracle Net[2] installation, *and* you have been authorized by the database administrator to connect to remote databases (that is, database servers running on other computers), you can connect to these other databases from SQL*Plus. Doing so requires knowing an Oracle Net *connect identifier* (also known as a *service name*) that you must supply along with your username and password. A connect identifier could look like this:

```
hqhr.WORLD
```

To use this identifier, you can append it to your username and password, separated by an at-sign (@):

```
SQL> CONNECT bob/swordfish@hqhr.WORLD
SQL> Connected.
```

When starting the pseudo-GUI version of SQL*Plus, supplying your credentials is straightforward, although it calls the connect identifier a *host string* (see Figure 2-2). If you want to connect to a database server running on the local machine, just leave the "Host String" field blank.

Once you have SQL*Plus running, you can do all kinds of things; here are the most common:

- Run a SQL statement.
- Compile and store a PL/SQL program in the database.
- Run a PL/SQL program.
- Issue a SQL*Plus-specific command.
- Run a script that contains a mix of the above.

---

2. Oracle Net is the current name for the product previously known as Net8 and SQL*Net.

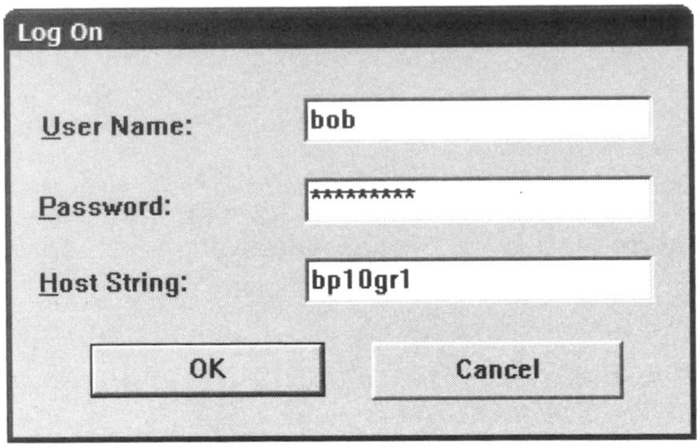

*Figure 2-2. The GUI login screen of SQL*Plus*

We'll take a look at these in the following sections.

## Running a SQL Statement

In the console version of SQL*Plus, the query:

```
SELECT isbn, author, title FROM books;
```

produces output similar to that shown in Figure 2-1.[3]

The default terminator in SQL*Plus for SQL statements is the semicolon, but you can change that terminator character.

## Running a PL/SQL Program

So, here we go (drum roll please). Let's type a short PL/SQL program into SQL*Plus:

```
SQL> BEGIN
  2      DBMS_OUTPUT.PUT_LINE('Hey look, ma!');
  3  END;
  4  /

PL/SQL procedure successfully completed.

SQL>
```

Oops. Although it has successfully completed, this particular program was supposed to invoke PL/SQL's built-in program that echoes back some text. SQL*Plus's somewhat annoying behavior is to suppress such output by default. To get it to display properly, you must use a SQL*Plus command to turn on SERVEROUTPUT:

---

3. Well, I cheated a bit in that figure because I used some column formatting commands. If this were a book about SQL*Plus or how to display database data, I would expound on the many ways SQL*Plus lets you control the appearance of the output by setting various formatting and display preferences. You can take my word for it, though; there are more options than you can shake a stick at.

```
SQL> SET SERVEROUTPUT ON
SQL> BEGIN
  2      DBMS_OUTPUT.PUT_LINE('Hey look, Ma!');
  3  END;
  4  /
Hey look, Ma!

PL/SQL procedure successfully completed.

SQL>
```

I generally put the SERVEROUTPUT command in my startup file (see "Loading your own custom environment automatically on startup" on page 35), causing it to be enabled until one of the following occurs:

- You disconnect, log off, or otherwise end your session.
- You explicitly set SERVEROUTPUT to OFF.
- The Oracle database discards session state either at your request or because of a compilation error (see "Recompiling Invalid Program Units" on page 731).
- In Oracle versions through Oracle9*i* Database Release 2, you issue a new CONNECT statement; in subsequent versions, SQL*Plus automatically reruns your startup file after each CONNECT.

When you enter SQL or PL/SQL statements into the console or pseudo-GUI SQL*Plus, the program assigns a number to each line after the first. There are two benefits to the line numbers: first, it helps you designate which line to edit with the built-in line editor (which you might actually use one day); and second, if the database detects an error in your code, it will usually report the error accompanied by a line number. You'll have plenty of opportunities to see *that* behavior in action.

To tell SQL*Plus that you're done entering a PL/SQL statement, you must usually include a trailing slash (see line 4 in the previous example). Although mostly harmless, the slash has several important characteristics:

- The meaning of the slash is "execute the most recently entered statement," regardless of whether the statement is SQL or PL/SQL.
- The slash is a command unique to SQL*Plus; it is *not* part of the PL/SQL language, nor is it part of SQL.
- It must appear on a line by itself; no other commands can be included on the line.
- In most versions of SQL*Plus prior to Oracle9*i* Database, if you accidentally precede the slash with any spaces, it doesn't work! Beginning with Oracle9*i* Database, SQL*Plus conveniently overlooks leading whitespace. Trailing space doesn't matter in any version.

As a convenience feature, SQL*Plus offers PL/SQL users an EXECUTE command, which saves typing the BEGIN, END, and trailing slash. So the following is equivalent to the short program I ran earlier:

```
SQL> EXECUTE DBMS_OUTPUT.PUT_LINE('Hey look, Ma!')
```

A trailing semicolon is optional, but I prefer to omit it. As with most SQL*Plus commands, EXECUTE can be abbreviated and is case-insensitive, so most interactive use gets reduced to:

```
SQL> EXEC dbms_output.put_line('Hey look, Ma!')
```

## Running a Script

Almost any statement that works interactively in SQL*Plus can be stored in a file for repeated execution. The easiest way to run such a script is to use the SQL*Plus "at-sign" (@) command.[4] For example, this runs all the commands in the file *abc.pkg*:

```
SQL> @abc.pkg
```

The file must live in my current directory (or on SQLPATH somewhere).

If you prefer words to at-signs, you can use the equivalent START command:

```
SQL> START abc.pkg
```

and you will get identical results. Either way, this command causes SQL*Plus to do the following:

1. Open the file named *abc.pkg*.
2. Sequentially attempt to execute all of the SQL, PL/SQL, and SQL*Plus statements in the file.
3. When complete, close the file and return you to the SQL*Plus prompt (unless the file invokes the EXIT statement, which will cause SQL*Plus to quit).

For example:

```
SQL> @abc.pkg

Package created.

Package body created.

SQL>
```

The default behavior is to display only the output from the individual statements on the screen; if you want to see the original source from the file, use the SQL*Plus command SET ECHO ON.

In my example, I've used a filename extension of *pkg*. If I leave off the extension, this is what happens:

```
SQL> @abc
SP2-0310: unable to open file "abc.sql"
```

---

4. START, @, and @@ commands are available in the non-browser versions of SQL*Plus. In *i*SQL*Plus, you can use the "Browse" and "Load Script" buttons for a similar result.

---

As you can see, the default file extension is *sql*. By the way, the "SP2-0310" is the Oracle-supplied error number, and "SP2" means that it is unique to SQL*Plus. (For more details about SQL*Plus error messages, refer to Oracle's *SQL*Plus User's Guide and Reference*.)

## What Is the "Current Directory"?

Any time you launch SQL*Plus from an operating system command prompt, SQL*Plus treats the operating system's then-current directory as its own current directory. In other words, if I were to start up using:

```
C:\BOB\FILES> sqlplus
```

then any file operations inside SQL*Plus (such as opening or running a script) will default to the directory *C:\BOB\FILES*.

If you use a shortcut or menu option to launch SQL*Plus, the current directory is the directory the operating system associates with the launch mechanism. So how would you change the current directory once you're inside SQL*Plus? It depends on the version. In the console program, you can't do it. You have to exit, change directories in the operating system, and restart SQL*Plus. In the GUI version, though, completing a File → Open or File → Save menu command will have the side effect of changing the current directory.

If your script file is in another directory, you can precede the filename with the path:[5]

```
SQL> @/files/src/release/1.0/abc.pkg
```

The idea of running scripts in other directories raises an interesting question. What if *abc.pkg* is located in this other directory and, in turn, calls other scripts? It might contain the lines:

```
REM  Filename: abc.pkg
@abc.pks
@abc.pkb
```

(Any line beginning with REM is a comment or "remark" that SQL*Plus ignores.) Executing the *abc.pkg* script is supposed to run *abc.pks* and *abc.pkb*. But because I have not included path information, where will SQL*Plus look for these other files? Let's see:

```
C:\BOB\FILES> sqlplus
...
SQL> @/files/src/release/1.0/abc.pkg
SP2-0310: unable to open file "abc.pks"
SP2-0310: unable to open file "abc.pkb"
```

It looks only in the directory where I started.

---

5. As a pleasant surprise, you can use forward slashes as directory delimiters on both Unix-Linux and Microsoft operating systems. This allows your scripts to port more easily between operating systems.

To address this problem, Oracle created the @@ command. This double at-sign means during this call, "pretend I have changed the current directory to be that of the currently executing file." So, the preferred way of writing the calls in the *abc.pkg* script is:

```
REM  Filename: abc.pkg
@@abc.pks
@@abc.pkb
```

Now I get:

```
C:\BOB\FILES> sqlplus
...
SQL> @/files/src/release/1.0/abc.pkg

Package created.

Package body created.
```

...just as I was hoping.

## Other SQL*Plus Tasks

There are dozens of commands specific to SQL*Plus, but I have space to mention only a few more that are particularly important or particularly confusing. For a thorough treatment of this venerable product, get a copy of Jonathan Gennick's book *Oracle SQL*Plus: The Definitive Guide* (O'Reilly) or, for quick reference, his *Oracle SQL*Plus Pocket Reference* (O'Reilly).

### Setting your preferences

You can change the behavior of SQL*Plus, as you can with many command-line environments, by changing the value of some of its built-in variables and settings. You have already seen one example, the SET SERVEROUTPUT statement. There are many options on the SQL*Plus SET command, such as SET SUFFIX (changes the default file extension) and SET LINESIZE *n* (sets the maximum number of characters in each displayed line before wrapping). To see all the SET values applicable to your current session, use the command:

```
SQL> SHOW ALL
```

SQL*Plus can also create and manipulate its own in-memory variables, and it sets aside a few special variables that will affect its behavior. Actually, there are two separate types of variables in SQL*Plus: DEFINEs and bind variables. To assign a value to a DEFINE variable, you can use the DEFINE command:

```
SQL> DEFINE x = "the answer is 42"
```

To view the value of x, specify:

```
SQL> DEFINE x
DEFINE X = "the answer is 42" (CHAR)
```

You would refer to such a variable using an ampersand (&). SQL*Plus does a simple substitution before sending the statement to the Oracle database, so you will need single-quote marks around the variable when you want to use it as a literal string.

```
SELECT '&x' FROM DUAL;
```

For bind variables, you first declare the variable. You can then use it in PL/SQL, and display it using the SQL*Plus PRINT command:

```
SQL> VARIABLE x VARCHAR2(10)
SQL> BEGIN
  2      :x := 'hullo';
  3  END;
  4  /

PL/SQL procedure successfully completed.

SQL> PRINT :x

X
--------------------------------
hullo
```

This can get a little bit confusing because there are now two different "x" variables, one that has been defined and one that has been declared.

```
SQL> SELECT :x, '&x' FROM DUAL;
old   1: SELECT :x, '&x' FROM DUAL
new   1: SELECT :x, 'the answer is 42' FROM DUAL

:X                               'THEANSWERIS42'
-------------------------------- ----------------
hullo                            the answer is 42
```

Just remember that DEFINEs are always character strings expanded by SQL*Plus, and declared variables are used as true bind variables in SQL and PL/SQL.

### Saving output to a file

Frequently, you will want to save output from a SQL*Plus session to a file—perhaps because you are generating a report, or because you want a record of your actions, or because you are dynamically generating commands to execute later. An easy way to do this in SQL*Plus is to use its SPOOL command:

```
SQL> SPOOL report
SQL> @run_report

    ...output scrolls past and gets written to the file report.lst...

SQL>SPOOL OFF
```

The first command, SPOOL report, tells SQL*Plus to save everything from that point forward into the file *report.lst*. The file extension of *.lst* is the default and can be overridden by supplying your own extension in the SPOOL command:

```
SQL> SPOOL report.txt
```

SPOOL OFF tells SQL*Plus to stop saving the output and to close the file.

### Exiting SQL*Plus

To exit SQL*Plus and return to the operating system, use the EXIT command:

```
SQL> EXIT
```

If you happen to be spooling when you exit, SQL*Plus will stop spooling and close the spool file.

What happens if you modify some table data during your session but then exit before ending the transaction with an explicit transaction control statement? By default, exiting SQL*Plus forces a COMMIT, unless your sessions end with a SQL error, and you have issued the SQL*Plus' WHENEVER SQLERROR EXIT ROLLBACK command (see the later section, "Error Handling in SQL*Plus" on page 36).

To disconnect from the database but remain connected to SQL*Plus, use the command DISCONNECT, which will look something like this in action:

```
SQL> DISCONNECT
Disconnected from Personal Oracle Database 10g Release 10.1.0.3.0 - Production
With the Partitioning, OLAP and Data Mining options
SQL>
```

You don't have to use DISCONNECT to change connections—you can just issue a CONNECT instead, and SQL*Plus will drop the first connection before connecting you to the new one. However, there is a good reason why you might want to disconnect before reconnecting: if you happen to be using operating system authentication,[6] the script might reconnect itself automatically...maybe to the wrong account. I've seen it happen.

### Editing a statement

SQL*Plus keeps the most recently issued statement in a buffer, and you can edit this statement using either the built-in line editor or an external editor of your choosing. To start with, I'll show how to set and use an external editor.

Use the EDIT command to have SQL*Plus save the current command buffer to a file, temporarily pause SQL*Plus, and invoke the editor:

```
SQL> EDIT
```

By default, the file will be saved with the name *afiedt.buf*, but you can change that with the SET EDITFILE command. Or, if you want to edit an existing file, just supply its name as an argument to EDIT:

---

6. Operating system authentication is a way that you can bypass the username/password prompt when you log in to SQL*Plus.

---

```
SQL> EDIT abc.pkg
```

Once you've saved the file and exited the editor, the SQL*Plus session will read the contents of the newly edited file into its buffer, and then resume.

The default external editors that Oracle assumes are:

- ed for Unix, Linux, and relatives
- Notepad For Microsoft Windows variants

Although the selection of default editors is actually hardcoded into the *sqlplus* executable file, you can easily change the current editor by assigning your own value to the SQL*Plus _EDITOR variable. Here's an example that I frequently use:

```
SQL> DEFINE _EDITOR = /bin/vi
```

where */bin/vi* is the full path to an editor that's popular among a handful of strange people. I recommend using the editor's full pathname here, for security reasons.

If you really want to use SQL*Plus' built-in line editor (and it *can* be really handy), the essential commands you need to know are:

L
> Lists the most recent statement.

*n*
> Makes the *n*th line of the statement the current line.

*DEL*
> Deletes the current line.

*C /old/new/*
> In the current line, changes the first occurrence of *old* to *new*. The delimiter (here a forward slash) can be any arbitrary character.

*n text*
> Makes *text* the current text of line *n*.

*I*

> Inserts a line below the current line. To insert a new line prior to line 1, use a line zero command (e.g., 0 *text*).

### Loading your own custom environment automatically on startup

To customize your SQL*Plus environment and have it assign your preferences from one session to the next, you will want to edit one or both of its auto-startup scripts. The way SQL*Plus behaves on startup is:

1. It searches for the file *$ORACLE_HOME/{S}qlplus/admin/glogin.sql* and, if found, executes any commands it contains. This "global" login script applies to everyone who executes SQL*Plus from that Oracle home, no matter which directory they start in.

2. Next, it runs the file *login.sql* in the current directory, if it exists.[7]

The startup script can contain the same kinds of statements as any other SQL*Plus script: SET commands, SQL statements, column formatting commands, and the like.

Neither file is required to be present. If both files are present, *glogin.sql* executes, followed by *login.sql*; in the case of conflicting preferences or variables, the last setting wins.

Here are a few of my favorite *login.sql* settings:

```
REM Number of lines of SELECT statement output before reprinting headers
SET PAGESIZE 999

REM Width of displayed page, expressed in characters
SET LINESIZE 132

REM Enable display of DBMS_OUTPUT messages. Use 1000000 rather than
REM "UNLIMITED" for databases earlier than Oracle Database 10g Release 2
SET SERVEROUTPUT ON SIZE UNLIMITED FORMAT WRAPPED

REM Change default to "vi improved" editor
DEFINE _EDITOR = /usr/local/bin/vim

REM Format misc columns commonly retrieved from data dictionary
COLUMN segment_name FORMAT A30 WORD_WRAP
COLUMN object_name FORMAT A30 WORD_WRAP

REM set the prompt (works in SQL*Plus
from Oracle9i Database or later)
SET SQLPROMPT "_USER'@'_CONNECT_IDENTIFIER > "
```

## Error Handling in SQL*Plus

The way SQL*Plus communicates success depends on the class of command you are running. With most SQL*Plus-specific commands, you can calibrate success by the absence of an error message. Successful SQL and PL/SQL commands, on the other hand, usually result in some kind of positive textual feedback.

If SQL*Plus encounters an error in a SQL or PL/SQL statement, it will, by default, report the error and continue processing. This behavior is desirable when you're working interactively. But when you're executing a script, there are many cases in which you want an error to cause SQL*Plus to terminate. Use the following command to make that happen:

```
SQL> WHENEVER SQLERROR EXIT SQL.SQLCODE
```

---

7. If it doesn't exist, and you have set the environment variable SQLPATH to one or more colon-delimited directories, SQL*Plus will search through those directories one at a time and execute the first *login.sql* that it finds. As a rule, I don't use SQLPATH because I am easily confused by this sort of skulking about.

Thereafter in the current session, SQL*Plus terminates if the database server returns any error messages in response to a SQL or PL/SQL statement. The SQL.SQLCODE part means that, when SQL*Plus terminates, it sets its return code to a nonzero value, which you can detect in the calling environment.[8] Otherwise, SQL*Plus always ends with a 0 return code, which may falsely imply that the script succeeded.

Another form of this command is:

```
SQL> WHENEVER SQLERROR EXIT SQL.SQLCODE ROLLBACK
```

which means that you also want SQL*Plus to roll back any uncommitted changes prior to exiting.

## Why You Will Love and Hate SQL*Plus

In addition to the features you just read about, the following are some particular features of SQL*Plus that you will come to know and love.

- With SQL*Plus, you can run "batch" programs, supplying application-specific arguments on the *sqlplus* command line, and referring to them in the script using &1 (first argument), &2 (second argument), etc.

- SQL*Plus provides complete and up-to-date support for all SQL and PL/SQL statements. This can be important when you're using features unique to Oracle. Third-party environments may not provide 100% coverage; for example, some have been slow to add support for Oracle's object types, which were introduced a number of years ago.

- SQL*Plus runs on all of the same hardware and operating system platforms on which the Oracle server runs.

But as with any tool, there are going to be some irritations:

- In console versions of SQL*Plus, the statement buffer is limited to the most recently used statement; SQL*Plus offers no further command history.

- With SQL*Plus, there are no modern command-interpreter features such as automatic completion of keywords or hints about which database objects are available while typing in a statement.

- Online help consists of minimal documentation of the SQL*Plus command set. (Use HELP *command* to get help on a specific command.)

- There is no ability to change the current directory once you've started SQL*Plus. This can be annoying when opening or saving scripts if you don't like typing full pathnames. If you discover that you're in an inconvenient directory, you have to quit SQL*Plus, change directories, and restart SQL*Plus.

---

8. Using, for example, $? in the Unix shell or %ERRORLEVEL% in Microsoft Windows.

- Unless I break down and use what I consider the dangerous SQLPATH feature, SQL*Plus looks only in the startup directory for *login.sql*; it would be better if it would fall back to look in my home directory for the startup script.

The bottom line is that SQL*Plus is something of a "real programmer's" tool that is neither warm nor fuzzy. But it is ubiquitous, doesn't crash, and is likely to be supported as long as there is an Oracle Corporation.

# Performing Essential PL/SQL Tasks

Let's turn to the highlights of creating, running, deleting, and otherwise managing PL/SQL programs, using SQL*Plus as the frontend. Don't expect to be overwhelmed with detail here; treat this section as a glimpse of topics that will be covered in much greater detail in the chapters ahead.

## Creating a Stored Program

To build a new stored PL/SQL program, you use one of SQL's CREATE statements. For example, if you want to create a stored function that counts words in a string, you can do so using a CREATE FUNCTION statement:

```
CREATE FUNCTION wordcount (str IN VARCHAR2)
   RETURN PLS_INTEGER
AS
   declare local variables here
BEGIN
   implement algorithm here
END;
/
```

As with the simple BEGIN-END blocks shown earlier, running this statement from SQL*Plus requires a trailing slash on a line by itself.

Assuming that the DBA has granted you Oracle's CREATE PROCEDURE privilege (which also gives you the privilege of creating functions), this statement causes Oracle to compile and store this stored function in your schema; if your code compiles, you'll probably see a success message such as:

```
Function created.
```

If another database object, such as a table or package, named wordcount already exists in your Oracle schema, CREATE FUNCTION will fail with the error message *ORA-00955: name is already used by an existing object*. That is one reason that Oracle provides the OR REPLACE option, which you will want to use probably 99% of the time.

```
CREATE OR REPLACE FUNCTION wordcount (str IN VARCHAR2)
   RETURN PLS_INTEGER
ASsame as before
```

---

The OR REPLACE option avoids the side effects of dropping and recreating the program; in other words, it preserves any object privileges you have granted to other users or roles. Fortunately, it replaces only objects of the same type, and it won't automatically drop a table named wordcount just because you decided to create a function by that name.

As with anonymous blocks used more than once, programmers generally store these statements in files in the operating system. I could create a file *wordcount.fun* for this function and use the SQL*Plus @ command to run it:

```
SQL> @wordcount.fun

Function created.
```

As mentioned earlier, SQL*Plus does not, by default, echo the contents of scripts. You can SET ECHO ON to see the source code scroll past the screen, including the line numbers that the database assigns; this setting can be helpful when troubleshooting. Let's introduce an error into the program by commenting out a variable declaration.

```
SQL> /* File on web: wordcount.fun */
SQL> SET ECHO ON
SQL> @wordcount.fun
SQL> CREATE OR REPLACE FUNCTION wordcount (str IN VARCHAR2)
  2      RETURN PLS_INTEGER
  3  AS
  4  /* words PLS_INTEGER := 0;   ***Commented out for intentional error*** */
  5      len PLS_INTEGER := NVL(LENGTH(str),0);
  6      inside_a_word BOOLEAN;
  7  BEGIN
  8      FOR i IN 1..len + 1
  9      LOOP
 10         IF ASCII(SUBSTR(str, i, 1)) < 33 OR i > len
 11         THEN
 12            IF inside_a_word
 13            THEN
 14               words := words + 1;
 15               inside_a_word := FALSE;
 16            END IF;
 17         ELSE
 18            inside_a_word := TRUE;
 19         END IF;
 20      END LOOP;
 21      RETURN words;
 22  END;
 23  /

Warning: Function created with compilation errors.

SQL>
```

This message tells us that the function was created, but that there were compilation errors that render it inoperable. We've succeeded in storing the source code in the database; now we need to tease the details of the error out of the database. The quickest way to see the full text of the error message is to use SQL*Plus' SHOW ERRORS command, abbreviated as SHO ERR:

```
SQL> SHO ERR

Errors for FUNCTION WORDCOUNT:

LINE/COL ERROR
-------- ------------------------------------------------
14/13    PLS-00201: identifier 'WORDS' must be declared
14/13    PL/SQL: Statement ignored
21/4     PL/SQL: Statement ignored
21/11    PLS-00201: identifier 'WORDS' must be declared
```

The compiler has detected both occurrences of the variable, reporting the exact line and column numbers. To see more detail about any server-based error, you can look it up by its identifier—PLS-00201 in this case—in Oracle's *Database Error Messages* document.

Behind the scenes, SHOW ERRORS is really just querying Oracle's USER_ERRORS view in the data dictionary. You can query that view yourself, but you generally don't need to (see the sidebar "Show Other Errors").

---

### Show Other Errors

Many Oracle programmers know only one form of the SQL*Plus command:

```
SQL> SHOW ERRORS
```

and they incorrectly believe that they must query the USER_ERRORS view directly to see anything but the error messages from the most recent compile. However, you can append to SHOW ERRORS an object category and a name, and it will display the latest errors for any object:

```
SQL> SHOW ERRORS category [schema.]object
```

For example, to view the latest errors for the wordcount function, specify:

```
SQL> SHOW ERRORS FUNCTION wordcount
```

Use caution when interpreting the output:

```
No errors.
```

This message actually means one of three things: (1) the object did compile successfully; (2) you gave it the wrong category (for example, function instead of procedure); or (3) no object by that name exists.

The complete list of categories this command recognizes varies by version, but includes the following:

---

```
DIMENSION
FUNCTION
JAVA SOURCE
JAVA CLASS
PACKAGE
PACKAGE BODY
PROCEDURE
TRIGGER
TYPE
TYPE BODY
VIEW
```

It's common practice to append a SHOW ERRORS command after every scripted CREATE statement that builds a stored PL/SQL program. So, a "good practices" template for building stored programs in SQL*Plus might begin with this form:

```
CREATE OR REPLACE program-type
AS
    your code
END;
/

SHOW ERRORS
```

(I don't usually include SET ECHO ON in scripts, but rather type it at the command line when needed.)

When your program contains an error that the compiler can detect, CREATE will still cause the Oracle database to store the program in the database, though in an invalid state. If, however, you mistype part of the CREATE syntax, the database won't be able to figure out what you are trying to do and won't store the code in the database.

## Executing a Stored Program

We've already looked at two different ways to invoke a stored program: wrap it in a simple PL/SQL block or use the SQL*Plus EXECUTE command. You can also use stored programs inside other stored programs. For example, you can invoke a function such as wordcount in any location where you could use an integer expression. Here is a short illustration of how I might test the wordcount function with a strange input (CHR(9) is an ASCII "tab" character):

```
BEGIN
    DBMS_OUTPUT.PUT_LINE('There are ' || wordcount(CHR(9)) || ' words in a tab');
END;
/
```

I have embedded wordcount as part of an expression and supplied it as an argument to DBMS_OUTPUT.PUT_LINE. Here, PL/SQL automatically casts the integer to a string so it can concatenate it with two other literal expressions; the result is:

```
There are 0 words in a tab
```

You can also invoke many PL/SQL functions inside SQL statements. Here are several examples of how you can use the wordcount function:

- Apply the function in a select list to compute the number of words in a table column:

```
SELECT isbn, wordcount(description) FROM books;
```

- Use the ANSI-compliant CALL statement, binding the function output to a SQL*Plus variable, and display the result:

```
VARIABLE words NUMBER
CALL wordcount('some text') INTO :words;
PRINT :words
```

- Same as above, but execute the function from a remote database as defined in the database link *test.newyork.ora.com*:

```
CALL wordcount@test.newyork.ora.com('some text') INTO :words;
```

- Execute the function, owned by schema bob, while logged in to any schema that has appropriate authorization:

```
SELECT bob.wordcount(description) FROM books WHERE id = 10007;
```

## Showing Stored Programs

Sooner or later you will want to get a list of the stored programs you own, and you may also need to view the most recent version of program source that Oracle has saved in its data dictionary. This is one task that you will find far easier if you use some kind of GUI-based navigation assistant, but if you lack such a tool, it's not too hard to write a few SQL statements that will pull the desired information out of the data dictionary.

For example, to see a complete list of your programs (and tables, indexes, etc.), query the USER_OBJECTS view, as in:

```
SELECT * FROM USER_OBJECTS;
```

This view shows name, type, creation time, latest compile times, status (valid or invalid), and other useful information.

If all you need is the summary of a PL/SQL program's callable interface in SQL*Plus, the easiest command to use is DESCRIBE:

```
SQL> DESCRIBE wordcount
FUNCTION wordcount RETURNS BINARY_INTEGER
 Argument Name                    Type                    In/Out Default?
 ------------------------------   ---------------------   ------ --------
 STR                              VARCHAR2                IN
```

DESCRIBE also works on tables, views, object types, procedures, and packages. To see the complete source code of your stored programs, query USER_SOURCE or TRIGGER_SOURCE. (Querying from these data dictionary views is discussed in further detail in Chapter 20.)

## Managing Grants and Synonyms for Stored Programs

When you first create a PL/SQL program, normally no one but you or the DBA can execute it. To give another user the authority to execute your program, issue a GRANT statement:

```
GRANT EXECUTE ON wordcount TO scott;
```

To remove the privilege, use REVOKE:

```
REVOKE EXECUTE ON wordcount FROM scott;
```

You could also grant the EXECUTE privilege to a role:

```
GRANT EXECUTE ON wordcount TO all_mis;
```

Or, if appropriate, you could allow any user on the current database to run the program:

```
GRANT EXECUTE ON wordcount TO PUBLIC;
```

If you grant a privilege to an individual like Scott, and to a role of which the user is a member, and also grant it to PUBLIC, the database remembers all three grants until they are revoked. Any one of the grants is sufficient to permit the individual to run the program, so if you ever decide you don't want Scott to run it, you must revoke the privilege from Scott, and revoke it from PUBLIC, and finally revoke it from the all_mis role (or revoke that role from Scott).

To view a list of privileges you have granted to other users and roles, you can query the USER_TAB_PRIVS_MADE data dictionary view. Somewhat counterintuitively, PL/SQL program names appear in the table_name column:

```
SQL> SELECT table_name, grantee, privilege
  2    FROM USER_TAB_PRIVS_MADE
  3   WHERE table_name = 'WORDCOUNT';

TABLE_NAME                     GRANTEE                        PRIVILEGE
------------------------------ ------------------------------ -----------
WORDCOUNT                      PUBLIC                         EXECUTE
WORDCOUNT                      SCOTT                          FXECUTE
WORDCOUNT                      MIS_ALL                        EXECUTE
```

When Scott does have the EXECUTE privilege on wordcount, he will probably want to create a synonym for the program to avoid having to prefix it with the name of the schema that owns it:

```
SQL> CONNECT scott/tiger
Connected.
SQL>CREATE OR REPLACE SYNONYM wordcount FOR bob.wordcount;
```

Now he can execute the program in his programs by referring only to the synonym:

```
IF wordcount(localvariable) > 100 THEN...
```

This is a good thing, because if the owner of the function changes, only the synonym (and not any stored program) needs modification.

It's possible to create a synonym for a procedure, function, package, or user-defined type. Synonyms for procedures, functions, or packages can hide not only the schema but also the actual database; you can create a synonym for remote programs as easily as local programs. However, synonyms can only hide schema and database identifiers; you cannot use a synonym in place of a packaged subprogram.

Removing a synonym is easy:

```
DROP SYNONYM wordcount;
```

## Dropping a Stored Program

If you really, truly don't need a particular stored program any more, you can drop it using SQL's DROP statement:

```
DROP FUNCTION wordcount;
```

You can drop a package, which can be composed of up to two elements (a specification and body), in its entirety:

```
DROP PACKAGE pkgname;
```

Or you can drop only the body without invalidating the corresponding specification:

```
DROP PACKAGE BODY pkgname;
```

Any time you drop a program that other programs call, the callers will be marked INVALID.

## Hiding the Source Code of a Stored Program

When you create a PL/SQL program as described above, the source code will be available in clear text in the data dictionary, and any DBA can view or even alter it. To protect trade secrets or to prevent tampering with your code, you might want some way to obfuscate your PL/SQL source code before delivering it.

Oracle provides a command-line utility called *wrap* that converts many CREATE statements into a combination of plain text and hex. It's not true encryption, but it does go a long way toward hiding your code. Here are a few extracts from a wrapped file:

```
FUNCTION wordcount wrapped
0
abcd
abcd
...snip...
1WORDS:
10:
1LEN:
1NVL:
1LENGTH:
1INSIDE_A_WORD:
1BOOLEAN:
...snip...
```

```
a5 b 81 b0 a3 a0 1c 81
b0 91 51 a0 7e 51 a0 b4
2e 63 37 :4 a0 51 a5 b a5
b 7e 51 b4 2e :2 a0 7e b4
2e 52 10 :3 a0 7e 51 b4 2e
d :2 a0 d b7 19 3c b7 :2 a0
d b7 :2 19 3c b7 a0 47 :2 a0
```

If you need true encryption—for example, to deliver information such as a password that really needs to be secure—you should not rely on this facility.[9]

To learn more about the *wrap* utility, see Chapter 20.

# Editing Environments for PL/SQL

As I mentioned earlier. you can use a "lowest common denominator" editing and execution environment like SQL*Plus or you can use a integrated development environment that offers extensive graphical interfaces to improve your productivity. This section lists some of the most popular of the IDE tools. I do not recommend any particular tool; you should carefully define the list of requirements and priorities you have for such a tool and then see which of them best meets your needs.

| Product | Description |
|---|---|
| Toad | Offered by Quest Software, Toad is far and away the most popular PL/SQL IDE. It is used by hundreds of thousands of developers, in both its free and commercial versions. For more information, see *http://www.quest.com/toad-for-oracle/*. |
| SQL Navigator | Also offered by Quest Software, SQL Navigator is also used by tens of thousands of developers who love the product's interface and productivity features. For more information, see *http://www.quest.com/sql-navigator/*. |
| PL/SQL Developer | This product is sold by Allround Automations, and is a favorite of many PL/SQL developers. It is built around a plug-in architecture, so third parties can offer extensions to the base product. For more information, see *http://www.allroundautomations.com/plsqldev.html*. |
| SQL Developer | After years of little or no support for PL/SQL editing, Oracle Corporation created SQL Developer as a "fork" of the foundation JDeveloper tool. SQL Developer is free and increasingly robust. For more information, see *http://www.oracle.com/technology/software/products/sql/index.html*. |

There are many other PL/SQL IDEs out there, but those listed above certainly offer choices from the best and most popular of these tools.

---

9. Oracle does provide a way of incorporating true encryption into your own applications using the built-in package DBMS_CRYPTO (or DBMS_OBFUSCATION_TOOLKIT) in releases before Oracle Database 10*g*; see Chapter 23 for information on DBMS_CRYPTO.

# Calling PL/SQL from Other Languages

Sooner or later, you will probably want to call PL/SQL from C, Java, Perl, PHP, or any number of other places. This seems like a reasonable request, but if you've ever done cross-language work before, you may be all too familiar with some of the intricacies of mating up language-specific datatypes—especially composite datatypes like arrays, records, and objects—not to mention differing parameter semantics or vendor extensions to "standard" application programming interfaces (APIs) like Microsoft's Open Database Connectivity (ODBC).

I will show a few very brief examples of calling PL/SQL from the outside world. Let's say that I've written a PL/SQL function that accepts an ISBN expressed as a string and returns the corresponding book title:

```
/* File on web: booktitle.fun */
FUNCTION booktitle (isbn_in IN VARCHAR2)
   RETURN VARCHAR2
IS
   l_title books.title%TYPE;
   CURSOR icur IS SELECT title FROM books WHERE isbn = isbn_in;
BEGIN
   OPEN icur;
   FETCH icur INTO l_title;
   CLOSE icur;
   RETURN l_title;
END;
```

In SQL*Plus, I could call this in several different ways. The shortest way would be as follows:

```
SQL> EXEC DBMS_OUTPUT.PUT_LINE(booktitle('0-596-00180-0'))
Learning Oracle PL/SQL

PL/SQL procedure successfully completed.
```

Let's see how I might call this function from the following environments:

- C, using Oracle's precompiler (Pro*C)
- Java, using JDBC
- Perl, using Perl DBI and DBD::Oracle
- PHP
- PL/SQL Server Pages

These examples are very contrived—for example, the username and password are hardcoded, and the programs simply display the output to stdout. Moreover, I'm not even going to pretend to describe every line of code. Still, these examples will give you an idea of some of the patterns you may encounter in different languages.

## C: Using Oracle's Precompiler (Pro*C)

Oracle supplies at least two different C-language interfaces to Oracle: one called OCI (Oracle Call Interface), which is largely the domain of rocket scientists, and the other called Pro*C. OCI provides hundreds of functions from which you must code low-level operations such as open, parse, bind, define, execute, fetch...and that's just for a single query. Because the simplest OCI program that does anything interesting is about 200 lines long, I thought I'd show a Pro*C example instead. Pro*C is a precompiler technology that allows you to construct source files containing a mix of C, SQL, and PL/SQL. You run the following through Oracle's *proc* program, and out will come C code.

```
/* File on web: callbooktitle.pc */
#include <stdio.h>
#include <string.h>

EXEC SQL BEGIN DECLARE SECTION;
    VARCHAR uid[20];
    VARCHAR pwd[20];
    VARCHAR isbn[15];
    VARCHAR btitle[400];
EXEC SQL END DECLARE SECTION;

EXEC SQL INCLUDE SQLCA.H;

int sqlerror();

int main()
{
    /* VARCHARs actually become a struct of a char array and a length */

    strcpy((char *)uid.arr,"scott");
    uid.len = (short) strlen((char *)uid.arr);
    strcpy((char *)pwd.arr,"tiger");
    pwd.len = (short) strlen((char *)pwd.arr);

    /* this is a cross between an exception and a goto */
    EXEC SQL WHENEVER SQLERROR DO sqlerror();

    /* connect and then execute the function */
    EXEC SQL CONNECT :uid IDENTIFIED BY :pwd;
    EXEC SQL EXECUTE
       BEGIN
          :btitle := booktitle('0-596-00180-0');
       END;
    END-EXEC;

    /* show me the money */
    printf("%s\n", btitle.arr);

    /* Disconnect from ORACLE. */
    EXEC SQL COMMIT WORK RELEASE;
    exit(0);
```

```
}

sqlerror()
{
    EXEC SQL WHENEVER SQLERROR CONTINUE;
    printf("\n% .70s \n", sqlca.sqlerrm.sqlerrmc);
    EXEC SQL ROLLBACK WORK RELEASE;
    exit(1);
}
```

As you can see, Pro*C is not an approach for which language purists will be pining away. And trust me, you don't want to mess with the C code that this generates. Nevertheless, many companies find that Pro*C (or Pro*Cobol or any of several other languages Oracle supports) serves a reasonable middle ground between, say, Visual Basic (too slow and clunky) and OCI (too hard).

Oracle's own documentation offers the best source of information regarding Pro*C.

## Java: Using JDBC

As with C, Oracle provides a number of different approaches to connecting to the database. The embedded SQL approach, known as SQLJ, is similar to Oracle's other precompiler technology, although a bit more debugger-friendly. A more popular and Java-centric approach is known as JDBC, which doesn't really stand for anything, but the usual interpretation is "Java Database Connectivity."

```
/* File on web: Book.java */
import java.sql.*;

public class Book
{
  public static void main(String[] args) throws SQLException
  {
    // initialize the driver and try to make a connection

    DriverManager.registerDriver (new oracle.jdbc.driver.OracleDriver ());
    Connection conn =
        DriverManager.getConnection("jdbc:oracle:thin:@localhost:1521:o92",
                            "scott", "tiger");

    // prepareCall uses ANSI92 "call" syntax
    CallableStatement cstmt = conn.prepareCall("{? = call booktitle(?)}");

    // get those bind variables and parameters set up
    cstmt.registerOutParameter(1, Types.VARCHAR);
    cstmt.setString(2, "0-596-00180-0");

    // now we can do it, get it, close it, and print it
    cstmt.executeUpdate();
    String bookTitle = cstmt.getString(1);
    conn.close();
    System.out.println(bookTitle);
```

```
        }
    }
```

This particular example uses the thin driver, which provides great compatibility and ease of installation (all the network protocol smarts exists in a Java library), at some expense of communications performance. An alternative approach would be to use what's known as the OCI driver. Don't worry: there's no rocket scientist programming required to use it, despite the name!

## Perl: Using Perl DBI and DBD::Oracle

Much beloved by the system administration community, Perl is something of the mother of all open source languages. Now in Version 5.10, it does just about everything and seems to run everywhere. And, with nifty auto-configuration tools such as CPAN (Comprehensive Perl Archive Network), it's a cinch to install community-supplied modules such as the DataBase Interface (DBI) and the corresponding Oracle driver, DBD::Oracle.

```perl
/* File on web: callbooktitle.pl */
#!/usr/bin/perl

use strict;
use DBI qw(:sql_types);

# either make the connection or die
my $dbh = DBI->connect(
    'dbi:Oracle:o92',
    'scott',
    'tiger',
    {
        RaiseError => 1,
        AutoCommit => 0
    }
) || die "Database connection not made: $DBI::errstr";

my $retval;

# make parse call to Oracle, get statement handle
eval {
    my $func = $dbh->prepare(q{
        BEGIN
            :retval := booktitle(isbn_in => :bind1);
        END;
    });

# bind the parameters and execute
    $func->bind_param(":bind1", "0-596-00180-0");
    $func->bind_param_inout(":retval", \$retval, SQL_VARCHAR);
    $func->execute;

};
```

```
if( $@ ) {
    warn "Execution of stored procedure failed: $DBI::errstr\n";
    $dbh->rollback;
} else {
    print "Stored procedure returned: $retval\n";
}

# don't forget to disconnect
$dbh->disconnect;
```

Perl is one of those languages in which it is shamelessly easy to write code that is impossible to read. It's not a particularly fast or small language, either, but there are compiled versions that at least address the speed problem.

For more information about Perl and Oracle, see *Programming the Perl DBI* by Alligator Descartes (O'Reilly). There are also many excellent books on the Perl language, not to mention the online information at *http://www.perl.com* (an O'Reilly site), *http://www.perl.org*, and *http://www.cpan.org*.

## PHP: Using Oracle Extensions

If you are the kind of person who might use the free and wildly popular web server known as Apache, you might also enjoy using the free and wildly popular programming language known as PHP. Commonly employed to build dynamic web pages, PHP can also be used to build GUI applications or to run command-line programs. As you might expect, Oracle is one of many database environments that work with PHP; Oracle Corporation has, in fact, partnered with Zend, in order to provide a "blessed" distribution of the Oracle database with PHP.[10]

This example uses the family of PHP functions known as OCI8. Don't let the "8" in the name fool you; it should work with everything from Oracle7 to Oracle Database 11*g*.

```
/* File on web: callbooktitle.php */
<?PHP
    // Initiate the connection to the o92 database
    $conn = OCILogon ("scott", "tiger", "o92");

    // Make parse call to Oracle, get statement identity
    $stmt = OCIParse($conn,
        "begin :res := booktitle('0-596-00180-0'); end;");

    // Show any errors
    if (!$stmt) {
        $err = OCIError();
        echo "Oops, you broke it: ".$err["message"];
        exit;
    }
```

---

10. Note that if you want support for PHP, you will need to get it from the user community or from a firm like Zend. Oracle Corporation does not take support calls for PHP.

---

```
    // Bind 200 characters of the variable $result to placeholder :res
    OCIBindByName($stmt, "res", &$result, 200);

    // Execute
    OCIExecute($stmt);

    // Stuff the value into the variable
    OCIResult($stmt,$result);

    // Display on stdout
    echo "$result\n";

    // Relax
    OCILogoff($conn);
?>
```

When executed at the command line, it looks something like this:

```
$ php callbooktitle.php
Learning Oracle PL/SQL
```

By the way, these Oracle OCI functions are not available in PHP by default, but it shouldn't be too difficult for your system administrator to rebuild PHP with the Oracle extensions.

You can find more information about PHP at *http://www.php.net* or in one of O'Reilly's many books on the subject. For PHP tips specific to Oracle, visit the Oracle Technology Network web site at *http://otn.oracle.com*.

## PL/SQL Server Pages

Although the PL/SQL Server Pages (PSP) environment is proprietary to Oracle, I thought I would mention it because it's a quick way to get a web page up and running. PSP is another precompiler technology; it lets you embed PL/SQL into HTML pages.

```
/* File on web: favorite_plsql_book.psp */
<%@ page language="PL/SQL" %>
<%@ plsql procedure="favorite_plsql_book" %>
<HTML>
   <HEAD>
      <TITLE>My favorite book about PL/SQL</TITLE>
   </HEAD>
   <BODY>
      <%= booktitle( '0-596-00180-0') %>
   </BODY>
</HTML>
```

That <%= %> construct means "process this as PL/SQL and return the result to the page." When properly installed on a web server connected to an Oracle database, this page displays as in Figure 2-3.

I'm rather fond of PL/SQL Server Pages as a good way to put together data-driven web sites fairly quickly.

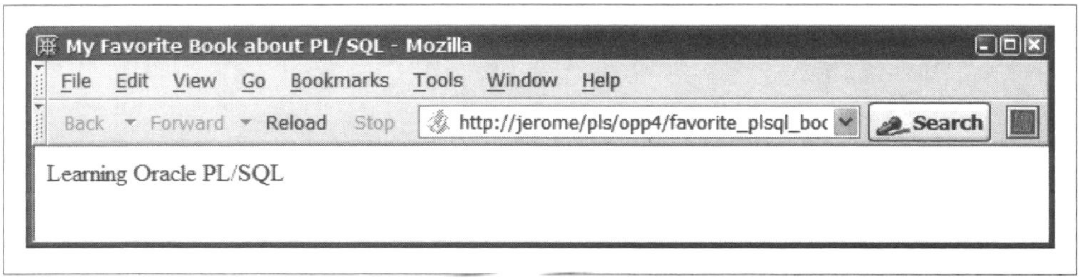

*Figure 2-3. Output from a PL/SQL Server Page*

For more information about PL/SQL Server Pages, see *Learning Oracle PL/SQL* (O'Reilly) by the authors of the book you're reading now.

## And Where Else?

You've seen how to use PL/SQL in SQL*Plus and in a number of other common environments and programming languages. There are still more places and ways that you can use PL/SQL:

- Embedded in COBOL or FORTRAN and processed with Oracle's precompiler.
- Called from Visual Basic, using some flavor of ODBC.
- Called from the Ada programming language, via a technology called SQL*Module.
- Executed automatically, as triggers on events in the Oracle database such as table updates.
- Scheduled to execute on a recurring basis inside the Oracle database, via the DBMS_SCHEDULER supplied package.
- The TimesTen database: an in-memory database acquired by Oracle Corporation, its contents can now be manipulated with PL/SQL code, just like the relational database.

I am not able, (un)fortunately, to address all these topics in this book.

# CHAPTER 3

# Language Fundamentals

Every language—whether human or computer—has a syntax, a vocabulary, and a character set. In order to communicate within that language, you have to learn the rules that govern its usage. Many of us are wary of learning a new computer language. Change is often scary, but in general, programming languages are very simple tongues, and PL/SQL is a relatively simple programming language. The difficulty of conversing in languages based on bytes is not with the language itself, but with the compiler or computer with which we are having the discussion. Compilers are, for the most part, rather dull-witted. They are not creative, sentient beings. They are not capable of original thought. Their vocabulary is severely limited. Compilers just happen to think their dull thoughts very, very rapidly—and very inflexibly.

If I hear someone ask "gottabuck?," I can readily interpret that sentence and decide how to respond. On the other hand, if I instruct PL/SQL to "gimme the next half-dozen records," I will not get very far in my application. To use the PL/SQL language, you must dot your i's and cross your t's—syntactically speaking. So, this chapter covers the fundamental language rules that will help you converse with the PL/SQL compiler— the PL/SQL block structure, character set, lexical units, and PRAGMA keyword.

## PL/SQL Block Structure

In PL/SQL, as in most other procedural languages, the smallest meaningful grouping of code is known as a *block*. A block is a unit of code that provides execution and scoping boundaries for variable declarations and exception handling. PL/SQL allows you to create *anonymous blocks* (blocks of code that have no name) and *named blocks*, which may be packages, procedures, functions, triggers, or object types.

A PL/SQL block has up to four different sections, only one of which is mandatory:

*Header*
> Used only for named blocks. The header determines the way the named block or program must be called. Optional.

*Declaration section*

Identifies variables, cursors, and subblocks that are referenced in the execution and exception sections. Optional.

*Execution section*

Statements the PL/SQL runtime engine will execute at runtime. Mandatory.

*Exception section*

Handles exceptions to normal processing (warnings and error conditions). Optional.

Figure 3-1 shows the structure of the PL/SQL block for a procedure.

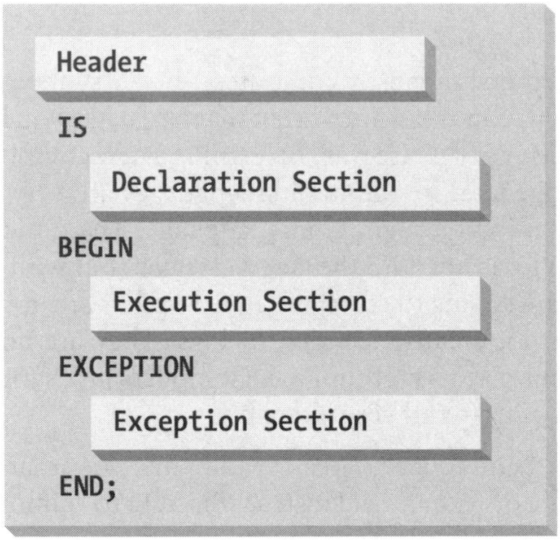

*Figure 3-1. The PL/SQL block structure*

Figure 3-2 shows a procedure containing all four sections of the elements of a block. This particular block begins with the keyword PROCEDURE, and, like all blocks, ends with the keyword END.

## Anonymous Blocks

When someone wishes to remain anonymous, that person goes unnamed. Same with the anonymous block in PL/SQL, which is shown in Figure 3-3: it lacks a header section altogether, beginning instead with either DECLARE or BEGIN. That means that it cannot be called by any other block—it doesn't have a handle for reference. Instead, anonymous blocks serve as containers that execute PL/SQL statements, usually including calls to procedures and functions. Because an anonymous block can have its own declaration and exception sections, developers often nest anonymous blocks to provide a scope for identifiers and exception handling within a larger program.

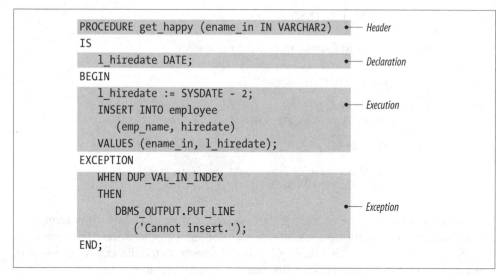

*Figure 3-2. A procedure containing all four sections*

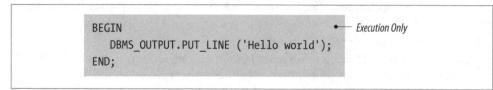

*Figure 3-3. An anonymous block without declaration and exception sections*

The general syntax of an anonymous PL/SQL block is as follows:

```
[ DECLARE   ... declaration statements ... ]
BEGIN   ... one or more executable statements ...
[ EXCEPTION
   ... exception handler statements ... ]
END;
```

The square brackets indicate an optional part of the syntax. You must have BEGIN and END statements, and you must have at least one executable statement. Here are a few examples:

- A bare minimum anonymous block:

  ```
  BEGIN
     DBMS_OUTPUT.PUT_LINE(SYSDATE);
  END;
  ```

- A functionally similar block, adding a declaration section:

  ```
  DECLARE
     l_right_now VARCHAR2(9);
  BEGIN
     l_right_now := SYSDATE;
  ```

```
        DBMS_OUTPUT.PUT_LINE (l_right_now);
    END;
```

- The same block, but including an exception handler:

```
DECLARE
    l_right_now VARCHAR2(9);
BEGIN
    l_right_now := SYSDATE;
    DBMS_OUTPUT.PUT_LINE (l_right_now);
EXCFPTTON
    WHEN VALUE_ERROR
    THEN
        DBMS_OUTPUT.PUT_LINE('I bet l_right_now is too small '
            || 'for the default date format!');
END;
```

Anonymous blocks execute a series of statements and then terminate, thus acting like procedures. In fact, all anonymous blocks are anonymous procedures. They are used in various environments where PL/SQL code is either executed directly or enclosed in some program in that environment. Common examples include:

*Database triggers*
> As discussed in Chapter 19, database triggers execute anonymous blocks when certain events occur.

*Ad hoc commands or script files*
> In SQL*Plus or similar execution environments, anonymous blocks run from hand-entered blocks or from scripts that call stored programs. Also, the SQL*Plus EXECUTE command translates its argument into an anonymous block by enclosing it between BEGIN and END statements.

*Compiled 3GL program*
> In Pro*C or OCI, anonymous blocks can be the means by which you can embed calls to stored programs.

In each case, the enclosing object—whether it's a trigger, a command-line environment, or a compiled program—provides the context and possibly a means of naming the program.

## Named Blocks

While anonymous PL/SQL blocks are indispensable, the majority of code you write will be in named blocks. You've seen a few short examples of stored procedures in this book already (as in Figure 3-1), so you probably know that the difference is in the header. A procedure header looks like this:

```
PROCEDURE [schema.]name [ ( parameter [, parameter ... ] ) ]
    [AUTHID {DEFINER | CURRENT_USER}]
```

A function header has similar syntax, but includes the RETURN keyword:

```
FUNCTION [schema.]name [ ( parameter [, parameter ... ] ) ]
   RETURN return_datatype
   [AUTHID {DEFINER | CURRENT_USER}]
   [DETERMINISTIC]
   [PARALLEL ENABLE ...]
   [PIPELINED [USING...] | AGGREGATE USING...]
```

Because Oracle allows you to invoke some functions from within SQL statements, the function header includes more optional components than the procedure header, corresponding to the functionality and performance dimensions of the SQL runtime environment.

For a more complete discussion of procedures and functions, see Chapter 17.

## Nested Blocks

PL/SQL shares with Ada and Pascal the additional definition of being a *block-structured language*, that is, blocks may "nest" within other blocks. In contrast, the C language has blocks, but standard C isn't strictly block-structured, because its subprograms cannot be nested.

Here's a PL/SQL example showing a procedure containing an anonymous, nested block:

```
PROCEDURE calc_totals
IS
   year_total NUMBER;
BEGIN
   year_total := 0;

   /* Beginning of nested block */
   DECLARE
      month_total NUMBER;
   BEGIN
      month_total := year_total / 12;
   END set_month_total;
   /* End of nested block */

END;
```

The /* and */ delimiters indicate comments (see "Comments" on page 75). You can nest anonymous blocks within anonymous blocks to more than one level, as shown in Figure 3-4.

Other terms you may hear for nested block are *enclosed block*, *child block*, or *subblock*; the outer PL/SQL block may be called the *enclosing block* or the *parent block*.

In general, the advantage of nesting a block is that it gives you a way to control both scope and visibility in your code.

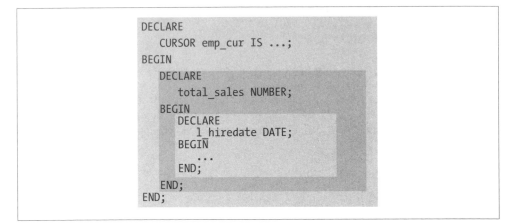

*Figure 3-4. Anonymous blocks nested three levels deep*

## Scope

In any programming language, the term *scope* refers to the way of identifying which "thing" is referred to by a given identifier. If you have more than one occurrence of an identifier, the language's scoping rules define which one will be used. Carefully controlling identifier scope not only will increase your control over runtime behavior but also will reduce the likelihood of a programmer accidentally modifying the wrong variable.

In PL/SQL, variables, exceptions, modules, and a few other structures are local to the block that declares them. When the block stops executing, you can no longer reference any of these structures. For example, in the earlier calc_totals procedure, I can reference elements from the outer block, like the year_total variable, anywhere in the procedure; however, elements declared within an inner block are not available to the outer block.

Every PL/SQL variable has a scope: the region of a program unit (block, subprogram, or package) in which that variable can be referenced. Consider the following package definition:

```
PACKAGE scope_demo
IS
   g_global   NUMBER;

   PROCEDURE set_global (number_in IN NUMBER);
END scope_demo;

PACKAGE BODY scope_demo
IS
   PROCEDURE set_global (number_in IN NUMBER)
   IS
      l_salary  NUMBER := 10000;
      l_count   PLS_INTEGER;
   BEGIN
```

```
      <<local_block>>
      DECLARE
         l_inner   NUMBER;
      BEGIN
         SELECT COUNT (*)
           INTO l_count
           FROM employees
          WHERE department_id = l_inner AND salary > l_salary;
      END local_block;

      g_global := number_in;
   END set_global;
END scope_demo;
```

The scope_demo.g_global variable can be referenced from any block in any schema that has EXECUTE authority on scope_demo.

The l_salary variable can be referenced only inside the set_global procedure.

The l_inner variable can be referenced only inside the local or nested block; note that I have used the label "local_block" to give a name to that nested block.

## Qualify all References to Variables and Columns in SQL Statements

None of the variables or column references in the last code example were *qualified* with the scope name. Here is another version of the same package body, but this time with qualified references (bold):

```
PACKAGE BODY scope_demo
IS
   PROCEDURE set_global (number_in IN NUMBER)
   IS
      l_salary   NUMBER := 10000;
      l_count    PLS_INTEGER;
   BEGIN

      <<local_block>>
      DECLARE
         l_inner   PLS_INTEGER;
      BEGIN
         SELECT COUNT (*)
           INTO set_global.l_count
           FROM employees e
          WHERE e.department_id = local_block.l_inner
            AND e.salary > set_global.l_salary;
      END local_block;

      scope_demo.g_global := set_global.number_in;
   END set_global;
END scope_demo;
```

With these changes, every single reference to a column and variable is qualified by the table alias, the package name, the procedure name, or the nested block label name.

So now you know that you can do this—and why bother? There are several very good reasons:

- Improve readability of your code.
- Avoid bugs that can arise when the names of variables are the same as the names of columns.
- Take full advantage of Oracle Database 11g's fine-grained dependency feature, which is explained in Chapter 20.

Let's take a closer look at the first two of these reasons. I'll describe the third in Chapter 20.

### Improve readability

Just about every SQL statement embedded in PL/SQL programs contains references to both columns and variables. In small, simple SQL statements, it is relatively easy to distinguish between these different references. In most applications, however, you will find very long, extremely complex SQL statements that contain dozens or even hundreds of references to columns and variables.

If you do not qualify these references, it is much harder to distinguish at a glance between variables and columns. With these qualifiers, the code self-documents quite clearly the source of those references.

"Wait a minute," I can hear my readers say. "We use clearly defined naming conventions to distinguish between columns and variables. All our local variables start with 'l_' so we know immediately if the identifier is a local variable."

That is a *really* good idea; we should all have (and follow) established conventions so that the names of our identifiers reveal additional information about them (Is it a parameter or a variable? What is its datatype? etc.).

Yet while helpful, naming conventions are not sufficient to *guarantee* that over time your identifiers will *always* be interpreted by the PL/SQL compiler as you intended.

### Avoid bugs through qualifiers

If you do not qualify references to all PL/SQL variables in your embedded SQL statements, code that works correctly today might in the future suddenly *not* work anymore. And it could be very difficult to figure out what went wrong.

Consider again this embedded SQL statement that does not qualify its references:

```
SELECT COUNT (*)
  INTO l_count
  FROM employees
 WHERE department_id = l_inner AND salary > l_salary;
```

Today, l_salary unambiguously refers to the l_salary variable declared in the set_global procedure. I test my program—it works! And then it goes into production and everyone is happy.

Two years go by, and then the users ask our DBA to add a column to the employees table to record something described as "limited salary". The DBA decides to name this column "l_salary".

Can you see the problem?

Within an embedded SQL statement, the Oracle database always attempts to resolve unqualified identifier references first as columns in one of the specified tables. If it cannot find a match, it then tries to resolve the reference as an in-scope PL/SQL variable. With the column, l_salary, added to the employees table, my unqualified reference to "l_salary" in the SELECT statement is no longer resolved to the PL/SQL variable. Instead, the database resolves it as the column in the table. The consequence?

My scope_demo package still compiles without any errors, but the WHERE clause of that query is *not* going to behave as I expect. The database will not use the value of the l_salary variable, but will instead compare the salary column's value in a row of the employees table to the value of the l_salary column in that same row.

This could be a *very* tricky bug to track down and fix!

Rather than rely solely on naming conventions to avoid "collisions" between identifiers, you should also qualify references to all column names *and* variables in those embedded SQL statements. Then your code will be much less likely to behave erratically in the future as your underlying tables evolve.

## Visibility

Once a variable is in scope, another important property is its *visibility*—that is, whether you can refer to it using only its name, or whether you need to attach a prefix in front of it.

### "Visible" identifiers

First, I'd like to make an observation about the trivial case:

```
DECLARE
   first_day DATE;
   last_day DATE;
BEGIN
   first_day := SYSDATE;
   last_day := ADD_MONTHS (first_day, 6);
END;
```

Because both the first_day and last_day variables are declared in the same block where they are used, I can conveniently refer to them using only their "unqualified" identifiers, which are also known as *visible identifiers*. A visible identifier might actually reference any of the following:

- An identifier declared in the current block.
- An identifier declared in a block that encloses the current block.
- A standalone database object (table, view, sequence, etc.) or PL/SQL object (procedure, function, type) that you own.
- A standalone database object or PL/SQL object on which you have appropriate privilege and that is the target of an Oracle synonym that you can see.
- A loop index variable (but it's visible and in-scope only inside the loop body).

PL/SQL also allows the possibility of referring to in-scope items that are not directly visible, as the next section describes.

### Qualified identifiers

A common example of an identifier that isn't visible is anything declared in a package specification, such as a variable, datatype, procedure, or function. To refer to one of these elements outside of that package, you merely need to prefix it with a dotted qualifier, similar to the way you would qualify a column name with the name of its table. For example:

*price_util.compute_means*
   A program named compute_means inside the price_util package

*math.pi*
   A constant named pi, declared and initialized in the math package

(Although the descriptions indicate what kinds of globals these are, you can't necessarily tell by looking—definitely an argument in favor of good naming conventions!)

You can use an additional qualifier to indicate the owner of the object. For example:

```
scott.price_util.compute_means
```

could refer to the compute_means procedure in the price_util package owned by the Oracle user account scott.

### Qualifying identifier names with module names

When necessary, PL/SQL offers many ways to qualify an identifier so that a reference to the identifier can be resolved. Using packages, for example, you can create variables with global scope. Suppose that I create a package called company_pkg and declare a variable named last_company_id in that package's specification, as follows:

```
PACKAGE company_pkg
IS
   last_company_id NUMBER;
   ...
END company_pkg;
```

Then, I can reference that variable outside of the package, as long as I prefix the identifier name with the package name:

```
IF new_company_id = company_pkg.last_company_id THEN
```

By default, a value assigned to one of these package-level variables persists for the duration of the current database session; it doesn't go out of scope until the session disconnects.

I can also qualify the name of an identifier with the module in which it is defined:

```
PROCEDURE calc_totals
IS
    salary NUMBER;
BEGIN
    ...
    DECLARE
      salary NUMBER;
    BEGIN
      salary := calc_totals.salary;
    END;
    ...
END;
```

The first declaration of salary creates an identifier whose scope is the entire procedure. In the nested block, however, I declare another identifier with the same name. So when I reference the variable "salary" inside the inner block, it will always be resolved first against the declaration in the inner block, where that variable is visible without any qualification. If I wish to make reference to the procedure-wide salary variable inside the inner block, I must qualify that variable name with the name of the procedure (cal_totals.salary).

This technique of qualifying an identifier also works in other contexts. Consider what will happen when you run a procedure such as this (order_id is the primary key of the orders table):

```
PROCEDURE remove_order (order_id IN NUMBER)
IS
BEGIN
    DELETE orders WHERE order_id = order_id; -- Oops!
END;
```

This code will delete everything in the orders table regardless of the order_id that you pass in. The reason: SQL's name resolution matches first on column names rather than on PL/SQL identifiers. The WHERE clause "order_id = order_id" is always true, so poof goes your data. One way to fix it would be:

```
PROCEDURE remove_order (order_id IN NUMBER)
IS
BEGIN
    DELETE orders WHERE order_id = remove_order.order_id;
END;
```

This forces the parser to do the right thing. (It will even work if you happen to have a packaged function called remove_order.order_id.)

PL/SQL goes to a lot of trouble and has established many rules for determining how to resolve such naming conflicts. While it is good to be aware of such issues, you are usually much better off never having to rely on these guidelines. Code defensively! If you don't want to qualify every variable to keep it unique, you will need to use careful naming conventions to avoid these kinds of name collisions.

### Nested programs

To conclude the discussion of nesting, scope, and visibility, PL/SQL also offers a particularly important feature known as a *nested program*. A nested program is a procedure or function that appears *completely inside* the declaration section of the enclosing block. Significantly, the nested program can reference any variables and parameters previously declared in the outer block, as demonstrated in this example:

```
PROCEDURE calc_totals (fudge_factor_in IN NUMBER)
IS
   subtotal NUMBER := 0;

   /* Beginning of nested block (in this case a procedure). Notice
   |  we're completely inside the declaration section of calc_totals.
   */
   PROCEDURE compute_running_total (increment_in IN PLS_INTEGER)
   IS
   BEGIN
      /* subtotal, declared above, is both in scope and visible */
      subtotal := subtotal + increment_in * fudge_factor_in;
   END;
   /* End of nested block */
BEGIN
   FOR month_idx IN 1..12
   LOOP
      compute_running_total (month_idx);
   END LOOP;
   DBMS_OUTPUT.PUT_LINE('Fudged total for year: ' || subtotal);
END;
```

Nested programs can make your program more readable and maintainable, and also allow you to reuse logic that appears in multiple places in the block. For more information about this topic, see Chapter 17.

## The PL/SQL Character Set

A PL/SQL program consists of a sequence of statements, each made up of one or more lines of text. The precise characters available to you will depend on what database character set you're using. For example, Table 3-1 illustrates the available characters in the US7ASCII character set.

*Table 3-1. Characters available to PL/SQL in the US7ASCII character set*

| Type | Characters |
| --- | --- |
| Letters | A–Z, a–z |
| Digits | 0–9 |
| Symbols | ~ ! @ # $ % * ( ) _ – + = | : ; " ' < > , . ? / ^ |
| Whitespace | Tab, space, newline, carriage return |

Every keyword, operator, and token in PL/SQL is made from various combinations of characters in this character set. Now you just have to figure out how to put them all together!

And now for some real PL/SQL trivia: Oracle's documentation—as well as earlier editions of this book—list the ampersand, curly braces, and square brackets as part of the default character set:

    & { } [ ]

While all characters are allowed in literal strings, Oracle does not seem to use these particular five characters anywhere in the visible portions of PL/SQL. Moreover, there is no direct way to use these characters in programmer-defined identifiers.

Regardless of your memory for such trivia, you'll definitely want to remember that *PL/SQL is a case-insensitive language.* That is, it doesn't matter how you type keywords and identifiers; uppercase letters are treated the same way as lowercase letters unless surrounded by delimiters that make them a literal string. By convention, the authors of this book prefer uppercase for built-in language keywords (and certain identifiers used by Oracle as built-in function and package names), and lowercase for programmer-defined identifiers.

A number of these characters—both singly and in combination with other characters—have a special significance in PL/SQL. Table 3-2 lists these special symbols.

*Table 3-2. Simple and compound symbols in PL/SQL*

| Symbol | Description |
| --- | --- |
| ; | Semicolon: terminates declarations and statements |
| % | Percent sign: attribute indicator (cursor attributes like %ISOPEN and indirect declaration attributes like %ROWTYPE); also used as a wildcard symbol with the LIKE condition |
| _ | Single underscore: single-character wildcard symbol in LIKE condition |
| @ | At-sign: remote location indicator |
| : | Colon: host variable indicator, such as :block.item in Oracle Forms |
| ** | Double asterisk: exponentiation operator |
| < > or != or ^= or ~= | Ways to denote the "not equal" relational operator |
| || | Double vertical bar: concatenation operator |

| Symbol | Description |
| --- | --- |
| << and >> | Label delimiters |
| <= and >= | Less than or equal, greater than or equal relational operators |
| := | Assignment operator |
| => | Association operator for positional notation |
| .. | Double dot: range operator |
| -- | Double dash: single-line comment indicator |
| /* and */ | Beginning and ending multiline comment block delimiters |

Characters are grouped together into *lexical units*, also called *atomics* of the language because they are the smallest individual components. A lexical unit in PL/SQL is any of the following:

- Identifier
- Literal
- Delimiter
- Comment

These are described in the following sections.

# Identifiers

An identifier is a name for a PL/SQL object, including any of the following:

- Constant or variable
- Exception
- Cursor
- Program name: procedure, function, package, object type, trigger, etc.
- Reserved word
- Label

Default properties of PL/SQL identifiers are summarized below:

- Up to 30 characters in length
- Must start with a letter
- Can include $ (dollar sign), _ (underscore), and # (hash sign)
- Cannot contain any "whitespace" characters

If the only difference between two identifiers is the case of one or more letters, PL/SQL normally treats those two identifiers as the same.[1] For example, the following identifiers are all considered by PL/SQL to be the same:

```
lots_of_$MONEY$
LOTS_of_$MONEY$
Lots_of_$Money$
```

The following strings are valid names of identifiers:

```
company_id#
primary_acct_responsibility
First_Name
FirstName
address_line1
S123456
```

The following identifiers are all illegal in PL/SQL:

```
1st_year                            -- Doesn't start with a letter
procedure-name                      -- Contains invalid character "-"
minimum_%_due                       -- Contains invalid character "%"
maximum_value_exploded_for_detail   -- Too long
company ID                          -- Has embedded whitespace
```

Identifiers are the handles for objects in your program and one of your chief means of communicating with other programmers. For this reason, many organizations adopt naming conventions; if your project doesn't require naming conventions, you will still want to choose variable names carefully...even if you are the only person who will ever see the code!

Although rarely done in practice, you can actually break some of these rules by surrounding identifiers with double quotation marks. I don't recommend programming like this, but you may one day have to deal with some "clever" code such as:

```
SQL> DECLARE
  2     "pi" CONSTANT NUMBER := 3.141592654;
  3     "PI" CONSTANT NUMBER := 3.14159265358979323846;
  4     "2 pi" CONSTANT NUMBER := 2 * "pi";
  5  BEGIN
  6     DBMS_OUTPUT.PUT_LINE('pi: ' || "pi");
  7     DBMS_OUTPUT.PUT_LINE('PI: ' || pi);
  8     DBMS_OUTPUT.PUT_LINE('2 pi: ' || "2 pi");
  9  END;
 10  /

pi: 3.141592654
PI: 3.14159265358979323846
2 pi: 6.283185308
```

---

1. The compiler accomplishes this internally by converting program text into uppercase during an early phase of compilation.

Notice that line 7 refers to pi without quotation marks. Because the compiler accomplishes its case-independence by defaulting identifiers and keywords to uppercase, the variable that line 7 refers to is the one declared on line 3 as "PI".

You may need to use the double-quote trick in SQL statements to refer to database objects that exist with mixed-case names. I've seen this happen when a programmer used Microsoft Access to create Oracle tables.

## Reserved Words

Of course, you don't get to (or have to) define all the identifiers in your programs. The PL/SQL language recognizes certain identifiers (such as BEGIN, IF, and THEN) as having special meaning.

PL/SQL provides two kinds of built-in identifiers:

- Reserved words
- Identifiers from the STANDARD package

In both cases you should not—and, in many cases, *cannot*—redefine the identifier for your program's own use.

### Reserved words

The PL/SQL compiler reserves certain identifiers for its use only. In other words, you cannot declare a variable with the name of that identifier. These are called *reserved words*. For example, one very important reserved word is END, which terminates blocks, IF statements, and loops. If you try to declare a variable named "end":

```
DECLARE
   end VARCHAR2(10) := 'blip';  /* Will not work; "end" is reserved. */
BEGIN
   DBMS_OUTPUT.PUT_LINE (end);
END;
/
```

you will receive this error message from the compiler:

```
PLS-00103: Encountered the symbol "END" when expecting one of the following:...etc...
```

### Identifiers from STANDARD package

In addition to avoiding identifiers that duplicate keywords, you should also avoid using identifiers that, in effect, *override* names that Oracle Corporation has defined in a special built-in package named STANDARD. STANDARD is one of two default packages in PL/SQL; Oracle defines in this package many of the basic building blocks of the PL/SQL language, including datatypes like PLS_INTEGER, exceptions like DUP_VAL_ON_INDEX, and functions like UPPER, REPLACE, and TO_DATE.

It may come as a surprise to many developers, but the identifiers defined in STANDARD (and DBMS_STANDARD, the other default package) are *not* reserved words. You *can* declare your own variables with the same name and your code will compile. You will, however, create lots of confusion if you do this.

The STANDARD package is explored in detail in Chapter 24.

### How to avoid using reserved words

Finding a valid name for your identifier should be the least of your problems, as there are thousands and thousands of permutations of the legal characters. The question is: how will you know if you inadvertently use a reserved word in your own program? First of all, the compiler will let you know if you try to use a name for an identifier that is actually reserved. If your curiosity compels you to investigate further, you could build a query against the V$RESERVED_WORDS view, and then try to compile a dynamically-constructed PL/SQL block that uses the reserved word as an identifier. I did precisely that; you will find the script in the *reserved_words.sql* file on the book's web site. The output from running this script is in *reserved.txt*

The results are very interesting. Here's the overall summary:

```
Reserved Word Analysis Summary
Total count in V$RESERVED_WORDS = 1733
Total number of reserved words = 118
Total number of non-reserved words = 1615
```

In other words, the vast majority of words that Oracle includes in this view are not truly reserved; that is, you can use them as the names of your own identifiers.

Generally, I recommend that you avoid using any words that Oracle Corporation uses as part of its own technology. Better yet, use naming conventions that employ consistent prefixes and suffixes, virtually guaranteeing that you will not encounter a true PL/SQL reserved word.

## Whitespace and Keywords

Identifiers must be separated by at least one space or by a delimiter, but you can format your text by adding additional spaces, line breaks (newlines and/or carriage returns), and tabs wherever you can put a space, without changing the meaning of your code.

The two statements shown here are therefore equivalent:

```
IF too_many_orders
THEN
   warn_user;
ELSIF no_orders_entered
THEN
   prompt_for_orders;
END IF;

IF too_many_orders THEN warn_user;
```

```
    ELSIF no_orders_entered THEN prompt_for_orders;
    END IF;
```

You may not, however, place a space or carriage return or tab within a lexical unit, such as the "not equals" symbol (!=). This statement results in a compile error:

```
    IF max_salary ! = min_salary THEN    -- yields PLS-00103 compile error
```

because the code contains a space between the ! and the =.

# Literals

A literal is a value that is not represented by an identifier; it is simply a value. Here is a smattering of literals you *could* see in a PL/SQL program:

*Number*
```
    415, 21.6, 3.141592654f, 7D, NULL
```
*String*
```
    'This is my sentence', '01-OCT-1986', q'!hello!', NULL
```
*Time interval*
```
    INTERVAL '25-6' YEAR TO MONTH, INTERVAL '-18' MONTH, NULL
```
*Boolean*
```
    TRUE, FALSE, NULL
```

The trailing "f" in number literal 3.14159f designates a 32-bit floating point number as defined by the IEEE 754 standard, which Oracle partially supports beginning with Oracle Database 10g Release 1. Similarly, 7D is the number 7 as represented in a 64-bit float.

The string q'!hello!' bears some explanation. The ! is a user-defined delimiter, also introduced in Oracle Database 10g; the leading q and the surrounding single quotes tell the compiler that the ! is the delimiter, and the string represented is simply the word hello.

The INTERVAL datatype allows you to manage amounts of time between dates or timestamps. The first example above represents "25 years and 6 months after"; the second represents "18 months before."

To specify literal values of dates and times, you can use the DATE or TIMESTAMP keyword:

```
    DATE '1986-10-01'
    TIMESTAMP '1986-10-01 00:00:00 -6:00'
```

Both expressions return October 1, 1986, with zero hours, zero minutes, and zero seconds; the first in the DATE datatype, and the second in the TIMESTAMP WITH TIME ZONE datatype. The second expression also includes time zone information; the -6 represents the number of hours' difference from UCT.

---

Alternatively, you can convert strings to date or timestamp datatypes using Oracle built-in functions. The following are the equivalent of the above literals:

```
TO_DATE('01-OCT-1986', 'DD-MON-YYYY')
TO_TIMESTAMP_TZ('01-OCT-1986 00:00:00 -6','DD-MON-YYYY HH24:MI:SS TZH')
```

In your code, a simple string such as '01-OCT-1986' *may* get converted to a date datatype; if that happens Oracle will apply the current session's value of the NLS_DATE_FORMAT parameter when attempting the conversion. In this case, only if the format were set to DD-MON-YYYY would you be guaranteed to get the desired result. You probably want to avoid such implicit conversions, since NLS_DATE_FORMAT can change.

Unlike identifiers, string literals in PL/SQL are case-sensitive. As you would probably expect, the following two literals are different.

```
'Steven'
'steven'
```

So the following condition evaluates to FALSE:

```
IF 'Steven' = 'steven'
```

## NULLs

The absence of a value is represented in the Oracle database by the keyword NULL. As shown in the previous section, variables of almost all PL/SQL datatypes can exist in a null state (the exception to this rule is any associative array type, instances of which are never null). Although it can be challenging for a programmer to handle NULL variables properly regardless of their datatype, strings that are null require special consideration.

In Oracle SQL and PL/SQL, a null string is *usually* indistinguishable from a literal of zero characters, represented literally as '' (two consecutive single quotes with no characters between them). For example, the following expression will evaluate to TRUE in both SQL and PL/SQL:

```
'' IS NULL
```

Assigning a zero-length string to a VARCHAR2($n$) variable in PL/SQL also yields a NULL result:

```
DECLARE
   str VARCHAR2(1) := '';
BEGIN
   IF str IS NULL   -- will be TRUE
```

This behavior is consistent with the database's treatment of VARCHAR2 table columns.

Let's look at CHAR data, though—it's a little quirky. If you create a CHAR(*n*) variable in PL/SQL and assign a zero-length string to it, the database *blank-pads the empty variable with space characters*, making it not null:

```
DECLARE
    flag CHAR(2) := '';  -- try to assign zero-length string to CHAR(2)
BEGIN
    IF flag = ' '  ...   -- will be TRUE
    IF flag IS NULL ...   -- will be FALSE
```

Strangely, PL/SQL is the only place you will see such behavior. In the database, when you insert a zero-length string into a CHAR(*n*) table column, the database does *not* blank-pad the contents of the column, but leaves it NULL instead!

These examples illustrate Oracle's partial adherence to the 92 and 99 versions of the ANSI SQL standard, which mandates a difference between a zero-length string and a NULL string. Oracle admits this difference, and says they may fully adopt the standard in the future. They've been issuing that warning for about 15 years, though, and it hasn't happened yet.

While NULL tends to behave as if its default datatype is VARCHAR2, the database will try to implicitly cast NULL to whatever type is needed for the current operation. Occasionally, you may need to make the cast explicit, using syntax such as TO_NUMBER(NULL) or CAST(NULL AS NUMBER).

## Embedding Single Quotes Inside a Literal String

An unavoidably ugly aspect of working with string literals occurs when you need to put the delimiter itself inside the string. Until Oracle Database 10*g* was released, you would write two single quotes next to each other if you wanted the string to contain a single quote in that position. Some examples:

| Literal (default delimiter) | Actual value |
| --- | --- |
| `'There''s no business like show business.'` | `There's no business like show business.` |
| `'"Hound of the Baskervilles"'` | `"Hound of the Baskervilles"` |
| `''''` | `'` |
| `'''hello'''` | `'hello'` |
| `''''''` | `''` |

The examples show, for instance, that it takes six single quotes to designate a literal containing two consecutive single quotes. In an attempt to simplify this type of construct, Oracle Database 10*g* introduced user-defined delimiters. Start the literal with "q" to mark your delimiter, and surround your delimited expression with single quotes. The table below shows this feature in action:

| Literal (delimiters highlighted) | Actual value |
|---|---|
| q'(There's no business like show business.)' | There's no business like show business. |
| q'{"Hound of the Baskervilles"}' | "Hound of the Baskervilles" |
| q'['}' | ' |
| q'!'hello'!' | 'hello' |
| q'\|''\|' | '' |

As the examples show, you can use plain delimiters such as ! or |, or you can use "mated" delimiters such as left and right parentheses, curly braces, and square brackets.

One final note: as you would expect, a double quote character does not have any special significance inside a string literal. It is treated the same as a letter or number.

## Numeric Literals

Numeric literals can be integers or real numbers (a number that contains a fractional component). Note that PL/SQL considers the number 154.00 to be a real number of type NUMBER, even though the fractional component is zero, and the number is actually an integer. Internally, integers and reals have a different representation, and there is some small overhead involved in converting between the two.

You can also use scientific notation to specify a numeric literal. Use the letter E (upper- or lowercase) to multiply a number by 10 to the nth power (e.g., 3.05E19, 12e-5).

Beginning with Oracle Database 10g, a real can be either an Oracle NUMBER type or an IEEE 754 standard floating-point type. Floating-point literals are either BINARY (32-bit) (designated with a trailing F) or BINARY DOUBLE (64-bit) (designated with a D).

In certain expressions, you may use the following named constants, as prescribed by the IEEE standard:

| Description | Binary float (32-bit) | Binary double (64-bit) |
|---|---|---|
| "Not a number" (NaN); result of divide by 0 or invalid operation | BINARY_FLOAT_NAN | BINARY_DOUBLE_NAN |
| Positive infinity | BINARY_FLOAT_INFINITY | BINARY_DOUBLE_INFINITY |
| Absolute maximum number that can be represented | BINARY_FLOAT_MAX_NORMAL | BINARY_DOUBLE_MAX_NORMAL |
| Smallest normal number; underflow threshold | BINARY_FLOAT_MIN_NORMAL | BINARY_DOUBLE_MIN_NORMAL |
| Maximum positive number that is less than the underflow threshold | BINARY_FLOAT_MAX_SUBNORMAL | BINARY_DOUBLE_MAX_SUBNORMAL |
| Absolute minimum positive number that can be represented | BINARY_FLOAT_MIN_SUBNORMAL | BINARY_DOUBLE_MIN_SUBNORMAL |

## Boolean Literals

PL/SQL provides two literals to represent Boolean values: TRUE and FALSE. These values are not strings; you should not put quotes around them. Use Boolean literals to assign values to Boolean variables, as in:

```
DECLARE
    enough_money BOOLEAN; -- Declare a Boolean variable
BEGIN
    enough_money := FALSE; -- Assign it a value
END;
```

You do not, on the other hand, need to refer to the literal value when checking the value of a Boolean expression. Instead, just let that expression speak for itself, as shown in the conditional clause of the following IF statement:

```
DECLARE
    enough_money BOOLEAN;
BEGIN
    IF enough_money
    THEN
        ...
```

A Boolean expression, variable, or constant may also evaluate to NULL, which is neither TRUE nor FALSE. For more information, see Chapter 4, particularly the sidebar "Three-Valued Logic" on page 82.

# The Semicolon Delimiter

A PL/SQL program is made up of a series of declarations and statements. These are defined logically, as opposed to physically. In other words, they are not terminated with the physical end of a line of code; instead, they are terminated with a semicolon (;). In fact, a single statement is often spread over several lines to make it more readable. The following IF statement takes up four lines and is indented to reinforce the logic behind the statement:

```
IF salary < min_salary (2003)
THEN
    salary := salary + salary * .25;
END IF;
```

There are two semicolons in this IF statement. The first semicolon indicates the end of the single executable statement within the IF-END IF construct. The second semicolon terminates the IF statement itself. This same statement could also be placed on a single physical line and have exactly the same result:

```
IF salary < min_salary (2003) THEN salary := salary + salary*.25; END IF;
```

The semicolons are still needed to terminate each logical, executable statement, even if they are nested inside one another. Unless you're *trying* to create unreadable code, I suggest that you not combine the different components of the IF statement on a single

---

line. I also recommend that you place no more than one statement or declaration on each line.

# Comments

Inline documentation, otherwise known as *comments*, is an important element of a good program. While this book offers many suggestions on how to make your program self-documenting through good naming practices and modularization, such techniques are seldom enough by themselves to communicate a thorough understanding of a complex program.

PL/SQL offers two different styles for comments: single-line and multiline block comments.

## Single-Line Comment Syntax

The single-line comment is initiated with two hyphens (--), which cannot be separated by a space or any other characters. All text after the double hyphen to the end of the physical line is considered commentary and is ignored by the compiler. If the double hyphen appears at the beginning of the line, the whole line is a comment.

Remember: the double hyphen comments out the remainder of a physical line, not a logical PL/SQL statement. In the following IF statement, I use a single-line comment to clarify the logic of the Boolean expression:

```
IF salary < min_salary (2003) -- Function returns min salary for year.
THEN
    salary := salary + salary*.25;
END IF;
```

## Multiline Comment Syntax

While single-line comments are useful for documenting brief bits of code or ignoring a line that you do not want executed at the moment, the multiline comment is superior for including longer blocks of commentary.

Multiline comments start with a slash-asterisk (/*) and end with an asterisk-slash (*/). PL/SQL considers all characters found between these two sequences of symbols to be part of the comment, and they are ignored by the compiler.

The following example of multiline comments shows a header section for a procedure. I use the vertical bars in the left margin so that, as the eye moves down the left edge of the program, it can easily pick out the chunks of comments:

```
PROCEDURE calc_revenue (company_id IN NUMBER) IS
/*
| Program: calc_revenue
| Author: Steven Feuerstein
| Change history:
```

```
|    10-JUN-2009 Incorporate new formulas
|    23-SEP-2008 - Program created
|*/
BEGIN
   ...
END;
```

You can also use multiline comments to block out lines of code for testing purposes. In the following example, the additional clauses in the EXIT statement are ignored so that testing can concentrate on the a_delimiter function:

```
EXIT WHEN a_delimiter (next_char)
/*
            OR
          (was_a_delimiter AND NOT a_delimiter (next_char))
*/
;
```

# The PRAGMA Keyword

A programming notion that is truly derived from Greek is *pragma*, which means "deed" or, by implication, an "action." In various programming languages, a pragma is generally a line of source code prescribing an action you want the compiler to take. It's like an option that you give the compiler; it can result in different runtime behavior for the program, but it doesn't get translated directly into bytecode.

PL/SQL has a PRAGMA keyword with the following syntax:

```
PRAGMA instruction_to_compiler;
```

The PL/SQL compiler will accept such directives anywhere in the declaration section, but most of them have certain additional requirements regarding placement.

PL/SQL offers several pragmas:

*AUTONOMOUS_TRANSACTION*
> Tells the PL/SQL runtime engine to commit or roll back any changes made to the database inside the current block without affecting the main or outer transaction. See Chapter 14 for more information.

*EXCEPTION_INIT*
> Tells the compiler to associate a particular error number with an identifier you have declared as an exception in your program. Must follow the declaration of the exception. See Chapter 6 for more information.

*RESTRICT_REFERENCES*
> Tells the compiler the purity level (freedom from side effects) of a packaged program. See Chapter 17 for more information.

*SERIALLY_REUSABLE*
> Tells the PL/SQL runtime engine that package-level data should not persist between references to that data. See Chapter 18 for more information.

The following block demonstrates the use of the EXCEPTION_INIT pragma to name a built-in exception that would otherwise have only a number:

```
DECLARE
    no_such_sequence EXCEPTION;
    PRAGMA EXCEPTION_INIT (no_such_sequence, -2289);
BEGIN
    ...
EXCEPTION
    WHEN no_such_sequence
    THEN
        q$error_manager.raise_error ('Sequence not defined');
END;
```

# Labels

A PL/SQL label is a way to name a particular part of your program. Syntactically, a label has the format:

```
<<identifier>>
```

where *identifier* is a valid PL/SQL identifier (up to 30 characters in length and starting with a letter, as discussed earlier in the section "Identifiers" on page 66). There is no terminator; labels appear directly in front of the thing they're labeling, which must be an executable statement—even if it is merely the NULL statement.

```
BEGIN
    ...
    <<the_spot>>
    NULL;
```

Because anonymous blocks are themselves executable statements, a label can "name" an anonymous block for the duration of its execution. For example:

```
<<insert_but_ignore_dups>>
BEGIN
    INSERT INTO catalog
    VALUES (...);
EXCEPTION
    WHEN DUP_VAL_ON_INDEX
    THEN
        NULL;
END insert_but_ignore_dups;
```

One reason you might label a block is to improve the readability of your code. When you give something a name, you self-document that code. You also clarify your own thinking about what that code is supposed to do, sometimes ferreting out errors in the process.

Another reason to use a block label is to allow you to qualify references to elements from an enclosing block that have duplicate names in the current, nested block. Here's a schematic example:

```
<<outerblock>>
DECLARE
    counter INTEGER := 0;
BEGIN
    ...
    DECLARE
        counter INTEGER := 1;
    BEGIN
        IF counter = outerblock.counter
        THEN
            ...
        END IF;
    END;
END;
```

Without the block label, there would be no way to distinguish between the two "counter" variables. Again, though, a better solution would probably have been to use distinct variable names.

A third function of labels is to serve as the target of a GOTO statement. See the discussion of GOTO in Chapter 4.

Although few programs I've seen or worked on require the use of labels, there is one final use of this feature that is more significant than the previous three combined: a label can serve as a target for the EXIT statement in nested loops. Here's the example code:

```
BEGIN
    <<outer_loop>>
    LOOP
        LOOP
            EXIT outer_loop;
        END LOOP;
        some_statement;
    END LOOP;
END;
```

Without the <<outer_loop>> label, the EXIT statement would have exited only the inner loop and would have executed *some_statement*. But I didn't want it to do that. So, in this case, the label provides functionality that PL/SQL does not offer in any other straightforward way.

# PART II

# PL/SQL Program Structure

This part of the book presents the basic PL/SQL programming elements and statement constructs. Chapters 4 through 6 describe conditional (IF and CASE) and sequential control statements (e.g., GOTO and NULL); loops and the CONTINUE statement introduced for loops in Oracle Database 11g; and exception handling in the PL/SQL language. When you complete this section of the book you will know how to construct blocks of code that correlate to the complex requirements in your applications.

Chapter 4, *Conditional and Sequential Control*
Chapter 5, *Iterative Processing with Loops*
Chapter 6, *Exception Handlers*

# Conditional and Sequential Control

This chapter describes two types of PL/SQL control statements: conditional control statements and sequential control statements. Almost every piece of code you write will require conditional control, which is the ability to direct the flow of execution through your program based on a condition. You do this with IF-THEN-ELSE and CASE statements. There are also CASE expressions; while not the same as CASE statements, they can sometimes be used to eliminate the need for an IF or CASE statement altogether. Far less often, you will need to tell PL/SQL to transfer control unconditionally via the GOTO statement, or explicitly to do nothing via the NULL statement.

## IF Statements

The IF statement allows you to implement conditional branching logic in your programs. With it, you'll be able to implement requirements such as:

- If the salary is between $10,000 and $20,000, apply a bonus of $1,500.
- If the collection contains more than 100 elements, truncate it.

The IF statement comes in three flavors, as shown in the following table:

| IF type | Characteristics |
|---|---|
| `IF THEN END IF;` | This is the simplest form of the IF statement. The condition between IF and THEN determines whether the set of statements between THEN and END IF should be executed. If the condition evaluates to FALSE or NULL, the code is not executed. |
| `IF THEN ELSE END IF;` | This combination implements an either/or logic: based on the condition between the IF and THEN keywords, execute the code either between THEN and ELSE or between ELSE and END IF. One of these two sections of executable statements is performed. |
| `IF THEN ELSIF ELSE END IF;` | This last and most complex form of the IF statement selects a condition that is TRUE from a series of mutually exclusive conditions and then executes the set of statements associated with that condition. If you're writing IF statements like this using any release from Oracle9*i* Database Release 1 onwards, you should consider using searched CASE statements instead. |

## The IF-THEN Combination

The general format of the IF-THEN syntax is as follows:

```
IF condition
THEN
   ... sequence of executable statements ...
END IF;
```

The *condition* is a Boolean variable, constant, or expression that evaluates to TRUE, FALSE, or NULL. If *condition* evaluates to TRUE, the executable statements found after the THEN keyword and before the matching END IF statement are executed. If *condition* evaluates to FALSE or NULL, those statements are not executed.

---

### Three-Valued Logic

Boolean expressions can return three possible results. When all values in a Boolean expression are known, the result is either TRUE or FALSE. For example, there is no doubt when determining the truth or falsity of an expression such as:

```
(2 < 3) AND (5 < 10)
```

Sometimes, however, you don't know all values in an expression. That's because databases allow for values to be NULL, or missing. What then, can be the result from an expression involving NULLs? For example:

```
2 < NULL
```

Because you don't know what the missing value is, the only answer you can give is "I don't know." This is the essence of so-called *three-valued logic*—that you can have not only TRUE and FALSE as a possible result, but also NULL.

To learn more about three-valued logic, I recommend Lex de Haan's and Jonathan Gennick's *Oracle Magazine* article "Nulls, Nothing to Worry About...", which you can find at *http://www.oracle.com/technology/oramag/oracle/05-jul/o45sql.html*. You might find C. J. Date's book *Database In Depth: Relational Theory for the Practitioner* (O'Reilly) helpful as well. I'll also have more to say about three-valued logic as you go through this chapter.

---

The following IF condition compares two different numeric values. Remember that if one of these two values is NULL, then the entire expression returns NULL. In the following example, the bonus is not given when salary is NULL:

```
IF salary > 40000
THEN
   give_bonus (employee_id,500);
END IF;
```

There are exceptions to the rule that a NULL in a Boolean expression leads to a NULL result. Some operators and functions are specifically designed to deal with NULLs in a way that leads to TRUE and FALSE (and not NULL) results. For example, you can use IS NULL to test for the presence of a NULL:

```
IF salary > 40000 OR salary IS NULL
THEN
   give_bonus (employee_id,500);
END IF;
```

In this example, "salary IS NULL" evaluates to TRUE in the event that salary has no value, and otherwise to FALSE. Employees whose salaries are missing will now get bonuses too. (As indeed they probably should, considering their employer was so inconsiderate as to lose track of their pay in the first place.)

> Using operators such as IS NULL and IS NOT NULL, or functions such as COALESCE and NVL2, are good ways to detect and deal with potentially NULL values. For every variable that you reference in every Boolean expression that you write, be sure to think carefully about the consequences if that variable is NULL.

It's not necessary to put the IF, THEN, and END IF keywords on their own lines. In fact, line breaks don't matter at all for any type of IF statement. You could just as easily write:

```
IF salary > 40000 THEN give_bonus (employee_id,500); END IF;
```

Putting everything on one line is perfectly fine for simple IF statements such as the one shown here. However, when writing IF statements of any complexity at all, you'll find that readability is much greater when you format the statement such that each keyword begins a new line. For example, the following code would be very difficult to follow if it were all crammed on a single line. Actually, it's difficult to follow as it appears on three lines:

```
IF salary > 40000 THEN INSERT INTO employee_bonus (eb_employee_id, eb_bonus_amt)
VALUES (employee_id, 500); UPDATE emp_employee SET emp_bonus_given=1 WHERE emp_
employee_id=employee_id; END IF;
```

Ugh! Who'd want to spend time figuring that out? It's much more readable when formatted nicely:

```
IF salary > 40000
THEN
   INSERT INTO employee_bonus
      (eb_employee_id, eb_bonus_amt)
      VALUES (employee_id, 500);
   UPDATE emp_employee
   SET emp_bonus_given=1
   WHERE emp_employee_id=employee_id;
END IF;
```

This readability issue becomes even more important when using the ELSE and ELSIF keywords, and when nesting one IF statement inside the other. Take full advantage of indents and formatting to make the logic of your IF statements easily decipherable. Future maintenance programmers will thank you.

## The IF-THEN-ELSE Combination

Use the IF-THEN-ELSE format when you want to choose between two mutually exclusive actions. The format of this either/or version of the IF statement is as follows:

```
IF condition
THEN
   ... TRUE sequence of executable statements ...
ELSE
   ... FALSE/NULL sequence of executable statements ...
END IF;
```

The *condition* is a Boolean variable, constant, or expression. If *condition* evaluates to TRUE, the executable statements found after the THEN keyword and before the ELSE keyword are executed (the "TRUE sequence of executable statements"). If *condition* evaluates to FALSE or NULL, the executable statements that come after the ELSE keyword and before the matching END IF keywords are executed (the "FALSE/NULL sequence of executable statements").

The important thing to remember is that one of the two sequences of statements will *always* execute, because IF-THEN-ELSE is an either/or construct. Once the appropriate set of statements has been executed, control passes to the statement immediately following the END IF keyword.

Following is an example of the IF-THEN-ELSE construct that builds upon the IF-THEN example shown in the previous section:

```
IF salary <= 40000
THEN
   give_bonus (employee_id, 0);
ELSE
   give_bonus (employee_id, 500);
END IF;
```

In this example, employees with a salary greater than $40,000 will get a bonus of $500 while all other employees will get no bonus at all. Or will they? What happens if salary, for whatever reason, happens to be NULL for a given employee? In that case, the statements following the ELSE will be executed, and the employee in question will get the bonus that is supposed to go only to highly paid employees. That's not good (well, it was good in the last section, but not now)! If the salary could be NULL, you can protect yourself against this problem using the NVL function:

```
IF NVL(salary,0) <= 40000
THEN
   give_bonus (employee_id, 0);
ELSE
   give_bonus (employee_id, 500);
END IF;
```

The NVL function will return zero any time salary is NULL, ensuring that any employees with a NULL salary also get a zero bonus (those poor employees).

## Using Boolean Flags

Often, it's convenient to use Boolean variables as flags so that you don't need to evaluate the same Boolean expression more than once. When doing so, remember that the result of a Boolean expression can be assigned directly to a Boolean variable. For example, rather than write:

```
IF :customer.order_total > max_allowable_order
THEN
    order_exceeds_balance := TRUE;
ELSE
    order_exceeds_balance := FALSE;
END IF;
```

you can instead (assuming neither variable could be NULL) write the following, much simpler expression:

```
order_exceeds_balance
    := :customer.order_total > max_allowable_order;
```

Now, whenever you need to test whether an order's total exceeds the maximum, you can write the following, easily understandable, IF statement:

```
IF order_exceeds_balance
THEN
...
```

If you have not had much experience with Boolean variables, it may take you a little while to learn how to integrate them smoothly into your code. It is worth the effort, though. The result is cleaner, more readable code.

## The IF-THEN-ELSIF Combination

This last form of the IF statement comes in handy when you have to implement logic that has many alternatives; it is not an either/or situation. The IF-ELSIF formulation provides a way to handle multiple conditions within a single IF statement. In general, you should use ELSIF with mutually exclusive alternatives (i.e., only one condition can be TRUE for any execution of the IF statement). The general format for this variation of IF is:

```
IF condition-1
THEN
    statements-1
ELSIF condition-N
THEN
    statements-N
[ELSE
    else_statements]
END IF;
```

Be very careful to use ELSIF, not ELSEIF. The inadvertent use of ELSEIF is a fairly common syntax error. ELSE IF (two words) doesn't work either.

Logically speaking, the IF-THEN-ELSIF construct is one way to implement CASE statement functionality in PL/SQL. Of course, if you are using Oracle9i Database onwards, you are probably better off actually using a CASE statement (discussed later in this chapter).

Each ELSIF clause must have a THEN after its *condition*. Only the ELSE keyword does not need the THEN keyword. The ELSE clause in the IF-ELSIF is the "otherwise" of the statement. If none of the conditions evaluate to TRUE, the statements in the ELSE clause are executed. But the ELSE clause is optional. You can code an IF-ELSIF that has only IF and ELSIF clauses. In such a case, if none of the conditions are TRUE, no statements inside the IF block are executed.

Following is an implementation of the complete bonus logic described at the beginning of this chapter using the IF-THEN-ELSEIF combination:

```
IF salary BETWEEN 10000 AND 20000
THEN
    give_bonus(employee_id, 1500);
ELSIF salary BETWEEN 20000 AND 40000
THEN
    give_bonus(employee_id, 1000);
ELSIF salary > 40000
THEN
    give_bonus(employee_id, 500);
ELSE
    give_bonus(employee_id, 0);
END IF;
```

## Avoiding IF Syntax Gotchas

Keep in mind these points about IF statement syntax:

*Always match up an IF with an END IF*
In all three variations of the IF statement, you must close off the executable statements associated with the conditional structure with an END IF keyword.

*You must have a space between the keywords END and IF*
If you type ENDIF instead of END IF, the compiler will get confused and give you the following hard-to-understand error messages:

```
ORA-06550: line 14, column 4:

PLS-00103: Encountered the symbol ";" when expecting one of the following:
```

*The ELSIF keyword should not have an embedded "E"*

If you type ELSEIF in place of ELSIF, the compiler will also get confused and not recognize the ELSEIF as part of the IF statement. Instead, the compiler will interpret ELSEIF as a variable or a procedure name.

*Place a semicolon (;) only after the END IF keywords*

The keywords THEN, ELSE, and ELSIF should not have a semicolon after them. They are not standalone executable statements, and, unlike END IF, do not complete a statement. If you include a semicolon after these keywords, the compiler will issue messages indicating that it is looking for a statement of some kind before the semicolon.

The conditions in the IF-ELSIF are always evaluated in the order of first condition to last condition. If two conditions evaluate to TRUE, the statements for the first such condition are executed. With respect to the current example, a salary of $20,000 will result in a bonus of $1,500 even though that $20,000 salary also satisfies the condition for a $1,000 bonus (BETWEEN is inclusive). Once a condition evaluates to TRUE, the remaining conditions are not evaluated at all.

The CASE statement represents a better solution to the bonus problem than the IF-THEN-ELSIF solution shown in this section. See "CASE Statements and Expressions" on page 90.

Even though overlapping conditions are allowed in an IF-THEN-ELSIF statement, it's best to avoid them when possible. In my example, the original spec is a bit ambiguous about how to handle boundary cases such as $20,000. Assuming that the intent is to give the highest bonuses to the lowest-paid employees (which seems like a reasonable approach to me), I would dispense with the BETWEEN operator and use the following less-than/greater-than logic. Note that I've also dispensed with the ELSE clause just to illustrate that it is optional:

```
IF salary >= 10000 AND salary <= 20000
THEN
   give_bonus(employee_id, 1500);
ELSIF salary > 20000 AND salary <= 40000
THEN
   give_bonus(employee_id, 1000);
ELSIF salary > 40000
THEN
   give_bonus(employee_id, 400);
END IF;
```

By taking steps to avoid overlapping conditions in an IF-THEN-ELSIF, I am eliminating a possible (probable?) source of confusion for programmers who come after me. I also eliminate the possibility of inadvertent bugs being introduced as a result of someone's reordering the ELSIF clauses. Note, though, that if salary is NULL, then no code will be executed, because there is no ELSE section.

The language does not require that ELSIF conditions be mutually exclusive. Always be aware of the possibility that two or more conditions might apply to a given value, and that consequently the order of those ELSIF conditions might be important.

## Nested IF Statements

You can nest any IF statement within any other IF statement. The following IF statement shows several layers of nesting:

```
IF condition1
THEN
   IF condition2
   THEN
      statements2
   ELSE
      IF condition3
      THEN
         statements3
      ELSIF condition4
      THEN
         statements4
      END IF;
   END IF;
END IF;
```

Nested IF statements are often necessary to implement complex logic rules, but you should use them carefully. Nested IF statements, like nested loops, can be very difficult to understand and debug. If you find that you need to nest more than three levels deep in your conditional logic, you should review that logic and see if there is a simpler way to code the same requirement. If not, then consider creating one or more local modules to hide the innermost IF statements.

A key advantage of the nested IF structure is that it defers evaluation of inner conditions. The conditions of an inner IF statement are evaluated only if the condition for the outer IF statement that encloses them evaluates to TRUE. Therefore, one obvious reason to nest IF statements is to evaluate one condition only when another condition is TRUE. For example, in my code to award bonuses, I might write the following:

```
IF award_bonus(employee_id) THEN
   IF print_check (employee_id) THEN
      DBMS_OUTPUT.PUT_LINE('Check issued for ' || employee_id);
   END IF;
END IF;
```

This is reasonable, because I want to print a message for each bonus check issued, but I don't want to print a bonus check for a zero amount in cases where no bonus was given.

## Short-Circuit Evaluation

PL/SQL uses *short-circuit evaluation*, which means that PL/SQL need not evaluate all of the expression in an IF statement. For example, when evaluating the expression in the following IF statement, PL/SQL stops evaluation and immediately executes the ELSE branch if the first operand is either FALSE or NULL:

```
IF condition1 AND condition2
THEN
   ...
ELSE
   ...
END IF;
```

PL/SQL can stop evaluation of the expression when *condition1* is FALSE or NULL, because the THEN branch is executed only when the result of the expression is TRUE, and that requires *both* operands to be TRUE. As soon as one operand is found to be other than TRUE, there is no longer any chance for the THEN branch to be taken.

 I found something interesting while researching PL/SQL's short-circuit behavior. The behavior that you get depends on the expression's context. Consider the following statement:

```
my_boolean := condition1 ANDcondition2
```

Unlike the case with an IF statement, when *condition1* is NULL, this expression will *not* short-circuit. Why not? Because the result could be either NULL or FALSE, depending on *condition2*. For an IF statement, NULL and FALSE both lead to the ELSE branch, so a short-circuit can occur. But for an assignment, the ultimate value must be known, and short-circuiting, in this case, can (and will) occur only when *condition1* is FALSE.

Similar to the case with AND, if the first operand of an OR operation in an IF statement is TRUE, PL/SQL immediately executes the THEN branch:

```
IF condition1 OR condition2
THEN
   ...
ELSE
   ...
END IF;
```

This short-circuiting behavior can be useful when one of your conditions is particularly expensive in terms of CPU or memory utilization. In such a case, be sure to place that condition at the end of the set of conditions:

```
IF low_CPU_condition AND high_CPU_condition
THEN
   ...
END IF;
```

The *low_CPU_condition* is evaluated first, and if the result is enough to determine the end result of the AND operation (i.e., the result is FALSE), the more expensive condition will not be evaluated, and your application's performance is the better for that evaluation's not happening.

 However, if you are *depending* on that second condition's being evaluated, perhaps because you want the side effects from a stored function that the condition invokes, then you have a problem and you need to reconsider your design. I don't believe it's good to depend on side effects in this manner.

You can achieve the effect of short-circuit evaluation in a much more explicit manner using a nested IF statement:

```
IF low_CPU_condition
THEN
   IF high_CPU_condition
   THEN
      ...
   END IF;
END IF;
```

Now, *high_CPU_condition* is evaluated only if *low_CPU_condition* evaluates to TRUE. This is the same effect as short-circuit evaluation, but it's more obvious at a glance what's going on. It's also more obvious that my intent is to evaluate *low_CPU_condition* first.

Short-circuiting also applies to CASE statements and CASE expressions. These are described in the next section.

## CASE Statements and Expressions

The CASE statement allows you to select one sequence of statements to execute out of many possible sequences. They have been part of the SQL standard since 1992, although Oracle SQL didn't support CASE until the release of Oracle8*i* Database, and PL/SQL didn't support CASE until Oracle9*i* Database Release 1. From this release onwards, the following types of CASE statements are supported:

*Simple CASE statement*
   Associates each of one or more sequences of PL/SQL statements with a value. Chooses which sequence of statements to execute based on an expression that returns one of those values.

*Searched CASE statement*
   Chooses which of one or more sequences of PL/SQL statements to execute by evaluating a list of Boolean conditions. The sequence of statements associated with the first condition that evaluates to TRUE is executed.

In addition to CASE statements, PL/SQL also supports CASE expressions. A CASE expression is very similar in form to a CASE statement and allows you to choose which of one or more expressions to evaluate. The result of a CASE expression is a single value, whereas the result of a CASE statement is the execution of a sequence of PL/SQL statements.

## Simple CASE Statements

A simple CASE statement allows you to choose which of several sequences of PL/SQL statements to execute based on the results of a single expression. Simple CASE statements take the following form:

```
CASE expression
WHEN result1 THEN
    statements1
WHEN result2 THEN
    statements2
...
ELSE
    statements_else
END CASE;
```

The ELSE portion of the statement is optional. When evaluating such a CASE statement, PL/SQL first evaluates *expression*. It then compares the result of *expression* with *result1*. If the two results match, *statements1* is executed. Otherwise, *result2* is checked, and so forth.

Following is an example of a simple CASE statement that uses the employee type as a basis for selecting the proper bonus algorithm:

```
CASE employee_type
WHEN 'S' THEN
    award_salary_bonus(employee_id);
WHEN 'H' THEN
    award_hourly_bonus(employee_id);
```

```
WHEN 'C' THEN
   award_commissioned_bonus(employee_id);
ELSE
   RAISE invalid_employee_type;
END CASE;
```

This CASE statement has an explicit ELSE clause; however, the ELSE is optional. When you do not explicitly specify an ELSE clause of your own, PL/SQL implicitly uses the following:

```
ELSE
   RAISE CASE_NOT_FOUND;
```

In other words, if you don't specify an ELSE clause, and none of the results in the WHEN clauses match the result of the CASE expression, PL/SQL raises a CASE_NOT_FOUND error. This behavior is different from what I'm used to with IF statements. When an IF statement lacks an ELSE clause, nothing happens when the condition is not met. With CASE, the analogous situation leads to an error.

By now you're probably wondering how, or even whether, the bonus logic shown earlier in this chapter can be implemented using a simple CASE statement. At first glance, it doesn't appear possible. However, a bit of creative thought yields the following solution:

```
CASE TRUE
WHEN salary >= 10000 AND salary <=20000
THEN
   give_bonus(employee_id, 1500);
WHEN salary > 20000 AND salary <= 40000
THEN
   give_bonus(employee_id, 1000);
WHEN salary > 40000
THEN
   give_bonus(employee_id, 500);
ELSE
   give_bonus(employee_id, 0);
END CASE;
```

The key point to note here is that the *expression* and *result* elements shown in the earlier syntax diagram can be either scalar values or expressions that evaluate to scalar values.

If you look back to the earlier IF-THEN-ELSIF statement implementing this same bonus logic, you'll see that I specified an ELSE clause for the CASE implementation, whereas I didn't specify an ELSE for the IF-THEN-ELSIF solution. The reason for the addition of the ELSE is simple: if no bonus conditions are met, the IF statement does nothing, effectively resulting in a zero bonus. A CASE statement, however, will raise an error if no conditions are met—hence the need to code explicitly for the zero bonus case.

To avoid CASE_NOT_FOUND errors, be sure that it's impossible for one of your conditions not to be met.

While my previous CASE TRUE statement may look like a clever hack, it's really an explicit implementation of the searched CASE statement, which I talk about in the next section.

## Searched CASE Statements

A searched CASE statement evaluates a list of Boolean expressions and, when it finds an expression that evaluates to TRUE, executes a sequence of statements associated with that expression. Essentially, a searched CASE statement is the equivalent of the CASE TRUE statement shown in the previous section.

Searched CASE statements have the following form:

```
CASE
WHEN expression1 THEN
   statements1
WHEN expression2 THEN
   statements2
...
ELSE
   statements_else
END CASE;
```

A searched CASE statement is a perfect fit for the problem of implementing the bonus logic. For example:

```
CASE
WHEN salary >= 10000 AND salary <=20000 THEN
   give_bonus(employee_id, 1500);
WHEN salary > 20000 AND salary <= 40000 THEN
   give_bonus(employee_id, 1000);
WHEN salary > 40000 THEN
   give_bonus(employee_id, 500);
ELSE
   give_bonus(employee_id, 0);
END CASE;
```

As with simple CASE statements, the following rules apply:

- Execution ends once a sequence of statements has been executed. If more than one expression evaluates to TRUE, only the statements associated with the first such expression are executed.

- The ELSE clause is optional. If no ELSE is specified, and no expressions evaluate to TRUE, then a CASE_NOT_FOUND exception is raised.

- WHEN clauses are evaluated in order, from top to bottom.

Following is an implementation of my bonus logic that takes advantage of the fact that WHEN clauses are evaluated in the order in which I write them. The individual expressions are simpler, but is the intent of the statement as easily grasped?

```
CASE
WHEN salary > 40000 THEN
   give_bonus(employee_id, 500);
WHEN salary > 20000 THEN
   give_bonus(employee_id, 1000);
WHEN salary >= 10000 THEN
   give_bonus(employee_id, 1500);
ELSE
   give_bonus(employee_id, 0);
END CASE;
```

If a given employee's salary is $20,000, then the first expression and second expression will evaluate to FALSE. The third expression will evaluate to TRUE, and that employee will be awarded a bonus of $1,500. If an employee's salary is $21,000, then the second expression will evaluate to TRUE, and the employee will be awarded a bonus of $1,000. Execution of the CASE statement will cease with the first WHEN condition that evaluates to TRUE, so a salary of $21,000 will never reach the third condition.

It's arguable whether you should take this approach to writing CASE statements. You should certainly be aware that it's possible to write such a statement, and you should watch for such order-dependent logic in programs that you are called upon to modify or debug.

Order-dependent logic can be a subtle source of bugs when you decide to reorder the WHEN clauses in a CASE statement. Consider the following searched CASE statement in which, assuming a salary of $20,000, both WHEN expressions evaluate to TRUE:

```
CASE
WHEN salary BETWEEN 10000 AND 20000 THEN
   give_bonus(employee_id, 1500);
WHEN salary BETWEEN 20000 AND 40000 THEN
   give_bonus(employee_id, 1000);
...
```

Imagine the results if a future programmer unthinkingly decides to make the code neater by reordering the WHEN clauses in descending order by salary. Don't scoff at this possibility! We programmers frequently fiddle with perfectly fine, working code to satisfy some inner sense of order. Following is the CASE statement rewritten with the WHEN clauses in descending order:

```
CASE
WHEN salary BETWEEN 20000 AND 40000 THEN
   give_bonus(employee_id, 1000);
WHEN salary BETWEEN 10000 AND 20000 THEN
   give_bonus(employee_id, 1500);
...
```

Looks good, doesn't it? Unfortunately, because of the slight overlap between the two WHEN clauses, I've introduced a subtle bug into the code. Now an employee with a salary of $20,000 gets a bonus of $1,000 rather than the intended $1,500. There may be cases where overlap between WHEN clauses is desirable, but avoid it when feasible. Always remember that order matters, and resist the urge to fiddle with working code. "If it ain't broke, don't fix it."

 Since WHEN clauses are evaluated in order, you may be able to squeeze some extra efficiency out of your code by listing the most likely WHEN clauses first. In addition, if you have WHEN clauses with "expensive" expressions (e.g., requiring lots of CPU and memory), you may want to list those last in order to minimize the chances that they will be evaluated. See "Nested IF Statements" on page 88 for an example of this issue.

Use searched CASE statements when you want to use Boolean expressions as a basis for identifying a set of statements to execute. Use simple CASE statements when you can base that decision on the result of a single expression.

## Nested CASE Statements

CASE statements can be nested just as IF statements can. For example, the following rather difficult-to-follow implementation of my bonus logic uses a nested CASE statement:

```
CASE
WHEN salary >= 10000 THEN
   CASE
   WHEN salary <= 20000 THEN
      give_bonus(employee_id, 1500);
   WHEN salary > 40000 THEN
      give_bonus(employee_id, 500);
   WHEN salary > 20000 THEN
      give_bonus(employee_id, 1000);
   END CASE;
WHEN salary < 10000 THEN
   give_bonus(employee_id,0);
END CASE;
```

Any type of statement may be used within a CASE statement, so I could replace the inner CASE statement with an IF statement. Likewise, any type of statement, including CASE statements, may be nested within an IF statement.

## CASE Expressions

CASE expressions do for expressions what CASE statements do for statements. Simple CASE expressions let you choose an expression to evaluate based on a scalar value that you provide as input. Searched CASE expressions evaluate a list of expressions to find the first one that evaluates to TRUE, and then return the results of an associated expression.

CASE expressions take the following two forms:

```
Simple_Case_Expression :=
   CASE expression
   WHEN result1 THEN
      result_expression1
   WHEN result2 THEN
      result_expression2
   ...
   ELSE
      result_expression_else
   END;
Searched_Case_Expression :=
   CASE
   WHEN expression1 THEN
      result_expression1
   WHEN expression2 THEN
      result_expression2
   ...
   ELSE
      result_expression_else
   END;
```

A CASE expression returns a single value, the result of whichever *result_expression* is chosen. Each WHEN clause must be associated with exactly one expression (no statements). Do not use semicolons or END CASE to mark the end of the CASE expression. CASE expressions are terminated by a simple END.

Following is an example of a simple CASE expression being used with the DBMS_OUTPUT package to output the value of a Boolean variable. (Recall that the PUT_LINE program is not overloaded to handle Boolean types.) In this example, the CASE expression converts the Boolean value into a character string, which PUT_LINE can then handle:

```
DECLARE
   boolean_true BOOLEAN := TRUE;
   boolean_false BOOLEAN := FALSE;
   boolean_null BOOLEAN;
   FUNCTION boolean_to_varchar2 (flag IN BOOLEAN) RETURN VARCHAR2 IS
   BEGIN
      RETURN
         CASE flag
            WHEN TRUE THEN 'True'
            WHEN FALSE THEN 'False'
            ELSE 'NULL'
         END;
   END;
BEGIN
   DBMS_OUTPUT.PUT_LINE(boolean_to_varchar2(boolean_true));
   DBMS_OUTPUT.PUT_LINE(boolean_to_varchar2(boolean_false));
   DBMS_OUTPUT.PUT_LINE(boolean_to_varchar2(boolean_null));
END;
```

A searched CASE expression can be used to implement my bonus logic, returning the proper bonus value for any given salary:

```
DECLARE
   salary NUMBER := 20000;
   employee_id NUMBER := 36325;
   PROCEDURE give_bonus (emp_id IN NUMBER, bonus_amt IN NUMBER) IS
   BEGIN
     DBMS_OUTPUT.PUT_LINE(emp_id);
     DBMS_OUTPUT.PUT_LINE(bonus_amt);
   END;
BEGIN
   give_bonus(employee_id,
         CASE
             WHEN salary >= 10000 AND salary <= 20000 THEN 1500
             WHEN salary > 20000 AND salary <= 40000 THEN 1000
             WHEN salary > 40000 THEN 500
             ELSE 0
         END);
END;
```

You can use a CASE expression anywhere you can use any other type of expression or value. The following example uses a CASE expression to compute a bonus amount, multiplies that amount by 10, and assigns the result to a variable that is displayed via DBMS_OUTPUT:

```
DECLARE
   salary NUMBER := 20000;
   employee_id NUMBER := 36325;
   bonus_amount NUMBER;
BEGIN
   bonus_amount :=
      CASE
          WHEN salary >= 10000 AND salary <= 20000 THEN 1500
          WHEN salary > 20000 AND salary <= 40000 THEN 1000
          WHEN salary > 40000 THEN 500
          ELSE 0
      END * 10;
   DBMS_OUTPUT.PUT_LINE(bonus_amount);
END;
```

Unlike with the CASE statement, no error is raised in the event that no WHEN clause is selected in a CASE expression. Instead, when no WHEN conditions are met, a CASE expression will return NULL.

# The GOTO Statement

The GOTO statement performs unconditional branching to another executable statement in the same execution section of a PL/SQL block. As with other constructs in the language, if you use GOTO appropriately and with care, your programs will be stronger for it.

The general format for a GOTO statement is:

```
GOTO label_name;
```

where *label_name* is the name of a label identifying the target statement. This GOTO label is defined in the program as follows:

```
<<label_name>>
```

You must surround the label name with double enclosing angle brackets (<< >>). When PL/SQL encounters a GOTO statement, it immediately shifts control to the first executable statement following the label. Following is a complete code block containing both a GOTO and a label:

```
BEGIN
   GOTO second_output;
   DBMS_OUTPUT.PUT_LINE('This line will never execute.');
   <<second_output>>
   DBMS_OUTPUT.PUT_LINE('We are here!');
END;
```

There are several restrictions on the GOTO statement:

- At least one executable statement must follow a label.
- The target label must be in the same scope as the GOTO statement.
- The target label must be in the same part of the PL/SQL block as the GOTO.

Contrary to popular opinion (including mine), the GOTO statement can come in handy. There are cases where a GOTO statement can simplify the logic in your program. On the other hand, because PL/SQL provides so many different control constructs and modularization techniques, you can almost always find a better way to do something than with a GOTO.

# The NULL Statement

Usually when you write a statement in a program, you want it to do something. There are cases, however, when you want to tell PL/SQL to do absolutely nothing, and that is where the NULL statement comes in handy. The NULL statement has the following format:

```
NULL;
```

Well, you wouldn't want a do-nothing statement to be complicated, would you? The NULL statement is simply the reserved word NULL followed by a semicolon (;) to indicate that this is a statement and not a NULL value. The NULL statement does nothing except pass control to the next executable statement.

Why would you want to use the NULL statement? There are several reasons, described in the following sections.

## Improving Program Readability

Sometimes, it's helpful to avoid any ambiguity inherent in an IF statement that doesn't cover all possible cases. For example, when you write an IF statement, you do not have to include an ELSE clause. To produce a report based on a selection, you can code:

```
IF :report_mgr.selection = 'DETAIL'
THEN
    exec_detail_report;
END IF;
```

What should the program be doing if the report selection is not 'DETAIL'? One might assume that the program is supposed to do nothing. But because this is not explicitly stated in the code, you are left to wonder if perhaps there was an oversight. If, on the other hand, you include an explicit ELSE clause that does nothing, you state very clearly, "Don't worry, I thought about this possibility and I really want nothing to happen:"

```
IF :report_mgr.selection = 'DETAIL'
THEN
    exec_detail_report;
ELSE
    NULL; -- Do nothing
END IF;
```

My example here was of an IF statement, but the same principle applies when writing CASE statements and CASE expressions. Similarly, if you want to temporarily remove all the code from a function or procedure, and yet still invoke that function or procedure, you can use NULL as a placeholder. Otherwise, you cannot compile a function or procedure without having any lines of code within it.

## Using NULL After a Label

In some cases, you can pair NULL with GOTO to avoid having to execute additional statements. Most of you will never have to use the GOTO statement; there are very few occasions where it is truly needed. If you ever do use GOTO, however, you should remember that when you GOTO a label, at least one executable statement must follow that label. In the following example, I use a GOTO statement to quickly move to the end of my program if the state of my data indicates that no further processing is required:

```
PROCEDURE process_data (data_in IN orders%ROWTYPE,
                        data_action IN VARCHAR2)
IS
    status INTEGER;
BEGIN
    -- First in series of validations.
    IF data_in.ship_date IS NOT NULL
    THEN
        status := validate_shipdate (data_in.ship_date);
        IF status != 0 THEN GOTO end_of_procedure; END IF;
```

```
      END IF;

      -- Second in series of validations.
      IF data_in.order_date IS NOT NULL
      THEN
         status := validate_orderdate (data_in.order_date);
         IF status != 0 THEN GOTO end_of_procedure; END IF;
      END IF;

      ... more validations ...

      <<end_of_procedure>>
      NULL;
   END;
```

With this approach, if I encounter an error in any single section, I use the GOTO to
bypass all remaining validation checks. Because I do not have to do anything at the
termination of the procedure, I place a NULL statement after the label because at least
one executable statement is required there. Even though NULL does nothing, it is still
an executable statement.

# CHAPTER 5

# Iterative Processing with Loops

This chapter explores the iterative control structures of PL/SQL, otherwise known as loops, which let you execute the same code repeatedly. It also describes the CONTINUE statement, introduced for loops in Oracle Database 11g. PL/SQL provides three different kinds of loop constructs:

- The simple or infinite loop
- The FOR loop (numeric and cursor)
- The WHILE loop

Each type of loop is designed for a specific purpose with its own nuances, rules for use, and guidelines for high-quality construction. As I explain each loop, I'll provide a table describing the following properties of the loop:

| Property | Description |
|---|---|
| How the loop is terminated | A loop executes code repetitively. How do you make the loop stop executing its body? |
| When the test for termination takes place | Does the test for termination take place at the beginning or end of the loop? What are the consequences? |
| Reason to use this loop | What are the special factors you should consider to determine if this loop is right for your situation? |

## Loop Basics

Why are there three different kinds of loops? To provide you with the flexibility you need to write the most straightforward code to handle any particular situation. Most situations that require a loop could be written with any of the three loop constructs. If you do not pick the construct that is best suited for that particular requirement, however, you could end up having to write many additional lines of code The resulting module would also be harder to understand and maintain.

## Examples of Different Loops

To give you a feeling for the way the different loops solve their problems in different ways, consider the following three procedures. In each case, the procedure makes a call to display_total_sales for a particular year, for each year number between the start and end argument values.

*The simple loop*

It's called simple for a reason: it starts simply with the LOOP keyword and ends with the END LOOP statement. The loop will terminate if you execute an EXIT, EXIT WHEN, or RETURN within the body of the loop (or if an exception is raised):

```
/* File on web: loop_examples.sql */
PROCEDURE display_multiple_years (
   start_year_in IN PLS_INTEGER
  ,end_year_in IN PLS_INTEGER
)
IS
   l_current_year PLS_INTEGER := start_year_in;
BEGIN
   LOOP
      EXIT WHEN l_current_year > end_year_in;
      display_total_sales (l_current_year);
      l_current_year :=  l_current_year + 1;
   END LOOP;
END display_multiple_years;
```

*The FOR loop*

Oracle offers a numeric and cursor FOR loop. With the numeric FOR loop, you specify the start and end integer values, and PL/SQL does the rest of the work for you, iterating through each intermediate value, and then terminating the loop:

```
/* File on web: loop_examples.sql */
PROCEDURE display_multiple_years (
    start_year_in IN PLS_INTEGER
   ,end_year_in IN PLS_INTEGER
 )
 IS
 BEGIN
   FOR l_current_year IN start_year_in .. end_year_in
   LOOP
      display_total_sales (l_current_year);
   END LOOP;
END display_multiple_years;
```

The cursor FOR loop has the same basic structure, but in this case you supply an explicit cursor or SELECT statement in place of the low-high integer range:

```
/* File on web: loop_examples.sql */
PROCEDURE display_multiple_years (
    start_year_in IN PLS_INTEGER
   ,end_year_in IN PLS_INTEGER
 )
 IS
```

```
BEGIN
   FOR sales_rec IN (
      SELECT *
        FROM sales_data
       WHERE year BETWEEN start_year_in AND end_year_in)
   LOOP
      display_total_sales (sales_rec.year);
   END LOOP;
END display_multiple_years;
```

*The WHILE loop*

The WHILE loop is very similar to the simple loop; a critical difference is that it checks the termination condition up front. It may not even execute its body a single time:

```
/* File on web: loop_examples.sql */
PROCEDURE display_multiple_years (
   start_year_in IN PLS_INTEGER
   ,end_year_in IN PLS_INTEGER
)
IS
   l_current_year PLS_INTEGER := start_year_in;
BEGIN
   WHILE (l_current_year <= end_year_in)
   LOOP
      display_total_sales (l_current_year);
      l_current_year :=  l_current_year + 1;
   END LOOP;
END display_multiple_years;
```

In this section, the FOR loop clearly requires the smallest amount of code. Yet I could use it in this case only because I knew that I would run the body of the loop a specific number of times. In many other situations, the number of times a loop must execute varies, so the FOR loop cannot be used.

## Structure of PL/SQL Loops

While there are differences among the three loop constructs, every loop has two parts: the loop boundary and the loop body:

*Loop boundary*

This is composed of the reserved words that initiate the loop, the condition that causes the loop to terminate, and the END LOOP statement that ends the loop.

*Loop body*

This is the sequence of executable statements inside the loop boundary that execute on each iteration of the loop.

Figure 5-1 shows the boundary and body of a WHILE loop.

In general, think of a loop much as you would a procedure or a function. The body of the loop is a black box, and the condition that causes loop termination is the interface

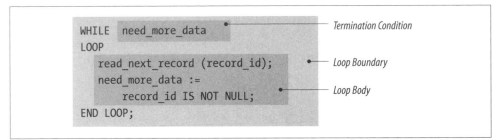

```
WHILE  need_more_data                      ← Termination Condition
LOOP
    read_next_record (record_id);          ← Loop Boundary
    need_more_data :=
        record_id IS NOT NULL;             ← Loop Body
END LOOP;
```

*Figure 5-1. The boundary and body of the WHILE loop*

to that black box. Code outside the loop should not have to know about the inner workings of the loop. Keep this in mind as you go through the different kinds of loops and examples in the rest of the chapter.

# The Simple Loop

The structure of the simple loop is the most basic of all the loop constructs. It consists of the LOOP keyword, the body of executable code, and the END LOOP keywords, as shown here:

```
LOOP
   executable statement(s)
END LOOP;
```

The loop boundary consists solely of the LOOP and END LOOP reserved words. The body must consist of at least one executable statement. The following table summarizes the properties of the simple loop:

| Property | Description |
| --- | --- |
| How the loop is terminated | The simple loop is terminated when an EXIT statement is executed in the body of the loop. If this statement is not executed, the simple loop becomes a true infinite loop. |
| When the test for termination takes place | The test takes place inside the body of the loop, and then only if an EXIT or EXIT WHEN statement is executed. Therefore, the body—or part of the body—of the simple loop always executes at least once. |
| Reason to use this loop | Use the simple loop when:<br><br>• You are not sure how many times you want the loop to execute.<br><br>• You want the loop to run at least once. |

This loop is useful when you want to guarantee that the body (or at least part of the body) will execute at least one time. Because there is no condition associated with the loop boundary that determines whether or not it should execute, the body of the loop will always execute the first time.

The simple loop will terminate only when an EXIT (or its close cousin, EXIT WHEN) statement is executed in its body, or when an exception is raised (and goes unhandled) within the body of the loop.

## Terminating a Simple Loop: EXIT and EXIT WHEN

Unless you want your loop to run "forever," you can put an EXIT or EXIT WHEN statement within the body of the loop. The syntax for these statements is as follows:

```
EXIT;
EXIT WHEN condition;
```

where *condition* is a Boolean expression.

The following example demonstrates how the EXIT forces the loop to immediately halt execution and pass control to the next statement after the END LOOP statement. The account_balance procedure returns the amount of money remaining in the account specified by the account ID. If there is less than $1,000 left, the EXIT statement is executed, and the loop is terminated. Otherwise, the program applies the balance to the outstanding orders for that account.

```
LOOP
    balance_remaining := account_balance (account_id);
    IF balance_remaining < 1000
    THEN
        EXIT;
    ELSE
        apply_balance (account_id, balance_remaining);
    END IF;
END LOOP;
```

You can use an EXIT statement only within a LOOP.

PL/SQL also offers the EXIT WHEN statement, which supports conditional termination of the loop. Essentially, the EXIT WHEN combines an IF-THEN statement with the EXIT statement. Using the same example, the EXIT WHEN changes the loop to:

```
LOOP
    /* Calculate the balance */
    balance_remaining := account_balance (account_id);

    /* Embed the IF logic into the EXIT statement */
    EXIT WHEN balance_remaining < 1000;

    /* Apply balance if still executing the loop */
    apply_balance (account_id, balance_remaining);
END LOOP;
```

Notice that the second form doesn't require an IF statement to determine when it should exit. Instead, that conditional logic is embedded inside the EXIT WHEN statement.

So when should you use EXIT WHEN, and when is the stripped-down EXIT more appropriate?

- EXIT WHEN is best used when there is a single conditional expression that determines whether or not a loop should terminate. The previous example demonstrates this scenario clearly.

- In situations with multiple conditions for exiting or when you need to set a "return value" coming out of the loop based on different conditions, you are probably better off using an IF or CASE statement, with EXIT statements in one or more of the clauses.

The following example demonstrates a preferred use of EXIT. It is taken from a function that determines if two files are equal (i.e., contain the same content):

```
   ...
   IF (end_of_file1 AND end_of_file2)
   THEN
      retval := TRUE;
      EXIT;
   ELSIF (checkline != againstline)
   THEN
      retval := FALSE;
      EXIT;
   ELSIF (end_of_file1 OR end_of_file2)
   THEN
      retval := FALSE;
      EXIT;
   END IF;
END LOOP;
```

## Emulating a REPEAT UNTIL Loop

PL/SQL does not provide a REPEAT UNTIL loop in which the condition is tested after the body of the loop is executed and thus guarantees that the loop always executes at least once. You can, however, emulate a REPEAT UNTIL with a simple loop, as follows:

```
LOOP
   ... body of loop ...
   EXIT WHEN boolean_condition;
END LOOP;
```

where *boolean_condition* is a Boolean variable or an expression that evaluates to a Boolean value of TRUE or FALSE (or NULL).

## The Intentionally Infinite Loop

Some programs, such as system monitoring tools, are not designed to be executed on demand but should always be running. In such cases, you may actually *want* to use an infinite loop:

```
LOOP
    data_gathering_procedure;
END LOOP;
```

Here, *data_gathering_procedure* goes out and, um, gathers data about the system. As anyone who has accidentally run such an infinite loop can attest, it's likely that the loop will consume large portions of the CPU. The solution for this, in addition to ensuring that your data gathering is performed as efficiently as possible, is to pause between iterations.

```
LOOP
    data_gathering_procedure;
        DBMS_LOCK.sleep(10); -- do nothing for 10 seconds
    END LOOP;
```

During the sleep period, the program uses virtually no cycles.

## Terminating an Intentionally Infinite Loop

As a practical matter, there will be times when you really *do* want to terminate intentionally infinite loops. If you're just working on an anonymous block in SQL*Plus, typing the terminal interrupt sequence (usually Ctrl-C) will probably do the job. But real programs generally run as stored procedures, and even killing the process that submitted the program (such as SQL*Plus) won't stop the background task. Aha, you say, what about ALTER SYSTEM KILL SESSION? Nice idea, but in some versions of the Oracle database this command doesn't actually kill sessions that are stuck in a loop (go figure).

So how can you put an executing program to sleep—permanently?

You may have to resort to operating system-level tools such as *kill* in Unix/Linux and *orakill.exe* in Microsoft Windows. These commands require you to discover the system process ID of the Oracle "shadow task," which is not hard if you have privileges to read V$SESSION and V$PROCESS views. But, even if the inelegance isn't an issue for you, your conscience could bother you for another reason: if you're running in shared server mode, you will probably end up killing other sessions as well. The best solution that I've come up with is to insert into the loop a kind of "command interpreter" that uses the database's built-in interprocess communication, known as a *database pipe*:

```
DECLARE
    pipename CONSTANT VARCHAR2(12) := 'signaler';
    result INTEGER;
    pipebuf VARCHAR2(64);
BEGIN
    /* create private pipe with a known name */
    result := DBMS_PIPE.create_pipe(pipename);

    LOOP
        data_gathering_procedure;
        DBMS_LOCK.sleep(10);

        /* see if there is a message on the pipe */
        IF DBMS_PIPE.receive_message(pipename, 0) = 0
        THEN
```

```
                    /* interpret the message and act accordingly */
                    DBMS_PIPE.unpack_message(pipebuf);
                    EXIT WHEN pipebuf = 'stop';
                END IF;
            END LOOP;
        END;
```

The DBMS_PIPE calls should have little impact on the overall CPU load.

A simple companion program can then kill the looping program by sending a "stop" message down the pipe:

```
    DECLARE
        pipename    VARCHAR2 (12) := 'signaler';
        result      INTEGER := DBMS_PIPE.create_pipe (pipename);
    BEGIN
        DBMS_PIPE.pack_message ('stop');
        result := DBMS_PIPE.send_message (pipename);
    END;
```

You can also send other commands down the pipe—for example, a command to increase or decrease the sleep interval. By the way, this example uses a private pipe, so the stop message needs to be sent by the same user account that is running the infinite loop. Also note that the database's namespace for private pipes is global across all sessions that the current user is running. So, if you want to have more than one program running the infinite loop, you need some extra logic to (1) create pipe names that are unique across sessions; and (2) determine the correct pipe name(s) through which you want to send the stop command.

# The WHILE Loop

The WHILE loop is a conditional loop that continues to execute as long as the Boolean condition defined in the loop boundary evaluates to TRUE. Because the WHILE loop execution depends on a condition and is not fixed, you should use a WHILE loop if you don't know in advance the number of times a loop must execute.

Here is the general syntax for the WHILE loop:

```
    WHILE condition
    LOOP
        executable statement(s)
    END LOOP;
```

where *condition* is a Boolean variable or an expression that evaluates to a Boolean value of TRUE, FALSE, or NULL. Each time an iteration of the loop's body is executed, the condition is checked. If it evaluates to TRUE, then the body is executed. If it evaluates to FALSE or NULL, then the loop terminates, and control passes to the next executable statement following the END LOOP statement.

The following table summarizes the properties of the WHILE loop:

| Property | Description |
|---|---|
| How the loop is terminated | The WHILE loop terminates when the Boolean expression in its boundary evaluates to FALSE or NULL. |
| When the test for termination takes place | The test for termination of a WHILE loop takes place in the loop boundary. This evaluation occurs prior to the first and each subsequent execution of the body. The WHILE loop, therefore, is not guaranteed to execute its loop even a single time. |
| Reason to use this loop | Use the WHILE loop when: |
| | • You are not sure how many times you must execute the loop body. |
| | • You will want to conditionally terminate the loop. |
| | • You don't have to execute the body at least one time. |

The WHILE loop's condition is tested at the beginning of the loop's iteration, before the body of the loop is executed. There are two consequences to this preexecution test:

• All the information needed to evaluate the condition must be set before the loop is executed for the first time.

• It is possible that the WHILE loop will not execute even a single time.

Here is an example of a WHILE loop from the *datemgr.pkg* file available on the book's web site. It shows a boundary condition consisting of a complex Boolean expression. There are two reasons for the WHILE loop to stop: either I have run out of date masks to attempt a conversion, or I have successfully performed a conversion (and date_converted is now TRUE):

```
/* File on web: datemgr.pkg */
WHILE mask_index <= mask_count AND NOT date_converted
LOOP
   BEGIN
      /* Try to convert string using mask in table row */
      retval := TO_DATE (value_in, fmts (mask_index));
      date_converted := TRUE;
   EXCEPTION
      WHEN OTHERS
      THEN
         mask_index:= mask_index+ 1;
   END;
END LOOP;
```

# The Numeric FOR Loop

There are two kinds of PL/SQL FOR loops: the numeric FOR loop and the cursor FOR loop. The numeric FOR loop is the traditional and familiar "counted" loop. The number of iterations of the FOR loop is known when the loop starts; it is specified in the range scheme found between the FOR and LOOP keywords in the boundary.

The range scheme implicitly declares the loop index (if it has not already been declared), specifies the start and end points of the range, and optionally dictates the order in which the loop index proceeds (from lowest to highest or highest to lowest).

Here is the general syntax of the numeric FOR loop:

```
FOR loop index IN [REVERSE] lowest number .. highest number
LOOP
    executable statement(s)
END LOOP;
```

You must have at least one executable statement between the LOOP and END LOOP keywords.

The following table summarizes the properties of the numeric FOR loop:

| Property | Description |
| --- | --- |
| How the loop is terminated | The numeric FOR loop terminates unconditionally when the number of times specified in its range scheme has been satisfied. You can also terminate the loop with an EXIT statement, but this is not recommended. |
| When the test for termination takes place | After each execution of the loop body, PL/SQL increments (or decrements if REVERSE is specified) the loop index and then checks its value. When it exceeds the upper bound of the range scheme, the loop terminates. If the lower bound is greater than the upper bound of the range scheme, the loop never executes its body. |
| Reason to use this loop | Use the numeric FOR loop when you want to execute a body of code a fixed number of times and do not want to halt that looping prematurely. |

## Rules for Numeric FOR Loops

Follow these rules when you use numeric FOR loops:

- Do not declare the loop index. PL/SQL automatically and implicitly declares it as a local variable with datatype INTEGER. The scope of this index is the loop itself; you cannot reference the loop index outside the loop.

- Expressions used in the range scheme (both for lowest and highest bounds) are evaluated once, when the loop starts. The range is not reevaluated during the execution of the loop. If you make changes within the loop to the variables that you used to determine the FOR loop range, those changes will have no effect.

- Never change the values of either the loop index or the range boundary from within the loop. This is an extremely bad programming practice. PL/SQL will either produce a compile error or ignore your instructions; in either case, you'll have problems.

- Use the REVERSE keyword to force the loop to decrement from the upper bound to the lower bound. You must still make sure that the first value in the range specification (the *lowest number* in *lowest number .. highest number*) is less than the second value. Do not reverse the order in which you specify these values when you use the REVERSE keyword.

## Examples of Numeric FOR Loops

These examples demonstrate some variations of the numeric FOR loop syntax:

- The loop executes 10 times; loop_counter starts at 1 and ends at 10:

```
FOR loop_counter IN 1 .. 10
LOOP
   ... executable statements ...
END LOOP;
```

- The loop executes 10 times; loop_counter starts at 10 and ends at 1:

```
FOR loop_counter IN REVERSE 1 .. 10
LOOP
   ... executable statements ...
END LOOP;
```

- Here is a loop that doesn't execute even once. I specified REVERSE, so the loop index, loop_counter, will start at the highest value and end with the lowest. I then mistakenly concluded that I should switch the order in which I list the highest and lowest bounds:

```
FOR loop_counter IN REVERSE 10 .. 1
LOOP
   /* This loop body will never execute even once! */
   ... executable statements ...
END LOOP;
```

Even when you specify a REVERSE direction, you must still list the lowest bound before the highest bound. If the first number is greater than the second number, the body of the loop will not execute at all. If the lowest and highest bounds have the same value, the loop will execute just once.

- The loop executes for a range determined by the values in the variable and expression:

```
FOR calc_index IN start_period_number ..
            LEAST (end_period_number, current_period)
LOOP
   ... executable statements ...
END LOOP;
```

In this example, the number of times the loop will execute is determined at runtime. The boundary values are evaluated once, before the loop executes, and then applied for the duration of loop execution.

## Handling Nontrivial Increments

PL/SQL does not provide a "step" syntax whereby you can specify a particular loop index increment. In all variations of the PL/SQL numeric FOR loop, the loop index is always incremented or decremented by one.

If you have a loop body that you want executed for a nontrivial increment (something other than one), you will have to write some cute code. For example, what if you want your loop to execute only for even numbers between 1 and 100? You can make use of the numeric MOD function, as follows:

```
FOR loop_index IN 1 .. 100
LOOP
   IF MOD (loop_index, 2) = 0
   THEN
      /* We have an even number, so perform calculation */
      calc_values (loop_index);
   END IF;
END LOOP;
```

Or you can use simple multiplication inside a loop with half the iterations:

```
FOR even_number IN 1 .. 50
LOOP
   calc_values (even_number*2);
END LOOP;
```

In both cases, the calc_values procedure executes only for even numbers. In the first example, the FOR loop executes 100 times; in the second example, it executes only 50 times.

Whichever approach you decide to take, be sure to document this kind of technique clearly. You are, in essence, manipulating the numeric FOR loop to do something for which it is not designed. Comments would be very helpful for the maintenance programmer who has to understand why you would code something like that.

# The Cursor FOR Loop

A cursor FOR loop is a loop that is associated with (and actually defined by) an explicit cursor or a SELECT statement incorporated directly within the loop boundary. Use the cursor FOR loop only if you need to fetch and process each and every record from a cursor, which is often the case with cursors.

The cursor FOR loop is one of my favorite PL/SQL features. It leverages fully the tight and effective integration of the procedural constructs with the power of the SQL database language. It reduces the volume of code you need to write to fetch data from a cursor. It greatly lessens the chance of introducing loop errors in your programming—and loops are one of the more error-prone parts of a program. Does this loop sound too good to be true? Well, it isn't—it's all true!

Here is the basic syntax of a cursor FOR loop:

```
FOR record IN { cursor_name | (explicit SELECT statement) }
LOOP
    executable statement(s)
END LOOP;
```

where *record* is a record declared implicitly by PL/SQL with the %ROWTYPE attribute against the cursor specified by *cursor_name*.

 Don't declare a record explicitly with the same name as the loop index record. It is not needed (PL/SQL declares one for its use within the loop implicitly) and can lead to logic errors. For tips on accessing information about a cursor FOR loop's record outside or after loop execution, see "Obtaining Information About FOR Loop Execution" on page 121.

You can also embed a SELECT statement directly in the cursor FOR loop, as shown in this example:

```
FOR book_rec IN (SELECT * FROM books)
LOOP
    show_usage (book_rec);
END LOOP;
```

You should, however, avoid this formulation because it results in the embedding of SELECT statements in "unexpected" places in your code, making it more difficult to maintain and enhance your logic.

The following table summarizes the properties of the cursor FOR loop where *record* is a record declared implicitly by PL/SQL with the %ROWTYPE attribute against the cursor specified by *cursor_name*:

| Property | Description |
| --- | --- |
| How the loop is terminated | The cursor FOR loop terminates unconditionally when all of the records in the associated cursor have been fetched. You can also terminate the loop with an EXIT statement, but this is not recommended. |
| When the test for termination takes place | After each execution of the loop body, PL/SQL performs another fetch. If the %NOTFOUND attribute of the cursor evaluates to TRUE, then the loop terminates. If the cursor returns no rows, then the loop never executes its body. |
| Reason to use this loop | Use the cursor FOR loop when you want to fetch and process every record in a cursor. |

You should use a cursor FOR loop whenever you need to unconditionally fetch all rows from a cursor (i.e., there are no EXITs or EXIT WHENs inside the loop that cause early termination). Let's take a look at how you can use the cursor FOR loop to streamline your code and reduce opportunities for error.

## Example of Cursor FOR Loops

Suppose I need to update the bills for all pets staying in my pet hotel, the Share-a-Din-Din Inn. The following example contains an anonymous block that uses a cursor, occupancy_cur, to select the room number and pet ID number for all occupants of the Inn. The procedure update_bill adds any new changes to that pet's room charges:

```
1    DECLARE
2       CURSOR occupancy_cur IS
3          SELECT pet_id, room_number
4             FROM occupancy WHERE occupied_dt = TRUNC (SYSDATE);
5       occupancy_rec occupancy_cur%ROWTYPE;
6    BEGIN
7       OPEN occupancy_cur;
8       LOOP
9          FETCH occupancy_cur INTO occupancy_rec;
10         EXIT WHEN occupancy_cur%NOTFOUND;
11         update_bill
12            (occupancy_rec.pet_id, occupancy_rec.room_number);
13       END LOOP;
14       CLOSE occupancy_cur;
15    END;
```

This code leaves nothing to the imagination. In addition to defining the cursor (line 2), you must explicitly declare the record for the cursor (line 5), open the cursor (line 7), start up an infinite loop (line 8), fetch a row from the cursor set into the record (line 9), check for an end-of-data condition with the %NOTFOUND cursor attribute (line 10), and finally perform the update (line 11). When you are all done, you have to remember to close the cursor (line 14).

If I convert this PL/SQL block to use a cursor FOR loop, then I have:

```
DECLARE
   CURSOR occupancy_cur IS
      SELECT pet_id, room_number
         FROM occupancy WHERE occupied_dt = TRUNC (SYSDATE);
BEGIN
   FOR occupancy_rec IN occupancy_cur
   LOOP
      update_bill (occupancy_rec.pet_id, occupancy_rec.room_number);
   END LOOP;
END;
```

Here you see the beautiful simplicity of the cursor FOR loop! Gone is the declaration of the record. Gone are the OPEN, FETCH, and CLOSE statements. Gone is the need to check the %NOTFOUND attribute. Gone are the worries of getting everything right. Instead, you say to PL/SQL, in effect:

> You and I both know that I want each row, and I want to dump that row into a record that matches the cursor. Take care of that for me, will you?

And PL/SQL does take care of it, just the way any modern programming language should.

As with all other cursors, you can pass parameters to the cursor in a cursor FOR loop. If any of the columns in the select list of the cursor is an expression, remember that you must specify an alias for that expression in the select list. Within the loop, the only way to access a particular value in the cursor record is with the dot notation (*record_name.column_name*, as in occupancy_rec.room_number), so you need a column name associated with the expression.

For more information about working with cursors in PL/SQL, check out Chapter 15.

## Loop Labels

You can give a name to a loop by using a label. (I introduced labels in Chapter 3.) A loop label in PL/SQL has the following format:

```
<<label_name>>
```

where *label_name* is the name of the label, and that loop label appears immediately before the LOOP statement:

```
<<all_emps>>
FOR emp_rec IN emp_cur
LOOP
   ...
END LOOP;
```

The label can also appear optionally after the END LOOP reserved words, as the following example demonstrates:

```
<<year_loop>>
WHILE year_number <= 1995
LOOP

   <<month_loop>>
   FOR month_number IN 1 .. 12
   LOOP
      ...
   END LOOP month_loop;
   year_number := year_number + 1;

END LOOPyear_loop;
```

The loop label is potentially useful in several ways:

- When you have written a loop with a large body (say one that starts at line 50, ends on line 725, and has 16 nested loops inside it), use a loop label to tie the end of the loop back explicitly to its start. This visual tag will make it easier for a developer to maintain and debug the program. Without the loop label, it can be very difficult to keep track of which LOOP goes with which END LOOP.

- You can use the loop label to qualify the name of the loop indexing variable (either a record or a number). Again, this can be helpful for readability. Here is an example:

```
<<year_loop>>
FOR year_number IN 1800..1995
LOOP
   <<month_loop>>
   FOR month_number IN 1 .. 12
   LOOP
      IF year_loop.year_number = 1900 THEN ... END IF;
   END LOOP month_loop;
END LOOP year_loop;
```

- When you have nested loops, you can use the label both to improve readability and to increase control over the execution of your loops. You can, in fact, stop the execution of a specific named outer loop by adding a loop label after the EXIT keyword in the EXIT statement of a loop, as follows:

```
EXIT loop_label;
EXIT loop_label WHEN condition;
```

While it is possible to use loop labels in this fashion, I recommend that you avoid it. It leads to very unstructured logic (quite similar to GOTOs) that is hard to debug. If you feel that you need to insert code like this, you should consider restructuring your loop, and possibly switching from a FOR loop to a simple or WHILE loop.

## The CONTINUE Statement

Oracle Database 11g offers a new feature for loops: the CONTINUE statement. Use this statement to exit the current iteration of a loop, and immediately continue on to the *next* iteration of that loop. This statement comes in two forms, just like EXIT: the unconditional CONTINUE and the conditional CONTINUE WHEN.

Here is a simple example of using CONTINUE WHEN to skip over loop body execution for even numbers:

```
BEGIN
   FOR l_index IN 1 .. 10
   LOOP
      CONTINUE WHEN MOD (l_index, 2) = 0;
      DBMS_OUTPUT.PUT_LINE ('Loop index = ' || TO_CHAR (l_index));
   END LOOP;
END;
/
```

The output is:

```
Loop index = 1
Loop index = 3
Loop index = 5
Loop index = 7
Loop index = 9
```

Of course, you can achieve the same effect with an IF statement, but CONTINUE may offer a more elegant and straightforward way to express the logic you need to implement.

CONTINUE is likely to come in handy mostly when you need to perform "surgery" on existing code, make some very targeted changes, and then immediately exit the loop body to avoid side effects.

You can also use CONTINUE to terminate an inner loop and continue immediately on to the next iteration of an outer loop's body. To do this, you will need to give names to your loops using labels. Here is an example:

```
BEGIN
   <<outer>>
   FOR outer_index IN 1 .. 5
   LOOP
      DBMS_OUTPUT.PUT_LINE (
         'Outer index = ' || TO_CHAR (outer_index));

      <<inner>>
      FOR inner_index IN 1 .. 5
      LOOP
         DBMS_OUTPUT.PUT_LINE (
            '   Inner index = ' || TO_CHAR (inner_index));
         CONTINUE outer;
      END LOOP inner;
   END LOOP outer;
END;
/
```

The output is:

```
Outer index = 1
   Inner index = 1
Outer index = 2
   Inner index = 1
Outer index = 3
   Inner index = 1
Outer index = 4
   Inner index = 1
Outer index = 5
   Inner index = 1
```

## Is CONTINUE as Bad as GOTO?

When I first learned about the CONTINUE statement, my instinctive reaction was that it represented another form of unstructured transfer of control, similar to GOTO, and should therefore be avoided whenever possible (I'd been doing just fine without it for years!). Charles Wetherell, a senior member of the PL/SQL development team, set me straight as follows:

"From a long time ago (the era of Dijkstra's 'goto' letter), exit and continue were discussed and understood to be structured transfers of control. Indeed, exit was directly recognized in one of Knuth's major programming language papers as a way to leave politely from a computation that you needed to abandon.

"Böhm and Jacopini proved that any program that uses any arbitrary synchronous control element (think of loop or goto) could be rewritten using only while loops, if statements, and Boolean variables in a completely structured way. Furthermore, the transformation between the bad unstructured version and the good structured version of a program could be automated. That's the good news. The bad news is that the new 'good' program might be exponentially larger than the old program because of the need to introduce many Booleans and the need to copy code into multiple if statement arms. In practice, real programs do not experience this exponential explosion. But one often sees 'cut-and-paste' code copies to simulate the effects of continue and exit. 'Cut-and-paste' causes maintenance headaches because if a change is needed, the programmer must remember to make a change in every copy of the pasted code.

"The continue statement is valuable because it makes code shorter, makes code easier to read, and reduces the need for Boolean variables whose exact meaning can be hard to decipher. The most common use is a loop where the exact processing that each item needs depends on detailed structural tests of the item. The skeleton of a loop might look like this; notice that it contains an exit to decide when enough items have been processed. Also notice that the last continue (after condition5) is not strictly necessary. But by putting a continue after each action, it is easy to add more actions in any order without breaking any other actions.

```
LOOP
    EXIT WHEN exit_condition_met;
    CONTINUE WHEN condition1;
    CONTINUE WHEN condition2;
    setup_steps_here;

    IF condition4 THEN
        action4_executed;
        CONTINUE;
    END IF;

    IF condition5 THEN
        action5_executed;
        CONTINUE; -- Not strictly required.
    END IF;
END LOOP;
```

"Without continue, I would have to implement the loop body like this:

```
LOOP
    EXIT WHEN exit_condition_met;

    IF condition1
    THEN
        NULL;
    ELSIF condition2
    THEN
        NULL;
    ELSE
        setup_steps_here;

        IF condition4 THEN
            action4_executed;
        ELSIF condition5 THEN
            action5_executed;
        END IF;
```

```
    END IF;
  END LOOP;
```

"Even with this simple example, continue avoids numerous elsif clauses, reduces nesting, and shows clearly which Boolean tests (and associated processing) are on the same level. In particular, the nesting depth is much less when continue is used. PL/SQL programmers can definitely write better code once they understand and use continue correctly."

# Tips for Iterative Processing

Loops are very powerful and useful constructs, but they are structures that you should use with care. Performance issues within a program often are traced back to loops, and any problem within a loop is magnified by its repeated execution. The logic determining when to stop a loop can be very complex. This section offers some tips on how to write loops that are clean, easy to understand, and easy to maintain.

## Use Understandable Names for Loop Indexes

Software programmers should not have to make Sherlock Holmes-like deductions about the meaning of the start and end range values of the innermost FOR loops in order to understand their purpose. Use names that self-document the purposes of variables and loops. That way, other people will understand your code, and you will remember what your own code does when you review it three months later.

How would you like to try to understand—much less maintain—code that looks like this?

```
FOR i IN start_id .. end_id
LOOP
   FOR j IN 1 .. 7
   LOOP
      FOR k IN 1 .. 24
      LOOP
         build_schedule (i, j, k);
      END LOOP;
   END LOOP;
END LOOP;
```

It is hard to imagine that someone would write code based on such generic integer variable names (right out of Algebra 101), yet it happens all the time. The habits we pick up in our earliest days of programming have an incredible half-life. Unless you are constantly vigilant, you will find yourself writing the most abominable code. In the case above, the solution is simple—use variable names for the loop indexes that are meaningful and therefore self-documenting:

```
FOR focus_account IN start_id .. end_id
LOOP
   FOR day_in_week IN 1 .. 7
```

```
        LOOP
           FOR month_in_biyear IN 1 .. 24
           LOOP
              build_schedule (focus_account, day_in_week, month_in_biyear);
           END LOOP;
        END LOOP;
     END LOOP;
```

Now that I have provided descriptive names for those index variables, I discover that the innermost loop actually spanned two sets of twelve months ($12 \times 2 = 24$).

## The Proper Way to Say Goodbye

One important and fundamental principle in structured programming is "one way in, one way out;" that is, a program should have a single point of entry and a single point of exit. A single point of entry is not an issue with PL/SQL: no matter what kind of loop you are using, there is always only one entry point into the loop—the first executable statement following the LOOP keyword. It is quite possible, however, to construct loops that have multiple exit paths. Avoid this practice. Having multiple ways of terminating a loop results in code that is much harder to debug and maintain.

In particular, you should follow these guidelines for loop termination:

- Do not use EXIT or EXIT WHEN statements within FOR and WHILE loops. You should use a FOR loop only when you want to iterate through all the values (integer or record) specified in the range. An EXIT inside a FOR loop disrupts this process and subverts the intent of that structure. A WHILE loop, on the other hand, specifies its termination condition in the WHILE statement itself.

- Do not use the RETURN or GOTO statements within a loop—again, these cause the premature, unstructured termination of the loop. It can be tempting to use these constructs because in the short run they appear to reduce the amount of time spent writing code. In the long run, however, you (or the person left to clean up your mess) will spend more time trying to understand, enhance, and fix your code over time.

Let's look at an example of loop termination issues with the cursor FOR loop. As you have seen, the cursor FOR loop offers many advantages when you want to loop through all of the records returned by a cursor. This type of loop is not appropriate, however, when you need to apply conditions to each fetched record to determine if you should halt execution of the loop. Suppose that you need to scan through each record from a cursor and stop when a total accumulation of a column (like the number of pets) exceeds a maximum, as shown in the following code. Although you can do this with a cursor FOR loop by issuing an EXIT statement inside the loop, it's an inappropriate use of this construct:

```
1   DECLARE
2      CURSOR occupancy_cur IS
3         SELECT pet_id, room_number
```

```
  4          FROM occupancy WHERE occupied_dt = TRUNC (SYSDATE);
  5      pet_count INTEGER := 0;
  6   BEGIN
  7      FOR occupancy_rec IN occupancy_cur
  8      LOOP
  9         update_bill
 10            (occupancy_rec.pet_id, occupancy_rec.room_number);
 11         pet_count := pet_count + 1;
 12         EXIT WHEN pet_count >= pets_global.max_pets;
 13      END LOOP;
 14   END;
```

The FOR loop explicitly states: "I am going to execute the body of this loop *n* times" (where *n* is a number in a numeric FOR loop, or the number of records in a cursor FOR loop). An EXIT inside the FOR loop (line 12) short-circuits this logic. The result is code that's difficult to follow and debug.

If you need to terminate a loop based on information fetched by the cursor FOR loop, you should use a WHILE loop or a simple loop in its place. Then the structure of the code will more clearly state your intentions.

## Obtaining Information About FOR Loop Execution

FOR loops are handy and concise constructs. They handle lots of the "administrative work" in a program; this is especially true of cursor FOR loops. There is, however, a tradeoff: by letting the database do so much of the work for you, you have limited access to information about the end results of the loop after it has been terminated.

Suppose that I want to know how many records I processed in a cursor FOR loop and then execute some logic based on that value. It would be awfully convenient to write code like this:

```
BEGIN
   FOR book_rec IN books_cur (author_in => 'FEUERSTEIN,STEVEN')
   LOOP
      ... process data ...
   END LOOP;
   IF books_cur%ROWCOUNT > 10 THEN ...
```

but if I try it, I get the runtime error *ORA-01001: invalid cursor*. This makes sense, because the cursor is implicitly opened and closed by the database. So how can you get this information from a loop that is closed? You need to declare a variable in the block housing that FOR loop, and then set its value inside the FOR loop so that you can obtain the necessary information about the FOR loop after it has closed. This technique is shown below:

```
DECLARE
   book_count PLS_INTEGER := 0;
BEGIN
   FOR book_rec IN books_cur (author_in => 'FEUERSTEIN,STEVEN')
   LOOP
      ... process data ...
```

```
      book_count := books_cur%ROWCOUNT;
   END LOOP;
   IF book_count > 10 THEN ...
```

## SQL Statement as Loop

You actually can think of a SQL statement such as SELECT as a loop. After all, such a statement specifies an action to be taken on a set of data; the SQL engine then "loops through" the data set and applies the action. In some cases, you will have a choice between using a PL/SQL loop and a SQL statement to do the same or similar work. Let's look at an example and then draw some conclusions about how you can decide which approach to take.

I need to write a program to move the information for pets who have checked out of the pet hotel from the occupancy table to the occupancy_history table. As a seasoned PL/SQL developer, I immediately settle on a cursor FOR loop. For each record fetched (implicitly) from the cursor (representing a pet who has checked out), the body of the loop first inserts a record into the occupancy_history table and then deletes the record from the occupancy table:

```
DECLARE
   CURSOR checked_out_cur IS
      SELECT pet_id, name, checkout_date
        FROM occupancy WHERE  checkout_date IS NOT NULL;
BEGIN
   FOR checked_out_rec IN checked_out_cur
   LOOP
      INSERT INTO occupancy_history (pet_id, name, checkout_date)
         VALUES (checked_out_rec.pet_id, checked_out_rec.name,
                 checked_out_rec.checkout_date);
      DELETE FROM occupancy WHERE pet_id = checked_out_rec.pet_id;
   END LOOP;
END;
```

This code does the trick. But was it necessary to do it this way? I can express precisely the same logic and get the same result with nothing more than an INSERT-SELECT FROM followed by a DELETE, as shown here:

```
BEGIN
   INSERT INTO occupancy_history (pet_id, NAME, checkout_date)
      SELECT pet_id, NAME, checkout_date
        FROM occupancy WHERE checkout_date IS NOT NULL;
   DELETE FROM occupancy WHERE checkout_date IS NOT NULL;
END;
```

What are the advantages to this approach? I have written less code, and my code will run more efficiently because I have reduced the number of "context switches" (moving back and forth between the PL/SQL and SQL execution engines). I execute just a single INSERT and a single DELETE.

There are, however, disadvantages to the 100% SQL approach. SQL statements are generally all-or-nothing propositions. In other words, if any one of those individual rows from occupancy_history fails, then the entire INSERT fails; no records are inserted or deleted. Also, the WHERE clause had to be coded twice. Although not a significant factor in this example, it may well be when substantially more complex queries are involved. The initial cursor FOR loop thus obviated the need to potentially maintain complex logic in multiple places.

PL/SQL offers more flexibility as well. Suppose, for example, that I want to transfer as many of the rows as possible, and simply write a message to the error log for any transfers of individual rows that fail. In this case, I really do need to rely on the cursor FOR loop, but with the added functionality of an exception section:

```
BEGIN
   FOR checked_out_rec IN checked_out_cur
   LOOP
      BEGIN
         INSERT INTO occupancy_history ...
         DELETE FROM occupancy ...
      EXCEPTION
         WHEN OTHERS THEN
            log_checkout_error (checked_out_rec);
      END;
   END LOOP;
END;
;
```

PL/SQL offers the ability to access and process a single row at a time, and to take action (and, perhaps, complex procedural logic based on the contents of that specific record). When that's what you need, use a blend of PL/SQL and SQL. If, on the other hand, your requirements allow you to use native SQL, you will find that you can use less code and that it will run more efficiently.

 You can continue past errors in SQL statements in two other ways: (1) use the LOG ERRORS clause with inserts, updates, and deletes in Oracle Database 10g Release 2 and later; and (2) use the SAVE EXCEPTIONS clause in your FORALL statements. See Chapter 21 for more details.

# CHAPTER 6

# Exception Handlers

It is a sad fact of life that many programmers rarely take the time to properly bullet-proof their programs. Instead, wishful thinking often reigns. Most of us find it hard enough—and more than enough work—to simply write the code that implements the positive aspects of an application: maintaining customers, generating invoices, and so on. It is devilishly difficult, from both a psychological standpoint and a resources perspective, to focus on the negative: for example, what happens when the user presses the wrong key? If the database is unavailable, what should I do?

As a result, we write applications that assume the best of all possible worlds, hoping that our programs are bug-free, that users will enter the correct data in the correct fashion, and that all systems (hardware and software) will always be a "go."

Of course, harsh reality dictates that no matter how hard you try, there will always be one more bug in your application. And your users will somehow always find just the right sequence of keystrokes to make a form implode. The challenge is clear: either you spend the time up-front to properly debug and bulletproof your programs, or you fight an unending series of rear-guard battles, taking frantic calls from your users and putting out the fires.

You know what you should do. Fortunately, PL/SQL offers a powerful and flexible way to trap and handle errors. It is entirely feasible within the PL/SQL language to build an application that fully protects the user and the database from errors.

## Exception-Handling Concepts and Terminology

In the PL/SQL language, errors of any kind are treated as *exceptions*—situations that should not occur—in your program. An exception can be one of the following:

- An error generated by the system (such as "out of memory" or "duplicate value in index").
- An error caused by a user action.
- A warning issued by the application to the user.

PL/SQL traps and responds to errors using an architecture of exception handlers. The exception handler mechanism allows you to cleanly separate your error processing code from your executable statements. It also provides an *event-driven* model, as opposed to a linear code model, for processing errors. In other words, no matter how a particular exception is raised, it is handled by the same exception handler in the exception section.

When an error occurs in PL/SQL, whether it's a system error or an application error, an exception is raised. The processing in the current PL/SQL block's execution section halts, and control is transferred to the separate exception section of the current block, if one exists, to handle the exception. You cannot return to that block after you finish handling the exception. Instead, control is passed to the enclosing block, if any.

Figure 6-1 illustrates how control is transferred to the exception section when an exception is raised.

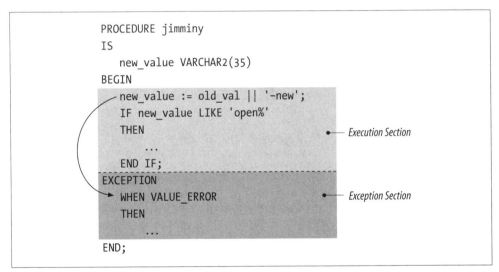

*Figure 6-1. Exception-handling architecture*

There are, in general, two types of exceptions:

*System exception*

An exception that is defined by Oracle and is usually raised by the PL/SQL runtime engine when it detects an error condition. Some system exceptions have names, such as NO_DATA_FOUND, while many others simply have numbers and descriptions.

*Programmer-defined exception*

An exception that is defined by the programmer and is therefore specific to the application at hand. You can associate exception names with specific Oracle errors using the EXCEPTION_INIT pragma (a compiler directive, requesting a specific behavior), or you can assign a number and description to that error using RAISE_APPLICATION_ERROR.

The following terms will be used throughout this chapter:

*Exception section*

The optional section in a PL/SQL block (anonymous block, procedure, function, trigger, or initialization section of a package) that contains one or more "handlers" for exceptions. The structure of an exception section is very similar to a CASE statement, which I discussed in Chapter 4.

*Raise*

Stops execution of the current PL/SQL block by notifying the runtime engine of an error. The database itself can raise exceptions, or your own code can raise an exception with either the RAISE or RAISE_APPLICATION_ERROR command.

*Handle (used as a verb), handler (used as a noun)*

"Traps" an error within an exception section. You can then write code in the handler to process that error, which might involve recording the error occurrence in a log, displaying a message to the user, or propagating an exception out of the current block.

*Scope*

The portion of code (whether in a particular block or for an entire session) in which an exception can be raised. Also, that portion of code for which an exception section can trap and handle exceptions that are raised.

*Propagation*

The process by which exceptions are passed from one block to its enclosing block if the exception goes unhandled in that block.

*Unhandled exception*

An exception is said to go "unhandled" when it propagates without being handled out of the outermost PL/SQL block. Control then passes back to the host execution environment, at which point that environment/program determines how to respond to the exception (roll back the transaction, display an error, ignore it, etc.).

*Un-named or anonymous exception*

An exception that has an error code and a description associated with it, but does not have a name that can be used in a RAISE statement or in an exception handler WHEN clause.

*Named exception*

An exception that has been given a name, either by Oracle in one of its built-in packages or by a developer. You can also associate a name with this exception through the use of the EXCEPTION_INIT pragma, or leave it defined only by its name (which can be used to both raise and handle the exception).

# Defining Exceptions

Before an exception can be raised or handled, it must be defined. Oracle predefines thousands of exceptions, mostly by assigning numbers and messages to those exceptions. Oracle also assigns names to a relative few of these thousands: the most commonly encountered exceptions.

These names are assigned in the STANDARD package (one of two default packages in PL/SQL; DBMS_STANDARD is the other), as well as in other built-in packages such as UTL_FILE and DBMS_SQL. The code Oracle uses to define exceptions like NO_DATA_FOUND is the same that you will write to define or declare your own exceptions. You can do this in two different ways, described in the following sections.

## Declaring Named Exceptions

The exceptions that PL/SQL has declared in the STANDARD package (and other built-in packages) cover internal or system-generated errors. Many of the problems a user will encounter (or cause) in an application, however, are specific to that application. Your program might need to trap and handle errors such as "negative balance in account" or "call date cannot be in the past." While different in nature from "division by zero," these errors are still exceptions to normal processing and should be handled gracefully by your program.

One of the most useful aspects of the PL/SQL exception-handling model is that it does not make any structural distinction between internal errors and application-specific errors. Once an exception is raised, it can and should be handled in the exception section, regardless of the type or source of error.

Of course, to handle an exception, you must have a name for that exception. Because PL/SQL cannot name these exceptions for you (they are specific to your application), you must do so yourself by declaring an exception in the declaration section of your PL/SQL block. You declare an exception by listing the name of the exception you want to raise in your program followed by the keyword EXCEPTION:

```
exception_name EXCEPTION;
```

The following declaration section of the calc_annual_sales procedure contains two programmer-defined exception declarations:

```
PROCEDURE calc_annual_sales
   (company_id_in IN company.company_id%TYPE)
IS
   invalid_company_id   EXCEPTION;
   negative_balance     EXCEPTION;

   duplicate_company    BOOLEAN;
BEGIN
   ... body of executable statements ...
EXCEPTION
```

```
WHEN NO_DATA_FOUND    -- system exception
  THEN
    ...
  WHEN invalid_company_id
  THEN

  WHEN negative_balance
  THEN
    ...
END;
```

The names for exceptions are similar in format to (and "read" just like) Boolean variable names, but can be referenced in only two ways:

- In a RAISE statement in the execution section of the program (to raise the exception), as in:

  ```
  RAISE invalid_company_id;
  ```

- In the WHEN clauses of the exception section (to handle the raised exception), as in:

  ```
  WHEN invalid_company_id THEN
  ```

## Associating Exception Names with Error Codes

Oracle has given names to just a handful of exceptions. Thousands of other error conditions within the database are defined by nothing more than an error number and a message. In addition, a developer can raise exceptions using RAISE_APPLICATION_ERROR (covered in "Raising Exceptions" on page 135) that consist of nothing more than an error number (between −20000 and −20999) and an error message.

Exceptions without names are perfectly legitimate, but they can lead to code that is hard to read and maintain. Suppose, for example, that I write a program in which I know the database might raise a date-related error, such as *ORA-01843: not a valid month*. I could write an exception handler to trap that error with code that looks like this:

```
EXCEPTION
  WHEN OTHERS THEN
    IF SQLCODE = -1843 THEN
```

but that is very obscure code, begging for a comment—or some sort of clarity. I can take advantage of the EXCEPTION_INIT statement to make this code's meaning transparent.

> SQLCODE is a built-in function that returns the number of the last error raised; it is discussed later in "Handling Exceptions" on page 138.

## Using EXCEPTION_INIT

EXCEPTION_INIT is a compile-time command or *pragma* used to associate a name with an internal error code. EXCEPTION_INIT instructs the compiler to associate an identifier, declared as an EXCEPTION, with a specific error number. Once you have made that association, you can then raise that exception by name and write an explicit WHEN handler that traps the error.

With EXCEPTION_INIT, I can replace the WHEN clause shown in the previous example with something like this:

```
PROCEDURE my_procedure
IS
   invalid_month EXCEPTION;
   PRAGMA EXCEPTION_INIT (invalid_month, -1843);
BEGIN
   ...
EXCEPTION
   WHEN invalid_month THEN
```

No more difficult to remember and understand hardcoded error numbers; instead, my code now explains itself.

The pragma EXCEPTION_INIT must appear in the declaration section of a block; the exception named must have already been defined in that same block, an enclosing block, or a package specification. Here is the syntax in an anonymous block:

```
DECLARE
   exception_name EXCEPTION;
   PRAGMA EXCEPTION_INIT (exception_name, integer);
```

where *exception_name* is the name of an exception and *integer* is a literal integer value, the number of the Oracle error with which you want to associate the named exception. The error number can be any integer value with these constraints:

- It cannot be −1403 (one of the two error codes for NO_DATA_FOUND). If for some reason you want to associate your own named exception with this error, you need to pass 100 to the EXCEPTION_INIT pragma.
- It cannot be 0 or any positive number besides 100.
- It cannot be a negative number less than −1000000.

Let's look at another example. In the following program code, I declare and associate an exception for this error:

```
ORA-2292 integrity constraint (OWNER.CONSTRAINT) violated  -
          child record found.
```

This error occurs if I try to delete a parent row while there are child rows still in that table. (A *child row* is a row with a foreign key reference to the parent table.)

```
PROCEDURE delete_company (company_id_in IN NUMBER)
IS
   /* Declare the exception. */
   still_have_employees EXCEPTION;

   /* Associate the exception name with an error number. */
   PRAGMA EXCEPTION_INIT (still_have_employees, -2292);
BEGIN
   /* Try to delete the company. */
   DELETE FROM company
     WHERE company_id = company_id_in;
EXCEPTION
   /* If child records were found, this exception is raised! */
   WHEN still_have_employees
   THEN
      DBMS_OUTPUT.PUT_LINE
         ('Please delete employees for company first.');
END;
```

### Recommended uses of EXCEPTION_INIT

You will find this pragma most useful in two circumstances:

- Giving names to otherwise anonymous system exceptions that you commonly reference in your code. In other words, Oracle did not predefine a name for the error; you have only the number with which to work.

- Assigning names to the application-specific errors you raise using RAISE_APPLI-CATION_ERROR (see "Raising Exceptions" on page 135). This allows you to handle such errors by name, rather than simply by number.

In both cases, I recommend that you centralize your usage of EXCEPTION_INIT into packages so that the definitions of exceptions are not scattered throughout your code. Suppose, for example, that I am doing lots of work with dynamic SQL (described in Chapter 16). I might then encounter "invalid column name" errors as I construct my dynamic queries. I don't want to have to remember what the code is for this error, and it's silly to define my pragmas in 20 different programs. So instead I predefine my own "system exceptions" in my own dynamic SQL package:

```
CREATE OR REPLACE PACKAGE dynsql
IS
   invalid_table_name EXCEPTION;
      PRAGMA EXCEPTION_INIT (invalid_table_name, -903);
   invalid_identifier EXCEPTION;
      PRAGMA EXCEPTION_INIT (invalid_identifier, -904);
```

and now I can trap for these errors in any program as follows:

```
WHEN dynsql.invalid_identifier THEN ...
```

I also suggest that you take this same approach when working with the −20,*NNN* error codes passed to RAISE_APPLICATION_ERROR (described later in this chapter). Avoid hardcoding these literals directly into your application; instead, build (or generate) a package that assigns names to those error numbers. Here is an example of such a package:

```
PACKAGE errnums
IS
    en_too_young CONSTANT NUMBER := -20001;
    exc_too_young EXCEPTION;
    PRAGMA EXCEPTION_INIT (exc_too_young, -20001);

    en_sal_too_low CONSTANT NUMBER := -20002;
    exc_sal_too_low EXCEPTION;
    PRAGMA EXCEPTION_INIT (exc_sal_too_low , -20002);
END errnums;
```

By relying on such a package, I can write code like the following, without embedding the actual error number in the logic:

```
PROCEDURE validate_emp (birthdate_in IN DATE)
IS
    min_years CONSTANT PLS_INTEGER := 18;
BEGIN
    IF ADD_MONTHS (SYSDATE, min_years * 12 * -1) < birthdate_in
    THEN
        RAISE_APPLICATION_ERROR
            (errnums.en_too_young,
            'Employee must be at least ' || min_years || ' old.');
    END IF;
END;
```

## About Named System Exceptions

Oracle gives names to a relatively small number of system exceptions by including EXCEPTION_INIT pragma statements in built-in package specifications.

The most important and commonly used set of named exceptions may be found in the STANDARD package in PL/SQL. Because this package is one of the two default packages of PL/SQL, you can reference these exceptions without including the package name as a prefix. So, for instance, if I want to handle the NO_DATA_FOUND exception in my code, I can do so with either of these statements:

```
WHEN NO_DATA_FOUND THEN
WHEN STANDARD.NO_DATA_FOUND THEN
```

You can find predefined exceptions in other built-in packages such as DBMS_LOB, the package used to manipulate large objects. Here is an example of one such definition in that package's specification:

```
invalid_argval EXCEPTION;
PRAGMA EXCEPTION_INIT(invalid_argval, -21560);
```

Because DBMS_LOB is not a default package, when I reference this exception, I need to include the package name:

```
WHEN DBMS_LOB.invalid_argval THEN...
```

Many of the STANDARD-based predefined exceptions are listed in Table 6-1, each with its Oracle error number, the value returned by a call to SQLCODE (a built-in function that returns the current error code, described in "Built-in Error Functions" on page 139), and a brief description. In all but one case (100, the ANSI standard error number for NO_DATA_FOUND), the SQLCODE value is the same as the Oracle error code.

*Table 6-1. Some of the predefined exceptions in PL/SQL*

| Name of exception/Oracle error/SQLCODE | Description |
|---|---|
| CURSOR_ALREADY_OPEN<br>ORA-6511 SQLCODE=-6511 | You tried to OPEN a cursor that was already open. You must CLOSE a cursor before you try to OPEN or re-OPEN it. |
| DUP_VAL_ON_INDEX<br>ORA-00001 SQLCODE= −1 | Your INSERT or UPDATE statement attempted to store duplicate values in a column or columns in a row that is restricted by a unique index. |
| INVALID_CURSOR<br>ORA-01001 SQLCODE=−1001 | You made reference to a cursor that did not exist. This usually happens when you try to FETCH from a cursor or CLOSE a cursor before that cursor is OPENed. |
| INVALID_NUMBER<br>ORA-01722 SQLCODE =−1722 | PL/SQL executes a SQL statement that cannot convert a character string successfully to a number. This exception is different from the VALUE_ERROR exception because it is raised only from within a SQL statement. |
| LOGIN_DENIED<br>ORA-01017 SQLCODE= −1017 | Your program tried to log into the database with an invalid username-password combination. This exception is usually encountered when you embed PL/SQL in a 3GL language. |
| NO_DATA_FOUND<br>ORA-01403 SQLCODE= +100 | This exception is raised in three different scenarios: (1) You executed a SELECT INTO statement (implicit cursor) that returned no rows. (2) You referenced an uninitialized row in a local associative array. (3) You read past end-of-file with the UTL_FILE package. |
| NOT_LOGGED ON<br>ORA-01012 SQLCODE= −1012 | Your program tried to execute a call to the database (usually with a DML statement) before it had logged into the database. |
| PROGRAM_ERROR<br>ORA-06501 SQLCODE= −6501 | PL/SQL encounters an internal problem. The message text usually also tells you to "Contact Oracle Support." |
| STORAGE_ERROR<br>ORA-06500 SQLCODE= −6500 | Your program ran out of memory, or memory was in some way corrupted. |
| TIMEOUT_ON_RESOURCE<br>ORA-00051 SQLCODE=-51 | A timeout occurred in the database while waiting for a resource. |
| TOO_MANY_ROWS<br>ORA-01422 SQLCODE= −1422 | A SELECT INTO statement returned more than one row. A SELECT INTO must return only one row; if your SQL statement returns more than one row, you should place the SELECT statement in an explicit CURSOR declaration and FETCH from that cursor one row at a time. |

| Name of exception/Oracle error/SQLCODE | Description |
| --- | --- |
| TRANSACTION_BACKED_OUT<br>ORA-00061 SQLCODE= −61 | The remote part of a transaction is rolled back, either with an explicit ROLLBACK command or as the result of some other action (such as a failed SQL/DML on the remote database). |
| VALUE_ERROR<br>ORA-06502 SQLCODE= −6502 | PL/SQL encountered an error having to do with the conversion, truncation, or invalid constraining of numeric and character data. This is a very general and common exception. If this type of error is encountered in a SQL DML statement within a PL/SQL block, then the INVALID_NUMBER exception is raised. |
| ZERO_DIVIDE<br>ORA-01476 SQLCODE= −1476 | Your program tried to divide by zero. |

Here is an example of how you might use the exceptions table. Suppose that your program generates an unhandled exception for error ORA-6511. Looking up this error, you find that it is associated with the CURSOR_ALREADY_OPEN exception. Locate the PL/SQL block in which the error occurs, and add an exception handler for CURSOR_ALREADY_OPEN, as shown here:

```
EXCEPTION
   WHEN CURSOR_ALREADY_OPEN
   THEN
      CLOSE my_cursor;
END;
```

Of course, you would be even better off analyzing your code to determine proactively which of the predefined exceptions might occur. You could then decide which of those exceptions you want to handle specifically, which should be covered by the WHEN OTHERS clause (discussed later in this chapter), and which would best be left unhandled.

## Scope of an Exception

The *scope* of an exception is that portion of the code that is "covered" by that exception. An exception covers a block of code if it can be raised in that block. The following table shows the scope for each of the different kinds of exceptions:

| Exception type | Description of scope |
| --- | --- |
| Named system exceptions | These exceptions are globally available because they are not declared in or confined to any particular block of code. You can raise and handle a named system exception in any block. |
| Named programmer-defined exceptions | These exceptions can be raised and handled only in the execution and exception sections of the block in which they are declared (and all nested blocks). If the exception is defined in a package specification, its scope is every program whose owner has EXECUTE privilege on that package. |
| Anonymous system exceptions | These exceptions can be handled in any PL/SQL exception section via the WHEN OTHERS section. If they are assigned a name, then the scope of that name is the same as that of the named programmer-defined exception. |

| Exception type | Description of scope |
| --- | --- |
| Anonymous program-mer-defined exceptions | These exceptions are defined only in the call to RAISE_APPLICATION_ERROR, and then are passed back to the calling program. |

Consider the following example of the exception overdue_balance declared in the procedure check_account. The scope of that exception is the check_account procedure, and nothing else:

```
PROCEDURE check_account (company_id_in IN NUMBER)
IS
   overdue_balance EXCEPTION;
BEGIN
   ... executable statements ...
   LOOP
      ...
      IF ... THEN
         RAISE overdue_balance;
      END IF;
   END LOOP;
EXCEPTION
   WHEN overdue_balance THEN ...
END;
```

I can RAISE the overdue_balance inside the check_account procedure, but I cannot raise that exception from a program that calls check_account. The following anonymous block will generate a compile error, as shown below:

```
DECLARE
   company_id NUMBER := 100;
BEGIN
   check_account (100);
EXCEPTION
   WHEN overdue_balance /* PL/SQL cannot resolve this reference. */
   THEN ...
END;
```

```
PLS-00201: identifier "OVERDUE_BALANCE" must be declared
```

The check_account procedure is a "black box" as far as the anonymous block is concerned. Any identifiers—including exceptions—declared inside check_account are invisible outside of that program.

# Raising Exceptions

There are three ways that an exception may be raised in your application:

- The database might raise the exception when it detects an error.
- You might raise an exception with the RAISE statement.
- You might raise an exception with the RAISE_APPLICATION_ERROR built-in procedure.

I've already looked at how the database raises exceptions. Now let's examine the different mechanisms you can use to raise exceptions.

## The RAISE Statement

Oracle offers the RAISE statement so that you can, at your discretion, raise a named exception. You can raise an exception of your own or a system exception. The RAISE statement can take one of three forms:

```
RAISE exception_name;
RAISE package_name.exception_name;
RAISE;
```

The first form (without a package name qualifier) can be used to raise an exception you have defined in the current block (or an outer block containing that block) or to raise a system exception defined in the STANDARD package. Here are two examples, first raising a programmer-defined exception:

```
DECLARE
    invalid_id EXCEPTION; -- All IDs must start with the letter 'X'.
    id_value VARCHAR2(30);
BEGIN
    id_value := id_for ('SMITH');
    IF SUBSTR (id_value, 1, 1) != 'X'
    THEN
        RAISE invalid_id;
    END IF;
    ...
END;
```

And then you can always raise a system exception as needed:

```
BEGIN
    IF total_sales = 0
    THEN
        RAISE ZERO_DIVIDE; -- Defined in STANDARD package
    ELSE
        RETURN (sales_percentage_calculation (my_sales, total_sales));
    END IF;
END;
```

The second form does require a package name qualifier. If an exception has been declared inside a package (other than STANDARD) and you are raising that exception outside that package, you must qualify your reference to that exception in your RAISE statement, as in:

```
IF days_overdue (isbn_in, borrower_in) > 365
THEN
    RAISE overdue_pkg.book_is_lost;
END IF;
```

The third form of the RAISE statement does not require an exception name, but can be used only within a WHEN clause of the exception section. Its syntax is simply:

```
RAISE;
```

Use this form when you want to re-raise (or propagate out) the same exception from within an exception handler, as you see here:

```
EXCEPTION
   WHEN NO_DATA_FOUND
   THEN
      -- Use common package to record all the "context" information,
      -- such as error code, program name, etc.
      errlog.putline (company_id_in);
      -- And now propagate NO_DATA_FOUND unhandled to the enclosing block.
      RAISE;
```

This feature is useful when you want to log the fact that an error occurred, but then pass that same error out to the enclosing block. That way, you record where the error occurred in your application but still stop the enclosing block(s) without losing the error information.

## Using RAISE_APPLICATION_ERROR

Oracle provides the RAISE_APPLICATION_ERROR procedure (defined in the default DBMS_STANDARD package) to raise application-specific errors in your application. The advantage to using RAISE_APPLICATION_ERROR instead of RAISE (which can also raise an application-specific, explicitly declared exception) is that you can associate an error message with the exception.

When this procedure is run, execution of the current PL/SQL block halts immediately, and any changes made to OUT or IN OUT arguments (if present and without the NOCOPY hint) will be reversed. Changes made to global data structures, such as packaged variables, and to database objects (by executing an INSERT, UPDATE, MERGE, or DELETE) will *not* be rolled back. You must execute an explicit ROLLBACK to reverse the effect of DML operations.

Here's the header for this procedure (defined in package DBMS_STANDARD):

```
PROCEDURE RAISE_APPLICATION_ERROR (
   num binary_integer,
   msg varchar2,
   keeperrorstack boolean default FALSE);
```

where *num* is the error number and must be a value between −20,999 and −20,000 (just think: Oracle needs all the rest of those negative integers for its *own* exceptions!); *msg* is the error message and must be no more than 2K characters in length (any text beyond that limit will be ignored); and *keeperrorstack* indicates whether you want to add the error to any already on the stack (TRUE) or replace the existing errors (the default, FALSE).

Oracle sets aside the range of −20999 and −20000 for use by its customers, but watch out! Several built-in packages, including DBMS_OUTPUT and DBMS_DESCRIBE, use error numbers between −20005 and −20000. See the *Oracle PL/SQL Packages and Types Reference* for documentation of the usages of these error numbers.

Let's take a look at one useful application of this built-in. Suppose that I need to support error messages in different languages for my user community. I create a separate error_table to store all these messages, segregated by the string_language value. I then create a procedure to raise the specified error, grabbing the appropriate error message from the table based on the language used in the current session:

```
/* File on web: raise_by_language.sp */
PROCEDURE raise_by_language (code_in IN PLS_INTEGER)
IS
   l_message error_table.error_string%TYPE;
BEGIN
   SELECT error_string
     INTO l_message
     FROM error_table
    WHERE error_number = code_in
      AND string_language  = USERENV ('LANG');

   RAISE_APPLICATION_ERROR (code_in, l_message);
END;
```

# Handling Exceptions

Once an exception is raised, the current PL/SQL block stops its regular execution and transfers control to the exception section. The exception is then either handled by an exception handler in the current PL/SQL block or passed to the enclosing block.

To handle or trap an exception once it is raised, you must write an exception handler for that exception. In your code, your exception handlers must appear after all the executable statements in your program but before the END statement of the block. The EXCEPTION keyword indicates the start of the exception section and the individual exception handlers:

```
DECLARE
   ... declarations ...
BEGIN
   ... executable statements ...
[ EXCEPTION
   ... exception handlers ... ]
END;
```

The syntax for an exception handler is as follows:

```
WHEN exception_name [ OR exception_name ... ]
THENexecutable statements
```

or:

```
WHEN OTHERS
THEN
    executable statements
```

You can have multiple exception handlers in a single exception section. The exception handlers are structured much like a conditional CASE statement, as shown in the following table:

| Property | Description |
| --- | --- |
| EXCEPTION<br>  WHEN NO_DATA_FOUND<br>  THEN *executable_statements1;* | If the NO_DATA_FOUND exception is raised, then execute the first set of statements. |
|   WHEN payment_overdue<br>  THEN *executable_statements2;* | If the payment is overdue, then execute the second set of statements. |
|   WHEN OTHERS<br>  THEN *executable_statements3;*<br>END; | If any other exception is encountered, then execute the third set of statements. |

An exception is handled if an exception that is named in a WHEN clause matches the exception that was raised. Notice that the WHEN clause traps errors only by exception name, not by error codes. If a match is found, then the executable statements associated with that exception are run. If the exception that has been raised is not handled or does not match any of the named exceptions, the executable statements associated with the WHEN OTHERS clause (if present) will be run. Only one exception handler can catch a particular error. After the statements for that handler are executed, control passes immediately out of the block.

The WHEN OTHERS clause is optional; if it is not present, then any unhandled exception is immediately propagated back to the enclosing block (if any). The WHEN OTHERS clause must be the last exception handler in the exception section. If you place any other WHEN clauses after WHEN OTHERS, you will receive the following compilation error:

```
PLS-00370: OTHERS handler must be last among the exception handlers of a block
```

## Built-in Error Functions

Before exploring the nuances of error handling, let's first review the built-in functions Oracle provides to help you identify, analyze, and respond to errors that occur in your PL/SQL application.

*SQLCODE*
> SQLCODE returns the error code of the most recently raised exception in your block. If there is no error, SQLCODE returns 0. SQLCODE also returns 0 when you call it outside of an exception handler.

The Oracle database maintains a stack of SQLCODE values. Suppose, for example, that function FUNC raises the VALUE_ERROR exception (–6502). Within the exception section of FUNC, you call a procedure PROC that raises DUP_VAL_ON_INDEX (–1). Within the exception section of PROC, SQLCODE returns –1. When control propagates back up to the exception section of FUNC, however, SQLCODE will still return –6502. Run the *sqlcode_test.sql* file (available on the book's web site) to see a demonstration of this behavior.

*SQLERRM*

SQLERRM is a function that returns the error message for a particular error code. If you do not pass an error code to SQLERRM, it returns the error message associated with the value returned by SQLCODE.

If SQLCODE is 0, SQLERRM returns this string:

```
ORA-0000: normal, successful completion
```

If SQLCODE is 1 (the generic user-defined exception error code), SQLERRM returns this string:

```
User-Defined Exception
```

Here is an example of calling SQLERRM to return the error message for a particular code:

```
1  BEGIN
2     DBMS_OUTPUT.put_line (SQLERRM (-1403));
3* END;
SQL> /
ORA-01403: no data found
```

The maximum length string that SQLERRM will return is 512 bytes (in some earlier versions of Oracle, only 255 bytes). Because of this restriction, Oracle Corporation recommends that you instead call DBMS_UTILITY.FORMAT_ERROR_STACK to ensure that you see the full error message string (this built-in will not truncate until 2,000 bytes).

The *oracle_error_info.pkg* and *oracle_error_info.tst* files on the book's web site provide an example of how you can use SQLERRM to validate error codes.

*DBMS_UTILITY.FORMAT_ERROR_STACK*

This built-in function, like SQLERRM, returns the message associated with the current error (i.e., the value returned by SQLCODE). It differs from SQLERRM in two ways:

- It will return up to 1,899 characters of error message, thereby avoiding truncation issues.

- You cannot pass an error code number to this function; it cannot be used to return the message for an arbitrary error code.

As a rule, you should call this function inside your exception handler logic to obtain the full error message.

Note that even though the name of the function includes the word "stack," it doesn't return a stack of errors leading back to the line on which the error was originally raised. That job falls to DBMS_UTILITY.FORMAT_ERROR_BACKTRACE.

*DBMS_UTILITY.FORMAT_ERROR_BACKTRACE*

Introduced in Oracle Database 10g, this function returns a formatted string that displays a stack of programs and line numbers leading back to the line on which the error was originally raised.

This function closed a significant gap in PL/SQL functionality. In Oracle9i Database and earlier releases, once you handled an exception inside your PL/SQL block, you were unable to determine the line on which the error had occurred (perhaps the most important piece of information to developers). If you wanted to see this information, you would have to allow the exception to go unhandled, at which point the full error backtrace would be displayed on the screen or otherwise presented to the user. This situation is explored in more detail in the following section.

*DBMS_UTILITY.FORMAT_CALL_STACK*

This function returns a formatted string showing the execution call stack inside your PL/SQL application. Its usefulness is not restricted to error management; you will also find it handy for tracing the execution of your code. This program is explored in more detail in Chapter 20.

## More on DBMS_UTILITY.FORMAT_ERROR_BACKTRACE

You should call the DBMS_UTILITY.FORMAT_ERROR_BACKTRACE function in your exception handler. It displays the execution stack at the point where an exception was raised. Thus, you can call DBMS_UTILITY.FORMAT_ERROR_BACKTRACE within an exception section at the top level of your stack and still find out where the error was raised deep within the call stack.

Consider the following scenario: I define a procedure proc3, which calls proc2, which in turns calls proc1. The proc1 procedure raises an exception:

```
CREATE OR REPLACE PROCEDURE proc1 IS
BEGIN
   DBMS_OUTPUT.put_line ('running proc1');
   RAISE NO_DATA_FOUND;
END;
/

CREATE OR REPLACE PROCEDURE proc2 IS
   l_str VARCHAR2 (30) := 'calling proc1';
BEGIN
   DBMS_OUTPUT.put_line (l_str);
   proc1;
END;
/

CREATE OR REPLACE PROCEDURE proc3 IS
```

```
BEGIN
   DBMS_OUTPUT.put_line ('calling proc2');
   proc2;
EXCEPTION
   WHEN OTHERS
   THEN
      DBMS_OUTPUT.put_line ('Error stack at top level:');
      DBMS_OUTPUT.put_line (DBMS_UTILITY.format_error_backtrace);
END;
/
```

The only program with an exception handler is the outermost program, proc3. I have placed a call to the backtrace function in proc3's WHEN OTHERS handler. When I run this procedure I see the following results:

```
SQL> SET SERVEROUTPUT ON
SQL> BEGIN
  2      DBMS_OUTPUT.put_line ('Proc3 -> Proc2 -> Proc1 backtrace');
  3      proc3;
  4  END;
  5  /

Proc3 -> Proc2 -> Proc1 backtrace
calling proc2
calling proc1
running proc1
Error stack at top level:
ORA-06512: at "SCOTT.PROC1", line 4
ORA-06512: at "SCOTT.PROC2", line 5
ORA-06512: at "SCOTT.PROC3", line 4
```

As you can see, the backtrace function shows at the top of its stack the line in proc1 on which the error was originally raised.

Often, an exception occurs deep within the execution stack. If you want that exception to propagate all the way to the outermost PL/SQL block, it may have to be re-raised within each exception handler in the stack of blocks. DBMS_UTILITY.FORMAT_ERROR_BACKTRACE shows the trace of execution back to the last RAISE in one's session. As soon as you issue a RAISE of a particular exception or re-raise the current exception, you restart the stack that the DBMS_UTILITY.FORMAT_ERROR_BACKTRACE function produces. This means that if you want to take advantage of this function, you should take one of the following two approaches:

- Call the function in the exception section of the block in which the error was raised. This way you have (and can log) that critical line number, even if the exception is re-raised further up in the stack.

- Avoid exception handlers in intermediate programs in your stack, and call the function in the exception section of the outermost program in your stack.

## Just the line number, please

In a real-world application, the error backtrace could be very long. Generally, the person doing the debugging or support doesn't really want to have to deal with the entire stack; he is mostly going to be interested only in that topmost entry. The developer of the application might even want to display that critical information to the user so that he can immediately and accurately report the problem to the support team.

In this case, it is necessary to parse the backtrace string and retrieve just the topmost entry. I built a utility to do this called the BT package; you can download it from the book's web site. In this package, I provide a simple, clean interface as follows:

```
/* File on web: bt.pkg */
PACKAGE bt
IS
  TYPE error_rt IS RECORD (
    program_owner all_objects.owner%TYPE
  , program_name all_objects.object_name%TYPE
  , line_number PLS_INTEGER
  );

  FUNCTION info (backtrace_in IN VARCHAR2)
    RETURN error_rt;

  PROCEDURE show_info (backtrace_in IN VARCHAR2);
END bt;
```

The record type, error_rt, contains a separate field for each element of the backtrace that I want to retrieve (owner of the program unit, name of the program unit, and line number within that program). Then, instead of calling and parsing the backtrace function in each exception section, I can call the bt.info function and report on the specifics of the error.

## Useful applications of SQLERRM

While it is true that you should use DBMS_UTILITY.FORMAT_ERROR_STACK in place of SQLERRM, that doesn't mean SQLERRM is totally irrelevant. In fact, you can use it to answer the following questions:

- Is a particular number a valid Oracle error?
- What is the error message corresponding to an error code?

As mentioned earlier in this chapter, SQLERRM will return the error message for an error code. If, however, you pass SQLERRM a code that is not valid, it does not raise an exception. Instead, it returns a string in one of the following two forms:

If the number is negative:

```
ORA-NNNNN: Message NNNNN not found; product=RDBMS; facility=ORA
```

If the number is positive or less than –65535:

```
-N: non-ORACLE exception
```

You can use these facts to build functions to neatly return information about whatever code you are currently working with. Here is the specification of a package with such programs:

```
/* File on web: oracle_error_info.pkg */
PACKAGE oracle_error_info
IS
   FUNCTION is_app_error (code_in IN INTEGER)
      RETURN BOOLEAN;

   FUNCTION is_valid_oracle_error (
      code_in            IN    INTEGER
    , app_errors_ok_in   IN    BOOLEAN DEFAULT TRUE
    , user_error_ok_in   IN    BOOLEAN DEFAULT TRUE
   )
      RETURN BOOLEAN;

   PROCEDURE validate_oracle_error (
      code_in            IN         INTEGER
    , message_out        OUT        VARCHAR2
    , is_valid_out       OUT        BOOLEAN
    , app_errors_ok_in   IN         BOOLEAN DEFAULT TRUE
    , user_error_ok_in   IN         BOOLEAN DEFAULT TRUE
   );
END oracle_error_info;
```

You will find the complete implementation on the book's web site.

## Combining Multiple Exceptions in a Single Handler

You can, within a single WHEN clause, combine multiple exceptions together with an OR operator, just as you would combine multiple Boolean expressions:

```
WHEN invalid_company_id OR negative_balance
THEN
```

You can also combine application and system exception names in a single handler:

```
WHEN balance_too_low OR ZERO_DIVIDE OR DBMS_LDAP.INVALID_SESSION
THEN
```

You cannot, however, use the AND operator because only one exception can be raised at a time.

## Unhandled Exceptions

If an exception is raised in your program, and it is not handled by an exception section in either the current or enclosing PL/SQL blocks, that exception is *unhandled*. PL/SQL returns the error that raised the unhandled exception all the way back to the application environment from which PL/SQL was run. That environment (a tool like SQL*Plus, Oracle Forms, or a Java program) then takes an action appropriate to the situation; in the case of SQL*Plus, a ROLLBACK of any DML changes from within that top-level block's logic is automatically performed.

One key decision to make about your application architecture is whether you want to allow unhandled exceptions to occur at all. They are handled differently by different frontends, and in some cases none too gracefully. If your PL/SQL programs are being called from a non-PL/SQL environment, you may want to design your outermost blocks or programs to do the following:

- Trap any exception that might have propagated out to that point.
- Log the error so that a developer can analyze what might be the cause of the problem.
- Pass back a status code, description, and any other information needed by the host environment to make a determination about an appropriate action to take.

## Propagation of Unhandled Exceptions

The scope rules for exceptions determine the block in which an exception can be raised. The rules for exception propagation address the way in which an exception is handled after it is raised.

When an exception is raised, PL/SQL looks for an exception handler in the current block (anonymous block, procedure, or function) of the exception. If it does not find a match, then PL/SQL propagates the exception to the enclosing block of that current block. PL/SQL then attempts to handle the exception by raising it once more in the enclosing block. It continues to do this in each successive enclosing block until there are no more blocks in which to raise the exception (see Figure 6-2). When all blocks are exhausted, PL/SQL returns an unhandled exception to the application environment that executed the outermost PL/SQL block. An unhandled exception halts the execution of the host program.

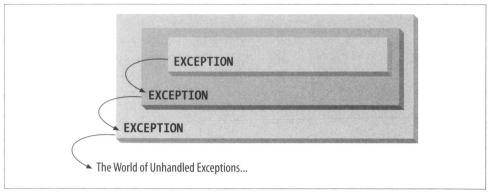

*Figure 6-2. Propagation of an exception through nested blocks*

### Losing exception information

The architecture of PL/SQL exception handling leads to an odd situation regarding local, programmer-defined exceptions: you can lose crucial information (what error occurred?) unless you are careful.

Consider the following situation. I declare an exception as follows:

```
BEGIN
    <<local_block>>
    DECLARE
        case_is_not_made EXCEPTION;
    BEGIN
        ...
    END local_block;
```

but neglect to include an exception section. The scope of the case_is_not_made exception is inside local_block's execution and exception sections. If the exception is not handled there and instead propagates to the enclosing block, then there is no way to know that the case_is_not_made exception was raised. You really don't know *which* error was raised, only that some error was raised. That's because all user-defined exceptions have an error code of 1 and an error message of "User Defined Exception"—unless you use the EXCEPTION_INIT pragma to associate a different number with that declared exception, and use RAISE_APPLICATION_ERROR to associate it with a different error message.

As a consequence, when you are working with locally defined (and raised) exceptions, you should include an exception handler specifically for that error by name.

### Examples of exception propagation

Let's look at a few examples of how exceptions propagate through enclosing blocks. Figure 6-3 shows how the exception raised in the inner block, too_many_faults, is handled by the next enclosing block. The innermost block has an exception section,

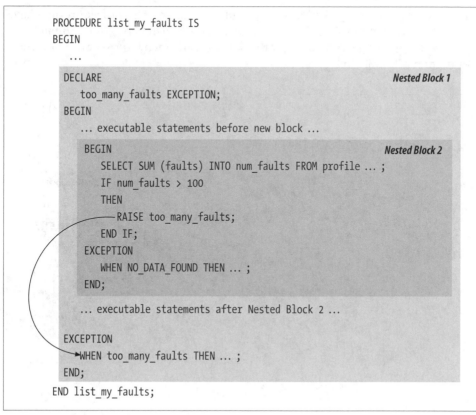

```
        PROCEDURE list_my_faults IS
        BEGIN
          ...
          DECLARE                                              Nested Block 1
             too_many_faults EXCEPTION;
          BEGIN
             ... executable statements before new block ...

             BEGIN                                             Nested Block 2
                SELECT SUM (faults) INTO num_faults FROM profile ... ;
                IF num_faults > 100
                THEN
                   RAISE too_many_faults;
                END IF;
             EXCEPTION
                WHEN NO_DATA_FOUND THEN ... ;
             END;

             ... executable statements after Nested Block 2 ...

          EXCEPTION
             WHEN too_many_faults THEN ... ;
          END;
        END list_my_faults;
```

*Figure 6-3. Propagation of exception handling to first nested block*

so PL/SQL first checks to see if too_many_faults is handled in this section. Because it is not handled, PL/SQL closes that block and raises the too_many_faults exception in the enclosing block, Nested Block 1. Control immediately passes to the exception section of Nested Block 1. (The executable statements after Nested Block 2 are not executed.) PL/SQL scans the exception handlers and finds that too_many_faults is handled in this block, so the code for that handler is executed, and control passes back to the main list_my_faults procedure.

Notice that if the NO_DATA_FOUND exception had been raised in the innermost block (Nested Block 2), then the exception section for Nested Block 2 would have handled the exception. Then control would pass back to Nested Block 1, and the executable statements that come after Nested Block 2 would be executed.

In Figure 6-4, the exception raised in the inner block is handled by the outermost block. The outermost block is the only one with an exception section, so when Nested Block 2 raises the too_many_faults exception, PL/SQL terminates execution of that block and raises that exception in the enclosing block, Nested Block 1. Again, this block has no exception section, so PL/SQL immediately terminates Nested Block 1 and passes control to the outermost block, the list_my_faults procedure. This procedure does have an exception section, so PL/SQL scans the exception handlers, finds a match for too_many_faults, executes the code for that handler, and then returns control to whatever program called list_my_faults.

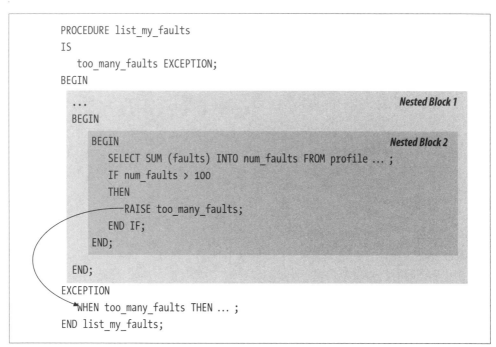

*Figure 6-4. Exception raised in nested block handled by outermost block*

## Continuing Past Exceptions

When an exception is raised in a PL/SQL block, normal execution is halted and control is transferred to the exception section. You can never return to the execution section once an exception is raised in that block. In some cases, however, the ability to continue past exceptions is exactly the desired behavior.

Consider the following scenario: I need to write a procedure that performs a series of DML statements against a variety of tables (delete from one table, update another, insert into a final table). My first pass at writing this procedure might produce code like the following:

```
PROCEDURE change_data IS
BEGIN
   DELETE FROM employees WHERE ... ;
   UPDATE company SET ... ;
   INSERT INTO company_history SELECT * FROM company WHERE ... ;
END;
```

This procedure certainly contains all the appropriate DML statements. But one of the requirements for this program is that, although these statements are executed in sequence, they are logically independent of each other. In other words, even if the DELETE fails, I want to go on and perform the UPDATE and INSERT.

With the current version of change_data, I can't make sure that all three DML statements will at least be attempted. If an exception is raised from the DELETE, for example, the entire program's execution will halt, and control will be passed to the exception section, if there is one. The remaining SQL statements won't be executed.

How can I get the exception to be raised and handled without terminating the program as a whole? The solution is to place the DELETE within its own PL/SQL block. Consider this next version of the change_data program:

```
PROCEDURE change_data IS
BEGIN
   BEGIN
      DELETE FROM employees WHERE ... ;
   EXCEPTION
      WHEN OTHERS THEN log_error;
   END;

   BEGIN
      UPDATE company SET ... ;
   EXCEPTION
      WHEN OTHERS THEN log_error;
   END;

   BEGIN
      INSERT INTO company_history SELECT * FROM company WHERE ... ;
   EXCEPTION
      WHEN OTHERS THEN log_error;
   END;
END;
```

With this new format, if the DELETE raises an exception, control is immediately passed to the exception section. But what a difference! Because the DELETE statement is now in its own block, it can have its own exception section. The WHEN OTHERS clause in that section smoothly handles the error by logging the occurrence of the error, *without re-raising that or any other error.* Control is then passed out of the DELETE's block and back to the enclosing change_data procedure. Since there is no longer an "active" exception, execution continues in this enclosing block.

Execution in this enclosing block then continues to the next statement in the procedure. A new anonymous block is then entered for the UPDATE statement. If the UPDATE statement fails, the WHEN OTHERS in the UPDATE's own exception section traps the problem and returns control to change_data, which blithely moves on to the INSERT statement (contained in its very own block).

Figure 6-5 shows this process for two sequential DELETE statements.

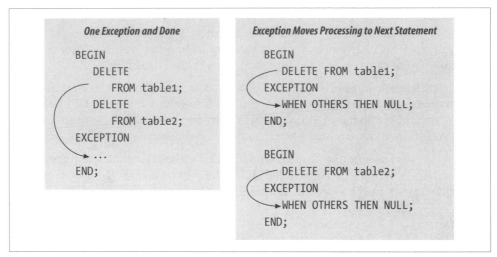

*Figure 6-5. Sequential DELETEs, using two different approaches to scope*

To summarize: an exception raised in the executable section will always be handled in the current block—if there is a matching handler present. You can create a "virtual block" around any statement(s) by prefacing it with a BEGIN and following it with an EXCEPTION section and an END statement. In this way you can control the scope of failure caused by an exception by establishing "buffers" of anonymous blocks in your code.

You can also take this strategy a step further and move the code you want to isolate into separate procedures or functions. Of course, these named PL/SQL blocks may also have their own exception sections and will offer the same protection from total failure. One key advantage of using procedures and functions is that you hide all the BEGIN-EXCEPTION-END statements from the mainline program. The program is then easier to read, understand, maintain, and reuse in multiple contexts.

There are other ways to continue past a DML exception. You can also use SAVE EXCEPTIONS with FORALL and LOG ERRORS in association with DBMS_ERROR-LOG to continue past exceptions raised by DML.

## Writing WHEN OTHERS Handling Code

Include the WHEN OTHERS clause in the exception section to trap any otherwise unhandled exceptions. Because you have not explicitly handled any specific exceptions, you will very likely want to take advantage of the built-in error functions, such as SQLCODE and DBMS_UTILITY.FORMAT_ERROR_STACK, to give you information about the error that has occurred.

Combined with WHEN OTHERS, SQLCODE provides a way for you to handle different, specific exceptions without having to use the EXCEPTION_INIT pragma. In the next example, I trap two parent-child exceptions, −1 and −2292, and then take an action appropriate to each situation:

```
PROCEDURE add_company (
    id_in      IN company.ID%TYPE
  , name_in    IN company.name%TYPE
  , type_id_in IN company.type_id%TYPE
)
IS
BEGIN
    INSERT INTO company (ID, name, type_id)
        VALUES (id_in, name_in, type_id_in);
EXCEPTION
    WHEN OTHERS
    THEN
        /*
        || Anonymous block inside the exception handler lets me declare
        || local variables to hold the error code information.
        */
        DECLARE
            l_errcode PLS_INTEGER := SQLCODE;
        BEGIN
            CASE l_errcode
            WHEN -1 THEN
                -- Duplicate value for unique index. Either a repeat of the
                -- primary key or name. Display problem and re-raise.
                DBMS_OUTPUT.put_line
                            (    'Company ID or name already in use. ID = '
                             || TO_CHAR (id_in)
                             || ' name = '
                             || name_in
                            );
                RAISE;
            WHEN -2291 THEN
                -- Parent key not found for type. Display problem and re-raise.
                DBMS_OUTPUT.put_line (
                    'Invalid company type ID: ' || TO_CHAR (type_id_in));
                RAISE;
            ELSE
                RAISE;
            END CASE;
        END; -- End of anonymous block.
END add_company;
```

You should use WHEN OTHERS with care, because it can easily "swallow up" errors and hide them from the outer blocks and the user. Specifically, watch out for WHEN OTHER handlers that do not re-raise the current exception or raise some other exception in its place. If WHEN OTHERS does not propagate out an exception, then the outer blocks of your application will never know that an error occurred.

Oracle Database 11*g* offers a new warning to help you identify programs that may be ignoring or swallowing up errors:

```
PLW-06009: procedure "string" OTHERS handler does not end in RAISE or RAISE_
APPLICATION_ERROR
```

Here is an example of using this warning:

```
/* File on web: plw6009.sql */
SQL> ALTER SESSION SET plsql_warnings = 'enable:all'
  2  /

SQL> CREATE OR REPLACE PROCEDURE plw6009_demo
  2  AS
  3  BEGIN
  4     DBMS_OUTPUT.put_line ('I am here!');
  5     RAISE NO_DATA_FOUND;
  6  EXCEPTION
  7     WHEN OTHERS
  8     THEN
  9        NULL;
 10  END plw6009_demo;
 11  /

SP2-0804: Procedure created with compilation warnings

SQL> SHOW ERRORS
Errors for PROCEDURE PLW6009_DEMO:

LINE/COL ERROR
-------- -----------------------------------------------------------------
7/9      PLW-06009: procedure "PLW6009_DEMO" OTHERS handler does not end
         in RAISE or RAISE_APPLICATION_ERROR
```

# Building an Effective Error Management Architecture

PL/SQL error raising and handling mechanisms are powerful and flexible, but they have some drawbacks that can present challenges to any development team that wants to implement a robust, consistent, informative architecture for error management.

Here are the some of the challenges you will encounter:

- The EXCEPTION is an odd kind of structure in PL/SQL. A variable declared to be EXCEPTION can only be raised and handled. It has at most two characteristics: an error code and an error message. You cannot pass an exception as an argument to a program; you cannot associate other attributes with an exception.

- It is very difficult to reuse exception-handling code. Directly related to the previous challenge is another fact: you cannot pass an exception as an argument; you end up cutting and pasting handler code, which is certainly not an optimal way to write programs.

- There is no formal way to specify which exceptions may be raised by a program. With Java on the other hand, this information becomes part of the specification of the program. The consequence is that you must look inside the program implementation to see what might be raised—or hope for the best.

- Oracle does not provide any way for you to organize and categorize your application-specific exceptions. It simply sets aside (for the most part) the 1,000 error codes between –20,999 and –20,000. You are left to manage those values.

Let's figure out how we can best meet most of these challenges.

## Decide on Your Error Management Strategy

It is extremely important that you establish a consistent strategy and architecture for error handling in your application before you write any code. To do that, you must answer questions like these:

- How and when do I log errors so that they can be reviewed and corrected? Should I write information to a file, to a database table, and/or to the screen?
- How and when do I report the occurrence of errors back to the user? How much information should the user see and have to keep track of? How do I transform often obscure database error messages into text that is understandable to my users?

Linked tightly to these very high-level questions are more concrete issues, such as:

- Should I include an exception-handling section in every one of my PL/SQL blocks?
- Should I have an exception-handling section only in the top-level or outermost blocks?
- How should I manage my transactions when errors occur?

Part of the complexity of exception handling is that there is no single right answer to any of these questions. It depends at least in part on the application architecture and the way it is used (batch process versus user-driven transactions, for example). However you answer these questions for your application, I strongly suggest that you "codify" the strategy and rules for error handling within a standardized package. I address this topic in a later section.

Here are some general principles you may want to consider:

- When an error occurs in your code, obtain as much information as possible about the context in which the error was raised. You are better off with more information than you really need, rather than with less. You can then propagate the exception to outer blocks, picking up more information as you go.
- Avoid hiding errors with handlers that look like WHEN *error* THEN NULL; (or, even worse: WHEN OTHERS THEN NULL;). There may be a good reason for you to write code like this, but do make sure it is really what you want and document the usage so that others will be aware of it.
- Rely on the default error mechanisms of PL/SQL whenever possible. Avoid writing programs that return status codes to the host environment or calling blocks. The only time you will want to use status codes is if the host environment cannot

gracefully handle Oracle errors (in which case, you might want to consider switching your host environment!).

## Standardize Handling of Different Types of Exceptions

An exception is an exception is an exception? Not really. Some exceptions, for example, indicate that the database is having very severe, low-level problems (such as ORA-00600). Other exceptions, like NO_DATA_FOUND, happen so routinely that we don't even really necessarily think of them as *errors*, but more as a conditional branching of logic ("If the row doesn't exist, then do this..."). Do these distinctions really matter? I think so, and Bryn Llewellyn, PL/SQL Product Manager as of the writing of this book, taught me a very useful way to categorize exceptions:

*Deliberate*
> The code architecture itself deliberately relies upon an exception in the way it works. This means you must (well, *should*) anticipate and code for this exception. An example is UTL_FILE.GET_LINE.

*Unfortunate*
> This is an error, but one that is to be expected and may not even indicate that a problem has occurred. An example is a SELECT INTO statement that raises NO_DATA_FOUND.

*Unexpected*
> This is a "hard" error indicating a problem in the application. An example is a SELECT INTO statement that is supposed to return a row for a given primary key, but instead raises TOO_MANY ROWS.

Let's take a close look at the examples of these exception categories. Then I will discuss how knowing about these categories can and should be useful to you.

### Deliberate exceptions

PL/SQL developers can use UTL_FILE.GET_LINE to read the contents of a file, one line at a time. When GET_LINE reads past the end of a file, it raises NO_DATA_FOUND. That's just the way it works. So if I want to read everything from a file and "do stuff," my program might look like this:

```
PROCEDURE read_file_and_do_stuff (
   dir_in IN VARCHAR2, file_in IN VARCHAR2
)
IS
   l_file   UTL_FILE.file_type;
   l_line   VARCHAR2 (32767);
BEGIN
   l_file := UTL_FILE.fopen (dir_in, file_in, 'R', max_linesize => 32767);

   LOOP
      UTL_FILE.get_line (l_file, l_line);
      do_stuff;
```

```
        END LOOP;
    EXCEPTION
       WHEN NO_DATA_FOUND
       THEN
           UTL_FILE.fclose (l_file);
           more_stuff_here;
    END;
```

You may notice something a bit strange about my loop; it has no EXIT statement. Also, I am running more application logic (more_stuff_here) in the exception section. I can rewrite my loop as follows:

```
    LOOP
       BEGIN
           UTL_FILE.get_line (l_file, l_line);
           do_stuff;
       EXCEPTION
          WHEN NO_DATA_FOUND
          THEN
              EXIT;
       END;
       END LOOP;

       UTL_FILE.flcose (l_file);
       more_stuff_here;
```

Now I have an EXIT statement in my loop, but that sure is some awkward code.

This is the kind of thing you need to do when you work with code that deliberately raises an exception as a part of its architecture. You'll find more in the next few sections about what I think you should do about this.

### Unfortunate and unexpected exceptions

I will cover these together because the two examples (NO_DATA_FOUND and TOO_MANY_ROWS) are tightly linked together. Suppose I need to write a function to return the full name of an employee (last comma first) for a particular primary key value.

I could write it most simply as follows:

```
    FUNCTION fullname (
       employee_id_in IN employees.employee_id%TYPE
    )
       RETURN VARCHAR2
    IS
       retval    VARCHAR2 (32767);
    BEGIN
       SELECT last_name || ',' || first_name
         INTO retval
         FROM employees
        WHERE employee_id = employee_id_in;

       RETURN retval;
    END fullname;
```

If I call this program with an employee ID that is not in the table, the database will raise the NO_DATA_FOUND exception. If I call this program with an employee ID that is found in more than one row in the table, the database will raise the TOO_MANY_ROWS exception.

One query, two different exceptions—should you treat them the same way? Perhaps not. Do these two exceptions truly reflect similar kinds of problems?

*NO_DATA_FOUND*

> With this exception I didn't find a match. That *could* be a serious problem, but is not necessarily the case. Perhaps I actually expect that most of the time I will not get a match, and therefore will simply insert a new employee. It is, shall we say, *unfortunate* that the exception was raised, but in this case it is not even an error.

*TOO_MANY_ROWS*

> With this exception we have a serious problem on our hands: something has gone wrong with our primary key constraint. I can't think of a circumstance in which this would be considered OK or simply "unfortunate." No, it is time to stop the program, and call attention to this very unexpected, "hard" error.

### How to benefit from this categorization

I hope you agree that this characterization sounds useful. I suggest that when you are about to build a new application, you decide as much as possible the standard approach you (and everyone else on the team) will take for each type of exception. Then, as you encounter (need to handle or write in anticipation of) an exception, decide into which category it falls, and then apply the already-decided approach. In this way, you will all write your code in a more consistent and productive manner.

Here are my guidelines for dealing with the three types of exceptions:

*Deliberate*

> You will need to write code in anticipation of this exception. The critical best practice in this case is to *avoid putting application logic in the exception section*. The exception section should only contain code needed to deal with the *error*: log the error data, re-raise the exception, etc. Programmers don't expect application-specific logic there, which means that it will be much harder to understand and maintain.

*Unfortunate*

> If there are circumstances under which a user of the code that raises this exception would not interpret the situation as an *error*, then don't propagate this exception out unhandled. Instead, return a value or status flag that indicates the exception was raised. You then leave it up to the user of the program to decide if that program should terminate with an error. Better yet, why not let the caller of your program tell it whether or not to raise an exception, and if not, what value should be passed to indicate that the exception occurred?

*Unexpected*

Now we are down to the hard stuff. All unexpected errors should be logged, recording as much of the application context as possible to help understand why it occurred. The program should then terminate with an unhandled exception (usually the same) that was raised within the program, which can be done with the RAISE statement, forcing the calling program to stop and deal with the error.

## Organize Use of Application-Specific Error Codes

When you use RAISE_APPLICATION_ERROR to raise application-specific errors, it is entirely up to you to manage the error codes and messages. This can get tricky and messy ("Gee, which number should I use? Well, I doubt that anyone would be using −20774!").

To help manage your error codes and provide a consistent interface with which developers can handle server errors, consider building a table to store all the −20,*NNN* error numbers you use, along with their associated exception names and error messages. Developers can then view these already defined errors via a screen and choose the one that fits their situation. See the *msginfo.sql* file on the book's web site for one such example of a table, along with code that will generate a package containing declarations of each of the "registered" exceptions.

Another approach you can take is to avoid the −20,*NNN* range entirely for application-specific errors. Why not use positive numbers instead? Oracle uses only 1 and 100 on the positive side of the integer range. While it is *possible* that Oracle will, over time, use other positive numbers, it is very unlikely. That leaves an awful lot of error codes for us to use.

I took this approach when designing the Quest Error Manager (QEM), a freeware error management utility (available at *www.ToadWorld.com* from the Downloads page). With Quest Error Manager, you can define your own errors in a special repository table. You can define an error by name and/or error code. The error codes can be negative or positive. If the error code is positive, then when you raise that exception, QEM uses RAISE_APPLICATION_ERROR to raise a generic exception (usually −20,000). The information about the current application error code is embedded in the error message, which can then be decoded by the receiving program.

You can also see a simpler implementation of this approach in the general error manager package, *errpkg.pkg*, which is described in the next section "Use Standardized Error Management Programs".

## Use Standardized Error Management Programs

Robust and consistent error handling is an absolutely crucial element of a properly constructed application. This consistency is important for two very different audiences: the user and the developer. If the user is presented with easy-to-understand, well-formatted information when an error occurs, she will be able to report that error more effectively to the support team and will feel more comfortable using the application. If the application handles and logs errors in the same way throughout the entire application, the support and maintenance programmers will be able to fix and enhance the code much more easily.

Sounds like a sensible approach, doesn't it? Unfortunately, and especially in development teams of more than a handful of people, the end result of exception handling is usually very different from what I just described. A more common practice is that each developer strikes out on his own path, following different principles, writing to different kinds of logs, and so on. Without standardization, debugging and maintenance become a nightmare. Here's an example of the kind of code that typically results:

```
EXCEPTION
    WHEN NO_DATA_FOUND
    THEN
        v_msg := 'No company for id '||TO_CHAR (v_id);
        v_err := SQLCODE;
        v_prog := 'fixdebt';
        INSERT INTO errlog VALUES
            (v_err,v_msg,v_prog,SYSDATE,USER);

    WHEN OTHERS
    THEN
        v_err := SQLCODE;
        v_msg := SQLERRM;
        v_prog := 'fixdebt';
        INSERT INTO errlog VALUES
            (v_err,v_msg,v_prog,SYSDATE,USER);
        RAISE;
```

At first glance, this code might seem quite sensible, and in fact explains itself clearly:

> If I don't find a company for this ID, grab the SQLCODE value, set the program name and message, and write a row to the log table. Then allow the enclosing block to continue (it's not a very severe error in this case). If any other error occurs, grab the error code and message, set the program name, write a row to the log table, and then propagate out the same exception, causing the enclosing block to stop (I don't know how severe the error is).

So what's wrong with all that? The mere fact that I can actually explain everything that is going on is an indication of the problem. I have exposed and hardcoded all the steps I take to get the job done. The result is that (1) I write a lot of code, and (2) if anything changes, I have to change a lot of code. Just to give you one example, notice that I am writing to a database table for my log. This means that the log entry has become a part of my logical transaction. If I need to roll back that transaction, I lose my error log.

There are several ways to correct this problem—for example, write to a file or use autonomous transactions to save my error log without affecting my main transaction. The problem is that, with the way I have written my code above, I have to apply my correction in potentially hundreds of different programs.

---

Now consider a rewrite of this same exception section using a standardized package:

```
EXCEPTION
   WHEN NO_DATA_FOUND
   THEN
      errpkg.record_and_continue (
         SQLCODE, 'No company for id ' || TO_CHAR (v_id));

   WHEN OTHERS
   THEN
      errpkg.record_and_stop;
END;
```

My error-handling package hides all the implementation details; I simply decide which of the handler procedures I want to use by viewing the specification of the package. If I want to record the error and then continue, I call the record_and_continue the program. If I want to record and then stop, clearly I want to use the record_and_stop the program. How does it record the error? How does it stop the enclosing block (i.e., how does it propagate the exception)? I don't know, and I don't care. Whatever it does, it does it according to the standards defined for my application.

All I know is that I can now spend more time building the interesting elements of my application, rather than worrying over the tedious, low-level administrivia.

The *errpkg.pkg* file available on the book's web site contains a prototype of such a standardized error-handling package. You will want to review and complete its implementation before using it in your application, but it will give you a very clear sense of how to construct such a utility.

Alternatively, you can take advantage of a much more complete error management utility (also free): the Quest Error Manager mentioned earlier. The most important concept underlying my approach with QEM is that you trap and log information about *instances* of errors, and not just the Oracle error. QEM consists of a PL/SQL package and four underlying tables that store information about errors that occur in an application.

## Work with Your Own Exception "Objects"

Oracle's implementation of the EXCEPTION datatype has some limitations, as described earlier. An exception consists of an identifier (a name) with which you can associate a number and a message. You can raise the exception, and you can handle it. That's it. Consider the way that Java approaches this same situation: all errors derive from a single Exception class. You can extend that class, adding other characteristics about an exception that you want to keep track of (error stack, context-sensitive data, etc.). An object instantiated from an Exception class is like any other kind of object in Java. You certainly can pass it as an argument to a method.

So PL/SQL doesn't let you do that with its native exceptions. This fact should not stop you from implementing your own exception "object." You can do so with Oracle object types or with a relational table of error information.

Regardless of implementation path, the key insight here is to distinguish between an error definition (error code is –1403, name is "no data found," cause is "implicit cursor did not find at least one row") and a particular *instance* of that error (I tried to select a company for this name and did not find any rows.). There is, in other words, just one definition of the NO_DATA_FOUND exception, but there are many different instances or occurrences of that exception. Oracle does not distinguish between these two representations of an error, but we certainly should—and we need to.

Here is an example of a simple exception object hierarchy to demonstrate the point. First, the base object type for all exceptions:

```
/* File on web: exception.ot */
CREATE TYPE exception_t AS OBJECT (
   name VARCHAR2(100),
   code INTEGER,
   description VARCHAR2(4000),
   help_text VARCHAR2(4000),
   recommendation VARCHAR2(4000),
   error_stack CLOB,
   call_stack CLOB,
   created_on DATE,
   created_by VARCHAR2(100)
   )
   NOT FINAL;
/
```

Next, I extend the base exception type for dynamic SQL errors by adding the sql_string attribute. When handling errors for dynamic SQL, it is very important to grab the string that is causing the problem, so it can be analyzed later.

```
CREATE TYPE dynsql_exception_t UNDER exception_t (
   sql_string CLOB )
   NOT FINAL;
/
```

Here is another subtype of exception_t, this time specific to a given application entity, the employee. An exception that is raised for an employee-related error will include the employee ID and the foreign key to the rule that was violated.

```
CREATE TYPE employee_exception_t UNDER exception_t (
   employee_id INTEGER,
   rule_id INTEGER );
/
```

The complete specification of an error object hierarchy will include methods on the exception supertype to display error information or write it to the repository. I leave it to the reader to complete the hierarchy defined in the *exception.ot* file.

If you do not want to work with object types, you can take the approach I developed for the Quest Error Manager: I define a table of error definitions (Q$ERROR) and another table of error instances (Q$ERROR_INSTANCE), which contains information about specific occurrences of an error. All the context-specific data for an error instance is stored in the Q$ERROR_CONTEXT table.

Here is an example of the kind of code you would write with the Quest Error Manager API:

```
WHEN DUP_VAL_ON_INDEX
THEN
   q$error_manager.register_error (
         error_name_in => 'DUPLICATE-VALUE'
         ,err_instance_id_out => l_err_instance_id
         );
   q$error_manager.add_context (
         err_instance_id_in => l_err_instance_id
         ,name_in => 'TABLE_NAME', value_in => 'EMPLOYEES'
         );
   q$error_manager.add_context (
         err_instance_id_in => l_err_instance_id
         ,name_in => 'KEY_VALUE', value_in => l_employee_id
         );
   q$error_manager.raise_error_instance (err_instance_id_in => l_err_instance_id);
END;
```

If the duplicate value error was caused by the unique name constraint, I obtain an error instance ID or handle for the "DUPLICATE-VALUE" error. (That's right. I use error *names* here, entirely sidestepping issues related to error numbers). Then I add context information for this instance (the table name and the primary key value that caused the problem). Finally, I raise the error instance, causing this block to fail and propagating the exception upwards.

Just as you can pass data from your application into the error repository through the API, you can also retrieve error information with the get_error_info procedure. Here is an example:

```
BEGIN
   run_my_application_code;
EXCEPTION
   WHEN OTHERS
   THEN
      DECLARE
         l_error    q$error_manager.error_info_rt;
      BEGIN
         q$error_manager.get_error_info (l_error);
         DBMS_OUTPUT.put_line ('');
         DBMS_OUTPUT.put_line ('Error in DEPT_SAL Procedure:');
         DBMS_OUTPUT.put_line ('Code = ' || l_error.code);
         DBMS_OUTPUT.put_line ('Name = ' || l_error.NAME);
         DBMS_OUTPUT.put_line ('Text = ' || l_error.text);
         DBMS_OUTPUT.put_line ('Error Stack = ' || l_error.error_stack);
```

```
      END;
   END;
```

These are just two of a number of different approaches to overcoming the limitations of the EXCEPTION type in PL/SQL. The bottom line is that there is no reason to accept the default situation, which is that you can only associate a code and message with the occurrence of an error.

## Create Standard Templates for Common Error Handling

You cannot pass an exception to a program, which makes it very difficult to share standard error-handling sections among different PL/SQL blocks. You may find yourself writing the same handler logic over and over again, particularly when working with specific areas of functionality, such as file I/O with UTL_FILE. In these situations, you should take the time to create templates or starting points for such handlers.

Let's take a closer look at UTL_FILE (described further in Chapter 22). Prior to Oracle9i Database Release 2, UTL_FILE defined a number of exceptions in its package specification. However, Oracle neglected to provide error numbers for those exceptions via the EXCEPTION_INIT pragma. Consequently, if you did not handle a UTL_FILE exception by name, it would be impossible via SQLCODE to figure out what had gone wrong. Given this situation, you would probably want to set up a template for UTL_FILE programs that looked in part like this:

```
/* File on web: utlflexc.sql */
DECLARE
   l_file_id   UTL_FILE.file_type;

   PROCEDURE cleanup (file_in IN OUT UTL_FILE.file_type
                     ,err_in IN VARCHAR2 := NULL)
   IS
   BEGIN
      UTL_FILE.fclose (file_in);

      IF err_in IS NOT NULL
      THEN
         DBMS_OUTPUT.put_line ('UTL_FILE error encountered:');
         DBMS_OUTPUT.put_line (err_in);
      END IF;
   END cleanup;
BEGIN
   -- Body of program here

   -- Then clean up before exiting...
   cleanup (l_file_id);
EXCEPTION
   WHEN UTL_FILE.invalid_path
   THEN
      cleanup (l_file_id, 'invalid_path');
      RAISE;
   WHEN UTL_FILE.invalid_mode
   THEN
```

```
        cleanup (l_file_id, 'invalid_mode');
        RAISE;
    END;
```

The key elements of this template include:

- A reusable cleanup program that ensures that the current file is closed before losing the handle to the file.
- The translation of the named exception to a string that can be logged or displayed so that you know precisely which error was raised.

 Starting with Oracle9i Database Release 2, UTL_FILE does assign error codes to each of its exceptions, but you still need to make sure that files are closed when an error occurs and report on the error as consistently as possible.

Let's take a look at another UTL_FILE-related need for a template. Oracle9i Database Release 2 introduced the FREMOVE program to delete a file. UTL_FILE offers the DELETE_FAILED exception, raised when FREMOVE is unable to remove the file. After trying out this program, I discovered that FREMOVE may, in fact, raise any of several exceptions, including:

*UTL_FILE.INVALID_OPERATION*
: The file you asked UTL_FILE to remove does not exist.

*UTL_FILE.DELETE_FAILED*
: You (or the Oracle process) do not have the necessary privileges to remove the file, or the attempt failed for some other reason.

Thus, whenever you work with UTL_FILE.FREMOVE, you should include an exception section that distinguishes between these two errors, as in:

```
BEGIN
   UTL_FILE.fremove (dir, filename);
EXCEPTION
   WHEN UTL_FILE.delete_failed
   THEN
      DBMS_OUTPUT.put_line (
         'Error attempting to remove: ' || filename || ' from ' || dir);
      -- Then take appropriate action....

   WHEN UTL_FILE.invalid_operation
   THEN
      DBMS_OUTPUT.put_line (
         'Unable to find and remove: ' || filename || ' from ' || dir);
      -- Then take appropriate action....
END;
```

The *fileIO.pkg* available on the book's web site offers a more complete implementation of such a template, in the context of an encapsulation of UTL_FILE.FREMOVE.

# Making the Most of PL/SQL Error Management

It will be very difficult to create applications that are easy to use and debug unless you take a consistent, high-quality approach to dealing with errors.

Oracle PL/SQL's error management capabilities allow you to define, raise and handle errors in very flexible ways. Limitations in its approach, however, mean that you will usually want to supplement the built-in features with your own application-specific code and tables.

I suggest that you meet this challenge by taking the following steps:

1. Study and understand how error raising and handling work in PL/SQL. It is not all completely intuitive. A prime example: an exception raised in the declaration section will *not* be handled by the exception section of that block.

2. Decide on the overall error management approach you will take in your application. Where and when do you handle errors? What information do you need to save and how will you do that? How are exceptions propagated to the host environment? How will you handle deliberate, unfortunate, and unexpected errors?

3. Build a standard framework to be used by all developers; that framework will include underlying tables, packages, and perhaps object types, along with a well-defined process for using these elements. Don't resign yourself to PL/SQL's limitations. Work around them by enhancing the error management model.

4. Create templates that everyone on your team can use, making it easier to follow the standard than to write one's own error-handling code.

# PART III

# PL/SQL Program Data

Just about every program you write will manipulate data—and much of that data is "local" to (i.e., defined in) your PL/SQL procedure or function. This part of the book concentrates on the various types of program data you can define in PL/SQL, such as numbers (including the datatypes introduced in Oracle Database 11*g*), strings, dates, timestamps, records, collections, XML datatypes, and user-defined datatypes. Chapters 7 through 13 also cover the various built-in functions provided by Oracle that allow you to manipulate and modify data.

Chapter 7, *Working with Program Data*
Chapter 8, *Strings*
Chapter 9, *Numbers*
Chapter 10, *Dates and Timestamps*
Chapter 11, *Records*
Chapter 12, *Collections*
Chapter 13, *Miscellaneous Datatypes*

# Working with Program Data

Almost every PL/SQL block you write will define and manipulate *program data*. Program data consists of data structures that exist only within your PL/SQL session (physically, within the Program Global Area, or PGA, for your session); they are not stored in the database. Program data can be:

*Variable or constant*
> The values of variables can change during a program's execution. The values of constants are static once they are set at the time of declaration.

*Scalar or composite*
> Scalars are made up of a single value, such as a number or a string. Composite data consists of multiple values, such as a record, a collection, or an object type instance.

*Containerized*
> Containers may contain information obtained from the database, or data that was never in the database and might not ever end up there.

Before you can work with program data inside your PL/SQL code, you must declare data structures, giving them names and datatypes.

This chapter describes how you declare program data. It covers the rules governing the format of the names you give them. It offers a quick reference to all the different types of data supported in PL/SQL and explores the concept of datatype conversion. The chapter finishes with some recommendations for working with program data. The remaining chapters in this part of the book describe specific types of program data.

## Naming Your Program Data

To work with a variable or a constant, you must first declare it, and when you declare it, you give it a name. Here are the rules that PL/SQL insists you follow when naming your data structures (these are the same rules applied to names of database objects, such as tables and columns):

- Names can be up to 30 characters in length.
- Names must start with a letter.
- After the first letter, names can then be composed of any of the following: letters, numerals, $, #, and _.
- All names are case-insensitive (unless those names are placed within double quotes).

Given these rules, the following names are valid:

```
l_total_count
first_12_years
total_#_of_trees
salary_in_$
```

These next two names are not only valid but considered identical by PL/SQL because it is *not* a case-sensitive language:

```
ExpertsExchange
ExpertSexChange
```

The next three names are invalid, for the reasons indicated:

```
1st_account  --Starts with a number instead of a letter
favorite_ice_cream_flavors_that_dont_contain_nuts  --Too long
email_address@business_loc  --Contains invalid character (@)
```

There are some exceptions to these rules (why am I not surprised?). If you embed a name within double quotes when you declare it, you can bypass all the above rules *except* the maximum length of 30 characters. For example, all of the following declarations are valid:

```
DECLARE
   "truly_lower_case" INTEGER;
   "     " DATE; -- Yes, a name consisting of five spaces!
   "123_go!" VARCHAR2(10);
BEGIN
   "123_go!"  := 'Steven';
END;
```

Note that when you reference these strange names in your execution section, you will need to do so within double quotes, as shown. Otherwise, your code will not compile.

Why would you use double quotes? There is little reason to do so in PL/SQL programs. It is a technique sometimes employed when creating database objects because it preserves case-sensitivity (in other words, if I CREATE TABLE "docs", then the name of the table is docs and not DOCS), but in general, you should avoid using double quotes in PL/SQL.

Another exception to these naming conventions has to do with the names of Java objects, which can be up to 4K in length. See the Java chapter included on the book's web site for more details about this variation and what it means for PL/SQL developers.

Here are two key recommendations for naming your variables, constants, and types:

*Ensure that each name accurately reflects its usage and is understandable at a glance*
You might even take a moment to write down—in noncomputer terms—what a variable represents. You can then easily extract an appropriate name from that statement. For example, if a variable represents the "total number of calls made about lukewarm coffee," a good name for that variable might be total_calls_on_cold_coffee, or tot_cold_calls, if you are allergic to five-word variable names. A bad name for that variable would be totcoffee, or t_#_calls_lwcoff, both too cryptic to get the point across.

*Establish consistent, sensible naming conventions*
Such conventions usually involve the use of prefixes and/or suffixes to indicate type and usage. For example, all local variables should be prefixed with "l_" while global variables defined in packages have a "g_" prefix. All record types should have a suffix of "_rt", and so on. You can download a comprehensive set of naming conventions from O'Reilly's Oracle page at *http://oracle.oreilly.com*. Click on "Oracle PL/SQL Best Practices," then "Examples." The download contains a standards document for your use. (Currently, the direct URL is *http://oreilly.com/catalog/9780596514105/*.)

# Overview of PL/SQL Datatypes

Whenever you declare a variable or a constant, you must assign it a datatype. PL/SQL is, with very few exceptions, a "statically typed programming language" (see the following sidebar for a definition). PL/SQL offers a comprehensive set of predefined scalar and composite datatypes, and you can create your own user-defined types (also known as *abstract datatypes*). Many of the PL/SQL datatypes are not supported by database columns, such as Boolean and NATURAL, but within PL/SQL code, these datatypes are quite useful.

Virtually all of these predefined datatypes are defined in the PL/SQL STANDARD package. Here, for example, are the statements that define the Boolean datatype and two of the numeric datatypes:

```
create or replace package STANDARD is

  type BOOLEAN is (FALSE, TRUE);

  type NUMBER is NUMBER_BASE;
  subtype INTEGER is NUMBER(38,);
```

When it comes to datatypes, PL/SQL supports the "usual suspects" and a whole lot more. This section provides a quick overview of the various predefined datatypes. They are covered in detail in Chapters 8 through 13, Chapter 15, and Chapter 26; you will find detailed references to specific chapters in the following sections.

## Character Data

PL/SQL supports both fixed- and variable-length strings as both traditional character and Unicode character data. CHAR and NCHAR are fixed-length datatypes; VARCHAR2 and NVARCHAR2 are variable-length datatypes. Here is a declaration of a variable-length string that can hold up to 2,000 characters:

```
DECLARE
    l_accident_description VARCHAR2(2000);
```

Chapter 8 explores the rules for character data, provides many examples, and explains the built-in functions provided to manipulate strings in PL/SQL.

For very large character strings PL/SQL has the CLOB (Character Large Object) and NCLOB (NLS Character Large Object) datatypes. For backward compatibility, PL/SQL also supports the LONG datatype. These datatypes allow you to store and manipulate very large amounts of data, in Oracle Database 11*g*, a LOB can hold up to 128 terabytes of information.

 There are many rules restricting the use of LONGs. I recommend that you avoid using LONGs (assuming that you are running Oracle8 Database or later).

Chapter 13 explores the rules for large objects, provides many examples, and explains the built-in functions and the DBMS_LOB package provided to manipulate large objects in PL/SQL.

## Numbers

PL/SQL supports an increasing variety of numeric datatypes. NUMBER has long been the workhorse of the numeric datatypes, and you can use it for decimal fixed- and floating-point values, and for integers. Following is an example of some typical NUMBER declarations:

```
/* File on web: numbers.sql */
DECLARE
    salary NUMBER(9,2); --fixed-point, seven to the left, two to the right
    raise_factor NUMBER; --decimal floating-point
    weeks_to_pay NUMBER(2); --integer
BEGIN
    salary := 1234567.89;
    raise_factor := 0.05;
    weeks_to_pay := 52;
END;
```

Because of its internal decimal nature, NUMBER is particularly useful when working with monetary amounts. You won't incur any rounding error as a result of binary representation. For example, when you store 0.95, you won't come back later to find only 0.949999968.

Prior to Oracle Database 10g, NUMBER was the only one of PL/SQL's numeric datatypes to correspond directly to a database datatype. You can see this subtyping by examining the package STANDARD. This exclusiveness is one reason you'll find NUMBER so widely used in PL/SQL programs.

Oracle Database 10g introduced two, binary floating-point types: BINARY_FLOAT and BINARY_DOUBLE. Like NUMBER, these binary datatypes are supported in both PL/SQL and the database. Unlike NUMBER, these binary datatypes are not decimal in nature—they have binary precision—so you can expect rounding. The BINARY_FLOAT and BINARY_DOUBLE types support the special values NaN (Not a Number) as well as positive and negative infinity. Given the right type of application, their use can lead to tremendous performance gains, as arithmetic involving these binary types is performed in hardware whenever the underlying platform allows.

Oracle Database 11g added two more variations on these floating-point types. SIMPLE_FLOAT and SIMPLE_DOUBLE are like BINARY_FLOAT and BINARY_DOUBLE, but they do not allow NULL values, nor do they raise an exception when an overflow occurs.

PL/SQL supports several numeric types and subtypes that do not correspond to database datatypes, but are nevertheless quite useful. Notable here are PLS_INTEGER and SIMPLE_INTEGER. PLS_INTEGER is an integer type with its arithmetic implemented in hardware. FOR loop counters are implemented as PLS_INTEGERs. SIMPLE_INTEGER, introduced in Oracle Database 11g, has the same range of values as PLS_INTEGER, but it does not allow NULL values, nor does it raise an exception when an overflow occurs. SIMPLE_INTEGER, like SIMPLE_FLOAT and SIMPLE_DOUBLE, is extremely speedy—especially with natively compiled code. I've measured stunning performance improvements using SIMPLE_INTEGER compared to other numeric datatypes.

Chapter 9 explores the rules for numeric data, provides many examples, and explains the built-in functions provided to manipulate numbers in PL/SQL.

## Dates, Timestamps, and Intervals

Prior to Oracle9*i* Database, the Oracle world of dates was limited to the DATE datatype, which stores both a date and a time (down to the nearest second). Oracle9*i* Database introduced two sets of new, related datatypes: INTERVALs and TIMESTAMPs. These datatypes greatly expand the capability of PL/SQL developers to write programs that manipulate and store dates and times with very high granularity, and also compute and store intervals of time.

Here is an example of a function that computes the age of a person as an interval with month granularity:

```
/* File on web: age.fnc */
FUNCTION age (dob_in IN DATE)
   RETURN INTERVAL YEAR TO MONTH
IS
BEGIN
   RETURN (SYSDATE - dob_in) YEAR TO MONTH;
END;
```

Chapter 10 explores the rules for date-related data, provides many examples, and explains the built-in functions provided to manipulate dates, timestamps, and intervals in PL/SQL.

## Booleans

PL/SQL supports a three-value Boolean datatype. A variable of this type can have one of only three values: TRUE, FALSE, and NULL.

Booleans help us write very readable code, especially involving complex logical expressions. Here's an example of a Boolean declaration, along with an assignment of a default value to that variable:

```
DECLARE
   l_eligible_for_discount BOOLEAN :=
      customer_in.balance > min_balance AND
      customer_in.pref_type = 'MOST FAVORED' AND
      customer_in.disc_eligibility;
```

Chapter 13 explores the rules for Boolean data and provides examples of usage.

## Binary Data

Oracle supports several forms of *binary data* (unstructured data that is not interpreted or processed by Oracle), including RAW, BLOB, and BFILE. The BFILE datatype stores unstructured binary data in operating-system files outside the database. RAW is a variable-length datatype like the VARCHAR2 character datatype, except that Oracle utilities do not perform character set conversion when transmitting RAW data.

The datatype LONG RAW is still supported for backward compatibility, but PL/SQL offers only limited support for LONG RAW data. In an Oracle database, a LONG RAW column can be up to 2 GB long, but PL/SQL will only be able to access the first 32,760 bytes of a LONG RAW. If, for example, you try to fetch a LONG RAW from the database into your PL/SQL variable which exceeds the 32,760 byte limit, you will encounter an *ORA-06502 PL/SQL numeric or value error* exception. To work with LONG RAWs longer than PL/SQL's limit, you need an OCI program; this is a good reason to migrate your legacy code from LONG RAWs to BLOBs, which have no such limit.

Chapter 13 explores the rules for binary data, provides many examples, and explains the built-in functions and the DBMS_LOB package provided to manipulate BFILEs and other binary data in PL/SQL.

## ROWIDs

Oracle provides two proprietary datatypes, ROWID and UROWID, used to represent the address of a row in a table. ROWID represents the unique physical address of a row in its table; UROWID represents the logical position of a row in an index-organized table (IOT). ROWID is also a SQL pseudocolumn that can be included in SQL statements.

Chapter 13 explores the rules for working with the ROWID and UROWID datatypes.

## REF CURSORs

The REF CURSOR datatype allows developers to declare cursor variables. A cursor variable can then be used with static or dynamic SQL statements to implement more flexible programs. There are two forms of REF CURSORs: the strong REF CURSOR and the weak REF CURSOR. PLSQL is a statically typed language, and the weak REF CURSOR is one of the few dynamically typed constructs supported.

Here is an example of a strong REF CURSOR declaration. I associate the cursor variable with a specific record structure (using a %ROWTYPE attribute):

```
DECLARE
    TYPE book_data_t IS REF CURSOR RETURN book%ROWTYPE;
    book_curs_var book_data_t;
```

And here are two weak REF CURSOR declarations in which I do not associate any particular structure with the resulting variable. The second declaration (line 4) showcases SYS_REFCURSOR, a predefined weak REF CURSOR type.

```
DECLARE
    TYPE book_data_t IS REF CURSOR;
    book_curs_var book_data_t;
    book_curs_var_b SYS_REFCURSOR;
```

Chapter 15 explores REF CURSORs and cursor variables in much more detail.

## Internet Datatypes

Beginning with Oracle Database 9*i*, there is native support for several Internet-related technologies and types of data, specifically XML (Extensible Markup Language) and URIs (Universal Resource Identifiers). The Oracle database provides datatypes for handling XML and URI data, as well as a class of URIs called DBUri-REFs that access data stored within the database itself. The database also includes a set of datatypes used to store and access both external and internal URIs from within the database.

The XMLType allows you to query and store XML data in the database using functions like SYS_XMLGEN and the DBMS_XMLGEN package. It also allows you to use native operators in the SQL language to search XML documents using the XPath language.

The URI-related types, including URIType and HttpURIType, are all part of an object type inheritance hierarchy and can be used to store URLs to external web pages and files, as well as to refer to data within the database.

Chapter 13 explores the rules for working with XMLType and URI types, provides some examples, and explains the built-in functions and packages provided to manipulate these datatypes.

## "Any" Datatypes

Most of the time, our programming tasks are fairly straightforward and very specific to the requirement at hand. At other times, however, we write more generic kinds of code. For those situations, the "Any" datatypes might come in very handy.

The "Any" types were introduced in Oracle9*i* Database and are very different from any other kind of datatype available in an Oracle database. They let you dynamically encapsulate and access type descriptions, data instances, and sets of data instances of any other SQL type. You can use these types (and the methods defined for them, as they are object types) to do things like determine the type of data stored in a particular nested table without having access to the actual declaration of that table type!

The "Any" datatypes include AnyType, AnyData, and AnyDataSet.

Chapter 13 explores the rules for working with the "Any" datatypes and provides some working examples of these dynamic datatypes.

## User-Defined Datatypes

You can use Oracle built-in datatypes and other user-defined datatypes to create arbitrarily complex types of your own that model closely the structure and behavior of data in your systems.

Chapter 26 explores this powerful feature in more detail and describes how to take advantage of the support for object type inheritance in Oracle9*i* Database through Oracle Database 11*g*.

# Declaring Program Data

With few exceptions, you must declare your variables and constants before you use them. These declarations are in the declaration section of your PLSQL program. (See Chapter 3 for more details on the structure of the PL/SQL block and its declaration section.)

Your declarations can include variables, constants, TYPEs (such as collection types or record types), and exceptions. This chapter focuses on the declarations of variables and constants. (See Chapter 11 for an explanation of TYPE statements for records and Chapter 12 for collection types. See Chapter 6 to learn how to declare exceptions.)

## Declaring a Variable

When you declare a variable, PL/SQL allocates memory for the variable's value and names the storage location so that the value can be retrieved and changed. The declaration also specifies the datatype of the variable; this datatype is then used to validate values assigned to the variable.

The basic syntax for a declaration is:

```
name datatype [NOT NULL] [ := | DEFAULT default_assignment];
```

where *name* is the name of the variable or constant to be declared, and *datatype* is the datatype or subtype that determines the type of data that can be assigned to the variable. You can include a NOT NULL clause, which tells the database to raise an exception if no value is assigned to this variable. The [*default_assignment*] clause tells the database to initialize the variable with a value; this is optional for all declarations except those of constants. If you declare a variable NOT NULL, you must assign a value to it in the declaration line.

The following examples illustrate declarations of variables of different datatypes:

```
DECLARE
    -- Simple declaration of numeric variable
    l_total_count NUMBER;

    -- Declaration of number that rounds to nearest hundredth (cent):
    l_dollar_amount NUMBER (10,2);

    -- A single datetime value, assigned a default value of the database server's
    -- system clock. Also, it can never be NULL
    l_right_now DATE NOT NULL  DEFAULT SYSDATE;

    -- Using the assignment operator for the default value specification
```

```
   l_favorite_flavor VARCHAR2(100) := 'Anything with chocolate, actually';

   -- Two-step declaration process for associative array.
   -- First, the type of table:
   TYPE list_of_books_t IS TABLE OF book%ROWTYPE INDEX BY BINARY_INTEGER;

   -- And now the specific list to be manipulated in this block:
   oreilly_oracle_books list_of_books_t;
```

The DEFAULT syntax (see l_right_now in the previous example) and the assignment operator syntax (see l_favorite_flavor in the previous example) are both equivalent and can be used interchangeably. So which should you use? I like to use the assignment operator (:=) to set default values for constants, and the DEFAULT syntax for variables. In the case of a constant, the assigned value is not really a default but an initial (and unchanging) value, so the DEFAULT syntax feels misleading to me.

## Declaring Constants

There are just two differences between declaring a variable and declaring a constant: for a constant, you include the CONSTANT keyword, and you must supply a default value (which isn't really a *default* at all, but rather is the *only* value). So the syntax for the declaration of a constant is:

```
name CONSTANT datatype [NOT NULL] := | DEFAULT default_value;
```

The value of a constant is set upon declaration and may not change thereafter.

Here are some examples of declarations of constants:

```
DECLARE
   -- The current year number; it's not going to change during my session.
   l_curr_year CONSTANT PLS_INTEGER :=
      TO_NUMBER (TO_CHAR (SYSDATE, 'YYYY'));

   -- Using the DEFAULT keyword
   l_author CONSTANT VARCHAR2(100) DEFAULT 'Bill Pribyl';

   -- Declare a complex datatype as a constant
   -- this isn't just for scalars!
   l_steven CONSTANT  person_ot :=
      person_ot ('HUMAN', 'Steven Feuerstein', 175,
               TO_DATE ('09-23-1958', 'MM-DD-YYYY') );
```

Unless otherwise stated, the information provided in the rest of this chapter for variables also applies to constants.

An unnamed constant is a literal value, such as 2 or 'Bobby McGee'. A literal does not have a name, although it does have an implied (undeclared) datatype.

---

## The NOT NULL Clause

If you do assign a default value, you can also specify that the variable must be NOT NULL. For example, the following declaration initializes the company_name variable to PCS R US and makes sure that the name can never be set to NULL:

```
company_name VARCHAR2(60) NOT NULL DEFAULT 'PCS R US';
```

If your code executes a line like this:

```
company_name := NULL;
```

then PL/SQL will raise the VALUE_ERROR exception. In addition, you will receive a compilation error with this next declaration, because the declaration does not include an initial or default value:

```
company_name VARCHAR2(60) NOT NULL; -- must assign a value if declared NOT NULL!
```

## Anchored Declarations

You can and often will declare variables using "hardcoded" or explicit datatypes, as follows:

```
l_company_name VARCHAR2(100);
```

A better practice for data destined for or obtained from a database table or other PLSQL program structure is to *anchor* your variable declaration to that object. When you "anchor" a datatype, you tell PL/SQL to set the datatype of your variable to the datatype of an already defined data structure: another PL/SQL variable, a predefined TYPE or SUBTYPE, a database table, or a specific column in a table.

PL/SQL offers two kinds of anchoring:

*Scalar anchoring*
> Use the %TYPE attribute to define your variable based on a table's column or some other PL/SQL scalar variable.

*Record anchoring*
> Use the %ROWTYPE attribute to define your record structure based on a table or a predefined PL/SQL explicit cursor.

The syntax for an anchored datatype is:

```
variable_name type_attribute%TYPE [optional default value assignment];
variable_name table_name | cursor_name%ROWTYPE [optional default value assignment];
```

where *variable name* is the name of the variable you are declaring, and *type attribute* is either a previously declared PL/SQL variable name or a table column specification in the format *table.column*.

This anchoring reference is resolved at the time the code is compiled; there is no runtime overhead to anchoring. The anchor also establishes a dependency between the code and the anchored element (the table, cursor, or package containing the variable referenced). This means that if those elements are changed, the code in which the anchoring takes place is marked INVALID. When it is recompiled, the anchor will again be resolved, thereby keeping the code current with the anchored element.

Figure 7-1 shows how the datatype is drawn from both a database table and a PL/SQL variable.

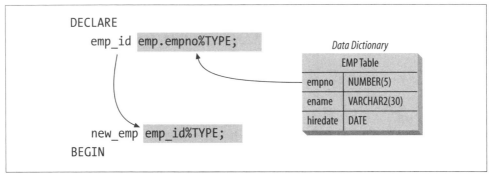

*Figure 7-1. Anchored declarations with %TYPE*

Here is an example of anchoring a variable to a database column:

```
l_company_id company.company_id%TYPE;
```

You can also anchor against PL/SQL variables; this is usually done to avoid redundant declarations of the same hardcoded datatype. In this case, the best practice is to create a "reference" variable in a package and then reference that package variable in %TYPE statements. (You could also create SUBTYPEs in your package; this topic is covered later in the chapter.) The following example shows just a portion of a package intended to make it easier to work with Oracle Advanced Queuing (AQ):

```
/* File on web: aq.pkg */
PACKAGE aq
IS

/* Standard datatypes for use with Oracle AQ. */
   v_msgid              RAW (16);
   SUBTYPE msgid_type IS v_msgid%TYPE;
   v_name               VARCHAR2 (49);
   SUBTYPE name_type IS v_name%TYPE;
   ...
END aq;
```

AQ message IDs are of type RAW(16). Rather than have to remember that (and hardcode it into my application again and again), I can simply declare an AQ message ID as follows:

```
DECLARE
   my_msg_id aq.msgid_type;
BEGIN
```

Then, if the database ever changes its datatype for a message ID, I can change the SUBTYPE definition in the AQ package, and all declarations will be updated with the next recompilation.

Anchored declarations provide an excellent illustration of the fact that PL/SQL is not just a procedural-style programming language, but was designed specifically as an extension to the Oracle SQL language. A very thorough effort was made by Oracle Corporation to tightly integrate the programming constructs of PL/SQL to the underlying SQL database.

Anchored declarations offer some important benefits when it comes to writing applications that adapt easily to change over time.

## Anchoring to Cursors and Tables

You've seen an example of anchoring to a database column and to another PL/SQL variable. Now let's take a look at the use of the %ROWTYPE anchoring attribute.

Suppose that I want to query a single row of information from the book table. Rather than declare individual variables for each column in the table (which, of course, I should do with %TYPE), I can simply rely on %ROWTYPE:

```
DECLARE
    l_book book%ROWTYPE;
BEGIN
    SELECT * INTO l_book
      FROM book
     WHERE isbn = '1-56592-335-9';
    process_book (l_book);
END;
```

Suppose, now, that I only want to retrieve the author and title from the book table. In this case, I build an explicit cursor and then %ROWTYPE against that cursor:

```
DECLARE
    CURSOR book_cur IS
        SELECT author, title FROM book
        WHERE  isbn = '1-56592-335-9';
    l_book book_cur%ROWTYPE;
BEGIN
    OPEN book_cur;
    FETCH book_cur INTO l_book;  END;
```

Finally, here is an example of an *implicit* use of the %ROWTYPE declaration: the cursor FOR loop.

```
BEGIN
    FOR book_rec IN (SELECT * FROM book)
    LOOP
        process_book (book_rec);
    END LOOP;
END;
```

Now let's explore some of the benefits of anchored declarations.

## Benefits of Anchored Declarations

Most of the declarations you have seen so far—character, numeric, date, Boolean—specify explicitly the type of data for the variable being declared. In each of these cases, the declaration contains a direct reference to a datatype and, in most cases, a constraint on that datatype. You can think of this as a kind of hardcoding in your program. While this approach to declarations is certainly valid, it can cause problems in the following situations:

*Synchronization with database columns*
> The PL/SQL variable "represents" database information in the program. If I declare explicitly and then change the structure of the underlying table, my program may not work properly.

*Normalization of local variables*
> The PL/SQL variable stores calculated values used throughout the application. What are the consequences of repeating (hardcoding) the same datatype and constraint for each declaration in all of our programs?

Let's take a look at each of these scenarios in detail.

### Synchronization with database columns

Databases hold information that needs to be stored and manipulated. Both SQL and PL/SQL perform these manipulations. Your PL/SQL programs often read data from a database into local program variables, and then write information from those variables back into the database.

Suppose that I have a company table with a column called NAME and a datatype of VARCHAR2(60). I can therefore create a local variable to hold this data as follows:

```
DECLARE
    cname VARCHAR2(60);
```

and then use this variable to represent this database information in my program. Now consider an application that uses the company entity. There may be a dozen different screens, procedures, and reports that contain this same PL/SQL declaration, VARCHAR2(60), over and over again. And everything works just fine...until the business requirements change, or the DBA has a change of heart. With a very small effort, the definition of the name column in the company table changes to VARCHAR2(100) in order to accommodate longer company names. Suddenly the database can store names that will raise VALUE_ERROR exceptions when FETCHed into the cname variable.

My programs have now become incompatible with the underlying data structures. All declarations of cname (and all the variations programmers employed for this data throughout the system) must be modified and retested—otherwise, my application is simply a ticking time bomb, just waiting to fail. My variable, which is a local representation of database information, is no longer synchronized with that database column.

### Normalization of local variables

Another drawback to explicit declarations arises when working with PL/SQL variables that store and manipulate calculated values not found in the database. Suppose that I hire some programmers to build an application to manage my company's finances. I am very bottom line-oriented, so many different programs make use of a total_revenue variable, declared as follows:

```
total_revenue NUMBER (10,2);
```

Yes, I like to track my total revenue down to the last penny. In 2002, when specifications for the application were first written, the maximum total revenue I ever thought I could possibly obtain was $99 million, so I used the NUMBER(10,2) declaration. Then, in 2005, business grew beyond my expectations and $99 million was not enough and we increased the maximum to NUMBER(14,2). But then we had a big job of finding and changing all the places where the variables where too small. I searched out any and all instances of the revenue variables so that I could change the declarations. This was a time-consuming and error-prone job—I initially missed a couple of the declarations, and the full regression test had to find them for me. I had spread equivalent declarations throughout the entire application. I had, in effect, denormalized my local data structures, with the usual consequences on maintenance. If only I had a way to define each of the local total_revenue variables in relation to a single datatype.

If only I had used %TYPE!

## Anchoring to NOT NULL Datatypes

When you declare a variable, you can also specify the need for the variable to be NOT NULL. This NOT NULL declaration constraint is transferred to variables declared with the %TYPE attribute. If I include a NOT NULL in my declaration of a source variable (one that is referenced afterwards in a %TYPE declaration), I must also make sure to specify a default value for the variables that use that source variable. Suppose that I declare max_available_date NOT NULL in the following example:

```
DECLARE
   max_available_date DATE NOT NULL :=
   ADD_MONTHS (SYSDATE, 3);
   last_ship_date max_available_date%TYPE;
```

The declaration of last_ship_date then fails to compile, with the following message:

```
PLS_00218: a variable declared NOT NULL must have an initialization assignment.
```

If you use a NOT NULL variable in a %TYPE declaration, the new variable must have a default value provided. The same is not true, however, for variables declared with

%TYPE where the source is a database column defined as NOT NULL. A NOT NULL constraint from a database table is *not* automatically transferred to a variable.

## Programmer-Defined Subtypes

With the SUBTYPE statement, PL/SQL allows you to define your own subtypes or aliases of predefined datatypes, sometimes referred to as *abstract datatypes*. In PL/SQL, a subtype of a datatype is a variation that specifies the same set of rules as the original datatype, but that might allow only a subset of the datatype's values.

There are two kinds of subtypes, constrained and unconstrained:

*Constrained subtype*
> A subtype that restricts or constrains the values normally allowed by the datatype itself. POSITIVE is an example of a constrained subtype of BINARY_ INTEGER. The package STANDARD, which predefines the datatypes and the functions that are part of the standard PL/SQL language, declares the subtype POSITIVE as follows:
>
> ```
> SUBTYPE POSITIVE IS BINARY_INTEGER RANGE 1 .. 2147483647;
> ```
>
> A variable that is declared POSITIVE can store only integer values greater than zero.

*Unconstrained subtype*
> A subtype that does not restrict the values of the original datatype in variables declared with the subtype. FLOAT is an example of an unconstrained subtype of NUMBER. Its definition in the STANDARD package is:
>
> ```
> SUBTYPE FLOAT IS NUMBER;
> ```
>
> In other words, an unconstrained subtype provides an alias or alternate name for the original datatype.
>
> ```
> PACKAGE utility
> AS
>    SUBTYPE big_string IS VARCHAR2(32767);
>    SUBTYPE big_db_string IS VARCHAR2(4000);
> END utility;
> ```

To make a subtype available, you first have to declare it in the declaration section of an anonymous PL/SQL block, procedure, function, or package. You've already seen the syntax for declaring a subtype used by PL/SQL in the STANDARD package. The general format of a subtype declaration is:

```
SUBTYPE subtype_name IS base_type;
```

where *subtype_name* is the name of the new subtype, and *base_type* is the datatype on which the subtype is based.

Be aware that an anchored subtype does not carry over the NOT NULL constraint to the variables it defines. Nor does it transfer a default value that was included in the original declaration of a variable or column specification.

# Conversion Between Datatypes

There are many different situations in which you need to convert data from one datatype to another. You can perform this conversion in two ways:

*Implicitly*
> By allowing the PL/SQL runtime engine to take its "best guess" at performing the conversion.

*Explicitly*
> By calling a PL/SQL function or operator to do the conversion.

In this section I will first review how and when PL/SQL performs implicit conversions, and then focus attention on the functions and operators available for explicit conversions.

## Implicit Data Conversion

Whenever PL/SQL detects that a conversion is necessary, it attempts to change the values as required to perform the operation. You would probably be surprised to learn how often PL/SQL performs conversions on your behalf. Figure 7-2 shows what kinds of implicit conversions PL/SQL can perform.

With implicit conversions you can specify a literal value in place of data with the correct internal format, and PL/SQL will convert that literal as necessary. In the following example, PL/SQL converts the literal string '125' to the numeric value 125 in the process of assigning a value to the numeric variable:

```
DECLARE
    a_number NUMBER;
BEGIN
    a_number := '125';
END;
```

You can also pass parameters of one datatype into a module and then have PL/SQL convert that data into another format for use inside the program. In the following procedure, the second parameter is a date. When I call that procedure, I pass a string value in the form DD-MON-YY, and PL/SQL converts that string automatically to a date:

```
PROCEDURE change_hiredate
    (emp_id_in IN INTEGER, hiredate_in IN DATE)

change_hiredate (1004, '12-DEC-94');
```

The implicit conversion from string to date datatype follows the NLS_DATE_FORMAT specification. The danger here is that if the NLS_DATE_FORMAT changes, your program breaks.

## Limitations of implicit conversion

As shown in Figure 7-2, conversions are limited; PL/SQL cannot convert any arbitrary datatype to any other datatype. Furthermore, some implicit conversions raise exceptions. Consider the following assignment:

```
DECLARE
   a_number NUMBER;
BEGIN
   a_number := 'abc';
END;
```

| From \ To | CHAR | VARCHAR2 | NCHAR | NVARCHAR2 | DATE | DATETIME/INTERVAL | NUMBER | BINARY_FLOAT | BINARY_DOUBLE | BINARY_INTEGER | PLS_INTEGER | SIMPLE_INTEGER | LONG | RAW | ROWID | CLOB | BLOB | NCLOB |
|---|---|---|---|---|---|---|---|---|---|---|---|---|---|---|---|---|---|---|
| CHAR | | ● | ● | ● | ● | ● | ● | ● | ● | ● | ● | ● | ● | ● | | ● | ● | ● |
| VARCHAR2 | ● | | ● | ● | ● | ● | ● | ● | ● | ● | ● | ● | ● | ● | ● | ● | | ● |
| NCHAR | ● | ● | | ● | ● | ● | ● | ● | ● | ● | ● | ● | ● | ● | ● | ● | | ● |
| NVARCHAR2 | ● | ● | ● | | ● | ● | ● | ● | ● | ● | ● | ● | ● | ● | ● | ● | | ● |
| DATE | ● | ● | ● | ● | | | | | | | | | | | | | | |
| DATETIME/INTERVAL | ● | ● | ● | ● | | | | | | | | | ● | | | | | |
| NUMBER | ● | ● | ● | ● | | | | ● | ● | ● | ● | ● | | | | | | |
| BINARY_FLOAT | ● | ● | ● | ● | | | ● | | ● | ● | ● | | | | | | | |
| BINARY_DOUBLE | ● | ● | ● | ● | | | ● | ● | | ● | ● | | ● | | | | | |
| BINARY_INTEGER | ● | ● | ● | ● | | | ● | ● | ● | | ● | ● | ● | | | | | |
| PLS_INTEGER | ● | ● | ● | ● | | | ● | ● | ● | ● | | ● | ● | | | | | |
| SIMPLE_INTEGER | ● | ● | ● | ● | | | ● | ● | ● | ● | ● | | | | | | | |
| LONG | ● | ● | ● | ● | ● | | | | | ● | ● | ● | | ● | | ● | | ● |
| RAW | ● | ● | ● | ● | | | | | | | | | ● | | | | ● | |
| ROWID | | ● | ● | ● | | | | | | | | | | | | | | |
| CLOB | ● | ● | ● | ● | | | | | | | | | ● | | | | | ● |
| BLOB | | | | | | | | | | | | | | ● | | | | |
| NCLOB | ● | ● | ● | ● | | | | | | | | | ● | | | ● | | |

Figure 7-2. Implicit conversions performed by PL/SQL

PL/SQL cannot convert 'abc' to a number and so will raise the VALUE_ERROR exception when it executes this code. It is up to you to make sure that if PL/SQL is going to perform implicit conversions, it is given values it can convert without error.

## Drawbacks of implicit conversion

There are several drawbacks to implicit conversion:

- PL/SQL is generally a static typing language. When your program performs an implicit conversion, you lose some of the benefits of the static typing, such as clarity and safety of your code.

- Each implicit conversion PL/SQL performs represents a loss, however small, in the control you have over your program. You do not expressly perform or direct the performance of the conversion; you simply make an assumption that it will take place and that it will have the intended effect. There is always a danger in making this assumption. If Oracle changes the way and circumstances under which it performs conversions or if the data itself no longer conforms to your (or the database's) expectations, your code is then affected.

- The implicit conversion that PL/SQL performs depends on the context in which the code occurs. The conversion that PL/SQL performs is not necessarily the one you might expect.

- Your code is easier to read and understand if you explicitly convert between datatypes where needed. Such conversions provide documentation of variances in datatypes between tables or between code and tables. By removing an assumption and a hidden action from your code, you remove a potential misunderstanding as well.

I strongly recommend that you avoid allowing either the SQL or PL/SQL languages to perform implicit conversions on your behalf, especially with datetime conversions. Instead, use conversion functions to guarantee that the right kinds of conversions take place.

## Explicit Datatype Conversion

Oracle provides a comprehensive set of conversion functions and operators to be used in SQL and PL/SQL; a complete list is shown in Table 7-1. Most of these functions are described in other chapters (for those, the table indicates the chapter number). For functions not described elsewhere, brief descriptions are provided later in this chapter.

*Table 7-1. The built-in conversion functions*

| Name | Description | Chapter |
|------|-------------|---------|
| ASCIISTR | Converts a string in any character set to an ASCII string in the database character set. | 8, 25 |
| CAST | Converts one built-in datatype or collection-typed value to another built-in datatype or collection-typed value; this very powerful conversion mechanism can be used as a substitute for traditional functions like TO_DATE. | 7, 9, 10 |
| CHARTOROWID | Converts a string to a ROWID. | 7 |
| CONVERT | Converts a string from one character set to another. | 7 |
| FROM_TZ | Adds time zone information to a TIMESTAMP value, thus converting it to a TIMESTAMP WITH TIME ZONE value. | 10 |
| HEXTORAW | Converts from hexadecimal to raw format. | 7 |

| Name | Description | Chapter |
|------|-------------|---------|
| MULTISET | Maps a database table to a collection. | 12 |
| NUMTODSINTERVAL | Converts a number (or numeric expression) to an INTERVAL DAY TO SECOND literal. | 10 |
| NUMTOYMINTERVAL | Converts a number (or numeric expression) to an INTERVAL YEAR TO MONTH literal. | 10 |
| RAWTOHEX, RAWTONHEX | Converts from a raw value to hexadecimal. | 7 |
| REFTOHEX | Converts a REF value into a character string containing the hexadecimal representation of the REF value. | 26 |
| ROWIDTOCHAR, ROWIDTONCHAR | Converts a binary ROWID value to a character string. | 7 |
| TABLE | Maps a collection to a database table; this is the inverse of MULTISET. | 12 |
| THE | Maps a single column value in a single row into a virtual database table. | 12 |
| TO_BINARY_FLOAT | Converts a number or a string to a BINARY_FLOAT. | 9 |
| TO_BINARY_DOUBLE | Converts a number or a string to a BINARY_DOUBLE. | 9 |
| TO_CHAR, TO_NCHAR (number version) | Converts a number to a string (VARCHAR2 or NVARCHAR2, respectively). | 9 |
| TO_CHAR, TO_NCHAR (date version) | Converts a date to a string. | 10 |
| TO_CHAR, TO_NCHAR (character version) | Converts character data between the database character set and the national character set. | 8 |
| TO_BLOB | Converts from a RAW value to a BLOB. | 13 |
| TO_CLOB, TO_NCLOB | Converts from a VARCHAR2, NVARCHAR2, or NCLOB value to a CLOB (or NCLOB). | 13 |
| TO_DATE | Converts a string to a date. | 10 |
| TO_DSINTERVAL | Converts a character string of a CHAR, VARCHAR2, NCHAR, or NVARCHAR2 datatype to an INTERVAL DAY TO SECOND type. | 10 |
| TO_LOB | Converts from a LONG to a LOB. | 13 |
| TO_MULTI_BYTE | Where possible, converts single-byte characters in the input string to their multibyte equivalents. | 8 |
| TO_NUMBER | Converts a string or a number (such as a BINARY_FLOAT) to a NUMBER. | 9 |
| TO_RAW | Converts from a BLOB to a RAW. | 13 |
| TO_SINGLE_BYTE | Converts multibyte characters in the input string to their corresponding single-byte characters. | 8 |
| TO_TIMESTAMP | Converts a character string to a value of type TIMESTAMP. | 10 |
| TO_TIMESTAMP_TZ | Converts a character string to a value of type TO_TIMESTAMP_TZ. | 10 |
| TO_YMINTERVAL | Converts a character string of a CHAR, VARCHAR2, NCHAR, or NVARCHAR2 datatype to an INTERVAL YEAR TO MONTH type. | 10 |
| TRANSLATE ... USING | Converts supplied text to the character set specified for conversions between the database character set and the national character set. | 8 |
| UNISTR | Takes as its argument a string in any character set and returns it in Unicode in the database Unicode character set. | 8, 25 |

## The CHARTOROWID function

The CHARTOROWID function converts a string of either type CHAR or type VARCHAR2 to a value of type ROWID. The specification of the CHARTOROWID function is:

```
FUNCTION CHARTOROWID (string_in IN CHAR) RETURN ROWID
FUNCTION CHARTOROWID (string_in IN VARCHAR2) RETURN ROWID
```

In order for CHARTOROWID to successfully convert the string, it must be an 18-character string of the format:

*OOOOOFFFBBBBBBRRR*

where *OOOOOO* is the data object number, *FFF* is the relative file number of the database file, *BBBBBB* is the block number in the file, and *RRR* is the row number within the block. All four numbers must be in base 64 format. If the input string does not conform to the above format, PL/SQL raises the VALUE_ERROR exception.

## The CAST function

The CAST function is a very handy and flexible conversion mechanism. It converts from one (and almost any) built-in datatype or collection-typed value to another built-in datatype or collection-typed value. CAST will be a familiar operator to anyone working with object-oriented languages in which it is often necessary to "cast" an object of one class into that of another.

With Oracle's CAST function, you can convert an unnamed expression (a number, a date, NULL, or even the result set of a subquery) or a named collection (a nested table, for instance) to a datatype or named collection of a compatible type.

Figure 7-3 shows the supported conversion between built-in datatypes. Note the following:

- You cannot cast LONG, LONG RAW, any of the LOB datatypes, or the Oracle-supplied types.
- "DATE" in the figure includes DATE, TIMESTAMP, TIMESTAMP WITH TIME-ZONE, INTERVAL DAY TO SECOND, and INTERVAL YEAR TO MONTH.
- To cast a named collection type into another named collection type, the elements of both collections must be of the same type.
- You cannot cast a UROWID to a ROWID if the UROWID contains the value of a ROWID of an index-organized table.

First let's take a look at using CAST as a replacement for scalar datatype conversion. You can use it in a SQL statement:

```
SELECT employee_id, cast (hire_date AS  VARCHAR2 (30))
  FROM employee;
```

and you can use it in native PL/SQL syntax:

```
DECLARE
   hd_display VARCHAR2 (30);
BEGIN
   hd_display := CAST (SYSDATE AS  VARCHAR2);
END;
```

| From \ To | BINARY_FLOAT, BINARY_DOUBLE | CHAR, VARCHAR2 | NUMBER | DATE, TIMESTAMP, INTERVAL | RAW | ROWID, UROWID | NCHAR, NVARCHAR2 |
|---|---|---|---|---|---|---|---|
| BINARY_FLOAT, BINARY_DOUBLE | ● | ● | ● | | | | ● |
| CHAR, VARCHAR2 | ● | ● | ● | ● | ● | ● | |
| NUMBER | ● | ● | ● | | | | ● |
| DATE, TIMESTAMP, INTERVAL | | ● | | ● | | | ● |
| RAW | | ● | | | ● | | ● |
| ROWID, UROWID | | ● | | | | | |
| NCHAR, NVARCHAR2 | ● | | ● | | | | ● |

*Figure 7-3. Casting built-in datatypes*

A much more interesting application of CAST comes into play when you are working with PL/SQL collections (nested tables and VARRAYs). For these datatypes, you use CAST to convert from one type of collection to another. You can also use CAST to manipulate (from within a SQL statement) a collection that has been defined as a PL/SQL variable.

Chapter 12 covers these topics in more detail, but the following example should give you a sense of the syntax and possibilities. First I create two nested table types and a relational table:

```
CREATE TYPE names_t AS TABLE OF VARCHAR2 (100);

CREATE TYPE authors_t AS TABLE OF VARCHAR2 (100);

CREATE TABLE favorite_authors (name VARCHAR2(200))
```

I would then like to write a program that blends together data from the favorite_ authors table with the contents of a nested table declared and populated in my program. Consider the following block:

```
/* File on web: cast.sql */
1   DECLARE
2       scifi_favorites   authors_t
```

```
 3            := authors_t ('Sheri S. Tepper', 'Orson Scott Card', 'Gene Wolfe');
 4    BEGIN
 5       DBMS_OUTPUT.put_line ('I recommend that you read books by:');
 6
 7       FOR rec IN  (SELECT column_value favs
 8                      FROM TABLE (CAST (scifi_favorites AS  names_t))
 9                    UNION
10                      SELECT NAME
11                        FROM favorite_authors)
12       LOOP
13          DBMS_OUTPUT.put_line (rec.favs);
14       END LOOP;
15    END;
```

On lines 2 and 3, I declare a local nested table and populate it with a few of my favorite science fiction/fantasy authors. In lines 7 through 11, I use the UNION operator to merge together the rows from favorite_authors with those of scifi_favorites. To do this, I *cast* the PL/SQL nested table (local and not visible to the SQL engine) as a type of nested table known in the database. Notice that I am able to cast a collection of type authors_t to a collection of type names_t; this is possible because they are of compatible types. Once the cast step is completed, I call the TABLE operator to ask the SQL engine to treat the nested table as a relational table. Here is the output I see on my screen:

```
I recommend that you read books by:
Gene Wolfe
Orson Scott Card
Robert Harris
Sheri S. Tepper
Tom Segev
Toni Morrison
```

### The CONVERT function

The CONVERT function converts strings from one character set to another character set. The specification of the CONVERT function is:

```
FUNCTION CONVERT
   (string_in IN VARCHAR2,
    new_char_set VARCHAR2
    [, old_char_set VARCHAR2])
RETURN VARCHAR2
```

The third argument, *old_char_set,* is optional. If this argument is not specified, then the default character set for the database instance is used.

The CONVERT function does *not* translate words or phrases from one language to another. CONVERT simply substitutes the letter or symbol in one character set with the corresponding letter or symbol in another character set. (Note that a character set is not the same thing as a human language.)

Two commonly used character sets are WE8MSWIN1252 (Microsoft Windows 8-bit Code Page 1252 character set) and AL16UTF16 (16-bit Unicode character set).

### The HEXTORAW function

The HEXTORAW function converts a hexadecimal string from type CHAR or VARCHAR2 to type RAW. The specification of the HEXTORAW function is:

```
FUNCTION HEXTORAW (string_in IN CHAR) RETURN RAW
FUNCTION HEXTORAW (string_in IN VARCHAR2) RETURN RAW
```

### The RAWTOHEX function

The RAWTOHEX function converts a value from type RAW to a hexadecimal string of type VARCHAR2. The specification of the RAWTOHEX function is:

```
FUNCTION RAWTOHEX (binary_value_in IN RAW) RETURN VARCHAR2
```

RAWTOHEX always returns a variable-length string value, even if its mirror conversion function is overloaded to support both types of input.

### The ROWIDTOCHAR function

The ROWIDTOCHAR function converts a binary value of type ROWID to a string of type VARCHAR2. The specification of the ROWIDTOCHAR function is:

```
FUNCTION ROWIDTOCHAR (row_in IN ROWID ) RETURN VARCHAR2
```

The string returned by this function has the format:

*OOOOOFFFBBBBBBRRR*

where *OOOOOO* is the data object number, *FFF* is the relative file number of the database file, *BBBBBB* is the block number in the file, and *RRR* is the row number within the block. All four numbers are in base 64 format. For example:

AAARYiAAEAAAEG8AAB

# Strings

Variables with character datatypes store text and are manipulated by character functions. Working with character data can range in difficulty from easy to quite challenging. In this chapter, I discuss PL/SQL's core string functionality largely in the context of single-byte character sets—for example, those that are commonly used in Western Europe and the United States. If you are working with Unicode or with multibyte character sets, or are dealing with multiple languages, be sure to read about globalization and localization issues in Chapter 25.

 CLOB (character large object) and LONG, while arguably character types, cannot be used in the same manner as the character types discussed in this chapter, and are more usefully thought of as *large object types*. I discuss large object types in Chapter 13.

## String Datatypes

Oracle supports four string datatypes, summarized in the following table. Which type you should use depends on your answers to the following two questions:

- Are you working with variable-length or fixed-length strings?
- Do you want to use the database character set or the national character set?

|  | Fixed-length | Variable-length |
|---|---|---|
| Database character set | CHAR | VARCHAR2 |
| National character set | NCHAR | NVARCHAR2 |

You will rarely need or want to use the fixed-length CHAR and NCHAR datatypes in Oracle-based applications; in fact, I recommend that you never use these types unless there is a specific requirement for fixed-length strings. See "Mixing CHAR and VARCHAR2 Values" on page 219 for a description of problems you may encounter when mixing fixed- and variable-length string variables. (The NCHAR and NVARCHAR2 datatypes are discussed in Chapter 25.)

## The VARCHAR2 Datatype

VARCHAR2 variables store variable-length character strings. When you declare a variable-length string, you must also specify a maximum length for the string, which can range from 1 to 32,767 bytes. You may specify the maximum length in terms of characters or bytes, but either way the length is ultimately defined in bytes. The general format for a VARCHAR2 declaration is:

```
variable_name VARCHAR2 (max_length [CHAR | BYTE]);
```

where:

*variable_name*
    Is the name of the variable you want to declare.

*max_length*
    Is the maximum length of the variable.

*CHAR*
    Indicates that *max_length* is expressed in terms of characters.

*BYTE*
    Indicates that *max_length* represents a number of bytes.

When you specify the maximum length of a VARCHAR2 string in terms of characters (using the CHAR qualifier), the actual length in bytes is determined using the largest number of bytes that the database character set uses to represent a character. For example, the Unicode UTF-8 character set uses up to four bytes for some characters; thus, if UTF-8 is your underlying character set, declaring a VARCHAR2 variable with a maximum length of 100 characters is equivalent to declaring the same variable with a maximum length of 400 bytes.

 You'll find the CHAR length qualifier most useful when working with multibyte character sets such as Unicode UTF-8. Read more about character semantics and character sets in Chapter 25.

If you omit the CHAR or BYTE qualifier when declaring a VARCHAR2 variable, then whether the size is in characters or bytes depends on the NLS_LENGTH_SEMANTICS initialization parameter. You can determine your current setting by querying NLS_SESSION_PARAMETERS.

Following are some examples of VARCHAR2 declarations:

```
DECLARE
    small_string VARCHAR2(4);
    line_of_text VARCHAR2(2000);
```

```
feature_name VARCHAR2(100 BYTE); -- 100 byte string
emp_name VARCHAR2(30 CHAR); -- 30 character string
```

The maximum length allowed for PL/SQL VARCHAR2 variables is 32,767 bytes, a much higher maximum than that for the VARCHAR2 datatype in the Oracle database (2,000 bytes prior to Oracle8*i* Database, and 4,000 bytes in Oracle8*i* Database and above). This size limit applies regardless of whether you declare a variable's size in terms of characters or bytes. As a result of PL/SQL's much higher size limit, if you plan to store a PL/SQL VARCHAR2 value in a VARCHAR2 database column, you must remember that only the first 2,000 or 4,000 bytes can be inserted, depending on which release of the database you are using. Neither PL/SQL nor SQL automatically resolves this inconsistency.

If you need to work with strings greater than 4,000 bytes in length, consider storing those strings in CLOB (character large object) columns. See Chapter 13 for information on CLOBs.

## The CHAR Datatype

The CHAR datatype specifies a fixed-length character string. When you declare a fixed-length string, you also specify a maximum length for the string, which can range from 1 to 32,767 bytes. (Again, this is much higher than that for the CHAR datatype in the Oracle database, which is only 2,000, or 255 prior to Oracle8*i* Database.) You can specify the length in terms of bytes or in terms of characters. For example, the following two declarations create strings of 100 bytes and 100 characters, respectively:

```
feature_name CHAR(100 BYTE);
feature_name CHAR(100 CHAR);
```

The actual number of bytes in a 100-character string depends on the underlying database character set. If you are using a variable-width character set, PL/SQL will allocate enough bytes to the string to accommodate the specified number of worst-case characters. For example, UTF-8 uses between one and four bytes per character, so PL/SQL will assume the worst and allocate 4 bytes × 100 characters, for a total of 400 bytes.

If you leave off the BYTE or CHAR qualifier, the results will depend on the setting of the NLS_LENGTH_SEMANTICS initialization parameter. When you compile your program, this setting is saved together with your program and may be reused or overwritten during later recompilation. (Compilation settings are discussed in Chapter 20.) Assuming the default setting, the following declaration results in a 100-byte string:

```
feature_name CHAR(100);
```

If you do not specify a length for the string, PL/SQL declares a string of one byte. Suppose you declare a variable as follows:

```
feature_name CHAR;
```

As soon as you assign a string of more than one character to the variable feature_name, PL/SQL will raise the generic VALUE_ERROR exception:

```
ORA-06502: PL/SQL:
    numeric or value error: character string buffer too small
```

Notice that the message does not indicate which variable was involved in the error. So if you do get this error after declaring some new variables or constants, check your declarations for a lazy use of CHAR. To avoid mistakes and to prevent future programmers from wondering about your intent, you should *always* specify a length when you use the CHAR datatype. Several examples follow:

```
yes_or_no CHAR (1) DEFAULT 'Y';
line_of_text    CHAR (80 CHAR); --Always a full 80 characters!
whole_paragraph CHAR (10000 BYTE); --Think of all the spaces...
```

Because CHAR is fixed-length, PL/SQL will right-pad any value assigned to a CHAR variable with spaces to the maximum length specified in the declaration.

## String Subtypes

PL/SQL supports several string subtypes, listed in Table 8-1, that you can use when declaring character string variables. Many of these subtypes exist for the ostensible purpose of providing compatibility with the ANSI SQL standard. It's unlikely that you'll ever need to use these—I never do—but you should be aware that they exist.

*Table 8-1. PL/SQL subtypes and their equivalents*

| Subtype | Equivalent PL/SQL type |
| --- | --- |
| CHAR VARYING | VARCHAR2 |
| CHARACTER | CHAR |
| CHARACTER VARYING | VARCHAR2 |
| NATIONAL CHAR | NCHAR |
| NATIONAL CHAR VARYING | NVARCHAR2 |
| NATIONAL CHARACTER | NCHAR |
| NATIONAL CHARACTER VARYING | NVARCHAR2 |
| NCHAR VARYING | NVARCHAR2 |
| STRING | VARCHAR2 |
| VARCHAR | VARCHAR2 |

Each subtype listed in the table is equivalent to the base PL/SQL type shown in the right column. For example, the following declarations all have the same effect:

```
feature_name VARCHAR2(100);
feature_name CHARACTER VARYING(100);
feature_name CHAR VARYING(100);
feature_name STRING(100);
```

The VARCHAR subtype deserves special mention. For years now Oracle Corporation has been threatening to change the meaning of VARCHAR (to something not equivalent to VARCHAR2) and warning against its use. I agree with Oracle's recommendation: If there is a possibility of VARCHAR's behavior being changed by Oracle (or the ANSI committee), it's senseless to depend on its current behavior. Don't use VARCHAR; use VARCHAR2.

# Working with Strings

Working with strings is largely a matter of manipulating those strings using Oracle's rich library of built-in string functions. To that end, I recommend that you become broadly familiar with the functions Oracle has to offer. In the subsections that follow, I'll begin by showing you how to write string constants, and then introduce you to the string manipulation functions that I have come to find most important in my own work.

## Specifying String Constants

One way to get strings into your PL/SQL programs is to issue a SELECT statement that returns character string values. Another way is to place string constants directly into your code. You write such constants by enclosing them within single quotes:

```
'Brighten the corner where you are.'
```

If you want to embed a single quote within a string constant, you can do so by typing the single quote twice:

```
'Aren''t you glad you''re learning PL/SQL with O''Reilly?'
```

If your program will be dealing with strings that contain embedded single quote characters, a more elegant approach is to specify your own string delimiters. Do this using the q prefix (uppercase Q may also be specified). For example:

```
q'!Aren't you glad you're learning PL/SQL with O'Reilly?!'
```

or:

```
q'{Aren't you glad you're learning PL/SQL with O'Reilly?}'
```

When you use the q prefix, you still must enclose the entire string within single quotes. The character immediately following the first quotation mark—an exclamation point (!) in the first of my two examples—then becomes the *delimiter* for the string. Thus, the first of my q-prefixed strings consists of all characters between the two exclamation points.

 Special rule: If your start delimiter character is one of [, {, <, or (, then your end delimiter character must be ], }, >, or ), respectively.

Normally, string constants are represented using the database character set. If such a string constant is assigned to an NCHAR or NVARCHAR2 variable, the constant will be implicitly converted to the national character set (see Chapter 25). The database performs such conversions when necessary, and you rarely need to worry about them. Occasionally, however, you may find yourself faced with the need to explicitly specify a string constant to be represented in the national character set. You can do so using the n prefix:

```
n'Pils vom faß: 1€'
```

If you need a string in the national character set, and you also want to specify some characters by their Unicode code point, you can use the u prefix:

```
u' Pils vom fa\00DF: 1\20AC'
```

00DF is the code point for the German letter "ß" while 20AC is the code point for the Euro symbol. The resulting string constant is the same as for the preceding n-prefixed example.

Using the assignment operator, you can store the value of a string constant within a variable:

```
DECLARE
    jonathans_motto VARCHAR2(50);
BEGIN
    jonathans_motto := 'Brighten the corner where you are.';
END;
```

You can also pass string constants to built-in functions. For example, to find out the number of characters in Jonathan's motto, you can use the LENGTH function:

```
BEGIN
    DBMS_OUTPUT.PUT_LINE(
        LENGTH('Brighten the corner where you are.')
    );
END;
```

Run this code, and you'll find that the number of characters is 34.

While this is not strictly a PL/SQL issue, you'll often find that ampersand (&) characters cause problems if you're executing PL/SQL code via SQL*Plus or SQL Developer. Both tools use ampersands to prefix substitution variables. When an ampersand is encountered, these tools "see" the next word as a variable and prompt you to supply a value:

```
SQL> BEGIN
  2    DBMS_OUTPUT.PUT_LINE ('Generating & saving test data.');
  3  END;
  4  /
Enter value for saving:
```

There are several solutions to this problem. One that works well with SQL*Plus and SQL Developer is to issue the command SET DEFINE OFF to disable the variable substitution feature. Other solutions can be found in Jonathan Gennick's book *Oracle SQL*Plus: The Definitive Guide* (O'Reilly).

## Using Nonprintable Characters

The built-in CHR function is especially valuable when you need to make reference to a nonprintable character in your code. Suppose you have to build a report that displays the address of a company. A company can have up to four address strings (in addition to city, state, and zip code). Your boss wants each address string on a new line. You can do that by concatenating all the address lines together into one, long text value, and using CHR to insert linefeeds where desired. The location in the standard ASCII collating sequence for the linefeed character is 10, so you can code:

```
SELECT name || CHR(10)
       || address1 || CHR(10)
       || address2 || CHR(10)
       || city || ', ' || state || ' ' || zipcode
       AS company_address
FROM company
```

And the results will end up looking like:

```
COMPANY_ADDRESS
--------------------
Harold Henderson
22 BUNKER COURT
SUITE 100
WYANDANCH, MN 66557
```

 Linefeed is the newline character for Linux and Unix systems. Windows uses the carriage return character together with the new line CHR(13)||CHR(10). In other environments, you may need to use some other character.

What? You say your boss doesn't want to see any blank lines? No problem. You can eliminate those with a bit of cleverness involving the NVL2 function:

```
SELECT name
       || NVL2(address1, CHR(10) || address1, '')
       || NVL2(address2, CHR(10) || address2, '')
       || CHR(10) || city || ', ' || state || ' ' || zipcode
       AS company_address
FROM company
```

Now the query returns a single formatted column per company. The NVL2 function returns the third argument when the first is NULL, and otherwise returns the second argument. In this example, when address1 is NULL, the empty string ('') is returned, and likewise for the other address columns. In this way, blank address lines are not returned so that the address will be scrunched down to:

```
COMPANY_ADDRESS
--------------------
Harold Henderson
22 BUNKER COURT
```

```
SUITE 100
WYANDANCH, MN 66557
```

The ASCII function, in essence, does the reverse of CHR: it returns the decimal representation of a given character in the database character set. For example, execute the following code to display the decimal code for the letter 'J':

```
BEGIN
    DBMS_OUTPUT.PUT_LINE(ASCII('J'));
END;
```

And you'll find that, in UTF-8 at least, the underlying representation of 'J' is the value 74.

 Watch for an interesting use of CHR later in the section "Traditional Searching, Extracting, and Replacing" on page 202.

## Concatenating Strings

There are two mechanisms for concatenating strings together: the CONCAT function and the concatenation operator—represented by two vertical bar characters ||. By far the more commonly used approach is the concatenation operator. Why, you may be asking yourself, are there two mechanisms? Well...there may be issues in translating the vertical bars in code between ASCII and EBCDIC servers, and some keyboards make typing the vertical bars a feat of finger agility. If you find it difficult to work with the vertical bars, use the CONCAT function, which takes two arguments as follows:

```
CONCAT (string1, string2)
```

CONCAT always appends *string2* to the end of *string1* and returns the result. If either string is NULL, CONCAT returns the non-NULL argument all by its lonesome. If both strings are NULL, CONCAT returns NULL. If the input strings are non-CLOB, the resulting string will be VARCHAR2. If one or more input strings is a CLOB, then the resulting datatype will be a CLOB as well. If one string is an NCLOB, the resulting datatype will be an NCLOB. In general, the return datatype will be the one that preserves the most information. Here are some examples of uses of CONCAT (where --> means that the function returns the value shown):

```
CONCAT ('abc', 'defg') --> 'abcdefg'
CONCAT (NULL, 'def') --> 'def'
CONCAT ('ab', NULL) --> 'ab'
CONCAT (NULL, NULL) --> NULL
```

Notice that you can concatenate only two stings together with the database function. With the concatenation operator, you can combine several strings. For example:

```
DECLARE
    x VARCHAR2(100);
BEGIN
```

```
      x := 'abc' || 'def' || 'ghi';
      DBMS_OUTPUT.PUT_LINE(x);
   END;
```

The output is:

```
abcdefghi
```

To perform the identical concatenation using CONCAT, you would need to nest one call to CONCAT inside another:

```
x := CONCAT(CONCAT('abc','def'),'ghi');
```

You can see that the || operator not only is much easier to use than CONCAT, but also results in much more readable code.

## Dealing with Case

Letter case is often an issue when working with strings. For example, you might want to compare two strings regardless of case. There are different approaches you can take to dealing with this problem depending partly on the database release you are running and partly on the scope that you want your actions to have.

### Forcing a string to all upper- or lowercase

One way to deal with case issues is to use the built-in UPPER and LOWER functions. These functions let you force case conversion on a string for a single operation. For example:

```
DECLARE
   name1 VARCHAR2(30) := 'Andrew Sears';
   name2 VARCHAR2(30) := 'ANDREW SEARS';
BEGIN
   IF LOWER(name1) = LOWER(name2) THEN
      DBMS_OUTPUT.PUT_LINE('The names are the same.');
   END IF;
END;
```

In this example, both strings are passed through LOWER so the comparison ends up being between 'andrew sears' and 'andrew sears'.

### Making comparisons case-insensitive

Starting with Oracle Database 10g Release 2 you can use the initialization parameters NLS_COMP and NLS_SORT to render all string comparisons case-insensitive. Set the NLS_COMP parameter to LINGUISTIC, which will tell the database to use NLS_SORT for string comparisons. Then set NLS_SORT to a case-insensitive setting, like BINARY_CI or XWEST_EUROPEAN_CI. The trailing _CI specifies **C**ase **I**nsensitivity. Here's a simple, SQL-based example that illustrates the kind of problem you can solve using NLS_COMP. The problem is to take a list of names and determine which should come first:

```
SELECT LEAST ('JONATHAN','Jonathan','jon') FROM dual
```

On my system the call to LEAST that you see here returns 'JONATHAN'. That's because the uppercase characters sort lower than the lowercase characters. By default, NLS_COMP is set to BINARY, meaning that string comparisons performed by functions such as LEAST are based on the underlying character code values.

You might like to see LEAST ignore case and return 'jon' instead of 'JONATHAN'. To that end, you can change NLS_COMP to specify that a linguistic sort (sensitive to the NLS_SORT settings) be performed:

```
ALTER SESSION SET NLS_COMP=LINGUISTIC
```

Next, you must change NLS_SORT to specify the sorting rules that you want. The default NLS_SORT value is often BINARY, but it may be otherwise depending on how your system is configured. For this example, use the sort BINARY_CI. The _CI suffix specifies a case-insensitive sort:

```
ALTER SESSION SET NLS_SORT=BINARY_CI
```

Now, try that call to LEAST one more time:

```
SELECT LEAST ('JONATHAN','Jonathan','jon') FROM dual
```

This time, the result is 'jon'. This seems like a simple exercise, but this result is not so easy to achieve without the linguistic sorting I've just described.

And it's not just functions that are affected by linguistic sorting. Simple string comparisons are affected as well. For example:

```
BEGIN
   IF 'Jonathan' = 'JONATHAN' THEN
      DBMS_OUTPUT.PUT_LINE('It is true!');
   END IF;
END;
```

With NLS_COMP and NLS_SORT set as I've described, the expression 'Jonathan' = 'JONATHAN' in this example evaluates to TRUE.

 NLS_COMP and NLS_SORT settings affect all string manipulation that you do. The settings "stick" until you change them, or until you terminate your session.

Oracle also supports accent-insensitive sorting, which you can get by appending _AI (rather than _CI) to a sort name. To find a complete list of linguistic sort names, refer to the *Oracle Database Globalization Support Guide*. That guide also explains the operation of NLS_COMP and NLS_SORT in detail. Also refer to Chapter 25 of this book, which presents more information on the various NLS parameters at your disposal.

### Case-insensitivity and indexes

When dealing with strings, you often want to do case-insensitive searching and comparisons. But when you implement this nifty technique, you find that your application stops using indexes and starts performing poorly. Take care that you don't inadvertently negate the use of indexes in your SQL. Let's look at an example using the demonstration table hr.employees to illustrate. The employees table has the index emp_name_ix on columns last_name, first_name. My code includes the following SQL:

```
SELECT * FROM employee WHERE last_name = lname
```

Initially the code is using the emp_name_ix index, but when I set NLS_COMP=LINGUISTIC and NLS_SORT=BINARY_CI to enable case-insensitivity I stop using the index and start doing full table scans instead—oops! One solution is to create a function-based, case-insensitive index, like this:

```
CREATE INDEX last_name_ci ON EMPLOYEES (NLSSORT(last_name, 'NLS_SORT=BINARY_CI'))
```

Now when I do my case-insensitive query, I use the case-insensitive index and keep my good performance.

### Capitalizing each word in a string

A third case-related function, after UPPER and LOWER, is INITCAP. This function forces the initial letter of each word in a string to uppercase, and all remaining letters to lowercase. For example:

```
DECLARE
    name VARCHAR2(30) := 'MATT williams';
BEGIN
    DBMS_OUTPUT.PUT_LINE(INITCAP(name));
END;
```

The output will be:

```
Matt Williams
```

It's wonderfully tempting to use INITCAP to properly format names, and all will be fine until you run into a case like:

```
DECLARE
    name VARCHAR2(30) := 'JOE mcwilliams';
BEGIN
    DBMS_OUTPUT.PUT_LINE(INITCAP(name));
END;
```

which generates this output:

```
Joe Mcwilliams
```

Joe McWilliams may not be so happy to see his last name written as "Mcwilliams," with a lowercase "w". INITCAP is handy at times but do remember that it doesn't yield correct results for words or names having more than just an initial capital letter.

## Traditional Searching, Extracting, and Replacing

Frequently, you'll find yourself wanting to search a string for a bit of text. Starting with Oracle Database 10g, you can use regular expressions for these textual manipulations; see the section later in this chapter on regular expressions for the full details. If you're not yet using Oracle Database 10g or later, you can use an approach that is backward-compatible to older database versions. The INSTR function returns the character position of a substring within a larger string. The following code finds the locations of all the commas in a list of names:

```
DECLARE
    names VARCHAR2(60) := 'Anna,Matt,Joe,Nathan,Andrew,Aaron,Jeff';
    comma_location NUMBER := 0;
BEGIN
    LOOP
        comma_location := INSTR(names,',',comma_location+1);
        EXIT WHEN comma_location = 0;
        DBMS_OUTPUT.PUT_LINE(comma_location);
    END LOOP;
END;
```

The output is:

```
5
10
14
21
28
34
```

The first argument to INSTR is the string to search. The second is the substring to look for, in this case a comma. The third argument specifies the character position at which to begin looking. After each comma is found, the loop begins looking again one character further down the string. When no match is found, INSTR returns zero, and the loop ends.

Having found the location of some text in a string, a natural next step is to extract it. I don't care about those commas. Let's extract the names instead. For that, I'll use the SUBSTR function:

```
DECLARE
    names VARCHAR2(60) := 'Anna,Matt,Joe,Nathan,Andrew,Aaron,Jeff';
    names_adjusted VARCHAR2(61);
    comma_location NUMBER := 0;
    prev_location NUMBER := 0;
BEGIN
    --Stick a comma after the final name
    names_adjusted := names || ',';
    LOOP
        comma_location := INSTR(names_adjusted,',',comma_location+1);
        EXIT WHEN comma_location = 0;
        DBMS_OUTPUT.PUT_LINE(
            SUBSTR(names_adjusted,
```

```
                prev_location+1,
                comma_location-prev_location-1));
        prev_location := comma_location;
    END LOOP;
END;
```

The list of names that I get is:

```
Anna
Matt
Joe
Nathan
Andrew
Aaron
Jeff
```

The keys to the preceding bit of code are twofold. First, a comma is appended to the end of the string to make the loop's logic easier to write. Every name in names_adjusted is followed by a comma. That simplifies life. Then, each time the loop iterates to DBMS_OUTPUT.PUT_LINE, the two variables named prev_location and comma_location point to the character positions on either side of the name to print. It's then just a matter of some simple math and the SUBSTR function. Three arguments are passed:

*names_adjusted*
> The string from which to extract a name.

*prev_location+1*
> The character position of the first letter in the name. Remember that prev_location will point to just before the name to display, usually to a comma preceding the name. That's why I add 1 to the value.

*comma_location-prev_location-1*
> The number of characters to extract. I subtract the extra 1 to avoid displaying the trailing comma.

All this searching and extracting is fairly tedious. Sometimes I can reduce the complexity of my code by cleverly using some of the built-in functions. Let's try the REPLACE function to swap those commas with newlines:

```
DECLARE
    names VARCHAR2(60) := 'Anna,Matt,Joe,Nathan,Andrew,Aaron,Jeff';
BEGIN
    DBMS_OUTPUT.PUT_LINE(
        REPLACE(names, ',', chr(10))
    );
END;
```

And the output is (!):

```
Anna
Matt
Joe
Nathan
```

```
Andrew
Aaron
Jeff
```

By using REPLACE I was able to avoid all that looping. I got the same results with code that is more simple and elegant. Of course, you won't always be able to avoid loop processing by using REPLACE, but it's good to know about alternative algorithms. With programming, there are always several ways to get the results you want!

---

## Negative String Positioning

Some of Oracle's built-in string functions, notably SUBSTR and INSTR, allow you to determine the position from which to begin extracting or searching by counting backwards from the right end of a string. For example, to extract the final 10 characters of a string:

```
SUBSTR('Brighten the corner where you are',-10)
```

This function call returns "re you are". The key is the use of a –10 as the starting position. By making the starting position negative, you instruct SUBSTR to count backwards from the end of the string.

INSTR adds an interesting twist to all of this. Specify a negative starting index, and INSTR will:

1. Count back from the end of the string to determine from whence to begin searching,
2. Then search backwards from that point towards the beginning of the string.

Step 1 is the same as for SUBSTR, but Step 2 proceeds in quite the opposite direction. For example, to find the occurrence of "re" that is second from the end:

```
INSTR('Brighten the corner where you are','re',-1,2)
```

To help illustrate these concepts, here are the letter positions in the string:

```
                    1111111111222222222223333
          12345678901234567890123456789012313
INSTR('Brighten the corner where you are','re',-1,2)
```

The result is 24. The fourth parameter, a 2, requests the second occurrence of "re". The third parameter is –1, so the search begins at the last character of the string (first character prior to the closing quote). The search progresses backwards towards the beginning, past the "re" at the end of "are" (the first occurrence) until reaching the occurrence of "re" at the end of "where".

There is one, subtle case in which INSTR with a negative position will search forward. Here's an example:

```
INSTR('Brighten the corner where you are','re',-2,1)
```

The –2 starting position means that the search begins with the "r" in "are". The result is 32. Beginning from the "r" in "are", INSTR looks forward to see whether it is pointing at an occurrence of "re". And it is, so INSTR returns the current position in the string,

---

which happens to be the 32nd character. Thus, the "re" in "are" is found even though it extends past the point at which INSTR began searching.

## Padding

Occasionally it's helpful to force strings to be a certain size. You can use LPAD and RPAD to add spaces (or some other character) to either end of a string in order to make the string a specific length. The following example uses the two functions to display a list of names two-up in a column, with the leftmost name being flush left and the rightmost name appearing flush right:

```
DECLARE
    a VARCHAR2(30) := 'Jeff';
    b VARCHAR2(30) := 'Eric';
    c VARCHAR2(30) := 'Andrew';
    d VARCHAR2(30) := 'Aaron';
    e VARCHAR2(30) := 'Matt';
    f VARCHAR2(30) := 'Joe';
BEGIN
    DBMS_OUTPUT.PUT_LINE(    RPAD(a,10) || LPAD(b,10)    );
    DBMS_OUTPUT.PUT_LINE(    RPAD(c,10) || LPAD(d,10)    );
    DBMS_OUTPUT.PUT_LINE(    RPAD(e,10) || LPAD(f,10)    );
END;
```

The output is:

```
Jeff            Eric
Andrew         Aaron
Matt             Joe
```

The default padding character is the space. If you like, you can specify a fill character as the third argument. Change the lines of code to read:

```
    DBMS_OUTPUT.PUT_LINE(    RPAD(a,10,'.') || LPAD(b,10,'.')    );
    DBMS_OUTPUT.PUT_LINE(    RPAD(c,10,'.') || LPAD(d,10,'.')    );
    DBMS_OUTPUT.PUT_LINE(    RPAD(e,10,'.') || LPAD(f,10,'.')    );
```

And the output changes to:

```
Jeff............Eric
Andrew.........Aaron
Matt............Joe
```

Your fill "character" can even be a string of characters:

```
    DBMS_OUTPUT.PUT_LINE(    RPAD(a,10,'-~-') || LPAD(b,10,'-~-')    );
    DBMS_OUTPUT.PUT_LINE(    RPAD(c,10,'-~-') || LPAD(d,10,'-~-')    );
    DBMS_OUTPUT.PUT_LINE(    RPAD(e,10,'-~-') || LPAD(f,10,'-~-')    );
```

And now the output looks like:

```
Jeff-~--~--~--~-Eric
Andrew-~---~--~Aaron
Matt-~--~--~--~--Joe
```

Fill characters, or strings are laid down from left to right, always, even when RPAD is used. You can see that that's the case if you study carefully the 10-character "column" containing Joe's name.

One possible problem to think about when using LPAD and RPAD is the possibility that some of your input strings may already be longer than (or equal to) the width that you desire. For example, change the column width to four characters:

```
DBMS_OUTPUT.PUT_LINE(   RPAD(a,4) || LPAD(b,4)   );
DBMS_OUTPUT.PUT_LINE(   RPAD(c,4) || LPAD(d,4)   );
DBMS_OUTPUT.PUT_LINE(   RPAD(e,4) || LPAD(f,4)   );
```

Now the output looks like:

```
JeffEric
AndrAaro
Matt Joe
```

Notice particularly the second row: both "Andrew" and "Aaron" were truncated to just four characters.

## Trimming

What LPAD and RPAD giveth, TRIM, LTRIM, and RTRIM taketh away. For example:

```
DECLARE
    a VARCHAR2(40) := 'This sentence has too many periods......';
    b VARCHAR2(40) := 'The number 1';
BEGIN
    DBMS_OUTPUT.PUT_LINE(   RTRIM(a,'.')   );
    DBMS_OUTPUT.PUT_LINE(
        LTRIM(b, 'ABCDEFGHIJKLMNOPQRSTUVWXYZ abcdefghijklmnopqrstuvwxyz')
    );
END;
```

And the output is:

```
This sentence has too many periods
1
```

As you can see, RTRIM removed all the periods. The second argument to that function was a period and specifies the character(s) to trim. My use of LTRIM is a bit absurd, but it demonstrates that you can specify an entire set of characters to trim. I asked that all letters and spaces be trimmed from the beginning of the string b, and I got what I asked for.

The default is to trim spaces from the beginning or end of the string. Specifying RTRIM(a) is the same as asking for RTRIM(a,' '). The same goes for LTRIM(a) and LTRIM(a,' ').

The other trimming function is just plain TRIM. Oracle added TRIM when Oracle8*i* Database was released in order to make the database more compliant with the ISO SQL standard. TRIM works a bit differently from LTRIM and RTRIM, as you can see:

---

```
DECLARE
   x VARCHAR2(30) := '.....Hi there!.....';
BEGIN
   DBMS_OUTPUT.PUT_LINE(   TRIM(LEADING '.' FROM x)   );
   DBMS_OUTPUT.PUT_LINE(   TRIM(TRAILING '.' FROM x)   );
   DBMS_OUTPUT.PUT_LINE(   TRIM(BOTH '.' FROM x)   );

   --The default is to trim from both sides
   DBMS_OUTPUT.PUT_LINE(   TRIM('.' FROM x)   );

   --The default trim character is the space:
   DBMS_OUTPUT.PUT_LINE(   TRIM(x)   );
END;
```

The output is:

```
Hi there!.....
.....Hi there!
Hi there!
Hi there!
.....Hi there!.....
```

One function, yet you can trim from either side, or from both sides. However, you can specify only a single character to remove. You cannot, for example, write:

```
TRIM(BOTH ',.;' FROM x)
```

Instead, to solve this particular problem, you can use a combination of RTRIM and LTRIM:

```
RTRIM(LTRIM(x,',.;'),',.;')
```

If you want to trim a set of characters, your options are RTRIM and LTRIM.

## Regular Expression Searching, Extracting, and Replacing

Oracle Database 10g introduced a very powerful change to string-manipulation: support for regular expressions. And I'm not talking the mundane, regular expression support involving the LIKE predicate that you find in other database management systems. Oracle has given us a well-thought-out and powerful feature set—just what PL/SQL needed.

Regular expressions form a sort of pattern language for describing and manipulating text. Those of you familiar with Perl doubtless know a bit about the topic already, as Perl has done more to spread the use of regular expressions than perhaps any other language. Regular expression support in Oracle Database 10g followed closely the Portable Operating System Interface (POSIX) regular expression standard. Oracle Database 10g Release 2 added support for many nonstandard, but quite useful operators from the world of Perl, and Oracle Database 11g augmented these features with yet more capabilities.

### Detecting a pattern

Regular expressions give you a pattern language you can use to describe text that you want to find and manipulate. To illustrate, let's revisit the example used throughout the earlier section on "Traditional Searching, Extracting, and Replacing" on page 202:

```
DECLARE
    names VARCHAR2(60) := 'Anna,Matt,Joe,Nathan,Andrew,Aaron,Jeff';
```

I will assign myself the task of determining programmatically whether names represents a list of comma-delimited elements. I can do that using the REGEXP_LIKE function, which detects the presence of a pattern in a string:

```
DECLARE
    names VARCHAR2(60) := 'Anna,Matt,Joe,Nathan,Andrew,Jeff,Aaron';
    names_adjusted VARCHAR2(61);
    comma_delimited BOOLEAN;
BEGIN
    --Look for the pattern
    comma_delimited := REGEXP_LIKE(names,'^([a-z A-Z]*,)+([a-z A-Z]*){1}$');

    --Display the result
    DBMS_OUTPUT.PUT_LINE(
        CASE comma_delimited
            WHEN true THEN 'We have a delimited list!'
            ELSE 'The pattern does not match.'
        END);
END;
```

The result is:

```
We have a delimited list!
```

To understand what's going on here, you must begin with the expression defining the pattern you seek. The general syntax for the REGEXP_LIKE function is:

```
REGEXP_LIKE (source_string, pattern [,match_modifier])
```

Where *source_string* is the character string to be searched; *pattern* is the regular expression pattern to search for in *source_string*; and *match_modifier* is one or more modifiers that apply to the search. If REGEXP_LIKE finds *pattern* in *source_string*, then it returns the Boolean TRUE; otherwise, it returns FALSE.

A recap of my thought process as I put the example together follows.

*[a-z A-Z]*
> Each entry in my list of names must consist of only letters and spaces. Square-brackets define a set of characters on which to match. I use a-z to gives us all lowercase letters, and I use A-Z to give all uppercase letters. The space sits in between those two parts of the expression. So any lowercase character, any uppercase character, or a space would match this pattern.

*[a-z A-Z]\**

> The asterisk is a *quantifier*, specifying that I want to see zero or more characters in each list item.

*[a-z A-Z]\*,*

> Each list item must terminate with a comma. An exception is the final item, but I can safely ignore that nuance for now.

*([a-z A-Z]\*,)*

> I use parentheses to define a subexpression that matches some number of characters terminated by a comma. I define this subexpression because I want to specify that the entire thing repeats.

*([a-z A-Z]\*,)+*

> The plus sign is another quantifier, and applies to the preceding element, which happens to be the subexpression. In contrast to the *, the + requires "one or more." A comma-delimited list consists of one or more of my subexpressions.

*([a-z A-Z]\*,)+([a-z A-Z]\*)*

> I add another subexpression: ([a-z A-Z]*). This is almost a duplicate of the first, but it doesn't include the comma. The final list item is not terminated by a comma.

*([a-z A-Z]\*,)+([a-z A-Z]\*){1}*

> I add the quantifier {1} to allow for exactly one list element with no trailing comma.

*^([a-z A-Z]\*,)+([a-z A-Z]\*){1}$*

> Finally, I use ^ and $ to anchor my expression to the beginning and end, respectively of the target string. I do this to require that the entire string, rather than some subset of the string, match my pattern.

Using REGEXP_LIKE, I examine the names string to see whether it matches the pattern. And it does:

```
We have a delimited list!
```

REGEXP_LIKE is optimized to detect the mere presence of a pattern within a string. Other functions let you do even more. Keep reading!

### Locating a pattern

You can use REGEXP_INSTR to locate occurrences of a pattern within a string. The general syntax for REGEXP_INSTR is:

```
REGEXP_INSTR (source_string, pattern [,beginning_position [,occurrence [,return_option
   [,match_modifier [,subexpression]]]]])
```

Where *source_string* is the character string to be searched; *pattern* is the regular expression pattern to search for in *source_string*; *beginning_position* is the character position at which to begin the search; *occurrence* is the ordinal occurrence desired (1 = first, 2 = second, etc.); *return_option* is either 0 for the beginning position or 1 for the ending position; and *match_modifier* is one or more modifiers that apply to the search, such as i for case insensitivity. Beginning with Oracle Database 11*g*, you can also specify a *subexpression* (1 = first subexpression, 2 = second subexpression, etc.), which causes REGEXP_INST to return the starting position for the specified subexpression. A sub-expression is a part of the pattern enclosed in parentheses.

For example, to find the first occurrence of a name beginning with the letter A and ending with a consonant, you might specify:

```
DECLARE
    names VARCHAR2(60) := 'Anna,Matt,Joe,Nathan,Andrew,Jeff,Aaron';
    names_adjusted VARCHAR2(61);
    comma_delimited BOOLEAN;
    j_location NUMBER;
BEGIN
    --Look for the pattern
    comma_delimited := REGEXP_LIKE(names,'^([a-z ]*,)+([a-z ]*)$', 'i');

    --Only do more if we do, in fact, have a comma-delimited list.
    IF comma_delimited THEN
        j_location := REGEXP_INSTR(names, 'A[a-z]*[^aeiou],|A[a-z]*[^aeiou]$');
        DBMS_OUTPUT.PUT_LINE(j_location);
    END IF;
END;
```

Execute this code and you'll find that the first A name ending with a consonant, which happens to be Andrew, begins at position 22. Here's how I worked out the pattern:

*A*

I begin with the letter A. No need to worry about commas, because I already know at this point that I am working with a delimited list.

*A[a-z ]\**

I follow that A with some number of letters or spaces. The * allows for zero or more such characters following the A.

*A[a-z ]\*[^aeiou]*

I add [^aeiou] because I want my name to end with anything but a vowel. The caret ^ creates an exclusion set—any character *except* a vowel will match. Because I specify no quantifier, exactly one such nonvowel is required.

*A[a-z ]\*[^aeiou],*

I require a comma to end the pattern. Otherwise, I'd have a match on the "An" of "Anna." While adding the comma solves that problem, it introduces another, because my pattern now will never match Aaron at the end of the string. Uh, oh...

*A[a-z ]\*[^aeiou],|A[a-z ]\*[^aeiou]$*

Here I've introduced a vertical-bar (|) into the mix. The | indicates alternation: I am now looking for a match with either pattern. The first pattern ends with a comma, whereas the second does not. The second pattern accommodates the possibility that the name I'm looking for is the final name in the list. The second pattern is thus anchored to the end of the string by the dollar sign ($).

Writing regular expressions is not easy! As a beginner, you'll discover subtleties to regular expression evaluation that will trip you up. I spent quite a bit of time working out just this one example, and went down several dead-end paths before getting it right. Don't despair, though. Writing regular expressions does become easier with practice.

While REGEXP_INSTR has its uses, I am often more interested in returning the text matching a pattern than I am in simply locating it.

### Extracting text matching a pattern

Let's use a different example to illustrate regular expression extraction. Phone numbers are a good example because they follow a pattern, but often there are several variations on this pattern. The phone number pattern includes the area code (three digits) followed by the exchange (three digits) followed by the local number (four digits). So, a phone number is a string of ten digits. But there are many optional and alternative ways to represent the number. The area code may be enclosed within parentheses and is usually, but not always, separated from the rest of the phone number with a space, dot, or dash character. The exchange is usually, but not always, separated from the rest of the phone number with a space, dot, or dash character. Thus, a legal phone number may include any of the following:

```
7735555253
773-555-5253
(773)555-5253
(773) 555 5253
773.555.5253
```

This kind of loosey-goosey pattern is easy work using regular expressions, but very hard without them. I'll use REGEXP_SUBSTR to extract a phone number from a string containing contact information:

```
DECLARE
   contact_info VARCHAR2(200) := '
     address:
     1060 W. Addison St.
     Chicago, IL 60613
     home 773-555-5253
   ';
   phone_pattern  VARCHAR2(90) :=
     '\(?\d{3}\)?[[:space:]\.\-]?\d{3}[[:space:]\.\-]?\d{4}';
BEGIN
   DBMS_OUTPUT.PUT_LINE('The phone number is: '||
     REGEXP_SUBSTR(contact_info,phone_pattern,1,1));
END;
```

This code shows me the phone number:

```
The phone number is: 773-555-5253
```

Whoa! That phone pattern is pretty intimidating with all those punctuation characters strung together. Let me break it down into manageable pieces:

\(?

> My phone pattern starts with an optional open parentheses character. Because the parentheses characters are metacharacters (have special meaning), I need to *escape* the open parenthesis by preceding it with a backslash. The question mark is a *quantifier*, specifying that the pattern allows zero or one of the preceding character. This portion of the pattern specifies an optional open parentheses character.

\d{3}

> The \d is one of those Perl-influenced operators introduced with Oracle Database 10*g* Release 2 and specifies a digit. The curly brackets are a *quantifier*, specifying that the pattern allows an exact number of preceding characters—in this case, three. This portion of the pattern specifies three digits.

\)?

> This portion of the pattern specifies an optional close parenthesis character.

[[:space:]\.\-]?

> The square brackets define a set of characters on which to match—in this case a whitespace character or a dot or a dash. The [:space:] notation is the POSIX character class for whitespace characters in our NLS character set—any whitespace character will match. A dot and dash are metacharacters, so I need to escape them in my pattern by preceding each with a backslash. Finally, the question mark specifies that the pattern allows zero or one of the preceding characters. This portion of the pattern specifies an optional whitespace, dot, or dash character.

\d{3}

> As described previously, this portion of the pattern specifies three digits.

[[:space:]\.\-]?

> As described previously, this portion of the pattern specifies an optional whitespace, dot, or dash character.

\d{4}

> As described previously, this portion of the pattern specifies four digits.

When you code with regular expressions, commenting your code becomes more important to someone (including yourself six months from now) wanting to understand your cleverness.

The general syntax for REGEXP_SUBSTR is:

```
REGEXP_SUBSTR (source_string, pattern [,position [,occurrence
   [,match_modifier [,subexpression]]]])
```

REGEXP_SUBSTR returns a string containing the portion of the source string matching the pattern or subexpression. If no matching pattern is found, a NULL is returned. *source_string* is the character string to be searched; *pattern* is the regular expression pattern to search for in *source_string*; *position* is the character position at which to begin the search; *occurrence* is the ordinal occurrence desired (1 = first, 2 = second, etc.); and *match_modifier* is one or more modifiers that apply to the search.

Beginning with Oracle Database 11g, you can also specify which *subexpression* to return (1 = first subexpression, 2 = second subexpression, etc.). A subexpression is a part of the pattern enclosed in parentheses. Subexpressions are useful when you need to match on the whole pattern but want only a portion of that patterned extracted. If I want to find the phone number, but only extract the area code, I enclose the area code portion of the pattern in parentheses, making it a subexpression:

```
DECLARE
  contact_info VARCHAR2(200) := '
    address:
    1060 W. Addison   St.
    Chicago, IL 60613
    home 773-555-5253
    work (312) 555-1234
    cell 224.555.2233
    ';
  phone_pattern  VARCHAR2(90) :=
    '\(?(\d{3})\)?[[:space:]\.\-]?\d{3}[[:space:]\.\-]?\d{4}';
  contains_phone_nbr BOOLEAN;
  phone_number VARCHAR2(15);
  phone_counter NUMBER;
  area_code VARCHAR2(3);
BEGIN
  contains_phone_nbr := REGEXP_LIKE(contact_info,phone_pattern);
  IF contains_phone_nbr THEN
    phone_counter := 1;
    DBMS_OUTPUT.PUT_LINE('The phone numbers are:');
    LOOP
      phone_number := REGEXP_SUBSTR(contact_info,phone_pattern,1,phone_counter);
      EXIT WHEN phone_number IS NULL;  -- NULL means no more matches
      DBMS_OUTPUT.PUT_LINE(phone_number);
      phone_counter := phone_counter + 1;
    END LOOP;
    phone_counter := 1;
    DBMS_OUTPUT.PUT_LINE('The area codes are:');
    LOOP
      area_code := REGEXP_SUBSTR(contact_info,phone_pattern,1,phone_counter,'i',1);
      EXIT WHEN area_code IS NULL;
      DBMS_OUTPUT.PUT_LINE(area_code);
      phone_counter := phone_counter + 1;
    END LOOP;
  END IF;
END;
```

This snippet of code extracts the phone numbers and area codes:

```
The phone numbers are:
773-555-5253
(312) 555-1234
224.555.2233
The area codes are:
773
```

312
224

## Counting regular expression matches

Sometimes, you just want a count of how many matches your regular expression has. Prior to Oracle Database 11g, you had to loop through and count each match. Now you can use the new function REGEXP_COUNT to tally up the number of matches. The general syntax for REGEXP_COUNT is:

```
REGEXP_COUNT (source_string, pattern [,position [,match_modifier]])
```

Where *source_string* is the character string to be searched; *pattern* is the regular expression pattern to search for in *source_string*; *position* is the character position at which to begin the search; and *match modifier* is one or more modifiers that apply to the search.

```
DECLARE
  contact_info VARCHAR2(200) := '
    address:
    1060 W. Addison   St.
    Chicago, IL 60613
    home 773-555-5253
    work (312) 123-4567';
  phone_pattern  VARCHAR2(90) :=
  '\(?(\d{3})\)?[[:space:]]\.\-]?(\d{3})[[:space:]]\.\-]?\d{4}';
BEGIN
  DBMS_OUTPUT.PUT_LINE('There are '
    ||REGEXP_COUNT(contact_info,phone_pattern)
    ||' phone numbers');
END;
```

The result is:

```
There are 2 phone numbers
```

## Replacing text

Regular expression search and replace is one of the best regular expression features. Your replacement text can refer to portions of your source text (called *back references*), enabling you to manipulate text in very powerful ways. Imagine that you're faced with the problem of displaying a comma-delimited list of names two to a line. One way to do that is to replace every second comma with a newline character. Again, this is hard to do with standard REPLACE, but easy using REGEXP_REPLACE.

The general syntax for REGEXP_REPLACE is:

```
REGEXP_REPLACE (source_string, pattern [,replacement_string
  [,position [,occurrence [,match_modifier]]])
```

Where *source_string* is the character string to be searched; *pattern* is the regular expression pattern to search for in *source_string*; *replacement_string* is the replace text for *pattern*; *position* is the character position at which to begin the search; and *match_modifier* is one or more modifiers that apply to the search.

Let's look at an example.

```
DECLARE
    names VARCHAR2(60) := 'Anna,Matt,Joe,Nathan,Andrew,Jeff,Aaron';
    names_adjusted VARCHAR2(61);
    comma_delimited BOOLEAN;
    extracted_name VARCHAR2(60);
    name_counter NUMBER;
BEGIN
    --Look for the pattern
    comma_delimited := REGEXP_LIKE(names,'^([a-z ]*,)+([a-z ]*){1}$', 'i');

    --Only do more if we do, in fact, have a comma-delimited list.
    IF comma_delimited THEN
        names := REGEXP_REPLACE(
                    names,
                    '([a-z A-Z]*),([a-z A-Z]*),',
                    '\1,\2' || chr(10)   );
    END IF;

    DBMS_OUTPUT.PUT_LINE(names);
END;
```

The output from this bit of code is:

```
Anna,Matt
Joe,Nathan
Andrew,Jeff
Aaron
```

I'll begin my explanation of this bit of wizardry by pointing out that I passed three arguments to REGEXP_REPLACE:

*names*

> The source string

*'([a-z A-Z]\*),([a-z A-Z]\*),'*

> An expression specifying the text that I want to replace. More on this in just a bit.

*\1,\2 ' || chr(10)*

> My replacement text. The \1 and \2 are back references and are what makes my solution work. I'll talk more about these in just a bit too.

The expression I'm searching for consists of two subexpressions enclosed within parentheses, plus two commas. Here's an explanation of how that expression works:

*([a-z A-Z]\*)*

> I want to begin by matching a name.

*,*

> I want that name to be terminated by a comma.

*([a-z A-Z]\*)*

> Then I want to match another name.

And I again want to match the terminating comma.

Remember that my goal is to replace every second comma with a newline. That's why I wrote my expression to match two names and two commas. There's a reason, too, why I kept the commas out of the subexpressions.

Following is the first match that will be found for my expression upon invoking REGEXP_REPLACE:

```
Anna,Matt,
```

The two subexpressions will correspond to "Anna" and "Matt" respectively. The key to my solution is that you can reference the text matching a given subexpression via a back reference. The two back references in my replacement text are \1 and \2, and they refer to the text matched by the first and second subexpressions. Here's how that plays out:

```
'\1,\2' || chr(10)      --our replacement text
'Anna,\2' || chr(10)    --fill in the value matched
                          by the first subexpression

'Anna,Matt' || chr(10)  --fill in the value matched
                          by the second subexpression
```

I hope you can begin to see the power at your disposal here. I don't even use the commas from the original text. I use only the text matching the two subexpressions, the names "Anna" and "Matt", and I insert those into a new string formatted with one comma and one newline.

I can do even more! I can easily change our replacement text to use a tab (an ASCII 9) rather than a comma:

```
names := REGEXP_REPLACE(
           names,
           '([a-z A-Z]*),([a-z A-Z]*),',
           '\1' || chr(9) || '\2' || chr(10)    );
```

And now I get my results in two, nice, neat columns:

```
Anna    Matt
Joe     Nathan
Andrew  Jeff
Aaron
```

I think regular expression search and replace is a wonderful thing. It's fun. It's powerful. You can do a lot with it.

### Groking greediness

*Greediness* is an important concept to understand when writing regular expressions. Consider the problem of extracting just the first name, *and its trailing comma*, from our comma-delimited list of names. Recall that the list looks like this:

```
names VARCHAR2(60) := 'Anna,Matt,Joe,Nathan,Andrew,Jeff,Aaron';
```

One solution that you might think of is to look for a series of characters ending in a comma:

```
.*,
```

Let's try this solution to see how it works:

```
DECLARE
    names VARCHAR2(60) := 'Anna,Matt,Joe,Nathan,Andrew,Jeff,Aaron';
BEGIN
    DBMS_OUTPUT.PUT_LINE(   REGEXP_SUBSTR(names, '.*,')   );
END;
```

My output is:

```
Anna,Matt,Joe,Nathan,Andrew,Jeff,
```

Well! This is certainly not what we were after. What happened? I was a victim of greediness. Not the sort of greediness your mother chastised you about, but rather a greediness of the regular-expression sort: each element of a regular expression will match as many characters as it possibly can. When you and I see:

```
.*,
```

our natural tendency often is to think in terms of *stopping* at the first comma and returning "Anna,". However, the database looks for the longest run of characters it can find that terminate with a comma; the database stops not at the first comma, but at the *last*.

In Oracle Database 10g Release 1, when regular expression support was first introduced, you had limited options for dealing with greediness problems. You may be able to reformulate an expression to avoid the problem. For example, you can use '[^,]*,' to return the first name and its trailing comma from your delimited string. Sometimes though, you are forced to change your whole approach to solving a problem, often to the point of using a completely different combination of functions than you first intended.

Starting with Oracle Database 10g Release 2 you get some relief from greed, in the form of nongreedy quantifiers inspired by those found in Perl. By adding a question-mark (?) to the quantifier for the period (.), changing that quantifier from an * to *?, I can request the shortest run of characters that precedes a comma, as follows:

```
DECLARE
    names VARCHAR2(60) := 'Anna,Matt,Joe,Nathan,Andrew,Jeff,Aaron';
BEGIN
    DBMS_OUTPUT.PUT_LINE(   REGEXP_SUBSTR(names, '(.*?,)')   );
END;
```

The output now is:

```
Anna,
```

The nongreedy quantifiers match as *soon* as they can, not as much as they can.

### Learning more about regular expressions

Regular expressions can seem deceptively simple, but end up being a surprisingly deep topic. They are simple enough that you'll be able to use them after just reading this chapter (I hope!), and yet there's so much more to learn. I'd like to recommend the following sources from Oracle and O'Reilly:

*Oracle Database Application Developer's Guide-Fundamentals*
Chapter 4 of this Oracle manual is the definitive source of information on regular expression support in Oracle.

*Oracle Regular Expression Pocket Reference*
A fine introduction to regular expressions written by Jonathan Gennick and Peter Linsley. Peter is one of the developers for Oracle's regular expression implementation.

*Mastering Oracle SQL*
Contains an excellent chapter introducing regular expressions in the context of Oracle SQL. Aside from regular expressions, this book by Sanjay Mishra and Alan Beaulieu is an excellent read if you want to hone your SQL skills.

*Mastering Regular Expressions*
Jeffrey Friedl's book stands tall as the definitive font of wisdom on using regular expressions. To really delve deeply into the topic, this is the book to read.

Finally, you'll find in Appendix A a table describing each of the regular expression metacharacters supported in Oracle's implementation of regular expressions.

## Working with Empty Strings

One issue that often causes great consternation, especially to people who come to Oracle after working with other databases, is that the Oracle database treats empty strings as NULLs. This is contrary to the ISO SQL standard, which recognizes the difference between an empty string and a string variable that is NULL.

The following code demonstrates the Oracle database's behavior:

```
/* File on web: empty_is_null.sql */
DECLARE
   empty_varchar2 VARCHAR2(10) := '';
   empty_char CHAR(10) := '';
BEGIN
   IF empty_varchar2 IS NULL THEN
      DBMS_OUTPUT.PUT_LINE('empty_varchar2 is NULL');
   END IF;

   IF '' IS NULL THEN
      DBMS_OUTPUT.PUT_LINE(''''' is NULL');
   END IF;

   IF empty_char IS NULL THEN
      DBMS_OUTPUT.PUT_LINE('empty_char is NULL');
```

```
      ELSIF empty_char IS NOT NULL THEN
         DBMS_OUTPUT.PUT_LINE('empty_char is NOT NULL');
      END IF;
   END;
```

The output is:

```
empty_varchar2 is NULL
'' is NULL
empty_char is NOT NULL
```

You'll notice in this example that the CHAR variable is not considered NULL. That's because CHAR variables, as fixed-length character strings, are never truly empty. The CHAR variable in this example is padded with blanks until it is exactly 10 characters in length. The VARCHAR2 variable, however, is NULL, as is the zero-length string literal.

You have to really watch for this behavior in IF statements that compare two VARCHAR2 values. Recall that a NULL is never equal to a NULL. Consider a program that queries the user for a name, and then compares that name to a value read in from the database:

```
DECLARE
   user_entered_name VARCHAR2(30);
   name_from_database VARCHAR2(30);
   ...
BEGIN
...
IF user_entered_name <> name_from_database THEN
...
```

If the user had entered an empty string instead of a name, the IF condition shown in this example would never be TRUE. That's because a NULL is never not-equal, nor equal, to any other value. One alternative approach to this IF statement is the following:

```
IF (user_entered_name <> name_from_database)
   OR (user_entered_name IS NULL) THEN
```

This is just one way of dealing with the "empty string is NULL" issue; it's impossible to provide a solution that works in all cases. You must think through what you are trying to accomplish, recognize that any empty strings will be treated as NULLs, and code appropriately.

## Mixing CHAR and VARCHAR2 Values

If you use both fixed-length (CHAR) and variable-length (VARCHAR2) strings in your PL/SQL code, you should be aware of how the database handles the interactions between these two datatypes, as described in the following sections.

### Database-to-variable conversion

When you SELECT or FETCH data from a CHAR database column into a VARCHAR2 variable, the trailing spaces are retained. If you SELECT or FETCH from a VARCHAR2 database column into a CHAR variable, PL/SQL automatically pads the value with spaces out to the maximum length. In other words, the type of the variable, not the column, determines the variable's resulting value.

### Variable-to-database conversion

When you INSERT or UPDATE a CHAR variable into a VARCHAR2 database column, the SQL kernel does not trim the trailing blanks before performing the change. When the following PL/SQL is executed, the company_name in the new database record is set to "ACME SHOWERS........" (where . indicates a space). It is, in other words, padded out to 20 characters, even though the default value was a string of only 12 characters.

```
DECLARE
    comp_id# NUMBER;
    comp_name CHAR(20) := 'ACME SHOWERS';
BEGIN
    SELECT company_id_seq.NEXTVAL
        INTO comp_id#
        FROM dual;
    INSERT INTO company (company_id, company_name)
        VALUES (comp_id#, comp_name);
END;
```

On the other hand, when you INSERT or UPDATE a VARCHAR2 variable into a CHAR database column, the SQL kernel automatically pads the variable-length string with spaces out to the maximum (fixed) length specified when the table was created, and places that expanded value into the database.

### String comparisons

Suppose your code contains a string comparison such as the following:

```
IF company_name = parent_company_name ...
```

PL/SQL must compare company_name to parent_company_name. It performs the comparison in one of two ways, depending on the types of the two variables:

- If a comparison is made between two CHAR variables, then PL/SQL uses *blank-padding* comparison.
- If at least one of the strings involved in the comparison is variable-length, then PL/SQL performs *non-blank-padding* comparison.

The following code snippet illustrates the difference between these two comparison methods:

```
DECLARE
   company_name CHAR(30)
      := 'Feuerstein and Friends';
   char_parent_company_name CHAR(35)
      := 'Feuerstein and Friends';
   varchar2_parent_company_name VARCHAR2(35)
      := 'Feuerstein and Friends';
BEGIN
   --Compare two CHARs, so blank-padding is used
   IF company_name = char_parent_company_name THEN
      DBMS_OUTPUT.PUT_LINE ('first comparison is TRUE');
   ELSE
      DBMS_OUTPUT.PUT_LINE ('first comparison is FALSE');
   END IF;

   --Compare a CHAR and a VARCHAR2, so nonblank-padding is used
   IF company_name = varchar2_parent_company_name THEN
      DBMS_OUTPUT.PUT_LINE ('second comparison is TRUE');
   ELSE
      DBMS_OUTPUT.PUT_LINE ('second comparison is FALSE');
   END IF;
END;
```

The output is:

```
first comparison is TRUE
second comparison is FALSE
```

The first comparison is between two CHAR values, so blank-padding is used: PL/SQL blank-pads the shorter of the two values out to the length of the longer value. It then performs the comparison. In this example, PL/SQL adds five spaces to the end of the value in company_name and then performs the comparison between company_name and char_parent_company_name. The result is that both strings are considered equal. Note that PL/SQL does not actually change the company_name variable's value. It copies the value to another memory structure and then modifies this temporary data for the comparison.

The second comparison involves a VARCHAR2 value, so PL/SQL performs a non-blank-padding comparison. It makes no changes to any of the values, uses the existing lengths, and performs the comparison. In this case, the first 22 characters of both strings are the same, "Feuerstein and Friends", but the fixed-length company_name is padded with eight space characters, whereas the variable-length VARCHAR2 company_name is not. Because one string has trailing blanks and the other does not, the two strings are not considered equal.

The fact that one VARCHAR2 value causes non-blank-padding comparisons is also true of expressions involving more than two variables, as well as of expressions involving the IN operator. For example:

```
IF menu_selection NOT IN
      (save_and_close, cancel_and_exit, 'OPEN_SCREEN')
   THEN ...
```

If any of the four strings in this example (menu_selection, the two named constants, and the single literal) is declared VARCHAR2, then exact comparisons without modification are performed to determine if the user has made a valid selection. Note that a literal like OPEN_SCREEN is always considered a fixed-length CHAR datatype.

### Character functions and CHAR arguments

A character function is a function that takes one or more character values as parameters and returns either a character value or a number value. When a character function returns a character value, that value is always of type VARCHAR2 (variable length), with the exceptions of UPPER and LOWER. These functions convert to uppercase and lowercase, respectively, and return CHAR values (fixed length) if the strings they are called on to convert are fixed-length CHAR arguments.

## String Function Quick Reference

As I have already pointed out, PL/SQL provides a rich set of string functions that allow you to get information about strings and modify the contents of those strings in very high-level, powerful ways. The following list gives you an idea of the power at your disposal and will be enough to remind you of syntax. For complete details on a given function, see Oracle's *SQL Reference* manual.

*ASCII(single_character)*
> Returns the NUMBER code that represents the specified character in the database character set.

*ASCIISTR(string1)*
> Takes a string in any character set and converts it into a string of ASCII characters. Any non-ASCII characters are represented using the form \*XXXX*, where *XXXX* represents the Unicode value for the character.

> For information on Unicode, including the underlying bytecodes used to represent characters in the Unicode character set, visit *http://unicode.org*.

*CHR(code_location)*
> Returns a VARCHAR2 character (length 1) that corresponds to the location in the collating sequence provided as a parameter. This is the reverse of ASCII. One variation is useful when working with national character set data:
>
> *CHR(code_location USING NCHAR_CS)*
> > Returns an NVARCHAR2 character from the national character set.

*COMPOSE(string1)*

Takes a Unicode string as input and returns that string in its fully normalized form. For example, you can use the unnormalized representation 'a\0303' to specify the character 'a' with a "~" on top (i.e., ã). COMPOSE('a\0303') will then return '\00E3', which is the Unicode code point (in hexadecimal) for the character ã.

In Oracle9*i* Database Release 1, COMPOSE must be called from a SQL statement; it cannot be used in a PL/SQL expression. From Oracle9*i* Database Release 2 onwards, you can invoke COMPOSE from a PL/SQL expression.

*CONCAT(string1, string2)*

Appends *string2* to the end of *string1*. You'll get the same results as from the expression *string1* || *string2*. I find the || operator so much more convenient that I almost never invoke the CONCAT function.

*CONVERT(string1, target_char_set)*

Converts a string from the database character set to the specified target character set. You may optionally specify a source character set:

```
CONVERT(string1, target_char_set, source_character_set)
```

*DECOMPOSE(string1)*

Takes a Unicode string as input and returns that string with any precomposed characters decomposed into their separate elements. This is the opposite of COMPOSE. For example, DECOMPOSE('ã') yields 'a~' (See COMPOSE).

Two variations are available:

*DECOMPOSE(string1 CANONICAL)*

Results in canonical decomposition, which gives a result that may be reversed using COMPOSE. This is the default.

*DECOMPOSE(string1)*

Results in decomposition in what is referred to as *compatibility mode*. Recomposition using COMPOSE may not be possible.

Like COMPOSE, DECOMPOSE cannot be invoked directly from a PL/SQL expression in Oracle9*i* Database Release 1; you must invoke it from a SQL statement. From Oracle9*i* Database Release 2 onwards, this restriction is removed.

*GREATEST(string1, string2, ...)*

Takes one or more strings as input, and returns the string that would come last (i.e., that is the greatest) if the inputs were sorted in ascending order. Also see the LEAST function, which is the opposite of GREATEST.

*INITCAP(string1)*

Reformats the case of the string argument, setting the first letter of each word to uppercase and the remainder of the letters to lowercase. This is sometimes called *title case*. A word is a set of characters separated by a space or non-alphanumeric character (such as # or _). For example, INITCAP('this is lower') gives 'This Is Lower'.

*INSTR(string1, string2)*

Returns the position at which *string2* is found within *string1*; otherwise, returns 0.

Several variations are available:

*INSTR(string1, string2, start_position)*

Begins searching for *string2* at the column in *string1* indicated by *start_position*. The default start position is 1, so INSTR(*string1*, *string2*, 1) is equivalent to INSTR(*string1*, *string2*).

*INSTR(string1, string2, negative_start_position)*

Begins searching from the end of *string1* rather than from the beginning.

*INSTR(string1, string2, start_position, nth)*

Finds the *nth* occurrence of *string2* after the start_position.

*INSTR(string1, string2, negative_start_position, nth)*

Finds the *nth* occurrence of *string2*, counting from the end of *string1*.

INSTR treats a string as a sequence of characters. The variations INSTRB, INSTR2, and INSTR4 treat a string as a sequence of bytes, Unicode code units, and Unicode code points, respectively. The variation INSTRC treats a string as a series of complete, Unicode characters. For example: 'a\0303', which is the decomposed equivalent of '\00E3', or ã, is treated and counted as a single character. INSTR, however, sees 'a\0303' as two characters.

*LEAST(string1, string2, ...)*

Takes one or more strings as input and returns the string that would come first (i.e., that is the least) if the inputs were sorted in ascending order. Also see GREATEST, which is the opposite of LEAST.

*LENGTH(string1)*

Returns the number of characters in a string. The variations LENGTHB, LENGTH2, and LENGTH4 return the number of bytes, the number of Unicode code units, and the number of Unicode code points, respectively. The variation LENGTHC returns the number of complete Unicode characters, normalizing (e.g., changing 'a\0303' to '\00E3') where possible.

LENGTH typically does not return zero. Remember that the Oracle database treats an empty string ('') as a NULL, so LENGTH('') is the same as trying to take the length of a NULL, and the result is NULL. The sole exception is when LENGTH is used against a CLOB. It is possible for a CLOB to hold zero bytes and yet not be NULL. In this one case, LENGTH returns zero.

*LOWER(string1)*

Converts all letters in the specified string to lowercase. This is the opposite of UPPER. The return datatype is the same as the input datatype (CHAR, VARCHAR2, CLOB). See also NLS_LOWER.

*LPAD(string1, padded_length)*

Returns the value from *string1*, but padded on the left with enough spaces to make the result *padded_length* characters long. There is one variation, shown next.

*LPAD(string1, padded_length, pad_string)*

Appends enough full or partial occurrences of *pad_string* to bring the total length up to *padded_length*. For example, LPAD('Merry Christmas!', 25, 'Ho! ') results in 'Ho! Ho! HMerry Christmas!'.

LPAD is the opposite of RPAD.

*LTRIM(string1)*

Removes, or trims, space characters from the left, or leading edge of *string1*. Also see TRIM (ISO standard) and RTRIM. There is one variation:

*LTRIM(string1, trim_string)*

Removes any characters found in *trim_string* from the left end of *string1*.

*NCHR(code_location)*

Returns an NVARCHAR2 character (length 1) that corresponds to the location in the national character set collating sequence specified by the *code_location* parameter. The CHR function's USING NCHAR_CS clause provides the same functionality as NCHR.

*NLS_INITCAP(string1)*

Returns a version of *string1*, which should be of type NVARCHAR2 or NCHAR, setting the first letter of each word to uppercase and the remainder of the letters to lowercase. This is sometimes called title case. The return value is a VARCHAR2. A *word* is a set of characters separated by a space or nonalphanumeric character.

You may specify a linguistic sorting sequence that affects the definition of "first letter:"

*NLS_INITCAP(string1, 'NLS_SORT=sort_sequence_name')*

When using this syntax, *sort_sequence_name* should be a valid, linguistic sort name as described in the *Oracle Database Globalization Support Guide*, Appendix A, under the heading "Linguistic Sorts."

The following example illustrates the difference between INITCAP and NLS_INITCAP:

```
BEGIN
    DBMS_OUTPUT.PUT_LINE(INITCAP('ijzer'));
    DBMS_OUTPUT.PUT_LINE(NLS_INITCAP('ijzer','NLS_SORT=XDUTCH'));
END;
```

The output is:

```
Ijzer
IJzer
```

In the Dutch language, the character sequence "ij" is treated as a single character. NLS_INITCAP correctly recognizes this as a result of the NLS_SORT specification, and uppercases the word "ijzer" (Dutch for "iron") appropriately.

*NLS_LOWER(string1) and NLS_LOWER(string1, 'NLS_SORT=sort_sequence_name')*
Returns *string1* in lowercase in accordance with language-specific rules. See NLS_INITCAP for a description of how the NLS_SORT specification can affect the results.

*NLS_UPPER(string1) and NLS_UPPER(string1, 'NLS_SORT=sort_sequence_name')*
Returns *string1* in uppercase in accordance with language-specific rules. See NLS_INITCAP for a description of how the NLS_SORT specification can affect the results.

*NLSSORT(string1) and NLSSORT(string1, 'NLS_SORT=sort_sequence_name')*
Returns a string of bytes that can be used to sort a string value in accordance with language-specific rules. The string returned is of the RAW datatype. For example, to compare two strings using French sorting rules:

```
IF NLSSORT(x, 'NLS_SORT=XFRENCH') > NLSSORT(y, 'NLS_SORT=XFRENCH') THEN...
```

When you omit the second parameter, the function uses the default sort sequence that you have established for your session. For a list of sort sequences, see the *Oracle Globalization Support Guide*, Appendix A, under the heading "Linguistic Sorts."

*REGEXP_COUNT, REGEXP_INSTR, REGEXP_LIKE, REGEXP_REPLACE, REGEXP_SUBSTR*
Refer to Appendix A of this book for these regular-expression functions.

*REPLACE(string1, match_string, replace_string)*
Returns a string in which all occurrences of *match_string* in *string1* are replaced by *replace_string*. REPLACE is useful for searching a pattern of characters, and then changing all instances of that pattern in a single function call.

*REPLACE(string1, match_string)*
Returns *string1* with all occurrences of *match_string* removed.

*RPAD(string1, padded_length)*
Returns the value from *string1*, but padded on the right with enough spaces to make the result *padded_length* characters long. There is one variation:

*RPAD(string1, padded_length, pad_string)*
Appends enough full or partial occurrences of *pad_string* to bring the total length up to *padded_length*. For example, RPAD('Merry Christmas! ', 25, 'Ho! ') results in 'Merry Christmas! Ho! Ho!'.

RPAD pads on the right, while its complement, LPAD, pads on the left.

*RTRIM(string1)*

> Removes, or trims, space characters from the right, or trailing edge of *string1*. See also TRIM (ISO standard) and LTRIM. There is one variation:

> *RTRIM(string1, trim_string)*

>> Removes any characters found in *trim_string* from the trailing edge of *string1*.

*SOUNDEX(string1)*

> Returns a character string that is the "phonetic representation" of the argument. For example:

```
SOUNDEX ('smith') --> 'S530'
SOUNDEX ('SMYTHE') --> 'S530'
SOUNDEX ('smith smith') --> 'S532'
SOUNDEX ('smith z') --> 'S532'
SOUNDEX ('feuerstein') --> 'F623'
SOUNDEX ('feuerst') --> 'F623'
```

> Keep the following SOUNDEX rules in mind when using this function:

> - The SOUNDEX value always begins with the first letter in the input string.

> - SOUNDEX uses only the first five consonants in the string to generate the return value.

> - Only consonants are used to compute the numeric portion of the SOUNDEX value. Except for leading vowels, all vowels are ignored.

> - SOUNDEX is not case-sensitive; uppercase and lowercase letters return the same SOUNDEX value.

> The SOUNDEX function is useful for ad hoc queries, and any other kinds of searches where the exact spelling of a database value is not known or easily determined.

 The SOUNDEX algorithm is English-centric and may not work well (or at all) for other languages.

*SUBSTR(string1, start, length)*

> Returns a substring from *string1*, beginning with the character at position *start* and going for *length* characters. If the end of *string1* is encountered before *length* characters are found, then all characters from *start* onward are returned. The following variations exist:

> *SUBSTR(string1, start)*

>> Returns all characters beginning from position *start* through to the end of *string1*.

> *SUBSTR(string1, negative_start, length)*

>> Counts backwards from the end of *string1* to determine the starting position from which to begin returning *length* characters.

*SUBSTR(string1, negative_start)*

Returns the last ABS(*negative_start*) characters from the string.

SUBSTR treats a string as a sequence of characters. The variations SUBSTRB, SUBSTR2, and SUBSTR4 treat a string as a sequence of bytes, Unicode code units, and Unicode code points, respectively. The variation SUBSTRC treats a string as a series of complete, Unicode characters. For example: 'a\0303', which is the decomposed equivalent of '\00E3', or ã, is treated and counted as a single character. SUBSTR, however, sees 'a\0303' as two characters.

*TO_CHAR(national_character_data)*

Converts data in the national character set to its equivalent representation in the database character set. See also TO_NCHAR.

 TO_CHAR may also be used to convert date and time values, as well as numbers, into human-readable form. These uses of TO_CHAR are described in Chapter 9 (for numbers) and Chapter 10 (for dates and times).

*TO_MULTI_BYTE(string1)*

Translates single-byte characters to their multibyte equivalents. Some multibyte character sets, notably UTF-8, provide for more than one representation of a given character. In UTF-8, for example, letters such as 'G' can be represented using one byte or using three bytes. TO_MULTI_BYTE lets you convert from the single to the multibyte representation. TO_MULTI_BYTE is the opposite of TO_SINGLE_BYTE.

*TO_NCHAR(database_character_data)*

Converts data in the database character set to its equivalent representation in the national character set. See also TO_CHAR and TRANSLATE...USING.

 TO_NCHAR may also be used to convert date and time values, as well as numbers, into human-readable form. These uses of TO_NCHAR are described in Chapter 9 (for numbers) and Chapter 10 (for dates and times).

*TO_SINGLE_BYTE(string1)*

Translates multibyte characters to their single-byte equivalents. This is the opposite of TO_MULTI_BYTE.

*TRANSLATE(string1, search_set, replace_set)*

Replaces every instance in *string1* of a character from *search_set* with the corresponding character from *replace_set*. For example:

```
TRANSLATE ('abcd', 'ab', '12') --> '12cd'
```

If the search set contains more characters than the replace set, then the "trailing" search characters that have no match in the replace set are not included in the result. For example:

```
TRANSLATE ('abcdefg', 'abcd', 'zyx') --> 'zyxefg'
```

The letter 'd' is removed, because it appears in *search_set* without a corresponding entry in *result_set*. TRANSLATE swaps individual characters, while REPLACE swaps strings.

**TRANSLATE(text USING CHAR_CS) and TRANSLATE(text USING NCHAR_CS)**

Translates character data to either the database character set (CHAR_CS) or the national character set (NCHAR_CS). The output datatype will be either VARCHAR2 or NVARCHAR2, depending on whether you are converting to the database or the national character set, respectively.

 TRANSLATE...USING is an ISO standard SQL function. Starting with Oracle9i Database Release 1, you can simply assign a VARCHAR2 to an NVARCHAR2 (and vice versa), and the database will handle the conversion implicitly. If you want to make such a conversion explicit, you can use TO_CHAR and TO_NCHAR to convert text to database and national character sets, respectively. Oracle Corporation recommends the use of TO_CHAR and TO_NCHAR over TRANSLATE...USING, because those functions support a greater range of input datatypes.

**TRIM(FROM string1)**

Returns a version of *string1* that omits any leading and trailing spaces. Variations include:

**TRIM(LEADING FROM ...)**

Trims only leading spaces.

**TRIM(TRAILING FROM ...)**

Trims only trailing spaces.

**TRIM(BOTH FROM ...)**

Explicitly specifies the default behavior of trimming *both* leading and trailing spaces.

**TRIM(...trim_character FROM string1)**

Removes occurrences of *trim_character*, which may be any one character that you want to specify.

Oracle added the TRIM function in Oracle8i Database to increase compliance with the ISO SQL standard. TRIM comes close to combining the functionality of LTRIM and RTRIM into one function. The difference is that with TRIM, you can specify only one trim character. When using LTRIM or RTRIM, you can specify a set of characters to trim.

*UNISTR(string1)*

Returns *string1* converted into Unicode. This is the opposite of ASCIISTR. You can represent nonprintable characters in the input string using the \XXXX notation, where *XXXX* represents the Unicode code point value for a character. For example:

```
BEGIN
  DBMS_OUTPUT.PUT_LINE(
    UNISTR('The symbol \20AC is the Euro.')
  );
END;

The symbol € is the Euro.
```

UNISTR gives you convenient access to the entire universe of Unicode characters, even those you cannot type directly from your keyboard. Chapter 25 discusses Unicode in more detail.

*UPPER(string1)*

Returns a version of *string1* with all letters made uppercase. The return datatype is the same as the datatype of *string1* (CHAR, VARCHAR2 or CLOB). UPPER is the opposite of LOWER. See also NLS_UPPER.

# CHAPTER 9

# Numbers

Where would we be without numbers? While those of us who are math-challenged might prefer a text-only view of the world, the reality is that much of the data in any database is numeric. How much inventory do we have? How much money do we owe? At what rate is our business growing? These are just some of the questions that we expect to answer using numbers from databases.

When working with numbers in PL/SQL, you need to have at least a passing familiarity with the following:

- The numeric datatypes at your disposal. It also helps to know in what situations they are best used.
- Conversion between numbers and their textual representations. How else do you expect to get those numbers into and out of your database?
- PL/SQL's rich library of built-in numeric functions. After all, you don't want to reinvent the wheel.

Each of these topics is discussed in this chapter. I'll begin by looking at the datatypes themselves.

## Numeric Datatypes

Like the Oracle database, PL/SQL offers a variety of numeric datatypes to suit different purposes:

*NUMBER*
> A true decimal datatype that is ideal for working with monetary amounts. NUMBER is also the only one of PL/SQL's numeric types to be implemented in a completely platform-independent fashion. Anything you do with NUMBERs should work the same regardless of the underlying hardware.

*PLS_INTEGER and BINARY_INTEGER*

Integer datatypes conforming to your hardware's underlying, integer representation. Arithmetic is performed using your hardware's native, machine instructions. You cannot store values of these types in the database.

*SIMPLE_INTEGER*

Introduced with Oracle Database 11*g*. Has the same range as BINARY_INTEGER, but does not allow for NULLs and does not raise an exception if an overflow occurs. The SIMPLE_INTEGER datatype results in significantly faster execution times for natively compiled code.

*BINARY_FLOAT and BINARY_DOUBLE*

Single- and double-precision, IEEE-754, binary floating-point types. I don't recommend these types for monetary amounts. They are useful, however, when you need fast, floating-point arithmetic.

*SIMPLE_FLOAT and SIMPLE_DOUBLE*

Introduced with Oracle Database 11*g*. Have the same range as BINARY_FLOAT and BINARY_DOUBLE, but do not allow for NULLs, do not raise an exception if an overflow occurs, and do not support special literals or predicates such as BINARY_FLOAT_MIN_NORMAL, IS NAN, or IS NOT INFINITE. These SIMPLE datatypes result in significantly faster execution times for natively compiled code.

In practice, you may encounter other numeric types, such as FLOAT, INTEGER, and DECIMAL. These are really nothing more than alternate names for the core numeric types just listed. I'll talk about these alternate names in "Numeric Subtypes" on page 246.

## The NUMBER Type

The NUMBER datatype is by far the most common numeric datatype you'll encounter in the world of Oracle and PL/SQL programming. Use it to store integer, fixed-point, or floating-point numbers of just about any size. Prior to Oracle Database 10*g*, NUMBER was the only numeric datatype supported directly by the Oracle database engine (later versions also support BINARY_FLOAT and BINARY_DOUBLE). NUMBER is implemented in a platform-independent manner, and arithmetic on NUMBER values yields the same result no matter what hardware platform you run on.

The simplest way to declare a NUMBER variable is simply to specify the keyword NUMBER:

```
DECLARE
    x NUMBER;
```

Such a declaration results in a floating-point NUMBER. The Oracle database will allocate space for up to the maximum of 40 digits, and the decimal point will float to best accommodate whatever values you assign to the variable. NUMBER variables can hold values as small as $10^{-130}$ (1.0E - 130) and as large as $10^{126}$ - 1 (1.0E126 - 1). Values smaller than $10^{-130}$ will get rounded down to 0, and calculations resulting in values larger than or equal to $10^{126}$ will be undefined, causing runtime problems but not raising an exception. This range of values is demonstrated by the following code block:

```
DECLARE
    tiny_nbr NUMBER := 1e-130;
    test_nbr NUMBER;
    --                          11111111111222222222233333333334
    --                 12345678901234567890123456789012345678901234567890
    big_nbr        NUMBER := 9.9999999999999999999999999999999999999999e125;
    --                          1111111111122222222223333333333334444444444
    --                 123456789012345678901234567890123456789012345678901234567890123456
    fmt_nbr VARCHAR2(50) := '9.99999999999999999999999999999999999999999EEEE';
BEGIN
    DBMS_OUTPUT.PUT_LINE('tiny_nbr          =' || TO_CHAR(tiny_nbr, '9.9999EEEE'));
    -- NUMBERs that are too small round down to zero
    test_nbr := tiny_nbr / 1.0001;
    DBMS_OUTPUT.PUT_LINE('tiny made smaller =' || TO_CHAR(test_nbr, fmt_nbr));
    -- NUMBERs that are too large throw an error
    DBMS_OUTPUT.PUT_LINE('big_nbr           =' || TO_CHAR(big_nbr, fmt_nbr));
    test_nbr := big_nbr * 1.0001;        -- too big
    DBMS_OUTPUT.PUT_LINE('big made bigger   =' || TO_CHAR(test_nbr, fmt_nbr));
END;
```

Output from this block is:

```
tiny_nbr          = 1.0000E-130
tiny made smaller =    .00000000000000000000000000000000000000000E+00
big_nbr           = 9.99999999999999999999999999999999999999900E+125
big made bigger   =#############################################
```

If you try to explicitly assign a number that is too large to your NUMBER variable, you'll raise a *numeric overflow or underflow* exception. But, if you assign calculation results that exceed the largest legal value, no exception is raised. If your application really needs to work with such large numbers, you will have to code validation routines that anticipate out-of-range values, or consider using BINARY_DOUBLE, which can be compared to BINARY_DOUBLE_INFINITY. Using binary datatypes has rounding implications, so be sure to read the sections on binary datatypes later in this chapter. For most applications, these rounding errors will probably cause you to choose the NUMBER datatype.

Often, when you declare a variable of type NUMBER, you will want to constrain its *precision* and *scale*, as follows

```
NUMBER (precision, scale)
```

Such a declaration results in a fixed-point number. The *precision* is the total number of significant digits in the number. The *scale* dictates the number of digits to the right (positive scale) or left (negative scale) of the decimal point, and also affects the point at which rounding occurs. Both the *precision* and the *scale* values must be literal, integer values; you cannot use variables or constants in the declaration. Legal values for *precision* range from 1 to 38, and legal values for *scale* range from –84 to 127.

When declaring fixed-point numbers, the value for *scale* is usually less than the value for *precision*. For example, you might declare a variable holding a monetary amount as NUMBER(9,2), which allows values up to and including 9,999,999.99. Figure 9-1 shows how to interpret such a declaration.

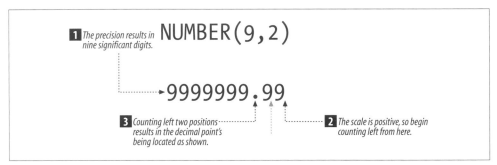

*Figure 9-1. A typical fixed-point NUMBER declaration*

As this figure illustrates, a declaration of NUMBER(9,2) results in a fixed-point number consisting of seven digits to the left of the decimal point and two digits to the right of the decimal point. Values stored in the variable will be rounded to a maximum of two decimal places, as shown in Table 9-1.

*Table 9-1. Rounding of NUMBER(9,2) values*

| Original value | Rounded value that is actually stored |
| --- | --- |
| 1,234.56 | 1,234.56 |
| 1,234,567.984623 | 1,234,567.98 |
| 1,234,567.985623 | 1,234,567.99 |
| 1,234,567.995623 | 1,234,568.00 |
| 10,000,000.00 | Results in an ORA-06502, numeric or value error, because the precision is too large for the variable |
| −10,000,000.00 | Same error as for 10,000,000.00 |

The last two values in the table result in an exception because they require more significant digits to represent than the variable can handle. Values in the tens of millions require at least eight significant digits to the left of the decimal point. You can't round such values to fit into only seven digits, so you get overflow errors.

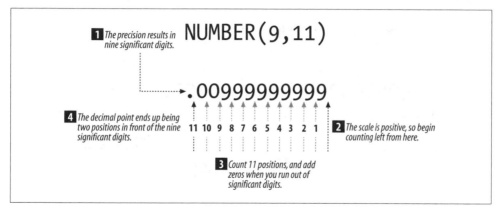

*Figure 9-2. The effect of scale exceeding precision*

Things get more interesting when you declare a variable with a *scale* that exceeds the variable's *precision* or when you use a negative value for *scale*. Figure 9-2 illustrates the effect of a *scale* exceeding a variable's *precision*.

The variable illustrated in this figure has the same number of significant digits as the variable in Figure 9-1, but those significant digits are used differently. Because the *scale* is 11, those nine significant digits can represent only absolute values less than 0.01. Values are rounded to the nearest hundred-billionth. Table 9-2 shows the results of storing some carefully chosen example values into a NUMBER(9,11) variable.

*Table 9-2. Rounding of NUMBER(9,11) values*

| Original value | Rounded value that is actually stored |
| --- | --- |
| 0.00123456789 | 0.00123456789 |
| 0.000000000005 | 0.00000000001 |
| 0.000000000004 | 0.00000000000 |
| 0.01 | Too large a number for the variable; requires a significant digit in the hundredth's position; results in an ORA-06502 error |
| −0.01 | Same as for 0.01 |

Negative *scale* values extend the decimal point out to the right, in the opposite direction of the positive scale. Figure 9-3 illustrates a variable declared NUMBER(9,-11).

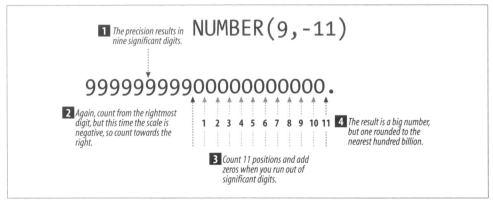

*Figure 9-3. The effect of negative scale*

Again I've used nine significant digits, but look where the decimal point is now! Rather than representing small values down to the hundred-billionth, the smallest value I can now represent precisely is 100 billion. Values less than 100 billion are rounded up or down to the nearest 100 billion, as illustrated in Table 9-3.

*Table 9-3. Rounding of NUMBER(9,-11) values*

| Original value | Rounded value that is actually stored |
| --- | --- |
| 50,000,000,000.123 | 100,000,000,000 |
| 49,999,999,999.999 | 0 |
| 150,000,975,230,001 | 150,000,000,000,000 |
| 100,000,000,000,000,000,000 or $1 \times 10^{20}$ | Too large a number for the variable; requires a significant digit in the hundred-quintillion's position; results in an ORA-06502 error |
| −100,000,000,000,000,000,000 or $−1 \times 10^{20}$ | Also results in an ORA-06502 error |

As Figure 9-3 and Table 9-3 illustrate, negative scales allows me to represent some very large numbers, but only at the sacrifice of precision in the less-significant digits. Any absolute value less than 50 trillion is rounded to zero when stored in a NUMBER(9,-11) variable.

When declaring NUMBER variables using *precision* and *scale*, bear in mind that *scale* is optional and defaults to zero. For example, the following declarations are equivalent:

```
x NUMBER(9,0);
x NUMBER(9);
```

Both of these declarations result in integer variables (i.e., zero digits past the decimal point) containing nine significant digits. The range of integer values that can be represented using nine significant digits is –999,999,999 through 999,999,999.

When used for fixed-point values, the range of NUMBER is constrained by the values that you are allowed to specify for *precision* and *scale*, as demonstrated in the following code block:

```
DECLARE
    low_nbr  NUMBER(38,127);
    high_nbr NUMBER(38,-84);
BEGIN
    /* 127 is largest scale, so begin with 1 and move
       decimal point 127 places to the left. Easy. */
    low_nbr := 1E-127;
    DBMS_OUTPUT.PUT_LINE('low_nbr = ' || low_nbr);

    /* -84 is smallest scale value. Add 37 to normalize
       the scientific-notation, and we get E+121. */
    high_nbr := 9.9999999999999999999999999999999999999E+121;
    DBMS_OUTPUT.PUT_LINE('high_nbr = ' || high_nbr);
END;
```

The output is:

```
low_nbr =
1.000000000000000000000000000000000000000000000000000000000000000000000000000
000000000000000E-127
high_nbr =
9.999999999999999999999999999999999999900000000000000000000000000000000000000
000000000000000E+121
```

As before, low_nbr represents the low end of the positive range and high_nbr the high end. One difference is that when working with fixed-point numbers, you are limited to 38 significant digits.

Given the wide range and versatility of the NUMBER datatype, it's no wonder that it's so widely used. Using simply NUMBER in your declarations, you can represent floating-point values. By constraining those numbers using *precision* and *scale*, you can represent fixed-point decimal numbers. By setting *scale* to zero or omitting it entirely, you can represent integer values. One datatype covers all the bases.

## The PLS_INTEGER Type

The PLS_INTEGER datatype stores signed integers in the range –2,147,483,648 through 2,147,483,647. Values are represented using your hardware platform's native integer format.

Following is an example of some PLS_INTEGER declarations:

```
DECLARE
    loop_counter PLS_INTEGER;
    days_in_standard_year CONSTANT PLS_INTEGER := 365;
    emp_vacation_days PLS_INTEGER DEFAULT 14;
```

The PLS_INTEGER datatype was designed for speed. Prior to Oracle Database 10g, PLS_INTEGER was the only integer datatype that used native machine arithmetic. All other numeric datatypes used the C language arithmetic library used with the NUMBER datatype. When you perform arithmetic using PLS_INTEGER values, the Oracle software uses native machine arithmetic. As a result, it's faster to manipulate PLS_INTEGER values than it is to manipulate integers in the NUMBER datatype. Because PLS_INTEGER values are integers, you generally won't run into any compatibility issues as you move from one hardware platform to the next.

I recommend that you consider using PLS_INTEGER whenever you're faced with intensive, integer arithmetic. Bear in mind, however, that if your use of PLS_INTEGER results in frequent conversions to and from the NUMBER type, you may be better off using NUMBER to begin with. You'll gain the greatest efficiency when you use PLS_INTEGER for integer arithmetic (and for loop counters) in cases where you can avoid conversions back and forth to the NUMBER type. When this datatype is used in integer arithmetic, the resulting values are rounded to whole numbers, as shown in this example:

```
DECLARE
 int1 PLS_INTEGER;
 int2 PLS_INTEGER;
 int3 PLS_INTEGER;
  nbr  NUMBER;
BEGIN
  int1 := 100;
  int2 := 49;
  int3 := int2/int1;
  nbr  := int2/int1;
  DBMS_OUTPUT.PUT_LINE('integer 49/100 =' || TO_CHAR(int3));
  DBMS_OUTPUT.PUT_LINE('number  49/100 =' || TO_CHAR(nbr));
  int2 := 50;
  int3 := int2/int1;
  nbr  := int2/int1;
  DBMS_OUTPUT.PUT_LINE('integer 50/100 =' || TO_CHAR(int3));
  DBMS_OUTPUT.PUT_LINE('number  50/100 =' || TO_CHAR(nbr));
END;
```

This gives the following output:

```
integer 49/100 =0
number  49/100 =.49
integer 50/100 =1
number  50/100 =.5
```

If the resultant value of integer arithmetic is out of the range of valid values (–2,147,483,648 through 2,147,483,647), you will encounter a *numeric overflow* error.

## The BINARY_INTEGER Type

The BINARY_INTEGER datatype also allows you to store signed integers in a binary format. The semantics of this datatype changed in Oracle Database 10g Release 1. Beginning with that release, BINARY_INTEGER is equivalent to PLS_INTEGER. In Oracle9i Database Release 2 and earlier releases, BINARY_INTEGER differed from

PLS_INTEGER in that Oracle implemented it using platform-independent library code.

Curiously, the package STANDARD looks like it constrains the BINARY_INTEGER type to the values –2,147,483,647 through 2,147,483,647, but I have encountered no exceptions assigning values from –2,147,483,648 through 2,147,483,647, which is a slightly larger range on the negative side.

```
subtype BINARY_INTEGER is INTEGER range '-2147483647'..2147483647;
```

I don't recommend using BINARY_INTEGER for new work. The only reason to use BINARY_INTEGER for new work is if you need your code to run on releases of Oracle prior to 7.3 (before PLS_INTEGER was introduced). I hope you're not running anything that old!

## The SIMPLE_INTEGER Type

The SIMPLE_INTEGER datatype is new to Oracle Database 11g. This datatype is a performance-enhanced version of PLS_INTEGER with a few caveats. The SIMPLE_INTEGER datatype has the same range of values as PLS_INTEGER (–2,147,483,648 through 2,147,483,647), but it does not support NULL values nor does it check for overflow conditions. So, you may be wondering why you would want to use this seemingly defective clone of PLS_INTEGER. Well, if you compile your code natively and your situation is such that your variable will never be NULL nor will it overflow, then the SIMPLE_INTEGER type will scream with better performance. Consider this example:

```
/* File on web: simple_integer_demo.sql */
-- First create a compute intensive procedure using PLS_INTEGER
CREATE OR REPLACE PROCEDURE pls_test (iterations IN PLS_INTEGER)
AS
   int1       PLS_INTEGER := 1;
   int2       PLS_INTEGER := 2;
   begints    timestamp;
   endts      timestamp;
BEGIN
   begints := SYSTIMESTAMP;

   FOR cnt IN 1 .. iterations
   LOOP
      int1 := int1 + int2;
   END LOOP;

   endts := SYSTIMESTAMP;
   DBMS_OUTPUT.put_line(   iterations
                        || ' iterations had run time of:'
                        || TO_CHAR (endts - begints));
END;
/

-- Next create the same procedure using SIMPLE_INTEGER
```

```
CREATE OR REPLACE PROCEDURE simple_test (iterations IN SIMPLE_INTEGER)
AS
   int1      SIMPLE_INTEGER := 1;
   int2      SIMPLE_INTEGER := 2;
   begints   timestamp;
   endts     timestamp;
BEGIN
   begints := SYSTIMESTAMP;

   FOR cnt IN 1 .. iterations
   LOOP
      int1 := int1 + int2;
   END LOOP;

   endts := SYSTIMESTAMP;
   DBMS_OUTPUT.put_line(   iterations
                        || ' iterations had run time of:'
                        || TO_CHAR (endts - begints));
END;
/

-- first recompile the procedures to as interpreted
ALTER PROCEDURE pls_test COMPILE PLSQL_CODE_TYPE=INTERPRETED;
/

ALTER PROCEDURE simple_test COMPILE PLSQL_CODE_TYPE=INTERPRETED
/

-- compare the run times
BEGIN pls_test(123456789); END;
/
123456789 iterations had run time of:+000000000 00:00:06.375000000

BEGIN simple_test(123456789); END;
/
123456789 iterations had run time of:+000000000 00:00:06.000000000

-- recompile with to native code
ALTER PROCEDURE pls_test COMPILE PLSQL_CODE_TYPE=NATIVE
/

ALTER PROCEDURE simple_test COMPILE PLSQL_CODE_TYPE= NATIVE
/

-- compare the run times
BEGIN pls_test(123456789); END;
/
123456789 iterations had run time of:+000000000 00:00:03.703000000

BEGIN simple_test(123456789); END;
/
123456789 iterations had run time of:+000000000 00:00:01.203000000
```

You can see from this example that SIMPLE_INTEGER gave a slight performance edge with interpreted code (6% in this test on a Microsoft Windows server). Both

PLS_INTEGER and SIMPLE_INTEGER are faster when compiled natively, but the native SIMPLE_INTEGER was over 300% faster than the native PLS_INTEGER! As a learning exercise, try this test with a NUMBER type also—I found SIMPLE_INTEGER over 1000% faster than NUMBER. On a Linux server running Oracle Database 11g Release 2, I measured similarly large performance differences using SIMPLE_INTEGER (often several hundred percent faster than alternative numeric types).

## The BINARY_FLOAT and BINARY_DOUBLE Types

Oracle Database 10g introduced two, new floating-point types: BINARY_FLOAT and BINARY_DOUBLE. These types conform to the single- and double-precision floating-point types defined in the IEEE-754 floating-point standard. They are implemented by both PL/SQL and the database engine itself, so you can use them in table definitions as well as in your PL/SQL code. Table 9-4 compares these new types to the venerable NUMBER type.

*Table 9-4. Comparison of floating-point types*

| Characteristic | BINARY_FLOAT | BINARY_DOUBLE | NUMBER |
|---|---|---|---|
| Maximum absolute value | 3.40282347E+38F | 1.7976931348623157E+308 | 9.999...999E+121 (38 9s total) |
| Minimum absolute value | 1.17549435E-38F | 2.2250748585072014E-308 | 1.0E-127 |
| Number of bytes used for the value | 4 (32 bits) | 8 (64 bits) | varies from 1 to 20 |
| Number of length bytes | 0 | 0 | 1 |
| Representation | Binary, IEEE-754 | Binary, IEEE-754 | Decimal |
| Literal suffix | f | d | None |

To write literals of these new types, you apply a suffix, either f or d depending on whether you want your literal to be interpreted as a BINARY_FLOAT or as a BINARY_DOUBLE. For example:

```
DECLARE
    my_binary_float  BINARY_FLOAT  := .95f;
    my_binary_double BINARY_DOUBLE := .95d;
    my_number        NUMBER        := .95;
```

There are also some special literals you can use when working with the IEEE-754 floating-point types. The following are supported by both PL/SQL and SQL:

*BINARY_FLOAT_NAN and BINARY_DOUBLE_NAN*
    Represents "not a number" in single or double precision, respectively.

*BINARY_FLOAT_INFINITY, BINARY_DOUBLE_INFINITY*
    Represents infinity in single or double precision, respectively.

This next batch of literals is supported *only* by PL/SQL:

*BINARY_FLOAT_MIN_NORMAL, BINARY_FLOAT_MAX_NORMAL*
Defines the normal range of values you should plan on storing in single- and double-precision variables, respectively.

*BINARY_FLOAT_MIN_SUBNORMAL, BINARY_FLOAT_MAX_SUBNORMAL*
Defines what is referred to as the *subnormal* range of values. Subnormal values are a part of the IEEE-754 standard that's designed to reduce problems caused by underflow to zero.

Finally, there are some predicates to use with these datatypes:

*IS NAN and IS NOT NAN*
Determines whether an IEEE-754 value is *not-a-number.*

*IS INFINITE and IS NOT INFINITE*
Determines whether an IEEE-754 value represents infinity.

It's *very* important to understand that these BINARY types are indeed binary. I do not recommend them for any situation in which exact, decimal representation is critical. The following code block illustrates why, for example, I would not use the new, binary types to represent monetary values:

```
BEGIN
    DBMS_OUTPUT.PUT_LINE(0.95f); --BINARY_FLOAT
    DBMS_OUTPUT.PUT_LINE(0.95d); --BINARY_DOUBLE
    DBMS_OUTPUT.PUT_LINE(0.95);  --NUMBER
END;
```

This example gives us:

```
9.49999988E-001
9.4999999999999996E-001
.95
```

Just as some fractions, such as 1/3, are not possible to represent precisely as decimal numbers, you'll often encounter cases where decimal numbers cannot be represented precisely as binary values. The decimal value 0.95 is just one such case. When dealing with money, use NUMBER.

 Be careful when mixing floating-point types in comparisons. For example:

```
BEGIN
    IF 0.95f = 0.95d
    THEN
        DBMS_OUTPUT.PUT_LINE('TRUE');
    ELSE
        DBMS_OUTPUT.PUT_LINE('FALSE');
    END IF;

    IF ABS(0.95f - 0.95d) < 0.000001d
    THEN
        DBMS_OUTPUT.PUT_LINE('TRUE');
    ELSE
        DBMS_OUTPUT.PUT_LINE('FALSE');
```

```
        END IF;
    END;
```

Which results in:

```
    FALSE
    TRUE
```

This output of FALSE and TRUE, respectively, illustrates the kind of subtle problem you can run into when representing decimal values in binary form. The BINARY_DOUBLE representation of 0.95 has more digits than the BINARY_FLOAT version, and thus the two values do not compare as equal. The second comparison is TRUE because, to compensate for the fact that 0.95 cannot be represented precisely in binary, we arbitrarily accept the two values being compared as equal whenever the magnitude of their difference is less than one one-millionth.

When would you want to use the IEEE-754 types? One reason to use them is performance, and another is conformance to IEEE standards. If you are performing extensive, numeric computations, you may see a significant increase in performance from using the IEEE-754 types. I ran the following code block, which reports the time needed to compute the area of 500,000 circles and to compute 5,000,000 sines. Both tasks are performed twice, once using BINARY_DOUBLE and once using NUMBER:

```
/* File on web: binary_performance.sql */
DECLARE
    bd BINARY_DOUBLE;
    bd_area BINARY_DOUBLE;
    bd_sine BINARY_DOUBLE;
    nm NUMBER;
    nm_area NUMBER;
    nm_sine NUMBER;
    pi_bd BINARY_DOUBLE := 3.1415926536d;
    pi_nm NUMBER := 3.1415926536;
    bd_begin TIMESTAMP(9);
    bd_end TIMESTAMP(9);
    bd_wall_time INTERVAL DAY TO SECOND(9);
    nm_begin TIMESTAMP(9);
    nm_end TIMESTAMP(9);
    nm_wall_time INTERVAL DAY TO SECOND(9);
BEGIN
    --Compute area 5,000,000 times using binary doubles
    bd_begin := SYSTIMESTAMP;
    bd := 1d;
    LOOP
        bd_area := bd * bd * pi_bd;
        bd := bd + 1d;
        EXIT WHEN bd > 5000000;
    END LOOP;
    bd_end := SYSTIMESTAMP;

    --Compute area 5,000,000 times using NUMBERs
    nm_begin := SYSTIMESTAMP;
```

```
      nm := 1;
      LOOP
         nm_area := nm * nm * 2 * pi_nm;
         nm := nm + 1;
         EXIT WHEN nm > 5000000;
      END LOOP;
      nm_end := SYSTIMESTAMP;

      --Compute and display elapsed, wall-clock time
      bd_wall_time := bd_end - bd_begin;
      nm_wall_time := nm_end - nm_begin;
      DBMS_OUTPUT.PUT_LINE('BINARY_DOUBLE area = ' || bd_wall_time);
      DBMS_OUTPUT.PUT_LINE('NUMBER        area = ' || nm_wall_time);

      --Compute sine 5,000,000 times using binary doubles
      bd_begin := SYSTIMESTAMP;
      bd := 1d;
      LOOP
         bd_sine := sin(bd);
         bd := bd + 1d;
         EXIT WHEN bd > 5000000;
      END LOOP;
      bd_end := SYSTIMESTAMP;

       --Compute sine 5,000,000 times using NUMBERs
      nm_begin := SYSTIMESTAMP;
      nm := 1;
      LOOP
         nm_sine := sin(nm);
         nm := nm + 1;
         EXIT WHEN nm > 5000000;
      END LOOP;
      nm_end := SYSTIMESTAMP;

      --Compute and display elapsed, wall-clock time for sine
      bd_wall_time := bd_end - bd_begin;
      nm_wall_time := nm_end - nm_begin;
      DBMS_OUTPUT.PUT_LINE('BINARY_DOUBLE sine = ' || bd_wall_time);
      DBMS_OUTPUT.PUT_LINE('NUMBER        sine = ' || nm_wall_time);
   END;
```

My results, which were reasonably consistent over multiple runs, look like this:

```
BINARY_DOUBLE area = +00 00:00:02.792692000
NUMBER        area = +00 00:00:08.942327000
BINARY_DOUBLE sine = +00 00:00:04.149930000
NUMBER        sine = +00 00:07:37.596783000
```

Be careful with benchmarks, including those I show above! As this example illustrates, the range of possible performance gains from using an IEEE-754 type over NUMBER is quite vast. Using BINARY_DOUBLE, you can compute the area of a circle 5 million times in approximately 40% of the time as when using NUMBER. If you decide to compute sine 5 million times, however, you can get that done in 0.9% of the time. The gain you get in a given situation depends on the computations involved. The message

---

to take away here is *not* that IEEE-754 will get things done a fixed percentage faster than NUMBER. It is that the potential performance improvement from using IEEE-754 over NUMBER is well worth considering and investigating when you're performing extensive calculations.

There are, however, a few areas in which Oracle's implementation of binary floating-point does not conform perfectly to the IEEE-754 standard. For example, Oracle co-erces –0 to +0, whereas the IEEE-754 standard does not call for that behavior. If con-formance is important to your application, check the section on "Datatypes" in Oracle's *SQL Reference* manual for the precise details on how and when Oracle diverges from the IEEE-754 standard.

---

### Mixing the Floating-Point Types

Oracle enforces an order of precedence on the implicit conversion of floating-point types. From highest to lowest priority, that precedence is BINARY_DOUBLE, BINARY_FLOAT, and NUMBER. When you write an expression containing a mix of these types, the database attempts to convert all values in the expression to the highest precedence type found in the expression. For example, if you mix BINARY_FLOAT and NUMBER, Oracle first converts all values to BINARY_FLOAT.

If you don't want the database to perform these implicit conversions, you should use the functions TO_NUMBER, TO_BINARY_FLOAT and TO_BINARY_DOUBLE. For example:

```
DECLARE
    nbr NUMBER := 0.95;
    bf BINARY_FLOAT := 2;
    nbr1 NUMBER;
    nbr2 NUMBER;
BEGIN
    --Default precedence, promote to binary_float
    nbr1 := nbr * bf;

    --Demote BINARY_FLOAT to NUMBER instead
    nbr2 := nbr * TO_NUMBER(bf);

    DBMS_OUTPUT.PUT_LINE(nbr1);
    DBMS_OUTPUT.PUT_LINE(nbr2);
END;
```

This results in:

```
1.89999998
1.9
```

To avoid the ambiguity and possible errors involving implicit conversions, I recom-mend explicit conversions, such as with the functions TO_NUMBER, TO_BINARY_FLOAT, and TO_BINARY_DOUBLE.

---

## The SIMPLE_FLOAT and SIMPLE_DOUBLE Types

The SIMPLE_FLOAT and SIMPLE_DOUBLE datatypes are new to Oracle Database 11g. These datatypes are performance-enhanced versions of the BINARY_FLOAT and BINARY_DOUBLE datatypes—but they do not support NULL values. Like the SIMPLE_INTEGER type, under the right conditions, these speedy cousins will make your code much faster when they are compiled natively.

## Numeric Subtypes

Oracle also provides several *numeric subtypes*. Most of the time, these subtypes are simply alternate names for the basic types I have just discussed. These alternate names offer compatibility with ISO SQL, SQL/DS, and DB2 datatypes, and usually have the same range of legal values as their base type. Sometimes, subtypes offer additional functionality by restricting values to a subset of those supported by their base type. These subtypes are described in Table 9-5.

*Table 9-5. Predefined numeric subtypes*

| Subtype | Compatibility | Corresponding Oracle datatype/notes |
| --- | --- | --- |
| DEC (*precision, scale*) | ANSI | NUMBER (*precision, scale*) |
| DECIMAL (*precision, scale*) | IBM | NUMBER (*precision, scale*) |
| DOUBLE PRECISION | ANSI | NUMBER, with 126 binary digits of precision |
| FLOAT | ANSI, IBM | NUMBER, with 126 binary digits of precision |
| FLOAT (*binary_precision*) | ANSI, IBM | NUMBER, with a *binary_precision* of up to 126 (the default) |
| INT | ANSI | NUMBER(38) |
| INTEGER | ANSI, IBM | NUMBER(38) |
| NATURAL | N/A | PLS_INTEGER,[a] but allows only nonnegative values (0 and higher) |
| NATURALN | N/A | Same as NATURAL, but with the additional restriction of never being NULL |
| NUMERIC (*precision, scale*) | ANSI | NUMBER (*precision, scale*) |
| POSITIVE | N/A | PLS_INTEGER,[a] but allows only positive values (1 and higher) |
| POSITIVEN | N/A | Same as POSITIVE, but with the additional restriction of never being NULL |
| REAL | ANSI | NUMBER, with 63 binary digits of precision |
| SIGNTYPE | N/A | PLS_INTEGER,[a] limited to the values −1, 0, and 1 |
| SMALLINT | ANSI, IBM | NUMBER (38) |

[a] BINARY_INTEGER prior to Oracle Database 10g

The NUMERIC, DECIMAL, and DEC datatypes can declare only fixed-point numbers. DOUBLE PRECISION and REAL are equivalent to NUMBER. FLOAT allows floating decimal points with binary precisions that range from 63 to 126 bits. I don't find it all that useful to define a number's precision in terms of bits rather than digits. I also don't find much use for the ISO/IBM compatible subtypes, and I don't believe you will either.

The subtypes that I sometimes find useful are the PLS_INTEGER subtypes. NATURAL and POSITIVE are both subtypes of PLS_INTEGER. These subtypes constrain the values you can store in a variable, and their use can make a program more self-documenting. For example, if you have a variable whose values must always be nonnegative, you can declare that variable to be NATURAL (0 and higher) or POSITIVE (1 and higher), improving the self-documenting aspect of your code.

# Number Conversions

Computers work with numbers best when those numbers are in some kind of binary format. We humans, on the other hand, prefer to see our numbers in the form of character strings containing digits, commas, and other punctuation. PL/SQL allows you to convert numbers back and forth between human- and machine-readable form. You'll usually perform such conversions using the TO_CHAR and TO_NUMBER functions.

When working with the IEEE-754, binary floating-point types, use TO_BINARY_FLOAT and TO_BINARY_DOUBLE. To simplify the discussion that follows, I'll generally refer only to TO_NUMBER. Please assume that any unqualified references to TO_NUMBER also apply to the TO_BINARY_FLOAT and TO_BINARY_DOUBLE functions.

## The TO_NUMBER Function

The TO_NUMBER function explicitly converts both fixed- and variable-length strings as well as IEEE-754 floating point types to the NUMBER datatype using an optional format mask. Use TO_NUMBER whenever you need to convert character string representations of numbers into their corresponding numeric value. Invoke TO_NUMBER as follows:

```
TO_NUMBER(string [,format [,nls_params]])
```

where:

*string*

Is a string or BINARY_DOUBLE expression containing the representation of a number.

When using TO_BINARY_FLOAT and TO_BINARY_DOUBLE, you may use the strings 'INF' and '-INF' to represent positive and negative infinity. You may also use 'NaN' to represent "not a number." These special strings are case-insensitive.

*format*

Is an optional format mask that specifies how TO_NUMBER should interpret the character representation of the number contained in the first parameter if it is a string expression.

*nls_params*

Is an optional string specifying various NLS parameter values. You can use this to override your current, session-level NLS parameter settings.

### Using TO_NUMBER with no format

In many straightforward cases, you can use TO_NUMBER to convert strings to numbers without specifying any format string at all. For example, all of the following conversions work just fine:

```
DECLARE
    a NUMBER;
    b NUMBER;
    c NUMBER;
    d NUMBER;
    e BINARY_FLOAT;
    f BINARY_DOUBLE;
    g BINARY_DOUBLE;

    n1 VARCHAR2(20) := '-123456.78';
    n2 VARCHAR2(20) := '+123456.78';
BEGIN
    a := TO_NUMBER('123.45');
    b := TO_NUMBER(n1);
    c := TO_NUMBER(n2);
    d := TO_NUMBER('1.25E2');
    e := TO_BINARY_FLOAT('123.45');
    f := TO_BINARY_DOUBLE('inf');
    g := TO_BINARY_DOUBLE('NAN');
END;
```

Generally, you should be able to use TO_NUMBER without specifying a format when the following conditions apply:

- Your number is represented using only digits and a single decimal point.

- Any sign is leading, and must be either minus (-) or plus (+). If no sign is present, the number is assumed to be positive.

- Scientific notation is used—for example, 1.25E2.

If your character strings don't meet these criteria or if you need to round values to a specific number of decimal digits, then you need to invoke TO_NUMBER with a format model.

## Using TO_NUMBER with a format model

Using TO_NUMBER with a format model enables you to deal with a much wider range of numeric representations than TO_NUMBER would otherwise recognize. Table B-1 (in Appendix B) gives a complete list of all supported number format model elements. For example, you can specify the location of group separators and the currency symbol:

```
a := TO_NUMBER('$123,456.78','L999G999D99');
```

You don't necessarily need to specify the exact number of digits in your format model. TO_NUMBER is forgiving in this respect as long as your model contains more digits than are in your actual value. For example, the following will work:

```
a := TO_NUMBER('$123,456.78','L999G999G999D99');
```

However, if you have more digits to the left or to the right of the decimal point than your format allows, the conversion will fail with an *ORA-06502: PL/SQL: numeric or value* error. The first of the following conversions will fail because the string contains ten digits to the left of the decimal, while the format calls for only nine. The second conversion will fail because there are too many digits to the right of the decimal point:

```
a := TO_NUMBER('$1234,567,890.78','L999G999G999D99');
a := TO_NUMBER('$234,567,890.789','L999G999G999D99');
```

You can force leading zeros using the 0 format element:

```
a := TO_NUMBER('001,234','000G000');
```

You can recognize angle-bracketed numbers as negative numbers using the PR element:

```
a := TO_NUMBER('<123.45>','999D99PR');
```

However, not all format elements can be used to convert strings to numbers. Some elements, such as RN for Roman numerals, are output only. The following attempt to convert the Roman numeral representation of a value to a number will fail:

```
a := TO_NUMBER('cxx111','rn');
```

EEEE is another output-only format, but that's OK because you don't need it to convert values that are correctly represented in scientific notation. You can simply do:

```
a := TO_NUMBER('1.23456E-24');
```

## Passing NLS settings to TO_NUMBER

Many of the number format model elements listed in Table B-1 ultimately derive their meaning from one of the NLS parameters. For example, the G element represents the numeric group separator, which is the second character in the NLS_NUMERIC_CHARACTERS setting in effect when the conversion takes place. You can view current NLS parameter settings by querying the NLS_SESSION_PARAMETERS view:

```
SQL> SELECT * FROM nls_session_parameters;

PARAMETER                   VALUE
------------------------    ----------------
NLS_LANGUAGE                AMERICAN
NLS_TERRITORY               AMERICA
NLS_CURRENCY                $
NLS_ISO_CURRENCY            AMERICA
NLS_NUMERIC_CHARACTERS      .,
NLS_CALENDAR                GREGORIAN
NLS_DATE_FORMAT             DD-MON-RR
```

Some NLS parameter settings are by default dependent on others. For example, set NLS_TERRITORY to AMERICA, and Oracle defaults NLS_NUMERIC_CHARACTERS TO ".,". If you need to, you can then override the NLS_NUMERIC_CHARACTERS setting (using an ALTER SESSION command, for example).

On rare occasions, you may want to override specific NLS parameter settings for a single call to TO_NUMBER. In the following example, I invoke TO_NUMBER and specify NLS settings corresponding to NLS_TERRITORY=FRANCE:

```
a := TO_NUMBER('F123.456,78','L999G999D99',
               'NLS_NUMERIC_CHARACTERS='',.'''
            || ' NLS_CURRENCY=''F'''
            || ' NLS_ISO_CURRENCY=FRANCE');
```

Because my NLS parameter string is so long, I've broken it up into three separate strings concatenated together so that our example fits nicely on the page. Note my doubling of quote characters. The setting I want for NLS_NUMERIC_CHARACTERS is:

```
NLS_NUMERIC_CHARACTERS=',.'
```

I need to embed this setting into our NLS parameter string, and to embed quotes within a string I must double them, so I end up with:

```
'NLS_NUMERIC_CHARACTERS='',.'''
```

The three NLS parameters set in this example are the only three you can set via TO_NUMBER. I don't know why that is. It certainly would be much more convenient if you could simply do the following:

```
a := TO_NUMBER('F123.456,78','L999G999D99','NLS_TERRITORY=FRANCE');
```

But unfortunately, NLS_TERRITORY is not something you can set via a call to TO_NUMBER. You are limited to specifying NLS_NUMERIC_CHARACTERS, NLS_CURRENCY, and NLS_ISO_CURRENCY.

 For detailed information on setting the various NLS parameters, see Oracle's *Globalization Support Guide*, which is part of the Oracle Database 11g documentation set.

Avoid using the third argument to TO_NUMBER; I believe it's better to rely on session settings to drive the way in which PL/SQL interprets format model elements such as L, G, and D. Instead of your having to hardcode such information throughout your programs, session settings can be controlled by the user outside the bounds of your code.

## The TO_CHAR Function

The TO_CHAR function is the converse of TO_NUMBER, and converts numbers to their character representations. Using an optional format mask, you can be quite specific about the form those character representations take. Invoke TO_CHAR as follows:

```
TO_CHAR(number [,format [,nls_params]])
```

where:

*number*

Is a number that you want to represent in character form. This number may be any of PL/SQL's numeric types: NUMBER, PLS_INTEGER, BINARY_INTEGER, BINARY_FLOAT, BINARY_DOUBLE, SIMPLE_INTEGER, SIMPLE_FLOAT, and SIMPLE_DOUBLE.

*format*

Is an optional format mask that specifies how TO_CHAR should present the number in character form.

*nls_params*

Is an optional string specifying various NLS parameter values. You can use this to override your current session-level NLS parameter settings.

 If you want your results to be in the national character set, you can use TO_NCHAR in place of TO_CHAR. In that case, be certain you provide your number format string in the national character set as well. Otherwise, you may receive output consisting of all number signs: #.

### Using TO_CHAR with no format

As with TO_NUMBER, you can invoke TO_CHAR without specifying a format mask:

```
DECLARE
   b VARCHAR2(30);
BEGIN
   b := TO_CHAR(123456789.01);
   DBMS_OUTPUT.PUT_LINE(b);
END;
```

The output is:

```
123456789.01
```

Unlike the situation with TO_NUMBER, you aren't likely to find this use of TO_CHAR very useful. At the very least, you may want to format your numeric output with group separators to make it more readable.

### Using TO_CHAR with a format model

When converting numbers to their character string equivalents, you'll most often invoke TO_CHAR with a format model. For example, you can output a monetary amount as follows:

```
DECLARE
    b VARCHAR2(30);
BEGIN
    b := TO_CHAR(123456789.01,'L999G999G999D99');
    DBMS_OUTPUT.PUT_LINE(b);
END;
```

The output (in the United States) is:

```
$123,456,789.01
```

The format model elements in Table B-1 (in Appendix B) give you a lot of flexibility, and you should experiment with them to learn the finer points of how they work. The following example specifies that leading zeros be maintained, but the B format element is used to force any zero values to blanks. Notice that the B element precedes the number elements (the 0s) but follows the currency indicator (the L):

```
DECLARE
    b VARCHAR2(30);
    c VARCHAR2(30);
BEGIN
    b := TO_CHAR(123.01,'LB000G000G009D99');
    DBMS_OUTPUT.PUT_LINE(b);

    c := TO_CHAR(0,'LB000G000G009D99');
    DBMS_OUTPUT.PUT_LINE(c);
END;
```

The output is:

```
$000,000,123.01
```

You see only one line of output from this example, and that's from the first conversion. The second conversion involves a zero value, and the B format element causes TO_CHAR to return that value as a blank string, even though the format otherwise specifies that leading zeros be returned. As an experiment, try this same example on your system, but leave off the B.

Not all combinations of format elements are possible. For example, you can't use LRN to place a currency symbol in front of a value expressed in Roman numerals. Oracle doesn't document every such nuance. It takes some experience and some experimenting to get a feel for what's possible and what's not.

### The V format element

The V format element is unusual enough to warrant a special explanation. The V element allows you to scale a value, and its operation is best explained through an illustration, which you'll find in Figure 9-4.

Why would you ever need such functionality? Look no further than the stock market for an example. The standard trading unit for stocks is 100 shares, and stock sales are sometimes reported in terms of the number of 100-share units sold. Thus, a sales figure of 123 actually represents 123 units of 100 shares, or 12,300 shares. The following example shows how V can be used to scale a value such as 123 in recognition of the fact that it really represents 100s:

```
DECLARE
   shares_sold NUMBER := 123;
BEGIN
   DBMS_OUTPUT.PUT_LINE(
      TO_CHAR(shares_sold,'999G9V99')
   );
END;
```

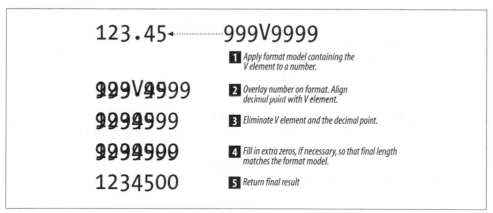

Figure 9-4. The V number format element

The output is:

```
12,300
```

Notice that the format model in this example includes the G element to specify the location of the group separator (the comma) in the displayed number. You can specify group separators only to the left of the V element, not to the right. This is unfortunate. Consider the following, perfectly reasonable format model:

```
TO_CHAR(123.45,'9G99V9G999');
```

You would hope to get the result formatted as 1,234,500. However, the G to the right of the V is invalid. You can use 9G99V9999 to get a result of 1,234500, or you can use 999V9999 to get a result of 1234500. Neither result is as readable as you would like it to be.

You probably won't use the V element very often, but it's worth knowing about this bit of interesting functionality.

### Rounding when converting numbers to character strings

When converting character strings to numbers, you'll get an error any time you have more digits to the left or right of the decimal point than the format model allows. When converting numbers to characters, however, you'll get an error only if the number requires more digits to the left of the decimal point than the format model allows. If you specify fewer decimal digits (i.e., digits to the right of the decimal point) in your format model than the number requires, the number will be rounded so that the fractional portion fits your model.

When a conversion fails because the model doesn't specify enough digits to the left of the decimal point, TO_CHAR returns a string of number signs (#). For example, the following conversion fails because 123 doesn't fit into two digits:

```
DECLARE
   b VARCHAR2(30);
BEGIN
   b := TO_CHAR(123.4567,'99.99');
   DBMS_OUTPUT.PUT_LINE(b);
END;

######
```

It's perfectly OK, however, for your model not to include enough digits to cover the fractional portion of a value. In such cases, rounding occurs. For example:

```
BEGIN
   DBMS_OUTPUT.PUT_LINE(TO_CHAR(123.4567,'999.99'));
   DBMS_OUTPUT.PUT_LINE(TO_CHAR(123.4567,'999'));
END;

123.46
123
```

Digits 5 and higher are rounded up, which is why 123.4567 is rounded up to 123.46. Digits less than 5 are rounded down, so 123.4xxx will always be rounded down to 123.

### Dealing with spaces when converting numbers to character strings

A reasonably common problem encountered when converting numbers to character strings is that TO_CHAR always leaves room for the minus sign even when numbers are positive. By default, TO_CHAR will leave one space in front of a number for use by a potential minus sign (-):

```
DECLARE
    b VARCHAR2(30);
    c VARCHAR2(30);
BEGIN
    b := TO_CHAR(-123.4,'999.99');
    c := TO_CHAR(123.4,'999.99');
    DBMS_OUTPUT.PUT_LINE(':' || b || ' ' || TO_CHAR(LENGTH(b)));
    DBMS_OUTPUT.PUT_LINE(':' || c || ' ' || TO_CHAR(LENGTH(c)));
END;
```

The output is:

```
:-123.40 7
: 123.40 7
```

Notice that both converted values have the same length, seven characters, even though the positive number requires only six characters when displayed in character form. That leading space can be a big help if you are trying to get columns of numbers to line up. However, it can be a bit of a pain if for some reason you need a compact number with no spaces whatsoever.

 Use the PR element, and your positive numbers will have one leading space and one trailing space to accommodate the potential enclosing angle brackets. Spaces will be left to accommodate whatever sign indicator you choose in your format model.

There are a couple of approaches you can take if you really need your numbers converted to characters without leading or trailing spaces. One approach is to use the TM format model element to get the "text minimum" representation of a number:

```
DECLARE
    b VARCHAR2(30);
    c VARCHAR2(30);
BEGIN
    b := TO_CHAR(-123.4,'TM9');
    c := TO_CHAR(123.4,'TM9');
    DBMS_OUTPUT.PUT_LINE(':' || b || ' ' || TO_CHAR(LENGTH(b)));
    DBMS_OUTPUT.PUT_LINE(':' || c || ' ' || TO_CHAR(LENGTH(c)));
END;
```

The output is:

```
:-123.4 6
:123.4 5
```

The TM approach works, but doesn't allow you to specify any other formatting information. You can't, for example, specify TM999.99 in order to get a fixed two decimal digits. If you need to specify other formatting information or if TM is not available in your release of PL/SQL, you'll need to trim the results of the conversion:

```
DECLARE
    b VARCHAR2(30);
    c VARCHAR2(30);
BEGIN
    b := LTRIM(TO_CHAR(-123.4,'999.99'));
    c := LTRIM(TO_CHAR(123.4,'999.99'));
    DBMS_OUTPUT.PUT_LINE(':' || b || ' ' || TO_CHAR(LENGTH(b)));
    DBMS_OUTPUT.PUT_LINE(':' || c || ' ' || TO_CHAR(LENGTH(c)));
END;
```

The output is:

```
:-123.40 7
:123.40 6
```

Here I've used LTRIM to remove any potential leading spaces, and I've successfully preserved our fixed two digits to the right of the decimal point. Use RTRIM if you are placing the sign to the right of the number (e.g., via the MI element) or TRIM if you are using something like PR that affects both sides of the number.

### Passing NLS settings to TO_CHAR

As with TO_NUMBER, you have the option of passing a string of NLS parameter settings to TO_CHAR. For example:

```
BEGIN
    DBMS_OUTPUT.PUT_LINE(
        TO_CHAR(123456.78,'999G999D99','NLS_NUMERIC_CHARACTERS='',.''')
    );
END;
```

The output is:

```
123.456,78
```

The three NLS parameters you can set this way are NLS_NUMERIC_CHARACTERS, NLS_CURRENCY, and NLS_ISO_CURRENCY. See "Passing NLS settings to TO_NUMBER" on page 249 for an example of all three being set at once.

## The CAST Function

The CAST function is used to convert numbers to strings and vice versa. The general format of the CAST function is as follows:

```
CAST (expression AS datatype)
```

The following example shows CAST being used first to convert a NUMBER to a VARCHAR2 string, and then to convert the characters in a VARCHAR2 string into their corresponding numeric value:

```
DECLARE
    a NUMBER := -123.45;
    a1 VARCHAR2(30);
    b VARCHAR2(30) := '-123.45';
    b1 NUMBER;
    b2 BINARY_FLOAT;
    b3 BINARY_DOUBLE;
BEGIN
    a1 := CAST (a AS VARCHAR2);
    b1 := CAST (b AS NUMBER);
    b2 := CAST (b AS BINARY_FLOAT);
    b3 := CAST (b AS BINARY_DOUBLE);
    DBMS_OUTPUT.PUT_LINE(a1);
    DBMS_OUTPUT.PUT_LINE(b1);
    DBMS_OUTPUT.PUT_LINE(b2);
    DBMS_OUTPUT.PUT_LINE(b3);
END;
```

The output is:

```
-123.45
-123.45
-1.23449997E+002
-1.2345E+002
```

CAST has the disadvantage of not supporting the use of number format models. An advantage to CAST, however, is that it is part of the ISO SQL standard, whereas the TO_CHAR and TO_NUMBER functions are not. If writing 100% ANSI-compliant code is important to you, you should investigate the use of CAST. Otherwise, I recommend using the traditional TO_NUMBER and TO_CHAR functions.

 Because PL/SQL is not part of the ISO standard, it is by definition not possible to write 100% ISO-compliant PL/SQL code, so CAST seems to bring no real benefit to PL/SQL number conversions. CAST can, however, be used in the effort to write 100% ISO-compliant SQL statements (such as SELECT, INSERT, etc.).

## Implicit Conversions

A final method of handling conversions between numbers and strings is to just leave it all to PL/SQL. Such conversions are referred to as *implicit conversions*, because you don't explicitly specify them in your code. Following are some straightforward implicit conversions that will work just fine:

```
DECLARE
    a NUMBER;
    b VARCHAR2(30);
```

```
BEGIN
   a := '-123.45';
   b := -123.45;
...
```

As I mentioned in Chapter 7, I have several problems with implicit conversions. I'm a strong believer in maintaining control over my code, and when you use an implicit conversion you are giving up some of that control. You should always know when conversions are taking place, and the best way to do that is to code them explicitly. Don't just let them happen. If you rely on implicit conversions, you lose track of when conversions are occurring, and your code is less efficient as a result. Explicit conversions also make your intent clear to other programmers, making your code more self-documenting and easier to understand.

Another problem with implicit conversions is that while they may work just fine (or seem to) in simple cases, sometimes they can be ambiguous. Consider the following:

```
DECLARE
   a NUMBER;
BEGIN
   a := '123.400' || 999;
```

What value will the variable "a" hold when this code executes? It all depends on how PL/SQL evaluates the expression on the right side of the assignment operator. If PL/SQL begins by converting the string to a number, you'll get the following result:

```
a := '123.400' || 999;
a := 123.4 || 999;
a := '123.4' || '999';
a := '123.4999';
a := 123.4999;
```

On the other hand, if PL/SQL begins by converting the number to a string, you'll get the following result:

```
a := '123.400' || 999;
a := '123.400' || '999';
a := '123.400999';
a := 123.400999;
```

Which is it? Do you know? Even if you *do* know, do you really want to leave future programmers guessing and scratching their heads when they look at your code? It would be much clearer, and therefore better, to write the conversion explicitly:

```
a := TO_NUMBER('123.400' || TO_CHAR(999));
```

This expression, by the way, represents how the database will evaluate the original example. Isn't it much easier to understand at a glance now that I've expressed the conversions explicitly?

## Numeric Operators

PL/SQL implements several operators that are useful when working with numbers. The operators that can be used with numbers are shown in Table 9-6 in order of precedence. The operators with lower precedence evaluate first while those with a higher precedence evaluate latter. For full details on a particular operator, consult Oracle's *SQL Reference* manual.

*Table 9-6. Numeric operators and precedence*

| Operator | Operation | Precedence |
|---|---|---|
| ** | Exponentiation | 1 |
| + | Identity | 2 |
| − | Negation | 2 |

| Operator | Operation | Precedence |
|---|---|---|
| * | Multiplication | 3 |
| / | Division | 3 |
| + | Addition | 4 |
| − | Subtraction | 4 |
| = | Equality | 5 |
| < | Less than | 5 |
| > | Greater than | 5 |
| <= | Less than or equal | 5 |
| >= | Greater than or equal | 5 |
| <>, !=, ~=, ^= | Not equal | 5 |
| IS NULL | Nullity | 5 |
| BETWEEN | Inclusive range | 5 |
| NOT | Logical negation | 6 |
| AND | Conjunction | 7 |
| OR | Inclusion | 8 |

# Numeric Functions

PL/SQL implements several functions that are useful when working with numbers. You've already seen the conversion functions TO_CHAR, TO_NUMBER, TO_BINARY_FLOAT, and TO_BINARY_DOUBLE. The next few subsections briefly describe several other useful functions. For full details on a particular function, consult Oracle's *SQL Reference* manual.

## Rounding and Truncation Functions

There are four different numeric functions that perform rounding and truncation actions: CEIL, FLOOR, ROUND, and TRUNC. It is easy to get confused about which to use in a particular situation. Table 9-7 compares these functions, and Figure 9-5 illustrates their use for different values and decimal place rounding.

*Table 9-7. Comparison of functions that perform rounding and truncation actions*

| Function | Summary |
|---|---|
| CEIL | Returns the smallest integer that is greater than or equal to the specified value. This integer is the "ceiling" over your value. |
| FLOOR | Returns the largest integer that is less than or equal to the specified value. This integer is the "floor" under your value. |

| Function | Summary |
|----------|---------|
| ROUND | Performs rounding on a number. You can round with a positive number of decimal places (the number of digits to the right of the decimal point) and also with a negative number of decimal places (the number of digits to the left of the decimal point). |
| TRUNC | Truncates a number to the specified number of decimal places. TRUNC simply discards all values beyond the decimal places provided in the call. |

| | 1.75 | 1.3 | 55.56 | 55.56 | 10 | Input |
|----------|------|-----|-------|-------|----|-------|
| **Function** | **0** | **0** | **1** | **-1** | **2** | Number of decimal places |
| **ROUND** | 2 | 1 | 55.6 | 60 | 10 | |
| **TRUNC** | 1 | 1 | 55.5 | 50 | 10 | |
| **FLOOR** | 1 | 1 | 55 | 55 | 10 | |
| **CEIL** | 2 | 2 | 56 | 56 | 10 | |

*Figure 9-5. Impact of rounding and truncation functions*

## Trigonometric Functions

Many trigonometric functions are available from PL/SQL. When using them, be aware that all angles are expressed in radians, not in degrees. You can convert between radians and degrees as follows:

```
radians = pi * degrees / 180 -- From degrees to radians
degrees = radians * 180 / pi -- From radians to degrees
```

PL/SQL does not implement a function for $\pi$ (pi) itself. However, you can obtain the value for $\pi$ through the following call:

```
ACOS (-1)
```

The inverse cosine (ACOS) of –1 is defined as exactly $\pi$. Of course, because $\pi$ is a never-ending decimal number, you always have to work with an approximation. Use the ROUND function if you want to round the results of ACOS(–1) to a specific number of decimal places.

## Numeric Function Quick Reference

The following list briefly describes each of PL/SQL's built-in numeric functions. Where applicable, functions are overloaded for different numeric types. For example:

*ABS*

Is overloaded for BINARY_DOUBLE, BINARY_FLOAT, NUMBER, SIMPLE_INTEGER, SIMPLE_FLOAT, SIMPLE_DOUBLE, and PLS_INTEGER, because you can take the absolute value of both floating-point and integer values.

*BITAND*

Is overloaded for PLS_INTEGER and INTEGER (a subtype of NUMBER), because the function is designed to AND only integer values.

*CEIL*

Is overloaded for BINARY_DOUBLE, BINARY_FLOAT, and NUMBER, because CEIL is a function that doesn't really apply to integers.

To check for what types a given function is overloaded, describe the built-in package SYS.STANDARD, like this:

```
SQL> DESCRIBE SYS.STANDARD
...full output trimmed for brevity...

FUNCTION CEIL RETURNS NUMBER
 Argument Name                    Type                    In/Out Default?
 ------------------------------   ----------------------- ------ --------
 N                                NUMBER                  IN
FUNCTION CEIL RETURNS BINARY_FLOAT
 Argument Name                    Type                    In/Out Default?
 ------------------------------   ----------------------- ------ --------
 F                                BINARY_FLOAT            IN
FUNCTION CEIL RETURNS BINARY_DOUBLE
 Argument Name                    Type                    In/Out Default?
 ------------------------------   ----------------------- ------ --------
 D                                BINARY_DOUBLE           IN
```

Almost all the functions in the following list are defined in the built-in package. SYS.STANDARD. BIN_TO_NUM is the one exception that I've noticed. For complete documentation of a given function, refer to Oracle's *SQL Reference* manual.

*ABS(n)*

Returns the absolute value of *n*.

*ACOS(n)*

Returns the inverse cosine of *n*, where *n* must be between –1 and 1. The value returned by ACOS is between 0 and $\pi$.

*ASIN(n)*

Returns the inverse sine, where *n* must be between –1 and 1. The value returned by ASIN is between $-\pi/2$ and $\pi/2$.

*ATAN(n)*

Returns the inverse tangent, where the number *n* must be between -infinity and infinity. The value returned by ATAN is between $-\pi/2$ and $\pi/2$.

*ATAN2(n, m)*

Returns the inverse tangent of *n/m*, where the numbers *n* and *m* must be between -infinity and infinity. The value returned by ATAN is between $–\pi$ and $\pi$. The result of ATAN2(*n,m*) is defined to be identical to ATAN(*n/m*).

*BIN_TO_NUM(b1, b2,...bn)*

Converts the bit vector represented by *b1* through *bn* into a number. Each of *b1* through *bn* must evaluate to either 0 or 1. For example, BIN_TO_NUM(1,1,0,0) yields 12.

*BITAND(n, m)*

Performs a logical AND between *n* and *m*. For example, BITAND(12,4) yields 4, indicating that the value 12 (binary 1100) has the 4-bit set. Similarly, BITAND(12,8) yields 8, indicating that the 8-bit is also set.

You'll find it easiest to work with BITAND if you confine yourself to positive integers. Values of type PLS_INTEGER, a good type to use in conjunction with BITAND, can store powers of two up to $2^{30}$, giving you 30 bits to work with.

*CEIL(n)*

Returns the smallest integer greater than or equal to *n*. For a comparison of CEIL with several other numeric functions, see Table 9-7 and Figure 9-5.

*COS(n)*

Returns the cosine of the angle *n*, which must be expressed in radians. If your angle is specified in degrees, then you should convert it to radians as described in "Trigonometric Functions" on page 261.

*COSH(n)*

Returns the hyperbolic cosine of *n*. If *n* is a real number, and *i* is the imaginary square root of –1, then the relationship between COS and COSH can be expressed as follows: COS ($i * n$) = COSH (*n*).

*EXP(n)*

Returns the value *e* raised to the *n*th power, where *n* is the input argument. The number *e* (approximately equal to 2.71828) is the base of the system of natural logarithms.

*FLOOR(n)*

Returns the largest integer that is less than or equal to *n*. For a comparison of FLOOR with several other numeric functions, see Table 9-7 and Figure 9-5.

*GREATEST(n1, n2,...n3)*

Returns the largest number among the list of input numbers; e.g., GREATEST (1, 0, –1, 20) yields 20.

*LEAST(n1, n2,...n3)*

Returns the lowest number among the list of input numbers; e.g., LEAST (1, 0, –1, 20) yields –1.

*LN(n)*

Returns the natural logarithm of *n*. The argument *n* must be greater than or equal to 0. If you pass LN a negative argument, you will receive the following error:

```
ORA-01428: argument '-1' is out of range
```

*LOG(b, n)*

Returns the base *b* logarithm of *n*. The argument *n* must be greater than or equal to 0. The base *b* must be greater than 1. If you pass LOG an argument that violates either of these rules, you will receive the following error:

```
ORA-01428: argument '-1' is out of range
```

*MOD(n, m)*

Returns the remainder of *n* divided by *m*. The remainder is computed using a formula equivalent to $n-(m*\text{FLOOR}(n/m))$ when *n* and *m* are both positive or both negative, and $n-(m*\text{CEIL}(n/m))$ when the signs of *n* and *m* differ. For example, MOD(10, 2.8) yields 1.6. If *m* is zero, then *n* is returned unchanged.

You can use MOD to determine quickly if a number is odd or even:

```
FUNCTION is_odd (num_in IN NUMBER) RETURN BOOLEAN
IS
BEGIN
   RETURN MOD (num_in, 2) = 1;
END;

FUNCTION is_even (num_in IN NUMBER) RETURN BOOLEAN
IS
BEGIN
   RETURN MOD (num_in, 2) = 0;
END;
```

*NANVL(n, m)*

Returns *m* if *n* is NaN (not a number); otherwise returns *n*. The value returned will be in the type of the argument with the highest numeric precedence: BINARY_DOUBLE, BINARY_FLOAT, or NUMBER, in that order.

*POWER(n, m)*

Raises *n* to the power *m*. If *n* is negative, then *m* must be an integer. The following example uses POWER to calculate the range of valid values for a PLS_INTEGER variable ($-2^{31}-1$ through $2^{31}-1$):

```
POWER (-2, 31) - 1 .. POWER (2, 31) - 1
```

The result is:

```
-2147483648 .. 2147483647
```

*REMAINDER(n, m)*

Returns the "remainder" of *n* divided by *m*. The remainder is defined as:

```
n - (m*ROUND(n/m))
```

For example: REMAINDER(10, 2.8) yields –1.2. Compare with MOD.

*ROUND(n)*

Returns *n* rounded to the nearest integer. For example:

```
ROUND (153.46) --> 153
```

*ROUND(n, m)*

Returns *n* rounded to *m* decimal places. The value of *m* can be less than zero. A negative value for *m* directs ROUND to round digits to the left of the decimal point rather than to the right. Here are some examples:

```
ROUND (153.46, 1) --> 153.5
ROUND (153, -1) --> 150
```

For a comparison of ROUND with several other numeric functions, see Figure 9-5 and Table 9-7 in "Rounding and Truncation Functions" on page 260.

*SIGN(n)*

Returns either a –1, 0, or +1, depending on whether *n* is less than zero, equal to zero, or greater than zero, respectively.

*SIN(n)*

Returns the sine of the specified angle, which must be expressed in radians. If your angle is specified in degrees, then you should convert it to radians as described in "Trigonometric Functions" on page 261.

*SINH(n)*

Returns the hyperbolic sine of *n*. If *n* is a real number, and *i* is the imaginary square root of –1, then the relationship between SIN and SINH can be expressed as follows: SIN $(i * n) = i *$ SINH $(n)$.

*SQRT(n)*

Returns the square root *n*, which must be greater than or equal to 0. If *n* is negative, you will receive the following error:

```
ORA-01428: argument '-1' is out of range
```

*TAN(n)*

Returns the tangent of the angle *n*, which must be expressed in radians. If your angle is specified in degrees, then you should convert it to radians as described in "Trigonometric Functions" on page 261.

*TANH(n)*

Returns the hyperbolic tangent of *n*. If *n* is a real number, and *i* is the imaginary square root of –1, then the relationship between TAN and TANH can be expressed as follows: TAN $(i * n) = i *$ TANH $(n)$.

*TRUNC(n)*

Truncates *n* to an integer. For example, TRUNC(10.51) yields the result 10.

*TRUNC(n, m)*

Truncates *n* to *m* decimal places. For example, TRUNC(10.789, 2) yields 10.78.

The value of *m* can be less than zero. A negative value for this argument directs TRUNC to truncate or zero-out digits to the left of the decimal point rather than to the right. For example, TRUNC(1264, –2) yields 1200.

For a comparison of TRUNC with several other numeric functions, see Table 9-7 and Figure 9-5.

# CHAPTER 10

# Dates and Timestamps

Most applications require the storage and manipulation of dates and times. Dates are quite complicated: not only are they highly formatted data, but there are myriad rules for determining valid values and valid calculations (leap days and years, daylight savings time changes, national and company holidays, date ranges, etc.). Fortunately, the Oracle database and PL/SQL provide a set of true datetime datatypes that store both date and time information using a standard, internal format.

For any datetime value, the database stores some or all of the following information:

- Year
- Month
- Day
- Hour
- Minute
- Second
- Time zone region
- Time zone hour offset from UTC
- Time zone minute offset from UTC

Support for true datetime datatypes is only half the battle. You also need a language that can manipulate those values in a natural and intelligent manner—as actual dates and times. To that end, Oracle provides you with support for SQL standard interval arithmetic, datetime literals, and a comprehensive suite of functions with which to manipulate date and time information.

## Datetime Datatypes

For a long time, the only datetime datatype available was DATE. Oracle9*i* Database shook things up by introducing three new TIMESTAMP and two new INTERVAL datatypes offering significant, new functionality while also bringing Oracle into closer compliance with the ISO SQL standard. I'll talk more about the INTERVAL datatypes later in this chapter. The four datetime datatypes are:

*DATE*
Stores a date and time, resolved to the second. Does not include time zone.

*TIMESTAMP*
Stores date and time without respect to time zone. Except for being able to resolve time to the billionth of a second (9 decimal places of precision), TIMESTAMP is the equivalent of DATE.

*TIMESTAMP WITH TIME ZONE*
Stores the time zone along with the date and time value allowing up to 9 decimal places of precision.

*TIMESTAMP WITH LOCAL TIME ZONE*
Stores a date and time with up to 9 decimal places of precision. This datatype is sensitive to time zone differences. Values of this type are automatically converted between the database time zone and the local (session) time zone. When values are stored in the database, they are converted to the database time zone, but the local (session) time zone is not stored. When a value is retrieved from the database, that value is converted from the database time zone to the local (session) time zone.

The nuances of these types, especially the TIMESTAMP WITH LOCAL TIME ZONE type, can be a bit difficult to understand at first. To help illustrate, let's look at the use of TIMESTAMP WITH LOCAL TIME ZONE in a calendaring application for users across multiple time zones. My database time zone is Coordinated Universal Time (UTC). (See the sidebar "Coordinated Universal Time" on page 270 for a description of UTC.) User Jonathan in Michigan (Eastern Daylight Time: UTC –4:00) has scheduled a conference call for 4:00–5:00 p.m. his time on Thursday. Donna in Denver (Mountain Daylight Time: UTC –6:00) needs to know this meeting is at 2:00–3:00 p.m. her time on Thursday. Selva in India (Indian Standard Time: UTC +5:30) needs to know this meeting is at 1:30-2:30 a.m. his time on Friday morning. Figure 10-1 shows how the meeting start time varies as it moves from a user in one time zone through the database to another user in a different time zone.

Figure 10-1 shows user Jonathan in the Eastern Daylight Time Zone, which is four hours behind UTC or UTC –4:00. Jonathan enters the meeting start time as 16:00 using 24-hour notation. This value gets converted to the database time zone (UTC) when the row is inserted. 20:00 is the value stored in the database. Donna is in Denver where daylight savings time is also observed as Mountain Daylight Time and is 6 hours behind Coordinated Universal Time (UTC –6:00). When Donna selects the start time, the value is converted to her session time zone and is displayed as 14:00. Selva is in India, which does not observe Daylight Savings Time—India Standard Time is five hours and 30 minutes ahead of UTC (UTC + 5:30). When Selva selects the meeting start time the value is converted to his session time zone and is displayed as 1:30 a.m. Friday.

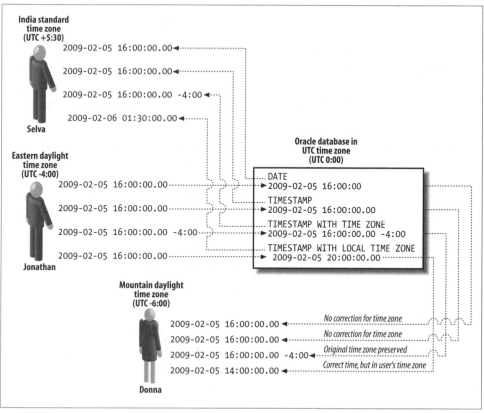

*Figure 10-1. Effect of different datetime datatypes*

By delegating the time zone management to the database via the TIMESTAMP WITH LOCAL TIME ZONE datatype, you don't have to burden your application with the complex rules surrounding time zones and daylight savings time (which sometimes change—as they did in the United States in 2007), nor do you have to burden your users with figuring out the time zone conversion. The correct time for the meeting is presented to each user simply and elegantly.

Sometimes you want the database to automatically change the display of the time and sometimes you don't. When you don't want the display of the timestamp to vary based on session settings, use the TIMESTAMP or TIMESTAMP WITH TIME ZONE datatypes.

## Coordinated Universal Time

Coordinated Universal Time, abbreviated UTC, is measured using highly accurate and precise atomic clocks, and forms the basis of our worldwide system of civil time. Time zones, for example, are all defined with respect to how far they are in terms of hours and minutes from UTC. UTC is atomic time, and is periodically adjusted through the mechanism of leap seconds to keep it in sync with time as determined by the rotation of the earth.

You may be familiar with Greenwich Mean Time (GMT) or Zulu Time. For most practical purposes, these references are equivalent to UTC.

Why the acronym UTC and not CUT? The standards body couldn't agree on whether to use the English acronym CUT or the French acronym TUC, so they compromised on UTC, which matches neither language. See *http://www.boulder.nist.gov/timefreq/general/misc.htm#Anchor-14550*.

For more information on UTC, see the National Institute of Standards and Technology document on UTC at *http://physics.nist.gov/GenInt/Time/world.html*.

## Declaring Datetime Variables

Use the following syntax to declare a datetime variable:

> *var_name* [CONSTANT] *datetime_type* [{:= | DEFAULT} *initial_value*]

Replace *datetime_type* with any one of the following:

```
DATE
TIMESTAMP [(precision)]
TIMESTAMP [(precision)] WITH TIME ZONE
TIMESTAMP [(precision)] WITH LOCAL TIME ZONE
```

The *precision* in these declarations refers to the number of decimal digits allocated for recording values to the fraction of a second. The default precision is 6, which means that you can track time down to 0.000001 seconds. The allowable range for precision is 0 through 9, giving you the ability to store very precise time-of-day values.

 Functions such as SYSTIMESTAMP that return timestamp values always return only six digits of subseconds precision.

Following are some example declarations:

```
DECLARE
   hire_date TIMESTAMP (0) WITH TIME ZONE;
   todays_date CONSTANT DATE := SYSDATE;
   pay_date TIMESTAMP DEFAULT TO_TIMESTAMP('20050204','YYYYMMDD');
BEGIN
```

```
        NULL;
    END;
    /
```

To specify a default, *initial_value*, you can use a conversion function such as TO_TIMESTAMP, or you can use a date or timestamp literal. Both are described in "Datetime Conversions" on page 278.

 A TIMESTAMP(0) variable behaves like a DATE variable.

## Choosing a Datetime Datatype

With such an abundance of riches, I won't blame you one bit if you ask for some guidance as to which datetime datatype to use when. To a large extent, the datatype you choose depends on the level of detail that you want to store:

- Use one of the TIMESTAMP types if you need to track time down to a fraction of a second.

- Use TIMESTAMP WITH LOCAL TIME ZONE if you want the database to automatically convert a time between the database and session time zones.

- Use TIMESTAMP WITH TIME ZONE if you need to keep track of the session time zone in which the data was entered.

- You can use TIMESTAMP in place of DATE. A TIMESTAMP that does not contain subsecond precision takes up 7 bytes of storage just like a DATE datatype does. When your TIMESTAMP does contain subsecond data, it takes up 11 bytes of storage.

Other considerations might also apply:

- Use DATE when it's necessary to maintain compatibility with an existing application written before any of the TIMESTAMP datatypes were introduced.

- In general, you should use datatypes in your PL/SQL code that correspond to, or are at least compatible with, the underlying, database tables. Think twice, for example, before reading a TIMESTAMP value from a table into a DATE variable, because you might lose information (in this case, the fractional seconds and perhaps time zone).

- If you're using a version older than Oracle9i Database, then you have no choice but to use DATE.

- When adding or subtracting years and months, you get different behavior from using ADD_MONTHS, which operates on values of type DATE, than from using interval arithmetic on the timestamp types. See "When to Use INTERVALs" on page 276 for more on this critical, yet subtle issue.

Be careful when using the DATE and TIMESTAMP datatypes together. Date arithmetic differs significantly between the two. Be careful when applying Oracle's traditional, built-in date functions (such as ADD_MONTHS or MONTHS_BETWEEN) to values from any of the timestamp types. See "Datetime Arithmetic" on page 300 for more on this topic.

# Getting the Current Date and Time

In any language, it's important to know how to get the current date and time. How to do that is often one of the first questions to come up, especially in applications that involve dates in any way, as most applications do.

Up through Oracle8i Database, you had one choice for getting the date and time in PL/SQL: you used the SYSDATE function, and that was it. Beginning with Oracle9i Database, you have all the functions in Table 10-1 at your disposal, and you need to understand how they work and what your choices are.

Table 10-1. Comparison of functions that return current date and time

| Function | Time zone | Datatype returned |
| --- | --- | --- |
| CURRENT_DATE | Session | DATE |
| CURRENT_TIMESTAMP | Session | TIMESTAMP WITH TIME ZONE |
| LOCALTIMESTAMP | Session | TIMESTAMP |
| SYSDATE | Database server | DATE |
| SYSTIMESTAMP | Database server | TIMESTAMP WITH TIME ZONE |

So which function should you use in a given situation? The answer depends on several factors, which you should probably consider in the following order:

1. Whether you are using a release prior to Oracle8i Database or need to maintain compatibility with such a release. In either case, your choice is simple: use SYSDATE.

2. Whether you are interested in the time on the database server or for your session. If for your session, then use a function that returns session time zone. If for the database server, then use a function that returns the database time zone.

3. Whether you need the time zone to be returned as part of the current date and time. If so, then call either SYSTIMESTAMP or CURRENT_TIMESTAMP.

If you decide to use a function that returns the time in the session time zone, be certain that you have correctly specified your session time zone. The functions SESSIONTIMEZONE and DBTIMEZONE will report your session and database time zones respectively. To report on the time in the database time zone, you must alter your session time zone to DBTIMEZONE and then use one of the session time zone functions. The following example illustrates some of these functions.

```
BEGIN
    DBMS_OUTPUT.PUT_LINE('Session Timezone='||SESSIONTIMEZONE);
    DBMS_OUTPUT.PUT_LINE('Session Timestamp='||CURRENT_TIMESTAMP);
    DBMS_OUTPUT.PUT_LINE('DB Server Timestamp='||SYSTIMESTAMP);
    DBMS_OUTPUT.PUT_LINE('DB Timezone='||DBTIMEZONE);
    EXECUTE IMMEDIATE 'ALTER SESSION SET TIME_ZONE=DBTIMEZONE';
    DBMS_OUTPUT.PUT_LINE('DB Timestamp='||CURRENT_TIMESTAMP);
    -- Revert session timezone to local setting
    EXECUTE IMMEDIATE 'ALTER SESSION SET TIME_ZONE=LOCAL';
END;
```

The output is:

```
Session Timezone=-04:00
Session Timestamp=23-JUN-08 12.48.44.656003000 PM -04:00
DB Server Timestamp=23-JUN-08 11.48.44.656106000 AM -05:00
DB Timezone=+00:00
DB Timestamp=23-JUN-08 04.48.44.656396000 PM +00:00
```

In this example, the session starts in U.S. Eastern Daylight Time (–4:00) while the server is on U.S. Central Daylight Time (–5:00). Although the database server is in Central Daylight Time, the database time zone is GMT (+00:00). To get the time in the database time zone, I first set the session time zone to match the database time zone, then call the session time zone function CURRENT_TIMESTAMP. Finally, I revert my session time zone back to the regular local setting that I started with.

What if there's no function to return a value in the datatype that you need? For example, what if you need the server time in a TIMESTAMP variable? You can let the database implicitly convert the types for you. But even better would be to use an explicit conversion with CAST. For example:

```
DECLARE
    ts1 TIMESTAMP;
    ts2 TIMESTAMP;
BEGIN
    ts1 := CAST(SYSTIMESTAMP AS TIMESTAMP);
    ts2 := SYSDATE;
    DBMS_OUTPUT.PUT_LINE(TO_CHAR(ts1,'DD-MON-YYYY HH:MI:SS AM'));
    DBMS_OUTPUT.PUT_LINE(TO_CHAR(ts2,'DD-MON-YYYY HH:MI:SS AM'));
END;
```

The output is:

```
24-FEB-2002 06:46:39 PM
24-FEB-2002 06:46:39 PM
```

The call to SYSTIMESTAMP uses CAST to make the conversion from TIMESTAMP WITH TIME ZONE to TIMESTAMP explicit. The call to SYSDATE allows the conversion from DATE to TIMESTAMP to happen implicitly.

Be aware of hardware and operating-system limitations if you are using these timestamp functions for subsecond timing purposes. The CURRENT_TIMESTAMP, LOCALTIMESTAMP, and SYSTIMESTAMP functions return values in either the TIMESTAMP WITH TIME ZONE or TIMESTAMP datatypes. These datatypes allow you to resolve time down to the billionth of a second.

That's all well and good, but think about where that time comes from. The database gets the time from the operating system via a call to GetTimeOfDay (Unix/Linux), GetSystemTime (Microsoft Windows), or other similar calls on other operating systems. The operating system, in turn, depends at some level on the hardware. If your operating system or underlying hardware tracks time only to the hundredth of a second, the database won't be able to return results any more granular than that. For example, when using Linux on an Intel x86 processor you can resolve time only to the millionth of a second (6 digits), whereas you can see resolution only to the thousandth of a second when the database runs on Microsoft Windows XP or Vista on the same hardware. In addition, while the operating system may report a timestamp with 6 digits of decimal precision, this number may not represent an accuracy of 1 microsecond.

# Interval Datatypes

The datetime datatypes let you record specific points in time. Interval datatypes, first introduced in Oracle9*i* Database, are all about recording and computing *quantities* of time. To better understand what the interval datatypes represent, step back a bit and think about the different kinds of datetime data you deal with on a daily basis:

*Instants*

An *instant* is a point in time with respect to a given granularity. When you plan to wake up at a given hour in the morning, that hour represents an instant. The granularity, then, would be to the hour, or possibly to the minute. DATE and all the TIMESTAMP datatypes allow you to represent instants of time.

*Intervals*

An *interval* refers not to a specific point in time, but to a specific *amount*, or quantity, of time. You use intervals all the time in your daily life. You work for eight hours a day (you hope), you take an hour for lunch (in your dreams!), and so forth. Oracle Database's two INTERVAL types allow you to represent time intervals.

*Periods*

A *period* (our definition) refers to an interval of time that begins or ends at a specific instant. For example: "I woke up at 8:00 a.m. today and worked for eight hours." Here, the 8-hour interval beginning at 8:00 a.m. today would be considered a period. The Oracle database has no datatype to directly support periods, nor does the SQL standard define one.

The database supports two interval datatypes. Both were introduced in Oracle9*i* Database, and both conform to the ISO SQL standard:

*INTERVAL YEAR TO MONTH*
> Allows you to define an interval of time in terms of years and months.

*INTERVAL DAY TO SECOND*
> Allows you to define an interval of time in terms of days, hours, minutes, and seconds (including fractional seconds).

---

### Why Two INTERVAL Datatypes?

I was initially puzzled about the need for two INTERVAL datatypes. I noticed that between the two datatypes, all portions of a TIMESTAMP value were accounted for, but the decision to treat year and month separately from days, hours, minutes, and seconds seemed at first rather arbitrary. Why not simply have one INTERVAL type that covers all possibilities? It turns out that we can blame this state of affairs on the long-dead Roman Emperor Julius Caesar, who designed our calendar and determined most of our month lengths.

The reason for having two INTERVAL types with a dividing line at the month level is that months are the only datetime component for which the length of time in question varies. Think about having an interval of 1 month and 30 days. How long is that, really? Is it less than two months? The same as two months? More than two months? If the one month is January, then 30 days gets you past February and into March, resulting in a 61-day interval that is a bit more than "two months" long. If the one month is February, then the interval is exactly two months (but only 59 or 60 days). If the one month is April, then the interval is slightly less than two months, for a total of 60 days.

Rather than sort out and deal with all the complications differing month lengths pose for interval comparison, date arithmetic, and normalization of datetime values, the ISO SQL standard breaks the datetime model into two parts, year and month, and everything else. (For more, see C. J. Date's *A Guide to the SQL Standard*, Addison-Wesley).

---

## Declaring INTERVAL Variables

Compared to other PL/SQL variable declarations, the syntax for declaring INTERVAL variables is a bit unusual. You not only have multiple-word type names, but in one case you specify not one, but two precisions:

```
var_name INTERVAL YEAR [(year_precision)] TO MONTH
```

or:

```
var_name INTERVAL DAY [(day_precision)] TO SECOND [(frac_sec_prec)]
```

where:

*var_name*
> Is the name of the INTERVAL variable that you want to declare.

*year_precision*

Is the number of digits (from 0 to 4) that you want to allow for a year value. The default is 2.

*day_precision*

Is the number of digits (from 0 to 9) that you want to allow for a day value. The default is 2.

*frac_sec_prec*

Is the number of digits (from 0 to 9) that you want to allow for fractional seconds (i.e., the fractional seconds precision). The default is 6.

It is the nature of intervals that you need only worry about precision at the extremes. INTERVAL YEAR TO MONTH values are always normalized such that the number of months is between 0 and 11. In fact, the database will not allow you to specify a month greater than 11; an interval of 1 year, 13 months must be expressed as 2 years, 1 month. The *year_precision* fixes the maximum size of the interval. Likewise, the *day_precision* in INTERVAL DAY TO SECOND fixes the maximum size of that interval.

You don't need to specify a precision for the hour, minute, and second values for an INTERVAL DAY TO SECOND variable for the same reason you don't specify a precision for month in an INTERVAL YEAR TO MONTH. The intervals are always normalized so that any values for hour, minute, and second are within the normal ranges of 0–23 for hours, 0–59 for minutes, and 0–59 for seconds (excluding fractional seconds).

The fractional second precision (*frac_sec_prec*) is necessary because INTERVAL DAY TO SECOND values can resolve intervals down to the fraction of a second. INTERVAL YEAR TO MONTH values don't handle fractional months, so no fractional month precision is necessary.

## When to Use INTERVALs

Use the INTERVAL types whenever you need to work with quantities of time. I provide two examples in this section, hoping to spark your natural creativity so that you can begin to think about how you might use INTERVAL types in systems you develop.

### Finding the difference between two datetime values

One use for INTERVAL types is when you need to look at the difference between two datetime values. Consider the following example, which computes an employee's length of service:

```
/* File on web: interval_between.sql */
DECLARE
   start_date TIMESTAMP;
   end_date TIMESTAMP;
   service_interval INTERVAL YEAR TO MONTH;
```

```
    years_of_service NUMBER;
    months_of_service NUMBER;
BEGIN
    --Normally, we would retrieve start and end dates from a database.
    start_date := TO_TIMESTAMP('29-DEC-1988','dd-mon-yyyy');
    end_date := TO_TIMESTAMP ('26-DEC-1995','dd-mon-yyyy');

    --Determine and display years and months of service:
    service_interval := (end_date - start_date) YEAR TO MONTH;
    DBMS_OUTPUT.PUT_LINE(service_interval);

    --Use the new EXTRACT function to grab individual
    --year and month components.
    years_of_service := EXTRACT(YEAR FROM service_interval);
    months_of_service := EXTRACT(MONTH FROM service_interval);
    DBMS_OUTPUT.PUT_LINE(years_of_service || ' years and '
                      || months_of_service || ' months');
END;
```

The line that performs the actual calculation to get years and months of service is:

```
service_interval := (end_date - start_date) YEAR TO MONTH;
```

The YEAR TO MONTH is part of the interval expression syntax. I talk more about that syntax in "Datetime Arithmetic" on page 300. You can see, however, that computing the interval is as simple as subtracting one timestamp from another. Had I not used an INTERVAL type, I would have had to code something like the following:

```
months_of_service := ROUND(months_between(end_date, start_date));
years_of_service := TRUNC(months_of_service/12);
months_of_service := MOD(months_of_service,12);
```

I believe the non-INTERVAL solution is more complex to code and understand.

 The INTERVAL YEAR TO MONTH type displays rounding behavior, and it's important you understand the ramifications of that. See "Datetime Arithmetic" on page 300 for details about this issue.

### Designating periods of time

For this example, I will explore a company with an assembly line. The time required to assemble each product (called *build time* in this example) is an important metric. Reducing this interval allows the assembly line to be more efficient, so management wants to track and report on this interval. In my example, each product has a tracking number used to identify it during the assembly process. The table I use to hold this assembly information looks like this:

```
TABLE assemblies (
    tracking_id NUMBER NOT NULL,
    start_time  TIMESTAMP NOT NULL,
    build_time  INTERVAL DAY TO SECOND
);
```

Next, I need a PL/SQL function to return the build time for a given tracking_id. The build time is calculated from the current timestamp minus the start time. I will cover date arithmetic in greater detail later in this chapter. This build time function is:

```
FUNCTION calc_build_time (
   esn IN assemblies.tracking_id%TYPE
)
   RETURN DSINTERVAL_UNCONSTRAINED
IS
   start_ts assemblies.start_time%TYPE;
BEGIN
   SELECT start_time INTO start_ts FROM assemblies
      WHERE tracking_id = esn;
   RETURN LOCALTIMESTAMP-start_ts;
END;
```

When I pass intervals into and out of PL/SQL programs I need to use the unconstrained keywords (see "Using Unconstrained INTERVAL Types" on page 306 for an explanation). With the build time recorded in a table, I can analyze the data more easily. I can calculate the minimum, maximum, and mean build time with simple SQL functions. I could answer questions like "Do I build any faster on Monday vs. Wednesday?" or how about first shift vs. second shift? But, I'm getting ahead of myself. This straightforward example simply demonstrates the basic concept of a day-to-second interval. Your job as a clever developer is to put these concepts to use in creative ways.

## Datetime Conversions

Now that you understand the Oracle database's array of datetime datatypes, it's time to look at how you get dates into and out of datetime variables. Human-readable datetime values are character strings such as "March 5, 2009" and "10:30 a.m.", so this discussion centers around the conversion of datetime values from character strings to Oracle's internal representation, and vice versa.

PL/SQL validates and stores dates that fall from January 1, 4712 B.C.E. through December 31, 9999 A.D. (Oracle documentation indicates a maximum date of December 31, 4712; run the *showdaterange.sql* script, available on the book's web site, to verify the range on your version.) If you enter a date without a time (many applications do not require the tracking of time, so PL/SQL lets you leave it off), the time portion of the value defaults to midnight (12:00:00 a.m.).

The database can interpret just about any date or time format you throw at it. Key to that flexibility is the concept of a *date format model*, which is a string of special characters that define a date's format to the database. For example, if your input date happens to be, for example, 15-Nov-1961, then that, rather obviously in this case, corresponds to the date format dd-mon-yyyy. You then use the string 'dd-mon-yyyy' in calls to conversion functions to convert dates to and from that format.

I show examples of several different format models in my conversion discussion, and I provide a complete reference to all the format model elements in Appendix C.

## From Strings to Datetimes

The first issue you'll face when working with dates is that of getting date (and time) values into your PL/SQL datetime variables. You do so by converting datetime values from character strings to the database's internal format. Such conversions can be done implicitly via assignment of a character string directly to a datetime variable, or better yet they should be done explicitly via one of Oracle's built-in conversion functions.

Implicit conversion is risky, and I don't recommend it. Following is an example of implicit conversion from a character string to a DATE variable:

```
DECLARE
    birthdate DATE;
BEGIN
    birthdate := '15-Nov-1961';
END;
```

Such a conversion relies on the NLS_DATE_FORMAT setting and will work fine until the day your DBA decides to change that setting. On that day, all your date-related code will break. Changing NLS_DATE_FORMAT at the session level can also break such code.

Rather than rely on implicit conversions and the NLS_DATE_FORMAT setting, it's far safer to convert dates explicitly via one of the built-in conversion functions, such as TO_DATE:

```
DECLARE
    birthdate DATE;
BEGIN
    birthdate := TO_DATE('15-Nov-1961','dd-mon-yyyy');
END;
```

Notice here the use of the format string 'dd-mon-yyyy' as the second parameter in the call to TO_DATE. That format string controls how the TO_DATE function interprets the characters in the first parameter.

PL/SQL supports the following functions to convert strings to dates and timestamps:

TO_DATE(*string*[, *format_mask*[, *nls_language*]])
Converts a character string to a value of type DATE.

TO_DATE(*number*[, *format_mask*[, *nls_language*]])
Converts a number representing a Julian date into a value of type DATE.

TO_TIMESTAMP(*string*[, *format_mask*[, *nls_language*]])
Converts a character string to a value of type TIMESTAMP.

```
TO_TIMESTAMP_TZ(string[, format_mask[, nls_language]])
```
Converts a character string to a value of type TIMESTAMP WITH TIME ZONE.
Also use this function when your target is TIMESTAMP WITH LOCAL TIME
ZONE.

Not only do these functions make it clear in your code that a type conversion is occurring, but they also allow you to specify the exact datetime format being used.

 The second version of TO_DATE can be used only with the format mask
of J for Julian date. The Julian date is the number of days that have
passed since January 1, 4712 B.C. Only in this use of TO_DATE can a
number be passed as the first parameter of TO_DATE.

For all other cases the parameters are as follows:

*string*
Is the string variable, literal, named constant, or expression to be converted.

*format_mask*
Is the format mask to be used in converting the string. The format mask defaults
to the NLS_DATE_FORMAT setting.

*nls_language*
Optionally specifies the language to be used to interpret the names and abbreviations of both months and days in the string. Here's the format of *nls_language*:

```
'NLS_DATE_LANGUAGE=language'
```

where *language* is a language recognized by your instance of the database. You can
determine the acceptable languages by checking the *Oracle Globalization Support
Guide*.

The format elements described in Appendix C apply when using the TO_ family of
functions. For example, the following calls to TO_DATE and TO_TIMESTAMP convert character strings of varying formats to DATE and TIMESTAMP values:

```
DECLARE
    dt DATE;
    ts TIMESTAMP;
    tstz TIMESTAMP WITH TIME ZONE;
    tsltz TIMESTAMP WITH LOCAL TIME ZONE;
BEGIN
    dt := TO_DATE('12/26/2005','mm/dd/yyyy');
    ts := TO_TIMESTAMP('24-Feb-2002 09.00.00.50 PM');
    tstz := TO_TIMESTAMP_TZ('06/2/2002 09:00:00.50 PM EST',
                'mm/dd/yyyy hh:mi:ssxff AM TZD');
    tsltz := TO_TIMESTAMP_TZ('06/2/2002 09:00:00.50 PM EST',
                'mm/dd/yyyy hh:mi:ssxff AM TZD');
    DBMS_OUTPUT.PUT_LINE(dt);
    DBMS_OUTPUT.PUT_LINE(ts);
    DBMS_OUTPUT.PUT_LINE(tstz);
```

```
    DBMS_OUTPUT.PUT_LINE(tsltz);
END;
```

The output is:

```
26-DEC-05
24-FEB-02 09.00.00.500000 PM
02-JUN-02 09.00.00.500000 PM -05:00
02-JUN-02 09.00.00.500000 PM
```

Note the decimal seconds (.50) and the use of XFF in the format mask. The X format element specifies the location of the radix character, in this case a period (.), separating the whole seconds from the fractional seconds. I could just as easily have specified a period, as in ".FF", but I chose to use X instead. The difference is that when X is specified, the database determines the correct radix character based on the current NLS_TERRITORY setting.

Any Oracle errors between ORA-01800 and ORA-01899 are related to date conversion. You can learn some of the date conversion rule nuances by perusing the different errors and reading about the documented causes of these errors. Some of these nuances are:

- A date literal passed to TO_CHAR for conversion to a date cannot be longer than 220 characters.

- You can't include both a Julian date element (J) and the day of year element (DDD) in a single format mask.

- You can't include multiple elements for the same component of the date/time in the mask. For example, the format mask YYYY-YYY-DD-MM is illegal because it includes two year elements, YYYY and YYY.

- You can't use the 24-hour time format (HH24) and a meridian element (e.g., a.m.) in the same mask.

As the preceding example demonstrates, The TO_TIMESTAMP_TZ function can convert character strings that include time zone information. And while time zones seem simple on the surface, they are anything but, as you'll see in "Working with Time Zones" on page 284.

## From Datetimes to Strings

Getting values into datetime variables is only half the battle. The other half is getting them out again in some sort of human-readable format. Oracle provides the TO_CHAR function for that purpose.

The TO_CHAR function can be used to convert a datetime value to a variable-length string. This single function works for DATE types as well as for all the types in the TIMESTAMP family. TO_CHAR is also used to convert numbers to character strings, as covered in Chapter 9. The following specification describes TO_CHAR for datetime values:

```
FUNCTION TO_CHAR
   (date_in IN DATE
   [, format_mask IN VARCHAR2
   [, nls_language IN VARCHAR2]])
RETURN VARCHAR2
```

where:

*date_in*
> Is the date to be converted to character format.

*format_mask*
> Is the mask made up of one or more of the date format elements. See Appendix C for a list of date format elements.

*nls_language*
> Is a string specifying a date language.

Both the *format_mask* and *nls_language* parameters are optional.

 If you want your results to be in the national character set, you can use TO_NCHAR in place of TO_CHAR. Be certain you provide your date format string in the national character set as well. Otherwise, you may receive *ORA-01821: date format not recognized* errors.

If *format_mask* is not specified, the default date format for the database instance is used. This format is `'DD-MON-RR'`, unless you have non-default NLS settings, such as NLS_DATE_FORMAT. The best practice, as mentioned elsewhere in this chapter, is to not rely on implicit conversions for dates. Changes to the server NLS settings and, for client-side code, changes to the client NLS settings, will cause logic bugs to creep into your programs if you rely on implicit conversions. As an example, in North America you write a routine assuming that the date 03-04-09 is 4 March 2009, but if your application is later deployed to Japan or Germany the implicit conversion will result in 3 April 2009 or 9 April 2003, depending on the NLS settings. If your application is always explicit in datatype conversions, you will not encounter these logic bugs.

Here are some examples of TO_CHAR being used for date conversion:

- Notice that there are two blanks between month and day and a leading zero for the fifth day:

    ```
    TO_CHAR (SYSDATE, 'Month DD, YYYY') --> 'February  05, 1994'
    ```

- Use the FM fill mode element to suppress blanks and zeros:

    ```
    TO_CHAR (SYSDATE, 'FMMonth DD, YYYY') --> 'February 5, 1994'
    ```

- Note the case difference on the month abbreviations of the next two examples. You get exactly what you ask for with Oracle date formats!

    ```
    TO_CHAR (SYSDATE, 'MON DDth, YYYY') --> 'FEB 05TH, 1994'
    TO_CHAR (SYSDATE, 'fmMon DDth, YYYY') --> 'Feb 5TH, 1994'
    ```

- The TH format is an exception to the capitalization rules. Even if you specify lowercase "th" in a format string, The database will use uppercase TH in the output.
- Show the day of the year, day of the month, and day of the week for the date (with fm used here as a toggle):

```
TO_CHAR (SYSDATE, 'DDD DD D ') --> '036 05 7'
TO_CHAR (SYSDATE, 'fmDDD fmDD D ') --> '36 05 7'
```

- Here's some fancy formatting for reporting purposes:

```
TO_CHAR (SYSDATE, '"In month "RM" of year "YEAR')
  --> 'In month II    of year NINETEEN NINETY FOUR'
```

- For TIMESTAMP variables, you can specify the time down to the millisecond using the FF format element:

```
TO_CHAR (A_TIMESTAMP, 'YYYY-MM-DD HH:MI:SS.FF AM TZH:TZM')
  --> a value like: 2002-02-19 01:52:00.123457000 PM -05:00
```

Be careful when dealing with fractional seconds. The FF format element represents fractional seconds in the output format model, and you'll be tempted to use the number of Fs to control the number of decimal digits in the output. Don't do that! Instead, use FF1 through FF9 to specify 1 through 9 decimal digits. For example, the following block uses FF6 to request six decimal digits of precision in the output:

```
DECLARE
   ts TIMESTAMP WITH TIME ZONE;
BEGIN
   ts := TIMESTAMP '2002-02-19 13:52:00.123456789 -5:00';
   DBMS_OUTPUT.PUT_LINE(TO_CHAR(ts,'YYYY-MM-DD HH:MI:SS.FF6 AM TZH:TZM'));
END;
```

The output is:

```
2002-02-19 01:52:00.123457 PM -05:00
```

Note the rounding that occurred. The number of seconds input was 00.123456789. That value was rounded (not truncated) to six decimal digits: 00.123457.

It's easy to slip up and specify an incorrect date format, and the introduction of TIMESTAMP types has made this even easier. Format elements that are valid with TIMESTAMP types are not valid for the DATE type. Look at the results in the following example when FF, TZH, and TZM are used to convert a DATE value to a character string:

```
DECLARE
   dt DATE;
BEGIN
   dt := SYSDATE;
   DBMS_OUTPUT.PUT_LINE(TO_CHAR(dt,'YYYY-MM-DD HH:MI:SS.FF AM TZH:TZM'));
END;
```

The output is:

```
   dt := SYSDATE;
  *
```

```
ORA-01821: date format not recognized
ORA-06512: at line 5
```

The error message you get in this case, *ORA-01821: date format not recognized*, is confusing and misleading. The date format is just fine. The problem is that it's being applied to the wrong datatype. Watch for this kind of problem when you write code. If you get an *ORA-01821* error, check *both* the date format and the datatype that you are trying to convert.

## Working with Time Zones

The inclusion of time zone information makes the use of TO_TIMESTAMP_TZ more complex than the TO_DATE and TO_TIMESTAMP functions. You may specify time zone information in any of the following ways:

- Using a positive or negative displacement of some number of hours and minutes from UTC time; for example, –5:00 is equivalent to U.S. Eastern Standard Time. Displacements must fall into the range –12:59 and +13:59. (I showed examples of this notation earlier in this chapter.)

- Using a time zone region name such as US/Eastern, US/Pacific, and so forth.

- Using a combination of time zone region name and abbreviation, as in US/Eastern EDT for U.S. Eastern Daylight Savings Time.

Let's look at some examples. I'll begin with a simple example that leaves off time zone information entirely:

```
TO_TIMESTAMP_TZ ('12312005 083015.50', 'MMDDYYYY HHMISS.FF')
```

The date and time in this example work out to be 31-Dec-2005 at 15 1/2 seconds past 8:30 a.m. Because no time zone is specified, the database will default to the current session time zone. With the time zone intentionally omitted, this code is less clear than it could be. If the application is designed to use the session time zone (as opposed to an explicit time zone), a better approach would be to first fetch the session time zone using the function SESSIONTIMEZONE and then explicitly use this value in the TO_TIMESTAMP_TZ function call. Being explicit in your intent helps the developer (who may be you) understand and correctly maintain this code two years down the road when some new feature or bug fix occurs.

---

### A Date or a Time?

Be aware that every datetime value is composed of both a date *and* a time. Forgetting this duality may lead to errors in your code. As an example, suppose that I write PL/SQL code to run on the first of the year, 2009:

```
IF SYSDATE = TO_DATE('1-Jan-2009','dd-Mon-yyyy')
THEN
    Apply2009PriceChange;
END IF;
```

---

The goal of this example is to run a routine to adjust prices for the new year, but the chance of that procedure's actually running is minimal. You'd need to run the code block exactly at midnight, to the second. That's because SYSDATE returns a time-of-day value along with the date.

To make the code block work as expected, you can truncate the value returned by SYSDATE to midnight of the day in question:

```
IF TRUNC(SYSDATE) = TO_DATE('1-Jan-2009','dd-Mon-yyyy');
```

Now, both sides of the comparison have a time of day, but that time of day is midnight. The TO_DATE function also returns a time of day, which, because no time of day was given, defaults to midnight (i.e., 00:00:00). Thus, no matter when on 1 Jan, 2009 you run this code block, the comparison will succeed, and the Apply2009PriceChange procedure will run.

This use of TRUNCATE to remove the time portion of a date stamp works equally well on timestamps.

Next, let's represent the time zone using a displacement of hours and minutes from UTC. Note the use of the TZH and TZM to denote the location of the hour and minute displacements in the input string:

```
TO_TIMESTAMP_TZ ('1231200 083015.50 -5:00', 'MMDDYY HHMISS.FF TZH:TZM')
```

In this example, the datetime value is interpreted as being an Eastern Standard Time value (regardless of your session time zone).

The next example shows the time zone being specified using a time zone region name. The example specifies EST, which is the region name corresponding to Eastern Time in the United States. Note the use of TZR in the format mask to designate where the time zone region name appears in the input string.

```
TO_TIMESTAMP_TZ ('01-Nov-2009 01:30:00 EST',
                 'dd-Mon-yyyy hh:mi:ss TZR')
```

This example is interesting in that it represents Eastern Time, not Eastern Standard Time. The difference is that "Eastern Time" can refer to either Eastern Standard Time or Eastern Daylight Time, depending on whether daylight savings time is in effect. And it might be in effect! I've carefully crafted this example to make it ambiguous. 01-Nov-2009 is the date on which Eastern Daylight Time ends, and at 2:00 a.m. time rolls back to 1:00 a.m. So on that date, 1:30 a.m. actually comes around twice! The first time it's 1:30 a.m. Eastern Daylight Time, and the second time it's 1:30 a.m. Eastern Standard Time. So what time is it, really, when I say it's 1:30 a.m. on 01-Nov-2009?

If you set the session parameter ERROR_ON_OVERLAP_TIME to TRUE (the default is FALSE), the database will give you an error whenever you specify an ambiguous time because of daylight savings time changes. Note that daylight savings time is also called *summer time* in some parts of the world.

The time zone region name alone doesn't distinguish between standard time and daylight savings time. To remove the ambiguity, you also must specify a time zone abbreviation, which I've done in the next two examples. Use the abbreviation EDT to specify Eastern Daylight Time:

```
TO_TIMESTAMP_TZ ('01-Nov-2009 01:30:00.00 US/Eastern EDT',
                       'dd-Mon-yyyy hh:mi:ssxff TZR TZD')
```

And use the abbreviation EST to specify Eastern Standard Time:

```
TO_TIMESTAMP_TZ ('01-Nov-2009 01:30:00.00 US/Eastern EST',
                       'dd-Mon-yyyy hh:mi:ssxff TZR TZD')
```

To avoid ambiguity, I recommend that you either specify a time zone offset using hours and minutes (as in –5:00) or use a combination of full region name and time zone abbreviation as in US/Eastern EDT). If you use region name alone, and there's ambiguity with respect to daylight savings time, the database will resolve the ambiguity by assuming that standard time applies.

If you're initially confused by the fact that EST, CST, or PST can be both a region name and an abbreviation, you're not alone. I was confused by this too. Depending on your time zone file version EST, CST, MST, and PST may appear as both region and abbreviation. You can further qualify each of those region names using the same string of three characters as a time zone abbreviation. The result (e.g., EST EST or CST CST) is standard time for the region in question. The best practice is to use the full region name, like US/Eastern or America/Detroit, instead of the three-letter abbreviation EST. See Oracle's Metalink Note 340512.1 *Timestamps & time zones—Frequently Asked Questions* for more information.

You can get a complete list of the time zone region names and time zone abbreviations that Oracle supports by querying the V$TIMEZONE_NAMES view. Any database user can access that view. When you query it, notice that time zone abbreviations are not unique (see the sidebar "A Time Zone Standard?" on page 287).

## Requiring a Format Mask to Match Exactly

When converting a character string to a datetime, the TO_* conversion functions normally make a few allowances:

- Extra blanks in the character string are ignored.
- Numeric values, such as the day number or the year, do not have to include leading zeros to fill out the mask.
- Punctuation in the string to be converted can simply match the length and position of punctuation in the format.

This kind of flexibility is great—until you want to actually restrict a user or even a batch process from entering data in a nonstandard format. In some cases, it simply is not OK when a date string has a caret (^) instead of a hyphen (-) between the day and month numbers. For these situations, you can use the FX modifier in the format mask to enforce an exact match between string and format model.

With FX, there is no flexibility in the interpretation of the string. It cannot have extra blanks if none are found in the model. Its numeric values must include leading zeros if the format model specifies additional digits. And the punctuation and literals must exactly match the punctuation and quoted text of the format mask (except for case, which is always ignored). In all of the following examples:

```
TO_DATE ('1-1-4', 'fxDD-MM-YYYY')
TO_DATE ('7/16/94', 'FXMM/DD/YY')
TO_DATE ('JANUARY^1^ the year of 94', 'FXMonth-dd-"WhatIsaynotdo"yy')
```

PL/SQL raises one of the following errors:

```
ORA-01861: literal does not match format string
ORA-01862: the numeric value does not match the length of the format item
```

However, the following example succeeds because case is always irrelevant, and FX does not change that:

```
TO_DATE ('Jan 15 1994', 'fxMON DD YYYY')
```

The FX modifier can be specified in upper-, lower-, or mixed-case; the effect is the same.

The FX modifier is a toggle, and can appear more than once in a format model. For example:

```
TO_DATE ('07-1-1994', 'FXDD-FXMM-FXYYYY')
```

Each time it appears in the format, FX changes the effect of the modifier. In this example, an exact match is required for the day number and the year number but not for the month number.

## Easing Up on Exact Matches

You can use FM (fill mode) in the format model of a call to a TO_DATE or TO_TIME-STAMP function to fill a string with blanks or zeros so that a date string that would otherwise fail the FX test will pass. For example:

```
TO_DATE ('07-1-94', 'FXfmDD-FXMM-FXYYYY')
```

This conversion succeeds, because FM causes the year 94 to be filled out with 00, so the year becomes 0094 (probably not behavior you would ever want). The day 1 is filled out with a single zero to become 01. FM is a toggle, just like FX.

Using FM as I've just described seems at first to defeat the purpose of FX. Why use both? One reason is that you might use FX to enforce the use of specific delimiters while using FM to ease up on the requirement that users enter leading zeros.

## Interpreting Two-Digit Years in a Sliding Window

The last millennium change caused an explosion of interest in using four-digit years as people suddenly realized the ambiguity inherent in the commonly used two-digit year. For example, does 1-Jan-45 refer to 1945 or 2045? The best practice is to use unambiguous four-digit years. But, despite this realization, habits are tough to break, and existing systems can be difficult to change, so you may find yourself still needing to allow your users to enter dates using two-digit years rather than four-digit years. To help, Oracle provides the RR format element to interpret two-digit years in a sliding window.

---

In the following discussion, I use the term "century" colloquially. RR's 20th century is composed of the years 1900–1999, and its 21st century is composed of the years 2000–2099. I realize this is not the proper definition of century, but it's a definition that makes it easier to explain RR's behavior.

If the current year is in the first half of the century (years 0 through 49), then:

- If you enter a date in the first half of the century (i.e., from 0 through 49), RR returns the current century.

- If you enter a date in the latter half of the century (i.e., from 50 through 99), RR returns the previous century.

On the other hand, if the current year is in the latter half of the century (years 50 through 99), then:

- If you enter a date in the first half of the century, RR returns the next century.

- If you enter a date in the latter half of the century, RR returns the current century.

Confusing? I had to think about it for awhile too. The RR rules are an attempt to make the best guess as to which century is intended when a user leaves off that information. Here are some examples of the impact of RR. Notice that for year 88 and year 18, SYSDATE returns a current date in the 20th and 21st centuries, respectively:

```
SELECT TO_CHAR (SYSDATE, 'MM/DD/YYYY') "Current Date",
       TO_CHAR (TO_DATE ('14-OCT-88', 'DD-MON-RR'), 'YYYY') "Year 88",
       TO_CHAR (TO_DATE ('14-OCT-18', 'DD-MON-RR'), 'YYYY') "Year 18"
  FROM dual;

Current Date Year 88 Year 18
------------ ------- -------
  02/25/2002    1988    2018
```

When we reach the year 2050, RR will interpret the same dates differently:

```
SELECT TO_CHAR (SYSDATE, 'MM/DD/YYYY') "Current Date",
       TO_CHAR (TO_DATE ('10/14/88', 'MM/DD/RR'), 'YYYY') "Year 88",
       TO_CHAR (TO_DATE ('10/14/18', 'MM/DD/RR'), 'YYYY') "Year 18"
  FROM dual;

Current Date Year 88 Year 18
------------ ------- -------
  02/25/2050    2088    2118
```

There are a number of ways you can activate the RR logic in your current applications. The cleanest and simplest way is to change the default format mask for dates in your database instance(s). In fact, Oracle has already done this for us. On a default Oracle install, you will find your NLS_DATE_FORMAT equivalent to the result of:

```
ALTER SESSION SET NLS_DATE_FORMAT='DD-MON-RR';
```

Then, if you have not hardcoded the date format mask anywhere else in your screens or reports, any two-digit years will be interpreted according to the windowing rules I've just described.

## Converting Time Zones to Character Strings

Time zones add complexity to the problem of converting datetime values to character strings. Time zone information consists of the following elements:

- A displacement from UTC in terms of hours and minutes
- A time zone region name
- A time zone abbreviation

All these elements are stored separately in a TIMESTAMP WITH TIME ZONE variable. The displacement from UTC is always present, but whether you can display the region name or abbreviation depends on whether you've specified that information to begin with. Look closely at this example:

```
DECLARE
    ts1 TIMESTAMP WITH TIME ZONE;
    ts2 TIMESTAMP WITH TIME ZONE;
    ts3 TIMESTAMP WITH TIME ZONE;
BEGIN
    ts1 := TO_TIMESTAMP_TZ('2002-06-18 13:52:00.123456789 -5:00',
                            'YYYY-MM-DD HH24:MI:SS.FF TZH:TZM');
    ts2 := TO_TIMESTAMP_TZ('2002-06-18 13:52:00.123456789 US/Eastern',
                            'YYYY-MM-DD HH24:MI:SS.FF TZR');
    ts3 := TO_TIMESTAMP_TZ('2002-06-18 13:52:00.123456789 US/Eastern EDT',
                            'YYYY-MM-DD HH24:MI:SS.FF TZR TZD');

    DBMS_OUTPUT.PUT_LINE(TO_CHAR(ts1,
        'YYYY-MM-DD HH:MI:SS.FF AM TZH:TZM TZR TZD'));
    DBMS_OUTPUT.PUT_LINE(TO_CHAR(ts2,
        'YYYY-MM-DD HH:MI:SS.FF AM TZH:TZM TZR TZD'));
    DBMS_OUTPUT.PUT_LINE(TO_CHAR(ts3,
        'YYYY-MM-DD HH:MI:SS.FF AM TZH:TZM TZR TZD'));
    END;
```

The output is:

```
2002-06-18 01:52:00.123457000 PM -05:00 -05:00
2002-06-18 01:52:00.123457000 PM -04:00 US/EASTERN EDT
2002-06-18 01:52:00.123457000 PM -04:00 US/EASTERN EDT
```

Note the following with respect to the display of time zone information:

- For ts1, I specified time zone in terms of a displacement from UTC. Thus, when ts1 was displayed, only the displacement could be displayed.
- In the absence of a region name for ts1, the database provided the time zone displacement. This is preferable to providing no information at all.

- For ts2, I specified a time zone region. That region was translated internally into an offset from UTC, but the region name was preserved. Thus, both the UTC offset and the region name could be displayed.

- For ts2, the database correctly recognized that daylight savings time is in effect during the month of June. As a result, the value of ts2 was implicitly associated with the EDT abbreviation.

- For ts3, I specified a time zone region and an abbreviation, and both those values could be displayed. No surprises here.

There's a one-to-many relationship between UTC offsets and time zone regions; the offset alone is not enough to get you to a region name. That's why you can't display a region name unless you specify one to begin with.

## Padding Output with Fill Mode

The FM modifier described in "Easing Up on Exact Matches" on page 288 can also be used when converting *from* a datetime *to* a character string, to suppress padded blanks and leading zeros that would otherwise be returned by the TO_CHAR function.

By default, the following format mask results in both padded blanks and leading zeros (there are five spaces between the month name and the day number):

```
TO_CHAR (SYSDATE, 'Month DD, YYYY') --> 'April     05, 1994'
```

With the FM modifier at the beginning of the format mask, however, both the extra blank and the leading zeros disappear:

```
TO_CHAR (SYSDATE, 'FMMonth DD, YYYY') --> April 5, 1994'
```

The modifier can be specified in upper-, lower-, or mixed-case; the effect is the same.

Remember that the FM modifier is a toggle, and can appear more than once in a format model. Each time it appears in the format, it changes the effect of the modifier. By default (that is, if FM is not specified anywhere in a format mask), blanks are not suppressed, and leading zeros are included in the result value.

# Date and Timestamp Literals

Date and timestamp literals, as well as the interval literals that appear later in this chapter, are part of the ISO SQL standard and have been supported since Oracle9i Database. They represent yet another option for you to use in getting values into datetime variables. A *date literal* consists of the keyword DATE followed by a date (and only a date) value in the following format:

```
DATE 'YYYY-MM-DD'
```

A *timestamp literal* consists of the keyword TIMESTAMP followed by a datetime value in a very specific format:

```
TIMESTAMP 'YYYY-MM-DD HH:MI:SS[.FFFFFFFFF] [{+|-}HH:MI]'
```

The *FFFFFFFFF* represents fractional seconds and is optional. If you specify fractional seconds, you may use anywhere from one to nine digits. The time zone displacement (*+HH:MI*) is optional and may use either a plus or a minus sign as necessary. The hours are always with respect to a 24-hour clock.

 If you omit the time zone displacement in a timestamp literal, the time zone will default to the session time zone.

The following PL/SQL block shows several valid date and timestamp literals:

```
DECLARE
   ts1 TIMESTAMP WITH TIME ZONE;
   ts2 TIMESTAMP WITH TIME ZONE;
   ts3 TIMESTAMP WITH TIME ZONE;
   ts4 TIMESTAMP WITH TIME ZONE;
   ts5 DATE;
BEGIN
   --Two digits for fractional seconds
   ts1 := TIMESTAMP '2002-02-19 11:52:00.00 -05:00';

   --Nine digits for fractional seconds, 24-hour clock, 14:00 = 2:00 PM
   ts2 := TIMESTAMP '2002-02-19 14:00:00.000000000 -5:00';

   --No fractional seconds at all
   ts3 := TIMESTAMP '2002-02-19 13:52:00 -5:00';

   --No time zone, defaults to session time zone
   ts4 := TIMESTAMP '2002-02-19 13:52:00';

   --A date literal
   ts5 := DATE '2002-02-19';
END;
```

The format for date and timestamp literals is prescribed by the ANSI/ISO standards, and cannot be changed by you or by the DBA. Thus, it's safe to use timestamp literals whenever you need to embed a specific datetime value (e.g., a constant) in your code.

 Oracle allows the use of time zone region names in timestamp literals—for example: TIMESTAMP '2002-02-19 13:52:00 EST'. However, this functionality goes above and beyond the SQL standard.

# Interval Conversions

An interval is composed of one or more datetime elements. For example, you might choose to express an interval in terms of years and months, or you might choose to speak in terms of hours and minutes. Table 10-2 lists the standard names for each of the datetime elements used to express intervals. These are the names you must use in conjunction with the conversion functions and expressions described in the subsections that follow. The names are not case-sensitive when used with the interval conversion functions. For example, YEAR, Year, and year are all equivalent.

*Table 10-2. Interval element names*

| Name | Description |
|------|-------------|
| YEAR | Some number of years, ranging from 1 through 999,999,999 |
| MONTH | Some number of months, ranging from 0 through 11 |
| DAY | Some number of days, ranging from 0 to 999,999,999 |
| HOUR | Some number of hours, ranging from 0 through 23 |
| MINUTE | Some number of minutes, ranging from 0 through 59 |
| SECOND | Some number of seconds, ranging from 0 through 59.999999999 |

## Converting from Numbers to Intervals

The NUMTOYMINTERVAL and NUMTODSINTERVAL functions allow you to convert a single numeric value to one of the interval datatypes. You do this by associating your numeric value with one of the interval elements listed in Table 10-2.

The function NUMTOYMINTERVAL (pronounced "num to Y M interval") converts a numeric value to an interval of type INTERVAL YEAR TO MONTH. The function NUMTODSINTERVAL (pronounced "num to D S interval") likewise converts a numeric value to an interval of type INTERVAL DAY TO SECOND.

Following is an example of NUMTOYMINTERVAL being used to convert 10.5 to an INTERVAL YEAR TO MONTH value. The second argument, Year, indicates that the number represents some number of years.

```
DECLARE
    y2m INTERVAL YEAR TO MONTH;
BEGIN
    y2m := NUMTOYMINTERVAL (10.5,'Year');
    DBMS_OUTPUT.PUT_LINE(y2m);
END;
```

The output is:

```
+10-06
```

In this example, 10.5 years was converted to an interval of 10 years, 6 months. Any fractional number of years (in this case 0.5) will be converted to an equivalent number of months, with the result being rounded to an integer. Thus, 10.9 years will convert to an interval of 10 years, 10 months.

The next example converts a numeric value to an interval of type INTERVAL DAY TO SECOND:

```
DECLARE
  an_interval INTERVAL DAY TO SECOND;
BEGIN
  an_interval := NUMTODSINTERVAL (1440,'Minute');
  DBMS_OUTPUT.PUT_LINE(an_interval);
END;
```

The output is:

```
+01 00:00:00.000000

PL/SQL procedure successfully completed.
```

As you can see, the database has automatically taken care of normalizing the input value of 1440 minutes to an interval value of 1 day. This is great, because now you don't need to do that work yourself. You can easily display any number of minutes (or seconds or days or hours) in a normalized format that makes sense to the reader. Prior to the introduction of the interval datatypes, you would have needed to write your own code to translate a minute value into the correct number of days, hours, and minutes.

## Converting Strings to Intervals

The NUMTO functions are fine if you are converting numeric values to intervals, but what about character string conversions? For those, you can use TO_YMINTERVAL and TO_DSINTERVAL, depending on whether you are converting to an INTERVAL YEAR TO MONTH or an INTERVAL DAY TO SECOND.

TO_YMINTERVAL converts a character string value into an INTERVAL YEAR TO MONTH value, and is invoked as follows:

```
TO_YMINTERVAL('Y-M')
```

where *Y* represents some number of years, and *M* represents some number of months. You must supply both values and separate them using a dash.

Likewise, TO_DSINTERVAL converts a character string into an INTERVAL DAY TO SECOND value. Invoke TO_DSINTERVAL using the following format:

```
TO_DSINTERVAL('D HH:MI:SS.FF')
```

where *D* is some number of days, and *HH:MI:SS.FF* represents hours, minutes, seconds and fractional seconds.

The following example shows an invocation of each of these functions:

```
DECLARE
  y2m INTERVAL YEAR TO MONTH;
  d2s1 INTERVAL DAY TO SECOND;
  d2s2 INTERVAL DAY TO SECOND;
BEGIN
  y2m := TO_YMINTERVAL('40-3'); --my age
  d2s1 := TO_DSINTERVAL('10 1:02:10');
  d2s2 := TO_DSINTERVAL('10 1:02:10.123'); --fractional seconds
END;
```

When invoking either function, you must supply all relevant values. You cannot, for example, invoke TO_YMINTERVAL specifying only a year, or invoke TO_DS_INTERVAL leaving off the seconds. You can, however, omit the fractional seconds.

## Formatting Intervals for Display

So far in this section on interval conversion, I've relied on the database's implicit conversion mechanism to format interval values for display. And that's pretty much the best that you can do. You can pass an interval to TO_CHAR, but TO_CHAR will ignore any format mask. For example:

```
DECLARE
    y2m INTERVAL YEAR TO MONTH;
BEGIN
    y2m := INTERVAL '40-3' YEAR TO MONTH;
    DBMS_OUTPUT.PUT_LINE(TO_CHAR(y2m,'YY "Years" and MM "Months"'));
END;
```

The output is the same as if no format mask had been specified:

```
+000040-03
```

If you're not satisfied with the default conversion of intervals to character strings, you can use the EXTRACT function:

```
DECLARE
    y2m INTERVAL YEAR TO MONTH;
BEGIN
    y2m := INTERVAL '40-3' YEAR TO MONTH;

    DBMS_OUTPUT.PUT_LINE(
        EXTRACT(YEAR FROM y2m) || ' Years and '
        || EXTRACT(MONTH FROM y2m) || ' Months'
    );
END;
```

The output is:

```
40 Years and 3 Months
```

EXTRACT is described in more detail in "CAST and EXTRACT" on page 297.

# Interval Literals

Interval literals are similar to timestamp literals and are useful when you want to embed interval values as constants within your code. Interval literals take the following form:

```
INTERVAL 'character_representation' start_element TOend_element
```

where:

*character_representation*
> Is the character string representation of the interval. See "Interval Conversions" on page 292 for a description of how the two interval datatypes are represented in character form.

*start_element*
> Specifies the leading element in the interval.

*end_element*
> Specifies the trailing element in the interval.

Unlike the TO_YMINTERVAL and TO_DSINTERVAL functions, interval literals allow you to specify an interval using any sequence of datetime elements from Table 10-2. There are only two restrictions:

- You must use a consecutive sequence of elements.
- You cannot transition from a month to a day within the same interval.

Following are several valid examples:

```
DECLARE
    y2ma INTERVAL YEAR TO MONTH;
    y2mb INTERVAL YEAR TO MONTH;
    d2sa INTERVAL DAY TO SECOND;
    d2sb INTERVAL DAY TO SECOND;
BEGIN
    /* Some YEAR TO MONTH examples */
    y2ma := INTERVAL '40-3' YEAR TO MONTH;
    y2mb := INTERVAL '40' YEAR;

    /* Some DAY TO SECOND examples */
    d2sa := INTERVAL '10 1:02:10.123' DAY TO SECOND;

    /* Fails in Oracle9i through 11gR2 because of a bug */
    --d2sb := INTERVAL '1:02' HOUR TO MINUTE;

    /* Following are two workarounds for defining intervals,
       such as HOUR TO MINUTE, that represent only a portion of the
       DAY TO SECOND range. */
    SELECT INTERVAL '1:02' HOUR TO MINUTE
    INTO d2sb
    FROM dual;

    d2sb := INTERVAL '1' HOUR + INTERVAL '02' MINUTE;
END;
```

In Oracle9*i* Database through Oracle Database 11*g* Release 2, expressions such as `INTERVAL '1:02' HOUR TO MINUTE` that don't specify a value for each possible element will work from a SQL statement but not from a PL/SQL statement. Furthermore, you'll get an error about using the keyword BULK in the wrong context. This is a bug that I hope to see fixed in a future release.

One very convenient thing that the database will do for you is to normalize interval values. In the following example, 72 hours and 15 minutes is normalized to 3 days, 0 hours, and 15 minutes:

```
DECLARE
    d2s INTERVAL DAY TO SECOND;
BEGIN
    SELECT INTERVAL '72:15' HOUR TO MINUTE INTO d2s FROM DUAL;
    DBMS_OUTPUT.PUT_LINE(d2s);
END;
```

The output is:

```
+03 00:15:00.000000
```

The database will normalize only the high-end value (hours in this example) of an interval literal. An attempt to specify an interval of 72:75 (72 hours and 75 minutes) results in an error.

# CAST and EXTRACT

CAST and EXTRACT are standard SQL functions that are sometimes useful when working with datetimes. CAST made its appearance in Oracle8 Database as a mechanism for explicitly identifying collection types, and it was enhanced in Oracle8*i* Database to enable conversion between built-in datatypes. With respect to date and time, you can use CAST to convert datetime values to and from character strings. The EXTRACT function introduced in Oracle9*i* Database allows you to pluck an individual datetime element from a datetime or interval value.

## The CAST Function

With respect to date and time, you can use the CAST function to:

- Convert a character string to a datetime value.
- Convert a datetime value to a character string.
- Convert one datetime type (e.g., DATE) to another (e.g., TIMESTAMP).

When used to convert datetimes to and from character strings, CAST respects the NLS parameter settings. Check your settings by querying V$NLS_PARAMETERS, and change them with an ALTER SESSION command. The NLS settings for datetimes are:

*NLS_DATE_FORMAT*
> When casting to or from a DATE

*NLS_TIMESTAMP_FORMAT*
> When casting to or from a TIMESTAMP or a TIMESTAMP WITH LOCAL TIME ZONE

*NLS_TIMESTAMP_TZ_FORMAT*
> When casting to or from a TIMESTAMP WITH TIME ZONE

The following example illustrates the use of CAST for each of these datetime types. The example assumes the default values of `'DD-MON-RR'`, `'DD-MON-RR HH.MI.SSXFF AM'`, and `'DD-MON-RR HH.MI.SSXFF AM TZR'` for NLS_DATE_FORMAT, NLS_TIME-STAMP_FORMAT, and NLS_TIMESTAMP_TZ_FORMAT, respectively.

```
DECLARE
   tstz TIMESTAMP WITH TIME ZONE;
   string VARCHAR2(40);
   tsltz TIMESTAMP WITH LOCAL TIME ZONE;
BEGIN
   -- convert string to datetime
   tstz := CAST ('24-Feb-2009 09.00.00.00 PM US/Eastern'
               AS TIMESTAMP WITH TIME ZONE);
   -- convert datetime back to string
   string := CAST (tstz AS VARCHAR2);
   tsltz := CAST ('24-Feb-2009 09.00.00.00 PM'
               AS TIMESTAMP WITH LOCAL TIME ZONE);

   DBMS_OUTPUT.PUT_LINE(tstz);
   DBMS_OUTPUT.PUT_LINE(string);
   DBMS_OUTPUT.PUT_LINE(tsltz);
END;
```

The output is:

```
24-FEB-09 09.00.00.000000 PM US/EASTERN
24-FEB-09 09.00.00.000000 PM US/EASTERN
24-FEB-09 09.00.00.000000 PM
```

This example generates a TIMESTAMP WITH TIME ZONE from a character string, converts that value to a VARCHAR2, and finally converts a character string to a TIME-STAMP WITH LOCAL TIME ZONE.

You might be asking yourself when you should use CAST. CAST does have some overlap with the TO_DATE, TO_TIMESTAMP, and TO_TIMESTAMP_TZ functions. However, the TO_TIMESTAMP function can take only a string as input, whereas CAST can take a string or a DATE as input and convert it to TIMESTAMP. So, use CAST when you have requirements that the TO_ functions can't handle. However, when there's a TO_ function that will fit the need, you should use the TO_ function as it generally leads to more readable code.

---

In a SQL statement, you can specify the size of a datatype in a CAST, as in `CAST (x AS VARCHAR2(40))`. However, PL/SQL does not allow you to specify the size of the target datatype.

## The EXTRACT Function

The EXTRACT function is used to extract date components from a datetime value. Use the following format when invoking EXTRACT:

```
EXTRACT (component_name, FROM {datetime | interval})
```

In this syntax, *component_name* is the name of a datetime element listed in Table 10-3. Component names are not case-sensitive. Replace *datetime* or *interval* with a valid datetime or interval value. The function's return type depends on the component you are extracting.

*Table 10-3. Datetime component names for use with EXTRACT*

| Component name | Return datatype |
|---|---|
| YEAR | NUMBER |
| MONTH | NUMBER |
| DAY | NUMBER |
| HOUR | NUMBER |
| MINUTE | NUMBER |
| SECOND | NUMBER |
| TIMEZONE_HOUR | NUMBER |
| TIMEZONE_MINUTE | NUMBER |
| TIMEZONE_REGION | VARCHAR2 |
| TIMEZONE_ABBR | VARCHAR2 |

The following example shows EXTRACT being used to check whether the current month is November:

```
BEGIN
   IF EXTRACT (MONTH FROM SYSDATE) = 11 THEN
      DBMS_OUTPUT.PUT_LINE('It is November');
   ELSE
      DBMS_OUTPUT.PUT_LINE('It is not November');
   END IF;
END;
```

Use EXTRACT when you need to use a datetime element to control program flow, as in this example, or when you need a datetime element as a numeric value.

# Datetime Arithmetic

Datetime arithmetic in an Oracle database can be reduced to the following types of operations:

- Adding or subtracting an interval to or from a datetime value.
- Subtracting one datetime value from another in order to determine the interval between the two values.
- Adding or subtracting one interval to or from another interval.
- Multiplying or dividing an interval by a numeric value.

For historical reasons, because of the way in which the database has been developed over the years, I draw a distinction between datetime arithmetic involving the DATE type and that involving the family of TIMESTAMP and INTERVAL types.

## Date Arithmetic with Intervals and Datetimes

Arithmetic with day to second intervals is easy when working with the TIMESTAMP family of datatypes. Simply create an INTERVAL DAY TO SECOND value and add or subtract it. For example, to add 1500 days, 4 hours, 30 minutes, and 2 seconds to the current date and time:

```
DECLARE
   current_date TIMESTAMP;
   result_date TIMESTAMP;
BEGIN
   current_date := SYSTIMESTAMP;
   result_date:= current_date + INTERVAL '1500 4:30:2' DAY TO SECOND;
   DBMS_OUTPUT.PUT_LINE(result_date);
END;
```

Date arithmetic with year and month values is not quite as straightforward. All days can be measured as 24 hours or 1440 minutes or even 86,400 seconds, but not all months have the same number of days. A month may have 28, 29, 30, or 31 days. (I'll ignore the goofy month when the Gregorian calendar was adopted). Because of this disparity in the number of days in a month, simply adding one month to a date can lead to an ambiguous resulting date. If you want to add one month to the last day of May, should you get the last day of June or the invalid value 31 June? Well, it all depends on what you need the dates or intervals to represent.

The Oracle database gives you the toolkit to build either result into your programs. You, the intelligent, clever developer, get to decide which behavior your system should implement. If you want an end of month to translate into an end of month (31 May + 1 month = 30 June), use the function ADD_MONTHS. If you do not want the database to alter day-of-month values, use an INTERVAL YEAR TO MONTH value. Thus 31May2008 + INTERVAL '1' MONTH will result in 31Jun2008, causing the database to throw an *ORA-01839: date not valid for month specified* error.

Date arithmetic using INTERVAL YEAR TO MONTH values is best reserved for those datetimes that are kept truncated to the beginning of a month, or perhaps to the 15th of the month—it is not appropriate for end-of-month values. If you need to add or subtract a number of months (and also years—you have the same end of month problem if you add one year to 29Feb2008) from a datetime that may include end-of-month values, look instead to the function ADD_MONTHS. This function, which returns a DATE datatype, will handle the end-of-month disparity by converting the resultant dates to the last day of the month instead of throwing an error. For example, ADD_MONTHS('31-May-2008',1) will return 30-Jun-2008. The resulting DATE will not have a time zone (or subsecond granularity), so if you need these components in your result, you will need to code some extra logic to extract and reapply these components to the computed results.

```
DECLARE
    end_of_may2008 TIMESTAMP;
    next_month TIMESTAMP;
BEGIN
    end_of_may2008 := TO_TIMESTAMP('31-May-2008', 'DD-Mon-YYYY');
    next_month := TO_TIMESTAMP(ADD_MONTHS(end_of_may2008, 1));
    DBMS_OUTPUT.PUT_LINE(next_month);
END;
```

The results are:

```
30-Jun-2008 00:00:00.000000
```

There is no SUBTRACT_MONTHS function, but you can call ADD_MONTHS with negative month values. For example, use ADD_MONTHS(current_date, -1) in the above example to go back one month to the last day of April.

## Date Arithmetic with DATE Datatypes

Date arithmetic with DATE datatypes can use INTERVAL values or can use numeric values representing days and fractions thereof. For example, to add one day to the current date and time, specify:

```
SYSDATE + 1
```

And to add four hours to the current date and time:

```
SYSDATE + (4/24)
```

Notice here my use of 4/24 rather than 1/6. I use this approach to make it plain that I am adding four hours to the value returned by SYSDATE. I could use 1/6, but then the next person to maintain the code has to figure out what is intended by 1/6. By using 4/24, I make my intent of adding four hours more explicit. Even more explicitly, I can use a meaningfully named constant like this:

```
DECLARE
    four_hours NUMBER := 4/24;
BEGIN
    DBMS_OUTPUT.PUT_LINE(
```

```
                'Now + 4 hours =' || TO_CHAR (SYSDATE + four_hours));
    END;
```

Table 10-4 shows the fractional values that you can use to represent hours, minutes, and seconds when working with DATEs. Table 10-4 also shows some easily understandable expressions that you can use to build those values, in case you prefer to use, say, 60/24/60 instead of 60/1440 to mean 60 minutes.

*Table 10-4. Fractional values in date arithmetic*

| Value | Expression | Represents |
|-------|-----------|-----------|
| 1/24 | 1/24 | One hour |
| 1/1440 | 1/24/60 | One minute |
| 1/86400 | 1/24/60/60 | One second |

Use the values in Table 10-4 consistently, and your code will be easier to understand. Once you learn three denominators, it becomes trivial to recognize that 40/86400 means 40 seconds. It's not so easy though, to recognize that 1/21610 means the same thing.

## Computing the Interval Between Two Datetimes

You can compute the interval between two TIMESTAMP family values by simply subtracting one value from the other. The result will always be of INTERVAL DAY TO SECOND. For example:

```
DECLARE
    leave_on_trip TIMESTAMP := TIMESTAMP '2005-03-22 06:11:00.00';
    return_from_trip TIMESTAMP := TIMESTAMP '2005-03-25 15:50:00.00';
    trip_length INTERVAL DAY TO SECOND;
BEGIN
    trip_length := return_from_trip - leave_on_trip;

    DBMS_OUTPUT.PUT_LINE('Length in days hours:minutes:seconds
 is ' || trip_length);
END;
```

The output is:

```
Length in days hours:minutes:seconds is +03 09:39:00.000000
```

Intervals can be negative or positive. A negative interval indicates that you've subtracted a more recent date from a date further in the past, as in:

```
18-Jun-1961 - 15-Nov-1961 = -150
```

Fundamentally, the sign of the result indicates the directionality of the interval. It's somewhat unfortunate that there is no absolute value function that applies to intervals in the same way that the ABS function applies to numeric values.

If you compute the interval between two DATE values, the result is a number representing how many 24-hour periods (not quite the same as days) are between the two values. If the number is an integer, then the difference is an exact number of days. If the number is a fractional number, then the difference includes some number of hours, minutes, and seconds as well. For example, here is the same computation as the one I specified previously, but this time using DATEs:

```
BEGIN
   DBMS_OUTPUT.PUT_LINE (
      TO_DATE('25-Mar-2005 3:50 pm','dd-Mon-yyyy hh:mi am')
      - TO_DATE('22-Mar-2005 6:11 am','dd-Mon-yyyy hh:mi am')
   );
END;
```

The output is:

```
3.40208333333333333333333333333333333333
```

The three days you can understand, but you probably wonder what exactly is represented by 0.40208333333333333333333333333333333333. Often the dates are TRUNCed before subtracting them, or the resulting number is truncated. Correctly translating a long decimal string into hours, minutes, and seconds is much easier using the INTERVAL and TIMESTAMP types.

Also useful for computing intervals between two DATEs is the MONTHS_BETWEEN function. The function syntax is:

```
FUNCTION MONTHS_BETWEEN (date1 IN DATE, date2 IN DATE)
   RETURN NUMBER
```

The following rules apply:

- If *date1* comes after *date2*, MONTHS_BETWEEN returns a positive number.

- If *date1* comes before *date2*, MONTHS_BETWEEN returns a negative number.

- If *date1* and *date2* are in the same month, MONTHS_BETWEEN returns a fraction (a value between –1 and +1).

- If *date1* and *date2* both fall on the last day of their respective months, MONTHS_BETWEEN returns a whole number (no fractional component).

- If *date1* and *date2* are in different months, and at least one of the dates is not the last day of the month, MONTHS_BETWEEN returns a fractional number. The fractional component is calculated on a 31-day month basis and also takes into account any differences in the time component of *date1* and *date2*.

Here are some examples of the uses of MONTHS_BETWEEN:

```
BEGIN
   --Calculate two ends of month, the first earlier than the second:
   DBMS_OUTPUT.PUT_LINE(
      MONTHS_BETWEEN ('31-JAN-1994', '28-FEB-1994'));

   --Calculate two ends of month, the first later than the second:
```

```
      DBMS_OUTPUT.PUT_LINE(
         MONTHS_BETWEEN ('31-MAR-1995', '28-FEB-1994'));

      --Calculate when both dates fall in the same month:
      DBMS_OUTPUT.PUT_LINE(
         MONTHS_BETWEEN ('28-FEB-1994', '15-FEB-1994'));

      --Perform months_between calculations with a fractional component:
      DBMS_OUTPUT.PUT_LINE(
         MONTHS_BETWEEN ('31-JAN-1994', '1-MAR-1994'));
      DBMS_OUTPUT.PUT_LINE(
         MONTHS_BETWEEN ('31-JAN-1994', '2-MAR-1994'));
      DBMS_OUTPUT.PUT_LINE(
         MONTHS_BETWEEN ('31-JAN-1994', '10-MAR-1994'));
   END;
```

The output is:

```
-1
13
.419354838709677419354838709677419354838
-1.032258064516129032258064516129032258065
-1.064516129032258064516129032258064516129
-1.322580645161290322580645161290322580065
```

If you think you detect a pattern here, you are right. As noted, MONTHS_BETWEEN
calculates the fractional component of the number of months by assuming that each
month has 31 days. Therefore, each additional day over a complete month counts for
1/31 of a month, and:

```
1 divided by 31 = .032258065--more or less!
```

According to this rule, the number of months between January 31, 1994 and February
28, 1994 is 1—a nice, clean integer. But the number of months between January 31,
1994 and March 1, 1994, has an additional .032258065 added to it. As with subtracting
DATEs, the TRUNC function is often used with MONTHS_BETWEEN.

## Mixing DATEs and TIMESTAMPs

The result of a subtraction involving two TIMESTAMPs is a value of type INTERVAL
DAY TO SECOND. The result of a subtraction involving two DATEs is a numeric
value. Consequently, if you want to subtract one DATE from another and return an
INTERVAL DAY TO SECOND value, you will need to CAST your DATEs into TIME-
STAMPs. For example:

```
DECLARE
   dt1 DATE;
   dt2 DATE;
   d2s INTERVAL DAY(3) TO SECOND(0);
BEGIN
   dt1 := TO_DATE('15-Nov-1961 12:01 am','dd-Mon-yyyy hh:mi am');
   dt2 := TO_DATE('18-Jun-1961 11:59 pm','dd-Mon-yyyy hh:mi am');
```

```
    d2s := CAST(dt1 AS TIMESTAMP) - CAST(dt2 AS TIMESTAMP);

    DBMS_OUTPUT.PUT_LINE(d2s);
END;
```

The output is:

```
+149 00:02:00
```

If you mix DATEs and TIMESTAMPs in the same subtraction expression, PL/SQL will implicitly cast the DATEs into TIMESTAMPs. For example:

```
DECLARE
    dt DATE;
    ts TIMESTAMP;
    d2s1 INTERVAL DAY(3) TO SECOND(0);
    d2s2 INTERVAL DAY(3) TO SECOND(0);
BEGIN
    dt := TO_DATE('15-Nov-1961 12:01 am','dd-Mon-yyyy hh:mi am');
    ts := TO_TIMESTAMP('18-Jun-1961 11:59 pm','dd-Mon-yyyy hh:mi am');

    d2s1 := dt - ts;
    d2s2 := ts - dt;

    DBMS_OUTPUT.PUT_LINE(d2s1);
    DBMS_OUTPUT.PUT_LINE(d2s2);
END;
```

The output is:

```
+149 00:02:00
-149 00:02:00
```

As with all datetime datatypes, it's best to use explicit casting and not rely on implicit datatype conversions.

## Adding and Subtracting Intervals

Unlike the case with datetime values, it makes perfect sense to add one interval to another. It also makes sense to subtract one interval from another. The one rule you need to keep in mind is that whenever you add or subtract two intervals, they must be of the same type. For example:

```
DECLARE
    dts1 INTERVAL DAY TO SECOND := '2 3:4:5.6';
    dts2 INTERVAL DAY TO SECOND := '1 1:1:1.1';

    ytm1 INTERVAL YEAR TO MONTH := '2-10';
    ytm2 INTERVAL YEAR TO MONTH := '1-1';

    days1 NUMBER := 3;
    days2 NUMBER := 1;
BEGIN
    DBMS_OUTPUT.PUT_LINE(dts1 - dts2);
    DBMS_OUTPUT.PUT_LINE(ytm1 - ytm2);
```

```
    DBMS_OUTPUT.PUT_LINE(days1 - days2);
  END;
```

The output is:

```
+000000001 02:03:04.500000000
+000000001-09
2
```

This example shows the results of three interval subtractions. The first two involve INTERVAL DAY TO SECOND and INTERVAL YEAR TO MONTH. The third shows the subtraction of two numbers. Remember: when working with DATE types, the interval between two DATE values is expressed as a NUMBER. Because months can have 28, 29, 30, or 31 days, if you add or subtract a day-to-second interval with a year-to-month interval, the database will raise an *ORA-30081: invalid datatype for datetime/interval arithmetic* exception.

## Multiplying and Dividing Intervals

Multiplication and division have no application to dates, but you can multiply an interval by a number and divide an interval by a number. Here are some examples:

```
DECLARE
    dts1 INTERVAL DAY TO SECOND := '2 3:4:5.6';
    dts2 INTERVAL YEAR TO MONTH := '2-10';
    dts3 NUMBER := 3;
BEGIN
    --Show some interval multiplication
    DBMS_OUTPUT.PUT_LINE(dts1 * 2);
    DBMS_OUTPUT.PUT_LINE(dts2 * 2);
    DBMS_OUTPUT.PUT_LINE(dts3 * 2);

    --Show some interval division
    DBMS_OUTPUT.PUT_LINE(dts1 / 2);
    DBMS_OUTPUT.PUT_LINE(dts2 / 2);
    DBMS_OUTPUT.PUT_LINE(dts3 / 2);
END;
```

The output is:

```
+000000004 06:08:11.200000000
+000000005-08
6
+000000001 01:32:02.800000000
+000000001-05
1.5
```

## Using Unconstrained INTERVAL Types

Intervals can be declared with varying levels of precision, and values of different precisions are not entirely compatible with each other. This becomes especially problematic when writing procedures and functions that accept INTERVAL values as parameters. The following example should help to visualize the problem. Notice the loss of precision when the value of dts is doubled via a call to the function double_my_interval:

```
DECLARE
   dts INTERVAL DAY(9) TO SECOND(9);

   FUNCTION double_my_interval (
      dts_in IN INTERVAL DAY TO SECOND) RETURN INTERVAL DAY TO SECOND
   IS
   BEGIN
      RETURN dts_in * 2;
   END;
BEGIN
   dts := '1 0:0:0.123456789';
   DBMS_OUTPUT.PUT_LINE(dts);
   DBMS_OUTPUT.PUT_LINE(double_my_interval(dts));
END;
```

The output is:

```
+000000001 00:00:00.123456789
+02 00:00:00.246914
```

Not only have I lost digits in my fractional seconds, but I've also lost digits where the number of days is concerned. Had dts been assigned a value of 100 days or more, the call to double_my_interval would have failed with an *ORA-01873: the leading precision of the interval is too small* error.

The issue here is that the default precision for INTERVAL types is not the same as the maximum precision. Usually, the calling program supplies the precision for parameters to a PL/SQL program, but with INTERVAL datatypes, the default precision of 2 is used. To work around this problem, I can use an explicitly unconstrained INTERVAL datatype:

*YMINTERVAL_UNCONSTRAINED*
  Accepts any INTERVAL YEAR TO MONTH value with no loss of precision

*DSINTERVAL_UNCONSTRAINED*
  Accepts any INTERVAL DAY TO SECOND value with no loss of precision

Using the DSINTERVAL_UNCONSTRAINED type, I can recode my earlier example as follows:

```
DECLARE
   dts INTERVAL DAY(9) TO SECOND(9);

   FUNCTION double_my_interval (
      dts_in IN DSINTERVAL_UNCONSTRAINED) RETURN DSINTERVAL_UNCONSTRAINED
   IS
   BEGIN
      RETURN dts_in * 2;
   END;
BEGIN
```

```
    dts := '100 0:0:0.123456789';
    DBMS_OUTPUT.PUT_LINE(dts);
    DBMS_OUTPUT.PUT_LINE(double_my_interval(dts));
END;
```

The output is:

```
+000000100 00:00:00.123456789
+000000200 00:00:00.246913578
```

Notice that I used DSINTERVAL_UNCONSTRAINED twice: once to specify the type of the formal parameter to double_my_interval, and once to specify the function's return type. As a result, I can now invoke the function on *any* INTERVAL DAY TO SECOND value with no loss of precision or ORA-01873 errors.

# Date/Time Function Quick Reference

Oracle implements a number of functions that are useful when working with datetime values. You've seen many of them used earlier in this chapter. I don't document them all here, but I do provide a list in Table 10-5 to help you become familiar with what's available. I encourage you to refer to Oracle's *SQL Reference* manual and read up on those functions that interest you.

 Avoid using Oracle's traditional date functions with the new TIME-STAMP types. Instead, use the new INTERVAL functionality whenever possible. Use date functions only with DATE values.

Many of the functions in Table 10-5 accept DATE values as inputs. ADD_MONTHS is an example of one such function. You must be careful when you consider using such functions to operate on any of the new TIMESTAMP datatypes. While you can pass a TIMESTAMP value to one of these functions, the database implicitly and silently converts that value to a DATE. Only then does the function perform its operation. For example:

```
DECLARE
    ts TIMESTAMP WITH TIME ZONE;
BEGIN
    ts := SYSTIMESTAMP;

    --Notice that ts now specifies fractional seconds
    --AND a time zone.
    DBMS_OUTPUT.PUT_LINE(ts);

    --Modify ts using one of the built-in date functions.
    ts := LAST_DAY(ts);

    --We've now LOST our fractional seconds, and the
    --time zone has changed to our session time zone.
    DBMS_OUTPUT.PUT_LINE(ts);
END;
```

The output is:

```
13-MAR-05 04.27.23.163826 PM -08:00
31-MAR-05 04.27.23.000000 PM -05:00
```

In this example, the variable ts contained a TIMESTAMP WITH TIME ZONE value. That value was implicitly converted into a DATE when it was passed to LAST_DAY. Because DATEs hold neither fractional seconds nor time zone offsets, those parts of ts's value were silently discarded. The result of LAST_DAY was assigned back to ts, causing a second, implicit conversion, this time from DATE to TIMESTAMP WITH TIME ZONE. This second conversion picked up the session time zone, and that's why you see –05:00 as the time zone offset in the final value.

This behavior is critical to understand! It's critical to avoid too. I'm sure you can imagine the kind of subtle program errors that can be induced by careless application of DATE functions to TIMESTAMP values. Frankly, I can't imagine why Oracle did not overload the built-in DATE functions so that they also worked properly for TIMESTAMPs. Be careful!

*Table 10-5. Built-in datetime functions*

| Name | Description |
| --- | --- |
| ADD_MONTHS | Returns a DATE containing the specified DATE incremented by the specified number of months. See the section "Adding and Subtracting Intervals" on page 305. |
| CAST | Converts between datatypes—for example, between DATE and the various TIMESTAMP datatypes. See the section "CAST and EXTRACT" on page 297. |
| CURRENT_DATE | Returns a DATE containing the current date and time in the session time zone. |
| CURRENT_TIMESTAMP | Returns a TIMESTAMP WITH TIME ZONE containing the current date and time in the session time zone. |
| DBTIMEZONE | Returns the time zone offset (from UTC) of the database time zone in the form of a character string (e.g., '-05:00'). The database time zone is only used with TIMESTAMP WITH LOCAL TIME ZONE datatypes. |
| EXTRACT | Returns a NUMBER or VARCHAR2 containing the specific datetime element, such as hour, year, or timezone_abbr. See the section "CAST and EXTRACT" on page 297. |
| FROM_TZ | Converts a TIMESTAMP and time zone to a TIMESTAMP WITH TIME ZONE. |
| LAST_DAY | Returns a DATE containing the last day of the month for the specified DATE. |
| LOCALTIMESTAMP | Returns the current date and time as a TIMESTAMP value in the local time zone. |
| MONTHS_ BETWEEN | Returns a NUMBER containing the quantity of months between two DATEs. See the section "Computing the Interval Between Two Datetimes" on page 302 for an example. |
| NEW_TIME | Shifts a DATE value from one time zone to another. This functionality exists to support legacy code. For any new applications, use the TIMESTAMP WITH TIME ZONE or TIMESTAMP WITH LOCAL TIME ZONE types. |
| NEXT_DAY | Returns the DATE of the first weekday specified that is later than a specified DATE. |
| NUMTODSINTERVAL | Converts a number of days, hours, minutes, or seconds (your choice) to a value of type INTERVAL DAY TO SECOND. |

| Name | Description |
| --- | --- |
| NUMTOYMINTERAL | Converts a number of years or months (your choice) to a value of type INTERVAL YEAR TO MONTH. |
| ROUND | Returns a DATE rounded to a specified level of granularity. |
| SESSIONTIMEZONE | Returns a VARCHAR2 containing the time zone offset (from UTC) of the session time zone in the form of a character string (e.g., '-05:00'). |
| SYSDATE | Returns the current date and time from the database server as a DATE value. |
| SYS_EXTRACT_UTC | Converts a TIMESTAMP WITH TIME ZONE value to a TIMESTAMP having the same date and time, but normalized to UTC. |
| SYSTIMESTAMP | Returns the current date and time from the database server as a TIMESTAMP WITH TIME ZONE value. |
| TO_CHAR | Converts datetime values to their character string representations. See the section "Datetime Conversions" on page 278. |
| TO_DATE | Converts a character string to a value of type DATE. See the section "Datetime Conversions" on page 278. |
| TO_DSINTERVAL | Converts a character string to a value of INTERVAL DAY TO SECOND. See the section "Interval Conversions" on page 292. |
| TO_TIMESTAMP | Converts a character string to a value of type TIMESTAMP. See the section "Datetime Conversions" on page 278. |
| TO_TIMESTAMP_TZ | Converts a character string to a value of type TIMESTAMP WITH TIME ZONE. See the section "Datetime Conversions" on page 278. |
| TO_YMINTERVAL | Converts a character string to a value of INTERVAL YEAR TO MONTH. See the section "Interval Conversions" on page 292. |
| TRUNC | Truncates a DATE or TIMESTAMP value to a specified level of granularity returning a DATE datatype. |
| TZ_OFFSET | Returns a VARCHAR2 containing the time zone offset from UTC (e.g., '-05:00') for a given time zone name, abbreviation, or offset. |

# CHAPTER 11

# Records

A *record* is a composite data structure, which means that it is composed of more than one element or component, each with its own value. Records in PL/SQL programs are very similar in concept and structure to the rows of a database table. The record as a whole does not have a value of its own; instead, each individual component or field has a value, and the record gives you a way to store and access these values as a group. Records can greatly simplify your life as a programmer, allowing you to write and fmanage your code more efficiently by shifting from field-level declarations and manipulation to record-level operations.

## Records in PL/SQL

Each row in a table has one or more columns of various datatypes. Similarly, a record is composed of one or more fields. There are three different ways to define a record, but once defined, the same rules apply for referencing and changing fields in a record.

The block below demonstrates the declaration of a record that is based directly on an underlying database table. Suppose that I have defined a table to keep track of my favorite books:

```
CREATE TABLE books (
   book_id        INTEGER,
   isbn           VARCHAR2(13),
   title          VARCHAR2(200),
   summary        VARCHAR2(2000),
   author         VARCHAR2(200),
   date_published DATE,
   page_count     NUMBER
);
```

I can then easily create a record based on this table, populate it with a query from the database, and then access the individual columns through the record's fields:

```
DECLARE
   my_book  books%ROWTYPE;
```

```
BEGIN
   SELECT *
     INTO my_book
     FROM books
    WHERE title = 'Oracle PL/SQL Programming, 5th Edition';

   IF my_book.author LIKE '%Feuerstein%'
   THEN
      DBMS_OUTPUT.put_line ('Our newest ISBN is ' || my_book.isbn);
   END IF;
END;
```

I can also define my own record type and use that as the basis for declaring records. Suppose, for example, that I want to work only with the author and title of a book. Rather than use %ROWTYPE to declare my record, I will instead create a record type:

```
DECLARE
   TYPE author_title_rt IS RECORD (
      author books.author%TYPE
      ,title books.title%TYPE
      );
   l_book_info author_title_rt;
BEGIN
   SELECT author, title INTO l_book_info
     FROM books WHERE isbn = '0-596-00977-1';
```

Let's take a look at some of the benefits of using records. Then I'll examine in more detail the different ways to define a record and finish up with examples of using records in my programs.

## Benefits of Using Records

The record data structure provides a high-level way of addressing and manipulating data defined inside PL/SQL programs (as opposed to stored in database tables). This approach offers several benefits, described in the following sections.

### Data abstraction

When you abstract something, you generalize it, distancing yourself from the nitty-gritty details and concentrating on the big picture. When you create modules, you abstract the individual actions of the module into a name. The name (and program specification) represents those actions.

When you create a record, you abstract all the different attributes or fields of the subject of that record. You establish a relationship between those different attributes and give that relationship a name by defining a record.

### Aggregate operations

Once you have stored information in records, you can perform operations on whole blocks of data at a time, rather than on each individual attribute. This kind of aggregate operation reinforces the abstraction of the record. Very often, you are not really interested in making changes to individual components of a record but instead to the object that represents all of those different components.

Suppose that in my job I need to work with companies. I don't really care about whether a company has two lines of address information or three; instead, I want to work at the level of the company itself, making changes to, deleting, or analyzing the status of a company. In all of these cases I am talking about a whole row in the database, not any specific column. The company record hides all that information from me, yet makes it accessible if and when I need it. This orientation brings you closer to viewing your data as a collection of objects, with rules applied to those objects.

### Leaner, cleaner code

Using records also helps you to write cleaner code and less of it. When I use records, I invariably produce programs that have fewer lines of code, are less vulnerable to change, and need fewer comments. Records also cut down on variable sprawl; instead of declaring many individual variables, I declare a single record. This lack of clutter creates aesthetically attractive code that requires fewer resources to maintain.

Use of PL/SQL records can have a dramatic, positive impact on your programs, both in initial development and in ongoing maintenance. To ensure that I get the most out of record structures, I have set the following guidelines for my code development:

*Create corresponding cursors and records*
> Whenever I create a cursor in my programs, I also create a corresponding record (except in the case of cursor FOR loops). I always FETCH into a record, rather than into individual variables. In those few instances when this involves a little extra work, I marvel at the elegance of the approach and compliment myself on my commitment to principle. And starting with Oracle9i Database Release 2, I can even use records with DML statements!

*Create table-based records*
> Whenever I need to store table-based data within my programs, I create a new (or use a predefined) table-based record to store that data. That way, I only have to declare a single variable. Even better, the structure of that record will automatically adapt to changes in the table with each compilation.

*Pass records as parameters*
> Whenever appropriate, I pass records rather than individual variables as parameters in my procedural interfaces. This way, my procedure calls are less likely to change over time, making my code more stable.

Cursors are discussed in more detail in Chapter 15. They are, however, used so commonly with records that they appear in many of the examples below.

# Declaring Records

You can declare a record in one of three ways:

*Table-based record*

Use the %ROWTYPE attribute with a table name to declare a record in which each field corresponds to—and has the same name as—a column in a table. In the following example, I declare a record named one_book with the same structure as the books table:

```
DECLARE
   one_book books%ROWTYPE;
```

*Cursor-based record*

Use the %ROWTYPE attribute with an explicit cursor or cursor variable in which each field corresponds to a column or aliased expression in the cursor SELECT statement. In the following example, I declare a record with the same structure as an explicit cursor:

```
DECLARE
   CURSOR my_books_cur IS
      SELECT * FROM books
       WHERE author LIKE '%FEUERSTEIN%';

   one_SF_book my_books_cur%ROWTYPE;
```

*Programmer-defined record*

Use the TYPE...RECORD statement to define a record in which each field is defined explicitly (with its name and datatype) in the TYPE statement for that record; a field in a programmer-defined record can even be another record. In the following example, I declare a record TYPE containing some information about my book writing career and an "instance" of that type, a record:

```
DECLARE
   TYPE book_info_rt IS RECORD (
      author books.author%TYPE,
      category VARCHAR2(100),
      total_page_count POSITIVE);

   steven_as_author book_info_rt;
```

Notice that when I declare a record based on a record TYPE, I do not use the %ROWTYPE attribute. The book_info_rt element already is a TYPE.

The general format of the %ROWTYPE declaration is:

```
record_name [schema_name.]object_name%ROWTYPE
   [ DEFAULT|:= compatible_record ];
```

The *schema_name* is optional (if not specified, then the schema under which the code is compiled is used to resolve the reference). The *object_name* can be an explicit cursor,

cursor variable, table, view, or synonym. You can provide an optional default value, which would be a record of the same or compatible type.

Here is an example of the creation of a record based on a cursor variable:

```
DECLARE
   TYPE book_rc IS REF CURSOR RETURN books%ROWTYPE;
   book_cv book_rc;

   one_book book_cv%ROWTYPE;
BEGIN
   ...
```

The other way to declare and use a record is to do so implicitly, with a cursor FOR loop. In the following block, the book_rec record is not defined in the declaration section; PL/SQL automatically declares it for me with the %ROWTYPE attribute against the loop's query:

```
BEGIN
   FOR book_rec IN (SELECT * FROM books)
   LOOP
      calculate_total_sales (book_rec);
   END LOOP;
END;
```

By far the most interesting and complicated way to declare a record is with the TYPE statement, so let's explore that feature in a bit more detail.

## Programmer-Defined Records

Table- and cursor-based records are great when you need to create program data matching those structures. Yet do these kinds of records cover all of our needs for composite data structures? What if I want to create a record that has nothing to do with either a table or a cursor? What if I want to create a record whose structure is derived from several different tables and views? Should I really have to create a "dummy" cursor just so I can end up with a record of the desired structure? For just these kinds of situations, PL/SQL offers programmer-defined records, declared with the TYPE...RECORD statement.

With the programmer-defined record, you have complete control over the number, names, and datatypes of fields in the record. To declare a programmer-defined record, you must perform two distinct steps:

1. Declare or define a record TYPE containing the structure you want in your record.

2. Use this record TYPE as the basis for declarations of your own actual records having that structure.

## Declaring programmer-defined record TYPEs

You declare a record type with the TYPE statement. The TYPE statement specifies the name of the new record structure, and the components or fields that make up that record. The general syntax of the record TYPE definition is:

```
TYPE type_name IS RECORD
   (field_name1 datatype1 [[NOT NULL]:=|DEFAULT default_value],
    field_name2 datatype2 [[NOT NULL]:=|DEFAULT default_value],
    ...
    field_nameN datatypeN [[NOT NULL]:=|DEFAULT default_value]
   );
```

where *field_nameN* is the name of the Nth field in the record, and *datatypeN* is the datatype of that Nth field. The datatype of a record's field can be any of the following:

- Hardcoded, scalar datatype (VARCHAR2, NUMBER, etc.).

- Programmer-defined SUBTYPE.

- Anchored declarations using %TYPE or %ROWTYPE attributes. In the latter case, I have created a *nested record*—one record inside another.

- PL/SQL collection type; a field in a record can be a list or even a collection.

- REF CURSOR, in which case the field contains a cursor variable.

Here is an example of a record TYPE statement:

```
TYPE company_rectype IS RECORD (
    comp# company.company_id%TYPE
  , list_of_names DBMS_SQL.VARCHAR2S
  , dataset SYS_REFCURSOR
  );
```

You can declare a record TYPE in a local declaration section or in a package specification; the latter approach allows you to globally reference that record type in any PL/SQL block compiled in the schema that owns the package or in the PL/SQL blocks of any schema that has EXECUTE privileges on the package.

## Declaring the record

Once you have created your own customized record types, you can use those types in declarations of specific records. The actual record declarations have the following format:

```
record_name record_type;
```

where *record_name* is the name of the record, and *record_type* is the name of a record type that you have defined with the TYPE...RECORD statement.

To build a customer sales record, for example, I first define a record type called customer_sales_rectype, as follows:

```
PACKAGE customer_sales_pkg
IS
```

```
TYPE customer_sales_rectype IS RECORD
  (customer_id   customer.customer_id%TYPE,
   customer_name customer.name%TYPE,
   total_sales   NUMBER (15,2)
  );
```

This is a three-field record structure that contains the primary key and name information for a customer, as well as a calculated, total amount of sales for the customer. I can then use this new record type to declare records with the same structure as this type:

```
DECLARE
   prev_customer_sales_rec customer_sales_pkg.customer_sales_rectype;
   top_customer_rec customer_sales_pkg.customer_sales_rectype;
```

Notice that I do not need the %ROWTYPE attribute, or any other kind of keyword, to denote this as a record declaration. The %ROWTYPE attribute is needed only for table and cursor records.

You can also pass records based on these types as arguments to procedures; simply use the record type as the type of the formal parameter as shown here:

```
PROCEDURE analyze_cust_sales (
   sales_rec_in IN customer_sales_pkg.customer_sales_rectype)
```

In addition to specifying the datatype, you can supply default values for individual fields in a record with the DEFAULT or := syntax. Finally, each field name within a record must be unique.

### Examples of programmer-defined record declarations

Suppose that I declare the following subtype, a cursor, and an associative array data structure.[1]

```
SUBTYPE long_line_type IS VARCHAR2(2000);

CURSOR company_sales_cur IS
   SELECT name, SUM (order_amount) total_sales
     FROM company c, orders o
    WHERE c.company_id = o.company_id;

TYPE employee_ids_tabletype IS
   TABLE OF employees.employee_id%TYPE
   INDEX BY BINARY_INTEGER;
```

I can then define the following programmer-defined record in that same declaration section:

- A programmer-defined record that is a subset of the company table, plus a PL/SQL table of employees. I use the %TYPE attribute to link the fields in the record directly

---

1. *Associative array* is the latest name for what used to be called a "PL/SQL table" or an "index-by table," as explained in detail in Chapter 12.

to the table. I then add a third field, which is actually an associative array of employee ID numbers.

```
TYPE company_rectype IS RECORD
   (company_id     company.company_id%TYPE,
    company_name   company.name%TYPE,
    new_hires_tab  employee_ids_tabletype);
```

- A mish-mash of a record that demonstrates the different kinds of field declarations in a record, including the NOT NULL constraint, the use of a subtype, the %TYPE attribute, a default value specification, an associative array, and a nested record. These varieties are shown here.

```
TYPE mishmash_rectype IS RECORD
   (emp_number NUMBER(10) NOT NULL := 0,
    paragraph_text long_line_type,
    company_nm company.name%TYPE,
    total_sales company_sales.total_sales%TYPE := 0,
    new_hires_tab employee_ids_tabletype,
    prefers_nonsmoking_fl BOOLEAN := FALSE,
    new_company_rec company_rectype
   );
```

As you can see, PL/SQL offers tremendous flexibility in designing your own record structures. Your records can represent tables, views, and SELECT statements in a PL/SQL program. They can also be arbitrarily complex, with fields that are actually records within records or associative arrays.

## Working with Records

Regardless of how you define a record (based on a table, cursor, or explicit record TYPE statement), you work with the resulting record in the same ways. You can work with the data in a record at the "record level," or you can work with individual fields of the record.

### Record-level operations

When you work at the record level, you avoid any references to individual fields in the record. Here are the record-level operations currently supported by PL/SQL:

- You can copy the contents of one record to another, as long as they are defined based on the same user-defined record types or compatible %ROWTYPE records (they have the same number of fields and the same or implicitly-convertible datatypes).
- You can assign a value of NULL to a record with a simple assignment.
- You can define and pass the record as an argument in a parameter list.
- You can RETURN a record back through the interface of a function.

Several record-level operations are not yet supported:

- You cannot use the IS NULL syntax to see if all fields in the record have NULL values. Instead, you must apply the IS NULL operator to each field individually.

- You cannot compare two records—for example, you cannot ask if the records (the values of their fields) are the same or different, or if one record is greater than or less than another. Unfortunately, to answer these kinds of questions, you must compare each field individually. I cover this topic and provide a utility that generates such comparison code in "Comparing Records" on page 325.

- Prior to Oracle9i Database Release 2, you could not insert into a database table with a record. Instead, you had to pass each individual field of the record for the appropriate column. For more information on record-based DML, see Chapter 14.

You can perform record-level operations on any records with compatible structures. In other words, the records must have the same number of fields and the same or convertible datatypes, but they don't have to be the same type. Suppose that I have created the following table:

```
CREATE TABLE cust_sales_roundup (
    customer_id NUMBER (5),
    customer_name VARCHAR2 (100),
    total_sales NUMBER (15,2)
    )
```

Then the three records defined as follows all have compatible structures, and I can "mix-and-match" the data in these records as shown:

```
DECLARE
    cust_sales_roundup_rec cust_sales_roundup%ROWTYPE;

    CURSOR cust_sales_cur IS SELECT * FROM cust_sales_roundup;
    cust_sales_rec cust_sales_cur%ROWTYPE;

    TYPE customer_sales_rectype IS RECORD
      (customer_id NUMBER(5),
       customer_name customer.name%TYPE,
       total_sales NUMBER(15,2)
       );
    preferred_cust_rec customer_sales_rectype;
BEGIN
    -- Assign one record to another.
    cust_sales_roundup_rec := cust_sales_rec;
    preferred_cust_rec := cust_sales_rec;
END;
```

Let's look at some other examples of record-level operations.

- In this example, I'll assign a default value to a record. You can initialize a record at the time of declaration by assigning it another, compatible record. In the following program, I assign an IN argument record to a local variable. I might do this so that I can modify the values of fields in the record:

```
PROCEDURE compare_companies
    (prev_company_rec IN company%ROWTYPE)
```

```
IS
   curr_company_rec company%ROWTYPE := prev_company_rec;
BEGIN
   ...
END;
```

- In this next initialization example, I create a new record type and record. I then create a second record type using the first record type as its single column. Finally, I initialize this new record with the previously defined record:

```
DECLARE
   TYPE first_rectype IS RECORD (var1 VARCHAR2(100) := 'WHY NOT');
   first_rec first_rectype;
   TYPE second_rectype IS RECORD (nested_rec first_rectype := first_rec);
BEGIN
   ...
END;
```

- I can also perform assignments within the execution section, as you might expect. In the following example I declare two different rain_forest_history records and then set the current history information to the previous history record:

```
DECLARE
   prev_rain_forest_rec rain_forest_history%ROWTYPE;
   curr_rain_forest_rec rain_forest_history%ROWTYPE;
BEGIN
   ... initialize previous year rain forest data ...

   -- Transfer data from previous to current records.
   curr_rain_forest_rec := prev_rain_forest_rec;
```

- The result of this aggregate assignment is that the value of each field in the current record is set to the value of the corresponding field in the previous record. I could also have accomplished this with individual direct assignments from the previous to current records. This would have required multiple, distinct assignments and lots of typing; whenever possible, use record-level operations to save time and make your code less vulnerable to change.

- I can move data directly from a row in a table to a record in a program by fetching directly into a record. Here are two examples:

```
DECLARE
   /*
   || Declare a cursor and then define a record based on that cursor
   || with the %ROWTYPE attribute.
   */
   CURSOR cust_sales_cur IS
      SELECT customer_id, customer_name, SUM (total_sales) tot_sales
        FROM cust_sales_roundup
       WHERE sold_on < ADD_MONTHS (SYSDATE, -3)
       GROUP BY customer_id, customer_name;
   cust_sales_rec cust_sales_cur%ROWTYPE;
BEGIN
   /* Move values directly into record by fetching from cursor */
```

```
   OPEN cust_sales_cur;
   FETCH cust_sales_cur INTO cust_sales_rec;
   CLOSE cust_sales_cur;
```

In this next block, I declare a programmer-defined TYPE that matches the data retrieved by the implicit cursor. Then I SELECT directly into a record based on that type.

```
DECLARE
   TYPE customer_sales_rectype IS RECORD
      (customer_id    customer.customer_id%TYPE,
       customer_name  customer.name%TYPE,
       total_sales    NUMBER (15,2)
      );
   top_customer_rec   customer_sales_rectype;
BEGIN
   /* Move values directly into the record: */
   SELECT customer_id, customer_name, SUM (total_sales)
     INTO top_customer_rec
     FROM cust_sales_roundup
    WHERE sold_on < ADD_MONTHS (SYSDATE, -3)
     GROUP BY customer_id, customer_name;
```

- I can set all fields of a record to NULL with a direct assignment.

```
/* File on web: record_assign_null.sql */
FUNCTION dept_for_name (
   department_name_in IN departments.department_name%TYPE
)
   RETURN departments%ROWTYPE
IS
   l_return    departments%ROWTYPE;

   FUNCTION is_secret_department (
      department_name_in IN departments.department_name%TYPE
   )
      RETURN BOOLEAN
   IS
   BEGIN
      RETURN CASE department_name_in
               WHEN 'VICE PRESIDENT' THEN TRUE
               ELSE FALSE
             END;
   END is_secret_department;
BEGIN
   SELECT *
     INTO l_return
     FROM departments
    WHERE department_name = department_name_in;

   IF is_secret_department (department_name_in)
   THEN
      l_return := NULL;
   END IF;
```

```
        RETURN l_return;
    END dept_for_name;
```

Whenever possible, try to work with records at the aggregate level: the record as a whole, and not individual fields. The resulting code is much easier to write and maintain. There are, of course, many situations in which you need to manipulate individual fields of a record. Let's take a look at how you would do that.

### Field-level operations

When you need to access a field within a record (to either read or change its value), you must use *dot notation*, just as you would when identifying a column from a specific database table. The syntax for such a reference is:

```
[[schema_name.]package_name.]record_name.field_name
```

You need to provide a package name only if the record is defined in the specification of a package that is different from the one you are working on at that moment. You need to provide a schema name only if the package is owned by a schema different from that in which you are compiling your code.

Once you have used dot notation to identify a particular field, all the normal rules in PL/SQL apply as to how you can reference and change the value of that field. Let's take a look at some examples.

The assignment operator (:=) changes the value of a particular field. In the first assignment, total_sales is zeroed out. In the second assignment, a function is called to return a value for the Boolean flag output_generated (it is set to TRUE, FALSE, or NULL):

```
BEGIN
    top_customer_rec.total_sales := 0;
    report_rec.output_generated := check_report_status (report_rec.report_id);
END;
```

In the next example I create a record based on the rain_forest_history table, populate it with values, and then insert a record into that same table:

```
DECLARE
    rain_forest_rec rain_forest_history%ROWTYPE;
BEGIN
    /* Set values for the record */
    rain_forest_rec.country_code  := 1005;
    rain_forest_rec.analysis_date := ADD_MONTHS (TRUNC (SYSDATE), -3);
    rain_forest_rec.size_in_acres := 32;
    rain_forest_rec.species_lost  := 425;

    /* Insert a row in the table using the record values */
    INSERT INTO rain_forest_history
            (country_code, analysis_date, size_in_acres, species_lost)
    VALUES
        (rain_forest_rec.country_code,
         rain_forest_rec.analysis_date,
         rain_forest_rec.size_in_acres,
         rain_forest_rec.species_lost);
```

```
    ...
END;
```

Notice that because the analysis_date field is of type DATE, I can assign any valid DATE expression to that field. The same goes for the other fields, and this is even true for more complex structures.

Starting with Oracle9i Database Release 2, you can also perform a record-level insert, simplifying the above INSERT statement into nothing more than this:

```
INSERT INTO rain_forest_history
   (country_code, analysis_date, size_in_acres, species_lost)
VALUES rain_forest_rec;
```

Record-level DML (for both inserts and updates) is covered fully in Chapter 14.

### Field-level operations with nested records

Suppose that I have created a nested record structure; that is, one of the fields in my "outer" record is actually another record. In the following example I declare a record TYPE for all the elements of a telephone number (phone_rectype), and then declare a record TYPE that collects all the phone numbers for a person together in a single structure (contact_set_rectype).

```
DECLARE
    TYPE phone_rectype IS RECORD
       (intl_prefix   VARCHAR2(2),
        area_code     VARCHAR2(3),
        exchange      VARCHAR2(3),
        phn_number    VARCHAR2(4),
        extension     VARCHAR2(4)
       );

    -- Each field is a nested record...
    TYPE contact_set_rectype IS RECORD
       (day_phone#    phone_rectype,
        eve_phone#    phone_rectype,
        fax_phone#    phone_rectype,
        home_phone#   phone_rectype,
        cell_phone#   phone_rectype
       );

    auth_rep_info_rec contact_set_rectype;
BEGIN
```

Although I still use the dot notation to refer to a field with nested records, now I might have to refer to a field that is nested several layers deep inside the structure. To do this I must include an extra dot for each nested record structure, as shown in the following assignment, which sets the fax phone number's area code to the home phone number's area code:

```
auth_rep_info_rec.fax_phone#.area_code :=
   auth_rep_info_rec.home_phone#.area_code;
```

### Field-level operations with package-based records

Finally, here is an example demonstrating references to packaged records (and package-based record TYPEs). Suppose that I want to plan out my summer reading (for all those days I will be lounging about in the sand outside my Caribbean hideaway). I create a package specification as follows:

```
CREATE OR REPLACE PACKAGE summer
IS
   TYPE reading_list_rt IS RECORD (
      favorite_author  VARCHAR2 (100),
      title            VARCHAR2 (100),
      finish_by        DATE);

   must_read reading_list_rt;
   wifes_favorite reading_list_rt;
END summer;

CREATE OR REPLACE PACKAGE BODY summer
IS
BEGIN  -- Initialization section of package
   must_read.favorite_author := 'Tepper, Sheri S.';
   must_read.title := 'Gate to Women''s Country';
END summer;
```

With this package compiled in the database, I can then construct my reading list as follows:

```
DECLARE
   first_book summer.reading_list_rt;
   second_book summer.reading_list_rt;
BEGIN
   summer.must_read.finish_by := TO_DATE ('01-AUG-2009', 'DD-MON-YYYY');
   first_book := summer.must_read;

   second_book.favorite_author := 'Hobb, Robin';
   second_book.title := 'Assassin''s Apprentice';
   second_book.finish_by := TO_DATE ('01-SEP-2009', 'DD-MON-YYYY');
END;
```

I declare two local book records. I then assign a "finish by" date to the packaged must-read book (notice the *package.record.field* syntax) and assign that packaged record to my first book of the summer record. I then assign values to individual fields for the second book of the summer.

Note that when you work with the UTL_FILE built-in package for file I/O in PL/SQL, you follow these same rules. The UTL_FILE.FILE_TYPE datatype is actually a record TYPE definition. So when you declare a file handle, you are really declaring a record of a package-based TYPE:

```
DECLARE
   my_file_id UTL_FILE.FILE_TYPE;
```

## Comparing Records

How can you check to see if two records are equal (i.e., that each corresponding field contains the same value)? It would be wonderful if PL/SQL would allow you to perform a direct comparison, as in:

```
DECLARE
   first_book summer.reading_list_rt := summer.must_read;
   second_book summer.reading_list_rt := summer.wifes_favorite;
BEGIN
   IF first_book = second_book /* THIS IS NOT SUPPORTED! */
   THEN
      lots_to_talk_about;
   END IF;
END;
```

Unfortunately, you cannot do that. Instead, to test for record equality, you must write code that compares each field individually. If a record doesn't have many fields, this isn't too cumbersome. For the reading list record, you would write something like this:

```
DECLARE
   first_book summer.reading_list_rt := summer.must_read;
   second_book summer.reading_list_rt := summer.wifes_favorite;
BEGIN
   IF  first_book.favorite_author = second_book.favorite_author
      AND first_book.title = second_book.title
      AND first_book.finish_by = second_book.finish_by
   THEN
      lots_to_talk_about;
   END IF;
END;
```

There is one complication to keep in mind. If your requirements indicate that two NULL records are equal (equally NULL), you will have to modify each comparison to something like this:

```
(first_book.favorite_author = second_book.favorite author
   OR( first_book.favorite_author IS NULL AND
      second_book.favorite_author IS NULL))
```

Any way you look at it, this is pretty tedious coding. Wouldn't it be great if you could generate code to do this for you? In fact, it's not all that difficult to do precisely that—at least if the records you want to compare are defined with %ROWTYPE against a table or view. In this case, you can obtain the names of all fields from the ALL_TAB_COLUMNS data dictionary view and then format the appropriate code out to the screen or to a file.

Better yet, you don't have to figure all that out yourself. Instead, you can download and run the "records equal" generator designed by Dan Spencer; you will find his package on the book's web site in the *gen_record_comparison.pkg* file.

## Trigger Pseudo-Records

When you are writing code inside database triggers for a particular table, the database makes available to you two structures, OLD and NEW, which are *pseudo-records*. These structures have the same format as table-based records declared with %ROW-TYPE: they have a field for every column in the table:

*OLD*

This pseudo-record shows the values of each column in the table *before* the current transaction started.

*NEW*

This pseudo-record reveals the new values of each column about to be placed in the table when the current transaction completes.

When you reference OLD and NEW within the body of the trigger, you must preface those identifiers with a colon; within the WHEN clause, however, do not use the colon. Here is an example:

```
TRIGGER check_raise
   AFTER UPDATE OF salary
   ON employee
   FOR EACH ROW
WHEN  (OLD.salary != NEW.salary) OR
      (OLD.salary IS NULL AND NEW.salary IS NOT NULL) OR
      (OLD.salary IS NOT NULL AND NEW.salary IS NULL)
BEGIN
   IF :NEW.salary > 100000 THEN ...
```

Chapter 19 offers a more complete explanation of how you can put the OLD and NEW pseudo-records to use in your database triggers. In particular, that chapter describes the many restrictions on how you can work with OLD and NEW.

# CHAPTER 12

# Collections

A *collection* is a data structure that acts like a list or a single-dimensional array. Collections are, in fact, the closest you can get in the PL/SQL language to traditional arrays. This chapter will help you decide which of the three different types of collections (associative array, nested table, and VARRAY) best fit your program requirements and show you how to define and manipulate those structures.

Here are some of the ways I've found collections handy:

*Maintain in-program lists of data*

> Most generally, I use collections to keep track of lists of data elements within my programs. Yes, you could use relational tables or global temporary tables (which would involve many context switches) or delimited strings, but collections are very efficient structures that can be manipulated with very clean, maintainable code.

*Improve multirow SQL operations by an order of magnitude or more*

> You can use collections in conjunction with FORALL and BULK COLLECT to dramatically improve the performance of multirow SQL operations. These "bulk" operations are covered in detail in Chapter 21.

*Cache database information*

> Collections are appropriate for caching database information that is static and frequently queried in a single session (or simply queried repeatedly in a single program) to speed up performance of those queries.

I have noticed over the years that relatively few developers know about and use collections. This always comes as a surprise, because I find them to be so handy. A primary reason for this limited usage is that collections are relatively complicated. Three different types of collections, multiple steps involved in defining and using them, usage in both PL/SQL programs and database objects, more complex syntax than simply working with individual variables: all of these factors conspire to limit usage of collections.

I have organized this chapter to be comprehensive in my treatment of collections, avoid redundancy in treatment of similar topics across different collection types, and offer guidance in your usage of collections. The resulting chapter is rather long, but I'm confident you will get lots out of it. Here is a quick guide to the remainder of its contents:

*Collections overview*

> I start by providing an introduction to collections and some orientation: a description of the different types, an explanation of the terminology specific to collections, a robust example of each type of collection, and guidelines for deciding which type of collection to use. If you read no further than this section, you will likely be able to start writing some basic collection logic. I strongly suggest, however, that you *do* read more than this section!

*Collection methods*

> Next, I explore the many methods (procedures and functions) that Oracle provides to help you examine and manipulate the contents of a collection. Virtually every usage of collections requires usage of these methods, so you want to make sure you are comfortable with what they do and how they work.

*Working with collections*

> Now it is time to build on all those "preliminaries" to explore some of the nuances of working with collections, including the initialization process necessary for nested tables and VARRAYs, different ways to populate and access collection data, the manipulation of collection columns through the SQL language, and string-indexed collections.

*Nested table multiset operations*

> Oracle Database 10*g* "filled out" the implementation of nested tables as "multisets" by providing the ability to manipulate the contents of nested tables as sets (union, intersection, minus, etc.). You can also compare two nested tables for equality and inequality.

*Maintaining schema-level collections*

> You can define nested table and VARRAY types within the database itself. The database provides a number of data dictionary views you can use to maintain those types.

# Collections Overview

Let's start with a review of collection concepts and terminology, a description of the different types of collections, and a number of examples to get you going.

## Collections Concepts and Terminology

The following explanations will help you understand collections and more rapidly establish a comfort level with these data structures.

*Element and index value*

A collection consists of multiple elements (chunks of data), each element of which is located at a certain index value in the list. You will sometimes see an element also referred to as a "row," and an index value referred to as the "row number."

*Collection type*

Each collection variable in your program must be declared based on a predefined collection *type*. As I mentioned earlier, there are, very generally, three types of collections: associative arrays, nested tables, and VARRAYs. Within those generic types, there are specific types that you define with a TYPE statement in a block's declaration section. You can then declare and use instances of those types in your programs.

*Collection or collection instance*

The term "collection" may refer to any of the following:

- A PL/SQL variable of type associative array, nested table, or VARRAY
- A table column of type nested table or VARRAY

Regardless of the particular type or usage, however, a collection is at its core a single-dimensional list of homogeneous elements.

A collection instance is an instance of a particular type of collection.

Partly due to the syntax and names Oracle has chosen to support collections, you will also find them referred to as *arrays* and *tables*.

*Homogeneous elements*

The datatype of each row element in a collection is the same; thus, its elements are *homogeneous*. This datatype is defined by the type of collection used to declare the collection itself. This datatype can, however, be a composite or complex datatype itself; you can declare a table of records, for example. And starting with Oracle9*i* Database, you can even define multilevel collections, in which the datatype of one collection is itself a collection type, or a record or object whose attribute contains a collection.

*One-dimensional or single-dimensional*

A PL/SQL collection always has just a single column of information in each row, and is in this way similar to a one-dimensional array. You cannot define a collection so that it can be referenced as follows:

```
my_collection (10, 44)
```

This is a two-dimensional structure and not currently supported with that traditional syntax. Instead, you can create multidimensional arrays by declaring collections of collections, in which case the syntax you use will be something like this:

```
my_collection (44) (10)
```

*Unbounded versus bounded*

A collection is said to be *bounded* if there are predetermined limits to the possible values for row numbers in that collection. It is *unbounded* if there are no upper or lower limits on those row numbers. VARRAYs or variable-sized arrays are always bounded; when you define them, you specify the maximum number of rows allowed in that collection (the first row number is always 1). Nested tables and associative arrays are only theoretically bounded. I describe them as unbounded, because from a theoretical standpoint, there is no limit to the number of rows you can define in them.

*Sparse versus dense*

A collection (or array or list) is called *dense* if all rows between the first and last row are defined and given a value (including NULL). A collection is *sparse* if rows are not defined and populated sequentially; instead, there are gaps between defined rows, as demonstrated in the associative array example in the next section. VARRAYs are always dense. Nested tables always start as dense collections but can be made sparse. Associative arrays can be sparse or dense, depending on how you fill the collection.

Sparseness is a very valuable feature, as it gives you the flexibility to populate rows in a collection using a primary key or other intelligent key data as the row number. By doing so, you can define an order on the data in a collection or greatly enhance the performance of lookups.

*Indexed by integers*

All collections support the ability to reference a row via the row number, an integer value. The associative array TYPE declaration makes that explicit with its INDEX BY clause, but the same rule holds true for the other collection types.

*Indexed by strings*

Starting with Oracle9*i* Database Release 2, it is possible to index an associative array by string values (currently up to 32K in length) instead of by numeric row numbers. This feature is not available for nested tables or VARRAYs.

*Outer table*

This refers to the *enclosing* table in which you have used a nested table or VARRAY as a column's datatype.

*Inner table*

This is the *enclosed* collection that is implemented as a column in a table; it is also known as a *nested table column*.

*Store table*

This is the physical table that Oracle creates to hold values of the inner table (a nested table column).

## Types of Collections

As mentioned earlier, Oracle supports three different types of collections. While these different types have much in common, they also each have their own particular characteristics, which are summarized below.

---

*Associative arrays*

These are single-dimensional, unbounded, sparse collections of homogeneous elements that are available only in PL/SQL. They were called *PL/SQL tables* in PL/SQL 2 (which shipped with Oracle 7) and *index-by tables* in Oracle8 Database and Oracle8*i* Database (because when you declare such a collection, you explicitly state that they are "indexed by" the row number). In Oracle9*i* Database Release 1, the name was changed to *associative arrays*. The motivation for the name change was that starting with that release, the INDEX BY syntax could be used to "associate" or index contents by VARCHAR2 or PLS_INTEGER.

*Nested tables*

These are also single-dimensional, unbounded collections of homogeneous elements. They are initially dense but can become sparse through deletions. Nested tables can be defined in both PL/SQL and the database (for example, as a column in a table). Nested tables are *multisets*, which means that there is no inherent order to the elements in a nested table.

*VARRAYs*

Like the other two collection types, VARRAYs (variable-sized arrays) are also single-dimensional collections of homogeneous elements. However, they are always bounded and never sparse. When you define a type of VARRAY, you must also specify the maximum number of elements it can contain. Like nested tables, they can be used in PL/SQL and in the database. Unlike nested tables, when you store and retrieve a VARRAY, its element order is preserved.

## Collection Examples

This section provides relatively simple examples of each different type of collection with explanations of the major characteristics.

### Using an associative array

In the following example, I declare an associative array type and then a collection based on that type. I populate it with four rows of data and then iterate through the collection, displaying the strings in the collection. A more thorough explanation appears after the code.

```
 1  DECLARE
 2     TYPE list_of_names_t IS TABLE OF person.first_name%TYPE
 3        INDEX BY PLS_INTEGER;
 4     happyfamily   list_of_names_t;
 5     l_row PLS_INTEGER;
 6  BEGIN
 7     happyfamily (2020202020) := 'Eli';
 8     happyfamily (-15070) := 'Steven';
 9     happyfamily (-90900) := 'Chris';
10     happyfamily (88) := 'Veva';
11
12     l_row := happyfamily.FIRST;
```

```
13
14     WHILE (l_row IS NOT NULL)
15     LOOP
16        DBMS_OUTPUT.put_line (happyfamily (l_row));
17        l_row := happyfamily.NEXT (l_row);
18     END LOOP;
19  END;
```

The output is:

```
Chris
Steven
Veva
Eli
```

| Line(s) | Description |
|---------|-------------|
| 2–3 | Declare the associative array TYPE, with its distinctive INDEX BY clause. A collection based on this type contains a list of strings, each of which can be as long as the first_name column in the person table. |
| 4 | Declare the happyfamily collection from the list_of_names_t type. |
| 9–10 | Populate the collection with four names. Notice that I can use virtually any integer value that I like. The row numbers don't have to be sequential in an associative array; they can even be negative! I hope, however, that *you* will never write code with such bizarre, randomly selected index values. I simply wanted to demonstrate the flexibility of an associative array. |
| 12 | Call the FIRST method (a function that is "attached" to the collection) to get the first or lowest defined row number in the collection. |
| 14–18 | Use a WHILE loop to iterate through the contents of the collection, displaying each row. Line 17 shows the NEXT method, which is used to move from the current defined row to the next defined row, "skipping over" any gaps. |

### Using a nested table

In the following example, I first declare a nested table type as a schema-level type. In my PL/SQL block, I declare three nested tables based on that type. I put the names of everyone in my family into the happyfamily nested table. I put the names of my children in the children nested table. I then use the set operator, MULTISET EXCEPT (introduced in Oracle Database 10*g*), to extract just the parents from the happyfamily nested table; finally, I display the names of the parents. A more thorough explanation appears after the code.

```
REM Section A
SQL> CREATE TYPE list_of_names_t IS TABLE OF VARCHAR2 (100);
  2  /
Type created.

REM Section B
  1  DECLARE
  2     happyfamily    list_of_names_t := list_of_names_t ();
  3     children       list_of_names_t := list_of_names_t ();
  4     parents        list_of_names_t := list_of_names_t ();
  5  BEGIN
  6     happyfamily.EXTEND (4);
```

```
 7        happyfamily (1) := 'Eli';
 8        happyfamily (2) := 'Steven';
 9        happyfamily (3) := 'Chris';
10        happyfamily (4) := 'Veva';
11
12        children.EXTEND;
13        children (1) := 'Chris';
14        children.EXTEND;
15        children (2) := 'Eli';
16
17        parents := happyfamily MULTISET EXCEPT children;
18
19        FOR l_row IN parents.FIRST .. parents.LAST
20        LOOP
21           DBMS_OUTPUT.put_line (parents (l_row));
22        END LOOP;
23   END;
```

The output is:

```
Steven
Veva
```

| Line(s) | Description |
| --- | --- |
| Section A | The CREATE TYPE statement creates a nested table type in the database itself. By taking this approach, I can use the type to declare nested tables from within any schema that has EXECUTE authority on the type. I can also declare columns in relational tables of this type. |
| 2–4 | Declare three different nested tables based on the schema-level type. Notice that in each case I also call a *constructor* function to initialize the nested table. This function always has the same name as the type and is created for us by Oracle. You must initialize a nested table before it can be used. |
| 6 | Call the EXTEND method to "make room" in my nested table for the members of my family. Here, in contrast to associative arrays, I must explicitly ask for a row in a nested table before I can place a value in that row. |
| 7–10 | Populate the happyfamily collection with our names. |
| 12–15 | Populate the children collection. In this case, I extend a single row at a time. |
| 17 | To obtain the parents in this family, I simply take the children out of the happyfamily. This is straightforward in releases from Oracle Database 10*g* onwards, where we have high-level set operators like MULTISET EXCEPT (very similar to the SQL MINUS). Notice that I do not need to call the EXTEND method before filling parents. The database will do this for me automatically, when populating a collection with set operators and SQL operations. |
| 19–22 | Because I know that my parents collection is *densely filled* from the MULTISET EXCEPT operation, I can use the numeric FOR loop to iterate through the contents of the collection. This construct will raise a NO_DATA_FOUND exception if used with a sparse collection. |

### Using a VARRAY

In the following example, I demonstrate the use of VARRAYs as columns in a relational table. First, I declare two different schema-level VARRAY types. I then create a relational table, family, that has two VARRAY columns. Finally, in my PL/SQL code, I populate two local collections and then use them in an INSERT into the family table. A more thorough explanation appears after the code.

```
REM Section A
SQL> CREATE TYPE first_names_t IS VARRAY (2) OF VARCHAR2 (100);
  2  /
Type created.

SQL> CREATE TYPE child_names_t IS VARRAY (1) OF VARCHAR2 (100);
  2  /
Type created.

REM Section B
SQL> CREATE TABLE family (
  2      surname VARCHAR2(1000)
  3    , parent_names first_names_t
  4    , children_names child_names_t
  5    );

Table created.

REM Section C
SQL>
  1  DECLARE
  2     parents    first_names_t := first_names_t ();
  3     children   child_names_t := child_names_t ();
  4  BEGIN
  5     parents.EXTEND (2);
  6     parents (1) := 'Samuel';
  7     parents (2) := 'Charina';
  8     --
  9     children.EXTEND;
 10     children (1) := 'Feather';
 11
 12     --
 13     INSERT INTO family
 14              ( surname, parent_names, children_names )
 15         VALUES ( 'Assurty', parents, children );
 16  END;
SQL> /

PL/SQL procedure successfully completed.

SQL> SELECT * FROM family
  2  /

SURNAME
PARENT_NAMES
CHILDREN_NAMES
--------------------------------------------
Assurty
FIRST_NAMES_T('Samuel', 'Charina')
CHILD_NAMES_T('Feather')
```

| Line(s) | Description |
|---|---|
| Section A | Use CREATE TYPE statements to declare two different VARRAY types. Notice that with a VARRAY, I must specify the maximum length of the collection. Thus, my declarations in essence dictate a form of social policy: you can have at most two parents and at most one child. |
| Section B | Create a relational table, with three columns: a VARCHAR2 column for the surname of the family and two VARRAY columns, one for the parents and another for the children. |
| Section C, lines 2–3 | Declare two local VARRAYs based on the schema-level type. As with nested tables (and unlike with associative arrays), I must call the constructor function of the same name as the TYPE to initialize the structures. |
| 5–10 | Extend and populate the collections with the names of parents and then the single child. If I try to extend to a second row, the database will raise the *ORA-06532: Subscript outside of limit* error. |
| 13–15 | Insert a row into the family table, simply providing the VARRAYs in the list of values for the table. Oracle certainly makes it easy for us to insert collections into a relational table! |

# Where You Can Use Collections

The following sections describe the different places in your code where a collection can be declared and used. Because a collection type can be defined in the database itself (nested tables and VARRAYs only), you can find collections not only in PL/SQL programs but also inside tables and object types.

## Collections as components of a record

Using a collection type in a record is similar to using any other type. You can use associative arrays, nested tables, VARRAYs, or any combination thereof in RECORD datatypes. For example:

```
CREATE OR REPLACE TYPE color_tab_t IS TABLE OF VARCHAR2(100)
/

DECLARE
    TYPE toy_rec_t IS RECORD (
        manufacturer INTEGER,
        shipping_weight_kg NUMBER,
        domestic_colors color_tab_t,
        international_colors color_tab_t
    );
```

## Collections as program parameters

Collections can also serve as parameters in functions and procedures. The format for the parameter declaration is the same as with any other (see Chapter 17 for more details):

```
parameter_name [ IN | IN OUT | OUT ] parameter_type
    [ [ NOT NULL ] [ DEFAULT | := default_value ] ]
```

PL/SQL does not offer generic, predefined collection types (except in certain supplied packages, such as DBMS_SQL and DBMS_UTILITY). This means that before you can pass a collection as an argument, you must have already defined the collection type that will serve as the parameter type. You can do this by:

- Defining a schema-level type with CREATE TYPE
- Declaring the collection type in a package specification
- Declaring that type in an outer scope from the definition of the module

Here is an example of using a schema-level type:

```
CREATE TYPE yes_no_t IS TABLE OF CHAR(1);
/
CREATE OR REPLACE PROCEDURE act_on_flags (flags_in IN yes_no_t)
IS
BEGIN
   ...
END act_on_flags;
/
```

Here is an example of using a collection type defined in a package specification: there is only one way to declare an associative array of Booleans (and all other base datatypes), so why not define them once in a package specification and reference them throughout my application?

```
/* File on web: aa_types.pks */
CREATE OR REPLACE PACKAGE aa_types
IS
   TYPE boolean_aat IS TABLE OF BOOLEAN INDEX BY PLS_INTEGER;
   ...
END aa_types;
/
```

Notice that when I reference the collection type in my parameter list, I must qualify it with the package name:

```
CREATE OR REPLACE PROCEDURE act_on_flags (
   flags_in IN aa_types.boolean_aat)
IS
BEGIN
   ...
END act_on_flags;
/
```

Finally, here is an example of declaring a collection type in an outer block and then using it in an inner block:

```
DECLARE
   TYPE birthdates_aat IS VARRAY (10) OF DATE;
   l_dates   birthdates_aat := birthdates_aat ();
BEGIN
   l_dates.EXTEND (1);
   l_dates (1) := SYSDATE;

   DECLARE
      FUNCTION earliest_birthdate (list_in IN birthdates_aat) RETURN DATE
      IS
```

```
      BEGIN
        ...
      END earliest_birthdate;
   BEGIN
      DBMS_OUTPUT.put_line (earliest_birthdate (l_dates));
   END;
END;
```

## Collection as datatype of a function's return value

In the next example, I have defined color_tab_t as the type of a function return value, and also used it as the datatype of a local variable. The same restriction about scope applies to this usage: types must be declared outside the module's scope.

```
FUNCTION true_colors (whose_id IN NUMBER) RETURN color_tab_t
AS
   l_colors color_tab_t;
BEGIN
   SELECT favorite_colors BULK COLLECT INTO l_colors
     FROM personality_inventory
    WHERE person_id = whose_id;
   RETURN l_colors;
END;
```

(You'll meet BULK COLLECT properly in Chapter 15.)

How would you use this function in a PL/SQL program? Because it acts in the place of a variable of type color_tab_t, you can do one of two things with the returned data:

1. Assign the entire result to a collection variable.

2. Assign a single element of the result to a variable (as long as the variable is of a type compatible with the collection's elements).

Option #1 is easy. Notice, by the way, that this is another circumstance where you don't have to initialize the collection variable explicitly:

```
DECLARE
   color_array color_tab_t;
BEGIN
   color_array := true_colors (8041);
END;
```

With Option #2, I put a subscript after the function call, as follows::

```
DECLARE
   one_of_my_favorite_colors VARCHAR2(30);
BEGIN
   one_of_my_favorite_colors := true_colors (8041) (1);
END;
```

Note that this code has a small problem: if there is no record in the database table where person_id is 8041, the attempt to read its first element will raise a COLLECTION_IS_NULL exception. I must therefore trap and deal with this exception in a way that makes sense to the application.

## Collection as "columns" in a database table

Using a nested table or VARRAY, you can store and retrieve nonatomic data in a single column of a table. For example, the employee table used by the HR department could store the date of birth for each employee's dependents in a single column, as shown in Table 12-1.

*Table 12-1. Storing a column of dependents as a collection in a table of employees*

| Id (NUMBER) | Name (VARCHAR2) | Dependents_ages (Dependent_birthdate_t) |
|---|---|---|
| 10010 | Zaphod Beeblebrox | 12-JAN-1763 |
| | | 4-JUL-1977 |
| | | 22-MAR-2021 |
| 10020 | Molly Squiggly | 15-NOV-1968 |
| | | 15-NOV-1968 |
| 10030 | Joseph Josephs | |
| 10040 | Cepheus Usrbin | 27-JUN-1995 |
| | | 9-AUG-1996 |
| | | 19-JUN-1997 |
| 10050 | Deirdre Quattlebaum | 21-SEP-1997 |

It's not terribly difficult to create such a table. First I define the collection type:

```
CREATE TYPE Dependent_birthdate_t AS VARRAY(10) OF DATE;
```

Now I can use it in the table definition:

```
CREATE TABLE employees (
    id NUMBER,
    name VARCHAR2(50),
    ...other columns...,
    dependents_ages dependent_birthdate_t
);
```

I can populate this table using the following INSERT syntax, which relies on the type's default *constructor* (discussed later in this chapter) to transform a list of dates into values of the proper datatype:

```
INSERT INTO employees VALUES (10010, 'Zaphod Beeblebrox', ...,
    dependent_birthdate_t( '12-JAN-1763', '4-JUL-1977', '22-MAR-2021'));
```

Now let's look at an example of a nested table datatype as a column. When I create the outer table personality_inventory, I must tell the database what I want to call the "store table."

```
CREATE TABLE personality_inventory (
    person_id NUMBER,
    favorite_colors color_tab_t,
    date_tested DATE,
```

```
    test_results BLOB)
 NESTED TABLE favorite_colors STORE AS favorite_colors_st;
```

The NESTED TABLE...STORE AS clause tells the database that I want the store table for the favorite_colors column to be called favorite_colors_st. There is no preset limit on how large this store table, which is located "out of line" (or separate from the rest of that row's data to accommodate growth) can grow.

You cannot directly manipulate data in the store table, and any attempt to retrieve or store data directly into favorite_colors_st will generate an error. The only path by which you can read or write the store table's attributes is via the outer table. (See the discussion of collection pseudo-functions in "Working with Collections in SQL" on page 382 for a few examples of doing so.) You cannot even specify storage parameters for the store table; it inherits the physical attributes of its outermost table.

One chief difference between nested tables and VARRAYs surfaces when you use them as column datatypes. Although using a VARRAY as a column's datatype can achieve much the same result as a nested table, VARRAY data must be predeclared to be of a maximum size, and is actually stored "inline" with the rest of the table's data. For this reason, Oracle Corporation says that VARRAY columns are intended for "small" arrays, and that nested tables are appropriate for "large" arrays.

### Collections as attributes of an object type

In this example, I am modeling automobile specifications. Each Auto_spec_t object will include a list of manufacturer's colors in which you can purchase the vehicle.

```
CREATE TYPE auto_spec_t AS OBJECT (
    make VARCHAR2(30),
    model VARCHAR2(30),
    available_colors color_tab_t
);
```

Because there is no data storage required for the object type, it is not necessary to designate a name for the companion table at the time I issue the CREATE TYPE ... AS OBJECT statement.

When the time comes to implement the type as, say, an object table, you could do this:

```
CREATE TABLE auto_specs OF auto_spec_t
    NESTED TABLE available_colors STORE AS available_colors_st;
```

This statement requires a bit of explanation. When you create a "table of objects," the database looks at the object type definition to determine what columns you want. When it discovers that one of the object type's attributes, available_colors, is in fact a nested table, the database treats this table as it did in earlier examples; in other words, it wants to know what to name the store table. So the phrase:

```
...NESTED TABLE available_colors STORE AS available_colors_st
```

says that you want the available_colors column to have a store table named available_colors_st.

See Chapter 25, *Object-Oriented Aspects of PL/SQL*, for more information about Oracle object types.

## Choosing a Collection Type

Which collection type makes sense for your application? In some cases, the choice is obvious. In others, there may be several acceptable choices. This section provides some guidance. Table 12-2 illustrates many of the differences between associative arrays, nested tables, and VARRAYs.

As a PL/SQL developer, I find myself leaning toward using associative arrays as a first instinct. Why is this? They involve the least amount of coding. You don't have to initialize or extend them. They have historically been the most efficient collection type (although this distinction will probably fade over time). However, if you want to store your collection within a database table, you cannot use an associative array. The question then becomes: nested table or VARRAY?

The following guidelines will help you make your choice; I recommend, however, that you read the rest of the chapter first if you are not very familiar with collections already.

- If you need sparse collections (for example, for "data-smart" storage), your only practical option is an associative array. True, you could allocate and then delete elements of a nested table variable (as illustrated in the later section on NEXT and PRIOR methods), but it is inefficient to do so for anything but the smallest collections.

- If your PL/SQL application requires negative subscripts, you also have to use associative arrays.

- If you are running Oracle Database 10*g* or later, and you'd find it useful to perform high-level set operations on your collections, choose nested tables over associative arrays.

- If you want to enforce a limit to the number of rows stored in a collection, use VARRAYs.

- If you intend to store large amounts of persistent data in a column collection, your only option is a nested table. The database will then use a separate table behind the scenes to hold the collection data, so you can allow for almost limitless growth.

- If you want to preserve the order of elements stored in the collection column and if your dataset will be small, use a VARRAY. What is "small?" I tend to think in terms of how much data you can fit into a single database block; if you span blocks, you get row chaining, which decreases performance.

- Here are some other indications that a VARRAY would be appropriate: you don't want to worry about deletions occurring in the middle of the data set; your data has an intrinsic upper bound; or you expect, in general, to retrieve the entire collection simultaneously.

Table 12-2. Comparing Oracle collection types

| Characteristic | Associative array | Nested table | VARRAY |
|---|---|---|---|
| Dimensionality | Single | Single | Single |
| Usable in SQL? | No | Yes | Yes |
| Usable as column datatype in a table? | No | Yes; data stored "out of line" (in separate table) | Yes; data stored "in line" (in same table) |
| Uninitialized state | Empty (cannot be null); elements un-defined | Atomically null; illegal to reference elements | Atomically null; illegal to reference elements |
| Initialization | Automatic, when de-clared | Via constructor, fetch, assignment | Via constructor, fetch, assignment |
| Index type | BINARY_INTEGER (and any of its sub-types) or VARCHAR2 | Positive integer between 1 and 2,147,483,647 | Positive integer between 1 and 2,147,483,647 |
| Sparse? | Yes | Initially, no; after deletions, yes | No |
| Bounded? | No | Can be extended | Yes |
| Can assign value to any element at any time? | Yes | No; may need to EXTEND first | No; may need to EXTEND first, and cannot EXTEND past upper bound |
| Means of extending | Assign value to ele-ment with a new subscript | Use built-in EXTEND procedure (or TRIM to condense), with no pre-defined maximum | EXTEND (or TRIM), but only up to declared maximum size |
| Can be compared for equality? | No | Yes, Oracle Database 10g and later | No |
| Can be manipulated with set operators | No | Yes, Oracle Database 10g and later | No |
| Retains ordering and sub-scripts when stored in and retrieved from database? | N/A | No | Yes |

# Collection Methods (Built-ins)

PL/SQL offers a number of built-in functions and procedures, known as *collection methods*, that let you obtain information about and modify the contents of collections. Table 12-3 contains the complete list of these programs.

*Table 12-3. Collection methods*

| Method (function or procedure) | Description |
|---|---|
| COUNT function | Returns the current number of elements in a collection. |
| DELETE procedure | Removes one or more elements from the collection. Reduces COUNT if the element is not already removed. With VARRAYs, you can delete only the entire contents of the collection. |
| EXISTS function | Returns TRUE or FALSE to indicate whether the specified element exists. |
| EXTEND procedure | Increases the number of elements in a nested table or VARRAY. Increases COUNT. |
| FIRST, LAST functions | Returns the smallest (FIRST) and largest (LAST) subscript in use. |
| LIMIT function | Returns the maximum number of elements allowed in a VARRAY. |
| PRIOR, NEXT functions | Returns the subscript immediately before (PRIOR) or after (NEXT) a specified subscript. You should always use PRIOR and NEXT to traverse a collection, especially if you are working with sparse (or potentially sparse) collections. |
| TRIM procedure | Removes collection elements from the end of the collection (highest defined subscript). |

These programs are referred to as *methods* because the syntax for using the collection built-ins is different from the normal syntax used to call procedures and functions. Collection methods employ a *member method* syntax that's common in object-oriented languages such as Java.

To give you a feel for member-method syntax, consider the LAST function. It returns the greatest index value in use in the associative array. Using standard function syntax, you might expect to call LAST as follows:

```
IF LAST (company_table) > 10 THEN ... /* Invalid syntax */
```

In other words, you'd pass the associative array as an argument. In contrast, by using the member-method syntax, the LAST function is a method that "belongs to" the object—in this case, the associative array. So the correct syntax for using LAST is:

```
IF company_table.LAST > 10 THEN ... /* Correct syntax */
```

The general syntax for calling these associative array built-ins is either of the following:

- An operation that takes no arguments:

      *table_name.operation*

- An operation that takes a row index for an argument:

      *table_name.operation(index_number [, index_number])*

The following statement, for example, returns TRUE if the 15th row of the company_tab associative array is defined:

```
company_tab.EXISTS(15)
```

The collection methods are not available from within SQL; they can be used only in PL/SQL programs.

## The COUNT Method

Use COUNT to compute the number of elements defined in an associative array, nested table, or VARRAY. If elements have been DELETEd or TRIMmed from the collection, they are not included in COUNT.

The specification for COUNT is:

```
FUNCTION COUNT RETURN PLS_INTEGER;
```

Let's look at an example. Before I do anything with my collection, I verify that it contains some information:

```
DECLARE
    volunteer_list volunteer_list_ar := volunteer_list_ar('Steven');
BEGIN
    IF volunteer_list.COUNT > 0
    THEN
        assign_tasks (volunteer_list);
    END IF;
END;
```

### Boundary considerations

If COUNT is applied to an initialized collection with no elements, it returns zero. It also returns zero if it's applied to an empty associative array.

### Exceptions possible

If COUNT is applied to an uninitialized nested table or a VARRAY, it raises the COLLECTION_IS_NULL predefined exception. Note that this exception is not possible for associative arrays, which do not require initialization.

## The DELETE Method

Use DELETE to remove one, a range of, or all elements of an associative array, nested table, or VARRAY. DELETE without arguments removes all of the elements of a collection. DELETE($i$) removes the $i$th element from the nested table or associative array. DELETE($i,j$) removes all elements in an inclusive range beginning with $i$ and ending with $j$. If the collection is a string-indexed associative array, then $i$ and $j$ are strings; otherwise, $i$ and $j$ are integers.

When you do provide actual arguments in your invocation of DELETE, it actually keeps a placeholder for the "removed" element, and you can later reassign a value to that element.

In physical terms, PL/SQL releases the memory only when your program deletes a sufficient number of elements to free an *entire page of memory* (unless you DELETE all the elements, which frees all the memory immediately).

 When DELETE is applied to VARRAYs, you can issue DELETE only without arguments (i.e., remove all rows). In other words, you cannot delete individual rows of a VARRAY, possibly making it sparse. The only way to remove a row from a VARRAY is to TRIM from the end of the collection.

The following procedure removes everything but the last element in the collection. It actually uses four collection methods: FIRST, to obtain the first defined row; LAST, to obtain the last defined row; PRIOR, to determine the next-to-last row; and DELETE to remove all but the last.

```
PROCEDURE keep_last (the_list IN OUT List_t)
AS
   first_elt PLS_INTEGER := the_list.FIRST;
   next_to_last_elt PLS_INTEGER := the_list.PRIOR(the_list.LAST);
BEGIN
   the_list.DELETE(first_elt, next_to_last_elt);
END;
```

Here are some additional examples:

- Delete all the rows from the names table:

    ```
    names.DELETE;
    ```

- Delete the 77th row from the globals table:

    ```
    globals.DELETE (77);
    ```

- Delete all the rows in the temperature readings table between the 0th row and the –15,000th row, inclusively:

    ```
    temp_readings.DELETE (-15000, 0);
    ```

### Boundary considerations

If *i* and/or *j* refer to nonexistent elements, DELETE attempts to "do the right thing" and will not raise an exception. For example, if you have defined elements in a nested table in index values 1, 2, and 3, then DELETE(–5,1), will remove only the item in position 1. DELETE(–5), on the other hand, will not change the collection.

### Exceptions possible

If DELETE is applied to an uninitialized nested table or a VARRAY, it raises the COLLECTION_ IS_NULL predefined exception.

## The EXISTS Method

Use the EXISTS method with nested tables, associative arrays, and VARRAYs to determine if the specified row exists within the collection. It returns TRUE if the element exists, FALSE otherwise. It never returns NULL. If you have used TRIM or DELETE to remove a row that existed previously, EXISTS for that row number returns FALSE.

In the following block, I check to see if my row exists, and if so I set it to NULL.

```
DECLARE
   my_list color_tab_t := color_tab_t();
   element PLS_INTEGER := 1;
BEGIN
   ...
   IF my_list.EXISTS(element)
   THEN
     my_list(element) := NULL;
   END IF;
END;
```

### Boundary considerations

If EXISTS is applied to an uninitialized (atomically null) nested table or a VARRAY, or an initialized collection with no elements, it simply returns FALSE. You can use EXISTS beyond the COUNT without raising an exception.

### Exceptions possible

There are no exceptions for EXISTS.

## The EXTEND Method

Adding an element to a nested table or VARRAY requires a separate allocation step. Making a "slot" in memory for a collection element is independent from assigning a value to it. If you haven't initialized the collection with a sufficient number of elements (null or otherwise), you must first use the EXTEND procedure on the variable. Do not use EXTEND with associative arrays.

EXTEND appends element(s) to a collection. EXTEND with no arguments appends a single null element. EXTEND($n$) appends $n$ null elements. EXTEND($n,i$) appends $n$ elements and sets each to the same value as the $i$th element; this form of EXTEND is required for collections with NOT NULL elements.

Here is the overloaded specification of EXTEND:

```
PROCEDURE EXTEND (n PLS_INTEGER:=1);
PROCEDURE EXTEND (n PLS_INTEGER, i PLS_INTEGER);
```

In the following example, the push procedure extends my list by a single row and populates it:

```
PROCEDURE push (the_list IN OUT List_t, new_value IN VARCHAR2)
AS
BEGIN
   the_list.EXTEND;
   the_list(the_list.LAST) := new_value;
END;
```

I can also use EXTEND to add 10 new rows to my list, all with the same value. First I extend a single row and populate explicitly. Then I extend again, this time by 9 rows, and specify the row number with new_value as the initial value for all my new rows.

```
PROCEDURE push_ten (the_list IN OUT List_t, new_value IN VARCHAR2)
AS
   l_copyfrom PLS_INTEGER;
BEGIN
   the_list.EXTEND;
   l_copyfrom := the_list.LAST;
   the_list(l_copyfrom) := new_value;
   the_list.EXTEND (9, l_copyfrom);
END;
```

### Boundary considerations

If *n* is null, EXTEND will do nothing.

### Exceptions possible

If EXTEND is applied to an uninitialized nested table or a VARRAY, it raises the COLLECTION_IS_NULL predefined exception. An attempt to EXTEND a VARRAY beyond its declared limit raises the SUBSCRIPT_OUTSIDE_LIMIT predefined exception.

## The FIRST and LAST Methods

Use the FIRST and LAST methods with nested tables, associative arrays, and VARRAYs to return, respectively, the lowest and highest index values defined in the collection. For string-indexed associative arrays, these methods return strings; "lowest" and "highest" are determined by the ordering of the character set in use in that session. For all other collection types, these methods return integers.

The specifications for these functions follow.

```
FUNCTION FIRST RETURN PLS_INTEGER | VARCHAR2;
FUNCTION LAST RETURN PLS_INTEGER | VARCHAR2;
```

For example, the following code scans from the start to the end of my collection:

```
FOR indx IN holidays.FIRST .. holidays.LAST
LOOP
   send_everyone_home (indx);
END LOOP;
```

Please remember that this kind of loop will only work (i.e., not raise a NO_DATA_FOUND exception) if the collection is densely populated.

In the next example, I use COUNT to concisely specify that I want to append a row to the end of an associative array. I use a cursor FOR loop to transfer data from the database to an associative array of records. When the first record is fetched, the companies collection is empty, so the COUNT operator will return 0.

```
FOR company_rec IN company_cur
LOOP
    companies ((companies.COUNT) + 1).company_id
        := company_rec.company_id;
END LOOP;
```

### Boundary considerations

FIRST and LAST return NULL when they are applied to initialized collections that have no elements. For VARRAYs, which have at least one element, FIRST is always 1, and LAST is always equal to COUNT.

### Exceptions possible

If FIRST and LAST are applied to an uninitialized nested table or a VARRAY, they raise the COLLECTION_ IS_NULL predefined exception.

## The LIMIT Method

Use the LIMIT method to determine the maximum number of elements that can be defined in a VARRAY. This function will return NULL if it is applied to initialized nested tables or to associative arrays. The specification for LIMIT is:

```
FUNCTION LIMIT RETURN PLS_INTEGER;
```

The following conditional expression makes sure that there is still room in my VARRAY before extending:

```
IF my_list.LAST < my_list.LIMIT
THEN
    my_list.EXTEND;
END IF;
```

### Boundary considerations

There are no boundary considerations for LIMIT.

### Exceptions possible

If LIMIT is applied to an uninitialized nested table or a VARRAY, it raises the COLLECTION_ IS_NULL predefined exception.

## The PRIOR and NEXT Methods

Use the PRIOR and NEXT methods with nested tables, associative arrays, and VAR-RAYs to navigate through the contents of a collection.

PRIOR returns the next-lower index value in use relative to *i*; NEXT returns the next higher. In the following example, this function returns the sum of elements in a list_t collection of numbers:

```
FUNCTION compute_sum (the_list IN list_t) RETURN NUMBER
AS
   row_index PLS_INTEGER := the_list.FIRST;
   total NUMBER := 0;
BEGIN
   LOOP
      EXIT WHEN row_index IS NULL;
      total := total + the_list(row_index);
      row_index := the_list.NEXT(row_index);
   END LOOP;
   RETURN total;
END compute_sum;
```

Here is that same program working from the last to the very first defined row in the collection:

```
FUNCTION compute_sum (the_list IN list_t) RETURN NUMBER
AS
   row_index PLS_INTEGER := the_list.LAST;
   total NUMBER := 0;
BEGIN
   LOOP
      EXIT WHEN row_index IS NULL;
      total := total + the_list(row_index);
      row_index := the_list.PRIOR(row_index);
   END LOOP;
   RETURN total;
END compute_sum;
```

In this case, it doesn't matter which direction you move through the collection. In other programs, though, it can make a big difference.

### Boundary considerations

If PRIOR and NEXT are applied to initialized collections that have no elements, they return NULL. If *i* is greater than or equal to COUNT, NEXT returns NULL; if *i* is less than or equal to FIRST, PRIOR returns NULL.

Through Oracle Database 11*g*, if the collection has elements, and *i* is greater than COUNT, PRIOR returns LIMIT; if *i* is less than FIRST, NEXT returns FIRST. However, do not rely on this behavior in future database versions.

### Exceptions possible

If PRIOR and NEXT are applied to an uninitialized nested table or a VARRAY, they raise the COLLECTION_ IS_NULL predefined exception.

## The TRIM Method

Use TRIM to remove *n* elements from the end of a nested table or VARRAY. Without arguments, TRIM removes exactly one element. As I've already mentioned, confusing behavior occurs if you combine DELETE and TRIM actions on a collection; for example, if an element that you are trimming has previously been DELETEd, TRIM "repeats" the deletion but counts this as part of *n*, meaning that you may be TRIMming fewer actual elements than you think.

 Attempting to TRIM an associative array will produce a compile-time error.

The specification for TRIM is:

```
PROCEDURE TRIM (n PLS_INTEGER:=1);
```

The following function pops the last value off of a list and returns it to the invoking block. The "pop" action is implemented by trimming the collection by a single row after extracting the value.

```
FUNCTION pop (the_list IN OUT list_t) RETURN VARCHAR2
AS
   l_value VARCHAR2(30);
BEGIN
   IF the_list.COUNT >= 1
   THEN
      /* Save the value of the last element in the collection
      || so it can be returned
      */
      l_value := the_list(the_list.LAST);
      the_list.TRIM;
   END IF;
   RETURN l_value;
END;
```

### Boundary considerations

If *n* is null, TRIM will do nothing.

### Exceptions possible

The TRIM method will raise the SUBSCRIPT_BEYOND_COUNT predefined exception if you attempt to TRIM more elements than actually exist. If TRIM is applied to an uninitialized nested table or a VARRAY, it raises the COLLECTION_IS_NULL predefined exception.

 If you use TRIM and DELETE on the same collection, you can get some very surprising results. Consider this scenario: if you DELETE an element at the end of a nested table variable and then do a TRIM on the same variable, how many elements have you removed? You might think that you have removed two elements, but, in fact, you have removed only one. The placeholder that is left by DELETE is what TRIM acts upon. To avoid confusion, Oracle Corporation recommends using either DELETE or TRIM, but not both, on a given collection.

# Working with Collections

You now know about the different types of collections and the collection methods. You have seen some examples of working with associative arrays, nested tables and VARRAYs. Now it is time to dive into the details of manipulating collections in your programs. Topics in this section include:

- Exception handling with collections
- Declaring collection types
- Declaring and initializing collection variables
- Assigning values to collections
- Using collections of complex datatypes, such as collections of other collections
- Working with sequential and nonsequential associative arrays
- The power of string-indexed collections
- Working with PL/SQL collections inside SQL statements

## Declaring Collection Types

Before you can work with a collection, you must declare it, and that declaration must be based on a collection type. So the first thing you must learn to do is define a collection type.

There are two ways to create user-defined collection types :

- You can declare the collection type within a PL/SQL program using the TYPE statement. This collection type will then be available for use within the block in which the TYPE is defined. If the TYPE is defined in a package specification, then it is available to any program whose schema has EXECUTE authority on the package.

- You can define a nested table type or VARRAY type as a schema-level object within the Oracle database by using the CREATE TYPE command. This TYPE can then be used as the datatype for columns in database tables and attributes of object types, and to declare variables in PL/SQL programs. Any program in a schema with EXECUTE authority on the TYPE can reference the TYPE.

## Declaring an associative array collection type

The TYPE statement for an associative array has the following format:

```
TYPE table_type_name IS TABLE OF datatype [ NOT NULL ]
    INDEX BY index_type;
```

where *table_type_name* is the name of the collection you are creating, *datatype* is the datatype of the single column in the collection, and *index_type* is the datatype of the index used to organize the contents of the collection. You can optionally specify that the collection be NOT NULL, meaning that every row in the table must have a value.

The rules for the table type name are the same as for any identifier in PL/SQL: the name may be up to 30 characters in length; it must start with a letter; and it may include a few special characters (hash sign, underscore, and dollar sign).

The datatype of the collection's single column can be any of the following:

*Scalar datatype*

Any PL/SQL-supported scalar datatype, such as VARCHAR2, CLOB, POSITIVE, DATE, or BOOLEAN.

*Anchored datatype*

A datatype inferred from a column, previously defined variable, or cursor expression using the %TYPE attribute. You can also define collections of records with the %ROWTYPE declaration or with a user-defined record type.

*Complex datatype*

Starting with Oracle9*i* Database Release 2, you can also use object types and collection types as the datatype of a collection. This means you can nest collections within collections. This topic is covered in more detail in "Collections of Complex Datatypes" on page 370.

The index_type of the collection determines the type of data you can use to specify the location of the data you are placing in the collection. Prior to Oracle9*i* Database Release 2, the only way you could specify an index for an associative array (a.k.a. index-by table) was:

```
INDEX BY PLS_INTEGER
```

Starting with Oracle9*i* Database Release 2, the INDEX BY datatype can be BINARY_INTEGER, any of its subtypes, VARCHAR2(*N*) or %TYPE against a VARCHAR2 column or variable. In other words, any of the following INDEX BY clauses are now valid:

```
INDEX BY BINARY_INTEGER
INDEX BY PLS_INTEGER
INDEX BY POSITIVE
INDEX BY NATURAL
```

```
INDEX BY SIGNTYPE /* Only three index values - -1, 0 and 1 - allowed! */
INDEX BY VARCHAR2(32767)
INDEX BY table.column%TYPE
INDEX BY cursor.column%TYPE
INDEX BY package.variable%TYPE
INDEX BYpackage.subtype
```

Here are some examples of associative array type declarations:

```
-- A list of dates
TYPE birthdays_tt IS TABLE OF DATE INDEX BY PLS_INTEGER;

-- A list of company IDs
TYPE company_keys_tt IS TABLE OF company.company_id%TYPE NOT NULL
   INDEX BY PLS_INTEGER;

-- A list of book records; this structure allows you to make a "local"
-- copy of the book table in your PL/SQL program.
TYPE booklist_tt IS TABLE OF books%ROWTYPE
   INDEX BY NATURAL;

-- Each collection is organized by the author name.
TYPE books_by_author_tt IS TABLE OF books%ROWTYPE
   INDEX BY books.author%TYPE;

-- A collection of collections
TYPE private_collection_tt IS TABLE OF books_by_author_tt
   INDEX BY VARCHAR2(100);
```

Notice that in the above example I declared a very generic type of collection (list of dates), but gave it a very specific name: birthdays_tt. There is, of course, just one way to declare an associative array type of dates. Rather than have a plethora of collection TYPE definitions that differ only by name scattered throughout your application, you might consider creating a single package that offers a set of predefined, standard collection types. Here is an example, available in the *colltypes.pks* file on the book's web site:

```
/* File on web: colltypes.pks */
PACKAGE collection_types
IS
   -- Associative array types
   TYPE boolean_aat IS TABLE OF BOOLEAN INDEX BY PLS_INTEGER;
   TYPE date_aat IS TABLE OF DATE INDEX BY PLS_INTEGER;
   TYPE pls_integer_aat IS TABLE OF PLS_INTEGER INDEX BY PLS_INTEGER;
   TYPE number_aat IS TABLE OF NUMBER INDEX BY PLS_INTEGER;
   TYPE identifier_aat IS TABLE OF VARCHAR2(30)
      INDEX BY PLS_INTEGER;
   TYPE vcmax_aat IS TABLE OF VARCHAR2(32767)
      INDEX BY PLS_INTEGER;

   -- Nested table types
   TYPE boolean_ntt IS TABLE OF BOOLEAN;
   TYPE date_ntt IS TABLE OF DATE;
   TYPE pls_integer_ntt IS TABLE OF PLS_INTEGER;
   TYPE number_ntt IS TABLE OF NUMBER;
```

```
    TYPE identifier_ntt IS TABLE OF VARCHAR2(30);
    TYPE vcmax_ntt IS TABLE OF VARCHAR2(32767)
END collection_types;
/
```

With such a package in place, you can grant EXECUTE authority to PUBLIC, and then all developers can use the packaged TYPEs to declare their own collections. Here is an example:

```
DECLARE
    family_birthdays collection_types.date_aat;
```

### Declaring a nested table or VARRAY

As with associative arrays, you must define a type before you can declare an actual nested table or VARRAY. You can define these types either in the database or in a PL/SQL block.

To create a nested table datatype that lives in the database (and not just your PL/SQL code), specify:

```
CREATE [ OR REPLACE ] TYPE type_name AS | IS
    TABLE OF element_datatype [ NOT NULL ];
```

To create a VARRAY datatype that lives in the database (and not just your PL/SQL code), specify:

```
CREATE [ OR REPLACE ] TYPE type_name AS | IS
    VARRAY (max_elements) OF element_datatype [ NOT NULL ];
```

To drop a type, specify:

```
DROP TYPE type_name [ FORCE ];
```

To declare a nested table datatype in PL/SQL, use the declaration:

```
TYPE type_name IS TABLE OF element_datatype [ NOT NULL ];
```

To declare a VARRAY datatype in PL/SQL, use the declaration:

```
TYPE type_name IS VARRAY (max_elements)
    OF element_datatype [ NOT NULL ];
```

where:

*OR REPLACE*

Allows you to rebuild an existing type. By including REPLACE, rather than dropping and re-creating the type, all existing grants of privileges will be preserved.

*type_name*

Is a legal SQL or PL/SQL identifier. This will be the identifier to which you refer later when you use it to declare variables or columns.

*element_datatype*

Is the type of the collection's elements. All elements are of a single type, which can be most scalar datatypes, an object type, or a REF object type. If the elements are objects, the object type itself cannot have an attribute that is a collection. In PL/SQL, if you are creating a collection with RECORD elements, its fields can be only scalars or objects. Explicitly disallowed collection datatypes are BOOLEAN, NCHAR, NCLOB, NVARCHAR2, REF CURSOR, TABLE, and VARRAY (non-SQL datatype).

*NOT NULL*

Indicates that a variable of this type cannot have any null elements. However, the collection can be atomically null (uninitialized).

*max_elements*

Is the maximum number of elements allowed in the VARRAY. Once declared, this cannot be altered.

*FORCE*

Tells the database to drop the type even if there is a reference to it in another type. For example, if an object type definition uses a particular collection type, you can still drop the collection type using the FORCE keyword.

 To execute the CREATE TYPE statement, you must follow it with a slash (/), just as if you were creating a procedure, function, or package.

Note that the only syntactic difference between declaring nested table types and declaring associative array types in a PL/SQL program is the absence of the INDEX BY clause for nested table types.

The syntactic differences between nested table and VARRAY type declarations are:

- The use of the keyword VARRAY.
- The limit on VARRAY's number of elements.

### Changing nested table of VARRAY characteristics

If you have created a nested table or VARRAY type in the database, you can use the ALTER TYPE command to change several of the type's characteristics.

Use the ALTER TYPE ... MODIFY LIMIT syntax to increase the number of elements of a VARRAY type. Here is an example:

```
ALTER TYPE list_vat MODIFY LIMIT 100 INVALIDATE;
/
```

When the element type of a VARRAY or nested table type is a variable character, RAW, or numeric, you can increase the size of the variable character or RAW type or increase the precision of the numeric type. Here is an example:

```
CREATE TYPE list_vat AS VARRAY(10) OF VARCHAR2(80);
/
```

```
ALTER TYPE list_vat MODIFY ELEMENT TYPE VARCHAR2(100) CASCADE;
/
```

The INVALIDATE and CASCADE options are provided to either invalidate all dependent objects or propagate the change to both the type and any table dependents.

## Declaring and Initializing Collection Variables

Once you have created your collection type, you can reference that collection type to declare an instance of that type: the actual collection variable. The general format for a collection declaration is:

```
collection_name collection_type [:= collection_type (...)];
```

where *collection_name* is the name of the collection, and *collection_type* is the name of both the previously declared collection type and (if nested table or VARRAY) a constructor function of the same name.

A constructor has the same name as the type, and accepts as arguments a comma-separated list of elements. When you are declaring a nested table or VARRAY, you *must* initialize the collection before using it. Otherwise, you will receive this error:

```
ORA-06531: Reference to uninitialized collection
```

In the following example I create a general collection type to emulate the structure of the company table. I then declare two different collections based on that type.

```
DECLARE
    TYPE company_aat IS TABLE OF company%ROWTYPE INDEX BY PLS_INTEGER;
    premier_sponsor_list company_aat;
    select_sponsor_list company_aat;
BEGIN
    ...
END;
```

If I declare a nested table or VARRAY, I can also immediately initialize the collection by calling its constructor function. Here is an example:

```
DECLARE
    TYPE company_aat IS TABLE OF company%ROWTYPE;
    premier_sponsor_list company_aat := company_aat();
BEGIN
    ...
END;
```

I could also choose to initialize the nested table in my executable section:

```
DECLARE
    TYPE company_aat IS TABLE OF company%ROWTYPE;
    premier_sponsor_list company_aat;
BEGIN
    premier_sponsor_list:= company_aat();
END;
```

I simply must ensure that it is initialized before I try to use the collection. Associative arrays do not need to be initialized before you assign values to them (and indeed cannot be initialized in this way). As you can see, declaring collection variables, or instances of a collection type, is no different from declaring other kinds of variables: simply provide a name, type, and optional default or initial value.

Let's take a closer look at nested table and VARRAY initialization.

The previous example showed you how to initialize a collection by calling a constructor function without any parameters. You can also provide an initial set of values. Suppose now that I create a schema-level type named color_tab_t:

```
CREATE OR REPLACE TYPE color_tab_t AS TABLE OF VARCHAR2(30)
```

Next, I declare some PL/SQL variables based on that type.

```
DECLARE
   my_favorite_colors color_tab_t := color_tab_t();
   his_favorite_colors color_tab_t := color_tab_t('PURPLE');
   her_favorite_colors color_tab_t := color_tab_t('PURPLE', 'GREEN');
```

In the first declaration, the collection is initialized as empty; it contains no rows. The second declaration assigns a single value, "PURPLE", to row 1 of the nested table. The third declaration assigns two values, "PURPLE" and "GREEN", to rows 1 and 2 of that nested table.

Because I have not assigned any values to my_favorite_colors in the call to the constructor, I will have to *extend* it before I can put elements into it. The his and her collections already have been extended implicitly as needed by the constructor values list.

Assignment via a constructor function is bound by the same constraints that you will encounter in direct assignments. If, for example, your VARRAY has a limit of five elements and you try to initialize it via a constructor with six elements, the database will raise the *ORA-06532: Subscript outside of limit* error.

### Initializing implicitly during direct assignment

You can copy the entire contents of one collection to another as long as both are built from the exact same collection type (two different collection types based on the same datatype will *not* work). When you do so, initialization comes along "for free."

Here's an example illustrating the implicit initialization that occurs when I assign wedding_colors to be the value of earth_colors.

```
DECLARE
   earth_colors color_tab_t := color_tab_t ('BRICK', 'RUST', 'DIRT');
   wedding_colors color_tab_t;
BEGIN
   wedding_colors := earth_colors;
   wedding_colors(3) := 'CANVAS';
END;
```

This code initializes wedding_colors and creates three elements that match those in earth_colors. These are independent variables rather than pointers to identical values; changing the third element of wedding_colors to CANVAS does not have any effect on the third element of earth_colors.

This kind of direct assignment is not possible when datatypes are merely "type-compatible." Even if you have created two different types with the exact same definition, the fact that they have different names makes them different types. Thus, the following block of code fails to compile:

```
DECLARE
   TYPE tt1 IS TABLE OF employees%ROWTYPE;
   TYPE tt2 IS TABLE OF employees%ROWTYPE;
   t1   tt1 := tt1();
   t2   tt2 := tt2();
BEGIN
   /* Fails with error "PLS-00382: expression is of wrong type" */
   t1 := t2;
END;
```

### Initializing implicitly via FETCH

If you use a collection as a type in a database table, the Oracle database provides some very elegant ways of moving the collection between PL/SQL and the table. As with direct assignment, when you use FETCH or SELECT INTO to retrieve a collection and drop it into a collection variable, you get automatic initialization of the variable. Collections can turn out to be incredibly useful!

Although I mentioned this briefly in an earlier example, let's take a closer look at how you can read an entire collection in a single fetch. First, I want to create a table containing a collection and populate it with a couple of values:

```
CREATE TABLE color_models (
    model_type VARCHAR2(12)
  , colors color_tab_t
  )
   NESTED TABLE colors STORE AS color_model_colors_tab
/

BEGIN
   INSERT INTO color_models
   VALUES ('RGB', color_tab_t ('RED','GREEN','BLUE'));
END;
/
```

Now I can show off the neat integration features. With one trip to the database, I can retrieve all the values of the colors column for a given row and deposit them into a local variable:

```
DECLARE
   l_colors color_tab_t;
BEGIN
   /* Retrieve all the nested values in a single fetch.
```

```
   || This is the cool part.
   */
   SELECT colors INTO l_colors FROM color_models
      WHERE model_type = 'RGB';
   ...
END;
```

Pretty neat, huh? Here are a few important things to notice:

- The database, not the programmer, assigns the subscripts of l_colors when fetched from the database.
- The database's assigned subscripts begin with 1 (as opposed to 0, as in some other languages) and increment by 1; this collection is always densely filled (or empty).
- Fetching satisfies the requirement to initialize the local collection variable before assigning values to elements. I didn't initialize l_colors with a constructor, but PL/SQL knew how to deal with it.

You can also make changes to the contents of the nested table and just as easily move the data back into a database table. Just to be mischievous, let's create a Fuschia-Green-Blue color model:

```
DECLARE
   color_tab color_tab_t;
BEGIN
   SELECT colors INTO color_tab FROM color_models
      WHERE model_type = 'RGB';

   FOR element IN 1..color_tab.COUNT
   LOOP
      IF color_tab(element) = 'RED'
      THEN
         color_tab(element) := 'FUSCHIA';
      END IF;
   END LOOP;

   /* Here is the cool part of this example. Only one insert
   || statement is needed -- it sends the entire nested table
   || back into the color_models table in the database. */

   INSERT INTO color_models VALUES ('FGB', color_tab);
END;
```

### VARRAY integration

Does this database-to-PL/SQL integration work for VARRAYs too? You bet, although there are a couple of differences.

First of all, realize that when you store and retrieve the contents of a nested table in the database, the Oracle database makes no promises about preserving the order of the elements. This makes sense because the server is just putting the nested data into a store table behind the scenes, and we all know that relational databases don't give two hoots about row order. By contrast, storing and retrieving the contents of a VARRAY *do* preserve the order of the elements.

Preserving the order of VARRAY elements is a fairly useful capability. It makes it possible to embed meaning in the order of the data, which is something you cannot do in a pure relational database. For example, if you want to store someone's favorite colors in rank order, you can do it with a single VARRAY column. Every time you retrieve the column collection, its elements will be in the same order as when you last stored it. In contrast, abiding by a pure relational model, you would need two columns: one for an integer corresponding to the rank and one for the color.

This order-preservation of VARRAYs suggests some possibilities for interesting utility functions. For example, you could fairly easily code a tool that would allow the insertion of a new "favorite" at the low end of the list by "shifting up" all the other elements.

A second difference between integration of nested tables and integration of VARRAYs with the database is that some SELECT statements you could use to fetch the contents of a nested table will have to be modified if you want to fetch a VARRAY. (See "Working with Collections in SQL" on page 382 for some examples.)

## Populating Collections with Data

A collection is empty after initialization. No elements are defined within it. A collection is, in this way, very much like a relational table. An element is defined by assigning a value to that element. This assignment can be done through the standard PL/SQL assignment operation, by fetching data from one or more relational tables into a collection, or by performing an aggregate assignment (in essence, copying one collection to another).

If you are working with associative arrays, you can assign a value (of the appropriate type) to any valid index value in the collection. If the index type of the associative array is an integer, then the index value must be between $-2^{31}$ and $2^{31} - 1$. The simple act of assigning the value creates the element and deposits the value at that index.

In contrast to associative arrays, you can't assign values to arbitrarily numbered subscripts of nested tables and VARRAYs; instead, the indexes (at least initially) are monotonically increasing integers, assigned by the PL/SQL engine. That is, if you initialize $n$ elements, they will have subscripts 1 through $n$—and those are the only rows to which you can assign a value.

Before you try to assign a value to an index value in a nested table or VARRAY, you must make sure that (1) the collection has been initialized, and (2) that index value has been defined. Use the EXTEND operator, discussed earlier in this chapter, to make new index values available in nested tables and VARRAYs.

### Using the assignment operator

You can assign values to a collection with the standard assignment operator of PL/SQL, as shown here:

```
countdown_test_list (43) := 'Internal pressure';
company_names_table (last_name_row + 10) := 'Johnstone Clingers';
```

You can use this same syntax to assign an entire record or complex datatype to an index value in the collection, as you see here:

```
DECLARE
   TYPE emp_copy_t IS TABLE OF employees%ROWTYPE;
   l_emps emp_copy_t := emp_copy_t();
   l_emprec employees%ROWTYPE;
BEGIN
   l_emprec.last_name := 'Steven';
   l_emprec.salary := 10000;
   l_emps.EXTEND;
   l_emps (l_emps.LAST) := l_emprec;
END;
```

As long as the structure of data on the right side of the assignment matches that of the collection type, the assignment will complete without error.

### What index values can I use?

When you assign data to an associative array, you must specify the location (index value) in the collection. The type of value, and valid range of values, you use to indicate this location depend on how you defined the INDEX BY clause of the associative array, and are explained in the following table:

| INDEX BY clause | Minimum value | Maximum value |
| --- | --- | --- |
| INDEX BY BINARY_INTEGER | $-2^{31}$ | $2^{31} - 1$ |
| INDEX BY PLS_INTEGER | $-2^{31}$ | $2^{31} - 1$ |
| INDEX BY SIMPLE_INTEGER | $-2^{31}$ | $2^{31} - 1$ |
| INDEX BY NATURAL | 0 | $2^{31} - 1$ |
| INDEX BY POSITIVE | 1 | $2^{31} - 1$ |
| INDEX BY SIGNTYPE | $-1$ | 1 |
| INDEX BY VARCHAR2(N) | Any string within specified length | Any string within specified length |

You can also index by any subtype of the above, or use a type anchored to a VARCHAR2 database column (e.g., *table_name.column_name*%TYPE).

### Aggregate assignments

You can also perform an "aggregate assignment" of the contents of an entire collection to another collection of exactly the same type. Here is an example of such a transfer:

---

```
 1  DECLARE
 2     TYPE name_t IS TABLE OF VARCHAR2(100) INDEX BY PLS_INTEGER;
 3     old_names name_t;
 4     new_names name_t;
 5  BEGIN
 6     /* Assign values to old_names table */
 7     old_names(1) := 'Smith';
 8     old_names(2) := 'Harrison';
 9
10     /* Assign values to new_names table */
11     new_names(111) := 'Hanrahan';
12     new_names(342) := 'Blimey';
13
14     /* Transfer values from new to old */
15     old_names := new_names;
16
17     /* This statement will display 'Hanrahan' */
18     DBMS_OUTPUT.PUT_LINE (
19        old_names.FIRST || ': ' || old_names(old_names.FIRST));
20  END;
```

The output is:

```
111: Hanrahan
```

A collection-level assignment completely replaces the previously defined rows in the collection. In the preceding example, rows 1 and 2 in old_names are defined before the last, aggregate assignment.

After the assignment, only rows 111 and 342 in the old_names collection have values.

### Assigning rows from a relational table

You can also populate rows in a collection by querying data from a relational table. The assignment rules described earlier in this section apply to SELECT-driven assignments. The following example demonstrates various ways you can copy data from a relational table into a collection

I can use an implicit SELECT INTO to populate a single row of data in a collection:

```
DECLARE
   TYPE emp_copy_t IS TABLE OF employees%ROWTYPE;
   l_emps emp_copy_t := emp_copy_t();
BEGIN
   l_emps.EXTEND;
   SELECT *
     INTO l_emps (1)
     FROM employees
    WHERE employee_id = 7521;
END;
```

I can use a cursor FOR loop to move multiple rows into a collection, populating those rows sequentially:

```
DECLARE
    TYPE emp_copy_t IS TABLE OF employees%ROWTYPE;
    l_emps emp_copy_t := emp_copy_t();
BEGIN
    FOR emp_rec IN (SELECT * FROM employees)
    LOOP
        l_emps.EXTEND;
        l_emps (l_emps.LAST) := emp_rec;
    END LOOP;
END;
```

I can also use a cursor FOR loop to move multiple rows into a collection, populating those rows *non*sequentially. In this case, I will switch to using an associative array, so that I can assign rows randomly, that is, using the primary key value of each row in the database as the row number in my collection:

```
DECLARE
    TYPE emp_copy_t IS TABLE OF employees%ROWTYPE INDEX BY PLS_INTEGER;
    l_emps emp_copy_t;
BEGIN
    FOR emp_rec IN (SELECT * FROM employees)
    LOOP
        l_emps (emp_rec.employee_id) := emp_rec;
    END  LOOP;
END;
```

I can also use BULK COLLECT (described in Chapter 21) to retrieve all the rows of a table in a single assignment step, depositing the data into any of the three types of collections. When using a nested tables or VARRAY, you do *not* need to explicitly initialize the collection. Here is an example:

```
DECLARE
    TYPE emp_copy_nt IS TABLE OF employees%ROWTYPE;
    l_emps emp_copy_nt;
BEGIN
    SELECT * BULK COLLECT INTO l_emps FROM employees;
END;
```

### Advantage of nonsequential population of collection

For anyone used to working with traditional arrays, the idea of populating your collection nonsequentially may seem strange. Why would you do such a thing? Consider the following scenario.

In many applications, you will find yourself writing and executing the same queries over and over again. In some cases, the queries are retrieving static data, such as codes and descriptions that rarely (if ever) change. Well, if the data isn't changing—especially during a user session—then why would you want to keep querying the information from the database? Even if the data is cached in the System Global Area (SGA), you still need to visit the SGA, confirm that the query has already been parsed, find that information in the data buffers, and finally return it to the session program area (the Program Global Area, or PGA).

Here's an idea: set as a rule that for a given static lookup table, a user will never query a row from the table more than once in a session. After the first time, it will be stored in the session's PGA and be instantly available for future requests. This is very easy to do with collections. Essentially, you use the collection's index as an intelligent key.

Let's take a look at an example. I have a hairstyles table that contains a numeric code (primary key) and a description of the hairstyle (e.g., "Pageboy"). These styles are timeless and rarely change.

Here is the body of a package that uses a collection to cache code-hairstyle pairs and that minimizes trips to the database:

```
 1 PACKAGE BODY justonce
 2 IS
 3     TYPE desc_t
 4     IS
 5        TABLE OF hairstyles.description%TYPE
 6           INDEX BY PLS_INTEGER;
 7
 8     descriptions   desc_t;
 9
10     FUNCTION description (code_in IN hairstyles.code%TYPE)
11        RETURN hairstyles.description%TYPE
12     IS
13        return_value   hairstyles.description%TYPE;
14
15        FUNCTION desc_from_database
16           RETURN hairstyles.description%TYPE
17        IS
18           l_description   hairstyles.description%TYPE;
19        BEGIN
20           SELECT description
21             INTO l_description
22             FROM hairstyles
23            WHERE code = code_in;
24           RETURN l_description;
25        END;
26     BEGIN
27        RETURN descriptions (code_in);
28     EXCEPTION
29        WHEN NO_DATA_FOUND
30        THEN
31           descriptions (code_in) := desc_from_database ();
32           RETURN descriptions (code_in);
33     END;
34 END justonce;
```

The table provides a description of the interesting aspects of this program:

| Line(s) | Description |
| --- | --- |
| 3–8 | Declare a collection type and the collection to hold my cached descriptions. |
| 10–11 | Header of my retrieval function. The interesting thing about the header is that it is not interesting at all. There is no indication that this function is doing anything but the typical query against the database to retrieve the description for the code. The implementation is hidden, which is just the way you want it. |
| 15–25 | That very traditional query from the database. But in this case, it is just a private function within my main function, which is fitting because it is not the main attraction. |
| 27 | The entire execution section! Simply return the description that is stored in the row indicated by the code number. The first time I run this function for a given code, the row will not be defined. So PL/SQL raises NO_DATA_FOUND (see lines 28–31). For all subsequent requests for this code, however, the row is defined, and the function returns the value immediately. |
| 29–32 | So the data hasn't yet been queried in this session. Fine. Trap the error, look up the description from the database, and deposit it in the collection. Then return that value. Now I am set to divert all subsequent lookup attempts. |

So how much of a difference does this caching make? I ran some tests on my laptop and found that it took just under two seconds to execute 10,000 queries against the hairstyles table. That's efficient, no doubt about it. Yet it took only 0.1 seconds to retrieve that same information 10,000 times using the above function. That's more than an order of magnitude improvement—and that's with a local database. The superiority of the collection caching technique would be even greater in a real-world situation.

Here are some final notes on the collection caching technique:

- This technique is a classic tradeoff between CPU and memory. Each session has its own copy of the collection (this is program data and is stored in the PGA). If you have 10,000 users, the total memory required for these 10,000 small caches could be considerable.

- Consider using this technique with any of the following scenarios: small, static tables in a multiuser application; large, static tables in which a given user will access only a small portion of the table; manipulation of large tables in a batch process (just a single connect taking up possibly a lot of memory).

The concept and implementation options for caching are explored in much greater depth in Chapter 21.

## Accessing Data Inside a Collection

There generally isn't much point to putting information into a collection unless you intend to use or access that data. There are several things you need to keep in mind when accessing data inside a collection:

- If you try to read an undefined index value in a collection, the database raises the NO_DATA_FOUND exception. One consequence of this rule is that you should avoid using numeric FOR loops to scan the contents of a collection unless you are certain it is, and always will be, densely-filled (no undefined index values between FIRST and LAST). If that collection is not densely filled, the database will fail with NO_DATA_FOUND as soon as it hits a gap between the values returned by the FIRST and LAST methods.

- If you try to read a row that is beyond the limit of EXTENDed rows in a table or VARRAY, the database raises the following exception:

  ```
  ORA-06533: Subscript beyond count
  ```

  When working with nested tables and VARRAYs, you should always make sure that you have extended the collection to encompass the row you want to assign or read.

- If you try to read a row whose index is beyond the limit of the VARRAY type definition, the database raises the following exception:

  ```
  ORA-06532: Subscript outside of limit
  ```

  Remember: you can always call the LIMIT method to find the maximum number of rows that are allowed in a VARRAY. Because the subscript always starts at 1 in this type of collection, you can then easily determine if you still have room for more data in the data structure.

Beyond these cautionary tales, it is very easy to access individual rows in a collection: simply provide the subscript (or subscripts—see "Collections of Complex Data-types" on page 370 for the syntax needed for collections of collections) after the name of the collection.

## Using String-Indexed Collections

Oracle9i Database Release 2 greatly expanded the datatypes developers can specify as the index type for associative arrays. VARCHAR2 offers the most flexibility and potential. Since with this datatype I can index by string, I can essentially index by just about *anything*, as long as it can be converted into a string of no more than 32,767 bytes.

Here is a block of code that demonstrates the basics:

```
/* File on web: string_indexed.sql */
DECLARE
   SUBTYPE location_t IS VARCHAR2(64);
   TYPE population_type IS TABLE OF NUMBER INDEX BY location_t;

   l_country_population population_type;
   l_continent_population population_type;

   l_count PLS_INTEGER;
   l_location location_t;
BEGIN
   l_country_population('Greenland') := 100000;
   l_country_population('Iceland') := 750000;
```

```
     l_continent_population('Australia') := 30000000;
     l_continent_population('Antarctica') := 1000;
     l_continent_population('antarctica') := 1001;

     l_count := l_country_population.COUNT;
     DBMS_OUTPUT.PUT_LINE ('COUNT = ' || l_count);

     l_location := l_continent_population.FIRST;
     DBMS_OUTPUT.PUT_LINE ('FIRST row = ' || l_location);
     DBMS_OUTPUT.PUT_LINE ('FIRST value = ' || l_continent_population(l_location));

     l_location := l_continent_population.LAST;
     DBMS_OUTPUT.PUT_LINE ('LAST row = ' || l_location);
     DBMS_OUTPUT.PUT_LINE ('LAST value = ' || l_continent_population(l_location));
   END;
```

Here is the output from the script:

```
COUNT = 2
FIRST row = Antarctica
FIRST value = 1000
LAST row = antarctica
LAST value = 1001
```

Points of interest from this code follow:

- With a string-indexed collection, the values returned by calls to the FIRST, LAST, PRIOR, and NEXT methods are *strings* and not integers.

- Notice that "antarctica" is last, coming after "Antarctica" and "Australia". That's because lowercase letters have a higher ASCII code than uppercase letters. The order in which *your* strings will be stored in your associative array will be determined by your character set.

- There is really no difference in syntax between using string-indexed and integer-indexed collections.

- I carefully defined a subtype, location_t, which I then used as the index type in my collection type declaration, and also to declare the l_location variable. You will find that when you work with string indexed collections, especially multilevel collections, subtypes will be very helpful reminders of precisely *what* data you are using for your index values.

The following sections offer other examples demonstrating the usefulness of this feature.

### Simplifying algorithmic logic with string indexes

Careful use of string indexed collections can greatly simplify your programs; in essence, you are transferring complexity from your algorithms to the data structure (and leaving it to the database) to do the "heavy lifting." The following example will give you a clear sense of that transfer.

---

Through much of 2006 and 2007, I led the effort to build an automated testing tool for PL/SQL, Quest Code Tester for Oracle. One key benefit of this tool is that it generates a test package from your descriptions of the expected behavior of a program. As I generate the test code, I need to keep track of the names of variables that I have declared, so that I do not inadvertently declare another variable with the same name.

My first pass at building a "string tracker" package looked like this:

```
/* File on web: string_tracker0.pkg */
 1  PACKAGE BODY string_tracker
 2  IS
 3     SUBTYPE name_t IS VARCHAR2 (32767);
 4     TYPE used_aat IS TABLE OF name_t INDEX BY PLS_INTEGER;
 5     g_names_used used_aat;
 6
 7     PROCEDURE mark_as_used (variable_name_in IN name_t) IS
 8     BEGIN
 9        g_names_used (g_names_used.COUNT + 1) := variable_name_in;
10     END mark_as_used;
11
12     FUNCTION string_in_use (variable_name_in IN name_t) RETURN BOOLEAN
13     IS
14        c_count   CONSTANT PLS_INTEGER := g_names_used.COUNT;
15        l_index            PLS_INTEGER := g_names_used.FIRST;
16        l_found            BOOLEAN     := FALSE;
17     BEGIN
18        WHILE (NOT l_found AND l_index <= c_count)
19        LOOP
20           l_found := variable_name_in = g_names_used (l_index);
21           l_index := l_index + 1;
22        END LOOP;
23
24        RETURN l_found;
25     END string_in_use;
26  END string_tracker;
```

Here is an explanation of the interesting parts of this package body:

| Line(s) | Description |
| --- | --- |
| 3–5 | Declare a collection of strings indexed by integer, to hold the list of variable names that I have already used. |
| 7–10 | Append the variable name to the end of the array, so as to mark it as "used." |
| 12–25 | Scan through the collection, looking for a match on the variable name. If found, then terminate the scan and return TRUE. Otherwise, return FALSE (string is not in use). |

Now, certainly, this is not a big, complicated package body. Still, I am writing more code than is necessary, and consuming more CPU cycles than necessary. How do I simplify things and speed them up? By using a string indexed collection.

Here's my second pass at the string_tracker package:

```
/* File on web: string_tracker1.pkg */
 1  PACKAGE BODY string_tracker
 2  IS
 3     SUBTYPE name_t IS VARCHAR2 (32767);
 4     TYPE used_aat IS TABLE OF BOOLEAN INDEX BY name_t;
 5     g_names_used used_aat;
 6
 7     PROCEDURE mark_as_used (variable_name_in IN name_t) IS
 8     BEGIN
 9        g_names_used (variable_name_in) := TRUE;
10     END mark_as_used;
11
12     FUNCTION string_in_use (variable_name_in IN name_t) RETURN BOOLEAN
13     IS
14     BEGIN
15        RETURN g_names_used.EXISTS (variable_name_in);
16     END string_in_use;
17  END string_tracker;
```

First of all, notice that my package body has shrunk from 26 lines to 17 lines. A reduction of almost 33%. And in the process, my code has been greatly simplified. The table below explains the changes:

| Line(s) | Description |
|---------|-------------|
| 3–5 | This time, I declare a collection of Booleans indexed by *strings*. Actcually, it doesn't really matter what kind of data the collection holds. I could create a collection of Booleans, dates, numbers, XML documents, whatever. The only thing that matters (as you will see below) is the index value. |
| 7–10 | Again, I mark a string as used, but in this version, the variable name serves as the *index value*, and not the value appended to the end of the collection. I assign a value of TRUE to that index value, but as I note above, I could assign whatever value I like: NULL, TRUE, FALSE. It doesn't matter because… |
| 12–16 | To determine if a variable name has already been used, I simply call the EXISTS method for the name of the variable. If an element is defined at that index value, then the name has already been used. In other words, I never actually look at or care about the value *stored* at that index value. |

Isn't that simple and elegant? I no longer have to write code to scan through the collection contents looking for a match. Instead, I zoom in directly on that index value and instantly have my answer.

Here's the lesson I took from the experience of building string_tracker: if as I write my program I find myself writing algorithms to search element by element through a collection to find a matching value, I should consider redesigning that collection (or creating a second collection) that uses string indexing to avoid the scan code. The result is a program that is leaner and more efficient, as well as easier to maintain in the future.

### Emulating primary keys and unique indexes

One very interesting application of string indexing is to emulate primary keys and unique indexes of a relational table in collections. Suppose that I need to do some heavy processing of employee information in my program. I need to go back and forth over the set of selected employees, searching by the employee ID number, last name, and email address.

Rather than query that data repeatedly from the database, I can cache it in a set of collections and then move much more efficiently through the data. Here is an example of the kind of code I would write:

```
DECLARE
   c_delimiter   CONSTANT CHAR (1) := '^';

   TYPE strings_t IS TABLE OF employees%ROWTYPE
                        INDEX BY employees.email%TYPE;

   TYPE ids_t IS TABLE OF employees%ROWTYPE
                   INDEX BY PLS_INTEGER;

   by_name        strings_t;
   by_email       strings_t;
   by_id          ids_t;

   ceo_name employees.last_name%TYPE
        := 'ELLISON' || c_delimiter || 'LARRY';

   PROCEDURE load_arrays
   IS
   BEGIN
      /* Load up all three arrays from rows in table. */
      FOR rec IN (SELECT *
                    FROM employees)
      LOOP
         by_name (rec.last_name || c_delimiter || rec.first_name) := rec;
         by_email (rec.email) := rec;
         by_id (rec.employee_id) := rec;
      END LOOP;
   END;
BEGIN
   load_arrays;

   /* Now I can retrieve information by name or by ID. */

   IF by_name (ceo_name).salary > by_id (7645).salary
   THEN
      make_adjustment (ceo_name);
   END IF;
END;
```

### Performance of string-indexed collections

What kind of price do you pay for using string indexing instead of integer indexing? It depends entirely on how long your strings are. When you use string indexes, the database takes your string and "hashes" (transforms) it into an integer value. So the overhead is determined by the performance of the hash function.

What I have found in my testing (see the *assoc_array_perf.tst* script on the book's web site) is the following:

```
Compare String and Integer Indexing, Iterations = 10000 Length = 100
   Index by PLS_INTEGER Elapsed: 4.26 seconds.
   Index by VARCHAR2 Elapsed: 4.75 seconds.
Compare String and Integer Indexing, Iterations = 10000 Length = 1000
   Index by PLS_INTEGER Elapsed: 4.24 seconds.
   Index by VARCHAR2 Elapsed: 6.4 seconds.
Compare String and Integer Indexing, Iterations = 10000 Length = 10000
   Index by PLS_INTEGER Elapsed: 4.06 seconds.
   Index by VARCHAR2 Elapsed: 24.63 seconds.
```

The conclusion: with relatively small strings (100 characters or less), there is no significant difference in performance between string and integer indexing. As the string index value gets longer, however, the overhead of hashing grows substantially. So be careful about what strings you use for indexes!

### Other examples of string-indexed collections

As you saw in the example of retrieving employee information, it doesn't take a whole lot of code to build multiple, highly efficient entry points into cached data transferred from a relational table. Still, to make it even easier for you to implement these techniques in your application, I have built a utility to generate such code for you.

The *genaa.sp* file on the book's web site accepts the name of your table as an argument, and from the information stored in the data dictionary for that table (primary key and unique indexes), generates a package to implement caching for that table. It populates a collection based on the integer primary key and another collection for each unique index defined on the table (indexed by PLS_INTEGER or VARCHAR2, depending on the type(s) of the column(s) in the index).

In addition, the file, *summer_reading.pkg*, also available on the book's web site, offers an example of the use of VARCHAR2-indexed associative arrays to manipulate lists of information within a PL/SQL program.

## Collections of Complex Datatypes

Starting with Oracle9*i* Database Release 2, you can define collection types of arbitrarily complex structures. All of the following structures are supported:

*Collections of records based on tables with %ROWTYPE*
   These structures allow you to quickly and easily mimic a relational table within a PL/SQL program.

*Collections of user-defined records*
   The fields of the record can be scalars or complex datatypes in and of themselves. For example, you can define a collection of records where the record TYPE contains a field that is itself another collection.

*Collections of object types and other complex types*
> The datatype of the collection can be an object type (Oracle's version of an object-oriented class, explored in Chapter 26) previously defined with the CREATE TYPE statement. You can also easily define collections of LOBs, XML documents, etc.

*Collections of collections (directly and indirectly)*
> You can define multilevel collections, including collections of collections and collections of datatypes that contain, as an attribute or a field, another collection.

Let's take a look at examples of each of these variations.

## Collections of records

You define a collection of records by specifying a record type (through either %ROWTYPE or a programmer-defined record type) in the TABLE OF clause of the collection definition. This technique applies only to collection TYPEs that are declared inside a PL/SQL program. Nested table and VARRAY TYPEs defined in the database cannot reference %ROWTYPE record structures.

Here is an example of a collection of records based on a custom record TYPE:

```
PACKAGE compensation_pkg
IS
   TYPE reward_rt IS RECORD (
      nm VARCHAR2(2000), sal NUMBER, comm NUMBER);

   TYPE reward_tt IS TABLE OF reward_rt INDEX BY PLS_INTEGER;

END compensation_pkg;
```

With these types defined in my package specification, I can declare collections in other programs like this:

```
DECLARE
   holiday_bonuses compensation_pkg.reward_tt;
```

Collections of records come in especially handy when you want to create in-memory (PGA) collections that have the same structure (and, at least in part, data) as database tables. Why would I want to do this? Suppose that I am running a batch process on Sunday at 3:00 a.m. against tables that are modified only during the week. I need to do some intensive analysis that involves multiple passes against the tables' data. I could simply query the data repetitively from the database, but that is a relatively slow, intensive process.

Alternately, I can copy the data from the table or tables into a collection and then move much more rapidly (and randomly) through my result set. I am, in essence, emulating bidirectional cursors in my PL/SQL code.

If you decide to copy data into collections and manipulate them within your program, you can choose between two basic approaches for implementing this logic:

- Embed all of the collection code in your main program.
- Create a separate package to encapsulate access to the data in the collection.

I generally choose the second approach for most situations. In other words, I find it useful to create separate, well-defined, and highly reusable APIs (application programmatic interfaces) to complex data structures and logic. Here is the package specification for my bidirectional cursor emulator:

```
/* File on web: bidir.pkg */
PACKAGE bidir
IS
   FUNCTION rowforid (id_in IN employee.employee_id%TYPE)
      RETURN employee%ROWTYPE;

   FUNCTION firstrow RETURN PLS_INTEGER;
   FUNCTION lastrow RETURN PLS_INTEGER;

   FUNCTION rowCount RETURN PLS_INTEGER;

   FUNCTION end_of_data RETURN BOOLEAN;

   PROCEDURE setrow (nth IN PLS_INTEGER);

   FUNCTION currrow RETURN employee%ROWTYPE;

   PROCEDURE nextrow;
   PROCEDURE prevrow;
END;
```

So how do you use this API? Here is an example of a program using this API to read through the result set for the employee table, first forward and then backward:

```
/* File on web: bidir.tst */
DECLARE
   l_employee   employees%ROWTYPE;
BEGIN
   LOOP
      EXIT WHEN bidir.end_of_data;
      l_employee := bidir.currrow;
      DBMS_OUTPUT.put_line (l_employee.last_name);
      bidir.nextrow;
   END LOOP;

   bidir.setrow (bidir.lastrow);

   LOOP
      EXIT WHEN bidir.end_of_data;
      l_employee := bidir.currrow;
      DBMS_OUTPUT.put_line (l_employee.last_name);
      bidir.prevrow;
   END LOOP;
END;
```

An astute reader will now be asking: when is the collection loaded up with the data? Or even better: where is the collection? There is no evidence of a collection anywhere in the code I have presented.

Let's take the second question first. The reason you don't see the collection is that I have hidden it behind my package specification. A user of the package never touches the collection and doesn't have to know anything about it. That is the whole point of the API. You just call one or another of the programs that will do all the work of traversing the collection (data set) for you.

Now, when and how is the collection loaded? This may seem a bit magical until you read about packages in Chapter 18. If you look in the package body, you will find that it has an initialization section as follows:

```
BEGIN -- Package initialization
   FOR rec IN  (SELECT * FROM employees)
   LOOP
      g_employees (rec.employee_id) := rec;
   END LOOP;
   g_currrow := firstrow;
END;
```

 Note that g_currrow is defined in the package body and therefore was not listed in the specification above.

This means that the very first time I try to reference any element in the package specification, this code is run automatically, transferring the contents of the employee table to my g_employees collection. When does that happen in my sample program shown earlier? Inside my loop, when I call the bidir.end_of_data function to see if I am done looking through my data set!

I encourage you to examine the package implementation. The code is very basic and easy to understand; the benefits of this approach can be dramatic.

### Collections of objects and other complex types

You can use an object type, LOB, XML document, and virtually any valid PL/SQL type as the datatype of a collection TYPE statement. The syntax for defining these collections is the same, but the way you manipulate the contents of the collections can be complicated, depending on the underlying type.

For more information on Oracle object types, see Chapter 26.

Here is an example of working with a collection of objects:

```
/* File on web: object_collection.sql */
TYPE pet_t IS OBJECT (
   tag_no   INTEGER,
```

```
    name       VARCHAR2 (60),
    MEMBER FUNCTION set_tag_no (new_tag_no IN INTEGER) RETURN pet_t);

DECLARE
   TYPE pets_t IS TABLE OF pet_t;

   pets    pets_t :=
      pets_t (pet_t (1050, 'Sammy'), pet_t (1075, 'Mercury'));
BEGIN
   FOR indx IN pets.FIRST .. pets.LAST
   LOOP
      DBMS_OUTPUT.put_line (pets (indx).name);
   END LOOP;
END;
```

And the output is:

```
Sammy
Mercury
```

Once I have my object type defined, I can declare a collection based on that type and then populate it with instances of those object types. You can just as easily declare collections of LOBs, XMLTypes, and so on. All the normal rules that apply to variables of those datatypes also apply to individual rows of a collection of that datatype.

## Multilevel Collections

Oracle9*i* Database Release 2 introduced the ability to nest collections within collections, a feature that is also referred to as *multilevel collections*. Let's take a look at an example and then discuss how you can use this feature in your applications.

Suppose that I want to build a system to maintain information about my pets. Besides their standard information, such as breed, name, and so on, I would like to keep track of their visits to the veterinarian. So I create a vet visit object type:

```
TYPE vet_visit_t IS OBJECT (
   visit_date  DATE,
   reason      VARCHAR2 (100)
   )
```

Notice that objects instantiated from this type are not associated with a pet (i.e., a foreign key to a pet table or object). You will soon see why I don't need to do that. Now I create a nested table of vet visits (we are supposed to go at least once a year):

```
TYPE vet_visits_t IS TABLE OF vet_visit_t;
```

With these data structures defined, I now declare my object type to maintain information about my pets:

```
TYPE pet_t IS OBJECT (
   tag_no   INTEGER,
   name     VARCHAR2 (60),
   petcare vet_visits_t,
   MEMBER FUNCTION set_tag_no (new_tag_no IN INTEGER) RETURN pet_t)
```

This object type has three attributes and one member method. Any object instantiated from this type will have associated with it a tag number, a name, and a list of visits to the vet. You can also modify the tag number for that pet by calling the set_tag_no program.

So I have now declared an object type that contains as an attribute a nested table. I don't need a separate database table to keep track of these veterinarian visits; they are a part of my object.

Now let's take advantage of the multilevel features of collections in the following example.

```
    /* File on web: multilevel_collections.sql */
 1 DECLARE
 2 TYPE bunch_of_pets_t
 3     IS
 4         TABLE OF pet_t INDEX BY PLS_INTEGER;
 5
 6     my_pets    bunch_of_pets_t;
 7 BEGIN
 8     my_pets (1) :=
 9         pet_t (
10             100
11           , 'Mercury'
12           , vet_visits_t (vet_visit_t ('01-Jan-2001', 'Clip wings')
13                         , vet_visit_t ('01-Apr-2002', 'Check cholesterol')
14                          )
15         );
16     DBMS_OUTPUT.put_line (my_pets (1).name);
17     DBMS_OUTPUT.put_line (my_pets (1).petcare (my_pets(1).petcare.LAST).reason);
18     DBMS_OUTPUT.put_line (my_pets.COUNT);
19     DBMS_OUTPUT.put_line (my_pets (1).petcare.LAST);
20 END;
```

The output from running this script is:

```
Mercury
Check cholesterol
1
2
```

The following table explains what's going on in the code:

| Line(s) | Description |
|---|---|
| 2–6 | Declare a local associative array TYPE, in which each row contains a single pet object. I then declare a collection to keep track of my "bunch of pets." |
| 8–15 | Assign an object of type pet_t to index 1 in this associative array. As you can see, the syntax required when working with nested, complex objects of this sort can be quite intimidating. So let's parse the various steps required. To instantiate an object of type pet_t, I must provide a tag number, a name, and a list of vet visits, which is a nested table. To provide a nested table of type vet_visits_t, I must call the associated constructor (of the same name). I can either provide a null or empty list, or initialize the nested table with some values. I do this in lines 8 and 9. Each row in the vet_visits_t collection is an object of type vet_visit_t, so again I must use the object constructor and pass in a value for each attribute (date and reason for visit). |

| Line(s) | Description |
|---------|-------------|
| 16 | Display the value of the name attribute of the pet object in row 1 of the my_pets associative array. |
| 17 | Display the value of the reason attribute of the vet visit object in row 2 of the nested table, which in turn resides in index 1 of the my_pets associative array. That's a mouthful, and it is a "line-full" of code. |
| 18–19 | Demonstrate how you can use the collection methods (in this case, COUNT and LAST) on both outer and nested collections. |

In this example I have the good fortune to be working with collections that, at each level, actually have names: the my_pets associative array and the petcare nested table. This is not always the case, as is illustrated in the next example.

### Unnamed multilevel collections: emulation of multidimensional arrays

You can use nested, multilevel collections to emulate multidimensional arrays within PL/SQL. Multidimensional collections are declared in stepwise fashion, adding a dimension at each step (quite different from the syntax used to declare an array in a 3GL).

I will start with a simple example and then step through the implementation of a generic three-dimensional array package. Suppose that I want to record temperatures within some three-dimensional space organized using some (X, Y, Z) coordinate system. The following block illustrates the sequential declarations necessary to accomplish this.

```
DECLARE
   SUBTYPE temperature IS NUMBER;
   SUBTYPE coordinate_axis IS PLS_INTEGER;

   TYPE temperature_x IS TABLE OF temperature INDEX BY coordinate_axis;
   TYPE temperature_xy IS TABLE OF temperature_x INDEX BY coordinate_axis;
   TYPE temperature_xyz IS TABLE OF temperature_xy INDEX BY coordinate_axis;

   temperature_3d temperature_xyz;
BEGIN
   temperature_3d (1) (2) (3) := 45;
END;
/
```

Here, the subtype and type names are used to provide clarity as to the usage of the contents of the actual collection (temperature_3d): the collection types (temperature_X, temperature_XY, temperature_XYZ) as well as the collection indexes (coordinate_axis).

Note that although my careful naming makes it clear what each of the collection types contains and is used for, I do not have corresponding clarity when it comes to referencing collection elements by subscript; in other words, in what order do I specify the dimensions? It is not obvious from my code whether the temperature 45 degrees is assigned to the point (X:1, Y:2, Z:3) or to (X:3, Y:2, Z:1).

Now let's move on to a more general treatment of a three-dimensional array structure.

The multdim package allows you to declare your own three-dimensional array, as well as set and retrieve values from individual cells. Here I create a simple package to encapsulate operations on a three-dimensional associative table storing VARCHAR2 elements indexed in all dimensions by PLS_INTEGER. The following declarations constitute some basic building blocks for the package:

```
/* Files on web: multdim.pkg, multdim.tst, multdim2.pkg */
CREATE OR REPLACE PACKAGE multdim
IS
   TYPE dim1_t IS TABLE OF VARCHAR2 (32767) INDEX BY PLS_INTEGER;
   TYPE dim2_t IS TABLE OF dim1_t INDEX BY PLS_INTEGER;
   TYPE dim3_t IS TABLE OF dim2_t INDEX BY PLS_INTEGER;

   PROCEDURE setcell (
      array_in    IN OUT    dim3_t,
      dim1_in               PLS_INTEGER,
      dim2_in               PLS_INTEGER,
      dim3_in               PLS_INTEGER,
      value_in    IN        VARCHAR2
   );

   FUNCTION getcell (
      array_in    IN    dim3_t,
      dim1_in           PLS_INTEGER,
      dim2_in           PLS_INTEGER,
      dim3_in           PLS_INTEGER
   )
      RETURN VARCHAR2;

   FUNCTION EXISTS (
      array_in    IN    dim3_t,
      dim1_in           PLS_INTEGER,
      dim2_in           PLS_INTEGER,
      dim3_in           PLS_INTEGER
   )
      RETURN BOOLEAN;
```

I have defined the three collection types progressively as before:

*Type dim1_t*
   A one-dimensional associative table of VARCHAR2 elements

*Type dim2_t*
   An associative table of Dim1_t elements

*Type dim3_t*
   An associative table of Dim2_t elements

Thus, three-dimensional space is modeled as cells in a collection of planes that are each modeled as a collection of lines. This is consistent with common understanding, which indicates a good model. Of course my collections are sparse and finite, while geometric three-dimensional space is considered to be dense and infinite, so the model has limitations. However, for my purposes, I am concerned only with a finite subset of points in three-dimensional space, and the model is adequate.

I equip my three-dimensional collection type with a basic interface to get and set cell values, as well as the ability to test whether a specific cell value exists in a collection.

### Exploring the multdim API

Let's look at the basic interface components. The procedure to set a cell value in a three-dimensional array given its coordinates could not be much simpler:

```
PROCEDURE setcell (
   array_in   IN OUT   dim3_t,
   dim1_in             PLS_INTEGER,
   dim2_in             PLS_INTEGER,
   dim3_in             PLS_INTEGER,
   value_in   IN   VARCHAR2
)
IS
BEGIN
   array_in(dim3_in )(dim2_in )(dim1_in) := value_in;
END;
```

Despite the simplicity of this code, there is significant added value in encapsulating the assignment statement, as it relieves me of having to remember the order of reference for the dimension indexes. It is not obvious when directly manipulating a dim3_t collection whether the third coordinate is the first index or the last. Whatever is not obvious in code will result in bugs sooner or later. The fact that all the collection indexes have the same datatype complicates matters because mixed-up data assignments will not raise exceptions but rather just generate bad results somewhere down the line. If my testing is not thorough, these are the kinds of bugs that make it to production code and wreak havoc on data and my reputation.

My function to return a cell value is likewise trivial but valuable:

```
FUNCTION getcell (
   array_in   IN   dim3_t,
   dim1_in         PLS_INTEGER,
   dim2_in         PLS_INTEGER,
   dim3_in         PLS_INTEGER
)
   RETURN VARCHAR2
IS
BEGIN
   RETURN array_in(dim3_in )(dim2_in )(dim1_in);
END;
```

If there is no cell in array_in corresponding to the supplied coordinates, then getcell will raise NO_DATA_FOUND. However, if any of the coordinates supplied are NULL, then the following, less friendly VALUE_ERROR exception is raised:

```
ORA-06502: PL/SQL: numeric or value error: NULL index table key value
```

In a more complete implementation, I should enhance the module to assert a precondition requiring all coordinate parameter values to be NOT NULL. At least the database's error message informs me that a null index value was responsible for the exception. It would be even better, though, if the database did not use the VALUE_ERROR exception for so many different error conditions.

With the EXISTS function, I get to some code that is a bit more interesting. EXISTS will return TRUE if the cell identified by the coordinates is contained in the collection and FALSE otherwise.

```
FUNCTION EXISTS (
   array_in   IN   dim3_t,
   dim1_in         PLS_INTEGER,
   dim2_in         PLS_INTEGER,
   dim3_in         PLS_INTEGER
 )
   RETURN BOOLEAN
IS
   l_value VARCHAR2(32767);
BEGIN
   l_value := array_in(dim3_in )(dim2_in )(dim1_in);
   RETURN TRUE;
EXCEPTION
   WHEN NO_DATA_FOUND THEN RETURN FALSE;
END;
```

This function traps the NO_DATA_FOUND exception raised when the assignment references a nonexistent cell and converts it to the appropriate Boolean. This is a very simple and direct method for obtaining my result, and illustrates a creative reliance on exception handling to handle the "conditional logic" of the function. You might think that you could and should use the EXISTS operator. You would, however, have to call EXISTS for each level of nested collections.

Here is a sample script that exercises this package:

```
/* File on web: multdim.tst */
DECLARE
   my_3d_array    multdim.dim3_t;
BEGIN
   multdim.setcell (my_3d_array, 1, 5, 800, 'def');
   multdim.setcell (my_3d_array, 1, 15, 800, 'def');
   multdim.setcell (my_3d_array, 5, 5, 800, 'def');
   multdim.setcell (my_3d_array, 5, 5, 805, 'def');

   DBMS_OUTPUT.PUT_LINE (multdim.getcell (my_3d_array, 1, 5, 800));
   /*
   Oracle11g Release 2 allows me to call PUT_LINE with a Boolean input!
   */
   DBMS_OUTPUT.PUT_LINE (multdim.EXISTS (my_3d_array, 1, 5, 800));
   DBMS_OUTPUT.PUT_LINE (multdim.EXISTS (my_3d_array, 6000, 5, 800));
   DBMS_OUTPUT.PUT_LINE (multdim.EXISTS (my_3d_array, 6000, 5, 807));

   /*
   If you are not on Oracle11g Release 2, then you can use this the
```

```
      procedure created in bpl.sp:

   bpl (multdim.EXISTS (my_3d_array, 1, 5, 800));
   bpl (multdim.EXISTS (my_3d_array, 6000, 5, 800));
   bpl (multdim.EXISTS (my_3d_array, 6000, 5, 807));
   */

   DBMS_OUTPUT.PUT_LINE (my_3d_array.COUNT);
END;
```

The *multdim2.pkg* file on the book's web site contains an enhanced version of the
multdim package that implements support for "slicing" of that three-dimensional collection, in which I fix one dimension and isolate the two-dimensional plane determined
by the fixed dimension. A slice from a temperature grid would give me, for example,
the range of temperatures along a certain latitude or longitude.

Beyond the challenge of writing the code for slicing, an interesting question presents
itself: will there be any differences between slicing out an XY plane, an XZ plane, or a
YZ plane in this fashion from a symmetric cube of data? If there are significant differences, it could affect how you choose to organize your multidimensional collections.

I encourage you to explore these issues and the implementation of the *multdim2.pkg*
package.

### Extending string_tracker with multilevel collections

Let's look at another example of applying multilevel collections: extending the
string_tracker package built-in the string indexing section to support *multiple lists* of
strings.

string_tracker is a handy utility, but it allows me to keep track of only one set of "used"
strings at a time. What if I need to track multiple lists, simultaneously? I can very easily
do this with multilevel collections.

```
/* File on web: string_tracker2.pks/pkb */
 1  PACKAGE BODY string_tracker
 2  IS
 3     SUBTYPE maxvarchar2_t IS VARCHAR2 (32767);
 4     SUBTYPE list_name_t IS maxvarchar2_t;
 5     SUBTYPE variable_name_t IS maxvarchar2_t;
 6
 7     TYPE used_aat IS TABLE OF BOOLEAN INDEX BY variable_name_t;
 8
 9     TYPE list_rt IS RECORD (
10        description      maxvarchar2_t
11      , list_of_values   used_aat
12     );
13
14     TYPE list_of_lists_aat IS TABLE OF list_rt INDEX BY list_name_t;
15
16     g_list_of_lists   list_of_lists_aat;
17
18     PROCEDURE create_list (
```

```
19          list_name_in        IN    list_name_t
20        , description_in     IN    VARCHAR2 DEFAULT NULL
21        )
22     IS
23     BEGIN
24        g_list_of_lists (list_name_in).description := description_in;
25     END create_list;
26
27     PROCEDURE mark_as_used (
28          list_name_in         IN    list_name_t
29        , variable_name_in    IN    variable_name_t
30        )
31     IS
32     BEGIN
33        g_list_of_lists (list_name_in)
34               .list_of_values (variable_name_in) := TRUE;
35     END mark_as_used;
36
37     FUNCTION string_in_use (
38          list_name_in         IN    list_name_t
39        , variable_name_in    IN    variable_name_t
40        )
41        RETURN BOOLEAN
42     IS
43     BEGIN
44        RETURN g_list_of_lists (list_name_in)
45                  .list_of_values.EXISTS (variable_name_in);
46     EXCEPTION
47        WHEN NO_DATA_FOUND
48        THEN
49           RETURN FALSE;
50     END string_in_use;
51  END string_tracker;
```

Here is an explanation of the multilevel collection-related changes to this package:

| Line(s) | Description |
| --- | --- |
| 7 | Once again, I have a collection type indexed by string to store the used strings. |
| 9–12 | Now I create a record to hold all the attributes of my list: the description and the list of used strings in that list. Notice that I do not have the list name as an attribute of my list. That may seem strange, except that the list name is the *index value* (see the next explanation). |
| 14–16 | Finally, I create a multilevel collection type: a list of lists, in which each element in this top level collection contains a record, which in turn contains the collection of used strings. |
| 33–34 | Now the mark_as_used procedure uses both the list name and the variable name as the index values into their respective collections: |

```
g_list_of_lists (list_name_in)
      .list_of_values(variable_name_in) := TRUE;
```

Notice that if I mark a variable name as used in a *new list*, the database creates a *new* element in the g_list_of_lists collection for that list. If I mark a variable name as used in a list previously created, it simply adds another element to the nested collection.

| Line(s) | Description |
|---------|-------------|
| 44–45 | Now to check to see if a string is used, I look to see if the variable name is defined as an element *within* an element of the list of lists collection: |

```
RETURN g_list_of_lists (list_name_in)
             .list_of_values.EXISTS (variable_name_in);
```

Finally, notice that in this third implementation of string_tracker I was very careful to use named subtypes in each of my formal parameter declarations and especially in the INDEX BY clause of the collection type declarations. By using subtypes instead of hardcoded VARCHAR2 declarations, my code is much more self-documenting. If you do not do this, you will find yourself scratching your head and asking "What am I using for the index of that collection?"

### How deeply can I nest collections?

As I played around with two- and three-dimensional arrays, I found myself wondering how deeply I could nest these multilevel collections. So I decided to find out. I built a small code generator that allows me to pass in the number of levels of nesting. It then constructs a procedure that declares *N* collection TYPEs, each one being a TABLE OF the previous table TYPE. Finally, it assigns a value to the string that is all the way at the heart of the nested collections.

I was able to create a collection of at least 250 nested collections before my computer ran into a memory error! I find it hard to believe that any PL/SQL developer will even come close to that level of complexity. If you would like to run this same experiment in your own system, check out the *gen_multcoll.sp* file available on the book's web site.

## Working with Collections in SQL

I've been working with Oracle's SQL for more than 22 years and PL/SQL for more than 18, but my brain has rarely turned as many cartwheels over SQL's semantics as it did when I first contemplated the *collection pseudo-functions* introduced in Oracle8 Database. These pseudo-functions exist to coerce database tables into acting like collections, and vice versa. Because there are some manipulations that work best when data is in one form versus the other, these functions give application programmers access to a rich and interesting set of structures and operations.

 The collection pseudo-functions are not available in PL/SQL proper, only in SQL. You can, however, employ these operators in SQL statements that appear in your PL/ SQL code, and it is extremely useful to understand how and when to do so. You'll see examples in the following sections.

The three collection pseudo-functions are as follows:

*CAST*
>   Maps a collection of one type to a collection of another type. This can encompass mapping a VARRAY to a nested table.

*MULTISET*
>   Maps a database table to a collection. With MULTISET and CAST, you can actually retrieve rows from a database table as a collection-typed column.

*TABLE*
>   Maps a collection to a database table. This is the inverse of MULTISET: it returns a single column that contains the mapped table.

Oracle introduced these pseudo-functions to manipulate collections that live in the database. They are important to your PL/SQL programs for several reasons, not the least of which is that they provide an incredibly efficient way to move data between the database and the application.

Yes, these pseudo-functions can be puzzling. But if you're the kind of person who gets truly excited by arcane code, these SQL extensions will make you jumping-up-and-down silly.

### The CAST pseudo-function

The CAST operator can be used in a SQL statement to convert from one built-in datatype or collection type to another built-in datatype or collection type. In other words, within SQL you can use CAST in place of TO_CHAR to convert from number to string.

Another very handy use of CAST is to convert between types of collections. Here is an example of casting a named collection. Suppose that I have created the color_ models table based on a VARRAY type as follows:

```
TYPE color_nt AS TABLE OF VARCHAR2(30)

TYPE color_vat AS VARRAY(16) OF VARCHAR2(30)

TABLE color_models (
   model_type VARCHAR2(12),
   colors color_vat);
```

I can CAST the VARRAY colors column as a nested table and apply the pseudo-function TABLE (explained shortly) to the result. An example is shown here. COLUMN_VALUE is the name that the database gives to the column in the resulting one-column virtual table. You can change it to whatever you want with a column alias:

```
SELECT COLUMN_VALUE my_colors
  FROM  TABLE (SELECT CAST(colors AS color_nt)
                 FROM color_models
                WHERE model_type = 'RGB')
```

CAST performs an on-the-fly conversion of the color_vat collection type to the color_nt collection type. CAST cannot serve as the target of an INSERT, UPDATE, or DELETE statement.

 Starting with Oracle Database 10g, you do not need to explicitly CAST a collection inside the TABLE operator. Instead, the database automatically determines the correct type.

It is also possible to cast a "bunch of table rows"—such as the result of a subquery—as a particular collection type. Doing so requires the MULTISET function, covered in the next section.

### The MULTISET pseudo-function

The MULTISET function exists only for use within CASTs. MULTISET allows you to retrieve a set of data and convert it on the fly to a collection type. (Note that the SQL MULTISET function is distinct from the PL/SQL MULTISET operators for nested tables, discussed in "Nested Table Multiset Operations" on page 387.)

The simplest form of MULTISET is this:

```
SELECT CAST (MULTISET (SELECT field FROM table) AS collection-type)
   FROM DUAL;
```

You can also use MULTISET in a correlated subquery in the select list:

```
SELECT outerfield,
   CAST(MULTISET(SELECT field FROM whateverTable
                 WHERE correlationCriteria)
     AS collectionTypeName)
   FROM outerTable
```

This technique is useful for making joins look as if they include a collection. For example, suppose that I had a detail table that listed, for each bird in my table, the countries where that species lives:

```
CREATE TABLE birds (
   genus VARCHAR2(128),
   species VARCHAR2(128),
   colors color_tab_t,
   PRIMARY KEY (genus, species)
);

CREATE TABLE bird_habitats (
   genus VARCHAR2(128),
   species VARCHAR2(128),
   country VARCHAR2(60),
   FOREIGN KEY (genus, species) REFERENCES birds (genus, species)
);

CREATE TYPE country_tab_t AS TABLE OF VARCHAR2(60);
```

I should then be able to smush the master and detail tables together in a single SELECT that converts the detail records into a collection type. This feature has enormous significance for client/server programs because the number of roundtrips can be cut down without incurring the overhead of duplicating the master records with each and every detail record:

```
DECLARE
   CURSOR bird_curs IS
      SELECT b.genus, b.species,
         CAST(MULTISET(SELECT bh.country FROM bird_habitats bh
                        WHERE bh.genus = b.genus
                          AND bh.species = b.species)
            AS country_tab_t)
        FROM birds b;
   bird_row bird_curs%ROWTYPE;
BEGIN
   OPEN bird_curs;
   FETCH bird_curs into bird_row;
   CLOSE bird_curs;
END;
```

As with the CAST pseudo-function, MULTISET cannot serve as the target of an INSERT, UPDATE, or DELETE statement.

### The TABLE pseudo-function

The TABLE operator casts or converts a collection-valued column into something you can SELECT from. It sounds complicated, but this section presents an example that's not too hard to follow.

Looking at it another way, let's say that you have a database table with a column of a collection type. How can you figure out which rows in the table contain a collection that meets certain criteria? That is, how can you select from the database table, putting a WHERE clause on the collection's contents? Wouldn't it be nice if you could just say:

```
SELECT *
  FROM table_name
 WHERE collection_column
       HAS CONTENTS 'whatever';    -- INVALID! Imaginary syntax!
```

Logically, that's exactly what you can do with the TABLE function. Going back to my color_models database table, how could I get a listing of all color models that contain the color RED? Here's the real way to do it:

```
SELECT *
  FROM color_models c
 WHERE 'RED' IN
       (SELECT * FROM TABLE(c.colors));
```

which, in SQL*Plus, returns:

```
MODEL_TYPE    COLORS
------------  -----------------------------------
RGB           COLOR_TAB_T('RED', 'GREEN', 'BLUE')
```

The query means "go through the color_models table and return all rows whose list of colors contains at least one RED element." Had there been more rows with a RED element in their colors column, these rows too would have appeared in my SQL*Plus result set.

As shown previously, TABLE accepts a collection as its only argument, which can be an alias-qualified collection column, as follows:

```
TABLE(alias_name.collection_name)
```

TABLE returns the contents of this collection coerced into a virtual database table. Hence, you can SELECT from it. In my example, it is used in a subquery.

To repeat an earlier admonition, none of the collection pseudo-functions is available from within PL/SQL, but PL/SQL programmers will certainly want to know how to use these gizmos in their SQL statements!

You will also find the pseudo-functions, particularly TABLE, very handy when you are taking advantage of the table function capability introduced in Oracle9i Database. A table function is a function that returns a collection, and it can be used in the FROM clause of a query. This functionality is explored in Chapter 17.

Personally, I find these features fascinating, and I enjoy the mental calisthenics required to understand and use them. Maybe mine isn't a global sentiment, but at least you must admit that Oracle hasn't let its language technology get tired!

### Sorting contents of collections

One of the wonderful aspects of pseudo-functions is that you can apply SQL operations against the contents of PL/SQL data structures (nested tables and VARRAYs, at least). You can, for example, use ORDER BY to select information from the nested table in the order you desire. Here, I populate a database table with some of my favorite authors:

```
TYPE names_t AS TABLE OF VARCHAR2 (100)

TYPE authors_t AS TABLE OF VARCHAR2 (100)

TABLE favorite_authors (name varchar2(200));

BEGIN
   INSERT INTO favorite_authors VALUES ('Robert Harris');
   INSERT INTO favorite_authors VALUES ('Tom Segev');
   INSERT INTO favorite_authors VALUES ('Toni Morrison');
END;
```

Now I would like to blend this information with data from my PL/SQL program:

```
DECLARE
   scifi_favorites   authors_t
      := authors_t ('Sheri S. Tepper', 'Orson Scott Card', 'Gene Wolfe');
BEGIN
   DBMS_OUTPUT.put_line ('I recommend that you read books by:');
```

```
      FOR rec IN  (SELECT COLUMN_VALUE favs
                     FROM TABLE (CAST (scifi_favorites AS  names_t))
                  UNION
                  SELECT NAME
                     FROM favorite_authors)
      LOOP
         DBMS_OUTPUT.put_line (rec.favs);
      END LOOP;
   END;
```

Notice that I can use UNION to combine data from my database table and collection.
I can also apply this technique only to PL/SQL data to sort the contents being retrieved:

```
   DECLARE
      scifi_favorites   authors_t
         := authors_t ('Sheri S. Tepper', 'Orson Scott Card', 'Gene Wolfe');
   BEGIN
      DBMS_OUTPUT.put_line ('I recommend that you read books by:');

      FOR rec IN  (SELECT COLUMN_VALUE Favs
                     FROM TABLE (CAST (scifi_favorites AS  names_t))
                  ORDER BY COLUMN_VALUE)
      LOOP
         DBMS_OUTPUT.put_line (rec.favs);
      END LOOP;
   END;
```

> COLUMN_VALUE in the above query is the system-defined name of
> the column created with the TABLE operator.

# Nested Table Multiset Operations

The essential advance made in collections starting with Oracle Database 10g is that the
database treats nested tables more like the multisets that they actually are. The database
provides high-level set operations that can be applied to nested tables and only, for the
time being, to nested tables. Here is a brief summary of these set-level capabilities:

| Operation | Return value | Description |
|---|---|---|
| = | BOOLEAN | Compares two nested tables, and returns TRUE if they have the same named type and cardinality and if the elements are equal. |
| <> or != | BOOLEAN | Compares two nested tables, and returns FALSE if they differ in named type, cardinality, or equality of elements. |
| [NOT] IN () | BOOLEAN | Returns TRUE [FALSE] if the nested table to the left of IN exists in the list of nested tables in the parentheses. |
| x MULTISET EXCEPT [DISTINCT] y | NESTED TABLE | Performs a MINUS set operation on nested tables x and y, returning a nested table whose elements are in x, but not in y. x, y, and the returned nested table must all be of the same type. The DISTINCT keyword instructs |

| Operation | Return value | Description |
|---|---|---|
| | | Oracle to eliminate any element in x which is also in y, regardless of the number of occurrences. |
| x MULTISET INTERSECT [DISTINCT] y | NESTED TABLE | Performs an INTERSECT set operation on nested tables x and y, returning a nested table whose elements are in both x and y. x, y, and the returned nested table must all be of the same type. The DISTINCT keyword forces the elimination of duplicates from the returned nested table, including duplicates of NULL, if they exist. |
| x MULTISET UNION [DISTINCT] y | NESTED TABLE | Performs a UNION set operation on nested tables x and y, returning a nested table whose elements include all those in x as well as those in y. x, y, and the returned nested table must all be of the same type. The DISTINCT keyword forces the elimination of duplicates from the returned nested table, including duplicates of NULL, if they exist. |
| SET(x) | NESTED TABLE | Returns nested table x without duplicate elements. |
| x IS [NOT] A SET | BOOLEAN | Returns TRUE [FALSE] if the nested table x is composed of unique elements. |
| x IS [NOT] EMPTY | BOOLEAN | Returns TRUE [FALSE] if the nested table x is empty. |
| e [NOT] MEMBER [OF] x | BOOLEAN | Returns TRUE [FALSE] if the expression e is a member of the nested table x. |
| y [NOT] SUBMULTISET [OF] x | BOOLEAN | Returns TRUE [FALSE] if the nested table y contains only elements that are also in nested table x. |

In the following sections, I will take a closer look at many of these features. As I do so, I'll make frequent references to this nested table type:

```
/* File on web: 10g_strings_nt.sql */
TYPE strings_nt IS TABLE OF VARCHAR2(100);
```

I'll also make repeated use of the following package:

```
/* File on web: 10g_authors.pkg */
CREATE OR REPLACE PACKAGE authors_pkg
IS
   steven_authors     strings_nt
      := strings_nt ('ROBIN HOBB'
                    , 'ROBERT HARRIS'
                    , 'DAVID BRIN'
                    , 'SHERI S. TEPPER'
                    , 'CHRISTOPHER ALEXANDER'
                    );
   veva_authors     strings_nt
      := strings_nt ('ROBIN HOBB'
                    , 'SHERI S. TEPPER'
                    , 'ANNE MCCAFFREY'
                    );

   eli_authors     strings_nt
      := strings_nt ( 'SHERI S. TEPPER'
                    , 'DAVID BRIN'
```

```
                     );

   PROCEDURE show_authors (
      title_in    IN   VARCHAR2
    , authors_in    IN    strings_nt
   );
END;
/

CREATE OR REPLACE PACKAGE BODY authors_pkg
IS
   PROCEDURE show_authors (
      title_in    IN   VARCHAR2
    , authors_in    IN    strings_nt
   )
   IS
   BEGIN
      DBMS_OUTPUT.put_line (title_in);

      FOR indx IN authors_in.FIRST .. authors_in.LAST
      LOOP
         DBMS_OUTPUT.put_line (indx || ' = ' || authors_in (indx));
      END LOOP;

      DBMS_OUTPUT.put_line ('_');
   END show_authors;
END;
/
```

## Testing Equality and Membership of Nested Tables

Prior to Oracle Database 10*g*, the only way to tell if two collections were identical (i.e., had the same contents) was to compare the values of each row for equality (and if the collection contained records, you would have to compare each field of each record); see the example in *10g_coll_compare_old.sql* for an example of this code. From Oracle Database 10*g* onwards, with nested tables, you only need to use the standard = and != operators as shown in the following example:

```
/* File on web: 10g_coll_compare.sql */
DECLARE
   TYPE clientele IS TABLE OF VARCHAR2 (64);

   group1   clientele := clientele ('Customer 1', 'Customer 2');
   group2   clientele := clientele ('Customer 1', 'Customer 3');
   group3   clientele := clientele ('Customer 3', 'Customer 1');
BEGIN
   IF group1 = group2
   THEN
      DBMS_OUTPUT.put_line ('Group 1 = Group 2');
   ELSE
      DBMS_OUTPUT.put_line ('Group 1 != Group 2');
   END IF;
```

```
        IF group2 != group3
        THEN
            DBMS_OUTPUT.put_line ('Group 2 != Group 3');
        ELSE
            DBMS_OUTPUT.put_line ('Group 2 = Group 3');
        END IF;
    END;
```

Note that the equality check implemented for nested tables treats NULLs consistently with other operators. It considers NULL to be "unknowable." Thus, one NULL is never equal to another NULL. As a consequence, if both of the nested tables you are comparing contain a NULL value at the same row, they will *not* be considered equal.

## Checking for Membership of an Element in a Nested Table

In a variation on that theme, you can use the MEMBER operator to determine if a particular element is in a nested table. Use SUBMULTISET to determine if an *entire* nested table is contained in another nested table. Here is an example:

```
/* File on web: 10g_submultiset.sql */
BEGIN
    bpl (authors_pkg.steven_authors
            SUBMULTISET OF authors_pkg.eli_authors
        , 'Father follows son?');
    bpl (authors_pkg.eli_authors
            SUBMULTISET OF authors_pkg.steven_authors
        , 'Son follows father?');

    bpl (authors_pkg.steven_authors
            NOT SUBMULTISET OF authors_pkg.eli_authors
        , 'Father doesn''t follow son?');
    bpl (authors_pkg.eli_authors
            NOT SUBMULTISET OF authors_pkg.steven_authors
        , 'Son doesn''t follow father?');
END;
/
```

Here are the results of running this code:

```
SQL> @10g_submultiset
Father follows son? - FALSE
Son follows father? - TRUE
Father doesn't follow son? - TRUE
Son doesn't follow father? - FALSE
```

## Performing High-Level Set Operations

Set operations like UNION, INTERSECT, and MINUS are extremely powerful and helpful, precisely because they are such simple, high-level concepts. You can write a very small amount of code to achieve great effects. Consider the following code, which shows a variety of set operators at work:

---

```
/* File on web: 10g_union.sql */
 1  DECLARE
 2     our_authors strings_nt := strings_nt();
 3  BEGIN
 4     our_authors := authors_pkg.steven_authors
 5                    MULTISET UNION authors_pkg.veva_authors;
 6
 7     authors_pkg.show_authors ('MINE then VEVA', our_authors);
 8
 9     our_authors := authors_pkg.veva_authors
10                    MULTISET UNION authors_pkg.steven_authors;
11
12     authors_pkg.show_authors ('VEVA then MINE', our_authors);
13
14     our_authors := authors_pkg.steven_authors
15                    MULTISET UNION DISTINCT authors_pkg.veva_authors;
16
17     authors_pkg.show_authors ('MINE then VEVA with DISTINCT', our_authors);
18
19     our_authors := authors_pkg.steven_authors
20                    MULTISET INTERSECT authors_pkg.veva_authors;
21
22     authors_pkg.show_authors ('IN COMMON', our_authors);
23
24     our_authors := authors_pkg.veva_authors
25                    MULTISET EXCEPT authors_pkg.steven_authors;
26
27     authors_pkg.show_authors (q'[ONLY VEVA'S]', our_authors);
28  END;
```

Here is the output from running this script:

```
SQL>  @10g_union
MINE then VEVA
1 = ROBIN HOBB
2 = ROBERT HARRIS
3 = DAVID BRIN
4 = SHERI S. TEPPER
5 = CHRISTOPHER ALEXANDER
6 = ROBIN HOBB
7 = SHERI S. TEPPER
8 = ANNE MCCAFFREY

VEVA then MINE
1 = ROBIN HOBB
2 = SHERI S. TEPPER
3 = ANNE MCCAFFREY
4 = ROBIN HOBB
5 = ROBERT HARRIS
6 = DAVID BRIN
7 = SHERI S. TEPPER
8 = CHRISTOPHER ALEXANDER

MINE then VEVA with DISTINCT
1 = ROBIN HOBB
2 = ROBERT HARRIS
```

```
       3 = DAVID BRIN
       4 = SHERI S. TEPPER
       5 = CHRISTOPHER ALEXANDER
       6 = ANNE MCCAFFREY

IN COMMON
       1 = ROBIN HOBB
       2 = SHERI S. TEPPER

ONLY VEVA'S
       1 = ANNE MCCAFFREY
```

Note that MULTISET UNION does not act precisely the same as the SQL UNION. It does not reorder the data, and it does not remove duplicate values. Duplicates are perfectly acceptable and, indeed, are significant in a multiset. If, however, you want to remove duplicates, use MULTISET UNION DISTINCT.

## Handling Duplicates in a Nested Table

So, a nested table can have duplicates (the same value stored more than once)—and those duplicates will persist even beyond a MULTISET UNION operation. Sometimes this is what you want; sometimes, you would much rather have a distinct set of values with which to work. Oracle provides the following operators:

*SET operator*
> Helps you transform a nondistinct set of elements in a nested table into a distinct set. You can think of it as a "SELECT DISTINCT" for nested tables.

*IS A SET and IS [NOT] A SET operators*
> Helps you answers questions like "Does this nested table contain any duplicate entries?"

The following script exercises these features of Oracle Database 10g and later:

```
/* Files on web: 10g_set.sql, bpl2.sp */
BEGIN
   -- Add a duplicate author to Steven's list
   authors_pkg.steven_authors.EXTEND;
   authors_pkg.steven_authors(authors_pkg.steven_authors.LAST) := 'ROBERT HARRIS';

   distinct_authors :=
      SET (authors_pkg.steven_authors);

   authors_pkg.show_authors (
      'FULL SET', authors_pkg.steven_authors);

   bpl (authors_pkg.steven_authors IS A SET, 'My authors distinct?');
   bpl (authors_pkg.steven_authors IS NOT A SET, 'My authors NOT distinct?');
   DBMS_OUTPUT.PUT_LINE ('');

   authors_pkg.show_authors (
      'DISTINCT SET', distinct_authors);
```

```
      bpl (distinct_authors IS A SET, 'SET of authors distinct?');
      bpl (distinct_authors IS NOT A SET, 'SET of authors NOT distinct?');
      DBMS_OUTPUT.PUT_LINE ('');

   END;
   /
```

And here are the results of this script:

```
SQL> @10g_set
FULL SET
1 = ROBIN HOBB
2 = ROBERT HARRIS
3 = DAVID BRIN
4 = SHERI S. TEPPER
5 = CHRISTOPHER ALEXANDER
6 = ROBERT HARRIS

My authors distinct? - FALSE
My authors NOT distinct? - TRUE

DISTINCT SET
1 = ROBIN HOBB
2 = ROBERT HARRIS
3 = DAVID BRIN
4 = SHERI S. TEPPER
5 = CHRISTOPHER ALEXANDER

SET of authors distinct? - TRUE
SET of authors NOT distinct? - FALSE
```

# Maintaining Schema-Level Collections

Here are some not-so-obvious bits of information that will assist you in using nested tables and VARRAYS. This kind of housekeeping is not necessary or relevant when working with associative arrays.

## Necessary Privileges

When they live in the database, collection datatypes can be shared by more than one database user (schema). As you can imagine, privileges are involved. Fortunately, it's not complicated; only one Oracle privilege—EXECUTE—applies to collection types.

If you are Scott, and you want to grant Joe permission to use color_tab_t in his programs, all you need to do is grant the EXECUTE privilege to him:

```
GRANT EXECUTE on color_tab_t TO JOE;
```

Joe can then refer to the type using *schema.type* notation. For example:

```
CREATE TABLE my_stuff_to_paint (
   which_stuff VARCHAR2(512),
   paint_mixture SCOTT.color_tab_t
```

```
)
NESTED TABLE paint_mixture STORE AS paint_mixture_st;
```

EXECUTE privileges are also required by users who need to run PL/SQL anonymous blocks that use the object type. That's one of several reasons that named PL/SQL modules—packages, procedures, functions—are generally preferred. Granting EXECUTE on the module confers the grantor's privileges to the grantee while executing the module.

For tables that include collection columns, the traditional SELECT, INSERT, UPDATE, and DELETE privileges still have meaning, as long as there is no requirement to build a collection for any columns. However, if a user is going to INSERT or UPDATE the contents of a collection column, that user must have the EXECUTE privilege on the type because that is the only way to use the default constructor.

## Collections and the Data Dictionary

The Oracle database offers several data dictionary views that provide information about your nested table and VARRAY collection types (see Table 12-4). The shorthand dictionary term for user-defined types is simply TYPE. Collection type definitions are found in the USER_SOURCE view (or DBA_SOURCE, or ALL_SOURCE).

*Table 12-4. Data dictionary entries for collection types*

| To answer the question ... | Use this view | As in |
|---|---|---|
| What collection types have I created? | USER_TYPES | SELECT type_name<br>  FROM user_types<br>WHERE typecode ='COLLECTION'; |
| What was the original type definition of collection Foo_t? | USER_SOURCE | SELECT text<br>  FROM user_source<br>WHERE name = 'FOO_T'<br>  AND type = 'TYPE'<br>ORDER BY line; |
| What columns implement Foo_t? | USER_TAB_ COLUMNS | SELECT table_name,column_name<br>  FROM user_tab_columns<br>WHERE data_type = 'FOO_T'; |
| What database objects are dependent on Foo_t? | USER_DEPENDENCIES | SELECT name, type<br>  FROM user_dependencies<br>WHERE referenced_name='FOO_T'; |

# CHAPTER 13

# Miscellaneous Datatypes

In this chapter, I'll explore all the native PL/SQL datatypes that have not yet been covered. These include the BOOLEAN, RAW, and UROWID/ROWID types, as well as the large object (LOB) family of types. I'll also discuss some useful, predefined object types, including XMLType, which allow you to store XML data in a database column, the URI types, which allow you store Uniform Resource Identifier (URI) information, and the Any types, which allow you to store, well, just about anything.

The terminology for the LOB implementation has changed in Oracle Database 11*g*. Oracle has re-engineered the implementation of LOBs using a technology called *SecureFiles*; the older pre-Oracle Database 11*g* LOB technology is now known as *BasicFiles*. In this chapter I'll also discuss SecureFiles and the performance benefits you can reap by using this updated technology.

## The BOOLEAN Datatype

Boolean values and variables are very useful in PL/SQL. Because a Boolean variable can only be TRUE, FALSE, or NULL, you can use that variable to explain what is happening in your code. With Booleans you can write code that is easily readable because it is more English-like. You can replace a complicated Boolean expression involving many different variables and tests with a single Boolean variable that directly expresses the intention and meaning of the text.

Here is an example of an IF statement with a single Boolean variable (or function—you really can't tell the difference just by looking at this short bit of code):

```
IF report_requested
THEN
   print_report (report_id);
END IF;
```

The beauty of this technique is that it not only makes your code a bit more self-documenting, it also has the potential to insulate your code from future change. For example, consider the human interface that needs to precede the previous code fragment. How do you know that a report was requested? Perhaps you ask the user to answer a question with a Y or an N, or perhaps the user must place a check in a checkbox or select an option from a drop-down list. The point is that it doesn't matter. You can freely change the human interface of your code, and, as long as that interface properly sets the report_requested Boolean variable, the actual reporting functionality will continue to work correctly.

 While PL/SQL supports a Boolean datatype, the Oracle database does not. You can create and work with Boolean variables from PL/SQL, but you cannot create tables having Boolean columns.

The fact that Boolean variables can be NULL has implications for IF...THEN...ELSE statements. For example, look at the difference in behavior between the following two statements:

```
IF report_requested
THEN
   NULL; --Executes if report_requested = TRUE
ELSE
   NULL; --Executes if report_requested = FALSE or IS NULL
END IF;

IF NOT report_requested
THEN
   NULL; --Executes if report_requested = FALSE
ELSE
   NULL; --Executes if report_requeste = TRUE or IS NULL
END IF;
```

If you need separate logic for each of the three possible cases, you can write a three-pronged IF statement as follows:

```
IF report_requested
THEN
   NULL;   --Executes if report_requested = TRUE
ELSIF NOT report_requested
THEN
   NULL;   --Executes if report_requested = FALSE
ELSE
   NULL;   --Executes if report_requested IS NULL
END IF;
```

For more details on the effects of NULLs in IF statements, refer back to Chapter 4.

# The RAW Datatype

The RAW datatype allows you to store and manipulate relatively small amounts of binary data. Unlike the case with VARCHAR2 and other character types, RAW data never undergoes any kind of character set conversion when traveling back and forth between your PL/SQL programs and the database. RAW variables are declared as follows:

```
variable_name RAW(maximum_size)
```

The value for *maximum_size* may range from 1 through 32767. Be aware that while a RAW PL/SQL variable can hold up to 32,767 bytes of data, a RAW database column can hold only 2,000 bytes.

RAW is not a type that you will use or encounter very often. It's useful mainly when you need to deal with small amounts of binary data. When dealing with the large amounts of binary data found in images, sound files, and the like, you should look into using the BLOB (binary large object) type. BLOB is described later in this chapter (see "Working with LOBs" on page 401).

## The UROWID and ROWID Datatypes

The UROWID and ROWID types allow you to work with database ROWIDs in your PL/SQL programs. A ROWID is a *row identifier*—a binary value that identifies the physical address for a row of data in a database table. A ROWID can be used to uniquely identify a row in table, even if that table does not have a unique key. Two rows with identical column values will have different ROWIDs or UROWIDs.

 Beware! ROWIDs in a table can change. In early Oracle releases (Oracle8 Database 8.0 and earlier) ROWIDs could not change during the life of a row. But starting with Oracle8i Database new features were added that violate this old rule. If row movement is enabled on a regular (heap organized) table or for any index-organized table, updates can cause a row's ROWID or UROWID to change. In addition, if someone alters the table to shrink, move, or perform some other operation that will cause a row to change from one physical data block to another, the ROWID will change.

With the caveat noted above, there can still sometimes be value in using ROWIDs. Referencing ROWIDs in SELECT, UPDATE, MERGE, and DELETE statements can lead to desirable improvements in processing speed, as access by ROWID is the fastest way to locate or retrieve a specific row in a table—faster than a search by primary key. Figure 13-1 contrasts the use of a ROWID in an UPDATE statement with the use of column values such as those for a primary key.

Historically, the ROWID type came before UROWID. As Oracle added functionality such as index-organized tables (IOTs) and gateways to other types of databases, Oracle developed new types of ROWIDs and hence had to develop a new datatype capable of holding them. Enter the UROWID datatype. The U in UROWID stands for Universal, and a UROWID variable can contain any type of ROWID from any type of table.

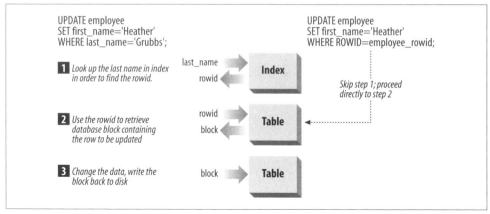

*Figure 13-1. ROWIDs take you directly to rows in a table*

 I recommend the use of UROWID for all new development involving ROWIDs. The ROWID type provides backward compatibility but can't accommodate all types of ROWIDs now encountered in an Oracle database. UROWID is safer because it accommodates any type of ROWID, while still providing the desired *access by rowid* execution plan.

## Getting ROWIDs

You can get the ROWID for a given table row by including the keyword ROWID in your select list. For example:

```
DECLARE
   employee_rowid UROWID;
   employee_salary NUMBER;
BEGIN
   --Retrieve employee information that we might want to modify
   SELECT rowid, salary INTO employee_rowid, employee_salary
     FROM employees
    WHERE last_name='Grubbs' AND first_name='John';
END;
```

Oracle calls the ROWID a *pseudo-column* because the ROWID value is not stored in the same sense that other column values are, yet you can refer to the ROWID as if it were a column. A ROWID is more akin to a pointer—it holds the physical address of a row in a table.

## Using ROWIDs

The main use of ROWIDs is in repeating access to a given database row. This use is particularly beneficial when accessing the row is costly or frequent. Recall the example from the previous section in which I retrieved the salary for a specific employee. What if I later want to modify that salary? One solution would be to issue an UPDATE statement with the same WHERE clause as the one I used in my original SELECT:

```
DECLARE
    employee_rowid UROWID;
    employee_salary NUMBER;
BEGIN
    --Retrieve employee information that we might want to modify
    SELECT rowid, salary INTO employee_rowid, employee_salary
      FROM employees
     WHERE last_name='Grubbs' AND first_name='John';

    /* Do a bunch of processing to compute a new salary */

    UPDATE employees
       SET salary = employee_salary
     WHERE last_name='Grubbs' AND first_name='John';
END;
```

While this code will certainly work, it has the disadvantage of having to repeat the same access path for the UPDATE as was used for the SELECT. Most likely, one or more indexes were accessed in order to find the employee row in question. But those indexes were just accessed for the SELECT statement, so why go through all the work of looking up the same ROWID twice? Internally, the purpose of accessing the index was to obtain the ROWID so that the row could be accessed directly. By including ROWID in my SELECT statement, I can simply supply that ROWID to the UPDATE statement, bypassing the index lookup:

```
DECLARE
    employee_rowid UROWID;
    employee_salary NUMBER;
BEGIN
    --Retrieve employee information that we might want to modify
    SELECT rowid, salary INTO employee_rowid, employee_salary
      FROM employees
     WHERE last_name='Grubbs' AND first_name='John';

    /* Do a bunch of processing to compute a new salary */

    UPDATE employees
       SET salary = employee_salary
     WHERE rowid = employee_rowid;
END;
```

Recall my caveat about ROWIDs changing. If in my multiuser system the ROWID for the John Grubbs row in the employee table in my example changes between the SELECT and the UPDATE, my code will not execute as intended. Why is that? Well, enabling row movement on a regular heap-organized table can allow a row's ROWID in that table to change. Row movement may be enabled because the DBA wants to do online table reorganizations, or the table may be partitioned and row movement will allow a row to migrate from one partition to another during an update.

Often, a better way to achieve the same effect as using ROWID in an UPDATE or DELETE statement is to use an explicit cursor to retrieve data, and then use the WHERE CURRENT OF CURSOR clause to modify or delete it. See Chapter 15 for detailed information on this technique.

Using ROWIDs is a powerful technique to improve the performance of your PL/SQL programs because they cut through to the physical management layer of the database. Good application programs don't usually get involved in how the data is physically managed. Instead they let the database and administrative programs work with the physical management and restrict application programs to logical management of data. Therefore, I don't generally recommend using ROWIDs in your application programs.

## The LOB Datatypes

Oracle and PL/SQL support several variations of large object datatypes. LOBs can store large amounts—from 8 to 128 terabytes—of binary data (such as images) or character text data.

Through Oracle9i Database Release 2, LOBs could store only up to 4 gigabytes. Starting with Oracle Database 10g, the limit was increased to a value between 8 and 128 terabytes that is dependent upon your database block size.

Within PL/SQL you can declare LOB variables of the following datatypes:

BFILE
    Binary file. Declares a variable that holds a file locator pointing to an operating-system file outside the database. The database treats the data in the file as binary data.

BLOB
    Binary large object. Declares a variable that holds a LOB locator pointing to a large binary object stored inside the database.

CLOB
    Character large object. Declares a variable that holds a LOB locator pointing to a large block of character data in the database character set, stored inside the database.

NCLOB
    National Language Support (NLS) character large object. Declares a variable that holds a LOB locator pointing to a large block of character data in the national character set, stored inside the database.

LOBs can be categorized as *internal* or *external*. Internal LOBs (BLOBs, CLOBs, and NCLOBs) are stored in the database and can participate in a transaction in the database server. External LOBs (BFILEs) represent binary data stored in operating-system files outside the database tablespaces. External LOBs cannot participate in transactions; in other words, you cannot commit or roll back changes to a BFILE. Instead, you must rely on the underlying filesystem for data integrity. Likewise, the database's read consistency model does not extend to BFILEs. Repeated reads of a BFILE may not give the same results, unlike internal LOBs which do follow the database read consistency model.

---

### LONG and LONG RAW

If you've been around Oracle for a few years, you've probably noticed that so far I've omitted any discussion of two datatypes: LONG and LONG RAW. This is intentional. In the database, LONG and LONG RAW allow you to store large amounts (up to 2 gigabytes) of character and binary data, respectively. The maximum lengths of the PL/SQL types, however, are much shorter: only 32,760 bytes, which is less than the 32,767 bytes supported by VARCHAR2 and RAW. Given this rather odd length limitation, I recommend using VARCHAR2 and RAW, instead of LONG and LONG RAW, in your PL/SQL programs.

If you're retrieving LONG and LONG RAW columns that may contain more than 32,767 bytes of data, you won't be able to store the returned values in VARCHAR2 or RAW variables. This is an unfortunate restriction and a good reason to avoid LONG and LONG RAW to begin with.

LONG and LONG RAW are obsolete types, maintained only for backward compatibility. Oracle doesn't recommend their use, and neither do I. For new applications where you have a choice, use CLOB and BLOB instead. For existing applications, Oracle's *SecureFiles and Large Objects Developer's Guide* provides guidance for migrating existing data from LONG to LOB columns.

---

# Working with LOBs

The topic of working with large objects is, well, large, and I can't begin to cover every aspect of LOB programming in this chapter. What I can and will do, however, is provide you with a good introduction to the topic of LOB programming aimed especially at PL/SQL developers. I'll discuss some of the issues to be aware of and show examples of fundamental LOB operations. All of this, I hope, will provide you with a good foundation for your future LOB programming endeavors.

Before getting into the meat of this section, please note that all LOB examples are based on the following table definition (which can be found in the *ch13_code.sql* file on the book's web site):

```
TABLE waterfalls (
   falls_name VARCHAR2(80),
```

```
    falls_photo BLOB,
    falls_directions CLOB,
    falls_description NCLOB,
    falls_web_page BFILE)
```

This table contains rows about waterfalls located in Michigan's Upper Peninsula. Figure 13-2 shows the Dryer Hose, a falls near Munising frequented by ice climbers in its frozen state.

*Figure 13-2. The Dryer Hose in Munising, Michigan*

The table implements one column for each of the four LOB types. Photos consist of large amounts of binary data, so the falls_photo column is defined as a BLOB. Directions and descriptions are text, so those columns are CLOB and NCLOB, respectively. Normally, you'd use either CLOB or NCLOB for both, but I wanted to provide an example that used each LOB type. Finally, the master copy of the web page for each waterfall is stored in an HTML file outside the database. I use a BFILE column to point to that HTML file. I'll use these columns in our examples to demonstrate various facets of working with LOB data in PL/SQL programs.

 In my discussion of large objects, I'll frequently use the acronym LOB to refer to CLOBs, BLOBs, NCLOBs, and BFILEs in general. I'll use specific type names only when discussing something specific to a type.

## Understanding LOB Locators

Fundamental to working with LOBs is the concept of a *LOB locator*. A LOB locator is a pointer to large object data in a database. Let's look at what happens when you select a BLOB column into a BLOB PL/SQL variable:

```
DECLARE
    photo BLOB;
BEGIN
    SELECT falls_photo
      INTO photo
      FROM waterfalls
     WHERE falls_name='Dryer Hose';
```

What, exactly, is in the photo variable after the SELECT statement executes? Is the photo itself retrieved? No. Only a pointer to the photo is retrieved. You end up with the situation shown in Figure 13-3.

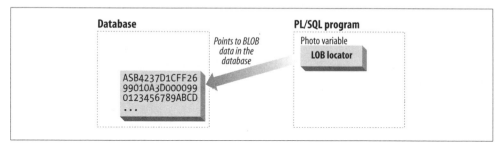

*Figure 13-3. A LOB locator points to its associated large object data within the database*

This is different from the way in which other datatypes work. Database LOB columns store LOB locators, and those locators point to the real data stored in a LOB segment elsewhere in the database. Likewise, PL/SQL LOB variables hold those same LOB locators, which point to LOB data within the database. To work with LOB data, you first retrieve a LOB locator, and you then use a built-in package named DBMS_LOB to retrieve and/or modify the actual LOB data. For example, to retrieve the binary photo data from the falls_photo BLOB column used in the previous example, you would go through the following steps:

1. Issue a SELECT statement to retrieve the LOB locator for the photo you wish to display.
2. Open the LOB via a call to DBMS_LOB.OPEN.
3. Make a call to DBMS_LOB.GETCHUNKSIZE to get the optimal chunk size to use when reading (and writing) the LOB's value.
4. Make a call to DBMS_LOB.GETLENGTH to get the number of bytes or characters in the LOB value.
5. Make multiple calls to DBMS_LOB.READ in order to retrieve the LOB data.
6. Close the LOB.

Not all of these steps are necessary, and don't worry if you don't understand them fully right now. I'll explain all the steps and operations shortly.

The use of locators might initially appear clumsy. It's a good approach, though, because it obviates the need to return all the data for a given LOB each time that you fetch a row from a table. Imagine how long a fetch would take if up to 128 terabytes of LOB data need to be transferred. Imagine the waste if you have to access only a small fraction of that data. With the Oracle database's approach, you fetch locators (a quick operation) and then you retrieve only the LOB data that you need. In addition, LOBs are not cached in the buffer cache by default, and LOBs do not generate undo like normal data. LOBs generate redo like normal data, unless you specify the NOLOGGING option. So loading 50 gigabytes of LOB data will not flush your buffer cache or flood your undo tablespace and degrade overall performance. This separate cache and undo management of LOBs gets ever better with SecureFiles in Oracle Database 11g...but more on that later.

---

### Oracle's LOB Documentation

If you are working with LOBs, I strongly recommend that you familiarize yourself with the following portions of Oracle's documentation set:

- *SecureFiles and Large Objects Developer's Guide*. Oracle Database 11g guide to LOB programming.
- *Application Developer's Guide—Large Objects*. Oracle Database 10g and earlier guide to LOB programming.
- *PL/SQL Packages and Types Reference*. See the chapter on the DBMS_LOB package.
- *SQL Reference*. The "Datatypes" section in Chapter 2, *Basic Elements of Oracle SQL*, contains important information about LOBs.

This is not an exhaustive list of LOB documentation, but you'll find all the essential information in these sources.

---

## Empty Versus NULL LOBs

Now that you understand the distinction between a LOB locator and the value to which it points, you need to wrap your mind around another key concept: the *empty LOB*. An empty LOB is what you have when a LOB locator doesn't point to any LOB data. This is not the same as a NULL LOB, which is a LOB column (or variable) that doesn't hold a LOB locator. Clear as mud, right? Let's look at some example code:

```
DECLARE
   directions CLOB;
BEGIN
   IF directions IS NULL THEN
     DBMS_OUTPUT.PUT_LINE('directions is NULL');
   ELSE
     DBMS_OUTPUT.PUT_LINE('directions is not NULL');
   END IF;
END;

directions is NULL
```

Here I have declared a CLOB variable, which is atomically NULL because I haven't yet assigned it a value. You're used to this behavior, right? It's the same with any other datatype: declare a variable without assigning a value and comparisons to NULL, such as `variable IS NULL`, evaluate to TRUE. In this regard, a LOB is similar to an object in that it must be initialized before data can be added to it. See Chapter 26 for more information on objects.

Let's press ahead with the example and initialize the LOB. The following code uses a call to EMPTY_CLOB to initialize (but not populate) the LOB variable.

First the code:

```
DECLARE
   directions CLOB;
BEGIN
   IF directions IS NULL THEN
     DBMS_OUTPUT.PUT_LINE('at first directions is NULL');
   ELSE
     DBMS_OUTPUT.PUT_LINE('at first directions is not NULL');
   END IF;
   DBMS_OUTPUT.PUT_LINE('Length = '
                       || DBMS_LOB.GETLENGTH(directions));

   -- initialize the LOB variable
   directions := EMPTY_CLOB();

   IF directions IS NULL THEN
     DBMS_OUTPUT.PUT_LINE('after initializing, directions is NULL');
   ELSE
     DBMS_OUTPUT.PUT_LINE('after initializing, directions is not NULL');
   END IF;
   DBMS_OUTPUT.PUT_LINE('Length = '
                       || DBMS_LOB.GETLENGTH(directions));
END;
```

The output is:

```
at first directions is NULL
Length =
after initializing, directions is not NULL
Length = 0
```

You can see that at first the CLOB variable is atomically NULL. It comes as no surprise then that the length of the NULL LOB is also NULL. After I initialize the CLOB variable with the built-in function EMPTY_CLOB, my variable is no longer NULL because it contains a value: the locator. DBMS_LOB.GETLENGTH shows that while initialized (NOT NULL) the CLOB is empty. This difference is important to understand because the way in which you test for the presence or absence of data is more complicated for a LOB than it is for scalar datatypes.

A simple IS NULL test suffices for traditional scalar datatypes:

```
IF some_number IS NULL THEN
   --You know there is no data
```

If an IS NULL test on a NUMBER or a VARCHAR2 (or any other scalar type) returns TRUE, you know that the variable holds no data. With LOBs, however, you not only need to check for nullity (no locator), but you also need to check the length:

```
IF some_clob IS NULL THEN
   --There is no data
ELSIF DBMS_LOB.GETLENGTH(some_clob) = 0 THEN
   --There is no data
ELSE
   --Only now is there data
END IF;
```

As illustrated in this example, you can't check the length of a LOB without first having a locator. Thus, to determine whether a LOB holds data, you must first check for the presence of a locator using an IS NULL test, and then check for a non-zero length or perform both checks together like this:

```
IF NVL(DBMS_LOB.GETLENGTH(some_clob),0) = 0 THEN
   -- There is no data
ELSE
   -- There is data
END IF;
```

The bottom line is that you need to check for two conditions, not just one.

 When working with BLOBs, use EMPTY_BLOB( ) to create an empty BLOB. Use EMPTY_CLOB( ) for CLOBs and NCLOBs.

# Writing into a LOB

Once you have a valid LOB locator, you can write data into that LOB using one of these procedures from the built-in DBMS_LOB package:

*DBMS_LOB.WRITE*
> Allows you to write data randomly into a LOB.

*DBMS_LOB.WRITEAPPEND*
> Allows you to append data to the end of a LOB.

Following is an extension of the previous examples in this chapter. It begins by creating a LOB locator for the directions column in the waterfalls table. After creating the locator, I use DBMS_LOB.WRITE to begin writing directions to Munising Falls into the CLOB column. I then use DBMS_LOB.WRITEAPPEND to finish the job:

```
/* File on web: munising_falls_01.sql */
DECLARE
   directions CLOB;
   amount BINARY_INTEGER;
   offset INTEGER;
   first_direction VARCHAR2(100);
   more_directions VARCHAR2(500);
BEGIN
   --Delete any existing rows for 'Munising Falls' so that this
   --example can be executed multiple times
   DELETE
     FROM waterfalls
    WHERE falls_name='Munising Falls';

   --Insert a new row using EMPTY_CLOB() to create a LOB locator
   INSERT INTO waterfalls
           (falls_name,falls_directions)
     VALUES ('Munising  Falls',EMPTY_CLOB());

   --Retrieve the LOB locator created by the previous INSERT statement
   SELECT falls_directions
     INTO directions
     FROM waterfalls
    WHERE falls_name='Munising Falls';

   --Open the LOB; not strictly necessary, but best to open/close LOBs.
   DBMS_LOB.OPEN(directions, DBMS_LOB.LOB_READWRITE);

   --Use DBMS_LOB.WRITE to begin
   first_direction := 'Follow I-75 across the Mackinac Bridge.';
   amount := LENGTH(first_direction);  --number of characters to write
   offset := 1; --begin writing to the first character of the CLOB
   DBMS_LOB.WRITE(directions, amount, offset, first_direction);

   --Add some more directions using DBMS_LOB.WRITEAPPEND
   more_directions := ' Take US-2 west from St. Ignace to Blaney Park.'
                   || ' Turn north on M-77 and drive to Seney.'
                   || ' From Seney, take M-28 west to Munising.';
```

```
      DBMS_LOB.WRITEAPPEND(directions,
                           LENGTH(more_directions), more_directions);

      --Add yet more directions
      more_directions := ' In front of the paper mill, turn right on H-58.'
                      || ' Follow H-58 to Washington Street. Veer left onto'
                      || ' Washington Street. You''ll find the Munising'
                      || ' Falls visitor center across from the hospital at'
                      || ' the point where Washington Street becomes'
                      || ' Sand Point Road.';
      DBMS_LOB.WRITEAPPEND(directions,
                           LENGTH(more_directions), more_directions);

      --Close the LOB, and we are done.
      DBMS_LOB.CLOSE(directions);
   END;
```

In this example, I used both WRITE and WRITEAPPEND solely to demonstrate the use of both procedures. Because my LOB had no data to begin with, I could have done all the work using only WRITE. Notice that I opened and closed the LOB; while this is not strictly necessary, it is a good idea, especially if you are using Oracle Text. Otherwise, any Oracle Text domain- and function-based indexes will be updated with each WRITE or WRITEAPPEND call, rather than being updated once when you call CLOSE.

 In the section on BFILEs, I show how to read LOB data directly from an external operating-system file.

When writing to a LOB, as I have done here, there is no need to update the LOB column in the table. That's because the LOB locator does not change. I did not change the contents of falls_directions (the LOB locator). Rather, I added data to the LOB to which the locator pointed.

Writing to an existing LOB requires a lock on the row containing the LOB value. In this example, the session implicitly obtained the needed lock on INSERT. However, unlike in conventional (non-LOB) updates, if I later need to write to an existing LOB, I'll need to do a SELECT...FOR UPDATE to obtain a lock explicitly. Otherwise Oracle will give a *ORA-22920 row containing the LOB value is not locked* error.

LOB updates take place within the context of a transaction. I did not COMMIT in my example code. You should issue a COMMIT after executing the PL/SQL block if you want the Munising Falls directions to remain permanently in your database. If you issue a ROLLBACK after executing the PL/SQL block, all the work done by this block will be undone.

My example writes to a CLOB column. You write BLOB data in the same manner, except that your inputs to WRITE and WRITEAPPEND should be of the RAW type instead of the VARCHAR2 type.

The following SQL*Plus example shows one way you can see the data just inserted by my example. The next section will show you how to retrieve the data using the various DBMS_LOB procedures.

```
SQL> SET LONG 2000
SQL> COLUMN falls_directions WORD_WRAPPED FORMAT A70
SQL> SELECT falls_directions
  2  FROM waterfalls
  3  WHERE falls_name='Munising Falls';
  4  /

FALLS_DIRECTIONS
----------------------------------------------------------------------
Follow I-75 across the Mackinac Bridge. Take US-2 west from St. Ignace
to Blaney Park. Turn north on M-77 and drive to Seney. From Seney,
take M-28 west to Munising. In front of the paper mill, turn right on
H-58. Follow H-58 to  Washington Street. Veer left onto Washington
Street. You'll find the Munising Falls visitor center across from the
hospital at the point where Washington Street becomes Sand Point Road.
```

## Reading from a LOB

To retrieve data from a LOB, you use the DBMS_LOB.READ procedure. First, of course, you must retrieve the LOB locator. When reading from a CLOB, you specify an offset in terms of characters. Reading begins at the offset that you specify, and the first character of a CLOB is always number 1. When you are working with BLOBs, offsets are in terms of bytes. Note that when you are calling DBMS_LOB.READ, you must specify the number of characters (or bytes) that you wish to read. Given that LOBs are large, it's reasonable to plan on doing more than one read to get at all the data.

The following example retrieves and displays the directions to Munising Falls. I have carefully chosen the number of characters to read both to accommodate DBMS_OUTPUT's line-length restriction and to ensure a nice-looking line break in the final output.

```
/* File on web: munising_falls_02.sql */
DECLARE
   directions CLOB;
   directions_1 VARCHAR2(300);
   directions_2 VARCHAR2(300);
   chars_read_1 BINARY_INTEGER;
   chars_read_2 BINARY_INTEGER;
   offset INTEGER;
BEGIN
   --Retrieve the LOB locator inserted previously
   SELECT falls_directions
     INTO directions
     FROM waterfalls
```

```
          WHERE falls_name='Munising Falls';

     --Begin reading with the first character
     offset := 1;

     --Attempt to read 229 characters of directions, chars_read_1 will
     --be updated with the actual number of characters read
     chars_read_1 := 229;
     DBMS_LOB.READ(directions, chars_read_1, offset, directions_1);

     --If we read 229 characters, update the offset and try to
     --read 255 more.
     IF chars_read_1 = 229 THEN
        offset := offset + chars_read_1;
        chars_read_2 := 255;
        DBMS_LOB.READ(directions, chars_read_2, offset, directions_2);
     ELSE
        chars_read_2 := 0;
        directions_2 := '';
     END IF;

     --Display the total number of characters read
     DBMS_OUTPUT.PUT_LINE('Characters read = ' ||
                          TO_CHAR(chars_read_1+chars_read_2));

     --Display the directions
     DBMS_OUTPUT.PUT_LINE(directions_1);
     DBMS_OUTPUT.PUT_LINE(directions_2);
  END;
```

The output from this code is as follows:

```
Characters read = 414
Follow I-75 across the Mackinac Bridge. Take US-2 west from St. Ignace to Blaney
Park. Turn north on M-77 and drive to Seney. From Seney, take M-28 west to
Munising. In front of the paper mill, turn right on H-58. Follow H-58 to
Washington Street. Veer left onto Washington Street. You'll find the Munising
Falls visitor center across from the hospital at the point where Washington
Street becomes Sand Point Road.
```

The chars_read_1 (amount to read) parameter, which is the second parameter you pass to DBMS_LOB.READ, is an IN OUT parameter, and DBMS_LOB.READ will update it to reflect the number of characters (or bytes) actually read. You'll know you've reached the end of a LOB when the number of characters or bytes read is less than the number you requested. It seems to me a bit inconvenient that the offset is not updated in the same manner. When reading several sequential portions of a LOB, you must update the offset each time based on the number of characters or bytes just read.

 You can use DBMS_LOB.GET_LENGTH (*lob_locator*) to retrieve the length of a LOB. The length is returned as a number of bytes for BLOBs and BFILEs, and as a number of characters for CLOBs.

## BFILEs Are Different

As mentioned earlier, the BLOB, CLOB, and NCLOB types represent *internal LOBs*, meaning that they are stored within the database. A BFILE, on the other hand, is an *external LOB* type. BFILEs are very different from internal LOBs in three important ways:

- The value of a BFILE is stored in an operating-system file, not within the database.
- BFILEs do not participate in transactions (i.e., changes to a BFILE cannot be rolled back or committed). However, changes to a BFILE locator can be rolled back and committed.
- From within PL/SQL and the Oracle database in general, you can only read BFILEs. The database does not allow you to write BFILE data. You must generate the external files—to which BFILE locators point—completely outside of the database.

When you work with BFILEs in PL/SQL, you still work with a LOB locator. In the case of a BFILE, however, the locator simply points to a file stored on the server. For this reason, two different rows in a database table can have a BFILE column that points to the same file.

A BFILE locator is composed of a directory alias and a filename. You use the BFILE-NAME function, which I will describe shortly, to return a locator based on those two pieces of information. A *directory alias* is simply a database-specific name for an operating-system directory. Directory aliases allow your PL/SQL programs to work with directories in an operating system-independent manner. If you have the CREATE ANY DIRECTORY privilege, you can create a directory alias (the directory must already exist in the filesystem) and grant access to it as follows:

```
CREATE DIRECTORY bfile_data AS 'c:\PLSQL Book\Ch13_Misc_Datatypes\'

GRANT READ ON DTRECTORY bfile_data TO gennick;
```

Creating directory aliases and dealing with access to those aliases are more database administration functions than PL/SQL issues, so I won't go too deeply into those topics. The examples here should be enough to get you started. To learn more about directory aliases, talk to your DBA or read the section in Oracle's *SQL Reference* on the CREATE DIRECTORY command. To see directories that you have access to, query the ALL_DIRECTORIES view.

### Creating a BFILE locator

BFILE locators are trivial to create; you simply invoke the BFILENAME function and pass it a directory alias and a filename. In the following example, I create a BFILE locator for the HTML file containing the Tannery Falls web page. I then store that locator into the waterfalls table.

```
DECLARE
    web_page BFILE;
```

```
BEGIN
   --Delete row for Tannery  Falls so this example can
   --be executed multiple times
   DELETE FROM waterfalls WHERE falls_name='Tannery Falls';

   --Invoke BFILENAME to create a BFILE locator
   web_page := BFILENMAE('BFILE_DATA','TanneryFalls.htm');

   --Save our new locator in the waterfalls table
   INSERT INTO waterfalls (falls_name, falls_web_page)
      VALUES ('Tannery  Falls',web_page);
END;
```

A BFILE locator is simply a combination of directory alias and filename. The actual file and directory don't even need to exist. That is, the database allows you to create directory aliases for directories that do not yet exist, and BFILENAME allows you to create BFILE locators for files that do not yet exist. There are times when it's convenient to do these things.

 The directory name you specify in calls to BFILENAME is case-sensitive, and its case must match that shown by the ALL_DIRECTORIES data dictionary view. I first used lowercase bfile_data in my example, only to be greatly frustrated by errors when I tried to access my external BFILE data (as in the next section). In most cases, you'll want to use all-uppercase for the directory name in a call to BFILENAME.

### Accessing BFILEs

Once you have a BFILE locator, you can access the data from an external file in much the same manner as you would access a BLOB. The following example retrieves the first 60 bytes of HTML from the Tannery Falls web page. The results, which are of the RAW type, are cast to a character string using the built-in UTL_RAW.CAST_TO_VARCHAR2 function.

```
DECLARE
   web_page BFILE;
   html RAW(60);
   amount BINARY_INTEGER := 60;
   offset INTEGER := 1;
BEGIN
   --Retrieve the LOB locator for the web page
   SELECT falls_web_page
     INTO web_page
     FROM waterfalls
    WHERE falls_name='Tannery Falls';

   --Open the locator, read 60 bytes, and close the locator
   DBMS_LOB.OPEN(web_page);
   DBMS_LOB.READ(web_page, amount, offset, html);
   DBMS_LOB.CLOSE(web_page);

   --Uncomment following line to display results in hex
```

```
  --DBMS_OUTPUT.PUT_LINE(RAWTOHEX(html));

  --Cast RAW results to a character string we can read
  DBMS_OUTPUT.PUT_LINE(UTL_RAW.CAST_TO_VARCHAR2(html));
END;
```

The output from this code will appear as follows:

```
<!DOCTYPE HTML PUBLIC "-//W3C//DTD HTML 4.0 Transitional//EN
```

The maximum number of BFILEs that can be opened within a session is established by the database initialization parameter, SESSION_MAX_OPEN_FILES. This parameter defines an upper limit on the number of files opened simultaneously in a session (not just BFILEs, but all kinds of files, including those opened using the UTL_FILE package).

Remember that from within the Oracle database, you can only read BFILEs. The BFILE type is ideal when you want to access binary data, such as a collection of images that is generated outside the database environment. For example, you might upload a collection of images from a digital camera to your server and create a BFILE locator to point to each of those images. You could then access the images from your PL/SQL programs.

### Using BFILEs to load LOB columns

In addition to allowing you to access binary file data created outside the Oracle database environment, BFILEs provide a convenient means to load data from external files into internal LOB columns. Up through Oracle9i Database Release 1, you could use the DBMS_LOB.LOADFROMFILE function to read binary data from a BFILE and store it into a BLOB column. Oracle9i Database Release 2 introduced the following, much improved, functions:

*DBMS_LOB.LOADCLOBFROMFILE*
> Loads CLOBs from BFILEs. Takes care of any needed character set translation.

*DBMS_LOB.LOADBLOBFROMFILE*
> Loads BLOBs from BFILEs. Does the same thing as DBMS_LOB.LOADFROM-FILE, but with an interface that is consistent with that of LOADCLOBFROMFILE.

Imagine that I had directions to Tannery Falls in an external text file named *TanneryFalls.directions* in a directory pointed to by the BFILE_DATA directory alias. The following example shows how I could use DBMS_LOB.LOADCLOBFROMFILE to load the directions into the falls_directions CLOB column in the waterfalls table:

```
/* File on web: munising_falls_03.sql */
DECLARE
   Tannery_Falls_Directions BFILE
      := BFILENAME('BFILE_DATA','TanneryFalls.directions');
   directions CLOB;
   destination_offset INTEGER := 1;
   source_offset INTEGER := 1;
   language_context INTEGER := DBMS_LOB.default_lang_ctx;
   warning_message INTEGER;
```

```
BEGIN
   --Delete row for Tannery Falls, so this example
   --can run multiple times.
   DELETE FROM waterfalls WHERE falls_name='Tannery Falls';

   --Insert a new row using EMPTY_CLOB() to create a LOB locator
   INSERT INTO waterfalls
              (falls_name,falls_directions)
      VALUES ('Tannery Falls',EMPTY_CLOB());

   --Retrieve the LOB locator created by the previous INSERT statement
   SELECT falls_directions
     INTO directions
     FROM waterfalls
    WHERE falls_name='Tannery Falls';

   --Open the target CLOB and the source BFILE
   DBMS_LOB.OPEN(directions, DBMS_LOB.LOB_READWRITE);
   DBMS_LOB.OPEN(Tannery_Falls_Directions);

   --Load the contents of the BFILE into the CLOB column
   DBMS_LOB.LOADCLOBFROMFILE
                 (directions, Tannery_Falls_Directions,
                             DBMS_LOB.LOBMAXSIZE,
                             destination_offset, source_offset,
                             NLS_CHARSET_ID('US7ASCII'),
                             language_context, warning_message);

   --Check for the only possible warning message.
   IF warning_message = DBMS_LOB.WARN_INCONVERTIBLE_CHAR THEN
       DBMS_OUTPUT.PUT_LINE (
          'Warning! Some characters couldn''t be converted.');
   END IF;

   --Close both LOBs
   DBMS_LOB.CLOSE(directions);
   DBMS_LOB.CLOSE(Tannery_Falls_Directions);
END;
```

The real work in this snippet of code is done by the call to DBMS_LOB.LOADCLOB-FROMFILE. That procedure reads data from the external file, performs any character set translation that's necessary, and writes the data to the CLOB column. I use the DBMS_LOB.LOBMAXSIZE constant to specify the amount of data to load. I really want *all* the data from the external file, and DBMS_LOB.LOBMAXSIZE is as much as a CLOB will hold.

The destination and source offsets both begin at 1. I want to begin reading with the first character in the BFILE, and I want to begin writing to the first character of the CLOB. To facilitate multiple, sequential calls to LOADCLOBFROMFILE, the procedure will update both these offsets to point one character past the most recently read character. Because they are IN OUT parameters, I must use variables and not constants in my procedure call.

---

The call to NLS_CHARSET_ID returns the character set ID number for the character set used by the external file. The LOADCLOBFROMFILE procedure will then convert the data being loaded from that character set to the database character set. The only possible warning message LOADCLOBFROMFILE can return is that some characters were not convertible from the source to the target character set. I check for this warning in the IF statement following the load.

 A warning is not the same as a PL/SQL error; the load will still have occurred, just as I requested.

The following SQL*Plus example shows the data loaded from my external file using LOADCLOBFROMFILE:

```
SQL>SET LONG 2000
SQL> COLUMN falls_directions WORD_WRAPPED FORMAT A70
SQL> SELECT falls_directions
  2  FROM waterfalls
  3  WHERE falls_name='Tannery Falls';
  4 /

FALLS_DIRECTIONS
------------------------------------------------------------------
From downtown Munising, take Munising Avenue east. It will
shortly turn into H-58. Watch for Washington Street veering
off to your left. At that intersection you'll see a wooden
stairway going into the woods on your right. Go up that
stairway and follow the trail to the falls. Do not park
on H-58! You'll get a ticket. You can park on Nestor Street,
which is just uphill from the stairway.
```

## SecureFiles Versus BasicFiles

SecureFiles, introduced with Oracle Database 11g, offer many improvements over the older implementation of LOBs, which are now known as BasicFiles. These improvements are internal and largely transparent to us as programmers—the same keywords, syntax, and programming steps are used. The internal implementation of SecureFiles involves improvements to many aspects of managing LOBs, including disk format, caching, locking, redo, and space management algorithms. This updated technology significantly improves performance and allows LOBs to be deduplicated, compressed, and encrypted using simple parameter settings. In addition, a new logging level, FILESYSTEM_LIKE_LOGGING, has been introduced to augment the existing LOGGING and NOLOGGING options. This new logging level logs only metadata changes, much as a journaled filesystem would do.

The SecureFiles features improve the performance of LOBs substantially. Oracle testing reports 200% to 900% improvements. In a simple test loading PDF files on a Microsoft

Windows server, I experienced a decrease in load times of 80% to 90%—from 169 seconds down to 20 to 30 seconds (depending on the options used and how many times I ran the load). I noted more moderate improvements on x86 Linux. Your experiences may differ, but expect improvements!

To use SecureFiles with your LOBs, your database initialization parameter DB_SECUREFILE must be set to PERMITTED (the default setting). In addition, the tablespace that will store the LOBs must use Automatic Segment Space Management (ASSM). If you are not sure about your database, ask your DBA. If you are the DBA, check in V$PARAMETER for initialization parameters and in DBA_TABLESPACES for Segment Space Management settings.

 While SecureFiles offers improvements, the default storage for Oracle Database 11g (both Release 1 and Release 2) is still BasicFiles, so make sure you specify SecureFiles if you want to use this technology.

### Deduplication

With the SecureFiles deduplication option, the database will store only one copy of each LOB. The database will generate a hash key for a LOB and compare it to existing LOBs in that table or partition of a table storing only one copy of each identical LOB. Note that deduplication does not work across partitions or subpartitions.

### Compression

The SecureFiles compression option causes the database to compress the LOB both on disk and in memory. Compression can be specified as MEDIUM (the default) or HIGH. HIGH compression will consume more CPU during the compression step, but will result in smaller LOBs. My simple test with PDF files showed that HIGH required about 25% longer to load than MEDIUM compression.

You can specify both deduplication and compression by including both options in the LOB clause, like this:

```
TABLE waterfalls
(
   falls_name          VARCHAR2 (80)
, falls_photo          BLOB
, falls_directions     CLOB
, falls_description    NCLOB
, falls_web_page       BFILE
)
LOB (falls_photo) STORE AS SECUREFILE (COMPRESS DEDUPLICATE)
LOB (falls_directions) STORE AS SECUREFILE (COMPRESS DEDUPLICATE)
LOB (falls_description) STORE AS SECUREFILE (COMPRESS DEDUPLICATE)
```

When you specify both options, deduplication occurs first, and then compression. Both deduplication and compression are part of the Advanced Compression Option of the database.

### Encryption

As with deduplication and compression, you specify the SecureFiles encryption option by telling the database to encrypt your LOB in the LOB clause of your CREATE TABLE statement. You can optionally specify the encryption algorithm you want to use. The valid algorithms, as of Oracle Database 11g, are 3DES168, AES128, AES192 (default), and AES256. You can use any combination of deduplication, compression, and encryption, as shown in this example:

```
TABLE waterfalls
(
   falls_name           VARCHAR2 (80)
, falls_photo          BLOB
, falls_directions     CLOB
, falls_description    NCLOB
, falls_web_page       BFILE
)
LOB (falls_photo) STORE AS SECUREFILE (COMPRESS DEDUPLICATE)
LOB (falls_directions) STORE AS SECUREFILE (ENCRYPT USING 'AES256')
LOB (falls_description) STORE AS SECUREFILE
   (ENCRYPT DEDUPLICATE COMPRESS HIGH
   )
```

If your database has not been configured for transparent data encryption (TDE, described in Chapter 23), you will have a couple of prerequisite steps to follow before you can start encrypting your LOBs. First, you need to create a *wallet*. This is where the master key will be stored. If you choose to use the default location for the wallet (*$ORACLE_BASE/admin/$ORACLE_SID/wallet*), you can create and open the wallet in one step like this:

```
ALTER SYSTEM SET ENCRYPTION KEY AUTHENTICATED BY "My-secret!passc0de";
```

If you want to store your wallet in a nondefault location, you will need to specify this location via the *SQLNET.ORA* file. If you want to store your wallet in the directory */oracle/wallet*, include these lines in your *SQLNET.ORA* file:

```
ENCRYPTION_WALLET_LOCATION=(SOURCE=(METHOD=file)
   (METHOD_DATA=(DIRECTORY=/oracle/wallet)))
```

Once the wallet has been created, it will need to be opened again after each instance restart. You open and close the wallet like this:

```
ALTER SYSTEM SET ENCRYPTION WALLET OPEN AUTHENTICATED BY "My-secret!passc0de";
-- now close the wallet
ALTER SYSTEM SET ENCRYPTION WALLET CLOSE;
```

## Temporary LOBs

So far, we've been talking about permanently storing large amounts of unstructured data by means of the various LOB datatypes. Such LOBs are known as *persistent LOBs*. Many applications have a need for *temporary LOBs* that act like local variables but do not exist permanently in the database. This section discusses temporary LOBs and the use of the DBMS_LOB built-in package to manipulate them.

Starting with Oracle8*i* Database, the database supports the creation, freeing, access, and update of temporary LOBs through the Oracle Call Interface (OCI) and DBMS_LOB calls. The default lifetime of a temporary LOB is the lifetime of the session that created it, but such LOBs may be explicitly freed sooner by the application. Temporary LOBs are ideal as transient workspaces for data manipulation, and because no logging is done, and no redo records are generated, they offer better performance than persistent LOBs do. In addition, whenever you rewrite or update a LOB, the Oracle database copies the entire LOB to a new segment. By avoiding all the associated redo logging, applications that perform lots of piecewise operations on LOBs should see significant performance improvements with temporary LOBs.

A temporary LOB is empty when it is created: you don't need to (and, in fact, you can't) use the EMPTY_CLOB and EMPTY_BLOB functions to initialize LOB locators for a temporary LOB. By default, all temporary LOBs are deleted at the end of the session in which they were created. If a process dies unexpectedly or if the database crashes, then temporary LOBs are deleted, and the space for temporary LOBs is freed.

Temporary LOBs are just like persistent LOBs in that they exist on disk inside your database. Don't let the word "temporary" fool you into thinking that they are memory structures. Temporary LOBs are written to disk, but instead of being associated with a specific LOB column in a specific table, they are written to disk in your session's temporary tablespace. Thus, if you use temporary LOBs, you need to make sure that your temporary tablespace is large enough to accommodate them.

Let's examine the processes for creating and freeing temporary LOBs. Then I'll explain how you can test to see whether a LOB locator points to a temporary or a permanent LOB. I'll finish up by covering some of the administrative details to consider when you're working with temporary LOBs.

### Creating a temporary LOB

Before you can work with a temporary LOB, you need to create it. One way to do this is with a call to the DBMS_LOB.CREATETEMPORARY procedure. This procedure creates a temporary BLOB or CLOB and its corresponding index in your default temporary tablespace. The header is:

```
DBMS_LOB.CREATETEMPORARY (
    lob_loc IN OUT NOCOPY [ BLOB | CLOB CHARACTER SET ANY_CS ],
    cache   IN BOOLEAN,
    dur     IN PLS_INTEGER := DBMS_LOB.SESSION);
```

The parameters to DBMS_LOB.CREATETEMPORARY are listed in Table 13-1.

*Table 13-1. CREATETEMPORARY parameters*

| Parameter | Description |
| --- | --- |
| *lob_loc* | Receives the locator to the LOB. |
| *cache* | Specifies whether the LOB should be read into the buffer cache. |
| *dur* | Controls the duration of the LOB. The *dur* argument can be one of these two named constants: |
| | *DBMS_LOB.SESSION*<br>Specifies that the temporary LOB created should be cleaned up (memory freed) at the end of the session. This is the default. |
| | *DBMS_LOB.CALL*<br>Specifies that the temporary LOB created should be cleaned up (memory freed) at the end of the current program call in which the LOB was created. |

Another way to create a temporary LOB is to declare a LOB variable in your PL/SQL code and assign a value to it. For example, the following code creates both a temporary BLOB and a temporary CLOB:

```
DECLARE
    temp_clob CLOB;
    temp_blob BLOB;
BEGIN
    --Assigning a value to a null CLOB or BLOB variable causes
    --PL/SQL to implicitly create a session-duration temporary
    --LOB for you.
    temp_clob :=' http://www.nps.gov/piro/';
    temp_blob := HEXTORAW('7A');
END;
```

I don't really have a strong preference as to which method you should use to create a temporary LOB, but I do believe the use of DBMS_LOB.CREATETEMPORARY makes the intent of your code a bit more explicit.

### Freeing a temporary LOB

The DBMS_LOB.FREETEMPORARY procedure explicitly frees a temporary BLOB or CLOB releasing the space from your default temporary tablespace. The header for this procedure is:

```
PROCEDURE DBMS_LOB.FREETEMPORARY (
    lob_loc IN OUT NOCOPY
        [ BLOB | CLOB CHARACTER SET ANY_CS ]);
```

In the following example, I again create two temporary LOBs. Then I explicitly free them:

```
DECLARE
    temp_clob CLOB;
    temp_blob BLOB;
```

```
BEGIN
   --Assigning a value to a null CLOB or BLOB variable causes
   --PL/SQL to implicitly create a session-duration temporary
   --LOB for you.
   temp_clob :='http://www.exploringthenorth.com/alger/alger.html';
   temp_blob := HEXTORAW('7A');

   DBMS_LOB.FREETEMPORARY(temp_clob);
   DBMS_LOB.FREETEMPORARY(temp_blob);
END;
```

After a call to FREETEMPORARY, the LOB locator that was freed (*lob_loc* in the previous specification) is marked as invalid. If an invalid LOB locator is assigned to another LOB locator through an assignment operation in PL/SQL, then the target of the assignment is also freed and marked as invalid.

 PL/SQL will implicitly free temporary LOBs when they go out of scope at the end of a block.

### Checking to see whether a LOB is temporary

The ISTEMPORARY function tells you if the LOB locator (*lob_loc* in the following specification) points to a temporary or a persistent LOB. The function returns an integer value: 1 means that it is a temporary LOB, and 0 means that it is not (it's a persistent LOB instead).

```
DBMS_LOB.ISTEMPORARY (
    lob_loc IN [ BLOB | CLOB CHARACTER SET ANY_CS ])
    RETURN INTEGER;
```

Note that while this function returns true (1) or false (0) it does not return a BOOLEAN datatype.

### Managing temporary LOBs

Temporary LOBs are handled quite differently from normal, persistent, internal LOBs. With temporary LOBs, there is no support for transaction management, consistent read operations, rollbacks, and so forth. There are various consequences of this lack of support:

- If you encounter an error when processing with a temporary LOB, you must free that LOB and start your processing over again.

- You should not assign multiple LOB locators to the same temporary LOB. Lack of support for consistent read and undo operations can cause performance degradation with multiple locators.

- If a user modifies a temporary LOB while another locator is pointing to it, a copy (referred to by Oracle as a *deep copy*) of that LOB is made. The different locators

---

will then no longer see the same data. To minimize these deep copies, use the NOCOPY compiler hint whenever you're passing LOB locators as arguments.

- To make a temporary LOB permanent, you must call the DBMS_LOB.COPY program and copy the temporary LOB into a permanent LOB.
- Temporary LOB locators are unique to a session. You cannot pass a locator from one session to another (through a database pipe, for example) in order to make the associated temporary LOB visible in that other session. If you need to pass a LOB between sessions, use a permanent LOB.

Oracle9i Database introduced a V$ view called V$TEMPORARY_LOBS that shows how many cached and uncached LOBs exist per session. Your DBA can combine information from V$TEMPORARY_LOBS and the DBA_SEGMENTS data dictionary view to see how much space a session is using for temporary LOBs.

## Native LOB Operations

Almost since the day Oracle unleashed LOB functionality to the vast hordes of database users, programmers and query-writers have wanted to treat LOBs as very large versions of regular, scalar variables. In particular, users wanted to treat CLOBs as very large character strings, passing them to SQL functions, using them in SQL statement WHERE clauses, and so forth. To the dismay of many, CLOBs originally could not be used interchangeably with VARCHAR2s. For example, in Oracle8 Database and Oracle8i Database, you could not apply a character function to a CLOB column:

```
SELECT SUBSTR(falls_directions,1,60)
  FROM waterfalls
```

Starting in Oracle9i Database, you can use CLOBs interchangeably with VARCHAR2s in a wide variety of situations:

- You can pass CLOBs to most SQL and PL/SQL VARCHAR2 functions— they are overloaded with both VARCHAR2 and CLOB parameters.
- In PL/SQL, but not in SQL, you can use various relational operators such as less-than (<), greater-than (>), and equals (=) with LOB variables.
- You can assign CLOB values to VARCHAR2 variables and vice versa. You can also select CLOB values into VARCHAR2 variables and vice versa. This is because PL/SQL now implicitly converts between the CLOB and VARCHAR2 types.

### SQL semantics

Oracle refers to the capabilities introduced in the previous section as offering *SQL semantics* for LOBs. From a PL/SQL developer's standpoint, it means that you can manipulate LOBs using native operators rather than a supplied package.

Following is an example showing some of the things you can do with SQL semantics:

```
DECLARE
   name CLOB;
   name_upper CLOB;
   directions CLOB;
   blank_space VARCHAR2(1) := ' ';
BEGIN
   --Retrieve a VARCHAR2 into a CLOB, apply a function to a CLOB
   SELECT falls_name, SUBSTR(falls_directions,1,500)
   INTO name, directions
   FROM waterfalls
   WHERE falls_name = 'Munising Falls';

   --Uppercase a CLOB
   name_upper := UPPER(name);

   -- Compare two CLOBs
   IF name = name_upper THEN
      DBMS_OUTPUT.PUT_LINE('We did not need to uppercase the name.');
   END IF;

   --Concatenate a CLOB with some VARCHAR2 strings
   IF INSTR(directions,'Mackinac Bridge') <> 0 THEN
      DBMS_OUTPUT.PUT_LINE('To get to ' || name_upper || blank_space
                           || 'you must cross the Mackinac Bridge.');
   END IF;
END;
```

The output is:

```
To get to MUNISING FALLS you must cross the Mackinac Bridge.
```

The small piece of code in this example does several interesting things:

- The falls_name column is a VARCHAR2 column, yet it is retrieved into a CLOB variable. This is a demonstration of implicit conversion between the VARCHAR2 and CLOB types.

- The SUBSTR function is used to limit retrieval to only the first 500 characters of the directions to Munising Falls. Further, the UPPER function is used to uppercase the falls name. This demonstrates the application of SQL and PL/SQL functions to LOBs.

- The IF statement that compares name to name_upper is a bit forced, but it demonstrates that relational operators may now be applied to LOBs.

- The uppercased falls name, a CLOB, is concatenated with some string constants and one VARCHAR2 string (blank_space). This shows that CLOBs may be concatenated.

There are many restrictions and caveats that you need to be aware of when using this functionality. For example, not every function that takes a VARCHAR2 input will accept a CLOB in its place; there are some exceptions. The regular expression functions notably work with SQL semantics, while aggregate functions do not. Likewise, not all relational operators are supported for use with LOBs. All of these restrictions and caveats are described in detail in the section called "SQL Semantics and LOBs" in Chapter 10 of the *SecureFiles and Large Objects Developer's Guide* manual for Oracle Database 11*g*. For Oracle Database 10*g* see Chapter 9, "SQL Semantics and LOBs," of the *Application Developers Guide – Large Objects* manual. If you're using SQL semantics, I strongly suggest that you take a look at this section of the manual for your database.

 SQL semantics for LOBs apply only to internal LOBs: CLOBs, BLOBs, and NCLOBs. SQL semantics support does not apply to BFILEs.

## SQL semantics may yield temporary LOBs

One issue you will need to understand when applying SQL semantics to LOBs is that the result is often the creation of a temporary LOB. Think about applying the UPPER function to a CLOB:

```
DECLARE
    directions CLOB;
BEGIN
    SELECT UPPER(falls_directions)
      INTO directions
      FROM waterfalls
     WHERE falls_name = 'Munising Falls';
END;
```

Because they are potentially very large objects, CLOBs are stored on disk. The database can't uppercase the CLOB being retrieved because that would mean changing its value on disk, in effect changing a value that you simply want to retrieve. Nor can the database make the change to an in-memory copy of the CLOB because the value may not fit in memory and also because what is being retrieved is only a locator that points to a value that must be on disk. The only option is for the database software to create a temporary CLOB in your temporary tablespace. The UPPER function then copies data from the original CLOB to the temporary CLOB, uppercasing the characters during the copy operation. The SELECT statement then returns a LOB locator pointing to the temporary CLOB, not to the original CLOB. There are two extremely important ramifications to all this:

- You cannot use the locator returned by a function or expression to update the original LOB. The directions variable in my example cannot be used to update the persistent LOB stored in the database because it really points to a temporary LOB returned by the UPPER function.

- Disk space and CPU resources are expended to create a temporary LOB, which can be of considerable size. I'll discuss this issue more in "Performance impact of using SQL semantics" on page 424.

If I want to retrieve an uppercase version of the directions to Munising Falls while still maintaining the ability to update the directions, I'll need to retrieve two LOB locators:

```
DECLARE
   directions_upper CLOB;
   directions_persistent CLOB;
BEGIN
   SELECT UPPER(falls_directions), falls_directions
     INTO directions_upper, directions_persistent
     FROM waterfalls
    WHERE falls_name = 'Munising Falls';
END;
```

Now I can access the uppercase version of the directions via the locator in directions_upper, and I can modify the original directions via the locator in directions_persistent. There's no performance penalty in this case from retrieving the extra locator. The performance hit comes from uppercasing the directions and placing them into a temporary CLOB. The locator in directions_persistent is simply plucked as-is from the database table.

In general, any character-string function to which you normally pass a VARCHAR2, and that normally returns a VARCHAR2 value, will return a temporary CLOB when you pass in a CLOB as input. Similarly, expressions that return CLOBs will most certainly return temporary CLOBs. Temporary CLOBs and BLOBs cannot be used to update the LOBs that you originally used in an expression or function.

### Performance impact of using SQL semantics

You'll need to give some thought to performance when you are using the new SQL semantics for LOB functionality. Remember that the "L" in LOB stands for "large," and that "large" can be as much as 128 terabytes (4 gigabytes prior to Oracle Database 10g). Consequently, you may encounter some serious performance issues if you indiscriminately treat LOBs the same as any other type of variable or column. Have a look at the following query, which attempts to identify all waterfalls for which a visit might require a trip across the Mackinac Bridge:

```
SELECT falls_name
  FROM waterfalls
 WHERE INSTR(UPPER(falls_directions),'MACKINAC BRIDGE') <> 0;
```

Think about what the Oracle database must do to resolve this query. For every row in the waterfalls table, it must take the falls_directions column, uppercase it, and place those results into a temporary CLOB (residing in your temporary tablespace). Then it must apply the INSTR function to that temporary LOB to search for the string 'MACKINAC BRIDGE'. In my examples, the directions have been fairly short. Imagine, however, that falls_directions were truly a large LOB, and that the average column size were one gigabyte. Think of the drain on your temporary tablespace as the database allocates the necessary room for the temporary LOBs created when uppercasing the directions. Then think of all the time required to make a copy of each CLOB in order to uppercase it, the time required to allocate and deallocate space for temporary CLOBs in your temporary tablespace, and the time required for the INSTR function to search character-by-character through an average of 1 GB per CLOB. Such a query would surely bring the wrath of your DBA down upon you.

---

### Oracle Text and SQL Semantics

If you need to execute queries that look at uppercase versions of CLOB values, and you need to do so efficiently, Oracle Text may hold the solution. For example, you might reasonably expect to write a query such as the following some day:

```
SELECT falls_name
  FROM waterfalls
 WHERE INSTR(UPPER(falls_directions), 'MACKINAC BRIDGE') <> 0;
```

If falls_directions is a CLOB column, this query may not be all that efficient. However, if you are using Oracle Text, you can define a case-insensitive Oracle Text index on that CLOB column, and then use the CONTAINS predicate to efficiently evaluate the query:

```
SELECT falls_name
  FROM waterfalls
 WHERE
       CONTAINS(falls_directions,'mackinac bridge') > 0;
```

For more information on CONTAINS and case-insensitive indexes using Oracle Text, see Oracle Corporation's *Text Application Developer's Guide*.

---

Because of all the performance ramifications of applying SQL semantics to LOBs, Oracle's documentation suggests that you limit such applications to LOBs that are 100 KB or less in size. I myself don't have a specific size recommendation to pass on to you; you should consider each case in terms of your particular circumstances and how much you need to accomplish a given task. I encourage you always to give thought to the performance implications of using SQL semantics for LOBs, and possibly to run some tests to experience these implications, so that you can make a reasonable decision based on your circumstances.

## LOB Conversion Functions

Oracle provides several conversion functions that are sometimes useful when working with large object data, described in Table 13-2.

*Table 13-2. LOB conversion functions*

| Function | Description |
| --- | --- |
| TO_CLOB (*character_data*) | Converts character data into a CLOB. The input to TO_CLOB can be any of the following character types: VARCHAR2, NVARCHAR2, CHAR, NCHAR, CLOB, and NCLOB. If necessary (for example, if the |

| Function | Description |
|---|---|
| | input is NVARCHAR2), input data is converted from the national character set into the database character set. |
| TO_BLOB(*raw_data*) | Similar to TO_CLOB, but converts RAW or LONG RAW data into a BLOB. |
| TO_NCLOB (*character_data*) | Does the same as TO_CLOB, except that the result is an NCLOB using the national character set. |
| TO_LOB (*long_data*) | Accepts either LONG or LONG RAW data as input, and converts that data to a CLOB or a BLOB, respectively. TO_LOB may be invoked only from the select list of a subquery in an INSERT... SELECT...FROM statement. |
| TO_RAW(*blob_data*) | Takes a BLOB as input and returns the BLOB's data as a RAW value. |

The TO_LOB function is designed specifically to enable one-time conversion of LONG and LONG RAW columns into CLOB and BLOB columns, because LONG and LONG RAW are now considered obsolete. The TO_CLOB and TO_NCLOB functions provide a convenient mechanism for converting character large object data between the database and national language character sets.

# Predefined Object Types

Starting with Oracle9i Database Release 1, Oracle provides a collection of useful, predefined object types:

*XMLType*
    Use this to store and manipulate XML data.

*URI types*
    Use these to store uniform resource identifiers (such as HTML addresses).

*Any types*
    Use these to define a PL/SQL variable that can hold any type of data.

The following subsections discuss these predefined object types in more detail.

## The XMLType Type

Oracle9i Database introduced a native object type called XMLType. You can use XMLType to define database columns and PL/SQL variables containing XML documents. Methods defined on XMLType enable you to instantiate new XMLType values, to extract portions of an XML document, and to otherwise manipulate the contents of an XML document in various ways.

XML is a huge subject that I can't hope to cover in detail in this book. However, if you're working with XML from PL/SQL, there are at least two things you need to know about:

*XMLType*
> A built-in object type that enables you to store XML documents in a database column or in a PL/SQL variable. XMLType was introduced in Oracle9*i* Database Release 1.

*XQuery*
> A query language used for retrieving and constructing XML documents. XQuery was introduced in Oracle Database 10*g* Release 2.

Starting with these two technologies and exploring further, you'll encounter many other XML related topics that will likely prove useful: XPath for referring to portions of an XML document, XML Schema for describing document structure, and so forth.

Using XMLType, you can easily create a table to hold XML data:

```
CREATE TABLE fallsXML (
    fall_id NUMBER,
    fall XMLType
);
```

The fall column in this table is of XMLType and can hold XML data. To store XML data into this column, you must invoke the static CreateXML method, passing it your XML data. CreateXML accepts XML data as input and instantiates a new XMLType object to hold that data. The new object is then returned as the method's result, and it is that object that you must store in the column. CreateXML is overloaded to accept both VARCHAR2 strings and CLOBs as input.

Use the following INSERT statements to create three XML documents in the falls table:

```
INSERT INTO fallsXML VALUES (1, XMLType.CreateXML(
    '<?xml version="1.0"?>
    <fall>
        <name>Munising Falls</name>
        <county>Alger</county>
        <state>MI</state>
        <url>
            http://michiganwaterfalls.com/munising_falls/munising_falls.html
        </url>
    </fall>'));

INSERT INTO fallsXML VALUES (2, XMLType.CreateXML(
    '<?xml version="1.0"?>
    <fall>
        <name>Au Train Falls</name>
        <county>Alger</county>
        <state>MI</state>
        <url>
            http://michiganwaterfalls.com/autrain_falls/autrain_falls.html
        </url>
    </fall>'));

INSERT INTO fallsXML VALUES (3, XMLType.CreateXML(
    '<?xml version="1.0"?>
    <fall>
```

```
     <name>Laughing Whitefish Falls</name>
     <county>Alger</county>
     <state>MI</state>
     <url>
       http://michiganwaterfalls.com/whitefish_falls/whitefish_falls.html
     </url>
   </fall>'));
```

You can query XML data in the table using various XMLType methods. The existsNode method used in the following example allows you to test for the existence of a specific XML node in an XML document. The built-in SQL EXISTSNODE function, also in the example, performs the same test. Whether you use the method or the built-in function, you identify the node of interest using an XPath expression.[1]

Both of the following statements produce the same output:

```
SQL> SELECT f.fall_id
  2  FROM fallsxml f
  3  WHERE f.fall.existsNode('/fall/url') > 0;

SQL> SELECT f.fall_id
  2  FROM fallsxml f
  3  WHERE EXISTSNODE(f.fall,'/fall/url') > 0;
  4  /

   FALL_ID
----------
         1
         2
```

You can, of course, also work with XML data from within PL/SQL. In the following example, I retrieve the fall column for Munising Falls into a PL/SQL variable that is also of XMLType. Thus, I retrieve the entire XML document into my PL/SQL program, where I can work further with it. After retrieving the document, I extract and print the text from the */fall/url* node.

```
<<demo_block>>
DECLARE
   fall XMLType;
   url VARCHAR2(100);
BEGIN
   --Retrieve XML for Munising Falls
   SELECT f.fall
     INTO demo_block.fall
     FROM fallsXML f
    WHERE f.fall_id = 1;

   --Extract and display the URL for Munising Falls
   url := fall.extract('/fall/url/text()').getStringVal;
   DBMS_OUTPUT.PUT_LINE(url);
END;
```

---

1. XPath is a syntax that describes parts of an XML document. Among other things, you can use XPath to specify a particular node or attribute value in an XML document.

---

The output is:

```
http://michiganwaterfalls.com/munising_falls/munising_falls.html
```

Pay special attention to the following two lines:

```
SELECT f.fall INTO demo_block.fall
```
> My variable name, fall, matches the name of the column in the database table. In my SQL query, therefore, I qualify my variable name with the name of my PL/SQL block.

```
url := fall.extract('/fall/url/text()').getStringVal;
```
> To get the text of the URL, I invoke two of XMLType's methods:

> extract
>> Returns an XML document, of XMLType, containing only the specified fragment of the original XML document. Use XPath notation to specify the fragment you want returned.

> getStringVal
>> Returns the text of an XML document.

In my example, I apply the getStringVal method to the XML document returned by the extract method, thus retrieving the text for the Munising Fall's URL. The extract method returns the contents of the <url> node as an XMLType object, and getStringVal then returns that content as a text string that I can display.

You can even index XMLType columns to allow for efficient retrieval of XML documents based on their content. You do this by creating a function-based index, for which you need the QUERY REWRITE privilege. The following example creates a function-based index on the first 80 characters of each falls name:

```
CREATE INDEX falls_by_name
   ON fallsxml f (
      SUBSTR(
         XMLType.getStringVal(
            XMLType.extract(f.fall,'/fall/name/text()')
         ),1,80
      ))
```

I had to use the SUBSTR function in the creation of this index. The getStringVal method returns a string that is too long to index, resulting in an *ORA-01450: maximum key length (3166) exceeded* error. Thus, when creating an index like this, I must use SUBSTR to restrict the results to some reasonable length.

If you decide to use XMLType in any of your applications, be sure to consult Oracle Corporation's documentation for more complete and current information. The *XML DB Developer's Guide* for Oracle Database 11g Release 2 is an important, if not critical, reference for developers working with XML. The *SQL Reference* also has some useful information on XMLType and on the built-in SQL functions that support XML. The *Database PL/SQL Packages and Types Reference* documents the programs, methods, and exceptions for each of the predefined object types, as well as several packages that work with XML data, such as DBMS_XDB, DBMS_XMLSCHEMA, and DBMS_XMLDOM.

## The URI Types

The URI types, introduced in Oracle9*i* Database, consist of a supertype and a collection of subtypes that provide support for storing URIs in PL/SQL variables and in database columns. UriType is the supertype, and a UriType variable can hold any instance of one of the subtypes:

*HttpUriType*
 A subtype of UriType that is specific to HTTP URLs, which usually point to web pages.

*DBUriType*
 A subtype of UriType that supports URLs that are XPath expressions.

*XDBUriType*
 A subtype of UriType that supports URLs that reference Oracle XML DB objects. XML DB is Oracle's name for a set of XML technologies built into the database.

To facilitate your work with URIs, the Oracle database also provides a UriFactory package that automatically generates the appropriate URI type for whatever URI you pass to it.

The URI types are created by the script named *$ORACLE_HOME/rdbms/admin/dbmsuri.sql*. All the types and subtypes are owned by the user SYS.

Starting with Oracle Database 11g, you need to create and configure Access Control Lists (ACLs) to allow network access. This security enhancement requires a few prerequisites before you can access the Internet. You have to create a network ACL, add privileges to it, and then define the allowable destinations to which the ACL permits access.

```
BEGIN
  -- create the ACL
  DBMS_NETWORK_ACL_ADMIN.CREATE_ACL(
     acl         => 'oreillynet-permissions.xml'
    ,description => 'Network permissions for www.oreillynet.com'
    ,principal   => 'WEBROLE'
    ,is_grant    => TRUE
    ,privilege   => 'connect'
    ,start_date  => SYSTIMESTAMP
    ,end_date    => NULL
  );
  -- assign privileges to the ACL
  DBMS_NETWORK_ACL_ADMIN.ADD_PRIVILEGE (
     acl         => 'oreillynet-permissions.xml'
    ,principal   => 'WEBROLE'
    ,is_grant    => TRUE
    ,privilege   => 'connect'
    ,start_date  => SYSTIMESTAMP
```

```
      ,end_date  => null
   );
   -- define the allowable destintions
   DBMS_NETWORK_ACL_ADMIN.ASSIGN_ACL (
       acl        => 'oreillynet-permissions.xml'
      ,host       => 'www.orillynet.com'
      ,lower_port => 80
      ,upper_port => 80
   );
   COMMIT;  -- you must commit the changes.
END;
```

Now I can retrieve my web pages using HttpUriType:

```
DECLARE
   WebPageURL HttpUriType;
   WebPage CLOB;
BEGIN
   --Create an instance of the type pointing
   --to Steven's Author Bio page at OReilly
   WebPageURL := HttpUriType.createUri('http://www.oreillynet.com/pub/au/344');

   --Retrieve the page via HTTP
   WebPage := WebPageURL.getclob();

   --Display the page title
   DBMS_OUTPUT.PUT_LINE(REGEXP_SUBSTR(WebPage,'<title>.*</title>'));
END;
```

The output from this code example is:

```
<title>Steven Feuerstein</title>
```

For more information on the use of the UriType family, see Chapter 20, *Accessing Data Through URIs*, of the *XML DB Developer's Guide* for Oracle Database 11g Release 2.

## The Any Types

Back in Chapter 7, I described PL/SQL as a statically typed language. For the most part this is true—datatypes must be declared and checked at compile time. There are the occasions when you really need the capabilities of dynamic typing and for those occasions, the *Any* types were introduced with Oracle9i Database Release 1. These dynamic datatypes enable you to write programs that manipulate data when you don't know the type of that data until runtime. Member functions support *introspection*, allowing you to determine the type of a value at runtime and to access that value.

 An introspection function is one that you can use in a program to examine and learn about variables declared by your program. In essence, your program learns about itself—hence the term introspection.

The Any types are opaque, meaning that you cannot manipulate the internal structures directly, but instead must use programs.

The following predefined types belong to this family:

*AnyData*
> Can hold a single value of any type, whether it's a built-in scalar datatype, a user-defined object type, a nested table, a large object, a varying array (VARRAY), or any other type not listed here.

*AnyDataSet*
> Can hold a set of values of any type, as long as all values are of the same type.

*AnyType*
> Can hold a description of a type. Think of this as an AnyData without the data.

The Any types are included with a starter database or can be created with the script named *dbmsany.sql* found in *$ORACLE_HOME/rdbms/admin*, and are owned by the user SYS.

In addition to creating the Any types, the *dbmsany.sql* script also creates a package named DBMS_TYPES that defines a set of named constants, such as TYPECODE_DATE. You can use these constants in conjunction with introspection functions such as GETTYPE in order to determine the type of data held by a given AnyData or AnyDataSet variable. The specific numeric values assigned to the constants are not important; you should always reference the named constants, not their underlying values.

The following example creates two user-defined types representing two kinds of geographic features. The subsequent PL/SQL block then uses SYS.AnyType to define a heterogeneous array of features (i.e., each array element can be of a different datatype).

First, I'll create the following two geographic feature types:

```
/* File on web: ch13_anydata.sql */
TYPE waterfall AS OBJECT (
   name VARCHAR2(30),
   height NUMBER
)

TYPE river AS OBJECT (
   name VARCHAR2(30),
   length NUMBER
)
```

Next, I'll execute the following PL/SQL code block:

```
DECLARE
   TYPE feature_array IS VARRAY(2) OF SYS.AnyData;
   features feature_array;
   wf waterfall;
   rv river;
   ret_val NUMBER;
BEGIN
```

```
          --Create an array where each element is of
          --a different object type
          features := feature_array(
                      AnyData.ConvertObject(
                          waterfall('Grand Sable Falls',30)),
                      AnyData.ConvertObject(
                          river('Manistique River', 85.40))
                  );

          --Display the feature data
          FOR x IN 1..features.COUNT LOOP
             --Execute code pertaining to whatever object type
             --we are currently looking at.
             --NOTE! GetTypeName returns SchemaName.TypeName
             --so, replace PLUSER with the schema you are using.
             CASE features(x).GetTypeName
             WHEN 'PLUSER.WATERFALL' THEN
                 ret_val := features(x).GetObject(wf);
                 DBMS_OUTPUT.PUT_LINE('Waterfall: '
                     || wf.name || ', Height = ' || wf.height || ' feet.');
             WHEN 'PLUSER.RIVER' THEN
                 ret_val := features(x).GetObject(rv);
                 DBMS_OUTPUT.PUT_LINE('River: '
                     || rv.name || ', Length = ' || rv.length || ' miles.');
             ELSE
                 DBMS_OUTPUT.PUT_LINE('Unknown type '||features(x).GetTypeName);
             END CASE;
          END LOOP;
      END;
```

Finally, my output should appear as follows:

```
Waterfall: Grand Sable  Falls, Height = 30 feet.
River: Manistique River, Length = 85.4 miles.
```

Let's look at this code one piece at a time. The features are stored in a VARRAY, which is initialized as follows:

```
features := feature_array(
            AnyData.ConvertObject(
                waterfall('Grand Sable Falls',30)),
            AnyData.ConvertObject(
                river('Manistique River, 85.40))
        );
```

Working from the inside out and focusing on Grand Sable Falls, this code can be interpreted as follows:

```
waterfall('Grand Sable Falls',30)
```

Invokes the constructor for the waterfall type to create an object of type waterfall.

```
AnyData.ConvertObject(
```

Converts (casts) the waterfall object into an instance of SYS.AnyData, allowing it to be stored in myarray of SYS.AnyData objects.

```
feature_array(
```
Invokes the constructor for the array. Each argument to feature_array is of type AnyData. The array is built from the two arguments I pass.

VARRAYs were discussed in Chapter 12, and you can read about object types in more detail in Chapter 26.

The next significant part of the code is the FOR loop in which each object in the features array is examined. A call to:

```
features(x).GetTypeName
```

returns the fully qualified type name of the current features object. For user-defined objects, the type name is prefixed with the schema name of the user who created the object. I had to include this schema name in my WHEN clauses; for example:

```
WHEN 'PLUSER.WATERFALL' THEN
```

If you're running this example on your own system, be sure to replace the schema I used (PLUSER) with the one that is valid for you. When creating TYPES that will be used with introspection, consider the type's owner carefully as that owner may need to be statically included in the code.

 For built-in types such as NUMBER, DATE, and VARCHAR2, GetTypeName will return just the type name. Schema names apply only to user-defined types (i.e., those created using CREATE TYPE).

Once I determined which datatype I was dealing with, I retrieved the specific object using the following call:

```
ret_val := features(x).GetObject(wf);
```

In my example, I ignored the return code. There are two possible return code values:

*DBMS_TYPES.SUCCESS*
The value (or object, in this case) was successfully returned.

*DBMS_TYPES.NO_DATA*
No data was ever stored in the AnyData variable in question, so no data can be returned.

Once I had the object in a variable, it was an easy enough task to write a DBMS_OUTPUT statement specific to that object type. For example, to print information about waterfalls, I used:

```
DBMS_OUTPUT.PUT_LINE('Waterfall: '
    || wf.name || ', Height = ' || wf.height || ' feet.');
```

For more information on the "Any" family of types:

- See Chapter 26, which examines the Any datatypes from an object-oriented perspective.
- Check out Oracle's *PL/SQL Packages and Types Reference*, and the *Object-Relational Developer's Guide*.
- Try out the *anynums.pkg* and *anynums.tst* scripts on the book's web site.

From an object-oriented design standpoint, there are better ways to deal with multiple feature types than the method I used in this section's example. In the real world, however, not everything is ideal, and my example does serve the purpose of demonstrating the utility of the SYS.AnyData predefined object type.

# PART IV

# SQL in PL/SQL

This part of the book addresses a central element of PL/SQL code construction: the connection to the underlying Oracle database, which takes places through SQL (Structured Query Language). Chapters 14 through 16 show you how to define transactions that update, insert, merge, and delete tables in the database; query information from the database for processing in a PL/SQL program; and execute SQL statements dynamically, using native dynamic SQL (NDS).

Chapter 14, *DML and Transaction Management*
Chapter 15, *Data Retrieval*
Chapter 16, *Dynamic SQL and Dynamic PL/SQL*

# DML and Transaction Management

PL/SQL is tightly integrated with the Oracle database via the SQL language. From within PL/SQL, you can execute any Data Manipulation Language (DML) statements—specifically INSERTs, UPDATEs, DELETEs, MERGEs, and, of course, queries.

 You cannot, however, execute Data Definition Language (DDL) statements in PL/SQL unless you run them as dynamic SQL. This topic is covered in Chapter 16.

You can also join multiple SQL statements together logically as a *transaction*, so that they are either saved ("committed" in SQL parlance) together, or rejected in their entirety ("rolled back"). This chapter examines the SQL statements available inside PL/SQL to establish and manage transactions. It focuses on exploring the intersection point of DML and PL/SQL, answering such questions as: How can you take full advantage of DML from within the PL/SQL language? And how do you manage transactions that are created implicitly when you execute DML statements? See "Transaction Management" on page 450.

To appreciate the importance of transactions in Oracle, it helps to consider the "ACID" principle: a transaction has Atomicity, Consistency, Isolation, and Durability. These concepts are defined as follows:

*Atomicity*

A transaction's changes to a state are atomic: either they all happen or none happens.

*Consistency*

A transaction is a correct transformation of state. The actions taken as a group do not violate any integrity constraints associated with that state.

*Isolation*

Many transactions may be executing concurrently, but from any given transaction's point of view, other transactions appear to have executed before or after its own execution.

*Durability*

Once a transaction completes successfully, the changes to the state are made permanent and survive any subsequent failures.

A transaction can either be saved by performing a COMMIT or erased by requesting a ROLLBACK. In either case, the affected locks on resources are released (a ROLLBACK TO might release only some locks). The session can then start a new transaction. The default behavior in a PL/SQL program is that there is one transaction per session, and all changes that you make are a part of that transaction. By using a feature called *autonomous transactions*, however, you can create nested transactions within the main, session-level transaction.

# DML in PL/SQL

From within any PL/SQL block of code you can execute DML statements (INSERTs, UPDATEs, DELETEs, and MERGEs) against any and all tables and views to which you have access.

 Access to these data structures is determined at the time of compilation when you're using the *definer rights model*. If you instead use the *invoker rights model* with the AUTHID CURRENT_USER compile option, access privileges are determined at runtime. See Chapter 24 for more details.

## A Quick Introduction to DML

It is outside the scope of this book to provide complete reference information about the features of DML statements in the Oracle SQL language. Instead, I present a quick overview of the basic syntax, and then explore special features relating to DML inside PL/SQL, including:

- Examples of each DML statement
- Cursor attributes for DML statements
- Special PL/SQL features for DML statements, such as the RETURNING clause

For detailed information, I encourage you to peruse Oracle documentation or a SQL-specific text.

Officially, the SELECT statement is considered a "DML" statement. Routinely, however, when developers refer to "DML" they almost always mean those statements that *modify* the contents of a database table. For the remainder of this chapter, DML will refer to the non-query statements of SQL.

There are four DML statements available in the SQL language:

*INSERT*
Inserts one or more new rows into a table.

*UPDATE*
Updates the values of one or more columns in one or more rows in a table.

*DELETE*
Removes one or more rows from a table.

*MERGE*
Offers non-declarative support for an "upsert"—that is, if a row already exists for the specified column values, do an update. Otherwise, do an insert.

### The INSERT statement

There are two basic types of INSERT statements; here is the syntax:

- Insert a single row with an explicit list of values:

    ```
    INSERT INTO table [(col1, col2, ..., coln)]
        VALUES (val1, val2, ..., valn);
    ```

- Insert one or more rows into a table as defined by a SELECT statement against one or more other tables:

    ```
    INSERT INTO table [(col1, col2, ..., coln)]
        SELECT ...;
    ```

Let's look at some examples of INSERT statements executed within a PL/SQL block. First, I insert a new row into the book table. Notice that I do not need to specify the names of the columns if I provide a value for each column.

```
BEGIN
   INSERT INTO books
        VALUES ('1-56592-335-9',
            'Oracle  PL/SQL Programming',
            'Reference for PL/SQL developers,' ||
            'including examples and best practice ' ||
            'recommendations.',
            'Feuerstein,Steven, with Bill Pribyl',
            TO_DATE ('01-SEP-1997','DD-MON-YYYY'),
            987);
   END;
```

I can also list the names of the columns and provide the values as variables (including a retrieval of the next available value from a sequence), instead of as literal values:

```
DECLARE
   l_isbn books.isbn%TYPE := '1-56592-335-9';
   ... other declarations of local variables
BEGIN
   INSERT INTO books (
        book_id, isbn, title, summary, author,
        date_published, page_count)
      VALUES (
        book_id_sequence.NEXTVAL, l_isbn, l_title, l_summary, l_author,
        l_date_published, l_page_count);
```

## Native PL/SQL Support for Sequences in Oracle Database 11g

Prior to Oracle Database 11g, if you wanted to get the next value from a sequence, you had to execute the call to the NEXTVAL function from within a SQL statement. You could do this directly inside the INSERT statement that needs the value, as in:

```
INSERT INTO table_name VALUES (sequence_name.NEXTVAL, ...);
```

or with a SELECT from the good old dual table, as in:

```
SELECT sequence_name.NEXTVAL INTO l_primary_key FROM SYS.dual;
```

From Oracle Database 11g onwards, however, you can now retrieve that next value (and the current value as well) with a native assignment operator—for example:

```
l_primary_key := sequence_name.NEXTVAL;
```

### The UPDATE statement

With the UPDATE statement you can update one or more columns in one or more rows. Here is the basic syntax:

```
UPDATE table
   SET col1 = val1
      [, col2 = val2, ... colN = valN]
[WHERE where_clause];
```

The WHERE clause is optional; if you do not supply one, all rows in the table are updated. Here are some examples of UPDATEs:

- Uppercase all the titles of books in the books table:

      ```
      UPDATE books SET title = UPPER (title);
      ```

- Run a utility procedure that removes the time component from the publication date of books written by specified authors (the argument in the procedure) and uppercases the titles of those books. As you can see, you can run an UPDATE statement standalone or within a PL/SQL block.

```
PROCEDURE remove_time (author_in IN VARCHAR2)
IS
BEGIN
   UPDATE books
      SET title = UPPER (title),
          date_published = TRUNC (date_published)
    WHERE author LIKE author_in;
END;
```

### The DELETE statement

You can use the DELETE statement to remove one, some, or all the rows in a table. Here is the basic syntax:

```
DELETE FROM table
 [WHERE where_clause];
```

The WHERE clause is optional in a DELETE statement. If you do not supply one, all rows in the table are deleted. Here are some examples of DELETEs:

- Delete all the books from the books table:

    ```
    DELETE FROM books;
    ```

- Delete all the books from the books table that were published prior to a certain date and return the number of rows deleted:

    ```
    PROCEDURE remove_books (
       date_in              IN       DATE,
       removal_count_out    OUT      PLS_INTEGER)
    IS
    BEGIN
       DELETE FROM books WHERE date_published < date_in;
       removal_count_out := SQL%ROWCOUNT;
    END;
    ```

Of course, all these DML statements can become qualitatively more complex as you deal with real-world entities. You can, for example, update multiple columns with the contents of a subquery. Starting with Oracle9i Database, you can replace a table name with a *table function* that returns a result set upon which the DML statement acts.

### The MERGE statement

With the MERGE statement, you specify the condition on which a match is to be evaluated, and then the two different actions to take for MATCHED and NOT MATCHED. Here is an example:

```
PROCEDURE time_use_merge (dept_in IN employees.department_id%TYPE
)
IS
BEGIN
   MERGE INTO bonuses d
       USING (SELECT employee_id, salary, department_id
                FROM employees
               WHERE department_id = dept_in) s
```

```
            ON (d.employee_id = s.employee_id)
      WHEN MATCHED
      THEN
         UPDATE SET d.bonus = d.bonus + s.salary * .01
      WHEN NOT MATCHED
      THEN
         INSERT (d.employee_id, d.bonus)
            VALUES (s.employee_id, s.salary * 0.2
   END;
```

The syntax and details of MERGE are all SQL-based, and I won't explore them further in this book. The *merge.sql* file, however, contains a more comprehensive example.

## Cursor Attributes for DML Operations

Oracle allows you to access information about the most recently executed implicit cursor by referencing one of the following special implicit cursor attributes:

Implicit cursor attributes return information about the execution of the most recent INSERT, UPDATE, DELETE, MERGE, or SELECT INTO statement. Cursor attributes for SELECT INTOs are covered in Chapter 15. In this section, I'll discuss how to take advantage of the SQL% attributes for DML statements.

First of all, remember that the values of implicit cursor attributes always refer to the most recently executed SQL statement, regardless of the block in which the implicit cursor is executed. And before Oracle opens the first SQL cursor in the session, all the implicit cursor attributes yield NULL. (The exception is %ISOPEN, which returns FALSE.)

Table 14-1 summarizes the significance of the values returned by these attributes for implicit cursors.

*Table 14-1. Implicit SQL cursor attributes for DML statements*

| Name | Description |
| --- | --- |
| SQL%FOUND | Returns TRUE if one or more rows were modified (created, changed, removed) successfully |
| SQL%NOTFOUND | Returns TRUE if no rows were modified by the DML statement |
| SQL%ROWCOUNT | Returns number of rows modified by the DML statement |
| SQL%ISOPEN | Always returns FALSE for implicit cursors (and, therefore, DML statements) because the Oracle database opens and closes their cursors automatically |

Now let's see how we can use cursor attributes with implicit cursors.

- Use SQL%FOUND to determine if your DML statement affected any rows. For example, from time to time an author will change his name and want a new name used for all of his books. So I create a small procedure to update the name and then report back via a Boolean variable whether any rows were modified:

```
PROCEDURE change_author_name (
   old_name_in        IN         books.author%TYPE,
   new_name_in        IN         books.author%TYPE,
   changes_made_out   OUT        BOOLEAN)
IS
BEGIN
   UPDATE books
      SET author = new_name_in
    WHERE author = old_name_in;

   changes_made_out := SQL%FOUND;
END;
```

- Use SQL%ROWCOUNT when you need to know exactly how many rows were affected by your DML statement. Here is a reworking of the above name-change procedure that returns a bit more information:

```
PROCEDURE change_author_name (
   old_name_in        IN         books.author%TYPE,
   new_name_in        IN         books.author%TYPE,
   rename_count_out   OUT        PLS_INTEGER)
IS
BEGIN
   UPDATE books
      SET author = new_name_in
    WHERE author = old_name_in;

   rename_count_out := SQL%ROWCOUNT;
END;
```

## RETURNING Information from DML Statements

Suppose that I perform an UPDATE or DELETE, and then need to get information about the results of that statement for future processing. Rather than perform a distinct query following the DML statement, I can add a RETURNING clause to an INSERT, UPDATE, DELETE, or MERGE and retrieve that information directly into variables in my program. With the RETURNING clause, I can reduce network round trips, consume less server CPU time, and minimize the number of cursors opened and managed in the application.

Here are some examples that demonstrate the capabilities of this feature.

- The following very simple block shows how I use the RETURNING clause to retrieve a value (the new salary) that was computed within the UPDATE statement:

```
DECLARE
   myname   employees.last_name%TYPE;
   mysal    employees.salary%TYPE;
BEGIN
   FOR rec IN (SELECT * FROM employees)
   LOOP
      UPDATE     employees
             SET salary = salary * 1.5
```

```
                WHERE employee_id = rec.employee_id
            RETURNING salary, last_name INTO mysal, myname;

            DBMS_OUTPUT.PUT_LINE ('New salary for ' ||
                myname || ' = ' || mysal);
        END LOOP;
    END;
```

- Suppose that I perform an UPDATE that modifies more than one row. In this case, I can return information not just into a single variable, but into a collection using the BULK COLLECT syntax. This technique is shown below in a FORALL statement:

```
DECLARE
    names name_varray;
    new_salaries number_varray;
BEGIN
    populate_arrays (names, new_salaries);

    FORALL indx IN names.FIRST .. names.LAST
        UPDATE compensation
            SET salary = new_salaries ( indx)
        WHERE last_name = names (indx)
        RETURNING salary BULK COLLECT INTO new_salaries;
    ...
END;
```

You can get lots more information about the FORALL (bulk bind) statement in Chapter 21.

## DML and Exception Handling

When an exception occurs in a PL/SQL block, the Oracle database does *not* roll back any of the changes made by DML statements in that block. You are the manager of the application's logical transaction, so you decide what kind of behavior should occur.

Consider the following procedure:

```
PROCEDURE empty_library (
    pre_empty_count OUT PLS_INTEGER)
IS
BEGIN

    /* tabcount implementation available in ch14_code.sql */
    pre_empty_count := tabcount ('books');

    DELETE FROM books;
    RAISE NO_DATA_FOUND;
END;
```

Notice that I set the value of the OUT parameter before I raise the exception. Now let's run an anonymous block that calls this procedure, and examine the after-effects:

```
DECLARE
    table_count    NUMBER := -1;
```

```
BEGIN
   INSERT INTO books VALUES (...);
   empty_library (table_count);
EXCEPTION
   WHEN OTHERS
   THEN
      DBMS_OUTPUT.put_line (tabcount ('books'));
      DBMS_OUTPUT.put_line (table_count);
END;
```

The output is:

```
0
-1
```

Notice that my rows remain deleted from the books table even though an exception was raised; the database did not perform an automatic rollback. My table_count variable, however, retains its original value.

So it is up to you to perform rollbacks—or rather, to decide if you *want* to perform a rollback—in programs that perform DML. Here are some things to keep in mind in this regard:

- If your block is an autonomous transaction (described later in this chapter), then you *must* perform a rollback or commit (usually a rollback) when an exception is raised.

- You can use *savepoints* to control the scope of a rollback. In other words, you can roll back to a particular savepoint and thereby preserve a portion of the changes made in your session. Savepoints are also explored later in this chapter.

- If an exception propagates past the outermost block (i.e., it goes "unhandled"), then in most host execution environments for PL/SQL like SQL*Plus, a rollback is automatically executed, reversing any outstanding changes.

## DML and Records

You can use records inside INSERT and UPDATE statements. Here is an example that demonstrates the use of records in both types of statements:

```
PROCEDURE set_book_info (book_in IN books%ROWTYPE)
IS
BEGIN
   INSERT INTO books VALUES book_in;
EXCEPTION
   WHEN DUP_VAL_ON_INDEX
   THEN
      UPDATE books SET ROW = book_in
       WHERE isbn = book_in.isbn;
END;
```

This enhancement offers some compelling advantages over working with individual variables or fields within a record:

*Very concise code*

You can "stay above the fray" and work completely at the record level. There is no need to declare individual variables or decompose a record into its fields when passing that data to the DML statement.

*More robust code*

By working with %ROWTYPE records and not explicitly manipulating fields in those records, your code is less likely to require maintenance as changes are made to the tables and views upon which the records are based.

In "Restrictions on record-based inserts and updates" on page 450, you will find a list of restrictions on using records in DML statements. First, let's take a look at how you can take advantage of record-based DML for the two supported statements, INSERT and UPDATE.

### Record-based inserts

You can INSERT using a record with both single-row inserts and bulk inserts (via the FORALL statement). You can also use records that are based on %ROWTYPE declarations against the table to which the insert is made, or on an explicit record TYPE that is compatible with the structure of the table.

Here are some examples.

- Insert a row into the books table with a %ROWTYPE record:

```
DECLARE
   my_book books%ROWTYPE;
BEGIN
   my_book.isbn := '1-56592-335-9';
   my_book.title := 'ORACLE PL/SQL PROGRAMMING';
   my_book.summary := 'General user guide and reference';
   my_book.author := 'FEUERSTEIN, STEVEN AND BILL PRIBYL';
   my_book.page_count := 1000;

   INSERT INTO books VALUES my_book;
END;
```

Notice that you do not include parentheses around the record specifier. If you use this format:

```
INSERT INTO books VALUES (my_book); -- With parentheses, INVALID!
```

then you will get an *ORA-00947: not enough values* exception, since the program is expecting a separate expression for each column in the table.

You can also use a record based on a programmer-defined record TYPE to perform the INSERT, but that record type must be 100% compatible with the table %ROWTYPE definition. You may not, in other words, INSERT using a record that covers only a subset of the table's columns.

- Perform record-based inserts with the FORALL statement. You can also work with collections of records and insert all those records directly into a table within the FORALL statement. See Chapter 21 for more information about FORALL.

### Record-based updates

You can also perform updates of an entire row using a record. The following example updates a row in the books table with a %ROWTYPE record. Notice that I use the keyword ROW to indicate that I am updating the entire row with a record:

```
/* File on web: record_updates.sql */
DECLARE
   my_book books%ROWTYPE;
BEGIN
   my_book.isbn := '1-56592-335-9';
   my_book.title := 'ORACLE PL/SQL PROGRAMMING';
   my_book.summary := 'General user guide and reference';
   my_book.author := 'FEUERSTEIN, STEVEN AND BILL PRIBYL';
   my_book.page_count := 1000;

   UPDATE books
      SET ROW = my_book
    WHERE isbn = my_book.isbn;
END;
```

There are some restrictions on record-based updates:

- You must update an entire row with the ROW syntax. You cannot update a subset of columns (although this may be supported in future releases). Any fields whose values are left NULL will result in a NULL value assigned to the corresponding column.
- You cannot perform an update using a subquery.

And, in case you are wondering, you cannot create a table column called ROW.

### Using records with the RETURNING clause

DML statements can include a RETURNING clause that returns column values (and expressions based on those values) from the affected row(s). You can return into a record, or even a collection of records:

```
/* File on web: record_updates.sql */
DECLARE
   my_book_new_info books%ROWTYPE;
   my_book_return_info books%ROWTYPE;
BEGIN
   my_book_new_info.isbn := '1-56592-335-9';
   my_book_new_info.title := 'ORACLE PL/SQL PROGRAMMING';
   my_book_new_info.summary := 'General user guide and reference';
   my_book_new_info.author := 'FEUERSTEIN, STEVEN AND BILL PRIBYL';
   my_book_new_info.page_count := 1000;
```

```
    UPDATE books
       SET ROW = my_book_new_info
     WHERE isbn = my_book_new_info.isbn
     RETURNING isbn, title, summary, author, date_published, page_count
           INTO my_book_return_info;
END;
```

Notice that I must list each of my individual columns in the RETURNING clause. Oracle does not yet support the * syntax.

### Restrictions on record-based inserts and updates

As you begin to explore these new capabilities and put them to use, keep in mind the following:

- You can use a record variable only (1) on the right side of the SET clause in UPDATEs; (2) in the VALUES clause of an INSERT; or (3) in the INTO subclause of a RETURNING clause.

- You must (and can only) use the ROW keyword on the left side of a SET clause. In this case, you may not have any other SET clauses (i.e., you may not SET a row and then SET an individual column).

- If you INSERT with a record, you may not pass individual values for columns.

- You cannot INSERT or UPDATE with a record that contains a nested record or with a function that returns a nested record.

- You cannot use records in DML statements that are executed dynamically (EXECUTE IMMEDIATE). This requires Oracle to support the binding of a PL/SQL record type into a SQL statement, and only SQL types can be bound in this way.

# Transaction Management

The Oracle database provides a very robust transaction model, as you might expect from a relational database. Your application code determines what constitutes a *transaction*, which is the logical unit of work that must be either saved with a COMMIT statement or rolled back with a ROLLBACK statement. A transaction begins implicitly with the first SQL statement issued since the last COMMIT or ROLLBACK (or with the start of a session), or continues after a ROLLBACK TO SAVEPOINT.

PL/SQL provides the following statements for transaction management:

*COMMIT*
 Saves all outstanding changes since the last COMMIT or ROLLBACK, and releases all locks.

*ROLLBACK*
 Reverses the effects of all outstanding changes since the last COMMIT or ROLL-BACK, and releases all locks.

---

*ROLLBACK TO SAVEPOINT*

Reverses the effects of all changes made since the specified savepoint was established, and releases locks that were established within that range of the code.

*SAVEPOINT*

Establishes a savepoint, which then allows you to perform partial ROLLBACKs.

*SET TRANSACTION*

Allows you to begin a read-only or read-write session, establish an isolation level, or assign the current transaction to a specified rollback segment.

*LOCK TABLE*

Allows you to lock an entire database table in the specified mode. This overrides the default row-level locking usually applied to a table.

These statements are explained in more detail in the following sections.

## The COMMIT Statement

When you COMMIT, you make permanent any changes made by your session to the database in the current transaction. Once you COMMIT, your changes will be visible to other database sessions or users. The syntax for the COMMIT statement is:

```
COMMIT [WORK] [COMMENT text];
```

The WORK keyword is optional and can be used to improve readability.

The COMMENT keyword lets you specify a comment that is then associated with the current transaction. The text must be a quoted literal and can be no more than 50 characters in length. The COMMENT text is usually employed with distributed transactions, and can be handy for examining and resolving in-doubt transactions within a two-phase commit framework. It is stored in the data dictionary along with the transaction ID.

Note that COMMIT releases any row and table locks issued in your session, such as with a SELECT FOR UPDATE statement. It also erases any savepoints issued since the last COMMIT or ROLLBACK.

Once you COMMIT your changes, you cannot roll them back with a ROLLBACK statement.

The following statements are all valid uses of COMMIT:

```
COMMIT;
COMMIT WORK;
COMMIT COMMENT 'maintaining account balance'.
```

## The ROLLBACK Statement

When you perform a ROLLBACK, you undo some or all changes made by your session to the database in the current transaction. Why would you want to undo changes? From an ad hoc SQL standpoint, the ROLLBACK gives you a way to erase mistakes you might have made, as in:

```
DELETE FROM orders;
```

"No, no! I meant to delete only the orders before May 2005!" No problem—just issue ROLLBACK. From an application coding standpoint, ROLLBACK is important because it allows you to clean up or restart from a clean state when a problem occurs.

The syntax for the ROLLBACK statement is:

```
ROLLBACK [WORK] [TO [SAVEPOINT] savepoint_name];
```

There are two basic ways to use ROLLBACK: without parameters or with the TO clause to indicate a savepoint at which the ROLLBACK should stop. The parameterless ROLLBACK undoes all outstanding changes in your transaction.

The ROLLBACK TO version allows you to undo all changes and release all acquired locks that were issued since the savepoint identified by *savepoint_name*. (See the next section on the SAVEPOINT statement for more information on how to mark a savepoint in your application.)

The *savepoint_name* is an undeclared Oracle identifier. It cannot be a literal (enclosed in quotes) or variable name.

All of the following uses of ROLLBACK are valid:

```
ROLLBACK;
ROLLBACK WORK;
ROLLBACK TO begin_cleanup;
```

When you roll back to a specific savepoint, all savepoints issued after the specified *savepoint_name* are erased, but the savepoint to which you roll back is not. This means that you can restart your transaction from that point and, if necessary, roll back to that same savepoint if another error occurs.

Immediately before you execute an INSERT, UPDATE, MERGE, or DELETE, PL/SQL implicitly generates a savepoint. If your DML statement then fails, a rollback is automatically performed to that implicit savepoint. In this way, only the last DML statement is undone.

## The SAVEPOINT Statement

SAVEPOINT gives a name to, and marks a point in, the processing of your transaction. This marker allows you to ROLLBACK TO that point, undoing any changes and releasing any locks issued after that savepoint, but preserving any changes and locks that occurred before you marked the savepoint.

The syntax for the SAVEPOINT statement is:

```
SAVEPOINT savepoint_name;
```

where *savepoint_name* is an undeclared identifier. This means that it must conform to the rules for an Oracle identifier (up to 30 characters in length, starting with a letter, containing letters, numbers, and #, $, or _), but that you do not need to (and are not able to) declare that identifier.

Savepoints are not scoped to PL/SQL blocks. If you reuse a savepoint name within the current transaction, that savepoint is "moved" from its original position to the current point in the transaction, regardless of the procedure, function, or anonymous block in which the SAVEPOINT statements are executed. As a corollary, if you issue a savepoint inside a recursive program, a new savepoint is executed at each level of recursion, but you can only roll back to the most recently marked savepoint.

## The SET TRANSACTION Statement

The SET TRANSACTION statement allows you to begin a read-only or read-write session, establish an isolation level, or assign the current transaction to a specified rollback segment. This statement must be the first SQL statement processed in a transaction, and it can appear only once. This statement comes in the following four flavors.

*SET TRANSACTION READ ONLY;*
> This version defines the current transaction as read-only. In a read-only transaction, all subsequent queries see only those changes that were committed before the transaction began (providing a read-consistent view across tables and queries). This statement is useful when you are executing long-running, multiple query reports, and you want to make sure that the data used in the report is consistent.

*SET TRANSACTION READ WRITE;*
> This version defines the current transaction as read-write and is the default setting

*SET TRANSACTION ISOLATION LEVEL SERIALIZABLE | READ COMMITTED;*
> This version defines how transactions that modify the database should be handled. You can specify a serializable or read-committed isolation level. When you specify SERIALIZABLE, a DML statement that attempts to modify a table already modified in an uncommitted transaction will fail. To execute this command, you must set the database initialization parameter COMPATIBLE to 7.3.0 or higher.
>
> If you specify READ COMMITTED, a DML statement that requires row-level locks held by another transaction will wait until those row locks are released. This is the default.

*SET TRANSACTION USE ROLLBACK SEGMENT rollback_segname;*
> This version assigns the current transaction to the specified rollback segment and establishes the transaction as read-write. This statement cannot be used with SET TRANSACTION READ ONLY.

Rollback segments were deprecated in favor of automatic undo management, introduced in Oracle9i Database

## The LOCK TABLE Statement

This statement allows you to lock an entire database table in the specified lock mode. By doing this, you can share or deny access to that table while you perform operations against it. The syntax for this statement is:

```
LOCK TABLE table_reference_list IN lock_mode MODE [NOWAIT | WAIT numseconds ]
```

where *table_reference_list* is a list of one or more table references (identifying either a local table/view or a remote entity through a database link), and *lock_mode* is the mode of the lock, which can be one of the following:

ROW SHARE
ROW EXCLUSIVE
SHARE UPDATE
SHARE
SHARE ROW EXCLUSIVE
EXCLUSIVE

If you specify the NOWAIT keyword, the database does not wait for the lock if the table has already been locked by another user, and instead reports an error. Beginning in Oracle Database 11g Release 1, you can set the number of seconds to wait by using the WAIT clause. If you want to wait forever, leave out both NOWAIT and WAIT. Locking a table never stops other users from querying or reading the table.

The following LOCK TABLE statements show valid variations:

```
LOCK TABLE emp IN ROW EXCLUSIVE MODE;
LOCK TABLE emp, dept IN SHARE MODE NOWAIT;
LOCK TABLE scott.emp@new_york IN SHARE UPDATE MODE;
```

 Whenever possible, you should rely on Oracle's default locking behavior. Use of LOCK TABLE in your application should be done as a last resort and with great care.

# Autonomous Transactions

When you define a PL/SQL block as an *autonomous transaction*, you isolate the DML in that block from the caller's transaction context. That block becomes an independent transaction that is started by another transaction, referred to as the *main transaction*.

Within the autonomous transaction block, the main transaction is suspended. You perform your SQL operations, commit or roll back those operations, and resume the main transaction. This flow of transaction control is illustrated in Figure 14-1.

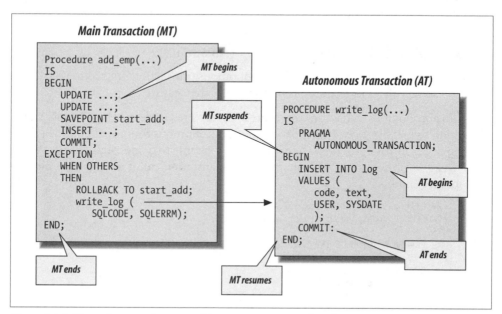

Figure 14-1. Flow of transaction control between main, nested, and autonomous transactions

## Defining Autonomous Transactions

There isn't much involved in defining a PL/SQL block as an autonomous transaction. You simply include the following statement in your declaration section:

```
PRAGMA AUTONOMOUS_TRANSACTION;
```

The pragma instructs the PL/SQL compiler to establish a PL/SQL block as autonomous or independent. For the purposes of the autonomous transaction, a PL/SQL block can be any of the following:

- Top-level (but not nested) anonymous PL/SQL blocks
- Functions and procedures, defined either in a package or as standalone programs
- Methods (functions and procedures) of an object type
- Database triggers

You can put the autonomous transaction pragma anywhere in the declaration section of your PL/SQL block. You would probably be best off, however, placing it before any data structure declarations. That way, anyone reading your code will immediately identify the program as an autonomous transaction.

This pragma is the only syntax change made to PL/SQL to support autonomous transactions. COMMIT, ROLLBACK, the DML statements—all the rest is as it was before. However, these statements have a different scope of impact and visibility when executed within an autonomous transaction, and you will need to include a COMMIT or ROLLBACK in your program.

## Rules and Restrictions on Autonomous Transactions

While it is certainly very easy to add the autonomous transaction pragma to your code, there are some rules and restrictions on the use of this feature.

- If an autonomous transaction attempts to access a resource held by the main transaction (which has been suspended until the autonomous routine exits), a deadlock can occur in your program. Here is a simple example to demonstrate the problem. I create a procedure to perform an update, and then call it after having already updated all rows:

```
/* File on web: autondlock.sql */
PROCEDURE update_salary (dept_in IN NUMBER)
IS
   PRAGMA AUTONOMOUS_TRANSACTION;

   CURSOR myemps IS
      SELECT empno FROM emp
       WHERE deptno = dept_in
          FOR UPDATE NOWAIT;
BEGIN
   FOR rec IN myemps
   LOOP
      UPDATE emp SET sal = sal * 2
       WHERE empno = rec.empno;
   END LOOP;
   COMMIT;
END;

BEGIN
   UPDATE emp SET sal = sal * 2;
   update_salary (10);
END;
```

The results are not pretty:

```
ERROR at line 1:
ORA-00054: resource busy and acquire with NOWAIT specified
```

- You cannot mark all the subprograms in a package (or all methods in an object type) as autonomous with a single PRAGMA declaration. You must indicate autonomous transactions explicitly in each program's declaration section in the package body. One consequence of this rule is that you cannot tell by looking at the package specification which (if any) programs will run as autonomous transactions.

- To exit without errors from an autonomous transaction program that has executed at least one INSERT, UPDATE, MERGE, or DELETE, you must perform an explicit commit or rollback. If the program (or any program called by it) has transactions pending, the runtime engine will raise the exception shown below—and then will roll back those uncommitted transactions.

  ```
  ORA-06519: active autonomous transaction detected and rolled back
  ```

- The COMMIT and ROLLBACK statements end the active autonomous transaction, but they do not force the termination of the autonomous routine. You can, in fact, have multiple COMMIT and/or ROLLBACK statements inside your autonomous block.

- You can roll back only to savepoints marked in the current transaction. When you are in an autonomous transaction, therefore, you cannot roll back to a savepoint set in the main transaction. If you try to do so, the runtime engine will raise this exception:

  ```
  ORA-01086: savepoint 'your savepoint' never established
  ```

- The TRANSACTIONS parameter in the database initialization file specifies the maximum number of transactions allowed concurrently in a session. If you use lots of autonomous transaction programs in your application, you might exceed this limit, in which case you will see the following exception:

  ```
  ORA-01574: maximum number of concurrent transactions exceeded
  ```

  In this case, increase the value for TRANSACTIONS. The default value is 75.

## Transaction Visibility

The default behavior of autonomous transactions is that once a COMMIT or a ROLL-BACK occurs in the autonomous transaction, those changes are visible immediately in the main transaction. But what if you want to hide those changes from the main transaction? You want them saved or undone—no question about that—but the information should not be available to the main transaction. To achieve this, use SET TRANSACTION as follows:

```
SET TRANSACTION ISOLATION LEVEL SERIALIZABLE;
```

The default isolation level of READ COMMITTED means that as soon as changes are committed, they are visible to the main transaction.

As is usually the case with the SET TRANSACTION statement, you must call it before you initiate your transactions (i.e., issue any SQL statements). In addition, the setting affects your entire session, not just the current program. The *autonserial.sql* script on the book's web site demonstrates use of the SERIALIZABLE isolation level.

## When to Use Autonomous Transactions

Where would you find autonomous transactions useful in your applications? First, let's reinforce the general principle: you will want to define your program module as an autonomous transaction whenever you want to isolate the changes made in that module from the caller's transaction context.

Here are some specific ideas:

*Logging mechanism*
> On the one hand, you need to log an error to your database log table. On the other hand, you need to roll back your core transaction because of the error. And you don't want to roll back over other log entries. What's a person to do? Go autonomous! This is probably the most common motivation for PL/SQL developers to use autonomous transactions and is explored at the end of this section.

*Perform commits and rollbacks in your database triggers*
> If you define a trigger as an autonomous transaction, then you can commit and/or roll back in that trigger, without affecting the transaction that fired the trigger. Why is this valuable? You may want to take an action in the database trigger that is not affected by the ultimate disposition of the transaction that caused the trigger to fire. For example, suppose that you want to keep track of each action against a table, whether or not the action completed. You might even want to be able to detect which actions failed. See the *autontrigger\*.sql* scripts on the book's web site for examples of how you can apply this technique.

*Reusable application components*
> This usage goes to the heart of the value of autonomous transactions. As we move more and more into the dispersed, multilayered world of the Internet, it becomes ever more important to be able to offer standalone units of work (also known as *cartridges*) that get their job done without any side effects on the calling environment. Autonomous transactions play a crucial role in this area.

*Avoid mutating table trigger errors for queries*
> Mutating table trigger errors occur when a row-level trigger attempts to read from or write to the table from which it was fired. If, however, you make your trigger an autonomous transaction by adding the PRAGMA AUTONOMOUS_TRANSACTION statement and committing inside the body of the trigger, then you will be able to *query* the contents of the firing table—but you can only see already-committed changes to the table. In other words, you will not see any changes made to the table that caused the firing of the trigger. In addition, you will still not be allowed to modify the contents of the table.

*Call user-defined functions in SQL that modify tables*
> Oracle lets you call your own functions inside a SQL statement, provided that this function does not update the database (and several other rules besides). If, however, you define your function as an autonomous transaction, you will then be able to insert, update, merge, or delete inside that function as it is run from within a

query. The *trcfunc.sql* script on the book's web site demonstrates an application of this capability, allowing you to audit which rows of a table have been queried.

*Retry counter*

Suppose that you want to let a user try to get access to a resource *N* times before an outright rejection; you also want to keep track of attempts between connections to the database. This persistence requires a COMMIT, but one that should remain independent of the main transaction. For an example of such a utility, see *retry.pkg* and *retry.tst* on the book's web site.

## Building an Autonomous Logging Mechanism

A very common requirement in applications is to keep a log of errors that occur during transaction processing. The most convenient repository for this log is a database table; with a table, all the information is retained in the database, and you can use SQL to retrieve and analyze the log.

One problem with a database table log, however, is that entries in the log become a part of your transaction. If you perform a ROLLBACK (or if one is performed for you), you can easily erase your log. How frustrating! You can get fancy and use savepoints to preserve your log entries while cleaning up your transaction, but that approach is not only fancy, it is complicated. With autonomous transactions, however, logging becomes simpler, more manageable, and less error prone.

Suppose that I have a log table defined as follows:

```
/* File on web: log.pkg */
CREATE TABLE logtab (
    code INTEGER, text VARCHAR2(4000),
    created_on DATE, created_by VARCHAR2(100),
    changed_on DATE, changed_by VARCHAR2(100)
    );
```

I can use it to store errors (SQLCODE and SQLERRM) that have occurred, or even for nonerror-related logging.

So I have my table. Now, how should I write to my log? Here's what you shouldn't do:

```
EXCEPTION
   WHEN OTHERS
   THEN
      DECLARE
         v_code PLS_INTEGER := SQLCODE;
         v_msg VARCHAR2(1000) := SQLERRM;
      BEGIN
         INSERT INTO logtab VALUES (
               v_code, v_msg, SYSDATE, USER, SYSDATE, USER);
      END;
END;
```

In other words, never expose your underlying logging mechanism by explicitly inserting into it your exception sections and other locations. Instead, you should build a layer of code around the table (this is known as *encapsulation*). There are three reasons to do this:

- If you ever change your table's structure, all those uses of the log table won't be disrupted.
- People can use the log table in a much easier, more consistent manner.
- You can then make that subprogram an autonomous transaction.

So here is my very simple logging package. It consists of two procedures:

```
PACKAGE log
IS
   PROCEDURE putline (code_in IN INTEGER, text_in IN VARCHAR2);
   PROCEDURE saveline (code_in IN INTEGER, text_in IN VARCHAR2);
END;
```

What is the difference between putline and saveline? The log.saveline procedure is an autonomous transaction routine; log.putline simply performs the insert. Here is the package body:

```
/* File on web: log.pkg */
PACKAGE BODY log
IS
   PROCEDURE putline (
      code_in IN INTEGER, text_in IN VARCHAR2)
   IS
   BEGIN
      INSERT INTO logtab
         VALUES (
            code_in,
            text_in,
            SYSDATE,
            USER,
            SYSDATE,
            USER
         );
   END;

   PROCEDURE saveline (
      code_in IN INTEGER, text_in IN VARCHAR2)
   IS
      PRAGMA AUTONOMOUS_TRANSACTION;
   BEGIN
      putline (code_in, text_in);
      COMMIT;
   EXCEPTION WHEN OTHERS THEN ROLLBACK;
   END;
END;
```

Here are some comments on this implementation that you might find helpful:

- The putline procedure performs the straight insert. You would probably want to add some exception handling to this program if you applied this idea in your production application.
- The saveline procedure calls the putline procedure (I don't want any redundant code), but does so from within the context of an autonomous transaction.

With this package in place, my error handler shown earlier can be as simple as this:

```
EXCEPTION
   WHEN OTHERS
   THEN
      log.saveline (SQLCODE, SQLERRM);
END;
```

No muss, no fuss. Developers don't have to concern themselves with the structure of the log table; they don't even have to know they are writing to a database table. And because I have used an autonomous transaction, they can rest assured that no matter what happens in their application, the log entry has been saved.

# CHAPTER 15

# Data Retrieval

One of the hallmarks of the PL/SQL language is its tight integration with the Oracle database, both for changing data in database tables and for extracting information from those tables. This chapter explores the many features available in PL/SQL to query data from the database and make that data available within PL/SQL programs.

When you execute a SQL statement from PL/SQL, the Oracle database assigns a private work area for that statement and also manages the data specified by the SQL statement in the System Global Area (SGA). The private work area contains information about the SQL statement and the set of data returned or affected by that statement.

PL/SQL provides a number of different ways to name this work area and manipulate the information within it; all of these ways involve defining and working with cursors. They include:

*Implicit cursors*

> A simple and direct SELECT...INTO retrieves a single row of data into local program variables. It's the easiest (and often the most efficient) path to your data, but it can often lead to coding the same or similar SELECTs in multiple places in your code.

*Explicit cursors*

> You can declare the query explicitly in your declaration section (local block or package). In this way, you can open and fetch from the cursor in one or more programs, with a granularity of control not available with implicit cursors.

*Cursor variables*

> Offering an additional level of flexibility, cursor variables (declared from a REF CURSOR type) allow you to pass a *pointer* to a query's underlying result set from one program to another. Any program with access to that variable can open, fetch from, or close the cursor.

*Cursor expressions*

> The CURSOR expression transforms a SELECT statement into a REF CURSOR result set and can be used with table functions to improve the performance of applications.

*Dynamic SQL queries*

> Oracle allows you to construct and execute queries dynamically at runtime using either native dynamic SQL (a.k.a., NDS, covered in Chapter 16) or DBMS_SQL. Details on this built-in package are available in the Oracle documentation as well as in *Oracle Built-in Packages* (O'Reilly).

This chapter explores implicit cursors, explicit cursors, cursor variables, and cursor expressions in detail.

# Cursor Basics

In its simplest form, you can think of a *cursor* as a pointer to the results of a query run against one or more tables in the database. For example, the following cursor declaration associates the entire employee table with the cursor named employee_cur:

```
CURSOR employee_cur IS SELECT * FROM employee;
```

Once I have declared the cursor, I can open it:

```
OPEN employee_cur;
```

Then I can fetch rows from it:

```
FETCH employee_cur INTO employee_rec;
```

Finally, I can close the cursor:

```
CLOSE employee_cur;
```

In this case, each record fetched from this cursor represents an entire record in the employee table. You can, however, associate any valid SELECT statement with a cursor. In the next example I have a join of three tables in my cursor declaration:

```
DECLARE
   CURSOR joke_feedback_cur
   IS
      SELECT J.name, R.laugh_volume, C.name
        FROM joke J, response R, comedian C
       WHERE J.joke_id = R.joke_id
         AND R.joker_id = C.joker_id;
BEGIN
   ...
END;
```

Here, the cursor does not act as a pointer into any actual table in the database. Instead, the cursor is a pointer into the virtual table or implicit view represented by the SELECT statement (SELECT is called a virtual table because the data it produces has the same structure as a table—rows and columns—but it exists only for the duration of the execution of the SQL statement). If the triple join returns 20 rows, each containing 3 columns, then the cursor functions as a pointer into those 20 rows.

## Some Data Retrieval Terms

You have lots of options in PL/SQL for executing SQL, and all of them occur as some type of cursor inside your PL/SQL program. Before diving into the details of the various approaches, this section will familiarize you with the types and terminology of data retrieval.

*Static SQL*
> A SQL statement is *static* if it is fully specified, or fixed, at the time the code containing that statement is compiled.

*Dynamic SQL*
> A SQL statement is *dynamic* if it is constructed at runtime and then executed, so you don't completely specify the SQL statement in the code you write. You can execute dynamic SQL either through the use of the built-in DBMS_SQL package or with native dynamic SQL.

*Result set*
> This is the set of rows identified by the database as fulfilling the request for data specified by the SQL statement. The result set is cached in the SGA to improve the performance of accessing and modifying the data in that set. The database maintains a pointer into the result set, which I will refer to in this chapter as the *current row*.

*Implicit cursor*
> PL/SQL declares and manages an implicit cursor every time you execute a SQL DML statement (INSERT, UPDATE, MERGE, or DELETE) or a SELECT INTO that returns a single row from the database directly into a PL/SQL data structure. This kind of cursor is called "implicit" because the database automatically handles many of the cursor-related operations for you, such as allocating a cursor, opening the cursor, fetching records, and even closing the cursor (although this is not an excuse to write code that relies on this behavior).

*Explicit cursor*
> This is a SELECT statement that you declare as a cursor explicitly in your application code. You then also explicitly perform each operation against that cursor (open, fetch, close, etc.). You will generally use explicit cursors when you need to retrieve multiple rows from data sources using static SQL.

*Cursor variable*
> This is a variable you declare that references or points to a cursor object in the database. As a true variable, a cursor variable can change its value (i.e., the cursor or result set it points to) as your program executes. The variable can refer to different cursor objects (queries) at different times. You can also pass a cursor variable as a parameter to a procedure or function. Cursor variables are very useful when

passing result set information from a PL/SQL program to another environment, such as Java or Visual Basic.

*Cursor attribute*

A cursor attribute takes the form %*attribute_name* and is appended to the name of a cursor or cursor variable. The attribute returns information about the state of the cursor, such as "is the cursor open?" and "how many rows have been retrieved for this cursor?" Cursor attributes work in slightly different ways for implicit and explicit cursors and for dynamic SQL. These variations are explored throughout this chapter.

*SELECT FOR UPDATE*

This statement is a special variation of the normal SELECT, which proactively issues row locks on each row of data retrieved by the query. Use SELECT FOR UPDATE only when you need to reserve data you are querying to ensure that no one changes the data while you are processing it.

*Bulk processing*

In Oracle8*i* Database and later, PL/SQL offers the BULK COLLECT syntax for queries that allows you to fetch multiple rows from the database in a single or bulk step.

## Typical Query Operations

Regardless of the type of cursor, PL/SQL performs the same operations to execute a SQL statement from within your program. In some cases, PL/SQL takes these steps for you. In others, such as with explicit cursors, you will code and execute these steps yourself.

*Parse*

The first step in processing a SQL statement is to parse it to make sure it is valid and to determine the execution plan (using either the rule- or cost-based optimizer, depending on how your DBA has set the OPTIMIZER_MODE parameter for your database, database statistics, query hints, etc.).

*Bind*

When you bind, you associate values from your program (host variables) with placeholders inside your SQL statement. With static SQL, the PL/SQL engine itself performs these binds. With dynamic SQL, you must explicitly request a binding of variable values if you want to use bind variables.

*Open*

When you open a cursor, the result set for the SQL statement is determined using any bind variables that have been set. The pointer to the active or current row is set to the first row. Sometimes you will not explicitly open a cursor; instead, the PL/SQL engine will perform this operation for you (as with implicit cursors or native dynamic SQL).

*Execute*

In the execute phase, the statement is run within the SQL engine.

*Fetch*

If you are performing a query, the FETCH command retrieves the next row from the cursor's result set. Each time you fetch, PL/SQL moves the pointer forward in the result set. When you are working with explicit cursors, remember that FETCH does nothing (does not raise an error) if there are no more rows to retrieve—you must use cursor attributes to identify this condition.

*Close*

This step closes the cursor and releases all memory used by the cursor. Once closed, the cursor no longer has a result set. Sometimes you will not explicitly close a cursor; instead, the PL/SQL engine will perform this operation for you (as with implicit cursors or native dynamic SQL).

Figure 15-1 shows how some of these different operations are used to fetch information from the database into your PL/SQL program.

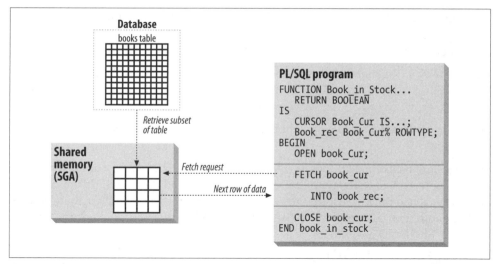

*Figure 15-1. Simplified view of cursor fetch operation*

## Introduction to Cursor Attributes

This section describes each of the different cursor attributes at a high level. They are explored in more detail for each of the kinds of cursors throughout this chapter, as well as in Chapters 14 and 16.

PL/SQL offers a total of six cursor attributes, as shown in Table 15-1.

*Table 15-1. Cursor attributes*

| Name | Description |
| --- | --- |
| %FOUND | Returns TRUE if the record was fetched successfully, FALSE otherwise |
| %NOTFOUND | Returns TRUE if the record was not fetched successfully, FALSE otherwise |
| %ROWCOUNT | Returns the number of records fetched from cursor at that point in time |
| %ISOPEN | Returns TRUE if cursor is open, FALSE otherwise |
| %BULK_ROWCOUNT | Returns the number of records modified by the FORALL statement for each collection element |
| %BULK_EXCEPTIONS | Returns exception information for rows modified by the FORALL statement for each collection element |

To reference a cursor attribute, attach it with "%" to the name of the cursor or cursor variable about which you want information, as in:

    cursor_name%attribute_name

For implicit cursors, the cursor name is hardcoded as "SQL", as in SQL%NOT-FOUND.

The following sections offer brief descriptions of each cursor attribute.

### The %FOUND attribute

The %FOUND attribute reports on the status of your most recent FETCH against the cursor. This attribute evaluates to TRUE if the most recent FETCH against the cursor returned a row, or FALSE if no row was returned.

If the cursor has not yet been opened, the database raises, the INVALID_CURSOR exception.

In the following example, I loop through all the callers in the caller_cur cursor, assign all calls entered before today to that particular caller, and then fetch the next record. If I have reached the last record, then the explicit cursor's %FOUND attribute is set to FALSE, and I exit the simple loop. After my UPDATE statement, I check the implicit cursor's %FOUND attribute as well.

```
FOR caller_rec IN caller_cur
LOOP
   UPDATE call
     SET caller_id = caller_rec.caller_id
   WHERE call_timestamp < SYSDATE;

   IF SQL%FOUND THEN
      DBMS_OUTPUT.PUT_LINE ('Calls updated for ' || caller_rec.caller_id);
   END IF;
END LOOP;
```

### The %NOTFOUND attribute

The %NOTFOUND attribute is the opposite of %FOUND. It returns TRUE if the most recent FETCH against the cursor did not return a row, often because the final row has already been fetched. If the cursor is unable to return a row because of an error, the appropriate exception is raised.

If the cursor has not yet been opened, the database raises the INVALID_CURSOR exception.

When should you use %FOUND and when should you use %NOTFOUND? Use whichever formulation fits most naturally in your code. In the previous example, I issued the following statement to exit my loop:

```
EXIT WHEN NOT caller_cur%FOUND;
```

An alternate and perhaps more readable formulation might use %NOTFOUND instead, as follows:

```
EXIT WHEN caller_cur%NOTFOUND;
```

### The %ROWCOUNT attribute

The %ROWCOUNT attribute returns the number of records fetched so far from a cursor at the time the attribute is queried. When you first open a cursor, its %ROWCOUNT is set to zero. If you reference the %ROWCOUNT attribute of a cursor that is not open, you will raise the INVALID_CURSOR exception. After each record is fetched, %ROWCOUNT is increased by one.

Use %ROWCOUNT to verify that the expected number of rows have been fetched (or updated, in the case of DML) or to stop your program from executing after a certain number of iterations.

Here is an example:

```
BEGIN
   UPDATE employees SET last_name = 'FEUERSTEIN';

   DBMS_OUTPUT.PUT_LINE (SQL%ROWCOUNT);
END;
```

### The %ISOPEN attribute

The %ISOPEN attribute returns TRUE if the cursor is open; otherwise, it returns FALSE. Here is an example of a common usage, making sure that cursors aren't left open when something unexpected occurs:

```
DECLARE
   CURSOR happiness_cur IS SELECT simple_delights FROM ...;
BEGIN
   OPEN happiness_cur;
   ...
   IF happiness_cur%ISOPEN THEN ...
```

```
EXCEPTION
   WHEN OTHERS THEN
      IF happiness_cur%ISOPEN THEN
         close happiness_cur;
      END IF;
END;
```

### The %BULK_ROWCOUNT attribute

The %BULK_ROWCOUNT attribute, designed for use with the FORALL statement, returns the number of rows processed by each DML execution. This attribute has the semantics of an associative array. It is covered in Chapter 21.

### The %BULK_EXCEPTIONS attribute

The %BULK_EXCEPTIONS attribute, designed for use with the FORALL statement, returns exception information that may have been raised by each DML execution. This attribute (covered in Chapter 21) has the semantics of an associative array of records.

 You can reference cursor attributes in your PL/SQL code, as shown in the preceding example, but you cannot use those attributes inside a SQL statement. For example, if you try to use the %ROWCOUNT attribute in the WHERE clause of a SELECT:

```
SELECT caller_id, company_id FROM caller
 WHERE company_id = company_cur%ROWCOUNT;
```

you will get the compile error *PLS-00229: Attribute expression within SQL expression.*

## Referencing PL/SQL Variables in a Cursor

Since a cursor must be associated with a SQL statement, every cursor must reference at least one table from the database and determine from that (and from the WHERE clause) which rows will be returned in the active set. This does not mean, however, that a PL/SQL cursor's SELECT may return only database information.

The list of expressions that appears after the SELECT keyword and before the FROM keyword is called the *select list*. In native SQL, this select list may contain both columns and expressions (SQL functions on those columns, constants, etc.). In PL/SQL, the select list of a SELECT may contain PL/SQL variables and complex expressions.

You can reference local PL/SQL program data (PL/SQL variables and constants), as well as host language bind variables in the WHERE, GROUP BY, and HAVING clauses of the cursor's SELECT statement. You can and should also *qualify* a reference to a PL/SQL variable with its scope name (procedure name, package name, etc.), especially within a SQL statement. For more information on this topic, check out "Scope" on page 58.

---

## Choosing Between Explicit and Implicit Cursors

In years past, it was common for "Oracle gurus" (including yours truly) to solemnly declare that you should *never* use implicit cursors for single-row fetches, and then explain that implicit cursors follow the ISO standard and always perform two fetches, making them less efficient than explicit cursors (for which you can just fetch a single time).

The first two editions of this book repeated that "wisdom," but in the third edition we broke from tradition (along with many others). The bottom line is that from Oracle8 Database onwards, as a result of very specific optimizations, it is very likely that your implicit cursor will now run *more*—not less—efficiently than the equivalent explicit cursor.

So does that mean that you should now always use implicit cursors, just as previously you should "always" have used explicit cursors? Not at all. There are still good reasons to use explicit cursors, including the following:

- In some cases, explicit cursors can still be more efficient. You should test your critical, often-executed queries in both formats to see which will be better in that particular situation.

- Explicit cursors offer much tighter programmatic control. If a row is not found, for example, the database will not raise an exception, instead forcing the execution block to shut down.

I suggest that the question to answer is not "implicit or explicit?," but rather, "encapsulate or expose?" And the answer is (new wisdom revealed):

> You should always encapsulate your single-row query, hiding the query behind a function interface, and passing back the data through the RETURN clause.

In other words, don't worry about explicit versus implicit. Instead, worry about how you can tune and maintain your code if single-row queries are duplicated throughout your code.

And *stop* worrying by taking the time to encapsulate them behind functions, preferably package-based functions. Then you and all other developers on your team can simply call the function whenever that data is needed. If Oracle ever changes its query behavior, rendering your previous "best practice" less than best, just change the implementation of that single function. Everyone's code will immediately benefit!

# Working with Implicit Cursors

PL/SQL declares and manages an implicit cursor every time you execute a SQL DML statement (INSERT, UPDATE, MERGE, or DELETE) or a SELECT INTO that returns data from the database directly into a PL/SQL data structure. This kind of cursor is called *implicit* because the database implicitly or automatically handles many of the cursor-related operations for you, such as allocating memory for a cursor, opening the cursor, fetching, and so on.

 The implicit DML statements are covered in Chapter 14, *DML and Transaction Management*. This chapter is concerned only with the implicit SQL query.

An implicit cursor is a SELECT statement that has these special characteristics:

- The SELECT statement appears in the executable section of your block; it is not defined in the declaration section, as explicit cursors are.
- The query contains an INTO clause (or BULK COLLECT INTO for bulk processing). The INTO clause is a part of the PL/SQL (not the SQL) language and is the mechanism used to transfer data from the database into local PL/SQL data structures.
- You do not open, fetch, or close the SELECT statement; all of these operations are done for you.

The general structure of an implicit query is as follows:

```
SELECT column_list
   [BULK COLLECT] INTO PL/SQL variable list...rest of SELECT statement...
```

If you use an implicit cursor, the database performs the open, fetches, and close for you automatically; these actions are outside your programmatic control. You can, however, obtain information about the most recently executed SQL statement by examining the values in the implicit SQL cursor attributes, as explained later in this chapter.

 In the following sections, the term *implicit cursor* means a SELECT INTO statement that retrieves (or attempts to retrieve) a single row of data. In Chapter 21, I'll discuss the SELECT BULK COLLECT INTO variation that allows you to retrieve multiple rows of data with a single implicit query.

## Implicit Cursor Examples

A common use of implicit cursors is to perform a lookup based on a primary key. In the following example, I look up the title of a book based on its ISBN number:

```
DECLARE
   l_title books.title%TYPE;
BEGIN
   SELECT title
     INTO l_title
     FROM books
    WHERE isbn = '0-596-00121-5';
```

Once I have fetched the title into my local variable, l_title, I can manipulate that information—for example, by changing the variable's value, displaying the title, or passing the title on to another PL/SQL program for processing.

Here is an example of an implicit query that retrieves an entire row of information into a record:

```
DECLARE
    l_book books%ROWTYPE;
BEGIN
    SELECT *
        INTO l_book
        FROM books
        WHERE isbn = '0-596-00121-5';
```

You can also retrieve group-level information from a query. The following single-row query calculates and returns the total salary for a department. Once again, PL/SQL creates an implicit cursor for this statement:

```
SELECT SUM (salary)
    INTO department_total
    FROM employees
    WHERE department_id = 10;
```

Because PL/SQL is so tightly integrated with the Oracle database, you can also easily retrieve complex datatypes, such as objects and collections, within your implicit cursor.

All of these illustrate the use of implicit queries to retrieve a single row's worth of information. If you want to retrieve more than one row, you must use either an explicit cursor for that query or the BULK COLLECT INTO clause (discussed in Chapter 21) in your query.

As mentioned earlier, I recommend that you always "hide" single-row queries like those shown above behind a function interface. This concept was explored in detail in "Choosing Between Explicit and Implicit Cursors" on page 471.

## Error Handling with Implicit Cursors

The implicit cursor version of the SELECT statement is kind of a black box. You pass the SQL statement to the SQL engine in the database, and it returns a single row of information. You can't get inside the separate operations of the cursor, such as the open, fetch, and close stages. You are also stuck with the fact that the Oracle database automatically raises exceptions from within the implicit SELECT for two common outcomes:

- The query does not find any rows matching your criteria. In this case, the database raises the NO_DATA_FOUND exception.

- The SELECT statement returns more than one row. In this case, the database raises the TOO_MANY_ROWS exception.

When either of these scenarios occurs (as well as any other exceptions raised when executing a SQL statement), execution of the current block terminates and control is passed to the exception section. You have no control over this process flow; you cannot tell the database that with this implicit cursor you actually expect not to find any rows, and it is not an error. Instead, whenever you code an implicit cursor (and, therefore, are expecting to retrieve just one row of data), you should include an exception section that traps and handles these two exceptions (and perhaps others, depending on your application logic).

In the following block of code, I query the title of a book based on its ISBN number, but I also anticipate the possible problems that arise:

```
DECLARE
   l_isbn books.isbn%TYPE := '0-596-00121-5';
   l_title books.title%TYPE;
BEGIN
   SELECT title
     INTO l_title
     FROM books
    WHERE isbn = l_isbn;
EXCEPTION
   WHEN NO_DATA_FOUND
   THEN
      DBMS_OUTPUT.PUT_LINE ('Unknown book: ' || l_isbn);
   WHEN TOO_MANY_ROWS
   THEN
      /* This package defined in errpkg.pkg */
      errpkg.record_and_stop ('Data integrity error for: ' || l_isbn);
      RAISE;
END;
```

One of the problems with using implicit queries is that there is an awesome temptation to make assumptions about the data being retrieved, such as:

- "There can never possibly be more than one row in the book table for a given ISBN; we have constraints in place to guarantee that."

- "There will always be an entry in the book table for Steven and Bill's *Oracle PL/SQL Programming*. I don't have to worry about NO_DATA_FOUND."

The consequence of such assumptions is often that we developers neglect to include exception handlers for our implicit queries.

Now, it may well be true that today, with the current set of data, a query will return only a single row. If the nature of the data ever changes, however, you may find that the SELECT statement that formerly identified a single row now returns several. Your program will raise an exception, the exception will not be properly handled, and this could cause problems in your code.

You should, as a rule, always include handlers for NO_DATA_FOUND and TOO_MANY_ROWS whenever you write an implicit query. More generally, you should include error handlers for any errors that you can reasonably anticipate will occur in your program. The action you take when an error does arise will vary. Consider the code that retrieves a book title for an ISBN. In the function below, notice that my two error handlers act very differently: NO_DATA_FOUND returns a value, while TOO_MANY_ROWS logs the error and re-raises the exception, causing the function to actually fail. (See Chapter 6 for more information about the *errpkg.pkg* package.)

```
FUNCTION book_title (isbn_in   IN   books.isbn%TYPE
)
   RETURN books.title%TYPE
IS
   return_value   book.title%TYPE;
BEGIN
  SELECT title
    INTO return_value
    FROM books
    WHERE isbn = isbn_in;

    RETURN return_value;
EXCEPTION
   WHEN NO_DATA_FOUND
   THEN
     RETURN NULL;
   WHEN TOO_MANY_ROWS
   THEN
     errpkg.record_and_stop ('Data integrity error for: '
              || isbn_in);
     RAISE;
END;
```

Here is the reasoning behind these varied treatments: the point of my function is to return the name of a book, which can never be NULL. The function can also be used to validate an ISBN (e.g., "does a book exist for this ISBN?"). For this reason, I really don't want my function to raise an exception when no book is found for an ISBN; that may actually constitute a successful condition, depending on how the function is being used. The logic may be, "If a book does not exist with this ISBN, then it can be used for a new book," which might be coded as:

```
IF book_title ('0-596-00121-7') IS NULL
THEN ...
```

In other words, the fact that no book exists for that ISBN is not an error and should not be treated as one within my general lookup function.

On the other hand, if the query raises the TOO_MANY_ROWS exception, I have a real problem: there should never be two different books with the same ISBN number. So in this case, I need to log the error and then stop the application.

## Implicit SQL Cursor Attributes

The Oracle database allows you to access information about the most recently executed implicit cursor by referencing the special implicit cursor attributes shown in Table 15-2. The table describes the significance of the values returned by these attributes for an implicit SQL query (SELECT INTO). Because the cursors are implicit, they have no name, and therefore, the keyword "SQL" is used to denote the implicit cursor.

*Table 15-2. Implicit SQL cursor attributes for queries*

| Name | Description |
|------|-------------|
| SQL%FOUND | Returns TRUE if one row (or more in the case of BULK COLLECT INTO) was fetched successfully, FALSE otherwise (in which case the database will also raise the NO_DATA_FOUND exception). |
| SQL%NOTFOUND | Returns TRUE if a row was not fetched successfully (in which case the database will also raise the NO_DATA_FOUND exception), FALSE otherwise. |
| SQL%ROWCOUNT | Returns the number of rows fetched from the specified cursor thus far. For a SELECT INTO, this will be 1 if a row was found and 0 if the database raises the NO_DATA_FOUND exception. |
| SQL%ISOPEN | Always returns FALSE for implicit cursors because the database opens and closes implicit cursors automatically. |

All the implicit cursor attributes return NULL if no implicit cursors have yet been executed in the session. Otherwise, the values of the attributes always refer to the most recently executed SQL statement, regardless of the block or program from which the SQL statement was executed. For more information about this behavior, see "Cursor Attributes for DML Operations" on page 444. You can also run the *query_implicit_attributes.sql* script on the book's web site to test out these values yourself.

Let's make sure you understand the implications of this last point. Consider the following two programs:

```
PROCEDURE remove_from_circulation
   (isbn_in in books.isbn%TYPE)
IS
BEGIN
   DELETE FROM book WHERE isbn = isbn_in;
END;

PROCEDURE show_book_count
IS
   l_count   INTEGER;
BEGIN
   SELECT COUNT (*)
     INTO l_count
     FROM books;

   -- No such book!
   remove_from_circulation ('0-000-00000-0');
```

```
        DBMS_OUTPUT.put_line (SQL%ROWCOUNT);
    END;
```

No matter how many rows of data are in the book table, I will always see "0" displayed in the output window. Because I call remove_from_circulation after my SELECT INTO statement, the SQL%ROWCOUNT reflects the outcome of my silly, impossible DELETE statement, and not the query.

If you want to make certain that you are checking the values for the right SQL statement, you should save attribute values to local variables immediately after execution of the SQL statement. I demonstrate this technique in the following example:

```
PROCEDURE show_book_count
IS
    l_count    INTEGER;
    l_numfound PLS_INTEGER;
BEGIN
    SELECT COUNT (*)
      INTO l_count
      FROM books;

    -- Take snapshot of attribute value:
    l_numfound := SQL%ROWCOUNT;

    -- No such book!
    remove_from_circulation ('0-000-00000-0');

    -- Now I can go back to the previous attribute value.
    DBMS_OUTPUT.put_line (l_numfound);
END;
```

# Working with Explicit Cursors

An explicit cursor is a SELECT statement that is explicitly defined in the declaration section of your code and, in the process, assigned a name. There is no such thing as an explicit cursor for INSERT, UPDATE, MERGE, and DELETE statements.

With explicit cursors, you have complete control over the different PL/SQL steps involved in retrieving information from the database. You decide when to OPEN the cursor, when to FETCH records from the cursor (and therefore from the table or tables in the SELECT statement of the cursor), how many records to fetch, and when to CLOSE the cursor. Information about the current state of your cursor is available through examination of cursor attributes. This granularity of control makes the explicit cursor an invaluable tool for your development effort.

Let's look at an example. The following function determines (and returns) the level of jealousy I should feel for my friends, based on their location.

```
1    FUNCTION jealousy_level (
2       NAME_IN   IN   friends.NAME%TYPE) RETURN NUMBER
3    AS
4       CURSOR jealousy_cur
```

```
 5        IS
 6           SELECT location FROM friends
 7            WHERE NAME = UPPER (NAME_IN);
 8
 9        jealousy_rec    jealousy_cur%ROWTYPE;
10        retval          NUMBER;
11     BEGIN
12        OPEN jealousy_cur;
13
14        FETCH jealousy_cur INTO jealousy_rec;
15
16        IF jealousy_cur%FOUND
17        THEN
18           IF jealousy_rec.location = 'PUERTO RICO'
19              THEN retval := 10;
20           ELSIF jealousy_rec.location = 'CHICAGO'
21              THEN retval := 1;
22           END IF;
23        END IF;
24
25        CLOSE jealousy_cur;
26
27        RETURN retval;
28     EXCEPTION
29        WHEN OTHERS THEN
30           IF jealousy_cur%ISOPEN THEN
31              CLOSE jealousy_cur;
32           END IF;
33     END;
```

This PL/SQL block performs the following cursor actions:

| Line(s) | Action |
| --- | --- |
| 4–7 | Declare the cursor |
| 9 | Declare a record based on that cursor |
| 12 | Open the cursor |
| 14 | Fetch a single row from the cursor |
| 16 | Check a cursor attribute to determine if a row was found |
| 18–22 | Examine the contents of the fetched row to calculate my level of jealousy |
| 25 | Close the cursor |
| 28–32 | Precautionary code to make sure that I clean up after myself in case something unexpected happens |

The next few sections examine each step in detail. In these sections, the word "cursor" refers to an explicit cursor unless otherwise noted.

# Declaring Explicit Cursors

To use an explicit cursor, you must first declare it in the declaration section of your PL/SQL block or in a package, as shown here:

```
CURSOR cursor_name [ ( [ parameter [, parameter ...] ) ]
   [ RETURN return_specification ]
   IS SELECT_statement
      [FOR UPDATE [OF [column_list]]];
```

where *cursor_name* is the name of the cursor, *return_specification* is an optional RETURN clause for the cursor, and *SELECT_statement* is any valid SQL SELECT statement. You can also pass arguments into a cursor through the optional parameter list described in "Cursor Parameters" on page 489. Finally, you can specify a list of columns that you intend to update after a SELECT...FOR UPDATE statement (also discussed later). Once you have declared a cursor, you can OPEN it and FETCH from it.

Here are some examples of explicit cursor declarations:

*A cursor without parameters*

The result set of this cursor contains all the company IDs in the table:

```
CURSOR company_cur IS
   SELECT company_id FROM company;
```

*A cursor with parameters*

The result set of this cursor is the name of the company that matches the company ID passed to the cursor via the parameter:

```
CURSOR name_cur (company_id_in IN NUMBER)
IS
   SELECT name FROM company
   WHERE company_id = company_id_in;
```

*A cursor with a RETURN clause*

The result set of this cursor is all columns (in the same structure as the underlying table) from all employee records in department 10:

```
CURSOR emp_cur RETURN employees%ROWTYPE
IS
   SELECT * FROM employees
   WHERE department_id = 10;
```

## Naming your cursor

The name of an explicit cursor can be up to 30 characters in length and follows the rules for any other identifier in PL/SQL. A cursor name is not a PL/SQL variable. Instead, it is an undeclared identifier used to point to or refer to the query. You cannot assign values to a cursor, nor can you use it in an expression. You can only reference that explicit cursor by name within OPEN, FETCH, and CLOSE statements, and use it to qualify the reference to a cursor attribute.

## Declaring cursors in packages

You can declare explicit cursors in any declaration section of a PL/SQL block. This means that you can declare such cursors within packages and at the package level, as well as within a subprogram in the package. I'll explore packages in general in Chapter 18. You may want to look ahead at that chapter to acquaint yourself with the basics of packages before plunging into the topic of declaring cursors in packages.

Here are two examples:

```
PACKAGE book_info
IS
   CURSOR titles_cur
   IS
      SELECT title
        FROM books;

   CURSOR books_cur (title_filter_in IN books.title%TYPE)
      RETURN books%ROWTYPE
   IS
      SELECT *
        FROM books
       WHERE title LIKE title_filter_in;
END;
```

The first cursor, titles_cur, returns just the titles of books. The second cursor, books_cur, returns a record for each row in the book table whose title passes the filter provided as a parameter (such as "All books that contain 'PL/SQL'"). Notice that the second cursor also utilizes the RETURN clause of a cursor, in essence declaring publicly the structure of the data that each FETCH against that cursor will return.

The RETURN clause of a cursor may be made up of any of the following datatype structures:

- A record defined from a database table, using the %ROWTYPE attribute
- A record defined from another, previously defined cursor, also using the %ROWTYPE attribute
- A record defined from a programmer-defined record

The number of expressions in the cursor's select list must match the number of columns in the record identified by *table_name*%ROWTYPE, *cursor*%ROWTYPE, or *record_type*. The datatypes of the elements must also be compatible. For example, if the second element in the select list is type NUMBER, then the second column in the RETURN record cannot be type VARCHAR2 or BOOLEAN.

Before exploring the RETURN clause and its advantages, let's first address a different question: why should you bother putting cursors into packages? Why not simply declare your explicit cursors wherever you need them directly in the declaration sections of particular procedures, functions, or anonymous blocks?

The answer is simple and persuasive. By defining cursors in packages, you can more easily reuse those queries and avoid writing the same logical retrieval statement over and over again throughout your application. By implementing that query in just one place and referencing it in many locations, you make it easier to enhance and maintain that query. You will also realize some performance gains by minimizing the number of times your queries will need to be parsed.

You should also consider creating a function that returns a cursor variable, based on a REF CURSOR. The calling program can then fetch rows through the cursor variable. See "Cursor Variables and REF CURSORs" on page 496 for more information.

 If you declare cursors in packages for reuse, you need to be aware of one important factor. Data structures, including cursors, that are declared at the "package level" (not inside any particular function or procedure) maintain their values or persist for your entire session. This means that a packaged cursor will stay open until you explicitly close it or until your session ends. Cursors declared in local blocks of code close automatically when that block terminates execution.

Now let's explore this RETURN clause and why you might want to take advantage of it. One of the interesting variations on a cursor declaration within a package involves the ability to separate the cursor's header from its body. The header of a cursor, much like the header of a function, is just that information a developer needs in order to write code to work with the cursor: the cursor's name, any parameters, and the type of data being returned. The body of a cursor is its SELECT statement.

Here is a rewrite of the books_cur in the book_info package that illustrates this technique:

```
PACKAGE book_info
IS
   CURSOR books_cur (title_filter_in IN books.title%TYPE)
      RETURN books%ROWTYPE;
END;

PACKAGE BODY book_info
IS
   CURSOR books_cur (title_filter_in IN books.title%TYPE)
      RETURN books%ROWTYPE
   IS
      SELECT *
        FROM books
       WHERE title LIKE title_filter_in;
END;
```

Notice that everything up to but not including the IS keyword is the specification, while everything following the IS keyword is the body.

There are two reasons that you might want to divide your cursor as shown above:

*Hide information*

> Packaged cursors are essentially black boxes. This is advantageous to developers because they never have to code or even see the SELECT statement. They only need to know what records the cursor returns, in what order it returns them, and which columns are in the column list. They simply use it as another predefined element in their application.

*Minimize recompilation*

> If I hide the query definition inside the package body, I can make changes to the SELECT statement without making any changes to the cursor header in the package specification. This allows me to enhance, fix, and recompile my code without recompiling my specification, which means that all the programs dependent on that package will not be marked invalid and will not need to be recompiled.

## Opening Explicit Cursors

The first step in using a cursor is to define it in the declaration section. The next step is to open that cursor. The syntax for the OPEN statement is simplicity itself:

```
OPEN cursor_name [ ( argument [, argument ...] ) ];
```

where *cursor_name* is the name of the cursor you declared, and the *argument*s are the values to be passed if the cursor was declared with a parameter list.

 Oracle also offers the OPEN *cursor* FOR syntax, which is utilized in both cursor variables (see "Cursor Variables") and native dynamic SQL (see Chapter 16).

When you open a cursor, PL/SQL executes the query for that cursor. It also identifies the active set of data—that is, the rows from all involved tables that meet the criteria in the WHERE clause and join conditions. The OPEN does not actually retrieve any of these rows; that action is performed by the FETCH statement.

Regardless of when you perform the first fetch, however, the read consistency model in the Oracle database guarantees that all fetches will reflect the data as it existed when the cursor was opened. In other words, from the moment you open your cursor until the moment that cursor is closed, all data fetched through the cursor will ignore any inserts, updates, and deletes performed by any active sessions after the cursor was opened.

Furthermore, if the SELECT statement in your cursor uses a FOR UPDATE clause, all the rows identified by the query are locked when the cursor is opened. (This feature is covered in the later section, "SELECT...FOR UPDATE.")

If you try to open a cursor that is already open, you will get the following error:

```
ORA-06511: PL/SQL: cursor already open
```

You can be sure of a cursor's status by checking the %ISOPEN cursor attribute before you try to open the cursor:

```
IF NOT company_cur%ISOPEN
THEN
    OPEN company_cur;
END IF;
```

The later section, "Explicit Cursor Attributes" on page 487, explains the different cursor attributes and how to best use them in your programs.

 If you are using a cursor FOR loop, you do not need to open (or fetch from or close) the cursor explicitly. Instead, the PL/SQL engine does that for you.

## Fetching from Explicit Cursors

A SELECT statement establishes a virtual table; its return set is a series of rows determined by the WHERE clause (or lack thereof), with columns determined by the column list of the SELECT. So a cursor represents that virtual table within your PL/SQL program. In almost every situation, the point of declaring and opening a cursor is to return, or fetch, the rows of data from the cursor and then manipulate the information retrieved. PL/SQL provides a FETCH statement for this action.

The general syntax for a FETCH is:

```
FETCH cursor_name INTO record_or_variable_list;
```

where *cursor_name* is the name of the cursor from which the record is fetched, and *record_or_variable_list* is the PL/SQL data structure(s) into which the next row of the active set of records is copied. You can fetch into a record structure (declared with the %ROWTYPE attribute or TYPE declaration statement), or you can fetch into a list of one or more variables (PL/SQL variables or application-specific bind variables such as Oracle Forms items).

### Examples of explicit cursors

The following examples illustrate the variety of possible fetches:

- Fetch into a PL/SQL record:

```
DECLARE
    CURSOR company_cur is SELECT ...;
    company_rec company_cur%ROWTYPE;
BEGIN
    OPEN company_cur;
    FETCH company_cur INTO company_rec;
```

- Fetch into a variable:

```
FETCH new_balance_cur INTO new_balance_dollars;
```

- Fetch into a collection row, a variable, and an Oracle Forms bind variable:

```
FETCH emp_name_cur INTO emp_name (1), hiredate, :dept.min_salary;
```

 You should always fetch into a record that was defined with %ROW-TYPE against the cursor; avoid fetching into lists of variables. Fetching into a record usually means that you write less code and have more flexibility to change the select list without having to change the FETCH statement.

### Fetching past the last row

Once you open an explicit cursor, you can FETCH from it until there are no more records left in the active set. Oddly enough, though, you can also continue to FETCH past the last record.

In this case, PL/SQL will not raise any exceptions. It just won't actually be doing anything. Because there is nothing left to fetch, it will not alter the values of the variables in the INTO list of the FETCH. More specifically, the FETCH operation will not set those values to NULL.

You should therefore never test the values of INTO variables to determine if the FETCH against the cursor succeeded. Instead, you should check the value of the %FOUND or %NOTFOUND attributes, as explained in the upcoming section, "Explicit Cursor Attributes" on page 487.

## Column Aliases in Explicit Cursors

The SELECT statement of the cursor includes the list of columns that are returned by that cursor. As with any SELECT statement, this column list may contain either actual column names or column expressions, which are also referred to as *calculated* or *virtual columns*.

A *column alias* is an alternative name you provide to a column or column expression in a query. You may have used column aliases in SQL*Plus to improve the readability of ad hoc report output. In that situation, such aliases are completely optional. In an explicit cursor, on the other hand, column aliases are required for calculated columns when:

- You FETCH into a record declared with a %ROWTYPE declaration against that cursor, and
- You want to reference the calculated column in your program.

Consider the following query. For all companies with sales activity during 2001, the SELECT statement retrieves the company name and the total amount invoiced to that company (assume that the default date format mask for this instance is DD-MON-YYYY):

```
SELECT company_name, SUM (inv_amt)
  FROM company c, invoice i
 WHERE c.company_id = i.company_id
   AND TO_CHAR (i.invoice_date, 'YYYY') = '2001';
```

The output is:

```
        COMPANY_NAME                          SUM (INV_AMT)
        ---------------                       -------------
        ACME TURBO INC.                       1000
        WASHINGTON HAIR CO.                   25.20
```

SUM (INV_AMT) does not make a particularly attractive column header for a report, but it works well enough for a quick dip into the data as an ad hoc query. Let's now use this same query in an explicit cursor and add a column alias:

```
DECLARE
    CURSOR comp_cur IS
        SELECT c.name, SUM (inv_amt) total_sales
          FROM company C, invoice I
         WHERE C.company_id = I.company_id
           AND TO_CHAR (i.invoice_date, 'YYYY') = '2001';
    comp_rec comp_cur%ROWTYPE;
BEGIN
    OPEN comp_cur;
    FETCH comp_cur INTO comp_rec;
    ...
END;
```

Without the alias, I have no way of referencing the column within the comp_rec record structure. With the alias in place, I can get at that information just as I would any other column or expression in the query:

```
IF comp_rec.total_sales > 5000
THEN
    DBMS_OUTPUT.PUT_LINE
        (' You have exceeded your credit limit of $5000 by ' ||
         TO_CHAR (comp_rec.total_sales - 5000, '$9999'));
END IF;
```

If you fetch a row into a record declared with %ROWTYPE, the only way to access the column or column expression value is by the column name; after all, the record obtains its structure from the cursor itself.

## Closing Explicit Cursors

Early on I was taught to clean up after myself, and I tend to be a bit obsessive (albeit selectively) about this later in life. Cleaning up after oneself is an important rule to follow in programming and can be crucial when it comes to cursor management. So be sure to close a cursor when you are done with it!

Here is the syntax for a CLOSE cursor statement:

```
CLOSE cursor_name;
```

where *cursor_name* is the name of the cursor you are closing.

Here are some special considerations regarding the closing of explicit cursors:

- If you declare and open a cursor in a program, be sure to close it when you are done. Otherwise, you may have just allowed a memory leak to creep into your code—and that's not good! Strictly speaking, a cursor (like any other data structure) should be automatically closed and destroyed when it goes out of scope. In fact, in many cases PL/SQL does check for and implicitly close any open cursors at the end of a procedure call, function call, or anonymous block. However, the overhead involved in doing that is significant, so for the sake of efficiency there are cases where PL/SQL does *not* immediately check for and close cursors opened in a PL/SQL block. In addition, REF CURSORs are, by design, never closed implicitly. The one thing you can count on is that whenever the outermost PL/SQL block ends and control is returned to SQL or some other calling program, PL/SQL will at that point implicitly close any cursors (but not REF CURSORs) left open by that block or nested blocks.

 Oracle Technology Network offers a detailed analysis of how and when PL/SQL closes cursors in an article titled "Cursor reuse in PL/SQL static SQL." Nested anonymous blocks provide an example of one case in which PL/SQL does not implicitly close cursors. For an interesting discussion of this issue see Jonathan Gennick's article, "Does PL/SQL Implicitly Close Cursors?" at *http://gennick .com/open_cursors.html*.

- If you declare a cursor in a package at the package level and then open it in a particular block or program, that cursor will stay open until you explicitly close it or until your session closes. Therefore, it is extremely important that you include a CLOSE statement for any packaged cursors as soon as you are done with them (and in the exception section as well), as in the following:

```
BEGIN
   OPEN my_package.my_cursor;

   ... Do stuff with the cursor

   CLOSE my_package.my_cursor;
EXCEPTION
   WHEN OTHERS
   THEN
      IF mypackage.my_cursor%ISOPEN THEN
```

```
                CLOSE my_package.my_cursor;
            END IF;
    END;
```

- You can close a cursor only if it is currently open. Otherwise, the database will raise an INVALID_CURSOR exception. You can check a cursor's status with the %ISOPEN cursor attribute before you try to close the cursor:

```
IF company_cur%ISOPEN
THEN
    CLOSE company_cur;
END IF;
```

Attempts to close a cursor that is already closed (or was never opened) will result in an *ORA-1001: Invalid cursor.*

- If you leave too many cursors open, you may exceed the value set by the database initialization parameter, OPEN_CURSORS (the value is on a per-session basis). If this happens, you will encounter the dreaded error message *ORA-01000: maximum open cursors exceeded.*

  If you get this message, check your usage of package-based cursors to make sure they are closed when no longer needed.

## Explicit Cursor Attributes

Oracle offers four attributes (%FOUND, %NOTFOUND, %ISOPEN, %ROWCOUNT) that allow you to retrieve information about the state of your cursor. Reference these attributes using this syntax:

```
cursor%attribute
```

where *cursor* is the name of the cursor you have declared.

Table 15-3 describes the significance of the values returned by these attributes for explicit cursors.

*Table 15-3. Values returned by cursor attributes*

| Name | Description |
| --- | --- |
| cursor%FOUND | Returns TRUE if a record was fetched successfully |
| cursor%NOTFOUND | Returns TRUE if a record was not fetched successfully |
| cursor%ROWCOUNT | Returns the number of records fetched from the specified cursor at that point in time |
| cursor%ISOPEN | Returns TRUE if the specified cursor is open |

Table 15-4 shows you the attribute values you can expect to see both before and after the specified cursor operations.

*Table 15-4. Cursor attribute values*

| Operation | %FOUND | %NOTFOUND | %ISOPEN | %ROWCOUNT |
|---|---|---|---|---|
| Before OPEN | ORA-01001 raised | ORA-01001 raised | FALSE | ORA-01001 raised |
| After OPEN | NULL | NULL | TRUE | 0 |
| Before first FETCH | NULL | NULL | TRUE | 0 |
| After first FETCH | TRUE | FALSE | TRUE | 1 |
| Before subsequent FETCH(es) | TRUE | FALSE | TRUE | 1 |
| After subsequent FETCH(es) | TRUE | FALSE | TRUE | Data-dependent |
| Before last FETCH | TRUE | FALSE | TRUE | Data-dependent |
| After last FETCH | FALSE | TRUE | TRUE | Data-dependent |
| Before CLOSE | FALSE | TRUE | TRUE | Data-dependent |
| After CLOSE | Exception | Exception | FALSE | Exception |

Here are some things to keep in mind as you work with cursor attributes for explicit cursors:

- If you try to use %FOUND, %NOTFOUND, or %ROWCOUNT before the cursor is opened or after it is closed, the database will raise an INVALID_CURSOR error (ORA-01001).

- If the result set is empty after the very first FETCH, then attributes will return values as follows: %FOUND = FALSE, %NOTFOUND = TRUE, and %ROWCOUNT = 0.

- If you are using BULK COLLECT, %ROWCOUNT will return the number of rows fetched into the associated collections. For more details, see Chapter 21.

The following code showcases many of these attributes:

```
PACKAGE bookinfo_pkg
IS
   CURSOR bard_cur
      IS SELECT title, date_published
    FROM books
    WHERE UPPER(author) LIKE 'SHAKESPEARE%';
END bookinfo_pkg;

DECLARE
   bard_rec    bookinfo_pkg.bard_cur%ROWTYPE;
BEGIN
   /* Check to see if the cursor is already opened.
      This may be the case as it is a packaged cursor.
      If so, first close it and then re-open it to
      ensure a "fresh" result set.
   */
   IF bookinfo_pkg.bard_cur%ISOPEN
   THEN
      CLOSE bookinfo_pkg.bard_cur;
```

```
      END IF;

      OPEN bookinfo_pkg.bard_cur;

      -- Fetch each row, but stop when I've displayed the
      -- first five works by Shakespeare or when I have
      -- run out of rows.
      LOOP
         FETCH bookinfo_pkg.bard_cur INTO bard_rec;
         EXIT WHEN bookinfo_pkg.bard_cur%NOTFOUND
              OR bookinfo_pkg.bard_cur%ROWCOUNT > 5;
         DBMS_OUTPUT.put_line (
              bookinfo_pkg.bard_cur%ROWCOUNT
           || ') '
           || bard_rec.title
           || ', published in '
           || TO_CHAR (bard_rec.date_published, 'YYYY')
         );
      END LOOP;

      CLOSE bookinfo_pkg.bard_cur;
   END;
```

## Cursor Parameters

In this book you've already seen examples of the use of parameters with procedures and functions. Parameters provide a way to pass information into and out of a module. Used properly, parameters improve the usefulness and flexibility of modules.

PL/SQL allows you to pass parameters into cursors. The same rationale for using parameters in modules applies to parameters for cursors:

*Makes the cursor more reusable*

Instead of hardcoding a value into the WHERE clause of a query to select particular information, you can use a parameter and then pass different values to the WHERE clause each time a cursor is opened.

*Avoids scoping problems*

When you pass parameters instead of hardcoding values, the result set for that cursor is not tied to a specific variable in a program or block. If your program has nested blocks, you can define the cursor at a higher-level (enclosing) block and use it in any of the subblocks with variables defined in those local blocks.

You can specify as many cursor parameters as you need. When you OPEN the cursor, you need to include an argument in the parameter list for each parameter, except for trailing parameters that have default values.

When should you parameterize your cursor? I apply the same rule of thumb to cursors as to procedures and functions; if I am going to use the cursor in more than one place with different values for the same WHERE clause, I should create a parameter for the cursor.

Let's take a look at the difference between parameterized and unparameterized cursors. First, here is a cursor without any parameters:

```
CURSOR joke_cur IS
   SELECT name, category, last_used_date
     FROM jokes;
```

The result set of this cursor is all the rows in the joke table. If I just wanted to retrieve all jokes in the HUSBAND category, I would need to add a WHERE clause:

```
CURSOR joke_cur IS
   SELECT name, category, last_used_date
     FROM jokes
    WHERE category = 'HUSBAND';
```

I didn't use a cursor parameter to accomplish this task, nor did I need to. The joke_cur cursor now retrieves only those jokes about husbands. That's all well and good, but what if I also wanted to see light-bulb jokes and then chicken-and-egg jokes and finally, as my 10-year-old niece would certainly demand, all my knock-knock jokes?

### Generalizing cursors with parameters

I really don't want to write a separate cursor for each category—that is definitely not a data-driven approach to programming. Instead, I would much rather be able to change the joke cursor so that it can accept different categories and return the appropriate rows. The best (though not the only) way to do this is with a cursor parameter:

```
PROCEDURE explain_joke (main_category_in IN joke_category.category_id%TYPE)
IS
   /*
   || Cursor with parameter list consisting of a single
   || string parameter.
   */
   CURSOR joke_cur (category_in IN VARCHAR2)
   IS
      SELECT name, category, last_used_date
        FROM joke
       WHERE category = UPPER (category_in);

   joke_rec joke_cur%ROWTYPE;

BEGIN
   /* Now when I open the cursor, I also pass the argument */
   OPEN joke_cur (main_category_in);
   FETCH joke_cur INTO joke_rec;
```

I added a parameter list after the cursor name and before the IS keyword. I took out the hardcoded "HUSBAND" and replaced it with "UPPER (category_in)" so that I could enter "HUSBAND", "husband", or "HuSbAnD" and the cursor would still work. Now when I open the cursor, I specify the value I want to pass as the category by including that value (which can be a literal, a constant, or an expression) inside parentheses. At the moment the cursor is opened, the SELECT statement is parsed and bound using the specified value for category_in. The result set is identified, and the cursor is ready for fetching.

### Opening cursors with parameters

I can OPEN that same cursor with any category I like. Now I don't have to write a separate cursor to accommodate this requirement:

```
OPEN joke_cur (jokes_pkg.category);
OPEN joke_cur ('husband');
OPEN joke_cur ('politician');
OPEN joke_cur (jokes_pkg.relation || '-IN-LAW');
```

The most common place to use a parameter in a cursor is in the WHERE clause, but you can make reference to it anywhere in the SELECT statement, as shown here:

```
DECLARE
    CURSOR joke_cur (category_in IN VARCHAR2)
    IS
        SELECT name, category_in, last_used_date
          FROM joke
         WHERE category = UPPER (category_in);
```

Instead of returning the category from the table, I simply pass back the category_in parameter in the select list. The result will be the same either way because my WHERE clause restricts categories to the parameter value.

### Scope of cursor parameters

The scope of the cursor parameter is confined to that cursor. You cannot refer to the cursor parameter outside of the SELECT statement associated with the cursor. The following PL/SQL fragment will not compile because the program_name identifier is not a local variable in the block. Instead, it is a formal parameter for the cursor and is defined only inside the cursor:

```
DECLARE
    CURSOR scariness_cur (program_name VARCHAR2)
    IS
        SELECT SUM (scary_level) total_scary_level
          FROM tales_from_the_crypt
         WHERE prog_name = program_name;
BEGIN
    program_name := 'THE BREATHING MUMMY'; /* Illegal reference */
    OPEN scariness_cur (program_name);
    ...
    CLOSE scariness_cur;
END;
```

### Cursor parameter modes

The syntax for cursor parameters is very similar to that of procedures and functions, with the restriction that a cursor parameter can be an IN parameter only. You cannot specify OUT or IN OUT modes for cursor parameters. The OUT and IN OUT modes are used to pass values out of a procedure through that parameter. This doesn't make sense for a cursor. Values cannot be passed back out of a cursor through the parameter list. Information is retrieved from a cursor only by fetching a record and copying values from the column list with an INTO clause. (See Chapter 17 for more information on the parameter mode.)

### Default values for parameters

Cursor parameters can be assigned default values. Here is an example of a parameterized cursor with a default value:

```
CURSOR emp_cur (emp_id_in NUMBER := 0)
IS
   SELECT employee_id, emp_name
     FROM employee
    WHERE employee_id = emp_id_in;
```

So if Joe Smith's employee ID is 1001, the following statements would set my_emp_id to 1001 and my_emp_name to JOE SMITH:

```
OPEN emp_cur (1001);
FETCH emp_cur INTO my_emp_id, my_emp_name;
```

Because the emp_id_in parameter has a default value, I can also open and fetch from the cursor without specifying a value for the parameter. If I do not specify a value for the parameter, the cursor uses the default value.

## SELECT...FOR UPDATE

When you issue a SELECT statement against the database to query some records, no locks are placed on the selected rows. In general, this is a wonderful feature because the number of records locked at any given time is kept to the absolute minimum: only those records that have been changed but not yet committed are locked. Even then, others are able to read those records as they appeared before the change (the "before image" of the data).

There are times, however, when you will want to lock a set of records even before you change them in your program. Oracle offers the FOR UPDATE clause of the SELECT statement to perform this locking.

When you issue a SELECT...FOR UPDATE statement, the database automatically obtains row-level locks on all the rows identified by the SELECT statement, holding the records "for your changes only" as you move through the rows retrieved by the cursor. It's as if you've issued an UPDATE statement against the rows, but you haven't—you've merely SELECTed them. No one else will be able to change any of these records until you perform a ROLLBACK or a COMMIT—but other sessions can still read the data.

Here are two examples of the FOR UPDATE clause used in a cursor:

```
CURSOR toys_cur IS
   SELECT name, manufacturer, preference_level, sell_at_yardsale_flag
     FROM my_sons_collection
    WHERE hours_used = 0
      FOR UPDATE;

CURSOR fall_jobs_cur IS
   SELECT task, expected_hours, tools_required, do_it_yourself_flag
     FROM winterize
    WHERE year_of_task = TO_CHAR (SYSDATE, 'YYYY')
      FOR UPDATE OF task;
```

The first cursor uses the unqualified FOR UPDATE clause, while the second cursor qualifies the FOR UPDATE with a column name from the query.

You can use the FOR UPDATE clause in a SELECT against multiple tables. In this case, rows in a table are locked only if the FOR UPDATE clause references a column in that table. In the following example, the FOR UPDATE clause does not result in any locked rows in the winterize table:

```
CURSOR fall_jobs_cur
IS
   SELECT w.task, w.expected_hours,
          w.tools_required,
          w.do_it_yourself_flag
     FROM winterize w, husband_config hc
    WHERE w.year_of_task = TO_CHAR (SYSDATE, 'YYYY')
      AND w.task_id = hc.task_id
    FOR UPDATE OF hc.max_procrastination_allowed;
```

The FOR UPDATE OF clause mentions only the max_procrastination_allowed column; no columns in the winterize table are listed. As a result, no rows in the winterize table will be locked. It is important to minimize the amount of data you lock, so that you decrease the impact you have on other sessions. Other sessions may be blocked by your locks, waiting for you to complete your transaction so they can proceed with their own DML statements.

If you simply state FOR UPDATE in the query and do not include one or more columns after the OF keyword, the database will then lock all identified rows across all tables listed in the FROM clause.

Furthermore, you do not have to actually UPDATE or DELETE any records just because you issue a SELECT...FOR UPDATE statement—that act simply states your intention to be able to do so (and prevents others from doing the same).

Finally, you can append the optional keyword NOWAIT to the FOR UPDATE clause to tell the database not to wait if the table has been locked by another user. In this case, control will be returned immediately to your program so that you can perform other work or simply wait for a period of time before trying again. You can also append WAIT to specify the maximum number of seconds the database should wait to obtain the lock. If no wait behavior is specified, then your session will be blocked until the table is available. For remote objects, the database initialization parameter, DISTRIBUTED_LOCK_TIMEOUT, is used to set the limit.

## Releasing Locks with COMMIT

As soon as a cursor with a FOR UPDATE clause is OPENed, all rows identified in the result set of the cursor are locked and remain locked until your session or your code explicitly issues either a COMMIT or a ROLLBACK. When either of these actions occurs, the locks on the rows are released. As a result, you cannot execute another FETCH against a FOR UPDATE cursor after you COMMIT or ROLLBACK. You will have lost your position in the cursor.

Consider the following program, which assigns winterization chores:[1]

```
DECLARE
    /* All the jobs in the Fall to prepare for the Winter */
    CURSOR fall_jobs_cur
    IS
       SELECT task, expected_hours, tools_required, do_it_yourself_flag
         FROM winterize
        WHERE year = TO_NUMBER (TO_CHAR (SYSDATE, 'YYYY'))
          AND completed_flag = 'NOTYET' FOR UPDATE;
BEGIN
    /* For each job fetched by the cursor... */
    FOR job_rec IN fall_jobs_cur
    LOOP
       IF job_rec.do_it_yourself_flag = 'YOUCANDOIT'
       THEN
          /*
          || I have found my next job. Assign it to myself (like someone
          || else is going to do it!) and then commit the changes.
          */
          UPDATE winterize SET responsible = 'STEVEN'
           WHERE task = job_rec.task
             AND year = TO_NUMBER (TO_CHAR (SYSDATE, 'YYYY'));
          COMMIT;
       END IF;
    END LOOP;
END;
```

Suppose this loop finds its first YOUCANDOIT job. It then commits an assignment of a job to STEVEN. When it tries to FETCH the next record, the program raises the following exception:

```
ORA-01002: fetch out of sequence
```

---

1. Caveat: I don't want to set false expectations, especially with my wife. The code in this block is purely an example. In reality, I set the max_procrastination_allowed to five years and let my house decay until I can afford to pay someone else to do something, or my wife does it, or she gives me an ultimatum. Now you know why I decided to write books and write software, rather than do things in the "real world."

If you ever need to execute a COMMIT or ROLLBACK as you FETCH records from a SELECT FOR UPDATE cursor, you should include code (such as a loop EXIT or other conditional logic) to halt any further fetches from the cursor.

## The WHERE CURRENT OF Clause

PL/SQL provides the WHERE CURRENT OF clause for both UPDATE and DELETE statements inside a cursor. This clause allows you to easily make changes to the most recently fetched row of data.

To update columns in the most recently fetched row, specify:

```
UPDATE table_name
   SET set_clause
 WHERE CURRENT OF cursor_name;
```

To delete the row from the database for the most recently fetched record, specify:

```
DELETE
  FROM table_name
 WHERE CURRENT OF cursor_name;
```

Notice that the WHERE CURRENT OF clause references the cursor, not the record into which the next fetched row is deposited.

The most important advantage to using WHERE CURRENT OF to change the last row fetched is that you do not have to code in two (or more) places the criteria used to uniquely identify a row in a table. Without WHERE CURRENT OF, you would need to repeat the WHERE clause of your cursor in the WHERE clause of the associated UPDATEs and DELETEs. As a result, if the table structure changed in a way that affected the construction of the primary key, you would have to update each SQL statement to support this change. If you use WHERE CURRENT OF, on the other hand, you modify only the WHERE clause of the SELECT statement.

This might seem like a relatively minor issue, but it is one of many areas in your code where you can leverage subtle features in PL/SQL to minimize code redundancies. Utilization of WHERE CURRENT OF, %TYPE and %ROWTYPE declaration attributes, cursor FOR loops, local modularization, and other PL/SQL language constructs can significantly reduce the pain of maintaining your Oracle-based applications.

Let's see how this clause would improve the example in the previous section. In the jobs cursor FOR loop, I want to UPDATE the record that was currently FETCHed by the cursor. I do this in the UPDATE statement by repeating the same WHERE used in the cursor because "(task, year)" makes up the primary key of this table:

```
WHERE task = job_rec.task
  AND year = TO_CHAR (SYSDATE, 'YYYY');
```

This is a less than ideal situation, as explained above: I have coded the same logic in two places, and this code must be kept synchronized. It would be so much more convenient and natural to be able to code the equivalent of the following statements:

- "Delete the row I just fetched."
- "Update these columns in that row I just fetched."

A perfect fit for WHERE CURRENT OF! The next version of my winterization program uses this clause. I have also switched from a FOR loop to a simple loop because I want to exit conditionally from the loop (possible but not recommended with a FOR loop):

```
DECLARE
   CURSOR fall_jobs_cur IS SELECT ... same as before ... ;
   job_rec fall_jobs_cur%ROWTYPE;
BEGIN
   OPEN fall_jobs_cur;
   LOOP
      FETCH fall_jobs_cur INTO job_rec;

      EXIT WHEN fall_jobs_cur%NOTFOUND;

      IF job_rec.do_it_yourself_flag = 'YOUCANDOIT'
      THEN
         UPDATE winterize SET responsible = 'STEVEN'
          WHERE CURRENT OF fall_jobs_cur;
         COMMIT;
         EXIT;
      END IF;
   END LOOP;
   CLOSE fall_jobs_cur;
END;
```

# Cursor Variables and REF CURSORs

A cursor variable is a variable that points to or references an underlying cursor. Unlike an explicit cursor, which names the PL/SQL work area for the result set, a cursor variable is a reference to that work area. Explicit and implicit cursors are static in that they are tied to specific queries. The cursor variable can be opened for any query, even for different queries within a single program execution.

The most important benefit of the cursor variable is that it provides a mechanism for passing results of queries (the rows returned by fetches against a cursor) between different PL/SQL programs—even between client and server PL/SQL programs. Prior to PL/SQL Release 2.3, you would have had to fetch all data from the cursor, store it in PL/SQL variables (perhaps a collection), and then pass those variables as arguments. With cursor variables, you simply pass the reference to that cursor. This improves performance and streamlines your code.

It also means that the cursor is, in effect, shared among the programs that have access to the cursor variable. In a client-server environment, for example, a program on the client side could open and start fetching from the cursor variable, and then pass that variable as an argument to a stored procedure on the server. This stored program could then continue fetching and pass control back to the client program to close the cursor.

You can also perform the same steps between different stored programs on the same or different database instances.

This process, shown in Figure 15-2, offers dramatic new possibilities for data sharing and cursor management in PL/SQL programs.

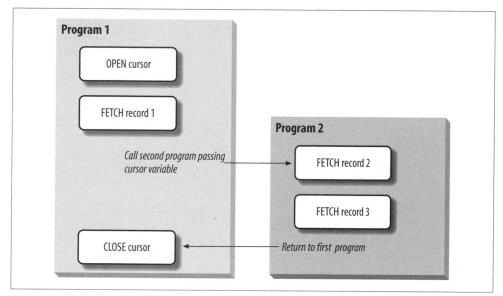

Figure 15-2. *Referencing a cursor variable across two programs*

## Why Cursor Variables?

Cursor variables allow you to do the following:

- Associate a cursor variable with different queries at different times in your program execution. In other words, a single cursor variable can be used to fetch from different result sets.

- Pass a cursor variable as an argument to a procedure or function. You can, in essence, share the results of a cursor by passing the reference to that result set.

- Employ the full functionality of static PL/SQL cursors for cursor variables. You can OPEN, CLOSE, and FETCH with cursor variables within your PL/SQL programs. You can also reference the standard cursor attributes—%ISOPEN, %FOUND, %NOTFOUND, and %ROWCOUNT—for cursor variables.

- Assign the contents of one cursor (and its result set) to another cursor variable. Because the cursor variable is a variable, it can be used in assignment operations. There are restrictions on referencing this kind of variable, however, as I'll discuss later in this chapter.

## Similarities to Static Cursors

One of the key design requirements for cursor variables was that, when possible, the semantics used to manage cursor objects would be the same as that of static cursors. While the declaration of a cursor variable and the syntax for opening it are enhanced, the following cursor operations for cursor variables are the same as for static cursors:

*The CLOSE statement*

In the following example, I declare a REF CURSOR type and a cursor variable based on that type. Then I close the cursor variable using the same syntax as for a static cursor:

```
DECLARE
    TYPE var_cur_type IS REF CURSOR;
    var_cur var_cur_type;
BEGIN
    OPEN var_cur FOR ...
    ...
    CLOSE var_cur;
END;
```

*Cursor attributes*

You can use any of the four cursor attributes with exactly the same syntax as for a static cursor. The rules governing the use and values returned by those attributes match those of explicit cursors. If I have declared a variable cursor as in the previous example, I could use all the cursor attributes as follows:

```
var_cur%ISOPEN
var_cur%FOUND
var_cur%NOTFOUND
var_cur%ROWCOUNT
```

*Fetching from the cursor variable*

You use the same FETCH syntax when fetching from a cursor variable into local PL/SQL data structures. There are, however, additional rules applied by PL/SQL to make sure that the data structures of the cursor variable's row (the set of values returned by the cursor object) match those of the data structures to the right of the INTO keyword. These rules are discussed in "Rules for Cursor Variables" on page 504.

Because the syntax for these aspects of cursor variables is the same as for the already familiar explicit cursors, the following sections will focus on features that are unique to cursor variables.

## Declaring REF CURSOR Types

Just as with a collection or a programmer-defined record, you must perform two distinct declaration steps in order to create a cursor variable:

1. Create a referenced cursor TYPE.
2. Declare the actual cursor variable based on that type.

The syntax for creating a referenced cursor type is as follows:

```
TYPE cursor_type_name IS REF CURSOR [ RETURN return_type ];
```

where *cursor_type_name* is the name of the type of cursor and *return_type* is the RE-TURN data specification for the cursor type. The *return_type* can be any of the data structures valid for a normal cursor RETURN clause, and is defined using the %ROW-TYPE attribute or by referencing a previously defined record type.

Notice that the RETURN clause is optional with the REF CURSOR type statement. Both of the following declarations are valid:

```
TYPE company_curtype IS REF CURSOR RETURN company%ROWTYPE;
TYPE generic_curtype IS REF CURSOR;
```

The first form of the REF CURSOR statement is called a *strong type* because it attaches a record type (or row type) to the cursor variable type at the moment of declaration. Any cursor variable declared using that type can only FETCH INTO data structures that match the specified record type. The advantage of a strong type is that the compiler can determine whether or not the developer has properly matched up the cursor variable's FETCH statements with its cursor object's query list.

The second form of the REF CURSOR statement, in which the RETURN clause is missing, is called a *weak type*. This cursor variable type is not associated with any record data structures. Cursor variables declared without the RETURN clause can be used in more flexible ways than the strong type. They can be used with any query, with any record type structure, and can vary even within the course of a single program.

Starting with Oracle9*i* Database, Oracle provides a predefined weak REF CURSOR type named SYS_REFCURSOR. You no longer need to define your own weak type; just use Oracle's:

```
DECLARE
    my_cursor SYS_REFCURSOR;
```

## Declaring Cursor Variables

The syntax for declaring a cursor variable is:

```
cursor_name cursor_type_name;
```

where *cursor_name* is the name of the cursor, and *cursor_type_name* is the name of the type of cursor previously defined with a TYPE statement.

Here is an example of the creation of a cursor variable:

```
DECLARE
    /* Create a cursor type for sports cars. */
    TYPE sports_car_cur_type IS REF CURSOR RETURN car%ROWTYPE;
```

```
    /* Create a cursor variable for sports cars. */
    sports_car_cur sports_car_cur_type;
BEGIN
    ...
END;
```

It is important to distinguish between declaring a cursor variable and creating an actual cursor object—the result set identified by the cursor SQL statement. A constant is nothing more than a value, whereas a variable points to its value. Similarly, a static cursor acts as a constant, whereas a cursor variable references or points to a cursor object. These distinctions are shown in Figure 15-3. Notice that two different cursor variables in different programs are both referring to the same cursor object.

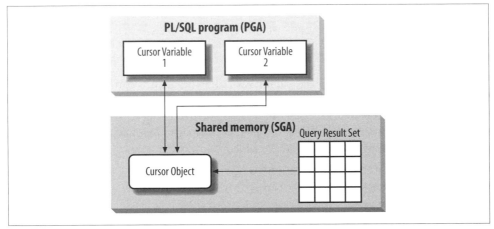

*Figure 15-3. The referencing character of cursor variables*

Declaration of a cursor variable does not create a cursor object. To do that, you must use the OPEN FOR syntax to create a new cursor object and assign it to the variable.

## Opening Cursor Variables

You assign a value (the cursor object) to a cursor variable when you OPEN the cursor. So the syntax for the traditional OPEN statement allows for cursor variables to accept a SELECT statement after the FOR clause, as shown below:

```
    OPEN cursor_name FOR select_statement;
```

where *cursor_name* is the name of a cursor variable, and *select_statement* is a SQL SELECT statement.

For strong REF CURSOR type cursor variables, the structure of the SELECT statement (the number and datatypes of the columns) must match or be compatible with the structure specified in the RETURN clause of the TYPE statement. Figure 15-4 shows an example of the kind of compatibility required. "Rules for Cursor Variables" on page 504 contains the full set of compatibility rules.

```
DECLARE
    TYPE emp_curtype IS
        REF CURSOR RETURN emp%ROWTYPE;
    emp_curvar emp_curtype;
BEGIN
    OPEN emp_curvar FOR
                SELECT * FROM emp;
END;
```

*Figure 15-4. Compatible REF CURSOR rowtype and select list*

If *cursor_name* is a cursor variable defined with a weak REF CURSOR type, you can OPEN it for any query, with any structure. In the following example, I open (assign a value to) the cursor variable three times, with three different queries:

```
DECLARE
    TYPE emp_curtype IS REF CURSOR;
    emp_curvar emp_curtype;
BEGIN
    OPEN emp_curvar FOR SELECT * FROM employees;
    OPEN emp_curvar FOR SELECT employee_id FROM employees;
    OPEN emp_curvar FOR SELECT company_id, name FROM company;
END;
```

That last OPEN didn't even have anything to do with the employee table!

If the cursor variable has not yet been assigned to any cursor object, the OPEN FOR statement implicitly creates an object for the variable. If at the time of the OPEN, the cursor variable is already pointing to a cursor object, OPEN FOR does not create a new object. Instead, it reuses the existing object and attaches a new query to that object. The cursor object is maintained separately from the cursor or query itself.

> If you associate a new result set with a cursor variable that was previously used in an OPEN FOR statement and you did not explicitly close that cursor variable, then the underlying cursor remains *open*. You should always explicitly close your cursor variables before repurposing them with another result set.

## Fetching from Cursor Variables

As mentioned earlier, the syntax for a FETCH statement using a cursor variable is the same as that for static cursors:

```
FETCH cursor_variable_name INTO record_name;
FETCH cursor_variable_name INTO variable_name, variable_name ...;
```

When the cursor variable is declared with a strong REF CURSOR type, the PL/SQL compiler makes sure that the data structures listed after the INTO keyword are compatible with the structure of the query associated with the cursor variable.

If the cursor variable is of the weak REF CURSOR type, the PL/SQL compiler cannot perform the same kind of check it performs for a strong REF CURSOR type. Such a cursor variable can FETCH into any data structures because the REF CURSOR type is not identified with a rowtype at the time of declaration. At compile time, there is no way to know which cursor object (and associated SQL statement) will be assigned to that variable.

Consequently, the check for compatibility must happen at runtime, when the FETCH is about to be executed. At this point, if the query and the INTO clause do not structurally match, then the PL/SQL runtime engine will raise the predefined ROWTYPE_MISMATCH exception. Note that PL/SQL will use implicit conversions if necessary and possible.

### Handling the ROWTYPE_MISMATCH exception

You can trap the ROWTYPE_MISMATCH exception and then attempt to FETCH from the cursor variable using a different INTO clause. But even though you are executing the second FETCH statement in your program, you will still retrieve the first row in the result set of the cursor object's query. This functionality comes in handy for weak REF CURSOR types, which can be easily defined using the predefined SYS_REFCURSOR type.

In the following example, a centralized real estate database stores information about properties in a variety of tables: one for homes, another for commercial properties, and so on. There is also a single, central table that stores addresses and building types (home, commercial, etc.). I use a single procedure to open a weak REF CURSOR variable for the appropriate table based on the street address. Each individual real estate office can then call that procedure to scan through the matching properties. Here are the steps:

1. Create the procedure. Notice that the mode of the cursor variable parameter is IN OUT:

```
/* File on web: rowtype_mismatch.sql */
PROCEDURE open_site_list
   (address_in IN VARCHAR2,
    site_cur_inout IN OUT SYS_REFCURSOR)
IS
   home_type CONSTANT PLS_INTEGER := 1;
   commercial_type CONSTANT PLS_INTEGER := 2;

   /* A static cursor to get building type. */
   CURSOR site_type_cur IS
      SELECT site_type FROM property_master
       WHERE address = address_in;
   site_type_rec site_type_cur%ROWTYPE;

BEGIN
   /* Get the building type for this address. */
   OPEN site_type_cur;
```

```
    FETCH site_type_cur INTO site_type_rec;
    CLOSE site_type_cur;

    /* Now use the site type to select from the right table.*/
    IF site_type_rec.site_type = home_type
    THEN
        /* Use the home properties table. */
        OPEN site_cur_inout FOR
            SELECT * FROM home_properties
            WHERE address LIKE '%' || address_in || '%';

    ELSIF site_type_rec.site_type = commercial_type
    THEN
        /* Use the commercial properties table. */
        OPEN site_cur_inout FOR
            SELECT * FROM commercial_properties
            WHERE address LIKE '%' || address_in || '%';
    END IF;
  END open_site_list;
```

2. Now that I have my open procedure, I can use it to scan properties.

In the following example, I pass in the address and then try to fetch from the cursor, assuming a home property. If the address actually identifies a commercial property, PL/SQL will raise the ROWTYPE_MISMATCH exception on account of the incompatible record structures. The exception section then fetches again, this time into a commercial building record, and the scan is complete.

```
/* File on web: rowtype_mismatch.sql */
DECLARE
    /* Declare a cursor variable. */
    building_curvar    sys_refcursor;

    address_string     property_master.address%TYPE;

    /* Define record structures for two different tables. */
    home_rec           home_properties%ROWTYPE;
    commercial_rec     commercial_properties%ROWTYPE;
BEGIN
    /* Retrieve the address from cookie or other source. */
    address_string := current_address ();

    /* Assign a query to the cursor variable based on the address. */
    open_site_list (address_string, building_curvar);

    /* Give it a try! Fetch a row into the home record. */
    FETCH building_curvar
    INTO home_rec;

    /* If I got here, the site was a home, so display it. */
    show_home_site (home_rec);
EXCEPTION
    /* If the first record was not a home... */
    WHEN ROWTYPE_MISMATCH
    THEN
```

```
        /* Fetch that same 1st row into the commercial record. */
        FETCH building_curvar
        INTO commercial_rec;

        /* Show the commercial site info. */
        show_commercial_site (commercial_rec);
    END;
```

# Rules for Cursor Variables

This section examines in more detail the rules and issues regarding the use of cursor variables in your programs. These include rowtype matching rules, cursor variable aliases, and scoping issues.

Remember that the cursor variable is a reference to a cursor object or query in the database. It is not the object itself. A cursor variable is said to refer to a given query if either of the following is true:

- An OPEN statement FOR that query was executed with the cursor variable.
- A cursor variable was assigned a value from another cursor variable that refers to that query.

You can perform assignment operations with cursor variables and also pass these variables as arguments to procedures and functions. In order to perform such actions between cursor variables (and to bind a cursor variable to a parameter), the different cursor variables must follow a set of compile-time and runtime rowtype matching rules.

### Compile-time rowtype matching rules

These are the rules that PL/SQL follows at compile time:

- Two cursor variables (including procedure parameters) are compatible for assignments and argument passing if any of the following are true:
  —Both variables (or parameters) are of a strong REF CURSOR type with the same *rowtype_name*.
  —Both variables (or parameters) are of a weak REF CURSOR type, regardless of the *rowtype_name*.
  —One variable (or parameter) is of any strong REF CURSOR type, and the other is of any weak REF CURSOR type.
- A cursor variable (or parameter) of a strong REF CURSOR type may be OPEN FOR a query that returns a rowtype that is structurally equal to the *rowtype_name* in the original type declaration.
- A cursor variable (or parameter) of a weak REF CURSOR type may be OPEN FOR any query. The FETCH from such a variable is allowed INTO any list of variables or record structure.

If either of the cursor variables is of the weak REF CURSOR type, then the PL/SQL compiler cannot really validate whether the two different cursor variables will be compatible. That will happen at runtime; the rules are covered in the next section.

### Runtime rowtype matching rules

These are the rules that PL/SQL follows at runtime:

- A cursor variable (or parameter) of a weak REF CURSOR type may be made to refer to a query of any rowtype regardless of the query or cursor object to which it may have referred earlier.

- A cursor variable (or parameter) of a strong REF CURSOR type may be made to refer only to a query that matches structurally the *rowtype_name* of the RETURN clause of the REF CURSOR type declaration.

- Two records (or lists of variables) are considered structurally matching with implicit conversions if both of the following are true:
  - The number of fields is the same in both records (or lists).
  - For each field in one record (or variable in one list), a corresponding field in the second list (or a variable in the second list) has the same PL/SQL datatype, or one that can be converted implicitly by PL/SQL to match the first.

- For a cursor variable (or parameter) used in a FETCH statement, the query associated with the cursor variable must structurally match (with implicit conversions) the record or list of variables of the INTO clause of the FETCH statement. This same rule is used for static cursors.

### Cursor variable aliases

If you assign one cursor variable to another cursor variable, they become *aliases* for the same cursor object; they share the reference to the cursor object (result set of the cursor's query). Any action taken against the cursor object through one variable is also available to and reflected in the other variable.

This anonymous block illustrates the way cursor aliases work:

```
1    DECLARE
2       TYPE curvar_type IS REF CURSOR;
3       curvar1 curvar_type;
4       curvar2 curvar_type;
5       story fairy_tales%ROWTYPE;
6    BEGIN
7       OPEN curvar1 FOR SELECT * FROM fairy_tales;
8       curvar2 := curvar1;
9       FETCH curvar1 INTO story;
10      FETCH curvar2 INTO story;
11      CLOSE curvar2;
12      FETCH curvar1 INTO story;
13   END;
```

The following table provides an explanation of the cursor variable actions:

| Line(s) | Description |
| --- | --- |
| 2–5 | Declare my weak REF CURSOR type and cursor variables. |
| 7 | Creates a cursor object and assigns it to curvar1 by opening a cursor for that cursor variable. |
| 8 | Assigns that same cursor object to the second cursor variable, curvar2. (Now I have two cursor variables that can be used to manipulate the same result set!) |
| 9 | Fetches the first record using the curvar1 variable. |
| 10 | Fetches the second record using the curvar2 variable. (Notice that it doesn't matter which of the two variables you use. The pointer to the current record resides with the cursor object, not with any particular variable.) |
| 11 | Closes the cursor object referencing curvar2. |
| 12 | Will raise the INVALID_CURSOR exception when I try to fetch again from the cursor object. (When I closed the cursor through curvar2, it also closed it as far as curvar1 was concerned.) |

Any change of state in a cursor object will be seen through any cursor variable that is an alias for that cursor object.

### Scope of cursor object

The scope of a cursor variable is the same as that of a static cursor: the PL/SQL block in which the variable is declared. The scope of the cursor object to which a cursor variable is assigned, however, is a different matter.

Once an OPEN FOR creates a cursor object, that cursor object remains accessible as long as at least one active cursor variable refers to that cursor object. This means that you can create a cursor object in one scope (PL/SQL block) and assign it to a cursor variable. Then, by assigning that cursor variable to another cursor variable with a different scope, the cursor object remains accessible even if the original cursor variable has gone out of scope.

In the following example, I use nested blocks to demonstrate how the cursor object can persist outside of the scope in which it was originally created:

```
DECLARE
   curvar1 SYS_REFCURSOR;
      do_you_get_it VARCHAR2(100);
BEGIN
   /*
   || Nested block which creates the cursor object and
   || assigns it to the curvar1 cursor variable.
   */
   DECLARE
      curvar2 SYS_REFCURSOR;
   BEGIN
      OPEN curvar2 FOR SELECT punch_line FROM joke;
      curvar1 := curvar2;
   END;
   /*
```

```
            || The curvar2 cursor variable is no longer active,
            || but "the baton" has been passed to curvar1, which
            || does exist in the enclosing block. I can therefore
            || fetch from the cursor object, through this other
            || cursor variable.
            */
            FETCH curvar1 INTO do_you_get_it;
            CLOSE curvar1;
        END;
```

## Passing Cursor Variables as Arguments

You can pass a cursor variable as an argument in a call to a procedure or a function. When you use a cursor variable in the parameter list of a program, you need to specify the mode of the parameter and the datatype (the REF CURSOR type).

### Identifying the REF CURSOR type

In your program header, you must identify the REF CURSOR type of your cursor variable parameter. To do this, that cursor type must already be defined.

If you are creating a local module within another program (see Chapter 17 for information about local modules), you can define the cursor type in the same program. It will then be available for the parameter. This approach is shown here:

```
DECLARE
    /* Define the REF CURSOR type. */
    TYPE curvar_type IS REF CURSOR RETURN company%ROWTYPE;

    /* Reference it in the parameter list. */
    PROCEDURE open_query (curvar_out OUT curvar_type)
    IS
        local_cur curvar_type;
    BEGIN
        OPEN local_cur FOR SELECT * FROM company;
        curvar_out := local_cur;
    END;
BEGIN
    ...
END;
```

If you are creating a standalone procedure or function, then the only way you can reference a preexisting REF CURSOR type is by placing that TYPE statement in a package. All variables declared in the specification of a package act as globals within your session, so you can then reference this cursor type using the dot notation shown in the second example:

- Create the package with a REF CURSOR type declaration:

```
PACKAGE company
IS
    /* Define the REF CURSOR type. */
```

```
    TYPE curvar_type IS REF CURSOR RETURN company%ROWTYPE;
END package;
```

- In a standalone procedure, reference the REF CURSOR type by prefacing the name of the cursor type with the name of the package:

```
PROCEDURE open_company (curvar_out OUT company.curvar_type) IS
BEGIN
   ...
END;
```

### Setting the parameter mode

Just like other parameters, a cursor variable argument can have one of the following three modes:

*IN*
    Can only be read by the program

*OUT*
    Can only be written to by the program

*IN OUT*
    Can be read or written to by the program

Remember that the value of a cursor variable is the reference to the cursor object, not the state of the cursor object. In other words, the value of a cursor variable does not change after you fetch from or close a cursor.

Only two operations, in fact, may change the value of a cursor variable (that is, the cursor object to which the variable points):

- An assignment to the cursor variable
- An OPEN FOR statement

If the cursor variable is already pointing to a cursor object, the OPEN FOR doesn't actually change the reference. It simply changes the query associated with the object.

The FETCH and CLOSE operations affect the state of the cursor object, but not the reference to the cursor object itself, which is the value of the cursor variable.

Here is an example of a program that has cursor variables as parameters:

```
PROCEDURE assign_curvar
   (old_curvar_in IN company.curvar_type,
    new_curvar_out OUT company.curvar_type)
IS
BEGIN
   new_curvar_out := old_curvar_in;
END;
```

This procedure copies the old company cursor variable to the new variable. The first parameter is an IN parameter because it appears only on the right side of the assignment. The second parameter must be an OUT (or IN OUT) parameter because its value is changed inside the procedure. Notice that the curvar_type is defined within the company package.

## Cursor Variable Restrictions

Cursor variables are subject to the following restrictions; note that Oracle may remove some of these in future releases:

- Cursor variables cannot be declared in a package because they do not have a persistent state.
- You cannot use remote procedure calls (RPCs) to pass cursor variables from one server to another.
- If you pass a cursor variable as a bind variable or host variable to PL/SQL, you will not be able to fetch from it from within the server unless you also open it in that same server call.
- The query you associate with a cursor variable in an OPEN FOR statement cannot use the FOR UPDATE clause if you are running Oracle8i Database or earlier.
- You cannot test for cursor variable equality, inequality, or nullity using comparison operators.
- You cannot assign NULLs to a cursor variable. Attempts to do so will result in a *PLS-00382 Expression is of wrong type* error message.
- Database columns cannot store cursor variable values. You will not be able to use REF CURSOR types to specify column types in statements to CREATE TABLEs.
- The elements in a nested table, associative array, or VARRAY cannot store the values of cursor variables. You will not be able to use REF CURSOR types to specify the element type of a collection.

## Cursor Expressions

Oracle provides a powerful feature in the SQL language: the cursor expression. A *cursor expression*, denoted by the CURSOR operator, returns a nested cursor from within a query. Each row in the result set of this nested cursor can contain the usual range of values allowed in a SQL query; it can also contain other cursors as produced by subqueries.

The CURSOR syntax, although first introduced in Oracle8i Database SQL, was not available from within PL/SQL programs. This deficiency was corrected in Oracle9i Database Release 1; since then, SQL statements within a PL/SQL procedure or function have been able to take advantage of the CURSOR expression.

You can therefore use cursor expressions to return a large and complex set of related values retrieved from one or more tables. You can then process the cursor expression result set using nested loops that fetch from the rows of the result set, and then additional rows from any nested cursors within those rows.

Cursor expressions can get complicated, given how complex the queries and result sets can be. Nevertheless, it's good to know all the possible ways to retrieve data from the Oracle database.

You can use cursor expressions in any of the following:

- Explicit cursor declarations
- Dynamic SQL queries
- REF CURSOR declarations and variables

You cannot use a cursor expression in an implicit query.

The syntax for a cursor expression is very simple:

```
CURSOR (subquery)
```

The database opens the nested cursor defined by a cursor expression implicitly as soon as it fetches the row containing the cursor expression from the parent or outer cursor. This nested cursor is closed when:

- You explicitly close the cursor.
- The outer, parent cursor is executed again, closed, or canceled.
- An exception is raised while fetching from a parent cursor. The nested cursor is closed along with the parent cursor.

## Using Cursor Expressions

You can use a CURSOR expression in two different, but very useful ways:

- To retrieve a subquery as a column in an outer query.
- To transform a query into a result set that can be passed as an argument to a streaming or transformative function.

### Retrieve a subquery as a column

The following procedure demonstrates the use of nested CURSOR expressions to retrieve a subquery as a column in an outer query. The top-level query fetches just two pieces of data: the city location and a nested cursor containing departments in that city. This nested cursor, in turn, fetches a nested cursor with a CURSOR expression—in this case, one containing the names of all the employees in each department.

I could have performed this same retrieval with separate explicit cursors, opened and processed in a nested fashion. The CURSOR expression gives us the option of using a different approach, and one that can be much more concise and efficient, given that all the processing takes place in the SQL statement executor and thus reduces context switching.

```
PROCEDURE emp_report (p_locid NUMBER)
IS
   TYPE refcursor IS REF CURSOR;

   -- The query returns only 2 columns, but the second column is
   -- a cursor that lets us traverse a set of related information.
   CURSOR all_in_one_cur is
      SELECT l.city,
             CURSOR (SELECT d.department_name,
                            CURSOR(SELECT e.last_name
                                     FROM employees e
                                    WHERE e.department_id =
                                                d.department_id)
                                AS ename
                       FROM departments d
                      WHERE l.location_id = d.location_id) AS dname
         FROM locations l
        WHERE l.location_id = p_locid;

   departments_cur    refcursor;
   employees_cur      refcursor;

   v_city     locations.city%TYPE;
   v_dname    departments.department_name%TYPE;
   v_ename    employees.last_name%TYPE;
BEGIN
   OPEN all_in_one_cur;

   LOOP
      FETCH all_in_one_cur INTO v_city, departments_cur;
      EXIT WHEN all_in_one_cur%NOTFOUND;

      -- Now I can loop through departments and I do NOT need to
      -- explicitly open that cursor. Oracle did it for me.
      LOOP
         FETCH departments_cur INTO v_dname, employees_cur;
         EXIT WHEN departments_cur%NOTFOUND;

         -- Now I can loop through employees for that department.
         -- Again, I do not need to open the cursor explicitly.
         LOOP
            FETCH employees_cur INTO v_ename;
            EXIT WHEN employees_cur%NOTFOUND;
            DBMS_OUTPUT.put_line (
                 v_city
               || '-'
               || v_dname
               || '-'
               || v_ename
            );
         END LOOP;
```

```
        END LOOP;
    END LOOP;

    CLOSE all_in_one_cur;
END;
```

### Implement a streaming function with the CURSOR expression

*Streaming functions*, also known as *transformative functions*, allow you to transform data from one state to another without using any local data structures as intermediate staging points. Suppose, for example, that I need to take the data in the StockTable and move it into TickerTable, pivoting one row in StockTable to two rows in TickerTable. Using the CURSOR expression and table functions, I can implement this solution as follows:

```
INSERT INTO TickerTable
    SELECT *
        FROM TABLE (StockPivot (CURSOR (SELECT * FROM StockTable)));
```

where the StockPivot function contains all the complex logic needed to perform the transformation. This technique is explained in depth in Chapter 17.

## Restrictions on Cursor Expressions

There are a number of restrictions on the use of cursor expressions:

- You cannot use a cursor expression with an implicit cursor because no mechanism is available to fetch the nested cursor INTO a PL/SQL data structure.
- Cursor expressions can appear only in the outermost SELECT list of the query specification.
- You can place cursor expressions only in a SELECT statement that is not nested in any other query expression, except when it is defined as a subquery of the cursor expression itself.
- Cursor expressions cannot be used when declaring a view.
- You cannot perform BIND and EXECUTE operations on cursor expressions when using the CURSOR expression in dynamic SQL (see Chapter 16).

# Dynamic SQL and Dynamic PL/SQL

*Dynamic SQL* refers to SQL statements that are constructed and executed at runtime. Dynamic is the opposite of static. *Static SQL* refers to SQL statements that are fully specified, or fixed, at the time the code containing that statement is compiled. *Dynamic PL/SQL* refers to entire PL/SQL blocks of code that are constructed dynamically, then compiled and executed.

Time for a confession: I have had more fun writing dynamic SQL and dynamic PL/SQL programs than just about anything else I have ever done with the PL/SQL language. By constructing and executing dynamically, you gain a tremendous amount of flexibility. You can also build extremely generic and widely useful reusable code.

So what can you do with dynamic SQL and dynamic PL/SQL?[1] Here are just a few ideas:

*Execute DDL statements*
> You can only execute queries and DML statements with static SQL inside PL/SQL. What if you want to create a table or drop an index? Time for dynamic SQL!

*Support ad hoc query and update requirements of web-based applications*
> A common requirement of Internet applications is that users may be able to specify which columns they want to see and vary the order in which they see the data (of course, users don't realize they are doing so).

*Softcode business rules and formulas*
> Rather than hardcoding business rules and formulas into your code, you can place that logic in tables. At runtime, you can generate and then execute the PL/SQL code needed to apply the rules.

Ever since Oracle7 Database, we PL/SQL developers have been able to use the built-in DBMS_SQL package to execute dynamic SQL. In Oracle8*i* Database, we were given a second option for executing dynamically constructed SQL statements: *native dynamic SQL* (NDS). NDS is a *native* part of the PL/SQL language; it is much easier to use than

---

1. For the remainder of this chapter, any reference to "dynamic SQL" also includes dynamic PL/SQL blocks, unless otherwise stated.

DBMS_SQL and, for many applications, it will execute more efficiently. There are still requirements for which DBMS_SQL is a better fit; they are described at the end of this chapter. For almost every situation you face, however, NDS will be the preferred implementation approach.

## NDS Statements

One of the nicest things about NDS is its simplicity. Unlike DBMS_SQL, which has dozens of programs and lots of rules to follow, NDS has been integrated into the PL/SQL language by adding one new statement, EXECUTE IMMEDIATE, which executes a specified SQL statement immediately, and by enhancing the existing OPEN FOR statement, which allows you to perform multiple-row dynamic queries.

 The EXECUTE IMMEDIATE and OPEN FOR statements will not be directly accessible from Oracle Forms Builder and Oracle Reports Builder until the PL/SQL version in those tools is upgraded to at least Oracle8i Database. For earlier versions, you will need to create stored programs that hide calls to these constructs; you will then be able to execute those stored programs from within your client-side PL/SQL code.

### The EXECUTE IMMEDIATE Statement

Use EXECUTE IMMEDIATE to execute (immediately!) the specified SQL statement. Here is the syntax of this statement:

```
EXECUTE IMMEDIATE SQL_string
   [INTO {define_variable[, define_variable]... | record}]
   [USING [IN | OUT | IN OUT] bind_argument
      [, [IN | OUT | IN OUT] bind_argument]...];
```

where:

*SQL_string*

Is a string expression containing the SQL statement or PL/SQL block.

*define_variable*

Is a variable that receives a column value returned by a query.

*record*

Is a record based on a user-defined TYPE or %ROWTYPE that receives an entire row returned by a query.

*bind_argument*

Is an expression whose value is passed to the SQL statement or PL/SQL block, or an identifier that serves as an input and/or output variable to the function or procedure that is called in the PL/SQL block.

*INTO clause*

> Is used for single-row queries; for each column value returned by the query, you must supply an individual variable or field in a record of a compatible type.

*USING clause*

> Allows you to supply bind arguments for the SQL string. This clause is used for both dynamic SQL and PL/SQL, which is why you can specify a parameter mode. This mode is relevant only for PL/SQL, however; the default is IN, which is the only kind of bind argument you would have for SQL statements.

You can use EXECUTE IMMEDIATE for any SQL statement or PL/SQL block except for multiple-row queries. If *SQL_string* ends with a semicolon, it will be treated as a PL/SQL block; otherwise, it will be treated as either DML (Data Manipulation Language) or DDL (Data Definition Language). The string may contain placeholders for bind arguments, but you cannot use bind values to pass in the names of schema objects, such as table names or column names.

> When you execute a DDL statement in your program, you will also perform a commit. If you don't want the DDL-driven commit to affect outstanding changes in the rest of your application, place the dynamic DDL statement within an autonomous transaction procedure. See the *auton_ddl.sql* file on the book's web site for a demonstration of this technique.

When the statement is executed, the runtime engine replaces each placeholder (an identifier with a colon in front of it, such as salary_value) in the SQL string with its corresponding bind argument in the USING clause. Note that you cannot pass a NULL literal value. Instead, you must pass a variable of the correct type that happens to have a value of NULL.

NDS supports all SQL datatypes. You can bind scalar values like strings, numbers, and dates, but you can also bind collections, LOBs, instances of an object type, XML documents, REFs, and more. You may not, however, bind values in the USING clause whose datatypes are specific to PL/SQL, such as Booleans, associative arrays, and user-defined record types. The INTO clause can, on the other hand, contain a PL/SQL record whose number and types of fields match the values fetched by the dynamic query.

Let's take a look at a few examples:

- Create an index:

```
BEGIN
   EXECUTE IMMEDIATE 'CREATE INDEX emp_u_1 ON employees (last_name)';
END;
```

It can't get much easier than that, can it?

- Create a stored procedure that will execute any DDL statement:

```
PROCEDURE exec_DDL (ddl_string IN VARCHAR2)
IS
BEGIN
   EXECUTE IMMEDIATE ddl_string;
END;
```

  With exec_ddl in place, I can create that same index as follows:

```
BEGIN
   exec_DDL ('CREATE INDEX emp_u_1 ON employees (last_name)');
END;
```

- Obtain the count of rows in any table for the specified WHERE clause:

```
/* File on web: tabcount_nds.sf */
FUNCTION tabcount (table_in IN VARCHAR2)
   RETURN PLS_INTEGER
IS
   l_query  VARCHAR2 (32767) := 'SELECT COUNT(*) FROM ' || table_in;
   l_return PLS_INTEGER;
BEGIN
   EXECUTE IMMEDIATE l_query INTO l_return;
   RETURN l_return;
END;
```

  So now I never again have to write SELECT COUNT(*), whether in SQL*Plus or within a PL/SQL program. Instead I can do the following:

```
BEGIN
   IF tabCount ('employees') > 100
   THEN
      DBMS_OUTPUT.PUT_LINE ('We are growing fast!');
   END IF;
END;
```

- Here's a function that lets you update the value of any numeric column in the employees table. It's a function because it returns the number of rows that have been updated.

```
/* File on web: updnval.sf */
FUNCTION updNVal (
   col IN VARCHAR2,
   val IN NUMBER,
   start_in IN DATE,
   end_in IN DATE)
   RETURN PLS_INTEGER
IS
BEGIN
   EXECUTE IMMEDIATE
      'UPDATE employees SET ' || col || ' = :the_value
         WHERE hire_date BETWEEN :lo AND :hi'
      USING val, start_in, end_in;
   RETURN SQL%ROWCOUNT;
END;
```

That is a very small amount of code to achieve all that flexibility! This example introduces the bind argument: after the UPDATE statement is parsed, the PL/SQL engine replaces the various placeholders (:the_value, :lo, and :hi) with the values in the USING clause. Notice also that I can rely on the SQL%ROWCOUNT cursor attribute that I have already been using for static DML statements.

- Suppose that I need to run a different stored procedure at 9:00 a.m. each day of the week. Each program's name has the structure DAYNAME_set_schedule. Each procedure has the same four arguments: you pass in employee_id and hour for the first meeting of the day; it returns the name of the employee and the number of appointments for the day. I can use dynamic PL/SQL to handle this situation:

```
/* File on web: run9am.sp */
PROCEDURE run_9am_procedure (
   id_in IN employee.employee_id%TYPE,
   hour_in IN INTEGER)
IS
   v_apptCount INTEGER;
   v_name VARCHAR2(100);
BEGIN
   EXECUTE IMMEDIATE
      'BEGIN ' || TO_CHAR (SYSDATE, 'DAY') ||
         '_set_schedule (:id, :hour, :name, :appts); END;'
      USING IN
         id_in, IN hour_in, OUT v_name, OUT v_apptCount;

   DBMS_OUTPUT.PUT_LINE (
      'Employee ' || v_name || ' has ' || v_apptCount ||
      ' appointments on ' || TO_CHAR (SYSDATE));
END;
```

As you can see, EXECUTE IMMEDIATE makes it very easy to execute dynamic SQL statements, with a minimum of syntactic fuss.

## The OPEN FOR Statement

The OPEN FOR statement was actually *not* introduced into PL/SQL for NDS; it was first offered in Oracle7 Database to support cursor variables. Now it is deployed in an especially elegant fashion to implement multiple-row dynamic queries. With DBMS_SQL, you go through a painful series of steps to implement multirow queries: parse, bind, define each column individually, execute, fetch, and extract each column value individually. That's a lot of code to write!

For native dynamic SQL, Oracle took an existing feature and syntax—that of cursor variables—and extended it in a very natural way to support dynamic SQL. The next section explores multirow queries in detail. Let's now look at the syntax of the OPEN FOR statement:

```
OPEN {cursor_variable | :host_cursor_variable} FOR SQL_string
   [USING bind_argument[, bind_argument]...];
```

where:

*cursor_variable*
>    Is a weakly typed cursor variable.

*:host_cursor_variable*
>    Is a cursor variable declared in a PL/SQL host environment such as an Oracle Call Interface (OCI) program.

*SQL_string*
>    Contains the SELECT statement to be executed dynamically.

*USING clause*
>    Follows the same rules as in the EXECUTE IMMEDIATE statement.

If you are not familiar with cursor variables, you might want to review Chapter 15. Here you will learn how to use cursor variables with NDS.

 You can also use EXECUTE IMMEDIATE with BULK COLLECT to retrieve multiple rows with a dynamic query. This approach requires much less code and can improve the performance of your query operation.

Following is an example that demonstrates the declaration of a weak REF CURSOR type, a cursor variable based on that type, and the opening of a dynamic query using the OPEN FOR statement:

```
PROCEDURE show_parts_inventory (
    parts_table IN VARCHAR2,
    where_in IN VARCHAR2)
IS
    TYPE query_curtype IS REF CURSOR;
    dyncur query_curtype;
BEGIN
    OPEN dyncur FOR
        'SELECT * FROM ' || parts_table
        ' WHERE ' || where_in;
    ...
```

Once you have opened the query with the OPEN FOR statement, the syntax rules used to fetch rows, close the cursor variable, and check the attributes of the cursor are all the same as for static cursor variables and hardcoded explicit cursors.

Let's now take a closer look at the OPEN FOR statement. When you execute an OPEN FOR statement, the PL/SQL runtime engine does the following:

1. Associates a cursor variable with the query found in the query string.

2. Evaluates any bind arguments and substitutes those values for the placeholders found in the query string.

3. Executes the query.

4. Identifies the result set.

5. Positions the cursor on the first row in the result set.

6. Zeros out the rows-processed count returned by %ROWCOUNT.

Note that any bind arguments (provided in the USING clause) in the query are evaluated only when the cursor variable is opened. This means that if you want to use a different set of bind arguments for the same dynamic query, you must issue a new OPEN FOR statement with those arguments.

To perform a multirow query, you follow these steps:

1. Declare a REF CURSOR type (or use the Oracle-defined SYS_REFCURSOR weak REF CURSOR type).

2. Declare a cursor variable based on the REF CURSOR.

3. OPEN the cursor variable FOR your query string.

4. Use the FETCH statement to fetch one row at a time from the query.

5. Check cursor attributes (%FOUND, %NOTFOUND, %ROWCOUNT, %ISOPEN) as necessary.

6. Close the cursor variable using the normal CLOSE statement. Generally, if and when you are done with your cursor variable, you should close it explicitly.

Here is a simple program to display the specified column of any table for the rows indicated by the WHERE clause (it will work for number, date, and string columns):

```
/* File on web: showcol.sp */
PROCEDURE showcol (
    tab IN VARCHAR2,
    col IN VARCHAR2,
    whr IN VARCHAR2 := NULL)
IS
    cv SYS_REFCURSOR;
    val VARCHAR2(32767);
BEGIN
    OPEN cv FOR
        'SELECT ' || col ||
        '  FROM ' || tab ||
        ' WHERE ' || NVL (whr, '1 = 1');

    LOOP
        /* Fetch and exit if done; same as with explicit cursors. */
        FETCH cv INTO val;
        EXIT WHEN cv%NOTFOUND;

        /* If on first row, display header info. */
        IF cv%ROWCOUNT = 1
        THEN
            DBMS_OUTPUT.PUT_LINE (RPAD ('-', 60, '-'));
            DBMS_OUTPUT.PUT_LINE (
                'Contents of ' || UPPER (tab) || '.' || UPPER (col));
            DBMS_OUTPUT.PUT_LINE (RPAD ('-', 60, '-'));
```

```
        END IF;

        DBMS_OUTPUT.PUT_LINE (val);
    END LOOP;

    /* Don't forget to clean up! Very important... */
    CLOSE cv;
END;
```

Here are some examples of output from this procedure:

```
SQL> EXEC showcol ('emp', 'ename', 'deptno=10')
-------------------------------------------------
Contents of EMP.ENAME
-------------------------------------------------
CLARK
KING
MILLER
```

I can even combine columns:

```
BEGIN
    showcol (
        'emp',
        'ename || ''-$'' || sal',
        'comm IS NOT NULL');
END;
/
-------------------------------------------------
Contents of EMP.ENAME || '-$' || SAL
-------------------------------------------------
ALLEN-$1600
WARD-$1250
MARTIN-$1250
TURNER-$1500
```

### FETCH into variables or records

The FETCH statement in the showcol procedure shown in the previous section fetches into an individual variable. You could also FETCH into a sequence of variables, as shown here:

```
DECLARE
    cv SYS_REFCURSOR;
    mega_bucks company.ceo_compensation%TYPE;
    achieved_by company.cost_cutting%TYPE;
BEGIN
    OPEN cv FOR
        'SELECT ceo_compensation, cost_cutting
           FROM ' || company_table_name (company_pkg.current_company_id);

    LOOP
        FETCH cv INTO mega_bucks, achieved_by;
        ...
    END LOOP;
```

```
      CLOSE cv;
   END;
```

Working with a long list of variables in the FETCH list can be cumbersome and inflexible; you have to declare the variables, keep that set of values synchronized with the FETCH statement, and so on. To ease our troubles, NDS allows us to fetch into a record, as shown here:

```
DECLARE
   cv SYS_REFCURSOR;
   ceo_info company%ROWTYPE;
BEGIN
   OPEN cv FOR
      'SELECT *
        FROM ' ||
             company_table_name (company_pkg.current_company_id);
   LOOP
      FETCH cv INTO ceo_info;
      ...
   END LOOP;
   CLOSE cv;
END;
```

Of course, in many situations you will not want to do a SELECT *; this statement can be very inefficient if your table has hundreds of columns, and you need to work with only three. A better approach is to create record TYPEs that correspond to different requirements. The best place to put these structures is in a package specification so that they can be used throughout your application. Here's one such package:

```
PACKAGE company_pkg
IS
   TYPE ceo_info_rt IS RECORD (
      mega_bucks company.ceo_compensation%TYPE,
      achieved_by company.cost_cutting%TYPE)
   ;

END company_pkg;
```

With this package in place, I can rewrite my CEO-related code as follows:

```
DECLARE
   cv SYS_REFCURSOR;
   rec company_pkg.ceo_info_rt;
BEGIN
   OPEN cv FOR
      'SELECT ceo_compensation, cost_cutting
        FROM ' || company_table_name (
                      company_pkg.current_company_id);
   LOOP
      FETCH cv INTO rec;
      ...
   END LOOP;
   CLOSE cv;
END;
```

### The USING clause in OPEN FOR

As with the EXECUTE IMMEDIATE statement, you can pass in bind arguments when you open a cursor. You can provide only IN arguments for a query. By using bind arguments, you can also improve the performance of your SQL and make it easier to write and maintain that code. In addition, you can potentially dramatically reduce the number of distinct parsed statements that are cached in the SGA, and thereby increase the likelihood that your preparsed statement is still in the SGA the next time you need it. (See the section "Binding Variables" on page 525 later in this chapter for information about this technique.)

Let's revisit the showcol procedure. That procedure accepted a completely generic WHERE clause. Suppose that I have a more specialized requirement: I want to display (or in some way process) all column information for rows that contain a date column with a value within a certain range. In other words, I want to be able to support this query:

```
SELECT last_name
  FROM employees
 WHERE hire_date BETWEEN x AND y;
```

as well as this query:

```
SELECT flavor
  FROM favorites
 WHERE preference_period BETWEEN x AND y;
```

I also want to make sure that the time component of the date column does not play a role in the WHERE condition.

Here is the header for the procedure:

```
/* File on web: showdtcol.sp */
PROCEDURE showcol (
    tab IN VARCHAR2,
    col IN VARCHAR2,
    dtcol IN VARCHAR2,
    dt1 IN DATE,
    dt2 IN DATE := NULL)
```

The OPEN FOR statement now contains two placeholders and a USING clause to match:

```
OPEN cv FOR
    'SELECT ' || col ||
    '  FROM ' || tab ||
    ' WHERE ' || dtcol ||
        ' BETWEEN TRUNC (:startdt)
             AND TRUNC (:enddt)'
    USING dt1, NVL (dt2, dt1+1);
```

I have crafted this statement so that if the user does not supply an end date, the WHERE clause returns rows whose date column is the same day as the dt1 provided. The rest of the showcol procedure remains the same, except for some cosmetic changes in the display of the header.

The following call to this new version of showcol asks to see the names of all employees hired in 1982:

```
BEGIN
    showcol ('emp',
        'ename', 'hiredate',
        TO_DATE ('01-01-1982', 'DD-MM-YYYY'),
        TO_DATE ('31-12-1982 23:59:59', 'DD-MM-YYYY HH23:MI:SS')
    );
END;
```

The output is:

```
-------------------------------------------------------------------
Contents of EMP.ENAME for HIREDATE between 01-JAN-82 and 31-DEC-82
-------------------------------------------------------------------
MILLER
```

## About the Four Dynamic SQL Methods

Now that you've been introduced to the two basic statements used to implement native dynamic SQL in PL/SQL, it's time to take a step back and review the four distinct types, or methods, of dynamic SQL, listed in Table 16-1, and the NDS statements you will need to implement those methods.

Table 16-1. The four methods of dynamic SQL

| Type | Description | NDS statements used |
| --- | --- | --- |
| Method 1 | No queries; just DDL statements and UPDATEs, INSERTs, MERGEs, or DELETEs, which have no bind variables | EXECUTE IMMEDIATE without USING and INTO clauses |
| Method 2 | No queries; just UPDATEs, INSERTs, MERGEs, or DELETEs, with a fixed number of bind variables | EXECUTE IMMEDIATE with a USING clause |
| Method 3 single row queried | Queries (SELECT statements) with a fixed numbers of columns and bind variables, retrieving a single row of data | EXECUTE IMMEDIATE with USING and INTO clauses |
| Method 3 multiple rows queried | Queries (SELECT statements) with a fixed numbers of columns and bind variables, retrieving or more rows of data | EXECUTE IMMEDIATE with USING and BULK COLLECT INTO clauses or OPEN FOR with dynamic string |
| Method 4 | A statement in which the number of columns selected (for a query) or the number of bind variables set is not known until runtime | For method 4, you will use the DBMS_SQL package |

### Method 1

The following DDL statement is an example of method 1 dynamic SQL:

```
EXECUTE IMMEDIATE 'CREATE INDEX emp_ind_1 on employees (salary, hire_date)';
```

And this UPDATE statement is also method 1 dynamic SQL because its only variation is in the table name; there are no bind variables:

```
EXECUTE IMMEDIATE
    'UPDATE ' || l_table || ' SET salary = 10000 WHERE employee_id = 1506'
```

## Method 2

I now replace both of my hardcoded values with placeholders (a colon preceded by an identifier) in the previous DML statement (indicated by the colon); I then have method 2 dynamic SQL:

```
EXECUTE IMMEDIATE
    'UPDATE ' || l_table || ' SET salary = :salary WHERE employee_id = :employee_id'
    USING 10000, 1506;
```

You can see that the USING clause contains the values that will be *bound* into the SQL string after parsing and before execution.

## Method 3

A method 3 dynamic SQL statement is a query with a fixed number of bind variables (or none). This likely is the type of dynamic SQL you will most often be writing. Here is an example:

```
EXECUTE IMMEDIATE
    'SELECT last_name, salary FROM employees
      WHERE department_id = :dept_id'
    INTO l_last_name, l_salary
    USING 10;
```

I am querying just two columns from the employee table and depositing them into the two local variables with the INTO clause. I also have a single bind variable. Because the numbers of these items are static at the time of compilation, I use method 3 dynamic SQL.

## Method 4

Finally, let's consider the most complex scenario: method 4 dynamic SQL. Consider this very generic query:

```
OPEN l_cursor FOR
    'SELECT ' || l_column_list ||
      'FROM employee';
```

At the time I compile my code, I don't have any idea how many columns will be queried from the employee table. This leaves me with quite a challenge: how do I write the FETCH INTO statement to handle that variability? Your choices are twofold: either fall back on DBMS_SQL to write relatively straightforward, though voluminous code, or switch to dynamic PL/SQL block execution.

Fortunately for many of you, scenarios requiring method 4 dynamic SQL are rare. If, you run into it, however, you should read "Meet Method 4 Dynamic SQL Requirements" on page 546.

# Binding Variables

You have seen several examples that use bind variables or arguments with NDS. Let's now go over the various rules and special situations you may encounter when binding.

You can bind into your SQL statement only those expressions (literals, variables, complex expressions) that replace placeholders for data values inside the dynamic string. You cannot bind in the names of schema elements (tables, columns, etc.) or entire chunks of the SQL statement (such as the WHERE clause). For those parts of your string, you must use concatenation.

For example, suppose you want to create a procedure that will truncate the specified view or table. Your first attempt might look something like this:

```
PROCEDURE truncobj (
   nm IN VARCHAR2,
   tp IN VARCHAR2 := 'TABLE',
   sch IN VARCHAR2 := NULL)
IS
BEGIN
   EXECUTE IMMEDIATE
      'TRUNCATE :trunc_type :obj_name'
      USING tp, NVL (sch, USER) || '.' || nm;
END;
```

This code seems perfectly reasonable. But when you try to run the procedure you'll get this error:

```
ORA-03290: Invalid truncate command - missing CLUSTER or TABLE keyword
```

If you rewrite the procedure to simply truncate tables, as follows:

```
EXECUTE IMMEDIATE 'TRUNCATE TABLE :obj_name' USING nm;
```

then the error becomes:

```
ORA-00903: invalid table name
```

Why does NDS (and DBMS_SQL) have this restriction? When you pass a string to EXECUTE IMMEDIATE, the runtime engine must first parse the statement. The parse phase guarantees that the SQL statement is properly defined. PL/SQL can tell that the following statement is valid:

```
'UPDATE emp SET sal = :xyz'
```

without having to know the value of :xyz. But how can PL/SQL know if the following statement is well formed?

```
'UPDATE emp SET :col_name = :xyz'
```

Even if you don't pass in nonsense for col_name, it won't work. For that reason, you must use concatenation:

```
PROCEDURE truncobj (
   nm IN VARCHAR2,
   tp IN VARCHAR2 := 'TABLE',
   sch IN VARCHAR2 := NULL)
IS
BEGIN
   EXECUTE IMMEDIATE
      'TRUNCATE ' || tp || ' ' || NVL (sch, USER) || '.' || nm;
END;
```

## Argument Modes

Bind arguments can have one of three modes:

*IN*
    Read-only value (the default mode)

*OUT*
    Write-only variable

*IN OUT*
    Can read the value coming in and write the value going out

When you are executing a dynamic query, all bind arguments must be of mode IN, except when you are taking advantage of the RETURNING clause, as shown here:

```
PROCEDURE wrong_incentive (
   company_in IN INTEGER,
   new_layoffs IN NUMBER
   )
IS
   sql_string VARCHAR2(32767);
   sal_after_layoffs NUMBER;
BEGIN
   sql_string :=
      'UPDATE ceo_compensation
          SET salary = salary + 10 * :layoffs
       WHERE company_id = :company
       RETURNING salary INTO :newsal';

   EXECUTE IMMEDIATE sql_string
     USING new_layoffs, company_in, OUT sal_after_layoffs;

   DBMS_OUTPUT.PUT_LINE (
      'CEO compensation after latest round of layoffs $' || sal_after_layoffs);
END;
```

Besides being used with the RETURNING clause, OUT and IN OUT bind arguments come into play mostly when you are executing dynamic PL/SQL. In this case, the modes of the bind arguments must match the modes of any PL/SQL program parameters, as well as the usage of variables in the dynamic PL/SQL block.

Here are some guidelines for the use of the USING clause with dynamic PL/SQL execution:

- A bind variable of mode IN can be provided as any kind of expression of the correct type: a literal value, named constant, variable, or complex expression. The expression is evaluated and then passed to the dynamic PL/SQL block.

- You must provide a variable to receive the outgoing value for a bind variable of mode OUT or IN OUT.

- You can bind values only to variables in the dynamic PL/SQL block that have a SQL type. If a procedure has a Boolean parameter, for example, that Boolean cannot be set (or retrieved) with the USING clause.

Let's take a look at how this works with a few examples. Here is a procedure with IN, OUT, and IN OUT parameters:

```
PROCEDURE analyze_new_technology (
    tech_name IN VARCHAR2,
    analysis_year IN INTEGER,
    number_of_adherents IN OUT NUMBER,
    projected_revenue OUT NUMBER
    )
```

Because I have four parameters, any dynamic invocation of this procedure must include a USING clause with four elements. Because I have two IN parameters, the first two of those elements can be literal values or expressions. The second two elements must be the names of variables because the parameter modes are OUT or IN OUT. Here is an example of a dynamic invocation of this procedure:

```
DECLARE
    devoted_followers NUMBER;
    est_revenue NUMBER;
BEGIN
    EXECUTE IMMEDIATE
        'BEGIN
            analyze_new_technology (:p1, :p2, :p3, :p4); END;'
    USING 'Java', 2002, IN OUT devoted_followers, OUT est_revenue;
END;
```

## Duplicate Placeholders

In a dynamically constructed and executed SQL string, NDS associates placeholders with USING clause bind arguments by *position* rather than by name. The treatment of multiple placeholders with the same name varies, however, according to whether you are using dynamic SQL or dynamic PL/SQL. You need to follow these rules:

- When you are executing a dynamic SQL string (DML or DDL—in other words, the string does *not* end in a semicolon), you must supply an argument for each placeholder, even if there are duplicates.

- When you are executing a dynamic PL/SQL block (the string ends in a semicolon), you must supply an argument for each unique placeholder.

Here is an example of a dynamic SQL statement with duplicate placeholders; notice the repetition of the val_in argument:

```
PROCEDURE updnumval (
   col_in      IN   VARCHAR2,
   start_in    IN   DATE, end_in  IN   DATE,
   val_in      IN   NUMBER)
IS
   dml_str VARCHAR2(32767) :=
      'UPDATE emp SET ' || col_in || ' = :val
         WHERE hiredate BETWEEN :lodate AND :hidate
         AND :val IS NOT NULL';
BEGIN
   EXECUTE IMMEDIATE dml_str
   USING val_in, start_in, end_in, val_in;
END;
```

And here is a dynamic PL/SQL block with a duplicate placeholder; notice that val_in is supplied only once:

```
PROCEDURE updnumval (
   col_in      IN   VARCHAR2,
   start_in    IN   DATE, end_in IN   DATE,
   val_in      IN   NUMBER)
IS
   dml_str VARCHAR2(32767) :=
      'BEGIN
          UPDATE emp SET ' || col_in || ' = :val
          WHERE hiredate BETWEEN :lodate AND :hidate
          AND :val IS NOT NULL;
      END;';
BEGIN
   EXECUTE IMMEDIATE dml_str
   USING val_in, start_in, end_in;
END;
```

## Passing NULL Values

You will encounter special moments when you want to pass a NULL value as a bind argument, as follows:

```
EXECUTE IMMEDIATE
   'UPDATE employee SET salary = :newsal
     WHERE hire_date IS NULL'
   USING NULL;
```

You will, however, get this error:

```
PLS-00457: in USING clause, expressions have to be of SQL types
```

Basically, this is saying that NULL has no datatype, and "no datatype" is not a valid SQL datatype.

So what should you do if you need to pass in a NULL value? You can do one of two things:

- Hide the NULL value behind a variable façade, most easily done with an uninitialized variable, as shown here:

```
DECLARE
   /* Default initial value is NULL */
   no_salary_when_fired NUMBER;
BEGIN
    EXECUTE IMMEDIATE
      'UPDATE employee SET salary = :newsal
        WHERE hire_date IS NULL'
       USING no_salary_when_fired;
END;
```

- Use a conversion function to convert the NULL value to a typed value explicitly:

```
BEGIN
    EXECUTE IMMEDIATE
      'UPDATE employee SET salary = :newsal
        WHERE hire_date IS NULL'
       USING TO_NUMBER (NULL);
END;
```

# Working with Objects and Collections

One of the most important advantages of NDS over DBMS_SQL is its support for datatypes such as objects and collections. You don't need to change the structure of the code you write in NDS to use it with these datatypes.

Suppose that I am building an internal administrative system for the national health management corporation Health$.Com. To reduce costs, the system will work in a distributed manner, creating and maintaining separate tables of customer information for each for-profit hospital owned by Health$.Com.

I'll start by defining an object type (person) and nested table type (preexisting_conditions), as follows:

```
/* File on web: health$.pkg */
CREATE OR REPLACE TYPE person AS OBJECT (
   name VARCHAR2(50), dob DATE, income NUMBER);
/
CREATE OR REPLACE TYPE preexisting_conditions IS TABLE OF VARCHAR2(25);
/
```

Once these types are defined, I can build a package to manage my most critical health-related information—data needed to maximize profits at Health$.Com. Here is the specification:

```
PACKAGE health$
AS
    PROCEDURE setup_new_hospital (hosp_name IN VARCHAR2);
```

```
    PROCEDURE add_profit_source (
       hosp_name IN VARCHAR2,
       pers IN Person,
       cond IN preexisting_conditions);

    PROCEDURE minimize_risk  (
       hosp_name VARCHAR2,
       min_income IN NUMBER := 100000,
       max_preexist_cond IN INTEGER := 0);

    PROCEDURE show_profit_centers (hosp_name VARCHAR2);
 END health$;
```

With this package, I can do the following:

- Set up a new hospital, which means create a new table to hold information about that hospital. Here's the implementation from the body:

```
FUNCTION tabname (hosp_name IN VARCHAR2) IS
BEGIN
   RETURN hosp_name || '_profit_center';
END;

PROCEDURE setup_new_hospital (hosp_name IN VARCHAR2) IS
BEGIN
   EXECUTE IMMEDIATE
      'CREATE TABLE ' || tabname (hosp_name) || ' (
         pers Person,
         cond preexisting_conditions)
         NESTED TABLE cond STORE AS cond_st';
END;
```

- Add a "profit source" (formerly known as a "patient") to the hospital, including her preexisting conditions. Here's the implementation from the body:

```
PROCEDURE add_profit_source (
   hosp_name IN VARCHAR2,
   pers IN Person,
   cond IN preexisting_conditions)
IS
BEGIN
   EXECUTE IMMEDIATE
      'INSERT INTO ' || tabname (hosp_name) ||
         ' VALUES (:revenue_generator, :revenue_inhibitors)'
      USING pers, cond;
END;
```

- The use of objects and collections is transparent. I could be inserting scalars like numbers and dates, and the syntax and code would be the same.

- Minimize the risk to the health maintenance organization's bottom line by removing any patients who have too many preexisting conditions or too little income. This is the most complex of the programs; here is the implementation:

```
PROCEDURE minimize_risk  (
   hosp_name VARCHAR2,
   min_income IN NUMBER := 100000,
```

```
      max_preexist_cond IN INTEGER := 1)
   IS
      cv RefCurTyp;
      human Person;
      known_bugs preexisting_conditions;

      v_table VARCHAR2(30) := tabname (hosp_name);
      v_rowid ROWID;
   BEGIN
      /* Find all rows with more than the specified number
         of preconditions and deny them coverage. */
      OPEN cv FOR
         'SELECT ROWID, pers, cond
            FROM ' || v_table || ' alias
           WHERE (SELECT COUNT(*) FROM TABLE (alias.cond))
                   > ' ||
                 max_preexist_cond ||
             ' OR
                 alias.pers.income < ' || min_income;
      LOOP
         FETCH cv INTO v_rowid, human, known_bugs;
         EXIT WHEN cv%NOTFOUND;
         EXECUTE IMMEDIATE
            'DELETE FROM ' || v_table || ' WHERE ROWID = :rid'
            USING v_rowid;
      END LOOP;
      CLOSE cv;
   END;
```

I decided to retrieve the ROWID of each profit source so that when I do
the DELETE it would be easy to identify the row. It would be awfully
convenient to make the query FOR UPDATE, and then use "WHERE
CURRENT OF cv" in the DELETE statement, but that is not possible
for two reasons: (1) The cursor variable would have to be globally accessible to be referenced inside a dynamic SQL statement; and (2) You
cannot declare cursor variables in packages because they don't have
persistent state. See "Dynamic PL/SQL" on page 531 for more details.

# Dynamic PL/SQL

Dynamic PL/SQL offers some of the most interesting and challenging coding opportunities. Think of it: while a user is running your application, you can take advantage
of NDS to do any of the following:

- Create a program, including a package that contains globally accessible data
  structures.

- Obtain (and modify) by name the value of global variables.

- Call functions and procedures whose names are not known at compile time.

I have used this technique to build very flexible code generators, softcoded calculation engines for users, and much more. Dynamic PL/SQL allows you to work at a higher level of generality, which can be both challenging and exhilarating.

There are some rules and tips you need to keep in mind when working with dynamic PL/SQL blocks and NDS:

- The dynamic string must be a valid PL/SQL block. It must start with the DECLARE or BEGIN keyword, and end with an END statement and semicolon. The string will not be considered PL/SQL code unless it ends with a semicolon.

- In your dynamic block, you can access only PL/SQL code elements that have global scope (standalone functions and procedures, and elements defined in the specification of a package). Dynamic PL/SQL blocks execute outside the scope of the local enclosing block.

- Errors raised within a dynamic PL/SQL block can be trapped and handled by the local block in which the string was run with the EXECUTE IMMEDIATE statement.

## Build Dynamic PL/SQL Blocks

Let's explore these rules. First, I will build a little utility to execute dynamic PL/SQL:

```
/* File on web: dynplsql.sp */
PROCEDURE dynPLSQL (blk IN VARCHAR2)
IS
BEGIN
   EXECUTE IMMEDIATE
      'BEGIN ' || RTRIM (blk, ';') || '; END;';
END;
```

This one program encapsulates many of the rules mentioned previously for PL/SQL execution. By enclosing the string within a BEGIN-END anonymous block, I guarantee that whatever I pass in will be executed as a valid PL/SQL block. For instance, I can execute the calc_totals procedure dynamically as simply as this:

```
SQL> exec dynPLSQL ('calc_totals');
```

Now let's use this program to examine what kind of data structures you can reference within a dynamic PL/SQL block. In the following anonymous block, I want to use dynamic SQL to assign a value of 5 to the local variable num:

```
<<dynamic>>
DECLARE
   num NUMBER;
BEGIN
   dynPLSQL ('num := 5');
END;
```

This string is executed within its own BEGIN-END block, which appears to be a nested block within the anonymous block named "dynamic". Yet when I execute this script, I receive the following error:

```
PLS-00201: identifier 'NUM' must be declared
ORA-06512: at "SCOTT.DYNPLSQL", line 4
```

The PL/SQL engine is unable to resolve the reference to the variable named num. I get the same error even if I qualify the variable name with its block name:

```
<<dynamic>>
DECLARE
   num NUMBER;
BEGIN
   /* Also causes a PLS-00302 error! */
   dynPLSQL ('dynamic.num := 5');
END;
```

Now suppose that I define the num variable inside a package as follows:

```
PACKAGE pkgvars
IS
   num NUMBER;
END pkgvars;
```

I can now successfully execute the dynamic assignment to this newly defined variable:

```
BEGIN
   dynPLSQL ('pkgvars.num := 5');
END;
```

What's the difference between these two pieces of data? In my first attempt, the variable num is defined locally in the anonymous PL/SQL block. In my second attempt, num is a public global variable defined in the pkgvars package. This distinction makes all the difference with dynamic PL/SQL.

It turns out that a dynamically constructed and executed PL/SQL block is not treated as a nested block; instead, it is handled as if it were a procedure or function called from within the current block. So any variables local to the current or enclosing blocks are not recognized in the dynamic PL/SQL block; you can make references only to globally defined programs and data structures. These PL/SQL elements include standalone functions and procedures and any elements defined in the specification of a package.

Fortunately, the dynamic block is executed within the context of the calling block. If you have an exception section within the calling block, it will trap exceptions raised in the dynamic block. So if I execute this anonymous block in SQL*Plus:

```
BEGIN
   dynPLSQL ('undefined.packagevar := ''abc''');
EXCEPTION
   WHEN OTHERS
   THEN
      DBMS_OUTPUT.PUT_LINE (SQLCODE);
END;
```

I will not get an unhandled exception.

 The assignment performed in this anonymous block is an example of indirect referencing. I don't reference the variable directly, but instead do so by specifying the name of the variable. The Oracle Forms Builder product (formerly known as SQL*Forms and Oracle Forms) offers an implementation of indirect referencing with the NAME_IN and COPY programs. This feature allows developers to build logic that can be shared across all forms in the application. PL/SQL does not support indirect referencing, but you can implement it with dynamic PL/SQL. See the *dynvar.pkg* file on the book's web site for an example of such an implementation.

The following sections offer a few more examples of dynamic PL/SQL to spark your interest and, perhaps, inspire your creativity.

## Replace Repetitive Code with Dynamic Blocks

This is a true story, I kid you not. During a consulting stint at an insurance company here in Chicago, I was asked to see what I could do about a particularly vexing program. It was very large and continually increased in size—soon it would be too large to even compile. Much to my amazement, this is what the program looked like:

```
PROCEDURE process_line (line IN INTEGER)
IS
BEGIN
   IF    line = 1 THEN process_line1;
   ELSIF line = 2 THEN process_line2;
   ...
   ELSIF line = 514 THEN process_line514;
   ...
   ELSIF line = 2057 THEN process_line2057;
   END IF;
END;
```

Each one of those line numbers represented fine print in an insurance policy that helped the company achieve its primary objective (minimizing the payment of claims). For each line number, there was a "process_line" program that handled those details. And as the insurance company added more and more exceptions to the policy, the program got bigger and bigger. Not a very scalable approach to programming!

To avoid this kind of mess, a programmer should be on the lookout for repetition of code. If you can detect a pattern, you can either create a reusable program to encapsulate that pattern, or you can explore the possibility of expressing that pattern as a dynamic SQL construction.

At the time, I fixed the problem using DBMS_SQL, but dynamic SQL would have been a perfect match. Here's the NDS implementation:

```
PROCEDURE process_line (line IN INTEGER)
IS
BEGIN
   EXECUTE IMMEDIATE
      'BEGIN process_line' || line || '; END;';
END;
```

From thousands of lines of code down to one executable statement! Of course, in most cases, identification of the pattern and conversion of that pattern into dynamic SQL will not be so straightforward. Still, the potential gains are enormous.

# Recommendations for NDS

By now, you should have a solid understanding of how native dynamic SQL works in PL/SQL. This section covers some topics you should be aware of as you start to build production applications with this PL/SQL feature.

## Use Invoker Rights for Shared Programs

I have created a number of useful generic programs in my presentation of NDS, including functions and procedures that do the following:

- Execute any DDL statement
- Return the count of rows in any table
- Return the count for each grouping by specified column

These are pretty darn useful utilities, and I want to let everyone on my development team use them. So I compile them into the COMMON schema and grant EXECUTE authority on the programs to PUBLIC.

However, there is a problem with this strategy. When Sandra connects to her SANDRA schema and executes this command:

```
SQL> EXEC COMMON.exec_DDL ('create table temp (x date)');
```

she will inadvertently create a table in the COMMON schema—unless I take advantage of the invoker rights model, which is described in detail in Chapter 24. The invoker rights model means that you define your stored programs so that they execute under the authority of and the privileges of the invoking schema rather than the defining schema (which is the default starting with Oracle8i Database and the only option prior to that release).

Fortunately, it's easy to take advantage of this new feature. Here is a version of my exec_ddl procedure that executes any DDL statement, but always has an impact on the calling or invoking schema:

```
PROCEDURE exec_DDL (ddl_string IN VARCHAR2)
   AUTHID CURRENT_USER
IS
```

```
BEGIN
   EXECUTE IMMEDIATE ddl_string;
END;
```

I recommend that you use the AUTHID CURRENT_USER clause in all of your dynamic SQL programs, particularly in those you plan to share among a group of developers.

## Anticipate and Handle Dynamic Errors

Any robust application needs to anticipate and handle errors. Error detection and correction with dynamic SQL can be especially challenging.

Sometimes the most challenging aspect of building and executing dynamic SQL programs is getting the string of dynamic SQL correct. You might be combining a list of columns in a query with a list of tables and then a WHERE clause that changes with each execution. You have to concatenate all that stuff, getting the commas right, the ANDs and ORs right, and so on. What happens if you get it wrong?

Well, the Oracle database raises an error. This error usually tells you exactly what is wrong with the SQL string, but that information can still leave much to be desired. Consider the following nightmare scenario: I am building the most complicated PL/SQL application ever. It uses dynamic SQL left and right, but that's OK. I am a pro at NDS. I can, in a flash, type EXECUTE IMMEDIATE, OPEN FOR, and all the other statements I need. I blast through the development phase, and rely on some standard exception-handling programs I have built to display an error message when an exception is encountered.

Then the time comes to test my application. I build a test script that runs through a lot of my code; I place it in a file named *testall.sql* (you'll find it on the book's web site). With trembling fingers, I start my test:

```
SQL> @testall
```

And, to my severe disappointment, here is what shows up on my screen:

```
ORA-00942: table or view does not exist
ORA-00904: invalid column name
ORA-00921: unexpected end of SQL command
ORA-00936: missing expression
```

Now, what am I supposed to make of all these error messages? Which error message goes with which SQL statement? Bottom line: when you do lots of dynamic SQL, it is very easy to get very confused and waste lots of time debugging your code—unless you take precautions as you write your dynamic SQL.

Here are my recommendations:

- Always include an error-handling section in code that calls EXECUTE IMMEDIATE and OPEN FOR.

- In each handler, record and/or display the error message and the SQL statement when an error occurs.
- You might also want to consider adding a "trace" in front of these statements so that you can easily watch the dynamic SQL as it constructed and executed.

How do these recommendations translate into changes in your code? First, let's apply these changes to the exec_ddl routine, and then generalize from there. Here is the starting point:

```
PROCEDURE exec_ddl (ddl_string IN VARCHAR2)
   AUTHID CURRENT_USER IS
BEGIN
   EXECUTE IMMEDIATE ddl_string;
END;
```

Now let's add an error-handling section to show us problems when they occur:

```
/* File on web: execddl.sp */
PROCEDURE exec_ddl (ddl_string IN VARCHAR2)
   AUTHID CURRENT_USER IS
BEGIN
   EXECUTE IMMEDIATE ddl_string;
EXCEPTION
   WHEN OTHERS
   THEN
      DBMS_OUTPUT.PUT_LINE (
         'Dynamic SQL Failure: ' || DBMS_UTILITY.FORMAT_ERROR_STACK);
      DBMS_OUTPUT.PUT_LINE (
         '   on statement: "' || ddl_string || '"');
      RAISE;
END;
```

When I use this version to attempt to create a table using really bad syntax, this is what I see:

```
SQL> EXEC execddl ('create table x')
Dynamic SQL Failure: ORA-00906: missing left parenthesis
   on statement: "create table x"
```

Of course, in your production version, you might want to consider something a bit more sophisticated than the DBMS_OUTPUT built-in package.

 With DBMS_SQL, if your parse request fails, and you do not explicitly close your cursor in the error section, that cursor remains open (and uncloseable), leading to possible *ORA-01000: maximum open cursors exceeded* errors. This will not happen with NDS; cursor variables declared in a local scope are automatically closed—and the memory released—when the block terminates.

Now let's broaden our view a bit: when you think about it, the exec_ddl procedure is not really specific to DDL statements. It can be used to execute any SQL string that does not require either USING or INTO clauses. From that perspective, you now have a single program that can and should be used in place of a direct call to EXECUTE IMMEDIATE; it has all that error handling built-in. I supply such a procedure in the ndsutil package.

I could even create a similar program for OPEN FOR—again, only for situations that do not require a USING clause. Because OPEN FOR sets a cursor value, I would probably want to implement it as a function, which would return a type of weak REF CURSOR. This leads right to a packaged implementation along these lines:

```
PACKAGE ndsutil
IS
    FUNCTION openFor (sql_string IN VARCHAR2) RETURN SYS_REFCURSOR;
END;
```

This NDS utility package contains the complete implementation of this function; the body is quite similar to the exec_dll procedure shown earlier.

## Use Binding Rather Than Concatenation

In most situations, you can take two different paths to insert program values into your SQL string: binding and concatenation. The following table contrasts these approaches for a dynamic UPDATE statement:

| Binding | Concatenation |
| --- | --- |
| EXECUTE IMMEDIATE<br>  'UPDATE ' \|\|<br>  tab \|\| 'SET sal =  :new_sal' USING v_sal; | EXECUTE IMMEDIATE<br>  'UPDATE ' \|\|<br>  tab \|\| 'SET sal = '\|\|<br>  v_sal; |

Binding involves the use of placeholders and the USING clause; concatenation short-cuts that process by adding the values directly to the SQL string. When should you use each approach? I recommend that you bind arguments whenever possible (see the next section for limitations on binding) rather than rely on concatenation. There are four reasons to take this approach:

*Binding is usually faster*
> When you bind in a value, the SQL string does not contain the value, just the placeholder name. Therefore, you can bind different values to the same SQL statement without changing that statement. Because it is the same SQL statement, your application can more likely take advantage of the preparsed cursors that are cached in the SGA of the database.
>
> Note that I included the phrase "more likely" here, because there are very few absolutes in the world of Oracle optimization. For example, one possible drawback with binding is that the cost-based optimizer has less information with which to work and might not come up with the best explain plan for your SQL statement.

*Binding is easier to write and maintain*

> When you bind, you don't have to worry about datatype conversion; it is all han-
> dled for you by the NDS engine. In fact, binding minimizes datatype conversion
> because it works with the native datatypes. If you use concatenation, you will often
> need to write very complex, error-prone string expressions involving multiple sin-
> gle quotes, TO_DATE and TO_CHAR function calls, and so on.

*Binding helps avoid implicit conversions*

> If you concatenate, you might inadvertently leave it up to the database to perform
> implicit conversions. Under some circumstances, the conversion that the database
> applies might not be the one you wanted; it could negate the use of indexes.

*Binding negates the chance of code injection*

> One of the greatest dangers with dynamic SQL is that you write very generalized
> code that is intended to be used in a certain way. Yet, depending on what the user
> passes in to your string, the resulting dynamic statement could perform very dif-
> ferent kinds of operations. That is, users can "inject" unwanted actions into your
> SQL statement. See the following section for an example.

There are some potential downsides to binding, however. Bind variables will negate
the use of any histogram statistics because the bind values are assigned only after the
statement has been parsed. The cost-based optimizer may, therefore, have less information to work with, and be unable to come up with the best execution plan for your
SQL statement.

For PL/SQL developers, I believe the primary emphasis should be how to write clean,
easy to understand, and maintainable code. If I rely on lots of concatenation, I end up
with statements that look like this:

```
EXECUTE IMMEDIATE
 'UPDATE employee SET salary = ' || val_in ||
 ' WHERE hire_date BETWEEN ' ||
    ' TO_DATE (''' || TO_CHAR (v_start)  || ''')' ||
    ' AND ' ||
    ' TO_DATE (''' || TO_CHAR (v_end)  || ''')';
```

A switch to binding makes my code much more understandable:

```
EXECUTE IMMEDIATE
   'UPDATE employee SET salary = :val
     WHERE hire_date BETWEEN :lodate AND :hidate'
   USING v_sal, v_start, v_end;
```

If there happen to be some scenarios in which concatenation is actually more efficient,
then don't worry about that until you or your DBA identify a particular dynamic SQL
statement with binding as the source of the problem. In other words, move from binding to concatenation only when a bottleneck is identified—on an exception basis.

## Minimize the Dangers of Code Injection

Many web-based applications offer wonderful flexibility to the end user. This flexibility is often accomplished through the execution of dynamic SQL and PL/SQL blocks. Consider the following example of a very general "get rows" procedure:

```
/* File on web: code_injection.sql */
PROCEDURE get_rows (
   table_in IN VARCHAR2, where_in IN VARCHAR2
)
IS
BEGIN
   EXECUTE IMMEDIATE
      'DECLARE
       l_row ' || table_in || '%ROWTYPE;
     BEGIN
         SELECT * INTO l_row
      FROM ' || table_in || ' WHERE ' || where_in || ';
     END;';
END get_rows;
```

This looks like such an innocent program, but in fact it opens up gaping holes in your application. Consider the following block:

```
BEGIN
   get_rows ('EMPLOYEE'
     ,'employee_id=7369;
        EXECUTE IMMEDIATE
          ''CREATE PROCEDURE backdoor (str VARCHAR2)
             AS BEGIN EXECUTE IMMEDIATE str; END;''' );
END;
/
```

After running this code, I have created a "back door" procedure that will execute any statement I pass in as a dynamic string. I could, for example, use UTL_FILE to retrieve the contents of any file on the system, then create (and drop) any table or object I desire, restricted only by whatever privileges are defined for the owner's schema.

*Code injection*, also known as *SQL injection*, can compromise seriously the security of any application. The execution of dynamic PL/SQL blocks offers the greatest opportunity for injection. While this is a very big topic that cannot be treated fully in this book, I offer the following recommendations to minimize the chances of injection occurring with your application. Chapter 23 providers additional security recommendations.

### Restrict privileges tightly on user schemas

The best way to minimize the risk of injection is to make sure that any schema to which an outside user connects has severely restricted privileges.

Do not let such a schema create database objects, remove database objects, or directly access tables. Do not allow the execution of supplied packages that interact (or can be used to interact) with the operating system, such as UTL_SMTP, UTL_FILE, UTL_TCP (and related packages), and DBMS_PIPE.

Such a schema should have privileges only to execute stored programs defined in *another* schema. This PL/SQL code may then be designed to carefully allow only a restricted set of operations. When defining programs in these executable schemas that use dynamic SQL, be sure to define the subprogram as AUTHID CURRENT_USER. That way, all SQL statements will be executed using the limited privileges of the currently-connected schema.

### Use bind variables whenever possible

Strict enforcement of the use of bind variables, plus built-in analysis and automated rejection of potentially dangerous strings, can help minimize the danger of injection.

By requiring binding, you can lose some flexibility. In the get_rows procedure, I would need to replace the completely dynamic WHERE clause with something less generic, but more tightly fitting the expected behavior of the application. Here's an example using a variation of the get_rows procedure:

```
PROCEDURE get_rows (
   table_in   IN   VARCHAR2, value1_in in VARCHAR2, value2_in IN DATE
)
IS
   l_where VARCHAR2(32767);
BEGIN
   IF table_in = 'EMPLOYEES'
   THEN
      l_where := 'last_name = :name AND hire_date < :hdate';
   ELSIF table_in = 'DEPARTMENTS'
   THEN
      l_where := 'name LIKE :name AND incorporation_date = :hdate';
   ELSE
      RAISE_APPLICATION_ERROR (
         -20000, 'Invalid table name for get_rows: ' || table_in);
   END IF;
   EXECUTE IMMEDIATE
      'DECLARE l_row ' || table_in || '%ROWTYPE;
      BEGIN
         SELECT * INTO l_row
      FROM ' || table_in || ' WHERE ' || l_where || ';
      END;'
      USING value1_in, value2_in;
END get_rows;
/
```

In this rewrite, the WHERE clause relies on two bind variables; there is no opportunity to concatenate a back-door entry point. I also check the table name and make sure it is one that I expect to see. This will help avoid calls to functions in the FROM clause (known as *table functions*), which could also cause aberrant behavior.

### Check dynamic text for dangerous text

The problem with the recommendations in the previous sections is that they rely on the proactive diligence of an individual developer or DBA to minimize the risk. That should be done, but perhaps something more could be offered to developers. It is also possible to include checks in your programs to make sure that the text provided by the user does not contain "dangerous" characters, such as the semicolon.

I created a utility named SQL Guard that takes another approach: analyze the string provided by the user to see if it contains a risk of SQL injection. The programmer can then decide whether or not to execute that statement and perhaps to log the problematic text. You will find the code and a user's guide for SQL Guard in the *sqlguard.zip* file on the book's web site.

With SQL Guard, the tests used to determine if there is a risk of SQL injection can be configured by the user. In other words, SQL Guard comes with a set of predefined tests. You can remove from or add to that list of tests to check for SQL injection patterns that may be specific to your own application environment.

It isn't possible to ever come up with a proactive mechanism that will trap, with 100% certainty, all possible SQL injection. Having said all that, if you decide to use SQL Guard, you *should* (it seems to me) be able to achieve the following:

- Increase awareness of SQL injection among your developers.
- Thwart the most common SQL injection attacks.
- More easily analyze your code base to identify possible injection pathways.

### Use DBMS_ASSERT to validate inputs

Use the supplied DBMS_ASSERT package to ensure that a user input that is *supposed* to be a valid SQL object name (for example, a schema name or table name) is, in fact, valid. The DBMS_ASSERT package was first documented in Oracle Database 11*g*. It has since been backported to each of these Oracle versions: 8.1, 9.2, 10.1, and 10.2. In some cases, it is available in the latest patchset; in others, it is available in a Critical Patch Update. You may need to contact Oracle Support before you can start using the package.

The DBMS_ASSERT.SIMPLE_SQL_NAME is purely an *asserter*: you pass it the string that should contain a valid SQL name. If it is valid, the function returns that string, unchanged. If it is *not* valid, Oracle raises the DBMS_ASSERT.INVALID_SQL_NAME exception.

For a much more comprehensive treatment of this issue, check out the whitepaper titled "How to write SQL injection proof PL/SQL," available on the Oracle Technology Network.

# When to Use DBMS_SQL

Native dynamic SQL should be your first choice (over DBMS_SQL) to satisfy dynamic SQL requirements in your PL/SQL programs for the following reasons:

- NDS is much easier to write; you need less code, and the code you write is more intuitive, leading to many fewer bugs. The code is also much easier to maintain.
- NDS works with all SQL datatypes, including user-defined objects and collection types (associative arrays, nested tables, and VARRAYs). DBMS_SQL works only with Oracle7 Database-compatible datatypes.

There are, however, situations when you will want or need to use DBMS_SQL. The following sections describe these situations.

## Parse Very Long Strings

Through Oracle Database 10*g*, EXECUTE IMMEDIATE executes the contents of a VARCHAR2 string, with a maximum length of 32K. (What if your SQL statement exceeds that length? While that scenario is unlikely for SQL statements you write yourself, *generated* dynamic SQL statements based on tables with many columns (you can now have up to 1,000 columns in a table) could easily exceed that limit. DBMS_SQL to the rescue!

 With Oracle Database 11*g*, EXECUTE IMMEDIATE can execute either a VARCHAR2 string or a CLOB. A new overloading of DBMS_SQL.PARSE also accepts a CLOB for parsing.

Use a special overloading of DBMS_SQL.PARSE to parse arbitrarily long SQL and PL/SQL statements by passing a collection to the built-in that contains the full text of the dynamic statement. The collection must be of type DBMS_SQL.VARCHAR2S (maximum bytes per line is 256) or DBMS_SQL.VARCHAR2A (maximum bytes per line is 32,676).

To demonstrate this approach, I show below a procedure that reads the contents of a file and executes it as a DDL statement or DML statement without any placeholders. As I am sure you have found with your own package definitions, such files can easily and often exceed 32K in length. I focus on the DBMS_SQL-specific steps; please check the file for the full implementation.

```
    /* File on web: compile_from_file.sp */
1  PROCEDURE compile_from_file (dir_in  IN VARCHAR2
2  , file_in IN VARCHAR2
3  )
4  IS
5     l_file    UTL_FILE.file_type;
6     l_lines   DBMS_SQL.varchar2s;
```

```
 7    l_cur     PLS_INTEGER := DBMS_SQL.open_cursor;
 8
 9    PROCEDURE read_file (lines_out IN OUT DBMS_SQL.varchar2s)
10    IS
11    BEGIN
12       l_file := UTL_FILE.fopen (dir_in, file_in, 'R');
13
14       LOOP
15          UTL_FILE.get_line (l_file, l_lines (lines_out.COUNT + 1));
16       END LOOP;
17    EXCEPTION
18       WHEN NO_DATA_FOUND
19       THEN
20          UTL_FILE.fclose (l_file);
21    END read_file;
22 BEGIN
23    read_file (l_lines);
24    /* Parse all the lines in the array (going from FIRST to LAST) */
25    DBMS_SQL.parse (l_cur
26                  , l_lines
27                  , l_lines.FIRST
28                  , l_lines.LAST
29                  , TRUE
30                  , DBMS_SQL.native
31                  );
32    DBMS_SQL.close_cursor (l_cur);
33 END compile_from_file;
```

Here is an explanation of the key sections of this program:

| Line(s) | Significance |
|---------|--------------|
| 6–7 | Declare the l_lines local collection based on the DBMS_SQL type; then declare and open a cursor for use by DBMS_SQL.PARSE |
| 9–21 | Transfer the contents of the file to the l_lines collection |
| 25–31 | Call the collection-based overloading of DBMS_SQL.PARSE, passing it the collection, and specifying that the entire contents of the collection be used (from l_lines.FIRST to l_lines.LAST) |

## Obtain Information About Query Columns

DBMS_SQL allows you to describe the columns of your dynamic cursor, returning information about each column in an associative array of records. This capability offers the possibility of writing very generic cursor-processing code; this program may come in particularly handy when you are writing method 4 dynamic SQL, and you are not certain how many columns are being selected.

When you call this program, you need to have declared a PL/SQL collection based on the DBMS_SQL.DESC_TAB collection type (or DESC_TAB2, if your query might return column names that are greater than 30 characters in length). You can then use collection methods to traverse the table and extract the needed information about the cursor. The following anonymous block shows the basic steps you will perform when working with this built-in:

```
DECLARE
   cur PLS_INTEGER := DBMS_SQL.OPEN_CURSOR;
   cols DBMS_SQL.DESC_TAB;
   ncols PLS_INTEGER;
BEGIN
   -- Parse the query.
   DBMS_SQL.PARSE
      (cur, 'SELECT hire_date, salary FROM employees', DBMS_SQL.NATIVE);
   -- Retrieve column information
   DBMS_SQL.DESCRIBE_COLUMNS (cur, ncols, cols);
   -- Display each of the column names
   FOR colind IN 1 .. ncols
   LOOP
      DBMS_OUTPUT.PUT_LINE (cols (colind).col_name);
   END LOOP;
   DBMS_SQL.CLOSE_CURSOR (cur);
END;
```

To simplify your use of DESCRIBE_COLUMNS, I have created a package that hides much of the underlying detail, making it easier to use this feature. Here is the package specification:

```
/* File on web: desccols.pkg */
PACKAGE desccols
IS

   FUNCTION for_query (sql_in IN VARCHAR2)
      RETURN DBMS_SQL.desc_tab;

   FUNCTION for_cursor (cur IN PLS_INTEGER)
      RETURN DBMS_SQL.desc_tab;

   PROCEDURE show_columns (
      col_list_in   IN   DBMS_SQL.desc_tab
   );
END desccols;
```

You can also use the for_query function when you want to get information about the columns of a dynamic query, but might not otherwise be using DBMS_SQL.

Here is a script demonstrating the usage of this package:

```
/* File on web: desccols.sql */
DECLARE
   cur    INTEGER          := DBMS_SQL.open_cursor;
   tab    DBMS_SQL.desc_tab;
BEGIN
   DBMS_SQL.parse (cur
                  , 'SELECT last_name, salary, hiredate FROM employees'
                  , DBMS_SQL.native
                  );
   tab := desccols.for_cursor (cur);
   desccols.show (tab);
```

```
    DBMS_SQL.close_cursor (cur);
    --
    tab := desccols.for_query ('SELECT * FROM employees');
    desccols.show (tab);
END;
/
```

# Meet Method 4 Dynamic SQL Requirements

DBMS_SQL supports method 4 dynamic SQL (variable number of columns selected of variables bound) more naturally than NDS. You have already seen that in order to implement method 4 with NDS, you must switch to dynamic PL/SQL, which is generally a higher level of abstraction than many developers want to deal with.

When would you run into method 4? It certainly arises when you build a frontend to support ad hoc query generation by users, or when you want to build a generic report program, which constructs the report format and contents dynamically at runtime. Let's step through the implementation of a variation on this theme: the construction of a PL/SQL procedure to display the contents of a table—any table, as specified by the user at runtime. Here I cover only those aspects pertaining to the dynamic SQL itself; check out the *intab.sp* file on the book's web site for the full implementation.

### The "in table" procedural interface

So I will use PL/SQL and DBMS_SQL. But before building any code, I need to come up with a specification. How will the procedure be called? What information do I need from my user (a developer, in this case)? What should a user have to type to retrieve the desired output? I want my procedure (which I call "intab" for "in table") to accept the inputs in the following table.

| Parameter | Description |
| --- | --- |
| Name of the table | Required. Obviously, a key input to this program. |
| WHERE clause | Optional. Allows you to restrict the rows retrieved by the query. If not specified, all rows are retrieved. You can also use this parameter to pass in ORDER BY and HAVING clauses, because they follow immediately after the WHERE clause. |
| Column name filter | Optional. If you don't want to display all columns in the table, provide a comma-delimited list, and only those columns will be used. |

Given these inputs, the specification for my procedure becomes the following:

```
PROCEDURE intab (
    table_in IN VARCHAR2
  , where_in IN VARCHAR2 DEFAULT NULL
  , colname_like_in IN VARCHAR2 := '%'
);
```

Here are some examples of calls to intab, along with their output. First, the entire contents of the emp table:

---

```
SQL> EXEC intab ('emp');
----------------------------------------------------------------------
_                        Contents of emp
----------------------------------------------------------------------
EMPNO ENAME      JOB        MGR  HIREDATE       SAL   COMM   DEPTNO
----------------------------------------------------------------------
 7369 SMITH      CLERK     7902 12/17/80 120000 800            20
 7499 ALLEN      SALESMAN  7698 02/20/81 120000 1600   300     30
 7521 WARD       SALESMAN  7698 02/22/81 120000 1250   500     30
 7566 JONES      MANAGER   7839 04/02/81 120000 2975           20
 7654 MARTIN     SALESMAN  7698 09/28/81 120000 1250  1400     30
 7698 BLAKE      MANAGER   7839 05/01/81 120000 2850           30
 7782 CLARK      MANAGER   7839 06/09/81 120000 2450           10
 7788 SCOTT      ANALYST   7566 04/19/87 120000 3000           20
 7839 KING       PRESIDENT      11/17/81 120000 5000           10
 7844 TURNER     SALESMAN  7698 09/08/81 120000 1500     0     30
 7876 ADAMS      CLERK     7788 05/23/87 120000 1100           20
 7900 JAMES      CLERK     7698 12/03/81 120000 950            30
 7902 FORD       ANALYST   7566 12/03/81 120000 3000           20
```

And now let's see just those employees in department 10, specifying a maximum length of 20 characters for string columns:

```
SQL> EXEC intab ('emp', 20, 'deptno = 10 ORDER BY sal');
----------------------------------------------------------------------
_                        Contents of emp
----------------------------------------------------------------------
EMPNO ENAME      JOB        MGR  HIREDATE       SAL   COMM   DEPTNO
----------------------------------------------------------------------
 7934 MILLER     CLERK     7782 01/23/82 120000 1300           10
 7782 CLARK      MANAGER   7839 06/09/81 120000 2450           10
 7839 KING       PRESIDENT      11/17/81 120000 5000           10
```

And now an entirely different table, with a different number of columns:

```
SQL> EXEC intab ('dept')
-------------------------------------
_        Contents of dept
-------------------------------------
DEPTNO DNAME          LOC
-------------------------------------
  10    ACCOUNTING    NEW   YORK
  20    RESEARCH      DALLAS
  30    SALES         CHICAGO
  40    OPERATIONS    BOSTON
```

Notice that the user does not have to provide any information about the structure of the table. My program will get that information itself—precisely the aspect of intab that makes it a method 4 dynamic SQL example.

### Steps for intab construction

To display the contents of a table, follow these steps:

1. Construct and parse the SELECT statement (using OPEN_CURSOR and PARSE).

2. Bind all local variables with their placeholders in the query (using BIND_VARIABLE).

3. Define each column in the cursor for this query (using DEFINE_COLUMN).

4. Execute and fetch rows from the database (using EXECUTE and FETCH_ ROWS).

5. Retrieve values from the fetched row, and place them into a string for display purposes (using COLUMN_VALUE). Then display that string with a call to the PUT_LINE procedure of the DBMS_OUTPUT package.

 My intab implementation does not currently support bind variables. I assume, in other words, that the *where_clause_in* argument does not contain any bind variables. As a result, I will not be exploring in detail the code required for step 2.

### Constructing the SELECT

To extract the data from the table, I have to construct the SELECT statement. The structure of the query is determined by the various inputs to the procedure (table name, WHERE clause, etc.) and the contents of the data dictionary. Remember that the user does not have to provide a list of columns. Instead, I must identify and extract the list of columns for that table from a data dictionary view. I have decided to use the ALL_TAB_COLUMNS view in the intab procedure so the user can view the contents not only of tables he owns (which are accessible in USER_TAB_COLUMNS), but also any table for which he has SELECT access.

Here is the cursor I use to fetch information about the table's columns:

```
CURSOR col_cur
   (owner_in IN VARCHAR2,
    table_in IN VARCHAR2)
IS
   SELECT column_name, data_type,
          data_length,
          data_precision, data_scale
     FROM all_tab_columns
    WHERE owner = owner_in
      AND table_name = table_in;
```

With this column cursor, I extract the name, datatype, and length information for each column in the table. How should I store all of this information in my PL/SQL program? To answer this question, I need to think about how that data will be used. It turns out that I will use it in many ways—for example:

- To build the select list for the query, I will use the column names.

- To display the output of a table in a readable fashion, I need to provide a column header that shows the names of the columns over their data. These column names must be spaced out across the line of data in, well, columnar format. So I need the column name and the length of the data for that column.

- To fetch data into a dynamic cursor, I need to establish the columns of the cursor with calls to DEFINE_COLUMN. For this, I need the column datatype and length.

- To extract the data from the fetched row with COLUMN_VALUE, I need to know the datatypes of each column, as well as the number of columns.

- To display the data, I must construct a string containing all the data (using TO_CHAR to convert numbers and dates). Again, I must pad out the data to fit under the column names, just as I did with the header line.

Therefore, I need to work with the column information several times throughout my program, yet I do not want to read repeatedly from the data dictionary. As a result, when I query the column data out of the ALL_TAB_COLUMNS view, I will store that data in three PL/SQL collections:

| Collection | Description |
| --- | --- |
| colname | The names of each column |
| coltype | The datatypes of each column, a string describing the datatype |
| collen | The number of characters required to display the column data |

So if the third column of the emp table is SAL, then colname(3) = 'SAL', coltype(3) = 'NUMBER', and collen(3) = 7, and so forth.

The name and datatype information is stored directly from the data dictionary. Calculating the column length is a bit trickier, but also not crucial to learning how to write method 4 dynamic SQL. I will leave it to the reader to study the file.

I apply all of my logic inside a cursor FOR loop that sweeps through all the columns for a table (as defined in ALL_COLUMNS). This loop (shown in the following example) fills my PL/SQL collection:

```
FOR col_rec IN col_cur (owner_nm, table_nm)
LOOP
   /* Construct select list for query. */
   col_list := col_list || ', ' || col_rec.column_name;

   /* Save datatype and length for calls to DEFINE_COLUMN. */
   col_count := col_count + 1;
   colname (col_count) := col_rec.column_name;
   coltype (col_count) := col_rec.data_type;

   /* Construct column header line. */
   col_header :=
      col_header || ' ' || RPAD (col_rec.column_name, v_length);
END LOOP;
```

When this loop completes, I have constructed the select list, populated my PL/SQL collections with the column information I need for calls to DBMS_SQL.DEFINE_COLUMN and DBMS_SQL.COLUMN_VALUE, and also created the column header line. Now that was a busy loop!

Now it is time to parse the query, and then construct the various columns in the dynamic cursor object.

### Defining the cursor structure

The parse phase is straightforward enough. I simply cobble together the SQL statement from its processed and refined components, including, most notably, the column list I just constructed (the col_list variable):

```
DBMS_SQL.PARSE
   (cur,
    'SELECT ' || col_list ||
    '  FROM ' || table_in || ' ' || where_clause,
   DBMS_SQL.NATIVE);
```

Of course, I want to go far beyond parsing. I want to execute this cursor. Before I do that, however, I must give some structure to the cursor. With DBMS_SQL, when you open a cursor, you have merely retrieved a handle to a chunk of memory. When you parse the SQL statement, you have associated a SQL statement with that memory. But as a next step, I must define the columns in the cursor so that it can actually store fetched data.

With method 4 dynamic SQL, this association process is complicated. I cannot hard-code the number or type of calls to DBMS_SQL.DEFINE_COLUMN in my program; I do not have all the information until runtime. Fortunately, in the case of intab, I *have* kept track of each column to be retrieved. Now all I need to do is issue a call to DBMS_SQL.DEFINE_COLUMN for each row defined in my *collection, colname*. Before we go through the actual code, here are some reminders about DBMS_SQL.DEFINE_COLUMN.

The header for this built-in procedure is as follows:

```
PROCEDURE DBMS_SQL.DEFINE_COLUMN
   (cursor_handle IN INTEGER,
    position IN INTEGER,
    datatype_in IN DATE|NUMBER|VARCHAR2)
```

There are three things to keep in mind with this built-in:

- The second argument is a number; DBMS_SQL.DEFINE_COLUMN does not work with column *names*—only with the sequential position of the column in the list.

- The third argument establishes the datatype of the cursor's column. It does this by accepting an expression of the appropriate type. You do not, in other words, pass a string such as "VARCHAR2" to DBMS_SQL.DEFINE_COLUMN. Instead, you would pass a variable defined as VARCHAR2.

- When you are defining a character-type column, you must also specify the maximum length of values retrieved into the cursor.

In the context of the intab procedure, the row in the collection is the Nth position in the column list. The datatype is stored in the coltype collection, but must be converted into a call to DBMS_SQL.DEFINE_COLUMN using the appropriate local variable. These complexities are handled in the following FOR loop:

```
FOR col_ind IN 1 .. col_count
LOOP
  IF is_string (col_ind)
  THEN
    DBMS_SQL.DEFINE_COLUMN
      (cur, col_ind, string_value, collen (col_ind));

  ELSIF is_number (col_ind)
  THEN
    DBMS_SQL.DEFINE_COLUMN (cur, col_ind, number_value);

  ELSIF is_date (col_ind)
  THEN
    DBMS_SQL.DEFINE_COLUMN (cur, col_ind, date_value);
  END IF;
END LOOP;
```

When this loop is completed, I will have called DEFINE_COLUMN for each column defined in the collections. (In my version, this is all columns for a table. In your enhanced version, it might be just a subset of all these columns.) I can then execute the cursor and start fetching rows. The execution phase is no different for method 4 than it is for any of the other simpler methods. Specify:

```
fdbk := DBMS_SQL.EXECUTE (cur);
```

where fdbk is the feedback returned by the call to EXECUTE.

Now for the finale: retrieval of data and formatting for display.

### Retrieving and displaying data

I use a cursor FOR loop to retrieve each row of data identified by my dynamic cursor. If I am on the first row, I will display a header (this way, I avoid displaying the header for a query that retrieves no data). For each row retrieved, I build the line and then display it:

```
LOOP
    fdbk := DBMS_SQL.FETCH_ROWS (cur);
    EXIT WHEN fdbk = 0;

    IF DBMS_SQL.LAST_ROW_COUNT = 1
    THEN
       /* We will display the header information here */
       ...
    END IF;

    /* Construct the line of text from column information here */
    ...
```

```
         DBMS_OUTPUT.PUT_LINE (col_line);
     END LOOP;
```

The line-building program is actually a numeric FOR loop in which I issue my calls to DBMS_SQL.COLUMN_VALUE. I call this built-in for each column in the table (information that is stored in—you guessed it—my collections). As you can see below, I use my is_* functions to determine the datatype of the column and therefore the appropriate variable to receive the value.

Once I have converted my value to a string (necessary for dates and numbers), I pad it on the right with the appropriate number of blanks (stored in the collen collection) so that it lines up with the column headers.

```
     col_line := NULL;
     FOR col_ind IN 1 .. col_count
     LOOP
        IF is_string (col_ind)
        THEN
           DBMS_SQL.COLUMN_VALUE (cur, col_ind, string_value);

        ELSIF is_number (col_ind)
        THEN
           DBMS_SQL.COLUMN_VALUE (cur, col_ind, number_value);
           string_value := TO_CHAR (number_value);

        ELSIF is_date (col_ind)
        THEN
           DBMS_SQL.COLUMN_VALUE (cur, col_ind, date_value);
           string_value := TO_CHAR (date_value, date_format_in);
        END IF;

        /* Space out the value on the line
           under the column headers. */
        col_line :=
           col_line || ' ' ||
           RPAD (NVL (string_value, ' '), collen (col_ind));
     END LOOP;
```

There you have it. A very generic procedure for displaying the contents of a database table from within a PL/SQL program. Again, check out *intab.sp* for the full details; the *intab_dbms_sql.sp* file also contains a version of this procedure that is updated to take advantage of more recent database features and is more fully documented.

## Minimize Parsing of Dynamic Cursors

One of the drawbacks of EXECUTE IMMEDIATE is that each time the dynamic string is executed it will be re-prepared, which will usually involve parsing, optimization, and plan generation. For most dynamic SQL requirements, the overhead of these steps will be compensated for by other benefits of NDS (in particular, the avoidance of calls to a PL/SQL API as happens with DBMS_SQL). In some cases, however, the parse phase may be quite expensive. For such scenarios, DBMS_SQL may be a better solution, precisely for the same reason that usually makes this built-in package unattractive: you have control over—and have to code for—each explicit step in the process.

With DBMS_SQL, you can explicitly avoid the parse phase when you know that the SQL string you are executing dynamically is changing only its bind variables. All you have to do is avoid calling DBMS_SQL.PARSE again, and simply rebind the variable values with calls to DBMS_SQL.BIND_VARIABLE. Let's look at a very simple example, demonstrating the specific calls you make to the DBMS_SQL package.

The following anonymous block executes a dynamic query inside a loop:

```
 1 DECLARE
 2 l_cursor   pls_INTEGER;
 3 l_result   pls_INTEGER;
 4 BEGIN
 5 FOR i IN 1 .. counter
 6 LOOP
 7    l_cursor := DBMS_SQL.open_cursor;
 8    DBMS_SQL.parse
 9       (l_cursor, 'SELECT ... where col = ' || i , DBMS_SQL.native);
10    l_result := DBMS_SQL.EXECUTE (l_cursor);
11    DBMS_SQL.close_cursor (l_cursor);
12 END LOOP;
13 END;
```

Within my loop, I take the following actions:

| Line(s) | Description |
| --- | --- |
| 7 | Obtain a cursor, simply a pointer to memory used by DBMS_SQL |
| 8–9 | Parse the dynamic query, after concatenating in the only variable element, the variable i |
| 10 | Execute the query |
| 11 | Close the cursor |

This is all valid (and, of course, you would usually follow up the execution of the query with fetch and retrieve steps), yet it also is a misuse of DBMS_SQL. Consider the following rewrite of the same steps:

```
DECLARE
    l_cursor   PLS_INTEGER;
    l_result   PLS_INTEGER;
BEGIN
    l_cursor := DBMS_SQL.open_cursor;
    DBMS_SQL.parse (l_cursor, 'SELECT ... WHERE col = :value'
                 , DBMS_SQL.native);

    FOR i IN 1 .. counter
    LOOP
       DBMS_SQL.bind_variable (l_cursor, 'value', i);
       l_result := DBMS_SQL.EXECUTE (l_cursor);
    END LOOP;
```

```
        DBMS_SQL.close_cursor (l_cursor);
   END;
```

In this usage of DBMS_SQL, I now declare the cursor only once, because I can reuse the same cursor with each call to DBMS_SQL.PARSE. I also move the parse call *outside of the cursor*. Because the structure of the SQL statement itself doesn't change, I don't need to reparse for each new value of i. So I parse once and then, within the loop, bind a new variable value into the cursor, and execute. When I am all done (after the loop terminates), I close the cursor.

The ability to perform each step explicitly and separately gives developers enormous flexibility (and also headaches from all the code and complexity of DBMS_SQL). If that is what you need, DBMS_SQL is hard to beat.

If you do use DBMS_SQL in your application, I encourage you to take advantage of the package found in the *dynalloc.pkg* file on the book's web site. This "dynamic allocation" package helps you to:

- Minimize cursor allocation through cursor reuse.
- Perform tight and useful error handling for all DBMS_SQL parse operations.
- Avoid errors trying to open or close cursors that are already opened or closed.

# Oracle Database 11g New Features

Oracle Database 11g adds interoperability between native dynamic SQL and DBMS_SQL: you can now take advantage of the best features of each of these approaches to obtain the best performance with the simplest implementation. Specifically, you can now convert a DBMS_SQL cursor to a cursor variable, and vice versa, as I describe in the following sections.

## DBMS_SQL.TO_REFCURSOR Function

Use the DBMS_SQL.TO_REFCURSOR function to convert a cursor *number* (obtained through a call to DBMS_SQL.OPEN_CURSOR) to a weakly-typed cursor variable (declared with the SYS_REFCURSOR type or a weak REF CURSOR type of your own). You can then fetch data from this cursor variable into local variables, or even pass that cursor variable to a non-PL/SQL host environment for data retrieval, having hidden all the complexities of the dynamic SQL processing in the backend.

Before passing a SQL cursor number to the DBMS_SQL.TO_REFCURSOR function, you must OPEN, PARSE, and EXECUTE it; otherwise, an error occurs. After you convert the cursor, you may not use DBMS_SQL any longer to manipulate that cursor, including the closing of the cursor. All operations must be done throught the cursor variable.

Why would you want to use this function? As noted in previous sections, DBMS_SQL is sometimes the preferred or only option for certain dynamic SQL operations, in particular method 4. Suppose I have a situation in which I know the specific columns that I am selecting, but the WHERE clause of the query has a unknown (at compile time) number of bind variables. I cannot use EXECUTE IMMEDIATE to execute the dynamic query because of this (it has a fixed USING clause).

I *could* use DBMS_SQL from start to finish, but using DBMS_SQL to retrieve rows and values from within the rows is an onerous amount of work. It is so much easier to use a regular, old static fetch and even BULK COLLECT.

The following example demonstrates precisely this scenario.

```
/* File on web: 11g_to_refcursor.sql */
DECLARE
   TYPE strings_t IS TABLE OF VARCHAR2 (200);

   l_cv             sys_refcursor;
   l_placeholders   strings_t     := strings_t ('dept_id');
   l_values         strings_t     := strings_t ('20');
   l_names          strings_t;

   FUNCTION employee_names (
      where_in            IN    VARCHAR2
    , bind_variables_in   IN    strings_t
    , placeholders_in     IN    strings_t
   )
      RETURN sys_refcursor
   IS
      l_dyn_cursor   NUMBER;
      l_cv           sys_refcursor;
      l_dummy        PLS_INTEGER;
   BEGIN
      /* Parse the retrieval of last names after appending the WHERE clause.

      NOTE: if you ever write code like this yourself, you MUST take steps
      to minimize the risk of SQL injection. This topic is also covered in
      this chapter. READ IT!
      */
      l_dyn_cursor := DBMS_SQL.open_cursor;
      DBMS_SQL.parse (l_dyn_cursor
                   , 'SELECT last_name FROM employees WHERE ' || where_in
                   , DBMS_SQL.native
                   );
      /*
         Bind each of the variables to the named placeholders;
         You cannot use EXECUTE IMMEDIATE for this step if you have
         a variable number of placeholders!
      */
      FOR indx IN 1 .. placeholders_in.COUNT
      LOOP
         DBMS_SQL.bind_variable (l_dyn_cursor
                              , placeholders_in (indx)
                              , bind_variables_in (indx)
```

```
                              );
         END LOOP;
         /*
         Execute the query now that all variables are bound.
         */
         l_dummy := DBMS_SQL.EXECUTE (l_dyn_cursor);
         /*
         Now it's time to convert to a cursor variable so that the frontend
         program or another PL/SQL program can easily fetch the values.
         */
         l_cv := DBMS_SQL.to_refcursor (l_dyn_cursor);
         /*
         Do not close with DBMS_SQL; you can ONLY manipulate the cursor
         through the cursor variable at this point.
         DBMS_SQL.close_cursor (l_dyn_cursor);
         */
         RETURN l_cv;
      END employee_names;
   BEGIN
      l_cv := employee_names ('DEPARTMENT_ID = :dept_id', l_values, l_placeholders);

      FETCH l_cv BULK COLLECT INTO l_names;

      FOR indx IN 1 .. l_names.COUNT
      LOOP
         DBMS_OUTPUT.put_line (l_names(indx));
      END LOOP;

      CLOSE l_cv;
   END;
   /
```

Another example of a scenario in which this function will come in handy is when you need to execute dynamic SQL that requires DBMS_SQL, but then you need to pass the result set back to the middle tier client (as with Java or .Net-based applications). You cannot pass back a DBMS_SQL cursor, but you definitely can return a cursor variable.

## DBMS_SQL.TO_CURSOR Function

Use the DBMS_SQL.TO_CURSOR function to convert a REF CURSOR variable (either strongly or weakly typed) to a SQL cursor number which you can then pass to DBMS_SQL subprograms. The cursor variable must already have been opened before you can pass it to the DBMS_SQL.TO_CURSOR function.

After you convert the cursor variable to a DBMS_SQL cursor, you will not be able to use native dynamic SQL operations to access that cursor or the data "behind" it.

This function comes in handy when you know at compile time how many variables you need to bind into the SQL statement, but you don't know how many items you are selecting (another example of dynamic SQL method 4!).

The following procedure demonstrates this application of the function.

---

```
/* File on web: 11g_to_cursorid.sql */
PROCEDURE show_data (
   column_list_in              VARCHAR2
, department_id_in     IN     employees.department_id%TYPE
)
IS
   sql_stmt    CLOB;
   src_cur     SYS_REFCURSOR;
   curid       NUMBER;
   desctab     DBMS_SQL.desc_tab;
   colcnt      NUMBER;
   namevar     VARCHAR2 (50);
   numvar      NUMBER;
   datevar     DATE;
   empno       NUMBER              := 100;
BEGIN
   /* Construct the query, embedding the list of columns to be selected,
      with a single bind variable.

      NOTE: this kind of concatenation leaves you vulnerable to SQL injection!
      Please read the section in this chapter on injection so that you can
      make sure your application is not vulnerable.
   */
   sql_stmt :=
         'SELECT '
      || column_list_in
      || ' FROM employees WHERE department_id = :dept_id';

   /* Open the cursor variable for this query, binding in the single value.
      MUCH EASIER than using DBMS_SQL for the same operations!
   */
   OPEN src_cur FOR sql_stmt USING department_id_in;

   /*
   To fetch the data, however, I can no longer use the cursor variable,
   since the number of elements fetched is unknown at complile time.

   This is, however, a perfect fit for DBMS_SQL and the DESCRIBE_COLUMNS
   procedure, so convert the cursor variable to a DBMS_SQL cursor number,
   and then take the necessary, if tedious steps.
   */
   curid := DBMS_SQL.to_cursor_number (src_cur);
   DBMS_SQL.describe_columns (curid, colcnt, desctab);

   FOR indx IN 1 .. colcnt
   LOOP
      IF desctab (indx).col_type = 2
      THEN
         DBMS_SQL.define_column (curid, indx, numvar);
      ELSIF desctab (indx).col_type = 12
      THEN
         DBMS_SQL.define_column (curid, indx, datevar);
      ELSE
         DBMS_SQL.define_column (curid, indx, namevar, 100);
      END IF;
```

```
      END LOOP;

      WHILE DBMS_SQL.fetch_rows (curid) > 0
      LOOP
         FOR indx IN 1 .. colcnt
         LOOP
            DBMS_OUTPUT.put_line (desctab (indx).col_name || ' = ');

            IF (desctab (indx).col_type = 1)
            THEN
               DBMS_SQL.COLUMN_VALUE (curid, indx, namevar);
               DBMS_OUTPUT.put_line ('   ' || namevar);
            ELSIF (desctab (indx).col_type = 2)
            THEN
               DBMS_SQL.COLUMN_VALUE (curid, indx, numvar);
               DBMS_OUTPUT.put_line ('   ' || numvar);
            ELSIF (desctab (indx).col_type = 12)
            THEN
               DBMS_SQL.COLUMN_VALUE (curid, indx, datevar);
               DBMS_OUTPUT.put_line ('   ' || datevar);
            END IF;
         END LOOP;
      END LOOP;

      DBMS_SQL.close_cursor (curid);
   END;
```

## Enhanced Security for DBMS_SQL

In 2006, security specialists identified a new class of vulnerability in which a program that uses DBMS_SQL and raises an exception allows an attacker to use the unclosed cursor to compromise the security of the database.[2]

Oracle Database 11g has introduced three security-related changes to DBMS_SQL to guard against this kind of attack:

- Generation of unpredictable, probably randomized, cursor numbers.
- Restriction of the use of the DBMS_SQL package whenever an invalid cursor number is passed to a DBMS_SQL program.
- Rejection of a DBMS_SQL operation when the current user attempting to use the cursor has changed from the user that opened the cursor.

### Unpredictable cursor numbers

Prior to Oracle Database 11g, calls to DBMS_SQL.OPEN_CURSOR returned a sequentially incremented number, usually between 1 and 300. This predictability could

---

2. For more details, visit David Litchfield's blog at *http://www.davidlitchfield.com/blog/archives/00000023 .htm.*

allow an attacker to iterate through integers and test them as valid, open cursors. Once found, a cursor could be repurposed and used by the attacker.

Now, it will be very difficult for an attacker to find a valid cursor through iteration. Here, for example, are five cursor numbers returned by OPEN_CURSOR in this block:

```
BEGIN
   FOR indx IN 1 .. 5
   LOOP
      DBMS_OUTPUT.put_line (DBMS_SQL.open_cursor ());
   END LOOP;
END;
/
1693551900
1514010786
1570905132
182110745
1684406543
```

### Denial of access to DBMS_SQL when bad cursor number is used (ORA-24971)

To guard against an attacker "fishing" for a valid cursor, the Oracle database will now deny access to the DBMS_SQL package as soon as an attempt is made to work with an invalid cursor number.

Consider the following block:

```
/* File on web: 11g_access_denied_1.sql */
DECLARE
   l_cursor    NUMBER;
   l_feedback  NUMBER;

   PROCEDURE set_salary
   IS
   BEGIN
      DBMS_OUTPUT.put_line ('Set salary = salary...');
      l_cursor := DBMS_SQL.open_cursor ();
      DBMS_SQL.parse (l_cursor
                     , 'update employees set salary - salary'
                     , DBMS_SQL.native
                     );
      l_feedback := DBMS_SQL.EXECUTE (l_cursor);
      DBMS_OUTPUT.put_line ('   Rows modified = ' || l_feedback);
      DBMS_SQL.close_cursor (l_cursor);
   END set_salary;
BEGIN
   set_salary ();

   BEGIN
      l_feedback := DBMS_SQL.EXECUTE (1010101010);
   EXCEPTION
      WHEN OTHERS
      THEN
         DBMS_OUTPUT.put_line (DBMS_UTILITY.format_error_stack ());
         DBMS_OUTPUT.put_line (DBMS_UTILITY.format_error_backtrace ());
```

```
        END;

    set_salary ();
EXCEPTION
   WHEN OTHERS
   THEN
      DBMS_OUTPUT.put_line (DBMS_UTILITY.format_error_stack ());
      DBMS_OUTPUT.put_line (DBMS_UTILITY.format_error_backtrace ());
END;
```

I execute a valid UPDATE statement, setting salary to itself for all rows in the employees table, within the set_salary local procedure. I call that procedure, then I attempt to execute an invalid cursor. Then I call set_salary again. Here are the results from running this block:

```
Set salary = salary...
   Rows modified = 106

ORA-29471: DBMS_SQL access denied
ORA-06512: at "SYS.DBMS_SQL", line 1501
ORA-06512: at line 22

Set salary = salary...
ORA-29471: DBMS_SQL access denied
ORA-06512: at "SYS.DBMS_SQL", line 980
ORA-06512: at line 9
ORA-06512: at line 30
```

The set_salary procedure worked the first time, but once I tried to execute an invalid cursor, I now get the ORA-29471 error when I try to run the set_salary program again. In fact, any attempt to call a DBMS_SQL program will raise that error.

The only way to re-enable access to DBMS_SQL again is by logging off and logging back on. Rather severe! But that makes sense, given the possibly dangerous nature of the situation that resulted in this error.

The database will also deny access to DBMS_SQL if the program in which you opened the cursor raised an exception (not necessarily related to the dynamic SQL). If you "swallow" that error (do not re-raise the exception), then it can be quite difficult to determine the source of the error.

### Rejection of DBMS_SQL operation when effective user changes (ORA-24970)

Oracle Database 11g provides a new overloading of the OPEN_CURSOR function that accepts an argument as follows:

```
DBMS_SQL.OPEN_CURSOR (security_level IN INTEGER) RETURN INTEGER;
```

This function allows you to specify security protection that Oracle enforces on the opened cursor when you perform operations on that cursor Here are the security levels that the database currently recognizes:

*0*

Turns off security checks for DBMS_SQL operations on this cursor. You can fetch from the cursor, re-bind and re-execute the cursor, with a different effective userid or roles than those in effect at the time the cursor was first parsed. This level of security is *not enabled by default*.

*1*

Requires that the effective userid and roles of the caller to DBMS_SQL for bind and execute operations on this cursor be the same as those of the caller of the most recent parse operation on this cursor.

*2*

Requires that the effective userid and roles of the caller to DBMS_SQL for all bind, execute, define, describe, and fetch operations on this cursor be the same as those of the caller.

Here is an example of how you might encounter the error caused by Oracle's new security check:

1. Create the user_cursor procedure in the HR schema. Note that this is a definer rights program, meaning that when another schema calls this program, the current or effective user is HR. I open a cursor and parse a query against ALL_SOURCE with this cursor. Then I return the DBMS_SQL cursor number as an OUT argument.

```
/* File on web: 11g_effective_user_id.sql */
PROCEDURE user_cursor (
   security_level_in    IN       PLS_INTEGER
 , cursor_out           IN OUT   NUMBER
 )
AUTHID DEFINER
IS
BEGIN
   cursor_out := DBMS_SQL.open_cursor (security_level_in);
   DBMS_SQL.parse (cursor_out
                  , 'select count(*) from all_source'
                  , DBMS_SQL.native
                  );
END;
```

2. Grant the ability to run this program to SCOTT:

```
GRANT EXECUTE ON use_cursor TO scott
```

3. Connect to SCOTT. Then run HR's use_cursor program, specifying level 2 security, and retrieve the dynamic SQL cursor. Then try to execute that cursor from the SCOTT schema.

```
SQL> DECLARE
  2     l_cursor    NUMBER;
  3     l_feedback number;
  4  BEGIN
  5     hr.use_cursor (2, l_cursor);
  6     l_feedback := DBMS_SQL.execute_and_fetch (l_cursor);
  7  END;
  8  /
DECLARE
*
ERROR at line 1:
ORA-29470: Effective userid or roles are not the same as when cursor was parsed
ORA-06512: at "SYS.DBMS_SQL", line 1513
ORA-06512: at line 6
```

Oracle raises the –29470 error because the cursor was opened and parsed under the HR schema (as a result of the AUTHID DEFINER clause), but executed under the SCOTT schema.

# PART V

# PL/SQL Application Construction

This part of the book is where it all comes together. By now, you've learned the basics. You know about declaring and working with variables. You're an expert on error handling and loop construction. Now it's time to build an application—and you do that by constructing the building blocks, made up of procedures, functions, packages, and triggers, as described in Chapters17 through 19. Chapter 20 discusses managing your PL/SQL code base, including testing and debugging programs and managing dependencies; it also provides an overview of the edition-based redefinition capability introduced in Oracle Database 11g Release 2. Chapter 21, new in the fifth edition, focuses on how you can use a variety of tools and techniques to get the best performance out of your PL/SQL programs. Chapter 22 describes I/O techniques for PL/SQL, from DBMS_OUTPUT (sending output to the screen) and UTL_FILE (reading and writing files) to UTL_MAIL (sending mail) and UTL_HTTP (retrieving data from a web page).

Chapter 17, *Procedures, Functions, and Parameters*
Chapter 18, *Packages*
Chapter 19, *Triggers*
Chapter 20, *Managing PL/SQL Code*
Chapter 21, *Optimizing PL/SQL Performance*
Chapter 22, *I/O and PL/SQL*

# Procedures, Functions, and Parameters

Earlier parts of this book have explored in detail all of the components of the PL/SQL language: cursors, exceptions, loops, variables, and so on. While you certainly need to know about these components when you write applications using PL/SQL, putting the pieces together to create well-structured, easily understood, and smoothly maintainable programs is even more important.

Few of our tasks are straightforward. Few solutions can be glimpsed in an instant and immediately put to paper or keyboard. The systems we build are usually large and complex, with many interacting and sometimes conflicting components. Furthermore, as users deserve, demand, and receive applications that are easier to use and vastly more powerful than their predecessors, the inner world of those applications becomes correspondingly more complicated.

One of the biggest challenges in our profession today is finding ways to reduce the complexity of our environment. When faced with a massive problem to solve, the mind is likely to recoil in horror. Where do I start? How can I possibly find a way through that jungle of requirements and features?

A human being is not a massively parallel computer. Even the brightest of our bunch have trouble keeping track of more than seven tasks (plus or minus two) at one time. We need to break down huge, intimidating projects into smaller, more manageable components, and then further decompose those components into individual programs with an understandable scope. We can then figure out how to build and test those programs, after which we can construct a complete application from these building blocks.

Whether you use "top-down design" (a.k.a. step-wise refinement, which is explored in detail in the section "Local or Nested Modules" on page 583) or some other methodology, there is absolutely no doubt that you will find your way to a high-quality and easily maintainable application by modularizing your code into procedures, functions, and object types.

# Modular Code

*Modularization* is the process by which you break up large blocks of code into smaller pieces (modules) that can be called by other modules. Modularization of code is analogous to normalization of data, with many of the same benefits and a few additional advantages. With modularization, your code becomes:

*More reusable*
> By breaking up a large program or entire application into individual components that "plug-and-play" together, you will usually find that many modules are used by more than one other program in your current application. Designed properly, these utility programs could even be of use in other applications!

*More manageable*
> Which would you rather debug: a 1,000-line program or five individual 200-line programs that call each other as needed? Our minds work better when we can focus on smaller tasks. You can also test and debug on a per-program scale (called *unit testing*) before individual modules are combined for a more complicated integration test.

*More readable*
> Modules have names, and names describe behavior. The more you move or hide your code behind a programmatic interface, the easier it is to read and understand what that program is doing. Modularization helps you focus on the big picture rather than on the individual executable statements. You might even end up with that most elusive kind of software: self-documenting code.

*More reliable*
> The code you produce will have fewer errors. The errors you do find will be easier to fix because they will be isolated within a module. In addition, your code will be easier to maintain because there is less of it and it is more readable.

Once you become proficient with the different iterative, conditional, and cursor constructs of the PL/SQL language (the IF statement, loops, etc.), you are ready to write programs. You will not really be ready to build an application, however, until you understand how to create and combine PL/SQL modules.

PL/SQL offers the following structures that modularize your code in different ways:

*Procedure*
> A program that performs one or more actions and is called as an executable PL/SQL statement. You can pass information into and out of a procedure through its parameter list.

*Function*

A program that returns data through its RETURN clause, and is used just like a PL/SQL expression. You can pass information into a function through its parameter list. You can also pass information out via the parameter list, but this is generally considered a bad practice.

*Database trigger*

A set of commands that are triggered to execute (e.g., log in, modify a row in a table, execute a DDL statement) when an event occurs in the database.

*Package*

A named collection of procedures, functions, types, and variables. A package is not really a module (it's more of a meta-module), but it is so closely related that I mention it here.

*Object type or instance of an object type*

Oracle's version of (or attempt to emulate) an object-oriented class. Object types encapsulate state and behavior, combining data (like a relational table) with rules (procedures and functions that operate on that data).

Packages are discussed in Chapter 18; database triggers are explored in Chapter 19. You can read more about object types in Chapter 26. This chapter focuses on how to build procedures and functions, and how to design the parameter lists that are an integral part of well-designed modules.

I use the term *module* to mean either a function or a procedure. As is the case with many other programming languages, modules can call other named modules. You can pass information into and out of modules with parameters. Finally, the modular structure of PL/SQL also integrates tightly with exception handlers to provide all-encompassing error-checking techniques (see Chapter 6).

This chapter explores how to define procedures and functions, and then dives into the details of setting up parameter lists for these programs. I also examine some of the more "exotic" aspects of program construction, including local modules, overloading, forward referencing, deterministic functions, and table functions.

# Procedures

A *procedure* is a module that performs one or more actions. Because a procedure call is a standalone executable statement in PL/SQL, a PL/SQL block could consist of nothing more than a single call to a procedure. Procedures are key building blocks of modular code, allowing you to both consolidate and reuse your program logic.

The general format of a PL/SQL procedure is as follows:

```
PROCEDURE [schema.]name[( parameter[, parameter...] ) ]
   [AUTHID DEFINER | CURRENT_USER]
IS
   [declarations]
```

```
BEGIN
   executable statements

[ EXCEPTION
     exception handlers]

 END [name];
```

where each element is used in the following ways:

*schema*

Optional name of the schema that will own this procedure. The default is the current user. If different from the current user, that user will need privileges to create a procedure in another schema.

*name*

The name of the procedure.

*parameters*

An optional list of parameters that you define to both pass information to the procedure, and send information out of the procedure back to the calling program.

*AUTHID clause*

Determines whether the procedure will execute with the privileges of the definer (owner) of the procedure or the current user. The former is known as the *definer rights model*, the latter as the *invoker rights model*. These models are described in detail in Chapter 24.

*declarations*

The declarations of local identifiers for that procedure. If you do not have any declarations, there will be no statements between the IS and BEGIN statements.

*executable statements*

The statements that the procedure executes when it is called. You must have at least one executable statement after the BEGIN and before the END or EXCEPTION keywords.

*exception handlers*

The optional exception handlers for the procedure. If you do not explicitly handle any exceptions, then you can leave out the EXCEPTION keyword and simply terminate the execution section with the END keyword.

Figure 17-1 shows the apply_discount procedure, which contains all four sections of the named PL/SQL block as well as a parameter list.

## Calling a Procedure

A procedure is called as an executable PL/SQL statement. In other words, a call to a procedure must end with a semicolon (;) and be executed before or after other SQL or PL/SQL statements (if they exist) in the execution section of a PL/SQL block.

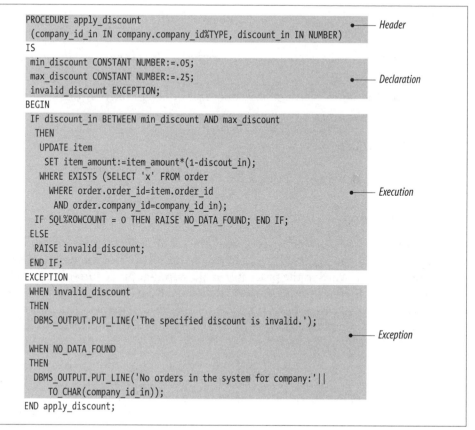

```
            PROCEDURE apply_discount
              (company_id_in IN company.company_id%TYPE, discount_in IN NUMBER)    ●——— Header
            IS
              min_discount CONSTANT NUMBER:=.05;
              max_discount CONSTANT NUMBER:=.25;                                   ●——— Declaration
              invalid_discount EXCEPTION;
            BEGIN
              IF discount_in BETWEEN min_discount AND max_discount
                THEN
                  UPDATE item
                  SET item_amount:=item_amount*(1-discout_in);
                  WHERE EXISTS (SELECT 'x' FROM order
                    WHERE order.order_id=item.order_id                             ●——— Execution
                      AND order.company_id=company_id_in);
               IF SQL%ROWCOUNT = 0 THEN RAISE NO_DATA_FOUND; END IF;
              ELSE
                RAISE invalid_discount;
              END IF;
            EXCEPTION
              WHEN invalid_discount
              THEN
                DBMS_OUTPUT.PUT_LINE('The specified discount is invalid.');
                                                                                   ●——— Exception
              WHEN NO_DATA_FOUND
              THEN
                DBMS_OUTPUT.PUT_LINE('No orders in the system for company:'||
                    TO_CHAR(company_id_in));
            END apply_discount;
```

*Figure 17-1. The apply_discount procedure*

The following executable statement runs the apply_discount procedure:

```
BEGIN
    apply_discount( new_company_id, 0.15 );      -- 15% discount
END;
```

If the procedure does not have any parameters, then you may call the procedure with or without parentheses, as shown here:

```
display_store_summary;
display_store_summary();
```

## The Procedure Header

The portion of the procedure definition that comes before the IS keyword is called the *procedure header* or *signature*. The header provides all the information a programmer needs to call that procedure, namely:

- The procedure name

- The AUTHID clause, if any
- The parameter list, if any

Ideally, a programmer should only need to see the header of the procedure in order to understand what it does and how it is to be called.

The header for the apply_discount procedure mentioned in the previous section is:

```
PROCEDURE apply_discount (
    company_id_in IN company.company_id%TYPE
  , discount_in IN NUMBER
)
```

It consists of the module type, the name, and a list of two parameters.

## The Procedure Body

The body of the procedure is the code required to implement that procedure, and consists of the declaration, execution, and exception sections of the function. Everything after the IS keyword in the procedure makes up that procedure's body. The exception and declaration sections are optional. If you have no exception handlers, leave off the EXCEPTION keyword and simply enter the END statement to terminate the procedure. If you have no declarations, the BEGIN statement simply follows immediately after the IS keyword.

You must supply at least one executable statement in a procedure. That is generally not a problem; instead, watch out for execution sections that become extremely long and hard to manage. You should work hard to keep the execution section compact and readable. See later sections in this chapter, especially "Improving readability" on page 592, for more specific guidance on this topic.

## The END Label

You can append the name of the procedure directly after the END keyword when you complete your procedure, as shown here:

```
PROCEDURE display_stores (region_in IN VARCHAR2) IS
BEGIN
   ...
END display_stores;
```

This name serves as a label that explicitly links the end of the program with its beginning. You should, as a matter of habit, use an END label. It is especially important to do so when you have a procedure that spans more than a single page, or is one in a series of procedures and functions in a package body.

## The RETURN Statement

The RETURN statement is generally associated with a function because it is required to RETURN a value from a function (or else raise an exception). Interestingly, PL/SQL also allows you to use a RETURN statement in a procedure. The procedure version of the RETURN does not take an expression; it therefore cannot pass a value back to the calling program unit. The RETURN simply halts execution of the procedure and returns control to the calling code.

You do not see this usage of RETURN very often, and for good reason. Use of the RETURN in a procedure usually leads to unstructured code because there would then be at least two paths out of the procedure, making execution flow harder to understand and maintain. Avoid using both RETURN and GOTO to bypass proper control structures and process flow in your program units.

# Functions

A *function* is a module that returns data through its RETURN clause, rather than in an OUT or IN OUT argument. Unlike a procedure call, which is a standalone executable statement, a call to a function can exist only as part of an executable statement, such as an element in an expression or the value assigned as the default in a declaration of a variable.

Because a function returns a value, it is said to have a datatype. A function can be used in place of an expression in a PL/SQL statement having the same datatype as the function.

Functions are particularly important constructs for building modular code. For example, every single business rule or formula in your application should be placed inside a function. Every single-row query should also be defined within a function, so that it can be easily and reliably reused.

 Some programmers prefer to rely less on functions, and more on procedures that return status information through the parameter list. If you are one of these programmers, make sure that your business rules, formulas, and single-row queries are tucked away into your procedures!

An application short on function definition and usage is likely to be difficult to maintain and enhance over time.

## Structure of a Function

The structure of a function is the same as that of a procedure, except that the function also has a RETURN clause. The general format of a function is as follows:

```
FUNCTION [schema.]name[( parameter[, parameter...] ) ]
   RETURN return_datatype
   [AUTHID DEFINER | CURRENT_USER]
   [DETERMINISTIC]
   [PARALLEL_ENABLE ...]
   [PIPELINED]
   [RESULT_CACHE ...]
IS
   [declaration statements]

BEGIN
   executable statements

[EXCEPTION
   exception handler statements]

END [name];
```

where each element is used in the following ways:

*schema*

Optional name of the schema that will own this function. The default is the current user. If different from the current user, that user will need privileges to create a function in another schema.

*name*

The name of the function.

*parameters*

An optional list of parameters that you define to both pass information into the function and send information out of the function back to the calling program.

*return_datatype*

The datatype of the value returned by the function. This is required in the function header and is explained in more detail in the next section.

*AUTHID clause*

Determines whether the function will execute with the privileges of the definer (owner) of the procedure or of the current user. The former is known as the *definer rights model*, the latter as the *invoker rights model*.

*DETERMINISTIC clause*

An optimization hint that lets the system use a saved copy of the function's return result, if available. The query optimizer can choose whether to use the saved copy or re-call the function.

*PARALLEL_ENABLE clause*

An optimization hint that enables the function to be executed in parallel when called from within a SELECT statement.

*PIPELINED clause*

Specifies that the results of this table function should be returned iteratively via the PIPE ROW command.

*RESULT_CACHE clause*

New to Oracle Database 11*g*. Specifies that the input values and result of this function should be stored in the new function result cache. This feature is explored in detail in Chapter 21, *Optimizing PL/SQL Performance*.

*declaration statements*

The declarations of local identifiers for that function. If you do not have any declarations, there will be no statements between the IS and BEGIN statements.

*executable statements*

The statements the function executes when it is called. You must have at least one executable statement after the BEGIN and before the END or EXCEPTION keywords.

*exception handler statements*

The optional exception handlers for the function. If you do not explicitly handle any exceptions, then you can leave out the EXCEPTION keyword and simply terminate the execution section with the END keyword.

Figure 17-2 illustrates the PL/SQL function and its different sections. Notice that the total_sales function does not have an exception section.

## The RETURN Datatype

A PL/SQL function can return virtually any kind of data known to PL/SQL, from scalars (single, primitive values like dates and strings) to complex structures such as collections, object types, cursor variables, and LOBs. You may not, however, return an exception through a function.

Here are some examples of RETURN clauses in functions:

- Return a string from a standalone function:

```
FUNCTION favorite_nickname (
    name_in IN VARCHAR2) RETURN VARCHAR2
IS
BEGIN
   ...
END;
```

- Return a number (age of a pet) from an object type member function:

```
TYPE pet_t IS OBJECT (
    tag_no              INTEGER,
    NAME                VARCHAR2 (60),
    breed               VARCHAR2(100),
    dob DATE,
    MEMBER FUNCTION age  RETURN NUMBER
)
```

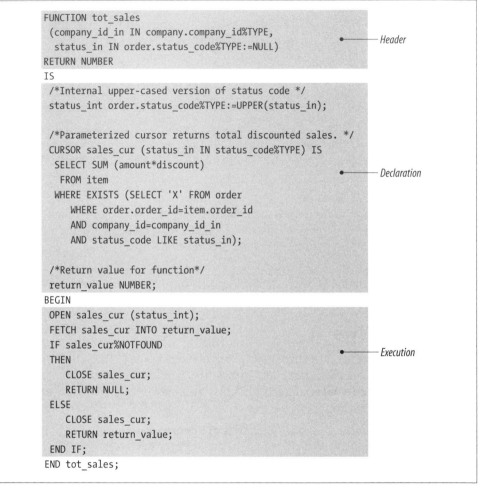

```
FUNCTION tot_sales
 (company_id_in IN company.company_id%TYPE,
  status_in IN order.status_code%TYPE:=NULL)
RETURN NUMBER                                              ──── Header
IS
 /*Internal upper-cased version of status code */
 status_int order.status_code%TYPE:=UPPER(status_in);

 /*Parameterized cursor returns total discounted sales. */
 CURSOR sales_cur (status_in IN status_code%TYPE) IS
  SELECT SUM (amount*discount)
    FROM item                                              ──── Declaration
  WHERE EXISTS (SELECT 'X' FROM order
      WHERE order.order_id=item.order_id
      AND company_id=company_id_in
      AND status_code LIKE status_in);

 /*Return value for function*/
 return_value NUMBER;
BEGIN
 OPEN sales_cur (status_int);
 FETCH sales_cur INTO return_value;
 IF sales_cur%NOTFOUND
 THEN                                                      ──── Execution
    CLOSE sales_cur;
    RETURN NULL;
 ELSE
    CLOSE sales_cur;
    RETURN return_value;
 END IF;
END tot_sales;
```

*Figure 17-2. The tot_sales function*

- Return a record with the same structure as the books table:

  ```
  PACKAGE book_info
  IS
     FUNCTION onerow (isbn_in IN books.isbn%TYPE)
       RETURN books%ROWTYPE;
  ...
  ```

- Return a cursor variable with the specified REF CURSOR type (based on a record type):

  ```
  PACKAGE book_info
  IS
     TYPE overdue_rt IS RECORD (
        isbn books.isbn%TYPE,
        days_overdue PLS_INTEGER);
  ```

```
TYPE overdue_rct IS REF CURSOR RETURN overdue_rt;

FUNCTION overdue_info (username_in IN lib_users.username%TYPE)
  RETURN overdue_rct;
```
...

## The END Label

You can append the name of the function directly after the END keyword when you complete your function, as shown here:

```
FUNCTION total_sales (company_in IN INTEGER) RETURN NUMBER
IS
BEGIN
   ...
END total_sales;
```

This name serves as a label that explicitly links the end of the program with its beginning. You should, as a matter of habit, use an END label. It is especially important to do so when you have a function that spans more than a single page or that is one in a series of functions and procedures in a package body.

## Calling a Function

A function is called as part of an executable PL/SQL statement wherever an expression can be used. The following examples illustrate how the various functions defined in the section "The RETURN Datatype" on page 573 can be invoked.

- Assign the default value of a variable with a function call:

```
DECLARE
   v_nickname VARCHAR2(100) :=
      favorite_nickname ('Steven');
```

- Use a member function for the pet object type in a conditional expression:

```
DECLARE
   my_parrot pet_t :=
      pet_t (1001, 'Mercury', 'African Grey',
             TO_DATE ('09/23/1996', 'MM/DD/YYYY'));
BEGIN
   IF my_parrot.age () < INTERVAL '50' YEAR
     THEN
        DBMS_OUTPUT.PUT_LINE ('Still a youngster!');
     END IF;
```

- Retrieve a single row of book information directly into a record:

```
DECLARE
   my_first_book books%ROWTYPE;
BEGIN
```

```
        my_first_book := book_info.onerow ('1-56592-335-9');
        ...
```

- Call a user-defined PL/SQL function from within a query:

```
DECLARE
  l_name employees.last_name%TYPE;
BEGIN

  SELECT last_name INTO l_name
    FROM employees
   WHERE employee_id = hr_info_pkg.employee_of_the_month ('FEBRUARY');
   ...
```

- Call a function of your own making from within a CREATE VIEW statement, utilizing a CURSOR expression to pass a result set as an argument to that function:

```
VIEW young_managers
AS
  SELECT managers.employee_id AS manager_employee_id
    FROM employees managers
   WHERE most_reports_before_manager
     (
       CURSOR ( SELECT reports.hire_date
                  FROM employees reports
                 WHERE reports.manager_id = managers.employee_id
              ),
       managers.hire_date
     ) = 1;
```

With PL/SQL, in contrast to some other programming languages, you cannot simply ignore the return value of a function if you don't need it. For example, this function call:

```
BEGIN
    favorite_nickname('Steven');
END;
```

will raise the error *PLS-00221: 'FAVORITE_NICKNAME' is not a procedure or is undefined*. You may not use a function as if it were a procedure.

## Functions Without Parameters

If a function has no parameters, the function call can be written with or without parentheses. The following code illustrates this with a call to a method named "age" of the pet_t object type:

```
IF my_parrot.age < INTERVAL '50' YEAR -- 9i INTERVAL type
IF my_parrot.age() < INTERVAL '50' YEAR
```

## The Function Header

The portion of the function definition that comes before the IS keyword is called the *function header* or *signature*. The header provides all the information a programmer needs to call that function, namely:

---

- The function name
- Modifiers to the definition and behavior of the function (e.g., is it deterministic? Does it run in parallel execution? Is it pipelined?)
- The parameter list, if any
- The RETURN datatype

Ideally, a programmer should need to look only at the header of the function in order to understand what it does and how it is to be called.

The header for the total_sales function discussed earlier is:

```
FUNCTION total_sales
    (company_id_in IN company.company_id%TYPE,
     status_in IN order.status_code%TYPE := NULL)
RETURN NUMBER
```

It consists of the module type, the name, a list of two parameters, and a RETURN datatype of NUMBER. This means that any PL/SQL statement or expression that references a numeric value can make a call to total_sales to obtain that value. Here is one such statement:

```
DECLARE
    v_sales NUMBER;
BEGIN
    v_sales := total_sales (1505, 'ACTIVE');
    ...
END;
```

## The Function Body

The body of the function is the code required to implement the function. It consists of the declaration, execution, and exception sections of the function. Everything after the IS keyword in the function makes up that function's body.

Once again, the declaration and exception sections are optional. If you have no exception handlers, simply leave off the EXCEPTION keyword and enter the END statement to terminate the function. If you have no declarations, the BEGIN statement simply follows immediately after the IS keyword.

A function's execution section should have a RETURN statement in it, although it is not necessary for the function to compile. If, however, your function finishes executing without executing a RETURN statement, Oracle will raise the following error (a sure sign of a very poorly designed function):

```
ORA-06503: PL/SQL: Function returned without value
```

 This error will *not* be raised if the function propagates an exception of its own unhandled out of the function.

# The RETURN Statement

A function must have at least one RETURN statement in its execution section of statements. It can have more than one RETURN, but only one is executed each time the function is called. The RETURN statement that is executed by the function determines the value that is returned by that function. When a RETURN statement is processed, the function terminates immediately and returns control to the calling PL/SQL block.

The RETURN clause in the header of the function is different from the RETURN statement in the execution section of the body. While the RETURN clause indicates the datatype of the return or result value of the function, the RETURN statement specifies the actual value that is returned. You have to specify the RETURN datatype in the header, but then also include at least one RETURN statement in the function. The datatype indicated in the RETURN clause in the header must be compatible with the datatype of the returned expression in the RETURN statement.

### RETURN any valid expression

The RETURN statement can return any expression compatible with the datatype indicated in the RETURN clause. This expression can be composed of calls to other functions, complex calculations, and even data conversions. All of the following usages of RETURN are valid:

```
RETURN 'buy me lunch';
RETURN POWER (max_salary, 5);
RETURN (100 - pct_of_total_salary (employee_id));
RETURN TO_DATE ('01' || earliest_month || initial_year, 'DDMMYY');
```

You can also return complex data structures such as object type instances, collections, and records.

An expression in the RETURN statement is evaluated when the RETURN is executed. When control is passed back to the calling block, the result of the evaluated expression is passed along, too.

### Multiple RETURNs

In the total_sales function shown in Figure 17-2, I used two different RETURN statements to handle different situations in the function, which can be described as follows:

> If I cannot obtain sales information from the cursor, I return NULL (which is different from zero). If I do get a value from the cursor, I return it to the calling program. In both of these cases, the RETURN statement passes back a value: in one case, the NULL value, and in the other, the return_value variable.

While it is certainly possible to have more than one RETURN statement in the execution section of a function, you are generally better off having just one: the last line in your execution section. The next section explains this recommendation.

### RETURN as last executable statement

Generally, the best way to make sure that your function always returns a value is to make the last executable statement your RETURN statement. Declare a variable named return_value (which clearly indicates that it will contain the return value for the function), write all the code to come up with that value, and then, at the very end of the function, RETURN the return_value, as shown here:

```
FUNCTION do_it_all (parameter_list) RETURN NUMBER IS
   return_value NUMBER;
BEGIN
   ... lots of executable statements ...
   RETURN return_value;
END;
```

Here is a rewrite of the logic in Figure 17-2 to fix the problem of multiple RETURN statements.

```
OPEN sales_cur;
IF sales_cur%NOTFOUND
THEN
   return_value:= NULL;
END IF;
CLOSE sales_cur;
RETURN return_value;
```

Beware of exceptions, though. An exception that gets raised might "jump" over your last statement straight into the exception handler. If your exception handler does not then have a RETURN statement, you will get an *ORA-06503: Function returned without value* error, regardless of how you handled the actual exception (unless you RAISE another).

## Parameters

Procedures and functions can both use *parameters* to pass information back and forth between the module and the calling PL/SQL block.

The parameters of a module, part of its header or signature, are at least as important as the code that implements the module (the module's body). In fact, the header of the program is sometimes described as a "contract"—between the author of the program and its users. Sure, you have to make certain that your module fulfills its promise. But the whole point of creating a module is that it can be called, ideally by more than one other module. If the parameter list is confusing or badly designed, it will be very difficult for other programmers to use the module, and the result is that few will bother. And it doesn't matter how well you implemented a program if no one uses it.

Many developers do not give enough attention to a module's set of parameters. Considerations regarding parameters include:

*Number of parameters*

Too few parameters can limit the reusability of your program; with too many parameters, no one will want to reuse your program. Certainly, the number of parameters is largely determined by program requirements, but there are different ways to define parameters (such as bundling multiple parameters in a single record).

*Types of parameters*

Should you use read-only, write-only, or read-write parameters?

*Names of parameters*

How should you name your parameters so that their purpose in the module is properly and easily understood?

*Default values for parameters*

How do you set defaults? When should a parameter be given defaults, and when should the programmer be forced to enter a value?

PL/SQL offers many different features to help you design parameters effectively. This section covers all elements of parameter definition.

## Defining Parameters

Formal parameters are defined in the parameter list of the program. A parameter definition parallels closely the syntax for declaring variables in the declaration section of a PL/SQL block. There are two important distinctions: first, a parameter has a passing mode while a variable declaration does not; and second, a parameter declaration must be unconstrained.

A *constrained declaration* is one that constrains or limits the kind of value that can be assigned to a variable declared with that datatype. An *unconstrained declaration* is one that does not limit values in this way. The following declaration of the variable company_name constrains the variable to 60 characters:

```
DECLARE
    company_name VARCHAR2(60);
```

When you declare a parameter, however, you must leave out the constraining part of the declaration:

```
PROCEDURE display_company (company_name IN VARCHAR2) IS ...
```

## Actual and Formal Parameters

We need to distinguish between two different kinds of parameters: actual and formal parameters. The *formal parameters* are the names that are declared in the parameter list of the header of a module. The *actual parameters* are the values or expressions placed in the parameter list of the actual call to the module.

Let's examine the differences between formal and actual parameters using the example of total_sales. Here, again, is the total_sales header:

```
FUNCTION total_sales
   (company_id_in IN company.company_id%TYPE,
    status_in IN order.status_code%TYPE := NULL)
RETURN std_types.dollar_amount;
```

The formal parameters of total_sales are:

*company_id_in*
   The primary key of the company.

*status_in*
   The status of the orders to be included in the sales calculation.

These formal parameters do not exist outside of the function. You can think of them as placeholders for real or actual parameter values that are passed into the function when it is used in a program.

When you use total_sales in your code, the formal parameters disappear. In their place, you list the actual parameters or variables whose values will be passed to total_sales. In the following example, the company_id variable contains the primary key pointing to a company record. In the first three calls to total_sales, a different, hardcoded status is passed to the function. The last call to total_sales does not specify a status; in this case, the function assigns the default value (provided in the function header) to the status_in parameter:

```
new_sales     := total_sales (company_id, 'N');
paid_sales    := total_sales (company_id, 'P');
shipped_sales := total_sales (company_id, 'S');
all_sales     := total_sales (company_id);
```

When total_sales is called, all the actual parameters are evaluated. The results of the evaluations are then assigned to the formal parameters inside the function to which they correspond (note that this is true only for IN and IN OUT parameters; parameters of OUT mode are not copied in).

The formal parameter and the actual parameter that corresponds to it (when called) must be of the same or compatible datatypes. PL/SQL will perform datatype conversions for you in many situations. Generally, however, you are better off avoiding all implicit datatype conversions. Use a formal conversion function like TO_CHAR (see "Numbers" on page 170) or TO_DATE (see Chapter 10), so that you know exactly what kind of data you are passing into your modules.

## Parameter Modes

When you define the parameter, you can also specify the way in which it can be used. There are three different modes of parameters:

| Mode | Description | Parameter usage |
|------|-------------|-----------------|
| IN | Read-only | The value of the actual parameter can be referenced inside the module, but the parameter cannot be changed. If you do not specify the parameter mode, then it is considered an IN parameter. |
| OUT | Write-only | The module can assign a value to the parameter, but the parameter's value cannot be referenced. |
| IN OUT | Read/write | The module can both reference (read) and modify (write) the parameter. |

The mode determines how the program can use and manipulate the value assigned to the formal parameter. You specify the mode of the parameter immediately after the parameter name and before the parameter's datatype and optional default value. The following procedure header uses all three parameter modes:

```
PROCEDURE predict_activity
   (last_date_in IN DATE,
    task_desc_inout IN OUT VARCHAR2,
    next_date_out OUT DATE)
```

The predict_activity procedure takes in two pieces of information: the date of the last activity and a description of the activity. It then returns or sends out two pieces of information: a possibly modified task description and the date of the next activity. Because the task_desc_inout parameter is IN OUT, the program can both read the value of the argument and change the value of that argument.

Let's look at each of these parameter modes in detail.

## IN mode

An IN parameter allows you to pass values into the module but will not pass anything out of the module and back to the calling PL/SQL block. In other words, for the purposes of the program, IN parameters function like constants. Just like constants, the value of the formal IN parameter cannot be changed within the program. You cannot assign values to the IN parameter or in any other way modify its value, without receiving a compilation error.

IN is the default mode; if you do not specify a parameter mode, the parameter is automatically considered IN. I recommend, however, that you always specify a parameter mode so that your intended use of the parameter is documented explicitly in the code itself.

IN parameters can be given default values in the program header (see the later section "Default Values" on page 589).

The actual value for an IN parameter can be a variable, a named constant, a literal, or a complex expression. All of the following calls to display_title are valid:

```
/* File on web: display_title.sql */
DECLARE
   happy_title CONSTANT VARCHAR2(30) := 'HAPPY BIRTHDAY';
   changing_title VARCHAR2(30) := 'Happy Anniversary';
   spc CONSTANT VARCHAR2(1) := CHR(32); -- ASCII code for a single space;
```

```
BEGIN
   display_title ('Happy Birthday');             -- a literal
   display_title (happy_title);                  -- a constant

   changing_title := happy_title;
   display_title (changing_title);               -- a variable
   display_title ('Happy' || spc || 'Birthday'); -- an expression
   display_title (INITCAP (happy_title));        -- another expression
END;
```

What if you want to transfer data out of your program? For that, you will need an OUT or an IN OUT parameter.

## OUT mode

An OUT parameter is the opposite of the IN parameter, but perhaps you already had that figured out. Use the OUT parameter to pass a value back from the program to the calling PL/SQL block. An OUT parameter is like the return value for a function, but it appears in the parameter list, and you can have as many as you like (disclosure: PL/SQL allows a maximum of 64K. parameters, but in practical terms, that is no limit at all).

Inside the program, an OUT parameter acts like a variable that has not been initialized. In fact, the OUT parameter has no value at all until the program terminates successfully (unless you have requested use of the NOCOPY hint, which is explored in detail in Chapter 21). During the execution of the program, any assignments to an OUT parameter are actually made to an internal copy of the OUT parameter. When the program terminates successfully and returns control to the calling block, the value in that local copy is then transferred to the actual OUT parameter. That value is then available in the calling PL/SQL block.

There are several consequences of these rules concerning OUT parameters:

- You cannot assign an OUT parameter's value to another variable or even use it in a reassignment to itself.

- You also cannot provide a default value to an OUT parameter. You can only assign a value to an OUT parameter inside the body of the module.

- Any assignments made to OUT parameters are rolled back when an exception is raised in the program. Because the value for an OUT parameter is not actually assigned until a program completes successfully, any intermediate assignments are therefore ignored. Unless an exception handler traps the exception and then assigns a value to the OUT parameter, no assignment is made to that parameter. The variable will retain the same value it had before the program was called.

- An actual parameter corresponding to an OUT formal parameter must be a variable. It cannot be a constant, literal, or expression because these formats do not provide a receptacle in which PL/SQL can place the OUTgoing value.

## IN OUT mode

With an IN OUT parameter, you can pass values into the program and return a value back to the calling program (either the original, unchanged value or a new value set within the program). The IN OUT parameter shares two restrictions with the OUT parameter:

- An IN OUT parameter cannot have a default value.
- An IN OUT actual parameter or argument must be a variable. It cannot be a constant, literal, or expression because these formats do not provide a receptacle in which PL/SQL can place the outgoing value.

Beyond these restrictions, none of the other restrictions apply.

You can use the IN OUT parameter in both sides of an assignment because it functions like an initialized, rather than uninitialized, variable. PL/SQL does not lose the value of an IN OUT parameter when it begins execution of the program. Instead, it uses that value as necessary within the program.

The combine_and_format_names procedure shown here combines the first and last names into a full name in the format specified ("LAST, FIRST" or "FIRST LAST"). I need the incoming names for the combine action, and I will uppercase the first and last names for future use in the program (thereby enforcing the application standard of all-uppercase for names of people and things). This program uses all three parameter modes: IN, IN OUT, and OUT.

```
PROCEDURE combine_and_format_names
   (first_name_inout IN OUT VARCHAR2,
    last_name_inout IN OUT VARCHAR2,
    full_name_out OUT VARCHAR2,
    name_format_in IN VARCHAR2 := 'LAST, FIRST')
IS
BEGIN
   /* Upper-case the first and last names. */
   first_name_inout := UPPER (first_name_inout);
   last_name_inout := UPPER (last_name_inout);

   /* Combine the names as directed by the name format string. */
   IF name_format_in = 'LAST, FIRST'
   THEN
      full_name_out := last_name_inout || ', ' || first_name_inout;

   ELSIF name_format_in = 'FIRST LAST'
   THEN
      full_name_out := first_name_inout || ' ' || last_name_inout;
   END IF;
END combine_and_format_names;
```

The first name and last name parameters must be IN OUT. The full_name_out is just an OUT parameter because I create the full name from its parts. If the actual parameter used to receive the full name has a value going into the procedure, I certainly don't want to use it! Finally, the name_format_in parameter is a mere IN parameter because it is used to determine how to format the full name, but is not changed or changeable in any way.

Each parameter mode has its own characteristics and purpose. You should choose carefully which mode to apply to your parameters so that they are used properly within the module.

> You should define formal parameters with OUT or IN OUT modes only in procedures. Functions should return all their information only through the RETURN clause. Following these guidelines will make it easier to understand and use those subprograms. In addition, functions with OUT or IN OUT parameters may not be called from within a SQL statement.

## Explicit Association of Actual and Formal Parameters in PL/SQL

How does PL/SQL know which actual parameter goes with which formal parameter when a program is executed? PL/SQL offers two ways to make the association:

*Positional notation*
Associate the actual parameter implicitly (by position) with the formal parameter.

*Named notation*
Associate the actual parameter explicitly with the formal parameter, using the formal parameter's name and the "=>" combination symbol.

### Positional notation

In every example so far, I have employed positional notation to guide PL/SQL through the parameters. With positional notation, PL/SQL relies on the relative positions of the parameters to make the correspondence: it associates the Nth actual parameter in the call to a program with the Nth formal parameter in the program's header.

With the following total_sales example, PL/SQL associates the first actual parameter, :order.company_id, with the first formal parameter, company_id_in. It then associates the second actual parameter, N, with the second formal parameter, status_in:

```
new_sales := total_sales (:order.company_id, 'N');

FUNCTION total_sales
    (company_id_in IN company.company_id%TYPE,
     status_in IN order.status_code%TYPE := NULL)
RETURN std_types.dollar_amount;
```

Positional notation, shown graphically in Figure 17-3, is the most common method for passing arguments to programs.

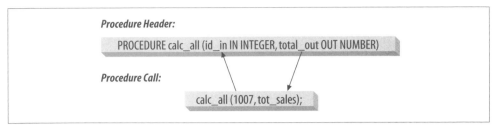

*Figure 17-3. Matching actual with formal parameters (positional notation)*

### Named notation

With named notation, you explicitly associate the formal parameter (the name of the parameter) with the actual parameter (the value of the parameter) right in the call to the program, using the combination symbol =>.

The general syntax for named notation is:

```
formal_parameter_name => argument_value
```

Because you provide the name of the formal parameter explicitly, PL/SQL no longer needs to rely on the order of the parameters to make the association from actual to formal. So, if you use named notation, you do not need to list the parameters in your call to the program in the same order as the formal parameters in the header. You can call total_sales for new orders in either of these two ways:

```
new_sales :=
   total_sales (company_id_in => order_pkg.company_id, status_in =>'N');

new_sales :=
   total_sales (status_in =>'N', company_id_in => order_pkg.company_id);
```

You can also mix named and positional notation in the same program call:

```
:order.new_sales := total_sales (order_pkg.company_id, status_in =>'N');
```

If you do mix notation, however, you must list all of your positional parameters before any named notation parameters, as shown in the preceding example. Positional notation has to have a starting point from which to keep track of positions, and the only starting point is the first parameter. If you place named notation parameters in front of positional notation, PL/SQL loses its place. Both of the following calls to total_sales will fail. The first statement fails because the named notation comes first. The second fails because positional notation is used, but the parameters are in the wrong order. PL/SQL will try to convert 'N' to a NUMBER (for company_id):

```
:order.new_sales := total_sales (company_id_in => order_pkg.company_id, 'N');
:order.new_sales := total_sales ('N', company_id_in => order_pkg.company_id);
```

## Benefits of named notation

Now that you are aware of the different ways to notate the order and association of parameters, you might be wondering why you would ever use named notation. Here are two possibilities:

*Named notation is self-documenting*

> When you use named notation, the call to the program clearly describes the formal parameter to which the actual parameter is assigned. The names of formal parameters can and should be designed so that their purpose is self-explanatory. In a way, the descriptive aspect of named notation is another form of program documentation. If you are not familiar with all of the modules called by an application, the listing of the formal parameters helps reinforce your understanding of a particular program call. In some development environments, the standard for parameter notation is named notation for just this reason. This is especially true when the formal parameters are named following the convention of appending the passing mode as the last token. Then, the direction of data can be clearly seen simply by investigating the procedure or function call.

*Named notation gives you complete flexibility over parameter specification*

> You can list the parameters in any order you want. (This does not mean, however, that you should randomly order your arguments when you call a program!) You can also include only the parameters you want or need in the parameter list. Complex applications may at times require procedures with literally dozens of parameters. Any parameter with a default value can be left out of the call to the procedure. Using named notation, the developer can use the procedure by passing only the values needed for that usage.

Let's see how these benefits can be applied. Consider the following program header:

```
/* File on web: namednot.sql */
PROCEDURE business_as_usual (
   advertising_budget_in    IN      NUMBER
 , contributions_inout    IN OUT NUMBER
 , merge_and_purge_on_in    IN      DATE DEFAULT SYSDATE
 , obscene_ceo_bonus_out    OUT     NUMBER
 , cut_corners_in           IN      VARCHAR2 DEFAULT 'WHENEVER POSSIBLE'
);
```

An analysis of the parameter list yields these conclusions:

- The minimum number of arguments that must be passed to business_as_usual is three. To determine this, add the number of IN parameters without default values to the number of OUT or IN OUT parameters.

- I can call this program with positional notation with either four or five arguments, because the last parameter has mode IN with a default value.

- You will need at least two variables to hold the values returned by the OUT and IN OUT parameters.

Given this parameter list, there are a number of ways that you can call this program:

- All positional notation, all actual parameters specified. Notice how difficult it is to recall the parameter (and significance) of each of these values.

```
DECLARE
   l_ceo_payoff          NUMBER;
   l_lobbying_dollars    NUMBER := 100000;
BEGIN
   /* All positional notation */
   business_as_usual (50000000
                     , l_lobbying_dollars
                     , SYSDATE + 20
                     , l_ceo_payoff
                     , 'PAY OFF OSHA'
                     );
```

- All positional notation, minimum number of actual parameters specified. Still hard to understand.

```
business_as_usual (50000000
                  , l_lobbying_dollars
                  , SYSDATE + 20
                  , l_ceo_payoff
                  );
```

- All named notation, keeping the original order intact. Now my call to business_as_usual is self-documenting.

```
business_as_usual
   (advertising_budget_in     => 50000000
   , contributions_inout       => l_lobbying_dollars
   , merge_and_purge_on_in     => SYSDATE
   , obscene_ceo_bonus_out     => l_ceo_payoff
   , cut_corners_in            => 'DISBAND OSHA'
   );
```

- Skip over all IN parameters with default values, another critical feature of named notation:

```
business_as_usual
   (advertising_budget_in     => 50000000
   , contributions_inout       => l_lobbying_dollars
   , obscene_ceo_bonus_out     => l_ceo_payoff
   );
```

- Change the order in which actual parameters are specified with named notation; also provide just a partial list:

```
business_as_usual
   (obscene_ceo_bonus_out     => l_ceo_payoff
   , merge_and_purge_on_in     => SYSDATE
   , advertising_budget_in     => 50000000
   , contributions_inout       => l_lobbying_dollars
   );
```

- Blend positional and named notation. You can start with positional, but once you switch to named notation, you can't go back to positional.

```
business_as_usual
  (50000000
  , l_lobbying_dollars
  , merge_and_purge_on_in      => SYSDATE
  , obscene_ceo_bonus_out      => l_ceo_payoff
  );
```

As you can see, there is lots of flexibility when it comes to passing arguments to a parameter list in PL/SQL. As a general rule, named notation is the best way to write code that is readable and more easily maintained. You just have to take the time to look up and write the parameter names.

## The NOCOPY Parameter Mode Qualifier

PL/SQL offers an option for modifying the definition of a parameter: the NOCOPY clause. NOCOPY requests that the PL/SQL compiler *not* make copies of OUT and IN OUT arguments. The main objective of using NOCOPY is to improve the performance of passing large constructs, such as collections, as IN OUT arguments. Because of its performance implications, this topic is covered in detail in Chapter 21.

## Default Values

As you have seen from previous examples, you can provide default values for IN parameters. If an IN parameter has a default value, you do not need to include that parameter in the call to the program. Likewise, a parameter's default value is used by the program only if the call to that program does not include that parameter in the list. You must, of course, include an actual parameter for any IN OUT parameters.

The parameter default value works the same way as a specification of a default value for a declared variable. There are two ways to specify a default value: either with the keyword DEFAULT or with the assignment operator (:=), as the following example illustrates:

```
PROCEDURE astrology_reading
  (sign_in IN VARCHAR2 := 'LIBRA',
   born_at_in IN DATE DEFAULT SYSDATE) IS
```

By using default values, you can call programs with different numbers of actual parameters. The program uses the default value of any unspecified parameters, and overrides the default values of any parameters in the list that have specified values. Here are all the different ways you can ask for your astrology reading using positional notation:

```
BEGIN
   astrology_reading ('SCORPIO',
      TO_DATE ('12-24-2009 17:56:10', 'MM-DD-YYYY HH24:MI:SS'));
   astrology_reading ('SCORPIO');
   astrology_reading;
```

```
        astrology_reading();
    END;
```

The first call specifies both parameters explicitly. In the second call, only the first actual parameter is included, so born_at_in is set to the current date and time. In the third call, no parameters are specified, so I omit the parentheses (or specify empty parentheses). Both of the default values are used in the body of the procedure.

What if you want to specify a birth time, but not a sign? To skip over leading parameters that have default values, you will need to use named notation. By including the name of the formal parameter, you can list only those parameters to which you need to pass values. In this (thankfully) last request for a star-based reading of my fate, I have successfully passed in a default of Libra as my sign and an overridden birth time of 5:56 p.m.

```
    BEGIN
        astrology_reading (
            born_at_in =>
                TO_DATE ('12-24-2009 17:56:10', 'MM-DD-YYYY HH24:MI:SS'));
    END;
```

## Local or Nested Modules

A *local or nested module* is a procedure or function that is defined in the declaration section of a PL/SQL block (anonymous or named). This module is considered local because it is defined only within the parent PL/SQL block. It cannot be called by any other PL/SQL blocks defined outside that enclosing block.

Figure 17-4 shows how blocks that are external to a procedure definition cannot "cross the line" into the procedure to directly invoke any local procedures or functions.

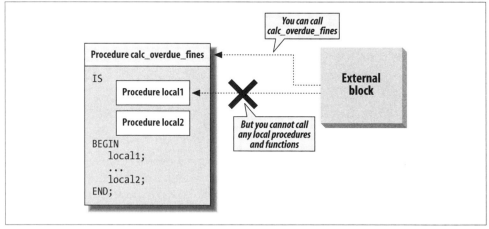

*Figure 17-4. Local modules are hidden and inaccessible outside the program*

The syntax for defining the procedure or function is exactly the same as that used for creating standalone modules.

The following anonymous block, for example, declares a local procedure:

```
DECLARE
   PROCEDURE show_date (date_in IN DATE) IS
   BEGIN
      DBMS_OUTPUT.PUT_LINE (TO_CHAR (date_in, 'Month DD, YYYY'));
   END show_date;
BEGIN
   ...
END ;
```

Local modules must be located after all of the other declaration statements in the declaration section. You must declare your variables, cursors, exceptions, types, records, tables, and so on before you type in the first PROCEDURE or FUNCTION keyword.

The following sections explore the benefits of local modules and offer a number of examples.

## Benefits of Local Modularization

There are two central reasons to create local modules:

*Reduce the size of the module by stripping it of repetitive code*
> This is the most common motivation to create a local module; you can see its impact in the next example. The code reduction leads to higher code quality because you have fewer lines to test and fewer potential bugs. It takes less effort to maintain the code because there is less to maintain. And when you do have to make a change, you make it in one place in the local module, and the effects are felt immediately throughout the parent module.

*Improve the readability of your code*
> Even if you do not repeat sections of code within a module, you still may want to pull out a set of related statements and package them into a local module. This can make it easier to follow the logic of the main body of the parent module.

The following sections examine these benefits.

### Reducing code volume

Let's look at an example of reducing code volume. The calc_percentages procedure takes numeric values from the sales package (sales_pkg), calculates the percentage of each sales amount against the total sales provided as a parameter, and then formats the number for display in a report or form. The example you see here has only three calculations, but I extracted it from a production application that actually performed 23 of these computations!

```
PROCEDURE calc_percentages (total_sales_in IN NUMBER)
IS
   l_profile sales_descriptors%ROWTYPE;
BEGIN
   l_profile.food_sales_stg :=
```

```
    TO_CHAR ((sales_pkg.food_sales / total_sales_in ) * 100,
             '$999,999');
 l_profile.service_sales_stg :=
    TO_CHAR ((sales_pkg.service_sales / total_sales_in ) * 100,
             '$999,999');
 l_profile.toy_sales_stg :=
    TO_CHAR ((sales_pkg.toy_sales / total_sales_in ) * 100,
             '$999,999');
END;
```

This code took a long time (relatively speaking) to write, is larger than necessary, and is maintenance-intensive. What if I need to change the format to which I convert the numbers? What if the calculation of the percentage changes? I will have to change each of the individual calculations.

With local modules, I can concentrate all the common, repeated code into a single function, which is then called repeatedly in calc_percentages. The local module version of this procedure is shown here:

```
PROCEDURE calc_percentages (total_sales_in IN NUMBER)
IS
    l_profile sales_descriptors%ROWTYPE;
    /* Define a function right inside the procedure! */
    FUNCTION pct_stg (val_in IN NUMBER) RETURN VARCHAR2
    IS
    BEGIN
       RETURN TO_CHAR ((val_in/total_sales_in ) * 100, '$999,999');
    END;
BEGIN
    l_profile.food_sales_stg := pct_stg (sales_pkg.food_sales);
    l_profile.service_sales_stg := pct_stg (sales_pkg.service_sales);
    l_profile.toy_sales_stg := pct_stg (sales_pkg.toy_sales);
END;
```

All of the complexities of the calculation, from the division by total_sales_in to the multiplication by 100 to the formatting with TO_CHAR, have been transferred to the function pct_stg. This function is defined in the declaration section of the procedure. By calling this function from within the body of calc_percentages, the executable statements of the procedure are much more readable and maintainable. Now, if the formula for the calculation changes in any way, I make the change just once in the function and it takes effect in all the assignments.

### Improving readability

You can use local modules to dramatically improve the readability and maintainability of your code. In essence, local modules allow you to follow *top-down design* or *stepwise refinement* methodologies very closely. You can also use the same technique to *decompose* or *refactor* an existing program so that it is more readable.

The bottom-line result of using local modules in this way is that you can dramatically reduce the size of your execution sections (you are transferring many lines of logic from an inline location in the execution section to a local module callable in that section).

By keeping your execution sections small, you will find that it is much easier to read and understand the logic.

 I suggest that you adopt as a guideline in your coding standards that execution sections of PL/SQL blocks be no longer than 60 lines (the amount of text that can fit on a screen or page). This may sound crazy, but if you follow the techniques in this section, you will find it not only possible but highly advantageous.

Suppose that I have a series of WHILE loops (some of them nested) whose bodies contain a series of complex calculations and deep nestings of conditional logic. Even with extensive commenting, it can be difficult to follow the program flow over several pages, particularly when the END IF or END LOOP of a given construct is not even on the same page as the IF or LOOP statement that began it.

In contrast, if you pull out sequences of related statements, place them in one or more local modules, and then call those modules in the body of the program, the result is a program that can literally document itself. The assign_workload procedure offers a simplified version of this scenario that still makes clear the gains offered by local modules:

```
/* File on web: local_modules.sql */
PROCEDURE assign_workload (department_in IN emp.deptno%TYPE)
IS
   CURSOR emps_in_dept_cur (department_in IN emp.deptno%TYPE)
   IS
      SELECT * FROM emp WHERE deptno = department_in;

   PROCEDURE assign_next_open_case
      (emp_id_in IN NUMBER, case_out OUT NUMBER)
   IS
   BEGIN ... full implementation ... END;

   FUNCTION next_appointment (case_id_in IN NUMBER)
      RETURN DATE
   IS
   BEGIN ... full implementation ... END;

   PROCEDURE schedule_case
      (case_in IN NUMBER, date_in IN DATE)
   IS
   BEGIN ... full implementation ... END;

BEGIN /* main */
   FOR emp_rec IN emps_in_dept_cur (department_in)
   LOOP
      IF analysis.caseload (emp_rec.emp_id) <
         analysis.avg_cases (department_in);
      THEN
         assign_next_open_case (emp_rec.emp_id, case#);
         schedule_case
```

```
                (case#, next_appointment (case#));
          END IF;
       END LOOP
    END assign_workload;
```

The assign_workload procedure has three local modules:

```
assign_next_open_case
next_appointment
schedule_case
```

It also relies on two packaged programs that already exist and can be easily plugged into this program: analysis.caseload and analysis.avg_cases. For the purposes of understanding the logic behind assign_workload, it doesn't really matter what code is executed in each of them. I can rely simply on the names of those modules to read through the main body of this program. Even without any comments, a reader can still gain a clear understanding of what each module is doing. Of course, if you want to rely on named objects to self-document your code, you'd better come up with very good names for the functions and procedures.

## Scope of Local Modules

The modularized declaration section looks a lot like the body of a package, as you will see in Chapter 18. A package body also contains definitions of modules. The big difference between local modules and package modules is their scope. Local modules can be called only from within the block in which they are defined; package modules can—at a minimum—be called from anywhere in the package. If the package modules are also listed in the package specification, they can be called by other program units from schemas that have EXECUTE authority on that package.

You should therefore use local modules only to encapsulate code that does not need to be called outside of the current program. Otherwise, go ahead, and create a package!

## Sprucing Up Your Code with Local Modules

These days it seems that whenever I write a program with more than 20 lines and any complexity whatsoever, I end up creating one or more local modules. Doing so helps me see my way through to a solution much more easily; I can conceptualize my code at a higher level of abstraction by assigning a name to a whole sequence of statements, and I can perform top-down design and stepwise refinement of my requirements. Finally, by modularizing my code even within a single program, I make it very easy to later extract a local module and make it a truly independent, reusable procedure or function.

You could also, of course, move that logic out of the local scope and make it a package body-level program of its own (assuming you are writing this code in a package). Taking this approach will reduce the amount of nesting of local procedures, which can be helpful. It also, however, can lead to package bodies with a very long list of programs, many of which are only used within another program. My general principle is to keep the definition of an element as close as possible to its usage, which naturally leads to the use of local modules.

I hope that as you read this, a program you have written comes to mind. Perhaps you can go back and consolidate some repetitive code, clean up the logic, and make the program actually understandable to another human being. Don't fight the urge. Go ahead, and modularize your code.

To help you define and work with local modules in your applications, I have created a package called TopDown. Using this package, you can spend a small amount of time placing "indicators" in your code, essentially instructions on what and how you want local modules created. You can then compile this sort-of-template into the database, call TopDown.Refactor for that program unit, and voila!, local modules are created as you requested.

You can then repeat that process for each level down through the complexities of your program, very quickly defining a highly modular architecture that you and others will appreciate for years to come.

You will find a more complete explanation of the TopDown package, the source code, and example scripts in the *TopDown.zip* file on the book's web site.

# Module Overloading

When more than one program in the same scope share the same name, the programs are said to be *overloaded*. PL/SQL supports the overloading of procedures and functions in the declaration section of a block (named or anonymous), package specifications and bodies, and object type definitions. Overloading is a very powerful feature, and you should exploit it fully to improve the usability of your software.

Here is a very simple example of three overloaded modules defined in the declaration section of an anonymous block (therefore, all are local modules):

```
DECLARE
   /* First version takes a DATE parameter. */
   FUNCTION value_ok (date_in IN DATE) RETURN BOOLEAN IS
   BEGIN
      RETURN date_in <= SYSDATE;
   END;

   /* Second version takes a NUMBER parameter. */
   FUNCTION value_ok (number_in IN NUMBER) RETURN BOOLEAN  IS
   BEGIN
      RETURN number_in > 0;
   END;

   /* Third version is a procedure! */
   PROCEDURE value_ok (number_in IN NUMBER) IS
   BEGIN
```

```
          IF number_in > O THEN
             DBMS_OUTPUT.PUT_LINE (number_in || 'is OK!');
          ELSE
             DBMS_OUTPUT.PUT_LINE (number_in || 'is not OK!');
          END IF;
       END;

   BEGIN
```

When the PL/SQL runtime engine encounters the following statement:

```
   IF value_ok (SYSDATE) THEN ...
```

the actual parameter list is compared with the formal parameter lists of the various overloaded modules, searching for a match. If one is found, PL/SQL executes the code in the body of the program with the matching header.

 Another name for overloading is *static polymorphism*. The term *polymorphism* refers to the ability of a language to define and selectively use more than one form of a program with the same name. When the decision on which form to use is made at compilation time, it is called static polymorphism. When the decision is made at runtime, it is called *dynamic polymorphism*; this type of polymorphism is available through inherited object types.

Overloading can greatly simplify your life and the lives of other developers. This technique consolidates the call interfaces for many similar programs into a single module name, transferring the burden of knowledge from the developer to the software. You do not have to try to remember, for instance, the six different names for programs adding values (dates, strings, Booleans, numbers, etc.) to various collections. Instead, you simply tell the compiler that you want to add a value and pass it that value. PL/SQL and your overloaded programs figure out what you want to do and then do it for you.

When you build overloaded modules, you spend more time in design and implementation than you might with separate, standalone modules. This additional time up-front will be repaid handsomely down the line because you and others will find it much easier and more efficient to use your programs.

## Benefits of Overloading

There are three different scenarios that benefit from overloading:

*Supporting many data combinations*
> When applying the same action to different kinds or combinations of data, overloading does not provide a single name for different activities, so much as it provides different ways of requesting the same activity. This is the most common motivation for overloading.

*Fitting the program to the user*

To make your code as useful as possible, you may construct different versions of the same program that correspond to different patterns of use. This often involves overloading functions and procedures. A good indicator of the need for this form of overloading is when you find yourself writing unnecessary code. For example, when working with DBMS_SQL, you will call the DBMS_SQL.EXECUTE function, but for DDL statements, the value returned by this function is irrelevant. Oracle should have overloaded this function as a procedure, so that I could simply execute a DDL statement like this:

```
BEGIN
    DBMS_SQL.EXECUTE ('CREATE TABLE xyz ...');
```

as opposed to:

```
DECLARE
    feedback PLS_INTEGER;
BEGIN
    feedback := DBMS_SQL.EXECUTE ('CREATE TABLE xyz ...');
```

and then ignoring the feedback.

*Overloading by type, not value*

This is the least common application of overloading. In this scenario, you use the type of data, not its value, to determine which of the overloaded programs should be executed. This really comes in handy only when you are writing very generic software. DBMS_SQL.DEFINE_COLUMN is a good example of this approach to overloading. I need to tell DBMS_SQL the type of each of my columns being selected from the dynamic query. To indicate a numeric column, I can make a call as follows:

```
DBMS_SQL.DEFINE_COLUMN (cur, 1, 1);
```

or I could do this:

```
DBMS_SQL.DEFINE_COLUMN (cur, 1, DBMS_UTILITY.GET_TIME);
```

It doesn't matter which I do; I just need to say "this is a number," but not any particular number. Overloading is an elegant way to handle this requirement.

Let's look at an example of the most common type of overloading and then review restrictions and guidelines on overloading.

## Supporting many data combinations

Use overloading to apply the same action to different kinds or combinations of data. As noted previously, this kind of overloading does not provide a single name for different activities so much as different ways of requesting the same activity. Consider DBMS_OUTPUT.PUT_LINE. You can use this built-in to display the value of any type of data that can be implicitly or explicitly converted to a string. Interestingly, in earlier versions of Oracle Database (7, 8, 8*i*, 9*i*), this procedure was overloaded. In Oracle

Database 10g and later, however, it is not overloaded at all! This means that if you want to display an expression that cannot be implicitly converted to a string, you cannot call DBMS_OUTPUT.PUT_LINE and pass it that expression.

You might be thinking: so what? PL/SQL implicitly converts numbers and dates to a string. What else might I want to display? Well, for starters, how about a Boolean? To display an expression of type Boolean variable's value, you must write an IF statement, as in:

```
IF l_student_is_registered
THEN
   DBMS_OUTPUT.PUT_LINE ('TRUE');
ELSE
   DBMS_OUTPUT.PUT_LINE ('FALSE');
END IF;
```

Now, isn't that silly? And a big waste of your time? Fortunately, it is very easy to fix this problem. Just build your own package, with lots of overloadings, on top of DBMS_OUTPUT.PUT_LINE. Here is a very abbreviated example of such a package. You can extend it easily, as I do with the do.pl procedure (why type all those characters just to say "show me," right?). A portion of the package specification is shown here:

```
/* File on web: do.pkg (also check out the p.* files) */
PACKAGE do
IS
   PROCEDURE pl (boolean_in IN BOOLEAN);

   /* Display a string. */
   PROCEDURE pl (char_in IN VARCHAR2);

   /* Display a string and then a Boolean value. */
   PROCEDURE pl (
      char_in      IN   VARCHAR2,
      boolean_in   IN   BOOLEAN
   );

   PROCEDURE pl (xml_in IN SYS.XMLType);
END do;
```

This package simply sits on top of DBMS_OUTPUT.PUT_LINE and enhances it. With do.pl, I can now display a Boolean value without writing my own IF statement, as in:

```
DECLARE
   v_is_valid BOOLEAN :=
      book_info.is_valid_isbn ('5-88888-66');
BEGIN
   do.pl (v_is_valid);
```

Better yet, I can get really fancy and even apply do.pl to complex datatypes like XMLType:

```
/* File on web: xmltype.sql */

DECLARE
```

```
   doc    xmltype;
BEGIN
   SELECT ea.report
   INTO doc
   FROM env_analysis ea
  WHERE company= 'ACME SILVERPLATING';

 do.pl (doc);
END;
```

## Restrictions on Overloading

There are several restrictions on how you can overload programs. When the PL/SQL engine compiles and runs your program, it has to be able to distinguish between the different overloaded versions of a program; after all, it can't run two different modules at the same time. So when you compile your code, PL/SQL will reject any improperly overloaded modules. It cannot distinguish between the modules by their names because by definition they are the same in all overloaded programs. Instead, PL/SQL uses the parameter lists of these sibling programs to determine which one to execute and/or the types of the programs (procedure versus function). As a result, the following restrictions apply to overloaded programs:

*The datatype "family" of at least one of the parameters of overloaded programs must differ*
INTEGER, REAL, DECIMAL, FLOAT, etc., are NUMBER subtypes. CHAR, VARCHAR2, and LONG are character subtypes. If the parameters differ only by datatype within the supertype or family of datatypes, PL/SQL does not have enough information to determine the appropriate program to execute.

> However, see the following section, which explains an improvement in Oracle Database 10g (and later) regarding overloading for numeric types.

*Overloaded programs with parameter lists that differ only by name must be called using named notation*
If you don't use the name of the argument, how can the compiler distinguish between calls to two overloaded programs? Please note, however, that it is always risky to use named notation as an enforcement paradigm. You should avoid situations where named notation yields different semantic meaning from positional notation.

*The parameter list of overloaded programs must differ by more than parameter mode*
Even if a parameter in one version is IN and that same parameter in another version is IN OUT, PL/SQL cannot tell the difference at the point at which the program is called.

*All of the overloaded programs must be defined within the same PL/SQL scope or block (anonymous block, standalone procedure or function, or package)*

You cannot define one version in one block (scope level) and define another version in a different block. You cannot overload two standalone programs; one simply replaces the other.

*Overloaded functions must differ by more than their return type (the datatype specified in the RETURN clause of the function)*

At the time that the overloaded function is called, the compiler doesn't know what type of data that function will return. The compiler therefore cannot determine which version of the function to use if all the parameters are the same.

## Overloading with Numeric Types

Starting with Oracle Database 10g, you can overload two subprograms if their formal parameters differ only in numeric datatype. Before getting into the details, let's look at an example. Consider the following block:

```
DECLARE
    PROCEDURE proc1 (n IN PLS_INTEGER) IS
    BEGIN
        DBMS_OUTPUT.PUT_LINE ('pls_integer version');
    END;

    PROCEDURE proc1 (n IN NUMBER) IS
    BEGIN
        DBMS_OUTPUT.PUT_LINE ('number version');
    END;
BEGIN
    proc1 (1.1);
    proc1 (1);
END;
```

When I try to run this code in Oracle9*i* Database, I get an error:

```
ORA-06550: line 14, column 4:
PLS-00307: too many declarations of 'PROC1' match this call
```

When I run this same block in Oracle Database 10g and Oracle Database 11g, however, I see the following results:

```
number version
pls_integer version
```

The PL/SQL compiler is now able to distinguish between the two calls. Notice that it called the "number version" when I passed a noninteger value. That's because PL/SQL looks for numeric parameters that match the value, and it follows this order of precedence in establishing the match: it starts with PLS_INTEGER or BINARY_INTEGER, then NUMBER, then BINARY_FLOAT, and finally BINARY_DOUBLE. It will use the first overloaded program that matches the actual argument values passed.

While it is very nice that the database now offers this flexibility, be careful when relying on this very subtle overloading—make sure that it is all working as you would expect. Test your code with a variety of inputs and check the results. Remember that you can pass a string such as "156.4" to a numeric parameter; be sure to try out those inputs as well.

You can also qualify numeric literals and use conversion functions to make explicit which overloading (i.e., which numeric datatype) you want to call. If you want to pass 5.0 as a BINARY_FLOAT, for example, you could specify the value 5.0f or use the conversion function, TO_BINARY_FLOAT(5.0).

# Forward Declarations

PL/SQL requires that you declare elements before using them in your code. Otherwise, how can PL/SQL be sure that the way you are using the construct is appropriate? Because modules can call other modules, however, you may encounter situations where it is completely impossible to define all modules before any references to those modules are made. What if program A calls program B and program B calls program A? PL/SQL supports *recursion*, including mutual recursion, in which two or more programs directly or indirectly call each other.

If you find yourself committed to mutual recursion, you will be very glad to hear that PL/SQL supports the *forward declaration* of local modules, which means that modules are declared in advance of the actual definition of that program. This declaration makes that program available to be called by other programs even before the program definition.

Remember that both procedures and functions have a header and a body. A forward declaration consists simply of the program header followed by a semicolon (;). This construction is called the *module header*. This header, which must include the parameter list (and a RETURN clause if it's a function), is all the information PL/SQL needs about a module in order to declare it and resolve any references to it.

The following example illustrates the technique of forward declaration. I define two mutually recursive functions within a procedure. Consequently, I have to declare just the header of my second function, total_cost, before the full declaration of net_profit:

```
PROCEDURE perform_calcs (year_in IN INTEGER)
IS
   /* Header only for total_cost function. */
   FUNCTION total_cost (...)  RETURN NUMBER;

   /* The net_profit function uses total_cost. */
   FUNCTION net_profit (...) RETURN NUMBER    IS
   BEGIN
      RETURN total_sales (...) - total_cost (...);
   END;
```

```
    /* The total_cost function uses net_profit. */
    FUNCTION total_cost (...)  RETURN NUMBER    IS
    BEGIN
       IF <condition based on parameters>
       THEN
          RETURN net_profit (...) * .10;
       ELSE
          RETURN <parameter value>;
       END IF;
    END;
 BEGIN
    ...
 END;
```

Here are some rules to remember concerning forward declarations:

- You cannot make forward declarations of a variable or cursor. This technique works only with modules (procedures and functions).
- The definition for a forwardly declared program must be contained in the declaration section of the same PL/SQL block (anonymous block, procedure, function, or package body) in which you code the forward declaration.

In some situations, forward declarations are absolutely required; in most situations, they just help make your code more readable and presentable. As with every other advanced or unusual feature of the PL/SQL language, use forward declarations only when you really need the functionality. Otherwise, the declarations simply add to the clutter of your program, which is the last thing you want.

# Advanced Topics

The following sections are most appropriate for experienced PL/SQL programmers. Here, I'll touch on a number of advanced modularization topics, including calling functions in SQL, using table functions, and using deterministic functions.

## Calling Your Function From Inside SQL

The Oracle database allows you to call your own custom-built functions from within SQL. In essence, this flexibility allows you to customize the SQL language to adapt to application-specific requirements.

 Whenever the SQL runtime engine calls a PL/SQL function, it must "switch" to the PL/SQL runtime engine. The overhead of this context switch can be substantial if the function is called many times.

## Requirements for calling functions in SQL

There are several requirements that a programmer-defined PL/SQL function must meet in order to be callable from within a SQL statement:

- All of the function's parameters must use the IN mode. Neither IN OUT nor OUT parameters are allowed in SQL-embedded stored functions.

- The datatypes of the function's parameters, as well as the datatype of the RETURN clause of the function, must be recognized within the Oracle server. While all of the Oracle server datatypes are valid within PL/SQL, PL/SQL has added new datatypes that are not (yet) supported in the database. These datatypes include BOOLEAN, BINARY_INTEGER, associative arrays, PL/SQL records, and programmer-defined subtypes.

- The function must be stored in the database. A function defined in a client-side PL/SQL environment cannot be called from within SQL; there would be no way for SQL to resolve the reference to the function.

 By default, user-defined functions that execute in SQL operate on a single row of data, not on an entire column of data that crosses rows, as the group functions SUM, MIN, and AVG do. It is possible to write aggregate functions to be called inside SQL, but this requires taking advantage of the ODCIAggregate interface, which is part of Oracle's Extensibility Framework. See the Oracle documentation for more details on this functionality.

## Restrictions on user-defined functions in SQL

In order to guard against nasty side effects and unpredictable behavior, the Oracle database applies many restrictions on what you can do from within a user-defined function executed inside a SQL statement:

- The function may not modify database tables. It may not execute any of the following types of statements: DDL (CREATE TABLE, DROP INDEX, etc.), INSERT, DELETE, MERGE, or UPDATE. Note that this restriction is relaxed if your function is defined as an autonomous transaction (described in Chapter 14); in this case, any changes made in your function occur independently of the outer transaction in which the query was executed.

- When called remotely or through a parallelized action, the function may not read or write the values of package variables. The Oracle server does not support side effects that cross user sessions.

- The function can update the values of package variables only if that function is called in a select list, or a VALUES or SET clause. If the stored function is called in a WHERE or GROUP BY clause, it may not write package variables.

- Prior to Oracle8 Database, you may not call RAISE_APPLICATION_ERROR from within the user-defined function.
- The function may not call another module (stored procedure or function) that breaks any of the preceding rules. A function is only as pure as the most impure module that it calls.
- The function may not reference a view that breaks any of the preceding rules. A view is a stored SELECT statement; that view's SELECT may use stored functions.
- Prior to Oracle Database 11g, you may use only positional notation to pass actual arguments to your function's formal parameters. In Oracle Database 11g, you may use named and mixed notation.

### Read consistency and user-defined functions

The read consistency model of the Oracle database is simple and clear: once I start a query, that query will only see data as it existed (was committed in the database) at the time the query was started. So if my query starts at 9:00 a.m. and runs for an hour, then even if another user comes along and changes data, my query will not see those changes.

Yet unless you take special precautions with user-defined functions in your queries, it is quite possible that your query will violate (or, at least, appear to violate) the read consistency model of the Oracle database. To understand this issue, consider the following function and the query that calls it:

```
FUNCTION total_sales (id_in IN account.account_id%TYPE)
   RETURN NUMBER
IS
   CURSOR tot_cur
   IS
      SELECT SUM (sales) total
        FROM orders
       WHERE account_id = id_in
         AND TO_CHAR (ordered_on, 'YYYY') = TO_CHAR (SYSDATE, 'YYYY');
   tot_rec tot_cur%ROWTYPE;
BEGIN
   OPEN tot_cur;
   FETCH tot_cur INTO tot_rec;
   CLOSE tot_cur;
   RETURN tot_rec.total;
END;

SELECT name, total_sales (account_id)
  FROM account
 WHERE status = 'ACTIVE';
```

The account table has 5 million active rows in it (a very successful enterprise!). The orders table has 20 million rows. I start the query at 10:00 a.m.; it takes about an hour to complete. At 10:45 a.m., somebody with the proper authority comes along, deletes all rows from the orders table, and performs a commit. According to the read consistency model of Oracle, the session running the query should not see all those deleted rows until the query completes. But the next time the total_sales function executes from within the query, it finds no order rows and returns NULL—and will do so until the query completes.

So if you are executing queries inside functions that are called inside SQL, you need to be acutely aware of read-consistency issues. If these functions are called in long-running queries or transactions, you will probably need to issue the following command to enforce read-consistency *between* SQL statements in the current transaction:

```
SET TRANSACTION READ ONLY
```

In this case, for read consistency to be possible, you need to ensure that you have sufficient undo tablespace.

## Table Functions

A *table function* is a function that can be called from within the FROM clause of a query, as if it were a relational table. Table functions return collections (nested tables or VAR-RAYs), which can then be transformed with the TABLE operator into a structure that can be queried using the SQL language. Table functions come in very handy when you need to:

- Perform very complex transformations of data, requiring the use of PL/SQL, but need to access that data from within an SQL statement.
- Pass complex result sets back to the host (that is, non-PLSQL) environment. You can open a cursor variable for a query based on a table function, and let the host environment fetch through the cursor variable.

There are two kinds of table functions that merit special mention and attention in our examples:

*Streaming table functions*
> *Data streaming* means that you can pass from one process or stage to another without having to rely on intermediate structures. Table functions, in conjunction with the CURSOR expression, enable you to stream data through multiple transformations, all within a single SQL statement.

*Pipelined table functions*
> These functions return a result set in *pipelined* fashion, meaning that data is returned while the function is still executing. Add the PARALLEL_ENABLE to a pipelined function's header, and you have a function that will execute in parallel within a parallel query.

Let's explore how to define table functions and put them to use in your application.

### Calling a function in a FROM clause

To call a function from within a FROM clause, you must do the following:

- Define the RETURN datatype of the function to be a collection (either a nested table or a VARRAY).
- Make sure that all of the other parameters to the function are of mode IN and have SQL datatypes. (You cannot, for example, call a function with a Boolean or record type argument inside a query.)
- Embed the call to the function inside the TABLE operator (if you are running Oracle8i Database, you will also need to use the CAST operator).

Here is a simple example of a table function. First, I will create a nested table type based on an object type of pets:

```
/* File on web: pet_family.sql */
CREATE TYPE pet_t IS OBJECT (
   name   VARCHAR2 (60),
   breed  VARCHAR2 (100),
   dob    DATE);

CREATE TYPE pet_nt IS TABLE OF pet_t;
```

Now I will create a function named pet_family. It accepts two pet objects as arguments: the mother and the father. Then, based on the breed, it returns a nested table with the entire family defined in the collection:

```
FUNCTION pet_family (dad_in IN pet_t, mom_in IN pet_t)
   RETURN pet_nt
IS
   l_count PLS_INTEGER;
   retval   pet_nt := pet_nt ();

   PROCEDURE extend_assign (pet_in IN pet_t) IS
   BEGIN
      retval.EXTEND;
      retval (retval.LAST) := pet_in;
   END;
BEGIN
   extend_assign (dad_in);
   extend_assign (mom_in);

   IF    mom_in.breed = 'RABBIT'   THEN l_count := 12;
   ELSIF mom_in.breed = 'DOG'      THEN l_count := 4;
   ELSIF mom_in.breed = 'KANGAROO' THEN l_count := 1;
   END IF;

   FOR indx IN 1 .. l_count
   LOOP
      extend_assign (pet_t ('BABY' || indx, mom_in.breed, SYSDATE));
   END LOOP;

   RETURN retval;
END;
```

The pet_family function is silly and trivial; the point to understand here is that your PL/SQL function may contain extremely complex logic—whatever is required within your application and can be accomplished with PL/SQL—that exceeds the expressive capabilities of SQL.

Now I can call this function in the FROM clause of a query, as follows::

```
SELECT pets.NAME, pets.dob
  FROM TABLE (pet_family (pet_t ('Hoppy', 'RABBIT', SYSDATE)
                        , pet_t ('Hippy', 'RABBIT', SYSDATE)
                        )
            ) pets;
```

And here is a portion of the output:

```
NAME        DOB
----------  ---------
Hoppy       27-FEB-02
Hippy       27-FEB-02
BABY1       27-FEB-02
BABY2       27-FEB-02
...
BABY11      27-FEB-02
BABY12      27-FEB-02
```

### Passing table function results with a cursor variable

Table functions help overcome a problem that developers have encountered in the past—namely, how do I pass data that I have produced through PL/SQL-based programming (i.e., the data is not intact inside one or more tables in the database) back to a non-PL/SQL host environment? Cursor variables allow me to easily pass back SQL-based result sets to, say, Java programs, because cursor variables are supported in JDBC. Yet if I first need to perform complex transformations in PL/SQL, how then do I offer that data to the calling program?

Now, we can combine the power and flexibility of table functions with the wide support for cursor variables in non-PL/SQL environments (explained in detail in Chapter 15) to solve this problem.

Suppose, for example, that I need to generate a pet family (bred through a call to the pet_family function, as shown in the previous section) and pass those rows of data to a frontend application written in Java. I can do this very easily as follows:

```
/* File on web: pet_family.sql */
FUNCTION pet_family_cv
   RETURN SYS_REFCURSOR
IS
   retval SYS_REFCURSOR;
BEGIN
   OPEN retval FOR
      SELECT *
        FROM TABLE (pet_family (pet_t ('Hoppy', 'RABBIT', SYSDATE)
```

```
                              , pet_t ('Hippy', 'RABBIT', SYSDATE)
                            )
                  );

        RETURN retval;
     END pet_family_cv;
```

In this program, I am taking advantage of the predefined weak REF CURSOR type, SYS_REFCURSOR (introduced in Oracle9i Database), to declare a cursor variable. I "OPEN FOR" this cursor variable, associating with it the query that is built around the pet_family table function.

I can then pass this cursor variable back to the Java frontend. Because JDBC recognizes cursor variables, the Java code can then easily fetch the rows of data and integrate them into the application.

### Creating a streaming function

A *streaming function* accepts as a parameter a result set (via a CURSOR expression) and returns a result set in the form of a collection. Because you can apply the TABLE operator to this collection and then query from it in a SELECT statement, these functions can perform one or more transformations of data within a single SQL statement.

Support for streaming functions was added in Oracle9i Database and can be used to hide algorithmic complexity behind a function interface and thus simplify the SQL in your application. I will walk through an example to explain the kinds of steps you will need to go through yourself to take advantage of table functions in this way.

Consider the following scenario. I have a table of stock ticker information that contains a single row for the open and close prices of stock:

```
/* File on web: tabfunc_streaming.sql */
TABLE stocktable (
   ticker VARCHAR2(10),
   trade_date DATE,
   open_price NUMBER,
   close_price NUMBER)
```

I need to transform (or *pivot*) that information into another table:

```
TABLE tickertable (
   ticker VARCHAR2(10),
   pricedate DATE,
   pricetype VARCHAR2(1),
   price NUMBER)
```

In other words, a single row in stocktable becomes two rows in tickertable. There are many ways to achieve this goal. A very traditional and straightforward approach in PL/SQL might look like this:

```
FOR rec IN  (SELECT * FROM stocktable)
LOOP
   INSERT INTO tickertable
```

```
                (ticker, pricetype, price)
          VALUES (rec.ticker, '0', rec.open_price);

      INSERT INTO tickertable
                (ticker, pricetype, price)
          VALUES (rec.ticker, 'C', rec.close_price);
   END LOOP;
```

There are also 100% SQL solutions, such as:

```
INSERT ALL
     INTO tickertable
          (ticker, pricedate, pricetype, price
          )
     VALUES (ticker, trade_date, '0', open_price
          )
     INTO tickertable
          (ticker, pricedate, pricetype, price
          )
     VALUES (ticker, trade_date, 'C', close_price
          )
     SELECT ticker, trade_date, open_price, close_price
       FROM stocktable;
```

Let's assume, however, that the transformation that I must perform to move data from stocktable to tickertable is very complex and requires the use of PL/SQL. In this situation, a table function used to stream the data as it is transformed would offer a much more efficient solution.

First of all, if I am going to use a table function, I will need to return a nested table or VARRAY of data. I will use a nested table because VARRAYs require the specification of a maximum size, and I don't want to have that restriction in my implementation. This nested table type must be defined as a schema-level element because the SQL engine must be able to resolve a reference to a collection of this type.

I would like to return a nested table based on the table definition itself. That is, I would like it to be defined as follows:

```
TYPE tickertype_nt IS TABLE of tickertype%ROWTYPE;
```

Unfortunately, this statement will fail because %ROWTYPE is not a SQL-recognized type. That attribute is available only inside a PL/SQL declaration section. So I must instead create an object type that mimics the structure of my relational table, and then define a nested table TYPE against that object type.

```
TYPE TickerType AS OBJECT (
   ticker VARCHAR2(10),
   pricedate DATE
   pricetype VARCHAR2(1),
   price NUMBER);

TYPE TickerTypeSet AS TABLE OF TickerType;
```

For my table function to stream data from one stage of transformation to the next, it will have to accept as its argument a set of data, in essence, a query. The only way to do that is to pass in a cursor variable, so I will need a REF CURSOR type to use in the parameter list of my function.

I create a package to hold the REF CURSOR type based on my new nested table type:

```
PACKAGE refcur_pkg
IS
    TYPE refcur_t IS REF CURSOR RETURN StockTable%ROWTYPE;
END refcur_pkg;
```

Finally, I can write my stock pivot function:

```
/* File on web: tabfunc_streaming.sql */
1    FUNCTION stockpivot (dataset refcur_pkg.refcur_t)
2        RETURN tickertypeset
3    IS
4        l_row_as_object tickertype := tickertype (NULL, NULL, NULL, NULL);
5        l_row_from_query  dataset%ROWTYPE;
6        retval tickertypeset := tickertypeset ();
7    BEGIN
8        LOOP
9           FETCH dataset
10            INTO l_row_from_query;
11
12            EXIT WHEN dataset%NOTFOUND;
13            --
14            l_row_as_object.ticker := l_row_from_query.ticker;
15            l_row_as_object.pricetype := 'O';
16            l_row_as_object.price := l_row_from_query.open_price;
17            l_row_as_object.pricedate := l_row_from_query.trade_date;
18            retval.EXTEND;
19            retval (retval.LAST) := l_row_as_object;
20            --
21            l_row_as_object.pricetype := 'C';
22            l_row_as_object.price := l_row_from_query.close_price;
23            retval.EXTEND;
24            retval (retval.LAST) := l_row_as_object;
25         END LOOP;
26
27         CLOSE dataset;
28
29         RETURN retval;
30    END stockpivot;
```

As with the pet_family function, the specifics of this program are not important, and your own transformation logic will be qualitatively more complex. The basic steps performed here, however, will likely be repeated in your own code, so I will review them.

| Line(s) | Description |
|---------|-------------|
| 1–2 | The function header: pass in a result set as a cursor variable, and return a nested table based on the object type. |
| 4 | Declare a local object, which will be used to populate the nested table. |
| 5 | Declare a local record based on the result set. This will be populated by the FETCH from the cursor variable. |
| 6 | The local nested table that will be returned by the function. |
| 8–12 | Start up a simple loop to fetch each row separately from the cursor variable, terminating the loop when no more data is in the cursor. |
| 14–19 | Use the "open" data in the record to populate the local object, and then place it in the nested table, after EXTENDing to define the new row. |
| 21–25 | Use the "closed" data in the record to populate the local object, and then place it in the nested table, after EXTENDing to define the new row. |
| 27–30 | Close the cursor and return the nested table. Mission completed. Really. |

And now that I have this function in place to do all the fancy, but necessary footwork, I can use it inside my query to stream data from one table to another:

```
BEGIN
   INSERT INTO tickertable
      SELECT *
        FROM TABLE (stockpivot (CURSOR (SELECT *
                                          FROM stocktable)));
END;
```

My inner SELECT retrieves all rows in the stocktable. The CURSOR expression around that query transforms the result set into a cursor variable, which is passed to stockpivot. That function returns a nested table, and the TABLE operator then translates it into a relational table format that can be queried.

It may not be magic, but it *is* a bit magical, wouldn't you say? Well, if you think a streaming function is special, check out pipelined functions!

### Creating a pipelined function

A *pipelined function* is a table function that returns a result set as a collection but does so asynchronous to the termination of the function. In other words, the database no longer waits for the function to run to completion, storing all the rows it computes in the PL/SQL collection, before it delivers the first rows. Instead, as each row is ready to be assigned into the collection, it is piped out of the function. This section describes the basics of pipelined table functions. The performance implications of these functions are explored in detail in Chapter 21.

Let's take a look at a rewrite of the stockpivot function and see more clearly what is needed to build pipelined functions:

```
     /* File on web: tabfunc_pipelined.sql */
1    FUNCTION stockpivot (dataset refcur_pkg.refcur_t)
2    RETURN tickertypeset PIPELINED
```

```
 3    IS
 4        l_row_as_object tickertype := tickertype (NULL, NULL, NULL, NULL);
 5        l_row_from_query  dataset%ROWTYPE;
 6    BEGIN
 7        LOOP
 8            FETCH dataset INTO l_row_from_query;
 9            EXIT WHEN dataset%NOTFOUND;
10
11            -- first row
12            l_row_as_object.ticker := l_row_from_query.ticker;
13            l_row_as_object.pricetype := 'O';
14            l_row_as_object.price := l_row_from_query.open_price;
15            l_row_as_object.pricedate := l_row_from_query.trade_date;
16            PIPE ROW (l_row_as_object);
17
18            -- second row
19            l_row_as_object.pricetype := 'C';
20            l_row_as_object.price := l_row_from_query.close_price;
21            PIPE ROW (l_row_as_object);
22        END LOOP;
23
24        CLOSE dataset;
25        RETURN;
26    END;
```

The following table notes several changes to our original functionality:

| Line(s) | Description |
|---|---|
| 2 | The only change from the original stockpivot function is the addition of the PIPELINED keyword. |
| 4–5 | Declare a local object and local record, as with the first stockpivot. What's striking about these lines is what I *don't* declare—namely, the nested table that will be returned by the function. A hint of what is to come…. |
| 7–9 | Start up a simple loop to fetch each row separately from the cursor variable, terminating the loop when no more data is in the cursor. |
| 12–15 and 19–21 | Populate the local object for the open and close tickertable rows to be placed in the nested table. |
| 16 and 21 | Use the PIPE ROW statement (valid only in pipelined functions) to "pipe" the objects immediately out from the function. |
| 25 | At the bottom of the executable section, the function doesn't return anything! Instead, it calls the unqualified RETURN (formerly allowed only in procedures) to return control to the calling block. The function already returned all of its data with the PIPE ROW statements. |

You can call the pipelined function as you would the nonpipelined version. You won't see any difference in behavior, unless you set up the pipelined function to be executed in parallel as part of a parallel query (covered in the next section) or include logic that takes advantage of the asynchronous return of data.

Consider, for example, a query that uses the ROWNUM pseudo-column to restrict the rows of interest:

```
BEGIN
   INSERT INTO tickertable
      SELECT *
        FROM TABLE (stockpivot (CURSOR (SELECT *
                                          FROM stocktable)))
        WHERE ROWNUM < 10;
END;
```

My tests show that on Oracle Database 10*g* and Oracle Database 11*g*, if I pivot 100,000 rows into 200,000, and then return only the first 9 rows, the pipelined version completes its work in 0.2 seconds, while the nonpipelined version took 4.6 seconds.

Clearly, piping rows back does work and does make a noticeable difference!

### Enabling a function for parallel execution

One enormous step forward for PL/SQL, introduced first in Oracle9*i* Database, is the ability to execute functions within a parallel query context. Prior to Oracle9*i* Database, a call to a PL/SQL function inside SQL caused serialization of that query—a major problem for data warehousing applications. You can now add information to the header of a pipelined function in order to instruct the runtime engine how the data set being passed into the function should be partitioned for parallel execution.

In general, if you would like your function to execute in parallel, it must have a single, strongly typed REF CURSOR input parameter.[1]

Here are some examples:

- Specify that the function can run in parallel and that the data passed to that function can be partitioned arbitrarily:

```
FUNCTION my_transform_fn (
     p_input_rows in employee_info.recur_t )
   RETURN employee_info.transformed_t
   PIPELINED
   PARALLEL_ENABLE ( PARTITION p_input_rows BY ANY )
```

In this example, the keyword ANY expresses the programmer's assertion that the results are independent of the order in which the function gets the input rows. When this keyword is used, the runtime system randomly partitions the data among the various query processes. This keyword is appropriate for use with functions that take in one row, manipulate its columns, and generate output rows based on the columns of this row only. If your program has other dependencies, the outcome will be unpredictable.

---

1. The input REF CURSOR need *not* be strongly typed to be partitioned by ANY.

- Specify that the function can run in parallel, that all the rows for a given department go to the same process, and that all of these rows are delivered consecutively:

```
FUNCTION my_transform_fn (
   p_input_rows in employee_info.recur_t )
RETURN employee_info.transformed_t
PIPELINED
CLUSTER P_INPUT_ROWS BY (department)
PARALLEL_ENABLE
   ( PARTITION P_INPUT_ROWS BY HASH (department) )
```

Oracle uses the term *clustered* to signify this type of delivery, and *cluster key* for the column (in this case, "department") on which the aggregation is done. But significantly, the algorithm does *not* care in what order of cluster key it receives each successive cluster, and Oracle doesn't guarantee any particular order here. This allows for a quicker algorithm than if rows were required to be clustered and delivered in the order of the cluster key. It scales as *order N* rather than *order N.log(N)*, where *N* is the number of rows.

In this example, I can choose between HASH (department) and RANGE (department), depending on what I know about the distribution of the values. HASH is quicker than RANGE and is the natural choice to be used with CLUSTER...BY.

- Specify that the function can run in parallel and that the rows that are delivered to a particular process, as directed by PARTITION ... BY (for that specified partition), will be locally sorted by that process. The effect will be to parallelize the sort:

```
FUNCTION my_transform_fn (
   p_input_rows in employee_info.recur_t )
RETURN employee_info.transformed_t
PIPELINED
ORDER P_INPUT_ROWS BY (C1)
PARALLEL_ENABLE
   ( PARTITION P_INPUT_ROWS BY RANGE (C1) )
```

Because the sort is parallelized, there should be no ORDER...BY in the SELECT used to invoke the table function. (In fact, an ORDER...BY clause in the SELECT statement would subvert the attempt to parallelize the sort.) Thus it's natural to use the RANGE option together with the ORDER...BY option. This will be slower than CLUSTER...BY, and so should be used only when the algorithm depends on it.

 The CLUSTER ... BY construct can't be used together with the ORDER...BY in the declaration of a table function. This means that an algorithm that depends on clustering on one key, c1, and then on ordering within the set row for a given value of c1 by, say, c2, would have to be parallelized by using the ORDER ... BY in the declaration in the table function.

## Deterministic Functions

A function is considered to be *deterministic* if it returns the same result value whenever it is called with the same values for its IN and IN OUT arguments. Another way to think about deterministic programs is that they have no *side effects*. Everything the program changes is reflected in the parameter list.

The following function (a simple encapsulation on top of SUBSTR) is a deterministic function:

```
FUNCTION betwnstr (
    string_in IN VARCHAR2, start_in IN PLS_INTEGER, end_in IN PLS_INTEGER)
    RETURN VARCHAR2 IS
BEGIN
    RETURN (SUBSTR (string_in, start_in, end_in - start_in + 1));
END betwnstr;
```

As long as I pass in, for example, "abcdef" for the string, 3 for the start, and 5 for the end, betwnStr will always return "cde". Now, if that is the case, why not have the database save the results associated with a set of arguments? Then when I next call the function with those arguments, it can return the result without executing the function!

You can achieve this effect when calling your function inside a SQL statement by adding the DETERMINISTIC clause to the function's header, as in the following:

```
FUNCTION betwnstr (
    string_in IN VARCHAR2, start_in IN PLS_INTEGER, end_in IN PLS_INTEGER)
    RETURN VARCHAR2 DETERMINISTIC
```

The decision to use a saved copy of the function's return result (if such a copy is available) is made by the Oracle query optimizer. Saved copies can come from a materialized view, a function-based index, or a repetitive call to the same function in the same SQL statement.

 You must declare a function as DETERMINISTIC in order for it to be called in the expression of a function-based index, or from the query of a materialized view if that view is marked REFRESH FIRST or ENABLE QUERY REWRITE. Also, deterministic caching of your function's inputs and results will occur only when the function is called inside a SQL statement.

A deterministic function can improve the performance of SQL statements that call such functions. For more information on using deterministic functions as a caching mechanism, see Chapter 21. That chapter also describes Oracle Database 11*g*'s new function result caching mechanism, specified using RESULT_CACHE.

Oracle has no way of reliably checking to make sure that the function you declare to be deterministic actually is free of any side effects. It is up to you to use this feature responsibly. Your deterministic function should not rely on package variables, nor should it access the database in a way that might affect the result set.

For a demonstration of the effect of a deterministic function (and its limitations), check out the *deterministic.sql* file on the book's web site.

## Go Forth and Modularize!

PL/SQL has a long history of establishing the foundation of code for large and complex applications. Companies run their businesses on PL/SQL-based applications, and they use these applications for *years and even decades*. To be quite honest, you don't have much of a chance of success building (and certainly maintaining) such large-scale, mission-critical systems without an intimate familiarity with (application of) the modularization techniques available in PL/SQL.

This book should provide you with some solid pointers and a foundation on which to build your code. There is still much more for you to learn, especially the awesome range of the supplied packages that Oracle Corporation provides with various tools and the database itself, such as DBMS_RLS (for row-level security) and UTL_TCP (for TCP-related functionality).

Behind all that technology, however, I strongly encourage you to develop a firm commitment to modularization and reuse. Develop a deep and abiding allergy to code redundancy and to the hardcoding of values and formulas. Apply a fanatic's devotion to the modular construction of true black boxes that easily plug-and-play in and across applications.

You will then find that you spend more time in the *design* phase of your development and less time debugging your code (joy of joys!). Your programs will be more readable and more maintainable. They will stand as elegant testimonies to your intellectual integrity. You will be the most popular kid in the class.

Go forth and modularize!

# CHAPTER 18

# Packages

A *package* is a grouping or packaging together of elements of PL/SQL code into a named scope. Packages provide a structure (both logically and physically) in which you can organize your programs and other PL/SQL elements such as cursors, TYPEs, and variables. They also offer significant, unique functionality, including the ability to hide logic and data from view, and to define and manipulate "global" or session-persistent data.

## Why Packages?

The package is a powerful and important element of the PL/SQL language. It should be the cornerstone of any application development project. What makes the package so powerful and important? Consider their advantages:

*Enhance and maintain applications more easily*

As more and more of the production PL/SQL code base moves into maintenance mode, the quality of PL/SQL applications will be measured as much by the ease of maintenance as they are by overall performance. Packages can make a substantial difference in this regard. From data encapsulation (hiding all calls to SQL statements behind a procedural interface to avoid repetition), to enumerating constants for literal or "magic" values, to grouping together logically related functionality, package-driven design and implementation lead to reduced points of failure in an application.

*Improve overall application performance*

By using packages, you can improve the performance of your code in a number of ways. Persistent package data can dramatically improve the response time of queries by caching static data, thereby avoiding repeated queries of the same information. Oracle's memory management also optimizes access to code defined in packages (see Chapter 24 for more details).

*Shore up application or built-in weaknesses*

> It is quite straightforward to construct a package on top of existing functionality where there are drawbacks. (Consider, for example, the UTL_FILE and DBMS_OUTPUT built-in packages in which crucial functionality is badly or partially implemented.) You don't have to accept these weaknesses; instead, you can build your own package on top of Oracle's to correct as many of the problems as possible. For example, the *do.pkg* script I described in Chapter 17 offers a substitute for the DBMS_OUTPUT.PUT_LINE built-in that adds an overloading for the XMLType datatype. Sure, you can get some of the same effect with standalone procedures or functions, but overloading and other package features make this approach vastly preferable.

*Minimize the need to recompile code*

> As you will read below, a package usually consists of two pieces of code: the specification and body. External programs (not defined in the package) can only call programs listed in the specification. If you change and recompile the package body, those external programs are not invalidated. Minimizing the need to recompile code is a critical factor in administering large bodies of application logic.

Packages are conceptually very simple. The challenge, I have found, is to figure out how to fully exploit them in an application. As a first step, I'll take a look at a simple package and see how, even in that basic code, we can reap many of the benefits of packages. Then I'll look at the special syntax used to define packages.

Before diving in, however, I would like to make an overall recommendation:

 *Always* construct your application around packages; avoid standalone (a.k.a., "schema-level") procedures and functions. Even if today you think that only one procedure is needed for a certain area of functionality, in the future you will almost certainly have two, then three, and then a dozen. At which point, you will find yourself saying, "Gee, I should really collect those together in a package!" That's fine, except that now you have to go back to all the invocations of those unpackaged procedures and functions and add in the package name. So start with a package and save yourself the trouble!

## Demonstrating the Power of the Package

A package consists of up to two chunks of code: the *specification* (required) and the *body* (optional, but almost always present). The specification defines how a developer can use the package: which programs can be called, what cursors can be opened, and so on. The body contains the implementation of the programs (and, perhaps, cursors) listed in the specification, plus other code elements as needed.

Suppose that I need to write code to retrieve the "full name" of an employee whose name is in the form "last, first." That seems easy enough to write:

```
PROCEDURE process_employee (
   employee_id_in IN employees.employee_id%TYPE)
IS
   l_fullname VARCHAR2(100);
BEGIN
   SELECT last_name || ',' || first_name
     INTO l_fullname
     FROM employees
    WHERE employee_id = employee_id_in;
     ...
END;
```

Yet there are many problems lurking in this seemingly transparent code:

- I have hardcoded the length of the l_fullname variable. I did this because it is a *derived* value, the concatenation of two column values. I did not, therefore, have a column against which I could %TYPE the declaration. This could cause difficulties over time if the size of last_name and/or first_name columns are expanded.

- I have also hardcoded or explicitly placed in this block the *formula* (an application rule, really) for creating a full name. What's wrong with that, you wonder? What if next week I get a call from the users: "We want to see the names in first-space-last format." Yikes! Time to hunt through all my code for the last-comma-first constructions.

- Finally, this very common query will likely appear in a variety of formats in multiple places in my application. This SQL redundancy can make it very hard to maintain my logic—and optimize its performance.

What's a developer to do? I would like to be able to change the way I write my code to avoid the above hardcodings. To do that, I need to write these things once (one definition of a "full name" datatype, one representation of the formula, one version of the query) and then call them wherever needed. Packages to the rescue!

Consider the following package specification:

```
/* Files on web: fullname.pkg, fullname.tst */
1    PACKAGE employee_pkg
2    AS
3        SUBTYPE fullname_t IS VARCHAR2 (200);
4
5        FUNCTION fullname (
6            last_in  employees.last_name%TYPE,
7            first_in  employees.first_name%TYPE)
8            RETURN fullname_t;
9
10       FUNCTION fullname (
11           employee_id_in IN employees.employee_id%TYPE)
12           RETURN fullname_t;
13   END employee_pkg;
```

What I have done here is essentially *list* the different elements I want to use. The following table summarizes the important elements of the code.

| Line(s) | Description |
|---|---|
| 3 | Declare a "new" datatype using SUBTYPE called fullname_t. It is currently defined to have a maximum of 200 characters, but that can be easily changed if needed. |
| 5–8 | Declare a function called fullname. It accepts a last name and a first name and returns the full name. Notice that the way the full name is constructed is not visible in the package specification. That's a good thing, as you will soon see. |
| 15–18 | Declare a second function, also called fullname; this version accepts a primary key for an employee and returns the full name for that employee. This repetition is an example of *overloading*, which I explored in Chapter 17. |

Now, before I even show you the implementation of this package, let's rewrite the original block of code using my packaged elements (notice the use of dot notation, which is very similar to its use in the form *table.column*):

```
DECLARE
   l_name employee_pkg.fullname_t;
   employee_id_in employees.employee_id%TYPE := 1;
BEGIN
   l_name := employee_pkg.fullname (employee_id_in);
   ...
END;
```

I declare my variable using the new datatype, and then simply call the appropriate function to do all the work for me. The name formula and the SQL query have been moved from my application code to a separate "container" holding employee-specific functionality. The code is cleaner and simpler. If I need to change the formula for last name or expand the total size of the full name datatype, I can go to the package specification or body, make the changes, and recompile any affected code, and the code will automatically take on the updates.

Speaking of the package body, here is the implementation of employee_pkg:

```
1    PACKAGE BODY employee_pkg
2    AS
3       FUNCTION fullname (
4          last_in employee.last_name%TYPE,
5          first_in employee.first_name%TYPE
6       )
7          RETURN fullname_t
8       IS
9       BEGIN
10         RETURN last_in || ', ' || first_in;
11      END;
12
13      FUNCTION fullname (employee_id_in IN employee.employee_id%TYPE)
14         RETURN fullname_t
15      IS
16         retval    fullname_t;
17      BEGIN
18         SELECT fullname (last_name, first_name) INTO retval
19            FROM employee
20          WHERE employee_id = employee_id_in;
21
```

```
22          RETURN retval;
23       EXCEPTION
24          WHEN NO_DATA_FOUND THEN RETURN NULL;
25
26          WHEN TOO_MANY_ROWS THEN errpkg.record_and_stop;
27       END;
28    END employee_pkg;
```

Note the following about this code:

| Line(s) | Description |
| --- | --- |
| 3–11 | These lines are nothing but a function wrapper around the last-comma-first formula. |
| 13–27 | Showcase a typical single-row query lookup built around an implicit query. |
| 18 | Here, though, the query calls that self-same fullname function to return the combination of the two name components. |

So now if my users call and say "first-space-last, please!", I will not groan and work late into the night, hunting down occurrences of || ', ' ||. Instead, I will change the implementation of my employee_pkg.fullname in about five seconds flat and astound my users by announcing that they are ready to go.

And that, dear friends, gives you some sense of the beauty and power of packages.

## Some Package-Related Concepts

Before diving into the details of package syntax and structure, you should be familiar with a few concepts:

*Information hiding*

Information hiding is the practice of removing from view information about one's system or application. Why would a developer ever want to hide information? Couldn't it get lost? Information hiding is actually quite a valuable principle and coding technique. First of all, humans can deal with only so much complexity at a time. A number of researchers have demonstrated that remembering more than seven (plus or minus two) items in a group for example, is challenging for the average human brain (this is known as the "human hrair limit," a term that comes from the book *Watership Down*). By hiding unnecessary detail, you can focus on the important stuff. Second, not everyone needs to know—or should be allowed to know—all the details. I might need to call a function that calculates CEO compensation, but the formula itself could very well be confidential. In addition, if the formula changes, the code is insulated from that change.

*Public and private*

Closely related to information hiding is the fact that packages are built around the concepts of public and private elements. *Public* code is defined in the package specification and is available to any schema that has EXECUTE authority on the package. *Private* code, on the other hand, is defined in and visible only from within the package. External programs using the package cannot see or use private code.

When you build a package, you decide which of the package elements are public and which are private. You also can hide all the details of the package body from the view of other schemas/developers. In this way, you use the package to hide the implementation details of your programs. This is most important when you want to isolate the most volatile aspects of your application, such as platform dependencies, frequently changing data structures, and temporary workarounds.

In early stages of development you can also implement programs in the package body as "stubs," containing just enough code to allow the package to compile. This technique allows you to focus on the interfaces of your programs and the way they connect to each other.

*Package specification*

The package specification contains the definition or specification of all the publicly available elements in the package that may be referenced outside of the package. The specification is like one big declaration section; it does not contain any PL/SQL blocks or executable code. If a specification is well designed, a developer can learn from it everything necessary to use the package. There should never be any need to go "behind" the interface of the specification and look at the implementation, which is in the body.

*Package body*

The body of the package contains all the code required to implement elements defined in the package specification. The body may also contain private elements that do not appear in the specification and therefore cannot be referenced outside of the package. The body of the package resembles a standalone module's declaration section. It contains both declarations of variables and the definitions of all package modules. The package body may also contain an execution section, which is called the *initialization section* because it is run only once, to initialize the package.

*Initialization*

Initialization should not be a new concept for a programmer. In the context of packages, however, it takes on a specific meaning. Rather than initializing the value of a single variable, you can initialize the entire package with arbitrarily complex code. Oracle takes responsibility for making sure that the package is initialized only once per session.

*Session persistence*

As a database programmer, the concept of persistence should also be familiar. After all, a database is all about persistence: I insert a row into the database on Monday, fly to the Bahamas for the rest of the week, and when I return to work on the following Monday, my row is still in the database. It persisted!

Another kind of persistence is *session persistence*. This means that if I connect to the Oracle database (establish a session) and execute a program that assigns a value to a package-level variable (i.e., a variable declared in a package specification or body, outside of any program in the package), that variable is set to persist for the length of my session, and it retains its value even if the program that performed the assignment has ended.

It turns out that the package is the construct that offers support in the PL/SQL language for session-persistent data structures.

## Diagramming Privacy

Let's go back to the public-private dichotomy for a moment. The distinction drawn between public and private elements in a package gives PL/SQL developers unprecedented control over their data structures and programs. A fellow named Grady Booch came up with a visual way to describe this aspect of a package (now called, naturally, the *Booch diagram*).

Take a look at Figure 18-1. Notice the two labels Inside and Outside. Outside consists of all the programs you write that are *not* a part of the package at hand (the *external programs*). Inside consists of the package body (the internals or implementation of the package).

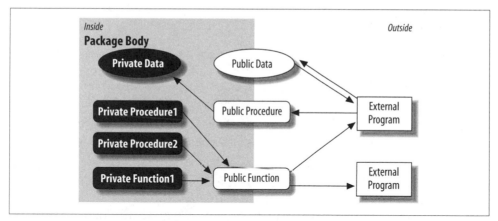

*Figure 18-1. Booch diagram showing public and private package elements*

Here are the conclusions we can draw from the Booch diagram:

- External programs cannot cross the boundary from outside to inside. That is, an external program may not reference or call any elements defined inside the package body. They are private and invisible outside of the package.

- Those elements defined in the package specification (labeled Public in the figure) straddle the boundary between inside and outside. These programs can be called by an external program (from the outside), can be called or referenced by a private program, and can, in turn, call or reference any other element in the package.

- Public elements of the package therefore offer the only path to the inside of the package. In this way, the package specification acts as a control mechanism for the package as a whole.

- If you find that a formerly private object (such as a module or a cursor) should instead be made public, simply add that object to the package specification and recompile. It will then be visible outside of the package.

# Rules for Building Packages

The package is a deceptively simple construct. In a small amount of time, you can learn all the basic elements of package syntax and rules, but you can spend weeks (or more) uncovering all the nuances and implications of the package structure. In this section, I review the rules you need to know in order to build packages. Later in the chapter, I will take a look at the circumstances under which you will want to build packages.

To construct a package, you must build a specification and, in almost every case, a package body. You must decide which elements go into the specification and which are hidden away in the body. You also can include a block of code that the database will use to initialize the package.

## The Package Specification

The specification of a package lists all the elements in that package that are available for use in applications, and provides all the information a developer needs in order to use elements defined in the package (often referred to as an API or application programming interface). A developer should never have to look at the implementation code in a package body to figure out how to use an element in the specification.

Here are some rules to keep in mind for package specification construction:

- You can declare elements of almost any datatype, such as numbers, exceptions, types, and collections, at the package level (i.e., not within a particular procedure or function in the package). This is referred to as *package-level data*; generally, you should avoid declaring variables in the package specification, although constants are always "safe."

  You cannot declare cursor variables (variables defined from a REF CURSOR type) in a package specification (or body). Cursor variables are not allowed to *persist* at the session level (see "Working with Package Data" on page 633 for more information about package data persistence).

- You can declare almost any type of data structure, such as a collection type, a record type, or a REF CURSOR type.

- You can declare procedures and functions in a package specification, but you can include only the header of the program (everything up to but not including the IS or AS keyword). The header must end with a semicolon.

- You can include explicit cursors in the package specification. An explicit cursor can take one of two forms: it can include the SQL query as a part of the cursor declaration, or you can "hide" the query inside the package body and provide only a RETURN clause in the cursor declaration. This topic is covered in more detail in the section, "Packaged Cursors" on page 635.

- If you declare any procedures or functions in the package specification or if you declare a CURSOR without its query, then you *must* provide a package body in order to implement those code elements.

- You can include an AUTHID clause in a package specification, which determines whether any references to data objects will be resolved according to the privileges of the owner of the package (AUTHID DEFINER) or of the invoker of the package (AUTHID CURRENT_USER). See Chapter 24 for more information on this feature.

- You can include an optional package name label after the END statement of the package, as in:

```
END my_package;
```

Here is a simple package specification illustrating these rules:

```
/* File on web: favorites.sql */
1    PACKAGE favorites_pkg
2       AUTHID CURRENT_USER
3    IS /* or AS */
4       -- Two constants; notice that I give understandable
5       -- names to otherwise obscure values.
6
7       c_chocolate CONSTANT PLS_INTEGER := 16;
8       c_strawberry CONSTANT PLS_INTEGER := 29;
9
10      -- A nested table TYPE declaration
11      TYPE codes_nt IS TABLE OF INTEGER;
12
13      -- A nested table declared from the generic type.
14      my_favorites codes_nt;
15
16      -- A REF CURSOR returning favorites information.
17      TYPE fav_info_rct IS REF CURSOR RETURN favorites%ROWTYPE;
18
19      -- A procedure that accepts a list of favorites
20      -- (using a type defined above) and displays the
21      -- favorite information from that list.
22      PROCEDURE show_favorites (list_in IN codes_nt);
23
24      -- A function that returns all the information in
25      -- the favorites table about the most popular item.
26      FUNCTION most_popular RETURN fav_info_rct;
27
28   END favorites_pkg; -- End label for package
```

As you can see, a package specification is, in structure, essentially the same as a declaration section of a PL/SQL block. One difference, however, is that a package specification may *not* contain any implementation code.

## The Package Body

The package body contains all the code required to implement the package specification. A package body is not always needed; see "When to Use Packages" on page 642 for examples of package specifications without bodies. A package body is required when any of the following conditions are true:

*The package specification contains a cursor declaration with a RETURN clause*
   You will then need to specify the SELECT statement in the package body.

*The package specification contains a procedure or function declaration*
   You will then need to complete the implementation of that module in the package body.

*You want to execute code in the initialization section of the package*
   The package specification does not support an execution section (executable statements within a BEGIN...END); you can do this only in the body.

Structurally, a package body is very similar to a procedure definition. Here are some rules particular to package bodies:

- A package body can have declaration, execution, and exception sections. The declaration section contains the complete implementation of any cursors and programs defined in the specification, and also the definition of any private elements (not listed in the specification). The declaration section can be empty as long as there is an initialization section.

- The execution section of a package is known as the *initialization section*; this optional code is executed when the package is instantiated for a session. I discuss this topic in the following section.

- The exception section handles any exceptions raised in the initialization section. You can have an exception section at the bottom of a package body only if you have defined an initialization section.

- A package body may consist of the following combinations: only a declaration section; only an execution section; execution and exception sections; or declaration, execution, and exception sections.

- You may not include an AUTHID clause in the package body; it must go in the package specification. Anything declared in the specification may be referenced (used) within the package body.

- The same rules and restrictions for declaring package-level data structures apply to the body as well as to the specification—for example, you cannot declare a cursor variable.

- You can include an optional package name label after the END statement of the package body, as in:

```
    END my_package;
```

Here is an implementation of the favorites_pkg body:

```
/* File on web: favorites.sql */
PACKAGE BODY favorites_pkg
IS
   -- A private variable
   g_most_popular    PLS_INTEGER := c_strawberry;

   -- Implementation of the function
   FUNCTION most_popular RETURN fav_info_rct
   IS
      retval fav_info_rct;
      null_cv fav_info_rct;
   BEGIN
      OPEN retval FOR
         SELECT *
           FROM favorites
          WHERE code = g_most_popular;
      RETURN retval;
   EXCEPTION
      WHEN NO_DATA_FOUND THEN RETURN null_cv;
   END most_popular;

  -- Implementation of the procedure
  PROCEDURE show_favorites (list_in IN codes_nt) IS
  BEGIN
     FOR indx IN list_in.FIRST .. list_in.LAST
     LOOP
        DBMS_OUTPUT.PUT_LINE (list_in (indx));
     END LOOP;
  END show_favorites;

END favorites_pkg; -- End label for package
```

See "When to Use Packages" on page 642 for other examples of package bodies.

## Initializing Packages

Packages can contain data structures that persist for your entire session (this topic is covered in more detail in "Working with Package Data" on page 633). The first time your session uses a package (whether by calling a program defined in the package, reading or writing a variable, or using a locally declared variable TYPE), the database initializes that package. This involves one or all of the following steps:

- Instantiate any package-level data (such as a number variable or a string constant).
- Assign default values to variables and constants as specified in their declarations.

- Execute a block of code, called the *initialization section*, which is specifically designed to initialize the package, complementing the preceding steps.

Oracle executes these steps just once per session, and not until you need that information (i.e., on the "first touch" of that package).

 A package may be reinitialized in a session if that package was recompiled since last use or if the package state for your entire session was reset, as is indicated by the following error:

```
ORA-04068: existing state of packages has been discarded
```

The initialization section of a package consists of all the statements following the BEGIN statement at the end of the package (and outside any procedure or function's definitions) and through to the END statement for the entire package body. Here is what an initialization section in favorites_pkg might look like:

```
/* File on web: favorites.sql */
PACKAGE BODY favorites_pkg
IS
   g_most_popular   PLS_INTEGER;

   PROCEDURE show_favorites (list_in IN codes_nt) ... END;

   FUNCTION most_popular RETURN fav_info_rct ... END;

   PROCEDURE analyze_favorites (year_in IN INTEGER) ... END;

-- Initialization section
BEGIN
   g_most_popular := c_chocolate;

   -- Use EXTRACT to get year number from SYSDATE!
   analyze_favorites (EXTRACT (YEAR FROM SYSDATE));
END favorites_pkg;
```

The initialization section is a powerful mechanism: PL/SQL automatically detects when this code should be run. You do not have to explicitly execute the statements, and you can be sure that they are run only once. Why would you use an initialization section? The following sections explore some specific reasons.

### Execute complex initialization logic

You can, of course, assign default values to package data directly in the declaration statement. This approach has several possible problems:

- The logic required to set the default value may be quite complex and not easily invoked as a default value assignment.

- If the assignment of the default value raises an exception, that exception cannot be trapped within the package: it will instead propagate out unhandled. This issue is covered in more detail in "When initialization fails" on page 630.

Using the initialization section to initialize data offers several advantages over default value assignments. For one thing, you have the full flexibility of an execution section in which to define, structure, and document your steps; and, if an exception is raised, you can handle it within the initialization section's exception section.

### Cache static session information

Another great motivation for including an initialization section in your package is to cache information that is static (unchanging) throughout the duration of your session. If the data values don't change, why endure the overhead of querying or recalculating those values again and again?

In addition, if you want to make sure that the information is retrieved just once in your session, then the initialization section is an ideal, automatically managed way to get this to happen.

There is an important and typical tradeoff when working with cached package data: memory versus CPU. By caching data in package variables, you can improve the elapsed time performance of data retrieval. This is accomplished by moving the data "closer" to the user, into the Program Global Area or PGA of *each* session. If there are 1,000 distinct sessions, then there are 1,000 copies of the cached data. This technique decreases the CPU usage, but consumes more, sometimes *much* more, memory.

See "Cache Static Session Data" on page 649 for more details on this technique.

### Avoid side effects when initializing

Avoid setting the values of global data in other packages within the initialization section (or anywhere else in those other packages, for that matter). This precaution can prevent havoc in code execution and potential confusion for maintenance programmers. Keep the initialization section code focused on the current package. Remember that this code is executed whenever your application first tries to use a package element. You don't want your users sitting idle while the package performs some snazzy, expensive setup computations that could be parceled out to different packages or triggers in the application.

```
PACKAGE BODY company IS
BEGIN
   /*
   || Initialization section of company_pkg updates the global
   || package data of a different package. This is a no-no!
   */
   SELECT SUM (salary)
     INTO employee_pkg.max_salary
```

```
        FROM employees;
    END company;
```

If your initialization requirements seem different from those we've illustrated, you should consider alternatives to the initialization section, such as grouping your startup statements together into a procedure in the package. Give the procedure a name like init_environment; then, at the appropriate initialization point in your application, call the init_environment procedure to set up your session.

### When initialization fails

There are several steps to initializing a package: declare data, assign default values, run the initialization section (if present). What happens when an error occurs, causing the failure of this initialization process? It turns out that even if a package fails to complete its initialization steps, the database marks the package as having been initialized and does *not* attempt to run the startup code again during that session. To verify this behavior, consider the following package:

```
/* File on web: valerr.pkg */
PACKAGE valerr
IS
    FUNCTION get RETURN VARCHAR2;
END valerr;

PACKAGE BODY valerr
IS
    -- A package-level, but private global variable
    v VARCHAR2(1) := 'ABC';

    FUNCTION get RETURN VARCHAR2
    IS
    BEGIN
        RETURN v;
    END;
BEGIN
    DBMS_OUTPUT.PUT_LINE ('Before I show you v...');
EXCEPTION
  WHEN OTHERS
  THEN
    DBMS_OUTPUT.PUT_LINE ('Trapped the error!');
END valerr;
```

Suppose that I connect to SQL*Plus and try to run the valerr.get function (for the first time in that session). This is what I see:

```
SQL> EXEC DBMS_OUTPUT.PUT_LINE (valerr.get) *
ERROR at line 1:
ORA-06502: PL/SQL: numeric or value error: character string buffer too small
```

In other words, my attempt in the declaration of the v variable to assign a value of "ABC" caused a VALUE_ERROR exception. The exception section at the bottom of the package did *not* trap the error; it can only trap errors raised in the initialization section itself. And so the exception goes unhandled. Notice, however, that when I call that function a second time in my session, I do not get an error:

```
SQL> BEGIN
  2    DBMS_OUTPUT.PUT_LINE ('V is set to ' || NVL (valerr.get, 'NULL'));
  3  END;
  4  /
  5  V is set to NULL
```

How curious! The statement "Before I show you v..." is never displayed; in fact, it is never executed. This packaged function fails the first time, but not the second or any subsequent times. Here I have one of those classic "unreproducible errors," and within the PL/SQL world, this is the classic cause of such a problem: a failure in package initialization.

These errors are very hard to track down. The best way to avoid such errors and also aid in detection is to move the assignments of default values to the initialization section, where the exception section can gracefully handle errors and report on their probable case, as shown here:

```
PACKAGE BODY valerr
IS
   v VARCHAR2(1);
   FUNCTION get RETURN VARCHAR2 IS BEGIN ... END;
BEGIN
   v := 'ABC';

EXCEPTION
  WHEN OTHERS
  THEN
    DBMS_OUTPUT.PUT_LINE ('Error initializing valerr:');
    DBMS_OUTPUT.PUT_LINE (DBMS_UTILITY.FORMAT_ERROR_STACK);
    DBMS_OUTPUT.PUT_LINE (DBMS_UTILITY.FORMAT_ERROR_BACKTRACE);
END valerr;
```

You may even want to standardize your package design to *always* include an initialization procedure to remind developers on your team about this issue. Here's an example:

```
/* File on web: package_template.sql */
PACKAGE BODY <package_name>
IS
   -- Place private data structures below.
   -- Avoid assigning default values here.
   -- Instead, assign in the initialization procedure and
   --   verify success in the verification program.

   -- Place private programs here.

   -- Initialization section (optional)
   PROCEDURE initialize IS
   BEGIN
      NULL;
   END initialize;
```

```
      PROCEDURE verify_initialization (optional)
      -- Use this program to verify the state of the package.
      -- Were default values assigned properly? Were all
      -- necessary steps performed?
      IS
      BEGIN
         NULL;
      END verify_initialization;

      -- Place public programs here.

BEGIN
   initialize;
   verify_initialization;
END <package_name>;
/
```

# Rules for Calling Packaged Elements

It doesn't really make any sense to talk about running or executing a package (after all, it is just a container for code elements). However, you will certainly want to run or reference those elements defined in a package.

A package owns its objects, just as a table owns its columns. To reference an element defined in the package specification *outside of* the package itself, you must use the same dot notation to fully specify the name of that element. Let's look at some examples.

The following package specification declares a constant, an exception, a cursor, and several modules:

```
PACKAGE pets_inc
IS
   max_pets_in_facility CONSTANT INTEGER := 120;
   pet_is_sick EXCEPTION;

   CURSOR pet_cur (pet_id_in IN pet.id%TYPE) RETURN pet%ROWTYPE;

   FUNCTION next_pet_shots (pet_id_in IN pet.id%TYPE) RETURN DATE;
   PROCEDURE set_schedule (pet_id_in IN pet.id%TYPE);

END pets_inc;
```

To reference any of these objects, I preface the object name with the package name, as follows:

```
DECLARE
   -- Base this constant on the id column of the pet table.
   c_pet CONSTANT pet.id%TYPE:= 1099;
   v_next_appointment DATE;
BEGIN
   IF pets_inc.max_pets_in_facility > 100
   THEN
      OPEN pets_inc.pet_cur (c_pet);
```

```
      ELSE
          v_next_appointment:= pets_inc.next_pet_shots (c_pet);
      END IF;
   EXCEPTION
      WHEN pets_inc.pet_is_sick
      THEN
          pets_inc.set_schedule (c_pet);
   END;
```

To summarize, there are two rules to follow in order to reference and use elements in a package:

- When you reference elements defined in a package specification from outside of that package (an external program), you must use dot notation in the form *package_name.element_name*.

- When you reference package elements from within the package (specification or body), you do not need to include the name of the package. PL/SQL will automatically resolve your reference within the scope of the package.

# Working with Package Data

Package data consists of variables and constants that are defined at the *package level*—that is, not within a particular function or procedure in the package. The scope of the package data is therefore not a single program, but rather the package as a whole. In the PL/SQL runtime architecture, package data structures *persist* (hold their values) for the duration of a session (rather than the duration of execution for a particular program).

If package data is declared inside the package body, then that data persists for the session but can be accessed only by elements defined in the package itself (private data).

If package data is declared inside the package specification, then that data persists for the session and is directly accessible (to both read and modify the value) by any program that has EXECUTE authority on that package (public data). Public package data is very similar to and potentially as dangerous as GLOBAL variables in Oracle Forms.

If a packaged procedure opens a cursor, that cursor remains open and is available throughout the session. It is not necessary to define the cursor in each program. One module can open a cursor while another performs the fetch. Additionally, package variables can carry data across the boundaries of transactions because they are tied to the session rather than to a single transaction.

## Global Within a Single Oracle Session

Package data structures act like globals within the PL/SQL environment. Remember, however, that they are accessible only within a single Oracle session or connection; package data is not shared across sessions. If you need to share data between different

Oracle sessions, you can use the DBMS_PIPE package or Oracle Advanced Queuing. (See the Oracle documentation or *Oracle Built-In Packages* (O'Reilly) for more information about these facilities.)

You need to be careful about assuming that different parts of your application maintain a single Oracle database connection. There are times when a tool may establish a new connection to the database to perform an action. If this occurs, the data you have stored in a package in the first connection will not be available.

For example, suppose that an Oracle Forms application has saved values to data structures in a package. When the form calls a stored procedure, this stored procedure can access the same package-based variables and values as the form can because they share a single database connection. But now suppose that the form kicks off a report using Oracle Reports. By default, Oracle Reports uses a second connection to the database (with the same username and password) to run the report. Even if this report accesses the same package and data structures, the values in those data structures will not match those used by the form. The report is using a different database connection and a new instantiation of the package data structures.

Just as there are two types of data structures in a package (public and private), there are also two types of global package data to consider: global public data and global private data. The next three sections explore the various ways that package data can be used.

## Global Public Data

Any data structure declared in the specification of a package is a global public data structure, meaning that any program outside of the package can access it. You can, for example, define a PL/SQL collection in a package specification and use it to keep a running list of all employees selected for a raise. You can also create a package of constants that are used throughout all your programs. Other developers will then reference the packaged constants instead of hardcoding the values in their programs. You are also allowed to change global public data structures unless they are declared as CONSTANTs in the declaration statement.

Global data is the proverbial "loose cannon" of programming. It is very convenient to declare and is a great way to have all sorts of information available at any point in time. However, reliance on global data structures leads to unstructured code that is full of side effects.

Recall that the specification of a module should give you all the information you need to understand how to call and use that module. However, it is not possible to determine if a package reads and/or writes to global data structures from the package's specification. Because of this, you cannot be sure of what is happening in your application and which program changes what data.

It is always preferable to pass data as parameters in and out of modules. That way, reliance on those data structures is documented in the specification and can be accounted for by developers. On the other hand, you should create named global data structures for information that truly is global to an application, such as constants and configuration information.

You can put all such data into a single, central package, which would be easiest to manage. Note, however, that such a design also builds a "single point of recompilation" into your application: every time you make a change to the package and recompile the specification, you will cause many programs in your application to be invalidated.

## Packaged Cursors

One particularly interesting type of package data is the explicit cursor, which was introduced in Chapter 14. I can declare a cursor in a package, in either the body or the specification. The state of this cursor (i.e., whether it is opened or closed, the pointer to the location in the result set) persists for the session, just like any other packaged data. This means that it is possible to open a packaged cursor in one program, fetch from it in a second, and close it in a third. This flexibility can be an advantage and also a potential problem.

Let's first look at some of the nuances of declaring packaged cursors, and then move on to how you can open, fetch, and close such cursors.

### Declaring packaged cursors

If you are declaring an explicit cursor in a package specification, you have two options:

- Declare the entire cursor, including the query, in the specification. This is exactly the same as if you were declaring a cursor in a local PL/SQL block.
- Declare only the header of the cursor and do not include the query itself. In this case, the query is defined in the package body only. You have, in effect, hidden the implementation of the cursor.

If you declare only the header, then you must add a RETURN clause to a cursor definition that indicates the data elements returned by a fetch from the cursor. Of course, these data elements are actually determined by the SELECT statement for that cursor, but the SELECT statement appears only in the body, not in the specification.

The RETURN clause may be made up of either of the following datatype structures:

- A record defined from a database table using the %ROWTYPE attribute
- A record defined from a programmer-defined record type

If you declare a cursor in a package body, the syntax is the same as if you were declaring it in a local PL/SQL block.

Here is a simple package specification that shows both of these approaches:

```
/* File on web: pkgcur.sql */
1    PACKAGE book_info
2    IS
3       CURSOR byauthor_cur (
4          author_in   IN   books.author%TYPE
5       )
6       IS
7          SELECT *
8            FROM books
9           WHERE author = author_in;
10
11       CURSOR bytitle_cur (
12          title_filter_in  IN   books.title%TYPE
13       ) RETURN books%ROWTYPE;
14
15       TYPE author_summary_rt IS RECORD (
16          author                    books.author%TYPE,
17          total_page_count          PLS_INTEGER,
18          total_book_count          PLS_INTEGER);
19
20       CURSOR summary_cur (
21          author_in   IN   books.author%TYPE
22       ) RETURN author_summary_rt;
23    END book_info;
```

The following table describes the logic of this program:

| Line(s) | Description |
|---------|-------------|
| 3–9 | This is a very typical explicit cursor definition, fully defined in the package specification. |
| 11–13 | Define a cursor without a query. In this case, I am telling whoever is looking at the specification that if they open and fetch from this cursor, they will receive a single row from the books table for the specified "title filter," the implication being that wildcards are accepted in the description of the title. |
| 15–18 | Define a new record type to hold summary information for a particular author. |
| 20–22 | Declare a cursor that returns summary information (just three values) for a given author. |

Let's take a look at the package body and then see what kind of code needs to be written to work with these cursors:

```
1    PACKAGE BODY book_info
2    IS
3       CURSOR bytitle_cur (
4          title_filter_in   IN   books.title%TYPE
5       ) RETURN books%ROWTYPE
6       IS
7          SELECT *
8          FROM books
9          WHERE title LIKE UPPER (title_filter_in);
10
11       CURSOR summary_cur (
12          author_in   IN   books.author%TYPE
13       ) RETURN author_summary_rt
14       IS
```

```
15          SELECT author, SUM (page_count), COUNT (*)
16            FROM books
17            WHERE author = author_in;
18     END book_info;
```

Because I had two cursors with a RETURN clause in my book information package specification, I must finish defining those cursors in the body. The select list of the query that I now add to the header must match, in number of items and datatype, the RETURN clause in the package specification; in this case, they do. If they do not match or the RETURN clause is not specified in the body, then the package body will fail to compile with one of the following errors:

```
20/11    PLS-00323: subprogram or cursor '<cursor>' is declared in a
         package specification and must be defined in the package body

5/13     PLS-00400: different number of columns between cursor SELECT
         statement and return value
```

### Working with packaged cursors

Now let's see how you can take advantage of packaged cursors. First of all, you do not need to learn any new syntax to open, fetch from, and close packaged cursors; you just have to remember to prepend the package name to the name of the cursor. So if I want to get information about all the books having to do with PL/SQL, I can write a block like this:

```
DECLARE
   onebook   book_info.bytitle_cur%ROWTYPE;
BEGIN
   OPEN book_info.bytitle_cur ('%PL/SQL%');

   LOOP
      EXIT WHEN book_info.bytitle_cur%NOTFOUND;
      FETCH book_info.bytitle_cur INTO onebook;
      book_info.display (onebook);
   END LOOP;

   CLOSE book_info.bytitle_cur;
END;
```

As you can see, I can %ROWTYPE a packaged cursor and check its attributes just as I would with a locally defined explicit cursor. Nothing new there!

There are some hidden issues lurking in this code, however. Because my cursor is declared in a package specification, its scope is not bound to any given PL/SQL block. Suppose that I run this code:

```
BEGIN -- Only open...
   OPEN book_info.bytitle_cur ('%PEACE%');
END;
```

and then, in the same session, I run the anonymous block with the LOOP shown above. I will then get this error:

```
ORA-06511: PL/SQL: cursor already open
```

This happened because in my "only open" block, I neglected to close the cursor. Even though the block terminated, my packaged cursor did not close.

Given the persistence of packaged cursors, you should always keep the following rules in mind:

- Never assume that a packaged cursor is closed (and ready to be opened).
- Never assume that a packaged cursor is opened (and ready to be closed).
- Always be sure to explicitly close your packaged cursor when you are done with it. You also will need to include this logic in exception handlers; make sure the cursor is closed through all exit points in the program.

If you neglect these rules, you might well execute an application that makes certain assumptions and then pays the price in unexpected and unhandled exceptions. So the question then becomes: how best can you remember and follow these rules? My suggestion is to build procedures that perform the open and close operations for you—and take all these nuances and possibilities into account.

The following package offers an example of this technique:

```
/* File on web: openclose.sql */
PACKAGE personnel
IS
   CURSOR emps_for_dept (
      department_id_in_in IN employees.department_id%TYPE)
   IS
      SELECT * FROM employees
       WHERE department_id = department_id_in;

   PROCEDURE open_emps_for_dept(
      department_id_in IN employees.department_id%TYPE,
      close_if_open IN BOOLEAN := TRUE
      );

   PROCEDURE close_emps_for_dept;

END personnel;
```

I have a packaged cursor along with procedures to open and close the cursor. So if I want to loop through all the rows in the cursor, I would write code like this:

```
DECLARE
   one_emp personnel.emps_for_dept%ROWTYPE;
BEGIN
   personnel.open_emps_for_dept (1055);

   LOOP
      EXIT WHEN personnel.emps_for_dept%NOTFOUND;
      FETCH personnel.emps_for_dept INTO one_emp;
      ...
   END LOOP;
```

```
        personnel.close_emps_for_dept;
    END;
```

I don't use explicit OPEN and CLOSE statements; instead, I call the corresponding procedures, which handle complexities related to packaged cursor persistence. I urge you to examine the *openclose.sql* file available on the book's web site to study the implementation of these procedures.

You have a lot to gain by creating cursors in packages and making those cursors available to the developers on a project. Crafting precisely the data structures you need for your application is hard and careful work. These same structures—and the data in them—are used in your PL/SQL programs, almost always via a cursor. If you do not package up your cursors and provide them "free of charge and effort" to all developers, each will write her own variations of these cursors, leading to all sorts of performance and maintenance issues. Packaging cursors is just one example of using packages to encapsulate access to data structures, which is explored further in "When to Use Packages" on page 642.

 One of the technical reviewers of this book, JT Thomas, offers the following alternative perspective:

> "Rather than working with packaged cursors, you can get exactly the same effect by encapsulating logic and data presentation into views and publishing these to the developers. This allows the developers to then be responsible for properly maintaining their own cursors; the idea is that it is not possible to enforce proper maintenance given the toolset available with publicly accessible package cursors. Specifically, as far as I know, there is no way to enforce the usage of the open/close procedures, but the cursors will always remain visible to the developer directly opening/closing it; thus, this construct is still vulnerable. To make matters worse, however, the acceptance of publicly accessible packaged cursors and the open/close procedures might lull a team into a false sense of security and reliability."

## Serializable Packages

As you have seen, package data by default persists for your entire session (or until the package is recompiled). This is an incredibly handy feature, but it has some drawbacks:

- Globally accessible (public *and* private) data structures persist, and that can cause undesired side effects. In particular, I can inadvertently leave packaged cursors open, causing "already open" errors in other programs.

- My programs can suck up lots of real memory (package data is managed in the user's memory area or User Global Area [UGA]) and then not release it if that data is stored in a package-level structure.

To help you manage the use of memory in packages, PL/SQL offers the SERIALLY_REUSABLE pragma. This pragma, which must appear in both the package specification and the body (if one exists), marks that package as *serially reusable*. For such packages, the duration of package state (the values of variables, the open status of a packaged cursor, etc.) can be reduced from a whole session to a single call of a program in the package.

To see the effects of this pragma, consider the following book_info package. I have created two separate programs: one to fill a list of books and another to show that list.

```
/* File on web: serialpkg.sql */
PACKAGE book_info
IS
   PRAGMA SERIALLY_REUSABLE;
   PROCEDURE fill_list;

   PROCEDURE show_list;
END;
```

As you can see in the following package body, that list is declared as a private, but global, associative array:

```
/* File on web: serialpkg.sql */
PACKAGE BODY book_info
IS
  PRAGMA SERIALLY_REUSABLE;

  TYPE book_list_t
  IS
     TABLE OF books%ROWTYPE
        INDEX BY PLS_INTEGER;
     my_books   book_list_t;

  PROCEDURE fill_list
  IS
  BEGIN
     FOR rec IN (SELECT *
                   FROM books
                  WHERE author LIKE '%FEUERSTEIN%')
     LOOP
        my_books (my_books.COUNT + 1) := rec;
     END LOOP;
  END fill_list;

  PROCEDURE show_list
  IS
  BEGIN
     IF my_books.COUNT = 0
     THEN
        DBMS_OUTPUT.PUT_LINE ('** No books to show you...');
     ELSE
        FOR indx IN 1 .. my_books.COUNT
        LOOP
           DBMS_OUTPUT.PUT_LINE (my_books (indx).title);
```

```
            END LOOP;
         END IF;
      END show_list;
   END;
```

To see the effect of this pragma, I fill and then show the list. In my first approach, these two steps are done in the same block, so the collection is still loaded and can be displayed:

```
SQL> BEGIN
  2      DBMS_OUTPUT.PUT_LINE (
  3          'Fill and show in same block:'
  4      );
  5      book_info.fill_list;
  6      book_info.show_list;
  7  END;
  8  /

Fill and show in same block:

   Oracle PL/SQL Programming
   Oracle PL/SQL Best Practices
   Oracle PL/SQL Built-in Packages
```

In my second attempt, I fill and show the list in two separate blocks. As a result, my collection is now empty:

```
SQL> BEGIN
  2      DBMS_OUTPUT.PUT_LINE ('Fill in first block');
  3      book_info.fill_list;
  4  END;
  5  /

Fill in first block

SQL> BEGIN
  2      DBMS_OUTPUT.PUT_LINE ('Show in second block:');
  3      book_info.show_list;
  4  END;
  5  /

Show in second block:
** No books to show you...
```

Here are some things to keep in mind for serialized packages:

- The global memory for serialized packages is allocated in the SGA, not in the user's UGA. This approach allows the package work area to be reused. Each time the package is reused, its package-level variables are initialized to their default values or to NULL, and its initialization section is re-executed.

- The maximum number of work areas needed for a serialized package is the number of concurrent users of that package. The increased use of SGA memory is offset by the decreased use of UGA or program memory. Finally, the database ages out work areas not in use if it needs to reclaim memory from the SGA for other requests.

# When to Use Packages

By now, I've covered the rules, syntax, and nuances of constructing packages. Let's now return to the list of reasons you might want to use PL/SQL packages and explore them in more detail. These scenarios include:

*Encapsulate (hide) data manipulation*
> Rather than have developers write SQL statements (leading to inefficient variations and maintenance nightmares), provide an interface to those SQL statements. This interface is known as a *table API* or *transaction API*.

*Avoid the hardcoding of literals*
> Use a package with constants to give a name to the literal ("magic") value and avoid hardcoding it into individual (and multiple) programs. You can, of course, declare constants within procedures and functions as well. The advantage of a constant defined in a package specification is that it can be referenced outside of the package.

*Improve the usability of built-in features*
> Some of Oracle's own utilities, such as UTL_FILE and DBMS_OUTPUT, leave lots to be desired. Build your own package on top of Oracle's to correct as many of the problems as possible.

*Group together logically related functionality*
> If you have a dozen procedures and functions that all revolve around a particular aspect of your application, put them all into a package so that you can manage (and find) that code more easily.

*Cache session-static data to improve application performance*
> Take advantage of persistent package data to improve the response time of your application by caching (and not requerying) static data.

The following sections describe each of these scenarios.

## Encapsulate Data Access

Rather than have developers write their own SQL statements, you should provide an interface to those SQL statements. This is one of the most important motivations for building packages, yet is only rarely employed by developers.

With this approach, PL/SQL developers as a rule will not write SQL in their applications. Instead, they will call predefined, tested, and optimized code that does all the work for them; for example, an "add" procedure (overloaded to support records) that issues the INSERT statement and follows standard error-handling rules; a function to retrieve a single row for a primary key; and a variety of cursors that handle the common requests against the data structure (which could be a single table or a "business entity" consisting of multiple tables).

If you take this approach, developers will not necessarily need to understand how to join three or six different highly normalized tables to get the right set of data. They can

---

just pick a cursor and leave the data analysis to someone else. They will not have to figure out what to do when they try to insert and the row already exists. The procedure has this logic inside it.

Perhaps the biggest advantage of this approach is that as your data structures change, the maintenance headaches of updating application code are both minimized and centralized. The person who is expert at working with that table or object type makes the necessary changes within that single package, and the changes are then "rolled out" more or less automatically to all programs relying on that package.

Data encapsulation is a big topic and can be very challenging to implement in a comprehensive way. You will find an example of a table encapsulation package (built around the employee table) in the *employee_tp.pks*, *employee_qp.\**, *employee_cp.\**, *department_tp.pks*, and *department_qp.\** files on the book's web site (these files were generated by the Quest CodeGen Utility, available from the Download page of ToadWorld, *http://www.ToadWorld.com*).

Let's take a look at what kind of impact this use of packages can have on your code. The *givebonus1.sp* file on the book's web site contains a procedure that gives the same bonus to each employee in the specified department, but only if he has been with the company for at least six months. Here are the parts of the give_bonus program that contains the SQL (see *givebonus1.sp* for the complete implementation):

```
/* File on web: givebonus1.sp */
PROCEDURE give_bonus (
   dept_in IN employees.department_id%TYPE,
   bonus_in IN NUMBER)
/*
|| Give the same bonus to each employee in the
|| specified department, but only if they have
|| been with the company for at least 6 months.
*/
IS
   l_name VARCHAR2(50);
   CURSOR by_dept_cur
   IS
      SELECT * FROM employees
      WHERE department_id = dept_in;

   fdbk INTEGER;
BEGIN
   /* Retrieve all information for the specified department. */
   SELECT department_name INTO l_name
     FROM departments
    WHERE department_id = dept_in;

   /* Make sure the department ID was valid. */
   IF l_name IS NULL
   THEN
      DBMS_OUTPUT.PUT_LINE (
         'Invalid department ID specified: ' || dept_in);
   ELSE
```

```
   /* Display the header. */
   DBMS_OUTPUT.PUT_LINE (
      'Applying Bonuses of ' || bonus_in ||
      ' to the ' || l_name || ' Department');
END IF;
/* For each employee in the specified department... */
FOR rec IN by_dept_cur
LOOP
   IF employee_rp.eligible_for_bonus (rec)
   THEN
      /* Update this column. */

      UPDATE employees
         SET salary = rec.salary + bonus_in
       WHERE employee_id = rec.employee_id;
       END IF;
   END LOOP;
END;
```

Now let's compare that to the encapsulation alternative, which you will find in its entirety in *givebonus2.sp*:

```
   /* File on web: givebonus2.sp */
1  PROCEDURE give_bonus (
2     dept_in     IN    employee_tp.department_id_t
3     , bonus_in   IN    employee_tp.bonus_t
4  )
5  IS
6     l_department      department_tp.department_rt;
7     l_employees       employee_tp.employee_tc;
8     l_rows_updated    PLS_INTEGER;
9  BEGIN
10    l_department := department_tp.onerow (dept_in);
11    l_employees := employee_qp.ar_fk_emp_department (dept_in);
12
13    FOR l_index IN 1 .. l_employees.COUNT
14    LOOP
15       IF employee_rp.eligible_for_bonus (rec)
16       THEN
17          employee_cp.upd_onecol_pky
18             (colname_in        => 'salary'
19             , new_value_in      =>   l_employees (l_index).salary
20                                      + bonus_in
21             , employee_id_in    => l_employees (l_index).employee_id
22             , rows_out          => l_rows_updated
23             );
24       END IF;
25    END LOOP;
26
27    ... more processing with name and other elements
28 END;
```

Here is an explanation of the changes made in this second version:

| Line(s) | Significance |
|---------|-------------|
| 2–7 | Declarations based on the underlying tables no longer use %TYPE and %ROWTYPE. Instead, a "types package" is provided that offers SUBTYPEs, which in turn rely on %TYPE and %ROWTYPE. By taking this approach, the application code no longer needs directly granted access to underlying tables (which would be unavailable in a fully encapsulated environment). |
| 10 | Replace the SELECT INTO with a call to a function that returns "one row" of information for the primary key. |
| 11 | Call a function that retrieves all the employee rows for the department ID foreign key. This function utilizes BULK COLLECT and returns a collection of records. This demonstrates how encapsulated code allows you to more easily take advantage of new features in PL/SQL. |
| 13–25 | The cursor FOR loop is replaced with a numeric FOR loop through the contents of the collection. |
| 17–23 | Use dynamic SQL to update any single column for the specified primary key. |

Overall, the SQL statements have been removed from the program and have been replaced with calls to reusable procedures and functions. Doing so optimizes the SQL in my application and allows me to write more robust code in a more productive manner.

It is by no means a trivial matter to build (or generate) such packages, and I recognize that most of you will not be willing or able to adopt a 100% encapsulated approach. You can, however, gain many of the advantages of data encapsulation without having to completely revamp your coding techniques. At a minimum, I suggest that you:

- Hide all your single-row queries behind a function interface. That way, you can make sure that error handling is performed and can choose the best implementation (implicit or explicit cursors, for example).

- Identify the tables that are most frequently and directly manipulated by developers and build layers of code around them.

- Create packaged programs to handle complex transactions. If "add a new order" involves inserting two rows, updating six others, and so on, make sure to embed this logic inside a procedure that handles the complexity. Don't rely on individual developers to figure it out (and write it more than once!).

## Avoid Hardcoding Literals

Virtually any application has a variety of *magic values*—literal values that have special significance in a system. These values might be type codes or validation limits. Your users will tell you that these magic values never change. "I will *always* have only 25 line items in my profit-and-loss," one will say. "The name of the parent company," swears another, "will *always* be ATLAS HQ." Don't take these promises at face value, and never code them into your programs. Consider the following IF statements:

```
IF footing_difference BETWEEN 1 and 100
THEN
    adjust_line_item;
END IF;
```

```
IF cust_status = 'C'
THEN
   reopen_customer;
END IF;
```

You are begging for trouble if you write code like this. You will be a much happier
developer if you instead build a package of named constants as follows:

```
PACKAGE config_pkg
IS
    closed_status      CONSTANT VARCHAR2(1) := 'C';
    open_status        CONSTANT VARCHAR2(1) := 'O';
    active_status      CONSTANT VARCHAR2(1) := 'A';
    inactive_status    CONSTANT VARCHAR2(1) := 'I';

    min_difference     CONSTANT PLS_INTEGER := 1;
    max_difference     CONSTANT PLS_INTEGER := 100;

    earliest_date      CONSTANT DATE := SYSDATE;
    latest_date        CONSTANT DATE := ADD_MONTHS (SYSDATE, 120);

END config_pkg;
```

Using this package, my two IF statements above now become:

```
IF footing_difference
   BETWEEN config_pkg.min_difference and config_pkg.max_difference
THEN
   adjust_line_item;
END IF;

IF cust_status = config_pkg.closed_status
THEN
   reopen_customer;
END IF;
```

If any of my magic values ever change, I simply modify the assignment to the appropriate constant in the configuration package. I do not need to change a single program
module. Just about every application I have reviewed (and many that I have written)
mistakenly includes hardcoded magic values in the program. In every single case (especially those that I myself wrote!), the developer had to make repeated changes to the
programs, during both development and maintenance phases. It was often a headache,
and sometimes a nightmare; I cannot emphasize strongly enough the importance of
consolidating all magic values into one or more packages.

You will find another example of such a package in the *utl_file_constants.pkg* file. This
package takes a different approach from that shown above. All values are hidden
in the package body. The package specification consists only of functions, which return
the values. This way, if and when I need to change a value, I do not have to recompile
the package specification, and I avoid the need to recompile dependent programs.

Finally, if *you* get to choose the literal values that you plan to hide behind constants,
you might consider using outlandish values that will further discourage any use of the

literals. Suppose, for example, that you need to return a status indicator from a procedure: success or failure? Typical values for such flags include 0 and 1, S and F, etc. The problem with such values is that they are intuitive and brief, making it easy for an undisciplined programmer to "cheat" and directly use the literal in his or her code. Consider the following:

```
PACKAGE do_stuff
IS
   c_success CONSTANT PLS_INTEGER := 0;
   c_failure CONSTANT PLS_INTEGER := 1;
   PROCEDURE big_stuff (stuff_key_in IN PLS_INTEGER, status_out OUT PLS_INTEGER);
END do_stuff;
```

With this definition, it is very likely indeed that you will encounter usages of big_stuff as follows:

```
do_stuff.big_stuff (l_stuff_key, l_status);

IF l_status = 0
THEN
   DBMS_OUTPUT.PUT_LINE ('Stuff went fine!');
END IF;
```

If, on the other hand, my package specification looks like this:

```
PACKAGE do_stuff
IS
   /* Entirely arbitrary literal values! */
   c_success CONSTANT PLS_INTEGER := -90845367;
   c_failure CONSTANT PLS_INTEGER := 55338292;
   PROCEDURE big_stuff (stuff_key_in IN PLS_INTEGER, status_out OUT PLS_INTEGER);
END do_stuff;
```

I predict that you will *never* see code like this:

```
do_stuff.big_staff (l_stuff_key, l_status);
IF l_status = -90845367
THEN
   DBMS_OUTPUT.PUT_LINE ('Stuff went fine!');
END IF;
```

It would be too embarrassing to write such code.

## Improve Usability of Built-in Features

Some of Oracle's own supplied packages, such as UTL_FILE and DBMS_OUTPUT, either contain very bothersome bugs or reflect design choices that are undesirable. We all have our pet peeves, and not just about how Oracle builds utilities for us. What about that "ace" consultant who blew into town last year? Are you still trying to deal with the code mess he left behind? Maybe you can't *replace* any of this stuff, but you can certainly consider building your own package on top of theirs (their packages, their poorly designed data structures, etc.) to correct as many of the problems as possible.

Rather than fill up the pages of this book with examples, I've listed the filenames of a number of packages available on the book's web site as companion code to this text. These demonstrate this use of packages and also offer some useful utilities. I suggest that you look through all the *.pkg* files on the site for other code you might find handy in your applications.

*filepath.pkg*
> Adds support for a path to UTL_FILE. This allows you to search through multiple, specified directories to find the desired file.

*xfile.pkg and JFile.java (alternatively, sf_file.pks/pkb and sf_file.java)*
> Extend the reach of UTL_FILE by providing a package that is built on top of a Java class that performs many tasks unsupported by UTL_FILE. The xfile ("eXtra File stuff") package also offers 100% support of the UTL_FILE interface. This means that you can do a global search and replace of "UTL_FILE" with "xfile" in your code and it will continue to work as it did before!

*sf_out.pks/pkb, bpl.sp, do.pkg*
> Substitutes for the "print line" functionality of DBMS_OUTPUT, which help you avoid the nuisances of its design drawbacks (inability to display Booleans or—prior to Oracle Dababase 10*g*—strings longer than 255 bytes, for instance).

## Group Together Logically Related Functionality

If you have a dozen procedures and functions that all revolve around a particular feature or aspect of your application, put them into a package so that you can manage (and find) that code more easily. This is most important when coding the business rules for your application. When implementing business rules, follow these important guidelines:

- Don't hardcode them (usually repeatedly) into individual application components.
- Don't scatter them across many different standalone, hard-to-manage programs.

Before you start building an application, construct a series of packages that encapsulate all of its rules. Sometimes these rules are part of a larger package, such as a table encapsulation package. In other cases, you might establish a package that contains nothing *but* the key rules. Here is one example:

```
/* File on web: custrules.pkg */
PACKAGE customer_rules
IS
    FUNCTION min_balance RETURN PLS_INTEGER;

    FUNCTION eligible_for_discount
        (customer_in IN customer%ROWTYPE)
        RETURN BOOLEAN;

    FUNCTION eligible_for_discount
        (customer_id_in IN customer.customer_id%TYPE)
```

```
    RETURN BOOLEAN;

  END customer_rules;
```

The "eligible for discount" function is hidden away in the package so that it can be easily managed. I also use overloading to offer two different interfaces to the formula: one that accepts a primary key and establishes eligibility for that customer in the database, and a second that applies its logic to customer information already loaded into a %ROWTYPE record. Why did I do this? Because if a person has already queried the customer information from the database, he can use the %ROWTYPE overloading and avoid a second query.

Of course, not all "logically related functionality" has to do with business rules. I might need to add to the built-in string manipulation functions of PL/SQL. Rather than create 12 different standalone functions, I will create a "string enhancements" package and put all of the functions there. Then I and others know where to go to access that functionality.

## Cache Static Session Data

Take advantage of persistent package data to improve the response time of your application by caching (and not requerying) static data. You can do this at a number of different levels; for each of the following items, I've listed a few helpful code examples available on the book's web site:

- Cache a single value, such as the name of the current user (returned by the USER function). Examples: *thisuser.pkg* and *thisuser.tst*.

- Cache a single row or set of information, such as the configuration information for a given user. Examples: *init.pkg* and *init.tst*.

- Cache a whole list of values, such as the contents of a static, reference code lookup table. Examples: *emplu.pkg* (employee lookup) and *emplu.tst*.

- Use the *.tst* files to compare cached and non-cached performance.

Package-based caching is just one type of caching available to PL/SQL developers. See Chapter 21, *Optimizing PL/SQL Performance*, for a more detailed presentation of all of your caching options.

 If you decide to take advantage of package-based caching, remember that this data is cached separately for each session that references the package (in the Program Global Area). This means that if your cache of a row in a table consumes 2MB and you have 1,000 simultaneously connected sessions, then you have just used up 2 GB of memory in your system—in addition to all the other memory consumed by the database.

# Packages and Object Types

Packages are containers that allow you to group together data and code elements. Object types are containers that allow you to group together data and code elements. Do you need both? Do object types supersede packages, especially now that Oracle has added support for inheritance? When should you use a package and when should you use an object type? All very interesting and pertinent questions.

It is true that packages and object types share some features:

- Each can contain one or more programs and data structures.
- Each can (and usually does) consist of both a specification and a body.

There are, however, key differences between the two, including:

- An object type is a *template* for data; you can instantiate multiple object type instances (a.k.a. "objects") from that template. Each one of those instances has associated with it all of the attributes (data) and methods (procedures and functions) from the template. These instances can be stored in the database. A package, on the other hand, is a one-off structure and, in a sense, a static object type: you cannot declare instances of it.
- Object types offer inheritance. That means that I can declare an object type to be "under" another type, and it *inherits* all the attributes and methods of that supertype. There is no concept of hierarchy or inheritance in packages. See Chapter 26 for lots more information about this.
- With packages, you can create private, hidden data and programs. This is not supported in object types, in which everything is publicly declared and accessible (although you can still hide the implementation of methods in the object type body).

So when should you use object types and when should you use packages? First of all, very few people use object types and even fewer attempt to take advantage of Oracle's "object-relational" model. For them, packages will remain the core building blocks of their PL/SQL-based applications.

If you do plan to exploit object types, I recommend that you consider putting much of your complex code into packages that are then called by methods in the object type. You then have more flexibility in designing the code that implements your object types, and you can share that code with other elements of your application.

# CHAPTER 19

# Triggers

Database triggers are named program units that are executed in response to events that occur in the database. Triggers are critical elements of a well-designed application built on the Oracle database and are used to do the following:

*Perform validation on changes being made to tables*
Because the validation logic is attached directly to the database object, database triggers offer a strong guarantee that the required logic will always be executed and enforced.

*Automate maintenance of the database*
Starting with Oracle8*i* Database, you can use database startup and shutdown triggers to automatically perform necessary initialization and cleanup steps. This is a distinct advantage over creating and running such steps as scripts external to the database.

*Apply rules concerning acceptable database administration activity in a granular fashion*
You can use triggers to tightly control what kinds of actions are allowed on database objects, such as dropping or altering tables. Again, by putting this logic in triggers, you make it very difficult, if not impossible, for anyone to bypass the rules you have established.

Five different types of events can have trigger code attached to them:

*Data Manipulation Language (DML) statements*
DML triggers are available to fire whenever a record is inserted into, updated in, or deleted from a table. These triggers can be used to perform validation, set default values, audit changes, and even disallow certain DML operations.

*Data Definition Language (DDL) statements*
DDL triggers fire whenever DDL is executed—for example, whenever a table is created. These triggers can perform auditing and prevent certain DDL statements from occurring.

*Database events*

Database event triggers fire whenever the database starts up or is shut down, whenever a user logs on or off, and whenever an Oracle error occurs. For Oracle8*i* Database and above, these triggers provide a means of tracking activity in the database.

*INSTEAD OF*

INSTEAD OF triggers are essentially alternatives to DML triggers. They fire when inserts, updates, and deletes are about to occur; your code specifies what to do in place of these DML operations. INSTEAD OF triggers control operations on views, not tables. They can be used to make nonupdateable views updateable and to override the behavior of views that are updateable.

*Suspended statements*

Oracle9*i* Database introduced the concept of suspended statements. Statements experiencing space problems (lack of tablespace or quota) can enter a suspended mode until the space problem is fixed. Triggers can be added to the mix to automatically alert someone of the problem or even to fix it.

This chapter describes these types of triggers; for each, I'll provide syntax details, example code, and suggested uses. I'll also touch on trigger maintenance at the end of the chapter.

If you need to emulate triggers on SELECT statements (queries), you should investigate the use of fine-grained auditing (FGA), which is described in Chapter 23 and in greater detail in *Oracle PL/SQL for DBAs* (O'Reilly).

# DML Triggers

Data Manipulation Language (DML) triggers fire when records are inserted into, updated within, or deleted from a particular table, as shown in Figure 19-1. These are the most common types of triggers, especially for developers; the other trigger types are used primarily by DBAs.

There are many options regarding DML triggers. They can fire after or before a DML statement, or they can fire after or before each row is processed within a statement. They can fire for INSERT, UPDATE, MERGE, or DELETE statements, or combinations of these three. Starting with Oracle Database 11*g*, you can bundle together several DML triggers into one compound trigger.

There are also many ways to actually configure DML triggers. To determine what works for your environment, you need to answer the following questions:

- Should the triggers fire once for the whole DML statement or once for each row involved in the statement?

- Should the triggers fire before or after the whole statement completes or before or after each row is processed?

- Should the triggers fire for inserts, updates, deletes, or a combination thereof?

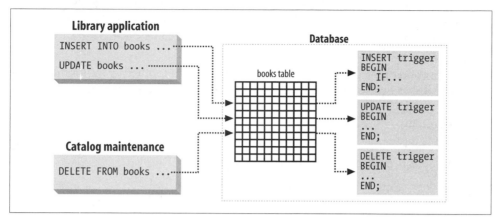

*Figure 19-1. DML trigger flow of control*

## DML Trigger Concepts

Before diving into the syntax and examples, you may find it useful to review these DML trigger concepts and associated terminology:

*BEFORE trigger*
    A trigger that executes before a certain operation occurs, such as BEFORE INSERT.

*AFTER trigger*
    A trigger that executes after a certain operation occurs, such as AFTER UPDATE.

*Statement-level trigger*
    A trigger that executes for a SQL statement as a whole (which may, in turn, affect one or more individual rows in a database table).

*Row-level trigger*
    A trigger that executes for a single row that has been affected by the execution of a SQL statement. Suppose that the books table contains 1,000 rows. Then the following UPDATE statement will modify 1,000 rows:

```
UPDATE books SET title = UPPER (title);
```

    And if I define a row-level update trigger on the books table, that trigger will fire 1,000 times.

*NEW pseudo-record*
    A data structure named NEW that looks like and (mostly) acts like a PL/SQL record. This pseudo-record is available only within update and insert DML triggers; it contains the values for the affected row after any changes were made.

*OLD pseudo-record*
> A data structure named OLD that looks like and (mostly) acts like a PL/SQL record. This pseudo-record is available only within update and delete DML triggers; it contains the values for the affected row before any changes were made.

*WHEN clause*
> The portion of the DML trigger that is run to determine whether or not the trigger code should be executed (allowing you to avoid unnecessary execution).

### DML trigger scripts

To explore some of the concepts presented in the previous section, I have made the following scripts available on the book's web site:

| Concept | Files | Description |
| --- | --- | --- |
| Statement-level and row-level triggers | *copy_tables.sql* | Creates two identical tables, one with data and one empty. |
| | *statement_vs_row.sql* | Creates two simple triggers, one statement-level and one row-level. After running these scripts, execute this statement and view the results (with SERVEROUTPUT turned on to watch the activity): <br><br>`INSERT INTO to_table`<br>`SELECT * FROM from_table;` |
| BEFORE and AFTER triggers | *before_vs_after.sql* | Creates BEFORE and AFTER triggers. After running the script, execute this statement and view the results: <br><br>`INSERT INTO to_table`<br>`SELECT * FROM from_table;` |
| Triggers for various DML operations | *one_trigger_per_type.sql* | Creates AFTER INSERT, UPDATE, and DELETE triggers on to_table. After running the script, execute these commands and view the results: <br><br>`INSERT INTO to_table`<br>`  VALUES (1);`<br>`UPDATE to_table`<br>`  SET col1 10;`<br>`DELETE to_table;` |

### Transaction participation

By default, DML triggers participate in the transaction from which they were fired. This means that:

- If a trigger raises an exception, that part of the transaction is rolled back.
- If the trigger performs any DML itself (such as inserting a row into a log table), then that DML becomes a part of the main transaction.
- You cannot issue a COMMIT or ROLLBACK from within a DML trigger.

If you define your DML trigger to be an autonomous transaction (discussed in Chapter 14), however, then any DML performed inside the trigger will be saved or rolled back—with your explicit COMMIT or ROLLBACK statement—without affecting the main transaction.

The following sections present the syntax for creating a DML trigger, provide reference information on various elements of the trigger definition, and explore an example that uses the many components and options for these triggers.

## Creating a DML Trigger

To create (or replace) a DML trigger, use the syntax shown here:

```
1   CREATE [OR REPLACE] TRIGGER trigger_name
2   {BEFORE | AFTER}
3   {INSERT | DELETE | UPDATE | UPDATE OF column_list } ON table_name
4   [FOR EACH ROW]
5   [WHEN (...)]
6   [DECLARE ... ]
7   BEGIN
8      ...executable statements...
9   [EXCEPTION ... ]
10  END [trigger_name];
```

The following table provides an explanation of these different elements:

| Line(s) | Description |
|---------|-------------|
| 1 | States that a trigger is to be created with the name supplied. Specifying OR REPLACE is optional. If the trigger exists and REPLACE is not specified, then your attempt to create the trigger anew will result in an ORA-4081 error. It is possible, by the way, for a table and a trigger (or a procedure and a trigger, for that matter) to have the same name. I recommend, however, that you adopt naming conventions to avoid the confusion that will result from this sharing of names. |
| 2 | Specifies if the trigger is to fire BEFORE or AFTER the statement or row is processed. |
| 3 | Specifies the combination of DML types to which the trigger applies: insert, update, or delete. Note that UPDATE can be specified for the whole record or just for a column list separated by commas. The columns can be combined (separated with an OR) and may be specified in any order. Line 3 also specifies the table to which the trigger is to apply. Remember that each DML trigger can apply to only one table. |
| 4 | If FOR EACH ROW is specified, then the trigger will activate for each row processed by a statement. If this clause is missing, the default behavior is to fire only once for the statement (a statement-level trigger). |
| 5 | An optional WHEN clause that allows you to specify logic to avoid unnecessary execution of the trigger. |
| 6 | Optional declaration section for the anonymous block that constitutes the trigger code. If you do not need to declare local variables, you do not need this keyword. Note that you should never try to declare the NEW and OLD pseudo-records. This is done automatically. |
| 7–8 | The execution section of the trigger. This is required and must contain at least one statement. |
| 9 | Optional exception section. This section will trap and handle (or attempt to handle) any exceptions raised in the execution section only. |

| Line(s) | Description |
| --- | --- |
| 10 | Required END statement for the trigger. You can include the name of the trigger after the END keyword to explicitly document which trigger you are ending. |

Here are a few examples of DML trigger usage:

- I want to make sure that whenever an employee is added or changed, all necessary validation is run. Notice that I pass the necessary fields of the NEW pseudo-record to individual check routines in this row-level trigger:

```
TRIGGER validate_employee_changes
   AFTER INSERT OR UPDATE
   ON employees
   FOR EACH ROW
BEGIN
   check_date (:NEW.hire_date);
   check_email (:NEW.email);
END;
```

- The following BEFORE INSERT trigger captures audit information for the CEO compensation table. It also relies on the autonomous transaction feature to commit this new row without affecting the "outer" or main transaction:

```
TRIGGER bef_ins_ceo_comp
   BEFORE INSERT
   ON ceo_compensation
   FOR EACH ROW
DECLARE
   PRAGMA AUTONOMOUS_TRANSACTION;
BEGIN
   INSERT INTO ceo_comp_history
       VALUES (:NEW.name,
               :OLD.compensation, :NEW.compensation,
               'AFTER INSERT', SYSDATE);
   COMMIT;
END;
```

### The WHEN clause

Use the WHEN clause to fine-tune the situations under which the body of the trigger code will actually execute. In the following example, I use the WHEN clause to make sure that the trigger code does not execute unless the new salary is changing to a *different* value:

```
TRIGGER check_raise
   AFTER UPDATE OF salary
   ON employees
   FOR EACH ROW
WHEN ((OLD.salary != NEW.salary) OR
      (OLD.salary IS NULL AND NEW.salary IS NOT NULL) OR
      (OLD.salary IS NOT NULL AND NEW.salary IS NULL))
BEGIN
   ...
```

In other words, if a user issues an UPDATE to a row and for some reason sets the salary to its current value, the trigger will and must fire, but the reality is that you really don't need any of the PL/SQL code in the body of the trigger to execute. By checking this condition in the WHEN clause, you avoid some of the overhead of starting up the PL/SQL block associated with the trigger.

The *genwhen.sp* file on the book's web site offers a procedure that will generate a WHEN clause to ensure that the new value is actually different from the old.

In most cases, you will reference fields in the OLD and NEW pseudo-records in the WHEN clause, as in the example shown above. You may also, however, write code that invokes built-in functions, as in the following WHEN clause that uses SYSDATE to restrict the INSERT trigger to fire only between 9 a.m. and 5 p.m.

```
TRIGGER valid_when_clause
BEFORE INSERT ON frame
FOR EACH ROW
WHEN ( TO_CHAR(SYSDATE,'HH24') BETWEEN 9 AND 17 )
    ...
```

Here are some things to keep in mind when using the WHEN clause:

- Enclose the entire logical expression inside parentheses. These parentheses are optional in an IF statement, but required in the trigger WHEN clause.
- Do *not* include the ":" in front of the OLD and NEW names. This colon (indicating a host variable) is required in the body of the trigger PL/SQL code, but cannot be used in the WHEN clause.
- You can invoke SQL built-in functions only from within the WHEN clause; you will not be able to call user-defined functions or functions defined in built-in packages (such as DBMS_UTILITY). Attempts to do so will generate an *ORA-04076: invalid NEW or OLD specification* error. If you need to invoke such functions, move that logic to the beginning of the trigger execution section.

The WHEN clause can be used only with row-level triggers. You will get a compilation error (ORA-04077) if you try to use it with statement-level triggers.

### Working with NEW and OLD pseudo-records

Whenever a row-level trigger fires, the PL/SQL runtime engine creates and populates two data structures that function much like records. They are the NEW and OLD pseudo-records ("pseudo" because they don't share all the properties of real PL/SQL records). OLD stores the original values of the record being processed by the trigger;

NEW contains the new values. These records have the same structure as a record declared using %ROWTYPE on the table to which the trigger is attached.

Here are some rules to keep in mind when working with NEW and OLD:

- With triggers on INSERT operations, the OLD structure does not contain any data; there *is* no "old" set of values.

- With triggers on UPDATE operations, both the OLD and NEW structures are populated. OLD contains the values prior to the update; NEW contains the values the row will contain after the update is performed.

- With triggers on DELETE operations, the NEW structure does not contain any data; the record is about to be erased.

- The NEW and OLD pseudo-records also contain the ROWID pseudo-column; this value is populated in both OLD and NEW with the same value, in all circumstances. Go figure!

- You cannot change the field values of the OLD structure; attempting to do so will raise the ORA-04085 error. You *can* modify the field values of the NEW structure.

- You can't pass a NEW or OLD structure as a "record parameter" to a procedure or function called within the trigger. You can pass only individual fields of the pseudo-record. See the *gentrigrec.sp* script for a program that will generate code transferring NEW and OLD values to records that *can* be passed as parameters.

- When referencing the NEW and OLD structures within the anonymous block for the trigger, you must preface those keywords with a colon, as in:

```
IF :NEW.salary > 10000 THEN...
```

- You cannot perform record-level operations with the NEW and OLD structures. For example, the following statement will cause the trigger compilation to fail:

```
BEGIN :new := NULL; END;
```

You can also use the REFERENCING clause to change the names of the pseudo-records within the database trigger; this allows you to write code that is more self-documenting and application-specific. Here is one example:

```
/* File on web: full_old_and_new.sql */
TRIGGER audit_update
   AFTER UPDATE
   ON frame
   REFERENCING OLD AS prior_to_cheat NEW AS after_cheat
   FOR EACH ROW
BEGIN
   INSERT INTO frame_audit
               (bowler_id,
                game_id,
                old_score,
                new_score,
                change_date,
                operation)
```

```
            VALUES (:after_cheat.bowler_id,
                    :after_cheat.game_id,
                    :prior_to_cheat.score,
                    :after_cheat.score,
                    SYSDATE,
                    'UPDATE');
   END;
```

Run the *full_old_and_new.sql* script to take a look at the behavior of the OLD and NEW pseudo-records.

### Determining the DML action within a trigger

Oracle provides a set of functions (also known as *operational directives*) that allow you to determine which DML action caused the firing of the current trigger. Each of these functions returns TRUE or FALSE, as described next:

*INSERTING*

> Returns TRUE if the trigger was fired by an insert into the table to which the trigger is attached, and FALSE if not.

*UPDATING*

> Returns TRUE if the trigger was fired by an update of the table to which the trigger is attached, and FALSE if not.

*DELETING*

> Returns TRUE if the trigger was fired by a delete from the table to which the trigger is attached, and FALSE if not.

Using these directives, it's possible to create a single trigger that consolidates the actions required for each different type of operations. Here's one such trigger:

```
/* File on web: one_trigger_does_it_all.sql */
TRIGGER three_for_the_price_of_one
BEFORE DELETE OR INSERT OR UPDATE ON account_transaction
FOR EACH ROW
BEGIN
  -- track who created the new row
  IF INSERTING
  THEN
    :NEW.created_by := USER;
    :NEW.created_date := SYSDATE;

  -- track deletion with special audit program
  ELSIF DELETING
  THEN
     audit_deletion(USER,SYSDATE);

  -- track who last updated the row
  ELSIF UPDATING
  THEN
    :NEW.UPDATED_BY := USER;
    :NEW.UPDATED_DATE := SYSDATE;
```

```
    END IF;
  END;
```

The UPDATING function is overloaded with a version that takes a specific column name as an argument. This is handy for isolating specific column updates.

```
/* File on web: overloaded_update.sql */
TRIGGER validate_update
BEFORE UPDATE ON account_transaction
FOR EACH ROW
BEGIN
  IF UPDATING ('ACCOUNT_NO')
  THEN
    errpkg.raise('Account number cannot be updated');
  END IF;
END;
```

Specification of the column name is not case-sensitive. The name is not evaluated until the trigger executes, and if the column does not exist in the table to which the trigger is attached, it will evaluate to FALSE.

 Operational directives can be called from within any PL/SQL block, not just triggers. They will, however, only evaluate to TRUE within a DML trigger or code called from within a DML trigger.

## DML Trigger Example: No Cheating Allowed!

One application function for which triggers are perfect is change auditing. Consider the example of Paranoid Pam (or Ms. Trustful as we call her), who runs a bowling alley and has been receiving complaints about people cheating on their scores. She recently implemented a complete Oracle application known as Pam's Bowl-A-Rama Scoring System, and now wants to augment it to catch the cheaters.

The focal point of Pam's application is the frame table that records the score of a particular frame of a particular game for a particular player:

```
/* File on web: bowlerama_tables.sql */
TABLE frame
(bowler_id    NUMBER,
 game_id      NUMBER,
 frame_number NUMBER,
 strike       VARCHAR2(1) DEFAULT 'N',
 spare        VARCHAR2(1) DEFAULT 'N',
 score        NUMBER,
 CONSTRAINT frame_pk
 PRIMARY KEY (bowler_id, game_id, frame_number))
```

Pam enhances the frame table with an audit version to catch all before and after values, so that she can compare them and identify fraudulent activity:

```
TABLE frame_audit
(bowler_id    NUMBER,
```

```
game_id       NUMBER,
frame_number  NUMBER,
old_strike    VARCHAR2(1),
new_strike    VARCHAR2(1),
old_spare     VARCHAR2(1),
new_spare     VARCHAR2(1),
old_score     NUMBER,
new_score     NUMBER,
change_date   DATE,
operation     VARCHAR2(6))
```

For every change to the frame table, Pam would like to keep track of before and after images of the affected rows. So she creates the following simple audit trigger:

```
/* File on web: bowlerama_full_audit.sql */
1    TRIGGER audit_frames
2    AFTER INSERT OR UPDATE OR DELETE ON frame
3    FOR EACH ROW
4    BEGIN
5      IF INSERTING THEN
6        INSERT INTO frame_audit(bowler_id,game_id,frame_number,
7                                new_strike,new_spare,new_score,
8                                change_date,operation)
9        VALUES(:NEW.bowler_id,:NEW.game_id,:NEW.frame_number,
10             :NEW.strike,:NEW.spare,:NEW.score,
11             SYSDATE,'INSERT');
12
13     ELSIF UPDATING THEN
14       INSERT INTO frame_audit(bowler_id,game_id,frame_number,
15                               old_strike,new_strike,
16                               old_spare,new_spare,
17                               old_score,new_score,
18                               change_date,operation)
19       VALUES(:NEW.bowler_id,:NEW.game_id,:NEW.frame_number,
20             :OLD.strike,:NEW.strike,
21             :OLD.spare,:NEW.spare,
22             :OLD.score,:NEW.score,
23             SYSDATE,'UPDATE');
24
25     ELSIF DELETING THEN
26       INSERT INTO frame_audit(bowler_id,game_id,frame_number,
27                               old_strike,old_spare,old_score,
28                               change_date,operation)
29       VALUES(:OLD.bowler_id,:OLD.game_id,:OLD.frame_number,
30             :OLD.strike,:OLD.spare,:OLD.score,
31             SYSDATE,'DELETE');
32     END IF;
33   END audit_frames;
```

Notice that for the INSERTING clause (lines 6–11), she relies on the NEW pseudo-record to populate the audit row. For UPDATING (lines 14–23), a combination of NEW and OLD information is used. For DELETING (lines 26–31), Pam has only OLD information with which to work. With this trigger in place, Pam can sit back and wait for action.

Of course, Pam doesn't announce her new auditing system. In particular, Sally Johnson (a very ambitious but not terribly skilled bowler) has no idea she is being watched. Sally has decided that she really wants to be the champion this year, and will stop at nothing to make it happen. Her father owns the bowling alley, she has access to SQL*Plus, and she knows that her bowler ID is 1. All that constitutes enough privilege and information to allow her to bypass the application GUI altogether, connect directly into SQL*Plus, and work some very unprincipled "magic."

Sally starts out by giving herself a strike in the first frame:

```
SQL> INSERT INTO frame
  2  (BOWLER_ID,GAME_ID,FRAME_NUMBER,STRIKE)
  3  VALUES(1,1,1,'Y');
1 row created.
```

But then she decides to be clever. She immediately downgrades her first frame to a spare to be less conspicuous:

```
SQL> UPDATE frame
  2  SET strike = 'N',
  3      spare = 'Y'
  4  WHERE bowler_id = 1
  5    AND game_id = 1
  6    AND frame_number = 1;
1 row updated.
```

Uh oh! Sally hears a noise in the corridor. She loses her nerve and tries to cover her tracks:

```
SQL> DELETE frame
  2  WHERE bowler_id = 1
  3    AND game_id = 1
  4    AND frame_number = 1;
1 row deleted.

SQL> COMMIT;
Commit complete.
```

She even verifies that her entries were deleted:

```
SQL> SELECT * FROM frame;
no rows selected
```

Wiping the sweat from her brow, Sally signs out, but vows to come back later and follow through on her plans.

Ever suspicious, Pam signs in and quickly discovers what Sally was up to by querying the audit table (Pam might also consider setting up an hourly job via DBMS_JOB to automate this part of the auditing procedure):

```
SELECT bowler_id, game_id, frame_number
     , old_strike, new_strike
     , old_spare, new_spare
     , change_date, operation
  FROM frame_audit
```

Here is the output:

```
BOWLER_ID GAME_ID FRAME_NUMBER O N O N CHANGE_DA OPERAT
--------- ------- ------------ - - - - --------- ------
        1       1            1   Y   N 12-SEP-00 INSERT
        1       1            1 Y N N Y 12-SEP-00 UPDATE
        1       1            1 N   N   12-SEP-00 DELETE
```

Sally is so busted! The audit entries show what Sally was up to even though no changes remain behind in the frame table. All three statements were audited by Pam's DML trigger: the initial insert of a strike entry, the downgrade to a spare, and the subsequent removal of the record.

### Applying the WHEN clause

After using her auditing system for many successful months, Pam undertakes an effort to further isolate potential problems. She reviews her application frontend and determines that the strike, spare, and score fields are the only ones that can be changed. Thus her trigger can be more specific:

```
TRIGGER audit_update
   AFTER UPDATE OF strike, spare, score
   ON frame
   REFERENCING OLD AS prior_to_cheat NEW AS after_cheat
   FOR EACH ROW
BEGIN
   INSERT INTO frame_audit (...)
     VALUES (...);
END;
```

After a few weeks of this implementation, Pam is still not happy with the auditing situation because audit entries are being created even when values are set equal to themselves. Updates like this one are producing useless audit records that show nothing changing:

```
SQL> UPDATE FRAME
  2  SET strike = strike;
  1 row updated.

SQL> SELECT old_strike,
  2         new_strike,
  3         old_spare,
  4         new_spare,
  5         old_score,
  6         new_score
  7    FROM frame_audit;

O N O N  OLD_SCORE  NEW_SCORE
- - - -  ---------- ----------
Y Y N N
```

Pam needs to further isolate the trigger so that it fires only when values actually change. She does this using the WHEN clause shown here:

```
/* File on web: final_audit.sql */
TRIGGER audit_update
AFTER UPDATE OF STRIKE, SPARE, SCORE ON FRAME
REFERENCING OLD AS prior_to_cheat NEW AS after_cheat
FOR EACH ROW
WHEN ( prior_to_cheat.strike != after_cheat.strike OR
       prior_to_cheat.spare != after_cheat.spare OR
       prior_to_cheat.score != after_cheat.score )
BEGIN
  INSERT INTO FRAME_AUDIT ( ... )
     VALUES ( ... );
END;
```

Now entries will appear in the audit table only if something did indeed change, allowing Pam to quickly identify possible cheaters. Pam performs a quick final test of her trigger.

```
SQL> UPDATE frame
  2  SET strike = strike;
1 row updated.

SQL> SELECT old_strike,
  2         new_strike,
  3         old_spare,
  4         new_spare,
  5         old_score,
  6         new_score
  7    FROM frame_audit;
no rows selected
```

### Using pseudo-records to fine-tune trigger execution

Pam has implemented an acceptable level of auditing in her system; now she'd like to make it a little more user-friendly. Her most obvious idea is to have her system add 10 to the score for frames recording a strike or spare. This allows the scorekeeper to track only the score for subsequent bowls while the system adds the strike score.

```
/* File on web: set_score.sql */
TRIGGER set_score
BEFORE INSERT ON frame
FOR EACH ROW
WHEN ( NEW.score IS NOT NULL )
BEGIN
  IF :NEW.strike = 'Y' OR :NEW.spare = 'Y'
  THEN
    :NEW.score := :NEW.score + 10;
  END IF;
END;
```

 Remember that field values in the NEW records can be changed only in BEFORE row triggers.

Being a stickler for rules, Pam decides to add score validation to her set of triggers:

```
/* File on web: validate_score.sql */
TRIGGER validate_score
   AFTER INSERT OR UPDATE
   ON frame
   FOR EACH ROW
BEGIN
   IF     :NEW.strike = 'Y' AND :NEW.score < 10
   THEN
      RAISE_APPLICATION_ERROR (
         -20001,
         'ERROR: Score For Strike Must Be >= 10'
      );
   ELSIF :NEW.spare = 'Y' AND :NEW.score < 10
   THEN
      RAISE_APPLICATION_ERROR (
         -20001,
         'ERROR: Score For Spare Must Be >= 10'
      );
   ELSIF :NEW.strike = 'Y' AND :NEW.spare = 'Y'
   THEN
      RAISE_APPLICATION_ERROR (
         -20001,
         'ERROR: Cannot Enter Spare And Strike'
      );
   END IF;
END;
```

Now when there is any attempt to insert a row that violates this condition, it will be rejected:

```
SQL> INSERT INTO frame VALUES(1,1,1,'Y',NULL,5);
2 INSERT INTO frame
              *
ERROR at line 1:
ORA-20001: ERROR: Score For Strike Must >= 10
```

## Multiple Triggers of the Same Type

Above and beyond all of the options presented for DML triggers, it is also possible to have multiple triggers of the same type attached to a single table. Switching from bowling to golf, consider the following example that provides a simple commentary of a golf score by determining its relationship to a par score of 72.

A single row-level BEFORE INSERT trigger would suffice:

```
/* File on web: golf_commentary.sql */
TRIGGER golf_commentary
   BEFORE INSERT
   ON golf_scores
   FOR EACH ROW
DECLARE
   c_par_score   CONSTANT PLS_INTEGER := 72;
BEGIN
```

```
      :new.commentary :=
        CASE
          WHEN :new.score < c_par_score THEN 'Under'
          WHEN :new.score = c_par_score THEN NULL
          ELSE 'Over' END || ' Par'
  END;
```

However, the requirement could also be satisfied with three separate row-level BEFORE INSERT triggers with mutually exclusive WHEN clauses:

```
TRIGGER golf_commentary_under_par
BEFORE INSERT ON golf_scores
FOR EACH ROW
WHEN (NEW.score < 72)
BEGIN
  :NEW.commentary := 'Under Par';
END;

TRIGGER golf_commentary_par
BEFORE INSERT ON golf_scores
FOR EACH ROW
WHEN (NEW.score = 72)
BEGIN
  :NEW.commentary := 'Par';
END;

TRIGGER golf_commentary_over_par
BEFORE INSERT ON golf_scores
FOR EACH ROW
WHEN (NEW.score > 72)
BEGIN
  :NEW.commentary := 'Over Par';
END;
```

Both implementations are perfectly acceptable and have advantages and disadvantages. A single trigger is easier to maintain because all of the code is in one place, while separate triggers reduce parse and execution time when more complex processing is required.

## Who Follows Whom

Prior to Oracle Database 11g there was no way to guarantee the order in which multiple DML triggers would fire. While this is not a concern in the previous example, it could be a problem in others, as shown in the next example.

What values will be shown by the final query?

```
/* File on web: multiple_trigger_seq.sql */

TABLE incremented_values
(value_inserted    NUMBER,
 value_incremented NUMBER);

TRIGGER increment_by_one
BEFORE INSERT ON incremented_values
```

```
FOR EACH ROW
BEGIN
  :NEW.value_incremented := :NEW.value_incremented + 1;
END;

TRIGGER increment_by_two
BEFORE INSERT ON incremented_values
FOR EACH ROW
BEGIN
  IF :NEW.value_incremented > 1 THEN
    :NEW.value_incremented := :NEW.value_incremented + 2;
  END IF;
END;

INSERT INTO incremented_values
 VALUES(1,1);

SELECT *
  FROM incremented_values;
```

Any guesses? On my database I got this result:

```
SQL> SELECT *
  2    FROM incremented_values;

VALUE_INSERTED VALUE_INCREMENTED
-------------- -----------------
             1                 2
```

So the increment_by_two trigger fired first and did nothing because the value_incremented column was not greater than 1; then the increment_by_one trigger fired to increase the value_incremented column by 1. Is this the result you will receive? The above example offers no guarantee. Will this always be the result? Again, there is no guarantee. Prior to Oracle Database 11g Oracle explicitly stated that there is no way to control or assure the order in which multiple triggers of the same type on a single table would fire. There are many theories, the most prevalent being that triggers fire in reverse order of creation or by order of object ID—but even those theories could not be relied upon.

Finally, in Oracle Database 11g, the firing order can be guaranteed using the FOLLOWS clause as shown in the following example.

```
TRIGGER increment_by_two
BEFORE INSERT ON incremented_values
FOR EACH ROW
FOLLOWS increment_by_one
BEGIN
  IF :new.value_incremented > 1 THEN
    :new.value_incremented := :new.value_incremented + 2;
  END IF;
END;
```

Now this trigger is guaranteed to fire after the increment_by_one trigger does. Thus guaranteeing the final result of the insert as well.

```
SQL> INSERT INTO incremented_values
  2  VALUES(1,1);
1 row created.
SQL> SELECT *
  2    FROM incremented_values;
VALUE_INSERTED VALUE_INCREMENTED
-------------- -----------------
             1                 4
```

The increment_by_one trigger made the inserted value 2 and then the increment_by_two trigger bumped it up to 4. This will always be the behavior because it is specified within the trigger itself—no need to rely on theories.

The link between triggers and their followers is viewable as a reference dependency in the dependencies view of the Oracle data dictionary.

```
SQL> SELECT referenced_name,
  2         referenced_type,
  3         dependency_type
  4    FROM user_dependencies
  5   WHERE name = 'INCREMENT_BY_TWO'
  6     AND referenced_type = 'TRIGGER';
REFERENCED_NAME    REFERENCED_TYPE    DEPE
------------------ ------------------ ----
INCREMENT_BY_ONE   TRIGGER            REF
```

Despite the behavior I've described here for Oracle Database 11g, triggers will not follow blindly—attempts to compile a trigger to follow one that is undefined are met with this error message.

```
Trigger "SCOTT"."BLIND_FOLLOWER" referenced in FOLLOWS or PRECEDES clause may
not exist
```

## Mutating Table Errors

When something mutates, it is changing. Something that is changing is hard to analyze and to quantify. A mutating table error (ORA-4091) occurs when a row-level trigger tries to examine or change a table that is already undergoing change (via an INSERT, UPDATE, or DELETE statement).

In particular, this error occurs when a row-level trigger attempts to read or write the table from which the trigger was fired. Suppose, for example, that I want to put a special check on my employee table to make sure that when a person is given a raise, that person's new salary is not more than 20% above the next-highest salary in his department.

I would therefore like to write a trigger like this:

```
TRIGGER brake_on_raises
   BEFORE UPDATE OF salary ON employees
   FOR EACH ROW
DECLARE
   l_curr_max NUMBER;
```

```
BEGIN
   SELECT MAX (salary) INTO l_curr_max
     FROM employees
     WHERE department_id = :NEW.department_id;
   IF l_curr_max * 1.20 < :NEW.salary
   THEN
      errpkg.RAISE (
         employee_rules.en_salary_increase_too_large,
         :NEW.employee_id,
         :NEW.salary
      );
   END IF;
END;
```

But when I try to perform an update that, say, doubles the salary of the PL/SQL programmer (yours truly), I get this error:

```
ORA-04091: table SCOTT.EMPLOYEE is mutating, trigger/function may not see it
```

Here are some guidelines to keep in mind regarding mutating table errors:

- In general, a row-level trigger may not read or write the table from which it has been fired. The restriction applies only to row-level triggers, however. Statement-level triggers are free to both read and modify the triggering table; this fact gives us a way to avoid the mutating table error.

- If you make your trigger an autonomous transaction (by adding the PRAGMA AUTONOMOUS TRANSACTION statement and committing inside the body of the trigger), then you will be able to *query* the contents of the firing table. However, you will still not be allowed to modify the contents of the table.

Because each release of the Oracle database renders mutating tables less and less of a problem, it's not really necessary to perform a full demonstration here. However a demonstration script named *mutation_zone.sql* is available on the book's web site. In addition, the file *mutating_template.sql* offers a package that can serve as a template for creating your own package to defer processing of row-level logic to the statement level.

## Compound Triggers: Putting It All In One Place

The age-old saying that "I finally got it all together, but I forgot where I put it" often applies to triggers. As you create more and more triggers containing more and more business logic, it becomes difficult to recall which triggers handle which rules and how all of the triggers interact. In the previous section I demonstrated how the three types of DML (insert, update, delete) can be put together in a single trigger, but wouldn't it be nice to be able to put row and statement triggers together in the same code object as well. Starting with Oracle Database 11g you can use the compound trigger to do just that.

Here's a very simple example to show the syntax.

```
/* File on web: compound_trigger.sql */
 1  TRIGGER compounder
 2  FOR UPDATE OR INSERT OR DELETE ON incremented_values
 3  COMPOUND TRIGGER
 4
 5    v_global_var NUMBER := 1;
 6
 7    BEFORE STATEMENT IS
 8    BEGIN
 9      DBMS_OUTPUT.PUT_LINE('Compound:BEFORE S:' || v_global_var);
10      v_global_var := v_global_var + 1;
11    END BEFORE STATEMENT;
12
13    BEFORE EACH ROW IS
14    BEGIN
15      DBMS_OUTPUT.PUT_LINE('Compound:BEFORE R:' || v_global_var);
16      v_global_var := v_global_var + 1;
17    END BEFORE EACH ROW;
18
19    AFTER EACH ROW IS
20    BEGIN
21      DBMS_OUTPUT.PUT_LINE('Compound:AFTER  R:' || v_global_var);
22      v_global_var := v_global_var + 1;
23    END AFTER EACH ROW;
24
25    AFTER STATEMENT IS
26    BEGIN
27      DBMS_OUTPUT.PUT_LINE('Compound:AFTER  S:' || v_global_var);
28      v_global_var := v_global_var + 1;
29    END AFTER STATEMENT;
30
31  END;
```

### Just like a package

Compound triggers look a lot like PL/SQL packages, don't they? All of the related code and logic is in one place, making it easy to debug and modify. Let's look at the syntax in detail.

The most obvious change is the COMPOUND TRIGGER statement, which advises Oracle that this trigger contains many triggers that it will need to fire and work together.

The next (and most eagerly awaited) change appears somewhat innocently on line 5— a global variable! Finally, global variables can be defined together with the code that manages them. No more special packages to manage them like this.

```
PACKAGE BODY yet_another_global_package AS
  v_global_var NUMBER := 1;
  PROCEDURE reset_global_var IS
  ...
END;
```

The remaining compound trigger syntax is very similar to standalone triggers but a bit more rigid.

*BEFORE STATEMENT*

The code in this section will fire before a DML statement executes, just like a standalone BEFORE statement trigger does.

*BEFORE EACH ROW*

The code in this section gets executed before each and every row is processed by the DML statement.

*AFTER EACH ROW*

The code in this section gets executed after each and every row is processed by the DML statement.

*AFTER STATEMENT*

The code in this section will fire after a DML statement executes, just like a standalone AFTER statement trigger does.

The rules for standalone triggers apply to compound triggers as well—for example, record values (OLD and NEW) cannot be modified in statement-level triggers.

### Not just like a package

So compound triggers look like packages, but do they behave in the same way? The short answer is no—they behave better! Consider this example:

```
SQL> BEGIN
  2     insert into incremented_values values(1,1);
  3     insert into incremented_values values(2,2);
  4  END;
  5  /
Compound:BEFORE  S:1
Compound:BEFORE  R:2
Compound:AFTER   R:3
Compound:AFTER   S:4
Compound:BEFORE  S:1
Compound:BEFORE  R:2
Compound:AFTER   R:3
Compound:AFTER   S:4

PL/SQL procedure successfully completed.
```

Notice that the output of the global variable was set back to 1 when the second statement executed. That's because the scope of the compound trigger is the DML statement that fires it. Once that statement completes, the compound trigger and its in-memory values start anew. That simplifies the logic.

A further benefit of the tight scoping is simplified error handling. I'll demonstrate by putting a primary key on the table just so I can try to violate it later:

```
SQL> ALTER TABLE incremented_values
  2 add constraint a_pk
  3primary key ( value_inserted );
```

Now to insert one record:

```
SQL> INSERT INTO incremented_values values(1,1);
Compound:BEFORE S:1
Compound:BEFORE R:2
Compound:AFTER  R:3
Compound:AFTER  S:4

1 row created.
```

No surprises so far. But the next INSERT should throw an error because it violates the new primary key:

```
SQL> INSERT INTO incremented_values values(1,1);
Compound:BEFORE S:1
Compound:BEFORE R:2
insert into incremented_values values(1,1)
*
ERROR at line 1:
ORA-00001: unique constraint (SCOTT.A_PK) violated
```

The next INSERT throws the primary key error again as expected. But that is not what's exceptional about this situation—what's exceptional is that the global variable was reinitialized back to 1 without any extra code having to be written. The firing DML completed so the compound trigger fell out of scope, and everything started anew for the next statement.

```
SQL> INSERT INTO incremented_values values(1,1);
Compound:BEFORE S:1
Compound:BEFORE R:2
insert into incremented_values values(1,1)
*
ERROR at line 1:
ORA-00001: unique constraint (DRH.A_PK) violated
```

I don't need to include extra exception handling or packages just to reset the values when exceptions occur.

## Compound following

Compound triggers also can be used with the FOLLOWS syntax: :

```
TRIGGER follows_compounder
BEFORE INSERT ON incremented_values
FOR EACH ROW
FOLLOWS compounder
BEGIN
   DBMS_OUTPUT.PUT_LINE('Following Trigger');
END;
```

Here's the output:

```
SQL> INSERT INTO incremented_values
  2  values(8,8);
Compound:BEFORE S:1
Compound:BEFORE R:2
Following Trigger
Compound:AFTER  R:3
Compound:AFTER  S:4

1 row created.
```

The specific triggers within the compound trigger cannot be defined to fire after any standalone or compound triggers.

> If a standalone trigger is defined to follow a compound trigger that does not contain a trigger to fire on the same statement or row, then the FOLLOWS clause is simply ignored.

# DDL Triggers

Oracle allows you to define triggers that will fire when DDL statements are executed. Simply put, DDL is any SQL statement used to create or modify a database object such as a table or an index. Here are some examples of DDL statements:

- CREATE TABLE
- ALTER INDEX
- DROP TRIGGER

Each of these statements results in the creation, alteration, or removal of a database object.

The syntax for creating these triggers is remarkably similar to that of DML triggers, except that the firing events differ, and they are not applied to individual tables.

> The INSTEAD OF CREATE TABLE trigger, described at the end of this section, allows the default behavior of a CREATE TABLE event to be manipulated and is a somewhat idiosyncratic DDL trigger. Not all of the aspects of syntax and usage described in the following subsections apply to this trigger type.

## Creating a DDL Trigger

To create (or replace) a DDL trigger, use the syntax shown here:

```
1    CREATE [OR REPLACE] TRIGGER trigger name
2    {BEFORE | AFTER } { DDL event} ON {DATABASE | SCHEMA}
3    [WHEN (...)]
4    DECLARE
```

```
5   Variable declarations
6   BEGIN
7   ...some code...
8   END;
```

The following table summarizes what is happening in this code:

| Line(s) | Description |
|---------|-------------|
| 1 | Specifies that a trigger is to be created with the name supplied. Specifying OR REPLACE is optional. If the trigger exists, and REPLACE is not specified, then good old Oracle error ORA-4081 will appear stating just that. |
| 2 | This line has a lot to say. It defines whether the trigger will fire before, after, or instead of the particular DDL event as well as whether it will fire for all operations within the database or just within the current schema. Note that the INSTEAD OF option is available only in Oracle9i Release 1 and higher. |
| 3 | An optional WHEN clause that allows you to specify logic to avoid unnecessary execution of the trigger. |
| 4–7 | These lines simply demonstrate the PL/SQL contents of the trigger. |

Here's an example of a somewhat uninformed town crier trigger that announces the creation of all objects:

```
/* File on web: uninformed_town_crier.sql */
SQL> CREATE OR REPLACE TRIGGER town_crier
  2    AFTER CREATE ON SCHEMA
  3    BEGIN
  4      DBMS_OUTPUT.PUT_LINE('I believe you have created something!');
  5    END;
  6  /
Trigger created.

SQL> SET SERVEROUTPUT ON
SQL> CREATE TABLE a_table
  2    (col1 NUMBER);
Table created.

SQL> CREATE INDEX an_index ON a_table(col1);
Index created.

SQL>
CREATE FUNCTION a_function RETURN BOOLEAN AS
  2    BEGIN
  3      RETURN(TRUE);
  4    END;
  5  /
Function created.

SQL> /*-- flush the DBMS_OUTPUT buffer */
SQL> BEGIN NULL; END;
  2  /
I believe you have created something!
I believe you have created something!
I believe you have created something!

PL/SQL procedure successfully completed.
```

Text displayed using the DBMS_OUTPUT built-in package within DDL triggers will not display until you successfully execute a PL/SQL block, even if that block does nothing.

Over time, this town crier would be ignored due to a lack of information, always proudly announcing that something had been created but never providing any details. Thankfully, there is a lot more information available to DDL triggers, allowing for a much more nuanced treatment, as shown in this version:

```
/* File on web: informed_town_crier.sql */
SQL> CREATE OR REPLACE TRIGGER town_crier
  2  AFTER CREATE ON SCHEMA
  3  BEGIN
  4     -- use event attributes to provide more info
  5     DBMS_OUTPUT.PUT_LINE('I believe you have created a ' ||
  6                          ORA_DICT_OBJ_TYPE || ' called ' ||
  7                          ORA_DICT_OBJ_NAME);
  8  END;
  9  /
Trigger created.

SQL> SET SERVEROUTPUT ON
SQL> CREATE TABLE a_table
  2  col1 NUMBER);
Table created.

SQL> CREATE INDEX an_index ON a_table(col1);
Index created.

SQL> CREATE FUNCTION a_function RETURN BOOLEAN AS
  2  BEGIN
  3     RETURN(TRUE);
  4  END;
  5  /
Function created.

SQL> /*-- flush the DBMS_OUTPUT buffer */

SQL> BEGIN NULL; END;
  2  /
I believe you have created a TABLE called A_TABLE
I believe you have created a INDEX called AN_INDEX
I believe you have created a FUNCTION called A_FUNCTION

PL/SQL procedure successfully completed.
```

Much more attention will be paid now that the town crier is more forthcoming. The above examples touch upon two important aspects of DDL triggers: the specific events to which they can be applied and the event attributes available within the triggers.

## Available Events

Table 19-1 lists the DDL events for which triggers can be coded. Each event can have a BEFORE and an AFTER trigger.

*Table 19-1. Available DDL events*

| DDL event | Fires when... |
|---|---|
| ALTER | Any database object is altered using the SQL ALTER command |
| ANALYZE | Any database object is analyzed using the SQL ANALYZE command |
| ASSOCIATE STATISTICS | Statistics are associated with a database object |
| AUDIT | Auditing is turned on using the SQL AUDIT command |
| COMMENT | Comments are applied to a database object |
| CREATE | Any database object is created using the SQL CREATE command |
| DDL | Any of the events listed here occur |
| DISASSOCIATE STATISTICS | Statistics are disassociated from a database object |
| DROP | Any database object is dropped using the SQL DROP command |
| GRANT | Privileges are granted using the SQL GRANT command |
| NOAUDIT | Auditing is turned off using the SQL NOAUDIT command |
| RENAME | A database object is renamed using the SQL RENAME command |
| REVOKE | Privileges are revoked using the SQL REVOKE command |
| TRUNCATE | A table is truncated using the SQL TRUNCATE command |

As with DML triggers, these DDL triggers fire when the event to which they are attached occurs within the specified database or schema. There is no limit to the number of trigger types that can exist in the database or schema.

## Available Attributes

Oracle provides a set of functions (defined in the DBMS_STANDARD package) that provide information about what fired the DDL trigger and other information about the trigger state (e.g., the name of the table being dropped). Table 19-2 displays these trigger attribute functions. The following sections offer some examples of usage.

*Table 19-2. DDL trigger event and attribute functions*

| Name | Returns... |
|---|---|
| ORA_CLIENT_IP_ADDRESS | IP address of the client. |
| ORA_DATABASE_NAME | Name of the database. |
| ORA_DES_ENCRYPTED_ PASSWORD | DES-encrypted password of the current user. |
| ORA_DICT_OBJ_NAME | Name of the database object affected by the firing DDL. |

| Name | Returns... |
| --- | --- |
| ORA_DICT_OBJ_NAME_LIST | Count of objects affected. It also returns a complete list of objects affected in the NAME_LIST parameter, which is a collection of type DBMS_STANDARD.ORA_NAME_LIST_T. |
| ORA_DICT_OBJ_OWNER | Owner of the database object affected by the firing DDL. |
| ORA_DICT_OBJ_OWNER_LIST | Count of objects affected. It also returns a complete list of object owners affected in the NAME_LIST parameter, which is a collection of type DBMS_STANDARD.ORA_NAME_LIST_T. |
| ORA_DICT_OBJ_TYPE | Type of database object affected by the firing DDL (e.g., TABLE or INDEX). |
| ORA_GRANTEE | Count of grantees. The USER_LIST argument contains the full list of grantees, which is a collection of type DBMS_STANDARD.ORA_NAME_LIST_T. |
| ORA_INSTANCE_NUM | Number of the database instance. |
| ORA_IS_ALTER_COLUMN | TRUE if the specified COLUMN_NAME argument is being altered, or FALSE if not. |
| ORA_IS_CREATING_NESTED_TABLE | TRUE if a nested table is being created, or FALSE if not. |
| ORA_IS_DROP_COLUMN | TRUE if the specified COLUMN_NAME argument is indeed being dropped, or FALSE if not. |
| ORA_LOGIN_USER | Name of the Oracle user for which the trigger fired. |
| ORA_PARTITION_POS | Position in the SQL command where a partitioning clause could be correctly added. |
| ORA_PRIVILEGE_LIST | Number of privileges being granted or revoked. The PRIVILEGE_LIST argument contains the full list of privileges affected, which is a collection of type DBMS_STANDARD.ORA_NAME_LIST_T. |
| ORA_REVOKEE | Count of revokees. The USER_LIST argument contains the full list of revokees, which is a collection of type DBMS_STANDARD.ORA_NAME_LIST_T. |
| ORA_SQL_TXT | Number of lines in the SQL statement firing the trigger. The SQL_TXT argument returns each line of the statement, which is an argument of type DBMS_STANDARD.ORA_NAME_LIST_T. |
| ORA_SYSEVENT | Type of event that caused the DDL trigger to fire (e.g., CREATE, DROP, or ALTER). |
| ORA_WITH_GRANT_OPTION | TRUE if privileges were granted with the GRANT option, or FALSE if not. |

Note the following about the event and attribute functions:

- The datatype ORA_NAME_LIST_T is defined in the DBMS_STANDARD package as:

```
TYPE ora_name_list_t IS TABLE OF VARCHAR2(64);
```

In other words, this is a nested table of strings, each of which can contain up to 64 characters.

- The DDL trigger event and attribute functions are also defined in the DBMS_STANDARD package. Oracle creates a standalone function (which adds the "ORA_" prefix to the function name) for each of the packaged functions by executing the *$ORACLE_HOME/rdbms/dbmstrig.sql* script during database creation. In some releases of the Oracle database, there are errors in this script that cause the standalone functions to not be visible or executable. If you feel that these elements have not been properly defined, you should ask your DBA to check the script for problems and make the necessary corrections.

- The USER_SOURCE data dictionary view does not get updated until after both BEFORE and AFTER DDL triggers are fired. In other words, you cannot use these functions to provide a "before and after" version control system built entirely within the database and based on database triggers.

## Working with Events and Attributes

The best way to demonstrate the possibilities offered by DDL trigger events and attributes is with a series of examples.

Here is a trigger that prevents any and all database objects from being created:

```
TRIGGER no_create
    AFTER CREATE ON SCHEMA
BEGIN
   RAISE_APPLICATION_ERROR (
       -20000,
       'ERROR : Objects cannot be created in the production database.'
   );
END;
```

After installing this trigger, attempts at creating anything meet with failure:

```
SQL> CREATE TABLE demo (col1 NUMBER);

*
ERROR at line 1:
ORA-20000: Objects cannot be created in the production database.
```

That is a rather terse and uninformative error message. There was a failure, but what failed? Wouldn't it be nice to have a little more information in the error message, such as the object I was attempting to create?

```
/* File on web: no_create.sql */
TRIGGER no_create
AFTER CREATE ON SCHEMA
BEGIN
  RAISE_APPLICATION_ERROR (-20000,
       'Cannot create the ' || ORA_DICT_OBJ_TYPE ||
       ' named '             || ORA_DICT_OBJ_NAME ||
       ' as requested by '   || ORA_DICT_OBJ_OWNER ||
       ' in production.');
END;
```

With this trigger installed, an attempt to create my table now offers much more diagnostic information:

```
SQL> CREATE TABLE demo (col1 NUMBER);
*
ERROR at line 1:
ORA-20000: Cannot create the TABLE named DEMO as requested by SCOTT in production
```

I could even place this logic within a BEFORE DDL trigger and take advantage of the ORA_SYSEVENT attribute to respond to specific events:

```
TRIGGER no_create
BEFORE DDL ON SCHEMA
BEGIN
   IF ORA_SYSEVENT = 'CREATE'
   THEN
      RAISE_APPLICATION_ERROR (-20000,
         'Cannot create the ' || ORA_DICT_OBJ_TYPE ||
         ' named '            || ORA_DICT_OBJ_NAME ||
         ' as requested by '  || ORA_DICT_OBJ_OWNER);
   ELSIF ORA_SYSEVENT = 'DROP'
   THEN
      -- Logic for DROP operations
      ...
   END IF;
END;
```

### What column did I touch?

I can use the ORA_IS_ALTER_COLUMN function to decipher which column was altered by an ALTER TABLE statement. Here is one example:

```
/* File on web: preserve_app_cols.sql  */
TRIGGER preserve_app_cols
   AFTER ALTER ON SCHEMA
DECLARE
   -- Cursor to get columns in a table
   CURSOR curs_get_columns (cp_owner VARCHAR2, cp_table VARCHAR2)
   IS
      SELECT column_name
        FROM all_tab_columns
       WHERE owner = cp_owner AND table_name = cp_table;
BEGIN
   -- if it was a table that was altered...
   IF ora_dict_obj_type = 'TABLE'
   THEN
      -- for every column in the table...
      FOR v_column_rec IN curs_get_columns (
                             ora_dict_obj_owner,
                             ora_dict_obj_name
                          )
      LOOP
         -- Is the current column one that was altered?
         IF ORA_IS_ALTER_COLUMN (v_column_rec.column_name)
         THEN
            -- Reject change to "core application" column
            IF mycheck.is_application_column (
                  ora_dict_obj_owner,
                  ora_dict_obj_name,
                  v_column_rec.column_name
               )
            THEN
               CENTRAL_ERROR_HANDLER (
```

```
                   'FAIL',
                   'Cannot alter core application attributes'
               );
          END IF; -- table/column is core
       END IF; -- current column was altered
    END LOOP; -- every column in the table
  END IF; -- table was altered
END;
```

Attempts to change core application attributes will now be stopped.

Remember that this logic will not work when the trigger is fired for the addition of new columns. That column information is not yet visible in the data dictionary when the DDL trigger fires.

I can check for attempts to drop specific columns as follows:

```
IF ORA_IS_DROP_COLUMN ('COL2')
THEN
  do something!
ELSE
  do something else!
END IF;
```

 The ORA_IS_DROP_COLUMN and ORA_IS_ALTER_COLUMN functions are blissfully unaware of the table to which the column is attached; they work on column name alone.

### Lists returned by attribute functions

Some of the attribute functions return two pieces of data: a list of items and a count of items. For example, the ORA_GRANTEE function returns a list and a count of users that were granted a privilege, and the ORA_PRIVILEGE_LIST function returns a list and a count of privileges granted. These two functions are perfect for use in AFTER GRANT triggers. The *what_privs.sql* file available on the book's web site offers an extended example of how to use both of these functions. Below is just a portion of the total code:

```
/* File on web: what_privs.sql */
TRIGGER what_privs
   AFTER GRANT ON SCHEMA
DECLARE
   v_grant_type      VARCHAR2 (30);
   v_num_grantees    BINARY_INTEGER;
   v_grantee_list    ora_name_list_t;
   v_num_privs       BINARY_INTEGER;
   v_priv_list       ora_name_list_t;
BEGIN
   -- Retrieve information about grant type and then the lists.
   v_grant_type := ORA_DICT_OBJ_TYPE;
   v_num_grantees := ORA_GRANTEE (v_grantee_list);
   v_num_privs := ORA_PRIVILEGE_LIST (v_priv_list);
```

```
          IF v_grant_type = 'ROLE PRIVILEGE'
          THEN
             DBMS_OUTPUT.put_line (
                'The following roles/privileges were granted');

             -- For each element in the list, display the privilege.
             FOR counter IN 1 .. v_num_privs
             LOOP
                DBMS_OUTPUT.put_line ('Privilege ' || v_priv_list (counter));
             END LOOP;
```

This trigger is great for detailing what privileges and objects are affected by grant operations, as shown below. In a more sophisticated implementation, you might consider storing this information in database tables so that you have a detailed history of changes that have occurred.

```
SQL> GRANT DBA TO book WITH ADMIN OPTION;
Grant succeeded.

SQL> EXEC DBMS_OUTPUT.PUT_LINE('Flush buffer');
        The following roles/privileges were granted
                Privilege UNLIMITED TABLESPACE
                Privilege DBA
        Grant Recipient BOOK
Flush buffer

SQL> GRANT SELECT ON x TO system WITH GRANT OPTION;
Grant succeeded.

SQL> EXEC DBMS_OUTPUT.PUT_LINE('Flush buffer');
        The following object privileges were granted
                Privilege SELECT
        On X with grant option
        Grant Recipient SYSTEM
Flush buffer
```

## Dropping the Undroppable

I have shown that one use for DDL triggers is preventing a particular type of DDL on a particular object or type of object. But what if I create a trigger that prevents DROP DDL and then attempt to drop the trigger itself? Will I be left with a trigger that is essentially undroppable? Fortunately, Oracle has thought of this scenario, as you can see here:

```
SQL> CREATE OR REPLACE TRIGGER undroppable
  2  BEFORE DROP ON SCHEMA
  3  BEGIN
  4    RAISE_APPLICATION_ERROR(-20000,'You cannot drop me! I am invincible!');
  5  END;

SQL> DROP TABLE employee;
  *
```

```
ERROR at line 1:
ORA-20000: You cannot drop me! I am invincible!

SQL> DROP TRIGGER undroppable;
Trigger dropped.
```

## The INSTEAD OF CREATE Trigger

Oracle provides the INSTEAD OF CREATE trigger to allow you to automatically partition a table. To do so, the trigger must trap the SQL statement being executed, insert the partition clause into it, and then execute it using the ORA_SQL_TXT function. The following trigger demonstrates these steps.

```
/* File on web: io_create.sql */
TRIGGER io_create
    INSTEAD OF CREATE ON DATABASE
WHEN (ORA_DICT_OBJ_TYPE = 'TABLE')
DECLARE
    v_sql      VARCHAR2 (32767);   -- sql to be built
    v_sql_t    ora_name_list_t;    -- table of sql
BEGIN
    -- get the SQL statement being executed
    FOR counter IN 1 .. ora_sql_txt (v_sql_t)
    LOOP
       v_sql := v_sql || v_sql_t (counter);
    END LOOP;

    -- Determine the partition clause and add it.
    -- We will call the my_partition function
    v_sql :=
          SUBSTR (v_sql, 1, ora_partition_pos)
       || magic_partition_function
       || SUBSTR (v_sql, ora_partition_pos + 1);

    /* Prepend table name with login username.
    |  Replace CRLFs with spaces.
    |  Requires an explicit CREATE ANY TABLE privilege,
    |  unless you switch to AUTHID CURRENT_USER.
    */
    v_sql :=
       REPLACE (UPPER (REPLACE (v_sql, CHR (10), ' '))
             , 'CREATE TABLE '
             , 'CREATE TABLE ' || ora_login_user || '.'
             );

    -- now execute the SQL
    EXECUTE IMMEDIATE v_sql;
END;
```

Now tables will be partitioned automatically, as determined by the logic in the my_partition function.

Oracle offers several partitioning options (e.g., range, hash) and logical partitioning choices (e.g., by primary key, by unique key). You must decide which of these you want to utilize in your partitioning function.

If you do not include the WHEN clause shown above, you will find that attempts to create objects that are *not* tables will fail with this error:

```
ORA-00604: error occurred at recursive SQL level 1
ORA-30511: invalid DDL operation in system triggers
```

Further, if you try to create an INSTEAD OF trigger for any other DDL operation besides CREATE, you will receive this compilation error:

```
ORA-30513: cannot create system triggers of INSTEAD OF type
```

 INSTEAD OF triggers for DML operations (insert, update, and delete) are addressed later in this chapter. These triggers share some syntax with the INSTEAD OF CREATE trigger for tables, but that is the extent of their similarity.

# Database Event Triggers

Database event triggers fire whenever database-wide events occur. There are six database event triggers:

*STARTUP*
Fires when the database is opened.

*SHUTDOWN*
Fires when the database is shut down normally.

*SERVERERROR*
Fires when an Oracle error is raised.

*LOGON*
Fires when an Oracle database session begins.

*LOGOFF*
Fires when an Oracle database session terminates normally.

*DB_ROLE_CHANGE*
Fires when a standby database is changed to be the primary database or vice versa.

As any DBA will immediately see, these triggers offer stunning possibilities for automated administration and very granular control.

## Creating a Database Event Trigger

The syntax used to create these triggers is quite similar to that used for DDL triggers:

```
1    CREATE [OR REPLACE] TRIGGER trigger_name
2    {BEFORE | AFTER} {database_event} ON {DATABASE | SCHEMA}
```

```
3    DECLARE
4      Variable declarations
5    BEGIN
6      ...some code...
7    END;
```

There are restrictions regarding what events can be combined with what BEFORE and AFTER attributes. Some situations just don't make sense:

*No BEFORE STARTUP triggers*

Even if such triggers could be created, when would they fire? Attempts to create triggers of this type will be met by this straightforward error message:

```
ORA-30500: database open triggers and server error triggers cannot have
BEFORE type
```

*No AFTER SHUTDOWN triggers*

Again, when would they fire? Attempts to create such triggers are deflected with this message:

```
ORA-30501: instance shutdown triggers cannot have AFTER type
```

*No BEFORE LOGON triggers*

It would require some amazingly perceptive code to implement these triggers: "Wait, I think someone is going to log on—do something!" Being strictly reality-based, Oracles stops these triggers with this message:

```
ORA-30508: client logon triggers cannot have BEFORE type
```

*No AFTER LOGOFF triggers*

"No wait, please come back! Don't sign off!" Attempts to create such triggers are stopped with this message:

```
ORA-30509: client logoff triggers cannot have AFTER type
```

*No BEFORE SERVERERROR*

These triggers would be every programmer's dream! Think of the possibilities....

```
CREATE OR REPLACE TRIGGER BEFORE_SERVERERROR
BEFORE SERVERERROR ON DATABASE
BEGIN
  diagnose_impending_error;
  fix_error_condition;
  continue_as_if_nothing_happened;
END;
```

Unfortunately, our dreams are shattered by this error message:

```
ORA-30500: database open triggers and server error triggers cannot have
BEFORE type
```

## The STARTUP Trigger

Startup triggers execute during database startup processing. This is a perfect place to perform housekeeping steps, such as pinning objects in the shared pool so that they do not "age out" with the least-recently-used algorithm.

 In order to create startup event triggers, users must have been granted the ADMINISTER DATABASE TRIGGER privilege.

Here is an example of creating a STARTUP event trigger:

```
CREATE OR REPLACE TRIGGER startup_pinner
AFTER STARTUP ON DATABASE
BEGIN
  pin_plsql_packages;
  pin_application_packages;
END;
```

## The SHUTDOWN Trigger

BEFORE SHUTDOWN triggers execute before database shutdown processing is performed. This is a great place to gather system statistics. Here is an example of creating a SHUTDOWN event trigger:

```
CREATE OR REPLACE TRIGGER before_shutdown
BEFORE SHUTDOWN ON DATABASE
BEGIN
  gather_system_stats;
END;
```

 SHUTDOWN triggers execute only when the database is shut down using NORMAL or IMMEDIATE mode. They do not execute when the database is shut down using ABORT mode or when the database crashes.

## The LOGON Trigger

AFTER LOGON triggers fire when an Oracle database session is begun. They are the perfect place to establish session context and perform other session setup tasks. Here is an example of creating a LOGON event trigger:

```
TRIGGER after_logon
AFTER LOGON ON SCHEMA
DECLARE
  v_sql VARCHAR2(100) := 'ALTER SESSION ENABLE RESUMABLE ' ||
                          'TIMEOUT 10 NAME ' || '''' ||
                          'OLAP Session'     || '''';
```

```
BEGIN
  EXECUTE IMMEDIATE v_sql;
  DBMS_SESSION.SET_CONTEXT('OLAP Namespace',
                           'Customer ID',
                           load_user_customer_id);
END;
```

## The LOGOFF Trigger

BEFORE LOGOFF triggers execute when sessions disconnect normally from the database. This is a good place to gather statistics regarding session activity. Here is an example of creating a LOGOFF event trigger:

```
TRIGGER before_logoff
BEFORE LOGOFF ON DATABASE
BEGIN
  gather_session_stats;
END;
```

## The SERVERERROR Trigger

AFTER SERVERERROR triggers fire after an Oracle error is raised, unless the error is one of the following:

*ORA-00600*
> Oracle internal error

*ORA-01034*
> Oracle not available

*ORA-01403*
> No data found

*ORA-01422*
> Exact fetch returns more than requested number of rows

*ORA-01423*
> Error encountered while checking for extra rows in an exact fetch

*ORA-04030*
> Out-of-process memory when trying to allocate $N$ bytes

In addition, the AFTER SERVERERROR trigger will *not* fire when an exception is raised *inside* this trigger (to avoid an infinite recursive execution of the trigger).

AFTER SERVERERROR triggers do not provide facilities to fix the error, only to log information about the error. It is therefore possible to build some powerful logging mechanisms around these triggers.

Oracle also provides built-in functions (again, defined in DBMS_STANDARD) that retrieve information about the error stack generated when an exception is raised:

*ORA_SERVER_ERROR*

Returns the Oracle error number at the specified position in the error stack. It returns 0 if no error is found at that position.

*ORA_IS_SERVERERROR*

Returns TRUE if the specified error number appears in the current exception stack.

*ORA_SERVER_ERROR_DEPTH*

Returns the number of errors on the stack.

*ORA_SERVER_ERROR_MSG*

Returns the full text of the error message at the specified position. It returns NULL if no error is found at the position.

*ORA_SERVER_ERROR_NUM_PARAMS*

Returns the number of parameters associated with the error message at the given position. It returns 0 if no error is found at the position.

*ORA_SERVER_ERROR_PARAM*

Returns the value for the specified parameter position in the specified error. It returns NULL if none found.

### SERVERERROR examples

Let's look at some examples of using the SERVERERROR functions. I'll start with a very simple example of a SERVERERROR trigger that echoes the fact that an error occurred.

```
TRIGGER error_echo
AFTER SERVERERROR
ON SCHEMA
BEGIN
  DBMS_OUTPUT.PUT_LINE ('You experienced an error');
END;
```

Whenever an Oracle error occurs (assuming that SERVEROUTPUT is ON), the coded message above will display:

```
SQL> SET SERVEROUTPUT ON
SQL> EXEC DBMS_OUTPUT.PUT_LINE(TO_NUMBER('A'));
You experienced an error
BEGIN DBMS_OUTPUT.PUT_LINE(TO_NUMBER('A')); END;

*
ERROR at line 1:
ORA-06502: PL/SQL: numeric or value error: character to number conversion error
ORA-06512: at line 1
```

Note that the Oracle error message was delivered after the trigger message. This allows the error to be accessed and logged prior to the actual failure, as shown in the next example.

SERVERERROR triggers are automatically isolated in their own autonomous transaction (autonomous transactions were covered in Chapter 14). This means that you can, for example, write error information out to a log table and save those changes with a COMMIT, while not affecting the session transaction in which the error occurred.

The error_logger trigger guarantees that information about all but a handful of errors listed earlier will be automatically logged regardless of the application, user, or program in which the error was raised:

```
/* File on web: error_log.sql */
TRIGGER error_logger
AFTER SERVERERROR
ON SCHEMA
DECLARE

   v_errnum    NUMBER;          -- the Oracle error #
   v_now       DATE := SYSDATE; -- current time

BEGIN

   -- for every error in the error stack...
   FOR e_counter IN 1..ORA_SERVER_ERROR_DEPTH LOOP

      -- write the error out to the log table; no
      -- commit is required because we are in an
      -- autonomous transaction
      INSERT INTO error_log(error_id,
                            username,
                            error_number,
                            sequence,
                            timestamp)
      VALUES(error_seq.nextval,
             USER,
             ORA_SERVER_ERROR(e_counter),
             e_counter,
             v_now);

   END LOOP;  -- every error on the stack

END;
```

Remember that all these new rows in the error_log have been committed by the time the END statement is reached, because the trigger is executed within an autonomous transaction. The following lines demonstrate this trigger in action:

```
SQL> EXEC DBMS_OUTPUT.PUT_LINE(TO_NUMBER('A'));
*
ERROR at line 1:
ORA-06502: PL/SQL: numeric or value error: character to number conversion error

SQL> SELECT * FROM error_log;
```

| USERNAME | ERROR_NUMBER | SEQUENCE | TIMESTAMP |
| --- | --- | --- | --- |
| BOOK | 6502 | 1 | 04-JAN-02 |
| BOOK | 6512 | 2 | 04-JAN-02 |

Why do two errors appear in the table when only one error was raised? The actual error stack generated by the database contains both ORA-06502 and ORA-06512, so they are both logged and denoted by their sequence of occurrence.

If you want to determine quickly if a certain error number is located in the stack without parsing it manually, use the companion function ORA_IS_SERVERERROR. This function is very useful for monitoring specific errors that may require extra handling, such as user-defined exceptions. This is the kind of code you might write:

```
-- Special handling of user defined errors
-- 20000 through 20010 raised by calls to
-- RAISE_APPLICATION_ERROR

FOR errnum IN 20000 .. 20010
LOOP
  IF ORA_IS_SERVERERROR (errnum)
  THEN
    log_user_defined_error (errnum);
  END IF;
END LOOP;
```

All Oracle error numbers are negative, except for 1 (user-defined exception) and 100 (synonymous with–1403, NO_DATA_FOUND). When you specify an error number in the call to ORA_IS_SERVERERROR, however, you must supply a positive number, as shown in the above example.

### Central error handler

While it is possible to implement separate SERVERERROR triggers in every schema in a database, I recommend creating a single central trigger with an accompanying PL/SQL package to provide the following features:

*Centralized error logging*
There is only one trigger and package to maintain and keep in Oracle's memory.

*Session-long searchable error log*
The error log can be accumulated over the course of a session rather than error by error. It can be searched to return details like the number of occurrences, the timestamp of the first and last occurrence, etc. The log can also be purged on demand.

*Option to save error log*
The error log can be saved to a permanent table in the database if desired.

*Viewable current log*
The current log of errors is viewable by specific error number and/or date range.

You can find the implementation of one such centralized error-handling package in the *error_log.sql* file on the book's web site. Once this package is in place, I can create the SERVERERROR trigger as follows:

```
CREATE OR REPLACE TRIGGER error_log
AFTER SERVERERROR
ON DATABASE
BEGIN
  central_error_log.log_error;
END;
```

Here are some example usages. First, I will generate an error:

```
SQL> EXEC DBMS_OUTPUT.PUT_LINE(TO_NUMBER('A'));
*
ERROR at line 1:
ORA-06502: PL/SQL: numeric or value error: character to number conversion error
```

Now I can search for a specific error number and retrieve that information in a record:

```
DECLARE
  v_find_record central_error_log.v_find_record;
BEGIN
  central_error_log.find_error(6502,v_find_record);
  DBMS_OUTPUT.PUT_LINE('Total Found   = ' || v_find_record.total_found);
  DBMS_OUTPUT.PUT_LINE('Min Timestamp = ' || v_find_record.min_timestamp);
  DBMS_OUTPUT.PUT_LINE('Max Timestamp = ' || v_find_record.max_timestamp);
END;
```

The output is:

```
Total Found   = 1
Min Timestamp = 04-JAN-02
Max Timestamp = 04-JAN-02
```

# INSTEAD OF Triggers

INSTEAD OF triggers control insert, update, merge, and delete operations on *views*, not tables. They can be used to make nonupdateable views updateable and to override the default behavior of views that are updateable.

## Creating an INSTEAD OF Trigger

To create (or replace) an INSTEAD OF trigger, use the syntax shown here:

```
1    CREATE [OR REPLACE] TRIGGER trigger_name
2    INSTEAD OF operation
3    ON view_name
4    FOR EACH ROW
5    BEGIN
6       ...code goes here...
7    END;
```

The table contains an explanation of this code:

| Line(s) | Description |
|---------|-------------|
| 1 | States that a trigger is to be created with the unique name supplied. Specifying OR REPLACE is optional. If the trigger exists, and REPLACE is not specified, then my attempt to create the trigger anew will result in an ORA-4081 error. |
| 2 | This is where we see differences between INSTEAD OF triggers and other types of triggers. Because INSTEAD OF triggers aren't really triggered by an event, I don't need to specify AFTER or BEFORE or provide an event name. What I do specify is the operation that the trigger is to fire in place of (or instead of). Stating INSTEAD OF followed by one of INSERT, UPDATE, MERGE, or DELETE accomplishes this. |
| 3 | This line is somewhat like the corresponding line for DDL and database event triggers in that the keyword ON is specified. The similarities end there: instead of specifying DATABASE or SCHEMA, I provide the name of the view to which the trigger is to apply. |
| 4–7 | Contains standard PL/SQL code. |

INSTEAD OF triggers are best explained with an example. Let's use one of my favorite topics: pizza delivery! Before I can start pounding the dough, I have to put a system in place to monitor my deliveries. I will need three tables: one to track actual deliveries, one to track delivery areas, and one to track my massive fleet of drivers (remember the first rule of business—always think big!).

```
/* File on web: pizza_tables.sql */
CREATE TABLE delivery
(delivery_id NUMBER,
 delivery_start DATE,
 delivery_end DATE,
 area_id NUMBER,
 driver_id NUMBER);

CREATE TABLE area
    (area_id NUMBER, area_desc   VARCHAR2(30));

CREATE TABLE driver
    (driver_id NUMBER, driver_name   VARCHAR2(30));
```

For the sake of brevity I will not create any primary or foreign keys.

I will also need three sequences to provide unique identifiers for our tables.

```
CREATE SEQUENCE delivery_id_seq;
CREATE SEQUENCE area_id_seq;
CREATE SEQUENCE driver_id_seq;
```

To avoid having to explain relational database design and normalization to my employees, I will simplify deliveries into a single view displaying delivery, area, and driver information:

```
VIEW delivery_info AS
SELECT d.delivery_id,
       d.delivery_start,
       d.delivery_end,
       a.area_desc,
       dr.driver_name
  FROM delivery        d,
```

```
      area       a,
      driver     dr
  WHERE a.area_id = d.area_id
    AND dr.driver_id = d.driver_id
```

Because my system relies heavily on this view for query functionality, why not make it available for insert, update, and delete as well? I cannot directly issue DML statements against the view; it is a join of multiple tables. How would the database know what to do with an INSERT? In fact, I need to tell the database very explicitly what to do when an insert, update, or delete operation occurs against the delivery_info view; in other words, I need to tell it what to do *instead of* trying to insert, update, or delete. Thus, I will use INSTEAD OF triggers. Let's start with the INSERT trigger.

## The INSTEAD OF INSERT Trigger

My INSERT trigger will perform four basic operations:

- Ensure that the delivery_end value is NULL. All delivery completions must be done via an update.
- Try to find the driver ID based on the name provided. If the name cannot be found, then assign a new ID and create a driver entry using the name and the new ID.
- Try to find the area ID based on the name provided. If the name cannot be found, then assign a new ID and create an area entry using the name and the new ID.
- Create an entry in the delivery table.

Bear in mind that this example is intended to demonstrate triggers—not how to effectively build a business system! After a while I will probably wind up with a multitude of duplicate driver and area entries. However, using this view speeds things up by not requiring drivers and areas to be predefined, and in the fast-paced world of pizza delivery, time is money!

```
/* File on web: pizza_triggers.sql */
TRIGGER delivery_info_insert
   INSTEAD OF INSERT
   ON delivery_info
DECLARE
   -- cursor to get the driver ID by name
   CURSOR curs_get_driver_id (cp_driver_name VARCHAR2)
   IS
      SELECT driver_id
        FROM driver
       WHERE driver_name = cp_driver_name;

   v_driver_id   NUMBER;

   -- cursor to get the area ID by name
   CURSOR curs_get_area_id (cp_area_desc VARCHAR2)
   IS
      SELECT area_id
        FROM area
```

```
               WHERE area_desc = cp_area_desc;

   v_area_id       NUMBER;
BEGIN
   /* Make sure the delivery_end value is NULL
    */
   IF :NEW.delivery_end IS NOT NULL
   THEN
      raise_application_error
               (-20000
               , 'Delivery end date value must be NULL when delivery created'
               );
   END IF;

/*
|| Try to get the driver ID using the name. If not found
|| then create a brand new driver ID from the sequence
*/
OPEN curs_get_driver_id (UPPER (:NEW.driver_name));

   FETCH curs_get_driver_id
    INTO v_driver_id;

   IF curs_get_driver_id%NOTFOUND
   THEN
      SELECT driver_id_seq.NEXTVAL
        INTO v_driver_id
        FROM DUAL;

      INSERT INTO driver
                  (driver_id, driver_name
                  )
           VALUES (v_driver_id, UPPER (:NEW.driver_name)
                  );
   END IF;

   CLOSE curs_get_driver_id;

/*
|| Try to get the area ID using the name. If not found
|| then create a brand new area ID from the sequence
*/
OPEN curs_get_area_id (UPPER (:NEW.area_desc));

   FETCH curs_get_area_id
    INTO v_area_id;

   IF curs_get_area_id%NOTFOUND
   THEN
      SELECT area_id_seq.NEXTVAL
        INTO v_area_id
        FROM DUAL;

      INSERT INTO area
                  (area_id, area_desc
```

```
                    )
          VALUES (v_area_id, UPPER (:NEW.area_desc)
                    );
   END IF;

   CLOSE curs_get_area_id;

   /*
     || Create the delivery entry
   */
   INSERT INTO delivery
               (delivery_id, delivery_start
               , delivery_end, area_id, driver_id
               )
         VALUES (delivery_id_seq.NEXTVAL, NVL (:NEW.delivery_start, SYSDATE)
               , NULL, v_area_id, v_driver_id
                 );
END;
```

## The INSTEAD OF UPDATE Trigger

Now let's move on to the UPDATE trigger. For the sake of simplicity, I will allow updating only of the delivery_end field, and only if it is NULL to start with. I can't have drivers resetting delivery times.

```
/* File on web: pizza_triggers.sql */
TRIGGER delivery_info_update
   INSTEAD OF UPDATE
   ON delivery_info
DECLARE
   -- cursor to get the delivery entry
   CURSOR curs_get_delivery (cp_delivery_id NUMBER)
   IS
      SELECT delivery_end
        FROM delivery
       WHERE delivery_id = cp_delivery_id
       FOR UPDATE OF delivery_end;

   v_delivery_end    DATE;
BEGIN
   OPEN curs_get_delivery (:NEW.delivery_id);
   FETCH curs_get_delivery INTO v_delivery_end;

   IF v_delivery_end IS NOT NULL
   THEN
      RAISE_APPLICATION_ERROR (
         -20000, 'The delivery end date has already been set');
   ELSE
      UPDATE delivery
         SET delivery_end = :NEW.delivery_end
       WHERE CURRENT OF curs_get_delivery;
   END IF;
```

```
        CLOSE curs_get_delivery;
END;
```

## The INSTEAD OF DELETE Trigger

The DELETE trigger is the simplest of all. It merely ensures that I am not deleting a completed entry and then removes the delivery record. The driver and area records remain intact.

```
/* File on web: pizza_triggers.sql */
TRIGGER delivery_info_delete
   INSTEAD OF DELETE
   ON delivery_info
BEGIN
  IF :OLD.delivery_end IS NOT NULL
  THEN
     RAISE_APPLICATION_ERROR (
        -20000,'Completed deliveries cannot be deleted');
  END IF;

  DELETE delivery
   WHERE delivery_id = :OLD.delivery_id;
END;
```

## Populating the Tables

Now, with a single INSERT focused on the delivery information I know (the driver and the area), all of the required tables are populated:

```
SQL> INSERT INTO delivery_info(delivery_id,
  2                            delivery_start,
  3                            delivery_end,
  4                            area_desc,
  5                            driver_name)
  6  VALUES
  7    NULL, NULL, NULL, 'LOCAL COLLEGE', 'BIG TED');

1 row created.

SQL> SELECT * FROM delivery;

DELIVERY_ID DELIVERY_ DELIVERY_    AREA_ID  DRIVER_ID
----------- --------- --------- ---------- ----------
          1 13-JAN-02                    1          1

SQL> SELECT * FROM area;

   AREA_ID AREA_DESC
---------- ------------------------------
         1 LOCAL COLLEGE

SQL> SELECT * FROM driver;
```

```
    DRIVER_ID DRIVER_NAME
    ---------- -----------------------------
            1 BIG TED
```

## INSTEAD OF Triggers on Nested Tables

Oracle has introduced many ways to store complex data structures as columns in tables or views. This is logically effective because the linkage between a table or view and its columns is obvious. Technically, it can require some not-so-obvious trickery to allow even the simplest of operations, like inserting records into these complex structures. One of these complex situations can be resolved with a special type of INSTEAD OF trigger, as shown in this section.

Consider the following view joining the chapters of a book with the lines in the chapter:

```
VIEW book_chapter_view AS
SELECT chapter_number,
       chapter_title,
       CAST(MULTISET(SELECT *
                        FROM book_line
                        WHERE chapter_number = book_chapter.chapter_number)
            AS book_line_t) lines
  FROM book_chapter;
```

I agree that the view is far too obtuse for its purpose (why not just join the tables directly?), but it easily demonstrates the use of INSTEAD OF triggers on nested table columns—or on any object or collection column in a view.

After creating a record in the BOOK_CHAPTER table and querying the view, I'll see the following, which explains that there are no lines in the chapter yet:

```
CHAPTER_NUMBER CHAPTER_TITLE
-------------- -----------------------------
LINES(CHAPTER_NUMBER, LINE_NUMBER, LINE_TEXT)
---------------------------------------------
            18 Triggers
BOOK_LINE_T()
```

So I then try to create the first line to get past my writer's block:

```
SQL> INSERT INTO TABLE(SELECT lines
  2                       FROM book_chapter_view
  3                      WHERE chapter_number = 18)
  4  VALUES(18,1,'Triggers are...');
INSERT INTO TABLE(SELECT lines
*
ERROR at line 1:
ORA-25015: cannot perform DML on this nested table view column
```

Apparently, the database has determined that there is not enough information available to just insert values into the BOOK_LINE table masquerading as the LINES column in the view. Thus, an INSTEAD OF trigger is required to make the intent crystal clear.

```
TRIGGER lines_ins
INSTEAD OF INSERT ON NESTED TABLE lines OF book_chapter_view
BEGIN
  INSERT INTO book_line
              (chapter_number,
               line_number,
               line_text)
  VALUES(:PARENT.chapter_number,
         :NEW.line_number,
         :NEW.line_text);
END;
```

Now I can add the first line:

```
SQL> INSERT INTO TABLE ( SELECT lines
  2                         FROM book_chapter_view
  3                        WHERE chapter_number = 18 )
  4  VALUES(18,1,'Triggers Are...');

1 row created.

SQL> SELECT *
  2    FROM book_chapter_view;

CHAPTER_NUMBER CHAPTER_TITLE
-------------- ------------------------------
LINES(CHAPTER_NUMBER, LINE_NUMBER, LINE_TEXT)
-----------------------------------------------------
            18 Triggers
BOOK_LINE_T(BOOK_LINE_O(18, 1, 'Triggers Are...'))
```

Note that the SQL used to create the trigger is just like what is used for other INSTEAD OF triggers except for two things:

- The ON NESTED TABLE COLUMN OF clause used to denote the involved column.

- The new PARENT pseudo-record containing values from the views parent record.

# AFTER SUSPEND Triggers

Oracle9*i* Database Release 1 introduced a new type of trigger that fires whenever a statement is suspended. This might occur as the result of a space issue such as exceeding an allocated tablespace quota. This functionality can be used to address the problem and allow the stalled operation to continue. AFTER SUSPEND triggers are a boon to busy developers tired of being held up by space errors, and to even busier DBAs who constantly have to resolve these errors.

The syntax used to create an AFTER SUSPEND trigger follows the same format as DDL and database event triggers. It declares the firing event (SUSPEND), the timing (AFTER), and the scope (DATABASE or SCHEMA):

```
1 CREATE [OR REPLACE] TRIGGER trigger_name
2 AFTER SUSPEND
3 ON {DATABASE | SCHEMA}
4 BEGIN
5 ... code...
6 END;
```

Let's take a closer look at AFTER SUSPEND, starting with an example of a scenario that would call for creation of this type of trigger.

For example, consider the situation faced by Batch Only, the star Oracle developer at Totally Controlled Systems. He is responsible for maintaining hundreds of programs that run overnight, performing lengthy transactions to summarize information and move it between disparate applications. At least twice a week, his pager goes off during the wee hours of the morning because one of his programs has encountered this Oracle error:

```
ERROR at line 1:
ORA-01536: space quota exceeded for tablespace 'USERS'
```

Batch then has the unenviable task of phoning Totally's Senior DBA, Don T. Planahead, and begging for a space quota increase. Don's usual question is, "How much do you need?" to which Batch can only feebly reply, "I don't know because the data load fluctuates so much." This leaves them both very frustrated, because Don wants control over the space allocation for planning reasons, and Batch doesn't want his night's sleep interrupted so often.

## Setting Up for the AFTER SUSPEND Trigger

Thankfully, an AFTER SUSPEND trigger can eliminate the dark circles under both Don's and Batch's eyes. Here is how they work through the situation.

Batch discovers a particular point in his code that encounters the error most frequently. It is an otherwise innocuous INSERT statement at the end of a program that takes hours to run:

```
INSERT INTO monthly_summary (
   acct_no, trx_count, total_in, total_out)
VALUES (
   v_acct, v_trx_count, v_total_in, v_total_out);
```

What makes this most maddening is that the values take hours to calculate, only to be immediately lost when the final INSERT statement fails. At the very least, Batch wants the program to suspend itself while he contacts Don to get more space allocated. He discovers that this can be done with a simple ALTER SESSION statement.

```
ALTER SESSION ENABLE RESUMABLE TIMEOUT 3600 NAME 'Monthly Summary';
```

This means that whenever this Oracle database session encounters an out-of-space error, it will go into a suspended (and potentially resumable) state for 3,600 seconds (1 hour). This provides enough time for Totally's monitoring system to page Batch, for

Batch to phone Don, and for Don to allocate more space. It's not a perfect system, but at least the hours spent calculating the data are no longer wasted.

Another problem faced by Batch and Don is that when they try to diagnose the situation in the middle of the night, they are both so tired and grumpy that time is wasted on misunderstandings. Thankfully, the need for explanations can be alleviated by another feature of suspended/resumable statements: the DBA_RESUMABLE view. This shows all sessions that have registered for resumable statements with the ALTER SESSION command shown above.

 The RESUMABLE system privilege must be granted to users before they can enable the resumable option.

Now, whenever Batch's programs go into the suspended state, he only has to phone Don and mumble "Check the resumable view." Don then queries it from his DBA account to see what is going on.

```
SQL> SELECT session_id,
  2         name,
  3         status,
  4         error_number
  5    FROM dba_resumable

SESSION_ID NAME                 STATUS    ERROR_NUMBER
---------- -------------------- --------- ------------
         8 Monthly Summary      SUSPENDED         1536

1 row selected.
```

This shows that session 8 is suspended because of ORA-01536: *space quota exceeded for tablespace* 'tablespace_name'. From past experience, Don knows which schema and tablespace are involved, so he corrects the problem and mumbles into the phone, "It's fixed." The suspended statement in Batch's code immediately resumes, and both Don and Batch can go back to sleep in their own beds.

---

### Invalid DDL Operation in System Triggers

AFTER SUSPEND triggers are not allowed to actually perform certain DDL (ALTER USER and ALTER TABLESPACE) to fix the problems they diagnose. They simply raise the error *ORA-30511: Invalid DDL operation in system triggers*. One way to work around this situation is as follows:

1. Have the AFTER SUSPEND trigger write the SQL statement necessary to fix a problem in a table.

2. Create a PL/SQL package that reads SQL statements from the table and executes them.

---

3. Submit the PL/SQL package to DBMS_JOB every minute or so.

## Looking at the Actual Trigger

After a few weeks, both Don and Batch are tired of their repetitive, albeit abbreviated late-night conversations, so Don sets out to automate things with an AFTER SUSPEND trigger. Here's a snippet of what he cooks up and installs in the DBA account:

```
/* File on web: smart_space_quota.sql */
TRIGGER after_suspend
AFTER SUSPEND
ON DATABASE
DECLARE
...
BEGIN

   -- if this is a space related error...
   IF ORA_SPACE_ERROR_INFO ( error_type => v_error_type,
                             object_type => v_object_type,
                             object_owner => v_object_owner,
                             table_space_name => v_tbspc_name,
                             object_name => v_object_name,
                             sub_object_name => v_subobject_name ) THEN

      -- if the error is a tablespace quota being exceeded...
      IF v_error_type = 'SPACE QUOTA EXCEEDED' AND
         v_object_type = 'TABLE SPACE' THEN
         -- get the username
         OPEN curs_get_username;
         FETCH curs_get_username INTO v_username;
         CLOSE curs_get_username;

         -- get the current quota for the username and tablespace
         OPEN curs_get_ts_quota(v_object_name,v_username);
         FETCH curs_get_ts_quota INTO v_old_quota;
         CLOSE curs_get_ts_quota;

         -- create an ALTER USER statement and send it off to
         -- the fixer job because if we try it here we will raise
         -- ORA-30511: invalid DDL operation in system triggers

         v_new_quota := v_old_quota + 40960;
         v_sql := 'ALTER USER ' || v_username  || ' ' ||
                  'QUOTA '      || v_new_quota || ' ' ||
                  'ON '         || v_object_name;
         fixer.fix_this(v_sql);

      END IF;  -- tablespace quota exceeded

   END IF;  -- space related error

END;
```

This creates a trigger that fires whenever a statement enters a suspended state and attempts to fix the problem. (Note that this particular example handles only tablespace quotas being exceeded.)

Now when Batch's programs encounter the tablespace quota problem, the database-wide AFTER SUSPEND trigger fires and puts a SQL entry in the "stuff to fix" table via the fixer package. In the background, a fixer job is running; it picks the SQL statement out of the table and executes it, thus alleviating the quota problem without requiring anyone to pick up the phone.

 A complete AFTER SUSPEND trigger and fixer package are available in the *fixer.sql* file on the book's web site.

## The ORA_SPACE_ERROR_INFO Function

Information on the cause of the statement suspension may be garnered using the ORA_SPACE_ERROR_INFO function shown in earlier examples. Now let's look at the syntax for specifying this function; the parameters are defined as shown in Table 19-3.

*Table 19-3. ORA_SPACE_ERROR_INFO parameters*

| Parameter | Description |
|---|---|
| error_type | Type of space error; will be one of the following: |
| | • SPACE QUOTA EXCEEDED: if a user has exceeded his quota for a tablespace |
| | • MAX EXTENTS REACHED: if an object attempts to go beyond its maximum extents specification |
| | • NO MORE SPACE: if there is not enough space in a tablespace to store the new information |
| object_type | Type of object encountering the space error |
| object_owner | Owner of the object encountering the space error |
| table_space_name | Tablespace encountering the space error |
| object_name | Name of the object encountering the space error |
| sub_object_name | Name of the subobject encountering the space error |

The function returns a Boolean value of TRUE if the suspension occurs because of one of the errors shown in the table, and FALSE if not.

The ORA_SPACE_ERROR_INFO function does not actually fix whatever space problems occur in your system; its role is simply to provide the information you need to take further action. In the earlier example, you saw how the quota error was addressed. Here are two additional examples of SQL you might supply to fix space problems diagnosed by the ORA_SPACE_ERROR_INFO function:

- Specify the following when your table or index has achieved its maximum extents and no more extents are available:

```
ALTER object_type object_owner.object_name STORAGE (MAXEXTENTS UNLIMITED);
```

- Specify the following when your tablespace is completely out of space:

```
/* Assume Oracle Managed Files (Oracle9i Database and later) being used so
   explicit datafile declaration not required */
ALTER TABLESPACE tablespace_name ADD DATAFILE;
```

## The DBMS_RESUMABLE Package

If the ORA_SPACE_ERROR_INFO function returns FALSE, then the situation causing the suspended statement cannot be fixed. Thus, there is no rational reason for remaining suspended. Unfixable statements can be aborted from within the AFTER_SUSPEND trigger using the ABORT procedure in the DBMS_RESUMABLE package. The following provides an example of issuing this procedure:

```
/* File on web: local_abort.sql */
TRIGGER after_suspend
AFTER SUSPEND
ON SCHEMA
DECLARE

  CURSOR curs_get_sid IS
  SELECT sid
    FROM v$session
   WHERE audsid = SYS_CONTEXT('USERENV','SESSIONID');
  v_sid       NUMBER;
  v_error_type VARCHAR2(30);
  ...

BEGIN

  IF ORA_SPACE_ERROR_INFO(...
    ...try to fix things...
  ELSE  -- cant fix the situation
    OPEN curs_get_sid;
    FETCH curs_get_sid INTO v_sid;
    CLOSE curs_get_sid;
    DBMS_RESUMABLE.ABORT(v_sid);
  END IF;

END;
```

The ABORT procedure takes a single argument, the ID of the session to abort. This allows ABORT to be called from a DATABASE- or SCHEMA-level AFTER SUSPEND trigger. The aborted session receives this error:

```
ORA-01013: user requested cancel of current operation
```

After all, the cancellation was requested by a user, but exactly which user is unclear.

---

In addition to the ABORT procedure, the DBMS_RESUMABLE package contains functions and procedures to get and set timeout values:

GET_SESSION_TIMEOUT
> Returns the timeout value of the suspended session by session ID:

```
FUNCTION DBMS_RESUMABLE.GET_SESSION_TIMEOUT (sessionid IN NUMBER)
      RETURN NUMBER;
```

SET_SESSION_TIMEOUT
> Sets the timeout value of the suspended session by session ID:

```
PROCEDURE DBMS_RESUMABLE.SET_SESSION_TIMEOUT (
    sessionid IN NUMBER, TIMEOUT IN NUMBER);
```

GET_TIMEOUT
> Returns the timeout value of the current session:

```
FUNCTION DBMS_RESUMABLE.GET_TIMEOUT RETURN NUMBER;
```

SET_SESSION_TIMEOUT
> Sets the timeout value of the current session:

```
PROCEDURE DBMS_REUSABLE.SET_TIMEOUT (TIMEOUT IN NUMBER);
```

 New timeout values take effect immediately but do not reset the counter to zero.

## Trapped Multiple Times

AFTER SUSPEND triggers fire whenever a statement is suspended. Therefore, they can fire many times during the same statement. For example, suppose that the following hardcoded trigger is implemented:

```
/* File on web: increment_extents.sql */
TRIGGER after_suspend
AFTER SUSPEND ON SCHEMA
DECLARE
   -- get the new max (current plus one)
   CURSOR curs_get_extents IS
   SELECT max_extents + 1
     FROM user_tables
    WHERE table_name = 'MONTHLY_SUMMARY';
   v_new_max NUMBER;

BEGIN
   - fetch the new maximum extent value
   OPEN curs_get_extents;
   FETCH curs_get_extents INTO v_new_max;
   CLOSE curs_get_extents;
```

```
        -- alter the table to take on the new value for maxextents
        EXECUTE IMMEDIATE 'ALTER TABLE MONTHLY_SUMMARY ' ||
                          'STORAGE ( MAXEXTENTS '         ||
                          v_new_max                       || ')';

        DBMS_OUTPUT.PUT_LINE('Incremented MAXEXTENTS to ' || v_new_max);
    END;
```

If you start with an empty table with MAXEXTENTS (maximum number of extents) specified as 1, inserting four extents' worth of data produces this output:

```
SQL> @test

Incremented MAXEXTENTS to 2
Incremented MAXEXTENTS to 3
Incremented MAXEXTENTS to 4

PL/SQL procedure successfully completed.
```

## To Fix or Not to Fix?

That is the question! The previous examples have shown how "lack of space" errors can be handled on the fly by suspending statements until intervention (human or automated) allows them to continue. Taken to an extreme, this approach allows applications to be installed with minimal tablespace, quota, and extent settings, and then to grow as required. While over-diligent DBAs may see this situation as nirvana, it does have its downsides:

*Intermittent pauses*
> Suspended statement pauses may wreak havoc with high-volume online transaction processing (OLTP) applications that require high throughput levels. This will be even more troublesome if the fix takes a long time.

*Resource contention*
> Suspended statements maintain their table locks, which may cause other statements to wait long periods of time or fail needlessly.

*Management overhead*
> The resources required to continuously add extents or datafiles, or increment quotas may wind up overwhelming those required to actually run the application.

For these reasons I recommend that AFTER SUSPEND triggers be used judiciously. They are perfect for long-running processes that must be restarted after failure, as well as for incremental processes that require DML to undo their changes before they can be restarted. However, they are not well suited to OLTP applications.

# Maintaining Triggers

Oracle offers a number of DDL statements that can help you manage your triggers. You can enable, disable, and drop triggers, view information about triggers, and check the status of triggers, as explained in the following sections.

## Disabling, Enabling, and Dropping Triggers

Disabling a trigger causes it not to fire when its triggering event occurs. Dropping a trigger causes it to be removed from the database altogether. The SQL syntax for disabling triggers is relatively simple compared to that for creating them:

```
ALTER TRIGGER trigger_name DISABLE;
```

For example:

```
ALTER TRIGGER emp_after_insert DISABLE;
```

A disabled trigger can also be reenabled as shown in the following example:

```
ALTER TRIGGER emp_after_insert ENABLE;
```

The ALTER TRIGGER command is concerned only with the trigger name; it does not require identifying the trigger type or anything else. You can also easily create stored procedures to handle these steps for you. The following procedure, for example, uses dynamic SQL to disable or enable all triggers on a table:

```
/* File on web: settrig.sp */
PROCEDURE settrig (
   tab      IN    VARCHAR2
 , sch      IN    VARCHAR DEFAULT NULL
 , action   IN    VARCHAR2
)
IS
   l_action        VARCHAR2 (10) := UPPER (action);
   l_other_action  VARCHAR2 (10) := 'DISABLED';
BEGIN
   IF l_action = 'DISABLE'
   THEN
      l_other_action := 'ENABLED';
   END IF;

   FOR rec IN (SELECT trigger_name FROM user_triggers
                 WHERE table_owner = UPPER (NVL (sch, USER))
                   AND table_name = tab AND status = l_other_action)
   LOOP
      EXECUTE IMMEDIATE
         'ALTER TRIGGER ' || rec.trigger_name || ' ' || l_action;
   END LOOP;
END;
```

The DROP TRIGGER command is just as easy; simply specify the trigger name, as shown in this example:

```
DROP TRIGGER emp_after_insert;
```

## Creating Disabled Triggers

Starting with Oracle Database 11g it is possible to create triggers in a disabled state so they don't fire. This is very helpful in situations where you want to validate a trigger but don't want it to start firing just yet. Here's a very simple example.

```
TRIGGER just_testing
AFTER INSERT ON abc
DISABLE
BEGIN
  NULL;
END;
```

Because the DISABLE keyword is included in the header, this trigger gets validated, compiled, and created, but it will not fire until it is explicitly enabled later on. Note that the DISABLE keyword is not present in what gets saved into the database though.

```
SQL> SELECT trigger_body
  2  FROM user_triggers
  3  WHERE trigger_name = 'JUST_TESTING';

TRIGGER_BODY
-------------------------------------------
BEGIN
  NULL;
END;
```

When you are using a GUI tool, be careful to avoid accidentally enabling triggers when they are recompiled.

## Viewing Triggers

You can find out lots of information about triggers by issuing queries against the following data dictionary views:

*DBA_TRIGGERS*
> All triggers in the database

*ALL_TRIGGERS*
> All triggers accessible to the current user

*USER_TRIGGERS*
> All triggers owned by the current user

Table 19-4 summarizes the most useful (and common) columns in these views.

*Table 19-4. Useful columns in trigger views*

| Name | Description |
|------|-------------|
| TRIGGER_NAME | Name of the trigger |

| Name | Description |
|---|---|
| TRIGGER_TYPE | Type of the trigger; you can specify: |
| | • For DML triggers: BEFORE_STATEMENT, BEFORE EACH ROW, AFTER EACH ROW, or AFTER STATEMENT |
| | • For DDL triggers: BEFORE EVENT or AFTER EVENT |
| | • For INSTEAD OF triggers: INSTEAD OF |
| | • For AFTER_SUSPEND triggers: AFTER EVENT |
| TRIGGERING_EVENT | Event that causes the trigger to fire: |
| | • For DML triggers: UPDATE, INSERT, or DELETE |
| | • For DDL triggers: DDL operation (see full list in the DDL trigger section of this chapter) |
| | • For database event triggers: ERROR, LOGON, LOGOFF, STARTUP, or SHUTDOWN |
| | • For INSTEAD OF triggers: INSERT, UPDATE, or DELETE |
| | • For AFTER SUSPEND triggers: SUSPEND |
| TABLE_OWNER | This column contains different information depending on the type of trigger: |
| | • For DML triggers: name of the owner of the table to which the trigger is attached |
| | • For DDL triggers: if database-wide, then SYS; otherwise, the owner of the trigger |
| | • For database event triggers: if database-wide, then SYS; otherwise, the owner of the trigger |
| | • For INSTEAD OF triggers: owner of the view to which the trigger is attached |
| | • For AFTER SUSPEND triggers: if database-wide, then SYS; otherwise, the owner of the trigger |
| BASE_OBJECT_TYPE | Type of object to which the trigger is attached: |
| | • For DML triggers: TABLE |
| | • For DDL triggers: SCHEMA or DATABASE |
| | • For database event triggers: SCHEMA or DATABASE |
| | • For INSTEAD OF triggers: VIEW |
| | • For AFTER SUSPEND triggers: SCHEMA or DATABASE |
| TABLE_NAME | For DML triggers: name of the table the trigger is attached to; other types of triggers: NULL |
| REFERENCING_NAMES | For DML (row-level) triggers: clause used to define the aliases for the OLD and NEW records |
| | For other types of triggers: text "REFERENCING NEW AS NEW OLD AS OLD" |
| WHEN_CLAUSE | For DML triggers: trigger's conditional firing clause |
| STATUS | Trigger's status (ENABLED or DISABLED) |
| ACTION_TYPE | Indicates whether the trigger executes a call (CALL) or contains PL/SQL (PL/SQL) |
| TRIGGER_BODY | Text of the trigger body (LONG column); this information is also available in the USER_SOURCE table starting with Oracle9i Database |

## Checking the Validity of Triggers

Oddly enough, the trigger views in the data dictionary do not display whether or not a trigger is in a valid state. If a trigger is created with invalid PL/SQL, it is saved in the database but marked as INVALID. You can query the USER_OBJECTS or ALL_OBJECTS views to determine this status, as shown here:

```
SQL> CREATE OR REPLACE TRIGGER invalid_trigger
  2  AFTER DDL ON SCHEMA
  3  BEGIN
  4    NULL
  5  END;
  6  /

Warning: Trigger created with compilation errors.

SQL> SELECT object_name,
  2         object_type,
  3         status
  4    FROM user_objects
  5   WHERE object_name = 'INVALID_TRIGGER';

OBJECT_NAME      OBJECT TYPE STATUS
-------------    ----------- -------
INVALID_TRIGGER  TRIGGER     INVALID
```

# CHAPTER 20

# Managing PL/SQL Code

Writing the code for an application is just one step toward putting that application into production and then maintaining the code base. It is not possible within the scope of this book to fully address the entire life cycle of application design, development, and deployment. I do have room, however, to offer some ideas and advice about the following topics:

*Managing and analyzing code in the database*

> When you compile PL/SQL program units, the source code is loaded into the data dictionary in a variety of forms (the text of the code, dependency relationships, parameter information, etc.). You can then use SQL statements to retrieve information about those program units, making it easier to understand and manage your application code.

*Using compile-time warnings*

> Starting with Oracle Database 10g, Oracle has added significant new and transparent capabilities to the PL/SQL compiler. The compiler will now automatically optimize your code, often resulting in substantial improvements in performance. In addition, the compiler will provide warnings about your code that will help you improve its readability, performance, and/or functionality.

*Manage dependencies and recompile code*

> Oracle automatically manages dependencies between database objects. It is very important to understand how these dependencies work, how to minimize invalidation of program units, and how best to recompile program units.

*Testing PL/SQL programs*

> Testing our programs to verify correctness is central to writing and deploying successful applications. You can strengthen your own homegrown tests with automated testing frameworks, both open source and commercial.

*Tracing PL/SQL code*

> Most of the applications we write are very complex—so complex, in fact, that we can get lost inside our own code. Code instrumentation (which means, mostly,

inserting trace calls in your programs) can provide the additional information needed to make sense of what we write.

*Debugging PL/SQL programs*

Many development tools now offer graphical debuggers based on Oracle's DBMS_DEBUG API. These provide the most powerful way to debug programs, but they are still just a small part of the overall debugging process. In this chapter I also discuss program tracing and explore some of the techniques and (dare I say) philosophical approaches you should utilize to debug effectively.

*Protecting stored code*

Oracle offers a way to "wrap" source code so that confidential and proprietary information can be hidden from prying eyes. This feature is most useful to vendors who sell applications based on PL/SQL stored code.

*Using edition-based redefinition*

New to Oracle Database 11g Release 2, this feature allows database administrators to "hot patch" PL/SQL application code. Prior to this release, if you needed to recompile a production package with "state" (package-level variables), you would risk the dreaded ORA-04068 error unless you scheduled downtime for the application—and that would require you to kick the users off the system. Now, new versions of code and underlying database tables can be compiled into the application while it is being used, reducing the downtime for Oracle applications. This is primarily a DBA feature, but it is covered lightly in this chapter.

# Managing Code in the Database

When you compile a PL/SQL program unit, its source code is stored in the database itself. Information about that program unit is then made available through a set of data dictionary views. This approach to compiling and storing code information offers two tremendous advantages:

*Information about that code is available via the SQL language*

You can write queries and even entire PL/SQL programs that read the contents of these data dictionary views, obtain lots of fascinating and useful information about your code, and even change the state of your application code.

*The database manages dependencies between your stored objects*

In the world of PL/SQL, you don't have to "make" an executable that is then run by users. There is no "build process" for PL/SQL. The database takes care of all such housekeeping details for you, letting you focus more productively on implementing business logic.

The following sections introduce you to some of the most commonly accessed sources of information in the data dictionary.

# Overview of Data Dictionary Views

The Oracle data dictionary is a jungle—lushly full of incredible information, but often with less than clear pathways to your destination. There are hundreds of views built on hundreds of tables, many complex interrelationships, special codes, and, all too often, nonoptimized view definitions. A subset of this multitude is particularly handy to PL/SQL developers; I will take a closer look at the key views in a moment. First, it is important to know that there are three types or levels of data dictionary views:

*USER_\**

Views that show information about the database objects owned by the currently connected schema.

*ALL_\**

Views that show information about all of the database objects to which the currently connected schema has access (either because it owns them or because it has been granted access to them). Generally they have the same columns as the corresponding USER view, with the addition of an OWNER column in the ALL views.

*DBA_\**

Views that show information about all the (non-SYS-owned) objects in the database. Generally they have the same columns as the corresponding ALL view.

I'll work with the USER views in this chapter; you can easily modify any scripts and techniques to work with the ALL views by adding an OWNER column to your logic. The following are some views a PL/SQL developer is most likely to find useful:

*USER_ARGUMENTS*

The arguments (parameters) in all the procedures and functions in your schema.

*USER_DEPENDENCIES*

The dependencies to and from objects you own. This view is mostly used by Oracle to mark objects INVALID when necessary, and also by IDEs to display the dependency information in their object browsers.

*USER_ERRORS*

The current set of compilation errors for all stored objects (including triggers) you own. This view is accessed by the SHOW ERRORS SQL*Plus command, described in Chapter 2. You can, however, write your own queries against it as well.

*USER_IDENTIFIERS (PL/Scope)*

Introduced in Oracle Database 11g and populated by the PL/Scope compiler utility. Once populated, this view provides you with information about all the identifiers (program names, variables, etc.) in your code base. This is a very powerful code analysis tool.

*USER_OBJECTS*

The objects you own. You can, for instance, use this view to see if an object is marked INVALID, find all the packages that have "EMP" in their names, etc.

*USER_OBJECT_SIZE*

The size of the objects you own. Actually, this view will show you the source, parsed, and compile sizes for your code. Although it is used mainly by the compiler and runtime engine, you can use it to identify the large programs in your environment, good candidates for pinning into the SGA.

*USER_PLSQL_OBJECT_SETTINGS*

Introduced in Oracle Database 10*g*. Information about the characteristics of a PL/SQL object that can be modified through the ALTER and SET DDL commands, such as the optimization level, debug settings, and more.

*USER_PROCEDURES*

Information about stored programs, such as the AUTHID setting, whether the program was defined as DETERMINISTIC, and so on.

*USER_SOURCE*

The text source code for all objects you own (in Oracle9*i* Database and above, including database triggers and Java source). This is a very handy view, because you can run all sorts of analysis of the source code against it using SQL and, in particular, Oracle Text.

*USER_STORED_SETTINGS*

PL/SQL compiler flags. Use this view to discover which programs have been compiled using native compilation.

*USER_TRIGGERS and USER_TRIG_COLUMNS*

The database triggers you own (including source code and description of triggering event) and any columns identified with the triggers. You can write programs against this view to enable or disable triggers for a particular table.

You can view the structures of each of these views either with a DESCRIBE command in SQL*Plus or by referring to the appropriate Oracle documentation. The following sections provide some examples of the ways you can use these views.

## Display Information About Stored Objects

The USER_OBJECTS view contains the following key information about an object:

*OBJECT_NAME*

Name of the object.

*OBJECT_TYPE*

Type of the object (e.g., PACKAGE, FUNCTION, TRIGGER).

*STATUS*

Status of the object: VALID or INVALID.

*LAST_DDL_TIME*

Timestamp indicating the last time that this object was changed.

The following SQL*Plus script displays the status of PL/SQL code objects:

```
/* File on web: psobj.sql */
SELECT object_type, object_name, status
  FROM user_objects
 WHERE object_type IN (
     'PACKAGE', 'PACKAGE BODY', 'FUNCTION', 'PROCEDURE',
     'TYPE', 'TYPE BODY', 'TRIGGER')
 ORDER BY object_type, status, object_name
```

The output from this script file will be similar to the following:

```
OBJECT_TYPE          OBJECT_NAME                      STATUS
-------------------  -------------------------------  ----------
FUNCTION             DEVELOP_ANALYSIS                 INVALID
                     NUMBER_OF_ATOMICS                INVALID

PACKAGE              CONFIG_PKG                       VALID
                     EXCHDLR_PKG                      VALID
```

Notice that two of my modules are marked as INVALID. See the section "Recompiling Invalid Program Units" on page 725 for more details on the significance of this setting and how you can change it to VALID.

## Display and Search Source Code

You should always maintain the source code of your programs in text files (or via a development tool specifically designed to store and manage PL/SQL code outside of the database). When you store these programs in the database, however, you can take advantage of SQL to analyze your source code across all modules, which may not be a straightforward task with your text editor.

The USER_SOURCE view contains all of the source code for objects owned by the current user. The structure of USER_SOURCE is as follows:

```
Name                          Null?     Type
----------------------------- --------- ----
NAME                          NOT NULL  VARCHAR2(30)
TYPE                                    VARCHAR2(12)
LINE                          NOT NULL  NUMBER
TEXT                                    VARCHAR2(4000)
```

where:

*NAME*
    Is the name of the object.

*TYPE*
    Is the type of the object (ranging from PL/SQL program units to Java source to trigger source).

*LINE*
    Is the line number.

*TEXT*
    Is the text of the source code.

USER_SOURCE is a very valuable resource for developers. With the right kind of queries, you can do things like:

- Display source code for a given line number.
- Validate coding standards.
- Identify possible bugs or weaknesses in your source code.
- Look for programming constructs not identifiable from other views.

Suppose, for example, that I have set as a rule that individual developers should never hardcode one of those application-specific error numbers between –20,999 and –20,000 (such hardcodings can lead to conflicting usages and lots of confusion). I can't stop a developer from writing code like this:

```
RAISE_APPLICATION_ERROR (-20306, 'Balance too low');
```

but I can create a package that allows me to identify all the programs that have such a line in them. I call it my "validate standards" package; it is very simple, and its main procedure looks like this:

```
/* Files on web: valstd.* */
PROCEDURE progwith (str IN VARCHAR2)
IS
   TYPE info_rt IS RECORD (
      NAME    user_source.NAME%TYPE
    , text    user_source.text%TYPE
   );
   TYPE info_aat IS TABLE OF info_rt
      INDEX BY PLS_INTEGER;

   info_aa    info_aat;
BEGIN
   SELECT NAME || '-' || line
        , text
   BULK COLLECT INTO info_aa
     FROM user_source
    WHERE UPPER (text) LIKE '%' || UPPER (str) || '%'
      AND NAME <> 'VALSTD'
      AND NAME <> 'ERRNUMS';

   disp_header ('Checking for presence of "' || str || '"');

   FOR indx IN info_aa.FIRST .. info_aa.LAST
   LOOP
      pl (info_aa (indx).NAME, info_aa (indx).text);
   END LOOP;
END progwith;
```

Once this package is compiled into my schema, I can check for usages of –20,NNN numbers with this command:

```
SQL> EXEC valstd.progwith ('-20')
====================
VALIDATE STANDARDS
```

```
==================
Checking for presence of "-20"
CHECK_BALANCE - RAISE_APPLICATION_ERROR (-20306, 'Balance too low');
MY_SESSION -    PRAGMA EXCEPTION_INIT(dblink_not_open,-2081);
VSESSTAT - CREATE DATE    : 1999-07-20
```

Notice that the second and third lines in my output are not really a problem; they show up only because I couldn't define my filter narrowly enough.

This is a fairly crude analytical tool, but you could certainly make it more sophisticated. You could also have it generate HTML that is then posted on your intranet. You could then run the valstd scripts every Sunday night through a DBMS_JOB-submitted job, and each Monday morning developers could check the intranet for feedback on any fixes needed in their code.

## Use Program Size to Determine Pinning Requirements

The USER_OBJECT_SIZE view gives you the following information about the size of the programs stored in the database:

*SOURCE_SIZE*
> Size of the source in bytes. This code must be in memory during compilation (including dynamic/automatic recompilation).

*PARSED_SIZE*
> Size of the parsed form of the object in bytes. This representation must be in memory when any object that references this object is compiled.

*CODE_SIZE*
> Code size in bytes. This code must be in memory when the object is executed.

Here is a query that allows you to show code objects that are larger than a given size. You might want to run this query to identify the programs that you will want to pin into the database using DBMS_SHARED_POOL (see Chapter 24 for more information on this package) in order to minimize the swapping of code in the SGA:

```
/* File on web: pssize.sql */
SELECT name, type, source_size, parsed_size, code_size
  FROM user_object_size
 WHERE code_size > &&1 * 1024
 ORDER BY code_size DESC
```

## Obtain Properties of Stored Code

The USER_PLSQL_OBJECT_SETTINGS view (introduced in Oracle Database 10*g*) provides information about the following compiler settings of a stored PL/SQL object:

*PLSQL_OPTIMIZE_LEVEL*
> Optimization level that was used to compile the object.

*PLSQL_CODE_TYPE*
Compilation mode for the object.

*PLSQL_DEBUG*
Indicates whether or not the object was compiled for debugging.

*PLSQL_WARNINGS*
Compiler warning settings that were used to compile the object.

*NLS_LENGTH_SEMANTICS*
NLS length semantics that were used to compile the object.

Possible uses for this view include:

- Identify any programs that are not taking full advantage of the optimizing compiler (an optimization level of 1 or 0):

```
/* File on web: low_optimization_level.sql */
SELECT owner, name
  FROM user_plsql_object_settings
 WHERE plsql_optimize_level IN (1,0);
```

- Determine if any stored programs have disabled compile-time warnings:

```
/* File on web: disable_warnings.sql */
SELECT NAME, plsql_warnings
  FROM user_plsql_object_settings
 WHERE plsql_warnings LIKE '%DISABLE%';
```

The USER_PROCEDURES view lists all functions and procedures, along with associated properties, including whether a function is pipelined, parallel enabled, or aggregate. USER_PROCEDURES will also show you the AUTHID setting for a program (DEFINER or CURRENT_USER). This can be very helpful if you need to see quickly which programs in a package or group of packages use invoker rights or definer rights. Here is an example of such a query:

```
/* File on web: show_authid.sql */
SELECT   AUTHID
       , p.object_name program_name
       , procedure_name subprogram_name
    FROM user_procedures p, user_objects o
   WHERE p.object_name = o.object_name
     AND p.object_name LIKE '<package or program name criteria>'
ORDER BY AUTHID, procedure_name;
```

## Analyze and Modify Trigger State Through Views

Query the trigger-related views (USER_TRIGGERS, USER_TRIG_COLUMNS) to do any of the following:

- Enable or disable all triggers for a given table. Rather than have to write this code manually, you can execute the appropriate DDL statements from within a PL/SQL program. See the section "Maintaining Triggers" on page 705 in Chapter 19 for an example of such a program.

- Identify triggers that execute only when certain columns are changed, but do not have a WHEN clause. A best practice for triggers is to include a WHEN clause to make sure that the specified columns actually *have* changed values (rather than simply writing the same value over itself).

Here is a query you can use to identify potentially problematic triggers lacking a WHEN clause:

```
/* File on web: nowhen_trigger.sql */
SELECT *
  FROM user_triggers tr
 WHERE when_clause IS NULL AND
       EXISTS (SELECT 'x'
                 FROM user_trigger_cols
                WHERE trigger_owner = USER
                AND trigger_name = tr.trigger_name);
```

## Analyze Argument Information

A *very* useful view for programmers is USER_ARGUMENTS. It contains information about each of the arguments of each of the stored programs in your schema. It offers, simultaneously, a wealth of nicely parsed information about arguments and a bewildering structure that is very hard to work with.

Here is a simple SQL*Plus script to dump the contents of USER_ARGUMENTS for all the programs in the specified package:

```
/* File on web: desctest.sql */
SELECT object_name, argument_name, overload
     , POSITION, SEQUENCE, data_level, data_type
  FROM user_arguments
 WHERE package_name = UPPER ('&&1');
```

A more elaborate PL/SQL-based program for displaying the contents of USER_ARGUMENTS may be found in the *show_all_arguments.sp* file on the book's web site.

You can also write more specific queries against USER_ARGUMENTS to identify possible quality issues with your code base. For example, Oracle recommends that you stay away from the LONG datatype and instead use LOBs. In addition, the fixed-length CHAR datatype can cause logic problems; you are much better off sticking with VARCHAR2. Here is a query that uncovers the usage of these types in argument definitions:

```
/* File on web: long_or_char.sql */
SELECT object_name, argument_name, overload
     , POSITION, SEQUENCE, data_level, data_type
  FROM user_arguments
 WHERE data_type IN ('LONG','CHAR');
```

You can even use USER_ARGUMENTS to deduce information about a package's program units that is otherwise not easily obtainable. Suppose that I want to get a list of all the procedures and functions defined in a package specification. You will say: "No problem! Just query the USER_PROCEDURES view." And that would be a fine answer, except that it turns out that USER_PROCEDURES doesn't tell you whether a program is a function or a procedure (in fact, it can be *both*, depending on how the program is overloaded!).

You might instead, want to turn to USER_ARGUMENTS. It does, indeed, contain that information, but it is far less than obvious. To determine whether a program is a function or a procedure, you must check to see if there is a row in USER_ARGUMENTS for that package-program combination that has a POSITION of 0. That is the value Oracle uses to store the RETURN "argument" of a function. If it is not present, then the program must be a procedure.

The following function uses this logic to return a string that indicates the program type (if it is overloaded with both types, the function returns "FUNCTION, PROCEDURE"). Note that the list_to_string function used in the main body is provided in the file.

```
/* File on web: program_type.sf */
FUNCTION program_type (
   owner_in     IN   VARCHAR2
 , package_in   IN   VARCHAR2
 , program_in   IN   VARCHAR2
)
   RETURN VARCHAR2
IS
   TYPE overload_aat IS TABLE OF all_arguments.overload%TYPE
      INDEX BY PLS_INTEGER;

   l_overloads  overload_aat;
   retval       VARCHAR2 (32767);

BEGIN
   SELECT   DECODE (MIN (POSITION), 0, 'FUNCTION', 'PROCEDURE')
   BULK COLLECT INTO l_overloads
      FROM all_arguments
     WHERE owner = owner_in
       AND package_name = package_in
       AND object_name = program_in
   GROUP BY overload;

   IF l_overloads.COUNT > 0
   THEN
      retval := list_to_string (l_overloads, ',', distinct_in => TRUE);
   END IF;

   RETURN retval;
END program_type;
/
```

Finally, you should also know that the built-in package, DBMS_DESCRIBE, provides a PL/SQL API to provide much of the same information as USER_ARGUMENTS. There are differences, however, in the way these two elements handle datatypes.

## Analyze Identifier Usage (Oracle Database 11g's PL/Scope)

It doesn't take long for the volume and complexity of our code base to present serious maintenance and evolutionary challenges. I might need, for example, to implement a new feature in some portion of an existing program. How can I be sure that I understand the impact of this feature *and* make all necessary changes? Prior to Oracle Database 11g, the tools I could use to perform impact analysis were largely limited to queries against ALL_DEPENDENCIES and ALL_SOURCE. Now, with PL/Scope, I can perform much more detailed and useful analyses.

PL/Scope collects data about identifiers in PL/SQL source code when it compiles your code, and makes it available in static data dictionary views. This collected data, accessible through USER_IDENTIFIERS, includes very detailed information about the types and usages (including declarations, references, assignments, etc.) of each identifier, plus information about the location of each usage in the source code.

You can then write queries against USER_IDENTIFIERS to mine your code for all sorts of information, including violations of naming conventions. PL/SQL editors, such as Toad, are likely to start offering user interfaces to PL/Scope, making it easy to analyze your code. Until that happens, you will need to construct your own queries (or use those produced and made available by others).

To use PL/Scope, you must first ask the PL/SQL compiler to analyze the identifiers of your program when it is compiled. You do this by changing the value of the PLSCOPE_SETTINGS compilation parameter; you can do this for a session or even an individual program unit, as shown here:

```
ALTER SESSION SET plscope_settings='IDENTIFIERS:ALL'
```

You can see the value of PLSCOPE_SETTINGS for any particular program unit with a query against USER_PLSQL_OBJECT_SETTINGS.

Once PL/Scope has been enabled, whenever you compile a program unit, Oracle will populate the data dictionary with detailed information about how each identifier in your program (variables, types, programs, etc.) is used.

Let's take a look at a few examples of using PL/Scope. Suppose I create the following package specification and procedure, with PL/Scope enabled:

```
/* File on web: 11g_plscope.sql */
ALTER SESSION SET plscope_settings='IDENTIFIERS:ALL'
/

CREATE OR REPLACE PACKAGE plscope_pkg
IS
   FUNCTION plscope_func (plscope_fp1 NUMBER)
```

```
     RETURN NUMBER;

   PROCEDURE plscope_proc (plscope_pp1 VARCHAR2);
END plscope_pkg;
/

CREATE OR REPLACE PROCEDURE plscope_proc1
IS
   plscope_var1   NUMBER := 0;
BEGIN
   plscope_pkg.plscope_proc (TO_CHAR (plscope_var1));
   DBMS_OUTPUT.put_line (SYSDATE);
   plscope_var1 := 1;
END plscope_proc1;
/
```

I can verify PL/Scope settings as follows:

```
SELECT name, plscope_settings
  FROM user_plsql_object_settings
 WHERE name LIKE 'PLSCOPE%'

NAME                           PLSCOPE_SETTINGS
------------------------------ ----------------
PLSCOPE_PKG                    IDENTIFIERS:ALL
PLSCOPE_PROC1                  IDENTIFIERS:ALL
```

Let's determine what has been *declared* in the process of compiling these two program units:

```
SELECT name, signature, TYPE
  FROM user_identifiers
 WHERE name LIKE 'PLSCOPE%' AND usage = 'DECLARATION'
ORDER BY type, usage_id

NAME            SIGNATURE                        TYPE
--------------- -------------------------------- -----------
PLSCOPE_FP1     864F31A5B51B94097568688379D5959C FORMAL IN
PLSCOPE_PP1     9124512252B0AB1320818EADAAD87162 FORMAL IN
PLSCOPE_FUNC    78168BCBE1511996C92DEA6FD93E0484 FUNCTION
PLSCOPE_PKG     7DFBE4474A77569165B7DCB606761B81 PACKAGE
PLSCOPE_PROC1   4A24FD31BEA28212C696235F192E6CEE PROCEDURE
PLSCOPE_PROC    F51FC44CA81F59C6B428AB27C6415B2E PROCEDURE
PLSCOPE_VAR1    401F008A81C7DCF48AD7B2552BF4E684 VARIABLE
```

Now I'll discover all locally-declared variables:

```
SELECT a.name variable_name, b.name context_name, a.signature
  FROM user_identifiers a, user_identifiers b
 WHERE      a.usage_context_id = b.usage_id
        AND a.TYPE = 'VARIABLE'
        AND a.usage = 'DECLARATION'
        AND a.object_name = 'PLSCOPE_PROC1'
        AND a.object_name = b.object_name
ORDER BY a.object_type, a.usage_id

VARIABLE_NAME  CONTEXT_NAME  SIGNATURE
```

```
-------------- ------------- --------------------------------
PLSCOPE_VAR1   PLSCOPE_PROC1 401F008A81C7DCF48AD7B2552BF4E684
```

Impressive, yet PL/Scope can do so much more. I would like to know all the locations in my program unit in which the variable is used, as well as the type of usage:

```
SELECT usage, usage_id, object_name, object_type
  FROM user_identifiers sig
     , (SELECT a.signature
          FROM user_identifiers a, user_identifiers b
         WHERE     a.usage_context_id = b.usage_id
               AND a.TYPE = 'VARIABLE'
               AND a.usage = 'DECLARATION'
               AND a.object_name = 'PLSCOPE_PROC1'
               AND a.object_name = b.object_name) variables
 WHERE sig.signature = variables.signature
 ORDER BY object_type, usage_id
```

```
USAGE        USAGE_ID  OBJECT_NAME                     OBJECT_TYPE
-----------  --------  ------------------------------  -------------
DECLARATION  3         PLSCOPE_PROC1                   PROCEDURE
ASSIGNMENT   4         PLSCOPE_PROC1                   PROCEDURE
REFERENCE    7         PLSCOPE_PROC1                   PROCEDURE
ASSIGNMENT   9         PLSCOPE_PROC1                   PROCEDURE
```

You should be able to see, even from these simple examples, that PL/Scope offers enormous potential in helping you better understand your code and analyze the impact of change on that code.

Lucas Jellama of AMIS has produced more interesting and complex examples of using PL/Scope to validate naming conventions. You can find these queries in the *11g_plscope_amis.sql* file on the book's web site.

# Managing Dependencies and Recompiling Code

Another very important phase of PL/SQL compilation and execution is the checking of program *dependencies*. A dependency (in PL/SQL) is a reference from a stored program to some database object outside that program. Server-based PL/SQL programs can have dependencies on tables, views, types, procedures, functions, sequences, synonyms, object types, package specifications, etc. Program units are not, however, dependent on package bodies or object type bodies; these are the "hidden" implementations.

Oracle's basic dependency principle for PL/SQL is, loosely speaking:

> Do not use the currently compiled version of a program if any of the objects on which it depends have changed since it was compiled.

The good news is that most dependency management happens automatically, from the tracking of dependencies to the recompilation required to keep everything synchronized. You can't completely ignore this topic, though, and the following sections should help you understand how, when, and why you'll need to intervene.

In Oracle Database 10g and earlier, these dependencies were tracked with a granularity of a program unit. So if a procedure was dependent upon a function within a package or a column within a table, the dependent unit was the package or the table. This granularity has been the standard from the dawn of PL/SQL—until recently.

Beginning with Oracle Database 11g, the granularity of dependency tracking has improved. Instead of tracking the dependency to the unit (for example; a package or a table), the grain is now the element within the unit (for example, the columns in a table or the packaged program together with the formal calling parameters and their mode). This *fine-grained dependency* tracking means that your program will not be invalidated if you add an additional program or overload an existing program in an existing package. Likewise, if you add a column to a table, the database will not automatically invalidate all PL/SQL programs that reference the table—only those programs that reference all columns, as in a SELECT * or by using the anchored declaration %ROWTYPE. The following sections explore this situation in detail.

In Chapter 3, the section titled "Qualify all References to Variables and Columns in SQL Statements" on page 59 provides an example of this fine-grained dependency management.

It would be nice to report on the fine-grained dependencies that Oracle Database 11g manages, but as of Oracle Database 11g Release 2, this data is not available in any of the data dictionary views. I hope that they will "published" for our use in the future.

If, however, you are not yet building and deploying applications on Oracle Database 11g, object-level dependency tracking means that almost any change to underlying database objects will cause a wide ripple effect of invalidations.

## Analyzing Dependencies with Data Dictionary Views

You can use several of the data dictionary views to analyze dependency relationships.

Let's take a look at a simple example. Suppose that I have a package named bookworm on the server. This package contains a function that retrieves data from the books table. After I create the table and then create the package, both the package specification and body are VALID:

```
SELECT object_name, object_type, status
  FROM USER_OBJECTS
 WHERE object_name = 'BOOKWORM';


OBJECT_NAME                      OBJECT_TYPE         STATUS
------------------------------   ------------------  -------
BOOKWORM                         PACKAGE             VALID
BOOKWORM                         PACKAGE BODY        VALID
```

Behind the scenes, when you compiled your PL/SQL program, the database determined a list of other objects that BOOKWORM needs in order to compile successfully. I can explore this dependency graph using a query of the data dictionary view USER_DEPENDENCIES:

```
SELECT name, type, referenced_name, referenced_type
  FROM USER_DEPENDENCIES
 WHERE name = 'BOOKWORM';
```

```
NAME              TYPE              REFERENCED_NAME  REFERENCED_TYPE
----------------  ----------------  ---------------  ----------------
BOOKWORM          PACKAGE           STANDARD         PACKAGE
BOOKWORM          PACKAGE BODY      STANDARD         PACKAGE
BOOKWORM          PACKAGE BODY      BOOKS            TABLE
BOOKWORM          PACKAGE BODY      BOOKWORM         PACKAGE
```

Figure 20-1 illustrates this information as a directed graph, where the arrows indicate a "depends-on" relationship. In other words, the figure shows that:

- The bookworm package specification and body both depend on the built-in package named STANDARD (see the sidebar "Flying the STANDARD" on page 725).

- The bookworm package body depends on its corresponding specification and on the books table.

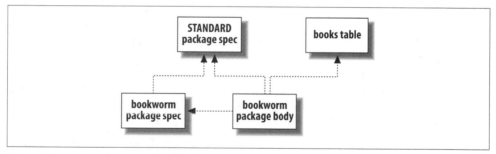

Figure 20-1. Dependency graph of the bookworm package

For purposes of tracking dependencies, the database records a package specification and body as two different entities. Every package body will have a dependency on its corresponding specification, but the specification will never depend on its body. Nothing depends on the body. Hey, it might not even have a body.

If you've been responsible for maintaining someone else's code during your career, you will know that performing impact analysis relies not so much on "depends-on" information as it does on "referenced-by" information. Let's say that I'm contemplating a change in the structure of the books table. Naturally, I'd like to know everything that might be affected:

```
SELECT name, type
  FROM USER_DEPENDENCIES
```

```
WHERE referenced_name = 'BOOKS'
  AND referenced_type = 'TABLE';

NAME                                  TYPE
------------------------------        -------------
ADD_BOOK                              PROCEDURE
TEST_BOOK                             PACKAGE BODY
BOOK                                  PACKAGE BODY
BOOKWORM                              PACKAGE BODY
FORMSTEST                             PACKAGE
```

As you can see, in addition to the bookworm package, there are some programs in my schema I haven't told you about, but fortunately the database never forgets. Nice!

As clever as the database is at keeping track of dependencies, it isn't clairvoyant: in the data dictionary, the database can only track dependencies of local stored objects written with static calls. There are plenty of ways that you can create programs that do not appear in the USER_DEPENDENCIES view. These include external programs that embed SQL or PL/SQL; remote stored procedures or client-side tools that call local stored objects; and any programs that use dynamic SQL.

As I was saying, if I alter the table's structure by adding a column:

```
ALTER TABLE books MODIFY popularity_index NUMBER (8,2);
```

then the database will immediately and automatically invalidate all program units that depend on the books table; or, in Oracle Database 11g, only those program units that reference this column. Any change in the DDL time of an object—even if you just rebuild it with no changes—will cause the database to invalidate dependent program units (see the later sidebar "Avoiding Those Invalidations" on page 735). Actually, the database's automatic invalidation is even more sophisticated than that; if you own a program that performs a particular DML statement on a table in another schema, and your privilege to perform that operation gets revoked, this action will also invalidate your program.

After the change, a query against USER_OBJECTS shows me the following information:

```
/* File on web: invalid_objects.sql */
SELECT object_name, object_type, status
  FROM USER_OBJECTS
 WHERE status = 'INVALID';

OBJECT_NAME                     OBJECT_TYPE            STATUS
------------------------------  --------------------   -------
ADD_BOOK                        PROCEDURE              INVALID
BOOK                            PACKAGE BODY           INVALID
BOOKWORM                        PACKAGE BODY           INVALID
FORMSTEST                       PACKAGE                INVALID
FORMSTEST                       PACKAGE BODY           INVALID
TEST_BOOK                       PACKAGE BODY           INVALID
```

By the way, this again illustrates a benefit of the two-part package arrangement: for the most part, the package bodies have been invalidated, but not the specifications. As long as the specification doesn't change, program units that depend on the package will not be invalidated. The only specification that has been invalidated here is for FORMSTEST, which depends on the books table because (as I happen to know) it uses the anchored declaration books%ROWTYPE.

One final note: another way to look at programmatic dependencies is to use Oracle's DEPTREE_FILL procedure in combination with the DEPTREE or IDEPTREE views. As a quick example, if I run the procedure using:

```
BEGIN DEPTREE_FILL('TABLE', USER, 'BOOKS'); END;
```

I can then get a nice listing by selecting from the IDEPTREE view:

```
SELECT * FROM IDEPTREE;

DEPENDENCIES
-------------------------------------------
TABLE SCOTT.BOOKS
   PROCEDUE SCOTT.ADD_BOOK
   PACKAGE BODY SCOTT.BOOK
   PACKAGE BODY SCOTT.TEST_BOOK
   PACKAGE BODY SCOTT.BOOKWORM
   PACKAGE SCOTT.FORMSTEST
      PACKAGE BODY SCOTT.FORMSTEST
```

This listing shows the result of a recursive "referenced-by" query. If you want to use these objects yourself, execute the *$ORACLE_HOME/rdbms/admin/utldtree.sql* script to build the utility procedure and views in your own schema. Or, if you prefer, you can emulate it with a query such as:

```
SELECT RPAD (' ', 3*(LEVEL-1)) || name || ' (' || type || ') '
   FROM user_dependencies
      CONNECT BY PRIOR RTRIM(name || type) =
               RTRIM(referenced_name || referenced_type)
         START WITH referenced_name = 'name' AND referenced_type = 'type'
```

Now that you've seen how the server keeps track of relationships among objects, let's explore one way that the database takes advantage of such information.

## Flying the STANDARD

All but the most minimal database installations will have a built-in package named STANDARD available in the database. This package gets created along with the data dictionary views from *catalog.sql* and contains many of the core features of the PL/SQL language, including:

- Functions such as INSTR and LOWER
- Comparison operators such as NOT, =, and >
- Predefined exceptions such as DUP_VAL_ON_INDEX and VALUE_ERROR

- Subtypes such as STRING and INTEGER

You can view the source code for this package by looking at the file *standard.sql*, which you would normally find in the *$ORACLE_HOME/rdbms/admin* subdirectory.

STANDARD's specification is the "root" of the PL/SQL dependency graph; that is, it depends upon no other PL/SQL programs, but most PL/SQL programs depend upon it. This package is explored in more detail in Chapter 24, *PL/SQL Architecture*.

## Fine-Grained Dependency (Oracle Database 11g)

One of the nicest features of PL/SQL is its automated dependency tracking. The Oracle database automatically keeps track of all database objects on which a program unit is dependent. If any of those objects are subsequently modified, the program unit is marked INVALID and must be recompiled. For example, in the case of the scope_demo package, the inclusion of the query from the employees table means that this package is marked as being dependent on that table.

As I mentioned earlier, prior to Oracle Database 11g, dependency information was recorded only with the granularity of the object as a whole. If *any* change at all is made to that object, all dependent program units are marked INVALID, *even if the change does not affect that program unit*.

Consider the scope_demo package. It is dependent on the employees table, but it refers only to the department_id and salary columns. In Oracle Database 10g, I can change the size of the first_name column and this package will be marked INVALID.

In Oracle Database 11g, Oracle fine-tuned its dependency tracking down to the element within an object. In the case of tables, the Oracle database now records that a program unit depends on specific columns within a table. With this approach, the database can avoid unnecessary recompilations, making it easier for you to evolve your application code base.

In Oracle Database 11g, I can indeed change the size of my first_name column, and this package is *not* marked INVALID, as you can see below:

```
ALTER TABLE employees MODIFY first_name VARCHAR2(2000)
/
Table altered.

SELECT object_name, object_type, status
  FROM all_objects
 WHERE owner = USER AND object_name = 'SCOPE_DEMO'
/

OBJECT_NAME                     OBJECT_TYPE           STATUS
------------------------------- --------------------- -------
SCOPE_DEMO                      PACKAGE               VALID
SCOPE_DEMO                      PACKAGE BODY          VALID
```

Note, however, that unless you fully qualify all references to PL/SQL variables inside your embedded SQL statements, you will not be able to take full advantage of this enhancement.

Specifically, qualification of variable names will avoid invalidation of program units when new columns are *added* to a dependent table.

Consider that original, unqualified SELECT statement in set_global:

```
SELECT COUNT (*)
   INTO l_count
   FROM employees
  WHERE department_id = l_inner AND salary > l_salary;
```

In Oracle Database 11g, fine-grained dependency means that the database will note that the scope_demo package is dependent only on department_id and salary.

Now suppose that the DBA adds a column to the employees table. Since there are unqualified references to PL/SQL variables in the SELECT statement, it is possible that the new column name will change the dependency information for this package. Namely, if the new column name is the same as an unqualified reference to a PL/SQL variable, the database will now resolve that reference to the *column name*. Thus, the database would need to update the dependency information for scope_demo, which means that it needs to invalidate the package.

If, conversely, you *do* qualify references to all your PL/SQL variables inside embedded SQL statements, then when the database compiles your program unit, it knows that there is no possible ambiguity. Even when columns are added, the program unit will remain VALID.

Note that the INTO list of a query is not actually a part of the SQL statement. As a result, variables in that list do not persist into the SQL statement that the PL/SQL compiler derives. Consequently, qualifying (or not qualifying) that variable with its scope name will have no bearing on the database's dependency analysis.

## Remote Dependencies

Server-based PL/SQL immediately becomes invalid whenever there is a change in a local object on which it depends. However, if it depends on an object in a remote database and that object changes, the local database does not attempt to invalidate the calling PL/SQL program in real time. Instead, the local database defers the checking until runtime.

Here is a program that has a remote dependency on the procedure recompute_prices, which lives across the database link *findat.ldn.world*:

```
PROCEDURE synch_em_up (tax_site_in IN VARCHAR2, since_in IN DATE)
IS
BEGIN
   IF tax_site_in = 'LONDON'
   THEN
```

```
        recompute_prices@findat.ldn.world(cutoff_time => since_in);
    END IF;
```

If you recompile the remote procedure and some time later try to run synch_em_up, you are likely to get an ORA-04062 error with accompanying text such as *timestamp* (or *signature*) *of package "SCOTT.recompute_prices" has been changed*. If your call is still legal, the database will recompile synch_em_up, and if it succeeds, its next invocation should run without error. To understand the database's remote procedure call behavior, you need to know that the PL/SQL compiler always stores two kinds of information about each referenced remote procedure: its timestamp and its signature:

*Timestamp*

The most recent date and time (down to the second) when an object's specification was reconstructed, as given by the TIMESTAMP column in the USER_OBJECTS view. For PL/SQL programs, this is not necessarily the same as the most recent compilation time because it's possible to recompile an object without reconstructing its specification. (Note that this column is of the DATE datatype, not the newer TIMESTAMP datatype.)

*Signature*

A footprint of the actual shape of the object's specification. Signature information includes the object's name and the ordering, datatype family, and mode of each parameter.

So when I compiled synch_em_up, the database retrieved both the timestamp and the signature of the remote procedure called recomputed_prices, and stored a representation of them with the bytecode of synch_em_up.

How do you suppose the database uses this information at runtime? The model is simple: it uses either the timestamp or the signature, depending on the current value of the parameter REMOTE_DEPENDENCIES_MODE. If that timestamp or signature information, which is stored in the local program's bytecode, doesn't match the actual value of the remote procedure at runtime, you get the ORA-04062 error.

Oracle's default remote dependency mode is the timestamp method, but this setting can sometimes cause unnecessary recompilations. The DBA can change the database's initialization parameter REMOTE_DEPENDENCIES_MODE, or you can change your session's setting, like this:

```
ALTER SESSION SET REMOTE_DEPENDENCIES_MODE = SIGNATURE;
```

or, inside PL/SQL:

```
EXECUTE IMMEDIATE 'ALTER SESSION SET REMOTE_DEPENDENCIES_MODE = SIGNATURE';
```

Thereafter, for the remainder of that session, every PL/SQL program run will use the signature method. As a matter of fact, Oracle's client-side tools always execute this ALTER SESSION...SIGNATURE command as the first thing they do after connecting to the database, overriding the database setting.

Oracle Corporation recommends using signature mode on client tools like Oracle Forms and timestamp mode on server-to-server procedure calls. Be aware that signature mode can cause false negatives—situations where the runtime engine thinks that the signature hasn't changed, but it really has—in which case the database does not force an invalidation of a program that calls it remotely. You can wind up with silent computational errors that are difficult to detect and even more difficult to debug. Here are several risky scenarios:

- Changing only the default value of one of the called program's formal parameters. The caller will continue to use the old default value.

- Adding an overloaded program to an existing package. The caller will not bind to the new version of the overloaded program even if it is supposed to.

- Changing just the name of a formal parameter. The caller may have problems if it uses named parameter notation.

In these cases, you will have to perform a manual recompilation of the caller. In contrast, the timestamp mode, while prone to false positives, is immune to false negatives. In other words, it won't miss any needed recompilations, but it may force recompilation that is not strictly required. This safety is no doubt why Oracle uses it as the default for server-to-server RPCs.

 If you do use the signature method, Oracle recommends that you add any new functions or procedures at the *end* of package specifications because doing so reduces false positives.

In the real world, minimizing recompilations can make a significant difference in application availability. It turns out that you can trick the database into thinking that a local call is really remote so that you can use signature mode. This is done using a loopback database link inside a synonym. Here is an example that assumes you have an Oracle Net service name "localhost" that connects to the local database:

```
CREATE DATABASE LINK loopback
    CONNECT TO bob IDENTIFIED BY swordfish USING 'localhost'
/
CREATE OR REPLACE PROCEDURE volatilecode AS
BEGIN
    -- whatever
END;
/
CREATE OR REPLACE SYNONYM volatile_syn FOR volatilecode@loopback
/
CREATE OR REPLACE PROCEDURE save_from_recompile AS
BEGIN
    ...
    volatile_syn;
    ...
```

```
END;
/
```

To take advantage of this arrangement, your production system would then include an invocation such as this:

```
BEGIN
   EXECUTE IMMEDIATE 'ALTER SESSION SET REMOTE_DEPENDENCIES_MODE=SIGNATURE';
   save_from_recompile;
END;
/
```

As long as you don't do anything that alters the signature of volatilecode, you can modify and recompile it without invalidating save_from_recompile or causing a run-time error. You can even rebuild the synonym against a different procedure entirely. This approach isn't completely without drawbacks; for example, if volatilecode outputs anything using DBMS_OUTPUT, you won't see it unless save_from_recompile retrieves it explicitly over the database link and then outputs it directly. But for many applications, such workarounds are a small price to pay for the resulting increase in availability.

## Limitations of Oracle's Remote Invocation Model

Through Oracle Database 11g Release 2, there is no direct way for a PL/SQL program to use any of the following package constructs on a remote server:

- Variables (including constants)
- Cursors
- Exceptions

This limitation applies not only to client PL/SQL calling the database server, but also to server-to-server RPCs.

The simple workaround for variables is to use "get-and-set" programs to encapsulate the data. In general, you should be doing that anyway because it is an excellent programming practice.

The workaround for cursors is to encapsulate them with open, fetch, and close subprograms. For example, if you've declared a book_cur cursor in the specification of the book_maint package, you could put this corresponding package body on the server:

```
PACKAGE BODY book_maint
AS
   prv_book_cur_status BOOLEAN;

   PROCEDURE open_book_cur IS
   BEGIN
      IF NOT book_maint.book_cur%ISOPEN
      THEN
         OPEN book_maint.book_cur;
      END IF;
```

```
      END;
      FUNCTION next_book_rec RETURN books%ROWTYPE
      IS
         l_book_rec books%ROWTYPE;
      BEGIN
         FETCH book_maint.book_cur INTO l_book_rec;
         prv_book_cur_status := book_maint.book_cur%FOUND;
         RETURN l_book_rec;
      END;

      FUNCTION book_cur_is_found RETURN BOOLEAN
      IS
      BEGIN
         RETURN prv_book_cur_status;
      END;

      PROCEDURE close_book_cur IS
      BEGIN
         IF book_maint.book_cur%ISOPEN
         THEN
            CLOSE book_maint.book_cur;
         END IF;
      END;
   END book_maint;
```

Unfortunately, this approach won't work around the problem of using remote exceptions; the exception "datatype" is treated differently from true datatypes. Instead, you can use the RAISE_APPLICATION_ERROR procedure with a user-defined exception number between –20000 and –20999. See Chapter 6 for a discussion of how to write a package to help your application manage this type of exception.

## Recompiling Invalid Program Units

In addition to becoming invalid when a referenced object changes, a new program may be in an invalid state as the result of a failed compilation. In any event, no PL/SQL program marked as INVALID will run until a successful recompilation changes its status to VALID. Recompilation can happen in one of three ways:

*Automatic runtime recompilation*
    The PL/SQL runtime engine will, under many circumstances, automatically recompile an invalid program unit when that program unit is called.

*ALTER...COMPILE recompilation*
    Use an explicit ALTER command to recompile the package.

*Schema-level recompilation*
    Use one of many alternative built-ins and custom code to recompile all invalid program units in a schema or database instance.

## Automatic runtime compilation

Since Oracle maintains information about the status of program units compiled into the database, it knows when a program unit is invalid and needs to be recompiled. When a user connected to the database attempts to execute (directly or indirectly) an invalid program unit, the database will automatically attempt to recompile that unit.

You might then wonder: why do we need to explicitly recompile program units at all? There are two reasons:

- In a production environment, "just in time" recompilation can have a ripple effect, in terms of both performance degradation and cascading invalidations of other database objects. The user experience will be much improved by recompiling all invalid program units when users are not accessing the application (if at all possible).

- Recompilation of a program unit that was previously executed by another user connected to the same instance can and usually *will* result in an error that looks like this:

```
ORA-04068: existing state of packages has been discarded
ORA-04061: existing state of package "SCOTT.P1" has been invalidated
ORA-04065: not executed, altered or dropped package "SCOTT.P1"
ORA-06508: PL/SQL: could not find program unit being called
```

This error occurs when a package that has "state" (one or more variables or constants declared at the package level) has been recompiled. All sessions that had previously initialized that package are now out of synch with the newly compiled package. When the database tries to reference or run an element of that package, it cannot "find program unit" and throws an exception.

The solution? Well, you (or the application) *could* trap the exception and then simply call that same program unit again. Now the package state will be reset (that's what the ORA-4068 error message is telling us), and the database *will* be able to execute the program. Unfortunately, the states of *all packages*, including DBMS_OUTPUT and other built-in packages, will have been reset in that session. It is very unlikely that users will be able to continue running the application successfully.

What this means for users of PL/SQL-based applications is that whenever the underlying code needs to be updated (recompiled), all users must stop using the application. That is *not* an acceptable scenario in today's world of "always on" Internet-based applications. Oracle Database 11g Release 2 finally addresses this problem by offering support for "hot patching" of application code through the use of edition-based redefinition. This topic is covered briefly at the end of this chapter.

The bottom line on automatic recompilation bears repeating: prior to Oracle Database 11g Release 2, in live production environments, do not do *anything* that will invalidate or recompile (automatically or otherwise) any stored objects for which sessions might have instantiations that will be referred to again.

Fortunately, development environments don't usually need to worry about ripple effects, and automatic recompilation outside of production can greatly ease our development efforts. While it might still be helpful to recompile all invalid program units (explored in the following sections), it is not as critical a step.

### ALTER...COMPILE recompilation

You can always recompile a program unit that has previously been compiled into the database using the ALTER...COMPILE command. In the case presented earlier, for example, I know by looking in the data dictionary that three program units were invalidated.

To recompile these program units in the hope of setting their status back to VALID, I can issue these commands:

```
ALTER PACKAGE bookworm COMPILE BODY REUSE SETTINGS;
ALTER PACKAGE book COMPILE BODY REUSE SETTINGS;
ALTER PROCEDURE add_book COMPILE REUSE SETTINGS;
```

Notice the inclusion of "REUSE SETTINGS". This clause ensures that all the compilation settings (optimization level, warnings level, etc.) previously associated with this program unit will remain the same. If you do not include REUSE SETTINGS, then the current settings of the session will be applied upon recompilation.

Of course, if you have many invalid objects, you will not want to type ALTER COMPILE commands for each one. You *could* write a simple query, like the one below, to *generate* all the ALTER commands:

```
SELECT 'ALTER ' || object_type || ' ' || object_name
       || ' COMPILE REUSE SETTINGS;'
  FROM user_objects
 WHERE status = 'INVALID'
```

The problem with this "bulk" approach is that as you recompile one invalid object, you may cause many others to be marked INVALID. You are much better off relying on more sophisticated methods for recompiling all invalid program units; these are covered next.

### Schema-level recompilation

Oracle offers a number of ways to recompile all invalid program units in a particular schema. Unless otherwise noted, the following utilities must be run from a schema with SYSDBA authority. All files listed below may be found in the *$ORACLE_HOME/ Rdbms/Admin* directory.

*utlip.sql*

> Invalidates and recompiles all PL/SQL code and views in the entire database. Actually, it sets up some data structures, invalidates the objects, and prompts you to restart the database and run *utlrp.sql*.

*utlrp.sql*

Recompiles all of the invalid objects in serial and is appropriate for single-processor hardware. If you have a multiprocessor machine, you probably want to use *utlrcmp.sql* instead.

*utlrcmp.sql*

Like *utlrp.sql*, recompiles all invalid objects, but in parallel; it works by submitting multiple recompilation requests into the database's job queue. You can supply the "degree of parallelism" as an integer argument on the command line. If you leave it null or supply "0", then the script will attempt to select the proper degree of parallelism on its own. However, even Oracle warns that this parallel version may not yield dramatic performance results because of write contention on system tables.

*DBMS_UTILITY.RECOMPILE_SCHEMA*

This procedure has been around since Oracle8 Database and can be run from any schema; SYSDBA authority is *not* required. It will recompile program units in the specified schema. Its header is defined as follows:

```
DBMS_UTILITY.COMPILE_SCHEMA (
    schema VARCHAR2
  , compile_all BOOLEAN DEFAULT TRUE,
  , reuse_settings BOOLEAN DEFAULT FALSE
);
```

Prior to Oracle Database 10g, this utility was poorly designed and often *invalidated* as many program units as it recompiled to VALID status. Now, it seems to work as one would expect.

*UTL_RECOMP*

This built-in package, first introduced in Oracle Database 10g, was designed for database upgrades or patches that require significant recompilation. It has two programs, one that recompiles invalid objects serially and one that uses DBMS_JOB to recompile in parallel. To recompile all of the invalid objects in a database instance in parallel, for example, a DBA only needs to run this single command:

```
UTL_RECOMP.recomp_parallel
```

When running this parallel version, it uses the DBMS_JOB package to queue up the recompile jobs. When this happens, all other jobs in the queue are temporarily disabled to avoid conflicts with the recompilation.

Here is an example of calling the serial version to recompile all invalid objects in the SCOTT schema:

```
SQL> CALL UTL_RECOMP.recomp_serial ('SCOTT');
```

If you have multiple processors, the parallel version may help you complete your recompilations more rapidly. As Oracle notes in its documentation of this package, however, compilation of stored programs results in updates to many catalog structures and is I/O-intensive; the resulting speedup is likely to be a function of the speed of your disks.

Here is an example of requesting recompilation of all invalid objects in the SCOTT schema, using up to four simultaneous threads for the recompilation steps:

```
SQL> CALL UTL_RECOMP.recomp_parallel ('SCOTT', 4);
```

 Solomon Yakobson, an outstanding Oracle DBA and general technologist, has also written a recompile utility that can be used by non-DBAs to recompile all invalid program units in dependency order. It handles stored programs, views (including materialized views), triggers, user-defined object types, and dimensions. You can find the utility in a file named *recompile.sql* on the book's web site.

---

### Avoiding Those Invalidations

When a database object's DDL time changes, the database's usual *modus operandi* is to immediately invalidate all of its dependents on the local database.

In Oracle Database 10g and later releases, recompiling a stored program via its original creation script will not invalidate dependents. This feature does not extend to re-compiling a program using ALTER...COMPILE or via automatic recompilation, which *will* invalidate dependents. Note that even if you use a script, the database is very picky; if you change anything in your source code—even just a single letter—that program's dependents will be marked INVALID.

---

# Compile-Time Warnings

Compile-time warnings can greatly improve the maintainability of your code and reduce the chance that bugs will creep into it. Compile-time warnings differ from compile-time errors; with warnings, your program will still compile and run. You may, however, encounter unexpected behavior or reduced performance as a result of running code that is flagged with warnings.

This section explores how compile-time warnings work and which issues are currently detected. Let's start with a quick example of applying compile-time warnings in your session.

## A Quick Example

A very useful compile-time warning is *PLW-06002: Unreachable code*. Consider the following program (available in the *cantgothere.sql* file on the book's web site). Because I have initialized the salary variable to 10,000, the conditional statement will *always* send me to line 9. Line 7 will never be executed.

```
      /* File on web: cantgothere.sql */
 1    PROCEDURE cant_go_there
 2    AS
 3       l_salary NUMBER := 10000;
 4    BEGIN
 5       IF l_salary > 20000
 6       THEN
 7          DBMS_OUTPUT.put_line ('Executive');
 8       ELSE
 9          DBMS_OUTPUT.put_line ('Rest of Us');
10       END IF;
11    END cant_go_there;
```

If I compile this code in any release prior to Oracle Database 10g, I am simply told "Procedure created." If, however, I have enabled compile-time warnings in my session on the new release and then try to compile the procedure, I get this response from the compiler:

```
SP2-0804: Procedure created with compilation warnings

SQL> SHOW err
Errors for PROCEDURE CANT_GO_THERE:

LINE/COL ERROR
-------- --------------------------------------
7/7      PLW-06002: Unreachable code
```

Given this warning, I can now go back to that line of code, determine why it is unreachable, and make the appropriate corrections.

---

### If You See a "No message file" Message

If you are running 10.1.0.2.0 on Windows, and try to reproduce what I showed in the section "A Quick Example" on page 735, you will see this message:

```
7/7      PLW-06002: Message 6002 not found;
            No message file for product=plsql, facility=PLW
```

The problem is that Oracle didn't ship the message file, *plwus.msb*, with the Oracle Database 10g software until 10.1.0.3.0, and the download available on OTN is 10.1.0.2.0. If you encounter this problem, you will need to contact Oracle Support to obtain this file (reference Bug 3680132) and place it in the *\plsql\mesg* subdirectory. You will then be able to see the actual warning message.

---

## Enabling Compile-Time Warnings

Oracle allows you to turn compile-time warnings on and off, and also to specify the type of warnings that interest you. There are three categories of warnings:

*Severe*
> Conditions that could cause unexpected behavior or actual wrong results, such as aliasing problems with parameters.

*Performance*

Conditions that could cause performance problems, such as passing a VARCHAR2 value to a NUMBER column in an UPDATE statement.

*Informational*

Conditions that do not affect performance or correctness, but that you might want to change to make the code more maintainable.

Oracle lets you enable/disable compile-time warnings for a specific category, for all categories, and even for specific, individual warnings. You can do this with either the ALTER DDL command or the DBMS_WARNING built-in package.

To turn on compile-time warnings in your system as a whole, issue this command:

```
ALTER SYSTEM SET PLSQL_WARNINGS='string'
```

The following command, for example, turns on compile-time warnings in your system for all categories:

```
ALTER SYSTEM SET PLSQL_WARNINGS='ENABLE:ALL';
```

This is a useful setting to have in place during development because it will catch the largest number of potential issues in your code.

To turn on compile-time warnings in your session for severe problems only, issue this command:

```
ALTER SESSION SET PLSQL_WARNINGS='ENABLE:SEVERE';
```

And if you want to alter compile-time warnings settings for a particular, already compiled program, you can issue a command like this:

```
ALTER PROCEDURE hello COMPILE PLSQL_WARNINGS='ENABLE:ALL' REUSE SETTINGS;
```

 Make sure to include REUSE SETTINGS to make sure that all *other* settings (such as the optimization level) are not affected by the ALTER command.

You can tweak your settings with a very high level of granularity by combining different options. For example, suppose that I want to see all performance-related issues, that I will not concern myself with server issues for the moment, and that I would like the compiler to treat *PLW-05005: function exited without a RETURN* as a compile error. I would then issue this command:

```
ALTER SESSION SET PLSQL_WARNINGS=
  'DISABLE:SEVERE'
,'ENABLE:PERFORMANCE'
,'ERROR:05005';
```

I especially like this "treat as error" option. Consider the *PLW-05005: function returns without value* warning. If I leave PLW-05005 simply as a warning, then when I compile my no_return function, shown below, the program does compile, and I *can* use it in my application.

```
SQL> CREATE OR REPLACE FUNCTION no_return
  2     RETURN VARCHAR2
  3  AS
  4  BEGIN
  5     DBMS_OUTPUT.PUT_LINE (
  6        'Here I am, here I stay');
  7  END no_return;
  8  /
SP2-0806: Function created with compilation warnings

SQL> SHOW ERR
Errors for FUNCTION NO_RETURN:

LINE/COL ERROR
-------- ----------------------------------------------------------------
1/1      PLW-05005: function NO_RETURN returns without value at line 7
```

If I now alter the treatment of that error with the ALTER SESSION command shown above and then recompile no_return, the compiler stops me in my tracks:

```
Warning: Procedure altered with compilation errors
```

By the way, I could also change the settings for that particular program only, to flag this warning as a "hard" error with a command like this:

```
ALTER PROCEDURE no_return COMPILE PLSQL_WARNINGS = 'error:6002' REUSE SETTINGS
/
```

You can, in each of these variations of the ALTER command, also specify ALL as a quick and easy way to refer to all compile-time warnings categories, as in:

```
ALTER SESSION SET PLSQL_WARNINGS='ENABLE:ALL';
```

Oracle also provides the DBMS_WARNING package, which provides the same capabilities to set and change compile-time warning settings through a PL/SQL API. DBMS_WARNING also goes beyond the ALTER command, allowing you to make changes to those warning controls that you care about while leaving all the others intact. You can also easily restore the original settings when you're done.

DBMS_WARNING was designed to be used in install scripts in which you might need to disable a certain warning, or treat a warning as an error, for individual program units being compiled. You might not have any control over the scripts surrounding those for which you are responsible. Each script's author should be able to set the warning settings he wants, while inheriting a broader set of settings from a more global scope.

## Some Handy Warnings

In the following sections, I present a subset of all the warnings Oracle has implemented, with an example of the type of code that will elicit the warning and some interesting behavior (where present) in the way that Oracle has implemented compile-time warnings.

To see the full list of warnings available in any given Oracle version, search for the "PLW" section of the *Error Messages* book of the Oracle documentation set, available at *http://tahiti.oracle.com*.

### PLW-05000: Mismatch in NOCOPY qualification between specification and body

The NOCOPY compiler hint tells the Oracle database that, if possible, you would like it to *not* make a copy of your IN OUT arguments. This can improve the performance of programs that pass large data structures, such as collections or CLOBs.

You need to include the NOCOPY hint in both the specification and the body of your program (relevant for packages and object types). If the hint is not present in both, the database will apply whatever is specified in the specification.

Here is an example of code that will generate this warning:

```
/* File on web: plw5000.sql */
PACKAGE plw5000
IS
   TYPE collection_t IS
      TABLE OF VARCHAR2 (100);

   PROCEDURE proc (
      collection_in IN OUT NOCOPY
         collection_t);
END plw5000;

PACKAGE BODY plw5000
IS
   PROCEDURE proc (
      collection_in IN OUT
         collection_t)
   IS
   BEGIN
      DBMS_OUTPUT.PUT_LINE ('Hello!');
   END proc;
END plw5000;
```

Compile-time warnings will display as follows:

```
SQL> SHOW ERRORS PACKAGE BODY plw5000
Errors for PACKAGE BODY PLW5000:

LINE/COL ERROR
-------- ----------------------------------------------------------------
3/20     PLW-05000: mismatch in NOCOPY qualification between specification
         and body

3/20     PLW-07203: parameter 'COLLECTION_IN' may benefit from use of the
         NOCOPY compiler hint
```

### PLW-05001: Previous use of 'string' (at line string) conflicts with this use

This warning will make itself heard when you have declared more than one variable or constant with the same name. It can also pop up if the parameter list of a program defined in a package specification is different from that of the definition in the package body.

You may be saying to yourself: I've seen that error before, but it is a compilation error, not a warning. And, in fact, you are right, in that the following program simply will not compile:

```
/* File on web: plw5001.sql */
PROCEDURE plw5001
IS
   a    BOOLEAN;
   a    PLS_INTEGER;
BEGIN
   a := 1;
   DBMS_OUTPUT.put_line ('Will not compile');
END plw5001;
```

You receive the following compile error: *PLS-00371: at most one declaration for 'A' is permitted in the declaration section.*

So why is there a *warning* for this situation? Consider what happens when I remove the assignment to the variable named a:

```
SQL> CREATE OR REPLACE PROCEDURE plw5001
  2  IS
  3     a    BOOLEAN;
  4     a    PLS_INTEGER;
  5  BEGIN
  6     DBMS_OUTPUT.put_line ('Will not compile?');
  7  END plw5001;
  8  /
Procedure created.
```

The program compiles! The database does not flag the PLS-00371 because I have not actually *used* either of the variables in my code. The PLW-05001 warning fills that gap by giving me a heads-up if I have declared, but not yet used, variables with the same name, as you can see here:

```
SQL> ALTER PROCEDURE plw5001 COMPILE plsql_warnings = 'enable:all';
SP2-0805: Procedure altered with compilation warnings

SQL> SHOW ERRORS
Errors for PROCEDURE PLW5001:

LINE/COL ERROR
-------- ----------------------------------------------------------------
4/4      PLW-05001: previous use of 'A' (at line 3) conflicts with this use
```

### PLW-05003: Same actual parameter (string and string) at IN and NOCOPY may have side effects

When you use NOCOPY with an IN OUT parameter, you are asking PL/SQL to pass the argument by reference, rather than by value. This means that any changes to the argument are made immediately to the variable in the outer scope. "By value" behavior (NOCOPY is not specified or the compiler ignores the NOCOPY hint), on the other hand, dictates that changes within the program are made to a local copy of the IN OUT parameter. When the program terminates, these changes are then copied to the actual parameter. (If an error occurs, the changed values are *not* copied back to the actual parameter.)

Use of the NOCOPY hint increases the possibility that you will run into the issue of argument aliasing, in which two different names point to the same memory location. Aliasing can be difficult to understand and debug; a compile-time warning that catches this situation will come in very handy.

Consider this program:

```
/* File on web: plw5003.sql */
PROCEDURE very_confusing (
   arg1    IN                VARCHAR2
 , arg2    IN OUT            VARCHAR2
 , arg3    IN OUT NOCOPY     VARCHAR2
 )
IS
BEGIN
   arg2 := 'Second value';
   DBMS_OUTPUT.put_line ('arg2 assigned, arg1 = ' || arg1);
   arg3 := 'Third value';
   DBMS_OUTPUT.put_line ('arg3 assigned, arg1 = ' || arg1);
END;
```

It's a simple enough program: pass in three strings, two of which are IN OUT; assign values to those IN OUT arguments; and display the value of the first IN argument's value after each assignment.

Now I will run this procedure, passing the very same local variable as the argument for each of the three parameters:

```
SQL> DECLARE
  2     str    VARCHAR2 (100) := 'First value';
  3  BEGIN
  4     DBMS_OUTPUT.put_line ('str before = ' || str);
  5     very_confusing (str, str, str);
  6     DBMS_OUTPUT.put_line ('str after = ' || str);
  7  END;
  8  /
str before = First value
arg2 assigned, arg1 = First value
arg3 assigned, arg1 = Third value
str after = Second value
```

Notice that while still running very_confusing, the value of the arg1 argument was not affected by the assignment to arg2. Yet when I assigned a value to arg3, the value of arg1 (an IN argument) was changed to "Third value"! Furthermore, when very_confusing terminated, the assignment to arg2 was applied to the str variable. Thus, when control returned to the outer block, the value of the str variable was set to "Second value", effectively writing over the assignment of "Third value".

As I said earlier, parameter aliasing can be very confusing. So, if you enable compile-time warnings, programs such as plw5003 may be revealed to have potential aliasing problems:

```
SQL> CREATE OR REPLACE PROCEDURE plw5003
  2  IS
  3     str   VARCHAR2 (100) := 'First value';
  4  BEGIN
  5     DBMS_OUTPUT.put_line ('str before = ' || str);
  6     very_confusing (str, str, str);
  7     DBMS_OUTPUT.put_line ('str after = ' || str);
  8  END plw5003;
  9  /
SP2-0804: Procedure created with compilation warnings

SQL> SHOW ERR

Errors for PROCEDURE PLW5003:
LINE/COL ERROR
-------- ---------------------------------------------------------------
6/4      PLW-05003: same actual parameter(STR and STR) at IN and NOCOPY
         may have side effects
6/4      PLW-05003: same actual parameter(STR and STR) at IN and NOCOPY
         may have side effects
```

### PLW-05004: Identifier string is also declared in STANDARD or is a SQL built-in

Many PL/SQL developers are unaware of the STANDARD package, and its implications for their PL/SQL code. For example, it is common to find programmers who assume that names like INTEGER and TO_CHAR are reserved words in the PL/SQL language. That is not the case. They are, respectively, a datatype and a function declared in the STANDARD package.

STANDARD is one of the two default packages of PL/SQL (the other is DBMS_STANDARD). Because STANDARD is a default package, you do not need to qualify references to datatypes like INTEGER, NUMBER, PLS_INTEGER, etc., with "STANDARD"—but you could, if you so desired.

PLW-5004 notifies you if you happen to have declared an identifier with the same name as an element in STANDARD (or a SQL built-in; most built-ins—but not all—are declared in STANDARD).

Consider this procedure definition:

```
     /* File on web: plw5004.sql
 1   PROCEDURE plw5004
 2   IS
 3      INTEGER   NUMBER;
 4
 5      PROCEDURE TO_CHAR
 6      IS
 7      BEGIN
 8         INTEGER := 10;
 9      END TO_CHAR;
10   BEGIN
11      TO_CHAR;
12   END plw5004;
```

Compile-time warnings for this procedure will display as follows:

```
LINE/COL ERROR
-------- -----------------------------------------------------------------
3/4      PLW-05004: identifier INTEGER is also declared in STANDARD
         or is a SQL builtin
5/14     PLW-05004: identifier TO_CHAR is also declared in STANDARD
         or is a SQL builtin
```

You should avoid reusing the names of elements defined in the STANDARD package unless you have a very specific reason to do so.

### PLW-05005: Function string returns without value at line string

This warning makes me happy. A function that does not return a value is a very badly designed program. This is a warning that I would recommend you ask the database to treat as an error with the "ERROR:5005" syntax in your PLSQL_WARNINGS setting.

You already saw one example of such a function—no_return. That was a very obvious chunk of code; there wasn't a single RETURN in the entire executable section. Your code will, of course, be more complex. The fact that a RETURN may not be executed could well be hidden within the folds of complex conditional logic.

At least in some of these situations, though, the database will *still* detect the problem. The following program demonstrates one of those situations:

```
 1 FUNCTION no_return (
 2    check_in IN BOOLEAN)
 3    RETURN VARCHAR2
 4 AS
 5 BEGIN
 6    IF check_in
 7    THEN
 8       RETURN 'abc';
 9    ELSE
10       DBMS_OUTPUT.put_line (
11       'Here I am, here I stay');
12    END IF;
13 END no_return;
```

Oracle has detected a branch of logic that will not result in the execution of a RETURN, so it flags the program with a warning. The *plw5005.sql* file on the book's web site contains even more complex conditional logic, demonstrating that the warning is raised for less trivial code structures as well.

### PLW-06002: Unreachable code

The Oracle database now performs static (compile-time) analysis of your program to determine if any lines of code in your program will never be reached during execution. This is extremely valuable feedback to receive, but you may find that the compiler warns you of this problem on lines that do not, at first glance, seem to be unreachable. In fact, Oracle notes in the description of the action to take for this error that you should "disable the warning if much code is made unreachable intentionally and the warning message is more annoying than helpful." I will come back to this issue at the end of the section.

You already saw an example of this compile-time warning in the section "A Quick Example" on page 735. Now consider the following code:

```
    /* File on web: plw6002.sql */
1   PROCEDURE plw6002
2   AS
3      l_checking BOOLEAN := FALSE;
4   BEGIN
5      IF l_checking
6      THEN
7         DBMS_OUTPUT.put_line ('Never here...');
8      ELSE
9         DBMS_OUTPUT.put_line ('Always here...');
10        GOTO end_of_function;
11     END IF;
12     <<end_of_function>>
13     NULL;
14  END plw6002;
```

In Oracle Database 10*g* and later, you will see the following compile-time warnings for this program:

```
LINE/COL  ERROR
--------  ------------------------------
5/7       PLW-06002: Unreachable code
7/7       PLW-06002: Unreachable code
13/4      PLW-06002: Unreachable code
```

I see why line 7 is marked as unreachable: l_checking is set to FALSE, and so line 7 can never run. But why is line 5 marked "unreachable." It seems as though, in fact, that code would *always* be run! Furthermore, line 13 will always be run as well because the GOTO will direct the flow of execution to that line through the label. Yet it is tagged as unreachable.

The reason for this behavior is that prior to Oracle Database 11*g* the unreachable code warning is generated after optimization of the code. In Oracle Database 11*g*, the analysis of unreachable code is much cleaner and more helpful.

The compiler does *not* give you false positives; when it says that line *N* is unreachable, it is telling you that the line truly will never be executed, accurately reflecting the optimized code.

There are currently scenarios of unreachable code that are *not* flagged by the compiler. Here is one example:

```
/* File on web: plw6002.sql */
FUNCTION plw6002 RETURN VARCHAR2
AS
BEGIN
   RETURN NULL;
   DBMS_OUTPUT.put_line ('Never here...');
END plw6002;
```

Certainly, the call to DBMS_OUTPUT.PUT_LINE is unreachable, but the compiler does not currently detect that state. This scenario, and others like it, may be covered in future releases of the compiler.

### PLW-07203: Parameter 'string' may benefit from use of the NOCOPY compiler hint

As mentioned earlier in relation to PLW-05005, use of NOCOPY with complex, large IN OUT parameters can improve the performance of programs under certain conditions. This warning will flag programs whose IN OUT parameters might benefit from NOCOPY. Here is an example of such a program:

```
/* File on web: plw7203.sql */
PACKAGE plw7203
IS
   TYPE collection_t IS TABLE OF VARCHAR2 (100);

   PROCEDURE proc (collection_in IN OUT collection_t);
END plw7203;
```

This is another one of those warnings that will be generated for lots of programs and may become a nuisance. The warning/recommendation is certainly valid, but for most programs the impact of this optimization will not be noticeable. Furthermore, you are unlikely to switch to NOCOPY without making other changes in your code to handle situations where the program terminates before completing, possibly leaving your data in an uncertain state.

### PLW-07204: Conversion away from column type may result in suboptimal query plan

This warning will surface when you call a SQL statement from within PL/SQL and rely on implicit conversions within that statement. Here is an example:

```
/* File on web: plw7204.sql */
FUNCTION plw7204
```

```
      RETURN PLS_INTEGER
   AS
      l_count PLS_INTEGER;
   BEGIN
      SELECT COUNT(*) INTO l_count
        FROM employees
       WHERE salary = '10000';
      RETURN l_count;
   END plw7204;
```

The salary column is numeric, but I am comparing it to a string value. The optimizer may well disable the use of an index on salary because of this implicit conversion.

Related tightly to this warning is *PLW-7202: bind type would result in conversion away from column type*.

### PLW-06009: Procedure "string" OTHERS handler does not end in RAISE or RAISE_APPLICATION_ERROR (Oracle Database 11g)

This warning (added in Oracle Database 11g) appears when your OTHERS exception handler does not execute some form of RAISE (re-raise the same exception or raise another) and does not call RAISE_APPLICATION_ERROR. In other words, there is a good possibility that you are "swallowing" up the error and ignoring it. Under certain, fairly rare circumstances, ignoring errors is the appropriate thing to do. Usually, however, you will want to pass an exception back to the enclosing block.

Here is an example:

```
   /* File on web: plw6009.sql */
   FUNCTION plw6009
      RETURN PLS_INTEGER
   AS
      l_count    PLS_INTEGER;
   BEGIN
      SELECT COUNT ( * ) INTO l_count
        FROM dual WHERE 1 = 2;

      RETURN l_count;
   EXCEPTION
      WHEN OTHERS
      THEN
         DBMS_OUTPUT.put_line ('Error!');
         RETURN 0;
   END plw6009;
```

# Testing PL/SQL Programs

I get great satisfaction out of creating new things, and that is one of the reasons I so enjoy writing software. I love to take an interesting idea or challenge, and then come up with a way of using the PL/SQL language to meet that challenge.

I have to admit, though, that I don't really like having to take the time to test my software (nor do I like to write documentation for it). I do it, but I don't really do enough of it. And I have this funny feeling that I am not alone. The overwhelming reality is that developers generally perform an inadequate number of inadequate tests and figure that if the users don't find a bug, there is no bug. Why does this happen? Let me count the ways....

*Psychology of success and failure*

We are so focused on getting our code to work correctly that we generally shy away from bad news—or from taking the chance of getting bad news. Better to do some cursory testing, confirm that everything seems to be working OK, and then wait for others to find bugs, if there are any (as if there were any doubt).

*Deadline pressures*

Hey, it's Internet time! Time to market determines all. We need everything yesterday, so let's release pre-beta software as production and let our users test/suffer through our applications.

*Management's lack of understanding*

IT management is notorious for not really understanding the software development process. If we aren't given the time and authority to write (and I mean "write" in the broadest sense, including testing, documentation, refinement, etc.) code properly, we will always end up with buggy junk that no one wants to admit ownership of.

*Overhead of setting up and running tests*

If it's a big deal to write and run tests, they won't get done. We'll decide that we don't have time; after all, there is always something else to work on. One consequence of this is that more and more of the testing is handed over to the QA department, if there is one. That transfer of responsibility is, on the one hand, positive. Professional quality assurance professionals can have a tremendous impact on application quality. Yet developers must take and exercise responsibility for unit testing their own code; otherwise, the testing/QA process is much more frustrating and extended.

The end result is that software almost universally needs more—much more—testing and fewer bugs. How can we test more effectively in the world of PL/SQL?

In the following sections, I answer that question by first taking a look at what I would consider to be a weak but typical manual testing process. Then I will draw some conclusions about the key problems with manual testing. From there, I will take a look at automated testing options for PL/SQL code.

## Typical, Tawdry Testing Techniques

When testing the effect of a program, you need to identify what has been changed by that program: for example, the string returned by a function, the table updated by a procedure. Then you need to decide, in advance, what the correct behavior of the program for a given set of inputs and setup (a test case) would be. Then after the program has run, you must compare the actual results (what was changed by the program) to the expected values. If they match, your program worked. If there is a discrepancy, the program failed.

That's a very general description of testing; the critical question is how you go about defining all needed test cases and implementing the tests. Let's start by looking at what I would consider to be a fairly typical and typically bad approach to testing.

Say that I am writing a big application with lots of string manipulation. I've got a "hangnail" called SUBSTR; this function bothers me, and I need to take care of it. What's the problem? SUBSTR is great when you know the starting location of a string and the number of characters you want. In many situations, though, I have only the start and end locations, and then I have to compute the number of characters. But which formula is it?

```
end - start
end - start + 1
end - start - 1
```

I can never remember (the correct answer is end – start + 1), so I write a program that will remember it for me—the betwnstr function:

```
/* File on web: betwnstr.sf */
FUNCTION betwnstr (string_in IN VARCHAR2
                , start_in IN INTEGER
                , end_in IN INTEGER
)
    RETURN VARCHAR2
IS
BEGIN
    RETURN (SUBSTR ( string_in,  start_in,  end_in - start_in + 1));
END betwnstr;
```

That was easy—and I am very certain that this formula is correct—I reverse engineered it from an example. Still, I should test it. The problem is that I am under a lot of pressure and this is just one little utility among many other programs I must write and test. So I throw together a crude "test script" built around DBMS_OUTPUT.PUT_LINE, and run it:

```
BEGIN
    DBMS_OUTPUT.put_line (NVL (betwnstr ('abcdefg', 3, 5)
                            , '**Really NULL**'));
END;

cde
```

It worked...how exciting! But I should run more tests than that one. Let's change the end value to 500. It should return the rest of the string, just like SUBSTR would:

```
BEGIN
    DBMS_OUTPUT.put_line (NVL (betwnstr ('abcdefg', 3, 500)
```

```
                               , '**Really NULL**'));
   END;

   cdefg
```

It worked again! This is my lucky day. Now, let's be sure to make sure it handles NULLs properly:

```
BEGIN
   DBMS_OUTPUT.put_line (NVL (betwnstr ('abcdefg', NULL, 5)
                               , '**Really NULL**'));
END;

**Really NULL**) );
```

Three in a row. This is one very correct function, wouldn't you say? No, you are probably (or, at the very least, *should* be) shaking your head and saying to yourself: "That's just pitiful. You haven't scratched the surface of all the scenarios you need to test. Why, you didn't even change the value of the first argument. Plus, every time you change your input values you threw away your last test."

Good points, all. So rather than just willy-nilly throw up some different argument values, I will come up with a list of test cases whose behavior I want to verify:

| String | Start | End | Result |
|---|---|---|---|
| abcdefg | 1 | 3 | abc |
| abcdefg | 0 | 3 | abc |
| <anything> | NULL | NOT NULL | NULL |
| <anything> | NOT NULL | NULL | NULL |
| NULL | <anything> | <anything> | NULL |
| abcdefg | Positive number | Smaller than start | NULL |
| abcdefg | 1 | Number larger than length of string | abcdefg |

From this grid, I will then construct a simple test script like the following:

```
/* File on web: betwnstr.tst */
BEGIN
   DBMS_OUTPUT.put_line ('Test 1: ' || betwnstr (NULL, 3, 5));
   DBMS_OUTPUT.put_line ('Test 2: ' || betwnstr ('abcdefgh', 0, 5));
   DBMS_OUTPUT.put_line ('Test 3: ' || betwnstr ('abcdefgh', 3, 5));
   DBMS_OUTPUT.put_line ('Test 4: ' || betwnstr ('abcdefgh', -3, -5));
   DBMS_OUTPUT.put_line ('Test 5: ' || betwnstr ('abcdefgh', NULL, 5));
   DBMS_OUTPUT.put_line ('Test 6: ' || betwnstr ('abcdefgh', 3, NULL));
   DBMS_OUTPUT.put_line ('Test 7: ' || betwnstr ('abcdefgh', 3, 100));
END;
```

And now whenever I need to test betwnstr, I simply run this script and check the results; based on that initial implementation, they are:

```
SQL> @betwnstr.tst
Test 1:
Test 2: abcdef
Test 3: cde
Test 4:
Test 5:
Test 6:
Test 7: cdefgh
```

Ah..."check the results." So easy to say, but how easy is it to do? Did this test work properly? I have to go through the results line by line and compare them to my grid. Plus, if I am going to test this code thoroughly, I will probably have more than 30 test cases (what about *negative* start and end values?). It will take me at least several minutes to scan the results of my test. This is a ridiculously simple piece of code. The thought of extending this technique to any "real" code is frightening. Imagine if my program modified two tables and returned two OUT arguments. I might have hundreds of test cases, plus non-trivial setup tasks and the challenge of figuring out how to make sure the contents of my tables are correct.

Yet this is the approach many developers take routinely when "testing" their code. To conclude, almost all the code testing we do suffers from these key drawbacks:

*Hand-written test code*

> We write the test code ourselves, which severely limits how much testing we can do. Who has time to write all that code?

*Incomplete testing*

> If we were completely honest with ourselves, we would be forced to admit that we don't actually *test* most of our code. Rather, we try a few of the most obvious cases to reassure ourselves that the program is not obviously broken. That's a far cry from actual testing.

*Throw-away testing*

> Our tests are not repeatable. We are so focused on getting the program to work *right now*, that we can't think ahead and realize that we—or someone else—will have to do the same tests, over and over again, in the future.

*Manual verification*

> If we rely on our own eyes and observational skills to verify test results, it will take way too much time and likely result in erroneous conclusions. We are so desperate for our programs to work that we will overlook minor issues or apparent failures, and explain them away.

*Testing after development*

> I believe that most programmers say to themselves "When I am done writing my program, I will test it." Sounds so reasonable, does it not? And yet it is a fatally flawed principle. First, we are never "done" writing our programs. So we inevitably run out of time for testing. Second, and more troubling, if we think about testing only after we finish implementing our program, we will subconsciously choose to

run tests that are most likely to succeed, and avoid those that we are pretty sure will cause problems. It's the way our brains are wired.

Clearly, if we are going to test effectively and thoroughly, we will need to take a different path. We need a way to define our tests so that they can easily be maintained over time. We need to be able to easily run our tests and then, most importantly, determine without lengthy analysis the outcome: success or failure. And we need to figure out a way to run tests without having to write enormous amounts of test code.

In the following sections, I first offer some advice on how to approach testing your code. Then I examine automated testing options for PL/SQL developers, with a focus on utPLSQL and Quest Code Tester for Oracle.

## General Advice for Testing PL/SQL Code

Whatever tool you choose to help you test, you should take the following into consideration if you hope to successfully transform the quality of your testing:

*Commit to testing*
> The most important change to make is inside our heads. We have to change our perspective from "I sure hope this program will work." to "I want to be able to *prove* that my program works." Once you commit to testing, you will find yourself writing more modular code that can be more easily tested. You will also then have to find tools to help you test more efficiently.

*Get those test cases out of your head before you start writing your program—and onto a piece of paper or into a tool that manages your tests*
> The important thing is to externalize your belief of what needs to be tested; otherwise, you are likely to lose or ignore that information. On Monday, when I start to build my program, I can easily think of 25 different scenarios (requirements) that need to be covered (implemented). Three days later I have run out of time, so I switch to testing. Suddenly and very oddly, I can only remember 5 test cases (the most obvious ones). If you make a list of your known test cases at the very beginning of the development process, you are much more likely to remember and verify them.

*Don't worry about 100% test coverage*
> I doubt that there has ever been a non-trivial software program that was *completely* tested. You should not set as your objective 100% coverage of all possible test cases. It is very unlikely to happen and will serve only to discourage you. The most important thing about testing is to get started. So what if you only implement 10% of your test cases in phase 1? That's 10% more than you were testing before. And once your test cases (and associated code) are in place, it is much easier to add to them.

*Integrate testing into development*

You cannot afford to put off testing until after you are "done" writing your software. Instead, you should think about testing as early as possible in the process. List out your test cases, construct your test code, and then run those tests *as you implement, debug, and enhance your program.* After every change, run your test again to verify that you are making progress. If you need a fancy name, a.k.a., a *methodology*, to be convinced about the value of this approach, check out the widely-adopted (in object-oriented circles) Test Driven Development (TDD).

*Get those regression tests in place*

All of the above, plus the tools described below, will help you build a *regression test.* This kind of test is intended to make sure that your code does not regress or move backwards. It's terribly embarrassing when we roll out V2 of our product and half the features of V1 are broken. "How can this happen?" wail our users. And if we gave them an honest answer, they would run screaming from the meeting room, because that answer would be: "Sorry, but we didn't have time to write a regression test. That means when we make a change in our spaghetti code we really don't have any idea what might have been broken." This is unacceptable, yes? Once you have a regression test in place, though, you can make changes and roll out new versions with confidence.

## Automated Testing Options for PL/SQL

Today, PL/SQL developers can choose from the following automated frameworks and tools for testing their code:

*utPLSQL*

The first framework for PL/SQL, utPLSQL is essentially the "JUnit for PL/SQL." It implements Extreme Programming testing principles, and automatically runs your handwritten test code, verifying results. The next section demonstrates a session with utPLSQL. For full details visit *http://utplsql.sourceforge.net.*

*PLUTO*

PLUTO is similar to utPLSQL, but it is implemented using Oracle object types. For more information see *http://code.google.com/p/pluto-test-framework.*

*dbFit*

This framework follows a very different approach to specifying tests: tabular scripts. dbFit "is a set of FIT fixtures which enables FIT/FitNesse tests to execute directly against a database." For more information visit *http://gojko.net/fitnesse/ dbfit.*

*Quest Code Tester for Oracle*

This commercial testing tool offers the highest level of test automation. It generates test code from UI-specified expected behaviors, runs that test, and displays the results using a red light-green light format. It is also demonstrated briefly in a later section. For full details check out *www.quest.com/code-tester-for-oracle.*

For both utPLSQL and Code Tester, I will build tests for the betwnstr function discussed earlier.

## Testing with utPLSQL

Way back in 1999, I discovered Extreme Programming and its associated testing frameworks, known generally as the XUnit family, with JUnit being its most famous member. I resolved to build a similar framework in PL/SQL and the result was utPLSQL. While it does not fully automate the testing process, utPLSQL offers many helpful testing capabilities that will save you lots of time over writing your own manual testing scripts.

This section provides a brief introduction to utPLSQL via a simple example. For all the details and software, visit *http://utplsql.sourceforge.net*.

utPLSQL (and the other Xunit tools) follows a cooperative paradigm: if you cooperate with utPLSQL by following its naming conventions and calling its backend API for test verification (a.k.a., *assertions*) in your test code, then utPLSQL will run your test code and automatically verify the results.

You do, however, have to build your own test package to be run by utPLSQL. Let's do that for betwnstr.

My test package specification is very simple. Using the "ut_" prefix of utPLSQL, I simply include programs to set up and tear down the test (even if they don't do anything, they need to be present), plus one procedure for each subprogram I want to test. If I am testing a schema-level function like betwnstr, then the test package contains just one test procedure:

```
/* File on web: ut_betwnstr.pks */
PACKAGE ut_betwnstr
IS
   PROCEDURE ut_setup;
   PROCEDURE ut_teardown;
   PROCEDURE ut_BETWNSTR;
END ut_betwnstr;
```

Inside the test package body, I need to implement each test case in the ut_betwnstr procedure. Here is the implementation of what I refer to as the "normal" test case: start and end values within the boundaries of the string:

```
    /* File on web: ut_betwnstr.pkb */
 1  PROCEDURE ut_betwnstr
 2  IS
 3     check_this      VARCHAR2 (32767);
 4     against_this    VARCHAR2 (32767);
 5  BEGIN
 6     /* "Normal usage" test case. Start and end values inside the string. */
 7
 8     /* Call program with to get actual results. */
 9     check_this :=
10        betwnstr (string_in      => 'abcdefgh'
11                 , start_in       => 3
```

```
12                    , end_in          => 5
13                    );
14
15      /* Define the "control" or expected value for this test case. */
16      against_this := 'cde';
17
18      /* Now use the assertion package to see if they are equal,
19          and record the results. */
20      utassert.eq ('Normal Usage', check_this, against_this);
21   END;
```

Here is a description of the significant lines of code:

| Line(s) | Description |
|---------|-------------|
| 3–4 | Declare two variables to hold the actual result (check_this) against the expected result (against_this). |
| 9–13 | Call betwnstr with input values that match the "normal" test case. |
| 16 | Set the expected or control value. |
| 20 | Use utPLSQL's assertion package, utassert, to *assert* that the expected value matches the actual value. If your assertion is correct, then the program worked and SUCCESS is recorded. Otherwise, FAILURE is the result for this test. |

So you build each test case in this way, compile the package, and then you run the test as follows (results are shown for a set of test cases, not demonstrated above):

```
SQL> EXEC utplsql.test ('betwnstr')
>   FFFFFFF   AA      III  L      U      U RRRRR    EEEEEE
>   F         A  A    I    L      U      U R      R E
>   F          A  A   I    L      U      U R        R E
>   F         A    A  I    L      U      U R        R E
>   FFFF      A    A  I    L      U      U RRRRRR  EEEE
>   F         AAAAAAAA I    L      U      U R    R   E
>   F         A    A  I    L      U      U R      R E
>   F         A    A  I    L       U    U R      R E
>   F         A    A  III  LLLLLLL  UUU    R        R EEEEEEE
>  .
>   FAILURE: "betwnstr"
>  .
> Individual Test Case Results:
>
FAILURE - EQ "Start at 0" Expected "abc" and got "abcd"
SUCCESS - EQ "Normal Usage" Expected "cde" and got "cde"
SUCCESS - ISNULL "null start" Expected "" and got ""
SUCCESS - ISNULL "null end" Expected "" and got ""
SUCCESS - ISNULL "null string" Expected "" and got ""
SUCCESS - ISNULL "big start small end" Expected "" and got ""
FAILURE - EQ "Negative values" Expected "def" and got ""
SUCCESS - EQ "end past string" Expected "abcdefgh" and got "abcdefgh"
```

Notice that you are shown the result for each test case. So if one of them failed, you can focus in on that case, more quickly identify the bug, and then run the test again—and again, until you get:

```
SQL> EXEC utplsql.test ('betwnstr')
.
>    SSSS   U    U  CCC    CCC  EEEEEEE  SSSS    SSSS
>    S    S U    U C    C C    C E        S    S  S    S
>    S       U    U C    C  C C    C E        S        S
>    S       U    U C       C     E        S        S
>    SSSS    U    U C       C     EEEE     SSSS    SSSS
>        S  U    U C       C     E            S        S
>        S U    U C    C C    C E            S        S
>    S    S U    U C    C C    C E        S    S  S    S
>    SSSS    UUU   CCC    CCC  EEEEEEE  SSSS    SSSS
```

This is a very brief introduction to utPLSQL, but you can see that this framework automatically runs my test, and then tells me whether or not my test succeeded. It even reports on individual test cases.

utPLSQL doesn't take all the pain out of building, but it provides a standardized process and a test harness from which you can run your tests and easily view results.

## Testing with Quest Code Tester for Oracle

I designed and built the first version of utPLSQL (it is now an independent, open source project) and yet, ironically and a bit hypocritically, I never really used utPLSQL very much. The reason was simple: I didn't have the time to build what would have to be very large test packages. So for most of my testing, I continued building crude scripts that relied on manual execution and verification. Bad boy!

In 2005, I accepted that I would never be disciplined enough to write comprehensive utPLSQL packages. Furthermore, I became fed up with my own hypocrisy and decided to make a second attempt at building an automated testing tool. So I asked myself a question: what kind of tool would allow lazy, undisciplined me to actually do lots of testing? And the answer was clear: a tool that generates test code, rather than forces me to write it. With that insight, I went back to the drawing board, and came up with designs for what eventually became Quest Code Tester for Oracle.

With Quest Code Tester, you describe the expected behavior of your program through a graphical interface. These descriptions are then stored in a set of Oracle tables (a true testing repository, which utPLSQL lacks). You can analyze the quality of testing by running reports against these tables, but, much more importantly, Code Tester generates test code from these descriptions. You may still need to write some code to set up the contents of tables and collections and so forth, but the vast majority of the test code is managed by Code Tester and regenerated whenever you change your test definition.

Figure 20-2 offers a screenshot of Test Builder, the main window for describing expected behavior. I have created eight test cases. Each test case has a set of inputs and outcomes. I press the Run button, and Code Tester saves this information to the repository, generates the test code, runs the test, and shows me the results, as shown in Figure 20-3.

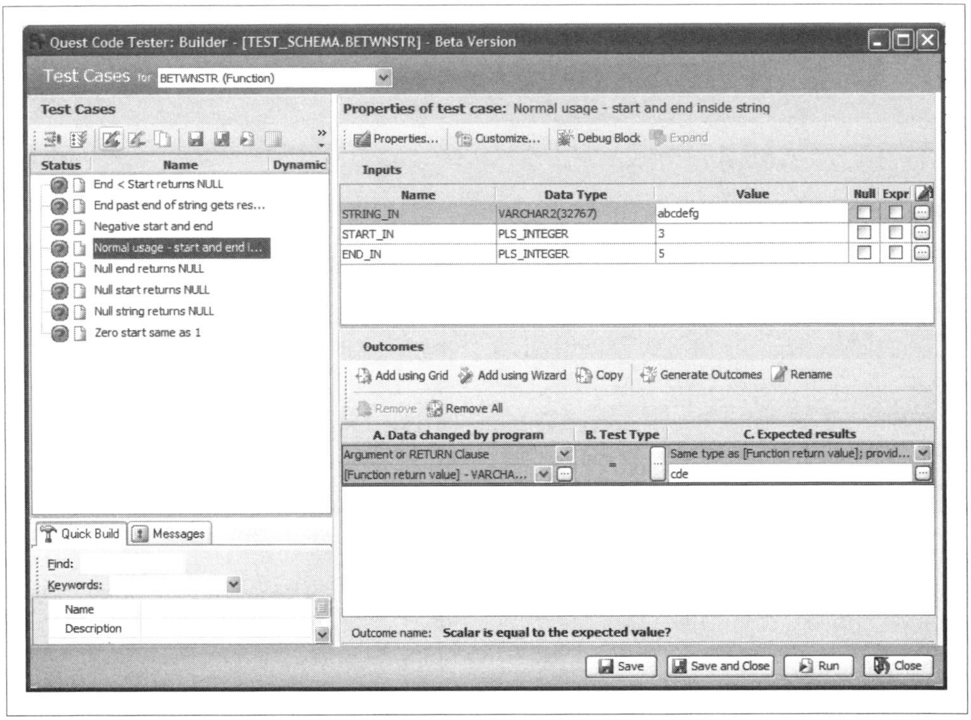

*Figure 20-2. List of defined test cases within Test Builder*

You can even ask Code Tester to generate test cases, based on sets of random values, lists of values, or queries, as shown in Figure 20-4.

You can also export test definitions to a file. You will find the test definition for betwnstr in the *Q##BETWNSTR.qut* file.

As you can see, Quest Code Tester is a rich and powerful testing tool, which takes on most of the heavy lifting required to test your programs. You can get more information about this product at *www.quest.com/code-tester-for-oracle*.

# Tracing PL/SQL Execution

You get your program to compile. You run your Quest Code Tester test definition—and it tells you that you have a failed test case: there's a bug somewhere in your program. How, then, do you find the cause of the problem? You can certainly dive right into your source code debugger (virtually all PL/SQL editors include visual debuggers with UI-settable breaks and watchpoints). You may, however, want to consider tracing execution of your program first.

Before exploring options for tracing PL/SQL code, let's first look at the difference between debugging and tracing. Developers often conflate these two processes into a

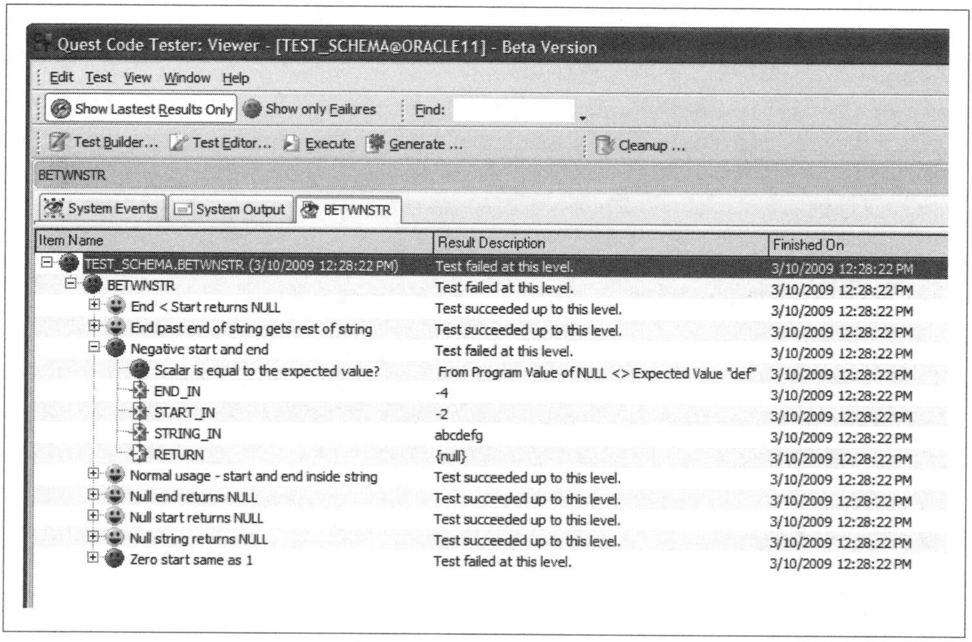

Figure 20-3. The Results Viewer shows the test results

single activity, yet they are quite different. To summarize, you first trace execution to obtain in-depth information about application behavior, helping you isolate the source of the problem; you then use a debugger to find the specific lines of code that cause a bug.

A key distinction between tracing and debugging is that tracing is a "batch" process, while debugging is interactive). That is, I turn on tracing and run my application code. When it is done, I open the trace log and use the information there to inform my debugging session. When I debug, I step through my code line by line (usually starting from a breakpoint that is close to the source of the problem, as indicated by trace data). A debug session is usually very time-consuming and tedious, so it makes an awful lot of sense to do everything I can to minimize the time spent debugging. Solid, proactive tracing will help me do this.

Every application should include programmer-defined tracing (also known as *instrumentation*). This section explores options for tracing, but before doing that, let's review some principles that we should follow when implementing tracing:

- Trace calls should remain in the code throughout all phases of development and deployment. In other words, do not insert trace calls while developing, and then remove them when the application goes into production. Tracing is often the best opportunity you have to understand what is happening in your application when it is run by a real, live user in a production environment.

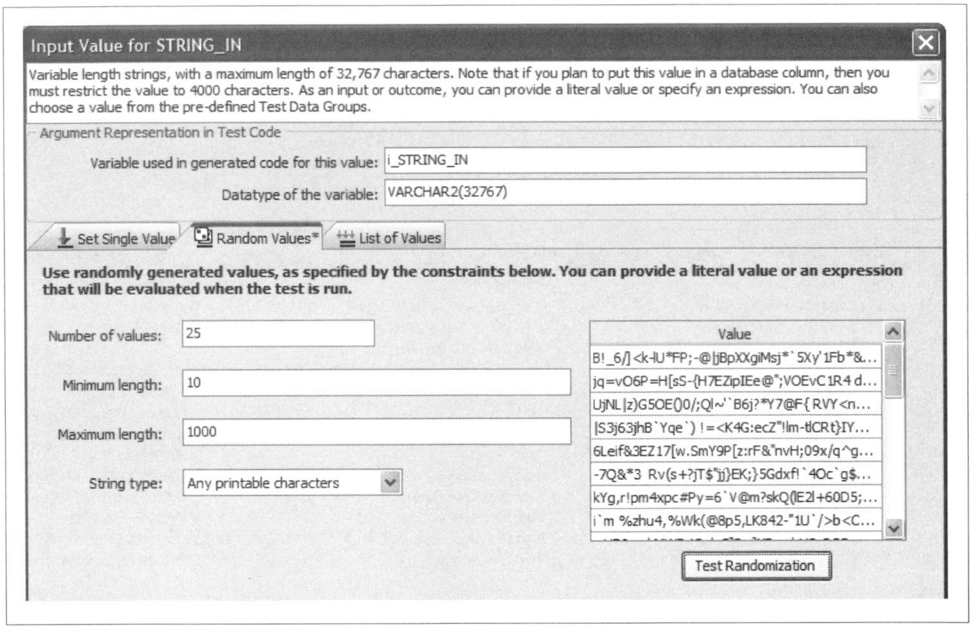

*Figure 20-4. Generating random values for boundary call testing*

- Keep the overhead of calls to your trace utility to an absolute minimum. When tracing is disabled, the user should see no impact on application performance.

- Do not call the DBMS_OUTPUT.PUT_LINE program directly within your application code as the trace mechanism. This built-in is not flexible or powerful enough for high-quality tracing.

- Make it easy for the end user to enable and disable tracing of your backend code. It should not require the intervention of the support organization to switch on tracing. Nor should you have to provide a different version of the application that includes tracing.

- If someone else has already created a trace utility that you can use (and meets these and your own principles), don't waste your time building your own trace mechanism.

Let's consider that last principle first. What tracing utilities already do exist?

*DBMS_APPLICATION_INFO*
This built-in package offers an API that allows applications to "register" their current execution status with the Oracle database. This tracing utility writes trace information to V$ dynamic views. It is described in the next section.

*Log4PLSQL*

This open source tracing framework is modeled after (and built upon) log4J, a very popular Java logging mechanism. You can get more information about Log4PLSQL at *http://log4plsql.sourceforge.net*.

*Quest Error Manager*

This is a freeware tool from Quest that you can use to raise, handle and log errors (discussed in Chapter 6), but also to trace program execution. I use the QEM trace facility in Quest Code Tester, and will demonstrate that usage in a later section.

*DBMS_TRACE*

This built-in utility traces the execution of PL/SQL code, but does not allow you to log as part of your trace any application data. You can, however, use this trace utility without making any changes to your source code. It is described in a later section.

 You can also use one of Oracle's built-in PL/SQL profilers to obtain information about the *performance* profile of each line and subprogram in your application. The profilers are discussed in Chapter 21.

## DBMS_APPLICATION_INFO

The DBMS_APPLICATION_INFO built-in package provides an API that allows applications to "register" their current execution status with the Oracle database. Once registered, information about the status of an application can be externally monitored through several of the V$ virtual tables. Using the V$ virtual tables as the trace repository is what distinguishes this package from all other tracing alternatives.

The DBMS_APPLICATION_INFO package is used to develop applications that can be monitored in various ways, including:

- Module usage (where do users spend their time in the application)
- Resource accounting by transaction and module
- End-user tracking and resource accounting in three-tier architectures
- Incremental recording of long-running process statistics

Applications registered using DBMS_APPLICATION_INFO can be analyzed for performance and resource consumption by DBAs and developers much more closely than is otherwise possible. This facilitates better application tuning as well as more accurate usage-based cost accounting.

Here are the subprograms in this package; all are procedures and none can be run in SQL:

| Name | Description |
|------|-------------|
| DBMS_APPLICATION_INFO.SET_MODULE | Sets name of module executing |
| DBMS_APPLICATION_INFO.SET_ACTION | Sets action within module |
| DBMS_APPLICATION_INFO.READ_MODULE | Reads module and action for current session |
| DBMS_APPLICATION_INFO.SET_CLIENT_INFO | Sets client information for session |
| DBMS_APPLICATION_INFO.READ_CLIENT_INFO | Reads client information for session |
| DBMS_APPLICATION_INFO.SET_SESSION_LONGOPS | Sets row in LONGOPS table (v8.0 only) |

For thorough coverage of this package, see the chapter from *Oracle Built-in Packages* (O'Reilly) that we have included on this book's web site.

Here is a demonstration of DBMS_APPLICATION_INFO:

```
/* File on web: dbms_application_info.sql */
PROCEDURE drop_dept (
    deptno_IN IN employees.department_id%TYPE
  , reassign_deptno_IN IN employees.department_id%TYPE
)
IS
   l_count PLS_INTEGER;
BEGIN
   DBMS_APPLICATION_INFO.SET_MODULE
      (module_name => 'DEPARTMENT FIXES'
      ,action_name => null);
   DBMS_APPLICATION_INFO.SET_ACTION (action_name => 'GET COUNT IN DEPT');

   SELECT COUNT(*)
     INTO l_count
     FROM employees
    WHERE department_id = deptno_IN;

   DBMS_OUTPUT.PUT_LINE ('Reassigning ' || l_count || ' employees');

   IF l_count > 0
   THEN
      DBMS_APPLICATION_INFO.SET_ACTION (action_name => 'REASSIGN EMPLOYEES');

      UPDATE employees
         SET department_id = reassign_deptno_IN
       WHERE department_id = deptno_IN;
   END IF;

   DBMS_APPLICATION_INFO.SET_ACTION (action_name => 'DROP DEPT');

   DELETE FROM departments WHERE department_id = deptno_IN;

   COMMIT;

   DBMS_APPLICATION_INFO.SET_MODULE(null,null);

EXCEPTION
```

```
      WHEN OTHERS THEN
          DBMS_APPLICATION_INFO.SET_MODULE(null,null);
    END drop_dept;
```

Notice in this example that DBMS_APPLICATION_INFO is called three times to distinguish between the three steps involved in the process of dropping the department. This gives a very fine granularity to the level at which the application can be tracked.

Be sure to set the action name to a name that can identify the current transaction or logical unit of work within the module.

When the transaction terminates, call DBMS_APPLICATION_INFO.SET_ACTION and pass a null value for the action_name parameter. This ensures that in case subsequent transactions do not register using DBMS_APPLICATION_INFO, they are not incorrectly counted as part of the current action. As in the example, if the program handles exceptions, the exception handler should probably reset the action information.

## Quest Error Manager Tracing

While Quest Error Manager (QEM) is intended primarily as a generalized exception management utility for PL/SQL applications, you can also use QEM to perform application tracing. I use QEM to implement tracing in the backend of Quest Code Tester. I demonstrate in this next section how I use QEM, and make it easy for users to start and stop tracing.

The following subprograms of the q$error_manager are helpful for tracing:

| Name | Description |
| --- | --- |
| set_trace | Turns tracing on or off |
| trace_enabled | Returns TRUE if tracing is currently enabled (turned on) |
| trace | Sends information from the application to the QEM log; you can specify a context (useful for filtering) and text (whatever information you want to trace) |
| totable | Directs trace output to the q$log table (default) |
| toscreen | Redirect trace output to the screen (default) |
| tofile | Directs output to the specified file using UTL_FILE |
| pl | Use instead of DBMS_OUTPUT.PUT_LINE to display strings, numbers, dates, CLOBs, and Booleans (not directly needed for tracing) |

Using the QEM API, I can enable tracing for all calls to trace as follows:

```
q$error_manager.set_tracing (TRUE);
```

In the next call to set_tracing, I enable tracing only for contexts that contain the string "balance":

```
q$error_manager.set_tracing (TRUE, 'balance');
```

As mentioned earlier, though, you don't want to have to instruct your users to execute PL/SQL statements to enable/disable tracing. Instead, you should build this capability directly into your user interface. In Quest Code Tester, for example, a user can start tracing by pressing Alt-Space to open the system menu and then choose "Start Tracing" (and "Stop Tracing"). They then see the window shown in Figure 20-5.

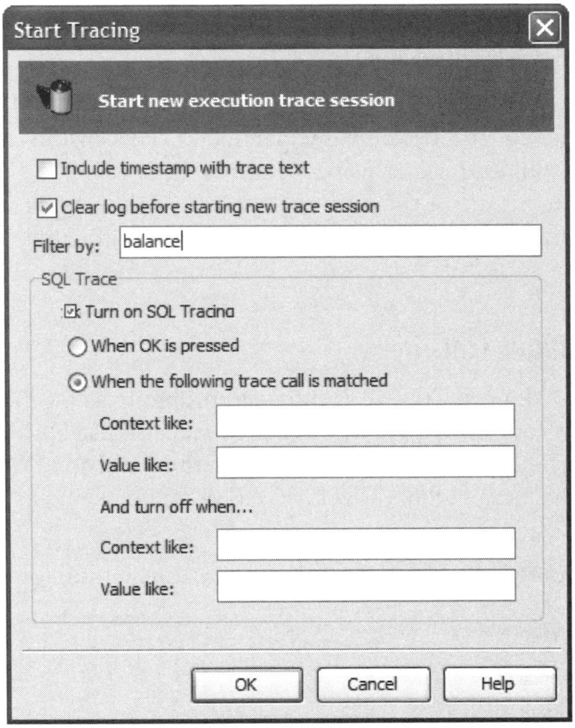

Figure 20-5. Start tracing from the Code Tester user interface

That covers enabling tracing. Now let's take a look at how I make calls to q$error_manager.trace in my stored programs.

I almost never call q$error_manager.trace directly. Instead, I nest it inside a call to q$error_manager.trace_enabled, as you see here:

```
IF q$error_manager.trace_enabled
THEN
   q$error_manager.trace (
        context_in => 'generate_test_code for program'
      , text_in    => qu_program_qp.name_for_id (l_program_key)
   );
END IF;
```

I call the trace program in this way to minimize the runtime overhead of tracing. The trace_enabled function returns the value of a single Boolean flag; it passes no actual arguments and finishes its work efficiently. If it returns TRUE, then the Oracle database will evaluate all the expressions in the parameter list and call the trace procedure, which will also make sure that tracing is enabled for this specific context.

If I call the trace procedure directly in my application code, then every time the runtime engine hits that line of code, it will evaluate all the actual arguments in the parameter list and call the trace procedure. The trace procedure will then make sure that tracing is enabled for this specific context. If tracing is disabled, then nothing more happens— but notice that the application will have wasted CPU cycles evaluating the arguments and passing them into trace.

Would a user ever notice the overhead of evaluating those arguments unnecessarily? Perhaps not, but as you add more and more trace calls to your code, you increase the probability of user impact. You should instead set as a habit and standard that you always hide your actual trace calls inside an IF statement that keeps overhead to a minimum.

## The DBMS_TRACE Facility

The DBMS_TRACE built-in package provides programs to start and stop PL/SQL tracing in a session. When tracing is turned on, the engine collects data as the program executes. The data is then written out to the Oracle server trace file.

The PL/SQL trace facility provides a trace file that shows you the specific steps executed by your code. DBMS_PROFILER and DBMS_HPROF (hierarchical profiler), which are described in Chapter 21, offer more comprehensive analyses of your application, including timing information and counts of the number of times a specific line was executed.

### Installing DBMS_TRACE

This package may not have been installed automatically with the rest of the built-in packages. To determine whether DBMS_TRACE is present, connect to SYS (or another account with SYSDBA privileges) and execute this command:

```
BEGIN DBMS_TRACE.CLEAR_PLSQL_TRACE; END;
```

If you see this error:

```
PLS-00201: identifier 'DBMS_TRACE.CLEAR_PLSQL_TRACE' must be declared
```

then you must install the package. Alternatively, you can use the DESCRIBE command in SQL*Plus.

To install DBMS_TRACE, remain connected as SYS (or another account with SYSDBA privileges), and run the following files in the order specified:

*$ORACLE_HOME/rdbms/admin/dbmspbt.sql*
*$ORACLE_HOME/rdbms/admin/prvtpbt.plb*

### DBMS_TRACE programs

The following subprograms are available in the DBMS_TRACE package:

| Name | Description |
| --- | --- |
| SET_PLSQL_TRACE | Starts PL/SQL tracing in the current session |
| CLEAR_PLSQL_TRACE | Stops the dumping of trace data for that session |
| PLSQL_TRACE_VERSION | Gets the major and minor version numbers of the DBMS_TRACE package |

To trace execution of your PL/SQL code, you must first start the trace with a call to:

```
DBMS_TRACE.SET_PLSQL_TRACE (trace_level INTEGER);
```

in your current session, where *trace_level* is one of the following values:

- Constants that determine which elements of your PL/SQL program will be traced:

```
DBMS_TRACE.trace_all_calls          constant INTEGER := 1;
DBMS_TRACE.trace_enabled_calls      constant INTEGER := 2;
DBMS_TRACE.trace_all_exceptions     constant INTEGER := 4;
DBMS_TRACE.trace_enabled_exceptions constant INTEGER := 8;
DBMS_TRACE.trace_all_sql            constant INTEGER := 32;
DBMS_TRACE.trace_enabled_sql        constant INTEGER := 64;
DBMS_TRACE.trace_all_lines          constant INTEGER := 128;
DBMS_TRACE.trace_enabled_lines      constant INTEGER := 256;
```

- Constants that control the tracing process:

```
DBMS_TRACE.trace_stop     constant INTEGER := 16384;
DBMS_TRACE.trace_pause    constant INTEGER := 4096;
DBMS_TRACE.trace_resume   constant INTEGER := 8192;
DBMS_TRACE.trace_limit    constant INTEGER := 16;
```

 By combining the DBMS_TRACE constants, you can enable tracing of multiple PL/SQL language features simultaneously. Note that the constants that control the tracing behavior (such as DBMS_TRACE.trace_pause) should not be used in combination with the other constants (such as DBMS_TRACE.trace_enabled_calls).

To turn on tracing from all programs executed in your session, issue this call:

```
DBMS_TRACE.SET_PLSQL_TRACE (DBMS_TRACE.trace_all_calls);
```

To turn on tracing for all exceptions raised during the session, issue this call:

```
DBMS_TRACE.SET_PLSQL_TRACE (DBMS_TRACE.trace_all_exceptions);
```

You then run your code. When you are done, you stop the trace session by calling:

```
DBMS_TRACE.CLEAR_PLSQL_TRACE;
```

You can then examine the contents of the trace file. The names of these files are generated by the database; you would usually look at the modification dates to figure out which file to examine. The location of the trace files is discussed in the later section, "Format of collected data" on page 766.

Note that you cannot use PL/SQL tracing with the shared server (formerly known as the multithreaded server, or MTS).

### Control trace file contents

The trace files produced by DBMS_TRACE can get *really* big. You can focus the output by enabling only specific programs for trace data collection. Note that you cannot use this approach with remote procedure calls.

To enable a specific program for tracing, you can alter the session to enable any programs that are created or replaced in the session. To take this approach, issue this command:

```
ALTER SESSION SET PLSQL_DEBUG=TRUE;
```

If you don't want to alter your entire session, you can recompile a specific program unit in debug mode as follows (not applicable to anonymous blocks):

```
ALTER [PROCEDURE | FUNCTION | PACKAGE BODY] program_name COMPILE DEBUG;
```

After you have enabled the programs you're interested in, issue the following call to initiate tracing just for those program units:

```
DBMS_TRACE.SET_PLSQL_TRACE (DBMS_TRACE.trace_enabled_calls);
```

You can also restrict the trace information to only those exceptions raised within enabled programs with this call:

```
DBMS_TRACE.SET_PLSQL_TRACE (DBMS_TRACE.trace_enabled_exceptions);
```

If you request tracing for all programs or exceptions and also request tracing only for enabled programs or exceptions, the request for "all" takes precedence.

### Pause and resume the trace process

The SET_PLSQL_TRACE procedure can do more than just determine which information will be traced. You can also request that the tracing process be paused and resumed. The following statement, for example, requests that no information be gathered until tracing is resumed:

```
DBMS_TRACE.SET_PLSQL_TRACE (DBMS_TRACE.trace_pause);
```

DBMS_TRACE will write a record to the trace file to show when tracing was paused and/or resumed.

Use the DBMS_TRACE.trace_limit constant to request that only the last 8,192 trace events of a run be preserved. This approach helps ensure that you can turn tracing on without overwhelming the database with trace activity. When the trace session ends, only the last 8,192 records are saved.

### Format of collected data

If you request tracing only for enabled program units, and the current program unit is not enabled, no trace data is written. If the current program unit is enabled, call tracing writes out the program unit type, name, and stack depth.

Exception tracing writes out the line number. Raising an exception records trace information on whether the exception is user-defined or predefined, and records the exception number in the case of predefined exceptions. If you raise a user-defined exception, you will always see an error code of 1.

Here is an example of the output from a trace of the showemps procedure:

```
***  1999.06.14.09.59.25.394
***  SESSION ID:(9.7) 1999.06.14.09.59.25.344
------------ PL/SQL TRACE INFORMATION -----------
Levels set :  1
Trace:  ANONYMOUS BLOCK: Stack depth = 1
Trace:   PROCEDURE SCOTT.SHOWEMPS: Call to entry at line 5 Stack depth = 2
Trace:    PACKAGE BODY SYS.DBMS_SQL: Call to entry at line 1 Stack depth = 3
Trace:     PACKAGE BODY SYS.DBMS_SYS_SQL: Call to entry at line 1 Stack depth = 4
Trace:     PACKAGE BODY SYS.DBMS_SYS_SQL: ICD vector index = 21 Stack depth = 4
Trace:    PACKAGE PLVPRO.P: Call to entry at line 26 Stack depth = 3
Trace:    PACKAGE PLVPRO.P: ICD vector index = 6 Stack depth = 3
Trace:    PACKAGE BODY PLVPRO.P: Call to entry at line 1 Stack depth = 3
Trace:    PACKAGE BODY PLVPRO.P: Call to entry at line 1 Stack depth = 3
Trace:     PACKAGE BODY PLVPRO.P: Call to entry at line 1 Stack depth = 4
```

# Debugging PL/SQL Programs

When you test a program, you find errors in your code. When you debug a program, you uncover the cause of an error and fix it. These are two very different processes and should not be confused. Once a program is tested, and bugs are uncovered, it is certainly the responsibility of the developer to fix those bugs. And so the debugging begins!

Many programmers find that debugging is by far the hardest part of programming. This difficulty often arises from the following factors:

*Lack of understanding of the problem being solved by the program*
Most programmers like to code. They tend to not like reading and understanding specifications, and will sometimes forgo this step so that they can quickly get down to writing code. The chance of a program meeting its requirements under these conditions is slim at best.

*Poor programming practice*
Programs that are hard to read (lack of documentation, too much documentation, inconsistent use of whitespace, bad choices for identifier names, etc.), programs that are not properly modularized, and programs that try to be too clever present a much greater challenge to debug than programs that are well designed and structured.

*The program simply contains too many errors*

Without the proper analysis and coding skills, your code will have a much higher occurrence of bugs. When you compile a program and get back five screens of compile errors, do you just want to scream and hide? It is easy to be so overwhelmed by your errors that you don't take the organized, step-by-step approach needed to fix those errors.

*Limited debugging skills*

There are many different approaches to uncovering the causes of your problems. Some approaches only make life more difficult for you. If you have not been trained in the best way to debug your code, you can waste many hours, raise your blood pressure, and upset your manager.

The following sections review the debugging methods that you will want to avoid at all costs, and then offer recommendations for more effective debugging strategies.

## The Wrong Way to Debug

As I present the various ways you shouldn't debug your programs, I expect that just about all of you will say to yourselves, "Well, that sure is obvious. Of course you shouldn't do that. I never do that."

And yet the very next time you sit down to do your work, you may very well follow some of these obviously horrible debugging practices.

If you happen to see little bits of yourself in the paragraphs that follow, I hope you will be inspired to mend your ways.

### Disorganized debugging

When faced with a bug, you become a whirlwind of frenzied activity. Even though the presence of an error indicates that you did not fully analyze the problem and figure out how the program should solve it, you do not now take the time to understand the program. Instead you place MESSAGE statements (in Oracle Forms) or SRW.MESSAGE statements (in Oracle Reports) or DBMS_OUTPUT.PUT_LINE statements (in stored modules) all over your program in the hopes of extracting more clues.

You do not save a copy of the program before you start making changes because that would take too much time; you are under a lot of pressure right now, and you are certain that the answer will pop right out at you. You will just remove your debug statements later.

You spend lots of time looking at information that is mostly irrelevant. You question everything about your program, even though most of it uses constructs you've employed successfully for years.

You skip lunch but make time for coffee, lots of coffee, because it is free and you want to make sure your concentration is at the most intense level possible. Even though you have no idea what is causing the problem, you think that maybe if you try this one change, it might help. You make the change and take several minutes to compile, generate, and run through the test case, only to find that the change didn't help. In fact, it seemed to cause another problem because you hadn't thought through the impact of the change on your application.

So you back out of that change and try something else in hopes that it might work. But several minutes later, you again find that it doesn't. A friend, noticing that your fingers are trembling, offers help. But you don't know where to start explaining the problem because you don't really know what is wrong. Furthermore, you are kind of embarrassed about what you've done so far (turned the program into a minefield of tracing statements) and realize you don't have a clean version to show your friend. So you snap at the best programmer in your group and call your family to let them know you aren't going to be home for dinner that night.

Why? Because you are determined to fix that bug!

### Irrational debugging

You execute your report, and it comes up empty. You spent the last hour making changes both in the underlying data structures and in the code that queries and formats the data. You are certain, however, that your modifications could not have made the report disappear.

You call your internal support hotline to find out if there is a network problem, even though File Manager clearly shows access to network drives. You further probe as to whether the database has gone down, even though you just connected successfully. You spend another 10 minutes of the support analyst's time running through a variety of scenarios before you hang up in frustration.

"They don't know anything over there," you fume. You realize that you will have to figure this one out all by yourself. So you dive into the code you just modified. You are determined to check every single line until you find the cause of your difficulty. Over the course of the next two hours, you talk aloud to yourself—a lot.

"Look at that! I called the stored procedure inside an IF statement. I never did that before. Maybe I can't call stored programs that way." So you remove the IF statement and instead use a GOTO statement to perform the branching to the stored procedure. But that doesn't fix the problem.

"My code seems fine. But it calls this other routine that Joe wrote ages ago." Joe has since moved on, making him a ripe candidate for the scapegoat. "It probably doesn't work anymore; after all, we did upgrade to a new voicemail system." So you decide to perform a standalone test of Joe's routine, which hasn't changed for two years and has no interface to voicemail. But his program seems to work fine—when it's not run from your program.

Now you are starting to get desperate. "Maybe this report should only run on weekends. Hey, can I put a local module in an anonymous block? Maybe I can use only local modules in procedures and functions! I think maybe I heard about a bug in this tool. Time for a workaround…."

You get angry and begin to understand why your eight-year-old hits the computer monitor when he can't beat the last level of Ultra Mystic Conqueror VII. And just as you are ready to go home and take it out on your dog, you realize that you are connected to the development database, which has almost no data at all. You switch to the test instance, run your report, and everything looks just fine.

Except, of course, for that GOTO and all the other workarounds you stuck in the report….

## Debugging Tips and Strategies

In this chapter, I do not pretend to offer a comprehensive primer on debugging. The following tips and techniques, however, should improve on your current set of error-fixing skills.

### Use a source code debugger

The single most effective thing you can do to minimize the time spent debugging your code is to use a source code debugger. One is now available in just about every PL/SQL Integrated Development Environment (IDE). If you are using Quest's Toad or SQL Navigator, Allround Automations' PL/SQL Developer, or Oracle SQL Developer (or any other such GUI tool), you will be able to set visual breakpoints in your code with the click of a mouse, step through your code line by line, watch variables as they change their values, and so on.

The other tips in this section apply whether or not you are using a GUI-based debugger, but there is no doubt that if you are still debugging the old-fashioned way (inserting calls to DBMS_OUTPUT.PUT_LINE in dozens of places in your code), you are wasting a lot of your time. (Unfortunately, if your code is deployed at some customer site, debugging with a GUI tool is not always possible, in which case you usually have to resort to some sort of logging mechanism.)

### Gather data

Gather as much data as possible about when, where, and how the error occurred. It is very unlikely that the first occurrence of an error will give you all the information you will want or need to figure out the source of that error. Upon noticing an error, the temptation is to show off one's knowledge of the program by declaring, "Got it! I know what's going on and exactly how to fix it." This can be very gratifying when it turns out that you do have a handle on the problem, and that may be the case for simple bugs. Some problems can appear simple, however, and turn out to require extensive testing and analysis. Save yourself the embarrassment of pretending (or believing) that you know more than you actually do. Before rushing to change your code, take these steps:

*Run the program again to see if the error is reproducible*
> This will be the first indication of the complexity of the problem. It is almost impossible to determine the cause of a problem if you are unable to get it to occur predictably. Once you work out the steps needed to get the error to occur, you will have gained much valuable information about its cause.

*Narrow the test case needed to generate the error*
> I recently had to debug a problem in one of my Oracle Forms modules. A pop-up window would lose its data under certain circumstances. At first glance, the rule seemed to be: "For a new call, if you enter only one request, that request will be lost." If I had stopped testing at that point, I would have had to analyze all code that initialized the call record and handled the INSERT logic. Instead, I tried additional variations of data entry and soon found that the data was lost only when I navigated to the pop-up window directly from a certain item. Now I had a very narrow test case to analyze, and it became very easy to uncover the error in logic.

*Examine the circumstances under which the problem does not occur*
> "Failure to fail" can offer many insights into the reason an error does occur. It also helps you narrow down the sections of code and the conditions you have to analyze when you go back to the program.

The more information you gather about the problem at hand, the easier it will be to solve that problem. It is worth the extra time to assemble the evidence. So even when you are absolutely sure you are on to that bug, hold off and investigate a little further.

### Remain logical at all times

Symbolic logic is the lifeblood of programmers. No matter which programming language you use, the underlying logical framework is a constant. PL/SQL has one particular syntax. The C language uses different keywords, and the IF statement looks a little different. The elegance of LISP demands a very different way of building programs. But underneath it all, symbolic logic provides the backbone on which you hang the statements that solve your problems.

The reliance on logical and rational thought in programming is one reason that it is so easy for a developer to learn a new programming language. As long as you can take the statement of a problem and develop a logical solution step by step, the particulars of a language are secondary.

With logic at the core of our being, it amazes me to see how often we programmers abandon this logic and pursue the most irrational path to solving a problem. We engage in wishful thinking and highly superstitious, irrational, or dubious thought processes.

Even though we know better—much better—we find ourselves questioning code that conforms to documented functionality, that has worked in the past, and that surely works at that moment. This irrationality almost always involves shifting the blame from oneself to the "other"—the computer, the compiler, Joe, the word processor, whatever. Anything and anybody but our own pristine selves!

When you attempt to shift blame, you only put off solving your problem. Computers and compilers may not be intelligent, but they're very fast and very consistent. All they can do is follow rules, and you write the rules in your program. So when you uncover a bug in your code, take responsibility for that error. Assume that *you* did something wrong—don't blame the PL/SQL compiler, Oracle Forms, or the text editor.

If you do find yourself questioning a basic element or rule in the compiler that has always worked for you in the past, it is time to take a break. Better yet, it is time to get someone else to look at your code. It is amazing how another pair of eyes can focus your own analytical powers on the real causes of a problem.

 Strive to be the Spock of Programming. Accept only what is logical. Reject that which has no explanation.

### Analyze instead of trying

So you have a pile of data and all the clues you could ask for in profiling the symptoms of your problem. Now it is time to analyze that data. For many people, analysis takes the following form: "Hmm, this looks like it could be the answer. I'll make this change, recompile, and try it to see if it works."

What's wrong with this approach? When you try a solution to see what will happen, what you are really saying is:

- You are not sure that the change really is a solution. If you were sure, you wouldn't "try" it to see what would happen. You would make the change and then test that change.

- You have not fully analyzed the error to understand its causes. If you know why an error occurs, then you know if a particular change will fix that problem. If you are unsure about the source of the error, you will be tempted to simply try a change and examine the impact. This is, unfortunately, very faulty logic.

- Even if the change stops the error from occurring, you can't be sure that your "solution" really solved anything. Because you aren't sure why the problem occurred, the simple fact that the problem doesn't reappear in your particular tests doesn't mean that you fixed the bug. The most you can say is that your change stopped the bug from occurring under certain, perhaps even most, circumstances.

To truly solve a problem, you must completely analyze the cause of the problem. Once you understand why the problem occurs, you have found the root cause and can take the steps necessary to make the problem go away in all circumstances.

When you identify a potential solution, perform a walk-through of your code based on that change. Don't execute your form. Examine your program, and mentally try out different scenarios to test your hypothesis. Once you are certain that your change actually does address the problem, you can then perform a test of that solution. You won't be *trying* anything; you will be *verifying* a fix.

Analyze your bug fully before you test solutions. If you say to yourself, "Why don't I try this?" in the hope that it will solve the problem, then you are wasting your time and debugging inefficiently.

### Take breaks, and ask for help

We are often our own biggest obstacles when it comes to sorting out our problems, whether a program bug or a personal crisis. When you are stuck on the inside of a problem, it is hard to maintain an objective distance and take a fresh look.

When you are making absolutely no progress and feel that you have tried everything, try these two radical techniques:

- Take a break
- Ask for help

When I have struggled with a bug for any length of time without success, I not only become ineffective, I also tend to lose perspective. I pursue irrational and superstitious leads. I lose track of what I have already tested and what I have assumed to be right. I get too close to the problem to debug it effectively.

My frustration level usually correlates closely to the amount of time I have sat in my ergonomic chair and perched over my wrist-padded keyboard and stared at my low-radiation screen. Often the very simple act of stepping away from the workstation will clear my head and leave room for a solution to pop into place. Did you ever wake up the morning after a very difficult day at work to find the elusive answer sitting there at the end of your dream?

Make it a rule to get up and walk around at least once an hour when you are working on a problem—heck, even when you are writing your programs. Give your brain a chance to let its neural networks make the connections and develop new options for your programming. There is a whole big world out there. Even when your eyes are glued to the monitor and your source code, the world keeps turning. It never hurts to remind yourself of the bigger picture, even if that only amounts to taking note of the weather outside your air-conditioned cocoon.

Even more effective than taking a break is asking another person to look at your problem. There is something entirely magical about the dynamic of adding another pair of eyes to the situation. You might struggle with a problem for an hour or two, and finally, at the exact moment that you break down and explain the problem to a coworker, the solution will jump out at you. It could be a mismatch on names, a false assumption, or a misunderstanding of the IF statement logic. Whatever the case, chances are that you yourself will find it (even though you couldn't for the last two hours) as soon as you ask someone else to find it for you.

And even if the error does not yield itself quite so easily, you still have lots to gain from the perspective of another person who (a) did not write the code and has no subconscious assumptions or biases about it, and (b) isn't mad at the program.

Other benefits accrue from asking for help. You improve the self-esteem and self-confidence of other programmers by showing that you respect their opinions. If you are one of the best developers in the group, then your request for help demonstrates that you, too, sometimes make mistakes and need help from the team. This builds the sense (and the reality) of teamwork, which will improve the overall development and testing efforts on the project.

### Change and test one area of code at a time

One of my biggest problems when I debug my code is that I am overconfident about my development and debugging skills, so I try to address too many problems at once. I make five or ten changes, rerun my test, and get very unreliable and minimally useful results. I find that my changes cause other problems (a common phenomenon until a program stabilizes, and a sure sign that lots more debugging and testing is needed), that some, but not all, of the original errors are gone, and that I have no idea which changes fixed which errors and which changes caused new errors.

In short, my debugging effort is a mess, and I have to back out of changes until I have a clearer picture of what is happening in my program.

Unless you are making very simple changes, you should fix one problem at a time and then test that fix. The amount of time it takes to compile, generate, and test may increase, but in the long run you will be much more productive.

Another aspect of incremental testing and debugging is performing unit tests on individual modules before you test a program that calls these various modules. If you test the programs separately and determine that they work, when you debug your application as a whole (in a system test), you do not have to worry about whether those modules return correct values or perform the correct actions. Instead, you can concentrate on the code that calls the modules. (See the earlier section "Testing PL/SQL Programs" on page 746, for more on unit testing.)

You will also find it helpful to come up with a system for keeping track of your troubleshooting efforts. Dan Clamage, a reviewer for this book, reports that he maintains a simple text file with running commentary of his efforts to reproduce the problem and what he has done to correct it. This file will usually include any SQL written to analyze the situation, setup data for test cases, a list of the modules examined, and any other items that may be of interest in the future. With this file in place, it's much easier to return at any time (e.g., after you have had a good night's sleep and are ready to try again) and follow your original line of reasoning.

# Protecting Stored Code

Virtually any application I write contains propriety information. If I write my application in PL/SQL and sell it commercially, I really don't want to let customers (or worse, competitors) see my secrets. Oracle offers a program known as *wrap* that hides or *obfuscates* most, if not all, of these secrets.

 Some people refer to "wrapping" code as "encrypting" code, but wrapping is not true encryption. If you need to deliver information, such as a password, that *really* needs to be secure, you should not rely upon this facility. Oracle does provide a way of incorporating true encryption into your own applications using the built-in package DBMS_CRYPTO (or DBMS_OBFUSCATION_TOOLKIT in releases before Oracle Database 10*g*). Chapter 23 describes encryption and other aspects of PL/SQL application security.

When you wrap PL/SQL source, you convert your readable ASCII text source code into unreadable ASCII text source code. This unreadable code can then be distributed to customers, regional offices, etc., for creation in new database instances. The Oracle database maintains dependencies for this wrapped code as it would for programs compiled from readable text. In short, a wrapped program is treated within the database just as normal PL/SQL programs are treated; the only difference is that prying eyes can't query the USER_SOURCE data dictionary to extract trade secrets.

Oracle has, for years, provided a *wrap* executable that performs the obfuscation of your code. Starting with Oracle Database 10*g* Release 2, you can also use the DBMS_DDL.WRAP and DBMS_DDL.CREATE_WRAPPED programs to wrap dynamically constructed PL/SQL code.

## Restrictions on and Limitations of Wrapping

You should be aware of the following issues when working with wrapped code:

- Wrapping makes reverse engineering of your source code difficult, but you should still avoid placing passwords and other highly sensitive information in your code.
- You cannot wrap the source code in triggers. If it is critical that you hide the contents of triggers, move the code to a package and then call the packaged program from the trigger.

- Wrapped code cannot be compiled into databases of a version lower than that of the *wrap* program. Wrapped code is upward-compatible only.
- You cannot include SQL*Plus substitution variables inside code that must be wrapped.

## Using the Wrap Executable

To wrap PL/SQL source code, you run the *wrap* executable. This program, named *wrap.exe*, is located in the *bin* directory of the Oracle instance. The format of the *wrap* command is:

```
wrap iname=infile [oname=outfile]
```

where *infile* points to the original, readable version of your program, and *outfile* is the name of the file that will contain the wrapped version of the code. If *infile* does not contain a file extension, then the default of *sql* is assumed.

If you do not provide an oname argument, then *wrap* creates a file with the same name as *infile* but with a default extension of *plb*, which stands for "PL/SQL binary" (a misnomer, but it gets the idea across: binaries are, in fact, unreadable).

Here are some examples of using the *wrap* executable:

- Wrap a program, relying on all the defaults:

    ```
    wrap iname=secretprog
    ```
- Wrap a package body, specifying overrides of all the defaults. Notice that the wrapped file doesn't have to have the same filename or extension as the original:

    ```
    wrap iname=secretbody.spb oname=shhhhhh.bin
    ```

## Dynamic Wrapping with DBMS_DDL

Oracle Database 10g Release 2 introduced a way to wrap code that is generated dynamically: the WRAP and CREATE_WRAPPED programs of the DBMS_DDL package:

*DBMS_DDL.WRAP*
    Returns a string containing an obfuscated version of your code.

*DBMS_DDL.CREATE_WRAPPED*
    Compiles an obfuscated version of your code into the database

Both programs are overloaded to work with a single string and with arrays of strings based on the DBMS_SQL.VARCHAR2A and DBMS_SQL.VARCHAR2S collection types. Here are two examples that use these programs:

- Obfuscate and display a string that creates a tiny procedure:

    ```
    SQL> DECLARE
      2     l_program   VARCHAR2 (32767);
    ```

```
3  BEGIN
4     l_program := 'CREATE OR REPLACE PROCEDURE dont_look IS BEGIN NULL; END;';
5     DBMS_OUTPUT.put_line (SYS.DBMS_DDL.wrap (l_program));
6  END;
7  /
```

The output is:

```
CREATE OR REPLACE PROCEDURE dont_look wrapped

a000000
369
abcd
....
XtQ19EnOI8a6hBSJmk2NebMgPHswg5nnm7+fMr2ywFy4CP6Z9P4I/v4rpXQruMAy/tJepZmB
CCor
uIHHLcmmpkOCnm4=
```

- Read a PL/SQL program definition from a file, obfuscate it, and compile it into the database:

```
/* File on web: obfuscate_from_file.sql */
PROCEDURE obfuscate_from_file (
   dir_in    IN   VARCHAR2
 , file_in   IN   VARCHAR2
)
IS
   l_file    UTL_FILE.file_type;
   l_lines   DBMS_SQL.varchar2s;

   PROCEDURE read_file (lines_out IN OUT NOCOPY DBMS_SQL.varchar2s)
   IS BEGIN ... not critical to the example ... END read_file;
BEGIN
   read_file (l_lines);
   SYS.DBMS_DDL.create_wrapped (l_lines, l_lines.FIRST, l_lines.LAST);
END obfuscate_from_file;
```

## Guidelines for Working with Wrapped Code

I have found the following guidelines useful in working with wrapped code:

- Create batch files so that you can easily, quickly, and uniformly wrap one or more files. In Windows, I create *bat* files that contain lines like this in my source code directories:

```
c:\orant\bin\wrap iname=plvrep.sps oname=plvrep.pls
```

Of course, you can also create parameterized scripts and pass in the names of the files you want to wrap.

- You can only wrap package specifications and bodies, object type specifications and bodies, and standalone functions and procedures. You can run the wrapped binary against any other kind of SQL or PL/SQL statement, but those files will not be changed.

---

- You can tell that a program is wrapped by examining the program header. It will contain the keyword WRAPPED, as in:

```
PACKAGE BODY package_name WRAPPED
```

Even if you don't notice the keyword WRAPPED on the first line, you will immediately know that you are looking at wrapped code because the text in USER_SOURCE will look like this:

```
LINE TEXT
------- ----------------------
   45 abcd
   46 95a425ff
   47 a2
   48 7 PACKAGE:
```

and no matter how bad your coding style is, it surely isn't *that* bad!

- Wrapped code is much larger than the original source. I have found in my experience that a 57 KB readable package body turns into a 153 KB wrapped package body, while an 86 KB readable package body turns into a 357 KB wrapped package body. These increases in file size do result in increased requirements for storing source code in the database. The size of compiled code stays the same, although the time it takes to compile may increase.

# Introduction to Edition-Based Redefinition (Oracle Database 11g Release 2)

One of the most significant enhancements in Oracle Database 11g Release 2 is surely *edition-based redefinition*, a new element of Oracle's high availability solution. This feature makes it possible to upgrade the database component of an application while it is being used; that is, Oracle now supports "hot patching" of PL/SQL-based applications. Edition-based redefinition will make it possible to minimize or completely eliminate downtime for maintenance.

With edition-based redefinition, when you need to upgrade an application while it is in use, you make a copy of any affected database objects in the application and *redefine* the copied objects in isolation from the running application. Any changes you make are not visible to nor have any effect on users. Users can continue to run the application as it existed before your changes (to this new edition). When you are certain that all changes are correct, you then make the upgraded application available to all users.

As you can imagine, adding this feature has had a sweeping impact on the Oracle database. For example, if you want to see a list of *all* the objects you have defined, instead of writing a query against ALL_OBJECTS, you can now query the contents of ALL_OBJECTS_AE ("All Editions"). The unique specifier for an object is now OWNER, OBJECT_NAME, and EDITION_NAME (assuming, in any case, that the owner is editions-enabled) This one aspect is just the tip of the iceberg of all the changes that edition-based redefinition has wrought in the Oracle database.

Other Oracle database capabilities in the high availability space can be adopted and deployed at particular sites where an application is installed without that application's needing special preparation and without its developers even knowing about the high availability capabilities that different sites use.

Edition-based redefinition is fundamentally different. To take advantage of this feature:

- The schema(s) that own the database objects that are the application's backend must be modified to prepare the application to use edition-based redefinition. This design work should be done by the application architect, and introduced into a new (or first) version of the application. Scripts need to be written to implement this preparatory upgrade step, and those scripts must run "old-style," that is to say, offline.

- Once the application is ready for edition-based redefinition, the development team programmers responsible for scripting patches and upgrades will then need to learn edition-based redefinition and write their scripts in a new way.

Given the complexity of this feature and the fact that, strictly speaking, it extends well beyond the PL/SQL language, we can do little more in this book than to offer below a very simple demonstration to give you a sense of how edition-based redefinition works (all code is available in the *11gR2_editions.sql* file on the book's web site).

Let's start by creating a new edition. Every edition must be defined as the child of an existing edition. Furthermore, all databases upgraded to or created in Oracle Database 11g Release 2 start with one edition named ora$base. This edition always must serve as the parent of the first edition created with a CREATE EDITION statement.

Suppose that I am enhancing my Human Resources application to reflect a change in the rule for displaying the full name of an employee. Historically, I displayed names in the format "first space last," as shown here:

```
/* File on web: 11gR2_editions.sql */
FUNCTION full_name (first_in IN employees.first_name%TYPE
                             , last_in IN employees.first_name%TYPE
                             )
      RETURN VARCHAR2
   IS
   BEGIN
      RETURN (first_in || ' ' || last_in);
   END full_name;
```

This function is defined in the ora$base edition. When I call it, I see the following output:

```
BEGIN
   DBMS_OUTPUT.put_line (full_name ('Steven', 'Feuerstein'));
END;
```

```
/
Steven Feuerstein
```

Unfortunately, our users have changed their minds (what a surprise!): they now want names displayed in the form "last comma first." Now, this function is called all day long in the application, and I don't want to have to force our users off that application. Thankfully, we recently upgraded to Oracle Database 11g Release 2. So I first create an edition for the new version of my function:

```
CREATE EDITION NEW_HR_PATCH_NAMEFORMAT
/
```

I then make this edition current in my session:

```
ALTER SESSION SET edition = HR_PATCH_NAMEFORMAT
/
```

Since this edition was based on ora$base, it inherits all the objects defined in that parent edition. I can, therefore, still call my function and get the same answer as before:

```
BEGIN
   DBMS_OUTPUT.put_line (full_name ('Steven', 'Feuerstein'));
END;
/
Steven Feuerstein
```

Now I change the implementation of this function to reflect the new rule:

```
CREATE OR REPLACE FUNCTION full_name (first_in IN employees.first_name%TYPE
                                    , last_in IN employees.first_name%TYPE
                                    )
   RETURN VARCHAR2
IS
BEGIN
   RETURN (last_in || ', ' || first_in);
END full_name;
/
```

Now when I run the function, I see a different result:

```
BEGIN
   DBMS_OUTPUT.put_line (full_name ('Steven', 'Feuerstein'));
END;
/
Feuerstein, Steven
```

But if I change the edition back to the base edition, I see my old format:

```
ALTER SESSION SET edition = ora$base
/

BEGIN
   DBMS_OUTPUT.put_line (full_name ('Steven', 'Feuerstein'));
END;
/
Steven Feuerstein
```

That's the basic idea behind edition-based redefinition, but of course your application architect and your development team will need to explore the many aspects of this feature, especially crossedition triggers and editioning views, both of which are needed when you change the structure of a table (which is *not* directly editionable),

You will find extensive documentation on edition-based redefinition in the Oracle Database 11*g* Release 2 *Advanced Application Developer's Guide*.

# CHAPTER 21

# Optimizing PL/SQL Performance

Optimizing the performance of an Oracle application is a complex process: you need to tune the SQL in your code base, make sure the System Global Area (SGA) is properly configured, optimize algorithmic logic, and so on. Tuning individual PL/SQL programs is a bit less daunting, but still more than enough of a challenge. Before spending lots of time changing your PL/SQL code in hopes of improving the performance of that code, you should first:

*Tune access to code and data in the SGA*

Before your code can be executed (and perhaps run too slowly), it must be loaded into the SGA of the Oracle instance. This process can benefit from a focused tuning effort, usually performed by a DBA. You will find more information about the SGA and other aspects of the PL/SQL architecture in Chapter 24.

*Optimize your SQL*

In virtually any application you write against the Oracle database, the vast majority of tuning will take place by optimizing the SQL statements executed against your data. The potential inefficiencies of a 16-way join dwarf the usual issues found in a procedural block of code. To put it another way, if you have a program that runs in 20 hours, and you need to reduce its elapsed time to 30 minutes, virtually your only hope will be to concentrate on the SQL within your code. There are many third-party tools available to both DBAs and developers that perform very sophisticated analyses of SQL within applications and recommend more efficient alternatives.

*Use the most aggressive compiler optimization level possible*

Oracle Database 10g introduced an optimizing compiler for PL/SQL programs. The default optimization level of 2 in that release took the most aggressive approach possible in terms of transforming your code to make it run faster (Oracle Database 11g has an even higher optimization level of 3. The default optimization level, however, is still 2 and that will be sufficient for the vast majority of your code). You should use this default level unless compilation time is unacceptably slow, and you are not seeing benefits from optimization.

Once you are confident that the *context* in which your PL/SQL code runs is not obviously inefficient, you should turn your attention to your packages and other code. I suggest the following steps:

*Write your application with best practices and standards in mind*
> While you shouldn't take clearly inefficient approaches to meeting requirements, you also shouldn't obsess about the performance implications of every line in your code. Remember that most of the code you write will never be a bottleneck in your application's performance, so optimizing it will not result in any user benefits. Instead, write the application with correctness and maintainability foremost in mind and then....

*Analyze your application's execution profile*
> Does it run quickly enough? If it does, great: you don't need to do any tuning (at the moment). If it's too slow, identify which specific elements of the application are causing the problem and then focus directly on those programs (or parts of programs). Once identified, you can then ...

*Tune your algorithms*
> As a procedural language, PL/SQL is often used to implement complex formulas and algorithms. You can use conditional statements, loops, perhaps even GOTOs and (I hope) reusable modules to get the job done. These algorithms can be written in many different ways, some of which perform very badly. How do you tune poorly written algorithms? This is a tough question with no easy answers. Tuning algorithms is much more complex than tuning SQL (which is "structured" and therefore lends itself more easily to automated analysis).

*Take advantage of any PL/SQL-specific performance features*
> Over the years, Oracle has added statements and optimizations that can make a substantial difference to the execution of your code. Consider using constructs ranging from the RETURNING clause to FORALL. Make sure you aren't living in the past and paying the price in application inefficiencies.

*Balance performance improvements against memory consumption*
> A number of the techniques that improve the performance of your code also consume more memory, usually in the Program Global Area (PGA), but also sometimes in the SGA. It won't do you much good to make your program blazingly fast if the resulting memory consumption is unacceptable in your application environment.

It's outside the scope of this book to offer substantial advice on SQL tuning and database/SGA configuration. I certainly *can*, on the other hand, tell you all about the most important performance optimization features of PL/SQL, and offer advice on how to apply those features to achieve the fastest PL/SQL code possible.

Finally, remember that overall performance optimization is a team effort. Work closely with your DBA, especially as you begin to leverage key features like collections, table functions and the function result cache.

# Tools to Assist in Optimization

In this section, I introduce the tools and techniques that can help optimize the performance of your code. These fall into several categories: analyzing memory usage, identifying bottlenecks in PL/SQL code, calculating elapsed time, choosing the fastest program, avoiding infinite loops, and using performance-related warnings.

## Analyzing Memory Usage

As I mentioned, as you go about optimizing code performance, you will also need to take into account the amount of memory your program consumes. Program data consumes PGA; each session connected to the Oracle database has its own PGA. Thus, the total memory required for your application is usually far greater than the memory needed for a single instance of the program. Memory consumption is an especially critical factor whenever you work with collections (array-like structures), as well as object types with a large number of attributes and records having a large number of fields.

For an in-depth discussion of this topic, check out the section "PL/SQL and Database Instance Memory" on page 996 in Chapter 24.

## Identifying Bottlenecks in PL/SQL Code

Before you can tune your application, you need to figure out what is running slowly and where you should focus your efforts. Oracle and third-party vendors offer a variety of products to help you do this; generally they focus on analyzing the SQL statements in your code, offering alternative implementations, and so on. These tools are very powerful, yet they can also be very frustrating to PL/SQL developers. They tend to offer an overwhelming amount of performance data without telling you what you really want to know: where are the bottlenecks in your code?

To answer these questions, Oracle offers a number of built-in utilities. Here are the most useful:

*DBMS_PROFILER*
> This built-in package allows you to turn on execution profiling in a session. Then, when you run your code, the Oracle database uses tables to keep track of detailed information about how long each line in your code took to execute. You can then run queries on these tables or—preferably—use screens in products like Toad or SQL Navigator to present the data in a clear, graphical fashion.

*DBMS_HPROF (hierarchical profiler)*
> Oracle Database 11*g* features a new *hierarchical profiler* that makes it easier to roll performance results up through the execution call stack. DBMS_PROFILER provides "flat" data about performance, which makes it difficult to answer questions

like "How much time altogether is spent in the ADD_ITEM procedure?" The hierarchical profiler makes it easy to answer such questions.

### DBMS_PROFILER

In case you do not have access to a tool that offers an interface to DBMS_PROFILER, here are some instructions and examples.

First of all, Oracle may not have installed DBMS_PROFILER for you automatically. To see if DBMS_PROFILER is installed and available, connect to your schema in SQL*Plus and issue this command:

```
SQL> DESC DBMS_PROFILER
```

If you then see the message:

```
ERROR:
ORA-04043: object dbms_profiler does not exist
```

then you (or your DBA) will have to install the program. To do this, run the *$ORACLE_HOME/rdbms/admin/profload.sql* file under a SYSDBA account.

You next need to run the *$ORACLE_HOME/rdbms/admin/proftab.sql* file in your own schema to create three tables populated by DBMS_PROFILER:

*PLSQL_PROFILER_RUNS*
> Parent table of runs

*PLSQL_PROFILER_UNITS*
> Program units executed in run

*PLSQL_PROFILER_DATA*
> Profiling data for each line in a program unit

Once all these objects are defined, you gather profiling information for your application by writing code like this:

```
BEGIN
   DBMS_PROFILER.start_profiler (
      'my application' || TO_CHAR (SYSDATE, 'YYYYMMDD HH24:MI:SS')
   );

   my_application_code;

   DBMS_PROFILER.stop_profiler;
END;
```

Once you have finished running your application code, you can run queries against the data in the PLSQL_PROFILER_ tables. Here is an example of such a query that displays those lines of code that consumed at least 1% of the total time of the run:

```
/* File on web: slowest.sql */
SELECT    TO_CHAR (
             p1.total_time / 10000000,
             '99999999')
```

```
               || '-'
               || TO_CHAR (p1.total_occur) AS time_count,
                   p2.unit_owner || '.' || p2.unit_name unit,
                   TO_CHAR (p1.line#)
               || '-'
               || p3.text text
          FROM plsql_profiler_data p1, plsql_profiler_units p2, all_source p3,
               plsql_profiler_grand_total p4
         WHERE p2.unit_owner NOT IN ('SYS', 'SYSTEM')
           AND p1.runid = &&firstparm
           AND (p1.total_time >= p4.grand_total / 100)
           AND p1.runid = p2.runid
           AND p2.unit_number = p1.unit_number
           AND p3.TYPE = 'PACKAGE BODY'
           AND p3.owner = p2.unit_owner
           AND p3.line = p1.line#
           AND p3.NAME = p2.unit_name
      ORDER BY p1.total_time DESC;
```

As you can see, these queries are fairly complex (I modified one of the canned queries from Oracle to produce the above four-way join). That's why it is far better to rely on a graphical interface in a PL/SQL development tool.

### Hierarchical profiler

Oracle Database 11*g* has introduced a second profiling mechanism: DBMS_HPROF, known as the hierarchical profiler. Use this profiler to obtain the execution profile of PL/SQL code, organized by the distinct subprogram calls in your application. "OK," I can hear you thinking, "but doesn't DBMS_PROFILER do that for me already?" Not really. Nonhierarchical (flat) profilers like DBMS_PROFILER record the time that your application spends within each subprogram, down to the execution time of each individual line of code. That's helpful, but in a limited way. Often, you also want to know how much time the application spends within a particular subprogram—that is, you need to "roll up" profile information to the subprogram level. That's what the new hierarchical profiler does for you.

The PL/SQL hierarchical profiler reports performance information about each subprogram in your application that is profiled, keeping SQL and PL/SQL execution times distinct. The profiler tracks a wide variety of information, including the number of calls to the subprogram, the amount of time spent in that subprogram, the time spent in the subprogram's subtree (that is, in its descendent subprograms), and detailed parent-children information.

The hierarchical profiler has two components:

*Data collector*
  Provides APIs that turn hierarchical profiling on and off. The PL/SQL runtime engine writes the "raw" profiler output to the specified file.

*Analyzer*

Processes the raw profiler output and stores the results in hierarchical profiler tables, which can then be queried to display profiler information.

To use the hierarchical profiler, do the following:

1. Make sure that you can execute the DBMS_HPROF package.

2. Make sure that you have WRITE privileges on the directory that you specify when you call DBMS_HPROF.START_PROFILING.

3. Create the three profiler tables (see details on this step below).

4. Call the DBMS_HPROF.START_PROFILING procedure to start the hierarchical profiler data collection in your session.

5. Run your application code long and repetitively enough to obtain sufficient code coverage to get interesting results.

6. Call the DBMS_HPROF.STOP_PROFILING procedure to terminate the gathering of profile data.

7. Analyze the contents and then run queries against the profiler tables to obtain results.

 To get the most accurate measurements of elapsed time for your subprograms, you should minimize any unrelated activity on the system on which your application is running.

Of course, on a production system other processes may slow down your program. You may also want to run these measurements while using Real Application Testing (RAT) in Oracle Database 11g to obtain real response times.

To create the profiler tables and other necessary database objects, run the *dbmshptab.sql* script (located in the *rdbms/admin* directory). This script will create these three tables:

*DBMSHP_RUNS*

Top-level information about each run of the ANALYZE utility of DBMS_HPROF.

*DBMSHP_FUNCTION_INFO*

Detailed information about the execution of each subprogram profiled in a particular run of the ANALYZE utility.

*DBMSHP_PARENT_CHILD_INFO*

Parent-child information for each subprogram profiled in DBMSHP_FUNCTION_INFO.

Here's a very simple example: I want to test the performance of my intab procedure (which displays the contents of the specified table using DBMS_SQL). So first I start profiling, specifying that I want the raw profiler data to be written to the *intab_trace.txt* file in the TEMP_DIR directory. This directory must have been previously defined with the CREATE DIRECTORY statement.

```
BEGIN
    DBMS_HPROF.start_profiling ('TEMP_DIR', 'intab_trace.txt');
END;
/
```

Then I call my program (run my application code):

```
BEGIN
    intab ('DEPARTMENTS');
END;
/
```

And then I terminate my profiling session:

```
BEGIN
    DBMS_HPROF.stop_profiling;
END;
/
```

I could have included all three statements in the same block of code; instead, I kept them separate because in most situations you are not going to include profiling commands in or near your application code.

So now that trace file is populated with data. I *could* open it and look at the data, and perhaps make a little bit of sense of what I find there. A much better use of my time and Oracle's technology, however, would be to call the ANALYZE utility of DBMS_HPROF. This function takes the contents of the trace file, transforms it, and places it into the three profiler tables. It returns a run number, which you must then use when querying the contents of these tables.

```
BEGIN
    DBMS_OUTPUT.PUT_LINE (
        DBMS_HPROF.ANALYZE ('TEMP_DIR', 'intab_trace.txt'));
END;
/
```

And that's it! The data has been collected and analyzed into the tables, and now I can choose from one of two approaches to obtaining the profile information:

1. Run the *plshprof* command-line utility (located in the directory *$ORACLE_HOME/bin/*). This utility generates simple HTML reports from either one or two raw profiler output files. For an example of a raw profiler output file, see the section titled "Collecting Profile Data" in the *Oracle Database Advanced Application Developer's Guide*. I can then peruse the generated HTML reports in the browser of my choice.

2. Run my own "home-grown" queries. Suppose, for example, that the above block returns 177 as the run number. First, here's a query that shows all current runs:

```
SELECT runid, run_timestamp, total_elapsed_time, run_comment
    FROM dbmshp_runs
```

Here's a query that shows me all the names of subprograms that have been profiled, across all runs:

```
SELECT symbolid, owner, module, type, function, line#, namespace
  FROM dbmshp_function_info
```

Here's a query that shows me information about subprogram execution for this specific run:

```
SELECT FUNCTION, line#, namespace, subtree_elapsed_time
     , function_elapsed_time, calls
  FROM dbmshp_function_info
 WHERE runid = 177
```

This query retrieves parent-child information for the current run, but not in a very interesting way, since I see only key values and not names of programs.

```
SELECT parentsymid, childsymid, subtree_elapsed_time, function_elapsed_time
     , calls
  FROM dbmshp_parent_child_info
 WHERE runid = 117
```

Here's a more useful query, joining with the function information table; now I can see the names of the parent and child programs, along with the elapsed time and number of calls.

```
SELECT    RPAD (' ', LEVEL * 2, ' ') || fi.owner || '.' || fi.module AS NAME
        , fi.FUNCTION, pci.subtree_elapsed_time, pci.function_elapsed_time
        , pci.calls
     FROM dbmshp_parent_child_info pci JOIN dbmshp_function_info fi
       ON pci.runid = fi.runid AND pci.childsymid = fi.symbolid
    WHERE pci.runid = 117
CONNECT BY PRIOR childsymid = parentsymid
START WITH pci.parentsymid = 1
```

The hierarchical profiler is a very powerful and rich utility. I suggest that you read Chapter 9 of the Oracle *Database Advanced Application Developer's Guide* for extensive coverage of this profiler.

## Calculating Elapsed Time

So you've found the bottleneck in your application; it's a function named CALC_TO-TALS, and it contains a complex algorithm that clearly needs some tuning. You work on the function for a little while, and now you want to know if it's faster. You certainly *could* profile execution of your entire application again, but it would certainly be much easier if you could simply run the original and modified versions "side by side" and see which is faster. To do this, you need a utility that computes the elapsed time of individual programs, even lines of code *within* a program.

The DBMS_UTILITY package offers two functions to help you obtain this information: DBMS_UTILITY.GET_TIME and DBMS_UTILITY.GET_CPU_TIME. Both are available for Oracle Database 10g and later.

You can easily use these functions to calculate the elapsed time (total and CPU, respectively) of your code down to the hundredth of a second. Here's the basic idea:

- Call DBMS_UTILITY.GET_TIME (or GET_CPU_TIME) before you execute your code. Store this "start time."
- Run the code whose performance you want to measure.
- Call DBMS_UTILITY.GET_TIME (or GET_CPU_TIME) to get the "end time." Subtract start from end; this difference is the number of hundredths of seconds that have elapsed between start and end.

Here is an example of this flow:

```
DECLARE
    l_start_time PLS_INTEGER;
BEGIN
    l_start_time := DBMS_UTILITY.get_time;

    my_program;

    DBMS_OUTPUT.put_line (
        'Elapsed: ' || DBMS_UTILITY.get_time - l_start_time);
END;
```

Now, here's something strange: I find these functions extremely useful, but I never (or rarely) call them directly in my performance scripts. Instead, I choose to *encapsulate* or hide the use of these functions—and their related "end – start" formula—inside a package or object type. In other words, when I want to test "my_program", I would write the following:

```
BEGIN
    sf_timer.start_timer ();

    my_program;

    sf_timer.show_elapsed_time ('Ran my_program');
END;
```

In other words, I capture the start time, run the code, and show the elapsed time.

I avoid direct calls to DBMS_UTILITY.GET_TIME, and instead use the SFTK timer package, sf_timer, for two reasons:

- To improve productivity: Who wants to declare those local variables, write all the code to call that mouthful of a built-in function, and do the math? I'd much rather have my utility do it for me.
- To get consistent results: If you rely on the simple "end – start" formula, you can sometimes end up with a *negative* elapsed time. Now, I don't care how fast your code is; you can't possibly go backwards in time!

How is it possible to obtain a negative elapsed time? The number returned by DBMS_UTILITY.GET_TIME represents the total number of seconds elapsed since an arbitrary point in time. When this number gets very big (the limit depends on your operating system), it rolls over to 0 and starts counting again. So if you happen to call GET_TIME right before the roll-over, end – start will come out negative!

What you really need to do to avoid the possible negative timing is to write code like this:

```
DECLARE
   c_big_number NUMBER := POWER (2, 32);
   l_start_time PLS_INTEGER;
BEGIN
   l_start_time := DBMS_UTILITY.get_time;
   my_program;
   DBMS_OUTPUT.put_line (
      'Elapsed: '
      || TO_CHAR (MOD (DBMS_UTILITY.get_time - l_start_time + c_big_number
                     , c_big_number)));
END;
```

Who in their right mind, and with the deadlines we all face, would want to write such code every time he or she needs to calculate elapsed time?

So instead I created the sf_timer package, to hide these details and make it easier to analyze and compare elapsed times.

## Choosing the Fastest Program

You'd think that choosing the fastest program would be clear and unambiguous. You run a script, you see which of your various implementations runs the fastest, and you go with that one. Ah, but under what scenario did you run those implementations? Just because you verified top speed for implementation C for one set of circumstances, that doesn't mean that your program will always or even mostly run faster than the other implementations.

When testing performance and especially when needing to choose among different implementations of the same requirements, you should consider and test all the following scenarios:

*Positive results*
   The program was given valid inputs and did what it was supposed to do.

*Negative results*
   The program was given invalid inputs (for example, a nonexistent primary key) and the program was not able to perform the requested tasks.

*The data neutrality of your algorithms*
   Your program works really well against a table of 10 rows, but what about for 10,000 rows? Your program scans a collection for matching data, but what if the matching row is at the beginning, middle, or end of the collection?

*Multiuser execution of program*

The program works fine for a single user, but you need to test it for simultaneous, multiuser access. You don't want to find out about deadlocks after the product goes into production, do you?

*Test on all supported versions of Oracle*

If your application needs to work well on Oracle Database 10*g* and Oracle Database 11*g*, for example, you must run your comparison scripts on instances of each version.

The specifics of each of your scenarios depend, of course, on the program you are testing. I suggest, though, that you create a procedure that executes each of your implementations and calculates the elapsed time for each. The parameter list of this procedure should include the number of times you want to run each program; you will very rarely be able to run each program just once and get useful results. You need to run your code enough times to ensure that the initial loading of code and data into memory does not skew the results. The other parameters to the procedure are determined by what you need to pass to each of your programs to run them.

Here is a template for such a procedure, with calls to sf_timer in place and ready to go:

```
/* File on web: compare_performance_template.sql */
PROCEDURE compare_implementations (
   title_in        IN VARCHAR2
 , iterations_in   IN INTEGER
 /*
 And now any parameters you need to pass data to the
 programs you are comparing....
 */
 )
IS
BEGIN
   DBMS_OUTPUT.put_line ('Compare Performance of <CHANGE THIS>: ');
   DBMS_OUTPUT.put_line (title_in);
   DBMS_OUTPUT.put_line ('Each program execute ' || iterations_in || ' times.');
   /*
   For each implementation, start the timer, run the program N times,
   then show elapsed time.
   */
   sf_timer.start_timer;

   FOR indx IN 1 .. iterations_in
   LOOP
      /* Call your program here. */
      NULL;
   END LOOP;

   sf_timer.show_elapsed_time ('<CHANGE THIS: Implementation 1');
   --
   sf_timer.start_timer;

   FOR indx IN 1 .. iterations_in
   LOOP
```

```
        /* Call your program here. */
        NULL;
    END LOOP;

    sf_timer.show_elapsed_time ('<CHANGE THIS: Implementation 2');
END compare_implementations;
```

You will see a number of examples of using sf_timer in this chapter.

## Avoiding Infinite Loops

If you are concerned about performance, you certainly want to avoid infinite loops! Infinite loops are less a problem for production applications (assuming that your team has done a decent job of testing!) and more a problem when you are in the process of building your programs. You may need to write some tricky logic to terminate a loop, and it certainly isn't productive to have to kill and restart your session as you test your program.

I have run into my own share of infinite loops and finally decided to write a utility to help me avoid this annoying outcome: the Loop Killer package. The idea behind sf_loop_killer is that while you may not yet be sure how to terminate the loop successfully, you know that if the loop body executes more than *N* times (e.g., 100, 1000, depending on your situation), you have a problem.

So you compile the Loop Killer package into your development schema and then write a small amount of code that will lead to a termination of the loop when it reaches a number of iterations you deem to be an unequivocal indicator of an infinite loop.

Here's the package spec (the full package is available on the book's web site):

```
/* File on web: sf_loop_killer.pks/pkb */
PACKAGE sf_loop_killer
IS
   c_max_iterations   CONSTANT PLS_INTEGER DEFAULT 1000;
   e_infinite_loop_detected    EXCEPTION;
   c_infinite_loop_detected    PLS_INTEGER := -20999;
   PRAGMA EXCEPTION_INIT (e_infinite_loop_detected, -20999);

   PROCEDURE kill_after (max_iterations_in IN PLS_INTEGER);

   PROCEDURE increment_or_kill (by_in IN PLS_INTEGER DEFAULT 1);

   FUNCTION current_count RETURN PLS_INTEGER;
END sf_loop_killer;
```

Let's look at an example of using this utility: I specify that I want the loop killed after 100 iterations. Then I call "increment or kill" at the end of the loop body. When I run this code (clearly an infinite loop), I then see the unhandled exception shown in Figure 21-1.

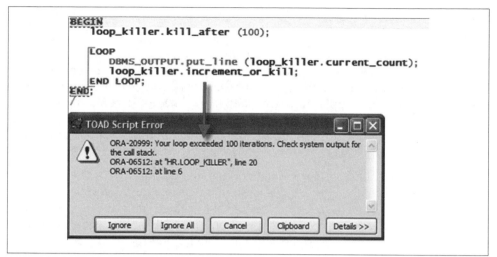

*Figure 21-1. Using the Loop Killer package*

## Performance-Related Warnings

Oracle introduced a compile-time warnings framework in Oracle Database 10g PL/SQL. When you turn on warnings in your session, Oracle will give you feedback on the quality of your code, and will offer advice for improving readability and performance. I recommend that you use compile-time warnings to help identify areas of your code that could be optimized.

You can enable warnings for the entire set of performance-related warnings with the following statement:

```
ALTER SESSION SET PLSQL_WARNINGS = 'ENABLE:PERFORMANCE'
```

Performance warnings include the following:

- PLW-06014: PLSQL_OPTIMIZE_LEVEL <= 1 turns off native code generation
- PLW-07203: parameter "string" may benefit from use of the NOCOPY compiler hint
- PLW-07204: conversion away from column type may result in suboptimal query plan

See "Compile-Time Warnings" on page 735 for additional warnings and more details about working with these warnings. All of the warnings are documented in the *Error Messages* book of your Oracle documentation set.

# The Optimizing Compiler

PL/SQL's optimizing compiler can improve runtime performance dramatically, with a relatively slight cost at compile time. The benefits of optimization apply to both interpreted and natively compiled PL/SQL because optimizations are applied by analyzing patterns in source code.

The optimizing compiler is enabled by default. However, you may want to alter its behavior, either by lowering its aggressiveness or by disabling it entirely. For example, if, in the course of normal operations, your system must perform recompilation of many lines of code, or if an application generates many lines of dynamically executed PL/SQL, the overhead of optimization may be unacceptable. Keep in mind, though, that Oracle's tests show that the optimizer doubles the runtime performance of computationally intensive PL/SQL.

In some cases, the optimizer may even alter program behavior. One such case might occur in code written for Oracle9i Database that depends on the relative timing of initialization sections in multiple packages. If your testing demonstrates such a problem, yet you wish to enjoy the performance benefits of the optimizer, you may want to rewrite the offending code or to introduce an initialization routine that ensures the desired order of execution.

The optimizer settings are defined through the PLSQL_OPTIMIZE_LEVEL initialization parameter (and related ALTER DDL statements), which can be set to 0, 1, 2, or 3 (3 is available only in Oracle Database 11g). The higher the number, the more aggressive is the optimization, meaning that the compiler will make a greater effort, and possibly restructure more of your code to optimize performance.

Set your optimization level according to the best fit for your application or program, as follows:

PLSQL_OPTIMIZE_LEVEL = 0
> Zero essentially turns off optimization. The PL/SQL compiler maintains the original evaluation order of statement processing of Oracle9i Database and earlier releases. Your code will still run faster than in earlier versions, but the difference will not be so dramatic.

PLSQL_OPTIMIZE_LEVEL = 1
> The compiler will apply many optimizations to your code, such as eliminating unnecessary computations and exceptions. It will not, in general, change the order of your original source code.

PLSQL_OPTIMIZE_LEVEL = 2
> This is the default value. It is also the most aggressive setting available prior to Oracle Database 11g. It will apply many modern optimization techniques beyond level 1, and some of those changes may result in moving source code relatively far from its original location. Level 2 optimization offers the greatest boost in performance. It may, however, cause the compilation time in some of your programs to increase substantially. If you encounter this situation (or, alternatively, if you are developing your code and want to minimize compile time, knowing that when you move to production, you will apply the highest optimization level), try cutting back the optimization level to 1.

*PLSQL_OPTIMIZE_LEVEL = 3*

New to Oracle Database 11g, this level of optimization adds inlining of nested or local subprograms. It may be of benefit in extreme cases (large numbers of local subprograms or recursive execution), but for most PL/SQL applications, the default level of 2 should suffice.

You can set the optimization level for the instance as a whole, but then override the default for a session or for a particular program. Here are some examples:

```
ALTER SESSION SET PLSQL_OPTIMIZE_LEVEL = 0;
```

Oracle retains optimizer settings on a module-by-module basis. When you recompile a particular module with nondefault settings, the settings will "stick," allowing you to recompile later using REUSE SETTINGS. For example:

```
ALTER PROCEDURE bigproc COMPILE PLSQL_OPTIMIZE_LEVEL = 0;
```

and then:

```
ALTER PROCEDURE bigproc COMPILE REUSE SETTINGS;
```

To view all the compiler settings for your modules, including optimizer level, interpreted versus native, and compiler warning levels, query the USER_PLSQL_OBJECT_SETTINGS view.

## Insights on How the Optimizer Works

In addition to doing things that mere programmers are not allowed to do, optimizers can also detect and exploit patterns in your code that you might not notice. One of the chief methods that optimizers employ is *reordering* the work that needs to be done, to improve runtime efficiency. The definition of the programming language circumscribes the amount of reordering an optimizer can do, but PL/SQL's definition leaves plenty of wiggle room—or "freedom"—for the optimizer. The rest of this section discusses some of the freedoms offered by PL/SQL, and gives examples of how code can be improved in light of them.

As a first example, consider the case of a "loop invariant," something that is inside a loop but that remains constant over every iteration. Any programmer worth his salt will take a look at this:

```
FOR e IN (SELECT * FROM employees WHERE DEPT = p_dept)
LOOP
   DBMS_OUTPUT.PUT_LINE('<DEPT>' || p_dept || '</DEPT>');
   DBMS_OUTPUT.PUT_LINE('<emp ID="' || e.empno || '">');
   etc.
END LOOP;
```

and tell you it would likely run faster if you pull the "invariant" piece out of the loop, so it doesn't re-execute needlessly:

```
l_dept_str := '<DEPT>' || p_dept || '</DEPT>'
FOR e IN (SELECT * FROM employees WHERE DEPT = p_dept)
```

```
LOOP
   DBMS_OUTPUT.PUT_LINE(l_dept_str);
   DBMS_OUTPUT.PUT_LINE('<emp ID="' || e.empno || '">');
   etc.
END LOOP;
```

Even a salt-worthy programmer might decide, however, that the clarity of the first version outweighs the performance gains that the second would give you. Starting with Oracle Database 10g, PL/SQL no longer forces you to make this decision. With the default optimizer settings, the compiler will detect the pattern in the first version and convert it to bytecode that implements the second version. The reason this can happen is that the language definition does not require that loop invariants be executed repeatedly; this is one of the freedoms the optimizer can, and does, exploit. You might think that this is optimization is a little thing, and it is; but it's the little things that can add up. I've never seen a database that got smaller over time. Plenty of PL/SQL programs loop over all of the records in a growing table, and a million-row table is no longer considered unusually large. Personally, I'd be quite happy if Oracle would automatically eliminate a million unnecessary instructions from my code.

As another example, consider a series of statements such as these:

```
result1 := r * s * t;
...
result2 := r * s * v;
```

If there is no possibility of modifying r and s between these two statements, PL/SQL is free to compile the code like this:

```
interim := r * s;
result1 := interim * t;
...
result2 := interim * v;
```

The optimizer would take such a step if it thinks that storing the value in a temporary variable would be faster than repeating the multiplication.

Oracle has revealed these and other insights into the PL/SQL optimizer in a whitepaper, "Freedom, Order, and PL/SQL Compilation," which is available on the Oracle Technology Network.[1] To summarize some of the paper's main points:

1. Unless your code requires execution of a code fragment in a particular order by the rules of short-circuit expressions or of statement ordering, PL/SQL may execute the fragment in some order other than the one in which it was originally written. Reordering has a number of possible manifestations. In particular, the optimizer may change the order in which package initialization sections execute, and if a calling program only needs access to a package constant, the compiler may simply store that constant with the caller.

---

1. "Freedom, Order, and PL/SQL Compilation," by Charles Wetherell, is available on OTN at *http://otn .oracle.com* (enter the paper title in the search box).

2. PL/SQL treats the evaluation of array indexes and the identification of fields in records as operators. If you have a nested collection of records and refer to a particular element and field such as *price(product)(type).settle*, PL/SQL must figure out an internal address that is associated with the variable. This address is treated as an expression; it may be stored and reused later in the program to avoid the cost of recomputation.

3. As shown earlier, PL/SQL may introduce interim values to avoid computations.

4. PL/SQL may completely eliminate operations such as *x\*0*. However, an explicit function call will not be eliminated; in the expression *f()\*0*, the function *f()* will always be called in case there are side effects. (In fact, the function will be called even if it is free of side effects and marked as DETERMINISTIC; the PL/SQL compiler ignores this keyword.)

5. PL/SQL does not introduce new exceptions.

6. PL/SQL may obviate the raising of exceptions. For example, the divide by 0 exception in this code can be dropped because it is unreachable:

```
IF FALSE THEN y := x/0; END IF;
```

7. PL/SQL does not have the freedom to change which exception handler will handle a given exception.

Point 1 deserves a bit of elaboration. In the applications that I write, I'm accustomed to taking advantage of package initialization sections, but I've never really worried about execution order. My initialization sections are typically small and involve the assignment of static lookup values (typically retrieved from the database), and these operations seem to be immune from the order of operations. If your application must guarantee the order of execution, you'll want to move the code out of the initialization section and put it into separate initialization routines you invoke explicitly; for example, call:

```
pkgA.init();
pkgB.init();
```

right where you need pkgA and then pkgB initialized. This advice holds true even if you are not using the optimizing compiler.

Point 2 also deserves some comment. The example is price(product)(type).settle. If this element is referenced several times where the value of the variable type is changing but the value of the variable product is not, then optimization might split the addressing into two parts—the first to compute price(product) and the second (used several places) to compute the rest of the address. The code will run faster because only the changeable part of the address is recomputed each time the entire reference is used. More importantly, this is one of those changes that the compiler can make easily, but that would be very difficult for the programmer to make in the original source code because of the semantics of PL/SQL. Many of the optimization changes are of this ilk; the compiler can operate "under the hood" to do something the programmer would find difficult.

PL/SQL includes other features to identify and speed up certain programming idioms. In this code:

```
counter := counter + 1;
```

the compiler does not generate machine code that does the complete addition. Instead, PL/SQL detects this programming idiom and uses a special PL/SQL Virtual Machine (PVM) "increment" instruction that runs much faster than the conventional addition.

A special instruction also exists to handle code that concatenates many terms:

```
str := 'value1' || 'value2' || 'value3' ...
```

Rather than treating this as a series of pair-wise concatenations, the compiler and PVM work together and do the series of concatenations in a single instruction.

Most of the rewriting that the optimizer does will be invisible to you. During an upgrade, you may find a program that is not as well behaved as you thought, because it relied on an order of execution that the new compiler has changed. It seems likely that a common problem area will be the order of package initialization, but of course your mileage may vary.

One final comment: the way the optimizer modifies code is deterministic, at least for a given value of PLSQL_OPTIMIZE_LEVEL. In other words, if you write, compile, and test your program using, say, the default optimizer level of 2, its behavior will not change when you move the program to a different computer or a different database—as long as the destination database version and optimizer level are the same.

## Runtime Optimization of Fetch Loops

For database versions up through and including Oracle9*i* Database Release 2, a cursor FOR loop such as the following would retrieve exactly one logical row per fetch.

```
FOR arow IN (SELECT something FROM somewhere)
LOOP
   ...
END LOOP;
```

So, if you had 500 rows to retrieve, there would be 500 fetches, and therefore 500 expensive "context switches" between PL/SQL and SQL.

However, starting with Oracle Database 10*g*, the database performs an automatic "bulkification" of this construct so that *each fetch retrieves (up to) 100 rows*. The cursor FOR loop above would use only five fetches to bring the 500 rows back from the SQL engine. It's as if the database automatically recodes your loop to use the BULK COLLECT feature (described later in this chapter).

This apparently undocumented feature also works for code of the form:

```
FOR arow IN cursorname
LOOP
```

```
      ...
   END LOOP;
```

However, it does *not* work with code of the form:

```
OPEN cursorname;
LOOP
   EXIT WHEN cursorname%NOTFOUND;
   FETCH cursorname INTO ...
END LOOP;
CLOSE cursorname;
```

Nevertheless, this internal optimization should be a big win for the cursor FOR loop case (which has the added benefit of conciseness).

# Data Caching Techniques

A very common technique for improving performance is to build caches for data that needs to be accessed repeatedly—and that is, at least for some period of time, static (does not change).

The SGA of the Oracle database is the "mother of all caches," Oracle-wise. It is a (usually) very large and (always) very complex area of memory that serves as the intermediary between the actual database (files on disk) and the programs that manipulate that database.

As described more thoroughly in Chapter 20, the SGA caches the following information (and much more, but these are the most relevant for PL/SQL programmers):

- Parsed cursors
- Data queried by cursors from the database
- Partially compiled representations of our programs

For the most part, however, the database does not use the SGA to cache *program data*. When you declare a variable in your program, the memory for that data is consumed in the PGA. Each connection to the database has its own PGA; the memory required to store your program data is, therefore, copied in *each* connection that calls that program.

Fortunately, there is a benefit to the use of PGA memory: your PL/SQL program can retrieve information more quickly from the PGA than it can from the SGA. Thus, PGA-based caching offers some interesting opportunities to improve performance. Oracle also provides other PL/SQL-specific caching mechanisms to help improve performance of your programs. In this section, you will learn about three types of PL/SQL caching:

*Package-based caching*
>   Use the PGA memory area to store static data that you need to retrieve many times. Use PL/SQL programs to avoid repeatedly accessing data via the SQL layer in the

SGA. This is the fastest caching technique, but also the most restrictive in terms of circumstances when it can be safely used.

*Deterministic function caching*

When you declare a function to be *deterministic* and call that function inside a SQL statement, Oracle will cache the inputs to the function and its return value. If you call the function with the same inputs, Oracle will return the previously stored value without calling the function.

*Function result caching (Oracle Database 11g )*

This latest advance in PL/SQL caching is the most exciting and useful. With a simple declarative clause in your function header, you can instruct the database to cache the function's input and return values. In contrast to the deterministic approach, however, the function result cache is used whenever the function is called (not just from within a SQL statement), and the cache is automatically invalidated when dependent data changes.

 Cache with care! When you cache, you store a copy of the data. You need to be very certain that your copy is accurate and up-to-date. It is quite possible to abuse each of these caching approaches and end up with "dirty data" being served up to users.

## Package-Based Caching

A package-based cache consists of one or more variables declared at the package-level, rather than in any subprogram of the package. Package-level data is a natural repository for a cache, because this kind of data persists throughout a session, even if programs in that session are not currently using the data or calling any of the subprograms in the package. In other words, if you declare a variable at the package level, then once you assign a value to that variable, it keeps that value until you disconnect, recompile the package, or change the value.

I will explore package-based caching by first describing the scenarios under which you will want to use this technique. Then I will look at a simple example of caching a single value. Finally, I will show you how you can cache all or part of a relational table in a package, and thereby greatly speed up access to the data in that table.

### When to use package-based caching

Consider using a package-based cache under the following circumstances:

- You are not yet using Oracle Database 11g or higher. If you are developing applications for recent releases, you will almost always be better off using the function result cache, not a package-based cache.

- The data you wish to cache does not change for the duration of time that the data is needed by a user. Examples of static data include small reference tables ("O" is for "Open", "C" is for "Closed", etc.) that rarely if ever change; and batch scripts that require a "snapshot" of consistent data taken at the time the script starts and used until the script ends.

- Your database server has enough memory to support a copy of your cache for each session connected to the instance (and using your cache). You can use the utility described earlier in this chapter to measure the size of the cache defined in your package.

Conversely, do *not* use a package-based cache if either of the following is true:

- The data you are caching could possibly change during the time the user accesses the cache.
- The volume of data cached requires too much memory per session, causing memory errors with large numbers of users.

### A simple example of package-based caching

Consider the USER function—it returns the name of the currently connected session. Oracle implements this function in the STANDARD package as follows:

```
function USER return varchar2 is
c varchar2(255);
begin
      select user into c from sys.dual;
      return c;
end;
```

Thus, every time you call USER, you execute a query. Sure, it's a fast query, but it should never be executed more than once in a session, since the value never changes. You are probably now saying to yourself: So what? Not only is a SELECT FROM dual very efficient, but the Oracle database will also cache the parsed query and the value returned, so it is already very optimized. Would package-based caching make any difference? Absolutely!

Consider the following package:

```
/* File on web: thisuser.pkg */
PACKAGE thisuser
IS
   cname CONSTANT VARCHAR2(30) := USER;
   FUNCTION name RETURN VARCHAR2;
END;

PACKAGE BODY thisuser
IS
   g_user VARCHAR2(30) := USER;

   FUNCTION name RETURN VARCHAR2 IS BEGIN RETURN g_user; END;
END;
```

I cache the value returned by USER in two different ways:

- A constant defined at the package level: the PL/SQL runtime engine calls USER to initialize the constant when the package is initialized (on first use).
- A function: the function returns the name of "this user"—the value returned by the function is a private (package body) variable also assigned the value returned by USER when the package is initialized.

Having now created these caches, I should see if they are worth the bother. Is either implementation noticeably faster than simply calling the highly optimized USER function over and over?

So I build a script utilizing sf_timer to compare performances:

```
/* File on web: thisuser.tst */
PROCEDURE test_thisuser (count_in IN PLS_INTEGER)
IS
   l_name all_users.username%TYPE;
BEGIN
   sf_timer.start_timer;
   FOR indx IN 1 .. count_in LOOP l_name := thisuser.NAME; END LOOP;
   sf_timer.show_elapsed_time ('Packaged Function');
   --
   sf_timer.start_timer;
   FOR indx IN 1 .. count_in LOOP l_name := thisuser.cname; END LOOP;
   sf_timer.show_elapsed_time ('Packaged Constant');
   --
   sf_timer.start_timer;
   FOR indx IN 1 .. count_in LOOP l_name := USER; END LOOP;
   sf_timer.show_elapsed_time ('USER Function');
END test_thisuser;
```

And when I run it for 100 and then 1,000,000 iterations, I see these results:

```
Packaged Function Elapsed: 0 seconds.
Packaged Constant Elapsed: 0 seconds.
USER Function Elapsed: 0 seconds.

Packaged Function Elapsed: .48 seconds.
Packaged Constant Elapsed: .06 seconds.
USER Function Elapsed: 32.6 seconds.
```

The results are clear: for small numbers of iterations, the advantage of caching is not apparent. For large numbers of iterations, the package-based cache is dramatically faster than going through the SQL layer and the SGA.

By the way, accessing the constant is faster than calling a function that returns the value. So why use a function? The function version offers this advantage over the constant: it *hides* the value. So if for any reason the value must be changed (not applicable to this scenario), you can do so without recompiling the package specification, which would force recompilation of all programs dependent on this package.

While it is unlikely that you will ever benefit from caching the value returned by the USER function, I hope you can see that package-based caching is clearly a very efficient way to store and retrieve data. Now let's take a look at a less trivial example.

## Caching table contents in a package

If your application includes a table that never changes during normal working hours (that is, it is static while a user accesses the table), you can rather easily create a package that caches the full contents of that table, boosting query performance by an order of magnitude or more.

Suppose that I have a table of products that is static, defined as follows:

```
/* File on web: package_cache_demo.sql */
TABLE products (
    product_number INTEGER PRIMARY KEY
  , description VARCHAR2(1000))
```

Here is a package body that offers two ways of querying data from this table; query each time or cache the data and retrieve from cache:

```
1   PACKAGE BODY products_cache
2   IS
3      TYPE cache_t IS TABLE OF products%ROWTYPE INDEX BY PLS_INTEGER;
4      g_cache    cache_t;
5
6      FUNCTION with_sql (product_number_in IN products.product_number%TYPE)
7         RETURN products%ROWTYPE
8      IS
9         l_row     products%ROWTYPE;
10     BEGIN
11        SELECT * INTO l_row FROM products
12         WHERE product_number = product_number_in;
13        RETURN l_row;
14     END with_sql;
15
16     FUNCTION from_cache (product_number_in IN products.product_number%TYPE)
17        RETURN products%ROWTYPE
18     IS
19     BEGIN
20        RETURN g_cache (product_number_in);
21     END from_cache;
22  BEGIN
23     FOR product_rec IN (SELECT * FROM products) LOOP
24        g_cache (product_rec.product_number) := product_rec;
25     END LOOP;
26  END products_cache;
```

Here is an explanation of the interesting parts of this package:

| Line(s) | Significance |
|---------|--------------|
| 3–4 | Declare an associative array cache, g_cache, that mimics the structure of my products table: every element in the collection is a record with the same structure as a row in the table. |
| 6–14 | The with_sql function returns one row from the products table for a given primary key, using the "traditional" SELECT INTO method. In other words, every time you call this function you run a query. |
| 16–21 | The from_cache function also returns one row from the products table for a given primary key, but it does so by using that primary key as the index value, thereby locating the row in g_cache. |

| Line(s) | Significance |
|---------|--------------|
| 23–25 | When the package is initialized, load the contents of the products table into the g_cache collection. Notice that I use the primary key value as the index into the collection. This emulation of the primary key is what makes the from_cache implementation possible (and so simple). |

With this code in place, the first time a user calls the from_cache (or with_sql) function, the database will first execute this code.

Next, I construct and run a block of code to compare the performance of these approaches:

```
DECLARE
   l_row    products%ROWTYPE;
BEGIN
   sf_timer.start_timer;
   FOR indx IN 1 .. 100000
   LOOP
      l_row := products_cache.from_cache (5000);
   END LOOP;
   sf_timer.show_elapsed_time ('Cache table');
   --
   sf_timer.start_timer;
   FOR indx IN 1 .. 100000
   LOOP
      l_row := products_cache.with_sql (5000);
   END LOOP;
   sf_timer.show_elapsed_time ('Run query every time');
END;
```

And here are the results I see:

```
Cache table Elapsed: .14 seconds.
Run query every time Elapsed: 4.7 seconds.
```

Again, it is very clear that package-based caching is much, much faster that executing a query repeatedly—even when that query is fully optimized by all the power and sophistication of the SGA.

### Just-in-time caching of table data

Suppose I have identified a static table to which I want to apply this caching technique. There is, however, a problem: the table has 100,000 rows of data. I can build a package like products_cache, shown in the previous section, but it uses 5 MB of memory in each session's PGA. With 500 simultaneous connections, this cache will consume 2.5 GB, which is unacceptable. Fortunately, I notice that even though the table has many rows of data, each user will typically query only the same 50 or so rows of that data (there are, in other words, hot spots of activity). So caching the full table in each session is wasteful in both CPU cycles (the initial load of 100,000 rows) and memory.

When your table is static, but you don't want or need *all* the data in that table, you should consider employing a "just in time" approach to caching. This means that you do *not* query the full contents of the table into your collection cache when the package initializes. Instead, whenever the user asks for a row, if it is in the cache, you return it immediately. If not, you query that single row from the table, add it to the cache, and then return the data.

The next time the user asks for that same row, it will be retrieved from the cache.

```
/* File on web: package_cache_demo.sql */
FUNCTION jit_from_cache (product_number_in IN products.product_number%TYPE)
   RETURN products%ROWTYPE
IS
   l_row    products%ROWTYPE;
BEGIN
   IF g_cache.EXISTS (product_number_in)
   THEN
      /* Already in the cache, so return it. */
      l_row := g_cache (product_number_in);
   ELSE
      /* First request, so query it from the database
         and then add it to the cache. */
      l_row := with_sql (product_number_in);
      g_cache (product_number_in) := l_row;
   END IF;

   RETURN l_row;
END jit_from_cache;
```

Generally, just-in-time caching is somewhat slower than the one-time load of all data to the cache, but it is still much faster than repeated database lookups.

## Deterministic Function Caching

A function is considered to be *deterministic* if it returns the same result value whenever it is called with the same values for its IN and IN OUT arguments. Another way to think about deterministic programs is that they have no side effects. Everything the program changes is reflected in the parameter list. See Chapter 17 for more details on deterministic functions.

Precisely because the deterministic function behaves so consistently, Oracle can build a cache from the function's inputs and outputs. After all, if the same inputs *always* result in the same outputs, then there is no reason to call the function a second time if the inputs match a previous invocation of that function.

Let's take a look at an example of the caching nature of deterministic functions. Suppose I define the following encapsulation on top of SUBSTR (return the string between start and end locations) as a deterministic function:

```
/* File on web: deterministic_demo.sql */
FUNCTION betwnstr (
   string_in IN VARCHAR2, start_in IN PLS_INTEGER, end_in IN PLS_INTEGER)
   RETURN VARCHAR2 DETERMINISTIC
IS
```

```
BEGIN
   RETURN (SUBSTR (string_in, start_in, end_in - start_in + 1));
END betwnstr;
```

I can then call this function inside a query (it does not modify any database tables, which would otherwise preclude using it in this way), such as:

```
SELECT betwnstr (last_name, 1, 5) first_five
   FROM employees
```

And when betwnstr is called in this way, the database will build a cache of inputs and the return value. So if I call the function with the same inputs, the database will return the value without calling the function. To demonstrate this optimization, I will change betwnstr to the following:

```
FUNCTION betwnstr (
   string_in IN VARCHAR2, start_in IN PLS_INTEGER, end_in IN PLS_INTEGER)
   RETURN VARCHAR2 DETERMINISTIC
IS
BEGIN
   DBMS_LOCK.sleep (.01);
   RETURN (SUBSTR (string_in, start_in, end_in - start_in + 1));
END betwnstr;
```

In other words, I will use the sleep subprogram of DBMS_LOCK to pause betwnstr 1/100th of a second.

If I call this function in a PL/SQL block of code (not from within a query), the database will *not* cache the function values, and so when I query the 107 rows of the employees table, it takes more than one second:

```
DECLARE
   l_string employees.last_name%TYPE;
BEGIN
   sf_timer.start_timer;

   FOR rec IN (SELECT * FROM employees)
   LOOP
      l_string := betwnstr ('FEUERSTEIN', 1, 5);
   END LOOP;

   sf_timer.show_elapsed_time ('Deterministic function in block');
END;
/
```

The output is:

```
Deterministic function in block Elapsed: 1.67 seconds.
```

If I now execute the same logic, but move the call to betwnstr *inside* the query, the performance is quite different:

```
BEGIN
   sf_timer.start_timer;

   FOR rec IN (SELECT betwnstr ('FEUERSTEIN', 1, 5) FROM employees)
```

```
   LOOP
      NULL;
   END LOOP;

   sf_timer.show_elapsed_time ('Deterministic function in query');
END;
/
```

The output is:

```
Deterministic function in query Elapsed: .05 seconds.
```

As you can see, caching with a deterministic function is a very effective path to optimization. Just be sure of the following:

- When you declare a function to be deterministic, make sure that it really *is*. The Oracle database does not analyze your program to determine if you are telling the truth. If you add the DETERMINISTIC keyword to a function that, for example, queries data from a table, the database might cache data inappropriately, with the consequence that a user sees "dirty data."

- You must call that function within a SQL statement to get the effects of deterministic caching; that is a significant constraint on the usefulness of this type of caching.

## Function Result Cache (Oracle Database 11g)

Prior to the release of Oracle Database 11g, package-based caching offered the best, most flexible option for caching data for use in a PL/SQL program. Sadly, the circumstances under which it can be used are quite limited, since the data source must be static and memory consumption grows with each session connected to the Oracle database.

Recognizing the performance benefit of this kind of caching (as well as that implemented for deterministic functions), Oracle implemented the *function result cache* in Oracle Database 11g. This feature offers a caching solution that overcomes the weaknesses of package-based caching and offers performance that is almost as fast.

When you turn on the function result cache for a function, you get the following benefits:

- Oracle stores both inputs and the return value in a separate cache for each function. The cache is shared among all sessions connected to this instance of the database; it is *not* duplicated for each session. And in Oracle Database 11g Release 2, the function result cache is even shared across instances in a RAC.

- Whenever the function is called, the database checks to see if it has already cached the same input values. If so, then the function is not executed. The values in the cache are simply returned.

- Whenever changes are made to tables that are identified as dependencies for the cache, the database automatically invalidates the cache. Subsequent calls to the function will then repopulate the cache with consistent data.
- Caching occurs whenever the function is called; you do not need to invoke it within a SQL statement.
- There is no need to write code to declare and populate a collection; instead, you use declarative syntax in the function header to specify the cache.

In the following sections, I will first describe the syntax of this feature. Then I will demonstrate some simple examples of the cache; discuss the circumstances under which you should use this cache; cover the DBA-related aspects of cache management; and review restrictions and gotchas for this feature.

### How to use the function result cache

Oracle has made it very easy to add function result caching to your functions. You simply need to add the RESULT_CACHE clause to the header of your function, and Oracle takes it from there.

The syntax of the RESULT_CACHE clause is:

```
RESULT_CACHE [ RELIES_ON (table_or_view [, table_or_view2 ...  table_or_viewN] ]
```

The RELIES_ON tells Oracle on which tables or views the contents of the cache rely. This clause can only be added to the headers of schema-level functions and the *implementation* of a packaged function (that is, in the package body).

Here are several examples of using this clause.

1. Schema-level function without RELIES_ON:

   ```
   CREATE OR REPLACE FUNCTION session_constant RETURN VARCHAR2
      RESULT_CACHE
   ```

2. Schema-level function with RELIES_ON clause indicating that the cache relies on the employees table:

   ```
   CREATE OR REPLACE FUNCTION name_for_id (id_in IN employees.employee_id%TYPE)
      RETURN employees.last_name%TYPE
      RESULT_CACHE RELIES ON (employees)
   ```

3. A packaged function without a RELIES_ON clause (needed in both specification and body):

   ```
   CREATE OR REPLACE PACKAGE get_data
   IS
      FUNCTION FUNCTION session_constant RETURN VARCHAR2
      RESULT_CACHE;
   END get_data;
   /

   CREATE OR REPLACE PACKAGE BODY get_data
   IS
   ```

```
        FUNCTION session_constant RETURN VARCHAR2
            RESULT_CACHE
        IS
        BEGIN
            ...
        END session_constant;
    END get_data;
    /
```

4. A packaged function with a RELIES_ON clause (it may appear *only* in the body):

```
    CREATE OR REPLACE PACKAGE get_data
    IS
        FUNCTION name_for_id (id_in IN employees.employee_id%TYPE)
            RETURN employees.last_name%TYPE
            RESULT_CACHE
    END get_data;
    /

    CREATE OR REPLACE PACKAGE BODY get_data
    IS
        FUNCTION name_for_id (id_in IN employees.employee_id%TYPE)
            RETURN employees.last_name%TYPE
            RESULT_CACHE RELIES ON (employees)
        IS
        BEGIN
            ...
        END name_for_id;
    END get_data;
    /
```

5. A RELIES_ON clause with multiple objects listed:

```
    CREATE OR REPLACE PACKAGE BODY get_data
    IS
        FUNCTION name_for_id (id_in IN employees.employee_id%TYPE)
            RETURN employees.last_name%TYPE
            RESULT_CACHE RELIES ON (employees, departments, locations)
    ...
```

That is all it takes! The only complicated element is RELIES_ON, so let's focus in on that before exploring this feature in more detail.

### The RELIES_ON clause

RELIES_ON is a critical element of the function result cache; it gives the database the information needed to correctly invalidate cached data. If you do not include this clause and/or list incorrectly the tables or views on which the function's returned data depends, that function could return out-of-date, incorrect data to a user.

The first thing to know about RELIES_ON is that it is no longer needed in Oracle Database 11g Release 2. Oracle will now *automatically* determine on which tables your returned data is dependent and correctly invalidate the cache when those tables' contents are changed. Run the *11Gr2_frc_no_relies_on.sql* script to verify this behavior.

In Oracle Database 11g Release 1, however, it is still up to you to explicitly list all tables and views from which returned data is queried. Determining which tables and views to include in the list is usually fairly straightforward. If your function contains a SELECT statement, then make sure that any tables or views in any FROM clause in that query are added to the list.

If you select from a view, you need to list only that view, not all the tables that are queried from within the view. The script named *11g_frc_views.sql* demonstrates how the database will determine from the view definition itself all the tables whose changes must invalidate the cache.

### Function result cache example: A deterministic function

In a previous section I talked about the caching associated with deterministic functions. In particular, I noted that this caching will only come into play when the function is called within a query. Let's now apply the Oracle Database 11g function result cache to the betwnstr function and see that it works when called natively in a PL/SQL block.

In the following function, I add the RESULT_CACHE clause to the header. I also add a call to DBMS_OUTPUT.PUT_LINE to show what inputs were passed to the function.

```
/* File on web: 11g_frc_simple_demo.sql */
FUNCTION betwnstr (
    string_in IN VARCHAR2, start_in IN INTEGER, end_in  IN INTEGER)
    RETURN VARCHAR2 RESULT_CACHE
IS
BEGIN
    DBMS_OUTPUT.put_line (
        'betwnstr for ' || string_in || '-' || start_in || '-' || end_in);
    RETURN (SUBSTR (string_in, start_in, end_in - start_in + 1));
END;
```

I then call this function for ten rows in the employees table. If the employee ID is even, then apply betwnstr to the employee last name; otherwise, pass it the same three input values.

```
DECLARE
    l_string   employees.last_name%TYPE;
BEGIN
    FOR rec IN (SELECT * FROM employees WHERE ROWNUM < 11)
    LOOP
        l_string :=
            CASE MOD (rec.employee_id, 2)
                WHEN 0 THEN betwnstr (rec.last_name, 1, 5)
                ELSE        betwnstr ('FEUERSTEIN', 1, 5)
            END;
    END LOOP;
END;
```

When I run this function, I see the following output:

```
betwnstr for OConnell-1-5
betwnstr for FEUERSTEIN-1-5
```

```
betwnstr for Whalen-1-5
betwnstr for Fay-1-5
betwnstr for Baer-1-5
betwnstr for Gietz-1-5
betwnstr for King-1-5
```

Notice that FEUERSTEIN appears only once, even though it was called five times. That demonstrates the function result cache in action.

### Function result cache example: Querying data from a table

You will mostly want to use the function result cache when you are querying data from a table, whose contents are queried more frequently than changed (in between changes, the data is static). Suppose, for example, that in my real estate management application, I have a table that contains the interest rates available for different types of loans. The contents of this table are updated via a scheduled job that runs once an hour throughout the day. Here is the structure of the table and the data I am using in my demonstration script:

```
/* File on web: 11g_frc_demo_table.sql */
CREATE TABLE loan_info (
    NAME VARCHAR2(100) PRIMARY KEY,
    length_of_loan INTEGER,
    initial_interest_rate NUMBER,
    regular_interest_rate NUMBER,
    percentage_down_payment INTEGER)
/
BEGIN
    INSERT INTO loan_info VALUES ('Five year fixed', 5, 6, 6, 20);
    INSERT INTO loan_info VALUES ('Ten year fixed', 10, 5.7, 5.7, 20);
    INSERT INTO loan_info VALUES ('Fifteen year fixed', 15, 5.5, 5.5, 10);
    INSERT INTO loan_info VALUES ('Thirty year fixed', 30, 5, 5, 10);
    INSERT INTO loan_info VALUES ('Two year balloon', 2, 3, 8, 0);
    INSERT INTO loan_info VALUES ('Five year balloon', 5, 4, 10, 5);
    COMMIT;
END;
/
```

Here is a function to retrieve all the information for a single row:

```
FUNCTION loan_info_for_name (NAME_IN IN VARCHAR2)
    RETURN loan_info%ROWTYPE
    RESULT_CACHE RELIES_ON (loan_info)
IS
    l_row    loan_info%ROWTYPE;
BEGIN
    DBMS_OUTPUT.put_line ('> Looking up loan info for ' || NAME_IN);

    SELECT * INTO l_row FROM loan_info WHERE NAME = NAME_IN;

    RETURN l_row;
END loan_info_for_name;
```

In this case, the RESULT_CACHE clause includes the RELIES_ON subclause to indicate that the cache for this function is based on data from ("relies on") the loan_info table. I then run the following script, which calls the function for two different names; then changes the contents of the table; and finally calls the function again for one of the original names.

```
DECLARE
   l_row    loan_info%ROWTYPE;
BEGIN
   DBMS_OUTPUT.put_line ('First time for Five year fixed...');
   l_row := loan_info_for_name ('Five year fixed');
   DBMS_OUTPUT.put_line ('First time for Five year balloon...');
   l_row := loan_info_for_name ('Five year balloon');
   DBMS_OUTPUT.put_line ('Second time for Five year fixed...');
   l_row := loan_info_for_name ('Five year fixed');

   UPDATE loan_info SET percentage_down_payment = 25
    WHERE NAME = 'Thirty year fixed';
   COMMIT;

   DBMS_OUTPUT.put_line ('After commit, third time for Five year fixed...');
   l_row := loan_info_for_name ('Five year fixed');
END;
```

Here's the output from running this script:

```
First time for Five year fixed...
> Looking up loan info for Five year fixed
First time for Five year balloon...
> Looking up loan info for Five year balloon
Second time for Five year fixed...
After commit, third time for Five year fixed...
> Looking up loan info for Five year fixed
```

And here is an explanation of what you see happening here:

- The *first* time I call the function for "Five year fixed", it executes the function, looks up the data, puts the data in the cache, and returns the data.

- The first time I call the function for "Five year balloon", it executes the function, looks up the data, puts the data in the cache, and returns the data.

- The *second* time I call the function for "Five year fixed", it does not execute the function (there is no "Looking up ..." for the second call). The function result cache at work...

- Then I change a column value for the row with name "Thirty year fixed" and commit that change.

- Finally, I call the function for the *third* time for "Five year fixed" and it calls the function this time to query the data. This happens because I have told Oracle that this RESULT_CACHE RELIES ON the loan_info table, and the contents of that table have changed.

## Function result cache example: Caching a collection

So far I have shown you examples of caching an individual value and an entire record. You can also cache an entire collection of data, even a collection of records. In the following code, I have changed the function to return all of the names of loans into a collection of strings (based on the predefined DBMS_SQL collection type). I then call the function repeatedly but the collection is populated only once. (BULK COLLECT is described later in this chapter.)

```
/* File on web: 11g_frc_table_demo.sql */
FUNCTION loan_names RETURN DBMS_SQL.VARCHAR2S
   RESULT_CACHE RELIES_ON (loan_info)
IS
   l_names    DBMS_SQL.VARCHAR2S;
BEGIN
   DBMS_OUTPUT.put_line ('> Looking up loan names....');

   SELECT name BULK COLLECT INTO l_names FROM loan_info;
   RETURN l_names;
END loan_names;
```

Here is a script that demonstrates that even when populating a complex type like this, the function result cache will come into play:

```
DECLARE
   l_names    DBMS_SQL.VARCHAR2S;
BEGIN
   DBMS_OUTPUT.put_line ('First time retrieving all names...');
   l_names := loan_names ();
   DBMS_OUTPUT.put_line('Second time retrieving all names...');
   l_names := loan_names ();

   UPDATE loan_info SET percentage_down_payment = 25
    WHERE NAME = 'Thirty year fixed';

   COMMIT;
   DBMS_OUTPUT.put_line ('After commit, third time retrieving all names...');
   l_names := loan_names ();
END;
/
```

The output is:

```
First time retrieving all names...
> Looking up loan names....
Second time retrieving all names...
After commit, third time retrieving all names...
> Looking up loan names....
```

## When to use the function result cache

Caching must always be done with the greatest of care. If you cache incorrectly, your application may deliver bad data to users. The function result cache is the most flexible and widely useful of the different types of caches you can use in PL/SQL code, but you can still get yourself in trouble with it.

You should consider adding RESULT_CACHE to your function header in any of the following circumstances:

- Data is queried from a table more frequently than it is updated. Suppose, for example, that in our Human Resources application, users query the contents of the employees table thousands of times a minute, but it is updated on average once every ten minutes. In between those changes, the employees table is static, so the data can be safely cached—and the query time reduced.

- A function that doesn't even query any data is called repeatedly (often in this scenario, recursively) with the same input values. One classic example from programming texts is the Fibonacci algorithm. To calculate the Fibonacci value for the integer, n (a.k.a., F(n)), you must compute F(1) through F(n–1) multiple times.

- Your application (or each user of an application) relies on a set of configuration values that are static during use of the application: a perfect fit for the function result cache!

### When *not* to use the function result cache

You cannot use the RESULT_CACHE clause if any of the following are true:

- The function is defined within the declaration section of an anonymous block. The function must be defined at the schema level or within a package.
- The function is a pipelined table function.
- The function has any OUT or IN OUT parameters. The function can only return data through the RETURN clause.
- Any of the function's IN parameters are of any of these types: BLOB, CLOB, NCLOB, REF CURSOR, collection, record, object type.
- The function RETURN type is any of the following: BLOB, CLOB, NCLOB, REF CURSOR, object type, or collection or record that contains the previously listed datatypes (for example, a collection of CLOBs would be a no-go for a function result cache).
- The function is an invoker rights function. In other words, your function is defined with the AUTHID CURRENT_USER clause (see Chapter 24 for more details on this clause). CURRENT_USER means that when the function is executed, any references to database objects like tables will be resolved according to the privileges of the *current user* of the function. So schemas USER1 and USER2 may actually need to query from *different tables* (for example, each has its own employees table). Yet if that function caches results and both those schemas call the function, then whoever calls it first will set the results wrongly for the second.

You should not use (or at a minimum very carefully evaluate your use of) the RESULT_CACHE clause if either of the following is true:

- Your function has side effects; for example, it modifies the contents of database tables or modifies the external state of your application (by, for example, sending data to sysout via DBMS_OUTPUT or sending email). Since you can never be sure when and if the body of the function will execute, your application will likely not perform correctly under all circumstances. This is an unacceptable tradeoff for improved performance.

- Your function executes a query against a table on which a Virtual Private Database security policy applies. I explore the ramifications of using VPD with function result caching later, in the section "The Virtual Private Database and function result caching" on page 816.

### Useful details of function result cache behavior

The following information should come in handy as you delve into the details of applying the function result cache to your application.

- When checking to see if the function has been called previously with the same inputs, Oracle considers NULL to be equal to NULL. In other words, if my function has one string argument and it is called with a NULL input value, then the next time it is called with a NULL value, Oracle will decide that it does not need to call the function and can instead return the cached outcome.

- Users never see dirty data. Suppose a result cache function returns the last name of an employee for an ID, and that the last name "Feuerstein" is cached for ID 400. Then if a user changes the contents of the employees table, but has not yet committed the change, the database will bypass the cache (and any other cache that relies on employees) for this user. All other users connected to the instance (RAC, in Oracle Database 11g Release 2) will continue to take advantage of the cache.

- When you define a function's cache as dependent on a particular table, then when that table is marked invalid, the function is also marked invalid and will need to be recompiled before it can be used.

- If the function propagates an unhandled exception, the database will not cache the input values for that execution. That is, the contents of the result cache for this function will not be changed.

### Managing the function result cache

The function result cache is an area of memory in the SGA. Oracle provides the usual cast of characters so that a database administrator can manage that cache:

*RESULT_CACHE_MAX_SIZE initialization parameter*

Maximum amount of SGA memory that the function result cache can use. When the cache fills up, Oracle will use the least-recently-used algorithm to age out of the cache the data that has been there the longest.

*DBMS_RESULT_CACHE package*

Supplied package that offers a set of subprograms to manage the contents of the cache. This package will mostly be of interest to database administrators.

*Dynamic performance views*

V$RESULT_CACHE_STATISTICS, V$RESULT_CACHE_MEMORY, V$RESULT_CACHE_OBJECTS, and V$RESULT_CACHE_DEPENDENCY

### The Virtual Private Database and function result caching

When you use the Virtual Private Database (VPD) (also known as *row level security* or *fine-grained access control*) in your application, you define *security policies* to SQL operations on tables. The Oracle database then automatically adds these polices in the form of WHERE clause predicates to restrict the rows that a user can query or change in that table. It is impossible to get around these policies, since they are applied *inside* the SQL layer—and they are invisible to the user. The bottom line: users connected to two different schemas can run what seems to be the same query (as in "SELECT last_name FROM employees") and get different results. For detailed information about VPD, see Chapter 23.

Let's take a look at a simplistic use of VPD and how it can lead to bad data for users (all the code in this section may be found in the *11g_frc_vpd.sql* file). Suppose I define the following package with two functions in my Human Resources application schema, one to return the last name of an employee for a given employee ID, and the other to be used as a VPD security policy:

```
/* File on web: 11g_frc_vpd.sql */
PACKAGE emplu11g
IS
   FUNCTION last_name (employee_id_in IN employees.employee_id%TYPE)
      RETURN employees.last_name%TYPE
      result_cache;

   FUNCTION restrict_employees (schema_in VARCHAR2, NAME_IN VARCHAR2)
      RETURN VARCHAR2;
END emplu11g;

PACKAGE BODY emplu11g
IS
   FUNCTION last_name (employee_id_in IN employees.employee_id%TYPE)
      RETURN employees.last_name%TYPE
      result_cache relies_on (employees)
   IS
      onerow_rec   employees%ROWTYPE;
   BEGIN
      DBMS_OUTPUT.PUT_LINE ( 'Looking up last name for employee ID '
```

```
                              || employee_id_in );
    SELECT * INTO onerow_rec
      FROM employees
     WHERE employee_id = employee_id_in;

    RETURN onerow_rec.last_name;
END last_name;

FUNCTION restrict_employees (schema_in VARCHAR2, NAME_IN VARCHAR2)
   RETURN VARCHAR2
IS
BEGIN
   RETURN (CASE USER
              WHEN 'HR' THEN '1 = 1'
              ELSE '1 = 2'
           END
          );
END restrict_employees;
END emplu11g;
```

The restrict_employees function states very simply: if you are connected to the HR schema, you can see all rows in the employees table; otherwise, you can see nothing.

I then assign this function as the security policy for all operations on the employees table:

```
BEGIN
   DBMS_RLS.add_policy
                  (object_schema        => 'HR'
                  , object_name         => 'employees'
                  , policy_name         => 'rls_and_rc'
                  , function_schema     => 'HR'
                  , policy_function     => 'emplu11g.restrict_employees'
                  , statement_types     => 'SELECT,UPDATE,DELETE,INSERT'
                  , update_check        => TRUE
                  );
END;
```

I then give the SCOTT schema the ability to execute this package and select from the underlying table:

```
GRANT EXECUTE ON emplu11g TO scott
/
GRANT SELECT ON employees TO scott
/
```

Before I run the result cache function, let's verify that the security policy is in place and affecting the data that HR and SCOTT can see.

I connect as HR and query from the employees table successfully:

```
SELECT last_name
  FROM employees
 WHERE employee_id = 198
/
LAST_NAME
```

```
------------------------
OConnell
```

Now I connect to SCOTT and execute the same query; notice the difference!

```
CONNECT scott/tiger@oracle11

SELECT last_name
  FROM hr.employees
 WHERE employee_id = 198
/
no rows selected.
```

The VPD at work: when connected as SCOTT, I cannot see rows of data that are visible from HR.

Now let's see what happens when I execute the same query from within a result cache function owned by HR. First, I connect as HR and execute the function, then display the name returned:

```
BEGIN
   DBMS_OUTPUT.put_line (emplu11g.last_name (198));
END;
/
Looking up last name for employee ID 198
OConnell
```

Notice the two lines of output:

1. "Looking up last name for employee ID 198" is displayed because the function was executed.

2. "OConnell" is displayed because the row of data was found and the last name returned.

Now I connect as SCOTT and run the same block of code. Since the function executes a SELECT INTO that *should* return no rows, I should expect to see an unhandled NO_DATA_FOUND exception. Instead...

```
BEGIN
   DBMS_OUTPUT.put_line (hr.emplu11g.last_name (198));
END;
/
OConnell
```

The function successfully returns "OConnell", but notice that the "Looking up..." text is not shown. That's because the PL/SQL engine did not actually execute the function (and the call to DBMS_OUTPUT.PUT_LINE inside the function). It simply returned the cached last name.

And this is precisely the scenario that makes VPD such a dangerous combination with the function result cache. Since the function was first called with the input value of 198 from HR, the last name was cached for use in all other sessions connected to this same instance. Thus, a user connected to SCOTT sees data that he is not supposed to see.

To verify that the function really should return NO_DATA_FOUND if caching were not in place, let's now connect to HR and invalidate the cache by committing a change to the employees table (any change will do):

```
BEGIN
   /* All us non-CEO employees deserve a 50% raise, don't we? */
   UPDATE employees SET salary = salary * 1.5;
   COMMIT;
END;/
```

And now when I connect to SCOTT and run the function, I get an unhandled NO_DATA_FOUND exception:

```
BEGIN
   DBMS_OUTPUT.put_line (hr.emplu11g.last_name (198));
END;
/
ORA-01403: no data found
ORA-06512: at "HR.EMPLU11G", line 10
ORA-06512: at line 3
```

So if you are working on one of those relatively rare applications that relies on the Virtual Private Database, be very wary of defining functions that use the function result cache.

## Caching Summary

If a value has not changed, you should seek ways to minimize the time it to takes to retrieve that value. As proven for years by the SGA of Oracle's database architecture, data caching is a critical technology when it comes to optimizing performance. We can learn from the SGA's transparent caching of cursors, data blocks, etc., to create our own caches or take advantage of non-transparent SGA caches (meaning that we need to change our code in some way to take advantage of them).

Here I briefly summarize the recommendations I've made for data caching. The options include:

*Package-based caching*
   Create a package-level cache, likely of a collection, that will store previously re-trieved data and make it available from PGA memory much more quickly than from the SGA. There are two major downsides of this cache: it is copied for each session connected to the Oracle database; and you cannot update the cache if a session makes changes to the table(s) from which the cached data is drawn.

*Deterministic function caching*
   Define a function as DETERMINISTIC. Specifying this keyword will cause caching of the function's inputs and return value within the scope of execution of a *single SQL query*.

*Function result cache (Oracle Database 11g)*

Use the Oracle Database 11g function result cache whenever you ask for data from a table that is queried much more frequently than it is changed. This declarative approach to function-based caching is *almost* as fast as the package-level cache. It is shared across all sessions connected to the instance, and can be automatically invalidated whenever a change is made to the table(s) from which the cached data is drawn.

# Bulk Processing for Multirow SQL

Oracle introduced a significant enhancement to PL/SQL's SQL-related capabilities with the FORALL statement and BULK COLLECT clause for queries. Together, these are referred to as *bulk processing* statements for PL/SQL. Why, you might wonder, would this be necessary? We all know that PL/SQL is tightly integrated with the underlying SQL engine in the Oracle database. PL/SQL is *the* database programming language of choice for Oracle—even though you can now use Java inside the database as well.

But this tight integration does not mean that there is no overhead associated with running SQL from a PL/SQL program. When the PL/SQL runtime engine processes a block of code, it executes the procedural statements within its own engine, but passes the SQL statements on to the SQL engine. The SQL layer executes the SQL statements and then returns information to the PL/SQL engine, if necessary.

This transfer of control (shown in Figure 21-2) between the PL/SQL and SQL engines is called a *context switch*. Each time a switch occurs, there is additional overhead. There are a number of scenarios in which many switches occur and performance degrades. As you can see, PL/SQL and SQL might be tightly integrated on the syntactic level, but "under the covers" the integration is not as tight as it could be.

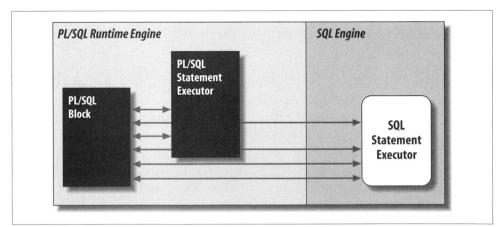

*Figure 21-2. Context switching between PL/SQL and SQL*

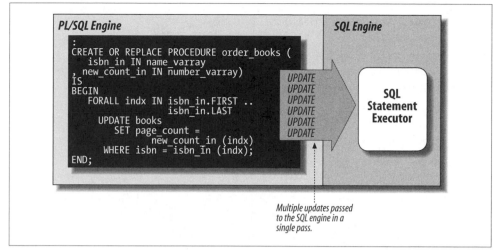

```
  :
CREATE OR REPLACE PROCEDURE order_books (
    isbn_in IN name_varray
, new_count_in IN number_varray)
IS
BEGIN
    FORALL indx IN isbn_in.FIRST ..
                   isbn_in.LAST
      UPDATE books
        SET page_count =
               new_count_in (indx)
        WHERE isbn = isbn_in (indx);
END;
```

*Figure 21-3. One context switch with FORALL*

With FORALL and BULK COLLECT, however, you can fine-tune the way these two engines communicate, effectively telling the PL/SQL engine to compress multiple context switches into a single switch, thereby improving the performance of your applications.

Consider the FORALL statement shown in the figure. Rather than use a cursor FOR loop or a numeric loop to iterate through the rows to be updated, I use a FORALL header to specify a total number of iterations for execution. At runtime, the PL/SQL engine "expands" the UPDATE statement into a set of statements incorporating all the iterations, and then passes them to the SQL engine with a single context switch. In other words, the same SQL statements are executed, but they are all run in the same round trip to the SQL layer, minimizing the context switches. This is shown in Figure 21-3.

This reduction in context switches leads to a surprisingly sharp reduction in elapsed time for multirow SQL statements executed in PL/SQL. Let's take a closer look at BULK COLLECT and FORALL.

## High Speed Querying with BULK COLLECT

With BULK COLLECT you can retrieve multiple rows of data through either an implicit or an explicit cursor with a single roundtrip to and from the database. BULK COLLECT reduces the number of context switches between the PL/SQL and SQL engines and thereby reduces the overhead of retrieving data.

Take a look at the following code snippet. I need to retrieve hundreds of rows of data on automobiles that have a poor environmental record. I place that data into a set of collections so that I can easily and quickly manipulate the data for both analysis and reporting.

```
DECLARE
   TYPE names_t IS TABLE OF transportation.name%TYPE;
   TYPE mileage_t IS TABLE OF transportation.mileage %TYPE;
   names names_t := names_t();
   mileages mileage_t := mileage_t();

   CURSOR major_polluters_cur
   IS
      SELECT name, mileage FROM transportation
       WHERE transport_type = 'AUTOMOBILE' AND mileage < 20;
BEGIN
   FOR bad_car IN major_polluters_cur
   LOOP
      names.EXTEND;
      names (major_polluters_cur%ROWCOUNT) := bad_car.NAME;
      mileages.EXTEND;
      mileages (major_polluters_cur%ROWCOUNT) := bad_car.mileage;
   END LOOP;
   -- Now work with data in the collections
END;
```

This certainly gets the job done, but the job might take a long time to complete. Consider this: if the transportation table contains 2,000 vehicles, then the PL/SQL engine issues 2,000 individual fetches against the cursor in the SGA.

To help out in this scenario, use the BULK COLLECT clause in the INTO element of your query. By using this clause in your cursor (explicit or implicit) you tell the SQL engine to bulk bind the output from the multiple rows fetched by the query into the specified collections before returning control to the PL/SQL engine. The syntax for this clause is:

```
... BULK COLLECT INTO collection_name[, collection_name] ...
```

where *collection_name* identifies a collection.

Here are some rules and restrictions to keep in mind when using BULK COLLECT:

- Prior to Oracle9i Database, you could use BULK COLLECT only with static SQL. Now you can use BULK COLLECT with both dynamic and static SQL.

- You can use BULK COLLECT keywords in any of the following clauses: SELECT INTO, FETCH INTO, and RETURNING INTO.

- The SQL engine automatically initializes and extends the collections you reference in the BULK COLLECT clause. It starts filling the collections at index 1, inserts elements consecutively (densely), and overwrites the values of any elements that were previously defined.

- You can't use the SELECT...BULK COLLECT statement in a FORALL statement.

- SELECT...BULK COLLECT will *not* raise NO_DATA_FOUND if no rows are found. Instead, you must check the contents of the collection to see if there is any data inside it.

- If the query returns no rows, the collection's COUNT method will return 0.

---

Let's explore these rules and the usefulness of BULK COLLECT through a series of examples. First, here is a rewrite of the major polluters example using BULK COLLECT:

```
DECLARE
   TYPE names_t IS TABLE OF transportation.name%TYPE;
   TYPE mileage_t IS TABLE OF transportation.mileage %TYPE;
   names names_t;
   mileages mileage_t;
BEGIN
   SELECT name, mileage BULK COLLECT INTO names, mileages
     FROM transportation
       WHERE transport_type = 'AUTOMOBILE'
         AND mileage < 20;

   /* Now work with data in the collections */
END;
```

I am now able to remove the initialization and extension code from the row-by-row fetch implementation.

I don't have to rely on implicit cursors to get this job done. Here is another reworking of the major polluters example, retaining the explicit cursor:

```
DECLARE
   TYPE names_t IS TABLE OF transportation.name%TYPE;
   TYPE mileage_t IS TABLE OF transportation.mileage %TYPE;
   names names_t;
   mileages mileage_t;

   CURSOR major_polluters_cur IS
      SELECT name, mileage FROM transportation
        WHERE transport_type = 'AUTOMOBILE' AND mileage < 20;
BEGIN
   OPEN major_polluters_cur;
   FETCH major_polluters_cur BULK COLLECT INTO names, mileages;
   CLOSE major_polluters_cur;
   ...
END;
```

I can also simplify my life and code by fetching into a collection of records, as you see here:

```
DECLARE
   TYPE transportation_aat IS TABLE OF transportation%ROWTYPE
      INDEX BY PLS_INTEGER;
   l_transportation transportation_aat;
BEGIN
   SELECT * BULK COLLECT INTO l_transportation
     FROM transportation
       WHERE transport_type = 'AUTOMOBILE'
         AND mileage < 20;

   -- Now work with data in the collections
END;
```

In Oracle Database 10g and later, the PL/SQL compiler will automatically optimize a cursor FOR loop so that it runs with performance comparable to BULK COLLECT. You do *not* need to explicitly transform this code yourself—unless the body of your loop executes, directly or indirectly, DML statements. The database does not optimize DML statements into FORALL, so you will need to explicitly convert your cursor FOR loop to use BULK COLLECT. You can then use the collections populated by the BULK COLLECT to "drive" the FORALL statement.

### Limiting rows retrieved with BULK COLLECT

Oracle provides a LIMIT clause for BULK COLLECT that allows you to limit the number of rows fetched from the database. The syntax is:

```
FETCH cursor BULK COLLECT INTO ... [LIMIT rows];
```

where *rows* can be any literal, variable, or expression that evaluates to an integer (otherwise, the database will raise a VALUE_ERROR exception).

LIMIT is very useful with BULK COLLECT, because it helps you manage how much memory your program will use to process data. Suppose, for example, that you need to query and process 10,000 rows of data. You *could* use BULK COLLECT to retrieve all those rows and populate a rather large collection. However, this approach will consume lots of memory in the PGA for that session. If this code is run by many separate Oracle schemas, your application performance may degrade because of PGA swapping.

The following block of code uses the LIMIT clause in a FETCH that is inside a simple loop.

```
DECLARE
   CURSOR allrows_cur IS SELECT * FROM employees;
   TYPE employee_aat IS TABLE OF allrows_cur%ROWTYPE
      INDEX BY BINARY_INTEGER;
   l_employees employee_aat;
BEGIN
   OPEN allrows_cur;
   LOOP
      FETCH allrows_cur BULK COLLECT INTO l_employees LIMIT 100;

      /* Process the data by scanning through the collection. */
      FOR l_row IN 1 .. l_employees.COUNT
      LOOP
         upgrade_employee_status (l_employees(l_row).employee_id);
      END LOOP;

      EXIT WHEN allrows_cur%NOTFOUND;
   END LOOP;

   CLOSE allrows_cur;
END;
```

Notice that I terminate the loop by checking the value of allrows_cur%NOTFOUND at the bottom of the loop. When querying data one row at a time, I usually put this code immediately after the FETCH statement. You should *not* do that when using BULK COLLECT, because when the fetch retrieves the last set of rows, the cursor will be exhausted (and %NOTFOUND will return TRUE) but you will still have some elements in the collection to process.

So either check the %NOTFOUND attribute at the *bottom* of your loop, or check the contents of the collection immediately after the fetch:

```
LOOP
   FETCH allrows_cur BULK COLLECT INTO l_employees LIMIT 100;
   EXIT WHEN l_employees.COUNT = 0;
```

The disadvantage of this second approach is that you will perform an extra fetch that returns no rows, compared to checking %NOTFOUND at the bottom of the loop body.

### Bulk fetching of multiple columns

As you have seen in previous examples, you certainly can bulk fetch the contents of more than one column. It would be most elegant if you could fetch those multiple columns into a single collection of records. In fact, Oracle made this feature available starting with Oracle9*i* Database Release 2.

Suppose that I would like to retrieve all the information in my transportation table for each vehicle whose mileage is less than 20 miles per gallon. I can do so with a minimum of coding fuss:

```
DECLARE
   -- Declare the type of collection
   TYPE VehTab IS TABLE OF transportation%ROWTYPE;

   -- Instantiate a particular collection from the TYPE.
   gas_guzzlers VehTab;
BEGIN
   SELECT *
     BULK COLLECT INTO gas_guzzlers
     FROM transportation
    WHERE mileage < 20;
   ...
```

Prior to Oracle9*i* Database Release 2, the above code would raise this exception:

```
PLS-00597: expression 'GAS_GUZZLERS' in the INTO list is of wrong type
```

You can use the LIMIT clause with a BULK COLLECT into a collection of records, just as you would with any other BULK COLLECT statement.

### Using the RETURNING clause with bulk operations

You have now seen BULK COLLECT used for both implicit and explicit query cursors. You can also use BULK COLLECT inside a FORALL statement, in order to take advantage of the RETURNING clause.

The RETURNING clause allows you to obtain information (such as a newly updated value for a salary) from a DML statement. RETURNING can help you avoid additional queries to the database to determine the results of DML operations that just completed.

Suppose that Congress has passed a law requiring that a company pay its highest-compensated employee no more than 50 times the salary of its lowest-paid employee. I work in the IT department of the newly merged company Northrop-Ford-Mattel-Yahoo-ATT, which employs a total of 250,000 workers. The word has come down from on high: the CEO is not taking a pay cut, so I need to increase the salaries of everyone who makes less than 50 times his 2008 total compensation package of $145 million—and decrease the salaries of all upper management except for the CEO. After all, somebody's got to make up for this loss in profit.

Wow! I have lots of updating to do, and I want to use FORALL to get the job done as quickly as possible. However, I also need to perform various kinds of processing on the employee data and then print a report showing the change in salary for each affected employee. That RETURNING clause would come in awfully handy here, so let's give it a try.

See the *onlyfair.sql* file on the book's web site for all of the steps shown here, plus table creation and INSERT statements.

First, I'll create a reusable function to return the compensation for an executive:

```
/* File on web: onlyfair.sql */
FUNCTION salforexec (title_in IN VARCHAR2) RETURN NUMBER
IS
   CURSOR ceo_compensation IS
      SELECT salary + bonus + stock_options +
             mercedes_benz_allowance + yacht_allowance
        FROM compensation
       WHERE title = title_in;
   big_bucks NUMBER;
BEGIN
   OPEN ceo_compensation;
   FETCH ceo_compensation INTO big_bucks;
   RETURN big_bucks;
END;
```

In the main block of the update program, I declare a number of local variables and the following query to identify underpaid employees and overpaid employees who are not lucky enough to be the CEO:

```
DECLARE
   big_bucks NUMBER := salforexec ('CEO');
   min_sal NUMBER := big_bucks / 50;
```

```
names name_tab;
old_salaries number_tab;
new_salaries number_tab;

CURSOR affected_employees (ceosal IN NUMBER)
IS
   SELECT name, salary + bonus old_salary
     FROM compensation
    WHERE title != 'CEO'
      AND ((salary + bonus < ceosal / 50)
             OR (salary + bonus > ceosal / 10)) ;
```

At the start of my executable section, I load all of this data into my collections with a
BULK COLLECT query:

```
OPEN affected_employees (big_bucks);
FETCH affected_employees
   BULK COLLECT INTO names, old_salaries;
```

Then I can use the names collection in my FORALL update:

```
FORALL indx IN names.FIRST .. names.L*
   UPDATE compensation
     SET salary =
         GREATEST(
           DECODE (
             GREATEST (min_sal, salary),
               min_sal, min_sal,
               salary / 5),
           min_sal )
   WHERE name = names (indx)
   RETURNING salary BULK COLLECT INTO new_salaries;
```

I use DECODE to give an employee either a major boost in yearly income or an 80%
cut in pay to keep the CEO comfy. I end it with a RETURNING clause that relies on
BULK COLLECT to populate a third collection: the new salaries.

Finally, because I used RETURNING and don't have to write another query against
the compensation table to obtain the new salaries, I can immediately move to report
generation:

```
FOR indx IN names.FIRST .. names.LAST
LOOP
   DBMS_OUTPUT.PUT_LINE (
     RPAD (names(indx), 20) ||
     RPAD (' Old: ' || old_salaries(indx), 15) ||
     ' New: ' || new_salaries(indx)
     );
END LOOP;
```

Here, then, is the report generated from the *onlyfair.sql* script:

```
John DayAndNight       Old: 10500     New: 2900000
Holly Cubicle          Old: 52000     New: 2900000
Sandra Watchthebucks Old: 22000000  New: 4000000
```

Now everyone can afford quality housing and health care. And tax revenue at all levels will increase, so public schools can get the funding they need.

 The RETURNING column values or expressions returned by each execution in FORALL are added to the collection after the values returned previously. If you use RETURNING inside a non-bulk FOR loop, previous values are overwritten by the latest DML execution.

## High Speed DML with FORALL

BULK COLLECT speeds up queries. FORALL does the same thing for inserts, updates, deletes and merges (FORALL with a merge is supported in Oracle Database 11g only) (I will refer to these statements collectively as "DML"). FORALL tells the PL/SQL runtime engine to bulk bind into the SQL statement all of the elements of one or more collections before sending its statements to the SQL engine.

Given the centrality of SQL to Oracle-based applications and the heavy impact of DML statements on overall performance, FORALL is probably the single most important optimization feature in the PL/SQL language.

So if you are not yet using FORALL, I have bad news and good news. The bad news is that your application code base has not been enhanced over the years to take advantage of critical Oracle features. The good news is that your users will experience some very pleasant (and relatively easy to achieve) boosts in performance.

You will find in the following pages explanations of all of the features and nuances of FORALL, along with plenty of examples.

### Syntax of the FORALL statement

Although the FORALL statement contains an iteration scheme (i.e., it iterates through all the rows of a collection), it is not a FOR loop. Consequently, it has neither a LOOP nor an END LOOP statement. Its syntax is as follows:

```
FORALL index IN
   [ lower_bound ... upper_bound |
     INDICES OF indexing_collection |
     VALUES OF indexing_collection
   ]
   [ SAVE EXCEPTIONS ]
   sql_statement;
```

where:

*index*

Is an integer, declared implicitly by Oracle, that is a defined index value in the collection.

*lower_bound*

Is the starting index value (row or collection element) for the operation.

*upper_bound*

Is the ending index value (row or collection element) for the operation.

*sql_statement*

Is the SQL statement to be performed on each collection element.

*indexing_collection*

Is the PL/SQL collection used to select the indices in the bind array referenced in the *sql_statement*; the INDICES OF and VALUES_OF alternatives are available starting in Oracle Database 10*g*.

*SAVE EXCEPTIONS*

Is an optional clause that tells FORALL to process all rows, saving any exceptions that occur.

You must follow these rules when using FORALL:

- The body of the FORALL statement must be a single DML statement—an INSERT, UPDATE, DELETE, or MERGE (in Oracle Database 11*g* and later).

- The DML statement must reference collection elements, indexed by the *index_row* variable in the FORALL statement. The scope of the *index_row* variable is the FORALL statement only; you may not reference it outside of that statement. Note, though, that the upper and lower bounds of these collections do not have to span the entire contents of the collection(s).

- Do not declare a variable for *index_row*. It is declared implicitly as PLS_INTEGER by the PL/SQL engine.

- The lower and upper bounds must specify a valid range of consecutive index numbers for the collection(s) referenced in the SQL statement. Sparsely filled collections will raise the following error:

  ```
  ORA-22160: element at index [3] does not exist
  ```

  See the *missing_element.sql* file on the book's web site for an example of this scenario.

  Starting with Oracle Database 10*g* you can use the INDICES OF and VALUES OF syntax to allow use of sparse collections (undefined elements between FIRST and LAST). These clauses are covered later in this chapter.

- Until Oracle Database 11*g*, fields within collections of records could not be referenced within the DML statement. Instead, you could only reference the row in the collection as a whole, whether the fields are collections of scalars or collections of more complex objects. For example, the code below:

  ```
  DECLARE
     TYPE employee_aat IS TABLE OF employees%ROWTYPE
        INDEX BY PLS_INTEGER;
     l_employees   employee_aat;
  ```

```
BEGIN
    FORALL l_index IN l_employees.FIRST .. l_employees.LAST
        INSERT INTO employee (employee_id, last_name)
            VALUES (l_employees (l_index).employee_id
                  , l_employees (l_index).last_name
            );
END;
```

will cause the following compilation error in releases prior to Oracle Database 11g:

```
PLS-00436: implementation restriction: cannot reference fields
of BULK In-BIND table of records
```

To use FORALL in this case, you would need to load the employee IDs and the last names into two separate collections. Thankfully, this restriction has been removed in Oracle Database 11g.

- The collection subscript referenced in the DML statement cannot be an expression. For example, the following script:

```
DECLARE
    names name_varray := name_varray ();
BEGIN
    FORALL indx IN names.FIRST .. names.LAST
        DELETE FROM emp WHERE ename = names(indx+10);
END;
```

will cause the following error:

```
PLS-00430: FORALL iteration variable INDX is not allowed in this context
```

### FORALL examples

Here are some examples of the use of the FORALL statement:

- Change the page count of all books whose ISBNs appear in the isbns_in collection:

```
PROCEDURE order_books (
    isbns_in IN name_varray,
    new_counts_in IN number_varray)
IS
BEGIN
    FORALL indx IN isbns_in.FIRST .. isbns_in.LAST
        UPDATE books
            SET page_count = new_counts_in (indx)
        WHERE isbn = isbns_in (indx);
END;
```

Notice that the only changes in this example are to change FOR to FORALL, and to remove the LOOP and END LOOP keywords. This use of FORALL accesses and passes to SQL each of the rows defined in the two collections. Refer back to Figure 21-3 for the change in behavior that results.

- The next example shows how the DML statement can reference more than one collection. In this case, I have three collections: denial, patient_name, and illnesses.

Only the first two are subscripted, and so individual elements of the collection are passed to each INSERT. The third column in health_coverage is a collection listing preconditions. Because the PL/SQL engine bulk binds only subscripted collections, the illnesses collection is placed in that column for each row inserted:

```
FORALL indx IN denial.FIRST .. denial.LAST
   INSERT INTO health_coverage
      VALUES (denial(indx), patient_name(indx), illnesses);
```

- Use the RETURNING clause in a FORALL statement to retrieve information about each separate DELETE statement. Notice that the RETURNING clause in FORALL must use BULK COLLECT INTO (the corresponding "bulk" operation for queries):

```
FUNCTION remove_emps_by_dept (deptlist IN dlist_t)
   RETURN enolist_t
IS
   enolist enolist_t;
BEGIN
   FORALL aDept IN deptlist.FIRST..deptlist.LAST
      DELETE FROM employees WHERE department_id IN deptlist(aDept)
         RETURNING employee_id BULK COLLECT INTO enolist;
   RETURN enolist;
END;
```

- Use the indices defined in one collection to determine which rows in the binding array (the collection referenced inside the SQL statement) will be used in the dynamic INSERT.

```
FORALL indx IN INDICES OF l_top_employees
   EXECUTE IMMEDIATE
      'INSERT INTO ' || l_table || ' VALUES (:emp_pky, :new_salary)'
      USING l_new_salaries(indx).employee_id,
            l_new_salaries(indx).salary;
```

## Cursor attributes for FORALL

You can use cursor attributes after you execute a FORALL statement to get information about the DML operation run within FORALL. Oracle also offers an additional attribute, %BULK_ROWCOUNT, to give you more granular information about the results of the bulk DML statement.

Table 21-1 describes the significance of the values returned by these attributes for FORALL.

*Table 21-1. Implicit SQL cursor attributes for FORALL statements*

| Name | Description |
|---|---|
| SQL%FOUND | Returns TRUE if the last execution of the SQL statement modified one or more rows. |
| SQL%NOTFOUND | Returns TRUE if the DML statement failed to change any rows. |
| SQL%ROWCOUNT | Returns the total number of rows processed by all executions of the SQL statement, not just the last statement. |

| Name | Description |
|------|-------------|
| SQL%ISOPEN | Always returns FALSE and should not be used. |
| SQL%BULK_ROWCOUNT | Returns a pseudo-collection that tells you the number of rows processed by each corresponding SQL statement executed via FORALL. Note that when %BULK_ROWCOUNT(*i*) is zero, %FOUND and %NOTFOUND are FALSE and TRUE, respectively. |
| SQL%BULK_EXCEPTIONS | Returns a pseudo-collection that provides information about each exception raised in a FORALL statement that includes the SAVE EXCEPTIONS clause. |

Let's now explore the %BULK_ROWCOUNT composite attribute. This attribute, designed specifically for use with FORALL, has the semantics of (acts like) an associative array or collection. The database deposits in the Nth element in this collection the number of rows processed by the Nth execution of the FORALL's INSERT, UPDATE, DELETE, or MERGE. If no rows were affected, the Nth row will contain a zero value.

Here is an example of using %BULK_ROWCOUNT (and the overall %ROWCOUNT attribute as well):

```
DECLARE
    TYPE isbn_list IS TABLE OF VARCHAR2(13);

    my_books  isbn_list
    := isbn_list (
        '1-56592-375-8', '0-596-00121-5', '1-56592-849-0',
        '1-56592-335-9', '1-56592-674-9', '1-56592-675-7',
        '0-596-00180-0', '1-56592-457-6'
    );
BEGIN
    FORALL book_index IN
        my_books.FIRST..my_books.LAST
        UPDATE books
            SET page_count = page_count / 2
        WHERE isbn = my_books (book_index);

    -- Did I update the total number of books I expected?
    IF SQL%ROWCOUNT != 8
    THEN
        DBMS_OUTPUT.PUT_LINE (
            'We are missing a book!');
    END IF;

    -- Did the 4th UPDATE statement affect any rows?
    IF SQL%BULK_ROWCOUNT(4) = 0
    THEN
        DBMS_OUTPUT.PUT_LINE (
            'What happened to Oracle PL/SQL Programming?');
    END IF;
END;
```

Here are some tips on how this attribute works:

- The FORALL statement and %BULK_ROWCOUNT use the same subscripts or row numbers in the collections. For example, if the collection passed to FORALL has data in rows 10 through 200, then the %BULK_ROWCOUNT pseudo-collection will also have rows 10 through 200 defined and populated. Any other rows will be undefined.

- When the INSERT affects only a single row (when you specify a VALUES list, for example), a row's value in %BULK_ROWCOUNT will be equal to 1. For IN-SERT...SELECT statements, however, %BULK_ROWCOUNT can be greater than 1.

- The value in a row of the %BULK_ROWCOUNT pseudo-array for deletes, updates and insert-selects may be any natural number (0 or positive); these statements can modify more than one row, depending on their WHERE clauses.

### ROLLBACK behavior with FORALL

The FORALL statement allows you to pass multiple SQL statements all together (in bulk) to the SQL engine. This means that you have a single context switch—but each statement still executes separately in the SQL engine.

What happens when one of those DML statements fails?

1. The DML statement that raised the exception is rolled back to an implicit savepoint marked by the PL/SQL engine before execution of the statement. Changes to all rows already modified by that statement are rolled back.

2. Any previous DML operations in that FORALL statement that already completed without error are *not* rolled back.

3. If you do not take special action (by adding the SAVE EXCEPTIONS clause to FORALL, discussed next), the entire FORALL statement stops and the remaining statements are not executed at all.

### Continuing past exceptions with SAVE EXCEPTIONS

By adding the SAVE EXCEPTIONS clause to your FORALL header, you instruct the Oracle database to continue processing even when an error has occurred. The database will then "save the exception" (or multiple exceptions, if more than one error occurs). When the DML statement completes, it will then raise the ORA-24381 exception. In the exception section, you can then access a pseudo-collection called SQL%BULK_EXCEPTIONS to obtain error information.

Here is an example, followed by an explanation of what is going on:

```
   /* File on web: bulkexc.sql */
1 DECLARE
2    bulk_errors   EXCEPTION;
3    PRAGMA EXCEPTION_INIT (bulk_errors, -24381);
4    TYPE namelist_t IS TABLE OF VARCHAR2(32767);
5
```

```
 6      enames_with_errors   namelist_t
 7         := namelist_t ('ABC',
 8             'DEF',
 9             NULL, /* Last name cannot be NULL */
10             'LITTLE',
11             RPAD ('BIGBIGGERBIGGEST', 250, 'ABC'), /* Value too long */
12             'SMITHIE'
13             );
14  BEGIN
15     FORALL indx IN enames_with_errors.FIRST .. enames_with_errors.LAST
16        SAVE EXCEPTIONS
17        UPDATE EMPLOYEES
18           SET last_name = enames_with_errors (indx);
19
20  EXCEPTION
21     WHEN bulk_errors
22     THEN
23        DBMS_OUTPUT.put_line ('Updated ' || SQL%ROWCOUNT || ' rows.');
24
25        FOR indx IN 1 .. SQL%BULK_EXCEPTIONS.COUNT
26        LOOP
27          DBMS_OUTPUT.PUT_LINE ('Error '
28             || indx
29             || ' occurred during '
30             || 'iteration '
31             || SQL%BULK_EXCEPTIONS (indx).ERROR_INDEX
32             || ' updating name to '
33             || enames_with_errors (SQL%BULK_EXCEPTIONS (indx).ERROR_INDEX);
34          DBMS_OUTPUT.PUT_LINE ('Oracle error is '
35                || SQLERRM ( -1 * SQL%BULK_EXCEPTIONS (indx).ERROR_CODE)
36                );
37        END LOOP;
38  END;
```

When I run this code with SERVEROUTPUT turned on, I see these results:

```
SQL> EXEC bulk_exceptions

Error 1 occurred during iteration 3 updating name to BIGBIGGERBIGGEST
Oracle error is ORA-01407: cannot update () to NULL

Error 2 occurred during iteration 5 updating name to
Oracle error is ORA-01401: inserted value too large for column
```

In other words, the database encountered two exceptions as it processed the DML for the names collection. It did not stop with the first exception, but continued on, cataloging a second.

The following table describes the error-handling functionality in this code:

| Line(s) | Description |
| --- | --- |
| 2–3 | Declare a named exception to make the exception section more readable. |
| 4–13 | Declare and populate a collection that will drive the FORALL statement. I have intentionally placed data in the collection that will raise two errors. |

| Line(s) | Description |
|---------|-------------|
| 15–18 | Execute an UPDATE statement with FORALL using the enames_with_errors collection. |
| 25–37 | Use a numeric FOR loop to scan through the contents of the SQL%BULK_EXCEPTIONS pseudo-collection. Note that I can call the COUNT method to determine the number of defined rows (errors raised), but I cannot call other methods, such as FIRST and LAST. |
| 31 and 33 | The ERROR_INDEX field of each pseudo-collection's row returns the row number in the driving collection of the FORALL statement for which an exception was raised. |
| 35 | The ERROR_CODE field of each pseudo-collection's row returns the error number of the exception that was raised. Note that this value is stored as a positive integer; you will need to multiple it by −1 before passing it to SQLERRM or displaying the information. |

## Driving FORALL with nonsequential arrays

Prior to Oracle Database 10g, the collection that is referenced inside the FORALL statement (the "binding array") had to be densely or consecutively filled. If there were any gaps between the low and high values specified in the range of the FORALL header, Oracle would raise an error as shown below:

```
1   DECLARE
2      TYPE employee_aat IS TABLE OF employees.employee_id%TYPE
3         INDEX BY PLS_INTEGER;
4      l_employees    employee_aat;
5   BEGIN
6      l_employees (1) := 100;
7      l_employees (100) := 1000;
8      FORALL l_index IN l_employees.FIRST .. l_employees.LAST
9         UPDATE employees SET salary = 10000
10           WHERE employee_id = l_employees (l_index);
11   END;
12   /
```

The error message looked like this:

```
DECLARE
*
ERROR at line 1:
ORA-22160: element at index [2] does not exist
```

Furthermore, there was no way for you to skip over rows in the binding array that you didn't want processed by the FORALL statement. These restrictions often led to the writing of additional code to compress collections to fit the limitations of FORALL. To help PL/SQL developers avoid this nuisance coding, starting with Oracle Database 10g, PL/SQL offers the INDICES OF and VALUES OF clauses, both of which allow you to specify the portion of the binding array to be processed by FORALL.

First, let's review the difference between these two clauses, and then I will explore examples to demonstrate their usefulness.

## INDICES OF

Use this clause when you have a collection (let's call it the *indexing array*) whose defined rows specify which rows in the binding array (referenced inside the FOR-ALL's DML statement) you would like to be processed. In other words, if the element at position *N* (a.k.a. the row number) is not defined in the indexing array, you want the FORALL statement to ignore the element at position *N* in the binding array.

## VALUES OF

Use this clause when you have a collection of integers (again, the indexing array) whose content (the value of the element at a specified position) identifies the position in the binding array that you want to be processed by the FORALL statement.

**INDICES OF example.** I would like to update the salaries of some employees to $10,000. Currently, no one has such a salary:

```
SQL> SELECT employee_id FROM employees WHERE salary = 10000;
no rows selected
```

I then write the following program.

```
     /* File on web: 10g_indices_of.sql */
 1   DECLARE
 2     TYPE employee_aat IS TABLE OF employees.employee_id%TYPE
 3        INDEX BY PLS_INTEGER;
 4
 5     l_employees           employee_aat;
 6
 7     TYPE boolean_aat IS TABLE OF BOOLEAN
 8        INDEX BY PLS_INTEGER;
 9
10     l_employee_indices   boolean_aat;
11   BEGIN
12     l_employees (1) := 7839;
13     l_employees (100) := 7654;
14     l_employees (500) := 7950;
15     --
16     l_employee_indices (1) := TRUE;
17     l_employee_indices (500) := TRUE;
18     l_employee_indices (799) := TRUE;
19
20     FORALL l_index IN INDICES OF l_employee_indices
21          BETWEEN 1 AND 500
22       UPDATE employees23            SET salary = 10000
24          WHERE employee_id = l_employees (l_index);
25   END;
```

The following table describes the logic of the program:

| Line(s) | Description |
| --- | --- |
| 2–5 | Define a collection of employee ID numbers. |
| 7–10 | Define a collection of Boolean values. |

| Line(s) | Description |
|---------|-------------|
| 12–14 | Populate (sparsely) three rows (1, 100, and 500) in the collection of employee IDs. |
| 16–18 | Define only two rows in the collection, 1 and 500. |
| 20–24 | In the FORALL statement, rather than specify a range of values from FIRST to LAST, I simply specify INDICES OF l_employee_indices. I also include an optional BETWEEN clause to restrict which of those index values will be used. |

After executing this code, I query the table to see that, in fact, only two rows of the table were updated; the employee with ID 7654 was skipped because the Boolean indices collection had no element defined at position 100.

```
SQL> SELECT employee_id FROM employee  WHERE salary = 10000;

EMPLOYEE_ID
-----------
       7839
       7950
```

With INDICES OF (line 20), the *contents* of the indexing array are ignored. All that matters are the positions or row numbers that are defined in the collection.

**VALUES OF example.** Again, I would like to update the salaries of some employees to $10,000, this time using the VALUES OF clause. Currently, no one has such a salary:

```
SQL> SELECT employee_id FROM employee WHERE salary = 10000;
no rows selected
```

I then write the following program:

```
     /* File on web: 10g_values_of.sql */
1    DECLARE
2      TYPE employee_aat IS TABLE OF employees.employee_id%TYPE
3        INDEX BY PLS_INTEGER;
4
5      l_employees             employee_aat;
6
7      TYPE indices_aat IS TABLE OF PLS_INTEGER
8        INDEX BY PLS_INTEGER;
9
10     l_employee_indices    indices_aat;
11   BEGIN
12     l_employees (-77) := 7820;
13     l_employees (13067) := 7799;
14     l_employees (99999999) := 7369;
15     --
16     l_employee_indices (100) := -77;
17     l_employee_indices (200) := 99999999;
18     --
19     FORALL l_index IN VALUES OF l_employee_indices
20        UPDATE employees
21           SET salary = 10000
22          WHERE employee_id = l_employees (l_index);
23   END;
```

The following table describes the logic of the program:

| Line(s) | Description |
|---------|-------------|
| 2–6 | Define a collection of employee ID numbers. |
| 7–10 | Define a collection of integers. |
| 12–14 | Populate (sparsely) three rows (–77, 13067, and 99999999) in the collection of employee IDs. |
| 16–17 | I want to set up the indexing array to identify which of those rows to use in my update. Because I am using VALUES OF, the row numbers that I use are unimportant. Instead, what matters is the *value* found in each of the rows in the indexing array. Again, I want to skip over that "middle" row of 13067, so here I define just two rows in the I_employee_indices array and assign them values –77 and 9999999, respectively. |
| 19–22 | Rather than specify a range of values from FIRST to LAST, I simply specify VALUES OF I_employee_indices. Notice that I populate rows 100 and 200 in the indices collection. VALUES OF does *not* require a densely filled indexing collection. |

After executing this code, I query the table to see that in fact only two rows of the table were updated; the employee with ID 7799 was skipped because the "values of" collection had no element whose value equaled 13067.

```
SQL> SELECT employee_id FROM employees WHERE salary = 10000;

EMPLOYEE_ID
-----------
       7369
       7820
```

# Improving Performance With Pipelined Table Functions

Pipelined functions are where the elegance and simplicity of PL/SQL converge with the performance of SQL. Complex data transformations are effortless to develop and support with PL/SQL, yet to achieve high-performance data processing, we often resort to set-based SQL solutions. Pipelined functions bridge the gap between the two methods effortlessly, but they also have some unique performance features of their own, making them a superb performance optimization tool.

In the following pages, I'll show some examples of typical data-processing requirements and how you might tune them with pipelined functions. I'll cover the following topics:

- How to tune typical data-loading requirements with pipelined functions. In each case, I'll convert legacy row-based solutions to set-based solutions that include parallel pipelined functions.

- How to exploit the parallel context of pipelined functions to improve the performance of data unloads.

- The relative performance of the partitioning and streaming options for parallel pipelined functions.

- How the cost-based optimizer (CBO) deals with both pipelined and standard table functions.
- How complex multitable loading requirements can be solved with multitype pipelined functions.

The basic syntax for pipelined table functions is covered in Chapter 17. To recap, a pipelined function is called in the FROM clause of a SQL statement and is queried as if it were a relational table or other rowsource. Unlike standard table functions (that have to complete all of their processing before passing a potentially large collection of data back to the calling context), pipelined table functions stream their results to the client almost as soon as they are prepared. In other words, pipelined functions do not materialize their entire result set, and this optimization feature dramatically reduces their PGA memory footprint. Another unique performance feature of pipelined functions is the ability to call them in the context of a parallel query. I have taken advantage of these unique performance features many times, and in the next few pages I will show you how and when to use pipelined functions to improve the performance of some of your own programs.

## Replacing Row-Based Inserts with Pipelined Function-Based Loads

To demonstrate the performance of pipelined functions, let's first imagine a typical legacy loading scenario that I want to bring into the 21st century. Using the stockpivot example, I have coded a simple row-by-row load to fetch the stockpivot source data and pivot each record into two rows for insert. It is contained in a package and is as follows:

```
/* File on web: stockpivot_setup.sql */
PROCEDURE load_stocks_legacy IS

   CURSOR c_source_data IS
      SELECT ticker, open_price, close_price, trade_date
      FROM   stocktable;

   r_source_data stockpivot_pkg.stocktable_rt;
   r_target_data stockpivot_pkg.tickertable_rt;

BEGIN
   OPEN c_source_data;
   LOOP
      FETCH c_source_data INTO r_source_data;
      EXIT WHEN c_source_data%NOTFOUND;

      /* Opening price... */
      r_target_data.ticker     := r_source_data.ticker;
      r_target_data.price_type := '0';
      r_target_data.price      := r_source_data.open_price;
      r_target_data.price_date := r_source_data.trade_date;
      INSERT INTO tickertable VALUES r_target_data;
```

```
        /* Closing price... */
        r_target_data.price_type := 'C';
        r_target_data.price      := r_source_data.close_price;
        INSERT INTO tickertable VALUES r_target_data;

    END LOOP;
    CLOSE c_source_data;
END load_stocks_legacy;
```

I regularly see code of this format and since Oracle8*i* Database I've typically used BULK COLLECT and FORALL as my primary tuning tool (when the logic is too complex for a set-based SQL solution). However, an alternative technique (that I first saw described by Tom Kyte[2]) is to use a set-based insert from a pipelined function. In other words, a pipelined function is used for all of the legacy data transformation and preparation logic, but the target-table load is handled separately as a set-based insert. Since reading about this powerful technique, I have used it successfully in my own performance optimization work, as described in the following sections.

### A pipelined function implementation

As demonstrated in Chapter 17, the first thing to consider when creating a pipelined function is the data that it will return. For this, I need to create an object type to define a single row of the pipelined function's return data.

```
/* File on web: stockpivot_setup.sql */
CREATE TYPE stockpivot_ot AS OBJECT
( ticker      VARCHAR2(10)
, price_type  VARCHAR2(1)
, price       NUMBER
, price_date  DATE
);
```

I also need to create a collection of this object as this defines the function's return type.

```
/* File on web: stockpivot_setup.sql */
CREATE TYPE stockpivot_ntt AS TABLE OF stockpivot_ot;
```

Transforming the legacy code into a pipelined function is quite simple. First I must define the function specification in the header (see the *stockpivot_setup.sql* file on the book's web site). I must also include a load procedure that I will describe later:

```
/* File on web: stockpivot_setup.sql */
CREATE PACKAGE stockpivot_pkg AS

   TYPE stocktable_rct IS REF CURSOR
     RETURN stocktable%ROWTYPE;

   <snip>

   FUNCTION pipe_stocks(
          p_source_data IN stockpivot_pkg.stocktable_rct
```

---

2. See his discussion in *Expert Oracle Database Architecture*, pp. 640–643.

```
            ) RETURN stockpivot_ntt PIPELINED;

    PROCEDURE load_stocks;

  END stockpivot_pkg;
```

My pipelined function takes a strong REF CURSOR as an input parameter (I could also use a weak REF CURSOR in this case). The cursor parameter itself is not necessarily required. It would be just as valid for me to declare the cursor in the function itself (as I did with the legacy procedure). However, the cursor parameter is going to be required for further iterations of this pipelined function, so I've introduced it from the outset.

The function's implementation follows.

```
          /* File on web: stockpivot_setup.sql */
    1     FUNCTION pipe_stocks(
    2             p_source_data IN stockpivot_pkg.stocktable_rct
    3             ) RETURN stockpivot_ntt PIPELINED IS
    4
    5       r_target_data stockpivot_ot := stockpivot_ot(NULL, NULL, NULL, NULL);
    6       r_source_data stockpivot_pkg.stocktable_rt;
    7
    8     BEGIN
    9       LOOP
    10        FETCH p_source_data INTO r_source_data;
    11        EXIT WHEN p_source_data%NOTFOUND;
    12
    13        /* First row... */
    14        r_target_data.ticker     := r_source_data.ticker;
    15        r_target_data.price_type := 'O';
    16        r_target_data.price      := r_source_data.open_price;
    17        r_target_data.price_date := r_source_data.trade_date;
    18        PIPE ROW (r_target_data);
    19
    20        /* Second row... */
    21        r_target_data.price_type := 'C';
    22        r_target_data.price      := r_source_data.close_price;
    23        PIPE ROW (r_target_data);
    24
    25       END LOOP;
    26       CLOSE p_source_data;
    27       RETURN;
    28     END pipe_stocks;
```

Other than the general pipelined function syntax (that you should by now be familiar with from Chapter 17), the majority of the pipelined function's code is recognizable from the legacy example. The main differences to consider are summarized here.

| Line(s) | Description |
| --- | --- |
| 2 | The legacy cursor is removed from the code and instead is passed as a REF CURSOR parameter. |
| 5 | My target data variable is no longer defined as the target table's ROWTYPE. It is now of the STOCKPIVOT_OT object type that defines the pipelined function's return data. |

| Line(s) | Description |
|---|---|
| 18 and 23 | Instead of inserting records into tickertable, I *pipe* records from the function. At this stage, the database will buffer a small number of my piped object rows into a corresponding collection. Depending on the client's array size, this buffered collection of data will be available almost immediately. |

## Loading from a pipelined function

As you can see, with only a small number of changes to the original load program, I now have a pipelined function that prepares and pipes all of the data that I need to load into tickertable. To complete the conversion of my legacy code, I only need to write an additional procedure to insert the piped data into my target table.

```
/* File on web: stockpivot_setup.sql */
   PROCEDURE load_stocks IS
   BEGIN

      INSERT INTO tickertable (ticker, price_type, price, price_date)
      SELECT ticker, price_type, price, price_date
      FROM   TABLE(
               stockpivot_pkg.pipe_stocks(
                  CURSOR(SELECT * FROM stocktable)));

   END load_stocks;
```

That completes the basic conversion of the row-by-row legacy code to a pipelined function solution. So how does this compare to the original? In my tests, I created the stocktable as an external table with a file of 500,000 records. The legacy row-by-row code completed in 57 seconds (inserting 1 million rows into tickertable) and the set-based insert using the pipelined function ran in just 16 seconds (test results for all examples are available on the book's web site).

Considering that this is my first and most basic pipelined function implementation, the improvement in performance shown above is quite respectable. However, it is not quite the performance I can get when using a simple BULK COLLECT and FORALL solution (which runs in just over 5 seconds in my tests), so I will need to make some modifications to my pipelined function load.

Before I do this, however, notice that I retained the single-row fetches off the main cursor and did nothing to reduce the "expensive" context-switching (which would require a BULK COLLECT fetch). So why is it faster than the legacy row-by-row code?

It is faster primarily because of the switch to set-based SQL. Set-based DML (such as the INSERT…SELECT I used in my pipelined load) is almost always considerably faster than a row-based, procedural solution. In this particular case, I have benefited directly from the Oracle database's internal optimization of set-based inserts. Specifically, the database writes considerably less redo information for set-based inserts (INSERT…SELECT) than it does for singleton inserts (INSERT…VALUES). That is to say, if I insert 100 rows in a single statement, it will generate less redo than if I inserted 100 rows one-by-one.

My original legacy load of 1 million tickertable rows generated over 270 MB of redo information. This was reduced to just over 37 MB when using the pipelined function-based load, contributing to a significant proportion of the time savings.

 I have omitted any complicated data transformations from my examples for the sake of clarity. You should assume in all cases that the data-processing rules are sufficiently complex to *warrant* a PL/SQL, pipelined function solution in the first place. Otherwise, I would probably just use a set-based SQL solution with analytic functions, subquery factoring, and CASE expressions to transform my high-volume data!

### Tuning pipelined functions with array fetches

Despite having tuned the legacy code with a pipelined function implementation, I am not done yet. There are further optimization possibilities and I need to make my processing at least as fast as a BULK COLLECT and FORALL solution. Notice that I used single-row fetches from the main source cursor. The first simple tuning possibility is therefore to use array fetches with BULK COLLECT.

I begin by adding a default array size to my package specification. The optimal array fetch size will vary according to your specific data-processing requirements, but I always prefer to start my tests with 100 and work from there. I also add an associative array type to the package specification (it could just as well be declared in the body); this is for bulk fetches from the source cursor. Finally, I add a second parameter to the pipelined function signature so that I can control the array fetch size (this isn't necessary of course: just good practice). My specification is now as follows.

```
/* File on web: stockpivot_setup.sql */
CREATE PACKAGE stockpivot_pkg AS
   <snip>
   c_default_limit CONSTANT PLS_INTEGER := 100;

   TYPE stocktable_aat IS TABLE OF stocktable%ROWTYPE
      INDEX BY PLS_INTEGER;

   FUNCTION pipe_stocks_array(
           p_source_data IN stockpivot_pkg.stocktable_rct,
           p_limit_size  IN PLS_INTEGER DEFAULT stockpivot_pkg.c_default_limit
           ) RETURN stockpivot_ntt PIPELINED;
   <snip>
END stockpivot_pkg;
```

The function itself is very similar to the original version.

```
/* File on web: stockpivot_setup.sql */
   FUNCTION pipe_stocks_array(
           p_source_data IN stockpivot_pkg.stocktable_rct,
           p_limit_size  IN PLS_INTEGER DEFAULT stockpivot_pkg.c_default_limit
           ) RETURN stockpivot_ntt PIPELINED IS

      r_target_data  stockpivot_ot := stockpivot_ot(NULL, NULL, NULL, NULL);
```

```
        aa_source_data stockpivot_pkg.stocktable_aat;

    BEGIN
      LOOP
        FETCH p_source_data BULK COLLECT INTO aa_source_data LIMIT p_limit_size;
        EXIT WHEN aa_source_data.COUNT = 0;

        /* Process the batch of (p_limit_size) records... */
        FOR i IN 1 .. aa_source_data.COUNT LOOP

          /* First row... */
          r_target_data.ticker     := aa_source_data(i).ticker;
          r_target_data.price_type := 'O';
          r_target_data.price      := aa_source_data(i).open_price;
          r_target_data.price_date := aa_source_data(i).trade_date;
          PIPE ROW (r_target_data);

          /* Second row... */
          r_target_data.price_type := 'C';
          r_target_data.price      := aa_source_data(i).close_price;
          PIPE ROW (r_target_data);
        END LOOP;
      END LOOP;
      CLOSE p_source_data;
      RETURN;
    END pipe_stocks_array;
```

The only difference from my original version is the use of BULK COLLECT...LIMIT
from the source cursor. The load procedure is the same as before, modified to reference
the array-version of the pipelined function. This reduced my loading time further to
just 6 seconds, purely because of the reduction in context-switching from array-based
PL/SQL. My pipelined function solution now has comparable performance to my
BULK COLLECT and FORALL solution.

## Exploiting parallel pipelined functions for ultimate performance

I've achieved some good performance gains from the switch to a set-based insert from
a pipelined function. Yet I have one more tuning option for my stockpivot load that
will give me better performance than any other solution: using the parallel capability
of pipelined functions described in Chapter 17. In this next iteration, I parallel-enable
my stockpivot function by adding another clause to the function signature:

```
/* File on web: stockpivot_setup.sql */
CREATE PACKAGE stockpivot_pkg AS
   <snip>
   FUNCTION pipe_stocks_parallel(
           p_source_data IN stockpivot_pkg.stocktable_rct
           p_limit_size  IN PLS_INTEGER DEFAULT stockpivot_pkg.c_default_limit
           ) RETURN stockpivot_ntt
             PIPELINED
             PARALLEL_ENABLE (PARTITION p_source_data BY ANY);
   <snip>
END stockpivot_pkg;
```

---

By using the ANY partitioning scheme, I have instructed the Oracle database to randomly allocate my source data to the parallel processes. This is because the order in which the function receives and processes the source data has no effect on the resulting output (i.e., there are no inter-row dependencies). That is not always the case, of course.

### Enabling parallel pipelined function execution

Aside from the parallel-enabling syntax in the specification and body, the function implementation is the same as the array-fetch example (see the *stockpivot_setup.sql* file on the web site for the full package). However, I need to ensure that my tickertable load is *executed* in parallel. First, I must enable parallel DML at the session level and once this is done, parallel query is invoked in one of the following ways:

- Using the PARALLEL hint
- Using parallel DEGREE settings on the underlying objects
- Forcing parallel query (ALTER SESSION FORCE PARALLEL (QUERY) PARALLEL *n*)

 Parallel query/DML is a feature of Oracle Database Enterprise Edition. If you use either Standard Edition or Standard Edition One, you are not licensed to use the parallel feature of pipelined functions.

In my load, I have enabled parallel DML at the session level and used hints to specify a degree of parallelism (DOP) of 4:

```
/* File on web: stockpivot_setup.sql */
PROCEDURE load_stocks_parallel IS
BEGIN

    EXECUTE IMMEDIATE 'ALTER SESSION ENABLE PARALLEL DML';

    INSERT /*+ PARALLEL(t, 4) */ INTO tickertable t
        (ticker, price_type, price, price_date)
    SELECT ticker, price_type, price, price_date
    FROM   TABLE(
            stockpivot_pkg.pipe_stocks_parallel(
                CURSOR(SELECT /*+ PARALLEL(s, 4) */ * FROM stocktable s)));

END load_stocks_parallel;
```

This reduces the load time to just over 3 seconds, a significant improvement on my original legacy code and all other versions of my pipelined function load. Of course, when dealing in small units of time such as this, the startup costs of parallel processes will impact the overall runtime, but I have still managed almost a 50% improvement on my array version. The fact that parallel inserts use direct path rather than conventional path also means that the redo generation dropped further still to just 25 KB!

In commercial systems, you might be tuning processes that run for an hour or more, so the gains you can achieve with parallel pipelined loads will be significant in both proportional and actual terms.

 When you are using parallel pipelined functions, your source cursor must be passed as a REF CURSOR parameter. In serial pipelined functions, the source cursor can be embedded in the function itself (although I have chosen not to do this in any of my examples).

Furthermore, the REF CURSOR can be either weakly or strongly typed for functions partitioned with the ANY scheme, but for HASH or RANGE based partitioning, it must be strongly typed. See Chapter 15 for more details on REF CURSORs and cursor variables.

## Tuning Merge Operations with Pipelined Functions

You might now be considering serial or parallel pipelined functions as a tuning mechanism for your own high-volume data loads. Yet not all loads involve inserts like the stockpivot example. Many data loads are incremental and require periodic merges of new and modified data. The good news is that the same principle of combining PL/SQL transformations with set-based SQL applies to merges (and updates) as well.

### Row-based PL/SQL merge processing

Consider the following procedure, taken from my *employee_pkg* example. I have a merge of a large number of employee records, but my legacy code uses an old PL/SQL technique of attempting an update first and inserting only when the update matches zero records in the target table.

```
/* File on web: employees_merge_setup.sql */
PROCEDURE upsert_employees IS
   n PLS_INTEGER := 0;
BEGIN
   FOR r_emp IN (SELECT * FROM employees_staging) LOOP
      UPDATE employees
      SET    <snip>
      WHERE  employee_id = r_emp.employee_id;

      IF SQL%ROWCOUNT = 0 THEN
         INSERT INTO employees (<snip>)
         VALUES (<snip>);
      END IF;
   END LOOP;
END upsert_employees;
```

I've removed some of the code for brevity, but you can clearly see the "upsert" technique in action. Note that I've used an implicit cursor FOR loop that will benefit from the array-fetch optimization introduced to PL/SQL in Oracle Database 10g.

To test this procedure, I created a staging table of 500,000 employees records (this is a massive corporation!) and inserted 250,000 of them into an employees table to manufacture an even split between updates and inserts. This PL/SQL "poor man's merge" solution completed in 46 seconds.

### Using pipelined functions for set-based MERGE

Converting this example to a set-based SQL MERGE from a pipelined function is, once again, quite simple. First, I create the supporting object and nested table types (see the *employees_merge_setup.sql* file for details) and declare the function in the package header.

```
/* File on web: employees_merge_setup.sql */
CREATE PACKAGE employee_pkg AS

   c_default_limit CONSTANT PLS_INTEGER := 100;

   TYPE employee_rct IS REF CURSOR RETURN employees_staging%ROWTYPE;
   TYPE employee_aat IS TABLE OF employees_staging%ROWTYPE
      INDEX BY PLS_INTEGER;
   <snip>

   FUNCTION pipe_employees(
            p_source_data IN employee_pkg.employee_rct
            p_limit_size  IN PLS_INTEGER DEFAULT employee_pkg.c_default_limit
            ) RETURN employee_ntt
              PIPELINED
              PARALLEL_ENABLE (PARTITION p_source_data BY ANY);
END employee_pkg;
```

I have parallel-enabled the pipelined function and used the ANY partitioning scheme as before. The function implementation is as follows:

```
/* File on web: employees_merge_setup.sql */
   FUNCTION pipe_employees(
            p_source_data IN employee_pkg.employee_rct,
            p_limit_size  IN PLS_INTEGER DEFAULT employee_pkg.c_default_limit
            ) RETURN employee_ntt
              PIPELINED
              PARALLEL_ENABLE (PARTITION p_source_data BY ANY) IS
      aa_source_data employee_pkg.employee_aat;
   BEGIN
     LOOP
        FETCH p_source_data BULK COLLECT INTO aa_source_data LIMIT p_limit_size;
        EXIT WHEN aa_source_data.COUNT = 0;
        FOR i IN 1 .. aa_source_data.COUNT LOOP
           PIPE ROW (
              employee_ot( aa_source_data(i).employee_id,
                           <snip>
                           SYSDATE ));
        END LOOP;
     END LOOP;
     CLOSE p_source_data;
```

```
        RETURN;
    END pipe_employees;
```

This function simply array-fetches the source data and pipes it out in the correct format. I can now use my function in a MERGE statement, which I wrap in a procedure in *employee_pkg*, as follows.

```
    /* File on web: employees_merge_setup.sql */
    PROCEDURE merge_employees IS
    BEGIN

        EXECUTE IMMEDIATE 'ALTER SESSION ENABLE PARALLEL DML';

        MERGE /*+ PARALLEL(e, 4) */
            INTO  employees e
            USING TABLE(
                    employee_pkg.pipe_employees(
                        CURSOR(SELECT /*+ PARALLEL(es, 4) */ *
                                FROM employees_staging es))) s
            ON    (e.employee_id = s.employee_id)
        WHEN MATCHED THEN
            UPDATE
            SET    <snip>
        WHEN NOT MATCHED THEN
            INSERT ( <snip> )
            VALUES ( <snip> );

    END merge_employees;
```

The SQL MERGE from my parallel pipelined function reduces the load time by over 50% to just 21 seconds. So using parallel pipelined functions as a rowsource for set-based SQL operations is clearly a valuable tuning technique for volume data loads.

## Asynchronous Data Unloading with Parallel Pipelined Functions

So far, I have demonstrated two types of data loads that have benefited from conversion to a parallel pipelined function. You might also want to exploit the parallel feature of pipelined functions for those times when you need to unload data (even well into the 21st century I have yet to see a corporate in-house ODS/DSS/warehouse that doesn't extract data for transfer to other systems).

### A typical data-extract program

Imagine the following scenario. I have a daily extract of all my trading data (held in tickertable) for transfer to a middle-office system, which expects a delimited flat file. To achieve this, I write a simple utility to unload data from a cursor:

```
    /* File on web: parallel_unload_setup.sql */
    PROCEDURE legacy_unload(
            p_source    IN SYS_REFCURSOR,
            p_filename  IN VARCHAR2,
            p_directory IN VARCHAR2,
```

```
            p_limit_size IN PLS_INTEGER DEFAULT unload_pkg.c_default_limit
            ) IS
    TYPE row_aat IS TABLE OF VARCHAR2(32767)
        INDEX BY PLS_INTEGER;
    aa_rows row_aat;
    v_name  VARCHAR2(128) := p_filename || '.txt';
    v_file  UTL_FILE.FILE_TYPE;
BEGIN
    v_file := UTL_FILE.FOPEN( p_directory, v_name, 'w', c_maxline );
    LOOP
        FETCH p_source BULK COLLECT INTO aa_rows LIMIT p_limit_size;
        EXIT WHEN aa_rows.COUNT = 0;
        FOR i IN 1 .. aa_rows.COUNT LOOP
            UTL_FILE.PUT_LINE(v_file, aa_rows(i));
        END LOOP;
    END LOOP;
    CLOSE p_source;
    UTL_FILE.FCLOSE(v_file);
END legacy_unload;
```

I simply loop through the source cursor parameter using an array fetch size of 100 and write each batch of rows to the destination file using UTL_FILE. The source cursor has just one column—the cursor is prepared with the source columns already concatenated/delimited.

In testing, 1 million delimited tickertable rows unloaded to a flat file in just 24 seconds (I ensured that tickertable was fully scanned a few times beforehand to reduce the impact of physical I/O). But tickertable has an average row length of just 25 bytes, and so unloads very quickly. Commercial systems will write significantly more data (in both row length and row counts) and potentially take tens of minutes.

### A parallel-enabled pipelined function unloader

If you recognize this scenario from your own systems, you should consider tuning with parallel pipelined functions. If you analyze the legacy example above, all of the data manipulation can be placed within a pipelined function (specifically, there are no DML operations). So how about if I take that cursor fetch logic and UTL_FILE management and put it inside a parallel pipelined function? If I do this, I can exploit Oracle's parallel query to unload the data to multiple files much faster.

Of course, pipelined functions usually return piped data, but in this case my source rows are being written to a file and I don't need them returned to the client. Instead, I will return one row per parallel process with some very basic metadata to describe the session information and number of rows it extracted. My supporting types are as follows:

```
/* File on web: parallel_unload_setup.sql */
CREATE TYPE unload_ot AS OBJECT
( file_name  VARCHAR2(128)
, no_records NUMBER
, session_id NUMBER );
```

```
        CREATE TYPE unload_ntt AS TABLE OF unload_ot;
```

My function implementation is based on the legacy processing with some additional
setup required for the metadata being returned.

```
        /* File on web: parallel_unload_setup.sql */
1       FUNCTION parallel_unload(
2               p_source    IN SYS_REFCURSOR,
3               p_filename  IN VARCHAR2,
4               p_directory IN VARCHAR2,
5               p_limit_size IN PLS_INTEGER DEFAULT unload_pkg.c_default_limit
6               )
7           RETURN unload_ntt
8           PIPELINED PARALLEL_ENABLE (PARTITION p_source BY ANY) AS
9           aa_rows row_aat;
10          v_sid   NUMBER := SYS_CONTEXT('USERENV','SID');
11          v_name  VARCHAR2(128) := p_filename || '_' || v_sid || '.txt';
12          v_file  UTL_FILE.FILE_TYPE;
13          v_lines PLS_INTEGER;
14      BEGIN
15          v_file := UTL_FILE.FOPEN(p_directory, v_name, 'w', c_maxline);
16          LOOP
17             FETCH p_source BULK COLLECT INTO aa_rows LIMIT p_limit_size;
18             EXIT WHEN aa_rows.COUNT = 0;
19             FOR i IN 1 .. aa_rows.COUNT LOOP
20                UTL_FILE.PUT_LINE(v_file, aa_rows(i));
21             END LOOP;
22          END LOOP;
23          v_lines := p_source%ROWCOUNT;
24          CLOSE p_source;
25          UTL_FILE.FCLOSE(v_file);
26          PIPE ROW (unload_ot(v_name, v_lines, v_sid));
27          RETURN;
28      END parallel_unload;
```

Note the following about this function:

| Line(s) | Description |
|---|---|
| 1 and 8 | My function is parallel-enabled and will partition the source data by ANY. Therefore, I am able to declare my source cursor based on the system-defined SYS_REFCURSOR type. |
| 10 | My return metadata will include the session ID (SID). This is available in the USERENV application context. You can derive the SID from views such as V$MYSTAT in versions prior to Oracle Database 10g. |
| 11 | I want to unload in parallel to multiple files so I create a unique filename for each parallel invocation. |
| 15–22 and 24–25 | I reuse all of the processing logic from the original legacy implementation. |
| 26 | For each invocation of the function, I pipe a single row containing the filename, number of rows extracted, and session identifier. |

With minimal effort, I have parallel-enabled my data unloader, using the pipelined function as an asynchronous forking mechanism. Let's see how to invoke this new version below. I've also included my test output from SQL*Plus.

```
/* File on web: parallel_unload_test.sql */
SELECT *
FROM   TABLE(
           unload_pkg.parallel_unload(
               p_source => CURSOR(SELECT /*+ PARALLEL(t, 4) */
                                   ticker     || ',' ||
                                   price_type || ',' ||
                                   price      || ',' ||
                                   TO_CHAR(price_date,'YYYYMMDDHH24MISS')
                               FROM   tickertable t),
               p_filename => 'tickertable',
               p_directory => 'DIR' ));
```

The output is:

```
FILE_NAME                     NO_RECORDS SESSION_ID
----------------------------- ---------- ----------
tickertable_144.txt               260788        144
tickertable_142.txt               252342        142
tickertable_127.txt               233765        127
tickertable_112.txt               253105        112

4 rows selected.

Elapsed: 00:00:12.21
```

On my test system, with four parallel processes, I have roughly halved my processing time. Remember that when dealing in small numbers of seconds, as in this example, the cost of parallel startup can have an impact on processing time. For extracts that take minutes or more to complete, your potential savings (in both actual and real terms) might be far greater.

 It is easy to improve further on this technique by "tuning" the UTL_FILE calls, using a buffering mechanism. See the PARALLEL_UNLOAD_BUFFERED function in the *parallel_unload_setup.sql* file on the book's web site for the implementation. Rather than write each line to file immediately, I instead append it to a large VARCHAR2 buffer (I could alternatively use a collection), and flush it to a file periodically. Reducing the UTL_FILE calls in such a way nearly halved the extract time of my parallel unloader to just under 7 seconds.

## Performance Implications of Partitioning and Streaming Clauses in Parallel Pipelined Functions

All of my parallel pipelined function examples so far have used the ANY partitioning scheme because there have been no dependencies between the rows of source data. As described in Chapter 17, there are several partitioning and streaming options to control how source input data is allocated and ordered in parallel processes. To recap, these are:

- Partitioning options (for allocating data to parallel processes):
    —PARTITION *p_cursor* BY ANY
    —PARTITION *p_cursor* BY RANGE(*cursor_column(s)*)
    —PARTITION *p_cursor* BY HASH(*cursor_column(s)*)
- Streaming options (for ordering data within a parallel process):
    —CLUSTER *p_cursor* BY (*cursor_column(s)*)
    —ORDER *p_cursor* BY (*cursor_column(s)*)

The particular method you choose depends on your specific data-processing requirements. For example, if you need to ensure that all orders for a specific customer are processed together, but in date order, you could use HASH partitioning with ORDER streaming. If you need to ensure that all of your trading data is processed in event order, you might use a RANGE/ORDER combination.

### Relative performance of partitioning and streaming combinations

These options have their own performance characteristics resulting from the sorting they imply. The following table summarizes the time taken to pipe 1 million tickertable rows through a parallel pipelined function (with a DOP of 4) using each of the partitioning and streaming options.[3]

| Partitioning option | Streaming option | Elapsed time (s) |
| --- | --- | --- |
| ANY | - | 5.37 |
| ANY | ORDER | 8.06 |
| ANY | CLUSTER | 9.58 |
| HASH | - | 7.48 |
| HASH | ORDER | 7.84 |
| HASH | CLUSTER | 8.10 |
| RANGE | - | 9.84 |
| RANGE | ORDER | 10.59 |
| RANGE | CLUSTER | 10.90 |

As you might expect, ANY and HASH partitioning are comparable (although the unordered ANY option is comfortably the quickest), but the RANGE partitioning mechanism is significantly slower. This is probably to be expected because the source data

---

3. To test the performance of these options for yourself, use the *parallel_options_*.sql* files available on the web site for this book.

---

must be ordered before the database can divide it among the slaves. Within the parallel processes themselves, ordering is quicker than clustering for all partitioning options (this is perhaps a surprising result as clustering doesn't need to order the entire set of data). Your mileage might vary, of course.

### Partitioning with skewed data

A further consideration with partitioning is the division of the workload among the parallel processes. The ANY and HASH options lead to a reasonably uniform spread of data among the parallel processes, regardless of the number of rows in the source. However, depending on your data characteristics, RANGE partitioning might lead to a very uneven allocation, especially if the values in the partitioning column(s) are skewed. If one parallel process receives too large a share of the data, this can negate any benefits of parallel pipelined functions. To test this yourself, use the files named *parallel_skew_*.sql* available on the book's web site.

All of my pipelined function calls include a REF CURSOR parameter supplied via the CURSOR(SELECT...) function. As an alternative, it is perfectly legal to prepare a REF CURSOR variable using the OPEN *ref cursor* FOR... construct and pass this variable in place of the CURSOR(SELECT...) call. If you choose to do this, beware bug 5349930! When you are using parallel-enabled pipelined functions, this bug can cause a parallel process to die unexpectedly with an ORA-01008: not all variables bound exception.

## Pipelined Functions and the Cost-Based Optimizer

The examples in this chapter demonstrate the use of pipelined functions as simple rowsources that generate data for loading and unloading scenarios. At some point, however, you might need to join a pipelined function to another rowsource (such as a table, a view, or the intermediate output of other joins within a SQL execution plan). Rowsource statistics (such as cardinality, data distribution, nulls, etc.) are critical to achieving efficient execution plans, but in the case of pipelined functions (or indeed any table function), the cost-based optimizer doesn't have much information to work with.

### Cardinality heuristics for pipelined table functions

Up to and including Oracle Database 11g Release 1, the CBO applies a heuristic cardinality to pipelined and table functions in SQL statements and this can sometimes lead to inefficient execution plans. The default cardinality appears to be dependent on the value of the DB_BLOCK_SIZE initialization parameter, but on a database with a standard 8Kb block size Oracle uses a heuristic of 8,168 rows. I can demonstrate this quite easily with a pipelined function that pipes a subset of columns from the employees table. Using Autotrace in SQL*Plus to generate an execution plan, I see the following.

```
/* Files on web: cbo_setup.sql and cbo_test.sql */
SQL> SELECT *
  2  FROM    TABLE(pipe_employees) e;

Execution Plan
----------------------------------------------------------
Plan hash value: 1802204150


----------------------------------------------------------------
| Id  | Operation                           | Name          | Rows  |
----------------------------------------------------------------
|   0 | SELECT STATEMENT                    |               |  8168 |
|   1 |  COLLECTION ITERATOR PICKLER FETCH| PIPE_EMPLOYEES |       |
----------------------------------------------------------------
```

This pipelined function actually returns 50,000 rows, so if I join this pipelined function to the departments table, I run the risk of getting a suboptimal plan.

```
/* File on web: cbo_test.sql */
SQL> SELECT *
  2  FROM    departments            d
  3  ,       TABLE(pipe_employees) e
  4  WHERE   d.department_id = e.department_id;

Execution Plan
----------------------------------------------------------
Plan hash value: 4098497386


----------------------------------------------------------------
| Id  | Operation                            | Name          | Rows  |
----------------------------------------------------------------
|   0 | SELECT STATEMENT                     |               |  8168 |
|   1 |  MERGE JOIN                          |               |  8168 |
|   2 |   TABLE ACCESS BY INDEX ROWID        | DEPARTMENTS   |    27 |
|   3 |    INDEX FULL SCAN                   | DEPT_ID_PK    |    27 |
|*  4 |   SORT JOIN                          |               |  8168 |
|   5 |    COLLECTION ITERATOR PICKLER FETCH| PIPE_EMPLOYEES |       |
----------------------------------------------------------------
```

As predicted, this appears to be a suboptimal plan; it is unlikely that a sort-merge join will be more efficient than a hash join in this scenario. So how do I influence the CBO? For this example I could use simple access hints such as LEADING and USE_HASH to effectively override the CBO's cost-based decision and secure a hash join between the table and pipelined function. However, for more complex SQL statements, it is quite difficult to provide all the hints necessary to "lock down" an execution plan. It is often far better to provide the CBO with better statistics with which to make its decisions. There are two ways to do this:

*Optimizer dynamic sampling*
   This feature was enhanced in Oracle Database 11g (11.1.0.7) to include sampling for table and pipelined functions.

*User-defined cardinality*
>   There are several ways to provide the optimizer with a suitable estimate of a pipe-lined function's cardinality.

I'll demonstrate both of these methods for my pipe_employees function below.

### Using optimizer dynamic sampling for pipelined functions

Dynamic sampling is an extremely useful feature that enables the optimizer to take a small statistics sample of one or more objects in a query during the parse phase. You might use dynamic sampling when you haven't gathered statistics on all of your tables in a query or when you are using transient objects such as global temporary tables. Starting with version 11.1.0.7, the Oracle database is able to use dynamic sampling for table or pipelined functions.

To see what difference this feature can make, I'll repeat my previous query but include a DYNAMIC_SAMPLING hint for the pipe_employees function.

```
/* File on web: cbo_test.sql */
SQL> SELECT /*+ DYNAMIC_SAMPLING(e 5) */
  2         *
  3  FROM   departments          d
  4  ,      TABLE(pipe_employees) e
  5  WHERE  d.department_id = e.department_id;

Execution Plan
------------------------------------------------------------
Plan hash value: 815920909

----------------------------------------------------------------------------
| Id | Operation                           | Name          | Rows  |
----------------------------------------------------------------------------
|  0 | SELECT STATEMENT                    |               | 50000 |
|* 1 |  HASH JOIN                          |               | 50000 |
|  2 |   TABLE ACCESS FULL                 | DEPARTMENTS   |    27 |
|  3 |   COLLECTION ITERATOR PICKLER FETCH | PIPE_EMPLOYEES |       |
----------------------------------------------------------------------------
```

This time, the CBO has correctly computed the 50,000 rows that my function returns and has generated a more suitable plan. Note that I used the word "computed" and not "estimated" because in version 11.1.0.7 and later, the optimizer takes a 100% sample of the table or pipelined function, regardless of the dynamic sampling level being used (this is also the case in Oracle Database 11g Release 2). I used level 5, but I could have used anything between level 2 and level 10 to get exactly the same result. This means, of course, that dynamic sampling can be potentially costly or time-consuming if it is being used for queries involving high-volume or long-running pipelined functions.

## Providing cardinality statistics to the optimizer

The only information that I can explicitly pass to the CBO for my pipelined function is its cardinality. As is often the case with Oracle, there are several ways to do this:

*CARDINALITY hint (undocumented)*
> Tells the Oracle database the cardinality of a rowsource in an execution plan. It is quite limited in use and effectiveness.

*OPT_ESTIMATE hint (undocumented)*
> Provides a scaling-factor to correct the estimated cardinality for a rowsource, join or index in an execution plan. This hint is used in SQL Profiles, a separately-licensed feature of Oracle Database 10g Enterprise Edition. SQL Profiles are used to store scaling factors for existing SQL statements to improve and stabilize their execution plans.

*Extensible Optimizer interface*
> Associates a pipelined or table function with an object type to calculate its cardinality and provides this information directly to the CBO (available starting with Oracle Database 10g).

The CARDINALITY and OPT_ESTIMATE hints are not officially supported by Oracle Corporation. For this reason, I prefer not to use them in production code. Other than SQL profiles (or dynamic sampling, as described earlier), the only officially supported method for supplying pipelined functions' cardinality estimates to the CBO is to use the optimizer extensibility features introduced in Oracle Database 10g.

### Extensible Optimizer and pipelined function cardinality

Optimizer extensibility is part of Oracle's Data Cartridge implementation—a set of well-formed interfaces that enable us to extend the database's built-in functionality with our own code and algorithms (typically stored in object types). For pipelined and table functions, the database provides a dedicated interface specifically for cardinality estimates. In the following simple example for my pipe_employees function, I will *associate* my pipelined function with a special object type that will tell the CBO about the function's cardinality. The pipe_employees function specification is as follows:

```
/* File on web: cbo_setup.sql */
FUNCTION pipe_employees(
        p_cardinality IN INTEGER DEFAULT 1
        ) RETURN employee_ntt PIPELINED
```

Note the p_cardinality parameter. My pipe_employees body doesn't use this parameter at all; instead, I am going to use this to tell the CBO the number of rows I expect my function to return. As the Extensible Optimizer needs this to be done via an interface type, I first create my interface object type specification:

```
     /* File on web: cbo_setup.sql */
   1 CREATE TYPE pipelined_stats_ot AS OBJECT (
   2
```

```
3       dummy INTEGER,
4
5       STATIC FUNCTION ODCIGetInterfaces (
6                       p_interfaces OUT SYS.ODCIObjectList
7                       ) RETURN NUMBER,
8
9       STATIC FUNCTION ODCIStatsTableFunction (
10                      p_function    IN  SYS.ODCIFuncInfo,
11                      p_stats       OUT SYS.ODCITabFuncStats,
12                      p_args        IN  SYS.ODCIArgDescList,
13                      p_cardinality IN INTEGER
14                      ) RETURN NUMBER
15  );
```

Note the following points about this type specification:

| Line(s) | Description |
|---------|-------------|
| 3 | All object types must have at least one attribute, so I've included one called "dummy" because it is not needed for this example. |
| 5 and 9 | These methods are part of the well-formed interface for the Extensible Optimizer. There are several other methods available, but the two I've used are the ones needed to implement a cardinality interface for my pipelined function. |
| 10–12 | These ODCIStatsTableFunction parameters are mandatory. The parameter names are flexible, but their positions and datatypes are fixed. |
| 13 | All parameters in a pipelined or table function must be replicated in its associated statistics type. In my example, pipe_employees has a single parameter, p_cardinality, which I must also include in my ODCIStatsTableFunction signature. |

My cardinality algorithm is implemented in the type body as follows:

```
/* File on web: cbo_setup.sql */
1   CREATE TYPE BODY pipelined_stats_ot AS
2
3       STATIC FUNCTION ODCIGetInterfaces (
4                       p_interfaces OUT SYS.ODCIObjectList
5                       ) RETURN NUMBER IS
6       BEGIN
7         p_interfaces := SYS.ODCIObjectList(
8                           SYS.ODCIObject ('SYS', 'ODCISTATS2')
9                           );
10        RETURN ODCIConst.success;
11      END ODCIGetInterfaces;
12
13      STATIC FUNCTION ODCIStatsTableFunction (
14                      p_function    IN  SYS.ODCIFuncInfo,
15                      p_stats       OUT SYS.ODCITabFuncStats,
16                      p_args        IN  SYS.ODCIArgDescList,
17                      p_cardinality IN INTEGER
18                      ) RETURN NUMBER IS
19      BEGIN
20        p_stats := SYS.ODCITabFuncStats(NULL);
21        p_stats.num_rows := p_cardinality;
22        RETURN ODCIConst.success;
```

```
 23     END ODCIStatsTableFunction;
 24
 25 END;
```

This is a very simple interface implementation. The key points to note are:

| Line(s) | Description |
|---|---|
| 3–11 | This mandatory assignment is needed by the Oracle database. No user-defined logic is required here. |
| 20–21 | This is my cardinality algorithm. The p_stats OUT parameter is how I tell the CBO the cardinality of my function. Any value that I pass to my pipe_employees' p_cardinality parameter will be referenced inside my statistics type. During query optimization (i.e., a "hard parse"), the CBO will invoke the ODCIStatsTableFunction method to retrieve the p_stats parameter value and use it in its calculations. |

To recap, I now have a pipelined function and a statistics type. All I need to do now is to associate the two objects using the ASSOCIATE STATISTICS SQL command. This association is what enables the "magic" I've described above to happen:

```
/* File on web: cbo_test.sql */
ASSOCIATE STATISTICS WITH FUNCTIONS pipe_employees USING pipelined_stats_ot;
```

Now I am ready to test. I'll repeat my previous query but include the number of rows I expect my pipelined function to return (this function pipes 50,000 rows).

```
/* File on web: cbo_test.sql */
SQL> SELECT *
  2  FROM    departments              d
  3  ,       TABLE(pipe_employees(50000)) e
  4  WHERE   d.department_id = e.department_id;

Execution Plan
-----------------------------------------------------------
Plan hash value: 815920909

---------------------------------------------------------------------
| Id  | Operation                         | Name          | Rows  |
---------------------------------------------------------------------
|   0 | SELECT STATEMENT                  |               | 50000 |
|*  1 |  HASH JOIN                        |               | 50000 |
|   2 |   TABLE ACCESS FULL               | DEPARTMENTS   |    27 |
|   3 |   COLLECTION ITERATOR PICKLER FETCH| PIPE_EMPLOYEES |       |
---------------------------------------------------------------------
```

This time, my expected cardinality has been picked up and used by the CBO, and I have the execution plan that I was expecting. I haven't even had to use any hints! In most cases, if the CBO is given accurate inputs, it will make a good decision, as demonstrated in this example. Of course, the example also highlights the "magic" of the Extensible Optimizer. I supplied my expected cardinality as a parameter to the pipe_employees function, and during the optimization phase, the database accessed this parameter via the associated statistics type and used it to set the rowsource cardinality accordingly (using my algorithm). I find this quite impressive.

As a final thought, note that it makes good sense to find a systematic way to derive pipelined function cardinalities. I have demonstrated one method—in fact, I should add a p_cardinality parameter to *all* my pipelined functions and associate them all with the pipelined_statistics_ot interface type. The algorithms you use in your interface types can be as sophisticated as you require. They might be based on other function parameters (for example, you might return different cardinalities based on particular parameter values). Perhaps you might store the expected cardinalities in a lookup table and have the interface type query this instead. There are many different ways that you can use this feature.

## Tuning Complex Data Loads with Pipelined Functions

My stockpivot example transformed each input row into two output rows of the same record structure. All of my other examples piped a single output row of a single record structure. But some transformations or loads are not so simple. It is quite common to load multiple tables from a single staging table—can pipelined functions be useful in such scenarios as well?

The good news is that they can; multitable loads can also be tuned with pipelined functions. The function itself can pipe as many different record types as you need, and conditional or unconditional multitable inserts can load the corresponding tables with the relevant attributes.

### One source, two targets

Consider an example of loading customers and addresses from a single-file delivery. Let's imagine that a single customer record has up to three addresses stored in his or her history. This means that as many as four records are generated for each customer. For example:

```
CUSTOMER_ID LAST_NAME  ADDRESS_ID STREET_ADDRESS                 PRIMARY
----------- ---------- ---------- ------------------------------ -------
       1060 Kelley          60455 7310 Breathing Street          Y
       1060 Kelley         119885 7310 Breathing Street          N
     103317 Anderson        65045 57 Aguadilla Drive             Y
     103317 Anderson        65518 117 North Union Avenue         N
     103317 Anderson        61112 27 South Las Vegas Boulevard   N
```

I have removed most of the detail, but this example shows that Kelley has two addresses in the system and Anderson has three. My loading scenario is that I need to add a single record per customer to the customers table, and all of the address records need to be inserted into the addresses table.

### Piping multiple record types from pipelined functions

How can a pipelined function generate a customer record and an address record at the same time? Surprisingly, there are two relatively simple ways to achieve this:

- Use substitutable object types (described in Chapter 26). Different subtypes can be piped out of a function in place of the supertype on which the function is based, meaning that each piped record can be inserted into its corresponding table in a conditional multitable INSERT FIRST statement.
- Use wide, denormalized records with all of the attributes for every target table stored in a single piped row. Each record being piped can be pivoted into multiple rows of target data and inserted using a multitable INSERT ALL statement.

### Using object-relational features

Let's take a look at the first method as it is the most elegant solution to this requirement. I first need to create four types to describe my data:

- An object "supertype" to head the type hierarchy. This will contain only the attributes that the subtypes need to inherit. In my case, this will be just the customer_id.
- A collection type of this supertype. I will use this as the return type for my pipelined function.
- A customer object "subtype" with the remaining attributes required for the customers table load.
- An address object "subtype" with the remaining attributes required for the addresses table load.

I've picked a small number of attributes for demonstration purposes. My types look like this:

```
/* File on web: multitype_setup.sql */
-- Supertype...
CREATE TYPE customer_ot AS OBJECT
( customer_id NUMBER
) NOT FINAL;

-- Collection of supertype...
CREATE TYPE customer_ntt AS TABLE OF customer_ot;

-- Customer detail subtype...
CREATE TYPE customer_detail_ot UNDER customer_ot
( first_name VARCHAR2(20)
, last_name  VARCHAR2(60)
, birth_date DATE
) FINAL;

-- Address detail subtype...
CREATE TYPE address_detail_ot UNDER customer_ot
( address_id     NUMBER
, primary        VARCHAR2(1)
, street_address VARCHAR2(40)
, postal_code    VARCHAR2(10)
) FINAL;
```

If you have never worked with object types, I suggest that you review the contents of Chapter 26. Briefly, however, Oracle's support for substitutability means that I can create rows of either customer_detail_ot or address_detail_ot, and use them wherever the customer_ot supertype is expected. So if I create a pipelined function to pipe a collection of the supertype, this means that I can also pipe rows of either of the subtypes. This is but one example of how an object-oriented type hierarchy can offer a simple and elegant solution.

## A multitype pipelined function

Let's take a look at the pipelined function body, and then I'll explain the key concepts.

```
    /* File on web: multitype_setup.sql */
 1  FUNCTION customer_transform_multi(
 2          p_source    IN customer_staging_rct,
 3          p_limit_size IN PLS_INTEGER DEFAULT customer_pkg.c_default_limit
 4          )
 5    RETURN customer_ntt
 6    PIPELINED
 7    PARALLEL_ENABLE (PARTITION p_source BY HASH(customer_id))
 8    ORDER p_source BY (customer_id, address_id) IS
 9
10      aa_source       customer_staging_aat;
11      v_customer_id customer_staging.customer_id%TYPE := -1;
12      /* Needs a non-null default */
13  BEGIN
14    LOOP
15      FETCH p_source BULK COLLECT INTO aa_source LIMIT p_limit_size;
16      EXIT WHEN aa_source.COUNT = 0;
17
18      FOR i IN 1 .. aa_source.COUNT LOOP
19
20        /* Only pipe the first instance of the customer details... */
21        IF aa_source(i).customer_id != v_customer_id THEN
22          PIPE ROW ( customer_detail_ot( aa_source(i).customer_id,
23                                         aa_source(i).first_name,
24                                         aa_source(i).last_name,
25                                         aa_source(i).birth_date ));
26        END IF;
27
28        PIPE ROW( address_detail_ot( aa_source(i).customer_id,
29                                     aa_source(i).address_id,
30                                     aa_source(i).primary,
31                                     aa_source(i).street_address,
32                                     aa_source(i).postal_code ));
33
34        /* Save customer ID for "control break" logic... */
35        v_customer_id := aa_source(i).customer_id;
36
37      END LOOP;
38    END LOOP;
39    CLOSE p_source;
40    RETURN;
41  END customer_transform_multi;
```

This function is parallel-enabled, and it processes the source data in arrays for maximum performance. The main concepts specific to multityping are:

| Line(s) | Description |
|---|---|
| 5 | My function's return is a collection of the customer supertype. This allows me to pipe subtypes instead. |
| 7–8 | I have data dependencies so have used hash partitioning with ordered streaming. I need to process each customer's records together, because I will need to pick off the customer attributes from the first record only, and then allow all addresses through. |
| 21–26 | If this is the first source record for a particular customer, pipe out a row of CUSTOMER_DETAIL_OT. Only one customer details record will be piped per customer. |
| 28–32 | For every source record, pick out the address information and pipe out a row of ADDRESS_DETAIL_OT. |

### Querying a multitype pipelined function

I now have a single function generating rows of two different types and structures. Using SQL*Plus, let's query a few rows from this function.

```
/* File on web: multitype_query.sql */
SQL> SELECT *
  2  FROM    TABLE(
  3              customer_pkg.customer_transform_multi(
  4                  CURSOR( SELECT * FROM customer_staging ) ) ) nt
  5  WHERE   ROWNUM <= 5;

CUSTOMER_ID
-----------
          1
          1
          1
          1
          2
```

That's a surprise—where's my data? Even though I used SELECT *, I have only the CUSTOMER_ID column in my results. The reason for this is simple: my function is defined to return a collection of the customer_ot supertype, which has only one attribute. So unless I code explicitly for the range of subtypes being returned from my function, the database will not expose any of their attributes. In fact, if I reference any of the subtypes' attributes using the above query format, the database will raise an *ORA-00904: invalid identifier* exception.

Fortunately, Oracle supplies two ways to access instances of object types: the VALUE function and the OBJECT_VALUE pseudo-column. Let's see what they do (they are interchangeable):

```
/* File on web: multitype_query.sql */
SQL> SELECT VALUE(nt) AS object_instance --could use "nt.OBJECT_VALUE" instead
  2  FROM    TABLE(
  3              customer_pkg.customer_transform_multi(
  4                  CURSOR( SELECT * FROM customer_staging ) ) ) nt
  5  WHERE   ROWNUM <= 5;
```

```
OBJECT_INSTANCE(CUSTOMER_ID)
----------------------------------------------------------------------------
CUSTOMER_DETAIL_OT(1, 'Abigail', 'Kessel', '31/03/1949')
ADDRESS_DETAIL_OT(1, 12135, 'N', '37 North Coshocton Street', '78247')
ADDRESS_DETAIL_OT(1, 12136, 'N', '47 East Sagadahoc Road', '90285')
ADDRESS_DETAIL_OT(1, 12156, 'Y', '7 South 3rd Circle', '30828')
CUSTOMER_DETAIL_OT(2, 'Anne', 'KOCH', '23/09/1949')
```

This is more promising. I now have the data as it is returned from the pipelined function, so I'm going to do two things with it. First I will determine the type of each record using the IS OF condition; this will be useful to me later on. Second, I will use the TREAT function to downcast each record to its underlying subtype (until I do this, the database thinks that my data is of the supertype and so will not allow me access to any of the attributes). The query now looks something like this:

```
/* File on web: multitype_query.sql */
SQL> SELECT CASE
  2            WHEN VALUE(nt) IS OF TYPE (customer_detail_ot)
  3            THEN 'C'
  4            ELSE 'A'
  5         END                                  AS record_type
  6  ,      TREAT(VALUE(nt) AS customer_detail_ot) AS cust_rec
  7  ,      TREAT(VALUE(nt) AS address_detail_ot)  AS addr_rec
  8  FROM   TABLE(
  9            customer_pkg.customer_transform_multi(
 10               CURSOR( SELECT * FROM customer_staging ) ) ) nt
 11  WHERE  ROWNUM <= 5;

RECORD_TYPE CUST_REC                          ADDR_REC
----------- --------------------------------- -----------------------------
C           CUSTOMER_DETAIL_OT(1, 'Abigail
            ', 'Kessel', '31/03/1949')

A                                             ADDRESS_DETAIL_OT(1, 12135, 'N
                                              ', '37 North Coshocton Street'
                                              , '78247')

A                                             ADDRESS_DETAIL_OT(1, 12136, 'N
                                              ', '47 East Sagadahoc Road', '
                                              90285')

A                                             ADDRESS_DETAIL_OT(1, 12156, 'Y
                                              ', '7 South 3rd Circle', '3082
                                              8')

C           CUSTOMER_DETAIL_OT(2, 'Anne',
            'KOCH', '23/09/1949')
```

I now have my data in the correct subtype format, which means that I can access the underlying attributes. I do this by wrapping the previous query in an inline view and accessing the attributes using dot notation, as follows.

```
/* File on web: multitype_query.sql */
SELECT ilv.record_type
```

```
         ,      NVL(ilv.cust_rec.customer_id,
                    ilv.addr_rec.customer_id) AS customer_id
         ,      ilv.cust_rec.first_name       AS first_name
         ,      ilv.cust_rec.last_name        AS last_name
                <snip>
         ,      ilv.addr_rec.postal_code      AS postal_code
    FROM   (
               SELECT CASE...
                      <snip>
               FROM   TABLE(
                          customer_pkg.customer_transform_multi(
                              CURSOR( SELECT * FROM customer_staging ) ) ) nt
               ) ilv;
```

### Loading multiple tables from a multitype pipelined function

I've removed some lines from the example above, but you should recognize the pattern.
I now have all the elements needed for a multitable insert into my customers and addresses tables. Here's the loading code:

```
    /* File on web: multitype_setup.sql */
       INSERT FIRST
          WHEN record_type = 'C'
          THEN
             INTO customers
             VALUES (customer_id, first_name, last_name, birth_date)
          WHEN record_type = 'A'
          THEN
             INTO addresses
             VALUES (address_id, customer_id, primary, street_address, postal_code)
       SELECT ilv.record_type
       ,      NVL(ilv.cust_rec.customer_id,
                    ilv.addr_rec.customer_id) AS customer_id
       ,      ilv.cust_rec.first_name       AS first_name
       ,      ilv.cust_rec.last_name        AS last_name
       ,      ilv.cust_rec.birth_date       AS birth_date
       ,      ilv.addr_rec.address_id       AS address_id
       ,      ilv.addr_rec.primary          AS primary
       ,      ilv.addr_rec.street_address   AS street_address
       ,      ilv.addr_rec.postal_code      AS postal_code
       FROM (
             SELECT CASE
                         WHEN VALUE(nt) IS OF TYPE (customer_detail_ot)
                         THEN 'C'
                         ELSE 'A'
                    END                                    AS record_type
                ,   TREAT(VALUE(nt) AS customer_detail_ot) AS cust_rec
                ,   TREAT(VALUE(nt) AS address_detail_ot)  AS addr_rec
                FROM   TABLE(
                           customer_pkg.customer_transform_multi(
                               CURSOR( SELECT * FROM customer_staging ))) nt
                ) ilv;
```

With this INSERT FIRST statement, I have a complex load that uses a range of object-relational features in a way that enables me to retain set-based principles. This approach might also work for you.

## An alternative multitype method

The alternative to this method is to create a single "wide" object record and pipe a single row for each set of customer addresses. I'll show you the type definition to clarify what I mean by this, but see the *multitype_setup.sql* files on the book's web site for the full example).

```
/* File on web: multitype_setup.sql */
CREATE TYPE customer_address_ot AS OBJECT
( customer_id          NUMBER
, first_name           VARCHAR2(20)
, last_name            VARCHAR2(60)
, birth_date           DATE
, addr1_address_id     NUMBER
, addr1_primary        VARCHAR2(1)
, addr1_street_address VARCHAR2(40)
, addr1_postal_code    VARCHAR2(10)
, addr2_address_id     NUMBER
, addr2_primary        VARCHAR2(1)
, addr2_street_address VARCHAR2(40)
, addr2_postal_code    VARCHAR2(10)
, addr3_address_id     NUMBER
, addr3_primary        VARCHAR2(1)
, addr3_street_address VARCHAR2(40)
, addr3_postal_code    VARCHAR2(10)
, CONSTRUCTOR FUNCTION customer_address_ot
     RETURN SELF AS RESULT
);
```

You can see that each of the three address instances per customer is "denormalized" into its respective attributes. Each row piped from the function is pivoted into four rows with a conditional INSERT ALL statement. The INSERT syntax is simpler and, for this particular example, quicker than the substitutable type method. The technique you choose will depend on your particular circumstances; note, however, that you may find that as the number of attributes increases, the performance of the denormalized method may degrade. Having said that, I've used this method successfully to tune a load that inserts up to nine records into four tables for every distinct financial transaction.

You can expect to experience a degradation in the performance of a pipelined function implementation when using wide rows or rows with many columns (pertinent to the denormalized multirecord example described above). For example, I tested a 50,000-row serial pipelined bulk load against row-by-row inserts using multiple columns of 10 bytes each. In Oracle9i Database, the row-based solution became faster than the pipelined solution at just 50 columns. Fortunately, this increases to somewhere between 100 and 150 columns in all major versions of Oracle Database 10g and Oracle Database 11g.

### A Final Word on Pipelined Functions

In this discussion of pipelined functions, I've shown several scenarios where such functions (serial or parallel) can help you improve the performance of your data loads and extracts. As a tuning tool, some of these techniques should prove to be useful. However, I do *not* recommend that you convert your entire code base to pipelined functions! They are a specific tool that is likely to apply to only a subset of your data-processing tasks. If you need to implement complex transformations that are too unwieldy when represented in SQL (typically as analytic functions, CASE expressions, subqueries, or even the frightening MODEL clause), then encapsulating them in pipelined functions, as I've shown in this section, may provide substantial performance benefits.

## Specialized Optimization Techniques

You should *always* proactively use FORALL and BULK COLLECT for all non-trivial multirow SQL operations (that is, those involving more than a few dozen rows). You should *always* look for opportunities to cache data. And for many data-processing tasks, you should strongly consider the use of pipelined functions. In other words, some techniques are so broadly effective that they should be used at every possible opportunity.

Other performance optimization techniques, however, really will only help you in relatively specialized circumstances. For example: the recommendation to use the PLS_INTEGER datatype instead of INTEGER is likely to do you little good unless you are running a program with a very large number of integer operations.

And that's what I cover in this section: performance-related features of PL/SQL that can make a noticeable difference, but only in more specialized circumstances. Generally, I suggest that you not worry too much about applying each and every one of these proactively. Instead, focus on building readable, maintainable code, and then if you identify bottlenecks in specific programs, see if any of these techniques might offer some relief.

## Using the NOCOPY Parameter Mode Hint

The NOCOPY parameter hint requests that the PL/SQL runtime engine pass an IN OUT argument by reference rather than by value. This can speed up the performance of your programs, because by-reference arguments are not copied within the program unit. When you pass large, complex structures like collections, records, or objects, this copy step can be expensive.

To understand NOCOPY and its potential impact, it will help to review how PL/SQL handles parameters. There are two ways to pass parameter values: by reference and by value.

*By reference*

> When an actual parameter is passed by reference, it means that a pointer to the actual parameter is passed to the corresponding formal parameter. Both the actual and the formal parameters then reference, or point to, the same location in memory that holds the value of the parameter.

*By value*

> When an actual parameter is passed by value, the value of the actual parameter is copied to the corresponding formal parameter. If the program then terminates without an exception, the formal parameter value is copied back to the actual parameter. If an error occurs, the changed values are not copied back to the actual parameter.

Parameter passing in PL/SQL without the use of NOCOPY follows these rules:

| Parameter mode | Passed by value or reference? (default behavior) |
| --- | --- |
| IN | By reference |
| OUT | By value |
| IN OUT | By value |

You can infer from these definitions and rules that when a large data structure (such as a collection, a record, or an instance of an object type) is passed as an OUT or IN OUT parameter, that structure will be passed by value, and your application could experience performance and memory degradation as a result of all this copying. The NOCOPY hint is a way for you to attempt to avoid this. This feature fits into a parameter declaration as follows:

```
parameter_name
  [ IN | IN OUT | OUT | IN OUT NOCOPY | OUT NOCOPY ]
parameter_datatype
```

You can specify NOCOPY only in conjunction with the OUT or IN OUT mode. Here is a parameter list that uses the NOCOPY hint for both of its IN OUT arguments:

```
PROCEDURE analyze_results (
   date_in IN DATE,
```

```
values IN OUT NOCOPY numbers_varray,
validity_flags IN OUT NOCOPY validity_rectype
);
```

There are two things you should keep in mind about NOCOPY:

- The corresponding actual parameter for an OUT parameter under the NOCOPY hint is set to NULL whenever the subprogram containing the OUT parameter is called.

- NOCOPY is a *hint*, not a command. This means that the compiler might silently decide that it can't fulfill your request for a NOCOPY parameter treatment. The next section lists the restrictions on NOCOPY that might cause this to happen.

### Restrictions on NOCOPY

A number of situations will cause the PL/SQL compiler to ignore the NOCOPY hint and instead use the default by-value method to pass the OUT or IN OUT parameter. These situations are the following:

*The actual parameter is an element of an associative array*
> You can request NOCOPY for an entire collection (each row of which could be an entire record), but not for an individual element in the table. A suggested work-around is to copy the structure to a standalone variable, either scalar or record, and then pass that as the NOCOPY parameter. That way, at least you aren't copying the entire structure.

*Certain constraints are applied to actual parameters*
> Some constraints will result in the NOCOPY hint's being ignored; these include a scale specification for a numeric variable and the NOT NULL constraint. You can, however, pass a string variable that has been constrained by size.

*The actual and formal parameters are record structures*
> One or both records were declared using %ROWTYPE or %TYPE, and the constraints on corresponding fields in these two records are different.

*In passing the actual parameter, the PL/SQL engine must perform an implicit datatype conversion*
> A suggested workaround is this: because you are always better off performing explicit conversions anyway, do that and then pass the converted value as the NOCOPY parameter.

*The subprogram requesting the NOCOPY hint is used in an external or remote procedure call*
> In these cases, PL/SQL will always pass the actual parameter by value.

### Performance benefits of NOCOPY

So how much can NOCOPY help you? To answer this question, I constructed a package with two procedures as follows:

---

```
/* File on web: nocopy_performance.tst */
PACKAGE nocopy_test
IS
   TYPE numbers_t IS TABLE OF NUMBER;

   PROCEDURE pass_by_value (numbers_inout IN OUT numbers_t);

   PROCEDURE pass_by_ref (numbers_inout IN OUT NOCOPY numbers_t);
END nocopy_test;
```

Each of them doubles the value in each element of the nested table, as in:

```
PROCEDURE pass_by_value (numbers_inout IN OUT numbers_t)
IS
BEGIN
   FOR indx IN 1 .. numbers_inout.COUNT
   LOOP
      numbers_inout (indx) := numbers_inout (indx) * 2;
   END LOOP;
END;
```

I then did the following for each procedure:

- Loaded the nested table with 100,000 rows of data.
- Called the procedure 1,000 times.

In Oracle Database 10*g*, I saw these results:

```
By value  (without NOCOPY) - Elapsed CPU : 20.49 seconds.
By reference (with NOCOPY) - Elapsed CPU : 12.32 seconds.
```

In Oracle Database 11*g*, however, I saw these results:

```
By value  (without NOCOPY) - Elapsed CPU : 13.12 seconds.
By reference (with NOCOPY) - Elapsed CPU : 12.82 seconds.
```

I ran similar tests of collections of strings, with similar results.

After running repeated tests, I conclude that prior to Oracle Database 11*g*, you can see a substantive improvement in performance, but in Oracle Database 11*g*, that advantage is very much narrowed, I assume by overall tuning of the PL/SQL engine in this new version.

### The downside of NOCOPY

Depending on your application, NOCOPY can improve the performance of programs with IN OUT or OUT parameters. These possible gains come, however, with a tradeoff: if a program terminates with an unhandled exception, you cannot trust the values in a NOCOPY actual parameter.

What do I mean by "trust?" Let's review how PL/SQL behaves concerning its parameters when an unhandled exception terminates a program. Suppose that I pass an IN OUT record to my calculate_totals procedure. The PL/SQL runtime engine first makes a copy of that record and then, during program execution, makes any changes to that copy. The actual parameter itself is not modified until calculate_totals ends successfully (without propagating back an exception). At that point, the local copy is copied back to the actual parameter, and the program that called calculate_totals can access that changed data. If calculate_totals terminates with an unhandled exception, however, the calling program can be certain that the actual parameter's value has not been changed.

That certainty disappears with the NOCOPY hint. When a parameter is passed by reference (the effect of NOCOPY), any changes made to the formal parameter are also made immediately to the actual parameter. Suppose that my calculate_totals program reads through a 10,000-row collection and makes changes to each row. If an error is raised at row 5,000 and propagated out of calculate_totals unhandled, my actual parameter collection will be only half-changed.

The *nocopy.tst* file on the book's web site demonstrate the challenges of working with NOCOPY. You should run this script and make sure you understand the intricacies of this feature before using it in your application.

Beyond that and generally, you should be judicious in your use of the NOCOPY hint. Use it only when you know that you have a performance problem relating to your parameter passing, and be prepared for the potential consequences when exceptions are raised.

 The PL/SQL Product Manager, Bryn Llewellyn, differs with me regarding NOCOPY. He is much more inclined to recommend broad usage of this feature. He argues that the side effect of partially modified data structures should not be a big concern, because this situation only arises when an unexpected error has occurred. When this happens, you will almost always stop application processing, log the error, and propagate the exception out to the enclosing block. The fact that a collection is in an uncertain state is likely to be of little importance at this point.

## Using the Right Datatype

When you are performing a small number of operations, it may not really matter if the PL/SQL engine needs to perform implicit conversions or if it uses a relatively slow implementation. On the other hand, if your algorithms require large amounts of intensive computations, the following advice could make a noticeable difference.

### Avoid implicit conversions

PL/SQL, just like SQL, will perform implicit conversions under many circumstances. In the following block, for example, PL/SQL must convert the integer 1 into a number (1.0) before adding it to another number and assigning the result to a number.

```
DECLARE
   l_number NUMBER := 2.0;
```

```
BEGIN
    l_number := l_number + 1;
END;
```

Most developers are aware that implicit conversions performed inside a SQL statement can cause performance degradation by turning off the use of indexes. Implicit conversion in PL/SQL can also affect performance, although usually not as dramatically as that found in SQL.

Run the *test_implicit_conversion.sql* script to see if you can verify an improvement in performance in your environment.

### Use PLS_INTEGER for intensive integer computations

When you declare an integer variable as PLS_INTEGER, it will use less memory than INTEGER and rely on machine arithmetic to get the job done more efficiently. In a program that requires intensive integer computations, simply changing the way that you declare your variables could have a noticeable impact on performance. See "The PLS_INTEGER Type" on page 237 for a more detailed discussion of the different types of integers.

### Use BINARY_FLOAT or BINARY_DOUBLE for floating-point arithmetic

Oracle Database 10g introduced two new floating-point types: BINARY_FLOAT and BINARY_DOUBLE. These types conform to the IEEE 754 floating-point standard and use native machine arithmetic, making them more efficient than NUMBER or INTEGER variables. See "The BINARY_FLOAT and BINARY_DOUBLE Types" on page 241 for details.

# Stepping Back for the Big Picture on Performance

This chapter offers numerous ways to improve the performance of your PL/SQL programs. Just about every one of them comes with a tradeoff: better performance for more memory, better performance for increased code complexity and maintenance costs, and so on. I offer these recommendations to ensure that you optimize code in ways that offer the most benefit to both your users and your development team:

- Make sure your SQL statements are properly optimized. Tuning PL/SQL code simply cannot compensate for the drag of unnecessary full table scans. If your SQL is running slowly, you cannot fix the problem in PL/SQL.

- Ensure that the PL/SQL optimization level is set to at least 2. That's the default, but developers can "mess" with this setting and end up with code that is not fully optimized by the compiler. You can enforce this optimization level with conditional compilation's $ERROR directive (covered in Chapter 20).

- Use BULK COLLECT and FORALL at every possible opportunity. This means that if you are executing row-by-row queries or DML statements, it's time to write a bunch more code to introduce and process your SQL via collections. Rewriting cursor FOR loops is less critical, but OPEN...LOOP...CLOSE constructs will always fetch one row at a time and really should be replaced.

- Keep an eye out for static datasets and when you find them, determine the best caching method to avoid repetitive, expensive retrievals of data. Even if you are not yet using Oracle Database 11g, start to encapsulate your queries behind function interfaces. That way, you can quickly and easily apply the function result cache when you upgrade to Oracle Database 11g.

- Your code doesn't have to be "as fast as possible." It simply has to be "fast enough." That is, don't obsess over optimization of every line of code. Instead, prioritize readability and maintainability over "blazing performance." Get your code to work properly (meet user requirements). Then stress test the code to identify bottlenecks. Get rid of the bottlenecks by applying some of the more specialized tuning techniques.

- Make sure that your DBA is aware of native compilation options, especially in Oracle Database 11g and higher. With these options, Oracle will transparently compile PL/SQL code down to machine code commands.

# CHAPTER 22

# I/O and PL/SQL

Many, perhaps most, of the PL/SQL programs you write need to interact only with the underlying Oracle database using SQL. However, there will inevitably be times when you will want to send information from PL/SQL to the external environment or read information from some external source (screen, file, etc.) into PL/SQL. This chapter explores some of the most common mechanisms for I/O in PL/SQL, including the following built-in packages:

*DBMS_OUTPUT*
    For displaying information on the screen
*UTL_FILE*
    For reading and writing operating system files
*UTL_MAIL and UTL_SMTP*
    For sending email from within PL/SQL
*UTL_HTTP*
    For retrieving data from a web page

It is outside the scope of this book to provide full reference information about the built-in packages introduced in this chapter. Instead, in this chapter, I will demonstrate how to use them to handle the most frequently encountered requirements. Check out Oracle's documentation for more complete coverage. You will also find *Oracle Built-in Packages* (O'Reilly) a helpful source for information on many packages; several chapters from that book are available on this book's web site.

## Displaying Information

Oracle provides the DBMS_OUTPUT package to give you a way to send information from your programs to a buffer. This buffer can then be read and manipulated by another PL/SQL program or by the host environment. DBMS_OUTPUT is most frequently used as a simple mechanism for displaying information on your screen.

Each user session has a DBMS_OUTPUT buffer of predefined size, which developers commonly set to UNLIMITED. Oracle versions prior to Oracle Database 10g Release 2 had a 1 million-byte limit. Once filled, you will need to empty it before you can reuse it; you can empty it programmatically, but more commonly you will rely on the host environment (such as SQL*Plus) to empty it and display its contents. This only occurs after the outermost PL/SQL block terminates; you cannot use DBMS_OUTPUT for real-time streaming of messages from your program.

The way to write information to this buffer is by calling the DBMS_OUTPUT.PUT and DBMS_OUTPUT.PUT_LINE programs. If you want to read from the buffer programmatically, you can use DBMS_OUTPUT.GET_LINE or DBMS_OUT-PUT.GET_LINES.

## Enabling DBMS_OUTPUT

Since the default setting of DBMS_OUTPUT is disabled, calls to the PUT_LINE and PUT programs are ignored and the buffer remains empty. To enable DBMS_OUTPUT, you generally execute a command in the host environment. For example, in SQL*Plus, you can issue this command:

```
SET SERVEROUTPUT ON SIZE UNLIMITED
```

In addition to enabling output to the console, this command has the side effect of issuing the following command to the database server:

```
BEGIN DBMS_OUTPUT.ENABLE (buffer_size => NULL); END;
```

(Null buffer_size equates to an unlimited buffer; otherwise the buffer_size is expressed in bytes.) SQL*Plus offers a variety of options for the SERVEROUTPUT command; check the documentation for the features for your release.

Developer environments such as Oracle's SQL Developer and Quest's Toad generally display the output from DBMS_OUTPUT in a designated portion of the screen (a "pane"), as long as you have properly enabled the display feature.

## Write Lines to the Buffer

There are two built-in procedures to choose from when you want to put information into the buffer. PUT_LINE appends a newline marker after your text; PUT places text in the buffer *without* a newline marker. If you're using PUT alone, the output will remain in the buffer, even when the call ends. In this case, call DBMS_OUTPUT.NEW_LINE to flush the buffer.

If the Oracle database knows implicitly how to convert your data to a VARCHAR2 string, then you can pass it in your call to the PUT and PUT_LINE programs. Here are some examples:

```
BEGIN
    DBMS_OUTPUT.put_line ('Steven');
```

```
      DBMS_OUTPUT.put_line (100);
      DBMS_OUTPUT.put_line (SYSDATE);
   END;
   /
```

Unfortunately, DBMS_OUTPUT does not know what to do with a variety of common PL/SQL types, most notably Booleans. You may therefore want to consider writing a small utility to make it easier to display Boolean values, such as the following procedure, which displays a string and then the Boolean:

```
/* File on web: bpl.sp */
PROCEDURE bpl (boolean_in IN BOOLEAN)
IS
BEGIN
   DBMS_OUTPUT.PUT_LINE(
      CASE boolean_in
         WHEN TRUE THEN 'TRUE'
         WHEN FALSE THEN 'FALSE'
         ELSE 'NULL'
      END
   );
END bpl;
/
```

The largest string that you can pass in one call to DBMS_OUTPUT.PUT_LINE is 32,767 bytes in the most recent releases of Oracle. With Oracle Database 10g Release 1 or earlier, the limit is 255 bytes. With any version, if you pass a value larger than the maximum allowed, the database will raise an exception (either VALUE_ERROR or *ORU-10028: line length overflow, limit of NNN chars per line*). To avoid this problem, you might want to use an encapsulation of DBMS_OUTPUT.PUT_LINE that automatically wraps long strings. The following files, available on the book's web site, offer variations on this theme.

*pl.sp*

> This standalone procedure allows you to specify the length at which your string will be wrapped.

*p.pks/pkb*

> The p package is a comprehensive encapsulation of DBMS_OUTPUT.PUT_LINE that offers many different overloadings (for example, you can display an XML document or an operating-system file by calling the p.l procedure) and also wraps long lines of text.

## Read the Contents of the Buffer

The typical usage of DBMS_OUTPUT is very basic: you call DBMS_OUTPUT.PUT_LINE and view the results on the screen. Behind the scenes, your client environment (e.g., SQL*Plus) calls the appropriate programs in the DBMS_OUTPUT package to extract the contents of the buffer and then display it.

If you need to obtain the contents of the DBMS_OUTPUT buffer, you can call the GET_LINE and/or GET_LINES procedures.

The GET_LINE procedure retrieves one line of information from the buffer in a first-in, first-out fashion, and returns a status value of 0 if successful. Here's an example that uses this program to extract the next line from the buffer into a local PL/SQL variable:

```
FUNCTION next_line RETURN VARCHAR2
IS
   return_value VARCHAR2(32767);
   status INTEGER;
BEGIN
   DBMS_OUTPUT.GET_LINE (return_value, status);
   IF status = 0
   THEN
      RETURN return_value;
   ELSE
      RETURN NULL;
   END IF;
END;
```

The GET_LINES procedure retrieves multiple lines from the buffer with one call. It reads the buffer into a PL/SQL collection of strings (maximum length 255 or 32,767, depending on your version of Oracle). You specify the number of lines you want to read, and it returns those. Here is a generic program that transfers the contents of the DBMS_OUTPUT buffer into a database log table:

```
/* File on web: move_buffer_to_log.sp */
PROCEDURE move_buffer_to_log
IS
   l_buffer      DBMS_OUTPUT.chararr;
   l_num_lines   PLS_INTEGER;
BEGIN
   LOOP
      l_num_lines := 100;
      DBMS_OUTPUT.get_lines (l_buffer, l_num_lines);

      EXIT WHEN l_buffer.COUNT = 0;

      FORALL indx IN l_buffer.FIRST .. l_buffer.LAST
         INSERT INTO logtab (text) VALUES (l_buffer (indx));
   END LOOP;
END;
```

# Reading and Writing Files

The UTL_FILE package allows PL/SQL programs to both read from and write to any operating-system files that are accessible from the server on which your database instance is running. You can load data from files directly into database tables while applying the full power and flexibility of PL/SQL programming. You can generate reports directly from within PL/SQL without worrying about the maximum buffer restrictions of DBMS_OUTPUT that existed prior to Oracle Database 10*g* Release 2.

UTL_FILE lets you read and write files accessible from the server on which your database is running. Sounds dangerous, eh? An ill-intentioned or careless programmer could theoretically use UTL_FILE to write over tablespace datafiles, control files, and so on. Oracle allows the DBA to place restrictions on where you can read and write your files in one of two ways:

- UTL_FILE reads and writes files in directories that are specified by the UTL_FILE_DIR parameter in the database initialization file.
- UTL_FILE also reads/writes files in locations specified by database "Directory" objects.

After explaining how to use these two approaches; I will examine the specific capabilities of the UTL_FILE package. Many of the UTL_FILE programs are demonstrated in a handy encapsulation package found in the *fileIO.pkg* file on the book's web site.

## The UTL_FILE_DIR Parameter

Although not officially deprecated, the UTL_FILE_DIR approach is rarely used with the latest versions of the Oracle database. Using directories is much easier and more flexible. If you have a choice, don't use UTL_FILE_DIR; just skip this section and jump ahead to "Work with Oracle Directories" on page 879.

When you call FOPEN to open a file, you must specify both the location and the name of the file in separate arguments. This file location is then checked against the list of accessible directories, which you can specify with an entry in the database initialization file such as:

```
UTL_FILE_DIR = directory
```

Include a parameter for UTL_FILE_DIR for each directory you want to make accessible for UTL_FILE operations. The following entries, for example, enable four different directories in Unix/Linux-like filesystems:

```
UTL_FILE_DIR = /tmp
UTL_FILE_DIR = /ora_apps/hr/time_reporting
UTL_FILE_DIR = /ora_apps/hr/time_reporting/log
UTL_FILE_DIR = /users/test_area
```

To bypass server security and allow read/write access to all directories, you can use this special syntax:

```
UTL_FILE_DIR = *
```

You should not use this option in production environments. In development environments, this entry certainly makes it easier for developers to get up and running on UTL_FILE, as well as to test their code. However, you should allow access to only a few specific directories when you move the application to production.

## Setting up directories

Here are some observations on working with and setting up accessible directories with UTL_FILE:

- Access is not recursive through subdirectories. Suppose that the following lines were in your database initialization file:

```
UTL_FILE_DIR = c:\group\dev1
UTL_FILE_DIR = c:\group\prod\oe
UTL_FILE_DIR = c:\group\prod\ar
```

You would not be able to open a file in the *c:\group\prod\oe\reports* subdirectory.

- Do not include the following entry on Unix or Linux systems:

```
UTL_FILE_DIR = .
```

This allows you to read/write on the current directory in the operating system.

- Do not enclose the directory names within single or double quotes.

- In a Unix/Linux environment, a file created by FOPEN has as its owner the shadow process running the Oracle instance. This is usually the "oracle" owner. If you try to access these files outside of UTL_FILE, you will need the correct privileges (or be logged in as "oracle") to access or change these files.

- You should not end your directory name with a delimiter, such as the forward slash in Unix/Linux. The following specification of a directory will result in problems when trying to read from or write to the directory:

```
UTL_FILE_DIR = /tmp/orafiles/
```

## Specifying file locations when opening files

The location of the file is an operating system-specific string that specifies the directory or area in which to open the file. When you pass the location in the call to UTL_FILE.FOPEN, you provide the location specification as it appears in the database initialization file. And remember that in case-sensitive operating systems, the case of the location specification in the initialization file must match that used in the call to UTL_FILE.FOPEN.

Here are some examples:

*In Windows*

```
file_id := UTL_FILE.FOPEN ('k:\common\debug', 'trace.lis', 'R');
```

*In Unix/Linux*

```
file_id := UTL_FILE.FOPEN ('/usr/od2000/admin', 'trace.lis', 'W');
```

Your location must be an explicit, complete path to the file. You cannot use operating system-specific parameters such as environment variables in Unix/Linux to specify file locations.

# Work with Oracle Directories

Prior to Oracle9*i* Database Release 2, whenever you opened a file, you needed to specify the location of the file, as in the examples above. Such a hardcoding of values is always to be avoided, however. What if the location of the accounts data changes? How many programs will you have to go fix to make sure everyone is looking in the right place? How many times will you have to make such changes?

A better approach is to declare a variable or constant and assign it the value of the location. If you do this in a package, the constant can be referenced by any program in a schema with the EXECUTE privilege on that package. Here is an example, followed by a recoding of the earlier FOPEN call:

```
PACKAGE accts_pkg
IS
   c_data_location
      CONSTANT VARCHAR2(30) := '/accts/data';
   ...
END accts_pkg;

DECLARE
   file_id   UTL_FILE.file_type;
BEGIN
   file_id := UTL_FILE.fopen (accts_pkg.c_data_location, 'trans.dat', 'R');
END;
```

That's great. But even better is to use a schema-level object that you can define in the database: a directory. This particular type of object is also used when working with BFILEs, so you can in effect "consolidate" file location references in both DBMS_LOB and UTL_FILE by using directories.

To create a directory, the DBA will need to grant you the CREATE ANY DIRECTORY privilege. You then define a new directory as shown in these examples:

```
CREATE OR REPLACE DIRECTORY development_dir AS '/dev/source';
```

```
CREATE OR REPLACE DIRECTORY test_dir AS '/test/source';
```

Here are some things to keep in mind about directories and UTL_FILE:

- The Oracle database does not validate the location you specify when you specify the name of a directory. It simply associates that string with the named database object.

- When you specify the name of a directory in a call to, say, UTL_FILE.FOPEN, it is not treated as the name of an Oracle object; instead, it is treated as a case-sensitive string. In other words, if you do not specify the name as an uppercase string, the operation will fail. This will work:

```
handle := UTL_FILE.FOPEN(
            location => 'TEST_DIR', filename => 'myfile.txt', open_mode => 'r');
```

...but this will not:

```
handle := UTL_FILE.FOPEN(
              location => test_dir, filename => 'myfile.txt', open_mode => 'r');
```

- Once created, you can grant permissions to specific users to work with that directory as follows:

```
GRANT READ ON DIRECTORY development_dir TO senior_developer;
```

- Finally, you can query the contents of ALL_DIRECTORIES to determine which directories are available in the currently connected schema. You can also leverage this view to build some useful utilities. Here is one example: print a list of all the directories defined in the database:

```
/* File on web: fileIO.pkg */
PROCEDURE fileIO.gen_utl_file_dir_entries
IS
BEGIN
   FOR rec IN (SELECT * FROM all_directories)
   LOOP
      DBMS_OUTPUT.PUT_LINE ('UTL_FILE_DIR = ' || rec.directory_path);
   END LOOP;
END gen_utl_file_dir_entries;
```

One advantage of building utilities like those found in *fileIO.pkg* is that you can easily add sophisticated handling of the case of the directory to avoid "formatting errors," such as forgetting to specify the directory name in uppercase.

## Open Files

Before you can read or write a file, you must open it. The UTL_FILE.FOPEN function opens the specified file and returns a file handle you can then use to manipulate the file. Here's the header for the function:

```
FUNCTION UTL_FILE.FOPEN (
       location      IN VARCHAR2
     , filename      IN VARCHAR2
     , open_mode     IN VARCHAR2
     , max_linesize IN BINARY_INTEGER DEFAULT NULL)
RETURN UTL_FILE.file_type;
```

Parameters are summarized in the following table:

| Parameter | Description |
| --- | --- |
| location | Location of the file (directory in UTL_FILE_DIR or a database directory). |
| filename | Name of the file. |
| open_mode | Mode in which the file is to be opened (see the following modes). |
| max_linesize | Maximum number of characters per line, including the newline character, for this file. Minimum is 1; maximum is 32767. The default of NULL means that UTL_FILE determines an appropriate value from the operating system (the value has historically been around 1,024 bytes). |
| UTL_FILE.file_type | Record containing all the information UTL_FILE needs to manage the file. |

You can open the file in one of three modes:

*R*

> Opens the file read-only. If you use this mode, use UTL_FILE's GET_LINE procedure to read from the file.

*W*

> Opens the file to read and write in replace mode. When you open in replace mode, all existing lines in the file are removed. If you use this mode, you can use any of the following UTL_FILE programs to modify the file: PUT, PUT_LINE, NEW_LINE, PUTF, and FFLUSH.

*A*

> Opens the file to read and write in append mode. When you open in append mode, all existing lines in the file are kept intact. New lines will be appended after the last line in the file. If you use this mode, you can use any of the following UTL_FILE programs to modify the file: PUT, PUT_LINE, NEW_LINE, PUTF, and FFLUSH.

Keep the following points in mind as you attempt to open files:

- The file location and the filename joined together must represent a legal filename on your operating system.
- The file location specified must be accessible and must already exist; FOPEN will not create a directory or subdirectory for you in order to write a new file:
- If you want to open a file for read access, the file must already exist. If you want to open a file for write access, the file will either be created if it does not exist or emptied of all its contents if it does exist.
- If you try to open with append, the file must already exist. UTL_FILE will not treat your append request like a write access request. If the file is not present, UTL_FILE will raise the INVALID_OPERATION exception.

The following example shows how to declare a file handle and then open a file for that handle in read-only mode:

```
DECLARE
    config_file UTL_FILE.FILE_TYPE;
BEGIN
    config_file := UTL_FILE.FOPEN ('/maint/admin', 'config.txt', 'R');
```

Notice that I did not provide a maximum line size when I opened this file. That parameter is, in fact, optional. If you do not provide it, the maximum length of a line you can read from or write to the file is approximately 1,024. Given this limitation, you probably want to include the max_linesize argument as shown below:

```
DECLARE
    config_file UTL_FILE.FILE_TYPE;
BEGIN
    config_file := UTL_FILE.FOPEN (
    '/maint/admin', 'config.txt', 'R', max_linesize => 32767);
```

Use the FOPEN_NCHAR function to open files written in multibyte character sets. In this case, Oracle recommends limiting max_linesize to 6400.

## Is the File Already Open?

The IS_OPEN function returns TRUE if the specified handle points to a file that is already open. Otherwise, it returns false. The header for the function is,

```
FUNCTION UTL_FILE.IS_OPEN (file IN UTL_FILE.FILE_TYPE) RETURN BOOLEAN;
```

where *file* is the file to be checked.

Within the context of UTL_FILE, it is important to know what this means. The IS_OPEN function does not perform any operating system checks on the status of the file. In actuality, it merely checks to see if the id field of the file handle record is not NULL. If you don't play around with these records and their contents, this id field is set to a non-NULL value only when you call FOPEN. It is set back to NULL when you call FCLOSE.

## Close Files

Use the UTL_FILE.FCLOSE and UTL_FILE.FCLOSE_ALL procedures to close a specific file and all open files in your session, respectively.

Use FCLOSE to close an open file. The header for this procedure is:

```
PROCEDURE UTL_FILE.FCLOSE (file IN OUT UTL_FILE.FILE_TYPE);
```

where *file* is the file handle.

Notice that the argument to UTL_FILE.FCLOSE is an IN OUT parameter because the procedure sets the id field of the record to NULL after the file is closed.

If there is buffered data that has not yet been written to the file when you try to close it, UTL_FILE will raise the WRITE_ERROR exception.

FCLOSE_ALL closes all the opened files. The header for this procedure is:

```
PROCEDURE UTL_FILE.FCLOSE_ALL;
```

This procedure will come in handy when you have opened a variety of files and want to make sure that none of them are left open when your program terminates.

In programs in which files have been opened, you may wish to call FCLOSE_ALL in the exception handlers of those programs. If there is an abnormal termination of the program, files will then still be closed.

```
EXCEPTION
   WHEN OTHERS
   THEN
      UTL_FILE.FCLOSE_ALL;
```

```
        ... other cleanup activities ...
    END;
```

When you close your files with the FCLOSE_ALL procedure, none of your file handles will be marked as closed (the id field, in other words, will still be non-NULL). The result is that any calls to IS_OPEN for those file handles will *still* return TRUE. You will not, however, be able to perform any read or write operations on those files (unless you reopen them).

## Read from Files

The UTL_FILE.GET_LINE procedure reads a line of data from the specified file, if it is open, into the provided line buffer. The header for the procedure is:

```
PROCEDURE UTL_FILE.GET_LINE
    (file IN UTL_FILE.FILE_TYPE,
     buffer OUT VARCHAR2);
```

where *file* is the file handle returned by a call to FOPEN, and *buffer* is the buffer into which the line of data is read. The variable specified for the *buffer* parameter must be large enough to hold all the data up to the next carriage return or end-of-file condition in the file. If not, PL/SQL will raise the VALUE_ERROR exception. The line terminator character is not included in the string passed into the buffer.

 Oracle offers additional GET programs to read NVARCHAR2 data (GET_LINE_NCHAR) and raw data (GET_RAW).

Here is an example that uses GET_LINE:

```
DECLARE
    l_file UTL_FILE.FILE_TYPE;
    l_line VARCHAR2(32767);
BEGIN
    l_file := UTL_FILE.FOPEN ('TEMP_DIR', 'numlist.txt', 'R', max_linesize => 32767);
    UTL_FILE.GET_LINE (l_file, l_line);
    DBMS_OUTPUT.PUT_LINE (l_line);
END;
```

Because GET_LINE reads data only into a string variable, you will have to perform your own conversions to local variables of the appropriate datatype if your file holds numbers or dates.

### GET_LINE exceptions

When GET_LINE attempts to read past the end of the file, the NO_DATA_FOUND exception is raised. This is the same exception that is raised when you:

* Execute an implicit (SELECT INTO) cursor that returns no rows

- Reference an undefined row of a PL/SQL collection
- Read past the end of a BFILE (binary file) with DBMS_LOB

If you are performing more than one of these operations in the same PL/SQL block, you may need to add extra logic to distinguish between the different sources of this error. See the *who_did_that.sql* file on the book's web site for a demonstration of this technique.

### Handy encapsulation for GET_LINE

The GET_LINE procedure is simple and straightforward. It gets the next line from the file. If the pointer to the file is already located at the last line of the file, UTL_FILE.GET_LINE does not return any kind of flag but instead raises the NO_DATA_FOUND exception. This design leads to poorly structured code; you might consider using an encapsulation on top of GET_LINE to improve that design, as explained in this section.

Here is a program that reads each line from a file and then processes that line:

```
DECLARE
   l_file   UTL_FILE.file_type;
   l_line   VARCHAR2 (32767);
BEGIN
   l_file := UTL_FILE.FOPEN ('TEMP', 'names.txt', 'R');

   LOOP
      UTL_FILE.get_line (l_file, l_line);
      process_line (l_line);
   END LOOP;
EXCEPTION
   WHEN NO_DATA_FOUND
   THEN
      UTL_FILE.fclose (l_file);
END;
```

Notice that the simple loop does not contain any explicit EXIT statement. The loop terminates *implicitly* and with an exception, as soon as UTL_FILE reads past the end of the file. In a small block like this one, the logic is clear. But imagine if my program is hundreds of lines long and much more complex. Suppose further that reading the contents of the file is just one step in the overall algorithm. If an exception terminates my block, I will then need to put the rest of my business logic in the exception section (bad idea) or put an anonymous BEGIN-END block wrapper around my read-file logic.

I am not comfortable with this approach. I don't like to code infinite loops without an EXIT statement; the termination condition is not structured into the loop itself. Furthermore, the end-of-file condition is not really an exception; every file, after all, must end at some point. Why must I be forced into the exception section simply because I want to read a file in its entirety?

I believe that a better approach to handling the end-of-file condition is to build a layer of code around GET_LINE that immediately checks for end-of-file and returns a Boolean value (TRUE or FALSE). The get_nextline procedure shown here demonstrates this approach:

```
/* File on web: getnext.sp */
PROCEDURE get_nextline (
   file_in IN UTL_FILE.FILE_TYPE
 , line_out OUT VARCHAR2
 , eof_out OUT BOOLEAN)
IS
BEGIN
   UTL_FILE.GET_LINE (file_in, line_out);
   eof_out := FALSE;
EXCEPTION
   WHEN NO_DATA_FOUND
   THEN
      line_out := NULL;
      eof_out  := TRUE;
END;
```

The get_nextline procedure accepts an already assigned file handle and returns two pieces of information: the line of text (if there is one) and a Boolean flag (set to TRUE if the end-of-file is reached, FALSE otherwise). Using get_nextline, I can now read through a file with a loop that has an EXIT statement:

```
DECLARE
   l_file   UTL_FILE.file_type;
   l_line   VARCHAR2 (32767);
   l_eof    BOOLEAN;
BEGIN
   l_file := UTL_FILE.FOPEN ('TEMP', 'names.txt', 'R');

   LOOP
      get_nextline (l_file, l_line, l_eof);
      EXIT WHEN l_eof;
      process_line (l_line);
   END LOOP;

   UTL_FILE.fclose (l_file);
END;
```

With get_nextline, I no longer treat end-of-file as an exception. I read a line from the file until I am done, and then I close the file and exit. This is, I believe, a more straightforward and easily understood program.

## Write to Files

In contrast to the simplicity of reading from a file, UTL_FILE offers a number of different procedures you can use to write to a file:

*UTL_FILE.PUT*

Adds the data to the current line in the opened file but does not append a line terminator. You must use the NEW_LINE procedure to terminate the current line or use PUT_LINE to write out a complete line with a line termination character.

*UTL_FILE.NEW_LINE*

Inserts one or more newline characters (default is 1) into the file at the current position.

*UTL_FILE.PUT_LINE*

Puts a string into a file, followed by a platform-specific line termination character. This is the program you are most likely to be using with UTL_FILE.

*UTL_FILE.PUTF*

Puts up to five strings out to the file in a format based on a template string, similar to the printf function in C.

*UTL_FILE.FFLUSH*

UTL_FILE writes are normally buffered; FFLUSH immediately writes the buffer out to the filesystem.

You can use these procedures only if you have opened your file with modes W or A; if you opened the file for read-only, the runtime engine raises the UTL_FILE.INVALID_OPERATION exception.

Oracle offers additional PUT programs to write NVARCHAR2 data (PUT_LINE_NCHAR, PUT_NCHAR, PUTF_NCHAR) and raw data (PUT_RAW).

Let's take a closer look at UTL_FILE.PUT_LINE. This procedure writes data to a file and then immediately appends a newline character after the text. The header for PUT_LINE is:

```
PROCEDURE UTL_FILE.PUT_LINE (
    file IN UTL_FILE.FILE_TYPE
   ,buffer IN VARCHAR2
   ,autoflush IN BOOLEAN DEFAULT FALSE)
```

Parameters are summarized in the following table:

| Parameter | Description |
| --- | --- |
| file | The file handle returned by a call to FOPEN |
| buffer | Text to be written to the file; maximum size allowed is 32,767 |
| autoflush | Pass TRUE if you want this line to be flushed out to the operating system immediately |

Before you can call UTL_FILE.PUT_LINE, you must have already opened the file.

Here is an example that uses PUT_LINE to dump the names of all our employees to a file:

```
PROCEDURE names_to_file
IS
    fileid   UTL_FILE.file_type;
BEGIN
    fileid := UTL_FILE.FOPEN ('TEMP', 'names.dat', 'W');

    FOR emprec IN (SELECT * FROM employee)
    LOOP
        UTL_FILE.put_line (fileid, emprec.first_name || ' ' || emprec.last_name);
    END LOOP;

    UTL_FILE.fclose (fileid);
END names_to_file;
```

A call to PUT_LINE is equivalent to a call to PUT followed by a call to NEW_LINE. It is also equivalent to a call to PUTF with a format string of "%s\n" (see the description of PUTF in the next section).

### Writing formatted text to file

Like PUT, PUTF puts data into a file, but it uses a message format (hence, the "F" in "PUTF") to interpret the different elements to be placed in the file. You can pass between one and five different items of data to PUTF. The header for the procedure is:

```
PROCEDURE UTL_FILE.putf
    (file IN FILE_TYPE
    ,format IN VARCHAR2
    ,arg1 IN VARCHAR2 DEFAULT NULL
    ,arg2 IN VARCHAR2 DEFAULT NULL
    ,arg3 IN VARCHAR2 DEFAULT NULL
    ,arg4 IN VARCHAR2 DEFAULT NULL
    ,arg5 IN VARCHAR2 DEFAULT NULL);
```

Parameters are summarized in the following table:

| Parameter | Description |
| --- | --- |
| file | The file handle returned by a call to FOPEN |
| format | The string that determines the format of the items in the file; see the following options |
| argN | An optional argument string; up to five may be specified |

The format string allows you to substitute the argN values directly into the text written to the file. In addition to "boilerplate" or literal text, the format string may contain the following patterns:

%s

Directs PUTF to put the corresponding item in the file. You can have up to five %s patterns in the format string because PUTF will take up to five items.

*\n*

Directs PUTF to put a newline character in the file. There is no limit to the number of \n patterns you may include in a format string.

The %s formatters are replaced by the argument strings in the order provided. If you do not pass in enough values to replace all of the formatters, then the %s is simply removed from the string before writing it to the file.

The following example illustrates how to use the format string. Suppose you want the contents of the file to look like this:

```
Employee: Steven Feuerstein
Soc Sec #: 123-45-5678
Salary: $1000
```

This single call to PUTF will accomplish the task:

```
UTL_FILE.PUTF
   (file_handle, 'Employee: %s\nSoc Sec #: %s\nSalary: %s\n',
    'Steven Feuerstein',
    '123-45-5678',
    TO_CHAR (:employee.salary, '$9999'));
```

If you need to write out more than five items of data, you can simply call PUTF twice consecutively to finish the job.

## Copy Files

UTL_FILE.FCOPY lets you easily copy the contents of one source file to another destination file. The following snippet, for example, uses UTL_FILE.FCOPY to perform a backup by copying a single file from the development directory to the archive directory:

```
DECLARE
   file_suffix   VARCHAR2 (100)
           := TO_CHAR (SYSDATE, 'YYYYMMDDHH24MISS');
BEGIN
   -- Copy the entire file...
   UTL_FILE.FCOPY (
      src_location      => 'DEVELOPMENT_DIR',
      src_filename      => 'archive.zip',
      dest_location     => 'ARCHIVE_DIR',
      dest_filename     =>   'archive'
                          || file_suffix
                          || '.zip'
   );
END;
```

You can also use FCOPY to copy just a *portion* of a file. The program offers two additional parameters that allow you to specify the starting and ending line numbers you want to copy from the file. Suppose that I have a text file containing the names of the winners of a monthly PL/SQL quiz that started in January 2008. I would like to transfer all the names in 2009 to another file. I can do that by taking advantage of the fifth and sixth arguments of the FCOPY procedure as shown below:

```
DECLARE
   c_start_year CONSTANT PLS_INTEGER := 2008;
   c_year_of_interest CONSTANT PLS_INTEGER := 2009;
   l_start PLS_INTEGER;
   l_end PLS_INTEGER;
BEGIN
   l_start := (c_year_of_interest - c_start_year)*12 + 1;
   l_end := l_start + 11;

   UTL_FILE.FCOPY (
      src_location       => 'WINNERS_DIR',
      src_filename       => 'names.txt',
      dest_location      => 'WINNERS_DIR',
      dest_filename      => 'names2008.txt',
      start_line         => l_start,
      end_line           => l_end
   );
END;
```

A useful encapsulation to UTL_FILE.FCOPY allows me to specify start and end strings instead of line numbers. I will leave the implementation of such a utility as an exercise for the reader (see the *infile.sf* file on the book's web site for an implementation of an "INSTR for files" that might give you some ideas on implementation).

## Delete Files

You can remove files using UTL_FILE.FREMOVE, as long as you are using Oracle9*i* Database Release 2 or later. The header for this procedure is:

```
PROCEDURE UTL_FILE.FREMOVE (
   location IN VARCHAR2,
   filcname IN VARCHAR2);
```

For example, here I can use UTL_FILE.FREMOVE to remove the original archive file shown previously:

```
BEGIN
   UTL_FILE.FREMOVE ('DEVELOPMENT_DIR', 'archive.zip');
END;
```

That's simple enough. You provide the location and name of the file, and UTL_FILE *attempts* to delete it. What if UTL_FILE encounters a problem? You might then see one of the following exceptions raised:

| Exception name | Meaning |
|---|---|
| UTL_FILE.invalid_path | Not a valid file handle |
| UTL_FILE.invalid_filename | File not found or filename NULL |
| UTL_FILE.file_open | File already open for writing/appending |

| Exception name | Meaning |
| --- | --- |
| UTL_FILE.access_denied | Access to the directory object is denied |
| UTL_FILE.remove_failed | Failed to delete file |

In other words, UTL_FILE will raise an exception if you try to remove a file that doesn't exist or if you do not have the privileges needed to remove the file. Many file-removal programs in other languages (for example, File.delete in Java) return a status code to inform you of the outcome of the removal attempt. If you prefer this approach, you can use (or copy) the fileIO.FREMOVE program found in the *fileIO.pkg* file on the book's web site.

## Rename and Move Files

I can combine copy and remove operations into a single step by calling the UTL_FILE.FRENAME procedure. This handy utility allows me to either rename a file in the same directory or to rename a file to another name *and* location (in effect, moving that file).

The header for FRENAME is:

```
PROCEDURE UTL_FILE.frename (
    src_location   IN VARCHAR2,
    src_filename   IN VARCHAR2,
    dest_location  IN VARCHAR2,
    dest_filename  IN VARCHAR2,
    overwrite      IN BOOLEAN DEFAULT FALSE);
```

This program may raise one of the following exceptions:

| Exception name | Meaning |
| --- | --- |
| UTL_FILE.invalid_path | Not a valid file handle |
| UTL_FILE.invalid_filename | File not found or filename NULL |
| UTL_FILE.rename_failed | Unable to perform the rename as requested |
| UTL_FILE.access_denied | Insufficient privileges to access directory object |

You will find an interesting application of FRENAME in the *fileIO.pkg*—the chgext procedure. This program changes the extension of the specified file.

## Retrieve File Attributes

Sometimes you need to get information about a particular file: How big is this file? Does a file even exist? What is the block size of the file? Such questions are not mysteries that can only be solved with the help of an operating system command (or, in the case of the file length, the DBMS_LOB package), as they were in early Oracle releases. UTL_FILE.FGETATTR provides that information in a single native procedure call.

The header for FGETATTR is:

```
PROCEDURE UTL_FILE.FGETATTR (
   location    IN VARCHAR2,
   filename    IN VARCHAR2,
   fexists     OUT BOOLEAN,
   file_length OUT NUMBER,
   block_size  OUT BINARY_INTEGER);
```

Thus, to use this program, you must declare three different variables to hold the Boolean flag (does the file exist?), the length of the file, and the block size. Here is a sample usage:

```
DECLARE
   l_fexists      BOOLEAN;
   l_file_length  PLS_INTEGER;
   l_block_size   PLS_INTEGER;
BEGIN
   UTL_FILE.FGETATTR (
      location    => 'DEVELOPMENT_DIR',
      filename    => 'bigpkg.pkg',
      fexists     => l_fexists,
      file_length => l_file_length,
      block_size  => l_block_size
   );
   ...
END;
```

This interface is a bit awkward. Suppose that you just want to find out the length of this file? You still have to declare all those variables, obtain the length, and then work with that value. Perhaps the best way to take advantage of FGETATTR is to build some of your own functions *on top of* this built-in that answer a single question, such as:

```
FUNCTION fileIO.flength (
   location_in  IN   VARCHAR2,
   file_in      IN   VARCHAR2
   )
   RETURN PLS_INTEGER;
```

or:

```
FUNCTION fileIO.fexists (
   location_in IN VARCHAR2,
   file_in IN VARCHAR2
   )
      RETURN BOOLEAN;
```

As a result, you do not have to declare unneeded variables, and you can write simpler, cleaner code.

# Sending Email

Over the years, Oracle has gradually made it easier to send email from within a stored procedure. Here's a short example:

```
/* Requires Oracle Database 10g or later */
BEGIN
   UTL_MAIL.send(
      sender     => 'me@mydomain.com'
      ,recipients => 'you@yourdomain.com'
      ,subject    => 'API for sending email'
      ,message    =>
'Dear Friend:

This is not spam. It is a mail test.

Mailfully Yours,
Bill'
      );

END;
```

When you run this block, the database will attempt to send this message using whatever SMTP[1] host the DBA has configured in the initialization file (see the discussion in the next section).

The header for UTL_MAIL.SEND is:

```
PROCEDURE send(sender     IN VARCHAR2,
               recipients IN VARCHAR2,
               cc         IN VARCHAR2 DEFAULT NULL,
               bcc        IN VARCHAR2 DEFAULT NULL,
               subject    IN VARCHAR2 DEFAULT NULL,
               message    IN VARCHAR2 DEFAULT NULL,
               mime_type  IN VARCHAR2
                             DEFAULT 'text/plain; charset=us-ascii',
               priority   IN PLS_INTEGER DEFAULT 3);
```

Most of the parameters are self-explanatory. One non-obvious usage hint: if you want to use more than one recipient (or cc or bcc), separate the addresses with commas, like this:

```
recipients => 'you@yourdomain.com, him@hisdomain.com'
```

Okay, so that's pretty good if you have a recent version of Oracle, but what if you only have access to earlier versions, or what if you just want a little more control? You can still use the UTL_SMTP package, which is a little more complicated but nevertheless workable. If you want to code at an even lower level, you can use UTL_TCP, an external procedure, or a Java stored procedure, but I'll leave those as an exercise for anyone who wants to write some entertaining code.

---

1. SMTP is one of many Internet acronyms governed by other acronyms. Simple Mail Transfer Protocol is governed by Request for Comment (RFC) 2821, which obsoletes RFC 821.

## Oracle Prerequisites

Unfortunately, not all versions of Oracle provide email-from-PL/SQL that works out of the box. The built-in UTL_SMTP is part of a default installation, so it will generally work right out of the box. If you are using Oracle Database 11g Release 2, there is one security hoop you will have to jump through, as explained below.

Starting with Oracle Database 10g, the default Oracle installation does not include the UTL_MAIL package. To set up and use UTL_MAIL, your DBA will have to perform the following tasks:

1. Set a value for the initialization parameter SMTP_OUT_SERVER. In Oracle Database 10g Release 2 and later, you can just do something like this:

   ```
   ALTER SYSTEM SET SMTP_OUT_SERVER = 'mailhost';
   ```

   In Oracle Database 10g Release 1, you need to edit your pfile by hand to set this parameter. The string you supply will be one or more (comma-delimited) mail hostnames that UTL_MAIL should try one at a time until it finds one it likes.

2. After setting this parameter, you must *bounce the database server* for the change to take effect. Amazing but true.

3. As SYS, run the installation scripts:

   ```
   @$ORACLE_HOME/rdbms/admin/utlmail.sql
   @$ORACLE_HOME/rdbms/admin/prvtmail.plb
   ```

4. Grant execute to the "privileged few" who need to use it:

   ```
   GRANT EXECUTE ON UTL_MAIL TO SCOTT;
   ```

## Configuring Network Security

In Oracle Database 11g Release 2, your DBA will need to jump through one more security hoop for any package that makes network callouts, including UTL_SMTP and UTL_MAIL. The DBA will need to create an Access Control List (ACL), put your username or role into it, and grant the network-level privilege to that list. Here is a simple cookbook ACL for this purpose:

```
BEGIN
   DBMS_NETWORK_ACL_ADMIN.CREATE_ACL (
      acl          => 'mail-server.xml'
      ,description => 'Permission to make network connections to mail server'
      ,principal   => 'SCOTT'  /* username or role */
      ,is_grant    => TRUE
      ,privilege   => 'connect'
   );

   DBMS_NETWORK_ACL_ADMIN.ASSIGN_ACL (
      acl          => 'mail-server.xml'
      ,host        => 'my-STMP-servername'
      ,lower_port  => 25    /* The default SMTP network port */
      ,upper_port  => NULL  /* Null here means open only port 25 */
```

```
      );
   END;
```

These days, your network administrator might also need to configure a firewall to allow port 25 outbound connections from your database server, and your email administrator might also have some permissions to set!

## Send a Short (32,767 or Less) Plaintext Message

In the previous section, the first example showed how to send a plaintext message if you have UTL_MAIL at your disposal. If, however, you are using UTL_SMTP, your program will have to communicate with the mail server at a lower programmatic level: opening the connection, composing the headers, sending the body of the message, and (ideally) examining the return codes. To give you a flavor of what this looks like, Figure 22-1 shows a sample conversation between a mail server and a PL/SQL mail client I've named send_mail_via_utl_smtp.

Here is the code for this simple stored procedure:

```
       /* File on web: send_mail_via_utl_smtp.sp */
 1    PROCEDURE send_mail_via_utl_smtp
 2     ( sender IN VARCHAR2
 3      ,recipient IN VARCHAR2
 4      ,subject IN VARCHAR2 DEFAULT NULL
 5      ,message IN VARCHAR2
 6      ,mailhost IN VARCHAR2 DEFAULT 'mailhost'
 7      )
 8    IS
 9      mail_conn UTL_SMTP.connection;
10      crlf CONSTANT VARCHAR2(2) := CHR(13) || CHR(10);
11      smtp_tcpip_port CONSTANT PLS_INTEGER := 25;
12    BEGIN
13      mail_conn := UTL_SMTP.OPEN_CONNECTION(mailhost, smtp_tcpip_port);
14      UTL_SMTP.HELO(mail_conn, mailhost);
15      UTL_SMTP.MAIL(mail_conn, sender);
16      UTL_SMTP.RCPT(mail_conn, recipient);
17      UTL_SMTP.DATA(mail_conn, SUBSTR(
18        'Date: ' || TO_CHAR(SYSTIMESTAMP, 'Dy, dd Mon YYYY HH24:MI:SS TZHTZM')
19        || crlf || 'From: ' || sender || crlf
20        || 'Subject: ' || subject || crlf
21        || 'To: ' || recipient || crlf
22        || message
23      , 1, 32767));
24
25      UTL_SMTP.QUIT(mail_conn);
26    END;
```

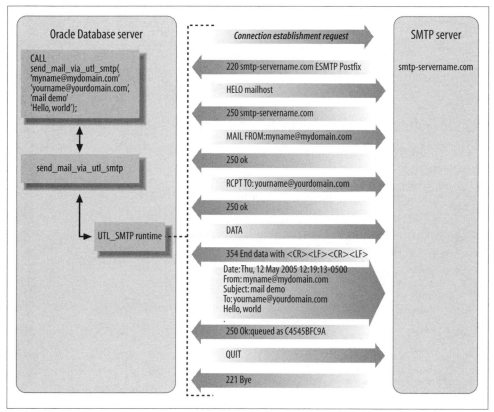

*Figure 22-1. A "conversation" between the PL/SQL mail client and SMTP server*

The following table explains a few concepts behind this code:

| Line(s) | Description |
|---------|-------------|
| 9 | You must define a variable to handle the "connection," which is a record of type UTL_SMTP.connection. |
| 10 | According to Internet mail standards, all header lines must end with a carriage return followed by a line feed, and you are responsible for making this happen (see lines 19–21). |
| 14–25 | These lines send specific instructions to the SMTP server in the sequence and form an Internet-compliant mail server expects. |
| 18 | This line uses SYSTIMESTAMP (introduced in Oracle9i Database) to gain access to time zone information. |

If you look at lines 17–23, you'll see that this procedure cannot send a message whose "DATA" part exceeds 32,767 bytes, which is the limit of PL/SQL variables. It's possible to send longer emails using UTL_SMTP, but you will need to stream the data using multiple calls to UTL_SMTP.WRITE_DATA, as shown later.

By convention, most email programs limit each line of text to 78 characters plus the two line-terminating characters. In general, you'll want to keep each line of text to a maximum of 998 characters exclusive of carriage return/line feed, or CRLF (that is, 1,000 bytes if you count the CRLF). Don't go over 1,000 bytes unless you're sure that your server implements the relevant SMTP "Service Extension."

## Include "Friendly" Names in Email Addresses

If I invoke the previous procedure like this:

```
BEGIN
   send_mail_via_utl_smtp('myname@mydomain.com',
      'yourname@yourdomain.com', 'mail demo', NULL);
END;
```

the "normally" visible headers of the email, as generated by lines 17–21, will show up something like this:

```
Date: Wed, 23 Mar 2005 17:14:30 -0600
From: myname@mydomain.com
Subject: mail demo
To: yourname@yourdomain.com
```

Most humans (and many antispam programs) prefer to see real names in the headers, in a form such as:

```
Date: Wed, 23 Mar 2005 17:14:30 -0600
From: Bob Swordfish <myname@mydomain.com>
Subject: mail demo
To:"Scott Tiger, Esq." <yourname@yourdomain.com>
```

There is, of course, more than one way to make this change; perhaps the most elegant would be to add some parsing to the sender and recipient parameters. This is what Oracle has done in UTL_MAIL. So, for example, I can call UTL_MAIL.SEND with addresses of the form:

```
["]Friendly name["] <email_address>
```

as in:

```
BEGIN
   UTL_MAIL.send('Bob Swordfish <myname@mydomain.com>',
      '"Scott Tiger, Esq." <yourname@yourdomain.com>',
      subject=>'mail demo');
END;
```

However, you need to realize that Oracle's package also adds character set information, so the previous code generates an email header that looks something like this:

```
Date: Sat, 24 Jan 2009 17:47:00 -0600 (CST)
From: Bob Swordfish <me@mydomain.com>
To: Scott Tiger, Esq. <you@yourdomain.com>
Subject: =?WINDOWS-1252?Q?mail=20demo?=
```

While that looks odd to most ASCII speakers, it is completely acceptable in Internet-standards-land; an intelligent mail client should interpret (rather than display) the character set information anyway.

One quick and dirty modification of the send_mail_via_utl_smtp procedure would simply be to add parameters for the friendly names (or change the existing parameters to record structures).

## Send a Plaintext Message of Arbitrary Length

UTL_MAIL is pretty handy, but if you want to send a text message larger than 32,767 bytes, it won't help you. One way around this limitation would be to modify the send_mail_via_utl_smtp procedure so that the "message" parameter is a CLOB data-type. Take a look at the other changes required:

```
/* File on web: send_clob.sp */
PROCEDURE send_clob_thru_email (
   sender     IN VARCHAR2
 , recipient IN VARCHAR2
 , subject   IN VARCHAR2 DEFAULT NULL
 , MESSAGE   IN CLOB
 , mailhost  IN VARCHAR2 DEFAULT 'mailhost'
)
IS
   mail_conn          UTL_SMTP.connection;
   crlf               CONSTANT VARCHAR2 (2) := CHR (13) || CHR (10);
   smtp_tcpip_port    CONSTANT PLS_INTEGER := 25;
   pos                PLS_INTEGER := 1;
   bytes_o_data       CONSTANT PLS_INTEGER := 32767;
   offset             PLS_INTEGER := bytes_o_data;
   msg_length         CONSTANT PLS_INTEGER := DBMS_LOB.getlength (MESSAGE);
BEGIN
   mail_conn := UTL_SMTP.open_connection (mailhost, smtp_tcpip_port);
   UTL_SMTP.helo (mail_conn, mailhost);
   UTL_SMTP.mail (mail_conn, sender);
   UTL_SMTP.rcpt (mail_conn, recipient);

   UTL_SMTP.open_data (mail_conn);
   UTL_SMTP.write_data (
      mail_conn
    ,  'Date: '
      || TO_CHAR (SYSTIMESTAMP, 'Dy, dd Mon YYYY HH24:MI:SS TZHTZM')
      || crlf
      || 'From: '
      || sender
      || crlf
      || 'Subject: '
      || subject
      || crlf
      || 'To: '
      || recipient
      || crlf
   );
```

```
      WHILE pos < msg_length
      LOOP
         UTL_SMTP.write_data (mail_conn, DBMS_LOB.SUBSTR (MESSAGE, offset, pos));
         pos := pos + offset;
         offset := LEAST (bytes_o_data, msg_length - offset);
      END LOOP;

      UTL_SMTP.close_data (mail_conn);

      UTL_SMTP.quit (mail_conn);
   END send_clob_thru_email;
```

Using open_data, write_data, and close_data allows you to transmit an arbitrary number of bytes to the mail server (up to whatever limit the server imposes on email size). Note the one big assumption that this code is making: that the CLOB has been properly split into lines of the correct length.

Let's next take a look at how to attach a file to an email.

## Send a Message with a Short (< 32,767) Attachment

The original email standard required all messages to be composed of seven-bit U.S. ASCII characters.[2] But we all know that emails can include attachments—such as viruses and word-processing documents—and these kinds of files are normally binary, not text. How can an ASCII message transmit a binary file? The answer, in general, is that attachments are transmitted using mail extensions known as MIME[3] in combination with a binary-to-ASCII translation scheme such as base64. To see MIME in action, let's take a look at an email that transmits a tiny binary file:

```
Date: Wed, 01 Apr 2009 10:16:51 -0600
From: Bob Swordfish <my@myname.com>
MIME-Version: 1.0
To: Scott Tiger <you@yourname.com>
Subject: Attachment demo
Content-Type: multipart/mixed;
 boundary="------------060903040208010603090401"

This is a multi-part message in MIME format.
--------------060903040208010603090401
Content-Type: text/plain; charset=us-ascii; format=fixed
Content-Transfer-Encoding: 7bit

Dear Scott:

I'm sending a gzipped file containing the text of the first
```

---

2. Modern mail programs generally support 8-bit character transfer per an SMTP extension known as 8BITMIME. You can discover whether it's supported via SMTP's EHLO directive.

3. Multipurpose Internet Mail Extensions, as set forth in RFC 2045, 2046, 2047, 2048, and 2049, and updated by 2184, 2231, 2646, and 3023. And then some....

```
paragraph. Hope you like it.

Bob
--------------06090304020801060309040l
Content-Type: application/x-gzip; name="hugo.txt.gz"
Content-Transfer-Encoding: base64
Content-Disposition: inline; filename="hugo.txt.gz"

H4sICDh/TUICA2xlc21pcy50eHQAPY5BDoJAEATvvqI/AJGDxjMaowcesbKNOwmZITsshhf7
DdGD105Vpe+K5tQcOJm6sGScU8gjvbrmoG8Tr1qhLtSCbs3CEa/gaMWTTbABF3kqa9z42+dE
RXhYmeHcpHmtBlmIoBEpREyZLpERtjB/aUSxns5/Ci7ac/uOP9a7Dw4FECSdAAAA
--------------06090304020801060309040l--
```

Although a lot of the text can be boilerplated, there are still a lot of details to handle when you generate the email. Fortunately, if you just want to send a "small" attachment (less than 32,767), and you have Oracle Database 10g or later, UTL_MAIL comes to the rescue. In this next example, I'll use UTL_MAIL.SEND_ATTACH_VARCHAR2, which sends attachments that are expressed as text.

The previous message and file can be sent as follows:

```
DECLARE
    b64 VARCHAR2(512) := 'H4sICDh/TUICA2xlc21...'; -- etc., as above
    txt VARCHAR2(512) := 'Dear Scott: ...'; -- etc., as above
BEGIN
    UTL_MAIL.send_attach_varchar2(
        sender => 'my@myname.com'
       ,recipients => 'you@yourname.com'
       ,message => txt
       ,subject => 'Attachment demo'
       ,att_mime_type => 'application/x-gzip'
       ,attachment => b64
       ,att_inline => TRUE
       ,att_filename => 'hugo.txt.gz'
    );
END;
```

Here are the new parameters:

| Parameter | Description |
|---|---|
| att_mime_type | Indication of the type of media and format of the attachment |
| att_inline | Directive to the mail-reading program as to whether the attachment should be displayed in the flow of the message body (TRUE) or as a separate thing (FALSE) |
| att_filename | Sender's designated name of the attached file |

The MIME type isn't just something you make up; it's loosely governed, like so many things on the Internet, by the Internet Assigned Numbers Authority (IANA). Common MIME content types include text/plain, multipart/mixed, text/html, application/pdf, and application/msword. For a complete list, visit IANA's web page at *http://www.iana.org/assignments/media-types/*.

You may have noticed that there was quite a bit of hand-waving earlier to attach a base64-encoded file to an email. Let's take a closer look at the exact steps required to convert a binary file into something you can send to an inbox.

## Send a Small File (< 32767) as an Attachment

To have the Oracle database convert a small binary file to something that can be emailed, you can read the contents of the file into a RAW variable, and use UTL_MAIL.SEND_ATTACH_RAW. This causes the database to convert the binary data to base64 and properly construct the MIME directives. If the file you want to send is in */tmp/hugo.txt.gz* (and is less than 32,767 in size), you might specify:

```
/* File on web: send_small_file.sql */
CREATE OR REPLACE DIRECTORY tmpdir AS '/tmp'
/
DECLARE
    the_file BFILE := BFILENAME('TMPDIR', 'hugo.txt.gz');
    rawbuf RAW(32767);
    amt PLS_INTEGER :=  32767;
    offset PLS_INTEGER := 1;
BEGIN
    DBMS_LOB.fileopen(the_file, DBMS_LOB.file_readonly);
    DBMS_LOB.read(the_file, amt, offset, rawbuf);
    UTL_MAIL.send_attach_raw
(
     sender => 'my@myname.com'
    ,recipients => 'you@yourname.com'
    ,subject => 'Attachment demo'
    ,message => 'Dear Scott...'
    ,att_mime_type => 'application/x-gzip'
    ,attachment => rawbuf
    ,att_inline => TRUE
    ,att_filename => 'hugo.txt.gz'
    );

    DBMS_LOB.close(the_file);
END;
```

If you don't have UTL_MAIL, follow the instructions in the next section.

## Attach a File of Arbitrary Size

To send a larger attachment, you can use the trusty UTL_SMTP package; if the attachment is not text, you can perform a base64 conversion with Oracle's built-in UTL_ENCODE package . Here is an example procedure that sends a BFILE along with a short text message:

```
        /* File on web: send_bfile.sp */
1    PROCEDURE send_bfile
2      ( sender IN VARCHAR2
3       ,recipient IN VARCHAR2
4       ,subject IN VARCHAR2 DEFAULT NULL
```

```
 5          ,message IN VARCHAR2 DEFAULT NULL
 6          ,att_bfile IN OUT BFILE
 7          ,att_mime_type IN VARCHAR2
 8          ,mailhost IN VARCHAR2 DEFAULT 'mailhost'
 9          )
10    IS
11       crlf CONSTANT VARCHAR2(2) := CHR(13) || CHR(10);
12       smtp_tcpip_port CONSTANT PLS_INTEGER := 25;
13       bytes_per_read CONSTANT PLS_INTEGER := 23829;
14       boundary CONSTANT VARCHAR2(78) := '-------5e9i1BxFQrgl9cOgs9O-------';
15       encapsulation_boundary CONSTANT VARCHAR2(78) := '--' || boundary;
16       final_boundary CONSTANT VARCHAR2(78) := '--' || boundary || '--';
17
18       mail_conn  UTL_SMTP.connection;
19       pos PLS_INTEGER := 1;
20       file_length PLS_INTEGER;
21
22       diralias VARCHAR2(30);
23       bfile_filename VARCHAR2(512);
24       lines_in_bigbuf PLS_INTEGER := 0;
25
26       PROCEDURE writedata (str IN VARCHAR2, crlfs IN PLS_INTEGER DEFAULT 1)
27       IS
28       BEGIN
29          UTL_SMTP.write_data(mail_conn, str || RPAD(crlf, 2 * crlfs, crlf));
30       END;
31
32    BEGIN
33       DBMS_LOB.fileopen(att_bfile, DBMS_LOB.LOB_READONLY);
34       file_length := DBMS_LOB.getlength(att_bfile);
35
36       mail_conn := UTL_SMTP.open_connection(mailhost, smtp_tcpip_port);
37       UTL_SMTP.helo(mail_conn, mailhost);
38       UTL_SMTP.mail(mail_conn, sender);
39       UTL_SMTP.rcpt(mail_conn, recipient);
40
41       UTL_SMTP.open_data(mail_conn);
42       writedata('Date: ' || TO_CHAR(SYSTIMESTAMP,
43                    'Dy, dd Mon YYYY HH24:MI:SS TZHTZM') || crlf
44          || 'MIME-Version: 1.0' || crlf
45          || 'From: ' || sender || crlf
46          || 'Subject: ' || subject || crlf
47          || 'To: ' || recipient || crlf
48          || 'Content-Type: multipart/mixed; boundary="' || boundary || '"', 2);
49
50       writedata(encapsulation_boundary);
51       writedata('Content-Type: text/plain; charset=ISO-8859-1; format=flowed');
52       writedata('Content-Transfer-Encoding: 7bit', 2);
53       writedata(message, 2);
54
55       DBMS_LOB.filegetname(att_bfile, diralias, bfile_filename);
56       writedata(encapsulation_boundary);
57       writedata('Content-Type: '
58          || att_mime_type || '; name="' || bfile_filename || '"');
59       writedata('Content-Transfer-Encoding: base64');
```

```
60      writedata('Content-Disposition: attachment; filename="'
61         || bfile_filename || '"', 2);
62
63      WHILE pos < file_length
64      LOOP
65         writedata(UTL_RAW.cast_to_varchar2(
66                     UTL_ENCODE.base64_encode
67                        DBMS_LOB.substr(att_bfile, bytes_per_read, pos))), 0);
68         pos := pos + bytes_per_read;
69      END LOOP;
70
71      writedata(crlf || crlf || final_boundary);
72
73      UTL_SMTP.close_data(mail_conn);
74      UTL_SMTP.QUIT(mail_conn);
75      DBMS_LOB.CLOSE(att_bfile);
76   END;
```

Let's take a look at a few highlights:

| Line(s) | Description |
| --- | --- |
| 13 | This constant governs how many bytes of the file to attempt to read at a time (see line 67), which should probably be as large as possible for performance reasons. It turns out that UTL_ENCODE.BASE64_ENCODE generates lines that are 64 characters wide. Because of the way base64 works, each 3 bytes of binary data gets translated into 4 bytes of character data. Add in 2 bytes of CRLF per emailed line of base64 text, and you get the largest possible read of 23,829 bytes (obtained from the expression TRUNC((0.75*64)*(32767/(64+2))-1). |
| 14–16 | You can reuse the same core boundary string throughout this email. As you can see from the code, MIME standards require that slightly different boundaries be used in different parts of the email. If you want to create an email with nested MIME parts, though, you will need a different boundary string for each level of nesting. |
| 26–30 | This is a convenience procedure to make the executable section a little cleaner. The crlfs parameter indicates the number of CRLFs to append to the line (generally 0, 1, or 2). |
| 55 | Instead of requiring a filename argument to send_bfile, you can just extract the filename from the BFILE itself. |
| 63–69 | This is the real guts of the program. It reads a portion of the file and converts it to base64, sending data out via the mail connection just before hitting the 32,767 limit. |

I know what you're thinking: I, too, used to think sending email was easy. And this procedure doesn't even provide much flexibility; it lets you send one text part and attach one file. But it provides a starting point that you can extend for your own application's needs.

One more point about crafting well-formed emails: rather than reading yourself to sleep with the RFCs, you may prefer to pull out the email client you use every day, send yourself an email of the form you are trying to generate, and then view the underlying "source text" of the message. It worked for me; I did that many times while writing this section of the book! Note, however, that some mail clients, notably Microsoft Outlook, don't seem to provide a way to examine all of the underlying "source."

# Working with Web-Based Data (HTTP)

Let's say you want to acquire some data from the web site of one of your business partners. There are lots of ways to retrieve a web page:

- "By hand," that is, by pointing your web browser to the right location.
- Using a scripting language such as Perl, which, incidentally, has lots of available gizmos and gadgets to interpret the data once you retrieve it.
- Via a command-line utility such as GNU *wget* (one of my favorite utilities).
- Using Oracle's built-in package UTL_HTTP.

Since this is a book about PL/SQL, guess which method I'll be discussing!

If you're running Oracle Database 11g Release 2 or later, you will need to set up a network ACL to permit outbound connections to any desired remote hosts, as mentioned in the previous section.

Let's start with a relatively simple means of coding the retrieval of a web page. This first method, which slices up the web page and puts the slices into an array, actually predates Oracle's support of CLOBs.

## Retrieve a Web Page in "Pieces"

One of the first procedures that Oracle ever released in the UTL_HTTP package retrieves a web page into consecutive elements of an associative array. Usage can be pretty simple:

```
DECLARE
   page_pieces UTL_HTTP.html_pieces; -- array of VARCHAR2(2000)
BEGIN
   page_pieces := UTL_HTTP.request_pieces(url => 'http://www.oreilly.com/');
END;
```

This format is not terribly fun to work with, because the 2,000-byte boundaries are unrelated to anything you would find on the text of the page. So if you have a parsing algorithm that needs a line-by-line approach, you will have to read and reassemble the lines. Moreover, Oracle says that it may not fill all of the (unending) pieces to 2,000 bytes; Oracle's algorithm does not use end-of-line boundaries as breaking points; and the maximum number of pieces is 32,767.

Even if an array-based retrieval meets your needs, you will likely encounter web sites where the above code just won't work. For example, some sites would refuse to serve their content to such a script, because Oracle's default HTTP "header" looks unfamiliar to the web server. In particular, the "User-Agent" header is a text string that tells the web server the browser software the client is using (or emulating), and many web sites are set up to provide content specific to certain browsers. But by default, Oracle does not send a User-Agent. A commonly used and supported header you might want to use is:

```
User-Agent: Mozilla/4.0 (compatible; MSIE 6.0; Windows NT 5.1)
```

Sending this header does increase the complexity of the code you must write, because doing so means you must code at a lower level of abstraction; in particular, you must initiate a "request," send your header, get the "response," and retrieve the page in a loop:

```
DECLARE
    req UTL_HTTP.req;     -- a "request object" (actually a PL/SQL record)
    resp UTL_HTTP.resp;   -- a "response object" (also a PL/SQL record)
    buf VARCHAR2(32767); -- buffer to hold data from web page
BEGIN
    req := UTL_HTTP.begin_request('http://www.oreilly.com/',
        http_version => UTL_HTTP.http_version_1_1);
    UTL_HTTP.set_header(req, 'User-Agent'
        , 'Mozilla/4.0 (compatible; MSIE 6.0; Windows NT 5.1)');
    resp := UTL_HTTP.get_response(req);

    BEGIN
        LOOP
            UTL_HTTP.read_text(resp, buf);
            -- process buf here; e.g., store in array
        END LOOP;
    EXCEPTION
        WHEN UTL_HTTP.end_of_body
        THEN
            NULL;
    END;
    UTL_HTTP.end_response(resp);
END;
```

The heart of the code above is this built-in:

```
PROCEDURE UTL_HTTP.read_text(
    r IN OUT NOCOPY UTL_HTTP.resp,
    data OUT NOCOPY VARCHAR2 CHARACTER SET ANY_CS,
    len IN PLS_INTEGER DEFAULT NULL);
```

If *len* is NULL, the Oracle database will fill the buffer up to its maximum size until reaching the end of the page, after which point the read operation raises the UTL_HTTP.end_of_body exception as above. (Yes, like UTL_FILE.GET_LINE discussed earlier, this goes against a coding practice that normal operations should not raise exceptions.) Each iteration through the loop, you will need to process the buffer, perhaps by appending it to a LOB.

You can also use the line-by-line retrieval using READ_LINE rather than READ_TEXT:

```
PROCEDURE UTL_HTTP.read_line(
r IN OUT NOCOPY UTL_HTTP.resp,
    data OUT NOCOPY VARCHAR2 CHARACTER SET ANY_CS,
    remove_crlf IN BOOLEAN DEFAULT FALSE);
```

This built-in reads one line of source text at a time, optionally cutting off the end-of-line characters. The caveat with READ_LINE is that each line you fetch from the HTTP server needs to be less than 32,767 in length. Such an assumption is not always a good one, so don't use READ_LINE unless you are sure this limit won't cause a problem.

## Retrieve a Web Page into a LOB

Because reading either by "pieces" or by lines can run into various size limits, you may decide that it would make more sense to read into LOBs. Again, Oracle provides a very simple call that may meet your needs. You can retrieve an entire page at once into a single data structure using the HTTPURITYPE built-in object type:

```
DECLARE
   text CLOB;
BEGIN
   text := HTTPURITYPE('http://www.oreilly.com').getclob;
END;
```

If you are retrieving a binary file and you want to put it in a BLOB, you can use getblob():

```
DECLARE
   image BLOB;
BEGIN
   image :=
      HTTPURITYPE('www.oreilly.com/catalog/covers/oraclep4.s.gif').getblob;
END;
```

The HTTPURITYPE constructor assumes HTTP as the transport protocol, and you can either include or omit the "http://"—but, unfortunately, this built-in does not support HTTPS, nor will it let you send a custom User-Agent.

The UTL_HTTP flavor of fetching a LOB looks like this:

```
/* File on web: url_to_clob.sql */
DECLARE
   req UTL_HTTP.req;
   rcsp UTL_HTTP.resp;
   buf VARCHAR2(32767);
   pagelob CLOB;
BEGIN
   req := UTL_HTTP.begin_request('http://www.oreilly.com/',
      http_version => UTL_HTTP.http_version_1_1);
   UTL_HTTP.set_header(req, 'User-Agent', 'Mozilla/4.0 (compatible;
 MSIE 6.0; Windows NT 5.1)');
   rcsp := UTL_HTTP.get_response(req);
   DBMS_LOB.createtemporary(pagelob, TRUE);
   BEGIN
      LOOP
         UTL_HTTP.read_text(resp, buf);
         DBMS_LOB.writeappend(pagelob, LENGTH(buf), buf);
      END LOOP;
   EXCEPTION
      WHEN UTL_HTTP.end_of_body
      THEN
         NULL;
   END;
END;
```

```
    UTL_HTTP.end_response(resp);

    ...here is where you parse, store, or otherwise process the LOB

    DBMS_LOB.freetemporary(pagelob);
END;
```

## Authenticate Using HTTP Username/Password

Although many web sites such as Amazon and eBay use a custom HTML form for login
and authentication, there are still a lot of sites that use *HTTP authentication*, more
precisely known as *basic authentication*. You will recognize such sites by your browser
client's behavior; it will pop up a modal dialog box requesting your username and
password.

It is sometimes possible to bypass the dialog by inserting your username and password
in the URL in the following form (although this approach is deprecated in the official
standards):

```
http://username:password@some.site.com
```

Both UTL_HTTP and HTTPURITYPE support this syntax, at least since 9.2.0.4. A
simple case:

```
DECLARE
    webtext clob;
    user_pass VARCHAR2(64) := 'bob:swordfish'; -- replace with your own
    url VARCHAR2(128) := 'www.encryptedsite.com/cgi-bin/login';
BEGIN
    webtext := HTTPURITYPE(user_pass || '@' || url).getclob;
END;
/
```

If encoding the username and password in the URL doesn't work, try something along
these lines:

```
    ...
    req := UTL_HTTP.begin_request('http://some.site.com/');
    UTL_HTTP.set_authentication(req, 'bob', 'swordfish');
    resp := UTL_HTTP.get_response(req);
    ...
```

This works as long as the site does not encrypt the login page.

## Retrieve an SSL-Encrypted Web Page (Via HTTPS)

Although HTTPURITYPE does not support SSL-encrypted retrievals, UTL_HTTP will
do the job if you set up an *Oracle wallet*. An Oracle wallet is just a catchy name for a
file that contains security certificates and, optionally, public/private key pairs. It's the
former (the certificates) that you need for HTTPS retrievals. You can store one or more
wallets as files in the database server's filesystem or in an LDAP directory service; Oracle

does not install any wallets by default. See Chapter 23 for more information on wallets and other Oracle security features.

To set up one of these wallet things, you'll want to fire up Oracle's GUI utility known as Oracle Wallet Manager, which is probably named *owm* on Unix/Linux hosts or will appear on your Start→Oracle... menu on Microsoft Windows. Once you have Oracle Wallet Manager running, the basic steps you need to follow[4] are:

1. Click on the "New" icon or select Wallet→New from the pull-down menu.

2. Give the wallet a password. In my example, the password will be "password1". Use the default wallet type ("standard").

3. If it asks you "Do you want to create a certificate request at this time?," the correct response is almost certainly "No." You don't need your own certificate to make an HTTPS retrieval.

4. Click on the Save icon or choose Wallet→Save As from the menu to designate the directory. Oracle will name the file for you (on my machine, *owm* named it "ewallet.p12").

5. Upload or copy the wallet file to some location on the Oracle server to which the oracle processes have read access. In the next example, the directory is */oracle/wallets*.

Now try something like this:

```
DECLARE
    req UTL_HTTP.req;
    resp UTL_HTTP.resp;
BEGIN
    UTL_HTTP.set_wallet('file:/oracle/wallets', 'password1');
    req := UTL_HTTP.begin_request('https://www.entrust.com/');
    UTL_HTTP.set_header(req, 'User-Agent', 'Mozilla/4.0');
    resp := UTL_HTTP.get_response(req);
    UTL_HTTP.end_response(resp);
END;
```

If you don't get an error message, you can reward yourself with a small jump for joy. This ought to work, because Entrust is one of the few authorities whose certificate Oracle includes by default when you create a wallet.

If you want to retrieve data from another HTTPS site whose public certificate doesn't happen to be on Oracle's list, you can fire up Oracle Wallet Manager again and "import" the certificate into your file, and again put it on the server. To download a certificate in a usable format, you can use Microsoft Internet Explorer and follow these steps:

1. Point your (Microsoft IE) browser to the HTTPS site.

2. Double-click on the yellow lock icon in the lower right corner of the window.

---

4. Thanks to Tom Kyte for spelling this out in plain English on *http://asktom.oracle.com*.

3. Click on Details → Copy to File.

4. Follow the prompts to export a base64-encoded certificate.

Or, if you have the OpenSSL package installed (typically on a Unix/Linux-based box), you could do this:

```
echo '' | openssl s_client -connect host:port
```

which will spew all kinds of information to stdout; just save the text between the BEGIN CERTIFICATE and END CERTIFICATE lines (inclusive) to a file. And by the way, the normal port for HTTPS is 443.

Now that you have your certificate, you can do this:

1. Open Oracle Wallet Manager.

2. Open your "wallet" file.

3. Import the certificate from the file you just created.

4. Save your wallet file, and upload it to the database server as before.

Remember that those certificates are not in an Oracle wallet until you import them via Oracle Wallet Manager. And in case you're wondering, a wallet can have more than one certificate, and a wallet directory can hold one or more wallets.

## Submit Data to a Web Page via GET or POST

Sometimes, you'll want to retrieve results from a web site as if you had filled out a form in your browser and pressed the Submit button. This section will show a few examples that use UTL_HTTP for this purpose, but many web sites are quirky and require quite a bit of fiddling about to get things working right. Some of the tools you may find useful while analyzing the behavior of your target site include:

- Familiarity with HTML source code (especially as it relates to HTML forms) and possibly with JavaScript.

- A browser's "view source" feature that lets you examine the source code of the site you're trying to use from PL/SQL.

- A tool such as GNU *wget* that easily lets you try out different URLs and has an ability to show the normally hidden conversation between web client and server (use the -d switch).

- Browser plug-ins such as Chris Pederick's Web Developer and Adam Judson's Tamper Data for Mozilla-based browsers.

First, let's look at some simple code you can use to query Google. As it turns out, Google's main page uses a single HTML form:

```
<form action=/search name=f>
```

Because the method tag is omitted, it defaults to GET. The single text box on the form is named "q" and includes the following properties (among others):

```
<input autocomplete="off" maxLength=2048 size=55 name=q value="">
```

You can encode the GET request directly in the URL as follows:

```
http://www.google.com/search?q=query
```

Given this information, here is the programmatic equivalent of searching for "oracle pl/sql programming" (including the double quotes) using Google:

```
DECLARE
   url VARCHAR2(64)
      := 'http://www.google.com/search?q=';
   qry VARCHAR2(128) := UTL_URL.escape('"oracle pl/sql programming"', TRUE);
   result CLOB;
BEGIN
   result := HTTPURITYPE(url || qry).getclob;
END;
```

Oracle's handy UTL_URL.ESCAPE function transforms the query by translating special characters into their hex equivalents. If you're curious, the escaped text from the example is:

```
%22oracle%20pl%2Fsql%20programming%22
```

Let's take a look at using POST in a slightly more complicated example. When I looked at the source HTML for *http://www.apache.org*, I found that their search form's "action" was *http://search.apache.org*, that the form uses the POST method, and that their search box is named "query". With POST, you cannot simply append the data to the URL as with GET; instead you send it to the web server in a particular form. Here is some code that POSTs a search for the string "oracle pl/sql" (relevant additions highlighted):

```
DECLARE
   req UTL_HTTP.req;
   resp UTL_HTTP.resp;
   qry VARCHAR2(512) := UTL_URL.escape('query=oracle pl/sql');
BEGIN
   req := UTL_HTTP.begin_request('http://search.apache.org/', 'POST', 'HTTP /1.0');
   UTL_HTTP.set_header(req, 'User-Agent', 'Mozilla/4.0');
   UTL_HTTP.set_header(req, 'Host', 'search.apache.org');
   UTL_HTTP.sct_header(req, 'Content-Type', 'application/x-www-form-urlencoded');
   UTL_HTTP.set_header(req, 'Content-Length', TO_CHAR(LENGTH(qry)));
   UTL_HTTP.write_text(req, qry);
   resp := UTL_HTTP.get_response(req);

   ...now we can retrieve the results as before (e.g., line by line)

   UTL_HTTP.end_response(resp);
END;
```

In a nutshell, the BEGIN_REQUEST includes the POST directive, and the code uses write_text to transmit the form data. While POST does not allow the name/value pairs to be appended to the end of the URL (like GET queries), this site allows the x-www-form-urlencoded content type, allowing name/value pairs in the qry variable that you send to the server.

The earlier Apache example shows one other additional header that my other examples don't use:

```
UTL_HTTP.set_header(req, 'Host', 'search.apache.org');
```

Without this header, Apache's site was responding with their main page, rather than their search page, The Host header is required for web sites that use the "virtual host" feature—that is, one IP address serves two or more hostnames—so the web server knows what site you're looking for. The good thing is that you can always include the Host header, even if the remote site does not happen to serve virtual hosts.

By the way, if you have more than one item in the form to fill out, URL encoding says that each name/value pair must be separated with an ampersand:

```
name1=value1&name2=value2&name3= ...
```

Okay, you've got all your GETs and POSTs working now, so you are all set to go forth and fetch...right? Possibly. It's likely your code will sooner or later run afoul of the HTTP "redirect." This is a special return code that web servers send, which means "sorry, you need to go *over there* to find what you are looking for." We are accustomed to letting our browsers handle redirects for us silently and automatically, but it turns out that the underlying implementation can be tricky: there are at least five different kinds of redirect, each with slightly different rules about what is "legal" for the browser to do. You may encounter redirects with any web page, but for many of them you should be able to use a feature in UTL_HTTP to follow redirects. That is:

```
UTL_HTTP.set_follow_redirect
  (max_redirects IN PLS_INTEGER DEFAULT 3);
```

Unfortunately, while testing code to retrieve a weather forecast page from the U.S. National Weather Service, I discovered that their server responds to a POST with a *302* "Found" redirect. This is an odd case in the HTTP standard, which holds that clients should *not* follow the redirect...and Oracle's UTL_HTTP adheres to the letter of the standard, at least in this case.

So, I have to ignore the standard to get something useful from the weather page. My final program to retrieve the weather in Sebastopol, California appears here:

```
/* File on web: orawx.sp */
PROCEDURE orawx
AS
    req UTL_HTTP.req;
    resp UTL_HTTP.resp;
    line VARCHAR2(32767);
    formdata VARCHAR2(512) := 'inputstring=95472';    -- zip code
    newlocation VARCHAR2(1024);
BEGIN
    req := UTL_HTTP.begin_request('http://www.srh.noaa.gov/zipcity.php',
```

```
                'POST', UTL_HTTP.http_version_1_0);
    UTL_HTTP.set_header(req, 'User-Agent', 'Mozilla/4.0');
    UTL_HTTP.set_header(req, 'Content-Type', 'application/x-www-form-urlencoded');
    UTL_HTTP.set_header(req, 'Content-Length', TO_CHAR(LENGTH(formdata)));
    UTL_HTTP.write_text(req, formdata);
    resp := UTL_HTTP.get_response(req);

    IF resp.status_code = UTL_HTTP.http_found
    THEN
      UTL_HTTP.get_header_by_name(resp, 'Location', newlocation);
      req := UTL_HTTP.begin_request(newlocation);
      resp := UTL_HTTP.get_response(req);     END IF;

    ...process the resulting page here, as before...

    UTL_HTTP.end_response(resp);
END;
```

Figure 22-2 shows the basic interaction between this code and the web server.

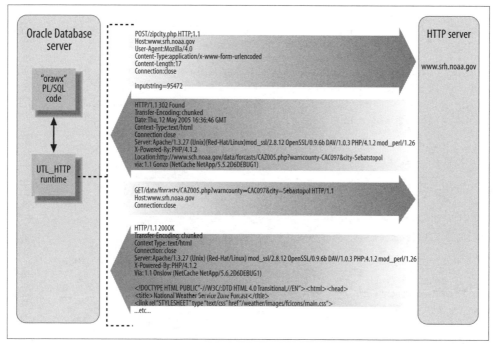

*Figure 22-2. Getting the Sebastopol weather from NOAA involves following a "302 found" redirection*

I don't know how common a problem that is, and my "fix" is not really a general-purpose solution for all redirects, but it gives you an idea of the kinds of quirks you may run into when writing this sort of code.

## Disable Cookies or Make Cookies Persistent

For better or for worse, session-level cookie support is *enabled by default* in recent versions of UTL_HTTP. Oracle has set a default of 20 cookies allowed per site and a total of 300 per session. To check whether this is true for your version of UTL_HTTP, use the following:

```
DECLARE
   enabled BOOLEAN;
   max_total PLS_INTEGER;
   max_per_site PLS_INTEGER;
BEGIN
   UTL_HTTP.get_cookie_support(enabled, max_total, max_per_site);
   IF enabled
   THEN
      DBMS_OUTPUT.PUT('Allowing ' || max_per_site || ' per site');
      DBMS_OUTPUT.PUT_LINE(' for total of ' || max_total || ' cookies. ');
   ELSE
      DBMS_OUTPUT.PUT_LINE('Cookie support currently disabled.');
   END IF;
END;
```

Cookie support is transparent; Oracle automatically stores cookies in memory and sends them back to the server when requested.

Cookies disappear when the session ends. If you'd like to make cookies persistent, you can save them into Oracle tables and then restore them when you start a new session. To do this, have a look at the sample code that Oracle provides in the UTL_HTTP section of the *Packages and Types* manual.

To completely disable cookie support for all your UTL_HTTP requests for the remainder of your session, use this code:

```
UTL_HTTP.set_cookie_support
(FALSE);
```

To disable cookies for a particular request, specify this:

```
UTL_HTTP.set_cookie_support(req, FALSE);
```

To change the number of cookies from Oracle's default values, specify this:

```
UTL_HTTP.set_cookie_support(TRUE,
   max_cookies => n,
   max_cookies_per_site => m);
```

## Retrieve Data from an FTP Server

Oracle does not provide out-of-the-box support for retrieving data from FTP sites via PL/SQL. However, if you need to send or receive files via FTP, there are several PL/SQL solutions available on the Internet. I've seen at least three different packages, authored, respectively, by Barry Chase, Tim Hall, and Chris Poole. These implementations typically use UTL_TCP and UTL_FILE (and possibly Java), and support most

---

of the commonly used FTP operations. You can find a link to some of these imple-mentations by visiting *http://plnet.org*.

In addition, some proxy servers support the retrieval of FTP via HTTP requests from the client, so you may be able to live without a true FTP package.

## Use a Proxy Server

For a variety of reasons, it is common in the corporate world for the network to force all web traffic through a proxy server. Fortunately, Oracle includes support for this kind of arrangement in UTL_HTTP. For example, if your proxy is running on port 8888 at 10.2.1.250, use the following:

```
DECLARE
   req UTL_HTTP.req;
   resp UTL_HTTP.resp;
BEGIN
   UTL_HTTP.set_proxy(proxy => '10.2.1.250:8888',
      no_proxy_domains => 'mycompany.com, hr.mycompany.com');

   req := UTL_HTTP.begin_request('http://some-remote-site.com');

   /* If your proxy requires authentication, use this: */
   UTL_HTTP.set_authentication(r => req,
      username => 'username',
      password => 'password',
      for_proxy => TRUE);

   resp := UTL_HTTP.get_response(req);...etc.
```

I happened to test this code on a proxy server that uses Microsoft NTLM-based au-thentication. After an embarrassing amount of trial and error, I discovered that I had to prefix my username with the Microsoft server "domain name" plus a backslash. That is, if I normally log in to the NTLM domain "mis" as user bill with password swordfish, I must specify:

```
username => 'mis\bill', password => 'swordfish'
```

# Other Types of I/O Available in PL/SQL

This chapter has focused on some of the types of I/O that I think are most useful in the real world and that aren't well covered elsewhere. But what about these other types of I/O?

- Database pipes, queues, and alerts
- TCP sockets
- Oracle's built-in web server

## Database Pipes, Queues, and Alerts

The DBMS_PIPE built-in package was originally designed as an efficient means of sending small bits of data between separate Oracle database sessions. With the introduction of autonomous transactions, database pipes are no longer needed if they are simply being used to isolate transactions from each other. Database pipes can also be used to manually parallelize operations.

Database queuing is a way to pass messages asynchronously among Oracle sessions. There are many variations on queuing: single versus multiple producers, single versus multiple consumers, limited-life messages, priorities, and more. The latest incarnation of Oracle's queuing features is covered in the Oracle manual called *Oracle Streams Advanced Queuing User's Guide*.

The DBMS_ALERT package allows synchronous notification to multiple sessions that various database events have occurred. My impression is that this feature is rarely used today; Oracle provides other products that fill a similar need but with more features.

You can read more about pipes and alerts in the chapter *Intersession Communication* in *Oracle Built-in Packages* (O'Reilly). For your convenience, that chapter is posted on this book's web site.

## TCP Sockets

As interesting a subject as low-level network programming may be to the geeks among us (including yours truly), it's just not a widely used feature. In addition to the UTL_TCP built-in package, Oracle also supports invocation of the networking features in Java stored procedures, which you can invoke from PL/SQL.

## Oracle's Built-in Web Server

Even if you haven't licensed the Oracle Application Server product, you still have access to an HTTP server built-in to the Oracle database. Configuration of the built-in server varies according to Oracle version, but the PL/SQL programming side of it, including the OWA_UTIL, HTP, and HTF packages, has remained relatively unchanged.

These packages let you generate database-driven web pages directly from PL/SQL. This is a fairly extensive topic, particularly if you want to generate and process HTML forms in your web page—not to mention the fact that HTTP is a stateless protocol, so you don't really get to set and use package-level variables from one call to the next. O'Reilly's *Learning Oracle PL/SQL* provides an introduction to PL/SQL that makes heavy use of the built-in web server and provides a number of code samples. The PL/SQL coding techniques are also applicable if you happen to be using Oracle's separate, full-blown application server product; for more information about this product, see *Oracle Application Server 10g Essentials* by Rick Greenwald, Robert Stackowiak, and Donald Bales (O'Reilly).

Although not an I/O method per se, Oracle Application Express, also known as Oracle APEX, deserves one final mention. This is a free add-on to the Oracle Database which lets you build full-blown, web-based applications that connect to an Oracle database. PL/SQL programmers can write their own stored programs that integrate into the GUI framework that Oracle APEX provides, which provides many convenient tools for exchanging data via a visible user interface.

# PART VI

# Advanced PL/SQL Topics

A language as mature and rich as PL/SQL is packed full of features that you may not use on a day-to-day basis, but that may make the crucial difference between success and failure. This part of the book focuses on those features. Chapter 23 explores the security-related challenges we face as we build PL/SQL programs. Chapter 24 contains an exploration of the PL/SQL architecture, including PL/SQL's use of memory. Chapter 25 provides guidance for PL/SQL developers who need to address issues of globalization and localization. Chapter 26 offers an introduction to the object-oriented features of Oracle.

Two additional chapters, describing invoking Java and C code from PL/SQL applications, are available in full on the book's web site.

Chapter 23, *Application Security and PL/SQL*
Chapter 24, *PL/SQL Architecture*
Chapter 25, *Globalization and Localization in PL/SQL*
Chapter 26, *Object-Oriented Aspects of PL/SQL*

# Application Security and PL/SQL

Many PL/SQL developers view security as an activity that only database administrators and security administrators need to be concerned about. It's certainly true that some aspects of security are the responsibility of DBAs—for example, performing user and privilege management and setting the password for the listener. However, it would be a gross mistake to believe that security is merely a DBA activity, one that does not belong on the plates of PL/SQL developers. For one thing, security is not an end unto itself; rather, it's an ongoing process and a means to an end. For another, a lot of administrators are more likely to spend their efforts securing the database as a whole rather than programming the security features of an individual application.

You've probably heard that "a chain is only as safe as its weakest link." This adage could have been written about application security. Every element of the entire infrastructure—application, architecture, middleware, database, operating system—contributes to the overall security of that infrastructure, and a failure of security in any single component compromises the security and increases the vulnerability of the entire system. Understanding the building blocks of security and incorporating them into your application design is not just desirable, it's essential.

## Security Overview

Oracle security topics fall into three general categories:

- Those that are exclusively in the DBA, system administrator, and network administrator domains. Topics in this category—for example, user and privilege management—are beyond the scope of this book.

- Those that are important to developers and application architects and that are not necessarily the responsibility of the DBA. One example is the issue of selecting invoker rights versus definer rights while creating stored code; this choice is typically made during the application design phase itself by the developer, not by the DBA. Topics in this category are covered elsewhere in this book; for example, the topic of rights is covered in Chapter 24.

- Those that are generally considered DBA topics but that developers and application architects need to know about and from which they can derive a good deal of unconventional value. These include encryption, row-level security (RLS), application contexts, and fine-grained auditing (FGA). These topics are the subject of this chapter.

How can the features and tools described in this chapter help PL/SQL developers and application architects? Let's answer that question by looking at each topic in turn:

*Encryption*

The answer here is obvious: encryption is vitally important to data protection and is actively applied in many application design situations. You need a working knowledge of the Oracle features and tools available to perform encryption, including Transparent Data Encryption (TDE), which was introduced in Oracle Database 10g Release 2, and Transparent Table Encryption (TTE), which was introduced in Oracle Database 11g.

*Row-level security (RLS)*

When you design an application, you must be aware of the architecture being used for access and authorization of data. RLS allows you to restrict the rows a user can see. A clear understanding of RLS helps you write better code, even if you don't implement RLS yourself. In many cases, RLS actually makes applications simpler to understand and easier to implement. In some special cases, it even allows an off-the-shelf application to be compliant with the established security practices followed in your organization.

*Application contexts*

Related to row-level security, application contexts are sets of name-value pairs that can be defined in a session through the execution of a specially defined stored procedure. Application contexts are most commonly used to control access to database resources according to rules that vary depending on the current user. They can be very useful application development resources.

*Fine-grained auditing (FGA)*

FGA provides a mechanism to record the fact that certain users have issued certain statements against a table and that certain conditions are met. FGA provides a number of features of value to developers. For example, FGA lets you implement what is in essence a *SELECT trigger*, a user-written procedure executed automatically every time a piece of data is selected from the table.

Oracle security is an enormous topic; this chapter can only touch on those aspects of most value to PL/SQL developers. For more information on these and related Oracle security operations, see *Oracle PL/SQL for DBAs* by Arup Nanda and Steven Feuerstein (O'Reilly). There are also many excellent security books on the market that you should also consult if you need to understand the intricacies of the security topics introduced in this chapter. Oracle's Security Technology Center (*otn.oracle.com/security*) provides several resources on this topic as well.

# Encryption

In the simplest terms, *encryption* means disguising data, or altering the contents in such a way that only the original user knows how to put them back together. Let's consider this very simple and ubiquitous example. I use my bank ATM card on a regular basis to withdraw money, perhaps a bit more than I should. Every time I do so, I need the PIN to access my account. Unfortunately, I am a rather forgetful person, so I decide that I will write down the PIN on something that I will always have when I use the ATM card—the ATM card itself.

Being a smart fellow, I realize that writing my PIN number on the card increases rather dramatically the vulnerability of the card; anyone who steals the card will see the PIN written right on it. Goodbye life savings! What can I do to prevent a thief from learning the PIN after stealing my card, yet also allow me to easily remember my PIN?

After a few minutes' consideration, I come up with a clever idea: I will alter the contents in some predetermined manner. In this case, I add a single-digit number to the PIN and write that new number on the ATM card. Let's say the single-digit number is 6. My PIN is 6523. After adding 6 to it, it becomes 6529, which is what I write on the card. If a thief gets my card, he will see 6529, but that's meaningless as a PIN. He will never be able to get the actual value even if he sees the number, because he needs to know how I altered the original number. Even if he knows that I add a number, he has to guess the number, 6 in this case. In other words, I just encrypted my PIN and made it difficult for a thief to know the actual value.

Let's pause for a moment here and examine the mechanics before I return to this example and admit that I haven't been terribly clever after all. I need to know two things to perform encryption (that is, to scramble my PIN beyond recognition):

- The method by which the value is altered—in this case, by adding a number to the source number.
- The specific number that I added—in this case, 6.

The first of these, the method part, is known as an *algorithm*. The second, the number part, is known as the *key*. These are the basic components of any encryption system, as shown in Figure 23-1. You can keep one component the same but vary the other to produce a different set of encrypted data.

With truly secure systems, the encryption algorithm is not, of course, as simplistic as the one I've described. The actual logic of the algorithm is extremely complex. It's beyond the scope of this chapter to delve into the exact mechanics of an encryption algorithm, and it's not necessary for you to understand the logic to start building an encryption system. You should, however, know the different basic types of algorithms and their relative merits. Most accepted encryption algorithms are in the public domain, so the choice of algorithm alone does not provide security. The security comes from varying the other variable you can control—the encryption key.

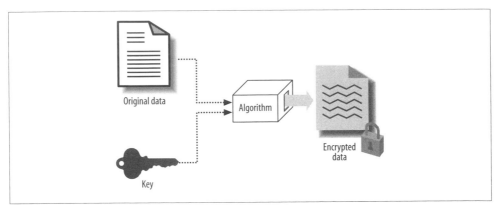

*Figure 23-1. Encryption basics*

One critical challenge when building an encryption infrastructure is to build an effective key management system. If the intruder gets access to the encryption keys, the encrypted data is vulnerable, regardless of the sophistication of the algorithm. On the other hand, some users (e.g., applications) will legitimately need access to the keys, and that access must be easy enough for the applications to run well. The challenge here is to balance the simplicity of access and the security of the keys. Later in this chapter, I'll provide an example showing how you can create and manage an effective key-management system.

## Key Length

In my earlier example of PIN encryption, there is a serious flaw. Because the algorithm is assumed to be universally known, the thief may know that I am simply adding a number to the PIN to encrypt it. Of course, he does not initially know *what* number. But suppose he starts guessing. It's not that difficult: all he has to do is guess 10 times—he's looking for a number between 0 and 9, because I'm using a single-digit number. It might be easier for the thief to decrypt my encrypted PIN, after all, merely by guessing a number up to a maximum of 10 times. But suppose I use a two-digit number. Now the thief will have to guess a number between 0 and 99, a total of 100 times, making it more difficult to guess. Increasing the number of digits of the key makes it more difficult to crack the code. Key length is extremely important in increasing the security of any encrypted system.

Of course, in real-life computer encryptions, the keys are not one or two digits, and they are not just numbers. Their length is typically at least 56 bits and may be as long as 256 bits. The length of the key depends upon the algorithm chosen, as I describe in the following section.

The longer the key, the more difficult it is to crack the encryption. However, longer keys also extend the elapsed time needed to do encryption and decryption because the CPU has to do more work.

## Algorithms

There are many widely used and commercially available encryption algorithms, but I'll focus here on those supported by Oracle for use in PL/SQL applications. All of these fall into the category of private key (sometimes called symmetric) algorithms; see the sidebar, "Public or Private?" on page 923, for a summary of the differences between these private key algorithms and the public key (sometimes called asymmetric) algorithms.

---

### Public or Private?

With *private key (symmetric)* encryption, you use a key to encrypt data and then use the *same* key to decrypt that data. During decryption, you must have access to the encryption key, which has to be transmitted to you somehow. This may not be convenient in situations where the data is transmitted from one location to the other, as the key management becomes complex and insecure.

In contrast, with *public key (asymmetric)* encryption, the intended receiver generates two keys. He keeps one—known as the *private* key—with him and sends the other one —known as the *public* key—to the intended sender. The sender then encrypts the data using the public key, but the encrypted data can only be decrypted using the private key, which is with the recipient. The sender never knows the private key and cannot tamper with the data. Public keys can be given out well in advance of any actual transfer and can be reused. Because there is no exchange of keys, key management becomes extremely easy, reducing the burden on one aspect of the encryption.

Public and private keys are statistically related, so theoretically it is possible to guess the private key from the public key, albeit rather laboriously. So, to reduce the risk of brute-force guessing, very high key lengths are used, typically 1,024-bit keys, instead of the 64-, 128,- or 256-bit keys used in symmetric encryption.

Oracle provides asymmetric encryption at two points:

- During transmission of data between the client and the database
- During authentication of users

Both of these functions require use of Oracle's Advanced Security Option, an extra-cost option that is not provided by default. This tool simply enables asymmetric key encryption on those functions; it does not provide a toolkit that PL/SQL developers can use to build an encryption solution for stored data.

---

The only developer-oriented encryption tool available in Oracle provides for symmetric encryption. For this reason, I focus on symmetric encryption, not asymmetric encryption, in this chapter.

The following algorithms are most commonly used with Oracle:

*Data Encryption Standard (DES)*

Historically, DES has been the predominant standard used for encryption. It was developed more than 20 years ago for the National Bureau of Standards (later renamed the National Institute of Standards and Technology (NIST) ) and has since become an ISO standard. There is a great deal to say about DES and its history, but my purpose here is not to describe the algorithm but simply to summarize its use inside the Oracle database. This algorithm requires a 64-bit key, but discards 8 of them, using only 56 bits. An intruder would have to use up to 72,057,594,037,927,936 combinations to guess the key.

DES was an adequate algorithm for decades, but it now shows signs of age. Today's powerful computers might find it easy to crack open even the large number of combinations needed to expose the key.

*Triple DES (DES3)*

NIST went on to solicit development of another scheme based on the original DES that encrypts data twice or thrice, depending upon the mode of calling. A hacker trying to guess a key would have to face 2,112, then 2,168 combinations in double- and triple-pass encryption routines respectively. DES3 uses a 128-bit or 192-bit key, depending on whether it is using a two-pass or three-pass scheme.

Triple DES was also acceptable for some time, but now it too shows signs of age and has become susceptible to determined attacks.

*Advanced Encryption Standard (AES)*

In November 2001, the Federal Information Processing Standards Publication (FIPS) 197 announced the approval of a new standard, the Advanced Encryption Standard, which became effective May 2002. The full text of the standard can be obtained from NIST at *http://csrc.nist.gov/publications/fips/fips197/fips-197.pdf*.

## Padding and Chaining

When a piece of data is encrypted, it is not encrypted as a whole by the algorithm. It's usually broken into chunks of 8 bytes each, and then each chunk is operated on independently. Of course, the length of the data may not be an exact multiple of 8. In that case the algorithm adds some characters to the last chunk to make it 8 bytes long. This process is known as *padding*. This padding also has to be done correctly so an attacker won't be able to figure out what was padded and then guess the key from there. To securely pad the values, you can use a predeveloped padding method implemented in Oracle, known as Public Key Cryptography System #5 (PKCS#5). There are several other padding options allowing for padding with zeros and for no padding at all. Later in this chapter, I'll show how you can use these options.

When data is divided into chunks, there needs to be a way to connect the adjacent chunks, a process known as *chaining*. The security of an encryption system also depends upon how chunks are connected and encrypted—independently or in conjunction with the adjacent chunks. The most common chaining format is Cipher Block Chaining (CBC); with the Oracle database, you can select that format via a constant defined in the CHAIN_CBC built-in package. Other chaining options are Electronic Code Book format (CHAIN_ECB), Cipher Feedback (CHAIN_CFB) and Output Feedback (CHAIN_OFB). Later in this chapter, I'll demonstrate these options.

## The DBMS_CRYPTO Package

Now that I've introduced the most basic building blocks of encryption, let's see how to create an encryption infrastructure in PL/SQL with Oracle's built-in package DBMS_CRYPTO.

 The DBMS_CRYPTO package was introduced in Oracle Database 10g. In earlier Oracle database versions, the DBMS_OBFUSCA-TION_TOOLKIT package provided similar (but not identical) functionality. That package is still available, but it has been deprecated in favor of the newer package.

Recall that to perform encryption, you need four components in addition to the input value:

- The encryption key
- The encryption algorithm
- The padding method
- The chaining method

The encryption key is something you supply. The other components are provided by Oracle. You choose them by selecting the appropriate constants from the DBMS_CRYPTO package, as described in the following sections.

### Algorithms

The constants listed in Table 23-1, defined in DBMS_CRYPTO, allow you to choose a specific algorithm and key length. Because these are defined as constants in the package, you must reference them in the form *PackageName.ConstantName*—for example, DBMS_CRYPTO.ENCRYPT_DES selects the Data Encryption Standard.

*Table 23-1. DBMS_CRYPTO algorithm constants*

| Constant | Effective key length | Description |
|---|---|---|
| ENCRYPT_DES | 56 | Data Encryption Standard (similar to the one provided in DBMS_OBFUSCATION_TOOLKIT) |
| ENCRYPT_3DES_2KEY | 112 | Modified Triple Data Encryption Standard; operates on a block three times with two keys |
| ENCRYPT_3DES | 156 | Triple Data Encryption Standard; operates on a block three times |
| ENCRYPT_AES128 | 128 | Advanced Encryption Standard |
| ENCRYPT_AES192 | 192 | Advanced Encryption Standard |
| ENCRYPT_AES256 | 256 | Advanced Encryption Standard |
| ENCRYPT_RC4 | | The only stream cipher, which is used to encrypt streaming data rather than discrete data being transmitted or data at rest. |

### Padding and chaining

For padding and chaining, the constants listed in Table 23-2 are available in the DBMS_CRYPTO package.

*Table 23-2. DBMS_CRYPTO padding and chaining constants*

| Constant | Padding/chaining method |
|---|---|
| PAD_PCKS5 | Padding with Public Key Cryptography System #5 |
| PAD_ZERO | Padding with zeros |
| PAD_NONE | No padding is done; when the data is assumed to be exactly 8 bytes (or a multiple thereof) in length, this padding method is chosen |
| CHAIN_CBC | Cipher Block Chaining, the most common method used |
| CHAIN_CFB | Cipher Feedback |
| CHAIN_ECB | Electronic Code Book |
| CHAIN_OFB | Output Feedback |

You will rarely need to be concerned about the exact padding or chaining methods to use; they offer advanced functionality seldom needed in typical system development. The most common choices are PKCS#5 for padding and CBC for chaining. In this chapter, I use these options unless otherwise noted.

## Encrypting Data

Let's move on to how you can actually use Oracle's encryption facilities in your applications. I'll start with a very simple example of encrypting the string Confidential Data using the DBMS_CRYPTO.ENCRYPT function. This function takes four arguments:

*src*

The source or the input data to be encrypted. It must be of the datatype RAW.

*key*

The encryption key, also in RAW. The length of this key must be as required by the algorithm chosen. For instance, if I choose DES, this key length must be at least 64 bits.

*typ*

Specification of the three static components—the algorithm, the padding mechanism, and the chaining method—by adding together the appropriate packaged constants.

*iv*

Specifies the optional initialization vector (IV), another component of the encryption that adds a little "salt" to the encrypted value, making the "pattern" more difficult to guess. (This topic is beyond the scope of this chapter.)

In the following examples, let's assume the following:

*Algorithm*
    Advanced Encryption Standard 128-bit

*Chaining method*
    Cipher Block Chaining

*Padding mechanism*
    Public Key Cryptography Standard #5

These three are specified in the *typ* parameter of the call to the function:

```
DBMS_CRYPTO.ENCRYPT_AES128
  + DBMS_CRYPTO.CHAIN_CBC
  + DBMS_CRYPTO.PAD_PKCS5;
```

Note how these have been added together. Had I chosen no padding instead of PKCS#5, I would have used:

```
DBMS_CRYPTO.ENCRYPT_AES128
  + DBMS_CRYPTO.CHAIN_CBC
  + DBMS_CRYPTO.PAD_NONE;
```

Similarly I can choose any specific algorithm and chaining method.

Next I must choose the key. Assume that I want to use "1234567890123456" for the key. The datatype of this value is VARCHAR2. To use it in the ENCRYPT function, I must first convert it to RAW. To do so, I use the STRING_TO_RAW function in the built-in package UTL_I18N (this package is explained later in the chapter). Here is a code snippet that does exactly that:

```
DECLARE
    l_raw    RAW (200);
    l_in_val VARCHAR2 (200) := 'Confidential Data';
BEGIN
```

```
        l_raw := utl_i18n.string_to_raw (l_in_val, 'AL32UTF8');
   END;
```

I have converted the VARCHAR2 variable l_in_val to RAW. Now, I'll encrypt the input value:

```
/* File on web: enc.sql */
1    DECLARE
2       l_key      VARCHAR2 (2000) := '1234567890123456';
3       l_in_val   VARCHAR2 (2000) := 'Confidential Data';
4       l_mod      NUMBER
5          :=     DBMS_CRYPTO.encrypt_aes128
6              + DBMS_CRYPTO.chain_cbc
7              + DBMS_CRYPTO.pad_pkcs5;
8       l_enc      RAW (2000);
9    BEGIN
10      l_enc :=
11         DBMS_CRYPTO.encrypt (utl_i18n.string_to_raw (l_in_val, 'AL32UTF8'),
12                              l_mod,
13                              utl_i18n.string_to_raw (l_key, 'AL32UTF8')
14                             );
15      DBMS_OUTPUT.put_line ('Encrypted=' || l_enc);
16   END;
```

The output is:

```
Encrypted=C0777257DFBF8BA9A4C1F724F921C43C70D0C0A94E2950BBB6BA2FE78695A6FC
```

Let's analyze the above code, line by line:

| Line(s) | Description |
| --- | --- |
| 2 | The key is defined here. As you can see, the key is exactly 16 characters, which AES requires. Here I specified a 128-bit key size. Most computers follow a 8-bit word size, which means that each byte is 8 bits long. Thus, 128 bits mean (128/8=) 16 bytes. Had I chosen AES192 instead, I would have specified a 192-bit or (192/8=) 24-byte long key. If the key length is not adequate, I will get the KeyBadSize exception. |
| 3 | The input value, which needs to be encrypted. This need not conform to any length restrictions, so you can use a value of any length. If it's not a multiple of 8 bytes, the input value is padded automatically by the algorithm. |
| 4–7 | I specify the algorithm, the padding method, and the chaining method. |
| 8 | I define a variable to hold the encrypted value. Note that the output is in RAW. |
| 11 | The input value is converted from VARCHAR2 to RAW. |
| 13 | As with the input value, the function also expects the key to be RAW. I convert it here. |
| 15 | Finally, I display the encrypted value, also in RAW, as a hexadecimal string. In a real system, you won't display the value as it is meaningless; you will probably do something else with the value, such as store it in a table or pass it to the calling procedure to be used elsewhere. |

You have now seen the basic workings of the ENCRYPT function. Using ENCRYPT, you can build a generic function to encrypt data. In this function, I will use the AES algorithm with a 128-bit key, PCKS#5 as the padding method, and CBC as the chaining

method. Consequently, the only variables a user of the function must provide are the
input value to be encrypted and the key.

```
/* File on web: get_enc_eval.sql */
FUNCTION get_enc_val (p_in_val IN VARCHAR2, p_key IN VARCHAR2)
    RETURN VARCHAR2
IS
    l_enc_val   RAW (4000);
BEGIN
    l_enc_val :=
        DBMS_CRYPTO.encrypt (src      => utl_i18n.string_to_raw (p_in_val,
                                                                  'AL32UTF8'
                                                                 ),
                             key      => utl_i18n.string_to_raw (p_key,
                                                                  'AL32UTF8'
                                                                 ),
                             typ      =>    DBMS_CRYPTO.encrypt_aes128
                                          + DBMS_CRYPTO.chain_cbc
                                          + DBMS_CRYPTO.pad_pkcs5
                            );
    RETURN l_enc_val;
END;
```

Before I close the section, there is one more thing to note. Here I have used the function
UTL_I18N.STRING_TO_RAW, rather than UTL_RAW.CAST_TO_RAW, to con-
vert the VARCHAR2 data to RAW. Why?

The ENCRYPT function requires the input to be RAW and also requires a specific
character set—AL32UTF8, which may not be the character set of the database. Therefore, while converting a VARCHAR2 string to RAW for use in encryption, I have to
perform two conversions:

- From the current database character set to the character set AL32UTF8
- From VARCHAR2 to RAW

Both of these conversions are performed by the STRING_TO_RAW function in the
built-in package UTL_IL8N; character set conversion is not performed by the
CAST_TO_RAW function.

 The UTL_IL8N package is provided as part of Oracle's Globalization
Support and is used to perform *globalization* (or *internationalization*,
which is often shortened to "i18n"; that name is made up of the starting
letter "i," the ending letter "n," and the 18 letters in between). For detailed information about globalization, see Chapter 25.

## Encrypting LOBs

Large object datatypes, such as CLOB and BLOB, can also be encrypted. Examples of
BLOB data include signature files and photocopies of legal documents. Because such
files are sensitive and are inside the database, you may need to encrypt them. Rather

than call the ENCRYPT *function* that I have been using in the previous examples, I have to use the overloaded *procedure* version of ENCRYPT, as shown in the next example.

```
/* File on web: enc_lob.sql */
DECLARE
   l_enc_val   BLOB;
   l_in_val    CLOB;
   l_key       VARCHAR2 (16) := '1234567890123456';
BEGIN
   DBMS_CRYPTO.encrypt (dst   => l_enc_val,
                        src   => l_in_val,
                        key   => utl_i18n.string_to_raw (l_key, 'AL32UTF8'),
                        typ   =>  DBMS_CRYPTO.encrypt_aes128
                                 + DBMS_CRYPTO.chain_cbc
                                 + DBMS_CRYPTO.pad_pkcs5
                       );
END;
```

The output is stored in the variable l_enc_val, which can then be passed on to a different program or stored in the table.

 For LOB data only, use the procedure version of ENCRYPT; for all other datatypes, use the function version. Make sure that you convert the values to RAW (and the CLOB to BLOB) before passing them to the ENCRYPT function.

## SecureFiles

Large objects (LOBs) have undergone a complete makeover in Oracle Database 11*g* and are now called *SecureFiles*. The traditional LOBs (now known as *BasicFiles*), such as CLOBs and BLOBs, are still available, but I recommend that you not use them any more. Wherever you used LOBs in the past, you should now use SecureFiles. Secure-Files offer the same functionality as LOBs, as well as additional features such as compression, deduplication, filesystem-like caching, the ability to stop redo logging, and more. For more information on using SecureFiles, see Chapter 13.

## Decrypting Data

There wouldn't be much point to encrypting data if I couldn't decrypt it at some point so that it could be read and used. To do this, I will use ENCRYPT's sister function, DECRYPT. Its calling structure is identical to ENCRYPT; it also takes four arguments:

*src*
    The encrypted value

*key*
    The key used previously to encrypt

*typ*

The combination of algorithm, padding, and chaining exactly as in ENCRYPT

*iv*

The initialization vector, as in ENCRYPT

The DECRYPT function also returns the unencrypted value in RAW; that value will need to be converted to another format for easy viewing.

While decrypting an encrypted value, you must use exactly the same algorithm, key, padding method, and chaining method used during encryption.

Let's see how decryption works. Here I have encrypted a value, stored the encrypted value in a SQL*Plus variable, and later used that as an input to the DECRYPT function.

```
1    /* File on the web decval.sql */
2    REM Define a variable to hold the encrypted value
3    VARIABLE enc_val varchar2(2000);
4    DECLARE
5       l_key      VARCHAR2 (2000) := '1234567890123456';
6       l_in_val   VARCHAR2 (2000) := 'Confidential Data';
7       l_mod      NUMBER
8          :=    DBMS_CRYPTO.encrypt_aes128
9                + DBMS_CRYPTO.chain_cbc
10               + DBMS_CRYPTO.pad_pkcs5;
11      l_enc      RAW (2000);
12   BEGIN
13      l_enc :=
14         DBMS_CRYPTO.encrypt (utl_i18n.string_to_raw (l_in_val, 'AL32UTF8'),
15                              l_mod,
16                              utl_i18n.string_to_raw (l_key, 'AL32UTF8')
17                             );
18      DBMS_OUTPUT.put_line ('Encrypted=' || l_enc);
19      :enc_val := RAWTOHEX (l_enc);
20   END;
21   /
22   DECLARE
23      l_key      VARCHAR2 (2000) := '1234567890123456';
24      l_in_val   RAW (2000)      := HEXTORAW (:enc_val);
25      l_mod      NUMBER
26         :=    DBMS_CRYPTO.encrypt_aes128
27               + DBMS_CRYPTO.chain_cbc
28               + DBMS_CRYPTO.pad_pkcs5;
29      l_dec      RAW (2000);
30   BEGIN
31      l_dec :=
32         DBMS_CRYPTO.decrypt (l_in_val,
33                              l_mod,
34                              utl_i18n.string_to_raw (l_key, 'AL32UTF8')
35                             );
```

```
36        DBMS_OUTPUT.put_line ('Decrypted=' || utl_i18n.raw_to_char (l_dec));
37     END;
```

This code needs some explanation, shown in the following table:

| Line(s) | Description |
|---|---|
| 23 | I declare the key for decryption. Note that the same key is used to encrypt and decrypt. |
| 24 | Because the variable enc_val is in hexadecimal, I convert it to RAW. |
| 26–28 | As with encryption, specify the algorithm, padding method, and chaining method as a single parameter. Note that they are the same as those used in encryption. They must be, in order for the decryption to work correctly. |
| 34 | As with encryption, the key must be in RAW, so I convert it from VARCHAR2 to RAW. |

The output of the above code segment is Confidential Data, the same as the input given.

 To decrypt an encrypted LOB value, you must use the overloaded procedure version of DECRYPT because you used the procedure version of ENCRYPT.

## Performing Key Generation

So far I have focused on the process of encryption and decryption, and have assumed a very simple key in the examples—"1234567890123456." The security of the encryption system depends entirely on the security of the key—that is, the difficulty a potential attacker would have to *guess* the value of the key. My key should therefore be random enough to be resistant to easy guessing.

There is a standard algorithm for creating a random number, defined by ANSI's standard X9.31: Pseudo-Random Number Generator (PRNG). Oracle implements this algorithm in the RANDOMBYTES function in the DBMS_CRYPTO package. The function takes one argument—the length of the random string generated—and returns a RAW value of that length. Here is how I use it to create a 16-byte value:

```
DECLARE
   l_key   RAW (16);
BEGIN
   l_key := DBMS_CRYPTO.randombytes (16);
END;
```

Of course, the generation of a string of random bytes has to be for some reason, and what better reason than to use it as an encryption key? Using this function, you can generate a key of any length suitable for the algorithm chosen.

## Performing Key Management

You've learned the basics of how to use encryption and decryption and to generate keys. But, that's the easy part; for the most part, I've simply shown how to use Oracle's supplied functionality to get the job done. Now comes the most challenging part in the encryption infrastructure—managing the key. Our applications will need to have access to the key to decrypt the encrypted values, and this access mechanism should be as simple as possible. On the other hand, because the key is literally the "key" to safeguard the encrypted values, it should not be too accessible. A proper key management system balances the simplicity of key access against prevention of unauthorized access to the keys.

There are essentially three different types of key management.

- A single key for the entire database.
- A single key for each row of tables with encrypted data.
- A combination of the above two.

The following sections describe these different approaches to key management.

### A single key for the database

With this approach, a single key can access any data in the database. As shown in Figure 23-2, the encryption routine reads only one key from the key location and encrypts all the data that needs to be protected.

This key could be stored in a variety of locations:

*In the database*
> This is the simplest strategy of all. The key is stored in a relational table, perhaps in a schema used specifically for this purpose. Because the key is inside the database, it is automatically backed up as a part of the database; older values can be obtained by flashback queries or the database, and the key is not vulnerable to theft from the operating system. The simplicity of this approach is also its weakness; because the key is just data in a table, anyone with the authority to modify that table (such as any DBA) could alter the key and disrupt the encryption infrastructure.

*In the filesystem*
> The key is stored in a file, which may then be read by the encryption procedure, using the UTL_FILE built-in package. By setting the appropriate privileges on that file, you can ensure that it cannot be changed from within the database.

*On some removable media controlled by the end user*
> This approach is the safest one; no one except the end user can decrypt the values or alter the key, not even the DBA or system administrator. Examples of removable media include a USB stick, a DVD, and a removable hard drive. A major disadvantage of removable media is the possibility of key loss. The responsibility of safekeeping the key lies with the end user. If the key is ever lost, the encrypted data is also lost—permanently.

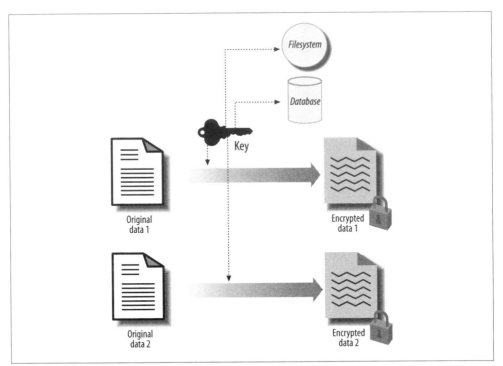

*Figure 23-2. Single database key approach*

The biggest disadvantage of this approach is its dependence on a single point of failure. If an intruder breaks into the database and determines the key, the entire database becomes immediately vulnerable. In addition, if you want to change the key, you will need to change all of the rows in all the tables, which may be quite an extensive task in a large database.

### A single key for each row

This approach calls for a single key per row of the table, as shown in Figure 23-3. If you use this approach, you create a different table to hold the keys. The source table and the key table are linked by the primary key of the source table.

The biggest advantage of this approach is the fact that each row is protected by a different key. If a single key is compromised, only one row, not the entire database, is vulnerable. When a key is changed, it does not affect the entire database; only one row is affected, and that row can be easily changed.

On the other hand, a major disadvantage of this approach is that the key must always be in the database. Storing keys on filesystems so that they are available to the database may not even be feasible. This approach also makes it difficult to protect against a database file theft in which both keys and encrypted data may be stolen.

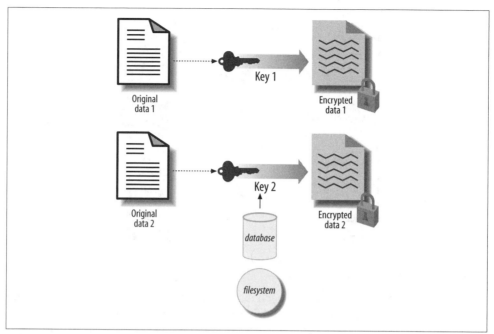

*Figure 23-3. Single key per row approach*

## A combined approach

The combined approach attempts to marry a high degree of security with the maximum possible flexibility. You create a different key for each row, but also have a *master key* (see Figure 23-4). The encryption process does not simply use the key stored for each row. Instead, the row key and a new, single, master key are combined using a bitwise XOR operation, and the resulting value is used as the encryption key for that row. To decrypt the value, you need to know the row key (stored in the database) and the master key (stored elsewhere). By storing these keys separately, you can increase the level of security for your encryption architecture.

The disadvantage of the combined approach is the same as that for the single key strategy: if the master key is lost, you have lost your ability to decrypt the data. However, this risk can be mitigated to some extent by backing up the master key to a different location.

 This approach is not the same as re-encrypting the encrypted value with a different key. The DBMS_CRYPTO package does not allow you to re-encrypt an encrypted value. If you attempt to do so, you will encounter the *ORA-28233 source data was previously encrypted* error.

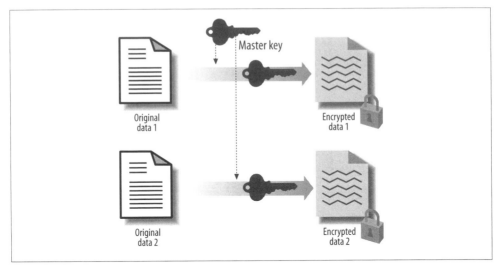

*Figure 23-4. Combined master key approach*

Now let's see how I can use this approach in a real application. Here I will use the same example shown earlier for decryption. I have added a new variable called l_master_key in line 6, which accepts a value from the user (the substitution variable &master_key). In lines 14 through 18, I have XORed the key and the master key, which was used as the encryption key in line 22, instead of the l_key variable.

```
/* File on web: combined_master_key.sql */
1    REM
2    REM Define a variable to hold the encrypted value
3    VARIABLE enc_val varchar2(2000);
4    DECLARE
5       l_key           VARCHAR2 (2000) := '1234567890123456';
6       l_master_key    VARCHAR2 (2000) := '&master_key';
7       l_in_val        VARCHAR2 (2000) := 'Confidential Data';
8       l_mod           NUMBER
9          :=   DBMS_CRYPTO.encrypt_aes128
10              + DBMS_CRYPTO.chain_cbc
11              + DBMS_CRYPTO.pad_pkcs5;
12      l_enc           RAW (2000);
13      l_enc_key       RAW (2000);
14   BEGIN
15      l_enc_key :=
16         UTL_RAW.bit_xor (utl_i18n.string_to_raw (l_key, 'AL32UTF8'),
17                          utl_i18n.string_to_raw (l_master_key, 'AL32UTF8')
18                         );
19      l_enc :=
20         DBMS_CRYPTO.encrypt (utl_i18n.string_to_raw (l_in_val, 'AL32UTF8'),
21                              l_mod,
22                              l_enc_key
23                             );
24      DBMS_OUTPUT.put_line ('Encrypted=' || l_enc);
25      :enc_val := RAWTOHEX (l_enc);
```

```
26      END;
27      /
28      DECLARE
29         l_key            VARCHAR2 (2000) := '1234567890123456';
30         l_master_key     VARCHAR2 (2000) := '&master_key';
31         l_in_val         RAW (2000)      := HEXTORAW (:enc_val);
32         l_mod            NUMBER
33            :=    DBMS_CRYPTO.encrypt_aes128
34               + DBMS_CRYPTO.chain_cbc
35               + DBMS_CRYPTO.pad_pkcs5;
36         l_dec            RAW (2000);
37         l_enc_key        RAW (2000);
38      BEGIN
39         l_enc_key :=
40            UTL_RAW.bit_xor (utl_i18n.string_to_raw (l_key, 'AL32UTF8'),
41                             utl_i18n.string_to_raw (l_master_key, 'AL32UTF8')
42                            );
43         l_dec := DBMS_CRYPTO.decrypt (l_in_val, l_mod, l_enc_key);
44         DBMS_OUTPUT.put_line ('Decrypted=' || utl_i18n.raw_to_char (l_dec));
45      END;
```

When I execute this block, I see the following output in SQL*Plus. Note that I supply the master key first to encrypt the value, and then provide the same master key while decrypting.

```
Enter value for master_key: MasterKey0123456
old   3:      l_master_key varchar2(2000) := '&master_key';
new   3:      l_master_key varchar2(2000) := 'MasterKey0123456';
Encrypted=C2CABD4FD4952BC3ABB23BD50849D0C937D3EE6659D58A32AC69EFFD4E83F79D

PL/SQL procedure successfully completed.

Enter value for master_key: MasterKey0123456
old   3:      l_master_key varchar2(2000) := '&master_key';
new   3:      l_master_key varchar2(2000) := 'MasterKey0123456';
Decrypted=ConfidentialData

PL/SQL procedure successfully completed.
```

It asked for the master key, which I supplied correctly, and the correct value came up. But what happens if I supply an incorrect master key?

```
Enter value for master_key: MasterKey0123456
old   3:      l_master_key varchar2(2000) := '&master_key';
new   3:      l_master_key varchar2(2000) := 'MasterKey0123456';
Encrypted=C2CABD4FD4952BC3ABB23BD50849D0C937D3EE6659D58A32AC69EFFD4E83F79D

PL/SQL procedure successfully completed.

Enter value for master_key: MasterKey0123455
old   3:      l_master_key varchar2(2000) := '&master_key';
new   3:      l_master_key varchar2(2000) := 'MasterKey0123455';
declare
*
ERROR at line 1:
ORA-28817: PL/SQL function returned an error.
```

```
ORA-06512: at "SYS.DBMS_CRYPTO_FFI", line 67
ORA-06512: at "SYS.DBMS_CRYPTO", line 41
ORA-06512: at line 15
```

Note the error here: the use of a wrong master key did not expose the encrypted data. This enhanced security mechanism relies on two different keys, and both keys must be present to successfully decrypt the data. If you hide the master key, it will be enough to prevent unauthorized decryption.

If the master key is stored with the client, and it is sent over the network, a potential attacker could use a tool to "sniff" the value as it passes by. To prevent this from occurring, you can use a variety of approaches.

- You could create a Virtual LAN (VLAN) between the application server and the database server that protects the network traffic between them to a great extent.

- You could modify the master key in some predetermined way, such as by reversing the characters so that an attacker could potentially get the master key that passed over the network but not the master key actually used.

- Finally, for a really secure solution, you could use Oracle's Advanced Security Option (an extra-cost option) to secure the network traffic between the client and the server.

There is no perfect key management solution. The approach you choose will be determined by the nature of your application and your best attempts to balance security against ease of access. The three approaches described in the previous sections represent three major types of key management techniques and are intended to give you a jump start on figuring out your own key management approach. You might very well come up with a better idea that could be more appropriate to your specific situation. For example, you might consider a hybrid approach, such as using different keys for critical tables.

## Cryptographic Hashing

Encryption provides a way to ensure that only authorized people can see your data. It does so by disguising sensitive data. In some cases, however, you may not be interested in disguising data but simply in protecting it from manipulation. A classic example is the need to store passwords securely. Another might have to do with making sure data is not unduly altered. Suppose that you have stored payment information for vendors. That data by itself may not be sensitive enough to require encryption, but you may want a way to ensure that someone does not alter the numbers to increase a payment amount. How can you do that?

The answer lies in a process known as *cryptographic hashing*. When you apply a cryptographic hash function to a value, you generate a new value that cannot be "reverse-engineered" to the original value *and* is very likely to be unique (see the warning below regarding the uniqueness of hash values). Hash functions are also deterministic, meaning that as long as you provide the same input value, the hash function will return the same hash value.

Hashing is not encryption because you can't decipher the original value from the hash value. Using hashing, you can generate an opaque representation of the input data and store it separate from the main data. When the time comes to validate the authenticity of the data, you simply generate the hash value again and compare it against the stored hash value. If the source data has been changed, the hash value will be different, and you can take appropriate action.

 It is theoretically possible that two different input values will produce the same hash value. However, by relying on widely used algorithms such as MD5 and SHA-1, you are ensured that the probability of a *hash conflict* is a statistically remote 1 in $10^{38}$. If you cannot afford to take even that chance, you will need to write conflict resolution logic around your use of the hash function.

There are two types of hashing available in Oracle: Message Digest (MD5) and Secure Hash Algorithm (SHA-1), both implemented in the HASH function of the DBMS_CRYTPO package. The HASH function takes two arguments:

*src*
> Input data for which the hash value should be generated. The value must be of datatype RAW, as with the ENCRYPT function. If the value to be hashed is a VARCHAR2 or NUMBER, you must convert it to RAW.

*typ*
> Type of hashing; it may be MD4, MD5, or SHA-1. The parameter is passed as a predefined constant in the DBMS_CRYPTO package, as in the encryption routines. The constants are:
>
> ```
> DBMS_CRYPTO.HASH_SH1
> DBMS_CRYPTO.HASH_MD5
> DBMS_CRYPTO.HASH_MD4
> ```

Let's look at an example. I declare a local variable with my source value and another to hold the hash value. I then call the HASH function, specifying SHA-1 as the hash method:

```
       /* File on web: hash.sql */
1   DECLARE
2      l_in_val   VARCHAR2 (2000) := 'CriticalData';
3      l_hash     RAW (2000);
4   BEGIN
5      l_hash :=
6         DBMS_CRYPTO.HASH (src      => utl_i18n.string_to_raw (
7                                        l_in_val, 'AL32UTF8'
8                                                             ),
9                           typ      => DBMS_CRYPTO.hash_sh1
10                         );
```

```
  11      DBMS_OUTPUT.put_line ('Hash=' || l_hash);
  12    * END;
```

The output is the following hash value;

```
Hash=9222DE984C1A7DD792F680FDFD3EA05CB6CA59A9
```

Of course, you will usually not display the hash value; you will either store it or send it to the recipient for further verification.

Hashing has many uses beyond cryptography. Web applications, for example, are stateless; an *application* session does not necessarily correspond to a "session" in the Oracle instance. Consequently, you cannot depend on the application of row-level locks to avoid lost updates. After a web page retrieves a row, another application might change it. How does a web session know whether a row retrieved earlier has been changed? One solution is to generate and cache the hash value of the row data. Then, at any later time, when the application needs to work with a row, it can do a second hash, compare the values, and quickly determine if the row is not current.

## Using Message Authentication Codes

Hashing is designed to verify the authenticity of data, not to protect it from prying eyes. The idea is to generate the hash value and store it in some place other than the data itself. You can later regenerate the hash value and compare against the stored data. There is a little problem, however: what if an intruder updates the main data, calculates the hash value as well, and updates the stored hash value?

To protect against that possibility, you can create a kind of password-protected hash value, known as a message authentication code (MAC). A MAC is a hash value combined with a key. If you use a different key, the same input data will produce a different MAC. As with a hash, you can't decipher the main data from the MAC; it is one-way encryption. The presence of the key makes it impossible for an intruder to come up with the same MAC value, unless he guesses the key (so don't use anything obvious!).

The MAC function in the DBMS_CRYPTO package implements the MAC algorithm. It accepts three parameters:

*src*
> Input value (RAW).

*key*
> Key used to calculate the MAC value.

*typ*
> Algorithm used. As with hashing, there are three choices: MD4, MD5, or SHA-1. The parameter is passed as a predefined constant in the DBMS_CRYPTO package (see the list in the previous section):

I'll use the same example shown for hashing, except that I will make it secure by adding a key—"SecretKey". Then I will compute second MAC value using another key. The key and input value both must be RAW; if they are not, I have to convert them.

```
DECLARE
    l_in_val   VARCHAR2 (2000) := 'Critical Data';
    l_key      VARCHAR2 (2000) := 'SecretKey';
    l_mac      RAW (2000);
BEGIN
    l_mac :=
        DBMS_CRYPTO.mac (src      => utl_i18n.string_to_raw (l_in_val,'AL32UTF8'),
                         typ      => DBMS_CRYPTO.hmac_sh1,
                         KEY      => utl_i18n.string_to_raw (l_key, 'AL32UTF8')
                        );
    DBMS_OUTPUT.put_line ('MAC=' || l_mac);
    -- let's use a different key
    l_key := 'Another Key';
    l_mac :=
        DBMS_CRYPTO.mac (src      => utl_i18n.string_to_raw (l_in_val,'AL32UTF8'),
                         typ      => DBMS_CRYPTO.hmac_sh1,
                         KEY      => utl_i18n.string_to_raw (l_key, 'AL32UTF8')
                        );
    DBMS_OUTPUT.put_line ('MAC=' || l_mac);
END;
```

The output is:

```
MAC=7A23524E8B665A57FE478FBE1D5BFE2406906B2E
MAC=0C0E467B588D2AD1DADE7393753E3D67FCCE800C
```

As expected, when a different key is used, the same input value provides a different MAC value. So if an intruder updates the MAC value, she may not know the key used initially; she will therefore generate a different MAC value, which won't match the previously generated value, and hence, will raise alarms.

 This example is very simplistic. In the real world, such an operation would require the generation of a much more complex and difficult-to-guess key.

## Using Transparent Data Encryption (TDE)

In the previous sections, you learned how to build an encryption infrastructure from the ground up. You may need such an infrastructure if your organization is to satisfy the many compliance-related regulations and directives in play these days, or you may simply want to protect your database from potential attacks. As we worked through the examples in these sections, I'm sure you noticed that building the encryption-related components (e.g., trigger, package) were relatively simple and straightforward. The most difficult part of the infrastructure was clearly the management of the encryption keys. While it's important to make these keys available to applications, access to the keys must be restricted to protect them from theft, and that can be tricky.

Starting with Oracle Database 10g Release 2, a feature known as *Transparent Data Encryption* (TDE) makes encrypting data extremely easy. All you have to do is to declare a column as encrypted; Oracle does the rest. The column value is intercepted when entered by the user, encrypted, and then stored in encrypted format. Afterwards, when the column is queried, the value is decrypted automatically, and then the decrypted text (cleartext) is returned to the user. The user does not even need to know that encryption and decryption are taking place—hence the term *transparent*. It's all done inside the Oracle code without any need for triggers or complex procedural logic.

Here is an example that uses TDE. To declare the column SSN of the table ACCOUNTS as being encrypted, simply specify:

```
ALTER TABLE accounts MODIFY (ssn ENCRYPT USING 'AES256')
```

The Oracle database instantly encrypts the column SSN using the AES algorithm and a 256-bit key. The key is stored in a data dictionary table, but to protect the key from theft, it is also encrypted using a master key, which is stored in a separate location known as a *wallet*. The wallet, by default, is in the location *$ORACLE_BASE/admin/ $ORACLE_SID/wallet*; however, you can always specify a different location in the file *SQLNET.ORA*. When a user inserts the data specifying:

```
INSERT INTO accounts (ssn) VALUES ('123456789')
```

the actual value is stored in encrypted format in the datafiles, the redo log files and their archives, and consequently the backup files. When a user subsequently queries the data, the encrypted value is automatically decrypted, and the original value is shown. The wallet must be opened by the DBA or a security administrator before the above statements are issued.

Given how easy TDE is to use, the big question is: does it make everything you've learned in this chapter about encryption obsolete?

---

### Encryption in a Nutshell

- Oracle provides two packages to implement encryption and related activities: DBMS_CRYPTO (available starting in Oracle Database 10g) and DBMS_OBFUSCATION_TOOLKIT. If you are now running Oracle Database 10g or Oracle Database 11g, you should be using DBMS_CRYPTO.

- Encryption needs four components to encrypt an input value: a key, an algorithm, a padding method, and a chaining method. Usually, the last three are kept the same. The key is hidden for each encrypted data.

- The longer the key, the more difficult it is to guess it and the more secure the encryption.

- To decrypt, you must use the same combination of algorithm, key, padding, and chaining used during encryption.

---

- The biggest challenge in building an encryption system is the management of the keys. Safekeeping the keys while making them easily accessible to applications is the key to a successful encryption system.
- Hashing is the generation of some seemingly random value from an input value. The input value cannot be guessed from the hash value. A hash function, when applied to a value, produces the same hash value every time.
- A message authentication code (MAC) is identical to a hash, except that a key is supplied during the generation of the MAC value.

Not at all! The goal of TDE is a limited one: to protect the database files mentioned earlier from potential theft by encrypting sensitive data using minimal effort. Note, however, that the emphasis is on the word transparent—that is, while encryption is done automatically, so is decryption. Within the database, Oracle does not differentiate between users. When a user queries the database, Oracle supplies the cleartext value regardless of who the authorized user may be.

In many cases, you will still need to build a more sophisticated system in which the cleartext value will be exposed only if the user making the request is actually authorized to see that value; in all other cases, the encrypted value will be returned. It is not possible to satisfy this requirement using TDE because TDE decrypts everything indiscriminately. You can, however, achieve this objective by building your own infrastructure using the techniques described in this chapter.

TDE comes with some limitations. For one thing, you can't have a foreign key column encrypted by TDE; that's quite a limitation in many business applications. For another, you can create only b*tree indexes on the columns under TDE. These restrictions are irrelevant, however, when you roll out your own encryption routine using PL/SQL.

When deciding whether TDE serves your purposes, the other aspect you must consider is automation. In TDE, the wallet (in which the master key is stored) must be opened by the DBA using a command such as the following:

```
ALTER SYSTEM SET ENCRYPTION WALLET OPEN AUTHENTICATED BY "pooh"
```

Here the password of the wallet is "pooh". If the database datafiles (or the redo logs or backups of those files) are stolen, the encrypted columns will remain encrypted because the thief will not know the password, "pooh", which would allow him to open the wallet.

After every database startup, the wallet must be explicitly opened by the DBA for the encrypted columns to be inserted or accessed. If the wallet is not open, the inserts and accesses to these columns fail. So, that is one extra step that needs to be performed after the database is opened. In addition, you will have to ensure that the person opening the database knows the wallet password.

To make such a process easier and more automatic, you might ordinarily consider creating a database startup trigger that calls the ALTER SYSTEM command (shown above) to open the wallet. If you do, however, this startup trigger will remove the only protection from the wallet and, subsequently, the encrypted columns. So, if you are using TDE, you should never use such a startup trigger, and you must be prepared to perform the extra step after each database startup. If you build your own encryption infrastructure, however, it is available as soon as the database is; no additional step is necessary, and no wallet passwords need to be remembered and entered.

In summary, TDE is a limited capability. It offers a quick and easy way to encrypt datafiles, redo logs, and backup files. However, it does not protect the data by discriminating among users; it always decrypts upon access. If you need to have more control over the decryption process, then you will have to rely on your own encryption infrastructure.

## Transparent Tablespace Encryption

The problems with TDE and, to a lesser extent, user-written encryption, on application performance can be summed up as follows:

- TDE negates the use of indexes for queries with a range scan, since there is no pattern correlation of the table data to the index entry. User-written encryption offers only limited opportunities to use indexes.

- Querying the encrypted data requires decryption of that data, which results in significant additional CPU consumption.

The impact of these problems means that in real-world application development, TDE is often rejected as unfeasible, while the extensive coding requirements for user-written encryption via DBMS_CRYPTO pose a significant challenge for many organizations.

To address these drawbacks, Oracle Database 11g has introduced a new feature: *TDE Tablespace Encryption*. With this feature, a user can define an entire tablespace, rather than an individual table, as encrypted. Here is an example of creating an encrypted tablespace:

```
TABLESPACE securets1
   DATAFILE '+DG1/securets1_01.dbf'
   SIZE 10M
   ENCRYPTION USING 'AES128'
   DEFAULT STORAGE (ENCRYPT)
```

Whenever you create an object in this tablespace, it will be converted to an encrypted format via an AES algorithm using a 128-bit key. You must have already set up the wallet and opened it as described in the TDE section. The encryption key is stored in the ENC$ table in an encrypted manner, and the key to that encryption is stored in the wallet, as it is in TDE. Of course, the wallet must be opened prior to tablespace creation.

You may be wondering how an encrypted tablespace can avoid the problems of table-based encryption. The key difference is that the data in the tablespace is only encrypted on disk; as soon as the data is read; the data is decrypted and placed in the SGA's buffer cache as cleartext. Index scans operate on the buffer cache, thereby bypassing the problem of unmatched encrypted data. Similarly, since the data is decrypted and placed in the buffer cache only once (at least until it is aged out), the decryption occurs just once, rather than every time that data is accessed. As a consequence, as long as the data remains in the SGA, performance is not affected by encryption. It's the best of both worlds—security by encryption and minimized performance impact.

Since the issues seem to have been resolved, does TDE tablespace encryption spell doom for the user-written encryption procedures shown in this chapter? Not at all!

When you encrypt a tablespace, *all* the objects—indexes and tables—are encrypted, regardless of whether you need them to be encrypted or not. That's fine when you need to encrypt all or most of the data in the tablespace. What if, on the other hand, you only need encryption for a fraction of the total data volume? With TDE tablespace encryption, your application will experience the performance impact of decryption for much more data than is really necessary. The Oracle database minimizes this impact, but it cannot completely avoid it. As a result, you may still choose to implement user-written encryption when you need to encrypt data selectively in your application's tables.

In addition, encrypted tablespaces can only be created; you can't convert an existing tablespace from cleartext to encrypted (nor can you change an encrypted tablespace to cleartext). Instead, you must create a tablespace as encrypted and then move your objects into it. If you decide to introduce encryption into an existing database, the TDE tablespace encryption approach may not be feasible, given the enormous volumes of many production databases. User-written encryption allows you to tightly control how much of the data will be encrypted—and then decrypted.

Clearly, user-written encryption still has its charm and its place in real-world applications. You can implement Transparent Tablespace Encryption much more quickly and easily, but you will need to validate that the "brute force" approach of total encryption works for your application.

# Row-Level Security

Row-level security (RLS) is a feature introduced in Oracle8*i* Database that allows you to define security policies on tables (and specific types of operations on tables) that have the effect of restricting which rows a user can see or change in a table. Much of the functionality is implemented with the built-in package DBMS_RLS.

Oracle has, for years, provided security at the table level and, to some extent, at the column level. Privileges may be granted to allow or restrict users to access only some tables or columns. For example, you can grant privileges to specific users to insert only into certain tables while allowing them to select from other tables. Or you can allow users to update certain columns of specific tables. Using views, you can also restrict how the tables get populated from the views, using INSTEAD OF triggers (described in Chapter 19). All of these privileges are based on one assumption; you can achieve security simply by restricting access to certain tables and columns. But when that access is granted, the users have access to see all the *rows* of the table. What if you need to limit the visibility of rows in a table, based on criteria such as the identity of the user or other application-specific characteristics?

Consider, for example, the demonstration table provided with the database—EMP in schema HR. The table has 14 rows of data, with primary keys (employee numbers) ranging from 7369 to 7934.

Suppose that you have given a user named Lora access to see this table, but you also want to add a further restriction so that Lora can see and modify only employees who get a commission (i.e., the COMM field is NOT NULL).

One way to solve this problem is to create a view on top of the table, but what if a user is able to (or needs to) gain access to the underlying table? In some cases, a user may have a legitimate need to access the table directly—for example, to create stored program units that work with the table. A view-based implementation simply won't work. Instead, you can turn to RLS. With RLS, you can instruct the Oracle database to limit the set of rows a user can see based on some arbitrary rules you define. It will be impossible for the user to evade these rules.

 In Oracle, RLS is also sometimes referred to as the Virtual Private Database (VPD) or fine-grained access control (FGAC).

If, for example, you enable RLS on the table EMP with the rule described above, then when Lora issues the following query:

```
SELECT * FROM emp
```

she sees only four rows—not 14—even though the query itself has no WHERE clause:

```
7499 ALLEN    SALESMAN    7698 20-FEB-81  1,600    300    30
7521 WARD     SALESMAN    7698 22-FEB-81  1,250    500    30
7654 MARTIN   SALESMAN    7698 28-SEP-81  1,250  1,400    30
7844 TURNER   SALESMAN    7698 08-SEP-81  1,500      0    30
```

Similarly when she updates the table without a WHERE clause, only those rows she is allowed to see are updated.

```
SQL> UPDATE hr.emp SET comm = 100
  2  /

4 rows updated.
```

It's as if the other 10 rows do not even exist for Lora. The database accomplishes this seeming act of magic ("Now you see it, now you don't!") by adding a *predicate* (a

WHERE clause) to any DML written by users against the table. In this case, the query SELECT * FROM EMP was *automatically* rewritten to:

```
SELECT * FROM emp WHERE comm IS NOT NULL
```

To achieve this kind of transparent, row-level security on a table, you must define an *RLS policy* on that table. This policy determines whether or not a restriction should be enabled during data access. You may want only UPDATEs to be restricted for users, while SELECTs from the table remain unrestricted, or you may want to restrict access for SELECTs only if the user selects a certain column (e.g., SALARY), not others. These instructions are placed in the policy. The policy is associated with a *policy function*, which generates the predicate (COMM IS NOT NULL, in this case) to be applied to the queries.

To summarize, at a high level, RLS consists of three main components:

*Policy*
> A declarative command that determines when and how to apply the policy: during queries, insertions, deletions, updates, or combinations of these operations.

*Policy function*
> A PL/SQL function that is called whenever the conditions specified in the policy are met.

*Predicate*
> A string that is generated by the policy function, and then applied to the users' SQL statements, indicating limiting conditions.

Conceptually, this behavior is illustrated in Figure 23-5. A policy is like a sieve that checks the rows of the table against the predicate generated. If they satisfy the predicate, they're allowed to pass through the sieve; otherwise, they are not shown to the user.

## Why Learn About RLS?

At first glance, row-level security may seem to be a topic for DBAs and security administrators, not for PL/SQL developers and not even for application architects. Why should a PL/SQL developer learn more about it?

*Security is everybody's business now*
> RLS was initially designed for security, and security has traditionally been the bailiwick of DBAs. In the 21st century, however, we all find ourselves in a more security-conscious environment. A myriad of laws, regulations, and guidelines constrain our applications. Increasingly, developers need to be aware of the security aspects of the various tools they use to construct their programs. Applications architects, in particular, need a working knowledge of how to apply RLS early in the design process.

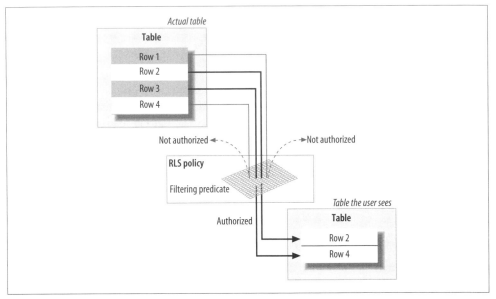

*Figure 23-5. Row-level security infrastructure*

### RLS is not just for security

Take a closer look at the RLS concept. It's a sieve, and the developer of the function controls how the sieve should filter. Suppose that you have a third-party application to support that now has two different functional areas going into the same table; you may have to make some changes in the application's queries to make sure that these functional areas are clearly delineated. But that means making changes to application, which may be undesirable. RLS may come to the rescue here. You can use RLS to create a logical separation of the rows inside the same table so that two applications will see different sets of data. This clearly benefits application development while keeping the overall system highly maintainable.

### You can use RLS to perform some tricks that aren't possible otherwise

Remember that RLS applies a function-generated predicate to your queries. If you generate a predicate 1=2, which always evaluates to FALSE, what will be the output of your queries? "No rows found," because the WHERE clause will always evaluate to FALSE. Thus, if you define a 1=2 policy on DELETEs, INSERTs, and UPDATEs, but not on SELECTs, you can effectively stop users from making changes to a table, while still allowing them to read the data. Oracle by default allows a tablespace, but not a specific table, to be read-only. But RLS gives you a way to make the table itself read-only.

Other approaches don't work here. If you simply revoke UPDATE or INSERT grants from the user, that will invalidate the procedures. If you define a procedure using the definer rights model (the default, described in Chapter 24), then you won't be able to revoke a privilege from the user itself.

---

Let's try to jump-start learning about RLS by looking at some examples.

## A Simple RLS Example

In this example, I'll use the same EMP table referenced earlier this chapter. The requirement that I will implement is as follows:

Users cannot see employees whose salaries are greater than $1,500.

I will therefore need to construct the following:

- A predicate that will be added automatically to the users' SQL statements.
- A policy function that generates the above predicate.
- A policy to call that function and apply the predicate transparently.

In this case, the predicate should be:

```
SALARY <= 1500
```

Next, I write the policy function to return this:

```
FUNCTION authorized_emps (
    p_schema_name    IN    VARCHAR2,
    p_object_name    IN    VARCHAR2
)
    RETURN VARCHAR2
IS
    l_return_val    VARCHAR2 (2000);
BEGIN
    l_return_val := 'SAL <= 1500';
    RETURN l_return_val;
END authorized_emps;
```

When the function is executed, it will return the string SAL <= 1500. Let's just confirm that using this code segment:

```
DECLARE
    l_return_string    VARCHAR2 (2000);
BEGIN
    l_return_string := authorized_emps ('X', 'X');
    DBMS_OUTPUT.put_line ('Return String = "' || l_return_string || '"');
END;
```

The output is:

```
Return String = "SAL <= 1500"
```

You might be wondering why I would pass in those arguments, if the function always returns the same value regardless of their values. This is actually a requirement of RLS, which I'll explain later.

Finally, I will create the policy using the ADD_POLICY function provided in Oracle's DBMS_RLS built-in package:

```
1    BEGIN
2       DBMS_RLS.add_policy (object_schema  => 'HR',
3                object_name        => 'EMP',
4                policy_name        => 'EMP_POLICY',
5                function_schema    => 'HR',
6                policy_function    => 'AUTHORIZED_EMPS',
7                statement_types    => 'INSERT, UPDATE, DELETE, SELECT'
8             );
9    END;
```

Here I am adding a policy named EMP_POLICY (line 4) on the table EMP (line 3) owned by the schema HR (line 2). The policy will apply the filter coming out of the function AUTHORIZED_EMPS (line 6) owned by schema HR (line 5) whenever any user performs INSERT, UPDATE, DELETE, or SELECT operations (line 7). Earlier I wrote the function AUTHORIZED_EMPS to create and return the predicate strings to be applied to the user queries.

Once this policy is in place, if the user selects from the table or tries to change it, she will be able to operate on only those rows where SAL <= 1500.

The policy EMP_POLICY is applied to the table EMP when a user performs SELECT, INSERT, DELETE, or UPDATE. The predicate of the policy function is applied to the policy. As long as the policy function returns a valid predicate string, it's applied to the query. Depending on the business needs, you can write the policy function in any way, as long as you follow certain rules:

- The policy may be a standalone or packaged function, but never a procedure.
- It must return a VARCHAR2 value, which will be applied as a predicate. Note that this means your predicates cannot be greater than 32,767 bytes in length.
- It must have exactly two input parameters in the following order:
  — *schema*, which owns the table on which the policy has been defined
  — *object_name*, which identifies the table(s) or view(s)

> To have no restrictions on access, you can specify a policy function that returns one of the following as a predicate.
> - NULL
> - 1=1 or some other expression that always evaluates to TRUE. Because the return value has to be VARCHAR2, you can't return the Boolean TRUE.
>
> Similarly to have a restriction for all rows, you can have a predicate that always evaluates to FALSE—for example, 1=2.

You can define more than one policy on the table. There is no precedence—that is, no defined order in which the policies are applied to the queries on the table. When you issue a SQL statement against the table, the query is appended to the predicates returned by all the policies.

To see the policies defined on a table, you can check the data dictionary view DBA_POLICIES, which shows the name of the policy, the object on which it is defined (and its owner), the policy function name (and its owner), and much more.

Starting with Oracle Database 10g, the parameter statement_types can have another value—INDEX. When you specify that, access to the rows even when creating indexes is also restricted. Suppose you are trying to create a function-based index on the SAL column; the index creation script will need all the values of the column, effectively bypassing the security. You specify INDEX as a value in the parameter as shown here:

```
1    BEGIN
2       DBMS_RLS.add_policy (object_schema  => 'HR',
3             object_name          => 'EMP',
4             policy_name          => 'EMP_POLICY',
5             function_schema      => 'HR',
6             policy_function      => 'AUTHORIZED_EMPS',
7             statement_types      => 'INSERT, UPDATE, DELETE, SELECT, INDEX'
8          );
9    END;
```

Then, if you attempt to create a function-based index, it will raise the following error:

```
ORA-28133: full table access is restricted by fine-grained security
```

Now you've seen how to create a policy. You can also drop a policy using the DROP_POLICY function in the DBMS_RLS package. To drop a policy using EMP_POLICY, I would issue the following statement:

```
BEGIN
    DBMS_RLS.drop_policy (object_schema   => 'HR',
                object_name         => 'EMP',
                policy_name         => 'EMP_POLICY'
             );
END;
```

Note that policies are not database schema objects—that is, no user owns them. Any user with the EXECUTE privilege on the DBMS_RLS package can create a policy. Similarly, any user with the EXECUTE privilege can drop that policy. Therefore it's important that you revoke EXECUTE privileges on the package from anyone who doesn't need this.

Let's examine a slight twist here. The user, instead of updating any other column, updates the SAL column, which is the column used in the predicate. It will be interesting to see the result:

```
SQL> UPDATE hr.emp SET sal = 1200;

7 rows updated.

SQL> UPDATE hr.emp SET sal = 1100;
```

```
7 rows updated.
```

Only seven rows are updated, as expected. Now let's change the updated amount. After all, everyone deserves a better salary.

```
SQL> UPDATE hr.emp SET sal = 1600;

7 rows updated.

SQL> UPDATE hr.emp SET sal = 1100;

0 rows updated.
```

As you may have predicted, the second update does not change any rows because the first update moved all of the rows in the table beyond the reach of a user whose RLS policy dictates a filtering predicate SAL <= 1500. Thus after the first update, all the rows were invisible to the user.

This is a potentially confusing situation in which the updates might themselves update the data to change the visibility of the table rows. During application development, this may create bugs or at least introduce some degree of unpredictability. To counter this behavior, let's take advantage of another parameter of DBMS_RLS.ADD_POLICY named update_check. Let's take a look at the impact of setting update_check to TRUE while creating a policy on the table:

```
BEGIN
   DBMS_RLS.add_policy (object_name          => 'EMP',
           policy_name          => 'EMP_POLICY',
           function_schema      => 'HR',
           policy_function      => 'AUTHORIZED_EMPS',
           statement_types      => 'INSERT, UPDATE, DELETE, SELECT',
           update_check         => TRUE
           );
END;
```

After this policy is placed on the table, if Lora performs the same update, she now gets an error:

```
SQL> UPDATE hr.emp SET sal = 1600;
UPDATE hr.emp SET sal = 1600
           *
ERROR at line 1:
ORA-28115: policy with check option violation
```

The ORA-28115 error is raised because the policy now prevents any updates to the column value that will make the rows move in and out of RLS coverage. Suppose that Lora updates SAL to a value that does not affect the visibility of the rows:

```
SQL> UPDATE hr.emp SET sal = 1200;

7 rows updated.
```

Because the new value of the SAL column—1200—will still make these 7 rows visible, this update is allowed.

 Set the update_check parameter to TRUE when defining a policy to avoid what may appear to be unpredictable behavior in the application.

## Using Dynamic Policies

In the earlier example, I talked about a policy that returns a predicate string that is a constant, SAL <= 1500. In real life that is not very common, except in some specialized applications such as goods warehouses. In most cases, you will need to build the filter based on the user's issuing the query. For example, the HR application may require that a user sees only records of his department. This is a *dynamic* requirement because it needs to be evaluated for each employee who is logged in.

And that isn't the only rule I need to apply to this situation. The table is protected by the RLS policy, which prevents users from seeing all the records. But what if the owner of that table, HR, selects from the table; it too will see only those records. That isn't right: the owner must be able to see all the records. To let HR see all the records, I have two options:

- Grant a special privilege to the user HR so that RLS policies do not apply to HR.
- Define the policy function so that if the calling user is the schema owner, the restrictive predicate is not applied.

Using the first approach, the policy function needs no change. The DBA can grant the following privilege to HR:

```
GRANT EXEMPT ACCESS POLICY TO hr;
```

This removes the application of any RLS policies from the user HR. Because no policy, regardless of which table it is defined on, will be applied, you should use this approach with great caution. In fact, considering the risk of a breach in security, it is probably something you should avoid altogether.

The other approach involves modifying the policy function to take care of this problem. Here is the policy function needed to handle this complexity:

```
1    FUNCTION authorized_emps (
2        p_schema_name    IN    VARCHAR2,
3        p_object_name    IN    VARCHAR2
4    )
5        RETURN VARCHAR2
6    IS
7        l_deptno         NUMBER;
8        l_return_val     VARCHAR2 (2000);
9    BEGIN
10       IF (p_schema_name = USER)
```

```
11        THEN
12           l_return_val := NULL;
13        ELSE
14           SELECT deptno
15             INTO l_deptno
16             FROM emp
17            WHERE ename = USER;
18
19           l_return_val := 'DEPTNO = ' || l_deptno;
20        END IF;
21
22        RETURN l_return_val;
23     END;
```

Let's examine this function in detail:

| Line(s) | Description |
|---------|-------------|
| 10 | I check to see whether the calling user is the owner of the table. If so, I return NULL as a predicate, which means that no restriction will be placed on the table during access. |
| 14–19 | I determine the department number of the user and then construct the predicate as "DEPTNO = *user's department number*". |
| 22 | Finally, I return the predicate. |

There is an interesting fringe benefit to this approach. The policy function returns DEPTNO as a limiting predicate, so I can apply this policy to any table that has a DEPTNO column.

The above example showed one extreme case of a dynamic policy function. When each record is returned, the policy executed the policy function, checked the predicate, and decided whether or not to pass the record. This is certainly an expensive approach because the database will go through the parse-execute-fetch cycle each time.

If the predicate remains the same, I can optimize performance of the application by eliminating unnecessary calls to the function. Starting with Oracle9*i* Database, the ADD_POLICY procedure has a parameter static_policy, which defaults to FALSE. If the parameter is set to TRUE, the policy function is executed only once at the beginning of the session. This value should only be used if you are absolutely sure that the predicate string will remain the same throughout the session.

Starting with Oracle Database 10*g*, there are several types of "dynamic" policies. You can set any of these policies in the parameter policy_type in the ADD_POLICY procedure. The valid values are:

```
DBMS_RLS.DYNAMIC
DBMS_RLS.CONTEXT_SENSTIVE
DBMS_RLS.SHARED_CONTEXT_SENSITIVE
DBMS_RLS.SHARED_STATIC
DBMS_RLS.STATIC
```

The default behavior is DYNAMIC. If the parameter static_policy (still available in Oracle Database 10g and Oracle Database 11g) is set to TRUE, the default value of policy_type is DBMS_RLS.STATIC. If static_policy is FALSE, then the policy_type is set to DBMS_RLS.DYNAMIC. In these two policy types—static and dynamic—the policies behave just as they would in Oracle9i Database with the parameter static_policy set to TRUE and FALSE, respectively.

In the following sections I'll show the other types of policies supported in Oracle Database 10g and later.

 The new policy types provide excellent performance benefits over the default dynamic type. However, beware of the side effects of these policy types. For example, because static polices do not re-execute the function, they may produce unexpected output.

### Shared static policy

A shared static policy type is similar to a static one, except that the same policy function is used in policies on multiple objects. In a previous example you saw how the function AUTHORIZED_EMPS was used as a policy function in the policies on both the DEPT and the EMP tables. Similarly, you can have the same policy defined on both tables, not merely the same function. This is known as a *shared policy*. If it can be considered static, then the policy is declared as *shared static* (DBMS_RLS.SHARED_STATIC). Using this type, here is how I can create the same policy on both the tables:

```
1   BEGIN
2      DBMS_RLS.drop_policy (object_schema    => 'HR',
3                            object_name      => 'DEPT',
4                            policy_name      => 'EMP_DEPT_POLICY'
5                            );
6      DBMS_RLS.add_policy (object_schema    -> 'HR',
7                           object_name      => 'DEPT',
8                           policy_name      => 'EMP_DEPT_POLICY',
9                           function_schema  => 'RLSOWNER',
10                          policy_function  => 'AUTHORIZED_EMPS',
11                          statement_types  => 'SELECT, INSERT, UPDATE, DELETE',
12                          update_check     => TRUE,
13                          policy_type      => DBMS_RLS.SHARED_STATIC
14                          );
15     DBMS_RLS.add_policy (object_schema    => 'HR',
16                          object_name      => 'EMP',
17                          policy_name      => 'EMP_DEPT_POLICY',
18                          function_schema  => 'RLSOWNER',
19                          policy_function  => 'AUTHORIZED_EMPS',
20                          statement_types  => 'SELECT, INSERT, UPDATE, DELETE',
21                          update_check     => TRUE,
22                          policy_type      => DBMS_RLS.SHARED_STATIC
23                          );
24  END;
```

By declaring a single policy on both tables, I have instructed the database to cache the result of the policy function once and then use it multiple times.

### Context-sensitive policy

As you learned earlier, static policies, although quite efficient, can be dangerous; because they do not re-execute the function every time, they may produce unexpected results. Hence, Oracle provides another type of policy—*context-sensitive*, which re-executes the policy function only when the application context changes in the session. (See "Application Contexts" on page 964.)

```
1    BEGIN
2       DBMS_RLS.drop_policy (object_schema    => 'HR',
3                             object_name      => 'DEPT',
4                             policy_name      => 'EMP_DEPT_POLICY'
5                            );
6       DBMS_RLS.add_policy (object_schema     => 'HR',
7                            object_name       => 'DEPT',
8                            policy_name       => 'EMP_DEPT_POLICY',
9                            function_schema   => 'RLSOWNER',
10                           policy_function   => 'AUTHORIZED_EMPS',
11                           statement_types   => 'SELECT, INSERT, UPDATE, DELETE',
12                           update_check      => TRUE,
13                           policy_type       => DBMS_RLS.CONTEXT_SENSITIVE
14                          );
15      DBMS_RLS.add_policy (object_schema     => 'HR',
16                           object_name       => 'EMP',
17                           policy_name       => 'EMP_DEPT_POLICY',
18                           function_schema   => 'RLSOWNER',
19                           policy_function   => 'AUTHORIZED_EMPS',
20                           statement_types   => 'SELECT, INSERT, UPDATE, DELETE',
21                           update_check      => TRUE,
22                           policy_type       => DBMS_RLS.CONTEXT_SENSITIVE
23                          );
24   END;
```

When you use the context-sensitive policy type (DBMS_RLS.CONTEXT_SENSITIVE), performance is generally not as good as SHARED_STATIC, but better than DYNAMIC. Here is an example of time differences for a particular query. To measure the time, I will use the built-in timer DBMS_UTILITY.GET_CPU_TIME.

```
DECLARE
   l_start time    PLS_INTEGER;
   l_count         PLS_INTEGER;
BEGIN
   l_start_time := DBMS_UTILITY.get_time;

   SELECT COUNT ( * )
     INTO l_count
     FROM hr.emp;
```

```
    DBMS_OUTPUT.put_line (DBMS_UTILITY.get_time - l_start_time);
END;
```

The difference in the output of the function call between the beginning and the end is the time elapsed in centiseconds (hundredths of a second). When this query is run under different conditions, I get different response times as shown in the table:

| Policy type | Response time (cs) |
| --- | --- |
| Dynamic | 133 |
| Context sensitive | 84 |
| Static | 37 |

### Shared context-sensitive policy

*Shared context sensitive policies* are similar to context-sensitive policies, except that the same policy is used for multiple objects, as you saw with shared static policies.

---

## Upgrade Strategy for Oracle Database 10g/11g Policy Types

When upgrading from Oracle9*i* Database to Oracle Database 10*g* or Oracle Database 11*g*, I recommend that you do the following:

1. Initially use the default type (dynamic).

2. Once the upgrade is complete, try to recreate the policy as context-sensitive and test the results thoroughly, with all possible scenarios, to eliminate any potential caching issues.

3. For those policies that can be made static, convert them to static and test thoroughly.

---

# Using Column-Sensitive RLS

Let's revisit the example of the HR application used in the previous sections. I designed the policy with the requirement that no user should have permission to see all records. A user can see only the data about the employees in her department. However, there may be cases in which that policy is too restrictive.

Suppose that you want to protect the data so people can't snoop around for salary information. Consider the following two queries:

```
SELECT empno, sal FROM emp
SELECT empno FROM emp
```

The first query shows salary information for employees, the very information you want to protect. In this case, you want to show only the employees in the user's own department. But the second query shows only the employee numbers. Should you filter that as well so that it shows only the employees in the same department?

The answer might vary depending upon the security policy in force at your organization. There may well be a good reason to let the second query show *all* employees, regardless of the department to which they belong. In such a case, will RLS be effective?

In Oracle9*i* Database, RLS doesn't help; in Oracle Database 10*g* and later, however, an ADD_POLICY parameter, sec_relevant_cols, makes it easy. In the above scenario, for example, you want the filter to be applied only when SAL and COMM columns are selected, not any other columns. You can write the policy as follows (note the new parameter):

```
BEGIN
    /* Drop the policy first. */
    DBMS_RLS.drop_policy (object_schema    => 'HR',
                          object_name      => 'EMP',
                          policy_name      => 'EMP_POLICY'
                         );
    /* Add the policy. */
    DBMS_RLS.add_policy (object_schema      => 'HR',
                         object_name        => 'EMP',
                         policy_name        => 'EMP_POLICY',
                         function_schema    => 'RLSOWNER',
                         policy_function    => 'AUTHORIZED_EMPS',
                         statement_types    => 'INSERT, UPDATE, DELETE, SELECT',
                         update_check       => TRUE,
                         sec_relevant_cols  => 'SAL, COMM'
                        );
END;
```

After this policy is put in place, queries on HR.EMP have different results.

```
SQL> -- harmless query, only EMPNO is selected
SQL> SELECT empno FROM hr.emp;
... rows are here ...

14 rows selected.

SQL> -- sensitive query, SAL is selected
SQL> SELECT empno, sal FROM hr.emp;
... rows are here ...

6 rows selected.
```

Note that when the column SAL is selected, the RLS policy kicks in, preventing the display of all rows; it filters out the rows where DEPTNO is something other than 30—that is, the DEPTNO of the user executing the query.

Column sensitivity does not just apply to being in the select list, but applies whenever the column is referenced, either directly or indirectly. Consider the following query:

```
SQL> SELECT deptno, count(*)
  2   FROM hr.emp
  3   WHERE sal> 0
  4   GROUP BY deptno;

   DEPTNO   COUNT(*)
```

```
---------- ----------
       30          6
```

Here, the SAL column has been referenced in the WHERE clause, so the RLS policy applies, causing only the records from department 30 to be displayed. Consider another example:

```
SQL> SELECT *
  2  FROM hr.emp
  3  WHERE deptno = 10;

no rows selected
```

Here the column SAL has not been referenced explicitly, but it is *implicitly* referenced by the SELECT * clause, so the RLS policy kicks in, filtering all but the rows from department 30. Because the query called for department 10, no rows were returned.

Let's examine a slightly different situation now. In the above case, I did protect the SAL column values from being displayed for those rows for which the user is not authorized. However, in the process, I suppressed the display of the *entire* row, not just the column. Now suppose that new requirements call for masking only the column, not the entire row, and for displaying all other non-sensitive columns. Can this be done?

It's easy, using another ADD_POLICY parameter, sec_relevant_cols_opt. Let's recreate the policy with the parameter set to DBMS_RLS.ALL_ROWS, as follows:

```
BEGIN
    DBMS_RLS.drop_policy (object_schema            => 'HR',
                          object_name              => 'EMP',
                          policy_name              => 'EMP_POLICY'
                         );
    DBMS_RLS.add_policy (object_schema             => 'HR',
                         object_name               => 'EMP',
                         policy_name               => 'EMP_POLICY',
                         function_schema           => 'RLSOWNER',
                         policy_function           => 'AUTHORIZED_EMPS',
                         statement_types           => 'SELECT',
                         update_check              => TRUE,
                         sec_relevant_cols         => 'SAL, COMM',
                         sec_relevant_cols_opt     => DBMS_RLS.all_rows
                        );
END;
```

If I issue the same type of query now, the results will be different:

```
SQL> -- Show a "?" for the NULL values in the output.
SQL> SET NULL ?
SQL> SELECT *
  2  FROM hr.emp
  3  ORDER BY deptno
  4  /

EMPNO ENAME      JOB        MGR HIREDATE    SAL   COMM DEPTNO
------ ---------- --------- ------ --------- ------ ------ ------
 7782 CLARK      MANAGER     7839 09-JUN-81 ?      ?         10
```

```
7839 KING      PRESIDENT ?        17-NOV-81 ?      ?           10
7934 MILLER    CLERK     7782 23-JAN-82 ?      ?           10
7369 SMITH     CLERK     7902 17-DEC-80 ?      ?           20
7876 ADAMS     CLERK     7788 12-JAN-83 ?      ?           20
7902 FORD      ANALYST   7566 03-DEC-81 ?      ?           20
7788 SCOTT     ANALYST   7566 09-DEC-82 ?      ?           20
7566 JONES     MANAGER   7839 02-APR-81 ?      ?           20
7499 ALLEN     SALESMAN  7698 20-FEB-81 1,600    300       30
7698 BLAKE     MANAGER   7839 01-MAY-81 2,850 ?           30
7654 MARTIN    SALESMAN  7698 28-SEP-81 1,250  1,400      30
7900 JAMES     CLERK     7698 03-DEC-81   950 ?           30
7844 TURNER    SALESMAN  7698 08-SEP-81 1,500      0       30
7521 WARD      SALESMAN  7698 22-FEB-81 1,250    500       30

14 rows selected.
```

Notice that *all* 14 rows have been shown, along with all the columns, but that the values for SAL and COMM have been made NULL for the rows that the user is not supposed to see—that is, the employees of the department other than 30.

RLS here lets you satisfy cases in which rows must be displayed, but sensitive values must be hidden. Prior to Oracle Database 10g, you would have had to use views to accomplish the same thing, and the operations were a good deal more complicated.

Use this feature with caution because in certain cases, it may produce unexpected results. Consider this query issued by, say, MARTIN:

```
SQL> SELECT COUNT(1), AVG(sal) FROM hr.emp;
COUNT(SAL)   AVG(SAL)
---------- ----------
        14 1566.66667
```

The result shows 14 employees and the average salary is 1,566, which is actually the average of the 6 employees MARTIN is authorized to see, not all 14 employees. This may create some confusion as to which values are correct. When the schema owner, HR, issues the same query, you see a different result:

```
SQL> CONN hr/hr
Connected.
SQL> SELECT COUNT(1), AVG(sal) FROM hr.emp;
COUNT(SAL)   AVG(SAL)
---------- ----------
        14 2073.21429
```

Because results vary by the user issuing the query, you need to be careful to interpret the results accordingly; otherwise, this feature may introduce difficult-to-trace bugs into your application.

## RLS Debugging

RLS is a somewhat complex feature, relying on a variety of elements in the Oracle architecture. You may encounter errors, either as a result of problems in the design or through misuse by users. Fortunately, for most errors, RLS produces a detailed trace

---

file in the directory specified by the database initialization parameter USER_DUMP_DEST.

## Interpreting errors

The most common error you will encounter, and the easiest to deal with, is *ORA-28110: Policy function or package has error*. The culprit here is a policy function with errors. Fixing your compilation errors and recompiling the function (or the package containing the function) cures the problem.

You may also encounter runtime errors, such as a datatype mismatch or a VALUE_ERROR exception. In these cases, Oracle raises the *ORA-28112: failed to execute policy function* error and produces a trace file. Here is an excerpt from a trace file:

```
------------------------------------------------------------
Policy function execution error:
Logon user      : MARTIN
Table/View      : HR.EMP
Policy name     : EMP_DEPT_POLICY
Policy function: RLSOWNER.AUTHORIZED_EMPS
ORA-01422: exact fetch returns more than requested number of rows
ORA-06512: at "RLSOWNER.AUTHORIZED_EMPS", line 14
ORA-06512: at line 1
```

The trace file shows that MARTIN was executing the query when this occurred. Here the policy function simply fetched more than one row. Examining the policy function, you notice that the policy function has a segment as follows:

```
SELECT deptno
  INTO l_deptno
  FROM hr.emp
 WHERE ename = USER
```

It seems that there is more than one employee with the name MARTIN: the number of rows fetched is more than one, which caused this problem. The solution is to either handle the error via an exception or just use something else as a predicate to get the department number.

The *ORA-28113: policy predicate has error* exception occurs when the policy function does not construct the predicate clause correctly. Here is an excerpt from the trace file for this error:

```
Error information for ORA-28113:
Logon user      : MARTIN
Table/View      : HR.EMP
Policy name     : EMP_DEPT_POLICY
Policy function: RLSOWNER.AUTHORIZED_EMPS
RLS predicate   :
DEPTNO = 10,
ORA-00907: missing right parenthesis
```

It shows that the predicate returned by the policy function is:

```
DEPTNO = 10,
```

This is syntactically incorrect, so the policy application failed and so did MARTIN's query. This can be fixed by correcting the policy function logic to return a valid value as the predicate.

### Performing direct path operations

If you are using direct path operations—for example, SQL*Loader's Direct Path Load or a Direct Path Insert using the APPEND hint (`INSERT /*+ APPEND */ INTO ...`), or Direct Path Export—you will have to take special precautions to achieve the desired result. That is because direct path operations attempt to bypass the SQL layer, but RLS needs the SQL layer to operate correctly.

In the case of exports, it's rather easy. Here is what happens when I export the table EMP, protected by one or more RLS policies, with the DIRECT=Y option:

```
About to export specified tables via Direct Path ...
EXP-00080: Data in table "EMP" is protected. Using conventional mode.
EXP-00079: Data in table "EMP" is protected. Conventional path may only be exporting
partial table.
```

The export is successfully done, but as you can see in the output, the output mode is *conventional*, not direct, as I wanted it to be. And in the process of performing the operation, the export still applied the RLS policies to the table—that is, the user can export only the rows he is authorized to see, not all of them.

 Because the operation of exporting a table under RLS may still successfully complete, you might get a false impression that all rows have been exported. However, be aware that only the rows the user is allowed to see, not all of them, are exported. In addition, even though the export was supposed to be run in direct mode, it runs in conventional mode.

Now, when you try to do a SQL*Loader Direct Path Load/Direct Path Insert, you get an error:

```
SQL> INSERT /*+ APPEND */
  2  INTO hr.EMP
  3  SELECT *
  4  FROM hr.emp
  5  WHERE rownum < 2;
from hr.emp
     *
ERROR at line 4:
ORA-28113: policy predicate has error
```

The error message is a little confusing—the policy predicate didn't actually have an error. The RLS policy was not applied because this was a direct path operation, but the error message didn't show that. You can fix this situation either by temporarily disabling the policy on the table EMP or by exporting through a user who has the EXEMPT ACCESS POLICY system privilege.

---

## Row-Level Security in a Nutshell

- RLS automatically applies a predicate (to be attached to a WHERE clause) to the queries issued by users so that only certain rows are visible.
- The predicate is generated by a policy function written by the user.
- A policy on a table determines under what circumstances the predicate should be imposed and what policy function to execute.
- More than one policy can be defined on a table.
- The same policy can be applied to more than one table.
- The type of policy (dynamic, static, etc.) determines how often to execute the policy function.
- Direct path operations do not work in combination with RLS. Oracle will force direct path exports to run in conventional mode, but imports & inserts will fail.

### Viewing SQL statements

During debugging, it may be necessary to see the exact SQL statement rewritten by Oracle when an RLS policy is applied. In this way you will leave nothing to chance or interpretation. You can see the rewritten statement through two different approaches:

*Use VPD views*

One option is to use the dictionary view V$VPD_POLICY. VPD in the name stands for Virtual Private Database, another name for row-level security. This view shows all the query transformations.

```
SELECT sql_text, predicate, POLICY, object_name
  FROM v$sqlarea, v$vpd_policy
 WHERE hash_value = sql_hash

SQL_TEXT                        PREDICATE
-----------------------------   -----------------------------
POLICY                          OBJECT_NAME
-----------------------------   -----------------------------
select count(*) from hr.emp     DEPTNO = 10
EMP_DEPT_POLICY                 EMP
```

The column SQL_TEXT shows the exact SQL statement issued by the user, while the column PREDICATE shows the predicate generated by the policy function and applied to the query. Using this view, you can identify the statements issued by the users and the predicates applied to them.

*Set an event*

The other option is to set an event in the session like this:

```
SQL> ALTER SESSION SET EVENTS '10730 trace name context forever, level 12';

Session altered.
```

```
SQL>SELECT COUNT(*) FROM hr.emp;
```

After the query finishes, you will see a trace file generated in the directory specified by the database initialization parameter USER_DUMP_DEST. Here is what the trace file shows:

```
Logon user     : MARTIN
Table/View     : HR.EMP
Policy name    : EMP_DEPT_POLICY
Policy function: RLSOWNER.AUTHORIZED_EMPS
RLS view :
SELECT  "EMPNO","ENAME","JOB","MGR","HIREDATE","SAL","COMM","DEPTNO"
FROM "HR"."EMP" "EMP" WHERE (DEPTNO = 10)
```

This clearly shows the statement as it was rewritten by the RLS policy.

Using either of these methods, you will be able to see the exact way that user queries are rewritten.

# Application Contexts

In the discussion of row-level security in the previous section, I made a critical assumption: the predicate (i.e., the limiting condition that restricts the rows of the table) was the same. In my examples, it was based on the department number of the user. What if I have a new requirement: users can now see employee records based not on department numbers but on a list of privileges maintained for that reason. A table named EMP_ACCESS maintains the information about which users can access which employee information.

```
SQL> DESC emp_access
Name                 Null?    Type
----------------     -------- ------------
USERNAME                      VARCHAR2(30)
DEPTNO                        NUMBER
```

Here is some sample data:

```
USERNAME                      DEPTNO
----------------------------- ----------
MARTIN                            10
MARTIN                            20
KING                              20
KING                              10
KING                              30
KING                              40
```

Here I observe that Martin can see departments 10 and 20, but King can see 10, 20, 30, and 40. If an employee's name is not here, he cannot see any records. This new requirement requires that I generate the predicate dynamically inside the policy function.

The requirements also state that users can be reassigned their privileges dynamically by updating the EMP_ACCESS table, and that it is not an option to log off and log in again. Hence, a LOGON trigger (see Chapter 19) will not help in this case.

Solution? One option is to create a package with a variable to hold the predicate and let the user execute a PL/SQL code segment to assign the value to the variable. Inside the policy function, you will be able to see the value of the packaged variable and apply that as the predicate. Is this an acceptable approach? Consider this option carefully: if the user can reassign another value to the package variable, what prevents him from assigning a very powerful value, such as that for King? Martin could log in, set the variable to all departments, and then SELECT from the table to see all the records. There is no security in this case, and that is unacceptable. This scenario is precisely why you should put the code for setting the variable values in the LOGON trigger, where the user will not have a chance to make a change.

## Using Application Contexts

The possibility that a user may change the value of the package variable dynamically requires us to rethink our strategy. We need a way to set a global variable by some secure mechanism so that unauthorized alteration will not be possible. Fortunately, Oracle provides this capability through *application contexts*. An application context is analogous to a global package variable; once set, it can be accessed throughout the session and reset. However, that's where the similarity ends. The important difference is that in contrast to a package variable, an application context is not set by mere value assignment; rather, it needs a call to a procedure to set the value—and that is what makes it more secure. Let's explore this further with an example.

An application context is similar to a structure in the C language or a record in PL/SQL: it has attributes, and attributes are assigned values. However, unlike its counterparts in C and PL/SQL, the attributes are not named during the creation of the context; instead, they are named and assigned at runtime. Application contexts reside in the Program Global Area, by default, unless they are defined as global contexts. Since the PGA is private to a session, the values are not visible to another session.

Here, I use the CREATE CONTEXT command to define a new context called dept_ctx:

```
SQL> CREATE CONTEXT dept_ctx USING set_dept_ctx;

Context created.
```

USING set_dept_ctx indicates that there is a procedure named set_dept_ctx, and that only that procedure can set or change attributes of the context dept_ctx; this cannot be done in any other way.

I have not yet specified any attributes of the context; I have simply defined the overall context (name and secure mechanism for changing it). To do that, I need to create the procedure. Inside this procedure, I will assign values to the context attributes using the

SET_CONTEXT function in the built-in package DBMS_SESSION, as shown in the following example.

```
PROCEDURE set_dept_ctx (p_attr IN VARCHAR2, p_val IN VARCHAR2)
IS
BEGIN
   DBMS_SESSION.set_context ('DEPT_CTX', p_attr, p_val);
END;
```

To set the attribute named DEPTNO to a value 10, I specify:

```
SQL> EXEC set_dept_ctx ('DEPTNO','10')

PL/SQL procedure successfully completed.
```

To obtain the current value of an attribute, I call the SYS_CONTEXT function, which accepts two parameters—the context name and the attribute name. Here is an example:

```
SQL> DECLARE
  2     l_ret    VARCHAR2 (20);
  3  BEGIN
  4     l_ret := SYS_CONTEXT ('DEPT_CTX', 'DEPTNO');
  5     DBMS_OUTPUT.put_line ('Value of DEPTNO = ' || l_ret);
  6  END;
  7  /

Value of DEPTNO = 10
```

I can use this function to get some predefined contexts—for example, to obtain the IP addresses and terminal names of the client:

```
BEGIN
   DBMS_OUTPUT.put_line (   'The Terminal ID is '
                            || SYS_CONTEXT ('USERENV', 'TERMINAL')
                         );
END;
```

The output is:

```
The Terminal ID is pts/0
```

I am taking advantage of the predefined application context USERENV, which has a set of attributes such as TERMINAL, IP_ADDRESS, OS_USER, whose values are assigned automatically by Oracle; I cannot modify the values for these context attributes. I can only obtain their values.

## Security in Contexts

All that the procedure set_dept_ctx does is call the supplied program DBMS_SESSION.SET_CONTEXT with appropriate parameters. Why do I need to use a procedure to do that? Can't I just call the built-in function directly? Let's see what happens if a user calls the same code segment to set the value of the attribute DEPTNO to 10:

```
SQL> BEGIN
  2     DBMS_SESSION.set_context
```

```
   3          ('DEPT_CTX', 'DEPTNO',10);
   4   END;
   5   /
begin
*
ERROR at line 1:
ORA-01031: insufficient privileges
ORA-06512: at "SYS.DBMS_SESSION", line 82
ORA-06512: at line 2
```

Note the error, *ORA-01031: insufficient privileges*; that's puzzling because the user Martin does have the EXECUTE privilege on DBMS_SESSION, so that is clearly not the issue here. You can verify this by regranting the EXECUTE privilege on this package and re-executing the same code segment; you will still get the same error.

The answer lies in the fact that application contexts cannot be assigned directly by calling the built-in package; they must be assigned through the program unit associated with the context at the time of its creation. This makes the program unit trusted for the context; hence, it's known as the *trusted program* of the application context.

 While creating an application context, you must specify its trusted program. Only the trusted program can set the values inside that context, and it cannot set values for any other context.

## Contexts as Predicates in RLS

So far you have learned that a procedure must be used to set a context value, which is akin to a global variable. You might be tempted to ask: how is that useful? Doesn't it increase the complexity rather unnecessarily without achieving any definite purpose?

The answer is no because the trusted procedure is the *only* way to set context values, it acts as a gatekeeper to the context. We can perform arbitrarily complex authentication and verification steps inside the trusted program to ensure that the attribute assignments are valid. We can even completely eliminate passing parameters and set the values from predetermined values without any input from the user. For example, from our requirement definition, we know that we need to set the application context value to a string of department numbers, picked from the table EMP_ACCESS, not passed by the user. This application context is then used in the policy function. Let's see how to meet this requirement.

First I need to modify the policy function:

```
/* File on web: authorized_emps_3.sql */
1     FUNCTION authorized_emps (
2        p_schema_name   IN   VARCHAR2,
3        p_object_name   IN   VARCHAR2
4     )
5        RETURN VARCHAR2
6     IS
```

```
 7        l_deptno        NUMBER;
 8        l_return_val    VARCHAR2 (2000);
 9     BEGIN
10        IF (p_schema_name = USER)
11        THEN
12           l_return_val := NULL;
13        ELSE
14           l_return_val := SYS_CONTEXT ('DEPT_CTX', 'DEPTNO_LIST');
15        END IF;
16
17        RETURN l_return_val;
18     END;
```

Here the policy function expects the department numbers to be passed through the attribute DEPTNO_LIST of the context dept_ctx (line 14). To set this value, I need to modify the trusted procedure of the context.

```
       /* File on web: set_dept_ctx_2.sql */
 1     PROCEDURE set_dept_ctx
 2     IS
 3        l_str    VARCHAR2 (2000);
 4        l_ret    VARCHAR2 (2000);
 5     BEGIN
 6        FOR deptrec IN (SELECT deptno
 7                          FROM emp_access
 8                         WHERE username = USER)
 9        LOOP
10           l_str := l_str || deptrec.deptno || ',';
11        END LOOP;
12
13        IF l_str IS NULL
14        THEN
15           -- No access records found, so no records
16           -- should be visible to this user.
17           l_ret := '1=2';
18        ELSE
19           l_str := RTRIM (l_str, ',');
20           l_ret := 'DEPTNO IN (' || l_str || ')';
21           DBMS_SESSION.set_context ('DEPT_CTX', 'DEPTNO_LIST', l_ret);
22        END IF;
23     END;
```

It's time to test the function. First Martin logs in and counts the number of employees. Before he issues the query, he needs to set the context:

```
SQL> EXEC rlsowner.set_dept_ctx

PL/SQL procedure successfully completed.

SQL> SELECT SYS_CONTEXT ('DEPT_CTX', 'DEPTNO_LIST') FROM DUAL;

SYS_CONTEXT('DEPT_CTX','DEPTNO_LIST')
-------------------------------------
DEPTNO IN (20,10)

SQL> SELECT DISTINCT deptno FROM hr.emp;
```

```
      DEPTNO
----------
          10
          20
```

Here Martin sees only the employees of departments 10 and 20, as per the EMP_ACCESS table. Suppose that Martin's department changes to Department Number 30, Martin's access should now be changed to department 30. The security administrator updates the table to reflect the changes.

```
SQL> DELETE emp_access WHERE username = 'MARTIN';

2 rows deleted.

SQL> INSERT INTO emp_access VALUES ('MARTIN',30);

1 row created.

SQL> COMMIT;

Commit complete.
```

When Martin issues the same queries, he will see different results:

```
SQL> EXEC rlsowner.set_dept_ctx

PL/SQL procedure successfully completed.

SQL> SELECT SYS_CONTEXT ('DEPT_CTX','DEPTNO_LIST') FROM DUAL;

SYS_CONTEXT('DEPT_CTX','DEPTNO_LIST')
------------------------------------------------------------

DEPTNO IN (30)

SQL> SELECT DISTINCT deptno FROM hr.emp;

      DEPTNO
----------
          30
```

This change takes effect automatically. Because Martin can't set the context attributes himself, this arrangement is inherently more secure than setting a global package variable would be. In addition, using the context-sensitive policy (in row-level security) in Oracle Database 10g and later improves the performance as well. The policy function is executed only when the context changes; the cached values are used until that happens. This makes the policy faster than the default dynamic policy type.

So, how is this approach different from creating a dynamically generated policy function on the fly from the emp_access table? In the case of a policy function, it must be executed to get the predicate value, the list of departments in this case. Consider a table with millions of queries against it; the policy function gets executed that many times, each time hitting the emp_access table—a sure shot to terrible performance. You can define the policy as static where the function is not executed as many times; but that means that if the emp_access table records change, the policy function will not pick the change and will produce the wrong result. Defining a context-sensitive policy with application contexts achieves the best of both words—the policy function is re-executed *unless* the context value changes. The context value resides in memory, so it can be accessed very quickly.

## Identifying Non-Database Users

Application contexts are useful well beyond the situations I've described so far. The most important use of application contexts is to distinguish between different users who cannot be identified through unique sessions. This is quite common in web applications that typically use a *connection pool*—a pool of connections to the database using a single user, named, for example, CONNPOOL. Web users connect to the application server, which, in turn, uses one of the connections from the pool to get to the database. This is shown in Figure 23-6.

Here the users Martin and King are not database users; they are web users, and the database has no knowledge of them. The connection pool connects to the database using the user id CONNPOOL, which is a database user. When Martin requests something from the database, the pool might decide to use the connection labeled 1 to get it from the database. After the request is complete, the connection becomes idle. If, at this point, King requests something, the pool might decide to use the same connection (labeled 1). Hence, from the database perspective, a session (which is actually the connection from the pool) is from the user CONNPOOL. As a consequence, the examples I showed earlier (where the USER function was used to identify the user) will not work to identify the user making the calls. The USER function will always return CONNPOOL because that is the connected user to the database.

This is where the application context comes into the picture. Assume that there is a context named WEB_CTX with the attribute name WEBUSER. This value is set to the name of the actual user (e.g., 'MARTIN') by the client when it sends the request to the connection pool as follows:

```
BEGIN
   set_web_ctx ('WEBUSER', 'MARTIN');
END;
```

The RLS policy can be based on this value instead of on the database username. In that case, the policy function will be slightly different, as shown below:

```
   /* File on web: authorized_emps_4.sql */
1    FUNCTION authorized_emps (
2       p_schema_name   IN   VARCHAR2,
3       p_object_name   IN   VARCHAR2
4    )
5       RETURN VARCHAR2
6    IS
7       l_deptno        NUMBER;
```

```
 8        l_return_val   VARCHAR2 (2000);
 9     BEGIN
10        IF (p_schema_name = USER)
11        THEN
12           l_return_val := NULL;
13        ELSE
14           SELECT deptno
15             INTO l_deptno
16             FROM emp
17            WHERE ename = SYS_CONTEXT ('WEB_CTX', 'WEBUSER');
18
19           l_return_val := 'DEPTNO = ' || l_deptno;
20        END IF;
21
22        RETURN l_return_val;
23     END;
```

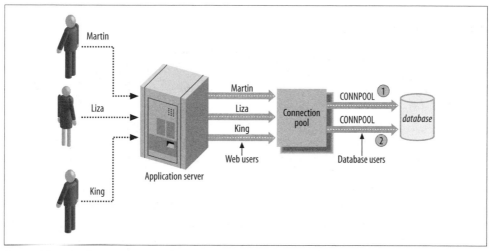

*Figure 23-6. Application users and RLS*

Note line 17. The original code showed the following:

```
WHERE ename = USER;
```

Now it is:

```
WHERE ename = SYS_CONTEXT ('WEB_CTX','WEBUSER');
```

That selects the name of the web user and matches it against the ENAME column.

# Fine-Grained Auditing

Fine-grained auditing (FGA) provides a mechanism to record the fact that some user has issued certain statements against a table and that certain conditions are met. The mechanism records the user's exact SQL statement as well as other details such as the time, terminal, and so on.

Traditional *auditing* in Oracle is the mechanism by which Oracle records which schema performed which action: Joe executed procedure X, John selected something from table Y, etc. The records of all these activities—known as the *audit trail*—go into a single table in the SYS schema, AUD$, which is exposed to users through several data dictionary views—for example, DBA_AUDIT_TRAIL. Audit trails can also be written to operating-system files instead of to database tables. Regardless of where this information is written, the basic problem with regular auditing still remains: it merely keeps track of who executed what statement, not specifically what was done. For example, it shows that Joe selected some records from table ACCOUNTS, but not which particular records. If you want to know the values changed, you can place DML triggers (discussed in Chapter 19) on the tables and capture the values in some table you have defined. But because it's not possible to define a trigger on SELECT statements, that option will not work either.

This is where Oracle's FGA comes in. FGA functionality is available via the built-in package DBMS_FGA. FGA was introduced in Oracle9*i* Database where it applied only to SELECT statements. Starting with Oracle Database 10*g*, it now applies to all DML statements.

 Don't confuse FGA with FGAC, which stands for fine-grained access control, a synonym for row-level security, which was discussed earlier in this chapter.

Using FGA you can now record the activity of SELECT, INSERT, UPDATE, and DE-LETE statements in the audit trail (albeit a different audit trail, not the AUD$ table). In this audit trail, you will find not only the information on who did what, but a whole lot of other information such as the exact SQL statement entered by the user, the System Change Number (SCN), the value of bind variables (if used), and more.

One of the best aspects of FGA is that it can be applied selectively, for specific activities. For example, you may want to perform an audit when someone selects the SAL column, but not any of the other columns. Or, you may want to record an audit trail only when someone selects the SAL column, and the value of SAL is at least 1500. This selective recording reduces the amount of audit information that is generated.

Another very useful feature of FGA is that it can be directed to execute a user-defined procedure automatically. This ability can be exploited in a variety of ways, as I'll describe in the following sections.

## Why Learn About FGA?

FGA is a close cousin of regular auditing, clearly a DBA-centric feature, so why should PL/SQL developers be interested in it? There are several reasons:

Security

> As I've noted for the other features described in this chapter, learning to leverage Oracle's built-in security features is simply part of good design for application developers and architects today. FGA should be a part of your overall design repertoire.

Performance

> A more immediately compelling reason is the practical value of the information returned by FGA. In addition to capturing information about who issues what statements, FGA is able to identify the exact SQL statements issued. If you enable FGA on a table, all of the SQL statements against that table will be captured in the FGA audit trails. You can later analyze this information to help you identify patterns in issuing these statements. This analysis can help you decide whether you need to add or modify indexes or make any other changes that will help improve performance.

Bind values

> FGA captures bind values as well, and any well-designed application uses a lot of bind variables. How do you know what different values are passed during the application run? The answer may help you decide whether or not you need to define an index. FGA trails will reveal the kind of information that will help you make such decisions.

Handler modules

> FGA can optionally execute a procedure, known as a *handler module*, whenever certain audit conditions are satisfied. If FGA is placed on SELECT statements, the

handler module will execute for each SELECT from the table. This is akin to specifying a trigger on a SELECT statement, something that Oracle does not support but that might be highly desirable. For example, suppose that whenever someone selects the salary of a company executive, a message should be sent to an advanced queue, which is then sent to a different database. You can implement a handler module to achieve the same objective that a trigger on SELECTs would provide you.

Let's take a closer look at how you can apply FGA in your application.

 For FGA to work correctly, your database must be in cost-based optimizer (CBO) mode, the queries must be using the CBO (i.e., they must not be using RULE hints), and the tables (or views) in the query must have been analyzed, at least with estimates. If these conditions are not met, FGA might produce *false positives*: it might write an audit trail even if the column was not actually selected.

## A Simple FGA Example

Let's start with a simple example—the same EMP table in the HR schema described in the earlier section on row-level security. Suppose that because of privacy regulations, you want to record a trail whenever someone selects the SAL and COMM columns. To reduce the size of the trail being generated, you may want to record the activity only when any of the selected records has a salary of $150,000 or more (not unreasonable considered the starting salary of executives today). Finally, you may also want to trigger auditing when someone queries the salary of employee 100 (you).

With these objectives in mind, let's start building the FGA infrastructure. As with RLS, there is an FGA policy defined on the table to be audited. The policy defines the conditions under which the auditing should be triggered and the actions taken. I add the policy using the ADD_POLICY procedure from the built-in package DBMS_FGA.

```
1 BEGIN
2    DBMS_FGA.add_policy (object_schema      => 'HR',
3                         object_name        => 'EMP',
4                         policy_name        => 'EMP_SEL',
5                         audit_column       => 'SAL, COMM',
6                         audit_condition    => 'SAL >= 150000 OR EMPID = 100'
7                        );
8 END;
```

Here I have defined an FGA policy named EMP_SEL in line 4, passed to the parameter policy_name. The policy is defined on the table EMP (line 3) owned by HR (line 2). That policy asks for the creation of an audit trail whenever any user selects two columns, SAL and COMM (audited columns, line 5). But the audit trail is written only if the value of SAL in that record is at least $150,000 or if the employee ID is 100 (audit condition, line 6).

The parameters audit_column and audit_condition can be omitted. If they are omitted, every SELECT from table EMP in the HR schema will be audited.

Starting with Oracle Database 10g, because FGA can be applied to regular DML as well, I can define the specific statements on which the policy should be effective, via a new parameter, statement_types:

```
1    BEGIN
2       DBMS_FGA.add_policy (object_schema    => 'HR',
3                            object_name       => 'EMP',
4                            policy_name       => 'EMP_DML',
5                            audit_column      => 'SALARY, COMM',
6                            audit_condition   => 'SALARY >= 150000 OR EMPID = 100,
7                            statement_types   => 'SELECT, INSERT, DELETE, UPDATE'
8                            );
9    END;
```

 Although both FGA and RLS rely on a *policy*, the significance of this element is quite different in each feature. They do have some similarities, though. Like its namesake in RLS, a policy in FGA is not a "schema object"—that is, no user owns it. Anyone with the EXECUTE privilege on the DBMS_FGA package can create a policy and drop one created by a different user. So ask your DBA to be very choosy while granting the EXECUTE privilege on this built-in package; granting to PUBLIC renders all of your auditing records suspect—at best.

In this case, the audit trail is written only when:

- The user selects one or both columns, SAL and COMM.
- The SAL value is at least 150,000, or the EMPID is 100.

*Both* conditions must be true for the audit record to be written. If one condition is true but the other one is not, then the action is not audited. If the user does not retrieve the SAL or the COMM columns in the query, either explicitly or implicitly, the trail is not generated even if the record being accessed has a value of 150,000 or more in the SAL column. For example, suppose that Jake's salary is $160,000, and his EMPID is 52. A user who merely wants to find his manager's name issues:

```
SELECT mgr
  FROM emp
 WHERE empid = 52;
```

Because the user has not selected the SAL or the COMM columns, the action is not audited. However the query:

```
SELECT mgr
  FROM emp
 WHERE sal >= 160000;
```

generates a trail. Why? Because the SAL column is present in the WHERE clause, the user has accessed it; hence, the audited column condition was fulfilled. The SAL of the records retrieved is more than 150,000; hence, the audit condition is fulfilled. Because both conditions have been fulfilled, the audit trail is triggered.

The audit condition need not reference the columns of the table on which the policy is defined; it can reference other values, such as pseudo-columns, as well. This becomes useful if you want to audit only a certain set of users, not all of them. Suppose you want to record accesses to table EMP made by Scott; you could define the policy as:

```
BEGIN
    DBMS_FGA.add_policy (object_schema      => 'HR',
                         object_name        => 'EMP',
                         policy_name        => 'EMP_SEL',
                         audit_column       => 'SALARY, COMM',
                         audit_condition    => 'USER=''SCOTT'''
                         );
END;
```

## Access How Many Columns?

In my example in the previous section, I have specified a list of relevant columns as follows

```
audit_column    => 'SAL, COMM'
```

This indicates that if a user accesses either the SAL or the COMM column, the action is logged. However, in some cases you may have a finer requirement that asks for logging only if *all* the columns named in the list are referenced, not just one of them. For example, in the employee database, you may want FGA to write a trail only if someone accesses SAL and EMPNAME together. If only one column is accessed, the action is not likely to uncover sensitive information because the user needs the name to match to a salary. Suppose the user issues a query:

```
SELECT salary FROM hr.emp;
```

This displays the salaries of all employees, but without a name next to the salary, the information is useless to a user who wants to know the salary of a particular employee. Similarly, if the user issues:

```
SELECT empname
    FROM hr.emp;
```

the query returns the names of the employees; without the SAL column, however, the salary information is protected. However, if the user issues:

```
SELECT empname, salary FROM hr.emp;
```

this query will enable the user to see the salaries of all employees, the very information that should be protected.

Of the three cases I've shown, the last one is the only one that will trigger generation of the audit trail (and the only one in which a trail would provide meaningful information). In Oracle9*i* Database, there was no provision to specify the combination of columns as an audit condition; in Oracle Database 10g and later, this is possible, through the audit_colum_opts parameter in the ADD_POLICY procedure. By default, the value of the parameter is DBMS_FGA.ANY_COLUMNS, which triggers an audit trail if any of the columns is referenced. If you specify DBMS_FGA.ALL_COLUMNS as the value of the parameter, the audit trail is generated only if *all* of the columns are referenced. In my example, if I want to have an FGA policy that creates an audit record only if the user selects both the SALARY and EMPNAME columns, I can create the policy as:

```
BEGIN
    DBMS_FGA.add_policy (object_schema          => 'HR',
            object_name          => 'EMP',
            policy_name          => 'EMP_DML',
            audit_column         => 'SALARY, EMPNAME',
            audit_condition      => 'USER=''SCOTT''',
            statement_types      => 'SELECT, INSERT, DELETE, UPDATE',
            audit_column_opts    => DBMS_FGA.all_columns
    );
END;
```

This feature is extremely useful in limiting audit records to only relevant ones and thus helping to limit the trail to a manageable size.

## Checking the Audit Trail

The FGA audit trails are recorded in the table FGA_LOG$ owned by SYS. A data dictionary view DBA_FGA_AUDIT_TRAIL is the external interface to this view, and you can check there for audit trails.

```
SELECT db_user, sql_text
  FROM dba_fga_audit_trail
 WHERE object_schema = 'HR' AND object_name = 'EMP'
```

This query produces the following output:

```
DB_USER SQL_TEXT
------- -------------------------------------------------
SCOTT   select salary from hr.emp where empid = 1
```

In addition to capturing the user and the SQL statement, the FGA trail also captures several other helpful pieces of information. Here are the important columns of the view:

*TIMESTAMP*
   The time when the activity occurred.

*SCN*
   The system change number when the activity occurred. This is useful when a value selected now is immaterial. You can use Oracle's flashback queries to look back at a previous SCN.

*OS_USER*
   The operating system user connected to the database.

*USERHOST*

The terminal or client machine from which the user is connected.

*EXT_NAME*

In some cases, the user may be externally authenticated, for example via LDAP. In such cases, the username in those external authentication mechanisms may be relevant and is captured in this column.

## Using Bind Variables

Back when I introduced FGA, I mentioned bind variables. Let's look more deeply into when you would use FGA with these variables. Let's assume that a user did *not* specify a statement such as the following:

```
SELECT salary
  FROM emp
 WHERE empid = 100;
```

but instead used:

```
DECLARE
   l_empid PLS_INTEGER;
BEGIN
   SELECT salary
     FROM emp
    WHERE empid = l_empid;
END;
```

FGA captures the values of bind variables along with the SQL text issued. The values recorded can be seen in the column SQL_BIND in the view DBA_FGA_AUDIT_TRAIL. In the above case, you specify the following code.

```
SQL> SELECT sql_text,sql_bind from dba_fga_audit_trail;

SQL_TEXT                                        SQL_BIND
----------------------------------------------  ----------------------
select * from hr.emp where empid = :empid       #1(3):100
```

Notice the format in which the captured bind variable is displayed:

```
#1(3):100
```

where:

*#1*

Indicates the first bind variable. If the query had more than one bind variable, the others would have been shown as #2, #3, and so on.

*(3)*

Indicates the actual length of the value of the bind variable. In this example, Scott used 100 as the value, so the length is 3.

*:100*

Indicates the actual value of the bind variable, which, in this case is 100.

The SQL_BIND column contains the string of values if more than one bind variable is used. For instance, if the query is:

```
DECLARE
    l_empid    PLS_INTEGER := 100;
    l_salary   NUMBER := 150000;

    TYPE emps_t IS TABLE OF emp%ROWTYPE;
    l_emps        empts_t;
BEGIN
    SELECT * BULK COLLECT INTO l_emps
      FROM hr.emp
     WHERE empid = l_empid OR salary > l_salary;
END;
```

the SQL_BIND column will look like this:

```
#1(3):100 #2(5):150000
```

 The SQL text and bind variable information are captured only if the audit_trail parameter in the ADD_POLICY procedure is set to DB_EXTENDED (the default), not to "DB".

---

### Fine-Grained Auditing in a Nutshell

- FGA can record SELECT accesses to a table (in Oracle9*i* Database) or all types of DML access (in Oracle Database 10*g* and later) into an audit table named FGA_LOG$ in the SYS schema.

- You can limit the generation of audit trail information so that the trail is produced only if certain columns are selected or certain conditions are met.

- For FGA to work correctly, the cost based optimizer must be used; otherwise, more false positives will occur.

- The recording of the trail is done through an autonomous transaction. Thus, if the DML fails, the trail will still exist, and that may also lead to false positives.

- The audit trails show the exact statement issued by the user, the value of the bind variables (if any), the System Change Number at the time of the query, and various attributes of the session, such as the database username, the operating system username, the timestamp, and much more.

- In addition to writing an entry into the audit trails, FGA can also automatically execute a procedure, known as handler module.

---

## Using Handler Modules

As I mentioned earlier, FGA can optionally execute PL/SQL stored program units such as stored procedures. If the stored procedure, in turn, encapsulates a shell or OS program, it can execute that as well. This stored program unit is known as the handler module. In the earlier example where I built the mechanism to audit accesses to the EMP table, I could optionally specify a stored procedure—standalone or packaged—to be executed as well. If the stored procedure is owned by user FGA_ADMIN and is named myproc, I will have to call the policy creation procedure, ADD_POLICY, with two new parameters, handler_schema and handler_module:

```
BEGIN
   DBMS_FGA.add_policy (object_schema    => 'HR',
                        object_name      => 'EMP',
                        policy_name      => 'EMP_SEL',
                        audit_column     => 'SALARY, COMM',
                        audit_condition  => 'SALARY >= 150000 OR EMPID = 100',
                        handler_schema   => 'FGA_ADMIN',
                        handler_module   => 'MYPROC'
                       );
END;
```

Whenever the policy's audit conditions are satisfied and the relevant columns are referenced, not only is the action recorded in the audit trails, but the procedure fga_admin.myproc is executed as well. The procedure is automatically executed every time the audit trails are written, as an *autonomous transaction*. (See the discussion of autonomous transactions in Chapter 14.) It has to have exactly three parameters—the schema name, the table name, and the policy name. Here is the structure of a handler module procedure:

```
PROCEDURE myproc (
   p_table_owner   IN   VARCHAR2,
   p_table_name    IN   VARCHAR2,
   p_fga_policy    IN   VARCHAR2
)
IS
BEGIN
   -- the code is here
END;
```

How is that useful? In several ways. For starters, this allows you to build your own audit handler program that can write to your own tables, not just to the standard audit trail tables. You can write the messages to a queue table to be placed in a different database, ask an email to be sent to security administrators, or simply count the number of times it happened. The possibilities are endless.

 If the handler module fails for any reason, FGA does not report an error when you query data from the table. Instead it simply silently stops retrieving the rows for which the handler module fails. This is a tricky situation because you will never know that a handler module failed. Not all rows will be returned, producing erroneous results. This makes it important that you thoroughly test your handler modules.

# CHAPTER 24

# PL/SQL Architecture

In my experience, relatively few PL/SQL developers exhibit a burning curiosity about the underlying architecture of the PL/SQL language. As a community, we seem to mostly be content with learning the basic syntax of PL/SQL, writing our programs, and going home to spend quality time with family and friends. That's a very healthy perspective!

I suggest, however, that all PL/SQL developers would benefit from a basic understanding of this architecture. Not only will you be able to write programs that utilize memory more efficiently, but you will be able to configure your programs and overall applications to behave in ways that you might have thought were impossible.

You will find in this chapter answers to the following questions...and many more:

- How does the PL/SQL runtime engine use memory, and what can I do to manage how much memory is used?
- Should I be running natively compiled code or stick with the default interpreted code? What does "native compilation" mean, anyway?
- Why do my programs become INVALID and how can I recompile them back to health?
- I have duplicated tables in 20 different schemas. Do I really have to maintain 20 copies of my code, in each of those schemas?
- And...who or what is *DIANA*?

## Who (or What) is DIANA?

In earlier editions of this book, the title of this chapter was *Inside PL/SQL*. I decided to change the name to *PL/SQL Architecture* for two reasons:

1. Most of what was in the chapter was not truly in any sense "internals." In fact, it is very difficult for PL/SQL developers (anyone outside of Oracle headquarters) to get information about "internal" aspects of PL/SQL.

2. I don't want to encourage you to try to uncover otherwise hidden aspects of PL/SQL. Developers, I believe, benefit most from learning the syntax of the language, not from trying to "game" or trick the PL/SQL compiler into doing something it wouldn't do of its own volition.

Having said that, a very common question that touches on the internal structures of the PL/SQL compiler is: "Who or what is DIANA?"

Asking a PL/SQL programmer *Who is Diana?* is like asking a San Francisco resident *Who's Bart?*. The answer to both questions is not so much a *who* as a *what*. For the San Francisco Bay Area resident, BART is the Bay Area Rapid Transit system—the subway. For the PL/SQL programmer, DIANA is the Distributed Intermediate Annotated Notation for Ada and is part of PL/SQL's heritage as an Ada-derived language. In some Ada compilers the output of the first part of the compilation is a DIANA. Likewise, PL/SQL was originally designed to output a DIANA in the first part of the compilation process.

As a PL/SQL programmer, however, you never really see or interact with your program's DIANA. Oracle Corporation may decide, like some Ada compiler publishers, that PL/SQL has outgrown DIANA, and another mechanism may be used. Changes in the internals of the database happen. For example, segment space management used to use free lists, but now uses bitmaps. So, while you might get an error if your DIANA grows too large (how embarrassing—your DIANA is showing!), you don't really do anything with DIANA and if she (it) goes away, you probably won't even know.

Knowing about DIANA might win you a T-shirt in a trivia contest at Oracle Open World, but it probably won't improve your programming skills— unless you are programming the PL/SQL compiler.

So ... enough with internals. Let's get on with our discussion of critical aspects of the PL/SQL architecture.

## How Does Oracle Execute PL/SQL Code?

Before I explore how an Oracle database executes PL/SQL programs, I first need to define a couple of terms of art:[1]

*PL/SQL runtime engine (a.k.a. PL/SQL Virtual Machine)*
    The PL/SQL Virtual Machine (PVM) is the database component that executes a PL/SQL program's bytecode. In this virtual machine, the bytecode of a PL/SQL program is translated to machine code that makes calls to the database server and returns results to the calling environment. The PVM itself is written in C. Historically, Oracle has included a PVM in some client-side tools such as Oracle Forms,

---

1. *http://en.wiktionary.org* defines a *term of art* as "A term whose use or meaning is specific to a particular field of endeavor."

where the runtime engine opens a session to a remote database, communicating with the SQL engine over a networking protocol.

*Database session*

For most (server-side) PL/SQL, the database session is the process and memory space associated with an authenticated user connection. Each session has its own memory area where it can hold an executing program's data. Sessions begin with logon and end with logoff. The sessions connected to a database are visible through the view V$SESSION.

To put these terms into context, let's take a look at several variations on running a trivial program from a very common frontend, SQL*Plus. This is a good representative of a session-oriented tool that gives you direct access to the PL/SQL environment inside the database server. (I introduced SQL*Plus and showed how to use it with PL/SQL back in Chapter 2.) Of course, you may be calling the server from other tools such as Oracle's other client-side tools or even a procedural language such as Perl, C, or Java. But don't worry: processing on the server side is relatively independent of the client environment.

PL/SQL execution launched directly from SQL*Plus always involves a top-level anonymous block. While you may know that the SQL*Plus EXECUTE command converts the call to an anonymous block, did you know that SQL's CALL statement uses a (simplified) kind of anonymous block? Actually, until Oracle9*i* Database's direct invocation of PL/SQL from SQL, *all* PL/SQL invocations from SQL used anonymous blocks.

## An Example

So let's begin with a look at the simplest possible anonymous block:

```
BEGIN
    NULL;
END;
```

...and find out just what happens when you send this block to the database server (Figure 24-1).

Let's step through the operations shown in this figure:

1. Starting on the left side of Figure 24-1, the user composes the source code for the block and then gives SQL*Plus the go-ahead command (a slash). As the figure shows, SQL*Plus sends the entire code block, exclusive of the slash, to the server. This transmission occurs over whatever connection the session has established (for example, Oracle Net or interprocess communication).

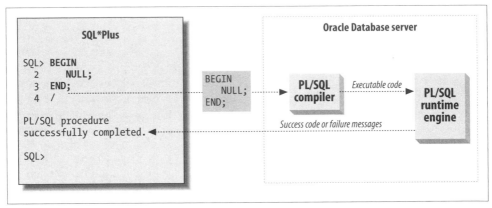

*Figure 24-1. Execution of a trivial anonymous block*

2. Next, the PL/SQL compiler attempts to compile this anonymous block to byte-code.[2] A first phase is to check the syntax to ensure that the program adheres to the grammar of the language. In this simple case, there are no identifiers to figure out, only language keywords. If compilation succeeds, the database puts the block's compiled form (the bytecode) into a shared memory area; if it fails, the compiler will return error messages to the SQL*Plus session.

3. Finally, the PVM interprets the bytecode and ultimately returns a success or failure code to the SQL*Plus session.

Let's add an embedded SQL query statement into the anonymous block and see how that changes the picture. Figure 24-2 introduces some of the SQL-related elements of the database server.

This example fetches a column value from the well-known table DUAL.[3]

After checking that the PL/SQL portions of the code adhere to the language's syntax, the PL/SQL compiler communicates with the SQL compiler to hand off any embedded SQL for execution. Likewise, PL/SQL programs called from SQL statements cause the SQL compiler to hand off the PL/SQL calls to the PL/SQL compiler. The SQL parser will resolve any expressions, look for opportunities to use the function result cache (starting with Oracle Database 11g), execute semantic and syntax checks, perform name resolution and determine an optimal execution plan. These steps are all part of the parse phase of the SQL execution and precede any substitution of bind variables and the execution and fetch of the SQL statement.

---

2. Actually, if some session previously needed the database to compile the block, there is a good chance that the compile phase won't need to be repeated. That is because the server caches the outputs of relatively expensive operations like compilation in memory and tries to share them.

3. According to a reputable source, the name DUAL is from its dual singularity: one row, one column.

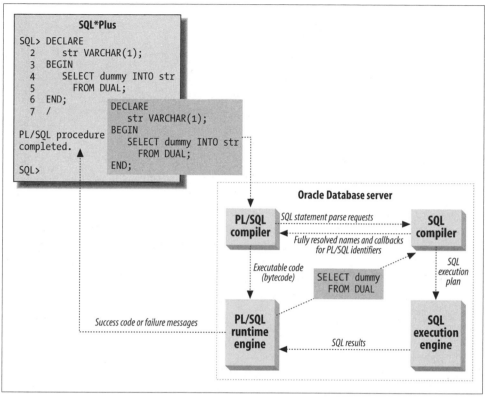

*Figure 24-2. Execution of an anonymous block that contains SQL*

While PL/SQL shares a SQL compiler with the database, this does not mean that every SQL function is available in PL/SQL. For example, SQL supports the NVL2 function:

```
SELECT NVL2(NULL, 1, 2) FROM DUAL;
```

But attempting to use NVL2 directly in PL/SQL results in *PLS-00201: identifier 'NVL2' must be declared.*

```
EXEC DBMS_OUTPUT.PUT_LINE(NVL2(NULL, 1, 2));

BEGIN DBMS_OUTPUT.PUT_LINE (NVL2(NULL, 1, 2)); END;

                     *
ERROR at line 1:
ORA-06550: line 1, column 28:
PLS-00201: identifier 'NVL2' must be declared
ORA-06550: line 1, column 7:
PL/SQL: Statement ignored
```

When a PL/SQL program is compiled, embedded SQL statements are modified slightly such that INTO clauses are removed, local program variables are replaced with bind variables, and some keywords are forced to uppercase. For example, if myvar is a local program variable, PL/SQL will change this:

```
select dummy into str from dual where dummy = myvar
```

into something like this in Oracle Database 10g or Oracle Database 11g:

```
SELECT DUMMY FROM DUAL WHERE DUMMY = :B1
```

There are two other kinds of callouts you can make from PL/SQL:

*Java stored procedures*
> The default database server installation includes not just a PL/SQL virtual machine but also a Java virtual machine. You can write a PL/SQL call spec whose logic is implemented as a static Java class. For details and examples, see Chapter 27 on the book's web site).

*External procedures*
> You can also implement the executable portion of a PL/SQL subprogram in custom C code, and at runtime the database will run your code in a separate process and memory space from the main database server. You are responsible for backing up these binaries and making sure each RAC node has a copy. Chapter 28 discusses external procedures and is also available on the book's web site.

You can learn more about the runtime architecture of these two approaches by consulting their respective chapters.

## Compiler Limits

Large PL/SQL programs may encounter the server error *PLS-00123: Program too large*. This means that the compiler bumped into the maximum allowed number of "nodes" in the parse tree. The normal workaround for this error is to split the program into several smaller programs or re-engineer it (for example to use a temporary table instead of 10,000 parameters). It's difficult to predict how many nodes a program will need because nodes don't directly correspond to anything easily measurable, such as tokens or lines of code.

Oracle advises that a "typical" stored program generates four parse tree nodes per line of code, and that this equates to the following approximate upper limits:

| PL/SQL program type | Upper limit (estimated) |
|---|---|
| Package and type bodies; standalone functions and procedures | 256M |
| Signature (header) of standalone functions and procedures | 128K |
| Package and type specifications; anonymous blocks | 128K |

These are only estimates, and there can be a fair amount of variance in either direction.

Other documented hard limits in the PL/SQL compiler include the following:

| PL/SQL elements | Upper limit (estimated) |
| --- | --- |
| Levels of block nesting | 255 |
| Parameters you can pass to a procedure or function | 65,536 |
| Levels of record nesting | 64 |
| Objects referenced in a program unit | 65,536 |
| Number of exception handlers in one program | 65,536 |
| Precision of a NUMBER (digits) | 38 |
| Size of a VARCHAR2 (bytes) | 32,767 |

Few of these are likely to cause a problem, but you can find a complete list of them in an appendix of Oracle's official PL/SQL documentation, *PL/SQL User's Guide and Reference*.

# The Default Packages of PL/SQL

A true object-oriented language like Java has a root class (in Java it is called Object, not surprisingly), from which all other classes are derived. PL/SQL is, officially, an object-relational language, but at its core it is a relational, procedural programming language and it has at *its* core a "root" package named STANDARD.

The packages you build are not derived from STANDARD, but almost every program you write will *depend on* and use this package. It is, in fact, one of the two *default* packages of PL/SQL, the other being DBMS_STANDARD.

To best understand the role that these packages play in your programming environment, it is worth traveling back in time to the late 1980s, before the days of Oracle7 and SQL*Forms 3, before Oracle PL/SQL even existed. Oracle had discovered that while SQL was a wonderful language, it couldn't do everything. Their customers found themselves writing C programs that executed the SQL statements, but those C programs had to be modified to run on each different operating system.

Oracle decided that it would create a programming language that could execute SQL statements natively and be portable across all operating systems on which the Oracle database was installed. The company also decided that rather than come up with a brand-new language on their own, they would evaluate existing languages and see if any of them could serve as the model for what became PL/SQL.

In the end, Oracle chose Ada as that model. Ada was originally designed for use by the U.S. Department of Defense, and was named after Ada Lovelace, an early and widely respected software programming pioneer. Packages are a construct adopted from Ada. In the Ada language, you can specify a "default package" in any given program unit. When a package is the default, you do not have to qualify references to elements in the package with the *package_name dot* syntax as in *my_package.call_procedure*.

When Oracle designed PL/SQL, they kept the idea of a default package, but changed the way it is applied. We (users of PL/SQL) are not allowed to specify a default package in a program unit. Instead, there are just two default packages in PL/SQL, STANDARD and DBMS_STANDARD. They are defaults for the entire language, not for any specific program unit.

You can (and almost always will) reference elements in either of these packages without using the package name as a dot-qualified prefix. Let's now explore how Oracle uses the STANDARD package (and to a lesser extent, DBMS_STANDARD) to, as stated in the *Oracle PL/SQL User Guide*, "define the PL/SQL environment."

STANDARD declares a set of types, exceptions, and subprograms that are automatically available to all PL/SQL programs and would be considered (mistakenly) by many PL/SQL developers to be "reserved words" in the language. When compiling your code, Oracle must resolve all unqualified identifiers; it first checks to see if an element with that name is declared in the current scope. If not, it then checks to see if there an element with that name defined in STANDARD or DBMS_STANDARD. If a match is found for all identifiers in your program, the code can be compiled (assuming there are no syntax errors).

To understand the role of STANDARD, consider the following, very strange-looking block of PL/SQL code. What do you think will happen when I execute this block?

```
    /* File on web: standard_demo.sql */
 1  DECLARE
 2     SUBTYPE DATE IS NUMBER;
 3     VARCHAR2 DATE := 11111;
 4     TO_CHAR      PLS_INTEGER;
 5     NO_DATA_FOUND EXCEPTION;
 6  BEGIN
 7     SELECT 1 INTO TO_CHAR
 8        FROM SYS.DUAL WHERE 1 = 2;
 9  EXCEPTION
10     WHEN NO_DATA_FOUND
11     THEN
12        DBMS_OUTPUT.put_line ('Trapped!');
13  END;
```

Most PL/SQL developers will say either "This block won't even compile," or "it will display the word 'Trapped!' since 1 is never equal to 2."

In fact, the block will compile, but when you run it, you will see an unhandled NO_DATA_FOUND exception:

```
ORA-01403: no data found
ORA-06512: at line 7
```

Now isn't that odd? NO_DATA_FOUND is the *only* exception I am actually handling, so how can it escape unhandled? Ah, but the question is: *which* NO_DATA_FOUND am I handling? You see, in this block, I have declared my *own* exception named NO_DATA_FOUND. This name is not a reserved word in the PL/SQL language (in contrast, BEGIN is a reserved word. You cannot name a variable "BEGIN"). Instead, it is an exception that is defined in the specification of the STANDARD package, as follows:

```
NO_DATA_FOUND exception;
  pragma EXCEPTION_INIT(NO_DATA_FOUND, 100);
```

Since I have a locally-declared exception with the name NO_DATA_FOUND, any *unqualified* reference to this identifier in my block will be resolved as *my* exception and not STANDARD's exception. A SELECT INTO that does not find any rows raises STANDARD.NO_DATA_FOUND, which is *not* the exception handled in the exception section.

If, on the other hand, line 12 in my exception section looked like this:

```
WHEN STANDARD.NO_DATA_FOUND
```

then the exception would be handled and the word "Trapped!" displayed.

In addition to the oddness of NO_DATA_FOUND, these lines also appear to be rather strange:

| Line(s) | Description |
| --- | --- |
| 2 | Define a new type of data named "DATE", which is actually of type NUMBER. |
| 3 | Declare a variable named "VARCHAR2" of type "DATA" and assign it a value of 11111. |
| 4 | Declare a variable named "TO_CHAR" of type PLS_INTEGER. |

I can "repurpose" these names of "built-in" elements of the PL/SQL language, because they are all defined in the STANDARD package. These names are not reserved by PL/SQL; they are simply and conveniently referenceable without their package name.

The STANDARD package contains the definitions of the supported datatypes in PL/SQL, the predefined exceptions, and the built-in functions, such as TO_CHAR, SYSDATE, and USER. The DBMS_STANDARD package contains transaction-related elements, such as COMMIT, ROLLBACK, and the trigger event functions INSERTING, DELETING, and UPDATING.

Here are a few things to note about STANDARD:

- You should never change the contents of this package. If you do, I suggest that you not contact Oracle Support and ask for help. You have likely just violated your maintenance agreement! Your DBA *should* give you read-only authority on the *RDBMS/Admin* directory so that you can examine this package, along with any of the supplied packages, like DBMS_OUTPUT (check out *dbmsotpt.sql*) and DBMS_UTILITY (check out *dbmsutil.sql*).

- Oracle even lets you read the package body of STANDARD; most package bodies, such as for DBMS_SQL, are wrapped or pseudo-encrypted. STANDARD is not. Look in the *stdbody.sql* script and you will see, for instance, that the USER function *always* executes a SELECT from SYS.dual, while SYSDATE will only execute a query if a C program to retrieve the system timestamp fails.

- Just because you see a statement in STANDARD doesn't mean you can write that same code in your own PL/SQL blocks. You cannot, for example, declare a subtype with a range of values, as is done for BINARY_INTEGER.

- Just because you see something defined in STANDARD doesn't mean you can use it in PL/SQL. For example, the DECODE function is declared in STANDARD, but it can be called only from within a SQL statement.

The STANDARD package is defined by the *stdspec.sql* and *stdbody.sql* files in *$ORA-CLE_HOME/RDBMS/Admin* (in some earlier versions of the database, this package may be found in the *standard.sql* file). You will find DBMS_STANDARD in *dbmsstdx.sql*.

If you are curious about which of the many predefined identifiers are actually reserved words in the PL/SQL language, check out the *reserved_words.sql* script on the book's web site. This script is explained in Chapter 3.

# Execution Authority Models

The Oracle database offers two different models for object permissions in your PL/SQL programs. The default (and only model way back in the days before Oracle8*i* Database) is *definer rights*. With this model, a stored program executes under the authority of its owner, or *definer*.[4] The other permission model uses the privileges of the user invoking the program and is referred to as *invoker rights*.

You need to understand the nuances of both the definer rights model and the invoker rights model because many PL/SQL applications rely on a combination of the two. Let's explore these in a little more detail, so you know when you want to use each model.

## The Definer Rights Model

Before a PL/SQL program can be executed from within a database instance, it must be compiled and stored in the database itself. Thus, a program unit is always stored within a specific schema or database account, even though the program might refer to objects in other schemas.

With the *definer rights model*, keep the following rules in mind:

- Any external reference in a program unit is resolved at compile time, using the directly granted privileges of the schema in which the program unit is compiled.

---

4. It was possible to get invoker rights by using a loopback database link.

- Database roles are ignored completely when compiling stored programs. All privileges needed for the program must be granted directly to the definer (owner) of the program.
- Whenever you run a program compiled with the definer rights model (the default), its SQL executes under the authority of the schema that owns the program.
- Although direct grants are needed to compile a program, you can grant EXECUTE authority to give other schemas and roles the ability to run your program.

Figure 24-3 shows how you can use the definer rights model to control access to underlying data objects. All the order entry data is stored in the OEData schema. All the order entry code is defined in the OECode schema. OECode has been granted the direct privileges necessary to compile the Order_Mgt package, which allows you to both place and cancel orders.

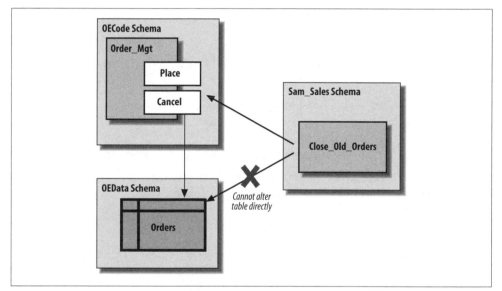

*Figure 24-3. Controlling access to data with the definer rights model*

To make sure that the orders table is updated properly, no direct access (either via roles or via privileges) is allowed to that table through any schema other than OECode. Suppose, for example, that the Sam_Sales schema needs to run through all the outstanding orders and close out old ones. Sam will not be able to issue a DELETE statement from the Close_Old_Orders procedure; instead, he will have to call Order_Mgt.cancel to get the job done.

### Advantages of definer rights

Certain situations cry out for definer rights. This model offers the following advantages:

- You are better able to control access to underlying data structures. You can guarantee that the only way the contents of a table can be changed is by going through a specific programmatic interface (usually a package).

- Application performance improves dramatically because the PL/SQL engine does not have to perform checks at runtime to determine if you have the appropriate privileges or—just as important—which object you should actually be manipulating (my accounts table may be quite different from yours!).

- You don't have to worry about manipulating the wrong table. With definer rights, your code will work with the same data structure you would be accessing directly in SQL in your SQL*Plus (or other execution) environment. It is simply more intuitive.

### Disadvantages of definer rights

But there are problems with the definer rights model as well. These are explored in the next sections.

**Where'd my table go.**   Let's see what all those definer rights rules can mean to a PL/SQL developer on a day-to-day basis. In many databases, developers write code against tables and views that are owned by other schemas, with public synonyms created for them to hide the schema. Privileges are then granted via database roles.

This very common setup can result in some frustrating experiences. Suppose that my organization relies on roles to grant access to objects. I am working with a table called accounts, and can execute this query without any problem in SQL*Plus:

```
SQL> SELECT account#, name FROM accounts;
```

Yet, when I try to use that same table (and the same query, even) inside a procedure, I get an error:

```
SQL> CREATE OR REPLACE PROCEDURE show_accounts
  2  IS
  3  BEGIN
  4     FOR rec IN (SELECT account#, name FROM accounts)
  5     LOOP
  6        DBMS_OUTPUT.PUT_LINE (rec.name);
  7     END LOOP;
  8  END;
  9  /

Warning: Procedure created with compilation errors.

SQL> sho err
Errors for PROCEDURE SHOW_ACCOUNTS:

LINE/COL ERROR
```

```
-------- --------------------------------------------------------
4/16      PL/SQL: SQL Statement ignored
4/43      PLS-00201: identifier 'ACCOUNTS' must be declared
```

This doesn't make any sense...or does it? The problem is that accounts is actually owned by another schema; I was unknowingly relying on a synonym and roles to get at the data. So if you are ever faced with this seemingly contradictory situation, don't bang your head against the wall in frustration. Instead, ask the owner of the object or the DBA to grant you the privileges you require to get the job done.

**How do I maintain all that code.**   Suppose that my database instance is set up with a separate schema for each of the regional offices in my company. I build a large body of code that each office uses to analyze and maintain its data. Each schema has its own tables with the same structure but different data, a design selected for both data security and ease of movement via transportable tablespaces.

Now, I would like to install this code so that I spend the absolute minimum amount of time and effort setting up and maintaining the application. The way to do that is to install the code in one schema and share that code among all the regional office schemas.

With the definer rights model, unfortunately, this goal and architecture are impossible to achieve. If I install the code in a central schema and grant EXECUTE authority to all regional schemas, then all those offices will be working with whatever set of tables is accessible to the central schema (perhaps one particular regional office or, more likely, a dummy set of tables). That's no good. I must instead install this body of code in each separate regional schema, as shown in Figure 24-4.

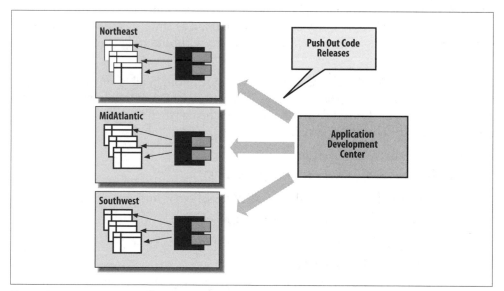

*Figure 24-4. Repetitive installations of code needed with definer rights*

The result is a maintenance and enhancement nightmare. Perhaps invoker rights will give us options for a better solution.

**Dynamic SQL and definer rights.** Another common source of confusion with definer rights occurs when using dynamic SQL (described in Chapter 16). Suppose that I create a generic "exec DDL" program (yes, this is a really bad idea security-wise, but it illustrates the unintended consequences of this learning exercise) as follows:

```
/* File on web: execddl.sp */
PROCEDURE execDDL (ddl_string IN VARCHAR2)
IS
BEGIN
    EXECUTE IMMEDIATE ddl_string;
EXCEPTION
    WHEN OTHERS
    THEN
        DBMS_OUTPUT.PUT_LINE ('Dynamic SQL Failure: ' || SQLERRM);
        DBMS_OUTPUT.PUT_LINE ('   on statement: "' || ddl_string || '"');
        RAISE;
END;
```

After testing it in my schema with outstanding results, I decide to share this neat utility with everyone else in my development organization. I compile it into the COMMON schema (where all reusable code is managed), grant EXECUTE to PUBLIC, and create a public synonym. Then I send out an email announcing its availability.

A few weeks later, I start getting calls from my coworkers. "Hey, I asked it to create a table, and it ran without any errors, but I don't have the table." "I asked it to drop my table, and the execddl procedure said that there is no such table. But I can do a DE-SCRIBE on it." You get the idea. I begin to have serious doubts about sharing my code with other people. Sheesh, if they can't use something as simple as the execddl procedure without screwing things up...but I decide to withhold judgment and do some research.

I log into the COMMON schema and find that, sure enough, all of the objects people were trying to create or drop or alter were sitting here in COMMON. And then it dawns on me: unless a user of execddl specifies his own schema when he asks to create a table, the results will be most unexpected.

In other words, this call to execddl:

```
EXEC execddl ('CREATE TABLE newone (rightnow DATE)')
```

would create the newone table in the COMMON schema. And this call to execddl:

```
EXEC execddl ('CREATE TABLE scott.newone (rightnow DATE)')
```

might solve the problem, but would fail with the following error:

```
ORA-01031: insufficient privileges
```

unless I grant CREATE ANY TABLE to the COMMON schema. Yikes...my attempt to share a useful piece of code got very complicated very fast! It sure would be nice to let people run the execddl procedure under their own authority and not that of COM-MON, without having to install multiple copies of the code.

**Privilege escalation and SQL injection.** The time to pause and review your design with a colleague is when your program executes dynamic SQL that relies on the owner's directly granted system privileges—and you think definer rights is appropriate to use. You should be very reluctant to create my execDDL procedure in the SYS schema or any other schema having system privileges that could serve as a gateway to privilege escalation if unexpected, but legal input is passed in. Please review Chapter 16 on how to prevent code injection.

## The Invoker Rights Model

Sometimes, your programs should execute using the privileges of the person running the program and not the owner of the program. In such cases, you should choose the *invoker rights model*. With this approach, all external references in the SQL statements in a PL/SQL program unit are resolved according to the privileges of the invoking schema, not those of the owning or defining schema.

Figure 24-5 demonstrates the fundamental difference between the definer and the invoker rights models. Recall that in Figure 24-4, it was necessary for me to push out copies of my application to each regional office so that the code would manipulate the correct tables. With invoker rights, this step is no longer necessary. Now I can compile the code into a single code repository. When a user from the Northeast region executes the centralized program (probably via a synonym), it will work automatically with tables in the Northeast schema.

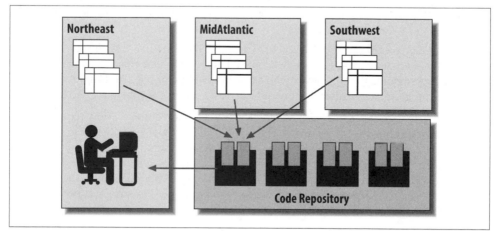

*Figure 24-5. Use of invoker rights model*

So that's the idea behind invoker rights. Let's see what is involved in terms of code, and then explore how best to exploit the feature.

### Invoker rights syntax

The syntax to support this feature is simple enough. You add the following clause before your IS or AS keyword in the program header:

```
AUTHID CURRENT_USER
```

Here, for example, is that generic "exec DDL" engine again, this time defined as an invoker rights program:

```
/* File on web: execddl.sql */
PROCEDURE execddl (ddl_in in VARCHAR2)
   AUTHID CURRENT_USER
IS
BEGIN
   EXECUTE IMMEDIATE ddl_in;
END;
```

The AUTHID CURRENT_USER clause before the IS keyword indicates that when execddl executes, it should run under the authority of the invoker or "current user," not the authority of the definer. And that's all you have to do. If you do not include the AUTHID clause, or if you include it and explicitly request definer rights as shown:

```
AUTHID DEFINER
```

then all references in your program will be resolved according to the directly granted privileges of the owning schema.

---

## Invoker Rights for Dynamic SQL

I have written hundreds of programs using dynamic SQL, and with definer rights I would have to worry about schema issues. Where is the program running? Who is running it? What will happen when someone runs it? These are serious questions to ask about your code!

You may be tempted to use the AUTHID CURRENT_USER clause with every stored program unit that uses any kind of dynamic SQL. Once you take this step, you reason, you can rest assured that no matter where the program is compiled and which schema runs the program, it will always act on the currently connected schema.

The problem with this approach, though, is twofold. First, your users now require the same privileges that the programs have (and you may not want the HR clerk to modify a salary outside the designated program). Second there is extra runtime checking that the database must perform for invoker rights programs—and that can be a drag on performance. Use invoker rights where it is appropriate—neither model should be adopted blindly. I like to *think* about which privilege model my program needs and deliberately code to that model.

---

### Rules and restrictions on invoker rights

There are a number of rules and restrictions to keep in mind when you are taking advantage of the invoker rights model:

- AUTHID DEFINER is the default option.
- The invoker rights model checks the privileges assigned to the invoker at the time of program execution to resolve any SQL-based references to database objects.
- With invoker rights, roles *are* in effect at runtime as long as the invoker rights program hasn't been called from a definer rights program.
- The AUTHID clause is allowed only in the header of a standalone subprogram (procedure or function), a package specification, or an object type specification. You cannot apply the AUTHID clause to individual programs or methods within a package or object type. So the whole package will be invoker rights or the whole package will be definer rights. If parts of your package should be invoker rights and parts should be definer rights, then you need two packages.
- Invoker rights resolution of external references will work for the following kinds of statements:
  — SELECT, INSERT, UPDATE, MERGE, and DELETE data manipulation statements
  — LOCK TABLE transaction control statement
  — OPEN and OPEN FOR cursor control statements
  — EXECUTE IMMEDIATE and OPEN FOR USING dynamic SQL statements
  — SQL statements parsed using DBMS_SQL.PARSE
- Definer rights will always be used to resolve all external references to PL/SQL programs and object type methods at compilation time.
- You can use invoker rights to change the resolution of static external data element references (tables and views).

You can also use invoker rights to resolve external references to PL/SQL programs. Here is one way to do it:

```
EXECUTE IMMEDIATE 'BEGIN someprogram; END;';
```

In this fragment, *someprogram* would get resolved at runtime according to the rights and namespace of the invoker. Alternatively, I could have used SQL's CALL statement instead of the anonymous block. (I can't just use a naked CALL statement because it is not directly supported within PL/SQL.)

## Combining Rights Models

What do you think would happen if a definer rights program called an invoker rights program? Or vice versa? The rules are simple:

- If a definer rights program calls an invoker rights program, the rights of the *calling* program's owner apply while the called program executes.

- If an invoker rights program calls a definer rights program, the rights of the *called* program's owner apply while the called program executes. When control returns to the caller, invoker rights resume.

To help keep all of this straight in your head, just remember that definer rights are "stronger" than (take precedence over) invoker rights.

Here are some files on the book's web site that you can use to explore the nuances of the invoker rights model in more detail:

*invdefinv.sql and invdefinv.tst*
   Two scripts that demonstrate the impact of the precedence of definer rights over invoker rights.

*invdef_overhead.tst*
   Examines the overhead of reliance on invoker rights (hint: runtime resolution is slower than compile-time resolution).

*invrole.sql*
   Demonstrates how a change in roles can affect how object references are resolved at runtime.

*irdynsql.sql*
   Explores some of the complexities involved in using invoker and definer rights with dynamic SQL.

## Conditional Compilation

Introduced in Oracle Database 10*g* Release 2, *conditional compilation* allows the compiler to compile selected parts of a program based on conditions you provide with the $IF directive.

Conditional compilation will come in very handy when you need to:

- Write a program that will run under different versions of Oracle, taking advantage of features specific to those versions. More specifically, you may want to take advantage of new features of the Oracle database where available, but you also need your program to compile and run in older versions. Without conditional compilation, you would have to maintain multiple files or use complex SQL*Plus substitution variable logic.

- Run certain code during testing and debugging, but then omit that code from the production code. Prior to conditional compilation, you would need to either comment out lines of code or add some overhead to the processing of your application—even in production.

- Install/compile different elements of your application based on user requirements, such as the components for which a user is licensed. Conditional compilation greatly simplifies the maintenance of a code base with this complexity.

You implement conditional compilation by placing compiler *directives* (commands) in your source code. When your program is compiled, the PL/SQL preprocessor evaluates the directives and selects those portions of your code that should be compiled. This pared-down source code is then passed to the compiler for compilation.

There are three types of directives:

*Selection directives*
> Use the $IF directive to evaluate expressions and determine which code should be included or avoided.

*Inquiry directives*
> Use the $$*identifier* syntax to refer to conditional compilation flags. These inquiry directives can be referenced within an $IF directive or used independently in your code.

*Error directives*
> Use the $ERROR directive to report compilation errors based on conditions evaluated when the preprocessor prepares your code for compilation.

First I'll show some simple examples, then delve more deeply into the capabilities of each directive. You'll also learn how to use two packages related to conditional compilation, DBMS_DB_VERSION and DBMS_PREPROCESSOR.

## Examples of Conditional Compilation

Let's start with some examples of several types of conditional compilation.

### Use application package constants in $IF directive

The $IF directive can reference constants defined in your own packages. In the example below, I vary the way that a bonus is applied depending on whether or not the location in which this third-party application is installed is complying with the Sarbanes-Oxley guidelines. Such a setting is unlikely to change for a long period of time. If I rely on the traditional conditional statement in this case, I will leave in place a branch of logic that should never be applied. With conditional compilation, the code is removed before compilation.

```
/* File on web: cc_my_package.sql */
PROCEDURE apply_bonus (
   id_in IN employee.employee_id%TYPE
   ,bonus_in IN employee.bonus%TYPE)
IS
BEGIN
   UPDATE employee
      SET bonus =
      $IF employee_rp.apply_sarbanes_oxley
      $THEN
         LEAST (bonus_in, 10000)
      $ELSE
```

```
        bonus_in
      $END
    WHERE employee_id = id_in;
  NULL;
END apply_bonus;
```

### Toggle tracing through conditional compilation flags

I can now set up my own debug/trace mechanisms and have them conditionally compiled into my code. This means that when my code rolls into production, I can have
this code completely removed so that there will be no runtime overhead to this logic.
Note that I can specify both Boolean and PLS_INTEGER values through the special
PLSQL_CCFLAGS compile parameter.

```
/* File on web: cc_debug_trace.sql */
ALTER SESSION SET PLSQL_CCFLAGS = 'oe_debug:true, oe_trace_level:10';

PROCEDURE calculate_totals
IS
BEGIN
$IF $$oe_debug AND $$oe_trace_level >= 5
$THEN
   DBMS_OUTPUT.PUT_LINE ('Tracing at level 5 or higher');
$END
   NULL;
END calculate_totals;
```

# The Inquiry Directive

An inquiry directive is a directive that makes an inquiry of the compilation environment. Of course, that doesn't really tell you much. So let's take a closer look at the
syntax for inquiry directives and the different sources of information available through
the inquiry directive.

The syntax for an inquiry directive is as follows:

```
$$identifier
```

where *identifier* is a valid PL/SQL identifier that can represent any of the following:

- Compilation environment settings: the values found in the USER_PLSQL_OB-
  JECT_SETTINGS data dictionary view.
- Your own custom-named directive: defined with the ALTER...SET
  PLSQL_CCFLAGS command, described in a later section.
- Implicitly defined directives: $$PLSQL_LINE and $$PLSQL_UNIT, providing you
  with the line number and program name.

Inquiry directives are designed for use within conditional compilation clauses, but they
can also be used in other places in your PL/SQL code. For example, I can display the
current line number in my program with this code:

```
DBMS_OUTPUT.PUT_LINE ($$PLSQL_LINE);
```

I can also use inquiry directives to define and apply application-wide constants in my code. Suppose, for example, that the maximum number of years of data supported in my application is 100. Rather than hardcode this value in my code, I can do the following:

```
ALTER SESSION SET PLSQL_CCFLAGS = 'max_years:100';

PROCEDURE work_with_data (num_years_in IN PLS_INTEGER)
IS
BEGIN
   IF num_years_in > $$max_years THEN ...
END  work_with_data;
```

Even more valuable, I can use inquiry directives in places in my code where a variable is not allowed. Here are two examples:

```
DECLARE
   l_big_string VARCHAR2($$MAX_VARCHAR2_SIZE);

   l_default_app_err EXCEPTION;
   PRAGMA EXCEPTION_INIT (l_default_app_err, $$DEF_APP_ERR_CODE);
BEGIN
```

### The DBMS_DB_VERSION package

The DBMS_DB_VERSION built-in package offers a set of constants that give you absolute and relative information about the version of your installed database. The constants defined in the Oracle Database 11g Release 2 version of this package are shown in Table 24-1. With each new version of Oracle, two new relative constants are added, and the values returned by the VERSION and RELEASE constants are updated.

*Table 24-1. DBMS_DB _VERSION constants*

| Name of packaged constant | Description | Value in Oracle Database 11g Release 2 |
| --- | --- | --- |
| DBMS_DB_VERSION.VERSION | The database version number, as in 11 for Oracle Database 11g | 11 |
| DBMS_DB_VERSION.RELEASE | The database release number, as in 2 for Oracle Database 11g Release 2 | 2 |
| DBMS_DB_VERSION.VER_LE_9 | TRUE if the current version is less than or equal to Oracle9i Database | FALSE |
| DBMS_DB_VERSION.VER_LE_9_1 | TRUE if the current version is less than or equal to Oracle9i Database Release 1 | FALSE |
| DBMS_DB_VERSION.VER_LE_9_2 | TRUE if the current version is less than or equal to Oracle9i Database Release 2 | FALSE |
| DBMS_DB_VERSION.VER_LE_10 | TRUE if the current version is less than or equal to Oracle Database 10g | FALSE |

| Name of packaged constant | Description | Value in Oracle Database 11g Release 2 |
|---|---|---|
| DBMS_DB_VERSION.VER_LE_10_1 | TRUE if the current version is less than or equal to Oracle Database 10g Release 1 | FALSE |
| DBMS_DB_VERSION.VER_LE_10_2 | TRUE if the current version is less than or equal to Oracle Database 10g Release 2 | FALSE |
| DBMS_DB_VERSION.VER_LE_11_1 | TRUE if the current version is less than or equal to Oracle Database 11g Release 1 | FALSE |
| DBMS_DB_VERSION.VER_LE_11_2 | TRUE if the current version is less than or equal to Oracle Database 11g Release 2 | TRUE |

While this package was designed for use with conditional compilation, you can, of course, use it for your own purposes.

Interestingly, you can write expressions that include references to as-yet undefined constants in the DBMS_DB_VERSION package. As long as they are not evaluated, as in the case below, they will not cause any errors. Here is an example:

```
$IF DBMS_DB_VERSION.VER_LE_10_2
$THEN
   Use this code.
$ELSEIF DBMS_DB_VERSION.VER_LE_12
   This is a placeholder for future.
$END
```

### Setting compilation environment parameters

The following information (corresponding to the values in the USER_PLSQL_OBJECT_SETTINGS data dictionary view) is available via inquiry directives:

*$$PLSQL_DEBUG*
    Debug setting for this compilation unit

*$$PLSQL_OPTIMIZE_LEVEL*
    Optimization level for this compilation unit

*$$PLSQL_CODE_TYPE*
    Compilation mode for this compilation unit

*$$PLSQL_WARNINGS*
    Compilation warnings setting for this compilation unit

*$$NLS_LENGTH_SEMANTICS*
    Value set for the NLS length semantics

See the *cc_plsql_parameters.sql* file on the book's web site for a demonstration that uses each of these parameters.

### Referencing unit name and line number

Oracle implicitly defines two very useful inquiry directives for use in $IF and $ERROR directives:

*$$PLSQL_UNIT*
Name of the compilation unit in which the reference appears

*$$PLSQL_LINE*
Line number of the compilation unit where the reference appears

You can call two built-in functions, DBMS_UTILITY.FORMAT_CALL_STACK and DBMS_UTILITY.FORMAT_ERROR_BACKTRACE, to obtain current line numbers, but then you must also parse those strings to find the line number and program unit name. These inquiry directives provide the information more directly. Here is an example:

```
BEGIN
   IF l_balance < 10000
   THEN
      raise_error (
         err_name => 'BALANCE TOO LOW'
        ,failed_in => $$plsql_unit
        ,failed_on => $$plsql_line
      );
   END IF;
   ...
END;
```

Run *cc_line_unit.sql* to see a demonstration of using these last two directives.

Note that when $$PLSQL_UNIT is referenced inside a package, it will return the name of the package, not the name of the individual procedure or function within the package.

### Using the PLSQL_CCFLAGS parameter

Oracle offers a parameter, PLSQL_CCFLAGS, which you can use with conditional compilation. Essentially, it allows you to define name-value pairs, and the name can then be referenced as an inquiry directive in your conditional compilation logic. Here is an example:

```
ALTER SESSION SET PLSQL_CCFLAGS = 'use_debug:TRUE, trace_level:10';
```

The flag name can be set to any valid PL/SQL identifier, including reserved words and keywords (the identifier will be prefixed with $$, so there will be no confusion with normal PL/SQL code). The value assigned to the name must be one of the following: TRUE, FALSE, NULL, or a PLS_INTEGER literal.

The PLSQL_CCFLAGS value will be associated with each program that is then compiled in that session. If you want to keep those settings with the program, then future compilations with the ALTER...COMPILE command should include the REUSE SET-TINGS clause.

Because you can change the value of this parameter and then compile selected program units, you can easily define different sets of inquiry directives for different programs.

Note that you can refer to a flag that is *not* defined in PLSQL_CCFLAGS; this flag will evaluate to NULL. If you enable compile-time warnings, this reference to an undefined flag will cause the database to report a *PLW-06003: unknown inquiry directive* warning (unless the source code is wrapped).

## The $IF Directive

Use the selection directive, implemented through the $IF statement, to direct the conditional compilation step in the preprocessor. Here is the general syntax of this directive:

```
$IF Boolean-expression
$THEN
   code_fragment
[ $ELSEIF Boolean-expression
$THEN
   code_fragment]
[ $ELSE
   code_fragment]
$END
```

where *Boolean-expression* is a static expression (it can be evaluated at the time of compilation) that evaluates to TRUE, FALSE, or NULL. The *code_fragment* can be any set of PL/SQL statements, which will then be passed to the compiler for compilation, as directed by the expression evaluations.

Static expressions can be constructed from any of the following elements:

- Boolean, PLS_INTEGER, and NULL literals, plus combinations of these literals.
- Boolean, PLS_INTEGER, and VARCHAR2 static expressions.
- Inquiry directives: identifiers prefixed with $$. These directives can be provided by Oracle (e.g., $$PLSQL_OPTIMIZE_LEVEL; the full list is provided in the section "The Optimizing Compiler" on page 793 in Chapter 21) or set via the PLSQL_CCFLAGS compilation parameter (explained earlier in this chapter).
- Static constants defined in a PL/SQL package.
- Most comparison operations (>, <, =, <> are fine, but you cannot use an IN expression), logical Boolean operations such as AND and OR, concatenations of static character expressions, and tests for NULL.

A static expression may not contain calls to procedures or functions that require execution; they cannot be evaluated during compilation, and therefore will render invalid the expression within the $IF directive. You will get a compile error as follows:

---

```
PLS-00174: a static boolean expression must be used
```

Here are examples of static expressions in $IF directives :

- If the user-defined inquiry directive controlling debugging is not NULL, then initialize the debug subsystem:

```
$IF $$app_debug_level IS NOT NULL $THEN
    debug_pkg.initialize;
$END
```

- Check the value of a user-defined package constant along with the optimization level:

```
$IF $$PLSQL_OPTIMIZE_LEVEL = 2 AND appdef_pkg.long_compilation
$THEN
    $ERROR 'Do not use optimization level 2 for this program!' $END
$END
```

 String literals and concatenations of strings are allowed only in the $ER-ROR directive; they may not appear in the $IF directive.

## The $ERROR Directive

Use the $ERROR directive to cause the current compilation to fail and return the error message provided. The syntax of this directive is:

```
$ERROR VARCHAR2_expression $END
```

Suppose that I need to set the optimization level for a particular program unit to 1, so that compilation time will be improved. In the following example, I use the $$ inquiry directive to check the value of the optimization level from the compilation environment. I then raise an error with the $ERROR directive as necessary.

```
/* File on web: cc_opt_level_check.sql */
SQL> CREATE OR REPLACE PROCEDURE long_compilation
  2  IS
  3  BEGIN
  4  $IF $$plsql_optimize_level != 1
  5  $THEN
  6      $ERROR 'This program must be compiled with optimization level = 1' $END
  7  $END
  8      NULL;
  9  END long_compilation;
 10  /

Warning: Procedure created with compilation errors.

SQL> SHOW ERRORS
Errors for PROCEDURE LONG_COMPILATION:

LINE/COL ERROR
```

```
-------- --------------------------------------------------------------
6/4      PLS-00179: $ERROR: This program must be compiled with
         optimization level = 1
```

## Synchronizing Code with Packaged Constants

Use of packaged constants within a selection directive allows you to easily synchronize multiple program units around a specific conditional compilation setting. This is possible because Oracle's automatic dependency management is applied to selection directives. In other words, if program unit PROG contains a selection directive that references package PKG, then PROG is marked as dependent on PKG. When the specification of PKG is recompiled, all program units using the packaged constant are marked INVALID and must be recompiled.

Suppose I want to use conditional compilation to automatically include or exclude debugging and tracing logic in my code base. I define a package specification to hold the required constants:

```
/* File on web: cc_debug.pks */
PACKAGE cc_debug
IS
   debug_active CONSTANT BOOLEAN := TRUE;
   trace_level CONSTANT PLS_INTEGER := 10;
END cc_debug;
```

I then use these constants in procedure calc_totals:

```
PROCEDURE calc_totals
IS
BEGIN
$IF cc_debug.debug_active AND cc_debug.trace_level > 5 $THEN
   log_info (...);
$END
   ...
END calc_totals;
```

During development, the debug_active constant is initialized to TRUE. When it is time to move the code to production, I change the flag to FALSE and recompile the package. The calc_totals program and all other programs with similar selection directives are marked INVALID and must then be recompiled.

## Program-Specific Settings with Inquiry Directives

Packaged constants are useful for coordinating settings across multiple program units. Inquiry directives, drawn from the compilation settings of individual programs, are a better fit when you need different settings applied to different programs.

Once you have compiled a program with a particular set of values, it will retain those values until the next compilation (from either a file or a simple recompilation using the ALTER...COMPILE command). Furthermore, a program is guaranteed to be recompiled with the same postprocessed source as was selected at the time of the *previous* compilation if all of the following conditions are TRUE:

- None of the conditional compilation directives refer to package constants. Instead, they rely only on inquiry directives.

- When the program is recompiled, the REUSE SETTINGS clause is used *and* the PLSQL_CCFLAGS parameter is not included in the ALTER...COMPILE command.

This capability is demonstrated by the *cc_reuse_settings.sql* script, whose output is shown below. I first set the value of app_debug to TRUE and then compile a program with that setting, A query against USER_PLSQL_OBJECT_SETTINGS shows that this value is now associated with the program unit:

```
/* File on web: cc_reuse_settings.sql */

SQL> ALTER SESSION SET plsql_ccflags = 'app_debug:TRUE';

SQL> CREATE OR REPLACE PROCEDURE test_ccflags
  2  IS
  3  BEGIN
  4     NULL;
  5  END test_ccflags;
  6  /

SQL> SELECT name, plsql_ccflags
  2    FROM user_plsql_object_settings
  3   WHERE NAME LIKE '%CCFLAGS%';

NAME                          PLSQL_CCFLAGS
----------------------------  ----------------------------
TEST_CCFLAGS                  app_debug:TRUE
```

I now alter the session, setting $$app_debug to evaluate to FALSE. I compile a new program with this setting:

```
SQL> ALTER SESSION SET plsql_ccflags = 'app_debug:FALSE';

SQL> CREATE OR REPLACE PROCEDURE test_ccflags_new
  2  IS
  3  BEGIN
  4     NULL;
  5  END test_ccflags_new;
  6/
```

Then I recompile my existing program with REUSE SETTINGS:

```
SQL> ALTER  PROCEDURE test_ccflags COMPILE REUSE SETTINGS;
```

A query against the data dictionary view now reveals that my settings are different for each program:

```
SQL> SELECT name, plsql_ccflags
  2    FROM user_plsql_object_settings
```

```
  3  WHERE NAME LIKE '%CCFLAGS%';

NAME                             PLSQL_CCFLAGS
-------------------------------  -----------------------------
TEST_CCFLAGS                     app_debug:TRUE
TEST_CCFLAGS_NEW                 app_debug:FALSE
```

## Working with Postprocessed Code

You can use the DBMS_PREPROCESSOR package to display or retrieve the source text of your program in its postprocessed form. DBMS_PREPROCESSOR offers two programs, overloaded to allow you to specify the object of interest in various ways, as well as to work with individual strings and collections:

*DBMS_PREPROCESSOR.PRINT_POST_PROCESSED_SOURCE*
Retrieves the postprocessed source and then displays it with the function DBMS_OUTPUT.PUTLINE.

*DBMS_PREPROCESSOR.GET_POST_PROCESSED_SOURCE*
Returns the postprocessed source as either a single string or a collection of strings.

When working with the collection version of either of these programs, you will need to declare that collection based on the following package-defined collection:

```
TYPE DBMS_PREPROCESSOR.source_lines_t IS TABLE OF VARCHAR2(32767)
   INDEX BY BINARY_INTEGER;
```

The following sequence demonstrates the capability of these programs. I compile a very small program with a selection directive based on the optimization level. I then display the postprocessed code, and it shows the correct branch of the $IF statement.

```
/* File on web: cc_postprocessor.sql
PROCEDURE post_processed
IS
BEGIN
$IF $$PLSQL_OPTIMIZE_LEVEL = 1
$THEN
   -- Slow and easy
  NULL;
$ELSE
   -- Fast and modern and easy
  NULL;
$END
END post_processed;


SQL> BEGIN
  2      DBMS_PREPROCESSOR.PRINT_POST_PROCESSED_SOURCE (
  3         'PROCEDURE', USER, 'POST_PROCESSED');
  4  END;
  5  /

PROCEDURE post_processed
IS
```

```
BEGIN
-- Fast and modern and easy
NULL;
END post_processed;
```

In the following block, I use the "get" function to retrieve the postprocessed code, and then display it using DBMS_OUTPUT.PUT_LINE:

```
DECLARE
   l_postproc_code   DBMS_PREPROCESSOR.SOURCE_LINES_T;
   l_row             PLS_INTEGER;
BEGIN
   l_postproc_code :=
      DBMS_PREPROCESSOR.GET_POST_PROCESSED_SOURCE (
         'PROCEDURE', USER, 'POST_PROCESSED');
   l_row := l_postproc_code.FIRST;

   WHILE (l_row IS NOT NULL)
   LOOP
      DBMS_OUTPUT.put_line (  LPAD (l_row, 3)
                           || ' - '
                           || rtrim ( l_postproc_code (l_row),chr(10))
                           );
      l_row := l_postproc_code.NEXT (l_row);
   END LOOP;
END;
```

Conditional compilation opens up all sorts of possibilities for PL/SQL developers and application administrators. And its usefulness only increases as new versions of the Oracle database are released and the DBMS_DB_VERSION constants can be put to full use, allowing us to take additional advantage of each version's unique PL/SQL features.

# PL/SQL and Database Instance Memory

By economizing on its use of machine resources such as memory and CPU, an Oracle database can support tens of thousands of simultaneous users on a single database. The databases's memory management techniques have become quite sophisticated over the years, and correspondingly difficult to understand. It's true that features such as Automatic Shared Memory Management ease the burden a bit for Oracle Database 10g and later, but administrators of busy databases still need a thorough knowledge of memory management, and advanced PL/SQL programmers should also have a good understanding of this topic. It's also true that the automation features introduced in recent versions ease the burden on DBAs considerably, but PL/SQL developers still risk wasting memory unless they understand how memory is used for cursors and package variables in particular.

## PGA, UGA, and CGA

When a client program such as SQL*Plus or SQL Developer interacts with the database, the database assigns a server process to service its calls. Each server process uses a memory area known as the Process Global Area (PGA) for its private data. Data needed only during a single database call is placed in an area of the PGA known as the Call Global Area (CGA). Data that needs to be retained between a session's database calls, like package variables and private SQL areas, is placed in the User Global Area (UGA).

The location of the UGA in memory depends on whether the session has connected to the database using a *dedicated* server or *shared* servers.

*Dedicated server*
> The database spawns a dedicated server process for each session. This is appropriate for workloads that are either intensive or involve long-running database calls. The UGA is placed in the PGA because no other server process will need to access it.

*Shared server*
> Database calls are queued to a group of shared server processes that can service calls on behalf of any session. This is appropriate if there are many hundreds of concurrent sessions making short calls with a lot of intervening idle time. The UGA is placed in the SGA so that it can be accessed by any of the shared server processes.

Figure 24-6 shows a simplified representation of these two different arrangements.[5]

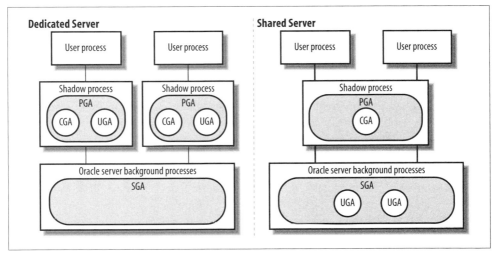

*Figure 24-6. Database instance memory and process architecture in dedicated vs. shared server configurations*

---

5. The figure doesn't show the shared server's dispatchers and request/response queues, which are somewhat ancillary to this discussion.

---

The total size of the PGA can vary quite a bit based on what kinds of operations your application requires the server to perform. For example, a SQL DML statement that requires a large sort can consume a lot of CGA memory; a PL/SQL package that populates a large PL/SQL collection in a package-level variable requires large amounts of UGA memory.

If your application uses shared servers, user processes may have to wait in a queue to be serviced. If any of your user processes invoke long-running PL/SQL blocks or SQL statements, the DBA may need to either configure the server with a greater number of shared processes or assign to those sessions a dedicated server.

Let's next consider what memory looks like to an individual running program.

## Cursors, Memory, and More

You may have written hundreds of programs that declare, open, fetch from, and close cursors. It's impossible to execute SQL or PL/SQL without cursors, and statements often automatically make recursive calls that open more cursors. Because every cursor, whether implicit or explicit, requires an allocation of memory on the database server, tuning the database sometimes involves reducing the number of cursors required by an application.

> Although this section is devoted to memory, keep in mind that memory is only one aspect of tuning the database; you may actually improve overall performance by increasing the number of cursors to avoid soft parses.

The database assigns cursors to anonymous PL/SQL blocks in much the same way that it assigns cursors to SQL statements. For example, on the first parse call from a session, the database opens an area in UGA memory (the "private SQL area") where it will put information specific to the run.

It turns out that some of the server-side data structures associated with cursors reside in the UGA, and some in the CGA. For example, because SELECT statements identify rows that need to be available during multiple fetches, the database allocates a work area for the cursor from UGA memory (SELECT statements also allocate a work area in the CGA). Because DML statements complete in a single call, the database allocates their work area only from CGA memory. Similarly, when executing PL/SQL, the database allocates UGA memory to store state information, and uses CGA for other processing.

When executing a SQL statement or a PL/SQL block, the server first looks in the library cache to see if it can find a reusable parsed representation of it. If it does find such a shared PL/SQL area, the runtime engine establishes an association between the private SQL area and the shared SQL area. The shared cursor has to be found or built before the private SQL area can be allocated. The private SQL area memory requirements are part of what is determined during compilation and cached in the shared cursor. If no reusable shared area exists, the database will "hard parse" the statement or the block. (As an aside, note that the database also prepares and caches a simple execution plan for anonymous PL/SQL blocks, which consists of calling the PL/SQL engine to interpret the bytecode.)

The database interprets the simplest of PL/SQL blocks—those that call no subprograms and include no embedded SQL statements—using only the memory allocated for its primary cursor. If your PL/SQL program includes SQL or PL/SQL calls, though, the database requires additional private SQL areas in the UGA. PL/SQL manages these on behalf of your application.

This brings us to another important fact about cursors: there are two ways a cursor can be closed. A *soft-closed* cursor is one that you can no longer use in your application without reopening it. This is what you get when you close a cursor using a statement such as this one:

```
CLOSE cursor_name;
```

or even when an implicit cursor closes automatically. However, PL/SQL does not immediately free the session memory associated with this cursor. Instead, it caches cursors to avoid a soft parse should the cursor be opened again, as often happens. You will see, if you look in the V$OPEN_CURSOR view, that the CLOSE alone does not reduce the count of this session's open cursors.

It turns out that PL/SQL maintains its own "session cursor cache"; that is, it decides when to close a cursor for good. This cache can hold a maximum number of cursors, as specified by the OPEN_CURSORS database initialization parameter. A least-recently-used (LRU) algorithm determines which of the soft-closed cursors need to be *hard-closed* and hence deallocated.

However, PL/SQL's internal algorithm works optimally only if your programs close their cursors immediately after they are through fetching with them. So remember:

> If you explicitly open a cursor, you should explicitly close it as soon as you are through using it (but not sooner).

There are a few ways that the database allows PL/SQL programmers to intervene in the default behavior. One way you can close all of your session cursors, of course, is to terminate the session! Less drastic ways include:

- Reset the package state, as discussed at the end of the later section "Large collections in PL/SQL" on page 1018.
- Use DBMS_SQL to gain explicit control over low-level cursor behavior. On the whole, though, memory gains provided by this approach are unlikely to offset the corresponding performance costs and programming challenges.

## Tips on Reducing Memory Use

Armed with a bit of theory, let's review some practical tips you can use in your day-to-day programming. Also check out the more general program tuning hints in Chapter 21. In addition, it helps to be able to *measure* the amount of memory your session is using at any given point of time in your application code. You can do this by querying the contents of various V$ views. The plsql_memory package (defined in the *plsql_memory.pkg* file on the book's web site) will help you do this.

### Statement sharing

The database can share the source and compiled versions of SQL statements and anonymous blocks, even if they are submitted from different sessions by different users. The optimizer determines the execution plan at parse time, so factors that affect the parse (including optimizer settings) will affect SQL statement sharing. For sharing to happen, certain conditions must be true:

1. Variable data values must be supplied via bind variables rather than literals so that the text of the statements will not differ. Bind variables themselves must match in name and datatype.

2. The letter case and formatting conventions of the source code must match exactly. If you are executing the same programs, this will happen automatically. Ad hoc statements may not match those in programs exactly.

3. References to database objects must resolve to the same underlying object.

4. For SQL, database parameters influencing the SQL optimizer must match. For example, the invoking sessions must be using the same "optimizer goal" (ALL_ROWS versus FIRST_ROWS).

5. The invoking sessions must be using the same language (Globalization Support, formerly National Language Support, or NLS) environment.

I'm not going to talk much about the SQL-specific rules; specific reasons for nonsharing of SQL statements that otherwise pass these rules can be found in the view V$SQL_SHARED_CURSOR. For now, let's explore the impact of the first three rules on your PL/SQL programs.

Rule #1, regarding bind variables, is so critical that it has a later section devoted it to it.

Rule #2, matching letter case and formatting, is a well-known condition to sharing statements. The text has to match because the database computes a hash value from its source text with which to locate and lock an object in the library cache.

Despite the fact that PL/SQL is normally a case-independent language, the block:

```
BEGIN NULL; END;
```

does not match:

```
begin null; end;
```

nor does it match:

```
BEGIN NULL;   END;
```

These statements will each hash to a different value and are inherently different SQL statements—they are logically the same but physically different. However, if all your anonymous blocks are short, and all your "real programs" are in stored code such as packages, there is much less chance of inadvertently disabling code sharing. The tip here is:

> Centralize your SQL and PL/SQL code in stored programs. Anonymous blocks should be as short as possible, generally consisting of a single call to a stored program.

In addition, an extension of this tip applies to SQL:

> To maximize the sharing of SQL statements, put SQL into programs. Then call these programs rather than write the SQL you need in each block.

I've always felt that trying to force statement sharing by adopting strict formatting conventions for SQL statements was just too impractical; it's much easier to put the SQL into a callable program.

Moving on, Rule #3 says that database object references (to tables, procedures, etc.) must resolve to the same underlying object. Say that Scott and I are connected to the same database, and we both run a block that goes like this:

```
BEGIN
   XYZ;
END;
```

The database's decision about whether to share the cached form of this anonymous block boils down to whether the name "xyz" refers to the same underlying stored procedure. If Scott has a synonym xyz that points to my copy of the procedure, then the database will share this anonymous block; if Scott and I own independent copies of xyz, the database will not share this anonymous block. So even if the two copies of the xyz procedure are line-by-line identical, the database caches these as different objects. The database also caches identical triggers on different tables as different objects. That leads to the following tip:

> Avoid proliferating copies of tables and programs in different accounts unless you have a good reason.

How far should you go with sharing of code at the application level? The conventional wisdom holds that you should identify and extract code that is common to multiple programs (especially triggers) and incorporate it by call rather than by duplicating it. In other words, set up one database account to own the PL/SQL programs, and grant EXECUTE privilege to any other users who need it. While sharing code in this manner is an excellent practice for code maintainability, it is not likely to save any memory. In fact, every caller has to instantiate the additional object at a cost of typically several KB per session. Of course, this won't be a huge burden unless you have enormous numbers of users.

There is another caveat on the conventional wisdom, and it applies if you are running in a high concurrency environment—that is, many users simultaneously executing the same PL/SQL program. Whenever common code is called, a "library cache latch" is needed to establish and then release a pin on the object. In high concurrency environments, this can lead to latch contention. In such cases, duplicating the code wherever it is needed may be preferred because doing so will avoid extra latching for the additional object and reduce the risk of poor performance due to latch contention.

But now, let's go back to Rule #1: use bind variables.

### Bind variables

In an Oracle database, a *bind variable* is an input variable to a statement whose value is passed by the caller's execution environment. Bind variables are especially significant to the sharing of SQL statements, regardless of whether the statements are submitted by PL/SQL, Java, SQL*Plus, or OCI. Application developers using virtually any environment should understand and use bind variables. Bind variables allow an application to scale, help prevent code injection, and allow SQL statement sharing.

A requirement for two different statements to be considered identical is that any bind variables must themselves match in name, datatype, and maximum length. So for example, the SQL statements given below do *not* match:

```
SELECT col FROM tab1 WHERE col = :bind1;
SELECT col FROM tab1 WHERE col = :bind_1;
```

But this requirement applies to the text of the statement as seen by the SQL engine. As mentioned much earlier in this chapter, PL/SQL rewrites your static SQL statements before SQL ever sees them! Here's an example:

```
FUNCTION plsql_bookcount (author IN VARCHAR2)
   RETURN NUMBER
IS
   titlepattern VARCHAR2(10) := '%PL/SQL%';
   lcount NUMBER;
BEGIN
   SELECT COUNT(*) INTO lcount
     FROM books
    WHERE title LIKE titlepattern
      AND author = plsql_bookcount.author;
   RETURN lcount;
END;
```

After executing plsql_bookcount, the V$SQLAREA view in Oracle Database 11g reveals that PL/SQL has rewritten the query as:

```
SELECT COUNT(*) FROM BOOKS WHERE TITLE LIKE :B2 AND AUTHOR = :B1
```

The parameter "author" and the local variable "titlepattern" have been replaced by the bind variables :B1 and :B2. This implies that, in static SQL, you don't need to worry about matching bind variable names; PL/SQL replaces your variable name with a generated bind variable name.

This automatic introduction of bind variables in PL/SQL applies to program variables that you use in the WHERE and VALUES clauses of static INSERT, UPDATE, MERGE, DELETE, and of course SELECT statements.

In additional experiments, I have found that changing the PL/SQL variable to have a different maximum length did not result in an additional statement in the SQL area, but that changing the variable's datatype can add a statement. But don't take my word for it; privileges permitting, you can run your own experiments to determine whether SQL statements are being shared in the way you think they are. Look in V$SQLAREA. For the code listed above (assuming that I am the only person running this particular code):

```
SELECT executions, sql_text FROM v$sqlarea
WHERE sql_text like 'SELECT COUNT(*) FROM BOOKS%';
/

EXECUTIONS SQL_TEXT
---------- --------------------------------------------------------
         1 SELECT COUNT(*) FROM BOOKS WHERE TITLE LIKE :B2
           AND AUTHOR = :B1
```

You might say, well, if PL/SQL is that smart, I don't need to worry about bind variables then, do I? Hang on there: even though PL/SQL automatically binds program variables into *static* SQL statements, this feature is not automatic when using *dynamic* SQL. Sloppy programming can easily result in statements getting built with literal values. For example:

```
FUNCTION count_recent_records (tablename_in IN VARCHAR2,
   since_in IN VARCHAR2)
RETURN PLS_INTEGER
AS
   count_l PLS_INTEGER;
BEGIN
   EXECUTE IMMEDIATE 'SELECT COUNT(*) FROM '
      || DBMS_ASSERT.SIMPLE_SQL_NAME(tablename_in)
      || ' WHERE lastupdate > TO_DATE('
      || DBMS_ASSERT.ENQUOTE_LITERAL(since_in)
      || ', ''YYYYMMDD'')'
      INTO count_l;
   RETURN count_l;
END;
```

This causes the dynamic construction of statements such as:

```
SELECT COUNT(*) FROM tabname WHERE lastupdate > TO_DATE('20090315','YYYYMMDD')
```

Repeated invocation with different since_in arguments can result in a lot of statements that are unlikely to be shared. For example:

```
SELECT COUNT(*) FROM tabname WHERE lastupdate > TO_DATE('20090105','YYYYMMDD')
SELECT COUNT(*) FROM tabname WHERE lastupdate > TO_DATE('20080704','YYYYMMDD')
SELECT COUNT(*) FROM tabname WHERE lastupdate > TO_DATE('20090101','YYYYMMDD')
```

This is wasteful of memory and other server resources.

A bind-variable version of this program would be:

```
FUNCTION count_recent_records (tablename_in IN VARCHAR2,
   since_in IN VARCHAR2)
RETURN PLS_INTEGER
AS
   count_l PLS_INTEGER;
BEGIN
   EXECUTE IMMEDIATE 'SELECT COUNT(*) FROM '
      || DBMS_ASSERT.SIMPLE_SQL_NAME(tablename_in)
      || ' WHERE lastupdate > :thedate'
      INTO count_l
      USING TO_DATE(since_in,'YYYYMMDD');
   RETURN count_l;
END;
```

which results in statements that look like this to the SQL compiler:

```
SELECT COUNT(*) FROM tabname WHERE lastupdate > :thedate
```

Not only is the second version prettier and easier to follow, but it will also perform much better over repeated invocations with the same tablename_in but with different since_in arguments.

The database offers the initialization parameter CURSOR_SHARING, which *may* provide some benefits to applications with a lot of non-bind-variable SQL. By setting this parameter to FORCE or to SIMILAR, you can ask the database to replace some or all SQL literals with bind variables at runtime, thus avoiding some of the hard-parse overhead. Unfortunately, this is one of those "sounds better in theory than in practice" features.

Even if you can derive some performance benefits from using CURSOR_SHARING, you should view it *only as a stopgap measure*. It's not nearly as efficient as using true bind variables and can have a number of unexpected and undesirable side effects. If you must use this feature with certain pathological (often third-party) software, do so only until the code can be modified to use true bind variables.

On the other hand, if you consistently exercise the small amount of discipline required to use true bind variables in your dynamic SQL, you will be rewarded, perhaps richly so, at runtime. Just remember to keep your CURSOR_SHARING parameter set to its default value of EXACT.

### Packaging to improve memory use and performance

When retrieving the bytecode of a stored PL/SQL program, the database reads the entire program. This rule applies not only to procedures and functions, but also to packages. In other words, you can't get the database to retrieve only a part of a package; the first time any session uses some element of a package, even just a single package variable, the database loads the compiled code for the entire package into the library cache. Having fewer large package instantiations requires less memory (and disk) overhead than more smaller instantiations. It also minimizes the number of pins taken and released, which is very important in high concurrency applications. So a logical grouping of package elements is not just a good design idea, it will also help your system's performance.

 Because the database reads an entire package into memory at once, design each of your packages with functionally related components that are likely to be invoked together.

### Large collections in PL/SQL

Sharing is a wonderful thing, but of course not everything can be shared at runtime. Even when two or more users are executing the same program owned by the same schema, each session has its own private memory area, which holds run-specific data such as the value of local or package variables, constants, and cursors. It wouldn't make much sense to try to share values that are specific to a given session.

Large collections are a case in point (Chapter 12 describes collections in detail). Imagine that I declare a PL/SQL associative array as follows:

```
DECLARE
    TYPE number_tab_t IS TABLE OF NUMBER INDEX BY PLS_INTEGER;
    number_tab number_tab_t;
    empty_tab number_tab_t;
```

Now I create a bunch of elements in this array:

```
FOR i IN 1..100000
LOOP
    number_tab(i) := i;
END LOOP;
```

The database has to put all of those elements somewhere. Following the rules discussed earlier, memory for this array will come from the UGA in the case of package-level data, or the CGA in the case of data in anonymous blocks or top-level procedures or functions. Either way, it's easy to see that manipulating large collections can require very large amounts of memory.

You may wonder how you can get that memory back once a program is through with it. This is a case where the natural and easy thing to do will help quite a bit. You can use one of these two forms:

```
number_tab.DELETE;
```

or:

```
number_tab := empty_tab;
```

Using either of these statements will cause the database to free the memory into its originating free list. That is, package-level memory frees into the session state heap, call-level memory frees into the CGA, and the CGA is freed into the PGA at the end of the call. The same thing happens when the collection passes out of scope; if you declare and use the collection only in a standalone procedure, the database realizes that you don't need it any more after the procedure finishes executing. Either way, though, this memory is not available to other sessions, nor is it available to the current session for CGA memory requirements. So, if a subsequent DML operation requires a large sort, you could wind up with some huge memory requirements. Not until the session ends will the database release this memory to its parent heap.

I should point out that it is no great hardship for a virtual memory operating system with plenty of paging/swap space if processes retain large amounts of inactive virtual memory in their address space. This inactive memory consumes only paging space, not real memory. There may be times, however, when you don't want to fill up paging space, and you would prefer that the database release the memory. For those times, the database supplies an on-demand "garbage collection" procedure. The syntax is simply:

```
DBMS_SESSION.FREE_UNUSED_USER_MEMORY;
```

This built-in procedure will find most of the UGA memory that is no longer in use by any program variables and release it back to the parent memory heap—the PGA in the case of dedicated server, or the SGA in the case of shared server.

I have run quite a few test cases to determine the effect of running garbage collection in different scenarios: for example, associative arrays versus nested tables, shared server versus dedicated server, and anonymous blocks versus package data. The conclusions and tips that are described next apply to using large collections.

- Merely assigning a NULL to a nested table or VARRAY will fail to mark its memory as unused. Instead, you can do one of three things: use the method *collection*.DELETE, assign a null but initialized collection to it, or wait for it to go out of scope.

- If you need to release memory to the parent heap, use DBMS_SESSION.FREE_UNUSED_USER_MEMORY when your program has

populated one or more large PL/SQL tables, marked them as unused, and is unlikely to need further large memory allocations for similar operations.

- Shared server mode can be more prone than dedicated server mode to memory-
  shortage errors. This is because the UGA is drawn from the SGA, which is limited
  in size. As discussed in the later section "What to Do if You Run Out of Memory" on page 1024, you may get an ORA-04031 error.

- If you must use shared server connections, you cannot release the memory occu-
  - pied by PL/SQL tables unless the table is declared at the package level.

As a practical matter, for a collection of NUMBER elements, there seems to be no
difference in storage required to store NULL elements versus, say, 38-digit number
elements. However, the database does seem to allocate memory for VARCHAR2 elements dynamically if the elements are declared larger than VARCHAR2(30).

When populating an associative array in dedicated server mode, a million-element associative array of NUMBERs occupies about 38 MB; even if the million elements are
just Booleans, almost 15 MB of memory is required. Multiply that by even 100 users,
and you're talking some big numbers, especially if you don't want the operating system
to start paging this memory out to disk.

If you'd like to discover for yourself how much UGA and PGA your current session
uses, you can run a query like the following:

```
SELECT n.name, ROUND(m.value/1024) kbytes
  FROM V$STATNAME n, V$MYSTAT m
 WHERE n.statistic# = m.statistic#
   AND n.name LIKE 'session%memory%'
```

(You'll need nondefault privileges to read the two V$ views in this query.) This will
show you the "current" and the "max" memory usage thus far in your session.

Incidentally, if you want to clear out the memory used by packaged collections but
don't want to terminate the session (for example, you are running scripts that test
memory usage), you can use one of these built-ins:

DBMS_SESSION.RESET_PACKAGE
> Frees all memory allocated to package state. This has the effect of resetting *all*
> package variables to their default values. For packages, this built-in goes beyond
> what FREE_UNUSED_USER_MEMORY does because RESET_PACKAGE
> doesn't care whether the memory is in use or not.

DBMS_SESSION.MODIFY_PACKAGE_STATE *(action_flag IN PLS_INTEGER)*
> You can supply one of two constants as the *action flag*:
> DBMS_SESSION.free_all_resources or DBMS_SESSION.reinitialize. The first has
> the same effect as using the RESET_PACKAGE procedure. Supplying the latter
> constant resets state variables to their defaults but doesn't actually free and recreate
> the package instantiation from scratch; also, it only soft-closes open cursors and

does not flush the cursor cache. If these behaviors are acceptable in your application, use the second constant because it will perform better than a complete reset.

### BULK COLLECT...LIMIT operations

Bulk binds are a great way to process data efficiently, but you should take care to limit your memory consumption and not let your collections grow too large. When you BULK COLLECT into a collection, the default is to fetch all the rows into the collection. When you have a lot of data, this results in a very large collection. That's where the LIMIT clause comes into play. It allows you to limit your memory consumption and make your programs faster.

When I benchmarked the LIMIT clause, I expected it to use less memory, but was surprised to find that it ran faster too. Here is the example benchmark, using a test table containing a million rows. To get good numbers for comparison, I ran it once to warm up the cache, reconnected to zero out my memory consumption, and then ran it a second time to compare. I've included calls to the plsql_memory package (see the *plsql_memory.pkg* file on the book's web site) to report on memory use:

```
/* File on web: LimitBulkCollect.sql */
DECLARE
  -- set up the collections
  TYPE numtab  IS TABLE OF NUMBER         INDEX BY PLS_INTEGER;
  TYPE nametab IS TABLE OF VARCHAR2(4000) INDEX BY PLS_INTEGER;
  TYPE tstab   IS TABLE OF TIMESTAMP      INDEX BY PLS_INTEGER;
  CURSOR test_c IS
    SELECT hi_card_nbr,hi_card_str ,hi_card_ts
    FROM data_test
  ;
  nbrs    numtab;
  txt     nametab;
  tstamps tstab;
  counter number;
  strt    number;
  fnsh    number;
BEGIN
  plsql_memory.start_analysis;   -- initialize memory reporting
  strt := dbms_utility.get_time; -- save starting time
  OPEN test_c;
  LOOP
    FETCH test_c BULK COLLECT INTO nbrs,txt,tstamps LIMIT 10000;
    EXIT WHEN nbrs.COUNT = 0;
    FOR i IN 1..nbrs.COUNT LOOP
      counter := counter + i;    -- do somthing with the data
    END LOOP;
  END LOOP;
  plsql_memory.show_memory_usage;
  CLOSE test_c;
  fnsh := dbms_utility.get_time;
  -- convert the centi-seconds from get_time to milliseconds
  DBMS_OUTPUT.PUT_LINE('Run time = '||(fnsh-strt)*10||' ms');
END;
```

```
/

Change in UGA memory: 0 (Current = 1366000)
Change in PGA memory: 1310720 (Current = 3555712)
Run time = 1530 ms
```

You can see that with a limit of 10,000 rows, I grew the PGA by 1,310,720 bytes. When I show the memory again after the PL/SQL block completes, you see that much (but not all) of this memory has been released:

```
-- report on memory again, after the program completes
EXEC  plsql_memory.show_memory_usage;

Change in UGA memory: 0 (Current = 1366000)
Change in PGA memory: -458752 (Current = 1786240)
```

Let's run it again, without the LIMIT clause, so I read the full complement of rows in one big slurp.

```
DECLARE
   -- set up the collections
   TYPE numtab  IS TABLE OF NUMBER          INDEX BY PLS_INTEGER;
   TYPE nametab IS TABLE OF VARCHAR2(4000)  INDEX BY PLS_INTEGER;
   TYPE tstab   IS TABLE OF TIMESTAMP       INDEX BY PLS_INTEGER;
   CURSOR test_c IS
     SELECT hi_card_nbr,hi_card_str ,hi_card_ts
     FROM data_test
   ;
   nbrs     numtab;
   txt      nametab;
   tstamps  tstab;
   counter  number;
   strt     number;
   fnsh     number;
BEGIN
   plsql_memory.start_analysis;   -- initialize memory reporting
   strt :=d bms_utility.get_time;  -- save starting time
   OPEN test_c;
   LOOP
     FETCH test_c BULK COLLECT INTO nbrs,txt,tstamps;
     EXIT WHEN nbrs.COUNT = 0;
     FOR i IN 1..nbrs.COUNT LOOP
       counter := counter + i;    -- do somthing with the data
     END LOOP;
   END LOOP;
   plsql_memory.show_memory_usage;
   CLOSE test_c;
   fnsh :=d bms_utility.get_time;
   -- convert the centi-seconds from get_time to milliseconds
   DBMS_OUTPUT.PUT_LINE ('Run time = '||(fnsh-strt)*10||' ms');
END;
/

Change in UGA memory: 0 (Current = 1366000)
Change in PGA memory: 134479872 (Current = 136724864)
Run time = 1940 ms
```

```
exec plsql_memory.show_memory_usage;

Change in UGA memory: 65464 (Current = 1431464)
Change in PGA memory: -458752 (Current = 1786240)
```

It is clear that the LIMIT reduced the memory usage from 131,328 KB to 1,280 KB. Wow! But the surprise was the 21% speedup from 1940 ms to 1530 ms—all from using less memory!

## Preservation of state

The database normally maintains the state of package-level constants, cursors, and variables in your UGA for as long as your session is running. Contrast this behavior with the variables instantiated in the declaration section of a standalone module. The scope of those variables is restricted to the module. When the module terminates, the memory and values associated with those variables are released. They are no more.

In addition to disconnecting, several other things can cause a package to obliterate its state:

- Someone recompiles the program, or the database invalidates it, as discussed earlier.
- The DBMS_SESSION.RESET_PACKAGE built-in procedure executes in your session.
- You include the SERIALLY_REUSABLE pragma (see Chapter 18) in your program, which causes the database to put the private SQL area into the SGA for reuse by other sessions. State will be retained only for the duration of the call, rather than for the entire session.[6]
- You are using the web gateway in the default mode that, by default, does not maintain persistent database sessions for each client.

Subject to these limitations, package data structures can act as "globals" within the PL/SQL environment. That is, they provide a way for different PL/SQL programs running in the same session to exchange data.

From an application design perspective, there are two types of global data: public and private:

*Public*

A data structure declared in the specification of a package is a global public data structure. Any calling program or user with the EXECUTE privilege has access to the data. Programs can assign even meaningless values to package variables not marked CONSTANT. Public global data is the proverbial "loose cannon" of

---

6. By the way, instances with many concurrent sessions can use this to save a *lot* of memory.

programming: convenient to declare but tempting to overuse, leading to a greater risk of unstructured code that is susceptible to ugly side effects.

The specification of a module should give you all the information you need to call and use that module. If the program reads and/or writes global data structures, you cannot tell this from the module specification; you cannot be sure of what is happening in your application and which program changes what data. It is always preferable to pass data as parameters in and out of modules. That way, the reliance on those data structures is documented in the specification and can be accounted for by the developer. In my own code, I try to limit global public data to those values that can truly be made CONSTANT.

*Private*

Not so problematic are global but private data structures (also called *package-level data*) that you might declare in the body of the package. Because it does not appear in the specification, this data cannot be referenced from outside the package—only from within the package, by other package elements.

 Packaged data items are global only within a single database session or connection. Package data is not shared across sessions. If you need to share data between different database sessions, there are other tools at your disposal, including the DBMS_PIPE package, Oracle Advanced Queuing, and the UTL_TCP package...not to mention database tables!

## What to Do if You Run Out of Memory

Let's say you're cruising along with your database running just fine, with lots of PL/SQL and SQL statements happily zipping by, and then it strikes: *ORA-04031: unable to allocate* n *bytes of shared memory*. This error is more common in shared server mode, which caps a shared server's UGA memory. In dedicated server mode, the database can usually grab more virtual memory from the operating system, but you may still encounter the analogous error *ORA-04030: out of process memory when trying to allocate* n *bytes*.

There are several ways to correct this condition. If you're the application developer, you can attempt to reduce your use of shared memory. Steps you could take include (more or less in order):

1. Modify code to ensure that the maximum number of SQL statements get shared.
2. Reduce the size or number of in-memory collections.
3. Reduce the amount of application code in memory.
4. Tune the database-wide settings and/or buy more server memory.

Steps 1 and 2 have already been covered; let's take a look at Step 3. How can you assess the size of your source code once it's loaded into memory? And how can you reduce it?

Before running a PL/SQL program, the database must load all of its bytecode into memory. You can see how much space a program object actually occupies in the shared pool by having your DBA run the built-in procedure DBMS_SHARED_POOL.SIZES, which lists all objects over a given size.

 Starting with Oracle Database 10g, the DBMS_SHARED_POOL package age is not installed by default; Oracle moved it into the Statspack set of tools, which your DBA can install by running the *spcreate.sql* script in *rdbms/admin*.

Here is an example that looks at the memory required by objects in the shared pool immediately after database startup:[7]

```
SQL> SET SERVEROUTPUT ON SIZE 1000000
SQL> EXEC DBMS_SHARED_POOL.sizes(minsize => 125)

SIZE(K) KEPT    NAME
------- ------  ----------------------------------------------------------------
433             SYS.STANDARD              (PACKAGE)
364             SYS.DBMS_RCVMAN           (PACKAGE BODY)
249             SYSMAN.MGMT_JOB_ENGINE    (PACKAGE BODY)
224             SYS.DBMS_RCVMAN           (PACKAGE)
221             SYS.DBMS_STATS_INTERNAL   (PACKAGE)
220             SYS.DBMS_BACKUP_RESTORE   (PACKAGE)
125             MERGE INTO cache_stats_1$ D USING (select * from table(dbms_sta
ts_internal.format_cache_rows(CURSOR((select dataobj# o, st
atistic# stat, nvl(value, 0) val from gv$segstat where stat
istic# in (0, 3, 5) and obj# > 0 and inst_id = 1) union all
(select obj# o, 7 stat,nvl(sum(num_buf), 0) val from x$kcb
oqh x where inst_id = 1 group by obj#) order by o))) wh
(20B5C934,3478682418)     (CURSOR)
```

The "minsize => 125" means "show only objects that are 125K or larger." This output shows that the package STANDARD occupies the most shared memory, 433K.[8]

Knowing the amount of memory your programs use is necessary, but not sufficient, information if you wish to reduce 4031 or 4030 errors; you must also know the size of the shared pool and how much of the shared pool is filled by "re-creatable" objects— that is, objects that can be aged out of memory and loaded again later when needed. Some of this information is difficult to tease out of the database and may require knowledge of the mysterious X$ views. However, versions 9.2.0.5 and later will automatically generate a heap dump in your USER_DUMP_DEST directory every time you

---

7. If you're wondering why the columns of data do not line up properly with their headings, it's probably because of the severe limitations of DBMS_OUTPUT. If you don't like it, write your own (grab the query from V$SQLAREA after running the package).

8. There is a bug in older versions of DBMS_SHARED_POOL.SIZES that results in the amount's being over-reported by about 2.3%. Oracle's package erroneously computed kilobytes by dividing bytes by 1000 instead of by 1024.

hit a 4031 error. See what you can discover from that, or just punt it over to Oracle Support. As a developer, you also need to figure out if your applications contain a large amount of unshared code that logically could be shared because this can have a big impact on memory requirements.

Natively compiled PL/SQL programs are linked to shared-library files, but the database still allocates some memory inside the database in order to run them. The same is true for external procedures. A privileged user can use operating-system-level utilities such as *pmap* on Solaris to measure the amount of memory they require outside of the database.

Now, on to Step 4: tune the database or buy more memory. A competent DBA (hey, don't look at me) will know how to tune the shared pool by adjusting parameters such as these:

SHARED_POOL_SIZE
    Bytes set aside for the shared pool.

DB_CACHE_SIZE
    Bytes of memory reserved to hold rows of data from the database (may need to be reduced in order to increase the size of the shared pool).

LARGE_POOL_SIZE
    Bytes of memory reserved for an optional region of memory that holds the UGA for shared server connections. This prevents the variable portion of the UGA from competing for use of the shared pool.

JAVA_POOL_SIZE
    Bytes used by the Java memory manager.

STREAMS_POOL_SIZE
    Bytes used by the Oracle Streams feature.

If that's too much to fuss with, and you are using Oracle Database 10g or later, the DBA can turn on the Automatic Shared Memory Management features:

SGA_TARGET
    Set to a nonzero number of bytes, which indicates the size of the SGA from which the database will automatically allocate the cache and pools indicated above.

PGA_AGGREGATE_TARGET
    Total amount of memory used by all of the server processes in the instance. Generally, it should be equal to the amount of server memory available to the database minus the SGA size.

You can also ask the DBA to force the shared pool to hold a PL/SQL program unit, sequence, table, or cursor in memory with the DBMS_SHARED_POOL.KEEP procedure.[9] For example, the following block would require that the database keep the STANDARD package pinned in memory:

```
BEGIN
    DBMS_SHARED_POOL.KEEP('SYS.STANDARD');
END;
```

It can be especially beneficial to pin into memory large program units that are executed relatively *infrequently*. Without pinning, the partially compiled code will likely be aged out of the shared pool. When called again, its loading could force many smaller objects out of the shared pool, and degrade performance.

It's probably obvious, but if you're encountering ORA-04031 errors resulting from a few users or applications, consider moving the offenders to dedicated server mode.

Another memory error you may find in shared server mode is *ORA-06500: PL/SQL: storage error*. Increasing the LARGE_POOL_SIZE usually makes this go away.

# Native Compilation

In its default mode (interpreted), your code is partially compiled, but also interpreted at runtime. PL/SQL executes in a virtual machine, and it first translates (compiles) your code into virtual machine code, sometimes called *bytecode* or *mcode*. This is basically the same model that Java uses. When it is time to actually run your code, however, that bytecode is translated (interpreted) into system calls.

However, once you have the code running well, you can choose to improve the runtime efficiency of your PL/SQL programs by having the database perform the bytecode to machine code translation early, at compile time. This second half compilation (called *native mode*) results in machine code in a shared library. The database will dynamically load this compiled machine code at runtime.

## When to Run Interpreted Mode

So, if native mode is faster, why run in interpreted mode? Let's look at this question from the other end. The goal of native mode is fast execution speed. So, to get the fastest execution speed, you crank up the optimization level and try to do as much work ahead of execution time as possible (including early translation to machine code). When you are developing and unit testing your code, you need the capabilities of the debugger more than you need fast execution speed. If you need to step through your source code and step over subprogram calls in a debugger, you surely can't have the optimizing compiler rearranging your source code (optimization level 2) or inlining subprograms

---

9. In the fine print, Oracle says that it may obsolete the feature when it comes up with better memory management algorithms.

(optimization level 3). So to debug, you have to revert to optimization level 0 or 1, at which point native mode is of questionable value. So I recommend running interpreted mode in development environments.

## When to Go Native

Native mode is built for speed. You run native mode when you have your program debugged and want to make it go as fast as possible. Native compilation goes hand in hand with higher optimization levels. This configuration is usually production and some test environments. With native mode, the compile times are slightly longer because you are doing more work in the compile, but the execution times will be faster or perhaps the same as in interpreted mode.

## Native Compilation and Database Release

Setting up native compilation and execution varies from major database release to major release. The details are spelled out in Chapter 20, but let's review a little native compilation and history here.

*Oracle9i Database*
> Native compilation was introduced with Oracle9i Database. Everything worked quite well with native compilation on this release, as long as you weren't running Real Application Clusters (RAC) and didn't mind complicated backups. RAC databases were a problem (they weren't supported) and database backups needed to include the shared libraries, which Oracle Recovery Manager (RMAN) didn't capture.

*Oracle Database 10g*
> Native compilation was improved with Oracle Database 10g. RAC databases and shared servers were supported, but you needed the C compiler and copies of the shared libraries on each RAC node. Database backups were still an issue though—they still needed to include the shared libraries, but RMAN didn't capture these shared libraries.

*Oracle Database 11g*
> Native compilation has again been improved with Oracle Database 11g. You no longer need a C compiler, and the shared libraries are stored in the data dictionary, where every backup tool on the planet (well, those that work with Oracle databases at least) locates and backs them up. So, with no issues related to backups or managing shared library files, there is little to hold you back from going native on your production and test databases. Try it, you'll like it, and you won't go back.

# What You Need to Know

So, do you really *need* to remember everything in this chapter? I certainly hope not, because I can't even remember it in my day-to-day work. Your database administrator, on the other hand, probably needs to know most of this stuff.

In addition to satisfying healthy curiosity, my goal in presenting this material was to help allay any misgivings programmers might have about the PL/SQL architecture. Whether or not you've ever had such concerns, there are a number of important points to remember about what goes on inside PL/SQL:

- To avoid compilation overhead, programs you plan to use more than a few times should be put in stored programs rather than stored in files as anonymous blocks.

- In addition to their unique ability to preserve state throughout a session, PL/SQL packages offer performance benefits. You should put most of your extensive application logic into package bodies.

- When upgrading Oracle versions, new features in the PL/SQL compiler warrant thorough application testing. In some (probably rare) cases when upgrading to Oracle Database 11g, slight changes in execution order, resulting from freedoms exploited by the optimizing compiler, could affect application results.

- While the Oracle database's automatic dependency management approach relieves a huge burden on developers, upgrading applications on a live production database should be undertaken with great care because of the need for object locking and package state reset.

- If you use signature-based remote dependency checking in remote procedure calls or with a loopback-link synonym as a way to avoid invalidations, you should institute (manual) procedures to eliminate the possibility of the signature check returning a false negative (which would cause a runtime error).

- Use definer rights to maximize performance and to help simplify the management and control of privileges on database tables. Use invoker rights only to address particular problems (for example, programs that use dynamic SQL and that create or destroy database objects).

- The database's sophisticated approaches aimed at minimizing the machine resources needed to run PL/SQL occasionally benefit from a little help from developers and DBAs—for example, by explicitly freeing unused user memory or pinning objects in memory.

- Where it makes sense to your application logic, use the cursor FOR loop idiom, rather than open/fetch loop/close, to take advantage of the automatic bulk binding feature in Oracle Database 10g and later versions.

- When your program does need to open an explicit cursor in a PL/SQL program, be sure to close the cursor as soon as fetching is complete.

- Native compilation of PL/SQL may not offer any performance advantages for SQL-intensive applications, but it can significantly improve the performance of compute-intensive programs.
- Calling remote packages entails some special programming considerations if you want to take advantage of anything in the package other than procedures, functions, types, and subtypes.
- Use program variables in embedded static SQL statements in PL/SQL, and bind variables in dynamic SQL statements, to avoid subverting the database's cursor sharing features.

# CHAPTER 25

# Globalization and Localization in PL/SQL

Businesses do not typically begin their operations on a global scale. They usually start as local or regional businesses with plans to expand. As they grow into new regions, or locales, critical applications need to adjust to new language and formatting requirements. If the applications are not designed to support multiple locales, this transition becomes very time-consuming and costly.

In a perfect development world, globalization would be an integral part of application design, and all design considerations would be accompanied by the question "Where in the world would this design fail?" In the real world, however, many companies do not include a globalization strategy in the initial design. Cost concerns, lack of globalization experience, or simply an inability to anticipate the global reach of the business are all common reasons for failing to analyze localization risks.

So, what's the big deal? It is just a matter of translating data, right? Not exactly. There are, in fact, many common PL/SQL programming tasks with localization implications that can disrupt your application's ability to function globally:

*Variable precision*
　　CHAR(1) handles "F" very nicely, but will it do the same for "民"?

*String sort order of result set*
　　ORDER BY is determined easily for English characters. Will Korean, Chinese, or Japanese be as straightforward? How are combined characters, or characters with accents, ordered?

*Information retrieval (IR)*
　　PL/SQL is often the language of choice for information retrieval applications. How can you store data in multiple languages and accurately retrieve information across languages using the same query?

*Date/time formatting*
> Different countries and regions use different calendars and date formats. How vulnerable is your code to these variations?

*Currency formatting*
> Currency considerations extend beyond basic currency conversion. A misused comma or period resulting from locale-specific formatting requirements can unintentionally change the cost of an item.

This chapter explores the ramifications of these kinds of issues and talks about how you can write PL/SQL code to anticipate and handle them. I begin with a discussion of Unicode and Oracle's Globalization Support architecture. Next, I demonstrate some problems using multibyte characters and describe how to handle them in your PL/SQL programs using character semantics. I then discuss some of the complexities associated with sorting character strings using various character sets, and demonstrate efficient multilingual information retrieval. Finally, I show how you can make your applications work using different date/time and currency formats.

---

## Globalization Strategy

As you develop with globalization in mind, you will find yourself anticipating localization problems much earlier in the development life cycle. There is no better time to think about globalization than during the design phase of your application. There is obviously far more to your overall globalization strategy than can be covered in this chapter, but your PL/SQL programs should be in good shape if you take into account:

- Character set
- NLS parameters
- Unicode functions
- Character versus byte semantics
- String sort order
- Multilingual information retrieval
- Date/time
- Currency

For additional information on globalization and localization within Oracle, see the globalization documentation at *http://otn.oracle.com/tech/globalization/index.html*. This site provides discussion forums, links to papers, and additional documentation on database and application server globalization. It also includes a Character Set Scanner download to assist with conversions.

---

Throughout this chapter, we will be working with a publication schema called g11n. If you want to install this catalog in your own environment, download the *G11N.ZIP* file from the book's web site and unzip to a local directory. Modify the header of *g11n.sql* with the correct environment details for your system, but *make sure when saving it again that your encoding is Unicode*. If the files are saved as ASCII or some other Western character set, the multibyte characters in the file will not save correctly and you will get errors when running the scripts. The *g11n.sql* script creates a user named g11n, grants necessary permissions to work through the samples, creates the sample objects, and adds seed data. Refer to the header of *g11n.sql* for additional instructions

# Overview and Terminology

Before I proceed, let's get some terminology straight. Globalization, internationalization, and localization are often used interchangeably, yet they actually have very different meanings. Table 25-1 defines each and explains how they are related.

*Table 25-1. Fundamental terms and abbreviation*

| Term | Abbreviation | Definition |
|---|---|---|
| Globalization | g11n | Application development strategy focused on making applications multilingual and locale-independent. Globalization is accomplished through internationalization and localization. |
| Internationalization | i18n | The design or modification of an application to work with multiple locales. |
| Localization | l10n | The process of actually making an application work in each specific locale. l10n includes text translation. It is made easier with a proper i18n implementation. |

If you haven't seen the abbreviations mentioned in Table 25-1 before, you may be confused about the numbers sandwiched between the two letters. These terms are often abbreviated by including the first letter and last letter, with the number of characters between them in the middle. Globalization, for example, has 11 letters between the "g" and the "n," making the abbreviation g11n.

It is true that Oracle supports localization to every region of the world. I have heard it suggested, though, that Oracle's localization support means that you can load English data and search it in Japanese. Not true! Oracle does not have a built-in linguistic translation engine that performs translations on the fly for you. If you have ever witnessed the results of a machine translation, you know that you would not want this kind of so-called functionality as a built-in "feature" anyway. Oracle *supports* localization, but it does not implement localization for you. That is still your job.

Additional terms used in this chapter are defined in Table 25-2; I'll expand on these in the following sections.

*Table 25-2. Detailed globalization, localization, and internationalization terms*

| Term | Definition |
| --- | --- |
| Character encoding | Each character is a representation of a code point. Character encoding is the mapping between character and code point. The type of character encoding chosen for the database determines the ability to store and retrieve these code points. |
| Character set | Characters are grouped by language or region. Each regionalized set of characters is referred to as a character set. |
| Code point | Each character in every character set is given a unique identifier called a code point. This identifier is determined by the Unicode Consortium. Code points can represent a character in its entirety or can be combined with other code points to form complex characters. An example of a code point is \0053. |
| Glyph | A glyph is the graphical display of a character that is mapped to one or more code points. The code point definition in this table used the \0053 code point. The glyph this code point is mapped to is the capital letter S. |
| Multibyte characters | Most Western European characters require only a single byte to store them. Multibyte characters, such as Japanese or Korean, require between 2 and 4 bytes to store a single character in the database. |
| NLS | National Language Support is the old name for Oracle's globalization architecture. Starting with Oracle9*i* Database, it is officially referred to as Globalization Support, but you will see documentation and parameters that make reference to NLS for some time to come. |
| Unicode | Unicode is a standard for character encoding. |

# Unicode Primer

Before the Unicode standard was developed, there were multiple character encoding schemes that were inadequate and that, at times, conflicted with each other. It was nearly impossible to develop global applications that were consistent because no single character encoding scheme could support all characters.

Unicode is a standard for character encoding that resolves these problems. It was developed and is maintained by the Unicode Consortium. The Unicode Standard and Unicode Character Database, or UCD, define what is included in each version.

Oracle's Unicode character sets allow you to store and retrieve more than 200 different individual character sets. Using a Unicode character set provides support for all character sets without making any engineering changes to an application.

Oracle Database 11g Release 2 supports Unicode version 5.0. First published in 2006, Unicode 5.0 includes the capacity to encode more than 1 million characters. This is enough to support all modern characters, as well as many ancient or minor scripts. At the time of this writing, Unicode 5.1 is the most current published Unicode version.

Unicode character sets in Oracle Database 11g include UTF-8 and UTF-16 encoding. UTF-8 stores characters in 1, 2, or 3 bytes, depending on the character. UTF-16 stores characters in 2 bytes regardless of character. Supplementary characters are supported with both encoding schemes, and these require 4 bytes per character regardless of the Unicode character set chosen.

Each Oracle database has two character sets. You can define one primary database character set that will be used for most application functions, and a separate NLS character set for NLS-specific datatypes and functions. Use the following query to determine the character sets you are using:

```
SELECT parameter, VALUE
  FROM nls_database_parameters
 WHERE parameter IN ('NLS_CHARACTERSET', 'NLS_NCHAR_CHARACTERSET')
```

This query returns the following results in my environment:

```
PARAMETER                   VALUE
------------------------    ----------
NLS_CHARACTERSET            AL32UTF8
NLS_NCHAR_CHARACTERSET      AL16UTF16
```

My NLS_CHARACTERSET, or primary character set for my database, has a value of AL32UTF8. This 32-bit UTF-8 Unicode character set is meant to encompass most common characters in the world. My NLS_NCHAR_CHARACTERSET, used primarily for NCHAR and NVARCHAR2 columns, is a 16-bit UTF-16 character set.

---

### Choosing a Character Set

Oracle now recommends that all new installations of the Oracle Database use a Unicode character set for the NLS_CHARACTERSET. Having performed a number of character set migrations, I agree that this recommendation is definitely a good one to follow. Your application may need to support only ASCII characters right now, but what about in two or three years? The performance implications of using Unicode are negligible, and space implications are minor since the encoding uses variable byte sizes based on the characters themselves.

Another consideration, even if you have no plans to work with multilingual data, is that you may still get multibyte characters in your database. Browser-based applications often support the copying and pasting of large amounts of text from word-processing applications. In doing so, they can take in more than simple ASCII characters. Bullets, for example, are multibyte characters. Unless you analyze everything that is posted to your data fields, it will be difficult to know whether the data going in is supported by your non-Unicode character set. Unicode ensures that your database will handle whatever characters are required today—and tomorrow.

---

The names Oracle gives to its character sets are structured to provide useful information about each character set. US7ASCII supports U.S. English characters, for example. For AL32UTF8, the character set is intended to support *all* languages. The second part of the string indicates the number of bits per character. US7ASCII uses 7 bits per character while AL32UTF8 uses up to 32 bits per character. The remainder of the string is the official character set name. Figure 25-1 illustrates this convention.

*Figure 25-1. Oracle's character set naming convention*

For more information on Unicode, refer to the Unicode Standard web site at:

*http://unicode.org/unicode/standard/standard.html*

## National Character Set Datatypes

The Globalization Support (national character set ) datatypes of NCLOB, NCHAR, and NVARCHAR2 use the character set defined for NLS_NCHAR_CHARACTERSET rather than the database default character set specified for the database using NLS_CHARACTERSET. These datatypes support only the use of a multibyte Unicode character set, so even when working with a database whose default is non-Unicode, they will store the characters using the national character set instead. Because the national character set supports only UTF-8 and UTF-16 encodings, NCLOB, NCHAR, and NVARCHAR2 are guaranteed to store the data as multibyte Unicode.

This used to cause a problem when comparing NCLOB/NCHAR/NVARCHAR2 columns with CLOB/CHAR/VARCHAR2 columns. For all currently supported releases, however, Oracle performs an implicit conversion, allowing the comparison to take place.

## Character Encoding

Your choice of a character set at database creation time determines the type of encoding your characters will have. Each encoded character is assigned a code value, or code point, that is unique to that character. This value is part of a Unicode character-mapping table whose values are controlled by the Unicode Consortium.

Code points appear as a U+ (or a backslash, \) followed by the hexadecimal value of the character, with the valid range of values from U+0000 to U+10FFFF$_{16}$. Combined characters, such as Ä, can be broken down into their individual components (A with an umlaut in this case) and recomposed again into their original state. The decomposition mapping for A is U+0041, and U+0308 for the umlaut. I will examine some Oracle functions in the next section that enable you to work with these code points.

A code unit is the byte size of the datatype that is used to store characters. The size of the code unit depends on the character set that is used. In certain circumstances, the code point is too large for a single code unit, so multiple code units are needed for a single code point.

Of course, users recognize characters, not code points and code units. The "word" \0053\0074\0065\0076\0065\006E doesn't mean a lot to average end users who recognize characters in their native language. For one thing, the text actually displayed on the user's screen is called a *glyph* and is simply a representation of the underlying code point. Your computer may not have the required fonts or may be otherwise unable to render the characters on the screen. This does not mean, however, that Oracle has stored the code point incorrectly.

## Globalization Support Parameters

Oracle relies on Globalization Support (NLS) parameters for its default behavior. These settings are configured at the time of database creation and encompass everything from your character sets to default currency symbols. I will refer to parameters that can be modified for your session throughout this chapter. Table 25-3 shows the parameters, example values, and an explanation of each. You can find the values on your system from the NLS_SESSION_PARAMETERS view.

---

### Unicode and Your Environment

Oracle supports all characters in the world but does your environment? Unless you work with Unicode characters on a regular basis, there is a good chance that your system is not set up to support certain multibyte characters (is unable, that is, to render the proper glyphs). Operating-system Unicode support does not guarantee that all applications on that operating system will work with all characters. The individual application vendors control their Unicode support. Even basic applications such as DOS have difficulty with certain characters if not properly configured.

If you require interaction with the Oracle database in a way that supports multibyte characters, but you do not want or need to adjust your operating system and applications, consider configuring *Oracle Application Express* from Oracle. You can access the database using your browser where Unicode encoding is easily configured. Oracle Application Express is free to install on top of any version of the Oracle database, and is actually preconfigured with Oracle Express Edition. *iSQL\*Plus* is another option for Oracle9*i* Database and later.

Many web-based tools have the appropriate encoding scheme listed in their page header so Unicode characters will display correctly by default, but in case you do not see the correct characters, set the encoding in your Internet Explorer browser as follows:

On the menu, select:

> *View → Encoding → Auto Select and UTF-8.*

Using Firefox, select:

> *View → Character Encoding → Unicode (UTF-8)*

---

*Table 25-3. NLS session parameters*

| Parameter | Description | Example |
|---|---|---|
| NLS_CALENDAR | Sets the default calendar for the database. | GREGORIAN |
| NLS_COMP | Works with NLS_SORT to define sort rules for characters. You must use a linguistic index when setting to ANSI. | BINARY |
| NLS_CURRENCY | Specifies the currency symbol and is based on the NLS_TERRITORY value unless explicitly overridden with another value. | $ |
| NLS_DATE_FORMAT | The default format of the date only. It is derived from NLS_TERRITORY and can be overridden. | DD-MON-RR |
| NLS_DATE_LANGUAGE | Determines the spelling of the day and month for date-related functions. | AMERICAN |
| NLS_DUAL_CURRENCY | Helps support the Euro and is derived from NLS_TERRITORY unless overridden. It is an alternate currency for a territory. | $ |
| NLS_ISO_CURRENCY | The ISO currency symbol whose default is derived from the NLS_TERRITORY. It can be overridden with any valid territory. | AMERICA |
| NLS_LANGUAGE | Sets the default language used within the database. It impacts everything from date formatting to server messages. | AMERICAN |
| NLS_LENGTH_SEMANTICS | Determines whether character or byte semantics are used. | BYTE |
| NLS_NCHAR_CONV_EXCP | Determines whether a character type conversion will report an error. | FALSE |
| NLS_NUMERIC_CHARACTERS | The default decimal character and group separator are derived from NLS_TERRITORY but can be overridden. | . , |
| NLS_SORT | Defines the character sort order for a given language. | BINARY |
| NLS_TERRITORY | Has a broad impact because many other NLS parameters depend on this value for their defaults. The value specifies the primary region supported by the database. | AMERICA |
| NLS_TIMESTAMP_FORMAT | Default timestamp format for TO_TIMESTAMP and TO_CHAR functions. | DD-MON-RR HH.MI.SSXF F AM |
| NLS_TIMESTAMP_TZ_FORMAT | Sets the timestamp with time zone format for TO_CHAR and TO_TIMESTAMP_TZ. | DD-MON-RR HH.MI.SSXF F AM TZR |
| NLS_TIME_FORMAT | Complements the NLS_DATE_FORMAT mentioned earlier. Sets the default time format for the database. | HH.MI.SSXF F AM |
| NLS_TIME_TZ_FORMAT | Defines the time format including the time zone region or UTC offset. | HH.MI.SSXF F AM TZR |

## Unicode Functions

Oracle's Unicode PL/SQL support begins with some basic string functions. However, you will notice slight variations in Table 25-4 for some well-known functions. Functions INSTR, LENGTH, and SUBSTR have a B, C, 2, or 4 appended to the end of the name indicating whether the function is byte, character, code unit, or code point-based.

INSTR, LENGTH, and SUBSTR use the length semantics associated with the datatype of the column or variable. These base functions and the variations ending in "C" will often return the same value until you begin work against NCHAR or NVARCHAR. Because your NLS_NCHAR_CHARACTERSET and NLS_CHARACTERSET can be different, INSTR, LENGTH, and SUBSTR can return different results (depending on the datatype) from their character counterparts.

Table 25-4. Unicode functions

| Unicode function | Description |
|---|---|
| ASCIISTR(string) | Converts string to ASCII characters. When the character is Unicode, it formats as the standard Unicode format \xxxx. |
| COMPOSE(string) | Converts a decomposed string to its fully composed form. |
| DECOMPOSE(string, [canonical \| compatibility]) | Takes string as an argument and returns a Unicode string in its individual code points. |
| INSTRB(string, substr, pos, occ) | Returns the byte position of substr in string beginning at position pos. You can also specify the occ occurrence of substr if it appears more than once. The default of pos and occ are both 1 if not specified. pos is in bytes. |
| INSTRC(string, substr, pos, occ) | Similar to INSTRB except that it returns the character position of substr in string beginning at position pos where pos is in characters. |
| INSTR2(string, substr, pos, occ) | Return position is based on UTF-16 code units. |
| INSTR4(string, substr, pos, occ) | Return position is based on UTF-16 code points. |
| LENGTHB(string) | Returns the number of bytes in string. |
| LENGTHC(string) | Returns the Unicode length of string. The length is in number of characters. |
| LENGTH2(string) | Length is based on UTF-16 code units. |
| LENGTH4(string) | Length is based on UTF-16 code points. |
| SUBSTRB(string, n, m) | Returns a portion of string beginning at position n for length m. n and m are in bytes. |
| SUBSTRC(string, n, m) | Returns a portion of string beginning at position n for length m. n and m are based on Unicode characters. |
| SUBSTR2(string, n, m) | n and m are in UTF-16 code units. |
| SUBSTR4(string, n, m) | n and m are in UTF-16 code points. |
| UNISTR | Converts string to an ASCII string representation of Unicode using backslash and hex digits. |

Let's take a closer look at these functions.

## ASCIISTR

ASCIISTR takes string as input and attempts to convert it to a string of ASCII characters. If string contains non-ASCII characters it formats them as \xxxx. As you will see with the DECOMPOSE function described later, this formatting comes in very handy.

```
BEGIN
   DBMS_OUTPUT.put_line ('ASCII Character: ' || ASCIISTR ('A'));
   DBMS_OUTPUT.put_line ('Unicode Character: ' || ASCIISTR ('Ä'));
END;
```

This returns the following:

```
ASCII Character: A
Unicode Character: \00C4
```

## COMPOSE

For some characters, there are multiple ways for code points to represent the same thing. This is a problem when you are comparing two values. An Ä can be created using a single code point U+00C4, or with multiple code points U+0041 (the letter A) and U+0308. U+00C4 is precomposed, while U+0041 and U+0308 are decomposed. On comparison, PL/SQL says these are not equal.

```
DECLARE
   v_precomposed    VARCHAR2 (20) := UNISTR ('\00C4');
   v_decomposed     VARCHAR2 (20) := UNISTR ('A\0308');
BEGIN
   IF v_precomposed = v_decomposed
   THEN
      DBMS_OUTPUT.put_line ('==EQUAL==');
   ELSE
      DBMS_OUTPUT.put_line ('<>NOT EQUAL<>');
   END IF;
END;
```

The following is displayed:

```
<>NOT EQUAL<>
```

Using the COMPOSE function I can make the decomposed value equal to the precomposed value:

```
DECLARE
   v_precomposed    VARCHAR2 (20) := UNISTR ('\00C4');
   v_decomposed     VARCHAR2 (20) := COMPOSE (UNISTR ('A\0308'));
BEGIN
   IF v_precomposed = v_decomposed
   THEN
      DBMS_OUTPUT.put_line ('==EQUAL==');
   ELSE
      DBMS_OUTPUT.put_line ('<>NOT EQUAL<>');
   END IF;
END;
```

This query returns the following:

```
==EQUAL==
```

## DECOMPOSE

As you might have guessed, DECOMPOSE is the opposite of COMPOSE. DECOM-POSE takes something that is precomposed and breaks it down into separate code points or elements:

```
DECLARE
    v_precomposed   VARCHAR2 (20) := ASCIISTR (DECOMPOSE ('Ä'));
    v_decomposed    VARCHAR2 (20) := 'A\0308';
BEGIN
    IF v_precomposed = v_decomposed
    THEN
        DBMS_OUTPUT.put_line ('==EQUAL==');
    ELSE
        DBMS_OUTPUT.put_line ('<>NOT EQUAL<>');
    END IF;
END;
```

The results are as follows:

```
==EQUAL==
```

## INSTR/INSTRB/INSTRC/INSTR2/INSTR4

All INSTR functions return the position of a substring within a string. The differences lie in how the position is determined:

*INSTR*
Finds the position by character.

*INSTRB*
Returns the position in bytes.

*INSTRC*
Determines the position by Unicode character.

*INSTR2*
Uses code units.

*INSTR4*
Returns the position by code point.

To illustrate, let's use the publication table in the **g11n** schema.

```
DECLARE
    v_instr     NUMBER (2);
    v_instrb    NUMBER (2);
    v_instrc    NUMBER (2);
    v_instr2    NUMBER (2);
    v_instr4    NUMBER (2);
BEGIN
    SELECT INSTR (title, 'グ'),
    INSTRB (title, 'グ'),
    INSTRC (title, 'グ
'),
    INSTR2 (title, 'グ'),
```

```
    INSTR4 (title, 'グ
')
        INTO v_instr, v_instrb, v_instrc,
            v_instr2, v_instr4
        FROM publication
    WHERE publication_id = 2;

    DBMS_OUTPUT.put_line ('INSTR of グ: ' || v_instr);
    DBMS_OUTPUT.put_line ('INSTRB of グ: ' || v_instrb);
    DBMS_OUTPUT.put_line ('INSTRC of グ: ' || v_instrc);
    DBMS_OUTPUT.put_line ('INSTR2 of グ: ' || v_instr2);
    DBMS_OUTPUT.put_line ('INSTR4 of グ: ' || v_instr4);
END;
/
```

The output is as follows:

```
INSTR of グ: 16
INSTRB of グ: 20
INSTRC of グ: 16
INSTR2 of グ: 16
INSTR4 of グ: 16
```

The position of character "グ" is different only for INSTRB in this case. One nice feature of INSTR2 and INSTR4 is that you can search for code points that do not represent complete characters. Returning to our character Ä, it is possible to include the umlaut as the substring for which to search.

### LENGTH/LENGTHB/LENGTHC/LENGTH2/LENGTH4

The LENGTH functions operate as follows:

*LENGTH*
> Returns the length in characters.

*LENGTHB*
> Returns the length in bytes of a string.

*LENGTHC*
> Returns the length in Unicode characters.

*LENGTH2*
> Is the number of code units.

*LENGTH4*
> Is the number of code points.

The LENGTH function matches the LENGTHC function when characters are precomposed.

```
DECLARE
    v_length    NUMBER (2);
    v_lengthb   NUMBER (2);
    v_lengthc   NUMBER (2);
    v_length2   NUMBER (2);
```

```
      v_length4    NUMBER (2);
   BEGIN
      SELECT LENGTH (title), LENGTHB (title), lengthc (title), length2 (title),
             length4 (title)
        INTO v_length, v_lengthb, v_lengthc, v_length2,
             v_length4
        FROM publication
       WHERE publication_id = 2;

      DBMS_OUTPUT.put_line ('LENGTH of string: ' || v_length);
      DBMS_OUTPUT.put_line ('LENGTHB of string: ' || v_lengthb);
      DBMS_OUTPUT.put_line ('LENGTHC of string: ' || v_lengthc);
      DBMS_OUTPUT.put_line ('LENGTH2 of string: ' || v_length2);
      DBMS_OUTPUT.put_line ('LENGTH4 of string: ' || v_length4);
   END;
```

This gives the following result:

```
LENGTH of string: 28
LENGTHB of string: 52
LENGTHC of string: 28
LENGTH2 of string: 28
LENGTH4 of string: 28
```

The only difference in this case is with the LENGTHB function. As expected, LENGTH
and LENGTHC returned the same result. My expectation changes when working with
decomposed characters, however. Note the following example:

```
DECLARE
   v_length    NUMBER (2);
BEGIN
   SELECT LENGTH (UNISTR ('A\0308'))
     INTO v_length
     FROM DUAL;

   DBMS_OUTPUT.put_line ('Decomposed string size using LENGTH: ' || v_length);

   SELECT lengthc (UNISTR ('A\0308'))
     INTO v_length
     FROM DUAL;

   DBMS_OUTPUT.put_line ('Decomposed string size using LENGTHC: ' || v_length);
END;
```

The length is returned as follows:

```
Decomposed string size using LENGTH: 2
Decomposed string size using LENGTHC: 1
```

In this case, LENGTH still returns the number of characters, but sees the A as separate
from the umlaut. LENGTHC returns the length of Unicode characters, so it sees only
one character.

### SUBSTR/SUBSTRB/SUBSTRC/SUBSTR2/SUBSTR4

The different versions of SUBSTR follow the same pattern as INSTR and LENGTH. SUBSTR returns a portion of a string beginning at a given position, for a specified length. The functions operate as follows:

*SUBSTR*

Determines position and length by character.

*SUBSTRB*

Determines position and length in bytes.

*SUBSTRC*

Determines position and length in Unicode characters.

*SUBSTR2*

Uses code units.

*SUBSTR4*

Uses code points.

The following example illustrates the use of these functions.

```
DECLARE
    v_substr     VARCHAR2 (20);
    v_substrb    VARCHAR2 (20);
    v_substrc    VARCHAR2 (20);
    v_substr2    VARCHAR2 (20);
    v_substr4    VARCHAR2 (20);
BEGIN
    SELECT SUBSTR (title, 13, 4), SUBSTRB (title, 13, 4),
           substrc (title, 13, 4), substr2 (title, 13, 4),
           substr4 (title, 13, 4)
      INTO v_substr, v_substrb,
           v_substrc, v_substr2,
           v_substr4
      FROM publication
     WHERE publication_id = 2;

    DBMS_OUTPUT.put_line ('SUBSTR of string: ' || v_substr);
    DBMS_OUTPUT.put_line ('SUBSTRB of string: ' || v_substrb);
    DBMS_OUTPUT.put_line ('SUBSTRC of string: ' || v_substrc);
    DBMS_OUTPUT.put_line ('SUBSTR2 of string: ' || v_substr2);
    DBMS_OUTPUT.put_line ('SUBSTR4 of string: ' || v_substr4);
END;
```

Notice the difference between SUBSTRB and the other functions in the output from the script.

```
SUBSTR of string: Lプログ
SUBSTRB of string: Lプ
SUBSTRC of string: Lプログ
SUBSTR2 of string: Lプログ
SUBSTR4 of string: Lプログ
```

### UNISTR

UNISTR takes a string and converts it to Unicode. I used this function in a few earlier examples to display the Unicode character of a decomposed string. In the section, "Character Encoding" on page 1036, I used a string of code points as an example when discussing glyphs. I can use UNISTR to make sense of all this:

```
DECLARE
    v_string    VARCHAR2 (20);
BEGIN
    SELECT UNISTR ('\0053\0074\0065\0076\0065\006E')
      INTO v_string
      FROM DUAL;

    DBMS_OUTPUT.put_line (v_string);
END;
```

The output is as follows:

```
Steven
```

 See *http://www.unicode.org/charts/* for a complete listing of characters and code points.

## Character Semantics

Undoubtedly, one of the first issues you will run into when localizing your application is support for multibyte characters. When you pass your first Japanese characters to a VARCHAR2 variable and experience an ORA-6502 error, you will likely spend an hour debugging your procedure that "should work."

At some point, you may realize that every declaration of every character variable or character column in your application will have to be changed to accommodate the multibyte character set. You will then, if you are anything like me, consider for a moment changing careers. Don't give up! Once you work through the initial challenges, you will be in a very strong position to guide application implementations in the future.

Consider the following example:

```
DECLARE
    v_title    VARCHAR2 (30);
BEGIN
    SELECT title
      INTO v_title
      FROM publication
     WHERE publication_id = 2;

    DBMS_OUTPUT.put_line (v_title);
EXCEPTION
    WHEN OTHERS
```

```
    THEN
        DBMS_OUTPUT.put_line (DBMS_UTILITY.format_error_stack);
    END;
```

It returns the following exception:

```
ORA-06502: PL/SQL: numeric or value error: character string buffer too small
```

It failed because the precision of 30 is in bytes, not in characters. A number of Asian character sets have up to 3 bytes per character, so it's possible that a variable with a precision of 2 will actually not support even a single character in your chosen character set!

Using the LENGTHB function I can determine the actual size of the string:

```
DECLARE
    v_length_in_bytes   NUMBER (2);
BEGIN
    SELECT LENGTHB (title)
      INTO v_length_in_bytes
      FROM publication
     WHERE publication_id = 2;

    DBMS_OUTPUT.put_line ('String size in bytes: ' || v_length_in_bytes);
END;
```

This returns the following result:

```
String size in bytes: 52
```

Prior to Oracle9i Database we were somewhat limited in what we could do. The approach I most frequently used in Oracle8i Database was to simply use the maximum number of characters expected and multiply by 3.

```
DECLARE
    v_title   VARCHAR2 (90);
BEGIN
    SELECT title
      INTO v_title
      FROM publication
     WHERE publication_id = 2;

    DBMS_OUTPUT.put_line (v_title);
EXCEPTION
    WHEN OTHERS
    THEN
        DBMS_OUTPUT.put_line (DBMS_UTILITY.format_error_stack);
END;
```

If you are using a display that can render the proper glyph, the following result is returned:

```
Oracle PL/SQL プログラミング 基礎編 第 3 版
```

This workaround does the job, but it is clumsy. Using byte semantics and simply multiplying the number of expected characters by 3 causes some undesired behaviors in your application:

- Many other database vendors use character rather than byte semantics by default, so porting applications to multiple databases becomes cumbersome.

- In cases where characters do not take the full 3 bytes, it is possible for the variable or column to store more than the expected number of characters.

- The padding that Oracle automatically applies to CHAR datatypes means that the full 90 bytes are used regardless of whether they are needed.

Character semantics were first introduced in Oracle9*i* Database. It is possible to declare a variable with precision in either bytes or characters. The following example is the same one that failed earlier—with one exception. Look at the declaration of the variable to see how I invoke character semantics:

```
DECLARE
   v_title    VARCHAR2 (30 CHAR);
BEGIN
   SELECT title
     INTO v_title
     FROM publication
    WHERE publication_id = 2;

   DBMS_OUTPUT.put_line (v_title);
EXCEPTION
   WHEN OTHERS
   THEN
      DBMS_OUTPUT.put_line (DBMS_UTILITY.format_error_stack);
END;
```

This returns the following complete string:

```
Oracle PL/SQL プログラミング 基礎編 第 3 版
```

This method still requires a change for every character variable or column declaration in your application. An easier solution is to change from byte semantics to character semantics for your entire database. To make this change, simply set NLS_LENGTH_SEMANTICS to CHAR. You can find your current setting by running:

```
SELECT parameter, VALUE
  FROM nls_session_parameters
 WHERE parameter = 'NLS_LENGTH_SEMANTICS'
```

The following is returned:

```
PARAMETER                      VALUE
------------------------------ ----------
NLS_LENGTH_SEMANTICS           BYTE
```

Also check the V$PARAMETER view:

```
SELECT NAME, VALUE
  FROM v$parameter
 WHERE NAME = 'nls_length_semantics'
```

This query returns the following:

```
NAME                      VALUE
------------------------- ----------
nls_length_semantics      BYTE
```

Modify your system NLS_LENGTH_SEMANTICS setting using the ALTER SYSTEM command:

```
ALTER SYSTEM SET NLS_LENGTH_SEMANTICS = CHAR
```

You can also modify this parameter for a session with the ALTER SESSION command:

```
ALTER SESSION SET NLS_LENGTH_SEMANTICS = CHAR
```

With this approach, modifying an existing application becomes a snap; now all existing declarations are automatically based on number of characters rather than bytes. After setting the system to character semantics, you can see the change in the data dictionary:

```
SELECT parameter, value
  FROM nls_session_parameters
 WHERE parameter = 'NLS_LENGTH_SEMANTICS'
```

The following is returned:

```
PARAMETER                 VALUE
------------------------- ----------
NLS_LENGTH_SEMANTICS      CHAR
```

Returning to the prior example, you can see that character semantics are used without specifying CHAR in the declaration.

```
DECLARE
   v_title   VARCHAR2 (30);
BEGIN
   SELECT title
     INTO v_title
     FROM publication
    WHERE publication_id = 2;

   DBMS_OUTPUT.put_line (v_title);
EXCEPTION
   WHEN OTHERS
   THEN
      DBMS_OUTPUT.put_line (DBMS_UTILITY.format_error_stack);
END;
```

The following is returned:

```
Oracle PL/SQL プログラミング 基礎編 第 3 版
```

Note that the maximum number of bytes allowed is not adjusted in any way with character semantics. While setting character semantics will allow 1,000 3-byte characters to go into a VARCHAR2(1000) without modification, you will not be able to put

---

32,767 3-byte characters in a VARCHAR2(32767). The VARCHAR2 variable limit is still set at 32,767 bytes and the VARCHAR2 column maximum is still 4,000 bytes.

 Include the use of character semantics in your initial application design and make your life infinitely easier. Unless you have an overwhelming need to use byte semantics in a portion of your application, set the parameter NLS_LENGTH_SEMANTICS = CHAR to make character semantics the default. If you change your NLS_LENGTH_SEMANTICS for an existing application, remember to recompile all objects so the change will take effect. *This includes rerunning the catproc.sql script to re-create all supplied packages too!*

# String Sort Order

Oracle provides advanced linguistic sort capabilities that extend far beyond the basic A-Z sorting you get with an ORDER BY clause. The complexities found in international character sets do not lend themselves to simple alphabetic sort, or collation, rules. Chinese, for example, includes approximately 70,000 characters (although many are not used regularly). Not exactly something you can easily put into song like the ABCs! Also, not something that can be defined by simple sort rules.

String sort order is an obvious programming problem that is often overlooked in globalization until a product makes its way to the test team. Ordering the names of employees, cities of operation, or customers is much more complicated than "A comes before B." Consider the following factors:

- Some European characters include accents that change the meaning of the base letter. The letter "a" is different from "ä." Which letter should come first in an ORDER BY?
- Each locale may have its own sort rules, so a multilingual application must be able to support different sort rules based on the text. Even regions that use the same alphabet may still have different sort rules.

Oracle provides three types of sorts: binary, monolingual, and multilingual.

The Unicode Consortium makes its collation algorithm public, so we can compare the output from our queries for these three types of sorts with the expected results shown at *http://www.unicode.org/charts/collation/*.

## Binary Sort

The binary sort is based on the character's encoding scheme, and the values associated with each character. It is very fast, and is especially useful if you know that all of your data is stored in uppercase. The binary sort is most useful for ASCII characters, sorting the English alphabet, but even then you may find some undesired results. ASCII encoding, for example, orders uppercase letters before their lowercase representation.

The following example from the g11n sample schema shows the results of a binary sort of German cities:

```
SELECT city
   FROM store_location
  WHERE country <> 'JP'
ORDER BY city;
```

The ordered list of results is as follows:

```
CITY
------------------------------------
Abdêra
Asselfingen
Astert
Auufer
Außernzell
Aßlar
Boßdorf
Bösleben
Bötersen
Cremlingen
Creuzburg
Creußen
Oberahr
Zudar
Zühlen
Ängelholm
...lsen
```

Note the order of the cities in the list. Ängelholm is ordered after Zühlen. Character codes are sorted in ascending order, providing the A–Z ordering you see above. These anomalies result from the inclusion of characters outside the English alphabet, here being treated as special characters.

## Monolingual Sort

Most European languages will benefit from monolingual sort capabilities within Oracle. Rather than using basic codes associated with the character's encoding scheme like the binary sort, two values are used to determine the relative position of a character in a monolingual sort. Each character has a major value, related to the base character, and a minor value, based on case and diacritic differences. If sort order can be determined by a difference in major value, the ordering is complete. Should there be a tie in major value, the minor value is used. This way, characters such as ö can be ordered relative to the character o accurately.

To see the impact this has on the ordering of these additional characters, let's return to the prior example and modify the session to use the German monolingual sort:

```
ALTER SESSION SET NLS_SORT = german;
```

Upon confirmation that the session has been altered, I run the following query:

```
SELECT city
  FROM store_location
 WHERE country <> 'JP'
ORDER BY city;
```

Notice that the order is different now that NLS_SORT is set to "german":

```
CITY
------------------------------------
Abdêra
Ängelholm
Aßlar
Asselfingen
Astert
Außernzell
Auufer
Boßdorf
Bösleben
Bötersen
Cremlingen
Creußen
Creuzburg
Oberahr
...lsen
Zudar
Zühlen
```

This is much better! The treatment of non-English characters is now in line with the expected German order of characters. By the way, if you do not want to (or cannot) alter your session NLS settings, you can use the NLSSORT function and the NLS_SORT parameter as part of your query. The following function demonstrates the use of this parameter:

```
FUNCTION city_order_by_func (v_order_by IN VARCHAR2)
   RETURN sys_refcursor
IS
   v_city    sys_refcursor;
BEGIN
   OPEN v_city
    FOR
       SELECT city
         FROM store_location
      ORDER BY NLSSORT (city, 'NLS_SORT=' || v_order_by);

   RETURN v_city;
END city_order_by_func;
```

As seen above, the NLSSORT function and the NLS_SORT parameter provide quick ways to change the results of an ORDER BY clause. For this function, which is used in the remaining examples, the NLS_SORT parameter is taken as input. Table 25-5 lists some of the available NLS_SORT parameter values in Oracle Database 11g.

*Table 25-5. Monolingual NLS_SORT parameter values*

| | | |
|---|---|---|
| arabic | xcatalan | japanese |
| arabic_match | german | polish |
| arabic_abj_sort | xgerman | punctuation |
| arabic_abj_match | german_din | xpunctuation |
| azerbaijani | xgerman_din | romanian |
| xazerbaijani | hungarian | russian |
| bengali | xhungarian | spanish |
| bulgarian | icelandic | xspanish |
| canadian french | indonesian | west_european |
| catalan | italian | xwest_european |

The list of parameters in this table includes some values prefixed with an x. These extended sort parameters allow for special cases in a language. In my cities example, some names have the character ß. This *sharp* s in German can be treated as ss for the purposes of the sort. I tried a sort using NLS_SORT = german. Let's try xgerman to see the difference:

```
VARIABLE v_city_order REFCURSOR
CALL city_order_by_func('xgerman') INTO :v_city_order;
PRINT v_city_order
```

This displays the following:

```
CITY
-----------------------------------
...
Abdêra
Ängelholm
Asselfingen
Aßlar
Astert
Außernzell
Auufer
...
```

Using xgerman rather than german, the word Aßlar drops to fourth in the list instead of third.

## Multilingual Sort

Monolingual sort, as you might guess from the use of "mono" in its name, has a major drawback. It can operate on only one language at a time based on the NLS_SORT parameter setting. Oracle also provides *multilingual* sort capabilities that allow you to sort for multiple locales.

The multilingual sort, based on the ISO 14651 standard, supports more than 1.1 million characters in a single sort. Not only does Oracle's multilingual support cover characters defined as part of the Unicode 4.0 standard, but it can also support supplementary characters.

Where binary sorts are determined by character encoding scheme codes, and monolingual sorts are developed in two stages, multilingual sorts use a three-step approach to determine the order of characters:

1. The first level, or primary level, separates base characters.
2. The secondary level distinguishes base characters from diacritics that modify the base characters.
3. Finally, the tertiary level separates by case.

For Asian languages, characters are also differentiated by number of strokes, PinYin, or radicals.

NLSSORT and NLS_SORT are still used for multilingual sorts, but the parameters change. GENERIC_M works well for most Western languages, and provides the base for the remaining list of values. Table 25-6 lists the NLS_SORT parameter values available for multilingual sorts.

*Table 25-6. Multilingual NLS_SORT parameter values*

| | | | |
|---|---|---|---|
| generic_m | | | |
| canadian_m | japanese_m | schinese_pinyin_m | tchinese_radical_m |
| danish_m | korean_m | schinese_radical_m | tchinese_stroke_m |
| french_m | schinese_stroke_m | spanish_m | thai_m |

To demonstrate the multilingual sort functionality, I can modify the call to use the generic_m value:

```
VARIABLE v_city_order REFCURSOR
CALL city_order_by_func('generic_m') INTO :v_city_order;
PRINT v_city_order
```

This returns the following ordered list of cities:

```
CITY
-----------------------------------
Abdêra
Ängelholm
Asselfingen
Aßlar
Astert
..
Zudar
Zühlen
尼崎市
旭川市
```

足立区
青森市

# Multilingual Information Retrieval

Application developers who work on catalogs, digital libraries, and knowledge repositories are no doubt familiar with information retrieval, or IR. An IR application takes in user-supplied criteria and searches for the items or documents that best match the *intent* of the user. This is one of the major ways that IR differs from standard SQL queries, which either do or do not find matches for the query criteria. Good IR systems can help determine what documents are about, and return those documents that are most relevant to the search, even if they don't match the search exactly.

Perhaps the most challenging task in IR is to support indexing and querying in multiple languages. English, for example, is a single-byte language that uses whitespace to separate words. Retrieval of information is substantially different when working with Japanese, which is a multibyte character set that does *not* use whitespace as delimiters.

Oracle Text, an option available in both the Oracle Enterprise Edition and the Oracle Standard Edition, provides full-text IR capabilities. Because Oracle Text uses SQL for index creation, search, and maintenance operations, it works very well in PL/SQL-based applications.

Called ConText and *inter*Media in prior releases, Oracle Text really came of age as an information retrieval solution with Oracle9*i* Database. With Oracle Text:

- All NLS character sets are supported.
- Searching across documents in Western languages, as well as in Korean, Japanese, and Traditional and Simplified Chinese, is possible.
- Unique characteristics of each language are accommodated.
- Searches are case-insensitive by default.
- Cross-language search is supported.

Before a PL/SQL application can be written that searches a data source, Oracle Text indexes must be created. As part of the g11n schema, I created an Oracle Text index on the publication.short_description column. To support multiple languages, I provided individual language preferences, as well as a MULTI_LEXER preference, that makes it possible to search across multiple languages with a single query.

---

### Oracle Text Indexes

There are four index types available with Oracle Text. The first, and most commonly used, is the CONTEXT index. The CONTEXT index can index any character or LOB column, including BFILEs. It uses a filter to extract text from different document types. The filter that is shipped with the data server can filter more than 350 different document types, including Word documents, PDFs, and XML documents.

---

Once the text is extracted from the document, it is broken into *tokens*, or individual terms and phrases, by a LEXER. Language-specific LEXERs are available where required. A MULTI_LEXER actually uses language-specific LEXERs (defined as SUB_LEXERs) to extract the tokens from a multilingual data source. The tokens are stored in Oracle Text index tables and are used during search operations to point to relevant documents. To see the tokens created in this chapter's examples, run the following:

```
SELECT token_text
  FROM dr$g11n_index$i
```

The result contains English, German, and Japanese tokens.

The other three Oracle Text index types are the CTXCAT, CTXRULE, and CTXXPATH indexes. For additional information regarding their structure, check out the *Oracle Text Application Developer's Guide*, and the *Oracle Text Reference* available at *http://otn.oracle.com*.

You can use the TEXT_SEARCH_FUNC function that is part of the **g11n** schema to test some of the multilingual features:

```
FUNCTION text_search_func (v_keyword IN VARCHAR2)
   RETURN sys_refcursor
IS
   v_title    sys_refcursor;
BEGIN
   OPEN v_title
    FOR
      SELECT    title, LANGUAGE, score (1)
        FROM publication
        WHERE contains (short_description, v_keyword, 1) > 0
      ORDER BY score (1) DESC;

   RETURN v_title;
END text_search_func;
```

A call to this function, passing "pl" as the keyword, yields the following result:

```
variable x refcursor;
call text_search_func('pl') into :x;
print x;
```

This returns the following result:

```
TITLE                                       LANGUAGE  SCORE(1)
------------------------------------------  --------  --------
Oracle PL/SQL プログラミング 基礎編 第 3 版             JA         18
Oracle PL/SQL Programming, 3rd Edition      EN        13
Oracle PL/SQL Programmierung, 2. Auflage    DE        9
```

You find this reference in all three languages because "pl" is common among them. Note that I searched on a lowercase "pl," but the "PL" in the record is uppercase. My search is case-insensitive by default even though no UPPER function was used.

It may be that some languages should be case-sensitive while others should not be. Language-specific case-sensitivity can be set as part of your language preference creation. Simply add a mixed_case attribute with a value of yes. The tokens will be created mixed case, just as they are stored in your document or column, but only for the language identified in that preference.

Oracle Database 11g makes multilingual IR easier with the introduction of the AUTO_LEXER. Although it has fewer language-specific features than the MULTI_LEXER, it provides a nearly effortless method of implementation. Instead of relying on a language column, the AUTO_LEXER identifies the text based on the code point.

Oracle also supports the WORLD_LEXER. It is not as full-featured as the MULTI_LEXER, and does not have language-specific features like the AUTO_LEXER. It is very easy to configure, however.

With the WORLD_LEXER, the text is broken into tokens based on the category in which it falls. Both Arabic and other categories are separated by whitespace because they're easily divided into tokens. Asian characters are more complex because they aren't whitespace delimited, so they are broken into overlapping tokens of two characters at a time. For example, the three-character string of 尼崎市 is broken into two tokens, 尼崎 and 崎市.

Oracle Text provides additional features as well, depending on the language. For details including language-specific features and restrictions, see the Oracle Text documentation provided on the OTN web site.

## IR and PL/SQL

I have designed and implemented some extremely large and complex record management systems and digital libraries. Based on my experiences, I have found that nothing beats PL/SQL for search and maintenance operations with Oracle Text. PL/SQL's tight integration to the database server, and its improved performance over the last few releases, makes stored PL/SQL program units the language of choice for these types of applications.

This is even more evident when working with multiple languages. The shared SQL and PL/SQL parser means that there is consistent handling of characters and character semantics, regardless of the language being indexed and searched.

One of the first projects most Oracle Text programmers undertake is to find a way to format strings for search. The following example creates a function that formats search strings for Oracle Text:

```
/* File on web: g11n.sql */
FUNCTION format_string (p_search IN VARCHAR2)
   RETURN VARCHAR2
AS
-- Define an associative array
   TYPE token_table IS TABLE OF VARCHAR2 (500 CHAR)
      INDEX BY PLS_INTEGER;

-- Define an associative array variable
   v_token_array          token_table;
   v_temp_search_string   VARCHAR2 (500 CHAR);
   v_final_search_string  VARCHAR2 (500 CHAR);
   v_count                PLS_INTEGER        := 0;
   v_token_count          PLS_INTEGER        := 0;
BEGIN
   v_temp_search_string := TRIM (UPPER (p_search));
   -- Find the max number of tokens
   v_token_count :=
        lengthc (v_temp_search_string)
      - lengthc (REPLACE (v_temp_search_string, ' ', ''))
      + 1;

   -- Populate the associative array
   FOR y IN 1 .. v_token_count
   LOOP
      v_count := v_count + 1;
      v_token_array (y) :=
           regexp_substr (v_temp_search_string, '[^[:space:]]+', 1, v_count);
      -- Handle reserved words
      v_token_array (y) := TRIM (v_token_array (y));

      IF v_token_array (y) IN ('ABOUT', 'WITHIN')
      THEN
         v_token_array (y) := '{' || v_token_array (y) || '}';
      END IF;
   END LOOP;

   v_count := 0;

   FOR y IN v_token_array.FIRST .. v_token_array.LAST
   LOOP
      v_count := v_count + 1;

      -- First token processed
      IF (    (v_token_array.LAST = v_count OR v_count = 1)
          AND v_token_array (y) IN ('AND', '&', 'OR', '|')
         )
```

```
      THEN
         v_final_search_string := v_final_search_string;
      ELSIF (v_count <> 1)
      THEN
         -- Separate by a comma unless separator already present
         IF    v_token_array (y) IN ('AND', '&', 'OR', '|')
            OR v_token_array (y - 1) IN ('AND', '&', 'OR', '|')
         THEN
            v_final_search_string :=
                     v_final_search_string || ' ' || v_token_array (y);
         ELSE
            v_final_search_string :=
                     v_final_search_string || ', ' || v_token_array (y);
         END IF;
      ELSE
         v_final_search_string := v_token_array (y);
      END IF;
   END LOOP;

   -- Escape special characters in the final string
   v_final_search_string :=
      TRIM (REPLACE (REPLACE (v_final_search_string,
                              '&',
                              ' & '
                             ),
                     ';',
                     ' ; '
                    )
           );
   RETURN (v_final_search_string);
END format_string;
```

This is designed to break *terms*, or tokens, from the string using the space between the characters. It uses character semantics for variable declarations, including the declaration of the associative array.

To test this with an English string, I run this SELECT:

```
SELECT format_string('oracle PL/SQL') AS "Formatted String"
   FROM dual
```

This returns the following result:

```
Formatted String
-----------------
ORACLE, PL/SQL
```

The FORMAT_STRING function separates terms with a comma by default, so an exact match is not required. A string of characters that is not whitespace-delimited will look exactly the way it was entered. The following example illustrates this using a mix of English and Japanese characters:

```
SELECT format_string('Oracle PL/SQL プログラミング 基礎編 第 3 版') AS
"Formatted String" FROM dual;
```

Passing this mixed character string to the FORMAT_STRING function returns the following result:

```
Formatted String
-----------------
ORACLE, PL/SQL プログラミング，基礎編，第 3 版
```

Where spaces delimit terms in the text, a comma is added regardless of the language.

The following CONTAINS search uses the FORMAT_STRING function:

```
SELECT score (1) "Rank", title
  FROM publication
  WHERE contains (short_description, format_string('プログラム'), 1) > 0;
```

This returns the following:

```
        Rank    TITLE
------------    ------------
          12    Oracle SQL*Plus デスクトップリファレンス
```

Using PL/SQL and Oracle Text, it is possible to index and perform full-text searches on data regardless of character set or language.

# Date/Time

My globalization discussion thus far has been focused on strings. Date/time issues, however, can be every bit as troublesome when localizing an application. Users may be on the other side of the world from your database and web server, but they still require accurate information relating to their time zone, and the format of the date and time must be in a recognized structure.

Consider the following issues related to date/time:

- There are different time zones around the world.
- Daylight savings time exists for some regions, and not for others.
- Certain locales use different calendars.
- Date/time formatting is not consistent throughout the world.

## Timestamp Datatypes

Until Oracle9i Database, working with dates and times was fairly straightforward. You had the DATE type and the TO_DATE function. The limited functionality of the DATE type made application development of global applications somewhat tedious, though. All time zone adjustments involved manual calculations. Sadly, if your application is to work with Oracle8i Database or earlier versions, I'm afraid you are still stuck with this as your only option.

Those of us working with Oracle9i Database and later, however, benefit greatly from the TIMESTAMP and INTERVAL datatypes discussed in detail in Chapter 10. If you have not read that chapter yet, I'll provide a quick overview here, but I do recommend that you go back and read that chapter to obtain a thorough understanding of the topic.

Lets take a look at an example of the TIMESTAMP, TIMESTAMP WITH TIME ZONE, AND TIMESTAMP WITH LOCAL TIME ZONE datatypes in action:

```
DECLARE
    v_date_timestamp        TIMESTAMP ( 3 )                      := SYSDATE;
    v_date_timestamp_tz     TIMESTAMP ( 3 ) WITH TIME ZONE       := SYSDATE;
    v_date_timestamp_ltz    TIMESTAMP ( 3 ) WITH LOCAL TIME ZONE := SYSDATE;
BEGIN
    DBMS_OUTPUT.put_line ('TIMESTAMP:  ' || v_date_timestamp);
    DBMS_OUTPUT.put_line ('TIMESTAMP WITH TIME ZONE:  ' || v_date_timestamp_tz);
    DBMS_OUTPUT.put_line (   'TIMESTAMP WITH LOCAL TIME ZONE:  '
                          || v_date_timestamp_ltz
                         );
END;
```

The following dates and times are returned:

```
TIMESTAMP:                        08-JAN-05 07.28.39.000 PM
TIMESTAMP WITH TIME ZONE:         08-JAN-05 07.28.39.000 PM -07:00
TIMESTAMP WITH LOCAL TIME ZONE:   08-JAN-05 07.28.39.000 PM
```

TIMEZONE and TIMEZONE WITH LOCAL TIMESTAMP are identical because the database time is in the same locale as my session. The value for TIMESTAMP WITH TIMEZONE shows that I am in the Mountain time zone. If I were in accessing my Colorado database via a session in California, the result would be slightly different.

```
TIMESTAMP:                        08-JAN-05 07.28.39.000 PM
TIMESTAMP WITH TIME ZONE:         08-JAN-05 07.28.39.000 PM -07:00
TIMESTAMP WITH LOCAL TIME ZONE:   08-JAN-05 06.28.39.000 PM
```

The value for TIMESTAMP WITH LOCAL TIMEZONE used the time zone of my session, which is now Pacific, or –08:00, and automatically converted the value.

## Date/Time Formatting

One localization challenge we face is related to date and time formatting. Japan, for example, may prefer the format *yyyy/MM/dd hh:mi:ssxff AM* while in the United States, you would expect to see *dd-MON-yyyy hh:mi:ssxff AM*.

A common way to handle this situation is to include a list of format masks in a locale table that maps to the user. When the user logs in, his assigned locale maps to the correct date/time format for his region.

The g11n schema has a USERS table and a LOCALE table, joined by a locale_id. Let's take a look at some examples using date/time functions (discussed in detail in Chapter 10), and the format masks provided in the g11n.locale table.

The registration_date column in the table uses the TIMESTAMP WITH TIME ZONE datatype. Using the TO_CHAR function and passing the format mask for each user's locale displays the date in the correct format.

```
/* File on web: g11n.sql */
FUNCTION date_format_func
   RETURN sys_refcursor
IS
   v_date   sys_refcursor;
BEGIN
   OPEN v_date
    FOR
       SELECT locale.locale_desc "Locale Description",
              TO_CHAR (users.registration_date,
                       locale.DATE_FORMAT
                      ) "Registration Date"
         FROM users, locale
         WHERE users.locale_id = locale.locale_id;

   RETURN v_date;
END date_format_func;
```

To execute it, I do the following:

```
variable v_format refcursor
CALL date_format_func() INTO :v_format;
PRINT v_format
```

This prints the following result set:

```
Locale Description              Registration Date
-----------------------         ------------------
English                         01-JAN-2005 11:34:21.000000 AM US/MOUNTAIN
Japanese                        2005/01/01 11:34:21.000000 AM JAPAN
German                          01 January 05 11:34:21.000000 AM EUROPE/WARSAW
```

The three locales have different date format masks assigned. Using this method allows each user to see an appropriate date format for his locale based on his profile. If I now add NLS_DATE_FORMAT, the dates and times will use the appropriate locale language. I have this mapped in my tables to ensure that each locale is displayed correctly.

```
/* File on web: g11n.sql */
FUNCTION date_format_lang_func
   RETURN sys_refcursor
IS
   v_date   sys_refcursor;
BEGIN
   OPEN v_date
    FOR
       SELECT locale.locale_desc "Locale Description",
              TO_CHAR (users.registration_date,
                       locale.DATE_FORMAT,
                       'NLS_DATE_LANGUAGE= ' || locale_desc
                      ) "Registration Date"
         FROM users, locale
         WHERE users.locale_id = locale.locale_id;

   RETURN v_date;
END date_format_lang_func;
```

I execute the function as follows:

```
variable v_format refcursor
CALL date_format_lang_func() INTO :v_format;
PRINT v_format
```

This prints the following:

```
Locale Description          Registration Date
----------------------      ------------------
English                     01-JAN-2005 11:34:21.000000 AM US/MOUNTAIN
Japanese                    2005/01/01 11:34:21.000000 午前  JAPAN
German                      01 Januar 05 11:34:21.000000 AM EUROPE/WARSAW
```

The same data is stored in the USERS table, but the time is displayed in locale-specific format. I can modify the function in the same way to use the time zone and timestamp functions to distinguish between time zones for various locales. NLS_DATE_LANGUAGE is customized for each territory, so AM is in Japanese for the Japanese locale, and the month for the German locale is displayed in German.

I can extend my function to include the session time zone either by converting the value to the TIMESTAMP WITH TIME ZONE datatype, or by converting the value to my session's local time zone with TIMESTAMP WITH LOCAL TIME ZONE. I do this with the CAST function (described in Chapter 7), which will change the datatype of the value stored in my table.

```
/* File on web: g11n.sql */
FUNCTION date_ltz_lang_func
    RETURN sys_refcursor
IS
   v_date   sys_refcursor;
BEGIN
   OPEN v_date
    FOR
       SELECT locale.locale_desc,
              TO_CHAR
                (CAST
                    (users.registration_date AS TIMESTAMP WITH LOCAL TIME ZONE
                    ),
                 locale.DATE_FORMAT,
                 'NLS_DATE_LANGUAGE= ' || locale_desc
                ) "Registration Date"
          FROM users, locale
         WHERE users.locale_id = locale.locale_id;

   RETURN v_date;
END date_ltz_lang_func;
```

The function is executed by doing the following:

```
variable v_format refcursor
CALL date_ltz_lang_func() INTO :v_format;
PRINT v_format
```

The registration dates are returned as follows:

```
Locale Description          Registration Date
----------------------      --------------------
English                     01-JAN-2005 11:34:21.000000 AM -07:00
Japanese                    2004/12/31 07:34:21.000000 午後 -07:00
German                      01 Januar 05 03:34:21.000000 AM -07:00
```

There is a lot going on here:

- Date/time language is converted to the locale-specific terms.
- Formatting is locale-specific.
- I use CAST to convert the values stored as TIMESTAMP WITH TIMEZONE to TIMESTAMP WITH LOCAL TIMEZONE.
- The displayed time is relative to my session's time zone, which is US/Mountain in this example, or –07:00.

Many of my examples thus far have shown the time zone as a UTC offset. This is not necessarily the easiest display for a user to understand. Oracle maintains a list of region names and abbreviations that can be substituted by modifying the format mask. In fact, the three records I have been working with were inserted using these region names rather than the UTC offset. For a complete list of time zones, query the V$TIMEZONE_NAMES view. Examine the INSERT statements into the USERS table in the g11n schema for more examples using region names.

I want to discuss one more NLS parameter related to date/time. My times are inserted into the table using the Gregorian calendar, which is the value for NLS_CALENDAR on my test system. Not all locales use the same calendar, however, and no amount of formatting will adjust the base calendar. With NLS_CALENDAR, I can change my default calendar from Gregorian to a number of other seeded calendars—Japanese Imperial for example. A simple SELECT of SYSDATE after setting the session results in the following:

```
ALTER SESSION SET NLS_CALENDAR = 'JAPANESE IMPERIAL';
ALTER SESSION SET NLS_DATE_FORMAT = 'E RR-MM-DD';
```

After altering the session, I run the following SELECT:

```
SELECT sysdate
  FROM dual;
```

The SELECT shows the modified SYSDATE:

```
SYSDATE
----------
H 17-02-08
```

Default values are controlled by your NLS settings. If you have a primary locale you are working with, you may find that setting your NLS parameters for your database is a much easier approach than explicitly stating them in your application. For applications in which these settings need to be dynamic, however, I recommend that you include NLS settings as part of your user/locale settings and store them with your application. This allows your code to function in any locale simply by setting a user's profile correctly.

# Currency Conversion

A discussion of globalization and localization would not be complete without addressing currency conversion issues. The most common approach to the conversion from dollars to yen, for example, is to use a rate table that tracks conversion rates between monetary units. But how does an application know how to display the resulting number? Consider the following:

- Are decimals and commas appropriate, and where should they be placed?
- Which symbol is used for each currency ($ for dollar, € for Euro, etc)?
- Which ISO currency symbol should be displayed (USD for example)?

Each publication in the g11n schema has a price and is associated with a locale. I can use the TO_CHAR function to format each string, but what about displaying the correct currency? I can use the NLS_CURRENCY parameter to format my prices correctly as follows:

```
/* File on web: g11n.sql */
FUNCTION currency_conv_func
   RETURN sys_refcursor
IS
   v_currency   sys_refcursor;
BEGIN
   OPEN v_currency
    FOR
       SELECT pub.title "Title",
              TO_CHAR (pub.price,
                       locale.currency_format,
                       'NLS_CURRENCY=' || locale.currency_symbol
                      ) "Price"
          FROM publication pub, locale
         WHERE pub.locale_id = locale.locale_id;

   RETURN v_currency;
END currency_conv_func;
```

I execute the currency conversion function as follows:

```
VARIABLE v_currency REFCURSOR
CALL currency_conv_func() INTO :v_currency;
PRINT v_currency
```

This returns the following list of prices:

```
Title                                              Price
-----------------------------------                ----------------
Oracle PL/SQL Programming, 3rd Edition             $54.95
Oracle PL/SQL プログラミング 基礎編 第 3 版         ¥5,800
Oracle PL/SQL Programmierung, 2. Auflage           €64
```

Note that no actual conversion is done here. If you need to automate the conversion from one currency to another, you will need to build your rate table and conversion rules.

The NLS_ISO_CURRENCY symbol is generally a three-character abbreviation. With a few exceptions, the first two characters refer to the country or locale, and the third character represents the currency. For example, the United States dollar and the Japanese yen are USD and JPY, respectively. Many European countries use the Euro, however, so the country/currency rule of thumb noted earlier cannot apply. It is simply represented as EUR.

The g11n schema includes ISO currency values to help us convert the prices of publications to their correct ISO abbreviations, as you can see in the ISO_CURRENCY_FUNC function:

```
/* File on web: g11n.sql */
FUNCTION iso_currency_func
    RETURN sys_refcursor
IS
    v_currency    sys_refcursor;
BEGIN
    OPEN v_currency
      FOR
         SELECT    title "Title",
                   TO_CHAR (pub.price,
                        locale.iso_currency_format,
                        'NLS_ISO_CURRENCY=' || locale.iso_currency_name
                   ) "Price - ISO Format"
            FROM publication pub, locale
           WHERE pub.locale_id = locale.locale_id
         ORDER BY publication_id;

    RETURN v_currency;
END iso_currency_func;
```

To execute the ISO_CURRENCY_FUNC function, I run the following:

```
VARIABLE v_currency REFCURSOR
CALL iso_currency_func() INTO :v_currency;
PRINT v_currency
```

The result set shows the following:

```
Title                                        Price - ISO Format
--------------------------------------       ----------------------
Oracle PL/SQL Programming, 3rd Edition        USD54.95
Oracle PL/SQL プログラミング 基礎編 第 3 版      JPY5,800
Oracle PL/SQL Programmierung, 2. Auflage      EUR64
```

USD, JPY, and EUR are included in my price display just as I expected based on the format mask.

# Globalization Development Kit for PL/SQL

Starting with Oracle Database 10g, Oracle provides a Globalization Development Kit (GDK) for Java and PL/SQL that simplifies the g11n development process. If you are developing a multilingual application, determining the locale of each user and presenting locale-specific feedback may be the most difficult programming task you will face. The PL/SQL components of the GDK help with this aspect of g11n development, and are delivered in two packages: UTL_I18N and UTL_LMS.

## UTL_I18N Utility Package

The UTL_I18N package is the workhorse of the GDK. Its subprograms are summarized in Table 25-7.

*Table 25-7. Programs in the UTL_I18N package*

| Name | Description |
| --- | --- |
| ESCAPE_REFERENCE | HTML and XML documents do not always support the same characters that are in the database. In such cases, it would be helpful to return an escape character. This function takes as input the source string, and the character set of the HTML or XML document. |
| GET_COMMON_TIME_ZONES | Returns a list of the most common time zones. This is particularly useful when presenting a user with a list of time zones he can select from to configure user settings. |
| GET_DEFAULT_CHARSET | Returns the default character set name or the email-safe name based on the language supplied to this function. |
| GET_DEFAULT_ISO_CURRENCY | Supplied with a territory, this function returns the appropriate currency code. |
| GET_DEFAULT_LINGUISTIC_SORT | Returns the most common sort for the supplied language. |
| GET_LOCAL_LANGUAGES | Returns local languages for a given territory. |
| GET_LOCAL_LINGUISTIC_SORTS | Returns a list of sort names based on a supplied language. |
| GET_LOCAL_TERRITORIES | Lists territory names based on a given language. |
| GET_LOCAL_TIMEZONES | Returns all time zones in a given territory. |
| GET_TRANSLATION | Translates the language and/or territory name for the specified language and returns the results. |
| MAP_CHARSET | Is particularly useful for applications that send data extracted from the database via email. Provides mapping between database character sets and email-safe character sets. |
| MAP_FROM_SHORT_LANGUAGE | Pass a short language name to this function, and it maps it to the Oracle language name. |

| Name | Description |
| --- | --- |
| MAP_LANGUAGE_FROM_ISO | Pass an ISO locale name to this function, and it returns the Oracle language name. |
| MAP_LOCALE_TO_ISO | Supply the Oracle language and territory to this function, and it returns the ISO locale name. |
| MAP_TERRITORY_FROM_ISO | Pass an ISO locale to this function, and it returns the Oracle territory name. |
| MAP_TO_SHORT_LANGUAGE | Reverse of the MAP_FROM_SHORT_LANGUAGE function. Supply the full Oracle language name to this function, and it returns the short name. |
| RAW_TO_CHAR | Overloaded function that takes a RAW type as input and returns a VARCHAR2. |
| RAW_TO_NCHAR | Identical to RAW_TO_CHAR except the return value is of type NVARCHAR2. |
| STRING_TO_RAW | Converts either VARCHAR2 or NVARCHAR2 to the specified character set and returns a value of type RAW. |
| TRANSLITERATE | Script translation, based on transliteration name, for Japanese Kana. |
| UNESCAPE_REFERENCE | Performs the reverse action of the ESCAPE_REFERENCE function. It recognizes escape characters and converts them back to their original characters. |

The GET_LOCAL_LANGUAGES function is one of the most useful in this package. If I know the territory of a user, I can reduce the list of values for valid languages for them to choose from in an application using the UTL_I18N.GET_LOCAL_LANGUAGES. This is great for applications in which the administrator must configure user-specific application settings. I can test it out using the following seed data.

```
CREATE TABLE user_admin (
    id NUMBER(10) PRIMARY KEY,
    first_name VARCHAR2(10 CHAR),
    last_name VARCHAR2(20 CHAR),
    territory VARCHAR2(30 CHAR),
    language VARCHAR2(30 CHAR))
/

BEGIN
INSERT INTO user_admin
    VALUES (1, 'Stan', 'Smith', 'AMERICA', 'AMERICAN');
INSERT INTO user_admin
    VALUES (2, 'Robert', 'Hammon', NULL, 'SPANISH');
INSERT INTO user_admin
    VALUES (3, 'Anil', 'Venkat', 'INDIA', NULL);
COMMIT;
END:
/
```

The territory is entered into the USER_ADMIN table. I can present a list of local languages for user Anil using the following anonymous block:

```
DECLARE
    -- Create array for the territory result set
    v_array   utl_i18n.string_array;
    -- Create the variable to hold the user record
    v_user    user_admin%ROWTYPE;
```

```
    BEGIN
       -- Populate the variable with the record for Anil
       SELECT *
         INTO v_user
         FROM user_admin
        WHERE ID = 3;

       -- Retrieve a list of languages valid for the territory
       v_array := utl_i18n.get_local_languages (v_user.territory);
       DBMS_OUTPUT.put (CHR (10));
       DBMS_OUTPUT.put_line ('=======================');
       DBMS_OUTPUT.put_line ('User: ' || v_user.first_name || ' '
                             || v_user.last_name
                            );
       DBMS_OUTPUT.put_line ('Territory: ' || v_user.territory);
       DBMS_OUTPUT.put_line ('=======================');

       -- Loop through the array
       FOR y IN v_array.FIRST .. v_array.LAST
       LOOP
          DBMS_OUTPUT.put_line (v_array (y));
       END LOOP;
    END;
```

This returns the following:

```
=======================
User: Anil Venkat
Territory: INDIA
=======================
ASSAMESE
BANGLA
GUJARATI
HINDI
KANNADA
MALAYALAM
MARATHI
ORIYA
PUNJABI
TAMIL
TELUGU
```

This list of values is much easier for a user to manage than a complete list of all languages. The same can be done for territories where the language is known. Suppose that Robert currently has a NULL territory, but his language is specified as SPANISH. The following anonymous block returns a list of valid territories for the SPANISH language:

```
DECLARE
   -- Create array for the territory result set
   v_array    utl_i18n.string_array;
   -- Create the variable to hold the user record
   v_user     user_admin%ROWTYPE;
BEGIN
   -- Populate the variable with the record for Robert
```

```
        SELECT *
          INTO v_user
          FROM user_admin
         WHERE ID = 2;

        -- Retrieve a list of territories valid for the language
        v_array := utl_i18n.get_local_territories (v_user.LANGUAGE);
        DBMS_OUTPUT.put (CHR (10));
        DBMS_OUTPUT.put_line ('=======================');
        DBMS_OUTPUT.put_line ('User: ' || v_user.first_name || ' '
                              || v_user.last_name
                             );
        DBMS_OUTPUT.put_line ('Language: ' || v_user.LANGUAGE);
        DBMS_OUTPUT.put_line ('=======================');

        -- Loop through the array
        FOR y IN v_array.FIRST .. v_array.LAST
        LOOP
           DBMS_OUTPUT.put_line (v_array (y));
        END LOOP;
     END;
```

The output is:

```
=======================
User: Robert Hammon
Language: SPANISH
=======================
SPAIN
CHILE
COLOMBIA
COSTA RICA
EL SALVADOR
GUATEMALA
MEXICO
NICARAGUA
PANAMA
PERU
PUERTO RICO
VENEZUELA
```

With a territory, I can present a list of languages, valid time zones, and currency to the end user and make configuration much easier. Once a language is selected, I can get the default character set, the default linguistic sort, the local territories, and the short language name, all using UTL_I18N.

## UTL_LMS Error-Handling Package

UTL_LMS is the second package that is part of the GDK. It includes two functions that retrieve and format an error message:

*GET_MESSAGE*
> Returns the raw message based on the language specified. By raw message, I mean that any parameters required for the message are not included in what is returned by GET_MESSAGE.

*FORMAT_MESSAGE*
> Adds detail to the message.

See the following example:

```
DECLARE
   v_bad_bad_variable   PLS_INTEGER;
   v_function_out       PLS_INTEGER;
   v_message            VARCHAR2 (500);
BEGIN
   v_bad_bad_variable := 'x';
EXCEPTION
   WHEN OTHERS
   THEN
      v_function_out :=
              utl_lms.GET_MESSAGE (06502, 'rdbms', 'ora', NULL, v_message);
      -- Output unformatted and formatted messages
      DBMS_OUTPUT.put (CHR (10));
      DBMS_OUTPUT.put_line ('Message - Not Formatted');
      DBMS_OUTPUT.put_line ('=======================');
      DBMS_OUTPUT.put_line (v_message);
      DBMS_OUTPUT.put (CHR (10));
      DBMS_OUTPUT.put_line ('Message - Formatted');
      DBMS_OUTPUT.put_line ('===================');
      DBMS_OUTPUT.put_line (utl_lms.format_message (v_message,
                                          ': The quick brown fox'
                                          )
                           );
END;
```

In the call to UTL_LMS.GET_MESSAGE, the value for language was left to the default value. In this case, the returned message will be in the default language, determined by NLS_LANGUAGE. My instance returns:

```
Message - Not Formatted
=======================
PL/SQL: numeric or value error%s

Message - Formatted
===================
PL/SQL: numeric or value error: The quick brown fox
```

Because a language value can be passed to UTL_LMS.GET_MESSAGE, I simply pass the application user's language when getting the message.

## GDK Implementation Options

The GDK functions allow for several different implementation options. If you are supporting only two or three locales, it might be easiest to separate your implementation

---

by locale. For your German system, set your database and application servers to the appropriate settings for that locale and have a completely separate environment for your users in France. More often than not, however, you will want to look at a true multilingual environment in which new locales can be added without purchasing and configuring a separate environment. This requires extra development effort up front, but is much easier to manage in the long run.

The method by which you determine your user's locale depends largely on who your users are and the type of application you are developing. In the following subsections I discuss three options for you to consider in your design.

## Method 1: Locale buttons

As a frequent surfer (of the Internet of course), I regularly see this method in action on web pages. Visit a company that does business in different locales and you might see buttons or links on the main page that look like the following:

> *in English | en Español | en Français | in Italiano*

This is great for web pages in which the business is restricted to a few locations and where date/time accuracy is not required. Users can choose their language and currency settings through the simple act of clicking the link, and should they choose incorrectly, they simply use the Back button on the browser to correct the problem.

In this scenario, you can either have separate pages and code for each locale or store session-specific selection in cookies or the database so all localization is controlled by the database. The most common approach here is to allow the application tier to control localization.

## Method 2: User administration

Applications that have a managed user base (not open to anonymous Internet users, for example) will find method 2 a great way to control locale settings. For a small number of users it is possible to use the UTL_I18N package to deliver a list of values (LOV) showing available time zones, locales, languages, and territories as I demonstrated earlier. The user or administrator simply selects the settings that are appropriate for the user, and every time that user logs in, that application reads these settings and delivers the appropriate localizations.

What about instances where there are a lot of users? It isn't feasible to manage each user's settings individually in all cases. We can take a lesson from the designers of the Oracle database (which is a global application, right?) and create profiles. Add to your application the ability to create a profile, and assign locale settings to it rather than to users. When you add a user, simply assign the profile. This cuts out many of the administrative headaches, especially if you ever have to go back and make a change later. You can simply change the profile rather than have to change all users.

### Method 3: Hybrid

Method 3 is a combination of methods 1 and 2. It is used frequently with Internet applications that have online stores. Most customers begin by browsing a site to see if it has something that they want. At this point, requiring them to fill out details about their location is premature, but they need locale-specific features such as data sorted and displayed in their language, and correct currency format. To make certain that basic locale information is correct, offer the solution discussed in method 1.

Once the decision to purchase is made, however, it is quite appropriate to have them enter a user profile including locale-specific information. The localization becomes more precise, using exact date/time and currency information from the database, all based on the customer's locale.

# CHAPTER 26
# Object-Oriented Aspects of PL/SQL

PL/SQL has always been a language that supports traditional procedural programming styles such as structured design and functional decomposition. Using PL/SQL packages, it is also possible to take an object-based approach, applying principles such as abstraction and encapsulation to the business of manipulating relational tables. Recent versions of the Oracle database have introduced direct support for *object-oriented programming* (OOP), providing a rich and complex type system, complete with support for type hierarchies and "substitutability."

In the interest of summarizing this book-sized topic into a modest number of pages, this chapter presents a few choice code samples to demonstrate the most significant aspects of object programming with PL/SQL. These cover the following areas:

- Creating and using object types
- Using inheritance and substitutability
- Type evolution
- Pointer (REF)-based retrieval
- Object views, including INSTEAD OF views

Among the things you will *not* find in this chapter are:

- Comprehensive syntax diagrams for SQL statements dealing with object types
- Database administration topics such as importing and exporting object data
- Low-level considerations such as physical data storage on disk

I'd like to introduce the topic with a brief history.

## Introduction to Oracle's Object Features

First released in 1997 as an add-on to the Oracle8 Database (the so-called "object-relational database"), the Objects Option allowed developers to extend Oracle's built-in datatypes to include *abstract datatypes*. The introduction of programmer-defined *collections* (described in Chapter 12) in that release also proved useful, not only because application developers had been looking for ways to store and retrieve arrays in the database, but also because PL/SQL provided a new way to query collections as if they were tables. While there were other interesting aspects of the new Oracle object model such as pointer-based navigation, there was no notion of inheritance or dynamic polymorphism, making the object-relational features of the Oracle8 Database an option that drew few converts from (or into) the camp of true OOP believers. The complexity of the object features, plus a perceived performance hit, also limited uptake in the relational camp.

The Oracle8*i* Database introduced support for Java Stored Procedures, which not only provided the ability to program the server using a less proprietary language than PL/SQL, but also made it easier for the OOP community to consider using stored procedures. Oracle provided a way to translate object type definitions from the server into Java classes, making it possible to share objects across the Java/database boundary. Oracle released the Oracle8*i* Database during a peak of market interest in Java, so hardly anyone really noticed that Oracle's core object features were not much enhanced, except that Oracle Corporation quietly began bundling the object features with the core database server. Around this time, I asked an Oracle representative about the future of object programming in PL/SQL, and the response was, "If you want real object-oriented programming in the database, use Java."

Nevertheless, with the Oracle9*i* Database release, Oracle significantly extended the depth of its native object support, becoming a more serious consideration for OOP purists. Inheritance and polymorphism have become available in the database, and PL/SQL has gained new object features. Does it finally make sense to extend the object model of your system into the structure of the database itself? Should you now repartition existing middleware or client applications to take advantage of "free stuff" in the database server? As Table 26-1 shows, Oracle has made great strides, and the move may be tempting. The table also shows that a few desirable features still aren't available.[1]

 Oracle Database 10*g*, although introducing several useful enhancements to collections (see Chapter 12), included only one new feature unique to object types: it is described in the sidebar "The OBJECT_VALUE Pseudo Column" on page 1111.

*Table 26-1. Significant object programming features in the Oracle database*

| Feature | 8.0 | 8.1 | 9.1 | 9.2 and later | 11g and later |
|---|---|---|---|---|---|
| Abstract datatypes as first-class database entity | ✓ | ✓ | ✓ | ✓ | ✓ |
| Abstract datatypes as PL/SQL parameter | ✓ | ✓ | ✓ | ✓ | ✓ |

1. Perhaps I should say *arguably* desirable features. The missing features are unlikely to be showstoppers.

| Feature | 8.0 | 8.1 | 9.1 | 9.2 and later | 11g and later |
|---|---|---|---|---|---|
| Collection-typed attributes | ✓ | ✓ | ✓ | ✓ | ✓ |
| REF-typed attributes for intra-database object navigation | ✓ | ✓ | ✓ | ✓ | ✓ |
| Implementing method logic in PL/SQL or C | ✓ | ✓ | ✓ | ✓ | ✓ |
| Programmer-defined object comparison semantics | ✓ | ✓ | ✓ | ✓ | ✓ |
| Views of relational data as object-typed data | ✓ | ✓ | ✓ | ✓ | ✓ |
| Compile-time or static polymorphism (method overloading) | ✓ | ✓ | ✓ | ✓ | ✓ |
| Ability to "evolve" type by modifying existing method logic (but not signature), or by adding methods | ✓ | ✓ | ✓ | ✓ | ✓ |
| Implementing method logic in Java | | ✓ | ✓ | ✓ | ✓ |
| "Static" methods (execute without having object instance) | | ✓ | ✓ | ✓ | ✓ |
| Relational primary key can serve as persistent object identifier, allowing declarative integrity of REFs | | ✓ | ✓ | ✓ | ✓ |
| Inheritance of attributes and methods from a user-defined type | | | ✓ | ✓ | ✓ |
| Dynamic method dispatch | | | ✓ | ✓ | ✓ |
| Noninstantiable supertypes, similar to Java-style "abstract classes" | | | ✓ | ✓ | ✓ |
| Ability to evolve type by removing methods (and adding to change signature) | | | ✓ | ✓ | ✓ |
| Ability to evolve type by adding and removing attributes, automatically propagating changes to associated physical database structures | | | ✓ | ✓ | ✓ |
| "Anonymous" types: ANYTYPE, ANYDATA, ANYDATASET | | | ✓ | ✓ | ✓ |
| Downcast operator (TREAT) and type detection operator (IS OF) available in SQL | | | ✓ | ✓ | ✓ |
| TREAT and IS OF available in PL/SQL | | | | ✓ | ✓ |
| User-defined constructor functions | | | | ✓ | ✓ |
| Supertype method invocation in a subtype | | | | | ✓ |
| "Private" attributes, variables, constants, and methods | | | | | |
| Inheritance from multiple supertypes | | | | | |
| Sharing of object types or instances across distributed databases without resorting to object views | | | | | |

Unless you're already a practicing object-oriented programmer, many of the terms in this table probably don't mean much to you. However, the remainder of this chapter should shed some light on these terms and give some clues about the larger architectural decisions you may need to make.

# Object Types by Example

In keeping with the sample general application area explored in the introductory book, *Learning Oracle PL/SQL Programming* (O'Reilly), I'd like to build an Oracle system that will use an object-oriented approach to modeling a trivial library catalog. The catalog can hold books, serials (such as magazines, proceedings, or newspapers), and, eventually, other artifacts.

A graphic portrayal of the top-level types appears in Figure 26-1. Later on, I might want to add to the type hierarchy, as the dotted-line boxes imply.

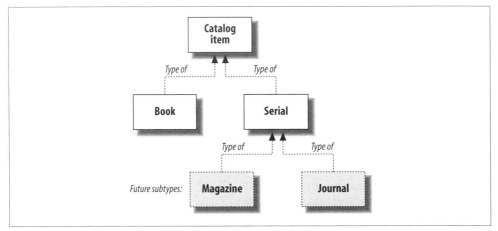

*Figure 26-1. Type hierarchy for a trivial library catalog*

## Creating a Base Type

The "root" or top of the hierarchy represents the common characteristics of all the subtypes. For now, let's assume that the only things that books and serials have in common are a library-assigned identification number and some kind of filing title. I can create an object type for catalog items using the following SQL statement from SQL*Plus:

```
CREATE OR REPLACE TYPE catalog_item_t AS OBJECT (
    id INTEGER,
    title VARCHAR2(4000),
    NOT INSTANTIABLE MEMBER FUNCTION ck_digit_okay
        RETURN BOOLEAN,
    MEMBER FUNCTION print
        RETURN VARCHAR2
) NOT INSTANTIABLE NOT FINAL;
```

This statement creates an object type, which is similar to a Java or C++ class. In relational terms, an object type is akin to a record type bundled with related functions and procedures. These subprograms are known collectively as *methods*.

The NOT FINAL keyword at the end flags the datatype as being able to serve as the *base type* or supertype from which you can derive other types. I needed to include NOT FINAL because I want to create subtypes for books and serials; if this keyword is omitted, the Oracle database defaults to FINAL, that is, no subtypes allowed.

Notice also that I've marked this type specification NOT INSTANTIABLE. Although PL/SQL will let me declare a variable of type catalog_item_t, I won't be able to give it a value—not directly, anyway. Similar to a Java *abstract class*, this kind of type exists only to serve as a base type from which to create subtypes, and objects of the subtype will, presumably, be instantiable.

For demonstration and debugging purposes, I've included a print method ("print" is *not* a reserved word, by the way) as a way to describe the object in a single string. When I create a subtype, it can (and probably should) override this method—in other words, the subtype will include a method with the same name, but will also print the subtype's attributes. Notice that instead of making print a procedure, which would have hard-coded a decision to use something like DBMS_OUTPUT.PUT_LINE, I decided to make it a function whose output can be redirected later. This decision isn't particularly object-oriented, just good design.

I've also defined a ck_digit_okay method that will return TRUE or FALSE depending on whether the "check digit" is OK. The assumption here (which is a bad one, I admit) is that all subtypes of catalog_item_t will be known by some identifier other than their library-assigned id, and these other identifiers include some concept of a check digit.[2] I'm only going to be dealing with books and serials, normally identified with an ISBN or ISSN, so the check digit concept applies to all the subtypes.

Here are a few further comments before moving on to the next part of the example:

- The CREATE TYPE statement above creates only an object type specification. The corresponding body, which implements the methods, will be created separately using CREATE TYPE BODY.

- Object types live in the same namespace as tables and top-level PL/SQL programs. This is one of the reasons I use the "_t" naming convention with types.

- Object types are owned by the Oracle user (schema) that created them, and this user may grant EXECUTE privilege to other users.

- You can attempt to create synonyms on object types, but unless you're using Oracle9i Database Release 2 or later, the synonyms won't work.

- As with conventional PL/SQL programs, you can create an object type using either definer rights (the default) or invoker rights (described in Chapter 24).

---

2. A *check digit* is a number incorporated into an identifier that is mathematically derived from the identifier's other digits. Its accuracy yields a small amount of confidence that the overall identifier has been correctly transcribed. The ISBN (International Standard Book Number) and ISSN (International Standard Serial Number)—identifiers assigned by external authorities—both contain check digits. So do most credit card numbers.

- Unlike some languages' object models, Oracle's model doesn't define a master root-level class from which all programmer-defined classes derive. Instead, you can create any number of standalone root-level datatypes such as catalog_item_t.
- If you see the compiler error *PLS-00103: Encountered the symbol ";" when expecting one of the following...*, you have probably made the common mistake of terminating the methods with a semicolon. The correct token in the type specification is a comma.

## Creating a Subtype

I made catalog_item_t impossible to instantiate, so now would be a good time to show how to create a subtype for book objects. In the real world, a book is a type of catalog item; this is also true in my example, in which all instances of this book_t subtype will have four attributes:

*id*
> Inherited from the base catalog_item_t type.

*title*
> Also inherited from the base type.

*isbn*
> Corresponds to the book's assigned ISBN, if any.

*pages*
> An integer giving the number of pages in the book.

In code, I can make the equivalent statement as follows:

```
1   TYPE book_t UNDER catalog_item_t (
2     isbn VARCHAR2(13),
3     pages INTEGER,
4
5     CONSTRUCTOR FUNCTION book_t (id IN INTEGER DEFAULT NULL,
6        title IN VARCHAR2 DEFAULT NULL,
7        isbn IN VARCHAR2 DEFAULT NULL,
8        pages IN INTEGER DEFAULT NULL)
9        RETURN SELF AS RESULT,
10
11     OVERRIDING MEMBER FUNCTION ck_digit_okay
12        RETURN BOOLEAN,
13
14     OVERRIDING MEMBER FUNCTION print
15        RETURN VARCHAR2
16   );
```

The interesting portions of this code are as follows:

| Line(s) | Description |
|---------|-------------|
| 1 | You can see that the syntax for indicating a subtype is the keyword UNDER in line 1, which makes a certain amount of intuitive sense. Oracle doesn't use the phrase AS OBJECT here because it would be redundant; the only thing that can exist "under" an object type is another object type. |
| 2–3 | I need to list only those attributes that are unique to the subtype; those in the parent type are implicitly included. Oracle orders the attributes with the base type first, then the subtype, in the same order as defined in the specification. |
| 5–15 | Here are the method declarations. I'll look at these methods more closely in the next section. |

## Methods

I've used two kinds of methods in the previous type definition:

*Constructor method*
   A function that accepts values for each attribute and assembles them into a typed object. Declared in lines 5–9 of the example.

*Member method*
   A function or procedure that executes in the context of an object instance—that is, it has access to the current values of each of the attributes. Declared in lines 11–12, as well as in lines 14–15 of the example.

My example shows a user-defined constructor, a feature that was introduced in Oracle9*i* Database Release 2. Earlier versions provided only a system-defined constructor. Creating your own constructor for each type gives you precise control over what happens at instantiation. That control can be very useful for doing extra tasks like validation and introducing controlled side effects. In addition, you can use several overloaded versions of a user-defined constructor, allowing it to adapt to a variety of calling circumstances.

To see some types and methods in action, take a look at this anonymous block:

```
1    DECLARE
2       generic_item catalog_item_t;
3       abook book_t;
4    BEGIN
5       abook := NEW book_t(title => 'Out of the Silent Planet',
6          isbn => '0-6848-238-02');
7       generic_item := abook;
8       DBMS_OUTPUT.PUT_LINE('BOOK: ' || abook.print());
9       DBMS_OUTPUT.PUT_LINE('ITEM: ' || generic_item.print());
10   END;
```

Interestingly, the objects' print invocations (lines 8 and 9) yield identical results for both abook and generic_item:

```
BOOK: id=; title=Out of the Silent Planet; isbn=0-6848-238-02; pages=
ITEM: id=; title=Out of the Silent Planet; isbn=0-6848-238-02; pages=
```

Let's walk through the code:

| Line(s) | Description |
|---|---|
| 5–6 | The constructor assembles a new object and puts it into a book. My example takes advantage of PL/SQL's named notation. It supplied values for only two of the four attributes, but the constructor creates the object anyway, which is what I asked it to do. |

The syntax to use any constructor follows the pattern:

```
[ NEW ] typename ( arg1, arg2, ... );
```

The NEW keyword, introduced in Oracle9*i* Database Release 2, is optional, but is nevertheless useful as a visual cue that the statement will create a new object.

| 7 | Even though a catalog item is not instantiable, I can assign to it an instance of a subtype, and it will even hold all the attributes that are unique to the subtype. This demonstrates one nifty aspect of "substitutability" that Oracle supports in PL/SQL, which is that by default, an object variable may hold an instance of any of its subtypes. Note to programmers of other languages: The assignment in line 7 is not simply creating a second reference to one object; instead, it's making a complete copy. |

In English, it certainly makes sense to regard a book as a catalog item. In computerese, it's a case of *widening* or *upcasting* the generic item by adding attributes from a more specific subtype. The converse operation, *narrowing*, is trickier but nevertheless possible, as you'll see later.

| 8–9 | Notice that the calls to print( ) use the graceful object-style invocation: |

```
object.methodname( arg1, arg2, ...)
```

because it is a member method executing on an already declared and instantiated object. Which version of the print method executes for objects of different types? The one in the *most specific subtype* associated with the currently instantiated object. The selection of the method gets deferred until runtime, in a feature known as *dynamic method dispatch*. This can be very handy, although it may incur a performance cost.

Let's turn now to the body of the book_t method, so you can better understand the result you've just seen. The implementation holds two important new concepts, which I'll describe afterwards.

```
1    TYPE BODY book_t
2    AS
3       CONSTRUCTOR FUNCTION book_t (id IN INTEGER,
4          title IN VARCHAR2,
5          isbn IN VARCHAR2,
6          pages IN INTEGER)
7          RETURN SELF AS RESULT
8       IS
9       BEGIN
10         SELF.id := id;
11         SELF.title := title;
12         SELF.isbn := isbn;
13         SELF.pages := pages;
14         IF isbn IS NULL OR SELF.ck_digit_okay
15         THEN
16            RETURN;
17         ELSE
18            RAISE_APPLICATION_ERROR(-20000, 'ISBN ' || isbn
19               || ' has bad check digit');
20         END IF;
```

```
21        END;
22
23        OVERRIDING MEMBER FUNCTION ck_digit_okay
24            RETURN BOOLEAN
25        IS
26            subtotal PLS_INTEGER := 0;
27            isbn_digits VARCHAR2(10);
28        BEGIN
29            /* remove dashes and spaces */
30            isbn_digits := REPLACE(REPLACE(SELF.isbn, '-'), ' ');
31            IF LENGTH(isbn_digits) != 10
32            THEN
33                RETURN FALSE;
34            END IF;
35
36            FOR nth_digit IN 1..9
37            LOOP
38                subtotal := subtotal +
39                    (11 - nth_digit) * TO_NUMBER(SUBSTR(isbn_digits, nth_digit, 1));
40            END LOOP;
41
42            /* check digit can be 'X' which has value of 10 */
43            IF UPPER(SUBSTR(isbn_digits, 10, 1)) = 'X'
44            THEN
45                subtotal := subtotal + 10;
46            ELSE
47                subtotal := subtotal + TO_NUMBER(SUBSTR(isbn_digits, 10, 1));
48            END IF;
49
50            RETURN MOD(subtotal, 11) = 0;
51
52        EXCEPTION
53            WHEN OTHERS
54            THEN
55                RETURN FALSE;
56        END;
57
58        OVERRIDING MEMBER FUNCTION print
59            RETURN VARCHAR2
60        IS
61        BEGIN
62            RETURN 'id=' || id || '; title=' || title
63                || '; isbn=' || isbn || '; pages=' || pages;
64        END;
65    END;
```

Note the following about lines 3–21:

- A user-defined constructor has several rules to follow:
    - It must be declared with keywords CONSTRUCTOR FUNCTION (line 3).
    - The return clause must be RETURN SELF AS RESULT (line 7).
    - It assigns values to any of the current object's attributes (lines 10–13).
    - It ends with a bare RETURN statement or an exception (line 16; lines 18–19).

- A constructor would typically assign values to as many of the attributes as it knows about. As you can see from line 14, my constructor tests the check digit before completing the construction. You will notice, if you skip ahead to line 30, that object attributes (such as SELF.isbn) are accessible even before validation is complete, an interesting and useful feature.

- Lines 18–19 are merely a placeholder; you should definitely take a more comprehensive approach to application-specific exceptions, as discussed in Chapter 6 in "Use Standardized Error Management Programs" on page 157.

Next, let's look at the use of the SELF keyword that appears throughout the type body; SELF is akin to Java's this keyword. Translation for non-Java programmers: SELF is merely a way to refer to the invoking (current) object when writing implementations of member methods. You can use SELF by itself when referring to the entire object, or you can use dot notation to refer to an attribute or a method:

```
IF SELF.id ...

IF SELF.ck_digit_okay() ...
```

The SELF keyword is not always required inside a member method, as you can see in lines 62–63, because the current object's attribute identifiers are always in scope. Using SELF can provide attribute visibility (as in lines 10–13, where the PL/SQL compiler interprets those unqualified identifiers as the formal parameters) and help to make your code SELF-documenting. (Ugh, sorry about that.)

There are a few more rules to note about this keyword:

- SELF isn't available inside static method bodies because static methods have no "current object." (I'll define static methods later in this section.)

- By default, SELF is an IN variable in functions and an IN OUT variable in procedures and constructor functions.

- You can change the default mode by including SELF as the first formal parameter.

Lines 23–56 of the previous example show the computing of the check digit, which is kind of fun, but my algorithm doesn't really exploit any new object-oriented features. I will digress to mention that the exception handler is quite important here; it responds to a multitude of problems such as the TO_NUMBER function encountering a character instead of a digit.

Next, on to creating a subtype for serials:

```
TYPE serial_t UNDER catalog_item_t (
   issn VARCHAR2(10),
   open_or_closed VARCHAR2(1),

   CONSTRUCTOR FUNCTION serial_t (id IN INTEGER DEFAULT NULL,
      title IN VARCHAR2 DEFAULT NULL,
      issn IN VARCHAR2 DEFAULT NULL,
      open_or_closed IN VARCHAR2 DEFAULT NULL)
      RETURN SELF AS RESULT,
```

```
    OVERRIDING MEMBER FUNCTION ck_digit_okay
       RETURN BOOLEAN,

    OVERRIDING MEMBER FUNCTION print
       RETURN VARCHAR2
) NOT FINAL;
```

Again, no new features appear in this type specification, but it does give another example of subtyping. A serial item in this model will have its own constructor, its own version of validating the check digit, and its own way to print itself.[3]

In addition to constructor and member methods, Oracle supports two other categories of methods:

*Static method*

> A function or procedure invoked independently of any instantiated objects. Static methods behave a lot like conventional PL/SQL procedures or functions.

*Comparison method*

> That is, a *map* or *order* method. These are special member methods that let you program what Oracle should do when it needs to compare two objects of this datatype—for example, in an equality test in PL/SQL or when sorting objects in SQL.

One final point before moving on. Objects follow PL/SQL's general convention that uninitialized variables are null;[4] the precise term for objects is *atomically null* (see Chapter 13 for more information).

As with collections, when an object is null, you cannot simply assign values to its attributes. Take a look at this short example:

```
DECLARE
    mybook book_t;        -- declared, but not initialized
BEGIN
    IF mybook IS NULL    -- this will be TRUE; it is atomically null
    THEN
        mybook.title := 'Learning Oracle PL/SQL'; -- this line raises...
    END IF;
EXCEPTION
    WHEN ACCESS_INTO_NULL    -- ...this predefined exception
    THEN
        ...
END;
```

Before assigning values to the attributes, you *must* initialize (instantiate) the entire object in one of three ways: by using a constructor method, via direct assignment from

---

3. In case you're curious, the open_or_closed attribute will be either (O)pen, meaning that the library can continue to modify the catalog entry (perhaps they do not own all the issues); (C)losed, meaning that the catalog entry is complete; or NULL, meaning we just don't know at the moment.

4. Associative arrays are a significant exception; they are non-null but empty when first declared.

another object, or via a fetch from the database, as described in "Storing, Retrieving, and Using Persistent Objects" on page 1085.

## Invoking Supertype Methods in Oracle Database 11g

One restriction in Oracle's object-oriented functionality that was lifted in Oracle Database 11g is the ability to invoke a method of a supertype that is overridden in the current (or higher-level) subtype.

Prior to Oracle Database 11g, if I overrode a supertype's method in a subtype, there was no way that I could call the supertype's method in an instance of the subtype. This is now possible, as I demonstrate below.

Suppose I create a root type to manage and display information about food (my favorite topic!):

```
/* File on web: 11g_gen_invoc.sql */
CREATE TYPE food_t AS OBJECT (
   NAME          VARCHAR2 (100),
   food_group    VARCHAR2 (100),
   grown_in      VARCHAR2 (100),
   MEMBER FUNCTION to_string RETURN VARCHAR2
)
NOT FINAL;
/
CREATE OR REPLACE TYPE BODY food_t
IS
   MEMBER FUNCTION to_string RETURN VARCHAR2
   IS
   BEGIN
      RETURN 'FOOD! ' || self.name || ' - '
            || self.food_group || ' - ' || self.grown_in;
   END;
END;
/
```

I then create a subtype of food, dessert, that overrides the to_string method. Now, when I display information about a dessert, I would like to include both dessert-specific information, as well as the more general food attributes, but I don't want to copy and paste the code from the food type. I want to reuse it. Prior to Oracle Database 11g, this was not possible. With the new *general invocation* feature (SELF AS *supertype*), however, I can define the type as follows:

```
CREATE TYPE dessert_t UNDER food_t (
   contains_chocolate CHAR (1)
 , year_created NUMBER (4)
 , OVERRIDING MEMBER FUNCTION to_string RETURN VARCHAR2
);
/

CREATE OR REPLACE TYPE BODY dessert_t
IS
```

```
OVERRIDING MEMBER FUNCTION to_string  RETURN VARCHAR2
IS
BEGIN
   /* Add the supertype (food) string to the subtype string.... */
   RETURN    'DESSERT! With Chocolate? '
          || contains_chocolate
          || ' created in '
          || SELF.year_created
          || chr(10)
          || (SELF as food_t).to_string;
END;
END;
/
```

Now, when I display the "to string" representation of a dessert, I see the food information as well:

```
DECLARE
   TYPE foodstuffs_nt IS TABLE OF food_t;

   fridge_contents foodstuffs_nt
         := foodstuffs_nt (
               food_t ('Eggs benedict', 'PROTEIN', 'Farm')
            , dessert_t ('Strawberries and cream'
                       , 'FRUIT', 'Backyard', 'N', 2001)
            );
BEGIN
   FOR indx in 1 .. fridge_contents.COUNT
   LOOP
      DBMS_OUTPUT.put_line (RPAD ('=', 60, '='));
      DBMS_OUTPUT.put_line (fridge_contents (indx).to_string);
   END LOOP;
END;
/
```

The output is:

```
==============================================================
FOOD! Eggs benedict - PROTEIN - Farm
==============================================================
DESSERT! With Chocolate? N created in 2001
FOOD! Strawberries and cream - FRUIT - Backyard
```

In Oracle's implementation of supertype invocation, you don't simply refer to the supertype with a generic SUPERTYPE keyword, as is done in some other object-oriented languages. Instead, you must specify the specific supertype from the hierarchy. This is more flexible (you can invoke whichever supertype method you like, but it also means that you must hardcode the name of the supertype in your subtype's code.

## Storing, Retrieving, and Using Persistent Objects

Thus far, I've only been discussing the definition of the datatypes and the instantiation of objects in the memory of running programs. Fortunately, that's not even half the story! Oracle wouldn't be Oracle if there were no way to store an object in the database.

There are at least two main ways that I could physically store the library catalog as modeled thus far: either as one big table of catalog objects or as a series of smaller tables, one for each subtype. I'll show the former arrangement, which could begin as follows:

```
CREATE TABLE catalog_items OF catalog_item_t
    (CONSTRAINT catalog_items_pk PRIMARY KEY (id));
```

This statement tells Oracle to build an *object table* called catalog_items, each row of which will be a *row object* of type catalog_item_t. An object table generally has one column per attribute:

```
SQL > DESC catalog_items
 Name                                 Null?    Type
 ------------------------------------ -------- -------------------------
 ID                                   NOT NULL NUMBER(38)
 TITLE                                         VARCHAR2(4000)
```

Remember, though, that catalog_item_t isn't instantiable, and each row in the table will actually be of a subtype such as a book or serial item. So where do the extra attributes go? Consider that these are legal statements:[5]

```
INSERT INTO catalog_items
    VALUES (NEW book_t(10003, 'Perelandra', '0-684-82382-9', 222));
INSERT INTO catalog_items
    VALUES (NEW serial_t(10004, 'Time', '0040-781X', '0'));.
```

---

## Method Chaining

An object whose type definition looks like this:

```
CREATE OR REPLACE TYPE chaindemo_t AS OBJECT (
    x NUMBER, y VARCHAR2(10), z DATE,
    MEMBER FUNCTION setx (x IN NUMBER) RETURN chaindemo_t,
    MEMBER FUNCTION sety (y IN VARCHAR2) RETURN chaindemo_t,
    MEMBER FUNCTION setz (z IN DATE) RETURN chaindemo_t);
```

provides the ability to "chain" its methods together. For example:

```
DECLARE
    c chaindemo_t := chaindemo_t(NULL, NULL, NULL);
BEGIN
    c := c.setx(1).sety('foo').setz(sysdate);  -- chained invocation
```

The executable statement above really just acts as the equivalent of:

```
c := c.setx(1);
c := c.sety('foo');
c := c.setz(sysdate);
```

Each function returns a typed object as the input to the next function in the chain. The implementation of one of the methods appears in the following code (the others are similar):

---

5. I would prefer to use named notation in these static function calls, but that was not supported until Oracle Database 11g, which now supports named notation for any user-defined PL/SQL function called within a SQL statement.

---

```
        MEMBER FUNCTION setx (x IN NUMBER) RETURN chaindemo_t IS
            l_self chaindemo_t := SELF;
        BEGIN
            l_self.x := x;
            RETURN l_self;
        END;
```

Here are some rules about chaining :

- You cannot use a function's return value as an IN OUT parameter to the next function in the chain. Functions return read-only values.
- Methods are invoked in order from left to right.
- The return value of a chained method must be of the object type expected by the method to its right.
- A chained call can include at most a single procedure.

If your chained call includes a procedure, it must be the rightmost method in the chain.

---

In fact, Oracle put the ISBN, ISSN, etc., into hidden columns on the catalog_items table. From an object programming point of view, that's pretty cool because it helps preserve the abstraction of the catalog item, yet provides a way to expose the additional subtype information when needed.

One more thing about the catalog_items table: the CONSTRAINT clause above designates the id column as the primary key. Yes, object tables can have primary keys too. And, if you exclude such a CONSTRAINT clause, Oracle will instead create a system-generated object identifier (OID), as described next.

### Object identity

If you're a relational database programmer, you know that conventional tables have a unique identifier for every row. If you're an object-oriented programmer, you know that OOP environments generally assign unique arbitrary identifiers that serve as object handles. If you're a programmer using object-relational features of the database, you have a mix of both approaches. The following table summarizes where you will find object identifiers:

| What and where | Has object identifier? |
| --- | --- |
| Row object in object table | Yes |
| Column object in any table (or fetched into PL/SQL program) | No; use row's primary key instead |
| Transient object created in PL/SQL program | No; use entire object instead |
| Row object fetched from object table into PL/SQL program | Yes, but available in program only if you explicitly fetch the "REF" ( See the later section "Using REFs" on page 1096) |

Here is an example of a table that can hold column objects:

```
CREATE TABLE my_writing_projects (
    project_id INTEGER NOT NULL PRIMARY KEY,
    start_date DATE,
    working_title VARCHAR2(4000),
    catalog_item catalog_item_t  -- this is a "column object"
);
```

Oracle Corporation takes the view that a column object is dependent on the row's primary key, and should not be independently identified.[6]

For any object table, the Oracle database can base its object identifier on one of two things:

*The primary key value*

> To use this feature, use the clause OBJECT IDENTIFIER IS PRIMARY KEY at the end of the CREATE TABLE statement.

*A system-generated value*

> If you omit the PRIMARY KEY clause, Oracle adds a hidden column named SYS_NC_OID$ to the table and populates it with a unique 16-byte RAW value for each row.

Which kind of OID should you use? Primary-key-based OIDs typically use less storage than system-generated OIDs, provide a means of enforcing referential integrity, and allow for much more convenient loading of objects. System-generated OIDs have the advantage that REFs to them cause "SCOPED" or limited to values from only one table. For a more complete discussion of the pros and cons of these two approaches, check out Oracle's *Application Developer's Guide—Object-Relational Features*. For now, you should know that a system-generated OID is:

*Opaque*

> Although your programs can use the OID indirectly, you don't typically see its value.

*Potentially globally unique across databases*

> The OID space makes provisions for up to $2^{128}$ objects (definitely "many" by the reckoning of the Hottentots).[7] In theory, these OIDs could allow object navigation across distributed databases without embedding explicit database links.

*Immutable*

> Immutable in this context means incapable of update. Even after export and import, the OID remains the same, unlike a ROWID. To "change" an OID, you would have to delete and recreate the object.

---

6. A contrary view is held by relational industry experts who assert that OIDs should not be used for row identification and that *only* column objects should have OIDs. See Hugh Darwen and C. J. Date, "The Third Manifesto," *SIGMOD Record*, Volume 24 Number 1, March 1995.

7. The Hottentots had a four-valued counting system: 1, 2, 3, and "many."

### The VALUE function

To retrieve an object from the database, Oracle provides the VALUE function in SQL. VALUE accepts a single argument, which must be a table alias in the current FROM clause, and returns an object of the type on which the table is defined. It looks like this in a SELECT statement:

```
SELECT VALUE(c)
  FROM catalog_items c;
```

I like short abbreviations as table aliases, which explains the c. The VALUE function returns an opaque series of bits to the calling program rather than a record of column values. SQL*Plus, however, has built-in features to interpret these bits, returning the following result from that query:

```
VALUE(C)(ID, TITLE)
-------------------------------------------------
BOOK_T(10003, 'Perelandra', '0-684-82382-9', 222)
SERIAL_T(10004, 'Time', '0040-781X', '0')
```

PL/SQL also has features to deal with fetching objects. Start with a properly typed local variable named catalog_item:

```
DECLARE
   catalog_item catalog_item_t;
   CURSOR ccur IS
      SELECT VALUE(c)
        FROM catalog_items c;
BEGIN
   OPEN ccur;
   FETCH ccur INTO catalog_item;
   DBMS_OUTPUT.PUT_LINE('I fetched item #' || catalog_item.id);
   CLOSE ccur;
END;
```

The argument to PUT_LINE uses *variable.attribute* notation to yield the attribute value, resulting in the output:

```
I fetched item #10003
```

The fetch assigns the object to the local variable catalog_item, which is of the base type; this makes sense because I don't know in advance which subtype I'll be retrieving. My fetch simply assigns the object into the variable.

In addition to substitutability, the example also illustrates (by displaying catalog_item.id) that I have direct access to the base type's attributes.

In case you're wondering, normal cursor attribute tricks work too; the previous anonymous block is equivalent to:

```
DECLARE
   CURSOR ccur IS
     SELECT VALUE(c) obj
        FROM catalog_items c;
   arec ccur%ROWTYPE;
```

```
BEGIN
   OPEN ccur;
   FETCH ccur INTO arec;
   DBMS_OUTPUT.PUT_LINE('I fetched item #' || arec.obj.id);
   CLOSE ccur;
END;
```

If I just wanted to print out all of the object's attributes, I could, of course, use the print method I've already defined. It's legal to use this because it has been defined at the root type level and implemented in the subtypes; at runtime, the database will find the appropriate overriding implementations in each subtype. Ah, the beauty of dynamic method dispatch.

As a matter of fact, the VALUE function supports dot notation, which provides access to attributes and methods—but only those specified on the base type. For example, the following:

```
SELECT VALUE(c).id, VALUE(c).print()
   FROM catalog_items c;
```

yields:

```
VALUE(C).ID VALUE(C).PRINT()
----------- -----------------------------------------------------------
      10003 id=10003; title=Perelandra; isbn=0-684-82382-9; pages=222
      10004 id=10004; title=Time; issn=0040-781X; open_or_closed=Open
```

If I happen to be working in a client environment that doesn't understand Oracle objects, I might want to take advantage of such features.

But what if I want to read only the attribute(s) unique to a particular subtype? I might first try something like this:

```
SELECT VALUE(c).issn    /* Error; subtype attributes are inaccessible */
   FROM catalog_items c;
```

This gives me *ORA-00904: invalid column name*. The Oracle database is telling me that an object of the parent type provides no direct access to subtype attributes. I might try declaring book of book_t and assigning the subtyped object to it, hoping that it will expose the "hidden" attributes:

```
book := catalog_item;  /* Error; Oracle won't do implied downcasts */
```

This time I get *PLS-00382: expression is of wrong type*. What's going on? The non-intuitive answer to that mystery appears in the next section.

Before I move on, here are a few final notes about performing DML on object relational tables:

- For object tables built on object types that lack subtypes, it is possible to select, insert, update, and delete all column values using conventional SQL statements. In this way, some object-oriented and relational programs can share the same underlying data.

---

- You cannot perform conventional relational DML on hidden columns that exist as a result of subtype-dependent attributes. You must use an "object DML" approach.

- To update an entire persistent object from a PL/SQL program, you can use an object DML statement such as:

```
UPDATE catalog_items c SET c = object_variable WHERE ...
```

This updates all the attributes (columns), including those unique to a subtype.

- The only good way I have found to update a specific column that is unique to a subtype is to update the entire object. For example, to change the page count to 1,000 for the book with id 10007:

```
UPDATE catalog_items c
   SET c = NEW book_t(c.id, c.title, c.publication_date, c.subject_refs,
                      (SELECT TREAT(VALUE(y) AS book_t).isbn
                         FROM catalog_items y
                        WHERE id = 10007),
                             1000)
   WHERE id = 10007;
```

Now let's go back and take a look at that last problem I mentioned.

### The TREAT function

If I'm dealing with a PL/SQL variable typed as a supertype, and it's populated with a value of one of its subtypes, how can I gain access to the subtype-specific attributes and methods? In my case, I want to treat a generic catalog item as the more narrowly defined book. This operation is called *narrowing* or *downcasting*, and is something the compiler can't, or won't, do automatically. What I need to use is the Oracle function called TREAT:

```
DECLARE
   book book_t;
   catalog_item catalog_item_t := NEW book_t();
BEGIN
   book := TREAT(catalog_item AS book_t);   /* Using 9i R2 or later */
END;
```

or, in SQL (note that in releases prior to Oracle9*i* Database Release 2 PL/SQL doesn't directly support TREAT):

```
DECLARE
   book book_t;
   catalog_item catalog_item_t := book_t(NULL, NULL, NULL, NULL);
BEGIN
   SELECT TREAT (catalog_item AS book_t)
     INTO book
     FROM DUAL;
END;
```

The general syntax of the TREAT function is:

```
TREAT (object_instance AS subtype) [ . { attribute | method( args...) } ]
```

where *object_instance* is any object with *subtype* as the name of one of its subtypes. Calls to TREAT won't compile if you attempt to treat one type as another from a different type hierarchy. One notable feature of TREAT is that if you have supplied an object from the correct type hierarchy, it will return either the downcasted object or NULL—but not an error.

As with VALUE, you can use dot notation with TREAT to specify an attribute or method of the TREATed object. For example:

```
DBMS_OUTPUT.PUT_LINE(TREAT (VALUE(c) AS serial_t).issn);
```

If I want to iterate over all the objects in the table in a type-aware fashion, I can do something like this:

```
DECLARE
    CURSOR ccur IS
        SELECT VALUE(c) item FROM catalog_items c;
    arec ccur%ROWTYPE;
BEGIN
    FOR arec IN ccur
    LOOP
        CASE
            WHEN arec.item IS OF (book_t)
            THEN
                DBMS_OUTPUT.PUT_LINE('Found a book with ISBN '
                    || TREAT(arec.item AS book_t).isbn);
            WHEN arec.item IS OF (serial_t)
            THEN
                DBMS_OUTPUT.PUT_LINE('Found a serial with ISSN '
                    || TREAT(arec.item AS serial_t).issn);
            ELSE
                DBMS_OUTPUT.PUT_LINE('Found unknown catalog item');
        END CASE;
    END LOOP;
END;
```

This block introduces the IS OF predicate to test an object's type. Although the syntax is somewhat exciting:

```
object IS OF ( [ ONLY ] typename )
```

the IS OF operator is much more limited than one would hope: it works only on object types, not on any of Oracle's core datatypes like NUMBER or DATE. Also, it will return an error if the *object* is not in the same type hierarchy as *typename*.

Notice the ONLY keyword. The default behavior—without ONLY—is to return TRUE if the object is of the given type *or any of its subtypes*. If you use ONLY, the expression won't check the subtypes and returns TRUE only if the type is an exact match.

Syntactically, you must always use the output from any TREAT expression as a function, even if you just want to call TREAT to invoke a member procedure. For example, you'd expect that if there were a set_isbn member procedure in the book_t, you could do this:

```
TREAT(item AS book_t).set_isbn('0140714154'); --wrong
```

But that gives the curious compiler error *PLS-00363: expression 'SYS_TREAT' cannot be used as an assignment target.*

Instead, you need to store the item in a temporary variable, and then invoke the member procedure:

```
book := TREAT(item AS book_t);
book.set_isbn('0140714154');
```

The IS OF predicate, like TREAT itself, became available in Oracle9*i* Database Release 1 SQL, although direct support for it in PL/SQL didn't appear until Oracle9*i* Database Release 2. As a Release 1 workaround, I could define one or more additional methods in the type tree, taking advantage of dynamic method dispatch to perform the desired operation at the correct level in the hierarchy. The "correct" solution to the narrowing problem depends not just on the version number, though, but also on what my application is supposed to accomplish.

For the moment, I'd like to move on to another interesting area: exploring the features Oracle offers when (not if!) you have to deal with changes in application design.

## Evolution and Creation

Oracle9*i* Database and later versions are light years beyond the Oracle8*i* Database in the area known as *type evolution*. That is, the later versions let you make a variety of changes to object types, even if you have created tables full of objects that depend on the type. Yippee!

Earlier in this chapter, I did a quick-and-dirty job of defining catalog_item_t. As almost any friendly librarian would point out, it might also be nice to carry publication date information[8] about all the holdings in the library. So I just hack out the following (no doubt while my DBA cringes):

```
ALTER TYPE catalog_item_t
    ADD ATTRIBUTE publication_date VARCHAR2(400)
    CASCADE INCLUDING TABLE DATA;
```

*Et voilà!* Oracle propagates this change to perform the needed physical alterations in the corresponding table(s). It appends the attribute to the bottom of the supertype's

---

8. I can't make this attribute an Oracle DATE type, though, because sometimes it's just a year, sometimes a month or a quarter, and occasionally something completely offbeat. I might get really clever and make this a nifty object type...well, maybe in the movie version.

attributes and adds a column after the last column of the supertype in the corresponding object table. A DESCRIBE of the type now looks like this:

```
SQL> DESC catalog_item_t
catalog_item_t is NOT FINAL
catalog_item_t is NOT INSTANTIABLE
Name                                     Null?    Type
---------------------------------------- -------- ----------------------------
 ID                                               NUMBER(38)
 TITLE                                            VARCHAR2(4000)
 PUBLICATION_DATE                                 VARCHAR2(400)

METHOD
------
 MEMBER FUNCTION CK_DIGIT_OKAY RETURNS BOOLEAN
 CK_DIGIT_OKAY IS NOT INSTANTIABLE

METHOD
------
 MEMBER FUNCTION PRINT RETURNS VARCHAR2
```

And a DESCRIBE of the table now looks like this:

```
SQL> DESC catalog_items
Name                                     Null?    Type
---------------------------------------- -------- ----------------------------
 ID                                      NOT NULL NUMBER(38)
 TITLE                                            VARCHAR2(4000)
 PUBLICATION_DATE                                 VARCHAR2(400)
```

In fact, the ALTER TYPE statement fixes *nearly* everything—though alas, it isn't smart enough to rewrite my methods. My constructors are a particular issue because I need to alter their signature. Hey, no problem! I can change a method signature by dropping and then recreating the method.

 When evolving object types, you may encounter the message *ORA-22337: the type of accessed object has been evolved.* This condition may prevent you from doing a DESCRIBE on the type. You might think that recompiling it will fix the problem, but it won't. Moreover, if you have hard dependencies on the type, the Oracle database won't let you recompile the object type specification. To get rid of this error, disconnect and then reconnect your Oracle session. This clears various buffers and enables DESCRIBE to see the new version.

To drop the method from the book type specification, specify:

```
ALTER TYPE book_t
   DROP CONSTRUCTOR FUNCTION book_t (id INTEGER DEFAULT NULL,
      title VARCHAR2 DEFAULT NULL,
      isbn VARCHAR2 DEFAULT NULL,
      pages INTEGER DEFAULT NULL)
      RETURN SELF AS RESULT
   CASCADE;
```

Notice that I supply the full function specification. That will guarantee that I'm dropping the correct method because multiple overloaded versions of it might exist. (Strictly speaking, though, the DEFAULTs are not required, but I left them in because I'm usually just cutting and pasting this stuff.)

The corresponding add-method operation is easy:

```
ALTER TYPE book_t
    ADD CONSTRUCTOR FUNCTION book_t (id INTEGER DEFAULT NULL,
        title VARCHAR2 DEFAULT NULL,
        publication_date VARCHAR2 DEFAULT NULL,
        isbn VARCHAR2 DEFAULT NULL,
        pages INTEGER DEFAULT NULL)
        RETURN SELF AS RESULT
    CASCADE;
```

Easy for me, anyway; the database is doing a lot more behind the scenes than I will probably ever know.

The next steps (not illustrated in this chapter) would be to alter the serial_t type in a similar fashion and then rebuild the two corresponding object type bodies with the CREATE OR REPLACE TYPE BODY statement. I would also want to inspect all the methods to see whether any changes would make sense elsewhere (for example, it would be a good idea to include the publication date in the print method).

By the way, you can drop a type using the statement:

```
DROP TYPE typename [ FORCE ];
```

Use the FORCE option with care because it cannot be undone. Any object types or object tables that depend on a force-dropped type will be rendered permanently useless. If there are any columns defined on a force-dropped type, the database marks them as UNUSED and makes them inaccessible. If your type is a subtype, and you have used the supertype in any table definitions, you might benefit from this form of the statement:

```
DROP TYPE subtypename VALIDATE;
```

VALIDATE causes the database to look through the table and drop the type as long as there are no instances of the subtype, avoiding the disastrous consequences of the FORCE option.

Now let's visit the strange and fascinating world of *object referencing*.

## Back to Pointers?

The object-relational features in Oracle include the ability to store an *object reference* or *REF value*. A REF is a *logical pointer* to a particular row in an object table. The Oracle database stores inside each reference the following information:

- The target row's primary key or system-generated object identifier.
- A unique identifier to designate the table.

- At the programmer's option, a hint on the row's physical whereabouts on disk, in the form of its ROWID.

The literal contents of a REF are not terribly useful unless you happen to like looking at long hex strings:

```
SQL> SELECT REF(c) FROM catalog_items c WHERE ROWNUM = 1;
REF(C)
--------------------------------------------------------------------------------
00002802099FC431FBE5F20599E0340003BA0F1F139FC431FBE5F10599E0340003BA0F1F130240000C0000
```

However, your queries and programs can use a REF to retrieve a row object without having to name the table where the object resides. Huh? Queries without table names? A pointer in a relational database? Let's take a look at how this feature might work in my library catalog.

### Using REFs

Libraries classify their holdings within a strictly controlled set of subjects. For example, the Library of Congress might classify the book you're reading now in the following three subjects:

- Oracle (Computer file)
- PL/SQL (Computer program language)
- Relational databases

The Library of Congress uses a hierarchical subject tree: "Computer file" is the broader subject or parent of "Oracle," and "Computer program language" is the broader subject for "PL/SQL."

When classifying things, any number of subjects may apply to a particular catalog item in a many-to-many (M:M) relationship between subjects and holdings. In my simple library catalog, I will make one long list (table) of all available subjects. While a relational approach to the problem would then establish an "intersection entity" to resolve the M:M relationship, I have other options out here in object-relational land.

I will start with an object type for each subject:

```
CREATE TYPE subject_t AS OBJECT (
   name VARCHAR2(2000),
   broader_term_ref REF subject_t
);
```

Each subject has a name and a broader term. However, I'm not going to store the term itself as a second attribute, but instead a reference to it. The third line of this type definition shows that I've typed the broader_term_ref attribute as a REF to a same-typed object. It's kind of like Oracle's old EMP table, with a MGR column whose value identifies the manager's record in the same table.

I now create a table of subjects:

```
CREATE TABLE subjects OF subject_t
  (CONSTRAINT subject_pk PRIMARY KEY (name),
   CONSTRAINT subject_self_ref FOREIGN KEY (broader_term_ref)
     REFERENCES subjects);
```

The foreign key begs a bit of explanation. Even though it references a table with a relational primary key, because the foreign key datatype is a REF, Oracle knows to use the table's object identifier instead. This support for the REF-based foreign key constraint is a good example of Oracle's bridge between the object and relational worlds.

Here are a few unsurprising inserts into this table (just using the default constructor):

```
INSERT INTO subjects VALUES (subject_t('Computer file', NULL));
INSERT INTO subjects VALUES (subject_t('Computer program language', NULL));
INSERT INTO subjects VALUES (subject_t('Relational databases', NULL));
INSERT INTO subjects VALUES (subject_t('Oracle',
  (SELECT REF(s) FROM subjects s WHERE name = 'Computer file')));
INSERT INTO subjects VALUES (subject_t('PL/SQL',
  (SELECT REF(s) FROM subjects s WHERE name = 'Computer program language')));
```

For what it's worth, you can list the contents of the subjects table, as shown here:

```
SQL> SELECT VALUE(s) FROM subjects s;

VALUE(S)(NAME, BROADER_TERM_REF)
--------------------------------------------------------------------------------
SUBJECT_T('Computer file', NULL)
SUBJECT_T('Computer program language', NULL)
SUBJECT_T('Oracle', 00002202089FC431FBE6FB0599E0340003BA0F1F139FC431FBE6690599E03
40003BA0F1F13)

SUBJECT_T('PL/SQL', 00002202089FC431FBE6FC0599E0340003BA0F1F139FC431FBE6690599E03
40003BA0F1F13)

SUBJECT_T('Relational databases', NULL)
```

Even if that's interesting, it's not terribly useful. However, what's both interesting and useful is that I can easily have Oracle automatically "resolve" or follow those pointers. For example, I can use the DEREF function to navigate those ugly REFs back to their target row in the table:

```
SELECT s.name, DEREF(s.broader_term_ref).name bt
  FROM subjects s;
```

Dereferencing is like an automatic join, although it's more of an outer join than an equi-join. In other words, if the reference is null or invalid, the driving row will still appear, but the target object (and column) will be null.

Oracle introduced a dereferencing shortcut that is really quite elegant. You only need to use dot notation to indicate what attribute you wish to retrieve from the target object:

```
SELECT s.name, s.broader_term_ref.name bt FROM subjects s;
```

Both queries produce the following output:

```
NAME                          BT
----------------------------  -----------------------------
Computer file
Computer program language
Oracle                        Computer file
PL/SQL                        Computer program language
Relational databases
```

As a point of syntax, notice that both forms require a table alias, as in the following:

```
SELECT table_alias.ref_column_name.column_name
  FROM tablenametable_alias
```

You can also use REF-based navigation in the WHERE clause. To show all the subjects whose broader term is "Computer program language," specify:

```
SELECT VALUE(s).name FROM subjects s
 WHERE s.broader_term_ref.name = 'Computer program language';
```

Although my example table uses a reference to itself, in reality a reference can point to an object in any object table in the same database. To see this in action, let's return to the definition of the base type catalog_item_t. I can now add an attribute that will hold a collection of REFs, so that each cataloged item can be associated with any number of subjects. First, I'll create a collection of subject references:

```
CREATE TYPE subject_refs_t AS TABLE OF REF subject_t;
```

Now I'll allow every item in the catalog to be associated with any number of subjects:

```
ALTER TYPE catalog_item_t
    ADD ATTRIBUTE subject_refs subject_refs_t
    CASCADE INCLUDING TABLE DATA;
```

And now (skipping gleefully over the boring parts about modifying any affected methods in the dependent types), I might insert a catalog record using the following exotic SQL statement:

```
INSERT INTO catalog_items
VALUES (NEW book_t(10007,
    'Oracle PL/SQL Programming',
    'Sept 1997',
    CAST(MULTISET(SELECT REF(s)
                    FROM subjects s
                   WHERE name IN ('Oracle', 'PL/SQL', 'Relational databases'))
      AS subject_refs_t),
    '1-56592-335-9',
    987));
```

The CAST/MULTISET clause performs an on-the-fly conversion of the subject REFs into a collection, as explained in the section "Working with Collections" on page 350.

Here is a slightly more understandable PL/SQL equivalent:

```
DECLARE
    subrefs subject_refs_t;
BEGIN
```

```
   SELECT REF(s)
     BULK COLLECT INTO subrefs
     FROM subjects s
    WHERE name IN ('Oracle', 'PL/SQL', 'Relational databases'));

   INSERT INTO catalog_items VALUES (NEW book_t(10007,
      'Oracle PL/SQL Programming', 'Sept 1997', subrefs, '1-56592-335-9', 987));
END;
```

In English, that code says "grab the REFs to three particular subjects, and store them with this particular book."

REF-based navigation is so cool that I'll show another example using some more of that long-haired SQL:

```
SELECT VALUE(s).name
   || ' (' || VALUE(s).broader_term_ref.name || ')' plsql_subjects
   FROM TABLE(SELECT subject_refs
               FROM catalog_items
              WHERE id=10007) s;
```

This example retrieves values from the subjects table, including the name of each broader subject term, without ever mentioning the subjects table by name. (The TABLE function converts a collection into a virtual table.) Here are the results:

```
PLSQL_SUBJECTS
------------------------------------
Relational databases ()
PL/SQL (Computer program language)
Oracle (Computer file)
```

Other than automatic navigation from SQL, what *else* does all this effort offer the PL/SQL programmer? Er, well, not a whole lot. References have a slight edge, at least because as theory goes, they are *strongly typed*—that is, a REF-typed column can point only to an object that is defined on the same object type as the REF. Contrast this behavior with conventional foreign keys, which can point to any old thing as long as the target is constrained to be a primary key or has a unique index on it.

### The UTL_REF package

The UTL_REF built-in package performs the dereferencing operation without an explicit SQL call, allowing your application to perform a programmatic lock, select, update, or delete of an object given only its REF. As a short example, I can add a method such as the following to the subject_t type:

```
MEMBER FUNCTION print_bt (str IN VARCHAR2)
   RETURN VARCHAR2
IS
   bt subject_t;
BEGIN
   IF SELF.broader_term_ref IS NULL
   THEN
       RETURN str;
   ELSE
```

```
        UTL_REF.SELECT_OBJECT(SELF.broader_term_ref, bt);
        RETURN bt.print_bt(NVL(str,SELF.name)) || ' (' || bt.name || ')';
      END IF;
    END;
```

This recursive procedure walks the hierarchy from the current subject to the "topmost" broader subject.

When using the procedures in UTL_REF, the REF argument you supply must be typed to match your object argument. The complete list of subprograms in UTL_REF follows:

UTL_REF.SELECT_OBJECT (*obj_ref* IN, *object_variable* OUT);
  Finds the object to which *obj_ref* points and retrieves a copy in *object_variable*.

UTL_REF.SELECT_OBJECT_WITH_CR (*obj_ref* IN, *object_variable* OUT);
  Like SELECT_OBJECT, but makes a copy ("snapshot") of the object. This version exists to avoid a mutating table error (ORA-4091), which can occur if you are updating an object table and setting the value to a function, but the function uses UTL_REF to dereference an object from the same table you're updating.

UTL_REF.LOCK_OBJECT (*obj_ref* IN);
  Locks the object to which *obj_ref* points but does not fetch it yet.

UTL_REF.LOCK_OBJECT (*obj_ref* IN, *object_variable* OUT);
  Locks the object to which *obj_ref* points and retrieves a copy in *object_variable*.

UTL_REF.UPDATE_OBJECT (*obj_ref* IN, *object_variable* IN);
  Replaces the object to which *obj_ref* points with the value supplied in *object_variable*. This operation updates all of the columns in the corresponding object table.

UTL_REF.DELETE_OBJECT (*obj_ref* IN);
  Deletes the object to which *obj_ref* points.

---

### In C, Better Support for REFs

While PL/SQL offers few overwhelming reasons to program with object references, you would find more benefits to this programming style with the Oracle Call Interface (OCI), Oracle's C/C++ language interface, or even with Pro*C. In addition to the ability to navigate REFs, similar to what you find in PL/SQL, OCI provides *complex object retrieval* (COR). With COR, you can retrieve an object and all its REFerenced neighbors in a single call. Both OCI and Pro*C support a client-side object cache, allowing an application to load objects into client memory and to manipulate (select, insert, update, merge, delete) them as if they were in the database. Then, in a single call, the application can flush all the changes back to the server. In addition to improving the programmer's functional repertoire, these features reduce the number of network round trips, improving overall performance. The downside: creating a cache of Oracle data outside the server invites a host of challenges relating to concurrency and locking.

---

### REFs and type hierarchies

All of the UTL_REF subprograms are procedures, not functions,[9] and the parameters have the unique characteristic of being semiweakly typed. In other words, the database doesn't need to know at compile time what the precise datatypes are, as long as the REF matches the object variable.

I'd like to mention a few more technical points about REFs when dealing with type hierarchies. Assume the following program declarations:

```
DECLARE
    book book_t;
    item catalog_item_t;
    itemref REF catalog_item_t;
    bookref REF book_t;
```

As you have seen, assigning a REF to an "exactly typed" variable works fine:

```
SELECT REF(c) INTO itemref
    FROM catalog_items c WHERE id = 10007;
```

Similarly, you can dereference an object into the exact type, using:

```
UTL_REF.select_object(itemref, item);
```

or:

```
SELECT DEREF(itemref) INTO item FROM DUAL;
```

However, you cannot directly narrow a REF:

```
SELECT REF(c)
    INTO bookref     /* Error */
    FROM catalog_items c WHERE id = 10007;
```

One way to narrow a REF would be to use TREAT, which understands how to narrow references:

```
SELECT TREAT(REF(c) AS REF book_t)
    INTO bookref
    FROM catalog_items c WHERE id = 10007;
```

You can always widen or upcast while dereferencing, whether you are using:

```
UTL_REF.select_object(TREAT(bookref AS ref catalog_item_t), item);
```

(notice the explicit upcast) or:

```
SELECT DEREF(bookref) INTO item FROM DUAL;
```

And, although you cannot narrow or downcast while dereferencing with DEREF, as shown here:

```
SELECT DEREF(itemref)
    INTO book    /* Error */
    FROM DUAL;
```

---

9. I'm somewhat mystified by this; it would be a lot handier if at least SELECT_OBJECT were a function.

TREAT can again come to the rescue:

```
SELECT DEREF(TREAT(itemref AS REF book_t))
    INTO book
    FROM catalog_items c WHERE id = 10007;
```

Or, amazingly enough, you can also perform an implicit downcast with UTL_REF:

```
UTL_REF.select_object(itemref, book);
```

Got all that?

### Dangling REFs

Here are a few final comments about object references:

- A REF may point to nothing, in which case it's known as a *dangling REF*. This can happen when you store a reference to an object and then delete the object. Oracle permits such nonsense if you fail to define a foreign key constraint that would prevent it.

- To locate references that point to nothing, use the IS DANGLING operator:

  ```
  SELECT VALUE(s) FROM subjects s
  WHERE broader_term_ref IS DANGLING;
  ```

Now let's move on and take a look at some Oracle features for dealing with data whose type is either unknown or varying.

## Generic Data: The ANY Types

As discussed in Chapter 13, Oracle provides the ANYDATA type, which can hold data in any other built-in or user-defined type. With ANYDATA, a PL/SQL program could, for instance, store, retrieve, and operate on a data item declared on any SQL type in the database—without having to create dozens of overloaded versions. Sounds pretty good, right? This feature was tailor-made for advanced queuing, where an application needs to put a "thing" in the queue, and you don't want the queue to have to know what the datatype of each item is.

The built-in packages and types in this family are:

*ANYDATA type*
    Encapsulation of any SQL-datatyped item in a self-descriptive data structure.

*ANYTYPE type*
    When used with ANYDATA, reads the description of the data structure. Can be used separately to create transient object types.

*DBMS_TYPES package*
    A package consisting only of constants that help interpret which datatype is being used in the ANYDATA object.

---

*ANYDATASET type*

Similar to an ANYDATA, but the contents are one or more instances of a datatype (like a collection).

## Preview: What ANYDATA is not

If I wanted to write a function that would print anything (that is, convert it to a string), I might start with this spec:

```
FUNCTION printany (whatever IN ANYDATA) RETURN VARCHAR2;
```

and hope to invoke the function like this:

```
DBMS_OUTPUT.PUT_LINE(printany(SYSDATE));          -- nope
DBMS_OUTPUT.PUT_LINE(printany(NEW book_t(111));   -- nada
DBMS_OUTPUT.PUT_LINE(printany('Hello world'));    -- nyet
```

Unfortunately, those calls won't work. ANYDATA is actually an encapsulation of other types, and you must first *convert* the data into the ANYDATA type using one of its built-in static methods:

```
DBMS_OUTPUT.PUT_LINE(printany(ANYDATA.ConvertDate(SYSDATE));
DBMS_OUTPUT.PUT_LINE(printany(ANYDATA.ConvertObject(NEW book_t(12345)));
DBMS_OUTPUT.PUT_LINE(printany(ANYDATA.ConvertVarchar2('Hello world')));
```

Don't think of ANYDATA as an exact replacement for overloading.

## Dealing with ANYDATA

Let's take a look at an implementation of the printany program and see how it figures out how to deal with data of different types. This code is not comprehensive; it deals only with numbers, strings, dates, objects, and REFs, but you could extend it to almost any other datatype.

```
     /* File on web: printany.fun */
1    FUNCTION printany (adata IN ANYDATA)
2       RETURN VARCHAR2
3    AS
4       aType ANYTYPE;
5       retval VARCHAR2(32767);
6       result_code PLS_INTEGER;
7    BEGIN
8       CASE adata.GetType(aType)
9       WHEN DBMS_TYPES.TYPECODE_NUMBER THEN
10         RETURN 'NUMBER: ' || TO_CHAR(adata.AccessNumber);
11      WHEN DBMS_TYPES.TYPECODE_VARCHAR2 THEN
12         RETURN 'VARCHAR2: ' || adata.AccessVarchar2;
13      WHEN DBMS_TYPES.TYPECODE_CHAR THEN
14         RETURN 'CHAR: ' || RTRIM(adata.AccessChar);
15      WHEN DBMS_TYPES.TYPECODE_DATE THEN
16         RETURN 'DATE: ' || TO_CHAR(adata.AccessDate, 'YYYY-MM-DD hh24:mi:ss');
17      WHEN DBMS_TYPES.TYPECODE_OBJECT THEN
18         EXECUTE IMMEDIATE 'DECLARE ' ||
19                        '  myobj ' || adata.GetTypeName || '; ' ||
```

```
20                          '   myad anydata := :ad; ' ||
21                          'BEGIN ' ||
22                          '   :res := myad.GetObject(myobj); ' ||
23                          '   :ret := myobj.print(); ' ||
24                          'END;'
25                          USING IN adata, OUT result_code, OUT retval;
26            retval := adata.GetTypeName || ': ' || retval;
27        WHEN DBMS_TYPES.TYPECODE_REF THEN
28            EXECUTE IMMEDIATE 'DECLARE ' ||
29                          '   myref ' || adata.GetTypeName || '; ' ||
30                          '   myobj ' || SUBSTR(adata.GetTypeName,
31                                      INSTR(adata.GetTypeName, ' ')) || '; ' ||
32                          '   myad anydata := :ad; ' ||
33                          'BEGIN ' ||
34                          '   :res := myad.GetREF(myref); ' ||
35                          '   UTL_REF.SELECT_OBJECT(myref, myobj);' ||
36                          '   :ret := myobj.print(); ' ||
37                          'END;'
38                          USING IN adata, OUT result_code, OUT retval;
39            retval := adata.GetTypeName || ': ' || retval;
40        ELSE
41            retval := '<data of type ' || adata.GetTypeName ||'>';
42        END CASE;
43
44        RETURN retval;
45
46    EXCEPTION
47      WHEN OTHERS
48      THEN
49        IF INSTR(SQLERRM, 'component ''PRINT'' must be declared') > 0
50        THEN
51          RETURN adata.GetTypeName || ': <no print() function>';
52        ELSE
53          RETURN 'Error: ' || SQLERRM;
54        END IF;
55    END;
```

Here are just a few highlights:

| Line(s) | Description |
|---------|-------------|
| 5 | In cases where I need a temporary variable to hold the result, I assume that 32K will be big enough. Remember that PL/SQL dynamically allocates memory for large VARCHAR2s, so it won't be a memory pig unless required. |
| 6 | The value of result_code (see lines 25 and 38) is irrelevant for the operations in this example, but is required by the ANYDATA API. |
| 8 | The ANYDATA type includes a method called GetType that returns a code corresponding to the datatype. Here is its specification: |

```
MEMBER FUNCTION ANYDATA.GetType
   (OUT NOCOPY ANYTYPE)
   RETURN typecode_integer;
```

To use this method, though, you have to declare an ANYTYPE variable into which Oracle will store detailed information about the type that you've encapsulated.

| Line(s) | Description |
| --- | --- |
| 9, 11, 13, 15, 17, 27 | These expressions rely on the constants that Oracle provides in the built-in package DBMS_TYPES. |
| 10, 12, 14, 16 | These statements use the ANYDATA.Access*NNN* member functions introduced in Oracle9*i* Database Release 2. In Release 1, you had to use the Get*NNN* member procedures for a similar result, although they required the use of a temporary local variable. |
| 18–25 | To get an object to print itself without doing a lot of data dictionary contortions, this little dynamic anonymous block will construct an object of the correct type and invoke its print() member method. You did give it a print(), didn't you? |
| 28–38 | The point of this is to dereference the pointer and return the referenced object's content. Well, it will work if there's a print(). |
| 49–51 | In the event that I'm trying to print an object with no print member method, the compiler will return an error at runtime that I can detect in this fashion. In this case the code will just punt and return a generic message. |

Running my earlier invocations:

```
DBMS_OUTPUT.PUT_LINE(printany(ANYDATA.ConvertDate(SYSDATE)));
DBMS_OUTPUT.PUT_LINE(printany(ANYDATA.ConvertObject(NEW book_t(12345))));
DBMS_OUTPUT.PUT_LINE(printany(ANYDATA.ConvertVarchar2('Hello world')));
```

yields:

```
DATE: 2005-03-10 16:00:25
SCOTT.BOOK_T: id=12345; title=; publication_date=; isbn=; pages=
VARCHAR2: Hello world
```

As you can see, using ANYDATA isn't as convenient as true inheritance hierarchies because ANYDATA requires explicit conversions. On the other hand, it does make possible the creation of a table column or object attribute that will hold any type of data.[10]

### Creating a transient type

Although PL/SQL still does not support defining new object types inside a program's declaration section, it is possible to use these ANY built-ins to create this kind of "transient" type—that is, one that exists only at runtime. Wrapped up as an ANYTYPE, you can even pass such a type as a parameter and create an instance of it as an ANYDATA. Here is an example:

```
/* Create (anonymous) transient type with two attributes: number, date */
FUNCTION create_a_type
   RETURN ANYTYPE
AS
   mytype ANYTYPE;
BEGIN
   ANYTYPE.BeginCreate(typecode => DBMS_TYPES.TYPECODE_OBJECT,
```

---

10. As of this writing, it is impossible to store in a table an ANYDATA encapsulating an object that has evolved or that is part of a type hierarchy.

```
                         atype => mytype);
       mytype.AddAttr(typecode => DBMS_TYPES.TYPECODE_NUMBER,
                      aname => 'just_a_number',
                      prec => 38,
                      scale => 0,
                      len => NULL,
                      csid => NULL,
                      csfrm => NULL);
       mytype.AddAttr(typecode => DBMS_TYPES.TYPECODE_DATE,
                      aname => 'just_a_date',
                      prec => 5,
                      scale => 5,
                      len => NULL,
                      csid => NULL,
                      csfrm => NULL);
       mytype.EndCreate;
       RETURN mytype;
    END;
```

As you can see, there are three main steps:

1. Begin the creation by calling the static procedure BeginCreate. This returns an initialized ANYTYPE.

2. One at a time, add the desired attributes using the AddAttr member procedure.

3. Call the member procedure EndCreate.

Similarly, when you wish to use the type, you will need to assign attribute values in a piecewise manner:

```
    DECLARE
       ltype ANYTYPE := create_a_type;
       l_any ANYDATA;
    BEGIN
       ANYDATA.BeginCreate(dtype => ltype, adata => l_any);
       l_any.SetNumber(num => 12345);
       l_any.SetDate(dat => SYSDATE);
       l_any.EndCreate;
    END;
```

If you don't know the structure of the datatype in advance, it is possible to discover it using ANYTYPE methods (such as GetAttrElemInfo) in combination with a piecewise application of the ANYDATA.Get methods. (See the *anyObject.sql* script on the book's web site for an example.)

## I Can Do It Myself

In object-oriented design, there is a school of thought that wants each object type to have the intelligence necessary to be self-sufficient. If the object needs to be stored persistently in a database, it would know how to save itself; similarly, it would include methods for update, delete, and retrieval. If I subscribed to this philosophy, here is one of the methods I would want to add to my type:

```
ALTER TYPE catalog_item_t
   ADD MEMBER PROCEDURE remove
   CASCADE;

TYPE BODY catalog_item_t
AS
   ...
   MEMBER PROCEDURE remove
   IS
   BEGIN
      DELETE catalog_items
       WHERE id = SELF.id;
       SELF := NULL;
   END;
END;
```

(Oracle does not offer a destructor method, by the way.) By defining this method at the supertype level, all my subtypes are taken care of too. This design assumes that corresponding objects will live in a single table; some applications might need some additional logic to locate the object. (Also, a real version of this method might include logic to perform ancillary functions like removing dependent objects and/or archiving the data before removing the object permanently.)

Assuming that my applications would always modify a transient object in memory before writing it to disk, I could combine insert and update into a single method I'll call "save":

```
ALTER TYPE catalog_item_t
   ADD MEMBER PROCEDURE save,
   CASCADE;

TYPE BODY catalog_item_t
AS
   ...
   MEMBER PROCEDURE save
   IS
   BEGIN
      UPDATE catalog_items c
         SET c = SELF
       WHERE id = SELF.id;
       IF SQL%ROWCOUNT = 0
       THEN
           INSERT INTO catalog_items VALUES (SELF);
       END IF;
   END;
```

You may correctly point out that this will replace all of the column values in the table even if they are unchanged, which could cause triggers to fire that shouldn't, and results in needless I/O. Alas, this is one of the unfortunate by-products of an object approach. It is true that with careful programming, you could avoid modifying columns from the supertype that haven't changed, but columns from any subtype are not individually accessible from any variation on the UPDATE statement that Oracle currently offers.

Retrieval is the most difficult operation to encapsulate because of the many WHERE-clause permutations and the multiset nature of the result. The specification of the query criteria can be a real rat's nest, as anyone who has ever built a custom query screen will attest. Considering only the result side, the options for what to return include:

- A collection of objects
- A collection of REFs
- A pipelined result set
- A cursor variable (strongly or weakly typed)

The requirements of the application and its programming environment will have the largest influence on how to choose from these options. Here's a stripped-down example that uses the fourth approach, a cursor variable:

```
ALTER TYPE catalog_item_t
    ADD STATIC FUNCTION cursor_for_query (typename IN VARCHAR2 DEFAULT NULL,
        title IN VARCHAR2 DEFAULT NULL,
        att1 IN VARCHAR2 DEFAULT NULL,
        val1 IN VARCHAR2 DEFAULT NULL)
        RETURN SYS_REFCURSOR
    CASCADE;
```

I use a static method that returns the built-in SYS_REFCURSOR type, which is a weak cursor type that Oracle provides (just something of a convenience feature), allowing the client program to iterate over the results. The "att1" and "val1" parameters provide a means of querying subtype-specific attribute/value pairs; a real version of this program would be better off accepting a collection of such attribute/value pairs to allow queries on multiple attributes of a given subtype.

Jumping ahead to how you might execute a query, let's look at this example:

```
DECLARE
    catalog_item catalog_item_t;
    l_refcur SYS_REFCURSOR;
BEGIN
    l_refcur := catalog_item_t.cursor_for_query(
        typename => 'book_t',
        title => 'Oracle PL/SQL Programming');
    LOOP
        FETCH l_refcur INTO catalog_item;
        EXIT WHEN l_refcur%NOTFOUND;
        DBMS_OUTPUT.PUT_LINE('Matching item:' || catalog_item.print);
    END LOOP;
    CLOSE l_refcur;
END;
```

which yields:

```
Matching item:id=10007; title=Oracle PL/SQL Programming;
 publication_date=Sept 1997;
 isbn=1-56592-335-9; pages=987
```

The implementation is:

```
1     MEMBER PROCEDURE save
2     IS
3     BEGIN
4        UPDATE catalog_items c
5           SET c = SELF
6         WHERE id = SELF.id;
7         IF SQL%ROWCOUNT = 0
8         THEN
9            INSERT INTO catalog_items VALUES (SELF);
10        END IF;
11    END;
12
13    STATIC FUNCTION cursor_for_query (typename IN VARCHAR2 DEFAULT NULL,
14        title IN VARCHAR2 DEFAULT NULL,
15        att1 IN VARCHAR2 DEFAULT NULL,
16        val1 IN VARCHAR2 DEFAULT NULL)
17        RETURN SYS_REFCURSOR
18    IS
19        l_sqlstr VARCHAR2(1024);
20        l_refcur SYS_REFCURSOR;
21    BEGIN
22        l_sqlstr := 'SELECT VALUE(c) FROM catalog_items c WHERE 1=1 ';
23        IF title IS NOT NULL
24        THEN
25          l_sqlstr := l_sqlstr || 'AND title = :t ';
26        END IF;
27
28        IF typename IS NOT NULL
29        THEN
30           IF att1 IS NOT NULL
31           THEN
32              l_sqlstr := l_sqlstr
33                 || 'AND TREAT(SELF AS ' || typename || ').' || att1 || ' ';
34              IF val1 IS NULL
35              THEN
36                 l_sqlstr := l_sqlstr || 'IS NULL ';
37              ELSE
38                 l_sqlstr := l_sqlstr || '=:v1 ';
39              END IF;
40           END IF;
41           l_sqlstr := l_sqlstr || 'AND VALUE(c) IS OF (' || typename ||') ';
42        END IF;
43
44        l_sqlstr := 'BEGIN OPEN :lcur FOR ' || l_sqlstr || '; END;';
45
46        IF title IS NULL AND att1 IS NULL
47        THEN
48           EXECUTE IMMEDIATE l_sqlstr USING IN OUT l_refcur;
49        ELSIF title IS NOT NULL AND att1 IS NULL
50        THEN
51           EXECUTE IMMEDIATE l_sqlstr USING IN OUT l_refcur, IN title;
52        ELSIF title IS NOT NULL AND att1 IS NOT NULL
53        THEN
54           EXECUTE IMMEDIATE l_sqlstr USING IN OUT l_refcur, IN title, IN att1;
55        END IF;
```

```
56
57          RETURN l_refcur;
58      END;
```

Because dynamic SQL is a little tricky to follow, here is what the function would have generated internally with the previous query:

```
BEGIN
    OPEN :lcur FOR
        SELECT VALUE(c)
          FROM catalog_items c
        WHERE 1=1
            AND title = :t
            AND VALUE(c) IS OF (book_t);
END;
```

One nice thing about this approach is that you don't have to modify the query code every time you add a subtype to the inheritance tree.

## Comparing Objects

So far, my examples have used object tables—tables in which each row constitutes an object built with the CREATE TABLE...OF type statement. As I've illustrated, such an arrangement enjoys some special features, such as REF-based navigation and the treatment of entire objects (rather than individual column values) as the unit of I/O.

You can also use an object type as the datatype for individual columns in a table (the relevant nomenclature is *column objects*, as mentioned earlier). For example, imagine that I want to create an historical record of changes in the catalog_items table, capturing all inserts, updates, and deletes.

```
CREATE TABLE catalog_history (
    id INTEGER NOT NULL PRIMARY KEY,
    action CHAR(1) NOT NULL,
    action_time TIMESTAMP DEFAULT (SYSTIMESTAMP) NOT NULL,
    old_item catalog_item_t,
    new_item catalog_item_t)
    NESTED TABLE old_item.subject_refs STORE AS catalog_history_old_subrefs
    NESTED TABLE new_item.subject_refs STORE AS catalog_history_new_subrefs;
```

As soon as you start populating a table with column objects, though, you raise some questions about how Oracle should behave when you ask it to do things like sort or index on one of those catalog_item_t columns. There are four ways you can compare objects; some are more useful than others:

*Attribute-level comparison*
> Include the relevant attribute(s) when sorting, creating indexes, or comparing.

*Default SQL*
> Oracle's SQL knows how to do a simple equality test. In this case, two objects are considered equal if they are defined on exactly the same type and every corresponding attribute is equal. This will work if the objects have only scalar attributes

(no collections or LOBs) and if you haven't already defined a MAP or ORDER member method on the object type.

*MAP member method*

You can create a special function method that returns a "mapping" of the object value onto a datatype that Oracle already knows how to compare, such as a number or a date. This will work only if no ORDER method exists.

*ORDER member method*

This is another special function that compares two objects and returns a flag value that indicates their relative ordering. This will work only if no MAP method exists.

Default SQL comparison is not terribly useful, so I won't say any more about it. The following sections describe the other, more useful ways to compare objects.

---

## The OBJECT_VALUE Pseudo Column

Curious readers may wonder how, precisely, one could automatically populate an audit-style table such as catalog_history, which includes column objects defined on a type that has subtypes. You might hope that it could be done with a table-level trigger.

The difficult question is how to capture the values of the attributes for all the subtypes. There is no obvious way to refer to them generically. No problem...Pseudo-Column Man comes to the rescue! Ponder this:

```
TRIGGER catalog_hist_upd_trg
AFTER UPDATE ON catalog_items
FOR EACH ROW
BEGIN
   INSERT INTO catalog_history (id,
      action,
      action_time,
      old_item,
      new_item)
   VALUES (catalog_history_seq.NEXTVAL,
      'U',
      SYSTIMESTAMP,
      :OLD.OBJECT_VALUE,
      :NEW.OBJECT_VALUE);
END;
```

Oracle provides access to the fully attributed subtypes via the pseudo-column OBJECT_VALUE. However, this works only if you have Oracle Database 10g or later; it's true that a similar pseudo-column SYS_NC_ROWINFO$ is available in earlier versions, but I have found that it does not work in this particular application.

OBJECT_VALUE can also be used for other purposes and is not limited to circumstances involving subtypes; for example, it can be useful when creating object views using the WITH OBJECT IDENTIFIER clause (discussed later in this chapter).

---

### Attribute-level comparison

Attribute-level comparison may not be precisely what you want, but it is fairly easy in PL/SQL, or even in SQL if you remember to use a table alias in the SQL statement. Oracle lets you expose attributes via dot notation:

```
SELECT * FROM catalog_history c
 WHERE c.old_item.id > 10000
 ORDER BY NVL(TREAT(c.old_item as book_t).isbn, TREAT
(c.old_item AS serial_t).issn)
```

Attribute-level index creation is equally easy:

```
CREATE INDEX catalog_history_old_id_idx ON catalog_history c (c.old_item.id);
```

### The MAP method

Both the MAP and the ORDER methods make it possible to perform statements such as the following:

```
SELECT * FROM catalog_history
 ORDER BY old_item;

IF old_item > new_item
THEN ...
```

First let's look at MAP. I can add a trivial MAP method to catalog_item_t as follows:

```
ALTER TYPE catalog_item_t
   ADD MAP MEMBER FUNCTION mapit RETURN NUMBER
   CASCADE;

TYPE BODY catalog_item_t
AS ...
   MAP MEMBER FUNCTION mapit RETURN NUMBER
   IS
   BEGIN
      RETURN id;
   END;
   ...
END;
```

Assuming, of course, that ordering by id makes sense, now I can order and compare catalog items to my heart's content, and the Oracle database will call this method automatically whenever necessary. The function needn't be so simple; for example, it could return a scalar value computed from all the object attributes, melded together in some way that actually might be of some value to librarians.

Creating a MAP method like this has a side effect, though: the equality comparison gets defined in a way you might not like. "Equality" now becomes a matter of the mapped value's being equal for the objects you're comparing. If you want an easy way to compare two objects for attribute-by-attribute equality, you will want to either create your own (non-MAP) method and invoke it by name when needed, or use an ORDER method.

## The ORDER method

The alternative to MAP is an ORDER member function, which compares two methods: SELF, and another object of the same type that you supply as an argument. You want to program the function to return an integer that is positive, zero, or negative, indicating the ordering relationship of the second object to SELF. Table 26-2 illustrates the behavior you need to incorporate.

*Table 26-2. Desired behavior of ORDER member functions*

| For these desired semantics... | Your ORDER member function must return |
|---|---|
| SELF < *argumentObject* | Any negative number (typically −1) |
| SELF = *argumentObject* | 0 |
| SELF > *argumentObject* | Any positive number (typically +1) |
| Undefined comparison | NULL |

Let's take a look at a nontrivial example of an ORDER method:

```
1    ALTER TYPE catalog_item_t
2       DROP MAP MEMBER FUNCTION mapit RETURN NUMBER
3       CASCADE;
4
5    ALTER TYPE catalog_item_t
6       ADD ORDER MEMBER FUNCTION orderit (obj2 IN catalog_item_t)
7          RETURN INTEGER
8       CASCADE;
9
10    TYPE BODY catalog_item_t
11    AS ...
12       ORDER MEMBER FUNCTION orderit (obj2 IN catalog_item_t)
13          RETURN INTEGER
14       IS
15          self_gt_o2 CONSTANT PLS_INTEGER := 1;
16          eq CONSTANT PLS_INTEGER := 0;
17          o2_gt_self CONSTANT PLS_INTEGER := -1;
18          l_matching_count NUMBER;
19       BEGIN
20          CASE
21             WHEN obj2 IS OF (book_t) AND SELF IS OF (serial_t) THEN
22                RETURN o2_gt_self;
23             WHEN obj2 IS OF (serial_t) AND SELF IS OF (book_t) THEN
24                RETURN self_gt_o2;
25             ELSE
26                IF obj2.title = SELF.title
27                   AND obj2.publication_date = SELF.publication_date
28                THEN
29                   IF obj2.subject_refs IS NOT NULL
30                      AND SELF.subject_refs IS NOT NULL
31                      AND obj2.subject_refs.COUNT = SELF.subject_refs.COUNT
32                   THEN
33                      SELECT COUNT(*) INTO l_matching_count FROM
34                         (SELECT *
```

```
35                          FROM TABLE(SELECT CAST(SELF.subject_refs AS subject_refs_t)
36                                      FROM dual)
37                      INTERSECT
38                      SELECT *
39                        FROM TABLE(SELECT CAST(obj2.subject_refs AS subject_refs_t)
40                                    FROM dual));
41                  IF l_matching_count = SELF.subject_refs.COUNT
42                  THEN
43                      RETURN eq;
44                  END IF;
45              END IF;
46          END IF;
47          RETURN NULL;
48      END CASE;
49   END;
50   ...
51 END;
```

Here are the important things to note:

| Line(s) | Description |
|---------|-------------|
| 21–24 | This means that "books sort higher than serials." |
| 26–46 | This is an equality test that uses a very cool feature. Because Oracle doesn't know how to compare collections, this code uses Oracle's ability to select from a collection as if it were a table. By checking to make sure that the relational intersection of these two collections has the expected number of elements, I can determine whether every element in the first collection has an equal counterpart in the second (which is my definition of "equality"). |

Overall, however, my ORDER method is still inadequate because it fails to treat the subtype-specific attributes, but anything longer would just be too unwieldy for this book.

### Additional comparison recommendations

To close out this discussion, here are a few additional rules and recommendations for comparison methods:

- MAP and ORDER cannot coexist in the same object type; use one or the other.
- Oracle recommends MAP when you have a large number of objects to sort or compare, as in a SQL statement. This is because of an internal optimization that reduces the number of function calls. With ORDER, the function must run once for every comparison.
- Oracle ignores the method names; you can call them anything you want.
- Subtypes can include MAP methods, but only if the supertype also has one.
- Subtypes cannot have ORDER methods; you'll have to put all the comparison "smarts" into the supertype.

# Object Views

Although Oracle's object extensions offer PL/SQL programmers rich possibilities for the design of new systems, it's unlikely that you will want to completely reengineer your existing systems to use objects. In part to allow established applications to take advantage of the new object features over time, Oracle provides *object views*. This feature offers several unique advantages:

*"Object-ification" of remote data*
> It's not yet possible to use the object tables and physical REFs across a distributed database, but you can create object views and virtual REFs that cast remote relational data as objects.

*Virtual denormalization*
> In a relational database or even an object-relational database, you will usually find relationships modeled in only one direction. For example, a book has some number of subjects. With an object view, it's easy to associate a column that provides the inverse mapping; for example, a subject object could include a collection of REFs that point to all of the books in that subject.

*Efficiency of object access*
> In Oracle Call Interface (OCI) applications, object programming constructs provide for the convenient retrieval, caching, and updating of object data. By reducing trips between application and database server, these programming facilities may provide performance improvements, with the added benefit that application code can be more succinct.

*Greater flexibility to change the object model*
> Although newer versions of Oracle have tremendous abilities in the area of type evolution, adding and removing object attributes still cause table bits to move around on the disk, which administrators may be loath to do. Recompiling object views suffers no such consequences.

On the other hand, there are some disadvantages to using object views:

*View performance*
> Object views are still views, and some Oracle shops are generally leery of the performance of any view.

*No virtual REFs*
> You cannot store virtual REFs in the database; instead, they get constructed on the fly. This may present some challenges if you someday want to convert those object views into object tables.

Other features of Oracle can improve the expressiveness of any types of views, not just object views. Two such features that are not strictly limited to object views are collections and INSTEAD OF triggers.

*Collections*

> Consider two relational tables with a simple master-detail relationship. You can create a view portraying the detail records as a single nonscalar attribute (collection) of the master.

*INSTEAD OF triggers*

> In addition, by using INSTEAD OF triggers, you can tell the Oracle database exactly how to perform inserts, updates, and deletes on the view.

From an object perspective, there is one slight disadvantage of object views when compared to comprehensive reengineering: object views cannot retrofit any benefits of encapsulation. Insofar as any applications apply INSERT, UPDATE, MERGE, and DELETE statements directly to the underlying relational data, they may subvert the benefits of encapsulation normally provided by an object approach. Object-oriented designs typically prevent free-form access directly to data. However, because Oracle supports neither private attributes nor private methods, the incremental sacrifice here is small.

If you do choose to layer object views on top of an existing system, it may be possible for new applications to enjoy incremental benefit, and your legacy systems are no worse off than they were before. Figure 26-2 illustrates this use of object views.

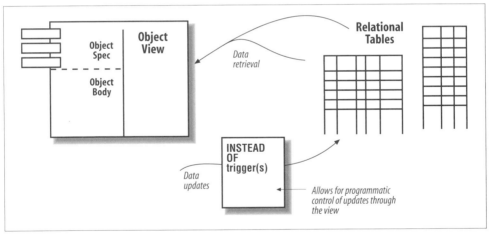

*Figure 26-2. Object views allow you to bind an object type definition to (existing) relational tables*

The following sections discuss aspects of using object views (including differences between object tables and object views) that PL/SQL programmers should find particularly useful and interesting.

## A Sample Relational System

For this chapter's second major example, let's look at how object views might be used in a database application that supports a graphic design firm. Their relational application includes information about images (GIF, JPEG, etc.) that appear on web sites they design. These images are stored in files, but data about them is stored in relational tables. To help the graphic artists locate the right image, each image has one or more associated keywords stored in a straightforward master-detail relationship.

The legacy system has a table of suppliers:

```
CREATE TABLE suppliers (
    id INTEGER NOT NULL PRIMARY KEY,
    name VARCHAR2(400) NOT NULL
);
```

Here is the table for image metadata:

```
CREATE TABLE images (
    image_id INTEGER NOT NULL PRIMARY KEY,
    file_name VARCHAR2(512) NOT NULL,
    file_type VARCHAR2(12) NOT NULL,
    supplier_id INTEGER REFERENCES suppliers (id),
    supplier_rights_descriptor VARCHAR2(256),
    bytes INTEGER
);
```

Not all images originate from suppliers; if the supplier id is null, then the image was created in-house.

Finally, there is one table for the keywords associated with the images:

```
CREATE TABLE keywords (
    image_id INTEGER NOT NULL REFERENCES images (image_id),
    keyword VARCHAR2(45) NOT NULL,
    CONSTRAINT keywords_pk PRIMARY KEY (image_id, keyword)
);
```

Let's assume that the following data exists in the underlying tables:

```
INSERT INTO suppliers VALUES (101, 'Joe''s Graphics');
INSERT INTO suppliers VALUES (102, 'Image Bar and Grill');
INSERT INTO images VALUES (100001, '/files/web/60s/smiley_face.png', 'image/png',
    101, 'fair use', 813);
INSERT INTO images VALUES (100002, '/files/web/60s/peace_symbol.gif', 'image/gif',
    101, 'fair use', 972);
INSERT INTO images VALUES (100003, '/files/web/00s/towers.jpg',
  'image/jpeg', NULL,
    NULL, 2104);
INSERT INTO KEYWORDS VALUES (100001, 'SIXTIES');
INSERT INTO KEYWORDS VALUES (100001, 'HAPPY FACE');
INSERT INTO KEYWORDS VALUES (100002, 'SIXTIES');
INSERT INTO KEYWORDS VALUES (100002, 'PEACE SYMBOL');
INSERT INTO KEYWORDS VALUES (100002, 'JERRY RUBIN');
```

In the next few sections, you'll see several object views defined on this data:

- The first view is defined on an image type that includes the keywords as a collection attribute.

- The second view is a "subview"—that is, defined on a subtype in an object type hierarchy. It will include characteristics for images that originate from suppliers.
- The final view includes keywords and their inverse references back to the relevant images.

## Object View with a Collection Attribute

Before creating an underlying type for the first view, I need a collection type to hold the keywords. Use of a nested table makes sense here, because keyword ordering is unimportant and because there is no logical maximum number of keywords.[11]

```
CREATE TYPE keyword_tab_t AS TABLE OF VARCHAR2(45);
```

At this point, it's a simple matter to define the image object type:

```
CREATE TYPE image_t AS OBJECT (
    image_id INTEGER,
    image_file BFILE,
    file_type VARCHAR2(12),
    bytes INTEGER,
    keywords keyword_tab_t
);
```

Assuming that the image files and the database server are on the same machine, I can use an Oracle BFILE datatype rather than the filename. I'll need to create a "directory," that is, an alias by which the database will know the directory that contains the images. In this case, I use the root directory (on the target Unix system, this is represented by a single forward slash), because I happen to know that the file_name column includes full pathnames.

```
CREATE DIRECTORY rootdir AS '/';
```

 You likely will not have privileges to work with files in the root directory; set your directory to a folder in which you can work.

So far, I have not defined a connection between the relational tables and the object type. They are independent organisms. It is in building the object view that I overlay the object definition onto the tables, as the next statement illustrates:

```
CREATE VIEW images_v
   OF image_t
   WITH OBJECT IDENTIFIER (image_id)
AS
   SELECT i.image_id, BFILENAME('ROOTDIR', i.file_name),
       i.file_type, i.bytes,
       CAST (MULTISET (SELECT keyword
```

11. If ordering were important or if there were a (small) logical maximum number of keywords per image, a VARRAY collection would be a better choice.

```
                        FROM keywords k
                        WHERE k.image_id = i.image_id)
            AS keyword_tab_t)
        FROM images i;
```

There are two components of this statement that are unique to object views:

*OF image_t*
>    This means that the view will return objects of type image_t.

*WITH OBJECT IDENTIFIER (image_id)*
>    To behave like a "real" object instance, data returned by the view will need some
>    kind of object identifier. By designating the primary key as the basis of a virtual
>    OID, I can enjoy the benefits of REF-based navigation to objects in the view.

In addition, the select list of an object view must correspond in number, position, and
datatype with the attributes in the associated object type.

OK, now that I've created an object view, what can I do with it? Most significantly, I
can retrieve data from it just as if it were an object table. So, from SQL*Plus, a query
like the following:

```
SQL> SELECT image_id, keywords FROM images_v;
```

yields:

```
   IMAGE_ID KEYWORDS
---------- --------------------------------------------------------
    100003 KEYWORD_TAB_T()
    100001 KEYWORD_TAB_T('HAPPY FACE', 'SIXTIES')
    100002 KEYWORD_TAB_T('JERRY RUBIN', 'PEACE SYMBOL', 'SIXTIES')
```

In the interest of deepening the object appearance, I could also add methods to the type
definition. Here, for example, is a print() method:

```
ALTER TYPE image_t
   ADD MEMBER FUNCTION print RETURN VARCHAR2
   CASCADE;

CREATE OR REPLACE TYPE BODY image_t
AS
   MEMBER FUNCTION print
      RETURN VARCHAR2
   IS
      filename images.file_name%TYPE;
      dirname VARCHAR2(30);
      keyword_list VARCHAR2(32767);
   BEGIN
      DBMS_LOB.FILEGETNAME(SELF.image_file, dirname, filename);
      IF SELF.keywords IS NOT NULL
      THEN
         FOR key_elt IN 1..SELF.keywords.COUNT
         LOOP
            keyword_list := keyword_list || ', ' || SELF.keywords(key_elt);
         END LOOP;
      END IF;
```

```
      RETURN 'Id=' || SELF.image_id || '; File=' || filename
         || '; keywords=' || SUBSTR(keyword_list, 3);
   END;
END;
```

This example illustrates a way to "flatten" the keyword list by iterating over the virtual collection of keywords.

---

## Is It Null, or Is It Not?

A null collection is not the same thing as an initialized collection with zero elements. Image 100003 has no keywords, but the object view is mistakenly returning an empty but initialized collection. To get a true NULL instead, I can use a DECODE to test the number of keywords:

```
CREATE OR REPLACE VIEW images_v
   OF image_t
   WITH OBJECT IDENTIFIER (image_id)
AS
   SELECT i.image_id, BFILENAME('ROOTDIR', i.file_name),
        i.file_type, i.bytes,
        DECODE((SELECT COUNT(*)
                   FROM keywords k2
                  WHERE k2.image_id = i.image_id),
              0, NULL,
              CAST (MULTISET (SELECT keyword
                               FROM keywords k
                              WHERE k.image_id = i.image_id)
                 AS keyword_tab_t))
     FROM images i;
```

In other words, if there are no keywords, return NULL; otherwise, return the CAST/MULTISET expression. From this view, "SELECT...WHERE image_id=100003" properly yields the following:

```
IMAGE_ID KEYWORDS
---------- -------------------------------------------------------
   100003
```

But you might conclude that this amount of conceptual purity is not worth the extra I/O (or having to look at the convoluted SELECT statement).

---

Other things you can do with object views include the following:

*Use virtual REFs*

These are pointers to virtual objects. They are discussed in detail in the later section, "Differences Between Object Views and Object Tables" on page 1125.

*Write INSTEAD OF triggers*

These will allow direct manipulation of the view's contents. You can read more about this topic in the earlier section, "INSTEAD OF Triggers" on page 690.

---

## Object Subview

In the case where I want to treat certain images differently from others, I might want to create a subtype. In my example, I'm going to create a subtype for those images that originate from suppliers. I'd like the subtype to include a REF to a supplier object, which is defined by:

```
CREATE TYPE supplier_t AS OBJECT (
    id INTEGER,
    name VARCHAR2(400)
);
```

and by a simple object view:

```
CREATE VIEW suppliers_v
    OF supplier_t
    WITH OBJECT IDENTIFIER (id)
AS
    SELECT id, name
      FROM suppliers;
```

I will need to alter or recreate the base type to be NOT FINAL:

```
ALTER TYPE image_t NOT FINAL CASCADE;
```

so that I can create the subtype under it:

```
CREATE TYPE supplied_images_t UNDER image_t (
    supplier_ref REF supplier_t,
    supplier_rights_descriptor VARCHAR2(256)
);
```

After all this preparation, I make the subview of this subtype and declare it to be UNDER the images_v view using the following syntax:

```
CREATE VIEW supplied_images_v
        OF supplied_images_t
        UNDER images_v
AS
    SELECT i.image_id, BFILENAME('ROOTDIR', i.file_name),
           i.file_type, i.bytes,
           CAST (MULTISET (SELECT keyword
                             FROM keywords k
                            WHERE k.image_id = i.image_id)
             AS keyword_tab_t),
           MAKE_REF(suppliers_v, supplier_id),
           supplier_rights_descriptor
      FROM images i
     WHERE supplier_id IS NOT NULL;
```

Oracle won't let a subview query through the superview, so this view queries the base table, adding the WHERE clause to restrict the records retrieved. Also notice that subviews don't use the WITH OBJECT IDENTIFIER clause because they inherit the same OID as their superview.

I have introduced the MAKE_REF function in this query, which Oracle provides as a way to compute a REF to a virtual object. Here, the virtual object is the supplier, as conveyed through suppliers_v. The specification of MAKE_REF is:

```
FUNCTION MAKE_REF (view, value_list) RETURN ref;
```

where:

*view*
> Is the object view to which you want *ref* to point.

*value_list*
> Is a comma-separated list of column values whose datatypes must match one-for-one with the OID attributes of *view*.

You should realize that MAKE_REF does not actually select through the view; it merely applies an internal Oracle algorithm to derive a REF. And, as with "real" REFs, virtual REFs may not point to actual objects.

Now I come to a surprising result. Although it seems that I have not changed the superview, images from suppliers now appear twice in the superview—that is, as duplicates:

```
SQL> SELECT COUNT(*), image_id FROM images_v GROUP BY image_id;

  COUNT(*)   IMAGE_ID
---------- ----------
         2     100001
         2     100002
         1     100003
```

The Oracle database is returning a logical UNION ALL of the query in the superview and that of the subview. This does sort of make sense; an image from a supplier is still an image. To eliminate the duplicates, add a WHERE clause on the parent that excludes records returned in the subview:

```
CREATE OR REPLACE VIEW images_v AS
   ...
   WHERE supplier_id IS NULL;
```

## Object View with Inverse Relationship

To demonstrate virtual denormalization, I can create a keyword type for a view that links keywords back to the images they describe:

```
CREATE TYPE image_refs_t AS TABLE OF REF image_t;

CREATE TYPE keyword_t AS OBJECT (
   keyword VARCHAR2(45),
   image_refs image_refs_t);
```

And here is a keywords view definition:

```
CREATE OR REPLACE VIEW keywords_v
   OF keyword_t
   WITH OBJECT IDENTIFIER (keyword)
AS
   SELECT keyword, CAST(MULTISET(SELECT MAKE_REF(images_v, image_id)
                                  FROM keywords
                                  WHERE keyword = main.keyword)
                   AS image_refs_t)
     FROM (SELECT DISTINCT keyword FROM keywords) main;
```

Now, I don't promise that queries on this view will run *fast*; the query is compensating for the fact that the database lacks a reference table of keywords by doing a SELECT DISTINCT operation. Even if I weren't using any object features, that would be an expensive query.

You may correctly point out that using MAKE_REF is not mandatory here; I could have retrieved a REF by making the inner query on images_v rather than on the keywords table. In general, MAKE_REF should be faster than a lookup through an object view; on occasion, you may not have the luxury of being able to perform that lookup.

Anyway, at this point I can run such pithy queries as this one:

```
SQL> SELECT DEREF(VALUE(i)).print()
  2    FROM keywords_v v, TABLE(v.image_refs) i
  3    WHERE keyword = 'SIXTIES';

DEREF(VALUE(I)).PRINT()
--------------------------------------------------------------------------------
Id=100001; File=/files/web/60s/smiley_face.gif; keywords=HAPPY FACE, SIXTIES
Id=100002; File=/files/web/60s/peace_symbol.gif; keywords=JERRY RUBIN, PEACE SYMBOL,
SIXTIES
```

That is, I can show a list of all the images tagged with the keyword SIXTIES, along with their other keywords and attributes. I admit that I'm not sure how groovy that really is!

# INSTEAD OF Triggers

Since Chapter 19 covered the syntax and use of INSTEAD OF triggers, I'm not going to discuss their mechanics here. Instead, I'll explore whether they are a good fit for the problem of updating object views. If your goal is to migrate toward an object approach, you may ask whether INSTEAD OF triggers are just a relational throwback that facilitates a free-for-all in which any application can perform DML.

Well, they are and they aren't.

Let's examine the arguments for both sides, and come up with some considerations so you can decide what's best for your application.

### The case against

On the one hand, you could use PL/SQL programs such as packages and object methods to provide a more comprehensive technique than triggers for encapsulating DML.

It is nearly trivial to take the logic from my INSTEAD OF trigger and put it into an alternate PL/SQL construct that has more universal application. In other words, if you've already standardized on some combination of packages and methods as the means of performing DML, you could keep your environment consistent without using view triggers. You might conclude that view triggers are just added complexity in an increasingly confusing equation.

Moreover, even Oracle cautions against the "excessive use" of triggers because they can cause "complex interdependencies." Imagine if your INSTEAD OF triggers performed DML on tables that had other triggers, which performed DML on still other tables with triggers...it's easy to see how this could get impossible to debug.

### The case for

On the other hand, you can put much of the necessary logic that you would normally put into a package or method body into an INSTEAD OF trigger instead. Doing this in combination with a proper set of privilege restrictions could protect your data just as well as, or even better than, methods or packages.

If you happen to use a client tool such as Oracle Forms, INSTEAD OF triggers allow you to use much more of the product's default functionality when you create a Forms "block" against a view rather than a table.

Finally, if you use OCI, INSTEAD OF triggers are *required* if the object view is not inherently modifiable, and you want to be able to easily "flush" cached object view data back to the server.

### The bigger question

The bigger question is this: what's the best place for the SQL statements that insert, update, and delete data, especially when using object views? Assuming that you want to localize these operations on the server side, you have at least three choices: PL/SQL packages, object methods, and INSTEAD OF triggers.

Table 26-3 summarizes some of the major considerations of the three techniques. Note that this table is not meant to compare these approaches for general-purpose use, but only as they apply to localizing DML on object views.

*Table 26-3. Assessment of techniques for encapsulating DML on object views*

| Consideration | PL/SQL package | Object method | INSTEAD OF trigger |
|---|---|---|---|
| Consistency with object-oriented approach | Potentially very good | Excellent | Potentially very good |
| Ability to modify when underlying schema changes | Excellent; can be easily altered and recompiled independently | Excellent in Oracle9i Database and later | Excellent |

| Consideration | PL/SQL package | Object method | INSTEAD OF trigger |
|---|---|---|---|
| Risk of unexpected interactions | Low | Low | High; triggers may have unpredictable interactions with each other |
| Ease of use with client tool default functionality (specifically Oracle Developer) | Acceptable; programmer must add code for all client-side transactional triggers | Acceptable; programmer must add code for all client-side transactional triggers | Excellent for top-level types (however, there is no INSTEAD OF LOCK server-side trigger) |
| Can be turned on and off at will | No | No | Yes (by disabling and enabling the trigger) |

As you can see, there is no clear "winner." Each technique has benefits that may be of more or less importance to your application.

One important point about using INSTEAD OF triggers in view hierarchies is that you will need a separate trigger for each level of the hierarchy. When you perform DML through a subview, the subview's trigger will fire; when you perform DML through the superview, the superview's trigger will fire.

And of course, you may decide that INSTEAD OF triggers make sense in combination with PL/SQL packages and/or object methods to provide layers of encapsulation. For example:

```
TRIGGER images_v_insert
INSTEAD OF INSERT ON images_v
FOR EACH ROW
BEGIN
   /* Call a packaged procedure to perform the insert. */
   manage_image.create_one(:NEW.image_id, :NEW.file_type,
      :NEW.file_name, :NEW.bytes, :NEW.keywords);
END;
```

In an ideal world, developers would select an overall architecture and design approach before hurling every Oracle feature at their application. Use a feature only if it make sense for your design. I agree with Oracle's advice that if you do use triggers, you should use them in moderation.

## Differences Between Object Views and Object Tables

In addition to the obvious difference between an object view and an object table, PL/SQL programmers should be aware of the more subtle differences. Areas of difference include the following:

- OID uniqueness
- "Storeability" of physical versus virtual REFs
- REFs to nonunique OIDs

Let's look at each difference in turn.

## OID uniqueness

An object table will always have a unique object identifier, either system-generated or derived from the primary key. It is technically possible—though poor practice—to create an object table with duplicate rows, but the instances will still be unique in their object identifier. This can happen in two different ways:

*Duplicate OIDs in a single view*
> An object view can easily contain multiple object instances (rows) for a given OID. You've already seen a case where the superview can accidentally contain duplicates.

*Duplicate OIDs across multiple views*
> If your object view is defined on an underlying object table or view *and* if you use the DEFAULT keyword to specify the OID, the view contains OIDs that match the OIDs of the underlying structure.

It seems more likely that this second possibility of duplication would be legitimate in your application because separate views are just separate stored queries.

## "Storeability" of physical versus virtual REFs

If you've built an application with physical object tables, you can store REFs to those objects persistently in other tables. A REF is a binary value that the database can use as a pointer to an object.

However, the database returns an error if you attempt to store a virtual REF—that is, a REF to a row of an object view—in an actual table. Because the reference depends on some column value(s), you will need to save the underlying column value(s) instead of the virtual reference. From one perspective, this is an irritant rather than a major obstacle. Still, it's a bit unpleasant that I cannot intermingle object tables with object views, nor can I perform a simple transformation from an object view into an object table. I would like to be able to create an object table:

```
CREATE TABLE images2 OF image_t
   NESTED TABLE keywords STORE AS keyword_tab;
```

and then populate it from the view:

```
INSERT INTO images2      /* invalid because images_v includes a REF */
  SELECT VALUE(i) FROM images_v i;
```

But alas, Oracle tells me *ORA-22979: cannot INSERT object view REF or user-defined REF*. Life goes on, however.

## REFs to nonunique OIDs

I don't believe that it is possible to have a REF to a non-unique OID when dealing with object tables. You may want to consider what will happen if you create a REF to an object in an object view, but the view has multiple object instances for the OID in question. Granted, this is a pretty weird case; you shouldn't be creating object views with ambiguous OIDs.

In my testing, DEREFing this type of virtual REF did indeed return an object—apparently, the first one Oracle found that matched.

# Maintaining Object Types and Object Views

If you work much with object types, you will learn a number of ways to get information about the types and views that you have created. Once you reach the limits of the SQL*Plus DESCRIBE command, this could involve direct queries from the Oracle data dictionary.

## Data Dictionary

The data dictionary term for user-defined types (objects and collections) is simply TYPE. Object type definitions and object type bodies are both found in the USER_SOURCE view (or DBA_SOURCE, or ALL_SOURCE), just as package specifications and bodies are. Table 26-4 lists a number of helpful queries you can use.

*Table 26-4. Data dictionary entries for object types*

| To answer the question... | Use a query such as |
| --- | --- |
| What object and collection types have I created? | `SELECT * FROM   user_types;`<br>`SELECT * FROM   user_objects`<br>`   WHERE object_type =   'TYPE';` |
| What do my object type hierarchies look like? | `SELECT RPAD(' ',   3*(LEVEL-1)) || type_name`<br>`   FROM user_types`<br>`WHERE typecode =   'OBJECT'`<br>`   CONNECT BY PRIOR   type_name = supertype_name;` |
| What are the attributes of type foo? | `SELECT * FROM   user_type_attrs`<br>`   WHERE type_name =   'FOO';` |
| What are the methods of type foo? | `SELECT * FROM   user_type_methods`<br>`   WHERE type_name =   'FOO';` |
| What are the parameters of foo's methods? | `SELECT * FROM   user_method_params`<br>`   WHERE type_name =   'FOO';` |
| What datatype is returned by foo's method called bar? | `SELECT * FROM   user_method_results`<br>`   WHERE type_name =   'FOO' AND method_name = 'BAR';` |
| What is the source code for foo, including all ALTER statements? | `SELECT text FROM   user_source`<br>`   WHERE name = 'FOO'`<br>`      AND type = 'TYPE'    /* or 'TYPE BODY' */`<br>`   ORDER BY line;` |
| What are the object tables that implement foo? | `SELECT table_name FROM   user_object_tables`<br>`   WHERE table_type =   'FOO';` |
| What are all the columns in an object table foo_tab, including the hidden ones? | `SELECT column_name,   data_type, hidden_column,`<br>`      virtual_column`<br>`   FROM user_tab_cols`<br>`   WHERE table_name =   'FOO_TAB';` |

| To answer the question... | Use a query such as |
|---|---|
| What columns implement foo? | ```SELECT table_name,    column_name
  FROM user_tab_columns
WHERE data_type =   'FOO';``` |
| What database objects depend on foo? | ```SELECT name, type FROM    user_dependencies
WHERE referenced_name    = 'FOO';``` |
| What object views have I created, using what OIDs? | ```SELECT view_name,    view_type, oid_text
  FROM user_views
WHERE type_text IS    NOT NULL;``` |
| What does my view hierarchy look like? (Requires a temporary table in Oracle versions that can't use a sub-query with CONNECT BY) | ```CREATE TABLE uvtemp AS
    SELECT    v.view_name, v.view_type,
        v.superview_name,    v1.view_type superview_type
        FROM user_views    v, user_views v1
      WHERE    v.superview_name = v1.view_name (+);
SELECT RPAD(' ',    3*(LEVEL-1)) || view_name
        || ' (' ||    view_type || ') '
    FROM uvtemp
    CONNECT BY PRIOR    view_type = superview_type;
DROP TABLE uvtemp;``` |
| What is the query on which I defined the foo_v view? | ```SET LONG 1000 -- or    greater
SELECT text FROM    user_views
    WHERE view_name =    'FOO_V';``` |
| What columns are in view foo_v? | ```SELECT column_name,    data_type_mod, data_type
    FROM    user_tab_columns
  WHERE table_name =    'FOO_V';``` |

One potentially confusing thing Oracle has done in the data dictionary is to make object tables invisible from the USER_TABLES view. Instead, a list of object tables appears in USER_OBJECT_TABLES (as well as in USER_ALL_TABLES).

## Privileges

There are a handful of system-level privileges associated with object types, summarized here:

*CREATE [ ANY ] TYPE*
> Create, alter, and drop object types and type bodies. ANY means in any schema.

*CREATE [ ANY ] VIEW*
> Create and drop views, including object views. ANY means in any schema.

*ALTER ANY TYPE*
> Use ALTER TYPE facilities on types in any schema.

*EXECUTE ANY TYPE*
> Use an object type from any schema for purposes including instantiating, executing methods, referencing, and dereferencing.

*UNDER ANY TYPE*
> Create a subtype in one schema under a type in any other schema.

*UNDER ANY VIEW*
> Create a subview in one schema under a view in any other schema.

There are three kinds of object-level privileges on object types: EXECUTE, UNDER, and DEBUG. It is also important to understand how the conventional DML privileges apply to object tables and views.

### The EXECUTE privilege

If you want your associate Joe to use one of your types in his own PL/SQL programs or tables, you can grant the EXECUTE privilege to him:

```
GRANT EXECUTE on catalog_item_t TO joe;
```

If Joe has the privilege needed to create synonyms and is running Oracle9i Database Release 2 or later, he will be able to create a synonym:

```
CREATE SYNONYM catalog_item_t FOR scott.catalog_item_t;
```

and use it as follows:

```
CREATE TABLE catalog_items OF catalog_item_t;
```

and/or:

```
DECLARE
    an_item catalog_item_t;
```

Joe can also use a qualified reference to the type scott.catalog_item_t.

If you refer to an object type in a stored program and grant EXECUTE privilege on that program to a user or role, having EXECUTE on the type is not required, even if the program is defined using invoker rights (described in Chapter 24). Similarly, if a user has a DML privilege on a view that has an INSTEAD OF trigger for that DML operation, that user doesn't need explicit EXECUTE privileges if the trigger refers to the object type because triggers run under the definer rights model. However, the EXECUTE privilege is required by users who need to run anonymous blocks that use the object type.

### The UNDER privilege

The UNDER privilege gives the grantee the right to create a subtype. You can grant it as follows:

```
GRANT UNDER ON image_t TO scott;
```

For a schema to be able to create a subtype, the supertype must be defined using invoker rights (AUTHID CURRENT_USER).

This privilege can also grant the recipient the right to create a subview:

```
GRANT UNDER ON images_v TO scott;
```

### The DEBUG privilege

If one of your associates is using a PL/SQL debugger to analyze code that uses a type you have created, you may want to grant him the DEBUG privilege:

```
GRANT DEBUG ON image_t TO joe;
```

Doing so will enable the grantee to look "under the covers" to examine the variables used in the type and to set breakpoints inside methods.

The DEBUG privilege also applies to object views, providing a way to debug the PL/SQL source code of INSTEAD OF triggers.

### The DML privileges

For object tables, the traditional SELECT, INSERT, UPDATE, and DELETE privileges still have some meaning. A user with only SELECT privilege on the object table may retrieve any relational columns in the base type on which the table is defined, but cannot retrieve the object-as-object. That is, VALUE, TREAT, REF, and DEREF are not available. Similarly, the other DML privileges, INSERT, UPDATE, and DELETE, also apply only to the relational interpretation of the table.

In the same fashion, the grantee will not have permission to use the constructor or other object methods unless the object type owner has granted the user EXECUTE privilege on the object type. Any columns defined on subtypes will be invisible.

# Concluding Thoughts from a (Mostly) Relational Developer

Over the years, I've seen no compelling evidence that any particular programming style has a monopoly on the fundamental things we care about—fidelity to requirements, performance efficiency, developer effectiveness, and system reliability. I have seen a lot of fads, bandwagons, hand-waving, and unsupported assumptions (OK, I'm probably not entirely innocent myself), and object-oriented programming seems to attract quite a lot of it. That isn't to say that OOP fails to help you solve problems; it's just that OOP is not the magic bullet that many would have you believe.

Take, for example, the principle of object-based decomposition, particularly as it tends to generate inheritance hierarchies. By accurately modeling objects as they exist in the real world, software artifacts should be easier to comprehend, faster to assemble, and more amenable to large-scale system development. Sounds fabulous, doesn't it? Well, there are a lot of different ways to decompose something drawn from the real world. It is a rare taxonomy that can exist in a simple hierarchy. My library catalog hierarchy could have been decomposed according to, say, media (print versus audio tape versus digital format ...). And, although Oracle provides wonderful tools for type evolution, it may still be so painful to make sweeping changes in a type hierarchy that it will never happen. This isn't really the tool's fault; reality has a way of circumventing even the best-laid plans.

Nor is it even clear that co-locating the programming logic (methods) with the data (attributes) in an abstract datatype yields any measurable benefits. It looks reasonable and makes for some great sound bites, but how exactly will coupling data and behavior be better than keeping data structures (logical and physical table design) separate from processes (procedures, functions, packages)? Many development methods acknowledge that an organization's business data structures have a much slower rate of change than do the algorithms that manipulate them. It is a design truism (even for OOP) that the more volatile elements of a system should be kept separate from the more stable elements.

There is considerable inconsistency on this last point. Rich and famous object evangelists, while emphasizing the value of bundling data with behaviors, simultaneously promote a model-view-controller approach that "separates business logic from data." Are these emperors wearing clothes, or not?

Many OOP proponents have argued for years that its greatest benefit is the reuse of software. It has been said so many times that it must be true! Unfortunately, few observers have hard evidence for this, in part because there is no consensus on what constitutes "reuse." Even object apologists began promoting higher-level "components" (whatever those may be) as a preferred unit of reuse precisely because objects proved very difficult to fit into situations beyond those for which they were designed. My sense is that OOP results in no more code reuse than well-designed subroutines.

It is certainly possible to use object-oriented approaches with PL/SQL and achieve reuse of software. Fellow author Don Bales, an accomplished object-oriented programmer, has been using PL/SQL packages as "types" for about a decade, and he says that he has been able to take entire packages (and any accompanying tables) and drop them into new software development projects without modification. He believes that the missing ingredient in most object approaches is an accurate model of the person who is actually executing the software—the user—whom Don models as an object with behaviors implemented in the actual program that is run.

Regardless of development method, some of the critical ingredients of software success are having prior expertise with similar problems, being able to employ seasoned project leaders, and incorporating a conscious software design phase. Introducing object methods or any other approach is likely to produce more positive results than an unplanned, organically grown system.

A few final thoughts on when to best use Oracle's object features:

- If you use the Oracle Call Interface (OCI), it's possible that the client-side cache and complex object retrieval would tip the scales in favor of heavy use of Oracle's object features. I'm not an OCI programmer, though, so I can't speak from experience in this regard.

- If your organization already uses object programming across the board, Oracle's object features will probably make it easier and more graceful to introduce database technology into your systems.

- Don't throw the collections baby out with the objects bathwater. Remember that you don't need to use object types or object views to take advantage of collections.

- If you've never used OOP before, these object features may seem quite complicated. I would encourage quite a bit of playing around before committing to an object approach. In particular, try out object views in conjunction with an existing system.

- I would caution against rejecting object types and object views on a vague performance argument. Oracle has made continuous progress in reducing overhead. If you perform some actual measurements, you might find OOP within acceptable bounds for your application.

- It turns out that Oracle delivers some of its built-in functionality, most notably XML_TYPE, but also Advanced Queuing, Oracle Spatial, and Rules Manager, using object types. As we have often learned in the past, once Oracle starts using some of its own features, bugs are more quickly fixed, performance is enhanced, and usability is improved. That has happened with object types, as well. More than that, however, it means that if you are going to fully leverage the Oracle feature set, you should become at least familiar with the object type syntax and basic features.

# Regular Expression Metacharacters and Function Parameters

This appendix describes the various regular expression metacharacters available starting with Oracle Database 10*g*. It also provides a summary of the syntax of the REGEXP_ functions. For more details on Oracle's regular expression support, see Chapter 8.

## Metacharacters

The Initial Release column in Table A-1 through Table A-3 indicates which metacharacters were introduced in Oracle Database 10*g* Release 1 and which in Release 2.

*Table A-1. Character-matching metacharacters*

| Syntax | Initial release | Description |
|--------|-----------------|-------------|
| . | 10gR1 | Matches any single character except for newline. Will match newline when the n flag is set. On Windows, Linux, and Unix platforms, chr(10) is recognized as the newline. |
| [ ... ] | 10gR1 | Defines a *matching list* that matches any character listed between the brackets. You may specify ranges of characters, as in a-z. These ranges are interpreted based on the NLS_SORT setting. |
|  |  | A dash (-) is a literal when it occurs first or last in the list (e.g., [abc-]). A closing-bracket (]) is a literal when it occurs first in the list (e.g., []abc]). A caret (^) in the first position makes the list a *nonmatching list* (see the next entry). |
| [^ ... ] | 10gR1 | Matches any character not listed between the brackets. Referred to as a "nonmatching list." |
| [:*class*:] | 10gR1 | Matches any character that belongs to the specified character class. May only be used within a matching list: [[:class:]abc] is a valid expression, [:class:]abc is not. Table A-5 lists the valid character class names. |
| [.*coll*.] | 10gR1 | Matches the specified collation element, which may be one or more characters. May only be used within a matching list. For example, the expression |

| Syntax | Initial release | Description |
|---|---|---|
| | | [[.ch.]] matches the Spanish letter "ch". Table A-4 lists the valid collation elements. |
| [=*char*=] | 10gR1 | Matches all characters that share the same base character as char. May be used only within a matching list. For example, [[=e=]] matches any of: "eéëèÉËÈ". |
| \d | 10gR2 | Matches any digit. Equivalent to [[:digit:]]. |
| \D | 10gR2 | Matches any nondigit. Equivalent to [^[:digit:]]. |
| \w | 10gR2 | Matches any "word character." Word characters are defined to be alphabetic characters, numeric characters, and the underscore. |
| \W | 10gR2 | Matches any nonword character. |
| \s | 10gR2 | Matches any whitespace character. Equivalent to [[:space:]]. |
| \S | 10gR2 | Matches nonwhitespace characters. Equivalent to [^[:space:]]. |

*Table A-2. Quantifiers*

| Syntax | Initial release | Description |
|---|---|---|
| ? | 10gR1 | Zero or one. |
| * | 10gR1 | Zero or more. |
| + | 10gR1 | One or more. |
| {*m*} | 10gR1 | Exactly *m* occurrences. |
| {*m*,} | 10gR1 | At least *m* occurrences. |
| {*m*,*n*} | 10gR1 | At least *m*, and at most *n* occurrences. |
| +? | 10gR2 | One or more, but nongreedy. |
| ?? | 10gR2 | Zero or one, but nongreedy. |
| {*m*}? | 10gR2 | The same as {*m*}. |
| {*m*,}? | 10gR2 | At least *m* occurrences, but nongreedy and stops as soon as *m* occurrences are reached. |
| {*m*,*n*}? | 10gR2 | At least *m*, and at most *n* occurrences, but nongreedy; when possible, *m* occurrences are matched. |

*Table A-3. Other metacharacters*

| Syntax | Initial release | Description |
|---|---|---|
| \| | 10gR1 | Specifies an alternation. An alternation within a subexpression doesn't extend beyond the subexpression. |
| ( ... ) | 10gR1 | Defines a subexpresson. |
| \\*n* | 10gR1 | References the text matched by the *n*th subexpression. Backreferences may range from \1 through \9. |
| \ | 10gR1 | When not followed by a digit, the \ is an escape character. For example, use the pattern \\1 to look for a single backslash followed by the digit |

| Syntax | Initial release | Description |
|---|---|---|
| | | 1, use \( to look for an opening-parentheses (rather than begin a sub-expression), etc. |
| ^ | 10gR1 | Anchors an expression to the beginning of the string (in multiline mode, to the beginning of a line). |
| $ | 10gR1 | Anchors an expression to the end of the string (in multiline mode, to the end of a line). |
| \A | 10gR2 | Anchors an expression to the beginning of the string regardless of whether multiline mode is specified. |
| \Z | 10gR2 | Anchors an expression to the end of the string, or a newline that happens to be ending a string, regardless of whether multiline mode is specified. |
| \z | 10gR2 | Anchors an expression to the end of the string regardless of whether multiline mode is specified. |

*Table A-4. Collation elements*

| NLS_SORT | Multicharacter collation elements | | |
|---|---|---|---|
| XCROATIAN | d_ | D_ | D_ |
| | lj | LJ | Lj |
| | nj | Nj | NJ |
| XCZECH | Ch | CH | Ch |
| XCZECH_PUNCTUATION | Ch | CH | Ch |
| XDANISH | aa | AA | Aa |
| | oe | OE | Oe |
| XHUNGARIAN | cs | CS | Cs |
| | gy | GY | Gy |
| | ly | LY | Ly |
| | ny | NY | Ny |
| | sz | SZ | Sz |
| | ty | TY | Ty |
| | zs | ZS | Zs |
| XSLOVAK | dz | DZ | Dz |
| | d_ | D_ | D_ |
| | ch | CH | Ch |
| XSPANISH | ch | CH | Ch |
| | ll | LL | Ll |

Table A-5. Supported character classes

| Class | Description |
|-------|-------------|
| [:alnum:] | Alphanumeric characters (same as [:alpha:] + [:digit:]) |
| [:alpha:] | Alphabetic characters only |
| [:blank:] | Blank space characters, such as space and tab |
| [:cntrl:] | Nonprinting, or control characters |
| [:digit:] | Numeric digits |
| [:graph:] | Graphical characters (same as [:punct:] + [:upper:] + [:lower:] + [:digit:]) |
| [:lower:] | Lowercase letters |
| [:print:] | Printable characters |
| [:punct:] | Punctuation characters |
| [:space:] | Whitespace characters such as space, formfeed, newline, carriage return, horizontal tab, and vertical tab |
| [:upper:] | Uppercase letters |
| [:xdigit:] | Hexadecimal characters |

# Functions and Parameters

The following syntax shows the function parameters for Oracle's regular expression functions. The meaning of the parameters is shown in "Regular Expression Parameters" on page 1137.

## Regular Expression Functions

The syntax for each regular expression function is shown below.

### REGEXP_COUNT (Oracle Database 11g Only)

Returns a tally of occurrences of an expression in a target string. The syntax is:

```
REGEXP_COUNT(source_string, expression
            [, position
            [, match_parameter]])
```

### REGEXP_INSTR

Returns the character position at which text can be found matching a regular expression in a target string. The syntax is:

```
REGEXP_INSTR(source_string, expression
            [, position [, occurrence
            [, return_option
            [, match_parameter
            [, subexpression]]]]])
```

### REGEXP_LIKE

Determines whether a given string contains text matching an expression. This is a Boolean function, returning TRUE, FALSE, or NULL. The syntax is:

```
REGEXP_LIKE (source_string, expression
          [, match_parameter])
```

### REGEXP_REPLACE

Performs a regular expression search-and-replace operation (see Chapter 8 for details). The syntax is:

```
REGEXP_REPLACE(source_string, expression
          [, replace_string
          [, position [, occurrence
          [, match_parameter]]]])
```

### REGEXP_SUBSTR

Extracts text matching a regular expression from a string. The syntax is:

```
REGEXP_SUBSTR(source_string, expression
          [, position [, occurrence
          [, match_parameter
          [, subexpression]]]])
```

## Regular Expression Parameters

These are the parameters that may be included in the regular expression functions described above.

*source_string*
> Is a string to be searched.

*expression*
> Is a regular expression describing the pattern of text that you seek.

*replace_string*
> Is a string generating the replacement text to be used in a search-and-replace operation.

*position*
> Is the character position within *source_string* at which to begin a search. This defaults to 1.

*occurrence*
> Is the occurrence of the pattern you want to locate. This defaults to 1, giving you the first possible match.

*return_option*

> Is valid only for REGEXP_INSTR, and determines whether the beginning or ending character position is returned for text matching a pattern. The default is 0, for the beginning. Use 1 to return the ending position.

*match_parameter*

> Is a text string through which you may specify options to vary the behavior of the regular expression matching engine.

*subexpression (Oracle Database 11g only)*

> Is a number (0 – 9) identifying which subexpression to match on. The default is 0 and signifies that subexpressions will not be used:

*i*

> Requests a case-insensitive search.

*c*

> Requests a case-sensitive search.

 By default, your NLS_SORT setting determines whether a search is case-sensitive.

*n*

> Allows the period to match newline characters. By default, the period does not match newlines.

*m*

> Changes the definition of *line* with respect to the ^ and $ metacharacters. By default, line means *the entire target string*. Using the m option, however, causes the definition of line to change from *the entire target string*, to *any line within that string*, where lines are delimited by newline characters.

You can specify multiple match parameters in any order. For example, `'in'` means the same as `'ni'`. If you specify conflicting options, such as `'ic'`, the last option, `'c'` in this case, is the one that takes precedence.

# Number Format Models

Number formats are used with both the TO_CHAR function and the TO_NUMBER function. You use number formats in calls to TO_CHAR to specify exactly how a numeric value should be translated into a VARCHAR2 string. You can specify the punctuation to use, the location of the positive or negative sign, and other useful items. Conversely, you use number formats in calls to TO_NUMBER to specify how a string representing a numeric value should be interpreted.

A number format mask can comprise one or more elements from Table B-1. The resulting character string (or the converted numeric value) reflects the combination of the format model elements you use. You will find examples of different applications of the format models in the descriptions of TO_CHAR and TO_NUMBER.

Format elements with a description starting with "Prefix:" can be used only at the beginning of a format mask; when a description starts with "Suffix:", the element can be used only at the end of a format mask. Most format elements are described in terms of their effect on a conversion of a number to its character string representation. Bear in mind that the majority of such elements may also be used in the converse manner, to specify the format of a character string to be converted into a number.

*Table B-1. Number format model elements*

| Format element | Description |
|---|---|
| $ | Prefix: puts a dollar sign in front of a number. (for currency symbol, see the C format element). |
| , (comma) | Places a comma into the return value. This comma is used as a group separator (see the G format element). |
| . (period) | Places a period into the return value. This period is used as a decimal point (see the D format element). |
| 0 | Each zero represents a significant digit to be returned. Leading zeros in a number are displayed as zeros. |
| 9 | Each 9 represents a significant digit to be returned. Leading zeros in a number are displayed as blanks. |
| B | Prefix: returns a zero value as blanks, even if the 0 format element is used to show leading zeros. |

| Format element | Description |
| --- | --- |
| C | Specifies the location of the ISO currency symbol in the returned value. The NLS_ISO_CURRENCY parameter specifies the ISO currency symbol. |
| D | Specifies the location of the decimal point in the returned value. All format elements to the left of the D format the integer component of the value. All format elements to the right of the D format the fractional part of the value. The character used for the decimal point is determined by the NLS_NUMERIC_CHARACTERS database parameter. |
| EEEE | Suffix: specifies that the value be returned in scientific notation. |
| FM | Prefix: removes any leading or trailing blanks from the return value. |
| G | Specifies the location of the group separator (for example, a comma or period to separate thousands as in 6,754 or 6.754) in the returned value. The character used for the group separator is determined by the database parameter NLS_NUMERIC_CHARACTERS. |
| L | Specifies the location of the local currency symbol (such as $ or €) in the return value. The NLS_CURRENCY parameter specifies the local currency symbol. |
| MI | Suffix: places a minus sign (-) after the number if it is negative. If the number is positive, a trailing space is placed after the number. |
| PR | Suffix: places angle brackets (< and >) around a negative value. Positive values are given a leading and a trailing space. |
| RN or rn | Specifies that the return value be converted to upper- or lowercase Roman numerals. The range of valid numbers for conversion to Roman numerals is between 1 and 3999. The value must be an integer. RN returns uppercase Roman numerals, while rn returns lowercase Roman numerals. |
| S | Prefix: places a plus sign (+) in front of a positive number and a minus sign (-) in front of a negative number. |
| TM | Prefix: returns a number using the minimum number of characters. TM stands for "text minimum." Follow TM with one 9 if you want a regular, decimal notation (the default). Follow TM with one E if you want scientific notation. |
| U | Places the dual currency symbol (often €) at the specified location. The NLS_DUAL_CURRENCY parameter controls the character returned by this format element. |
| V | Multiplies the number to the left of the V in the format model by 10 raised to the *n*th power, where *n* is the number of 9s found after the V in the format model. |
| X | Returns a number in hexadecimal value. You can precede this element with 0s to return leading zeros or with FM to trim leading and trailing blanks. X cannot be used in combination with any other format elements. |

Notice that sometimes two elements can specify the same thing, or seemingly the same thing. For example, you can use the dollar sign ($), comma (,), and period (.), or you can use the L, G, and D elements, respectively. The letter elements respect your current NLS settings, and return the proper characters for whatever language you are using. For example, some European languages use a comma rather than a period to represent the decimal point. The dollar sign, comma, and period format elements are U.S.-centric and always return those three characters. We recommend that you use the

NLS-sensitive format model elements such as L, G, and D unless you have a specific reason to do otherwise.

---

## Denoting Monetary Units

Table B-1 shows four format elements you can use to denote currency symbols . These elements are $, L, C, and U, and you may be wondering about the differences among them:

*The $ format element*
> Is U.S.-centric and always returns a dollar sign ($).

*The L format element*
> Respects your current NLS_CURRENCY setting, which specifics your local currency indicator. If, for example, you set your NLS_TERRITORY to indicate that you're in the United Kingdom, NLS_CURRENCY will default to £, and the L format element will result in the £ being used as the currency indicator.

*The C format element*
> Is similar to the L element but it results in the ISO currency indicator, as specified by your current NLS_ISO_CURRENCY setting. For the United Kingdom, you'll get GBP (for Great Britain pounds), while for the United States, you'll get USD (for U.S. dollars), and so forth.

*The U format element*
> Was added to support the Euro and uses the currency indicator specified by NLS_DUAL_CURRENCY. For countries that support the Euro, the NLS_DUAL_CURRENCY setting defaults to the Euro symbol (€).

To view your current NLS_CURRENCY and NLS_ISO_CURRENCY settings, you can query the NLS_SESSION_PARAMETERS or V$NLS_PARAMETERS system views.

---

# Date Format Models

Table C-1 lists the date format model elements that you can use with the conversion functions TO_CHAR, TO_DATE, TO_TIMESTAMP, and TO_TIMESTAMP_TZ. Some of the model elements in Table C-1 are also used with ROUND and TRUNC.

You have the option of specifying default date and timestamp formats at the session level, a capability that can come in handy if your particular needs differ from those of the majority of database users. Use the ALTER SESSION command to specify session-level default date and timestamp formats. The following example works in Oracle8*i* Database or higher, and sets the default date format to MM/DD/YYYY:

```
BEGIN
    EXECUTE IMMEDIATE 'ALTER SESSION SET NLS_DATE_FORMAT=''MM/DD/YYYY''';
END;
```

To check the default date format in effect for your session at any given time, issue the following query against the NLS_SESSION_PARAMETERS data dictionary view:

```
SELECT value
FROM nls_session_parameters
WHERE parameter='NLS_DATE_FORMAT';
```

To set or check default timestamp formats, use NLS_TIMESTAMP_FORMAT and NLS_TIMESTAMP_TZ_FORMAT.

Some elements in Table C-1 apply only when translating datetime values from Oracle's internal format into character strings, and not vice versa. Such elements can't be used in a default date model (e.g., with NLS_DATE_FORMAT) because the default date model applies to conversions in both directions. These elements are noted as "Output-only" in the table.

*Table C-1. Date format model elements*

| Element | Description |
|---------|-------------|
| Other text | Any punctuation, such as a comma (,) or slash (/) or hyphen (-), will be reproduced in the formatted output of the conversion. You can also include text within double quotes (" ") and the text will be represented as entered in the converted value. |
| A.M. or P.M. | The meridian indicator (morning or evening) with periods. |
| AM or PM | The meridian indicator (morning or evening) without periods. |
| B.C. or A.D. | The B.C. or A.D. indicator, with periods. |
| BC or AD | The B.C. or A.D. indicator, without periods. |
| CC and SCC | The century. If the SCC format is used, any B.C. dates are prefaced with a minus sign (-). Output-only. |
| D | The day of the week, from 1 through 7. The day of the week that is decreed the first day is specified implicitly by the NLS_TERRITORY initialization parameter for the database instance. |
| DAY, Day, or day | The name of the day in upper-, mixed-, or lowercase format. |
| DD | The day of the month, from 1 through 31. |
| DDD | The day of the year, from 1 through 366. |
| DL | Long date format. Depends on the current values of NLS_TERRITORY and NLS_LANGUAGE. May be used alone or with TS, but not with any other elements. |
| DS | Short date format. Depends on the current values of NLS_TERRITORY and NLS_LANGUAGE. May be used alone or with TS, but not with any other elements. |
| DY, Dy, or dy | The abbreviated name of the day, as in TUE for Tuesday. |
| E | The abbreviated era name. Valid only for the following calendars: Japanese Imperial, ROC Official, and Thai Buddha. Input-only. |
| EE | The full era name. |
| FF | The fractional seconds. Only valid when used with TIMESTAMP values. The number of digits returned will correspond to the precision of the datetime being converted. |
| | Always use FF (two Fs) regardless of the number of decimal digits you wish to see or use. Any other number of Fs is invalid. |
| FF1..FF9 | Same as FF, but the digit (1..9) controls the number of decimal digits used for fractional seconds. Use FF1 to see one digit past the decimal point, FF2 to see two digits past, and so forth. |
| FM | Element that toggles suppression of blanks in output from conversion. (FM stands for Fill Mode.) |
| FX | Element that requires exact pattern matching between data and format model. (FX stands for Format eXact.) |
| HH or HH12 | The hour of the day, from 1 through 12. Output only. |
| HH24 | The hour of the day, from 0 through 23. |
| IW | The week of the year, from 1 through 52 or 1 through 53, based on the ISO standard. Output-only. |
| IYY or IY or I | The last three, two, or one digits of the ISO standard year. Output only. |
| IYYY | The four-digit ISO standard year. Output only. |
| J | The Julian day format of the date (counted as the number of days since January 1, 4712 B.C., the earliest date supported by the Oracle database). |

| Element | Description |
| --- | --- |
| MI | The minutes component of the datetime value, from 0 through 59. |
| MM | The number of the month in the year, from 01 through 12. January is month number 01, September is 09, etc. |
| MON, Mon, or mon | The abbreviated name of the month, as in JAN for January. This also may be in upper-, mixed-, or lowercase format. |
| MONTH, Month, or month | The name of the month, in upper-, mixed-, or lowercase format. |
| Q | The quarter of the year, from 1 through 4. January through March are in the first quarter, April through June in the second quarter, etc. Output only. |
| RM | The Roman numeral representation of the month number, from I through XII. January is I, September is IX, etc. Output only. |
| RR | The last two digits of the year. This format displays years in centuries other than our own. |
| RRRR | Same as RR when used for output; accepts four-digit years when used for input. |
| SCC or CC | The century. If the SCC format is used, any B.C. dates are prefaced with a minus sign (-). Output only. |
| SP | Suffix that converts a number to its spelled format. This element can appear at the end of any element that results in a number. For example, a model such as "DDth-Mon-Yyyysp" results in output such as "15th-Nov-One Thousand Nine Hundred Sixty-One". The return value is always in English, regardless of the date language. (Note that Yyyy resulted in mixed-case words.) |
| SPTH or THSP | Suffix that converts a number to its spelled and ordinal format; for example, 4 becomes FOURTH and 1 becomes FIRST. This element can appear at the end of any element that results in a number. For example, a model such as "Ddspth Mon, Yyyysp" results in output such as "Fifteenth Nov, One Thousand Nine Hundred Sixty-One". The return value is always in English, regardless of the date language. |
| SS | The seconds component of the datetime value, from 0 through 59. |
| SSSSS | The number of seconds since midnight of the time component. Values range from 0 through 86399, with each hour comprising 3,600 seconds. |
| SYEAR, YEAR, SYear, Year, syear, or year | The year spelled out in words (e.g., "two thousand two"). The S prefix places a negative sign in front of B.C. dates. The format may be upper-, mixed-, or lowercase. Output only. |
| SYYYY or YYYY | The four-digit year. If the SYYYY format is used, any B.C. dates are prefaced with a minus sign (-). |
| TH | Suffix that converts a number to its ordinal format; for example, 4 becomes 4th and 1 becomes 1st. This element can appear at the end of any element that results in a number. For example, "DDth-Mon-YYYY" results in output such as "15th-Nov-1961". The return value is always in English, regardless of the date language. |
| TS | Short time format. Depends on the current values of NLS_TERRITORY and NLS_LANGUAGE. May be used alone or with either DL or DS, but not with any other elements. |
| TZD | The abbreviated time zone name; for example, EST, PST, etc. This is an input-only format, which may seem odd at first. |
| TZH | The time zone hour displacement. For example, −5 indicates a time zone five hours earlier than UTC. |
| TZM | The time zone minute displacement. For example, −5:30 indicates a time zone that is five hours, thirty minutes earlier than UTC. A few such time zones do exist. |

| Element | Description |
|---|---|
| TZR | The time zone region. For example, "US/Eastern" is the region in which EST (Eastern Standard Time) and EDT (Eastern Daylight Time) are valid. |
| W | The week of the month, from 1 through 5. Week 1 starts on the first day of the month and ends on the seventh. Output only. |
| WW | The week of the year, from 1 through 53. Output only. |
| X | The local radix character. In American English, this is a period (.). This element can be placed in front of FF so that fractional seconds are properly interpreted and represented. |
| Y,YYY | The four-digit year with a comma. |
| YYY or YY or Y | The last three, two, or one digits of the year. The current century is the default when using these elements to convert a character string value into a date. |

Whenever a date format returns a spelled value (words rather than numbers, as with MONTH, MON, DAY, DY, AM, and PM), the language used to spell these words is determined by the Globalization Support, formerly National Language Support parameters, NLS_DATE_LANGUAGE and NLS_LANGUAGE, or by the optional date language argument you can pass to both TO_CHAR and TO_DATE.

---

### ISO Dates

The IYY and IW elements represent the ISO (International Standards Organization) year and week. The ISO calendar is a good example of "design by committee." The first day of the ISO year is always a Monday and is determined by the following rules:

- When January 1 falls on a Monday, the ISO year begins on the same day.
- When January 1 falls on a Tuesday through Thursday, the ISO year begins on the preceding Monday.
- When January 1 falls on a Friday through Sunday, the ISO year begins on the following Monday.

These rules lead to some strange situations. For example, 31-Dec-2008 is considered to be the first day of ISO year 2009, and if you display that date using the IYYY format, 31-Dec-2009 is exactly what you'll get.

ISO weeks always begin on Mondays and are numbered from the first Monday of the ISO year.

---

Here are some examples of date format models composed of the above format elements:

```
'Month DD, YYYY'
'MM/DD/YY Day A.M.'
'Year Month Day HH24:MI:SS'
'J'
'SSSSS-YYYY-MM-DD'
'"A beautiful summer morning on the" DDth" day of "Month'
```

You can use the format elements in any combination, in any order. Older releases of Oracle allowed you to specify the same date element twice. For example, the model "Mon (MM) DD, YYYY" specifies the month twice. However, you can specify an element only once in a format model. For example, you can specify only one of MONTH, MON, and MM because all three refer to the month.

See the description of the TO_CHAR and TO_DATE functions in Chapter 10 for more examples of the use and resulting values of date format models.

# Index

## Symbols

! (exclamation mark)
  != (not equal) operator, 65, 259, 387
    testing nested tables, 389
  user-defined string literal delimiter, 70
\# (hash sign) in identifiers, 66
$ (dollar sign)
  $$identifier syntax for inquiry directive, 1000
  in identifiers, 66
% (percent sign)
  attribute indicator, 65
  in cursor attribute names, 468
  wildcard symbol in LIKE condition, 65
& (ampersand)
  problems with, executing PL/SQL code in SQL*Plus, 196
  referring to SQL*Plus variables, 33
" " (quotation marks, double)
  data structure names enclosed in, 168
  inside string literals, 73
  surrounding identifiers, 67
' ' (quotation marks, single)
  embedding inside literal strings, 72
  indicating null strings, 71
  SQL*Plus variables used as literal strings, 33
  in string constants, 195
( ) (parentheses)
  as string literal delimiters, 73
  functions without parameters, 576
* (asterisk)
  ** (exponentiation) operator, 65, 259
  multiplication operator, 259

+ (plus sign)
  addition operator, 259
  identity operator, 259
- (hyphen), -- (double hyphen) delimiting single-line comments, 65, 75
- (minus sign)
  negation operator, 259
  subtraction operator, 259
. (dot)
  .. (range) operator, 65
  component selector, xxxii
  dot notation component selector, 115, 322
  dot notation for fields in nested records, 323
  dot notation referencing package elements, 620, 632
... (ellipses) in syntax descriptions, xxxii
/ (slash)
  /* */ multiline comment block delimiters, 65
  division operator, 259
  following CREATE TYPE statement, 354
: (colon)
  := (assignment) operator, 65, 176
    assigning values to a collection, 360
    storing string constant in a variable, 196
  host variable indicator, 65
; (semicolon)
  placing only after END IF keywords in IF statements, 87
  terminating declarations and statements, 65, 74
< > (angle brackets)
  < (less than) operator, 259

---

We'd like to hear your suggestions for improving our indexes. Send email to *index@oreilly.com*.

<%= %>, embedding PL/SQL into HTML page, 51

<< >> label delimiters, 65, 98

<= (less than or equal to) operator, 65, 259

<> (not equal) operator, 65, 259, 387

> (greater than) operator, 259

>= (greater than or equal to) operator, 65, 259

= (equals sign)
   => association operator, 65, 585
     using for named notation, 586
   equality operator, 259, 387
     testing nested tables for equality, 389

? (question mark)
   nongreedy quantifiers in regular expressions, 217

@ (at sign)
   SQL*Plus at-sign command, 30

@ (at-sign)
   remote location indicator, 65

[ ] (square brackets) in syntax descriptions, xxxii

^ (caret)
   ^= (not equal) operator, 65, 259

_ (underscore)
   in identifiers, 66
   single-character wildcard in LIKE condition, 65

{ } curly braces in syntax descriptions, xxxii

| (vertical bar)
   in code examples, xxxii
   as string literal delimiter, 73
   || (concatenation) operator, 65, 198

~ (tilde)
   ~= (not equal) operator, 65, 259

## A

ABORT procedure (DBMS_RESUMABLE), 702

abstract datatypes, 169

ACLs (access control lists), 430, 893

actual and formal parameters, 580
   association in PL/SQL, 585–589

Ada, xxv, 987
   DIANA (Distributed Intermediate Annotated Notation for Ada), 981

ADD_MONTHS function, 300

Advanced Encryption Standard (AES), 924

Advanced Queuing (AQ), 178, 634

AFTER GRANT triggers, 680

AFTER SUSPEND triggers, 697–704
   aborting unfixable statements using DBMS_RESUMABLE, 702
   downsides to using, 704
   example of, 700
   ORA_SPACE_ERROR_INFO function, 701
   setting up, 698
   trapped multiple times, 703

AFTER triggers, 653

aggregate assignments
   entire collection contents to another collection, 360
   in record-level operations, 320

alerts, 914

algorithms (encryption), 921, 923
   AES (Advanced Encryption Standard), 924, 927
   DBMS_CRYPTO algorithm constants, 925
   DES (Data Encryption Standard), 924
   Triple DES (DES3), 924

ALL_* views, 711

ALL_DEPENDENCIES view, 719

ALL_IDENTIFIERS view, PL/Scope information in, 15

ALL_OBJECTS_AE view, 778

ALL_SOURCE view, 719

ALTER command, enabling compile-time warnings, 737

ALTER INDEX statements, 673

ALTER SESSION...SIGNATURE command, 728

ALTER TRIGGER command, 705

ALTER TYPE command, 354, 1093–1095

ALTER...COMPILE recompilation, 733

anchored datatypes, 351

anchored declarations, 177
   anchoring to cursors and tables, 179
   benefits of, 180

AND operator
   exception handler for multiple exceptions, 144
   short-circuit evaluation in IF statements, 89

anonymous blocks, 53, 54
   general syntax, 55
   labeling, 77

nested, 57
uses of, 56
anonymous exceptions, 127
ANSI/ISO standards for date and timestamp
    literal format, 292
ANY keyword, 613
ANY types, 431–435, 1102
    creating a transient type, 1105
    resources for information, 435
ANYDATA type, 174, 432, 1103–1105
ANYDATASET type, 174, 432, 1103
ANYTYPE type, 174, 432, 1102
    creating transient type, 1105
application contexts, 920, 964–972
    contexts as predicates in RLS, 967
    creating and setting, 965
    identifying non-database users, 970
    security in, 966
application security, 919–980
    application contexts, 964–972
    encryption, 921–945
    fine-grained auditing (FGA), 972–980
    row-level security (RLS), 945–964
    security overview, 919
AQ (Advanced Queuing), 178, 634
architecture of PL/SQL, 981–1030
    conditional compilation, 998–1009
    default packages, 987
    DIANA, 981
    execution authority models, 990–998
    native compilation, 1027
    Oracle execution of PL/SQL code, 982
    PL/SQL and databse instance memory,
        1009–1027
arguments, 581
    (see also parameters)
    information about, 717
array fetches, tuning pipelined functions with,
    843
arrays, 327
    (see also associative arrays; collections;
    VARRAYs)
    collection, 329
    multidimensional, creating with collections
        of collections, 329
    multidimensional, emulation with
        unnamed multilevel collections,
        376

nonsequential arrays with FORALL
    statements, 835
ASCII function, 198, 222
ASCII, US7ASCII character set, 64
ASCIISTR function, 222, 1039
assignment
    of entire collection contents to another
        collection, 360
    in record-level operations, 319
    rows from relational table to a collection,
        361
assignment operator (:=), 65, 176
    assigning values to a collection, 360
    storing string constant in a variable, 196
ASSM (Automatic Segment Space
    Management), 416
association operator (=>), 65
associative arrays, 331
    assigning data to, specifying index value for,
        360
    collection using, 331
    comparison to other collection types, 340
    declaring associative array collection type,
        351
asymmetric encryption, 923
attribute-level comparison, 1110, 1112
audit trail, 972
    checking, 977
auditing (see fine-grained auditing)
authentication
    external, captured in FGA, 978
    MACs (method authentication codes), 940
    operating system, 34
    proxy server requiring authentication, 913
    using HTTP username and password, 906
AUTHID clause, 6
    AUTHID CURRENT_USER, 996
    AUTHID DEFINER, 996
    in package specification, 625
    settings for programs, 716
automatic runtime recompilation, 732
autonomous transactions, 454–461
    building autonomous logging mechanism,
        459
    defining, 455
    DML triggers as, 655, 669
    rules and restrictions on, 456
    visibility of, 457
    when to use, 458

AUTONOMOUS_TRANSACTION pragma, 76, 455

# B

basic authentication, 906
BasicFiles, 415, 930
BEFORE INSERT triggers, 656, 665
BEFORE triggers, 653
BETWEEN operator, 259
BFILE datatype, 173, 400, 411–415
    accessing BFILEs, 412
    creating BFILE locator, 411
    sending as email attachment, 900
    using BFILEs to load LOB columns, 413
BFILENAME function, 411
binary (32-bit) floating-point literals, 73
binary data, 173
binary double (64-bit) floating-point literals, 73
binary files (see BFILE datatype)
binary sort, 1050
BINARY type, 73
BINARY_FLOAT and BINARY_DOUBLE datatypes, 171, 241
    literals used with, 241
    performance improvements with, 871
    performance, NUMBER type versus, 243
    predicates used with, 242
BINARY_INTEGER datatype, 239
bind values, 973
bind variables
    reducing memory use with, 1015–1018
    in SQL*Plus, 32
        declaring and displaying with PRINT command, 33
    using in FGA, 978
binding variables, 525–529
    argument modes, 526
    duplicate placeholders, 527
    passing NULL values, 528
    using bind variables to prevent code injection, 541
    using instead of concatenation in NDS, 538
blank-padding comparison, 220
BLOBs (Binary Large Objects), 173, 400, 403
    (see also LOBs)
    creating empty BLOBs, 406
    writing into, 409

block-structured language, 57
blocks, 53–64
    anonymous, 54
    exception section, 127
    labeling, 77
    named, 56
    nested, 57
    scope, 58
    visibility of variables, 61–64
body of a function, 577
body of a loop, 103
body of a package, 618, 622
    example implementation, 620
    rules for construction, 626
body of a procedure, 570
books on PL/SQL programming, 17
BOOLEAN datatypes, 172, 395
Boolean expressions, 82
    NULL versus UNKNOWN results, 91
Boolean literals, 70, 74
Boolean values, displaying with DBMS_OUTPUT, 875
Boolean variables, 74
    using as flags for expression evaluation, 85
boundary (loop), 103
    simple loops, 104
bounded collections, 330
bugs, avoiding through use of qualifiers, 60
BULK COLLECT clause, 821–828
    array fetches with, using to tune pipelined functions, 843
    bulk fetching of multiple columns, 825
    LIMIT clause with, reducing memory usage, 1021
    limiting rows retrieved, 824
bulk processing for multirow SQL, 820–838
    DML using FORALL statement, 828–838
    querying using BULK COLLECT, 821–828
bulk processing, defined, 466
%BULK_EXCEPTIONS attribute, 470
%BULK_ROWCOUNT attribute, 470
bytecode, 1027

# C

C language, 48
    (see also External Procedures chapter on book web site)
    calling PL/SQL function from, 47
    support for REFs, 1100

caching, 799–820
  deterministic functions, 805
  function result cache, 807
  function results (see function result cache)
  package-based, 800–805
  recommendations for data caching, 819
  static session data, 629, 649
  types available to PL/SQL developers, 649
calculated or virtual columns, 484
calendar (ISO), 1146
Call Global Area (CGA), 1010
CALL statements, 983
cardinality for pipelined table functions, 853–859
CASCADE option (ALTER TYPE), 354
case in strings, 199
  capitalizing each word, 201
  case-insensitivity and indexes, 201
  forcing string to all upper- or lowercase, 199
  making comparisons case-insensitive, 199
CASE statements, 8
CASE statements and expressions, 90–97
  CASE expressions, 95
  CASE in SQL statements, 97
  nested CASE statements, 95
  searched CASE statements, 93
  simple CASE statements, 91
case-insensitivity in PL/SQL, 65
CASE_NOT_FOUND errors, 92
CAST function, 187
  converting numbers to and from strings, 256
  using to convert between numbers and strings, 256
  using with date and time values, 297
CAST pseudo-function, 383
CBO (cost-based optimizer), 853–859
certificates, 907
CGA (Call Global Area), 1010
chaining, 925
  CBC (Cipher Block Chaining), 927
  DBMS_CRYPTO chaining constants, 926
chaining (method), 1086
CHAR datatype, 170, 191, 193
  assigning zero-length string to, 72
  converting hexadecimal string to type RAW, 190
  empty strings and, 219

mixing with VARCHAR2 values, 219–222
character encodings
  defined, 1034
  Unicode, 1036
character functions, CHAR arguments, 222
Character Large Objects (see CLOBs)
character semantics, 1045–1049
character sets, 64
  conversions, 929
  converting strings between, 189
  defined, 1034
  national character set datatypes, 1036
  translating, 229
characters
  dangerous characters in dynamic text, 542
  nonprintable, in code, 197
CHARTOROWID function, 187
child blocks, 57
CHR function, 222
  referencing nonprintable characters in code, 197
client-side PL/SQL, 4
CLOBs (Character Large Objects), 170, 400, 403
  (see also LOBs)
  applying SQL semantics to, temporary CLOB yielded by, 423
  empty versus NULL, 405
  reading from, 409
  using interchangeably with VARCHAR2, 421
  writing into, 407
CLOSE cursor statements, 464, 486
  closing cursor variable, 498
CLUSTER ... BY clause, 614
clustered, 614
code examples
  conventions used in, xxxi
  web site for downloads, xxxiii
code injection (see SQL injection)
code management, 709–780
  compile-time warnings, 735–746
  data dictionary views for PL/SQL developers, 710–721
  in the database, 710
  debugging, 766–774
  edition-based redefinition, 777–780
  managing dependencies and recompiling code, 721–735

protecting stored code, 774
testing PL/SQL programs, 746
tracing PLSQL execution, 756–766
code points, 1036
defined, 1034
code units, 1037
code, creating and running, 23–52
calling PLSQL from other languages, 46–52
creating and editing source code, 24
creating stored program, 38
database navigation, 23
dropping stored programs, 44
editing environments for PL/SQL, 45
error handling in SQL*Plus, 36
executing stored program in SQL*Plus, 41
grants and synonyms for stored programs, 43
hiding source code of stored program, 44
other SQL*Plus tasks, 32
editing a statement, 34
exiting SQL*Plus, 34
loading custom environment at startup, 35
saving output to file, 33
setting your preferences, 32
reasons to love and hate SQL*Plus, 37
showing stored programs, 42
using SQL*Plus, 25
code, minimizing redundancies in, 495
CodeGen utility, 19
collection instance, 329
collections, 327–394
accessing data in, 364
as attributes of object type, 339
built-in methods, 341
caching, using function result cache, 813
choosing collection type, 340
as columns in database table, 338
comparison of collection types, 340
of complex datatypes, 370–374
objects and other types, 373
records, 371–373
as components of a record, 335
concepts and terminology, 328
converting types, 188
COUNT method, 343
as datatype of function return value, 337

declaring and initializing collection variables, 355–359
initializing implicitly during direct assignment, 356
initializing implicitly via FETCH, 357
declaring collection types, 350
DELETE method, 343
EXISTS method, 345
EXTEND method, 345
FIRST and LAST methods, 346
large, memory use and, 1018
LIMIT method, 347
multilevel, 374–382
extending string_tracker (example), 380
multidimensional API (example), 378
nesting of collections, levels of, 382
unnamed, emulating multidimensional arrays, 376
multiset operations on nested tables
checking element membership, 390
high-level set operations, 390
nested table multiset operations, 387–393
handling duplicates, 392
testing equality and membership, 389
NULL, 1120
populating with data, 359–364
advantages of nonsequential population, 362
aggregate assignments, 360
assigning rows from relational table, 361
specifying index values, 360
using assignment operator, 360
PRIOR and NEXT methods, 348
as program parameters, 335
schema-level, maintaining, 393
data dictionary entries for collections, 394
string-indexed, 365–370
TRIM procedure, 349
types of, 330
using a nested table, 332
using a VARRAY, 333
using an associative array, 331
working with in SQL, 382–387
CAST pseudo-function, 383
MULTISET pseudo-function, 384
sorting collection contents, 386
TABLE pseudo-function, 385

working with using NDS, 529–531
COLLECTION_IS_NULL exception, 343
column aliases in explicit cursors, 484
column objects, 1110
columns
    bulk fetching of multiple columns, 825
    determining which column was altered, 679
    object types as datatype for, 1110
    RLS sensitive to, 957
    synchronization of local variables with, 180
command-line interpreters, 25
comments, 75
    multiline, 75
    single-line, 75
    specifying for current transaction, 451
COMMIT statements, 451
    releasing locks with, 494
compilation
    conditional (see conditional compilation)
    native, 14, 1027
    recompiling invalid program units, 731–735
compilation environment parameters, 1002
compile-time warnings, 735–746
    enabling and specifying category, 736
    reference listing of handy warnings, 739–746
compiler directives, 999–1001
compiler settings for stored code, 715
compilers
    limits on PL/SQL program size, 986
    optimizing compiler, 794–799
    PL/SQL and SQL, 984
complex datatypes, 351
    collections of, 370–374
COMPOSE function, 223, 1040
composite data, 167
compound triggers, 15, 652, 670–673
    differences from packages, 671
    order of firing, 672
    resemblance to packages, 670
CONCAT function, 198, 223
concatenation
    binding versus, for dynamic SQL strings, 538
    inserting program values into SQL strings, 526

concatenation operator (||), 65, 198
conditional compilation, 998–1009
    $ERROR directive, 1005
    examples of, 999
    $IF directive, 1004
    inquiry directives, 1000
    program-specific settings with inquiry directives, 1006
    synchronizing code with packaged constants, 1006
    toggle tracing through conditional compilation flags, 1000
    working with postprocessed code, 1008
conditional control statements, 8
    CASE statements and expressions, 90–97
        CASE expressions, 95
        nested CASE statements, 95
        searched CASE statements, 93
        simple CASE statements, 91
    IF statements, 81–90
        IF-THEN, 82
        IF-THEN-ELSE, 84
        IF-THEN-ELSIF, 85
connect identifiers (Oracle Net), 27
connection pools, 970
constants, 167
    declaring, 176
    name conflicts in, 740
    naming, 167
    specifying string constants, 195
constrained declarations, 580
constrained subtypes, 182
CONSTRUCTOR FUNCTION keywords, 1081
constructor methods, 1079
    user-defined, 1081
containers, 167
CONTAINS predicate, 425
context-sensitive policies, 956
CONTINUE statements, 13, 116
    understanding and using correctly, 117
contributors to this book, listed, xxviii
control statements, 8
CONVERT function, 189, 223
cookies, disabling or making persistent, 912
Coordinated Universal Time (see UTC)
cost-based optimizer (CBO), 853–859
COUNT function, 341, 343

CPAN (Comprehensive Perl Archive Network), 49
CREATE statements
    CREATE FUNCTION, 38
    wrapping in plain text and hex to hide source code, 44
CREATE TABLE statements, 673
CREATE TYPE statements, 353
    creating object type, 1076
    creating schema-level type, 336
    FORCE option, 13
cryptographic hashing, 938
cryptography (see DBMS_CRYPTO package; encryption)
currency conversions, 1064–1066
currency symbols, 1141
CURRENT_DATE function, 272
CURRENT_TIMESTAMP function, 272
cursor attributes, 467–470
    %BULK_EXCEPTIONS, 470
    %BULK_ROWCOUNT, 470
    %FOUND, 468
    %ISOPEN, 469
    %NOTFOUND, 469
    %ROWCOUNT, 469
    defined, 466
    explicit cursor attributes, 487
    for FORALL statements, 831
    implicit cursor attributes for DML statements, 444
        SQL%FOUND, 444
        SQL%ROWCOUNT, 445
    implicit SQL cursor attributes, 476
    listed, 467
    using with cursor variables, 498
cursor expressions, 464, 509–512
    restrictions on, 512
    using, 510
cursor FOR loops, 102, 112–115
    declaring records, 315
    exiting properly, 120
    getting information on loop execution, 121
    implicit use of %ROWTYPE declaration, 179
    runtime optimization of, 798
CURSOR operator, 509
cursor variables, 173, 463, 496
    benefits of using, 497
    declaring, 499

declaring REF CURSOR types, 498
defined, 466
fetching from, 501
    handling ROWTYPE_MISMATCH exception, 502
opening, 500
packages and, 624
passing as arguments in procedure or function calls, 507
passing table function results with, 607
restrictions on, 509
rules for, 504
    aliases, 505
    rowtype matching at compile-time, 504
    rowtype matching at runtime, 505
    scope of cursor object, 506
similarities to static cursors, 498
using with NDS, 517
cursor-based records, declaring, 314
cursors, 464
    anchoring to, 179
    choosing between explicit and implicit, 471
    closing, 1012
    data retrieval terminology, 465
    DBMS_SQL.TO_CURSOR function, 556
    defining structure in method 4 dynamic SQL using DBMS_SQL, 550
    explicit, 463, 465, 477–492
        attributes, 487
        closing, 486
        column aliases in, 484
        declaring, 479–482
        fetching from, 483
        opening, 482
        parameters, 489–492
    implicit, 463, 465
    memory usage, 1011
    minimizing parsing of dynamic cursors, 553
    opening and closing, DBMS_SQL versus NDS, 537
    in package specification, 625
    packaged, 635–639
        alternative to, 639
        declaring, 635
        opening and closing, 638
        taking advantage of, 637
    remote invocation and, 730

security enhancements for DBMS_SQL
package, 559
SELECT FOR UPDATE statements, 492–
496
typical query operations, 466
working with implicit cursors, 472
CURSOR_SHARING initialization parameter,
1017

# D

D, designating 64-bit floating-point literals, 73
dangling REFs, 1102
Data Definition Language (see DDL)
data dictionary
entries for object types, 1127
views providing information on collections,
394
data dictionary views, 711–721
analyzing identifier usage (PL/Scope), 719–
721
dependency analysis with, 722
overview of, 711
for triggers, 706
USER_ARGUMENTS view, 717
USER_OBJECTS view, 712
USER_OBJECT_SIZE view, 715
USER_PLSQL_OBJECT_SETTINGS view,
715
USER_PROCEDURES view, 716
USER_SOURCE view, 713
USER_TRIGGERS and
USER_TRIG_COLUMNS, 716
data encapsulation, 20
Data Encryption Standard (DES), 924
Triple DES (DES3), 924
Data Manipulation Language (see DML)
data streaming, 605
Database Error Messages document, 40
database event triggers, 652, 683–690
(see also triggers)
creating, 683
LOGOFF, 686
LOGON, 685
SERVERERROR, 686–690
SHUTDOWN, 685
STARTUP, 685
database languages, 4
database pipes, 107, 914

Database PL/SQL Packages and Types
Reference, 430
database queuing, 914
database sessions, 983
database triggers (see triggers)
datatypes, 169–175
anchored, 177
benefits of, 180
ANY, 174
binary data, 173
Boolean, 172, 395
character data, 170
conversions between, 183–190
compile-time warning about, 745
explicit conversion, 185
implicit conversion, 183
dates, timestamps, and intervals, 172
FORCE option with CREATE TYPE
statements, 13
Internet-related, 174
interval, 274
LOBs (large objects), 400
matching in cross-language work, 46
naming, 169
national character set, 1036
NOT NULL, anchoring to, 181
numeric, 171, 231
overloading by type, not value, 597
performance improvement using right type,
870
predefined object types, 426
ANY types, 431–435
URI types, 430
XMLType, 426–430
programmer-defined subtypes, 182
RAW, 397
REF CURSOR, 173
return value for functions, 573
ROWID and UROWID, 173, 397–400
SIMPLE types in Oracle Database 11g, 14
string, 191
supertype invocation from subtype, 16
user-defined, 175
DATE datatype, 172, 268
converting strings to, 279
converting to strings, 281
DATE values as inputs to datetime
functions, 308
format elements used with, 283

when to use, 271
date format models, 278, 1143–1147
    DATE versus TIMESTAMP types, 283
    NLS_DATE_FORMAT setting, 279
    requiring exact format mask match with FX, 287
    RR element, interpreting two-digit years, 288
    using FM (fill mode), 288
dates and time, 267–310, 1059–1064
    arithmetic operations on, 300
        adding and subtracting intervals, 305
        computing intervals between datetimes, 302
        date arithmetic with DATE datatypes, 301
        intervals and datetimes, 300
        mixing DATEs and TIMESTAMPs, 304
        multiplying and dividing intervals, 306
        unconstrained INTERVAL types, 307
    calculating elapsed time, 788
    choosing a datetime datatype, 271
    conversions, 278–291
        from datetimes to strings, 281
        from strings to datetimes, 279
        interpreting two-digit years, 288
        not requiring exact match for format mask, 288
        padding output with FM (fill mode), 291
        requiring exact match for format mask, 287
        time zones to character strings, 290
        working with time zones, 284
    date and timestamp literals, 291
    datetime datatypes, 172, 268
    declaring datetime variables, 270
    formatting in localization efforts, 1060–1064
    getting current date and time, 272
    interval conversions, 293–295
    interval datatypes, 274–278
    interval literals, 295
    literals in PL/SQL, 70
    time differences for a query, 956
    TIMESTAMP datatypes, 1059
    using CAST function with, 297
    using EXTRACT function with, 299
DBA_* views, 711

DBD::Oracle module, 49
dbFit testing framework, 752
DBI (DataBase Interface) module (Perl), 49
DBMS_ALERT package, 914
DBMS_APPLICATION_INFO package, 759
DBMS_ASSERT package, 1016
    using to validate user inputs, 542
DBMS_CRYPTO package, 925
    algorithm constants, 925
    DECRYPT function, 930
    ENCRYPT function, 926
    ENCRYPT procedure, 930
    HASH function, 939
    MAC function, 940
    padding and chaining constants, 926
    RANDOMBYTES function, 932
DBMS_DB_VERSION package, 1001
DBMS_DDL package, 775
DBMS_DESCRIBE package, information about arguments, 719
DBMS_FGA package, 972
    ADD_POLICY procedure, 974
DBMS_HPROF package, 16, 784, 785
DBMS_LOB package, 173
    CREATETEMPORARY procedure, 418
    FREETEMPORARY procedure, 419
    GET_LENGTH procedure, 410
    LOADBLOBFROMFILE package, 413
    LOADCLOBFROMFILE procedure, 413
    predefined exceptions in, 132
    READ procedure, 409
    WRITE and WRITEAPPEND procedures, 407–409
DBMS_OUTPUT package
    CASE expression used with, 96
    enabling, 874
    PUT_LINE function, overloading, 598
    reading buffer contents, 875
    writing lines to the buffer, 874
DBMS_PIPE package, 634
    calls, CPU load and, 108
DBMS_PREPROCESSOR package, 1008
DBMS_PROFILER package, 783
DBMS_RESULT_CACHE package, 816
DBMS_RESUMABLE package
    ABORT procedure, 702
    functions and procedures for timeout values, 703
DBMS_RLS package, 945

ADD_POLICY function, 949
 policy_type parameter, 955
 sec_relevant_cols parameter, 958
 sec_relevant_cols_opt parameter, 959
 statement_type parameter, 951
 static_policy parameter, 954
 update_check parameter, 952
 DROP_POLICY function, 951
DBMS_SESSION package
 clearing out memory used by packaged
  collection, 1020
 SET_CONTEXT function, 966
DBMS_SQL package
 DEFINE_COLUMN function, overloading
  by type, 597
 dynamic SQL, 514
 new features in Oracle Database 11g, 554–
  562
  enhanced security, 558–562
  TO_CURSOR function, 556
  TO_REFCURSOR function, 554
 when to use, 543–554
  meeting method 4 dynamic SQL
   requirements, 546–552
  minimizing parsing of dynamic cursors,
   553
  obtaining information about query
   columns, 544
  parsing very long strings, 543
DBMS_STANDARD package, 987
 DDL event and attribute functions, 676
 functions for error stack information, 686
DBMS_TRACE package, 763–766
DBMS_TYPES package, 1102
DBMS_TYPES.NO_DATA, 434
DBMS_TYPES.SUCCESS, 434
DBMS_UTILITY package
 FORMAT_CALL_STACK function, 141
 FORMAT_ERROR_BACKTRACE
  function, 141–143
 FORMAT_ERROR_STACK function, 140
 functions to calculate elapsed time, 788
 RECOMPILE_SCHEMA procedure, 734
DBMS_WARNING package, 738
DBTIMEZONE function, 273
DBURITYPE datatype, 430
DB_ROLE_CHANGE triggers, 683
DDL (Data Definition Language), 515

invalid DDL operation in system triggers,
 699
stored procedure to execute DDL
 statements, 516
triggers, 673–683
 available attributes, 676
 available events, 676
 creating, 673
 dropping undroppable triggers, 681
 INSTEAD OF CREATE, 682
 working with events and triggers, 678–
  681
deadline pressures on developers, resisting, 20
deadlock, 456
DEBUG privilege (for object types), 1129
debugging, 766–774
 row-level security (RLS), 961
 tips and strategies for
  analyzing instead of trying, 771
  changing and testing single code area,
   773
  gathering data, 770
  remaining logical, 770
  taking breaks and asking for help, 772
  using source code debugger, 769
 tracing versus, 757
 wrong way to debug, 767
  disorganized debugging, 767
  traditional debugging, 768
DEC datatype, 246
DECIMAL datatype, 246
declaration section, 54
declarations, 175–182
 anchored, 177
  benefits of, 180
 anchoring to cursors and tables, 179
 anchoring to NOT NULL datatypes, 181
 constants, 176
 constrained and unconstrained, 580
 forward, 601
 NOT NULL clause, 177
 termination with semicolon (;), 74
 variables, 175
  NOT NULL clause, 177
DECOMPOSE function, 223, 1041
decrypting data, 930
dedicated server, 1010
DEFAULT operator, setting default values for
 variables, 176

DEFINE command (SQL*Plus), 32
definer rights model, 990–995
  advantages of, 992
  combining with invoker rights, 997
  defined, 990
  disadvantages of, 992
  dynamic SQL and, 994
DELETE procedure, 341, 343
DELETE statements, 441, 443
  continuing past errors, 149
  as loops, 122
  WHERE CURRENT OF clause, 495
DELETE triggers, INSTEAD OF DELETE,
    695
DELETING clause in DML triggers, 661
DELETING function, 659
deliberate exceptions, 154
  guidelines for handling, 156
denormalization, virtual, 1122
dense collections, 330
dependencies, 721–730
  analyzing using data dictionary views, 722
  fine-grained (Oracle Database 11g), 16,
    726
  invalidation of dependents through
    recompilation, 735
  Oracle's basic dependency principle, 721
  remote, 727
  USER_DEPENDENCIES view, 711
DEPTREE view, 725
DEPTREE_FILL procedure, 725
DES (Data Encryption Standard), 924
DES3 (Triple DES), 924
DESCRIBE command (SQL*Plus), 42
design, planning before coding, 20
DETERMINISTIC clause, 572
deterministic functions, 615
  caching, 805
  caching using function result cache, 810
development in PL/SQL, advice for, 19
  asking for help, 21
  planning and design before coding, 20
  taking creative approach, 22
DIANA (Distributed Intermediate Annotated
    Notation for Ada), 981
direct path operations, 962
directories
  current directory for SQL*Plus, 31
  setting up using UTL_FILE, 878

working with Oracle directories, 879
DISABLE keyword, 706
DISCONNECT command (SQL*Plus), 34
DML (Data Manipulation Language), 439–
    450
  cursor attributes for DML operations, 444
  DELETE statement, 443
  DML statements in SQL, 441
  encapsulation on object views, 1124
  exception handling and, 446
  high speed statement execution using
    FORALL, 828–838
  INSERT statement, 441
  MERGE statement, 443
  order of firing, 666
  records and, 447
  RETURNING clause, retrieving
    information from DML
    statements, 445
  triggers, 652
    compound, 670–673
    concepts and associated terminology,
      653
    creating, 655–660
    example, 660–665
    multiple triggers of same type, 665
    mutating table errors, 668
    participation in transactions, 654
    scripts, 654
  UPDATE statement, 442
DML privileges for object types, 1130
DOUBLE PRECISION datatype, 246
downcasting, 1091
DROP statements, dropping stored programs,
    44
DROP TRIGGER command, 673, 681, 705
DROP TYPE statements, 1095
DSINTERVAL_UNCONSTRAINED
    datatype, 307
duplicates
  handling in nested tables, 392
  SecureFiles deduplication option, 416
dynamic PL/SQL, 513, 531–535
  replacing repetitive code with dynamic
    block, 534
dynamic sampling, 855
dynamic SQL, 465, 513, 514
  (see also NDS)
  defined, 464

definer rights and, 994

enhancements in Oracle Database 11g, 14

invoker rights for, 996

methods, 523

new features in Oracle Database 11g, 554–562

when to use DBMS_SQL, 543–554

dynamically typed programming languages, 170

# E

echoing content of scripts in SQL*Plus, 39

ed editor (Unix/Linux), 35

EDIT command (SQL*Plus), 34

edition-based redefinition, 12, 710, 777–780

_EDITOR variable (SQL*Plus), 35

editors

default external editors assumed by Oracle, 35

for source code, 24

SQL*Plus line editor, 35

element and index value (collections), 329

ELSE clauses

IF-THEN-ELSE statements, 84

using to prevent errors in simple CASE statements, 92

ELSIF keyword, 87

common syntax errors with, 86

email, sending, 891–902

attaching file of arbitrary size, 900

configuring network security, 893

including friendly names in addresses, 896

message with short attachment, 898

Oracle prerequisites for, 893

plaintext message of arbitrary length, 897

short plaintext message, 894

small file as attachment, 900

embedded languages, 23

empty LOBs, 405

empty strings, 218

encapsulation, 460

data encapsulation in packages, 642–645

of DML on object views, 1124

single-row queries behind function interface, 471

enclosed blocks, 57

encryption, 921–945

algorithms, 923

DBMS_CRYPTO package, 925

decrypting data, 930

encrypting data, 926–929

encrypting LOBs, 930

key generation, 932

key length, 922

key management, 933–938

padding and chaining, 925

SecureFiles, 417

SSL-encrypted web page, 907

TDE (Transparent Data Encryption), 942

TDE tablespace encryption, 944

wrapping versus, 774

END IF keywords

avoiding syntax errors in IF statements, 86

line breaks and, 83

END IF statements, 82

END label

for functions, 575

for packages, 625

for procedures, 570

END LOOP statement, 102

equality

comparing records for, 325

comparison of collection types for, 340

object type comparisons for, 1083, 1111

MAP method and, 1112

ORDER method, 1113

testing nested tables for, 389

error codes

application specific, organizing use of, 157

associating exception names with, 129–132

set aside for users versus in built-in packages, 137

$ERROR directive, 1005

error directives, 999

error messages

retrieving and formatting with UTL_LMS, 1069

returning for error codes, 140

errors

anticipating and handling in NDS, 536

date conversions, 281

handling in SQL*Plus, 36

handling with implicit cursors, 473

interpreting RLS errors, 961

logging errors occurring during transaction processing, 459

mutating table errors, 668

ORA_SPACE_ERROR_INFO function,
701
raising and handling, 9
SERVERERROR database event trigger,
686–690
showing error messages in SQL*Plus, 40
treatment as exceptions in PL/SQL, 125
event-driven model for error processing, 126
evolution, object types, 1093
EXCEPTION datatype, 152, 159
exception handling, 125–164
building effective error management
architecture, 152
deciding on strategy, 153
standard templates for common error
handling, 162
standardizing for different types of
exceptions, 154
use of application-specific error codes,
157
using standardized programs, 158
writing your own exception objects,
159
built-in error functions, 139–144
combining multiple exceptions in single
handler, 144
concepts and terminology, 125
continuing past exceptions, 148
defining exception handlers, 138
defining exceptions, 128–135
DML and, 446
handling exceptions, 138–152
making most of PL/SQL error management,
164
propagation of unhandled exceptions, 145
losing exception information, 146
raising exceptions, 135–138
unhandled exceptions, 145
writing WHEN OTHERS handling code,
150
EXCEPTION keyword, 138
exception section, 54
exception handlers in, 138
exceptions, 10, 125
continuing past in FORALL statements,
833
OTHERS handler not executing RAISE,
746
remote invocation and, 730

system and programmer-defined, 126
EXCEPTION_INIT pragma, 76, 127, 130–
132
associating exception names with error
codes, 130
recommended uses of, 131
EXECUTE command (SQL*Plus), 29, 41
EXECUTE IMMEDIATE statements, 514–517
length of strings executed, 543
using in dynamic SQL, 523
EXECUTE privileges
for object types, 1129
RLS policies and, 951
in SQL*Plus, 43
execution authority models, 990–998
combining, 997
definer rights, 990–995
invoker rights, 995–997
execution authority, improvements in, 5
execution section, 54
EXISTS function, 341, 345
EXISTSNODE function, 428
EXIT command (SQL*Plus), 34
EXIT statements
label as target for, 78
loop label after, 116
terminating simple loops, 105
using properly with loops, 120
EXIT WHEN statements, 105
explicit cursors
attributes, 487
choosing between implicit cursors and, 471
closing, 486
column aliases in, 484
declaring, 479–482
defined, 465
fetching from, 483
opening, 482
parameters, 489–492
exponentiation operator (**), 65, 259
EXTEND procedure, 341, 345
extent settings, 704
external LOBs, 401
external procedures, 986, 1026
(see also External Procedures chapter on
book web site)
EXTRACT function
conversions of intervals to character strings,
295

listing of datetime component names used with, 299

using with date and time values, 299

## F

F, denoting binary (32-bit) floating-point literals, 73

FALSE values, 172

FETCH statements
  cursor variables used in, rowtype matching rules, 505
  fetching from cursor variables, 498, 501
  fetching from explicit cursors, 483
  fetching into variables or records, 520
  initializing collections implicitly via, 357
  using BULK COLLECT with LIMIT clause, 824

Feuerstein, Steven, PL/SQL portal, 18

FF format element, 283

fine-grained access control (FGAC), 946

fine-grained auditing (FGA), 920, 972–980
  checking the audit trail, 977
  number of columns to access, 976
  reasons to learn FGA, 973
  simple example, 974
  using bind variables, 978
  using handler modules, 980

Firefox browser, setting Unicode character encoding, 1037

FIRST and LAST functions, 341, 346

FLOAT datatype, 246

floating-point datatypes, 171, 232, 241–246
  BINARY_FLOAT and BINARY_DOUBLE, 241–245
  floating-point arithmetic with, 871
  mixing in comparisons, 242
  mixing, Oracle order of precedence on implicit conversions, 245
  SIMPLE_FLOAT and SIMPLE_DOUBLE, 246

floating-point literals, 73

FLOOR function, 260

FM (fill mode) element, 282, 288
  padding output in datetime conversions, 291

FOLLOWS clause, 667, 672

FOR loops, 102
  cursor FOR loop, 112–115
  exiting properly, 120

numeric FOR loop, 109–112
  examples of, 111
  nontrivial increments, 112
  rules for, 110
  obtaining information about execution, 121

FORALL statements, 820, 828–838
  cursor attributes for, 831
  examples of, 830
  INDICES OF clause, 829, 836
  nonsequential arrays with, 835
  returning information into a collection using BULK COLLECT syntax, 446
  ROLLBACK behavior with, 833
  rules for use, 829
  SAVE EXCEPTIONS clause, 833
  syntax, 828
  using BULK COLLECT and RETURNING clause, 826
  VALUES OF clause, 829, 837

FORCE keyword, 354

FORCE option, CREATE TYPE statements, 13

formal parameters, 580
  association with actual parameters, 585–589

FORMAT_STRING function, 1058

forward declarations, 601

%FOUND attribute, 468
  using with explicit cursors, 487

fractional seconds, FF format element, 283

fractional values in date arithmetic, 302

FREMOVE utility, 163

FROM clauses
  table functions in, 386, 541, 605–615
    calling function, 605

FTP server, retrieving data from, 913

function result cache (Oracle Database 11g), 13, 807–819
  example caching a collection, 813
  example querying data from table, 811
  example using deterministic function, 810
  how to use, 808
  managing, 815
  RELIES_ON clause, 809
  Virtual Private Database (VPD) and, 816–819
  when not to use, 814
  when to use, 814

functions, 571–579
  body of, 577
  built-in error functions, 139–144
  calling, 575
  calling from within SQL, 602
  collection as datatype of return value, 337
  conversion functions, built-in, 185–190
  converting strings to dates and timestamps, 279
  creating in SQL*Plus, 38
  date/time, 308
  datetime, built-in, 309
  DDL trigger event and attribute, 676
  declared in package specification, 625
  defined, 567
  determining DML action within a trigger, 659
  deterministic, 615
  END label, 575
  error stack generated when exception is raised, 686
  forward declaration, 601
  getting current date and time, 272
  header, 576
  information about, in USER_PROCEDURES view, 716
  LOB conversion, 425
  not returning value, compile-time warning for, 743
  numeric, 260–265
  overloaded, requirements for, 600
  overloading, 595
  parameters, 579–590
  passing cursor variables as arguments in function calls, 507
  PL/SQL, invoking within SQL statements, 42
  RETURN datatype, 573
  RETURN statement, 578
  streaming or transformative, 512
  string, quick reference, 222–230
  structure of, 571
  table functions, 605–615, 839
    (see also pipelined table functions)
  Unicode, 1038–1045
  without parameters, 576
FX modifier in format masks, 287

**G**

GDK (Globalization Development Kit), 1066–1072
  implementation options, 1071
  UTL_I18N package, 1066
  UTL_LMS error-handling package, 1069
GET method (HTTP), 909
global data, 634
  package data structures acting as, 1023
globalization and localization, 1031–1072
  character semantics, 1045–1049
  currency conversion, 1064–1066
  dates and time, 1059–1064
  development kit for PL/SQL, 1066–1072
  globalization strategy, 1032
  multilingual information retrieval, 1054–1059
  overview and terminology, 1033
  string sort order, 1049–1054
  Unicode primer, 1034–1045
glyphs, 1034
GOTO statements, 8, 97
  restrictions on, 98
  using NULL after a label, 99
GRANT statements, 43
GREATEST function, 223
greediness in regular expression matching, 216

**H**

habits in programming, reassessing, 22
handler modules, 974
  using in FGA, 980
handlers (exception), 127
hashing, 938
headers
  function, 56, 576
  for named PLSQL blocks, 53
  procedure, 56, 569
help, asking for, 21
HEXTORAW function, 190
hierarchical profiler (see DBMS_IIPROF)
homogenous elements, 329
hot patching of PL/SQL-based applications, 777
HTML pages, embedding PL/SQL using PSP, 51
HTTP authentication, 906

HTTP data, working with, 903–913
    authentication, 906
    cookies, disabling or making persistent,
        912
    HTTP headers, 903
    retrieval of FTP via HTTP, 913
    retrieving web page in pieces, 903
    retrieving web page into a LOB, 905
    submitting data to web page via GET or
        POST methods, 908–911
HTTP server built into Oracle database, 914
HTTPS protocol, retrieving SSL-encrypted web
        page via, 907
HTTPURITYPE datatype, 174, 430, 905
    HTTP authentication, 906
    retrieving web pages, 431

## I

I Love PL/SQL And web site, 18
I/O (input/output), 873–915
    database pipes, queues, and alerts, 914
    displaying information, 873–877
        enabling DBMS_OUTPUT, 874
        reading buffer contents, 875
        writing lines to the buffer, 874
    Oracle's built-in web server, 914
    reading and writing files, 877–891
        closing files, 882
        copying files, 888
        deleting files, 889
        determining if file is open, 882
        opening files, 880
        reading from files, 883
        renaming and moving files, 890
        retrieving file attributes, 890
        UTL_FILE_DIR parameter, 877
        working with Oracle directories, 879
        writing to files, 885
    saving output to file using SQL*Plus, 33
    sending email, 891–902
        file attachment of arbitrary size, 900
        network security, 893
        Oracle friendly names in addresses, 896
        Oracle prerequisites, 893
        plaintext message of arbitrary length,
            897
        short plaintext message, 894
        small file attachment, 900
    TCP sockets, 914

working with web-based data, 903–913
    cookies, 912
    FTP data, 913
    HTTP authentication, 906
    retrieving SSL-encrypted web page, 907
    retrieving web page in pieces, 903
    retrieving web page into a LOB, 905
    submitting data to web page, 908–911
IANA (Internet Assigned Numbers Authority),
        899
identifiers, 66–70
    $$identifier syntax for inquiry directives,
        1000
    avoiding incorrect use of reserved words,
        69
    built-in, 68
        reserved words, 68
        from STANDARD package, 68
    case-insensitivity in names, 67
    object, 1087
    PL/Scope information about, 719
    qualified, visibility and, 62
    qualifying with module names, 62
    scope of, 58
    separating with whitespace, 69
    valid and invalid names for, 67
    visible, 61
IDEPTREE view, 725
IDEs (integrated development environments)
    listing of popular IDEs for PL/SQL, 45
    source code debuggers, 769
    Toad IDE, 24
    using for database navigation, 23
IEEE-754 floating-point standard, 241–246
    converting types, 247
    floating-point literals, 73
    Oracle binary floating-point
        implementation versus, 245
$IF directive, 999, 1004
IF statements, 8, 81–90
    avoiding syntax gotchas, 86
    comparing two VARCHAR2 values, issue
        with NULLs and empty strings,
        219
    IF-THEN statements, 82
    IF-THEN-ELSE statements, 84
    IF-THEN-ELSIF statements, 85
    line breaks and, 83
    listing of types, 81

nested, 88
short-circuit evaluation, 89
IF...THEN...ELSE statements, implications of
NULL Boolean variables, 396
implicit conversions, 183, 257
avoiding to improve performance, 870
drawbacks of, 184
limitations of, 184
problems with, 259
implicit cursors
choosing between explicit cursors and, 471
defined, 465
error handling, 473
examples of use, 472
SELECT statement with special
characteristics, 472
SQL cursor attributes, 476
IN mode, 582
bind arguments, 526
IN OUT mode, 492, 584
bind arguments, 526
NOCOPY qualifier, compile-time warning
about, 739, 741
INDEX BY clause
associative arrays, index values, 360
datatypes for collection indexes, 351
specifying index values for assignment to
associative array, 360
index values, 329
assigning data to associative array, 360
assigning values to, in nested table or
VARRAY collections, 359
defined for collection, getting lowest and
highest, 346
greatest value in use in an associative array,
342
returned by PRIOR and NEXT collection
methods, 348
trying to read undefined index value in
collection, 365
index-organized table (IOT), 173
indexed by integers (collections), 330
indexed by strings (collections), 330
indexes
case-insensitive indexes using Oracle Text,
425
case-insensitivity and, 201
collection, datatypes, 351
collection, string indexes, 365–370

creating using EXECUTE IMMEDIATE,
515
creating, restricted row access in RLS, 951
determining which rows in binding array to
use in dynamic INSERT, 831
indexing in multiple languages, 1054
numeric FOR loop, 110
handling nontrivial increments, 112
Oracle Text, 1054
understandable names for loop indexes,
119
INDICES OF clause (FORALL statement),
829
example, 836
VALUES OF clause versus, 835
infinite loops, 106
avoiding, 792
terminating, 107
information hiding with packages, 621
information retrieval (IR), multilingual, 1054–
1059
and PL/SQL, 1056
informational compile-time warnings, 737
INITCAP function, 201, 224
initialization of packages, 622, 627–632
avoiding side effects, 629
caching static session information, 629
executing complex initialization logic, 628
failure of, 630
initialization procedure included in
packages, 631
initialization section, 628
steps in process, 627
inner table, 330
inquiry directives, 999, 1000
DBMS_DB_VERSION package, 1001
program-specific settings with, 1006
referencing unit name and line number,
1003
setting compilation environmental
parameters, 1002
using PLSQL_CCFLAGS parameter, 1003
INSERT statements, 441
as loops, 122
populating tables with single INSERT, 695
record-based, 448
restrictions on, 450
using records, 447
INSERT triggers, 656

INSTEAD OF INSERT trigger, 692
INSERTING clause in DML triggers, 659, 661
instantiable types, 1077
instants, 274
INSTEAD OF CREATE triggers, 682
INSTEAD OF triggers, 652, 690–697
    creating, 690
    INSTEAD OF DELETE, 695
    INSTEAD OF INSERT, 692
    INSTEAD OF UPDATE, 694
    on nested tables, 696
    populating tables with single INSERT, 695
    using in object views, 1123
INSTR function, 202, 224, 1041
    negative string positioning, 204
instrumentation, 757
integer datatypes, 171
    BINARY_INTEGER, 239
    PLS_INTEGER, 237
        subtypes, 247
        using for intensive integer computations, 871
    SIMPLE_INTEGER, 239
internal LOBs, 401
    SQL semantics for, 423
internationalization, 1033
Internet Assigned Numbers Authority (IANA), 899
Internet Explorer
    retrieving data from HTTPS site, 907
    setting Unicode encoding, 1037
Internet resources for PL/SQL, 18
Internet-related datatypes, 174
interpreted mode, 1028
INTERVAL datatypes, 172, 274–278
    declaring INTERVAL variables, 275
    unconstrained, 307
    when to use, 276
        designating periods of time, 277
        finding difference between datetime values, 276
INTERVAL DAY TO SECOND datatype, 275
interval literals, 295
INTERVAL YEAR TO MONTH datatype, 275
intervals, 274
    adding and subtracting, 305
    computing between two datetimes, 302
    conversions, 293

converting numbers to, 293
converting strings to, 294
date arithmetic with, 300
element names, 293
formatting for display, 295
as literals, 70
multiplying and dividing, 306
INTO clause
    EXECUTE IMMEDIATE statement, 515
    FETCH INTO statements, 501
        runtime rowtype matching rules, 505
    INSERT INTO statements, 441
    SELECT INTO or BULK COLLECT INTO, 472
    SELECT INTO statement, 7
INVALIDATE option (ALTER TYPE), 354
invoker rights for shared programs, 535
invoker rights model, 995–997
    combining with definer rights, 998
    rules and restrictions, 996
    syntax, 996
IR (information retrieval), multilingual, 1054–1059
    and PL/SQL, 1056
IS NULL operator, 259
    testing scalar datatypes and LOBs, 406
IS OF operator, 1092
ISO dates, 1146
isolation levels for transactions, 453
    READ COMMITTED, 457
    SERIALIZABLE, 457
%ISOPEN attribute, 469
    using with explicit cursors, 487
ISO_CURRENCY_FUNC function, 1065

## J

Java, 46
    (see also Calling Java from PL/SQL chapter on book web site)
    abstract classes, 1077
    calling PL/SQL from, using JDBC, 48
    stored procedures, 986, 1074
JDBC (Java Database Connectivity), 48

## K

keys (cryptographic), 921
    combined master key approach, 935
    generating, 932

key management, 933
single database key approach, 933
single key per row approach, 934

# L

label delimiters (<< >>), 65
labels, 77
    as targets for GOTO statements, 98
        NULL after, 99
    loop, 115
large objects (see LOBs)
LAST function, 341
    member-method syntax, 342
    using (example), 347
LEAST function, 224
    linguistic sorting and, 200
LENGTH function, 224, 1042
    passing string constants to, 196
LENGTHB function, 1046
lexical units, 66
    error caused by whitespace in, 70
LIMIT clause for BULK COLLECT, 824, 844
LIMIT function, 347
line breaks, IF statements and, 83
line numbers (compilation unit), 1003
linefeed character, 197
Linux
    ed editor, 35
    killing a process, 107
    opening files, specifying locations for, 878
    retrieving SSL-encrypted web page via
        HTTPS, 908
lists
    collections of, 382
    returned by DDL trigger attribute functions,
        680
literals, 70–74
    avoiding hardcoding of, 645
    Boolean, 74
    date and timestamp, 291
    embedding single quotes within, 72
    NULLs, 71
    numeric, 73
LOBs (large objects), 170
    BFILEs, 411–415
    conversion functions, 425
    datatypes, 400
    empty versus NULL, 405
    encrypting, 930

examples, table definition for, 401
function return values containing, 814
internal and external, 401
locators, 403
native LOB operations, 421
    performance impact of SQL semantics,
        424
    SQL semantics for, 421
    temporary LOBs yielded by SQL
        semantics, 423
Oracle documentation for, 404
reading from, 409
retrieving web page into a LOB, 905
SecureFiles, 930
SecureFiles versus BasicFiles, 415
temporary, 418–421
writing into, 407–409
local modules, 590–595
    benefits of using, 591
        improving readability, 592
        reducing code volume, 591
    forward declaration of, 601
    scope of, 594
    sprucing up your code with, 594
local variables
    normalization of, 181
    synchronization with database columns,
        180
localization (see globalization and localization)
LOCALTIMESTAMP function, 272
locators (LOB), 403
    BFILE locator, 411
    creating BFILE locator, 411
    temporary LOBs yielded by application of
        SQL semantics, 423
LOCK TABLE statements, 454
locking
    releasing locks with COMMIT statement,
        494
    using SELECT FOR UPDATE statement,
        492
logging
    building autonomous logging mechanism,
        459
    errors, then continuing past error, 149
LOGOFF triggers, 683, 686
LOGON triggers, 683, 685, 965
LONG datatype, 170, 401
LONG RAW datatype, 173, 401

---

LOOP keyword, 104
Loop Killer package, 792
loops, 8, 101–123
    avoiding infinite loops, 792
    CONTINUE statement, 13, 116
    cursor FOR loop, 112–115
    FOR loop, 102
    infinite loop, 106
    labels, 115
    listing of loop types with descriptions, 101
    numeric FOR loop, 109–112
    runtime optimization of fetch loops, 798
    simple loop, 102, 104–108
    SQL statement as, 122
    structure of, 103
    tips on writing, 119–123
        exiting properly, 120
        getting execution information on FOR
            loops, 121
        understandable names for indexes, 119
    WHILE loop, 103, 108
Looseline, 430
Lovelace, Ada, xxv
LOWER function, 199, 225
LPAD function, 205, 225
LTRIM function, 206, 225

## M

MACs (message authentication codes), 940
main transaction, 454
managing code (see code management)
many-to-many (MM) relationships, 1096
MAP method, 1111, 1112
mcode, 1027
MD5 (Message Digest), 939
member methods, 1079
member-method syntax, collection methods,
    342
membership, testing nested table collections
    for, 389
memory
    analyzing usage, 783
    cached packaged data memory versus CPU,
        629
    database instance memory and PL/SQL,
        1009–1027
        cursors and, 1011
        PGA, UGA, and CGA, 1010
        reducing memory use, 1013–1024

    running out of memory, 1024
    serialized packages and, 641
merge operations, tuning with pipelined
        functions, 846–848
MERGE statements, 441, 443
message authentication codes (MACs), 940
method chaining, 1086
methods, 1076, 1079
    collection, 341–350
    constructor, 1079
    invoking supertype methods from subtype,
        1084
    member, 1079
Microsoft, 25
    (see also Windows systems)
    ODBC (Open Database Connectivity), 46
MIME (Multipurpose Internet Mail
        Extensions), 898
MIME types, 899
MOD function, 112
modular code, 566
    forward declarations, 601
    functions, 571–579
    local or nested modules, 590–595
    module overloading, 595–601
    parameters, 579–590
    procedures, 567
modularization, 566
    importance of, 616
module names, qualifying identifer names with,
    62
monolingual sort, 1050
MONTHS_BETWEEN function, 303
multibyte characters, 1034, 1045
multilevel collections (see collections,
    multilevel)
multilingual data retrieval, 1054–1059
multilingual sort, 1052
multiset operations on nested tables (see nested
    tables)
MULTISET pseudo-function, 384
    MULTISET UNION, 392

## N

name conflicts in variables or constants, 740
named blocks, 53, 56
named exceptions, 127
    declaring, 128
    system exceptions, 132

named notation, associating actual and formal
    parameters, 586
  benefits of named notation, 587
naming conventions for program data, 167
narrowing, 1091
national character set datatypes, 1036
native compilation, 1027
  new features in Oracle Database 11g, 14
native dynamic SQL (see NDS)
NCHAR datatype, 170, 191, 1036
  NLS_NCHAR_CHARACTERSET, 1035
NCLOBs (NLS Character Large Objects), 170,
    400, 1036
  creating empty NCLOBs, 406
NDS (native dynamic SQL), 514–525
  binding variables, 525–529
  dynamic PL/SQL, 531–535
  EXECUTE IMMEDIATE statement, 514–
    517
  OPEN FOR statement, 517–523
  recommendations for, 535–542
    errors, 536
    minimizing danger of code injection,
      540–542
    using binding instead of concatenation,
      538
    using invoker rights for shared programs,
      535
  working with objects and collections, 529–
    531
nested blocks, 57
nested modules (see local modules)
nested programs, scope and visibility of
    variables, 64
nested tables, 331
  changing characteristics of, 354
  collection using, 332
  comparison to other table types, 340
  database-to-PL/SQL integration, 358
  declaring and initializing collection
    variables of type, 355
  declaring nested table collection type, 353
  INSTEAD OF triggers on, 696
  multiset operations on, 387–393
    checking element membership, 390
    handling duplicates, 392
    high-level set operations, 390
    testing equality and membership, 389
  using as column datatype, 339

NEW pseudo-records, 326, 653
  working with, in DML triggers, 658
NEXT function, 341, 348
NLS (National Language Support), 1034
NLS Character Large Objects (see NCLOBs)
NLS Large Objects (see NCLOBs)
NLS settings
  for datetimes, 297
  determining by querying
    NLS_SESSION_PARAMETERS,
    192
  NLS_CALENDAR parameter, 1063
  NLS_COMP parameter, 199
  NLS_CURRENCY parameter, 1064
  NLS_DATE_FORMAT parameter, 279,
    289
  NLS_DATE_LANGUAGE parameter,
    1062
  NLS_LENGTH_SEMANTICS parameter,
    192, 1047
  NLS_SORT parameter
    monolingual values, 1051
    multilingual values, 1053
  NLS_SORTparameter, 199
  NLS_TERRITORY parameter, 281
  passing to TO_CHAR function, 256
  passing to TO_NUMBER function, 249
  session parameters, listed, 1037
NLSSORT function, 226, 1051
NLS_INITCAP function, 225
NLS_LOWER function, 226
NLS_UPPER function, 226
NOCOPY parameter mode hint, 589, 867–
    870
  compile-time warnings about, 739, 741,
    745
  downside of, 869
  performance benefits of, 868
  restrictions on, 868
non-blank-padding comparison, 220
nongreedy quantifiers in regular expressions,
    217
normalization
  interval values, 297
  of local variables, 181
NOT FINAL keyword, 1077
NOT INSTANTIABLE keyword, 1077
NOT operator, 259
Notepad editor, 35

%NOTFOUND attribute, 469
    using with explicit cursors, 487
NOWAIT keyword, using with LOCK TABLE,
    454
NO_DATA_FOUND exception, 156
    definition in STANDARD package, 989
    raised by implicit cursor SELECT statement,
        473
NULL statements, 98
    improving readability with, 99
    using after GOTO statement label, 99
NULLs, 71, 172
    in Boolean expressions, 82
    Boolean variables as, implications for
        IF...THEN...ELSE statements,
        396
    collection, 1120
    comparing NULL records, 325
    empty strings as, 218
    equality check for nested tables, 390
    NULL LOB, 405
    passing as bind arguments, 528
    UNKNOWN versus, 91
NUMBER datatype, 73, 171, 232
    constraining precision and scale, 233
    converting strings and IEEE-754 floating-
        point types to, 247–251
    dealing with money, 242
    mixing with other floating-point types, 245
    negative scale values, 235
    performance, BINARY_DOUBLE versus,
        243
    range of, 237
    rounding of values, 234
    using for floating-point numbers, 241
number format models, 1139
    CAST function and, 257
    using with TO_CHAR function, 252
    using with TO_NUMBER function, 249
        passing NLS settings, 249
    V element, 253
numbers
    conversions, 247–259
        implicit conversions, 257
        using CAST function, 256
        using TO_CHAR function, 251–256
        using TO_NUMBER function, 247–251
    converting to intervals, 293
NUMERIC datatype, 246

numeric datatypes, 231
    BINARY_DOUBLE, 241
    BINARY_FLOAT, 241
    BINARY_INTEGER, 239
    NUMBER, 232
    overloading with, 600
    PLS_INTEGER, 237
    SIMPLE_INTEGER, 239
    subtypes, 246
numeric FOR loops, 109–112
    examples of, 111
    nontrivial increments, 112
    rules for, 110
numeric functions, 260–265
    quick reference, 261–265
    rounding and truncation, 260
    trigonometric, 261
numeric literals, 70, 73
numeric operators, 259
NUMTOYMINTERVAL function, 293
NVARCHAR2 datatype, 170, 191, 1036
    NLS_NCHAR_CHARACTERSET, 1035
NVL2 function, 197

## O

object identifiers (OIDs), 1087, 1119
    primary-key-based, 1088
    REFs to nonunique OIDs, 1127
    system-generated, 1088
    uniqueness, 1126
object tables, 1110
    object views versus, 1125
    views, 1128
object types, 567, 1076–1114
    ANY types, 431–435, 1102–1106
    comparing objects, 1110
        additional recommendations, 1114
        attribute-level comparison, 1112
        MAP method, 1112
        ORDER method, 1113
    creating base type, 1076
    creating self-sufficient type, 1106–1110
    evolution and creation, 1093
    invoking sypertype methods from subtype,
        1084
    maintaining object types and object views,
        1127
    methods, 1079
    object views, 1115–1127

packages and, 650
predefined, 426
privileges, 1128
REFs (object references), 1095–1102
storing, retrieving, and using persistent
    objects, 1085
URI types, 430
XMLType, 426–430
object views, 1115–1127
  with collection attribute, 1118
  example relational system, 1117
  INSTEAD OF triggers, 1123
  with inverse relationship, 1122
  maintaining, 1127
  object subview, 1121
  object tables versus, 1125
object-oriented programming, 1073–1132
  concluding thoughts on, 1130
  Oracle's object features, 1074
    best situations for use, 1131
objects
  collections of, 373
  stored, displaying information about, 712
  viewing all objects you have defined, 778
  working with using NDS, 529–531
OBJECT_VALUE pseudo-column, 1111
OCI (Oracle Call Interface), 47
  creation of temporary LOBs, 418
  support for REFs, 1100
ODBC (Open Database Connectivity), 46
OIDs (see object identifiers)
OLD pseudo-records, 326, 654
  working with, in DML triggers, 658
ON NESTED TABLE COLUMN OF clause,
  697
one-dimensional or single-dimensional, 329
ONLY keyword, 1092
Open Directory Project, 19
OPEN FOR statements, 517–523
  fetching into variables or records, 520
  method 4 dynamic SQL, 524
  USING clause, 522
OPEN statements
  opening cursor variables, 500
  opening explicit cursors, 482
OPEN_CURSORS initialization parameter,
  1012
operating systems
  starting up SQL*Plus, 26

terminating intentionally infinite loop, 107
time values from, 273
operational directives, 659
optimizing compiler, 794–799
  how optimizer works, 795
  runtime optimization of fetch loops, 798
optimizing performance (see performance
  optimization)
OR operator
  combining multiple exceptions in single
    handler, 144
  short-circuit evaluation in IF statements,
    89
Oracle Advanced Queuing (AQ), 178, 634
Oracle Application Express (Oracle APEX),
  915
Oracle Call Interface (see OCI)
Oracle Database 11g, 11, 12–16
  automatic subprogram inlining, 15
  compile-time warning, OTHERS handler
    not ending in RAISE, 746
  compound triggers, 15, 652, 670–673
  CONTINUE statement, 13
  creating disabled triggers, 706
  dynamic SQL enhancements, 14, 554–562
  fine-grained dependency tracking, 16, 726
  firing order of DML triggers, using
    FOLLOWS clause, 667
  function result cache, 13, 807–819
  hierarchical profiler, DBMS_HPROF, 16,
    784, 785
  native compilation, 14, 1028
  PL/Scope, 15, 719–721
  REGEXP_COUNT function, 214
  regular expressions, specifying which
    subexpression to return, 213
  SecureFiles, 15
  sequences in expressions, 14
  SIMPLE datatypes, 14
  SQL*Plus, 25
  supertype invocation from subtype, 16,
    1084
  TDE tablespace encryption, 944
  upgrade strategy for policy types, 957
Oracle Database 11g Release 2
  configuring network security, 893
  DBMS_DB_VERSION constants, 1001
  edition-based redefinition, 12, 710, 777–
    780

FORCE option with CREATE TYPE, 13
Oracle databases
    native compilation and database release, 1028
    version information in DBMS_DB_VERSION, 1001
    versions, xxxii
    versions, and corresponding PL/SQL versions, 11
Oracle Globalization Support Guide, 280
Oracle Net, 27
Oracle Technology Network web site, 19, 51
Oracle Text, 425, 1054
    indexes, 1055
Oracle Wallet Manager utility, 907
ORA_GRANTEE function, 680
ORA_IS_ALTER_COLUMN function, 679
ORA_SPACE_ERROR_INFO function, 701
ORA_SQL_TXT function, 682
ORDER BY clause
    international character sets and, 1049
    using with CLUSTER BY in table functions, 614
ORDER method, 1111, 1113
OUT mode, 492, 583
    bind arguments, 526
out-of-space errors, 698
outer table, 330
overloading, module, 595–601
    benefits of, 596
        supporting many data combinations, 598
    overloading with numeric types, 600
    restrictions on, 599

## P

package body (see body of a package)
package specification (see specification)
packaged constants, synchronizing code with, 1006
packages, 617–650
    advantages of using, 617
    available on book web site, 648
    body of, 626
    caching based on, 800–805
        caching table contents, 803
        just-in-time caching of table data, 804
    compound triggers and, 670
    concepts related to, 621

creating with REF CURSOR type declaration, 507
declaring explicit cursors in, 480
default PL/SQL packages, 987
defined, 567
demonstrating power of, 618
dependencies, analyzing, 722
improving memory use and performance by using, 1018
initializing, 627–632
object types and, 650
preservation of state of constants, cursors, and variables, 1023
public and private elements, diagram of, 623
records based on, 324
rules for calling elements, 632
specification, 624
when to use, 642
    avoiding hardcoding of literals, 645
    caching static session data, 649
    encapsulating data access, 642–645
    grouping logically related functionality, 648
    improving usability of built-in features, 647
working with package data, 633–641
    cursors, 635–639
    global public data, 634
    global within Oracle session, 634
    serializable packages, 639–641
padding (encryption), 925
    DBMS_CRYPTO padding constants, 926
    PKCS#5, 927
padding strings, 205
    string comparisons and, 220
parallel execution of table function, 613
parallel pipelined functions, 844
    asynchronous data unloading with, 848–851
    enabling execution, 845
    performance implications of partitioning and streaming clauses, 852
PARALLEL_ENABLE clause, 572
parameters, 579–590
    actual and formal, 580
        association in PL/SQL, 585–589
    considerations for, 579
    cursor, 489–492

cursor variable arguments, setting mode, 508
default values, 589
defining, 580
modes of, 581
  IN mode, 582
  IN OUT mode, 584
  OUT mode, 583
  NOCOPY parameter mode qualifier, 589, 739, 741
overloaded modules, 599
passing by reference and by value, 867
parent block, 57
PARENT pseudo-records, 697
PARTITION...BY clause, 614
partitioning
  parallel pipelined functions, performance and, 852
  with skewed data, 853
pattern matching (see regular expressions)
peer code review process, 21
performance
  comple-time warnings about, 737
  impact of using SQL semantics, 424
  improving with ROWIDs, 400
  information returned by FGA, 973
  string-indexed collections, 369
performance optimization, 781–872
  analyzing memory usage, 783
  avoiding infinite loops, 792
  big picture on performance, 871
  bulk processing for multirow SQL, 820–838
    DML using FORALL, 828–838
    querying with BULK COLLECT, 821–828
  calculating elapsed time, 788
  choosing fastest program, 790
  data caching techniques, 799–820
    deterministic function caching, 805
    function result cache, 807–819
    package-based caching, 800–805
  identifying bottlenecks in PL/SQL code, 783
  using DBMS_HPROF, 785
  using DBMS_PROFILER, 784
  optimizing compiler, 794–799
  specialized techniques, 866–871

NOCOPY parameter mode hint, 867–870
  using right datatype, 870
  using pipelined table functions, 838–866
  warnings about performance, 793
periods, 274
  designating periods of time, 277
Perl
  calling PL/SQL from, 49
  resources for information, 50
persistent LOBs, 418
PGA (Program Global Area), 167, 362, 1010
  data caching in, 799
PHP
  calling PL/SQL from, 50
  resources for information, 51
PIPELINED clause, 572
pipelined table functions, 605, 838–866
  cost-based optimizer and, 853–859
  creating, 611
  parallel
    asynchronous data unloading with, 848–851
    partitioning and streaming clauses, performance and, 852
    replacing row-based inserts with loads from, 839–846
    loading from pipelined function, 842
    parallel pipelined functions, 844
    pipelined function implementation, 840
    tuning with array fetches, 843
  summary of performance tuning use, 866
  tuning complex data loads with, 859–865
  tuning merge operations with, 846–848
PKCS#5 (Public Key Cryptography Standard #5), 925, 927
PL/Net.org, 19
PL/Scope, 15, 719–721
  USER_IDENTIFIERS view, 711
PL/SQL, xxv
  advice for developers, 19
  application construction
    code management, 709–780
    I/O, 873–915
    modular programming, 590–616
    optimizing performance, 781–872
    packages, 617–650
    procedures, functions, and parameters, 565–590

triggers, 651–708
architecture, 981–1030
block structure, 53–64
calling from C language, 47
calling from Java, 48
calling from other languages, 46
calling from Perl, 49
calling from PHP, 50
character set, 64
comments, 75
control and conditional logic, 8
creating and running code, 23–52
defining characteristics, 3
ease of learning, 7
errors, raising and handling, 9
globalization and localization, 1031–1072
identifiers, 66–70
integration with SQL, 7
literals, 70–74
object-oriented aspects, 1073–1132
online resources, 18
origins and brief history of, 4
other languages or environments to use it
 from, 52
procedural language capabilities, xxv
program data
  collections, 327–394
  dates and timestamps, 267–310
  miscellaneous datatypes, 395–435
  numbers, 231
  records, 311–326
  strings, 191–230
  working with, 167–190
program structure
  conditional and sequential control, 81–
   100
  exception handlers, 125–164
  iterative processing with loops, 101–
   123
resources for developers, 17
security, 919–980
semicolon (;), terminating statements and
 declarations, 74
SQL in
  data retrieval, 463–512
  DML and transaction management,
   439–461
  dynamic SQL and PL/SQL, 513–562
versions, xxxii, 11

PL/SQL Developer IDE, 45
PL/SQL User's Guide and Reference, 987
PL/SQL Virtual Machine (PVM), 983
PLSQL_CCFLAGS compile parameter, 1000
PLSQL_CCFLAGS parameter, 1003
PLS_INTEGER datatype, 171, 237
  subtypes, 247
  using for intensive integer computations,
   871
PLUTO testing framework, 752
pointers, 463
  (see also cursor variables; cursors)
  LOB locators, 403
  object references (REFs), 1095
  similarity of ROWIDs to, 398
policies (FGA), 974
policies (RLS), 947
  context-sensitive policy, 956
  creating, 949
  dropping, 951
  dynamic, 953
  shared context-sensitive policy, 957
  shared static policy, 955
  upgrade strategy for policy types, 957
  viewing policies defined on a table, 951
policy function, 947
  errors in, 961
  RLS example, 949
  rules for, 950
polymorphism, 596
portability, application, 5
positional notation, associating actual and
  formal parameters, 585
POST method (HTTP), 909
postprocessed code, 1008
PRAGMA keyword, 76
pragmas
  AUTONOMOUS_TRANSACTION, 455
  types of pragmas in PL/SQL, 76
precision
  datetime variables, 270
  NUMBER datatype, 233
predicates, 947
  contexts as predicates in RLS, 967
  RLS example, 949
  used with BINARY_FLOAT AND
   BINARY_DOUBLE types, 242
primary keys

emulating with string indexes in collections, 369

using ROWIDs instead of, 397

PRINT command (SQL*Plus), 33

PRIOR and NEXT functions, 341, 348

private code, 622

Booch diagram showing private package elements, 623

private key, 923

privilege escalation and SQL injection, 995

privileges

CREATE ANY DIRECTORY, 879

granting and removing for stored programs, 43

listing with DDL trigger attribute functions, 680

object types, 1128

rejection of DBMS_SQL operations when effective user changes, 560

restriction on user schemas to prevent code injection, 540

for schema-level collections, 393

PRNG (Pseudo-Random Number Generator), 932

Pro*C precompiler, 47

procedures, 567–571

body of, 570

declared in package specification, 625

defined, 566

defining in local modules, 590

END label, 570

forward declaration, 601

header, 56, 569

overloading, 595

parameters, 579–590

passing cursor variables as arguments in procedure calls, 507

RETURN statement, 571

standalone, referencing REF CURSOR type, 508

USER_PROCEDURES view, 716

profilers, 783–788

DBMS_HPROF package, 16, 785

DBMS_PROFILER package, 784

program data, 167–190

conversions between datatypes, 183–190

datatypes in PL/SQL, 169–175

declaring, 175–182

defined, 167

naming, 167

programmer-defined subtypes, 182

Program Global Area (see PGA)

programmer-defined exceptions, 127

losing information about, 146

programmer-defined records, 314, 315–318

declaring record TYPEs, 316

declaring records, 316

examples of declarations, 317

programmer-defined tracing, 757

programming habits, reassessing, 22

programming languages

calling PL/SQL from other languages, 46–52

database, 4

static and dynamic typing, 170

programs

compiler limits on size of, 986

nested, 64

stored in database, size of, 715

propagation of exceptions, 127

unhandled exceptions, 145

examples of propagation, 147

losing exception information, 146

proxy servers, 913

pseudo-columns

OBJECT_VALUE, 1111

ROWID, 398

pseudo-records, 326

changing names in DML triggers, 658

PARENT, 697

using to fine-tune trigger execution, 664

PSP (PL/SQL Server Pages), 51

public code, 622

Booch diagram showing public package elements, 623

global public package data, 634

public key, 923

Public Key Cryptography Standard #5 (see PKCS#5)

PVM (PL/SQL Virtual Machine), 983

## Q

qualifying references, 59

labels as aid in, 77

Quest Code Tester for Oracle, 752

testing with, 755

Quest CodeGen utility, 19

Quest Error Manager (QEM) framework, 19

tracing with, 761
queuing, 914

# R

raising exceptions, 127, 135–138
    RAISE statement, 136
    RAISE_APPLICATION_ERROR
        procedure, 137
random numbers, 932
range operator (..), 65
ranges, numeric FOR loops, 110
RAW datatype, 173, 397
    AQ message IDs, 178
    casting to VARCHAR2, 412
    converting hexadecimal string from type
        CHAR or VARCHAR2 to, 190
    converting VARCHAR2 value to, 927
    UTL_MAIL.SEND_ATTACH_RAW, 900
RAWTOHEX function, 190
READ COMMITTED isolation level, 457
read consistency and user-defined functions,
    604
READ procedure (DBMS_LOB), 409
REAL datatype, 246
real numbers, 73
recompiling code, invalid program units, 731–
    735
record anchoring, 177
records, 311–326
    benefits of using, 312
    collections as components of, 335
    collections of, 371–373
    comparing, 325
    in cursor RETURN clause, 480
    declaring, 314
    defining your own type, 312
    fetching into, 521
    field-level operations, 322–324
        nested records, 323
        package-based records, 324
    programmer-defined, 315–318
    record-level operations, 318–322
        fetching directly into a record, 320
        initializations, 319
        setting all fields to NULL with direct
            assignment, 321
    trigger pseudo-records, 326
    using with DML statements, 447
        record-based inserts, 448

record-based updates, 449
    restrictions on inserts and updates, 450
    RETURNING clause, 449
records equal generator, 325
recursion, 601
redefinition capability (see edition-based
    redefinition)
REF CURSOR datatype, 173
REF CURSOR types
    compatible rowtype and select list, 500
    converting to SQL cursor number using
        DBMS_SQL.TO_CURSOR, 556
    DBMS_SQL.TO_REFCURSOR function,
        554
    declaring, 498
    FETCH INTO statements, compatible
        rowtype, 501
    identifying for cursor variable used as
        argument, 507
    rowtype matching at compile time, 504
    rowtype matching at runtime, 505
    strong and weak, 499
references, qualifying with scope, 59
REFERENCING clause, changing names of
    pseudo-records in DML triggers, 658
REFs (object references), 1095–1102
    better support in C, 1100
    dangling REFs, 1102
    to nonunique OIDs, 1127
    storing, physical versus virtual REFs, 1126
    type hierarchies and, 1101
    using, 1096
    UTL_REF package, 1099
    virtual REFs, 1120, 1122
REGEXP_COUNT function, 214, 1136
REGEXP_INSTR function, 1136
    locating a pattern, 209
REGEXP_LIKE function, 208, 1137
REGEXP_REPLACE function, 214, 1137
REGEXP_SUBSTR function, 211, 1137
regular expressions, 207–218, 1133–1138
    counting matches, 214
    detecting a pattern, 208
    extracting text matching a pattern, 211
    functions and parameters, 1136
    greediness in matching and nongreedy
        quantifiers, 216
    locating a pattern, 209
    metacharacters, 1133–1136

replacing text, 214
resources for information, 218
RELIES_ON clause (function result cache),
808, 809
using (example), 812
remote dependencies, 727
remote invocation, limitations of Oracle's
model, 730
REMOTE_DEPENDENCIES_MODE
initialization parameter, 728
REPEAT UNTIL loop, emulating, 106
REPLACE function, 203, 226
reserved words, 68
avoiding incorrect use of, 69
information on, 990
resources for PL/SQL developers, 17
books from O'Reilly, 17
online resources, 18
RESTRICT_REFERENCES pragma, 76
result sets, 465
RESULT_CACHE clause, 573, 808
RELIES_ON subclause, 809, 812
using with deterministic function
(example), 810
when not to use, 814
when to use, 814
RESULT_CACHE_MAX_SIZE initialization
parameter, 816
resumable statements, 699
DBMS_RESUMABLE package, 702
RETURN clauses
cursor
datatype structures, 480
declaring cursor with RETURN clause,
479
function, 567
return datatype, 573
packaged cursors, 635
RETURN SELF AS RESULT clause, 1081
RETURN statements
functions, 578
as last executable statement, 579
multiple RETURNs, 578
returning any valid expression, 578
use with procedures, 571
RETURNING clause
DML statements, using records with, 449
using in FORALL statement with BULK
COLLECT, 826

using in FORALL statements, 831
using with DML statements, 445
REVERSE keyword, 111
REVOKE statements, 43
RLS (see row-level security)
rollback segment, assigning current transaction
to, 453
ROLLBACK statements, 452
rollbacks
considerations in programs performing
DML, 447
with FORALL statements, 833
ROUND function, 260
rounding functions, 260
row-based merge processing, 846
row-level security (RLS), 920, 945–964
column-sensitive RLS, 957–961
contexts as predicates in, 967
debugging, 961
direct path operations, 962
interpreting errors, 961
viewing SQL statements, 963
dynamic policies, 953
main components, 947
reasons to learn about, 947
simple example, 949–953
row-level triggers, 653
%ROWCOUNT attribute, 469
using with explicit cursors, 487
ROWID datatype, 173, 397–400
changes in, 397
converting CHAR or VARCHAR2 values to,
187
getting ROWIDs, 398
using ROWIDs, 399
ROWIDTOCHAR function, 190
%ROWTYPE attribute, 173
anchoring to cursors and tables, 179
packaged cursors, 637
use in record declarations, 314
using in record anchoring, 177
ROWTYPE_MISMATCH exception, 502
RPAD function, 205, 226
RR date format element, 288
RTRIM function, 206, 227

## S

SAVE EXCEPTIONS clause (FORALL
statement), 829, 833

SAVEPOINT statements, 452
savepoints
    erasure by COMMIT, 451
    indicating for ROLLBACK statement, 452
scalar anchoring, 177
scalar datatypes, 351
    IS NULL test, 406
scalars, 167
scale, NUMBER datatype, 233
schema-level recompilation, 733
scope, 58
    of compound triggers, 671
    cursor object to which cursor variable is
        assigned, 506
    cursor parameters, 491
    exceptions, 127, 134
    local modules, 594
    qualified references with scope name, 59
scripts, running from SQL*Plus, 30
search strings, formatting for multilingual IR,
    1057
searched CASE statements, 93
SecureFiles, 15, 395, 930
    BasicFiles versus, 415
    compression, 416
    deduplication, 416
    encryption, 417
security, 919
    (see also application security)
    in application contexts, 966
    enhancements for DBMS_SQL package,
        558
security policies (see policies)
SELECT FOR UPDATE statements, 466, 492–
        496
    releasing locks with COMMIT, 494
    WHERE CURRENT OF clause, 495
SELECT statements
    explicit cursor, 477
    explicit cursor body, 481
    implicit cursor, 472
selection directives, 999
SELF keyword, 1082
sequences
    in expressions, 14
    native PL/SQL support for in Oracle
        Database 11g, 442
sequential control statements, 81
    GOTO, 97

SERIALIZABLE isolation level, 457
SERIALLY_REUSABLE pragma, 76, 640
SERVERERROR triggers, 683, 686–690
    central error handler, 689
    examples of, 687
SERVEROUTPUT command (SQL*Plus), 28
session persistence with packages, 622
sessions
    caching static data, 629, 649
    database, 983
    package data as global within, 634
SESSIONTIMEZONE function, 273
SET command (SQL*Plus), 32
SET DEFINE OFF command (SQL*Plus), 196
SET ECHO ON command (SQL*Plus), 39
SET EDITFILE command (SQL*Plus), 34
set operations (see nested tables, multiset
        operations on)
SET TRANSACTION statements, 453
    isolation level of SERIALIZABLE, 457
set-based MERGE, using pipelined functions,
        847
severe compile-time warnings, 736
SFTK timer package, 789
SGA (System Global Area), 362, 782
    data caching in, 799
SHA-1 (Secure Hash Algorithm), 939
shared context-sensitive policies, 957
shared server, 1010
shared static policies, 955
short-circuit evaluation, 89
SHOW ERRORS command (SQL*Plus), 40
    list of categories recognized by, 40
SHUTDOWN triggers, 683, 685
signature mode (remote dependencies), 728
SIMPLE datatypes, 14
simple loops, 102, 104–108
    emulating REPEAT UNTIL loop, 106
    exiting, 105
    infinite loop (intentional), 106
SIMPLE_DOUBLE datatype, 171, 246
SIMPLE_FLOAT datatype, 171, 246
SIMPLE_INTEGER datatype, 171, 239
SMTP (Simple Mail Transfer Protocol), 892
    8BITMIME, 898
    UFL_SMTP, 893
SMTP server, conversation with PL/SQL mail
        client, 895
SOUNDEX function, 227

source code
    displaying and searching in
        USER_SOURCE view, 713
    managing (see code management)
sparse collections, 330
specification (packages), 618, 622
    example, 619
    referencing element defined in from outside
        the package, 632
    rules for construction, 624
SPOOL command (SQL*Plus), 33
SQL (Structured Query Language)
    calling functions from, 602
    DML statements in, 441
    dynamic and static SQL, 513
    dynamic SQL enhancements in Oracle
        Database 11g, 14
    execution of anonymous PL/SQL block
        containing SQL statement, 984
    integration with PL/SQL, xxvi, 7
    native dynamic SQL (see NDS)
    object comparisons, 1111
    semantics for LOBs, 421–425
        performance impact of, 424
        yielding temporary LOBs, 423
    working with collections, 382–387
        CAST pseudo-function, 383
        MULTISET pseudo-function, 384
        sorting collection contents, 386
        TABLE pseudo-function, 385
SQL Developer IDE, 45
SQL injection
    avoiding in dynamic SQL and PL/SQL, 540–
        542
    preventing by using DBMS_ASSERT, 1016
    privilege escalation and, 995
SQL Navigator IDE, 45
SQL statements
    calling deterministic functions within, 615
    as loops, 122
    qualifying references to variables and
        columns in, 59
SQL%BULK_EXCEPTIONS attribute, 832,
    833
SQL%BULK_ROWCOUNT attribute, 832
SQL%FOUND attribute, 444, 476, 832
SQL%ISOPEN attribute, 476, 832
SQL%NOTFOUND attribute, 476, 832
SQL%ROWCOUNT attribute, 445, 476, 832

SQL*Plus, 25–38, 983
    benefits and limitations of, 37
    creating stored programs, 38
    current directory, 31
    editing statements, 34
    error handling, 36
    executing stored programs, 41
    exiting, 34
    loading custom environment automatically
        on startup, 35
    problems with & (ampersand) in PLSQL
        code, 196
    running a PL/SQL program, 28
    running a script, 30
    running a SQL statement, 28
    saving output to file, 33
    setting your preferences, 32
    showing stored programs, 42
    starting up, 26
        pseudo-GUI version, 27
    versions, 25
SQL*Plus User's Guide and Reference, 31
SQLCODE function, 129, 139
    combining with WHEN OTHERS clause,
        151
SQLERRM function, 140
    useful applications of, 143
SQLPATH environment variable, 30
SSL-encrypted web page, retrieving via HTTPS,
    907
STANDARD package, 987
    compile-time warning about, 742
    core features of PL/SQL language and
        dependencies, 725
    defining PL/SQL environment, 988
    identifiers from, 68
    important points about, 989
    predefined datatypes in, 169
    predefined exceptions in, 128
START command (SQL*Plus), 30
STARTUP triggers, 683, 685
statement sharing, 1013
statement-level triggers, 653
statements, 81
    (see also conditional control statements;
    sequential control statements; SQL
    statements)
    PL/SQL, termination with semicolon (;),
        74

static polymorphism, 596
static SQL, 465, 513
static typing, 170
stepwise refinement in application design, 20
stepwise refinement methodologies, 592
store table, 330
streaming functions, 512
    parallel pipelined functions, performance and, 852
streaming table functions, 605
    creating, 608–611
string literals, 71
string-indexed collections, 365–370
    emulating primary keys and unique indexes, 369
    other examples of, 370
    performance, 369
    simplifying algorithmic logic with, 366
strings, 191–230
    CHAR datatype, 193
    concatenating, 198
    converting datetimes to, 281
    converting numbers to, 251–256
    converting time zones to, 290
    converting to and from numbers, 256
    converting to datetimes, 279
    converting to intervals, 294
    datatypes, listed, 191
    dealing with case, 199
    empty strings, 218
    mixing CHAR and VARCHAR2 values, 219–222
    nonprintable characters, 197
    null and zero-length, 71
    padding, 205
    quick reference for string functions, 222–230
    searching, extracting, and replacing, traditional, 202
    searching, extracting, and replacing, using regular expressions, 207–218
    sort order, globalization and, 1049–1054
    specifying string constants, 195
    subtypes, 194
    trimming, 206
    VARCHAR2 datatype, 192
strong type, 499
sub-blocks, 57
subprograms

automatic inlining in Oracle Database 11g, 15
execution profile of code, 16
overloading, 600
SUBSTR function, 202, 227, 1044
    negative string positioning, 204
subtypes
    creating for object type, 1078
    numeric, 246
    programmer-defined, 182
    string, 194
subviews, 1121
supertype methods, invoking, 16, 1084
suspendable/resumable statements, 699
suspended statements, 652
symmetric encryption, 923
synchronization with database columns, 180
synonyms for stored programs, 43
SYS.STANDARD package, numeric functions in, 262
SYSDATE function, 272, 301
system exceptions, 126
    named, listing of predefined exceptions, 132
System Global Area (SGA), 362, 782
    data caching in, 799
system-generated object identifiers, 1088
SYSTIMESTAMP function, 272
    precision of timestamps returned, 273
SYS_REFCURSOR datatype, 173, 499, 1108

## T

table functions, 386, 605–615, 839
    (see also pipelined table functions)
    calling in a FROM clause, 605
    creating pipelined function, 611
    creating streaming function, 608–611
    enabling for parallel execution, 613
    passing results with a cursor variable, 607
TABLE operator, 605
TABLE pseudo-function, 385
table-based records, declaring, 314
tables
    anchoring to, 179
    locking, 454
TCP sockets, 914
TDE (Transparent Data Encryption), 417, 942
TDE tablespace encryption, 944
temporary LOBs, 418–421

creating, 418
freeing, 419
managing, 420
yielded by SQL semantics for LOBs, 423
testing PL/SQL programs, 746–756
automated testing options, 752
general advice for, 751
reasons for inadequate testing, 747
typically bad approach to testing, 748
key drawbacks of, 750
using Quest Code Tester for Oracle, 755
using utPLSQL, 753–755
testing, planning and developing tests, 20
text, 408
(see also Oracle Text)
checking dynamic text for dangerous
content, 542
TEXT_SEARCH_FUNC function, 1055
THEN keyword, 82
requirement after ELSIF clause, 86
three-valued logic, 82
time zones, 268
converting to character strings, 290
region names and time zone abbreviations,
286
session and database, 272
working with, 284
timeout values, DBMS_RESUMABLE package
functions for, 703
TIMESTAMP datatypes, 172, 268, 1059
arithmetic with intervals, 300
caution using DATE with, 271
considerations when choosing, 271
conversions between, 273
conversions using CAST function, 298
converting strings to, 279
converting to strings, 281
date formats and, 283
as inputs for datetime functions, 308
mixing with DATEs in datetime arithmetic,
304
timestamp literals, 291
timestamp mode (remote dependencies), 728
TIMESTAMP WITH LOCAL TIME ZONE
datatype, 268
considerations when choosing, 271
TIMESTAMP WITH TIME ZONE datatype,
268
considerations when choosing, 271

time zone information in, 290
Toad IDE, 24, 45
TOO_MANY_ROWS exception, 156
raised by implicit cursor SELECT statement,
473
top-down design, 20, 592
TO_CHAR function, 228, 251–256
converting datetime values to strings, 281
dealing with spaces, 255
examples of use for date conversions, 282
interval format masks and, 295
passing NLS settings to, 256
rounding when converting, 254
V format element, 253
TO_DATE function, 279
TO_DSINTERVAL function, 294
TO_MULTI_BYTE function, 228
TO_NCHAR function, 228
TO_NUMBER function, 247–251
passing NLS settings to, 249
using with format model, 249
using with no format, 248
TO_TIMESTAMP function, 279
TO_TIMESTAMP_TZ function, 279
TO_YMINTERVAL function, 294
tracing program execution, 756–766
using DBMS_APPLICATION_INFO
package, 759
using DBMS_TRACE package, 763–766
using Quest Error Manager (QEM), 761
transactions, 439, 450–461
autonomous, 454–461
building autonomous logging
mechanism, 459
defining, 455
rules and restrictions for, 456
visibility of, 457
when to use, 458
COMMIT statement, 451
defined, 450
exiting SQL*Plus before completion of, 34
integrity of, 5
LOCK TABLE statement, 454
participation of DML triggers, 654
PL/SQL statements for transaction
management, 450
ROLLBACK statement, 452
SAVEPOINT statement, 452
SET TRANSACTION statement, 453

transformative functions, 512
transient types, 1105
TRANSLATE function, 228
Transparent Data Encryption (TDE), 417, 942
TREAT function, 1091
triggers, 651–708
    AFTER SUSPEND, 697–704
    checking validity of, 708
    compound, 670–673
    creating disabled triggers, 706
    database event, 683–690
    DDL, 673–683
    defined, 567
    disabling, enabling, and dropping, 705
    DML, 652
        creating, 655–660
        example, 660–665
        multiple triggers of same type, 665
        mutating table errors, 668
        order of firing, 666
    enhancements in Oracle Database 11g, 15
    events with trigger code attached, 651
    INSTEAD OF, 690–697
    pseudo-records, 326
    USER_TRIGGERS and
        USER_TRIG_COLUMNS views,
        712
        analyzing and modifying triggers, 716
    uses of, 651
    viewing, 706
trigonometric functions, 261
TRIM function, 206, 229
TRIM procedure, 341, 349
trimming strings, 206
Triple DES (DES3), 924
TRUE values, 172
TRUNC function, 260
    with MONTHS_BETWEEN function, 304
    using with dates and times, 285
%TYPE attribute, 177
    anchoring to NOT NULL datatypes, 182
type evolution, 1093
type hierarchies
    object types, 1076
    REFs and, 1101
TYPE statements, declaring programmer-
    defined records, 315
TYPE...RECORD statements, 314

**U**

UGA (User Global Area), 1010
unbounded collections, 330
unconstrained declarations, 580
unconstrained subtypes, 182
UNDER privilege (for objct types), 1129
unexpected exceptions, 154
    exception handling for, 155
    guidelines for handling, 156
unfortunate exceptions, 154
    exception handling for, 155
    guidelines for handling, 156
unhandled exceptions, 127, 145
    propagation of, 145
        examples, 147
        losing exception information, 146
Unicode, 1034–1045
    character encoding, 1036
    defined, 1034
    globalization support (NLS) parameters,
        1037
    national character set datatypes, 1036
    PL/SQL functions for, 1038–1045
    support in your environment, 1037
    Unicode Standard web site, 1036
    UTF-8 character set, 192
UNISTR function, 230, 1045
units (compilation), 1003
Unix
    ed editor, 35
    killing a process, 107
    opening files, specifying locations for, 878
    retrieving SSL-encrypted web page via
        HTTPS, 908
UNKNOWN values, NULL versus, 91
unnamed (anonymous) exceptions, 127
unreachable code, compile-time warning
    about, 744
UPDATE statements, 441, 442
    record-based, 449
        restrictions on, 450
    using in dynamic SQL, 524
    using records, 447
    using RETURNING clause, 445
    WHERE CURRENT OF clause, 495
UPDATE triggers, INSTEAD OF UPDATE,
    694
UPDATING clause in DML triggers, 661
UPDATING function, 659

UPPER function, 199, 230
URI types, 430
URIs (Universal Resource Identifiers), 174
URITYPE datatype, 174
UROWID datatype, 173, 397
US7ASCII character set, 64
USER function, 801
User Global Area (UGA), 1010
user-defined datatypes, 169, 175
    collection, 350
user-defined functions
    calling from within SQL
        read consistency and, 604
    calling from within SQL, restrictions on,
        603
USER_* views, 711
USER_ARGUMENTS view, 711
USER_DEPENDENCIES view, 711, 723
USER_DUMP_DEST initialization parameter,
    961
USER_ERRORS view, 40, 711
USER_IDENTIFIERS view, 711, 719
USER_OBJECTS view, 711
    information about stored objects, 712
    showing stored programs in, 42
USER_OBJECT_SIZE view, 712, 715
USER_PLSQL_OBJECT_SETTINGS view,
    712, 715, 1002, 1007
USER_PROCEDURES view, 712, 716
USER_SOURCE view, 712, 713
USER_STORED_SETTINGS view, 712
USER_TAB_PRIVS_MADE view, 43
USER_TRIGGERS view, 712, 716
USER_TRIG_COLUMNS view, 712, 716
USING clause
    association of placeholders with bind
        arguments, 527
    EXECUTE IMMEDIATE statement, 515
    OPEN FOR statements, 522
USSR_ARGUMENTS view, 717
UTC (Coordinated Universal Time), 268, 270
    time zone information, 290
UTL_ENCODE package, 900
UTL_FILE package, 877–891
    closing files with FCLOSE and
        FCLOSE_ALL procedures, 882
    copying files with FCOPY procedure, 888
    DELETE_FAILED exception, 163

deleting files with FREMOVE procedure,
    889
error codes for exceptions, 163
INVALID_OPERATION exception, 163
IS_OPEN function, 882
opening files with FOPEN function, 880
    specifying locations, 878
reading from files with GET_LINE
    procedure, 883
renaming and moving files with FRENAME
    procedure, 890
retrieving file attributes with FGETATTR
    procedure, 890
UTL_FILE_DIR parameter, 877
    setting up directories, 878
working with Oracle directories, 879
writing formatted text to file with PUTF
    procedure, 887
writing to files, procedures for, 885
UTL_HTTP package, 903–913
    authentication using HTTP username and
        password, 906
    cookies, disabling or making persistent,
        912
    end_of_body exception, 904
    fetching a LOB, 905
    proxy servers, 913
    READ_LINE procedure, 904
    READ_TEXT procedure, 904
    retrieving SSL-encrypted web page via
        HTTPS, 907
UTL_I18N package
    listing of programs in, 1066
    STRING_TO_RAW function, 927, 929
UTL_LMS package, 1069
UTL_MAIL package
    SEND procedure, 892
        friendly names in addresses, 896
    SEND_ATTACH_RAW procedure, 900
    SEND_ATTACH_VARCHAR2 procedure,
        899
    setting up and using, 893
UTL_RAW package
    CAST_TO_VARCHAR2 function, 412
UTL_RECOMP package, 734
UTL_REF package, 1099
UTL_SMTP package, 893
    sending plaintext method of arbitrary
        length, 897

UTL_URL.ESCAPE function, 909
utPLSQL testing framework, 752
    testing with, 753–755

# V

V number format element, 253
V$TEMPORARY_LOBS view, 421
V$TIMEZONE_NAMES view, 286
validation of user input, using DBMS_ASSERT
    package, 542
validity of triggers, checking, 708
VALUE function, 1089
VALUES OF clause (FORALL statement), 829,
    836
    example, 837
VALUE_ERROR exception, 177, 180
VARCHAR2 datatype, 170, 192
    assigning zero-length string to, 71
    casting RAW type to, 412
    converting binary value of type ROWID to,
        190
    converting hexadecimal string to type RAW,
        190
    converting to RAW, using
        UTL_I18N.STRING_TO_RAW
        function, 927
    converting type RAW to hexadecimal string
        of, 190
    empty strings and, 219
    mixing with CHAR values, 219–222
    sending file as email attachment, 899
    using CLOBs interchangeably with, 421
variable attribute notation, 1089
variables, 167
    binding, 525–529
    declaring, 175
        default values, NOT NULL clause, 177
    declaring datetime variables, 270
    declaring INTERVAL variables, 275
    name conflicts in, 740
    naming, 167
    qualifying references to, 59
    remote invocation and, 730
    scope, 58
    SQL*Plus, declared and bind variables, 32
VARRAYs, 331
    accessing data in, 364
    bounded collections, 330
    changing characteristics of, 354

    collection using, 333
    comparison to other collection types, 340
    database-to-PL/SQL integration, 358
    declaring and initializing collection
        variables of type, 355
    declaring VARRAY collection type, 353
    using as column datatype, 339
versions
    of installed database, 1001
    Oracle database and PL/SQL, xxxii, 11
virtual columns, 484
virtual denormalization, 1122
Virtual Private Database (VPD), 946, 963
    function result caching and, 816–819
visibility of variables, 61–64
    identifier names qualified with module
        names, 62
    qualified identifiers, 62
    visible identifiers, 61

# W

wallets, 907
    TDE master key storage, 943
warnings
    compile-time, 735–746
    about performance, 793
WE8MSWIN1252 character set, 189
weak type, 499
web site for this book, xxxv
    DML trigger scripts, 654
    packages available on, 648
web sites for PL/SQL, 18
WHEN clauses
    CASE expressions and, 97
    in DML triggers, 654, 656
        applying (example), 663
    evaluation in searched CASE statements,
        93
    exceptions named in, 139
    simple CASE statements and, 92
    in triggers, getting information about, 716
WHEN OTHERS clause, 139, 150
WHERE clause
    DELETE statement, 443
    UPDATE statement, 442
WHERE CURRENT OF clause, 495
WHILE loops, 103, 108
    exiting properly, 120
whitespace

dealing with spaces in number to character
string conversions, 255
keywords and, 69
not allowed in identifiers, 66
wildcards
% (percent sign), used in LIKE condition,
65
_ (underscore) in LIKE condition, 65
Windows systems
carriage return and new line characters,
197
killing a process, 107
Notepad editor, 35
opening files, specifying locations for, 878
retrieving SSL-encrypted web page via
HTTPS, 907
WORK keyword, 451
wrap utility, 44
WRAPPED keyword, 777
wrapping code, 774
guidelines for wrapped code, 776
restrictions and limitations, 774
using DBMS_DDL package, 775
using wrap executable, 775
WRITE and WRITEAPPEND procedures
(DBMS_LOB), 407–409

# X

XDBURITYPE datatype, 430
XML DB Developer's Guide for Oracle
Database 11g Release 2, 430
XMLType, 174, 426–430
CreateXML method, 427
documentation, 430
existsNode method, 428
indexing columns, 429
using INSERT statements to create XML
documents, 427
XQuery language, 427

# Y

YMINTERVAL_UNCONSTRAINED
datatype, 307

# Z

zero-length strings, 71

# About the Authors

**Steven Feuerstein** is considered one of the world's leading experts on the Oracle PL/SQL language, having written 10 books on PL/SQL, including *Oracle PL/SQL Programming* and *Oracle PL/SQL Best Practices* (both published by O'Reilly). Steven has been developing software since 1980, spent five years with Oracle (1987–1992), and has served as PL/SQL Evangelist for Quest Software since January 2001. He is an Oracle ACE Director and writes regularly for *Oracle Magazine*, which named him the PL/SQL Developer of the Year in both 2002 and 2006. He is also the first recipient of ODTUG's Lifetime Achievement Award (2009). Since 2005, he has focused his attention on improving the testing of PL/SQL programs, primarily through the creation of Quest Code Tester for Oracle, which automates PL/SQL code testing. Steven's online technical cyberhome is located at *http://www.ToadWorld.com/SF*. You can also catch up on his latest, mostly non-PLSQL rants at *http://feuerthoughts.blogspot.com*.

**Bill Pribyl** is the primary author of *Learning Oracle PL/SQL* and the coauthor of *Oracle PL/SQL Programming* and its companion pocket reference (all from O'Reilly). He thrives on writing oddball PL/SQL code such as TCP/IP networking clients, transcendental functions, and XML-based web scrapers. Bill holds a degree in physics from Rice University and now works full-time for an energy trading firm in Houston, Texas.

# Colophon

Ants are featured on the cover of *Oracle PL/SQL Programming*, Fifth Edition. At least 8,000 different species of ants can be found everywhere on Earth except the North and South Poles. Ants preserved in amber suggest that these insects existed 50 million years before humans.

Humans have long been fascinated by ants, because these tiny insects are accomplished builders, nurses, miners, and even farmers. Fables such as "The Ant and the Grasshopper" extol the virtues of hardworking, forward-looking ants. (Hail ants!) It is true that individual ants are able to perform amazing feats: an ant can carry up to 50 times its body weight, can travel the human equivalent of 40 miles a day, and can climb vertical heights the equivalent of Mount Everest. However, the greatest accomplishments of ants are those performed together for the good of their community.

Queen ants establish new communities, or nests, after their mating flight. On this flight the queen mates with several males. After mating, the males fall to Earth and die. The queen then finds an uninhabited nest, settles into it, and pulls her wings off. She will never fly again, and after removing her wings she is able to absorb the wing muscles as nutrients for her eggs. She will continue to lay eggs, thousands of them, for years.

During the three-stage development process, which takes about two months, the eggs, larvae, and pupae are cared for by the nurse ants, who feed, clean, and carefully move the young to warmer or cooler places in the nest, depending on the temperature. These nurse ants are, in turn, cared for by other worker ants, who feed the nurses with regurgitated food. The workers and the nurses will fight together to defend the young against enemies if the nest is invaded, either by another group of ants or by a larger animal.

The cover image is is a 19th-century engraving from the Dover Pictorial Archive. The cover font is Adobe ITC Garamond. The text font is Linotype Birka; the heading font is Adobe Myriad Condensed; and the code font is LucasFont's TheSansMonoCondensed.

# Get even more for your money.

**Join the O'Reilly Community, and register the O'Reilly books you own. It's free, and you'll get:**

- $4.99 ebook upgrade offer
- 40% upgrade offer on O'Reilly print books
- Membership discounts on books and events
- Free lifetime updates to ebooks and videos
- Multiple ebook formats, DRM FREE
- Participation in the O'Reilly community
- Newsletters
- Account management
- 100% Satisfaction Guarantee

**Signing up is easy:**

1. Go to: oreilly.com/go/register
2. Create an O'Reilly login.
3. Provide your address.
4. Register your books.

Note: English-language books only

**To order books online:**

oreilly.com/store

**For questions about products or an order:**

orders@oreilly.com

**To sign up to get topic-specific email announcements and/or news about upcoming books, conferences, special offers, and new technologies:**

elists@oreilly.com

**For technical questions about book content:**

booktech@oreilly.com

**To submit new book proposals to our editors:**

proposals@oreilly.com

**O'Reilly books are available in multiple DRM-free ebook formats. For more information:**

oreilly.com/ebooks

Spreading the knowledge of innovators        oreilly.com

# Have it your way.

## O'Reilly eBooks

- Lifetime access to the book when you buy through oreilly.com
- Provided in up to four DRM-free file formats, for use on the devices of your choice: PDF, .epub, Kindle-compatible .mobi, and Android .apk
- Fully searchable, with copy-and-paste and print functionality
- Alerts when files are updated with corrections and additions

oreilly.com/ebooks/

## Safari Books Online

- Access the contents and quickly search over 7000 books on technology, business, and certification guides
- Learn from expert video tutorials, and explore thousands of hours of video on technology and design topics
- Download whole books or chapters in PDF format, at no extra cost, to print or read on the go
- Get early access to books as they're being written
- Interact directly with authors of upcoming books
- Save up to 35% on O'Reilly print books

See the complete Safari Library at safari.oreilly.com

# O'REILLY®